Sunset

Western Garden Book

By the Editors of Sunset Books and Sunset Magazine

Bright ranunculus and blue Dutch irises herald spring in the West.

Lane Publishing Co. ▪ Menlo Park, California

Silklike Shirley poppies (Papaver rhoeas) create a garden painting with their varied combinations of warm colors.

Cover: Galium odoratum (sweet woodruff). Design by Joe di Chiarro. Photography by Ells Marugg.

Editor, Sunset Books: Elizabeth L. Hogan

First printing October 1988

 Library of Congress Catalog Card Number 88-80952. Hardcover edition: ISBN 0-376-03853-5. Softcover edition: ISBN 0-376-03891-8. Lithographed in the United States.

Foreword

Over its 55-year lifetime, this book has become an indispensable part of gardening in the West, a region that extends from the Pacific Ocean to the eastern slope of the Rocky Mountains.

Horticulturally, this region is known primarily for the mildness of the winters in its lower elevations. But in recent times another aspect of the Western climate has claimed special significance: the limited availability of water in relation to a seemingly unlimited population growth. Today, the drought tolerance of any plant being considered for placement in a garden must be routinely assessed.

This fifth edition tells you in which Western climates any listed plant will grow; it also identifies each plant's degree of drought tolerance. Wet years may come and go, but eras of water scarcity will evermore be with us. It becomes increasingly important to choose more drought-resistant plants, be more careful about how and where we place high-water-need plants, and learn how we can be more water-thrifty in the ways we irrigate all plants.

Our updated Western Plant Encyclopedia includes a helpful new aid: the family name of every plant. Knowing what family a plant belongs to can help you anticipate what to expect from it.

Another new feature, beginning on page 8, is the "The Spirit of Western Gardening," where scores of beautiful color photographs show what specific Western garden plants look like as they mature and flower. Also, at the back of the book is a new index that gives *all* the page numbers on which a plant is listed or described.

The editors of *Sunset Magazine* and *Sunset Books* hope that this book will make gardening more deeply satisfying for you than ever before.

For their helpful advice and continuing good will, we offer special thanks to our consultants.

Joseph F. Williamson

Managing Editor, *Sunset Magazine*

Staff

Editorial Director

Joseph F. Williamson
Managing Editor, *Sunset Magazine*

Editor, Western Plant Encyclopedia

John R. Dunmire
Senior Editor, *Sunset Magazine*

Coordinating Editors

Suzanne Normand Mathison
Linda J. Selden

Assistant Editor

Philip Edinger

Contributing Editors

Susan Warton
Rebecca La Brum
Lance Walheim
Jim McCausland

Garden Editor, *Sunset Magazine*

Kathleen Norris Brenzel

Design

Joe di Chiarro

Illustrations

Lois Lovejoy
Mary Davey Burkhardt
Ireta Cooper
Dennis Nolan

Climate Maps

Joe Seney

Consultants

Special Consultants

Bob Cowden
Walter L. Doty
Warren Jones
Elsa Uppman Knoll
Nevin Smith

Pacific Northwest

Arthur L. Antonelli
Bob Badger
Noble Bashor
Wilbur L. Bluhm
Bruce Briggs
Ralph Byther
Andrew A. Duncan
Roger Gossler
Harold Greer
L. Keith Hellstrom
Harold T. Hopkins
Anton S. Horn
Stott Howard
Wallace K. Huntington
Francis J. Lawrence
Whitney Lawrence
John Mitsch
Patrick P. Moore
Robert Norton
Earl L. Phillips
Wallace M. Ruff
Ellie Sather
George Schenk
R. M. Snodgrass
Robert L. Stebbins
Eleanor Stubbs
Ted Van Veen

California & Nevada

A. D. Ali
William Aplin
John Boething
Gerald Bol
Worth Brown
Charles Burr
John Catlin
Philip E. Chandler
Francis Ching
Barrie Coate
Stephen Cohan
Clifford Comstock
Al Condit
Ira J. Condit
Dave Cudney
Dan Davids
Jerry C. Davids
Donald F. Dillon
Roger Duer
Clyde Elmore
Morgan Evans
Percy Everett
Everett Farwell
Stan Farwig
George Haight
Richard A. Haubrich
Don Hodel
Barbara Joe Hoshizaki
Colin Jackson
Myron W. Kimnach
Carlton Koehler
Frederick M. Lang
Andrew T. Leiser
Peter J. Lert
Robert Ludekens
James M. Lyons
Arthur H. McCain
Elizabeth McClintock
Rod McLellan
Ralph D. McPheeters
Rex Marsh
Mildred Mathias
Lynne Meyer
Ray Miller
Craig Minor
W. S. Moore
Dennison Morey
Bill Moynier
Kathy Musial
Howard D. Ohr
Hadley Osborne
Arthur Otis
Glenn Park
Owen Pearce
Dennis Perry
James C. Perry
Eleanor Philp
Robert G. Platt
Harold Prickett
Robert Raabe
Chris Rosmini
Robert H. Ruf
Roy Rydell
Saratoga Horticultural Foundation
R. H. Sciaroni
George Harmon Scott
Joe Seals
Lily Singer
Ted Sjulin
L. K. Smith
Soil and Plant Laboratory, Inc.
Ray Sodomka
Vernon T. Stoutemyer
Strybing Arboretum
Peter Sugawara
Harold Swanton
John Van Barneveld
James Wilson
Donald P. Woolley
Carl Zangger

Rockies & Southwest

James Behnken
William M. Brown, Jr.
Whitney Cranshaw
Mark Dimmitt
Rodney Engard
Boyce Foerman
Ron Gass
Stan Heathman
Dick Hildreth
Richard Hine
Panayoti Kelaidis
James Klett
David Langston
Terry Mikel
Irene Mitchell
Ernest F. Reimschussel
Jackie H. Richner
Michael Rowland
Bill G. Scott
Harvey F. Tate
Larry E. Watson
Gayle Weinstein
Ric Wogisch

Contents

The Spirit of Western Gardening

April garden in southern California explodes with color. Gray dusty miller (Centaurea cineraria) and pink dianthus mingle with sweet alyssum (Lobularia maritima), callas (Zantedeschia), and red valerian (Centranthus ruber).

Gardens in the West are famous for their color and vitality. And they exhibit immense variety over a territory that spans both wide differences in climate and thousands of plant possibilities.

Near Tucson, western gardening might take the shape of a sculptural cactus tableau. Northward, in the state of Washington, it might feature deep pink rhododendrons glowing through rain-misted air. In any urban locale, from Denver to San Diego, you're likely to see gardens flourish on a small scale in clay pots, hanging baskets, or planter boxes.

In this opening chapter, we invite you to enjoy the exuberant spirit of western gardens by taking an armchair tour through a selection of colorful examples. Among the tempting home-grown edibles, dazzling floral displays, and sumptuous foliage, perhaps you'll see ideas that you'd like to try for yourself.

Textures, Patterns & Tones

Foliage in western gardens displays a profusion of colors and forms, from velvety ground covers underfoot to high, shimmering treetops.

Private streetside garden is swathed in greenery from various foliage plants. Coral tree (Erythrina), in foreground at right, screens fence behind it with its spreading branches.

Slender stalks of blooming blue fescue (Festuca ovina glauca) etch fine, feathery lines that accent neighboring clump of vivid pink geraniums and red petunias.

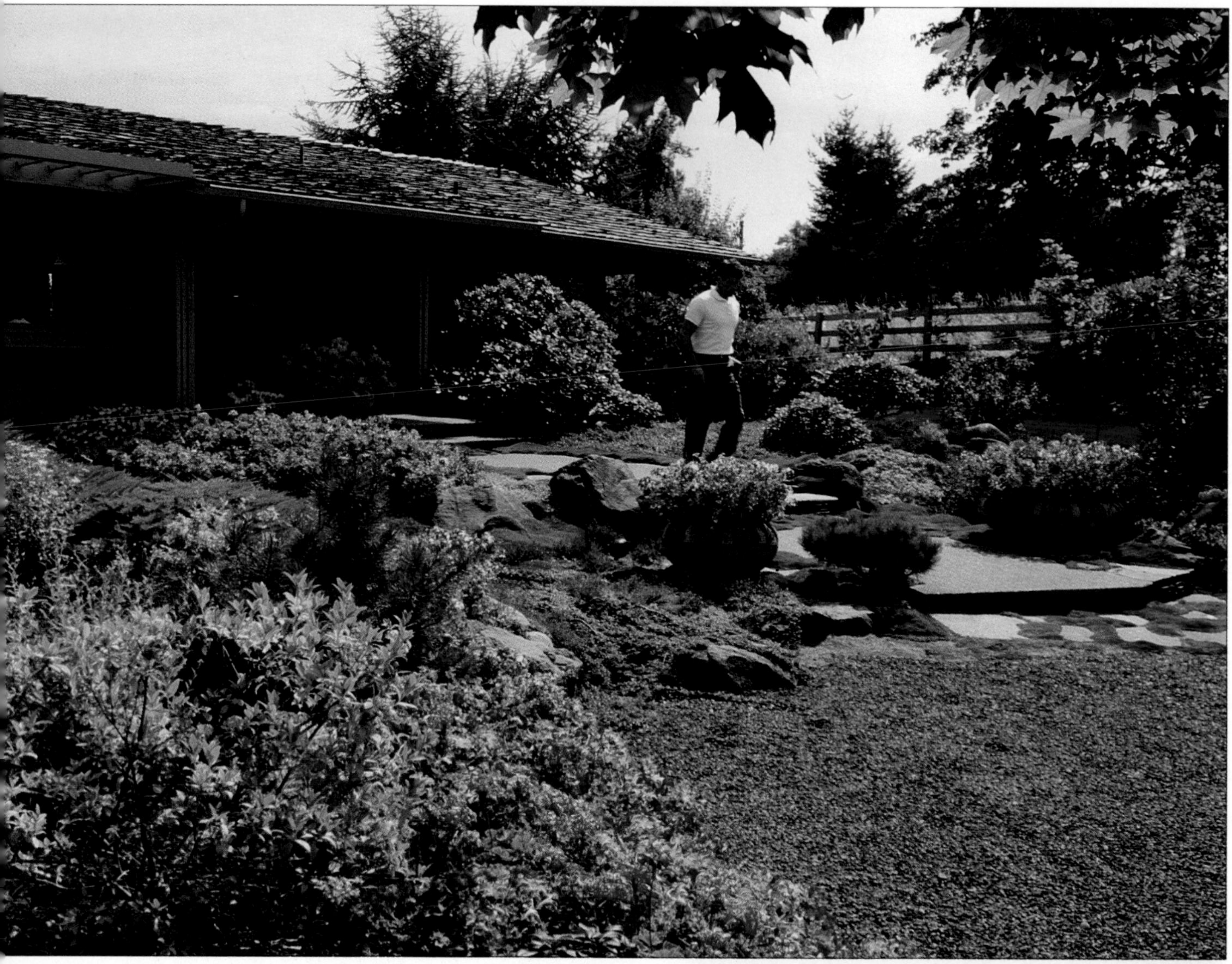

Gently rolling "alpine" topography spreads variegated tapestry in front of house. Shrubs include azaleas, Swiss mountain pine (Pinus mugo), heath (Erica), rhododendrons, Viburnum davidii, and junipers. Annuals in beds and containers contribute color.

Amid profusion of perennials and herbs, woolly thyme surrounds broken concrete pavers. As ground cover, it provides soft, treadable, and fragrance-releasing surface.

All but smothered in heavily fragrant Jasminum polyanthum, old arbor frames tranquil, easygoing garden where bulbs and perennials pop up as they please. Design: Garry Bernhardt.

Woolly-leafed Crete dittany (Origanum dictamnus) grows alongside yellow- and orange-flowered sunrose (Helianthemum), dark blue Veronica incana, and lavender catmint (Nepeta faassenii).

A compact and evergreen ground cover, Oxalis crassipes fills spaces between pavers with garlands of green.

Splashes of Color

Clear, vivid flower color from bulbs, annuals, and perennials creates a splashy display that, in the West, may continue all year.

Bursting with red, orange, and salmon bloom, papery Iceland poppies (Papaver nudicaule) bask in sunlight. Top western performers, they put on superstar show from winter through early spring in mild-climate areas.

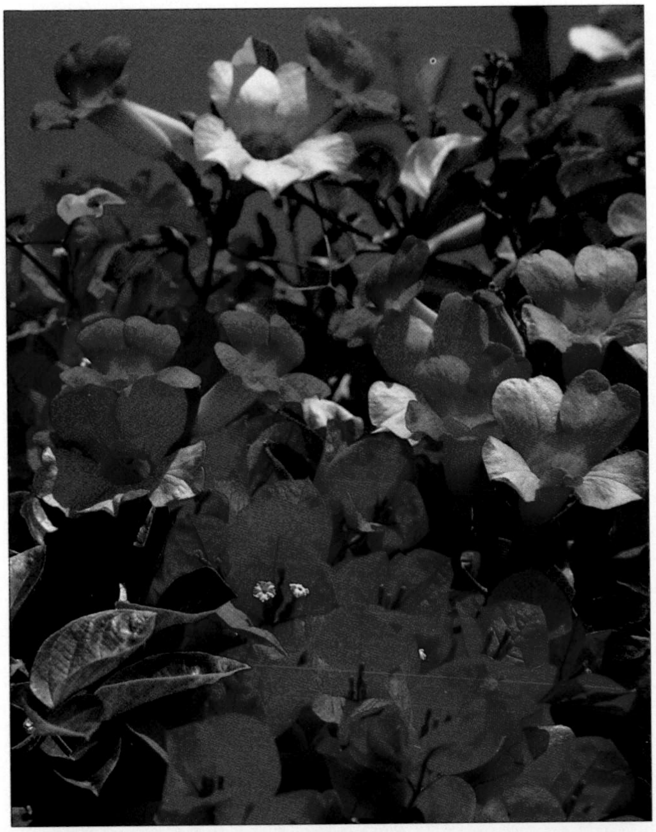

Sun-loving vines meet and mix at middle of garden fence. Blooming intermittently all summer, pinkish purple royal trumpet vine (Distictis 'Rivers') and red bougainvillea are trained from opposite ends.

Glorious gerberas (Transvaal daisies) in hot pink, red, orange, and yellow add drama to summer garden. These are compact Happipot strain.

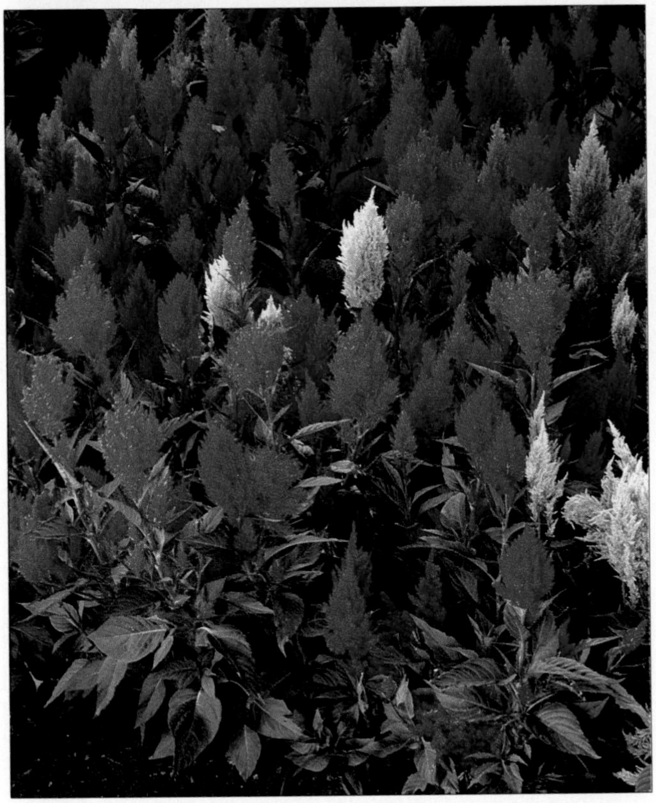

Like candle flames, Celosia's plumes seem to blaze against green foliage. This is grouping of Century Mixed strain.

Abundance of golden blooms characterizes perennial coreopsis, an easygoing plant that dazzles throughout summer with little attention.

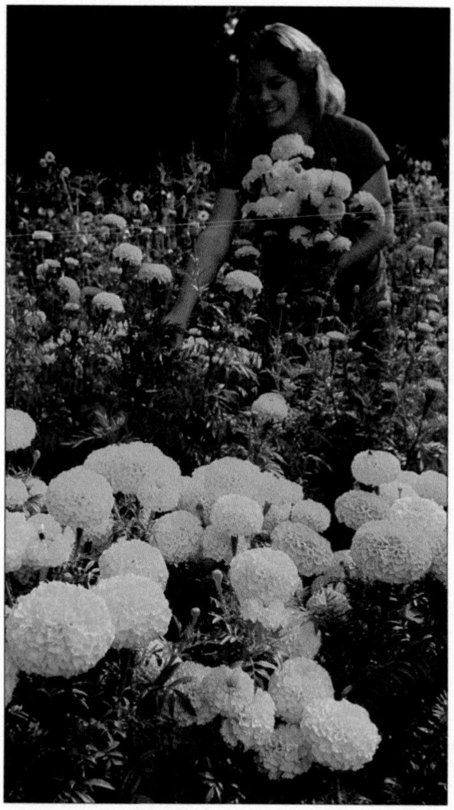

On warm October day, this sunny field of marigolds offers armloads of cheerful yellow and orange blooms.

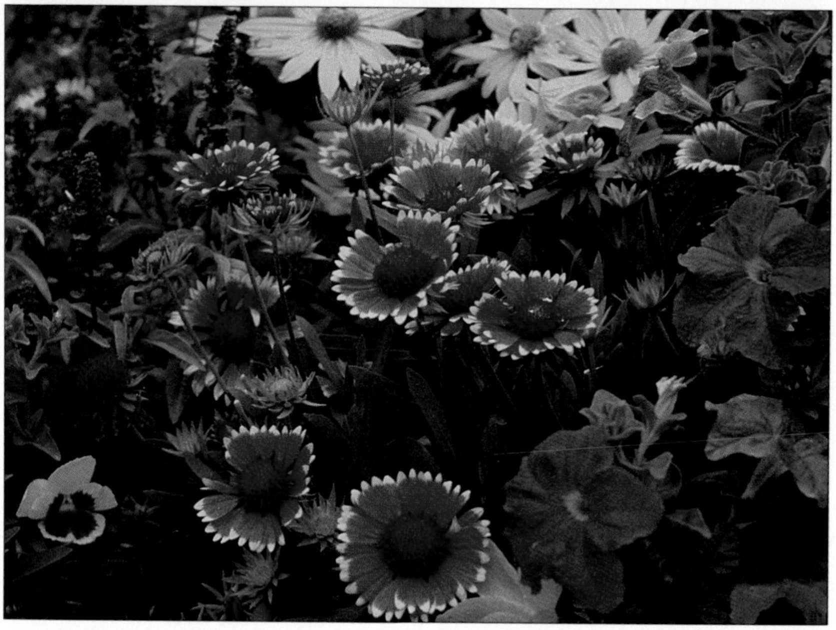

Long-blooming Gaillardia grandiflora 'Goblin', with yellow-tipped red flowers, mingles with purple petunias, yellow pansies, and golden cosmos.

Lavender to deep purple iris, tall bearded hybrids, stand gracefully in springtime garden. The popular perennial occurs in many types, of which tall bearded is best known.

Woodland charm comes to shaded patio in grouping of blue hydrangeas, ageratum, streptocarpus, ferns, and Persian violets (Exacum affine).

Blue and white salvia (S. farinacea) combine handsomely in border planting. Vibrant shades of blue are this salvia's trademark.

Floral Tapestries

Varied heights, hues, and flower forms appear to weave a harmonious tapestry when plants combine in a cottage garden or perennial border.

Riot of color results from tall yellow and orange Alstroemeria aurantiaca, behind fence, and slightly shorter Ligtu hybrids; Iceland poppies (Papaver nudicaule), at foot of fence; and nemesia, in foreground. Design: Terry and Eve Allan Baldwin.

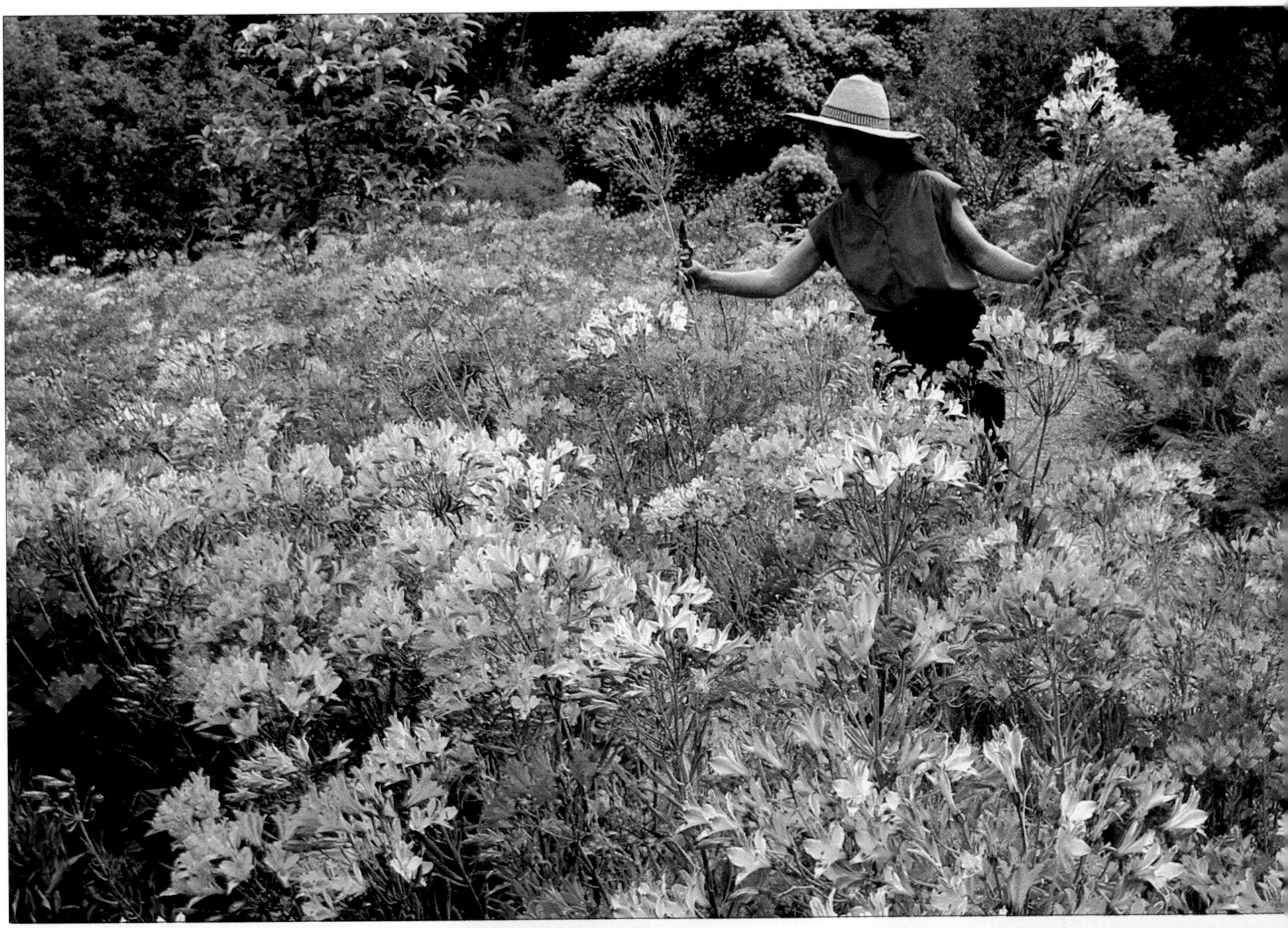

Summertime profusion of waist-high blooms turns field into colorful vision. Mature Ligtu hybrid alstroemerias spread by seed and underground stems. Single stalk in her hand has 41 flowers and buds.

Sweeping border combines perennials of different heights and shapes. In foreground are baby's breath (Gypsophila paniculata), Shasta daisies (Chrysanthemum maximum), and Sedum spectabile.

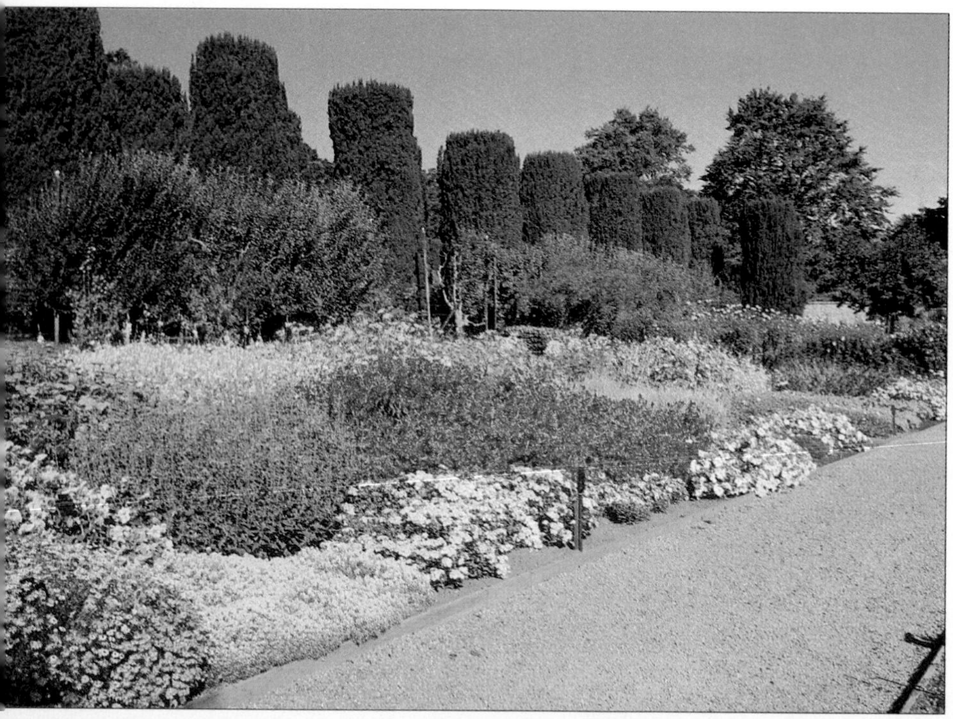

Colorful palette of massed annuals imitates perennial border along path; included are cosmos, petunias, Swan River daisies (Brachycome iberidifolia), sweet alyssum (Lobularia maritima), and zinnias.

Vertical garden grows in wall of wire, soil mix, and moss. Soaking up sun are sweet alyssum (Lobularia maritima), pansies, ornamental kale, parsley, lobelia, stonecrop (Sedum), and (across top) fern asparagus (Asparagus setaceus).

Festive flowers create colorful backdrop for late-summer garden party. Border boasts such show-offs as marigolds, zinnias, and Gloriosa daisies (Rudbeckia hirta).

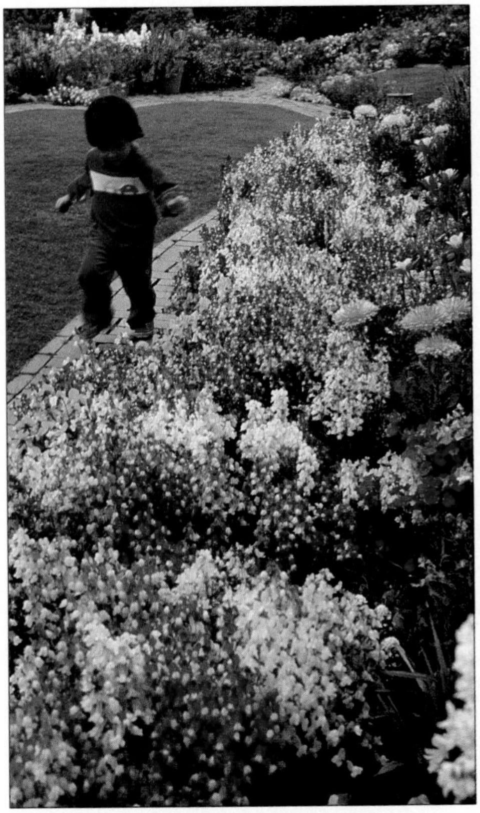

Like miniature snapdragons, masses of Fairy Bouquet linaria stand 8 to 10 inches high. Tapestry of rich pastels includes 13 color variations. Sow seeds like wildflowers; new plants volunteer year after year.

Ablaze with bloom, 4-year-old border displays basket-of-gold (Aurinia saxatilis), white evergreen candytuft (Iberis sempervirens), miniature daisies (Chrysanthemum paludosum), red nemesia, and pink and gold linaria, as well as green leaves of agapanthus, daylilies (Hemerocallis), and iris (not yet in bloom).

Small-scale Gardens

From sunny Albuquerque to cool, drizzling Seattle, many western gardens thrive in the few square feet of a patio, balcony, or deck.

Soaking up mist, container-grown bouquets brighten deck with yellow and orange marigolds, white marguerites (Chrysanthemum frutescens), purple petunias, and red-orange zinnias. Design: Kienholz/Kunkle, Inc.

Brimming over wall around deck, dwarf French marigolds, nasturtiums (Tropaeolum majus), and lobelia grow in inset metal planter.

A miniature bulb like Chionodoxa luciliae makes a sure-to-please gift in spring.

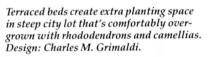

Terraced beds create extra planting space in steep city lot that's comfortably overgrown with rhododendrons and camellias. Design: Charles M. Grimaldi.

Kitchen garden in wooden box offers lettuce, several kinds of peppers, basil, parsley, and even flowers for the table.

Collectors' Showpieces

Whether rose, camellia, azalea, or hibiscus, certain dramatically beautiful plants are prized by gardeners for their ornamental blooms.

Cascading garlands of white Japanese wisteria (Wisteria floribunda 'Longissima Alba'), draping from vine over 25 years old, stage brief but spectacular show each spring.

Vibrant pink-tinged blossoms of stately Rhododendron 'Point Defiance' look almost tropical. Actually, rhododendrons do thrive in moist air, but they also prefer cool temperatures.

Pale pink 'Climbing Dainty Bess' is hybrid tea rose that vigorously scales fence—or can be left to form fountainlike shrub.

Soft masses of ruffled bloom on Rhododendron 'Purple Splendour' glow luminously through rain-washed air.

A fairyland cloud of pink-to-white flowers, Rhododendron davidsonianum blooms in Northwest garden in April and May. Its upright habit shows off display.

Luscious, rose-shaded 'Hana Jiman', semidouble Sasanqua camellia, is not only lovely to look at but mildly fragrant as well.

Vibrant flowers of 'Wildfire' camellias provide Christmas cheer at entryway, greens and ribbons dressing up their terra-cotta pots.

Symbol of Hawaii, flamboyant hibiscus also performs beautifully in mild mainland climates. 'Cherie' has striking neon-orange blossoms, 5 inches across, with wavy petal edges.

Soaking up sun, bougainvillea spills over huge boulder. Its hot pink blossoms contrast richly with the cool gray stone.

Lavender hue, ruffled petals, and heady fragrance make 'Angel Face' exceptionally romantic double floribunda rose.

The Garden Cornucopia

"It tastes best if grown in the West"—while that slogan may exaggerate in a few cases, most fruits and vegetables do perform magnificently here.

Herbal knot garden features central oval of dwarf gray sage enclosing English lavender and its dwarf, purple-flowered variety, 'Hidcote'. Rimming brick walk are golden sage, woolly thyme, more lavender, golden oregano, lamb's ears, yarrows, and sage.

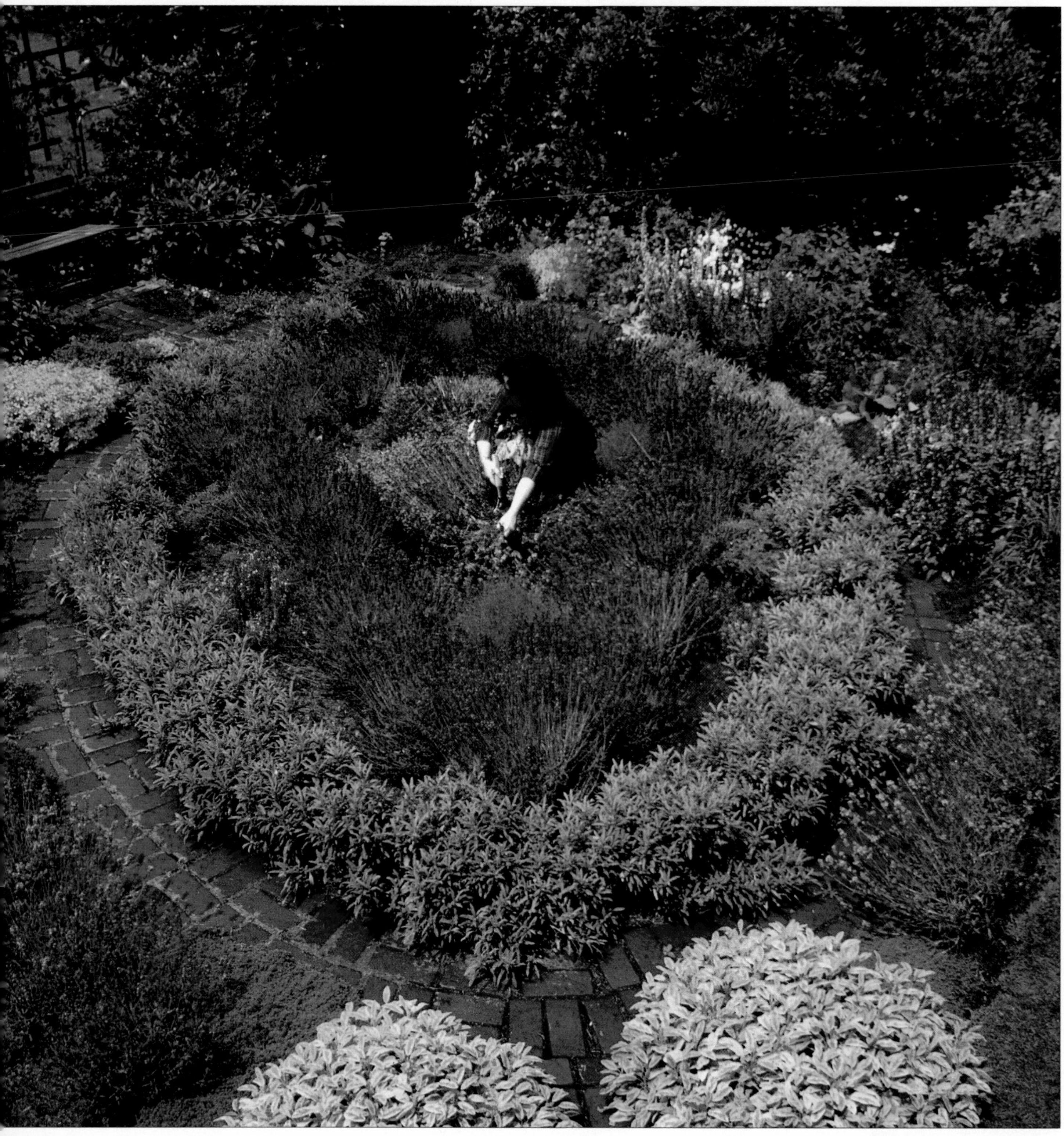

Sunny California's citrus, once inspired an agricultural "gold rush." Here's one attraction: plump, juicy grapefruit (which also does well in Arizona and Texas).

Luscious raspberries thrive especially well in the Northwest, though they also grow in other regions.

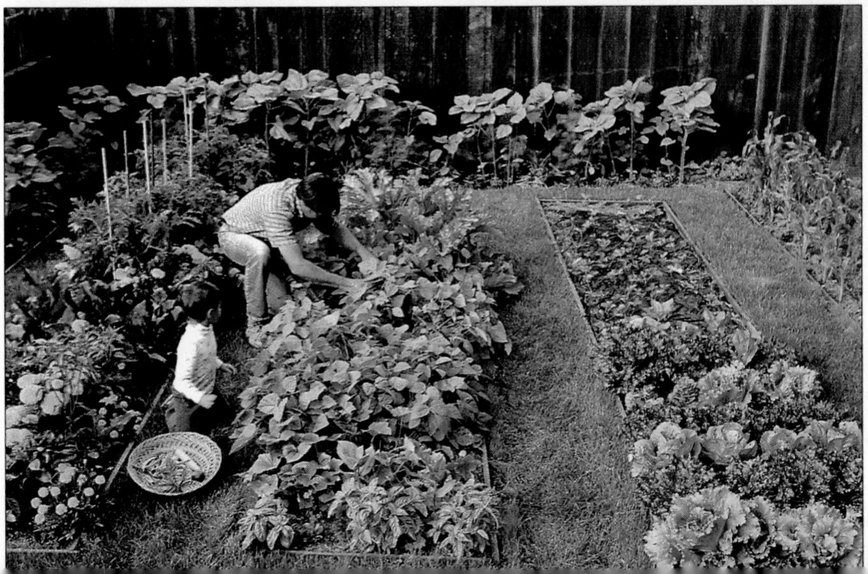

Picking vine-ripened bush beans, Dad and young helper enjoy time together in garden that also provides salad greens, strawberries, tomatoes, and eggplant.

Natives of Western Soil

The West's diverse climates support a great variety of native plants, all likely to grow easily and attractively where they already feel at home.

Old oaks, native to garden site, contribute privacy, shade, and natural grace. Since too much water harms oaks, landscaper selected drought-resistant companion plants.

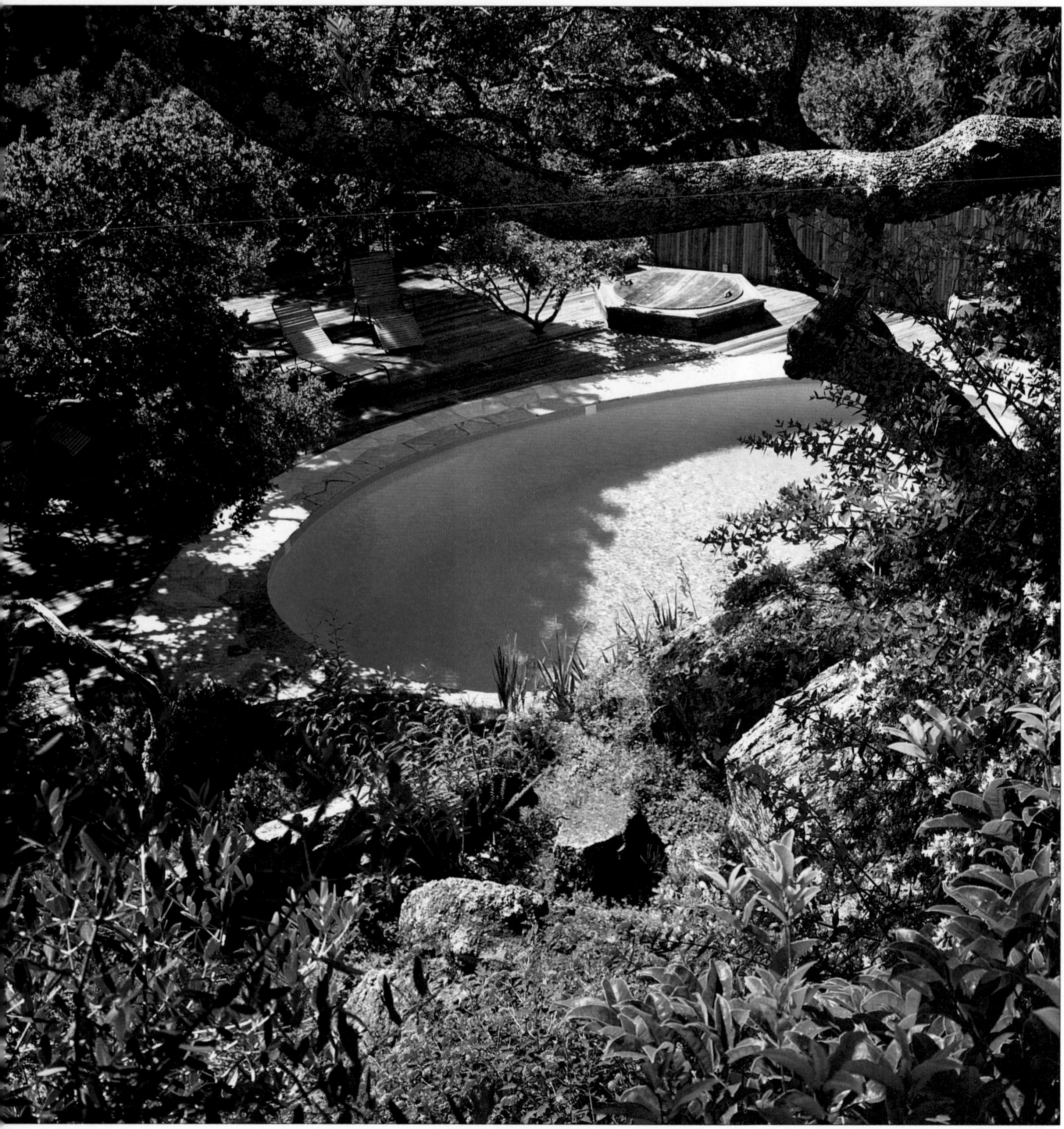

Big, white Matilija poppies (Romneya coulteri) thrive anywhere in West on benign neglect and little water. The British fuss over this Southwest native, one of their prized perennials.

Nature landscaped sculptural Southwest garden, which features ocotillo (Fouquieria splendens), saguaro (Carnegiea gigantea), Opuntia, and barrel cactus. It needs no maintenance beyond occasional grooming.

Baby blue eyes (Nemophila menziesii) sparkles in early spring sunshine. This low-grower can turn garden into wild meadow.

Bright orange California poppies grow alongside 'Blue Ribbon' Dutch iris in an eye-catching combination of complementary colors.

The Garden's Four Seasons

Each season stages an annual spectacle of garden color. In many parts of the West, even winter brings astonishing bloom.

Symphony in pink transforms garden in spring, as 200 'Palestrina' tulips bloom simultaneously with flowering cherry (Prunus yedoensis 'Akebono').

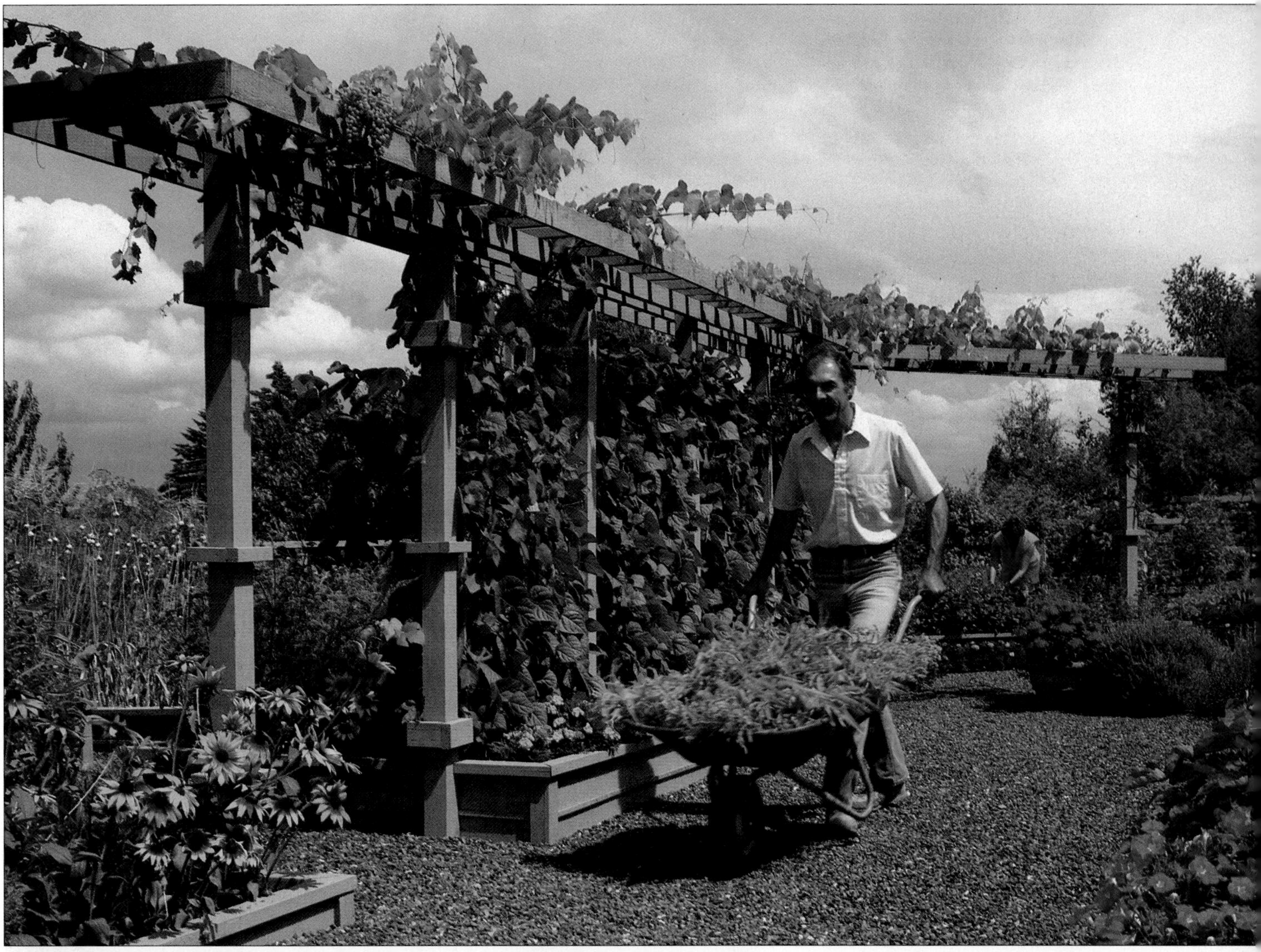

Summer in garden is busy time of year. Here, grapevines and beans clamber vigorously over trellis; Gloriosa daisies (Rudbeckia hirta) soak up sun, and dozens of other edibles and flowers pack nearby raised beds.

Brilliant autumn leaves of liquidambar, birch (Betula), and Japanese maple (Acer palmatum) screen front of house with warm color.

Western winters bring snow to some areas, elsewhere look like spring. Here, early Narcissus 'February Gold' bloom against still-leafless birches (Betula), echoing yellow of Acacia baileyana in background.

The West's 24 Climate Zones

In the sections titled "Western Plant Encyclopedia" (beginning on page 199) and "Planting for a Purpose" (pages 113 to 176), you will find climate zones assigned to almost every listed plant.

If you've been gardening for any time at all, you know why such climate assignments are necessary. The plants we grow in western gardens come from all parts of the world. Because of their greatly varied backgrounds, they differ immensely in their response to the different climates of the West. Many can't live through a cold winter; others require cold winters. Some can't perform well in coastal humidity; others depend on damp air—and so it goes. Many factors combine and interplay to establish climates. These factors form so many different combinations in the West that we have identified two dozen different plant climate zones.

A plant climate zone is an area in which a common set of temperature ranges, humidity patterns, and other geographic and seasonal characteristics allow certain plants to succeed and cause others to fail.

Remember, there's a difference between *weather* and *climate*. Weather is what is going on in the atmosphere outside your window at the moment you read this. Climate is the accumulation of weather effects in your area throughout the cycle of seasons.

Six important factors combine to make up western plant climate zones:

1. ***Distance from the equator (latitude).*** Generally, the farther a spot is from the equator, the longer and colder are its winters. The number of hours of daylight increases in summer and decreases in winter as you progress from the equator toward the pole.

2. ***Elevation.*** High elevations mean longer and colder winters, and comparatively lower night temperatures all through the year.

3. ***Influence of the Pacific Ocean.*** Weather in the western United States derives almost exclusively from two sources. The Pacific Ocean is one of them. The more an area is dominated by the Pacific Ocean's weather, the moister its atmosphere in all seasons, the milder its winters, the cooler its summers, and the more its rainfall is limited to fall, winter, and spring.

4. ***Influence of the continental air mass.*** This is the other major source of our weather in the West. The North American continent creates its own weather (quite different from that created by the ocean). The farther inland you live, the more the continental air mass influences your weather. The more such influence an area gets, the colder its winters, the hotter its summers, and the more likely its precipitation to come at any time of the year.

5. ***Mountains and hills.*** Our systems of mountains and hills act as barriers that determine whether areas beyond them will be influenced mostly by marine air or mostly by continental air—or, as happens in some places, by some of each. The Coast Ranges take some of the marine influence out of air that passes west to east across them. The marine influence that remains is effectively weakened or blocked altogether by the lofty second barrier—the Sierra-Cascades and southern California's interior mountains. Beyond the Rocky Mountains, marine influence is virtually nil—here, arctic air plays a role in the climate. In

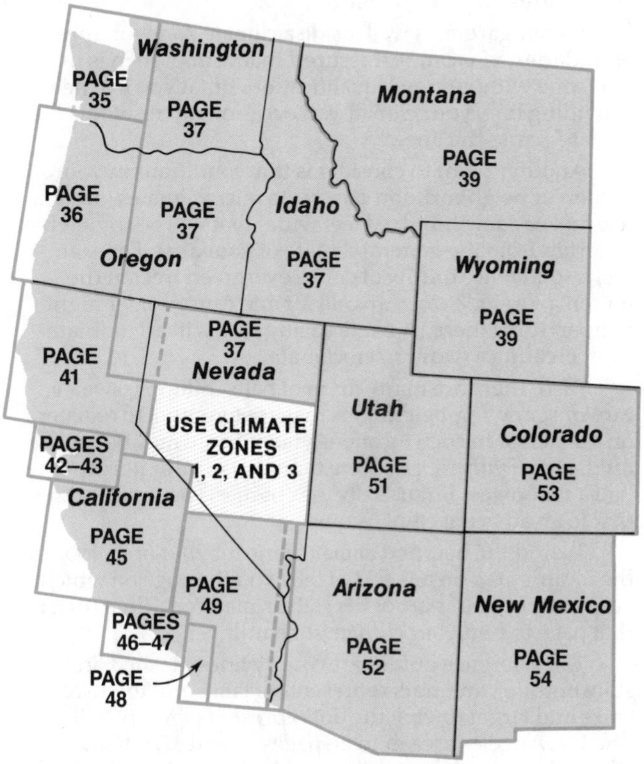

exactly the opposite order, first the Rockies, then the interior ranges, and then the Coast Ranges lessen or eliminate the westward influence of the continental air mass.

6. Local terrain. The five factors mentioned above operate at all seasons. Local terrain has its major effect on the cold air and frosts of fall, winter, and spring.

Warm air rises; cold air sinks. Experienced gardeners understand the practical applications of these physical facts: they know that cold air flows downhill. If yours is a hillside garden—or if your entire community is on sloping ground—your garden will never be quite as cold in winter as will the gardens on the lower ground beyond. The bands of a hillside or slope are called *thermal belts*. The lowlands and river bottoms into which the cold air flows are called *cold-air basins*. Above the thermal belt, winter air can be so cold (because of the elevation influence mentioned on page 33) that the temperature is as low as in the cold-air basin at the base—or even lower.

The 24 plant climate zones used in this book were mapped by drawing lines at certain latitudes (distances from the equator), drawing other lines representing the typical penetrations of marine and continental air, and drawing still more lines for elevations and the major thermal belts and cold basins. The resulting climate areas are relatively constant within their boundaries.

Do not consider the lines on the maps to be rigid. Only in a very few places in the West are the climate-controlling factors so consistent that we can draw a line on the ground with a stick and say, "On this side of the line is climate X and on the other side, climate Y." In most cases, such a line would be nonsense. As the influence of each of the factors listed previously rises or falls, the lines shift gradually back and forth.

If your garden is well inside a climate zone's mapped boundaries, you can rest assured that your garden is in that zone without much qualification. But if you live near a dividing line, your climate can occasionally resemble the climate across the line.

Another point to consider is that conditions in your garden or neighborhood can create microclimates (areas a few feet or a few hundred feet wide) that will be somewhat different from the general climate of your area. For example, a solid fence or row of dense evergreen trees at the bottom of a slope can trap cold air and cause colder night temperatures there. A south-facing wall will accumulate heat, creating a warm microclimate.

Also, there are many thermal belts, hilltops, swales, canyons, and fog-belt fingers that are too small to register on the maps. In such locations your climate may be *slightly* milder or *slightly* more severe than that of your neighbors half a mile away. But usually the change is no greater than that to an adjacent climate zone.

To find the mapped climate zone for your area, look at the locator map on page 33. It tells you the page on which your state or your part of the state is mapped. Then turn to that page to find your climate zone number.

The reference guides are county lines (dashed lines), state borders, and dots representing cities and towns. In cities and larger towns, the dot represents the city hall. The Los Angeles area map on pages 46 and 47, where county lines are few and cities are big, is further oriented by freeway routes. Communities shown on the maps are not necessarily the largest or most important. Many smaller towns are included because they happen to be on or near a transition line between two zones.

Descriptions of the plant climate zones follow. Zones are arranged from harshest (Zone 1) to mildest (Zone 24). In the chapter of this book called "Planting for a Purpose" and in the "Western Plant Encyclopedia," climate adaptability is repeatedly indicated by two zone numbers connected by a dash (as "Zones 4–9"). This means that the plant is recommended for all the zones from first to second number, inclusive. Temperatures are in degrees Fahrenheit.

ZONE 1 *Coldest Winters in the West*

Zones 1, 2, and 3 are the snowy parts of the West—the regions where snow falls and stays on the ground (a day, a week, or all winter) every year. Of the three snowy-winter climates, Zone 1 is the coldest.

The extreme winter cold of Zone 1 can be caused by any or all of the three factors that can make cold winters: latitude, influence of continental air mass, and elevation. Most of Zone 1 in the Northwest and Rocky Mountain states does indeed get its cold winter temperatures from all three contributing factors.

In this zone, the typical growing season (period between last frost in springtime and first frost in fall) lasts for not much longer than 100 days—although it may average as high as 180 days in some parts. Throughout most of Zone 1, frosts can occur on any day of the year.

ZONE 2 *Second-Coldest Western Climate*

Here, too, snow is to be expected in winter. The chief difference between Zone 2 and Zone 1 is that the record low temperatures and the average annual low temperatures are not as low in Zone 2 as in Zone 1. And this makes a difference with many desirable garden plants.

In Zone 2, protection in winter can make it possible to grow plants that ordinarily would perish from the effects of wind, cold, and winter sun. Areas of Utah sheltered by the Wasatch Range and moderated by the Great Salt Lake have milder winters than surrounding areas.

In the northerly latitudes and interior areas where the continental air mass rules supreme, the difference between Zone 2 and Zone 1 is mostly one of elevation. Notice that some Zone 2 exists along parts of the Snake River of Idaho, and the Grande Ronde and Burnt rivers of Oregon, along the Columbia and Spokane rivers in eastern Washington, and in the lakes region of the Idaho panhandle. In Colorado, Zone 2 comprises the river valleys of the western portion of the state and the low-elevation plains of the south-east corner of the state. Zone 2 includes

(Continued on page 38)

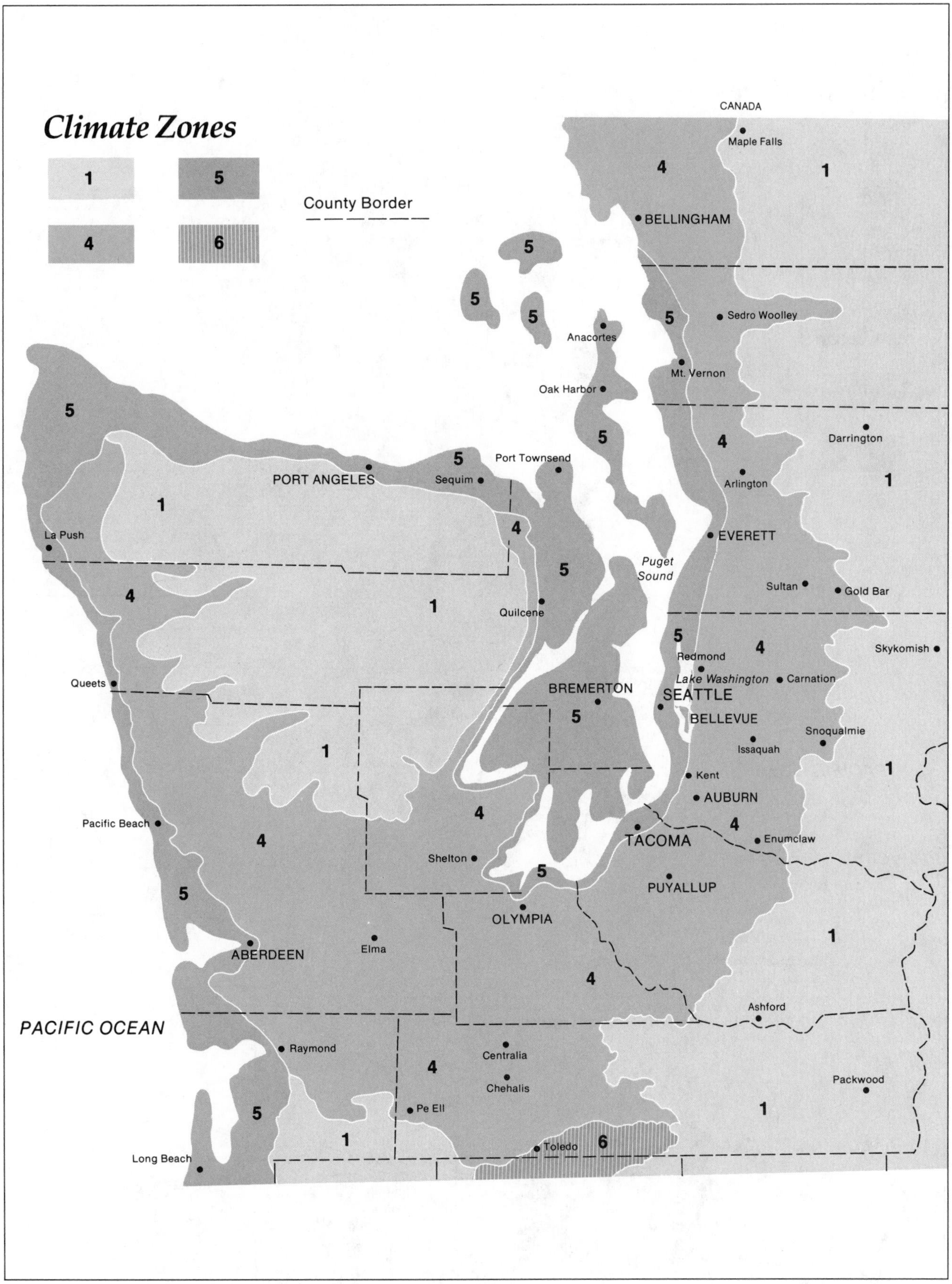
Climate Zones
1
5
4
6
County Border
CANADA
Maple Falls
BELLINGHAM
Sedro Woolley
Anacortes
Mt. Vernon
Oak Harbor
Darrington
Port Townsend
PORT ANGELES
Sequim
Arlington
La Push
EVERETT
Puget Sound
Sultan
Gold Bar
Quilcene
Skykomish
Redmond
Lake Washington
Carnation
Queets
BREMERTON
SEATTLE
BELLEVUE
Snoqualmie
Issaquah
Kent
AUBURN
Pacific Beach
TACOMA
Enumclaw
Shelton
PUYALLUP
OLYMPIA
ABERDEEN
Elma
Ashford
PACIFIC OCEAN
Raymond
Centralia
Chehalis
Packwood
Pe Ell
Toledo
Long Beach

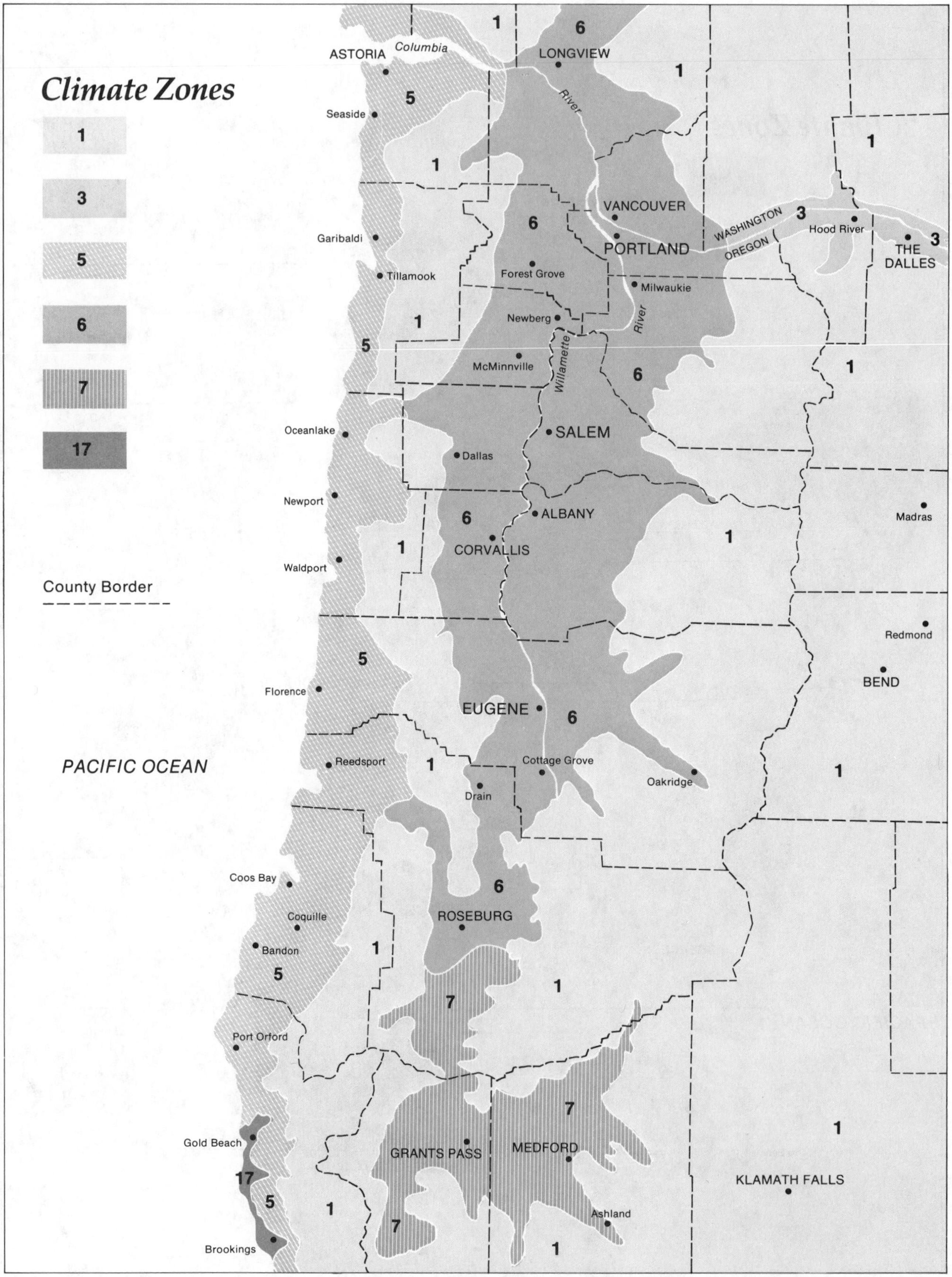
Climate Zones
1
3
5
6
7
17
County Border
PACIFIC OCEAN
ASTORIA
Columbia
River
LONGVIEW
Seaside
VANCOUVER
PORTLAND
WASHINGTON
OREGON
Hood River
THE DALLES
Garibaldi
Tillamook
Forest Grove
Milwaukie
Newberg
McMinnville
Willamette
River
Oceanlake
SALEM
Dallas
Newport
ALBANY
CORVALLIS
Madras
Waldport
Redmond
BEND
Florence
EUGENE
Reedsport
Cottage Grove
Oakridge
Drain
Coos Bay
Coquille
ROSEBURG
Bandon
Port Orford
Gold Beach
GRANTS PASS
MEDFORD
KLAMATH FALLS
Ashland
Brookings

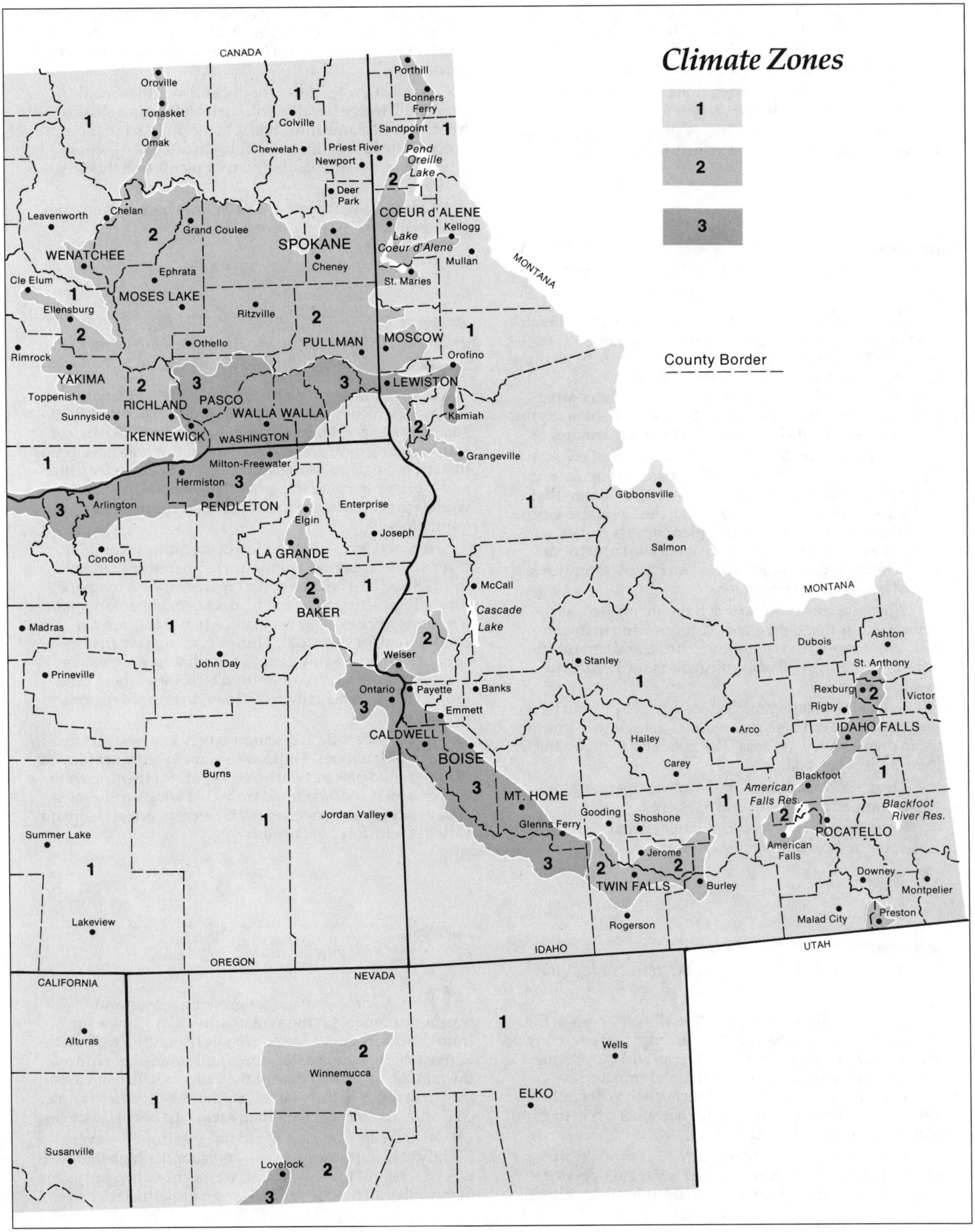

Climate Zones
1
2
3
County Border
CANADA
MONTANA
WASHINGTON
OREGON
IDAHO
NEVADA
CALIFORNIA
UTAH
Oroville
Tonasket
Omak
Colville
Chewelah
Porthill
Bonners Ferry
Sandpoint
Priest River
Newport
Pend Oreille Lake
Deer Park
Leavenworth
Chelan
Grand Coulee
WENATCHEE
Ephrata
Cle Elum
Ellensburg
MOSES LAKE
SPOKANE
Cheney
COEUR d'ALENE
Lake Coeur d'Alene
Kellogg
Mullan
St. Maries
Ritzville
Othello
PULLMAN
MOSCOW
Orofino
Rimrock
YAKIMA
Toppenish
Sunnyside
RICHLAND
PASCO
KENNEWICK
WALLA WALLA
LEWISTON
Kamiah
Grangeville
Milton-Freewater
Hermiston
Arlington
PENDLETON
Enterprise
Elgin
Joseph
Gibbonsville
Salmon
Condon
LA GRANDE
BAKER
McCall
Cascade Lake
Madras
Prineville
John Day
Weiser
Ontario
Payette
Banks
Emmett
Stanley
CALDWELL
BOISE
Burns
Jordan Valley
MT. HOME
Glenns Ferry
Hailey
Carey
Arco
Gooding
Shoshone
Jerome
TWIN FALLS
Burley
Rogerson
Dubois
Ashton
St. Anthony
Rexburg
Rigby
Victor
IDAHO FALLS
Blackfoot
American Falls Res.
Blackfoot River Res.
POCATELLO
American Falls
Downey
Montpelier
Malad City
Preston
Summer Lake
Lakeview
Alturas
Susanville
Winnemucca
Wells
ELKO
Lovelock

most of the high territory of New Mexico—only a small portion of the state lies in Zone 1. The Zone 2 areas in California and Arizona are at higher elevations, which are nevertheless not as cold as the higher areas of Zone 1.

During a 20-year period in Zone 2, annual low temperatures ranged from −3° to −34°F.

The growing season averages about 150 days. Some places can count on almost 200 frost-free days in a row.

ZONE 3 *Mildest of High-Elevation and Interior Climates*

This is the mildest of the snowy-winter climates. East of the Cascades in the Northwest, the Zone 3 areas are the ones that often are called "banana belts." Of course, the only place you can grow the real, fruiting banana satisfactorily outdoors is in the tropics. But the comparatively mild winter lows of Zone 3 allow gardeners to grow such plants as English boxwood and winter jasmine.

The portion of Zone 3 from Hood River to Lewiston is slightly lower in elevation than the surrounding Zone 2. This fact, combined with the influence of Pacific air that spills over the Cascades and through the Columbia Gorge, moderates most winters. Much planting is based on winter lows of 10° to 15°F. In an occasional winter, arctic air forces temperatures much lower. Such winters limit selection of broad-leafed evergreens.

Absolute cold is not so much the enemy here as drying winds that dehydrate plants growing in frozen soil. Wind protection, mulching, shade, and careful late autumn watering will help you grow many borderline evergreens.

In California, the Zone 3 areas often happen to be the lowest parts of the high mountains—areas where many cabin owners keep gardens. The zone also includes the Reno area of Nevada.

Over a 20-year period, minimum temperatures in Zone 3 ranged from 13° to −24°F.

Average growing season is about 160 days. In Walla Walla, the season lasts almost 220 days.

ZONE 4 *Cold-Winter Parts of Western Washington*

This is one of the smallest climate zones in the West. It is the region west of the Cascades that gets considerable influence from the Pacific Ocean and Puget Sound —but also is affected by the continental air mass, by higher elevation, or by both. It touches salt water only in Whatcom County, but in some higher spots it is in distant view of the ocean or the sound.

It differs from neighboring Zone 5 principally in greater frequency of extremely low winter temperatures, a shorter growing season, and considerably more rainfall.

The two Puget Sound climates (Zones 4 and 5) can be found in the same neighborhood, a fact that is behind much of the familiar northwestern talk about warm or cold gardens.

Some of the tenderer rhododendrons that Seattle grows will freeze here, as will some of the rarer shrubs from New Zealand and Chile. On the other hand, no zone grows better perennials and bulbs than Zone 4. People who like woodland plants and rock plants find this area a paradise.

Over a 20-year period, winter lows here ranged from 19° down to −7°F.

ZONE 5 *Marine Influence Along the Northwest Coast and Puget Sound*

Mild ocean air brings relatively warm winters to this area, which is on the same latitude as Duluth, Minnesota, and Bangor, Maine. The climate is much like that of southern England, and the gardens in this area have benefited from England's long and successful search for better and more varied garden plants. The region is one of the world's great centers of rhododendron culture and rock gardening.

Temperatures of 0°F. or lower are quite uncommon. Over a 20-year period, minimum temperatures ranged from 28° to 1°F. The occasional big freeze, with temperatures plummeting to near 0°F., does considerable damage if it comes very early or very late, when plants are not conditioned for such cold. These occasional big freezes should not serve as the gauge of hardiness; even native plants have been killed or injured by some of them. The growing season may run to 250 days in favored regions near salt water.

Many waterside areas show a very low heat accumulation in the summer. Those who want to grow heat-loving plants should pick out the hottest spots for them; a south wall or a west wall sheltered from cold winds will almost always supply such needed heat. Select peach and tomato varieties with low heat needs.

ZONE 6 *Willamette Valley*

A somewhat longer growing season and warmer summers set the Willamette Valley climate off from the coast–Puget Sound climate (Zone 5). The Coast Range tempers the coastal winds and somewhat reduces the rainfall, but the climate of the valley is still essentially maritime much of the year, hence getting much less winter cold and less summer heat than areas east of the Cascades.

Average lows are similar to those of Zone 5—even slightly colder in some places—but summer high temperatures average 5° to 9°F. warmer, warm enough to put sugar in the 'Elberta' peaches and to speed growth of such evergreens as abelia and nandina. The long, mild growing season has made the Willamette Valley one of the West's great growing areas for nursery stock. Many of the West's (and the nation's) fruit and shade trees, deciduous shrubs, and broad-leafed evergreens start life here.

Any mention of the Willamette Valley must include roses and rhododendrons, both of which attain near-perfection here. Broad-leafed evergreens generally are at their clean, green best; choice rhododendrons, azaleas, and pieris grow as basic landscaping shrubs.

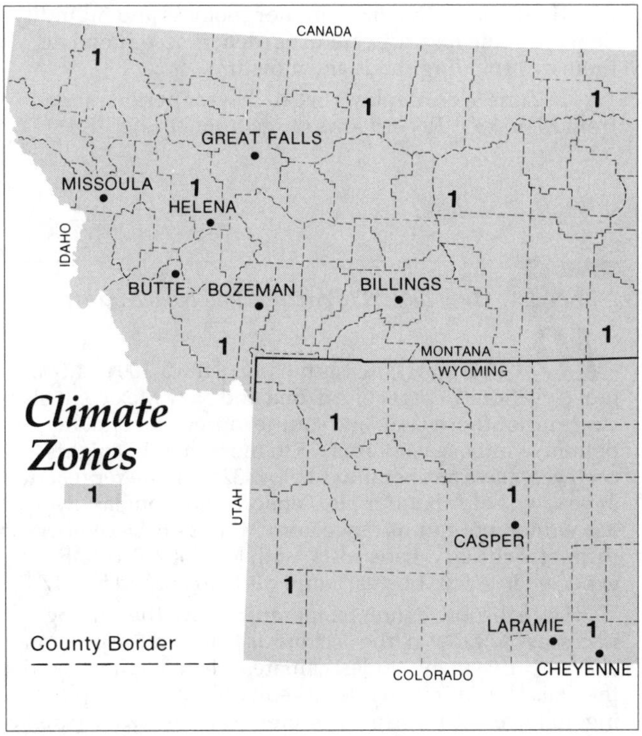

ZONE 7 *Oregon's Rogue River Valley and California's Digger Pine Belt*

Zone 7 appears over quite a few thousand square miles in the regions west of the Sierra-Cascades. Because of the influence of latitude, this climate is found at low elevations in a valley in Oregon (the Rogue Valley) but at middle elevations in California (the low mountains, most of which can be identified by native Digger pines).

Hot summers and mild but pronounced winters give this area sharply defined seasons without severe winter cold or enervating humidity. The climate pleases plants that require a marked seasonal pattern to do well—peony, iris, lilac, and flowering cherry, for example. Deciduous fruit trees that require a marked seasonal pattern do well also; the region is noted for its pears, apples, peaches, and cherries.

Gardeners in a few spots in the Coast Ranges near San Francisco Bay will be surprised to find their gardens mapped in Zone 7—there isn't a Digger pine to be seen. These are hilltop and ridge-top areas that are too high (and hence too cold in winter) to be included in milder Zones 15 and 16.

For such a big area, it is of course impossible to state exact low temperatures. But at weather-recording stations in the Zone 7 area, the typical winter lows range from 23° to 9°F., the record lows from 15° to −1°F.

ZONE 8 *Cold-Air Basins of California's Central Valley*

Only a shade of difference exists between Zone 8 and Zone 9, but it's an important difference—crucial in some cases. Zone 9 is a thermal belt, meaning that cold air can flow from it to lower ground—and the lower ground is here in Zone 8. Citrus furnish the most meaningful illustration. Lemons, oranges, and grapefruit cannot be grown commercially in Zone 8 because winter nights frequently are cold enough to injure or even kill the trees, and the trees would need regular heating. The same winter cold can damage many garden plants.

Zone 8 differs from Zone 14, which it joins near the latitudes of North Sacramento and Modesto, in that Zone 14 occasionally gets some marine influence.

Low temperatures in Zone 8 over a 20-year period ranged from 29° to 13°F.

Certain features that Zone 8 and 9 share are described under Zone 9.

ZONE 9 *Thermal Belts of California's Central Valley*

Repeating the example cited for Zone 8, the biggest readily apparent difference between Zones 8 and 9 is that Zone 9 is a safer climate for citrus. Most of the valley's commercial citrus crops are grown in Zone 9. The same distinction, thermal belt versus cold basin, is reflected for certain species and varieties—hibiscus, melaleuca, pittosporum, and other plants—recommended for Zone 9 but not for Zone 8.

Zones 8 and 9 have these features in common: summer daytime temperatures are high, sunshine is almost constant during the growing season, and growing seasons are long. Deciduous fruits and vegetables of nearly every kind thrive in these long, hot summers; winter cold is just adequate to satisfy dormancy requirements of the fruit trees. Fiercely cold, piercing north winds blow for several days at a time in winter, but they are more distressing to gardeners than to garden plants. Tule fogs (dense fogs that rise from the ground under certain peculiar weather conditions) appear and stay for hours or days during winter. The fogs usually hug the ground at night and rise to 800 to 1,000 feet by afternoon. Heat-loving plants such as oleander and crape myrtle perform at their peak in Zones 8 and

9 (and 14). Plants that like summer coolness and humidity demand some fussing; careful gardeners accommodate them by providing shade and moisture.

In Zone 9, winter lows over a 20-year period ranged from 28° to 18°F. Record lows range from 21° to 15°F.

ZONE 10 *High Desert of Arizona and New Mexico*

This zone consists mostly of the 3,300 to 4,500-foot elevations in parts of Arizona and New Mexico. It also exists in southern Utah and southern Nevada. It has a definite winter season: from 75 to more than 100 nights each year have temperatures below 32°F. In the representative towns of Albuquerque, Benson, and Douglas, average winter minimums range from 31° to 24°F. December through February. Late frosts, with lows of 25° to 22°F., are expected in April. Lowest temperature recorded is – 17°F.

Here the low winter temperatures give the chilling necessary to grow all the deciduous fruit and the perennials that thrive in the coldest climates—lilacs, spiraea, and the like. The definite winter season calls for spring planting, followed by a spring–summer growing season (unlike neighboring Zones 12 and 13, where most planting should be done in fall).

Distinguishing this climate from Zone 11 are more rainfall and less wind. Annual rainfall averages 12 inches, with half of that amount falling in July and August. In the eastern parts of Zone 10, summer's precipitation provides more water than winter's.

ZONE 11 *Medium to High Desert of California and Southern Nevada*

In varying degrees, this climate has similarities to its two extremely different neighboring climates—the cold-winter Zones 1, 2, and 3 and the subtropical low desert, Zone 13.

It is characterized by wide swings in temperature, both between summer and winter and between day and night. Winter lows of 11° to 0°F. have occurred within the area. Highest summer temperatures recorded range from 111° to 117°F. On the average, there are 110 days in summer with temperatures above 90°F. and about 85 nights in winter with temperatures below 32°F.

Hot summer days are followed by cool nights; freezing nights are often followed by daytime temperatures of 60°F.

The hazards of the climate are late spring frosts and desert winds. Wind protection greatly increases the chance of plant survival and the rate of plant growth.

If soil moisture is inadequate, the characteristic winter winds and bright sunlight may combine to kill or badly injure normally hardy evergreen plants by desiccation.

ZONE 12 *Arizona's Intermediate Desert*

The crucial difference between Arizona's intermediate desert climate and the low desert (Zone 13) is in the number of days of killing frost. Tucson has an average of 22 nights with temperatures below 32°F.; Wickenburg, 65. Extreme low temperatures of 6°F. have been recorded. The mean maximum temperatures in July and August are 5° or 6°F. cooler than the highs of Zone 13.

Many of the subtropicals that do well in Zone 13 are not reliably hardy here. However, the average winter temperatures are high enough to encourage growing of many such plants, with protection in extreme winters.

Although winter temperatures are lower than in Zone 13, the total hours of cold are not enough to provide sufficient winter chilling for some of the deciduous fruits and deciduous flowering shrubs.

Between March and May, strong wind (25–40 miles per hour) can cause damage to young tender growth.

Here, as in Zone 13 and the eastern parts of Zone 10, summer rains are to be expected. In some cases they are more dependable than winter rains. And, as in Zone 13, the growing season starts in September or October (often the best planting season).

ZONE 13 *Low or Subtropical Desert Areas*

The low desert, from below sea level in the Imperial Valley to 1,100 feet in the Phoenix area, is rightly classified as subtropical desert. Mean daily maximum temperatures in the hottest month (July) range from 106° to 108°F. The winters are short and mild. Frosts, which can be expected from December 1 to February 15, are of short duration. There are rarely more than 6 to 10 nights with temperatures below 32°F. Although the average minimum temperature in the winter months is 37°F., lows of 19° to 13°F. have been recorded.

Winter lows and summer highs exclude some of the subtropicals grown in southern California's mild-winter zones (22 to 24). However, numerous subtropicals with high heat requirements thrive in this climate. Some examples are dates, grapefruit, bauhinia, beaumontia, many cassias, and thevetia.

As in Zone 12, spring winds and summer storms are a factor in gardening: the rains supply some soil moisture but not enough to support a garden. And on many afternoons dense clouds shield plants from the hot sun.

The gardening year begins in September and October for most vegetables and annual flowers, although corn and melons are planted in late winter. Growth of the fall-planted plants is slow through the short winter, picks up speed in mid-February, and races through the increasing temperatures of March and April.

The lack of winter cold rules out fruits and flowering fruits with high chilling requirements, such as most apples.

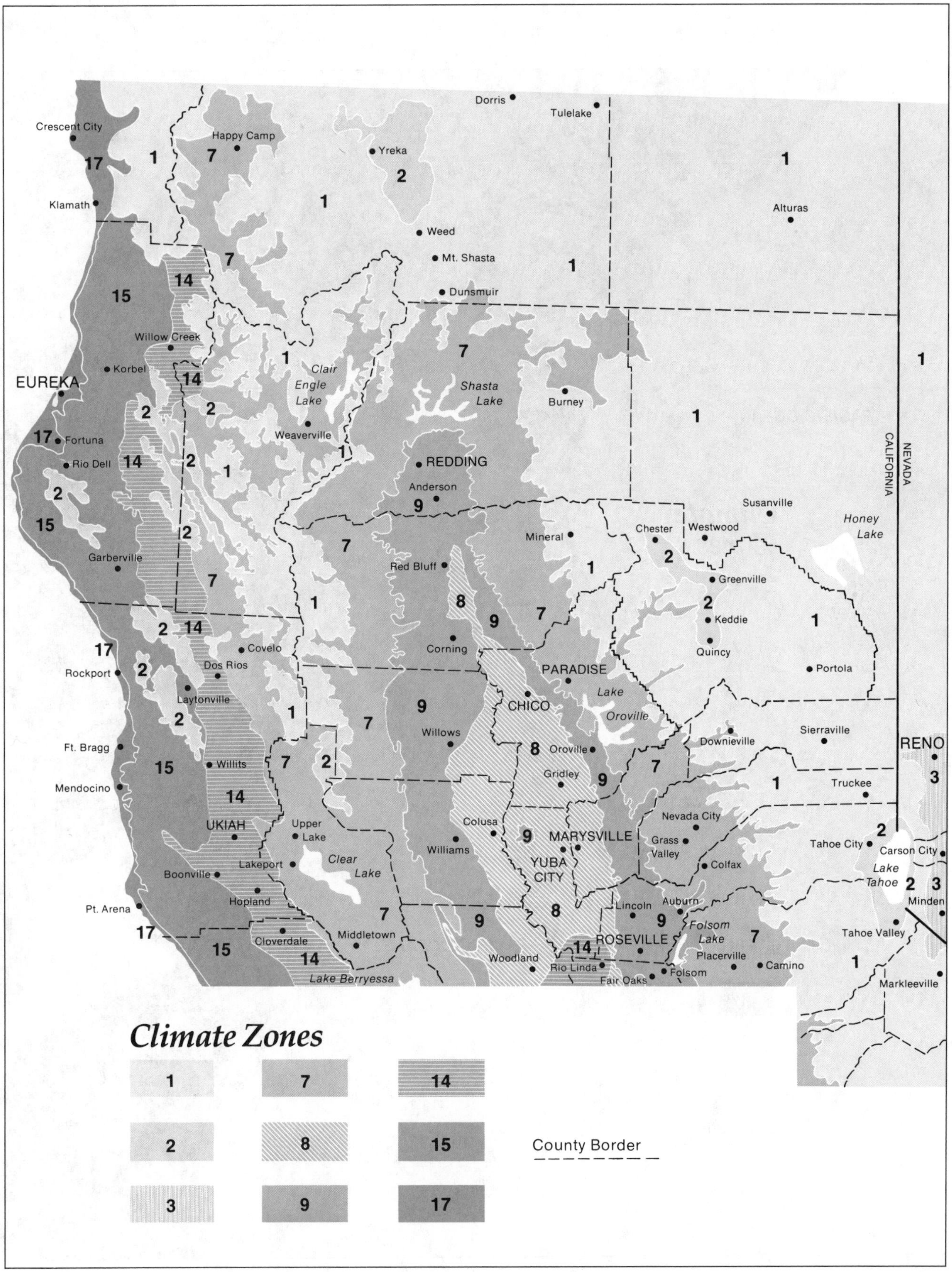
Crescent City
Happy Camp
Yreka
Dorris
Tulelake
Klamath
Weed
Mt. Shasta
Dunsmuir
Alturas
Willow Creek
Korbel
EUREKA
Clair Engle Lake
Shasta Lake
Burney
Fortuna
Rio Dell
Weaverville
REDDING
Anderson
NEVADA
CALIFORNIA
Susanville
Honey Lake
Mineral
Chester
Westwood
Garberville
Red Bluff
Greenville
Keddie
Quincy
Corning
Covelo
Rockport
Dos Rios
Laytonville
PARADISE
Lake Oroville
CHICO
Portola
Willows
Downieville
Sierraville
Ft. Bragg
Oroville
Willits
Gridley
RENO
Mendocino
Truckee
UKIAH
Upper Lake
Colusa
MARYSVILLE
Nevada City
Grass Valley
Williams
Clear Lake
Lakeport
YUBA CITY
Colfax
Tahoe City
Carson City
Lake Tahoe
Boonville
Hopland
Auburn
Minden
Pt. Arena
Lincoln
Folsom Lake
Tahoe Valley
Cloverdale
Middletown
ROSEVILLE
Placerville
Woodland
Rio Linda
Camino
Lake Berryessa
Fair Oaks
Folsom
Markleeville
Climate Zones
1
7
14
2
8
15
3
9
17
County Border

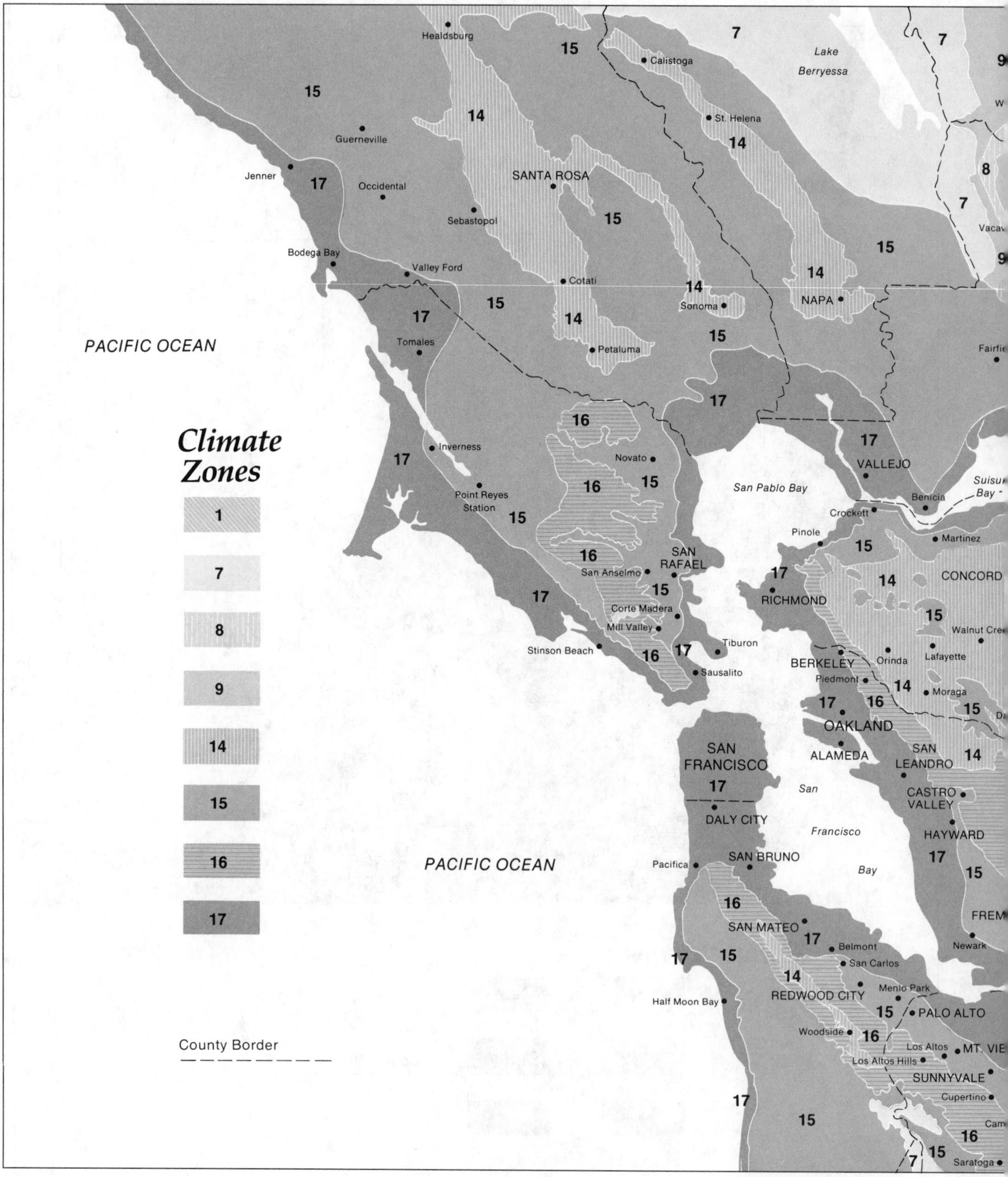
Climate Zones
1
7
8
9
14
15
16
17
County Border
PACIFIC OCEAN
PACIFIC OCEAN
Healdsburg
Calistoga
Lake Berryessa
St. Helena
Guerneville
Jenner
Occidental
SANTA ROSA
Sebastopol
Bodega Bay
Valley Ford
Cotati
Sonoma
NAPA
Tomales
Petaluma
Inverness
Novato
VALLEJO
Benicia
San Pablo Bay
Point Reyes Station
Crockett
Pinole
Martinez
CONCORD
San Anselmo
SAN RAFAEL
RICHMOND
Corte Madera
Mill Valley
Stinson Beach
Tiburon
Sausalito
BERKELEY
Orinda
Lafayette
Piedmont
Moraga
OAKLAND
ALAMEDA
SAN FRANCISCO
SAN LEANDRO
CASTRO VALLEY
San Francisco Bay
DALY CITY
HAYWARD
Pacifica
SAN BRUNO
SAN MATEO
Newark
Belmont
San Carlos
Menlo Park
REDWOOD CITY
Half Moon Bay
PALO ALTO
Woodside
Los Altos
Los Altos Hills
SUNNYVALE
Cupertino
Saratoga

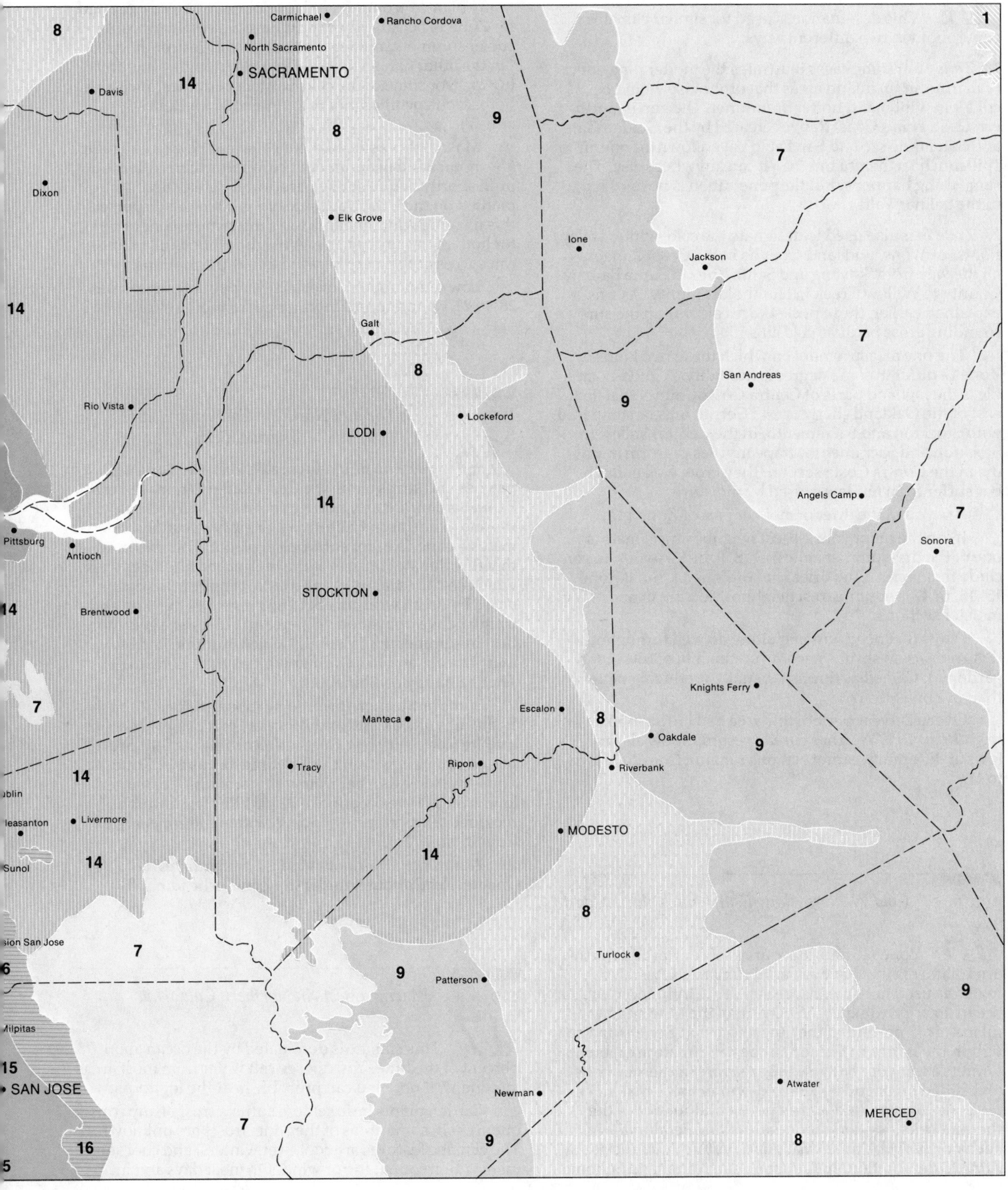
Carmichael
Rancho Cordova
1
8
North Sacramento
SACRAMENTO
Davis
14
9
8
7
Dixon
Elk Grove
Ione
Jackson
14
Galt
7
8
San Andreas
Rio Vista
9
Lockeford
LODI
14
Angels Camp
7
Pittsburg
Antioch
Sonora
STOCKTON
14
Brentwood
Knights Ferry
7
Escalon
Manteca
8
Oakdale
9
14
Tracy
Ripon
Riverbank
ublin
leasanton
Livermore
MODESTO
Sunol
14
14
8
sion San Jose
7
Turlock
6
9
Patterson
9
ilpitas
15
SAN JOSE
Atwater
Newman
MERCED
7
16
9
8
5

ZONE 14 *Northern California's Inland Areas with Some Ocean Influence*

This designation is used for similar climates that come about in two different ways:

1. ***Zone 14*** in some cases illustrates the moderating effect of marine air on inland areas that otherwise would be colder in winter and hotter in summer. The gap in northern California's Coast Ranges created by the Golden Gate and San Francisco and San Pablo bays allows marine air to spill much farther inland than it can anywhere else. The same thing happens, but the penetration is not as deep, in the Salinas Valley.

2. ***Zone 14*** is also used to designate the cold-winter valley floors, canyons, and land-troughs in the Coast Ranges—all the way from Solvang and Santa Ynez in Santa Barbara County to Willow Creek in Humboldt County. As was explained earlier, these pockets are colder than the surrounding areas because cold air sinks.

The one measurement on which these two kinds of Zone 14 differ in some degree is humidity. A good example is the lowland parts of Contra Costa County that lie east of the Oakland–Berkeley–El Cerrito hills as compared with Stockton and Sacramento, in the Central Valley. In Stockton and Sacramento, crape myrtles perform mightily; in the Contra Costa section, they grow well enough but suffer from mildew caused by moisture.

Are you in the drier or moister part of Zone 14?

If, on the map, your closest neighboring climate is one of the dry-summer zones—7, 8, 9, or 18—you can conclude that yours is the drier kind of Zone 14. But if Zone 15, 16, or 17 is your nearest neighbor, you are in one of the moister sections.

Fruits that need winter chilling do well throughout this zone, as do shrubs needing summer heat (oleander, gardenia). Camellias flourish, usually producing better than in Zones 15–17.

Over a 20-year period, this area had lows ranging from 26° to 16°F. Weather bureau records show all-time lows at different weather stations ranging from 20° down to 11°F.

ZONE 15 *Cold Winters Along California's North Coast*

Zones 15 and 16 are areas of central and northern California that have a coastal climate. "Coastal climate" as used here means areas that are influenced by ocean air approximately 85 percent of the time and by inland air 15 percent of the time. Note that Zone 16 is also within the northern California coastal climate area, but its winters are milder because the areas are in thermal belts (explained on page 34). The cold-winter areas that make up Zone 15 are in cold-air basins, on hilltops above the thermal belts, or—as is the case north of Petaluma—in such northerly latitudes that plant performance dictates a Zone 15 designation. In Contra Costa, Napa, and Sonoma counties, Zone 15 exists on hills above the colder valley floors, which are designated Zone 14.

In Zone 15 the finest climate for fuchsias begins. Many plants recommended for Zone 15 are not suggested for Zone 14 because they must have a moister atmosphere, cooler summers, milder winters, or all three conditions. On the other hand, Zone 15 also gets enough winter chilling to favor some of the cold-winter specialties, such as herbaceous peonies (not recommended for Zones 16 and 17).

Most of this zone, like Zones 16 and 17, gets a regular afternoon wind in summer. It blows from early afternoon until shortly before sunset. Trees and dense shrubs planted on the windward side of a garden can disperse this nagging wind, making the garden more comfortable for both plants and people. A neighborhood full of trees can successfully keep the wind above the rooftops.

Low temperatures over a 20-year period range from 28° to 21°F., and record lows range from 26° to 16°F.

ZONE 16 *Central and Northern California Coast Thermal Belts*

Here's a much-favored climate that exists in patches and strips along the Coast Ranges from western Santa Barbara County north to northern Marin County. It's one of northern California's finest horticultural climates—especially for subtropical plants. The reason is that this climate consists of the thermal belts (slopes from which cold air drains) in the coastal climate area (dominated by ocean weather about 85 percent of the time and by inland weather about 15 percent). This zone gets more heat in summer than Zone 17, which is dominated by maritime air, and has warmer winters than Zone 15. That's a happy combination.

Some of the more favored portions of Zone 16, such as the hills of Oakland and Berkeley, practically never see a white frost. Very few weather-recording stations are placed squarely within the indefinite borders of Zone 16. Those that do exist there show a typical range of winter lows over a 20-year period of 32° to 19°F. The lowest recorded temperatures at points within the zone range from 25° to 18°F.

A summer afternoon wind is an integral part of this climate. Read about it under the Zone 15 heading.

ZONE 17 *Marine Effects in Northern California*

This climate is dominated by the ocean about 98 percent of the time. You can see salt water from most areas in Zone 17; if not, you can probably hear the foghorns.

Garden plants here seldom suffer a frost of any consequence—in some areas of the zone, frosts are unknown. The climatic features are cool, wet winters, and cool summers with frequent fog or wind. On most days and in

(Continued on page 50)

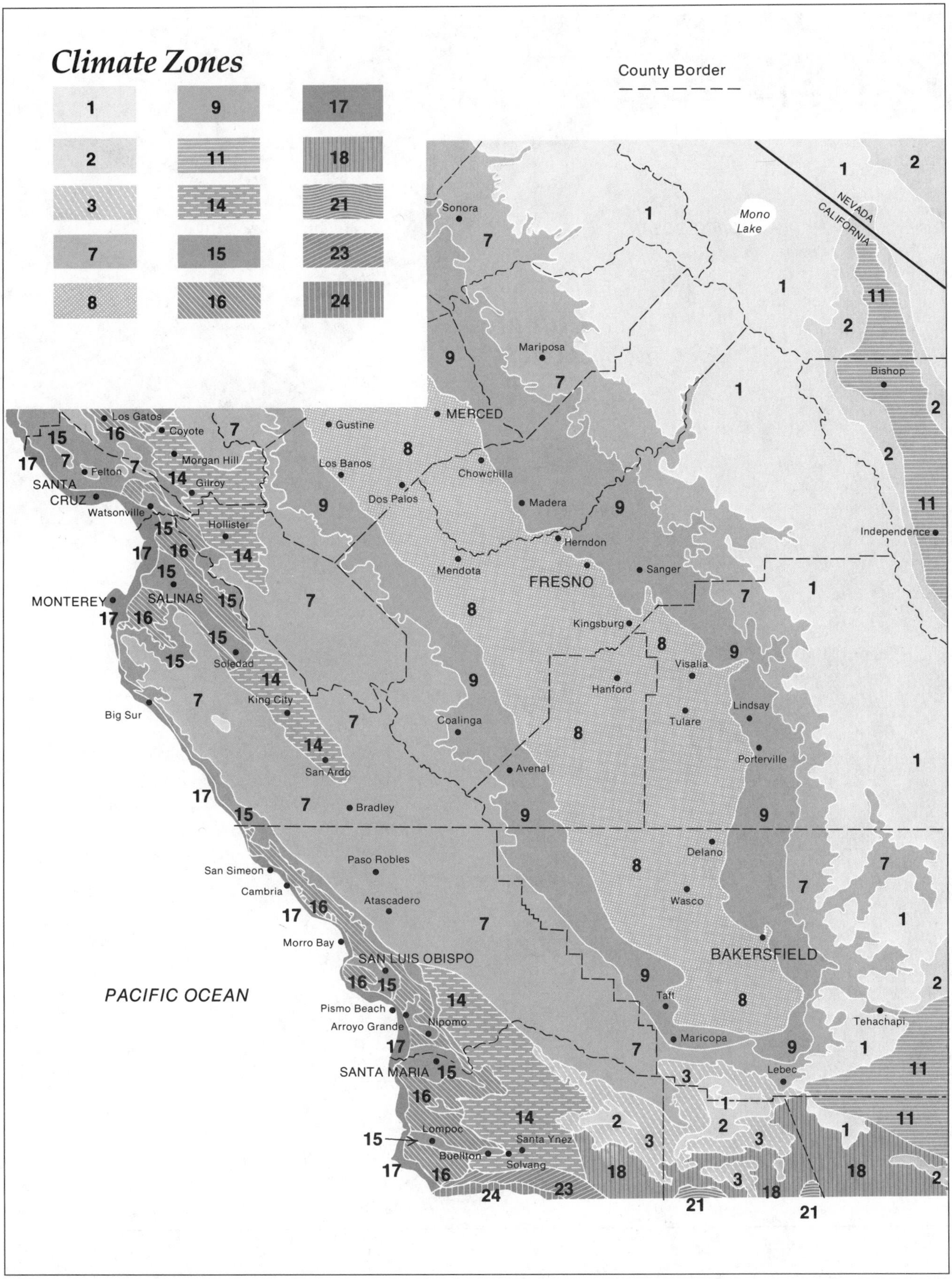
Climate Zones
1
2
3
7
8
9
11
14
15
16
17
18
21
23
24
County Border
NEVADA
CALIFORNIA
Mono Lake
Sonora
Mariposa
MERCED
Bishop
Independence
Los Gatos
Coyote
Gustine
Morgan Hill
Felton
SANTA CRUZ
Gilroy
Watsonville
Los Banos
Chowchilla
Dos Palos
Madera
Hollister
Herndon
Mendota
Sanger
FRESNO
MONTEREY
SALINAS
Kingsburg
Soledad
Visalia
Hanford
King City
Big Sur
Tulare
Lindsay
Coalinga
Porterville
San Ardo
Avenal
Bradley
Delano
Paso Robles
San Simeon
Cambria
Atascadero
Wasco
Morro Bay
BAKERSFIELD
SAN LUIS OBISPO
PACIFIC OCEAN
Taft
Pismo Beach
Arroyo Grande
Nipomo
Tehachapi
Maricopa
SANTA MARIA
Lebec
Lompoc
Santa Ynez
Buellton
Solvang

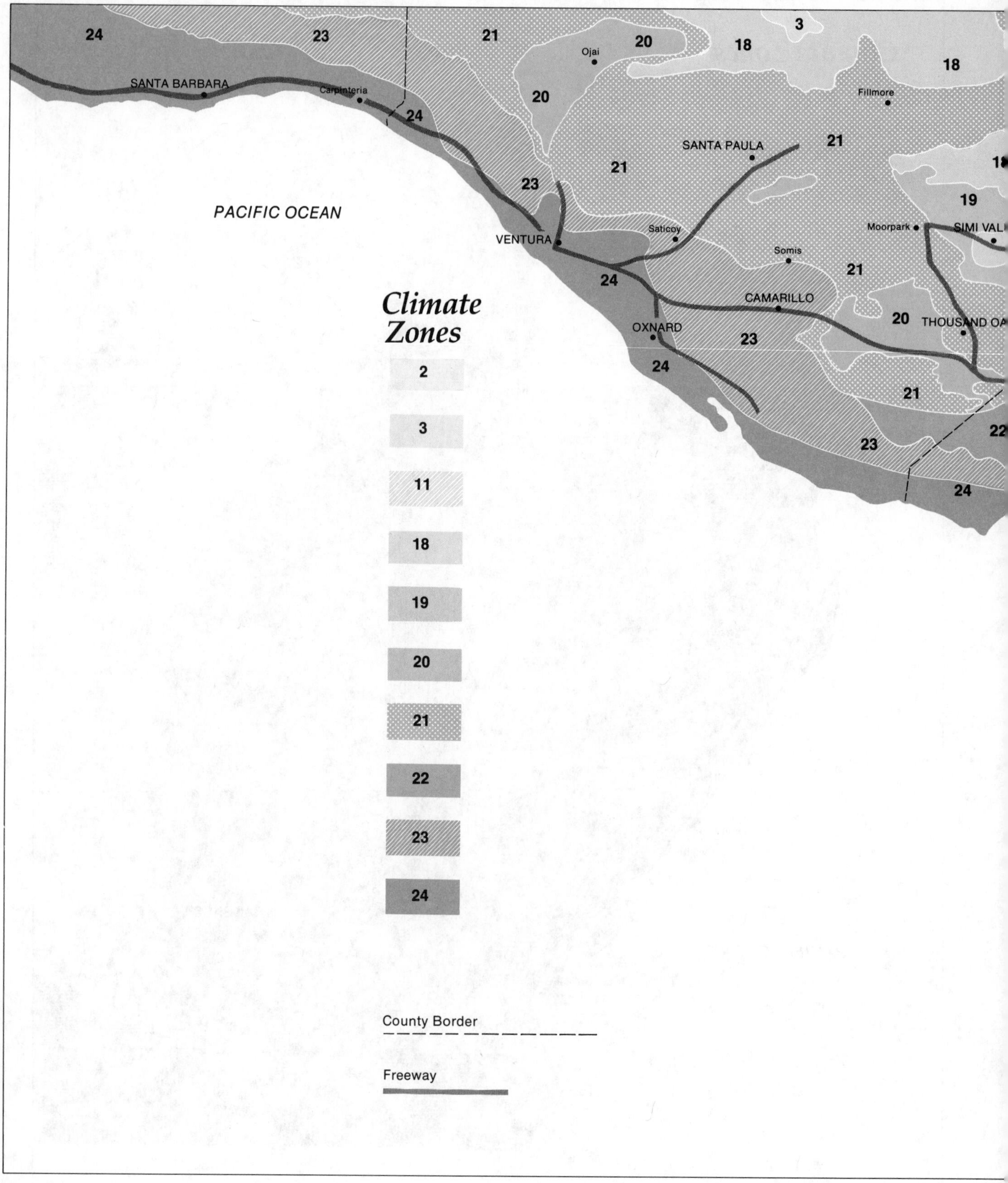
24
23
21
20
3
18
18
Ojai
SANTA BARBARA
Carpinteria
24
20
Fillmore
SANTA PAULA
21
21
23
19
PACIFIC OCEAN
VENTURA
Saticoy
Moorpark
SIMI VAL
Somis
21
24
CAMARILLO
20
THOUSAND OA
OXNARD
23
24
21
23
22
24
Climate Zones
2
3
11
18
19
20
21
22
23
24
County Border
Freeway

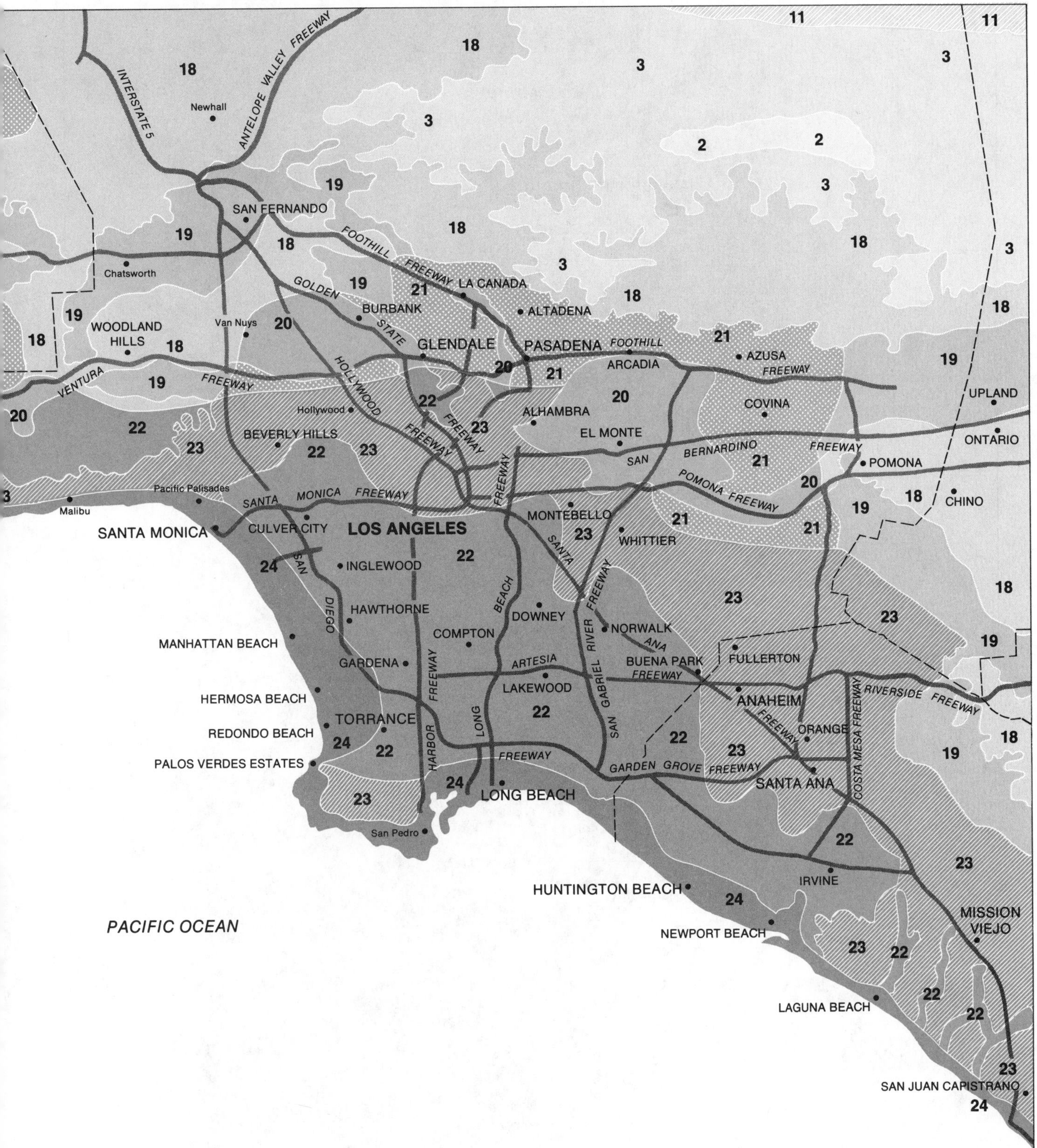
INTERSTATE 5
ANTELOPE VALLEY FREEWAY
Newhall
SAN FERNANDO
FOOTHILL FREEWAY
Chatsworth
GOLDEN STATE
LA CANADA
BURBANK
ALTADENA
Van Nuys
WOODLAND HILLS
GLENDALE
PASADENA
FOOTHILL FREEWAY
AZUSA
ARCADIA
VENTURA FREEWAY
HOLLYWOOD FREEWAY
UPLAND
Hollywood
ALHAMBRA
COVINA
BEVERLY HILLS
EL MONTE
SAN BERNARDINO FREEWAY
ONTARIO
POMONA
Pacific Palisades
SANTA MONICA FREEWAY
POMONA FREEWAY
CHINO
Malibu
MONTEBELLO
SANTA MONICA
CULVER CITY
LOS ANGELES
WHITTIER
SAN DIEGO
INGLEWOOD
SANTA ANA FREEWAY
LONG BEACH FREEWAY
HAWTHORNE
DOWNEY
NORWALK
MANHATTAN BEACH
COMPTON
SAN GABRIEL RIVER FREEWAY
FULLERTON
GARDENA
ARTESIA FREEWAY
BUENA PARK
LAKEWOOD
ANAHEIM
RIVERSIDE FREEWAY
HERMOSA BEACH
HARBOR FREEWAY
COSTA MESA FREEWAY
TORRANCE
ORANGE
REDONDO BEACH
PALOS VERDES ESTATES
GARDEN GROVE FREEWAY
SANTA ANA
LONG BEACH
San Pedro
IRVINE
HUNTINGTON BEACH
MISSION VIEJO
PACIFIC OCEAN
NEWPORT BEACH
LAGUNA BEACH
SAN JUAN CAPISTRANO

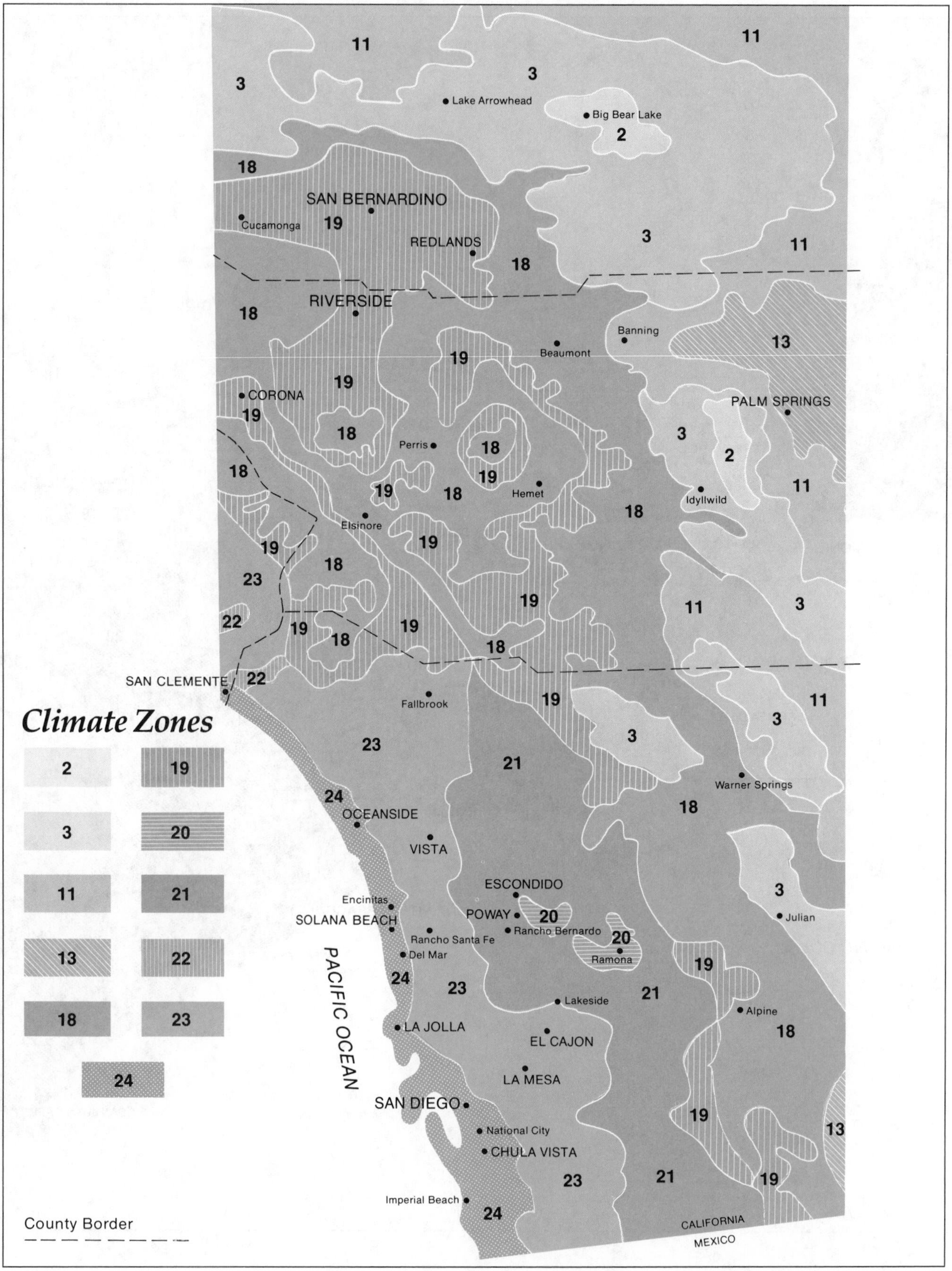

Lake Arrowhead
Big Bear Lake
SAN BERNARDINO
Cucamonga
REDLANDS
RIVERSIDE
Banning
Beaumont
PALM SPRINGS
CORONA
Perris
Hemet
Idyllwild
Elsinore
SAN CLEMENTE
Fallbrook
Warner Springs
OCEANSIDE
VISTA
ESCONDIDO
Encinitas
SOLANA BEACH
POWAY
Rancho Bernardo
Rancho Santa Fe
Ramona
Del Mar
Julian
PACIFIC OCEAN
Lakeside
Alpine
LA JOLLA
EL CAJON
LA MESA
SAN DIEGO
National City
CHULA VISTA
Imperial Beach
CALIFORNIA
MEXICO
Climate Zones
2
3
11
13
18
19
20
21
22
23
24
County Border

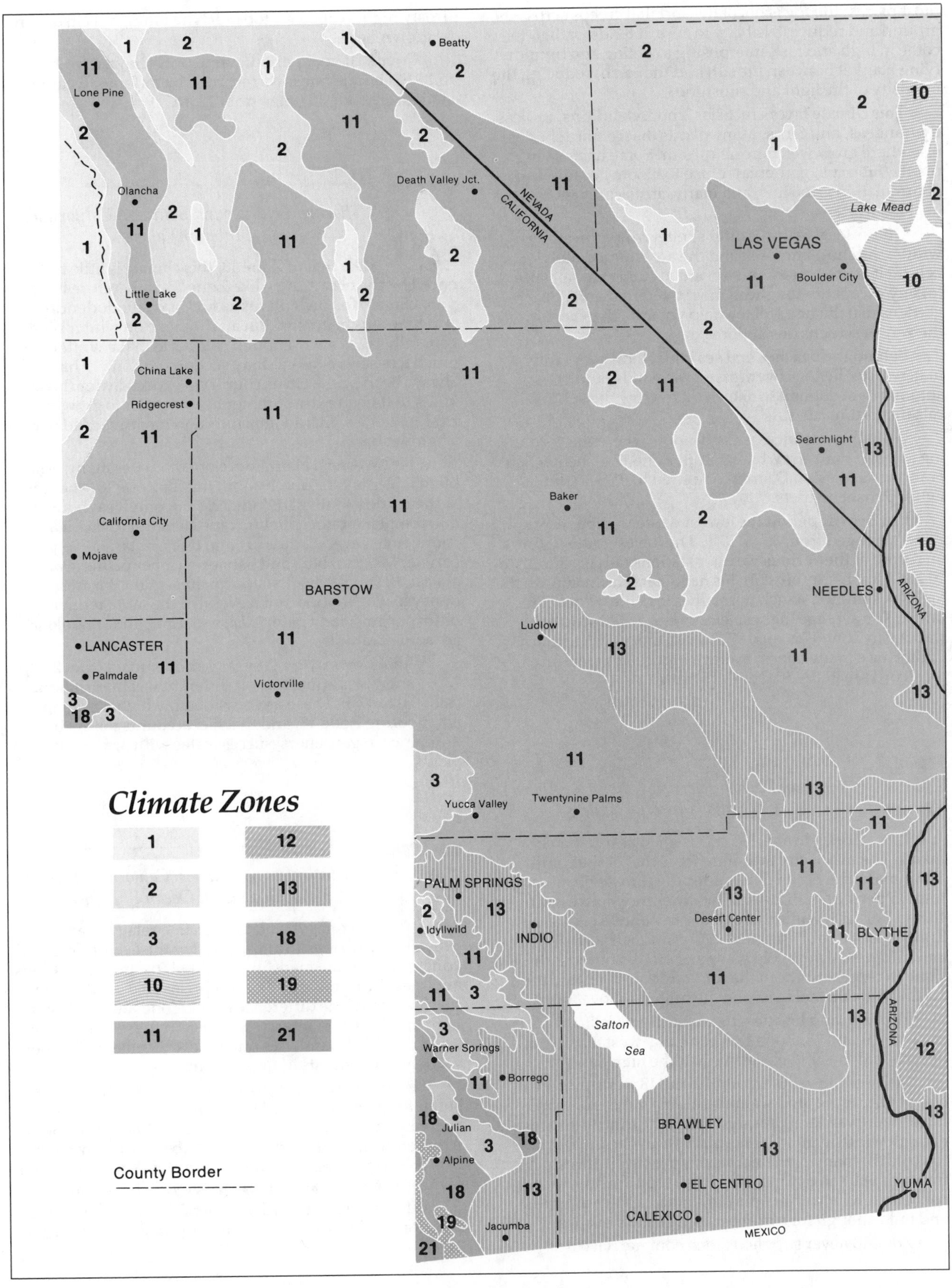
Beatty
Lone Pine
Olancha
Little Lake
Death Valley Jct.
NEVADA
CALIFORNIA
Lake Mead
LAS VEGAS
Boulder City
China Lake
Ridgecrest
Searchlight
Baker
California City
Mojave
BARSTOW
NEEDLES
ARIZONA
Ludlow
LANCASTER
Palmdale
Victorville
Yucca Valley
Twentynine Palms
PALM SPRINGS
Idyllwild
INDIO
Desert Center
BLYTHE
Salton Sea
Warner Springs
Borrego
Julian
Alpine
Jacumba
BRAWLEY
EL CENTRO
CALEXICO
MEXICO
YUMA
Climate Zones
1
2
3
10
11
12
13
18
19
21
County Border

most places, the fog is not of the sort that creeps across the ground and reduces visibility to zero; it tends, rather, to come in high and fast, interposing a cooling and humidifying blanket between the sun and the earth, reducing the intensity of the light and sunshine.

This climate favors fuchsias, rhododendrons, azaleas, hydrangeas, and ferns. Many plants that require shade elsewhere grow well here in full sun. Some heat-loving plants (hibiscus, gardenia) refuse to bloom because heat accumulation is too low; and many citrus varieties find the heat insufficient.

Unless local features offer shelter from prevailing winds, the shoreline itself and the area immediately behind it are too gusty and too much subject to salt spray for any except the toughest, most tolerant plants. Beach gardens usually need all the help you can give them in the way of screens or windbreaks.

Behind the beaches and sea cliffs, local geography may reduce the fog cover, lessen the winds, and boost summer heat enough to allow you to grow the subtropicals that ordinarily sulk.

What this produces is many spots where the gardening is easier than elsewhere within Zone 17—such as San Francisco's Mission District compared to its Sea Cliff or Outer Sunset districts.

In a 20-year period the lowest winter temperatures in Zone 17 ranged from 36° to 23°F. The lowest temperatures on record at the various weather stations range from 30° to 20°F. Of further interest in this heat-starved climate are the highs of summer, which normally are in the 60° to 75°F. range. The average highest temperature of 12 weather stations in Zone 17 is only 97°F. In all the other northern California climate zones, average highest temperatures on record are in the 104° to 116°F. range.

ZONE 18 *Above and Below Thermal Belts in Southern California's Interior Valleys*

Zones 18 and 19 are classified as interior climates. The major climate influence is that of the continental air mass; the ocean determines the climate no more than 15 percent of the time. The difference between Zones 18 and 19 is that winters are colder in Zone 18 because Zone 19 is favorably situated in thermal belts (on slopes and hillsides, where cold air drains off on winter nights). Zone 18 represents both the cold-air basins beneath the air-drained thermal belts and the hilltops above them.

The high and low deserts of southern California are in Zones 11 and 13. Zone 18 is generally west of the low deserts and lower in elevation than the high deserts.

Many of the valley floors of Zone 18 were once apricot, peach, apple, and walnut regions, but the orchards have given way to homes. Although the climate supplies enough winter chill for some plants that need it, it is not too cold for many of the hardier subtropicals. It is too hot, too cold, and too dry for fuchsias but, on the other hand, cold enough for tree peonies and many apple varieties, and mild enough for a number of avocado varieties.

Zone 18 never supplied much commercial citrus (frosty nights called for too much heating), but citrus can be grown here.

Over a 20-year period, winter lows ranged from 28° to 10°F. The all-time lows recorded by different weather stations in Zone 18 range from 22° to 7°F.

ZONE 19 *Thermal Belts around Southern California's Interior Valleys*

Like that of Zone 18, this climate is little influenced by the ocean. Also like Zone 18, it therefore has a poor climate for such plants as fuchsias, rhododendrons, and tuberous begonias. But air drainage on winter nights generally takes away enough cold air to make winter lows much less severe here. Many sections of Zone 19 have always been prime citrus country—especially for those kinds that need extra summer heat in order to grow sweet fruit. Likewise, macadamia nuts and most avocados can be grown here.

Our "Western Plant Encyclopedia" cites many ornamental plants for Zone 19—but not for Zone 18—because of the milder winters in Zone 19. Bougainvillea, bouvardia, bromelia, calocephalus, cape chestnut (*Calodendrum*), chorizema, several kinds of coral tree (*Erythrina*), leucocoryne, Mexican blue and San Jose hesper palms (*Brahea armata, B. brandegeei*), livistona palms, giant Burmese honeysuckle, myoporum, several of the more tender pittosporums, lady palm (*Rhapis excelsa*), and rondeletia are some examples.

Winter lows over a 20-year period ranged from 27° to 22°F., and the all-time lows at different weather stations from 23° to 17°F. These are considerably higher than in neighboring Zone 18, and that fact accounts for the big difference in gardeners' success rates with ornamental plants.

ZONE 20 *Cold Winters in Southern California's Sections of Occasional Ocean Influence*

In Zones 20 and 21 the same relative pattern prevails as in Zones 18 and 19, in that the even-numbered zone is the climate made up of cold-air basins and hilltops and the odd-numbered one comprises cold-air-drained thermal belts. The difference is that Zones 20 and 21 get both maritime and interior weather. In these transitional areas, climate boundaries often move 20 miles in 24 hours with the movements of these air masses.

Because of the greater ocean influence, this climate is better for plants that need moisture—fuchsias, tuberous begonias, and the like. The Los Angeles State and County Arboretum at Arcadia is in Zone 20 (bordering on Zone 21). The array of plants grown there gives some indication of the great choice available to gardeners in this zone.

Winter lows over a 20-year period ranged from 28° to 23°F. Record lows at various weather stations range from 21° to 14°F.

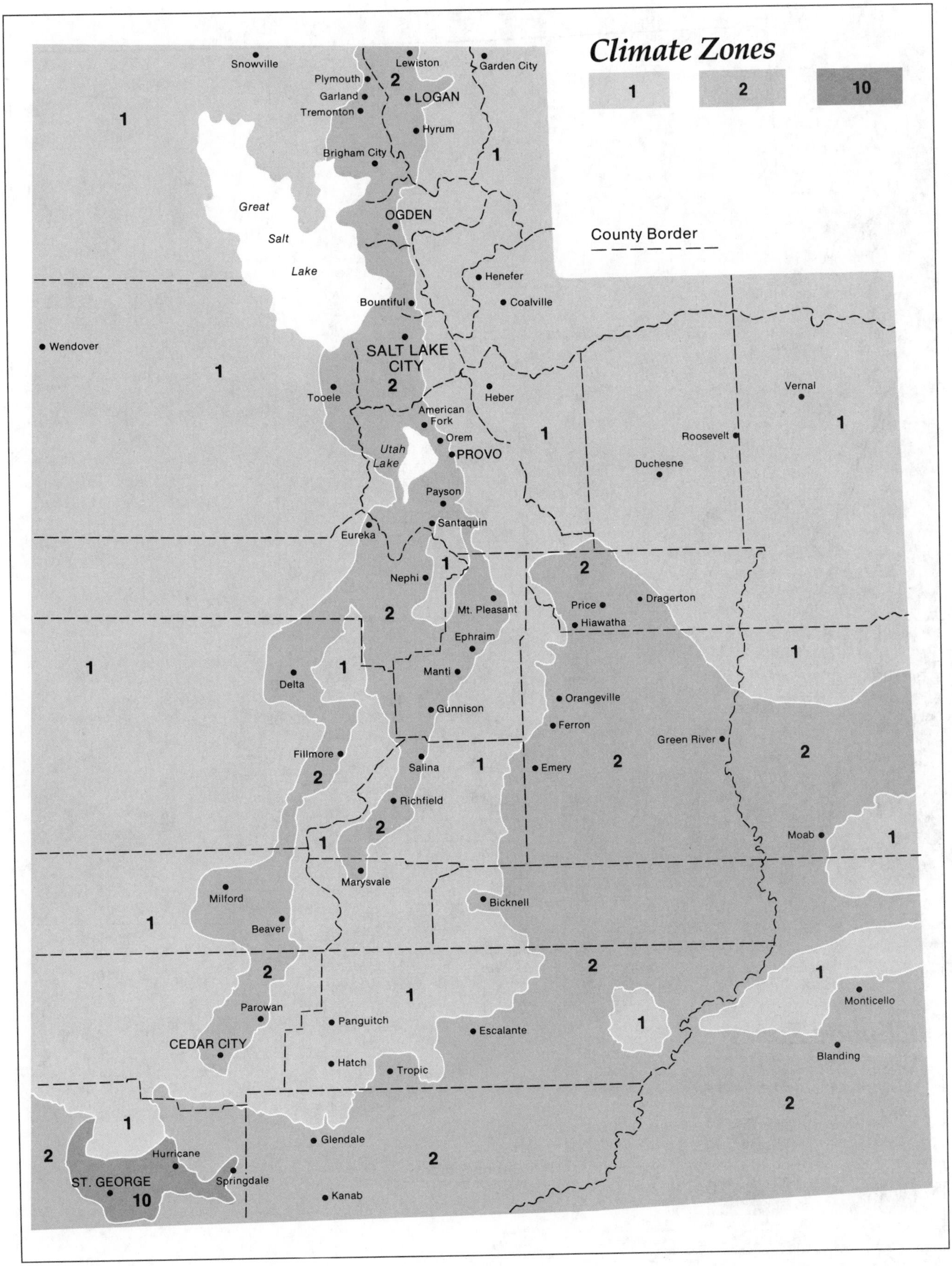
Climate Zones
1
2
10
County Border
Snowville
Lewiston
Garden City
Plymouth
Garland
LOGAN
Tremonton
Hyrum
Brigham City
Great
Salt
Lake
OGDEN
Henefer
Coalville
Bountiful
Wendover
SALT LAKE
CITY
Tooele
Heber
American
Fork
Orem
Utah
Lake
PROVO
Vernal
Roosevelt
Duchesne
Payson
Santaquin
Eureka
Nephi
Mt. Pleasant
Price
Dragerton
Hiawatha
Ephraim
Manti
Delta
Gunnison
Orangeville
Ferron
Green River
Fillmore
Salina
Emery
Richfield
Moab
Marysvale
Milford
Bicknell
Beaver
Parowan
Panguitch
Escalante
Monticello
CEDAR CITY
Hatch
Tropic
Blanding
Glendale
Hurricane
ST. GEORGE
Springdale
Kanab

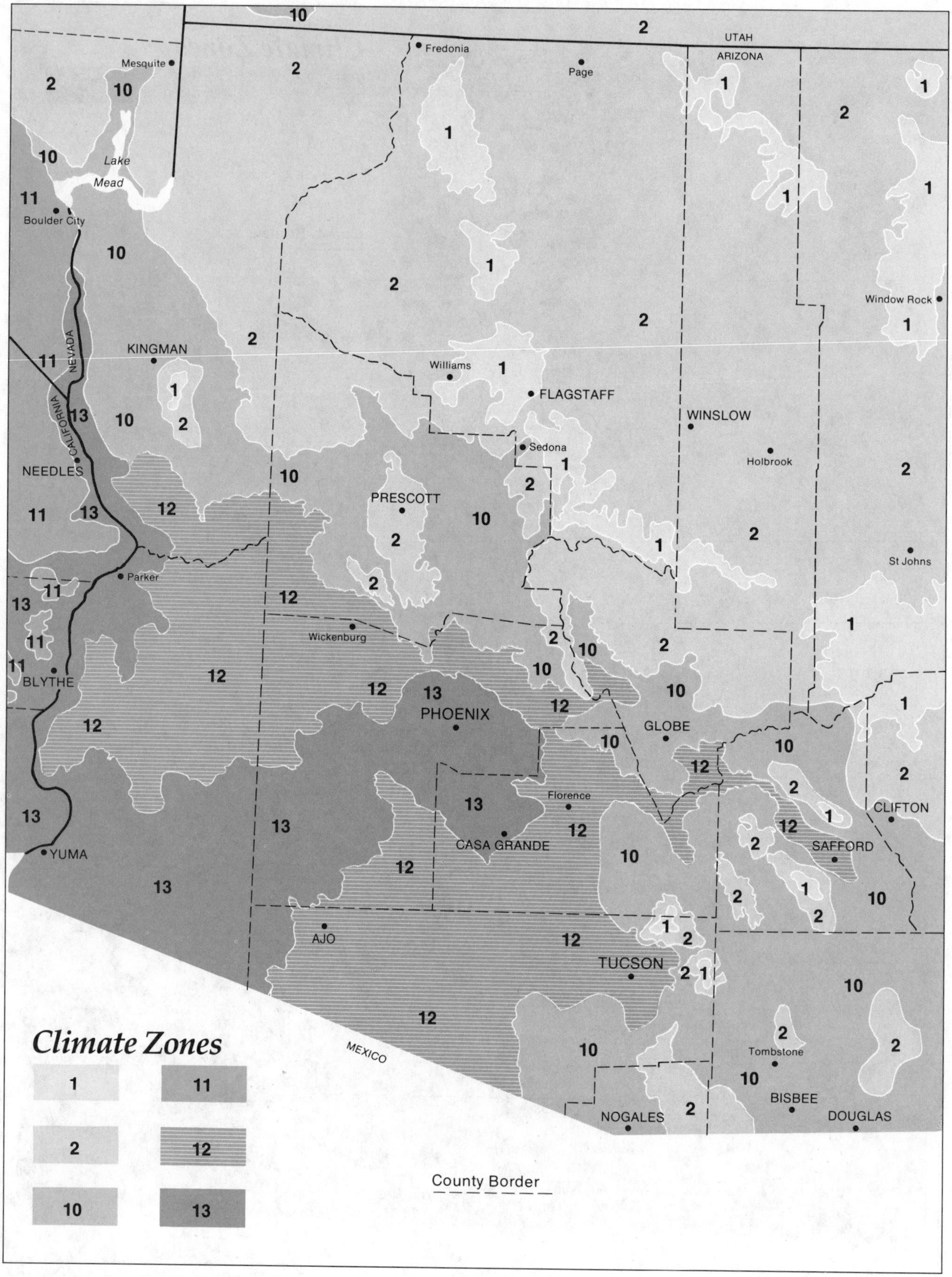

Climate Zones
1
2
10
11
12
13
County Border
UTAH
ARIZONA
NEVADA
CALIFORNIA
MEXICO
Lake Mead
Mesquite
Fredonia
Page
Boulder City
KINGMAN
Williams
FLAGSTAFF
WINSLOW
Holbrook
Window Rock
Sedona
NEEDLES
PRESCOTT
St Johns
Parker
Wickenburg
BLYTHE
PHOENIX
GLOBE
Florence
CASA GRANDE
CLIFTON
SAFFORD
YUMA
AJO
TUCSON
Tombstone
BISBEE
DOUGLAS
NOGALES

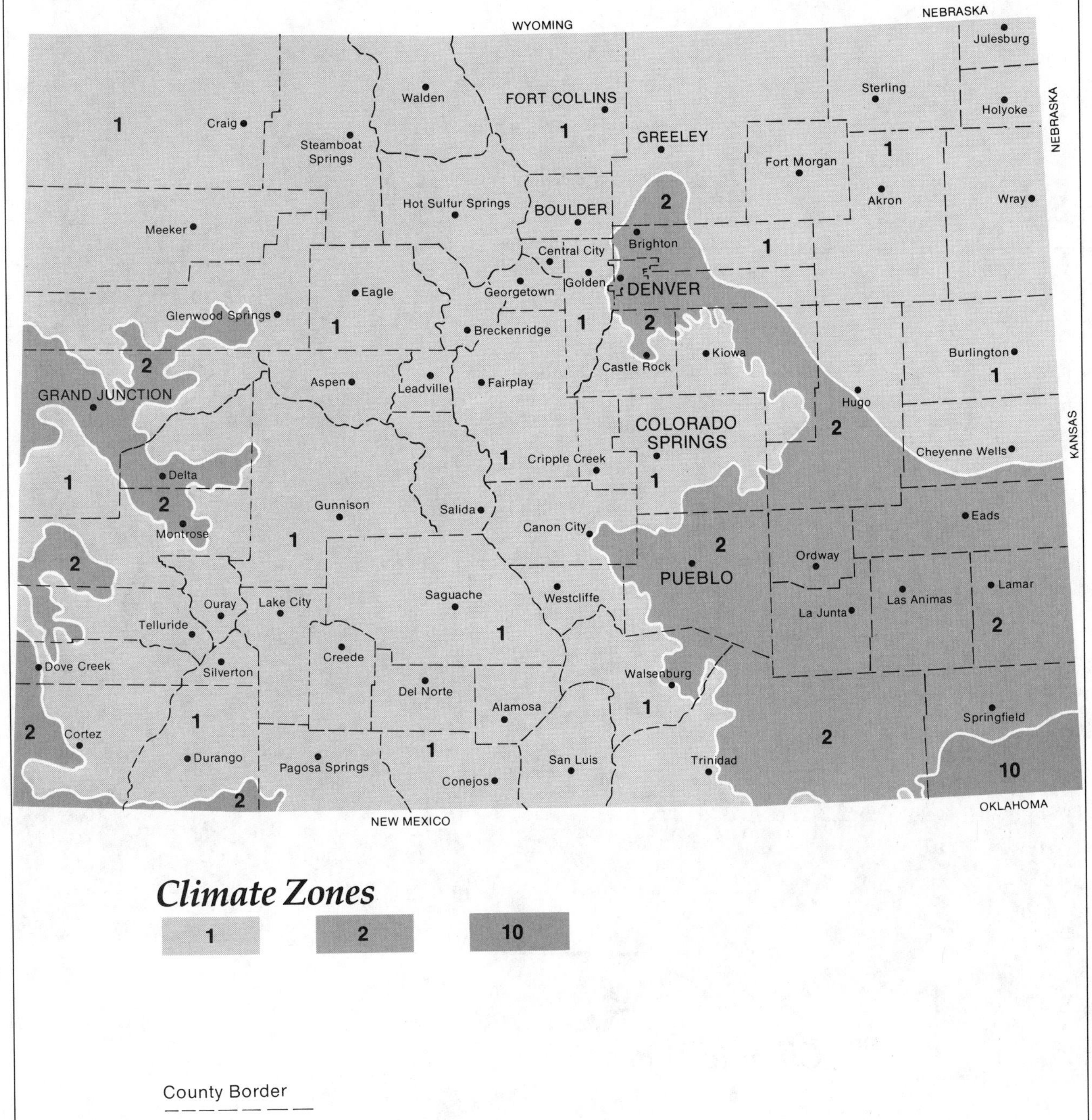
WYOMING
NEBRASKA
NEBRASKA
KANSAS
OKLAHOMA
NEW MEXICO
Julesburg
Sterling
Holyoke
Walden
FORT COLLINS
GREELEY
Craig
Steamboat Springs
Fort Morgan
Akron
Wray
Hot Sulfur Springs
BOULDER
Meeker
Brighton
Central City
Golden
DENVER
Georgetown
Eagle
Glenwood Springs
Breckenridge
Castle Rock
Kiowa
Burlington
Aspen
Leadville
Fairplay
GRAND JUNCTION
Hugo
COLORADO SPRINGS
Cheyenne Wells
Cripple Creek
Delta
Gunnison
Salida
Montrose
Canon City
Eads
Ordway
PUEBLO
Lamar
Ouray
Lake City
Saguache
Westcliffe
Las Animas
La Junta
Telluride
Creede
Dove Creek
Silverton
Del Norte
Walsenburg
Alamosa
Springfield
Cortez
Durango
Pagosa Springs
San Luis
Trinidad
Conejos
1
2
10
Climate Zones
1
2
10
County Border

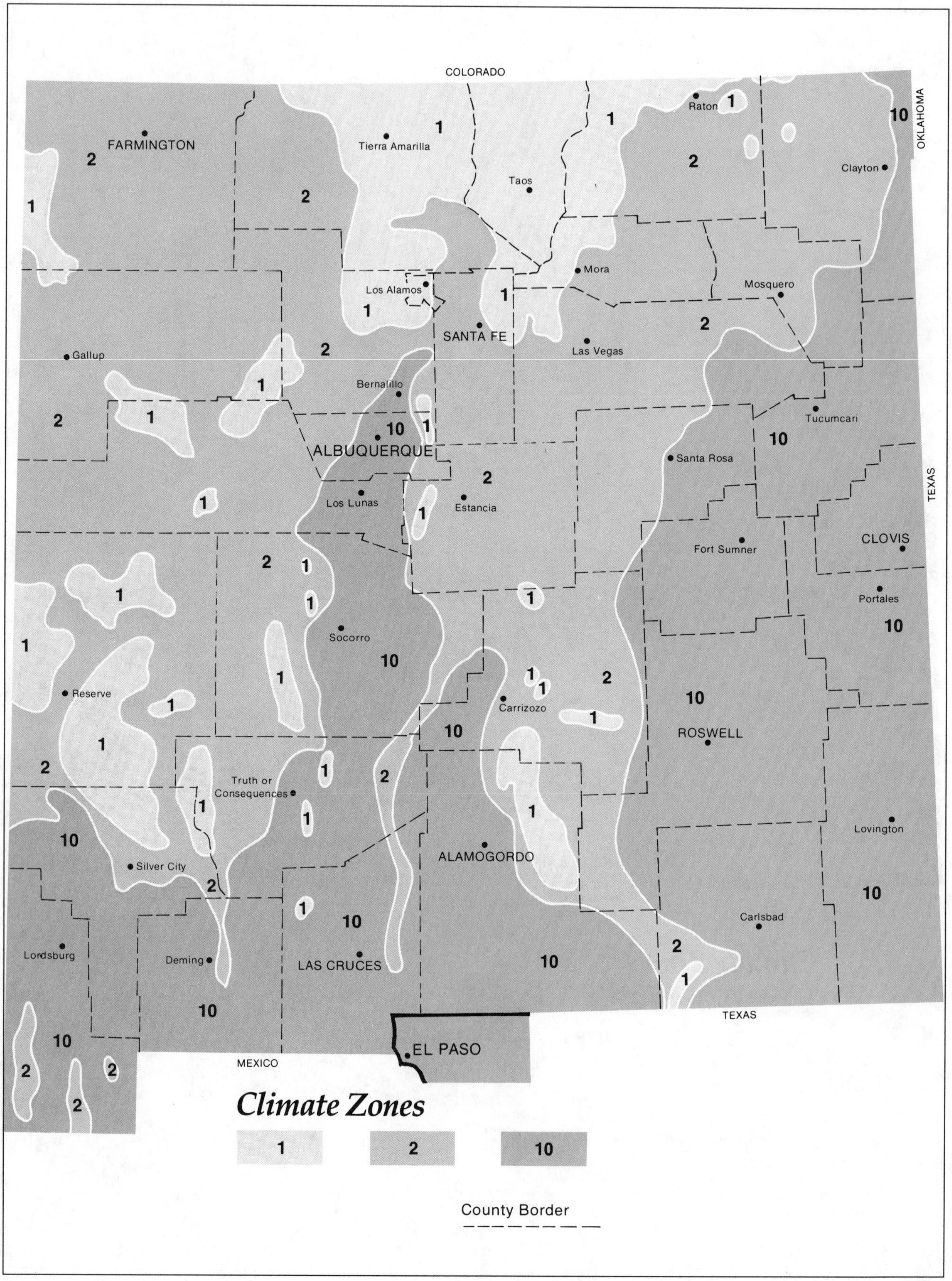
COLORADO
OKLAHOMA
TEXAS
TEXAS
MEXICO
FARMINGTON
Tierra Amarilla
Taos
Raton
Clayton
Los Alamos
Mora
Mosquero
SANTA FE
Las Vegas
Gallup
Bernalillo
ALBUQUERQUE
Tucumcari
Santa Rosa
Los Lunas
Estancia
Fort Sumner
CLOVIS
Portales
Socorro
Reserve
Carrizozo
ROSWELL
Truth or Consequences
Lovington
ALAMOGORDO
Silver City
Carlsbad
Lordsburg
Deming
LAS CRUCES
EL PASO
Climate Zones
1
2
10
County Border

ZONE 21 *Thermal Belts in Southern California's Sections of Occasional Ocean Influence*

The interplay of weather influences described for Zone 20 applies to Zone 21 as well. Your garden can be in ocean air or a high fog one day and in a mass of interior air (perhaps a drying Santa Ana wind from the desert) the next day. On the other hand, Zone 21 is a thermal belt: cold winter air drains off, making it possible to grow plants here that are too tender for Zone 20.

This area is fine citrus-growing country. Its mild winters favor a number of other tender plants, because temperatures never dip very far below 30°F. Over a 20-year period, winter lows at the weather-recording stations in Zone 21 ranged from 36° to 23°F. Record lows for different stations range from 27° to 17°F.

This is the mildest zone that gets winter chilling adequate for most forms of lilac and certain other plants.

ZONE 22 *Cold-Winter Portions of Southern California's Coastal Climate*

Areas falling in Zone 22 have a coastal climate (they are influenced by the ocean approximately 85 percent of the time) and in winter are either cold-air basins or hilltops above the air-drained slopes. Zone 22 has lower winter temperatures than neighboring Zone 23.

Actually, the winters are so mild here that winter lows are not of much significance, seldom below 28°F. The coldest temperatures generally are experienced in canyons and near canyon mouths where considerable cold air drainage may cause fairly heavy frost damage. Annual winter lows recorded over 20 years range from 21° to 24°F.

Gardeners who take advantage of building overhangs or the protection of tree branches can grow an impressive variety of subtropical plants—bananas, gingers, tree ferns, and the like. The lack of a pronounced chilling period during the winter limits the use of such deciduous woody plants as flowering cherry and lilac. Many herbaceous perennials from colder regions fail to thrive because winters are too warm for them to go dormant.

ZONE 23 *Thermal Belts of Southern California's Coastal Climate*

Found here is one of the most favored climates in North America for the growing of subtropical plants. This zone could be called the avocado belt, for it has always been southern California's best strip for growing that crop. Frosts don't amount to much in these air-drained thermal belts, and most of the time (approximately 85 percent) they are under the influence of Pacific Ocean weather; only 15 percent of the time is the determining influence from the interior. A notorious portion of this 15 percent consists of those days when hot and extremely drying Santa Ana winds blow down the hills and canyons from the mountains and deserts.

Zone 23 lacks either the summer heat or the winter cold necessary to grow successfully some plants such as pears, most apples, and most peaches. On the other hand, it enjoys more heat than the neighboring maritime climate, Zone 24. As an example of that difference, gardenias and oleanders are recommended for Zone 23 but not Zone 24.

Temperature records prove the mildness of Zone 23. But severe winters have descended on some sections of Zone 23 at times, and the net result has been a surprising spread of low temperatures. Over a 20-year period, lows ranged from 38° to 23°F. In recorded history, the lows for different stations range from 28° to 23°F.

ZONE 24 *Marine Influence Along the Southern California Coast*

This is the climate zone along southern California's beaches that is almost completely dominated by the ocean. Where the beach runs along high cliffs or palisades, Zone 24 extends only to that barrier. But where hills are low or nonexistent, it runs inland several miles.

This is a mild marine climate (milder than northern California's maritime Zone 17), because south of Point Conception the Pacific is comparatively warm. The winters are mild, the summers are cool and often of limited sunshine because of daily high fogs, and the air is seldom really dry. This is southern California's best fuchsia and tuberous begonia climate. Scores of less-well-known plants from Chile, New Zealand, the Canary Islands, and the moister parts of South Africa do well here for the same reason—*Leucodendron argenteum* and *Corynocarpus laevigata* are examples. Very tender plants find a good home here, but they must be able to get along with only moderate summer heat. In this climate, gardens planted with certain kinds of plants can become jungles.

Areas of Zone 24 that are close to the mouths of canyons can suffer from cold air that comes down the canyons on some winter nights. Several such canyons are big enough to be shown on the map; you will see them on the map along the coast south of Laguna Beach. Partly because of the unusually low temperatures created by this canyon action, the scope of winter lows in Zone 24 is broader than you might think. In a 20-year period, lows ranged from 44° to 24°F. The all-time record lows of different stations range from 33° to 20°F. This shows that there are some weather stations in Zone 24 that have never recorded a freezing temperature (32°F. or below).

The all-time high temperatures here are interesting in that they help define the total climate, but they aren't greatly significant in terms of plant growth. Average all-time high of weather stations in Zone 24 is 105°F. Compare this with temperatures of northern California's marine climate, Zone 17, which average 97°F., and southern California's inland climates—Zone 22 at 111°F., Zone 20 at 114°F., and Zone 18 at 115°F.

Gardening Basics

How Plants Grow

Knowledge about how plants grow is an important key to becoming a successful gardener. This knowledge will give you the background understanding that will make all aspects of plant culture more immediately understandable.

Green plants that grow in soil share certain characteristics with animals: both are composed of protoplasm (largely water and proteins); both have tissues of various kinds that serve various functions; both consume and store energy; and both are capable of reproducing themselves. But there is one significant difference: green plants are able to manufacture their own food from essentially inorganic materials.

The Seed

A plant's life cycle typically begins with a seed (exceptions are the ferns, mosses, fungi, and algae, which develop from spores). Depending on its kind, a seed may be very large (like sunflower seeds) or of dustlike smallness (like begonia seeds). But each seed contains inside its protective coating an embryo plant and, in most cases, a supply of stored food (starch, proteins, oils) to start the embryo growing and sustain the new plant until it is capable of manufacturing its own food.

Seeds sprout, or *germinate,* when conditions are favorable. Such conditions include moisture and a certain amount of warmth. In addition, some seeds have other special needs before they can germinate: light or absence of light; a period of dormancy; very high or very low temperatures; or weathering, exposure to acids, or grinding to soften and crack the seed coat. Some seeds may remain viable (able to germinate) for a very brief time period; others may remain sound for many years.

When germination occurs, the seed coat splits, a rootlet starts downward, and a sprout (*hypocotyl*) bearing one or more seed leaves (*cotyledons*) makes its way toward the soil surface (see illustration on page 58). The majority of garden plants have two seed leaves. Botanists refer to these plants collectively as *dicotyledons,* or "dicots" for short. But a number of familiar plants—grasses, corn, orchids, lilies, irises, palms—have only one cotyledon; these are classed as *monocotyledons* ("monocots"). All the conifers (such as pines, spruces, and firs and the cycads) have many seed leaves.

The Roots

The first single root sent down by the germinating seed soon begins to send out tiny white rootlets, which draw in the chemical substances needed for growth and the water needed to carry these substances to the aboveground part of the plant. If no moisture is available to a plant's roots, the plant dies.

As a woody plant grows and matures, its roots take on different functions and a different appearance. The older portions grow a skinlike covering similar to bark. These larger, older roots act as vessels to transport water and nutrients to the rest of the plant, and sometimes serve as storage vessels for food. In addition, the entire root system anchors the plant in the soil.

At the roots' ends are tender root tips. Each contains a growing point that continually produces elongating cells; these cells push the roots deeper and farther out into the moist soil.

Immediately behind the root tip (or cap) is a zone of cells that produce single-celled root hairs. These very delicate root hairs perform the actual absorption of water and nutrients. Exposed to sunshine or dry air, the root hairs quickly shrivel and die. In a new transplant, the loss of root hairs causes wilting: until roots grow a new set of hairs, they cannot meet the needs for water and food imposed by the leaves. For this reason, gardeners plant and transplant leafy plants as quickly as possible, without exposing roots to the air any more than is necessary.

The Stem

A woody dicotyledon can illustrate the complex internal system of plants. Between the cotyledons is the growth tip, which—through its *terminal bud*—elongates to form the main stem. *Lateral buds* develop along this stem and open to produce the first true leaves. The stem continues to elongate as the plant grows, producing additional lateral buds; these buds develop into leaves or, as the plant becomes larger, into branches.

If a terminal bud is removed or damaged, the lateral buds take over the growth of the main stem. On the other hand, if the lateral buds are removed, energy is temporarily directed to the growth of the terminal bud. The gardener's art of pinching puts this growth characteristic to use

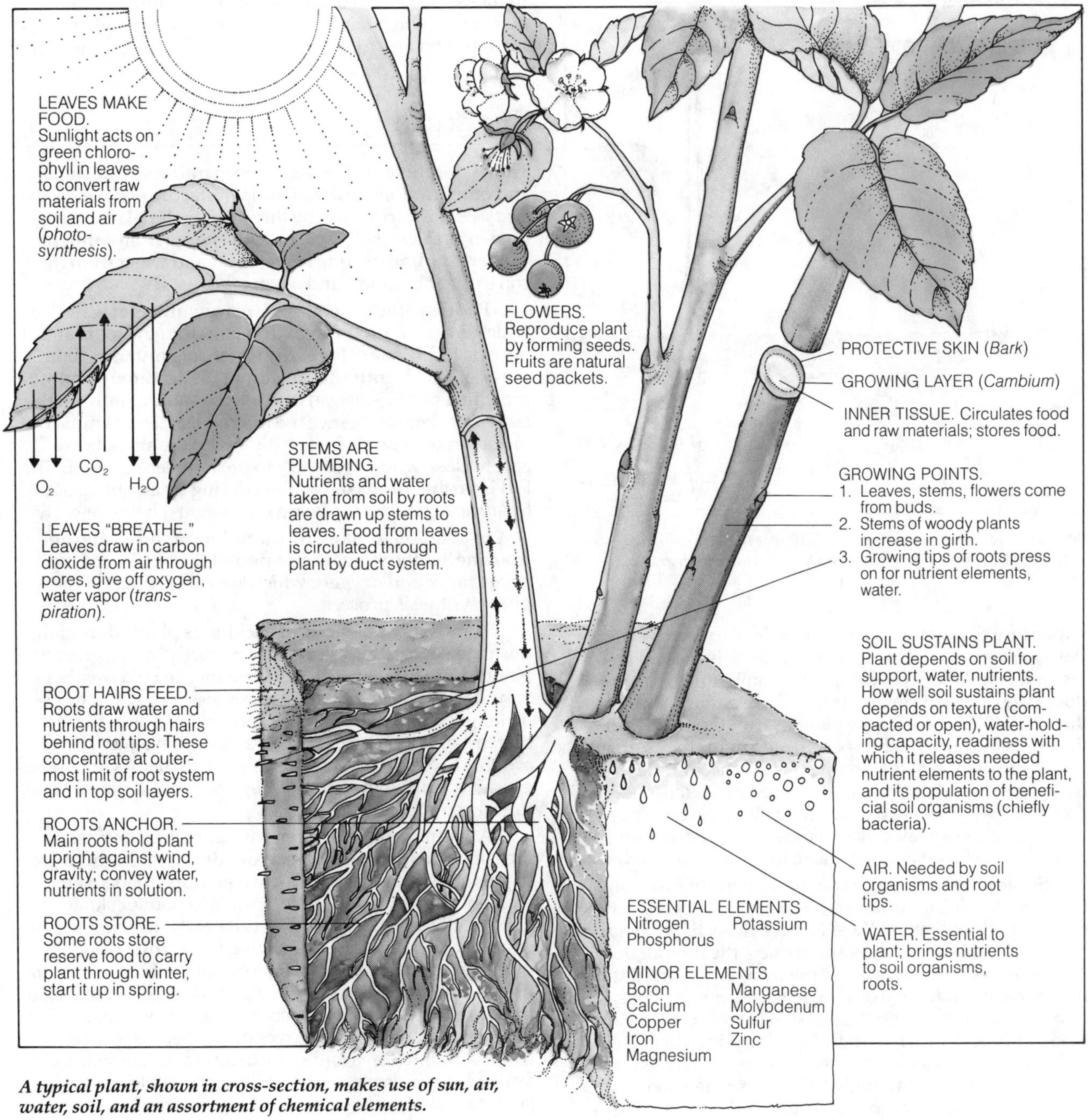
LEAVES MAKE FOOD.
Sunlight acts on green chlorophyll in leaves to convert raw materials from soil and air (*photosynthesis*).
O_2
CO_2
H_2O
LEAVES "BREATHE."
Leaves draw in carbon dioxide from air through pores, give off oxygen, water vapor (*transpiration*).
FLOWERS.
Reproduce plant by forming seeds. Fruits are natural seed packets.
STEMS ARE PLUMBING.
Nutrients and water taken from soil by roots are drawn up stems to leaves. Food from leaves is circulated through plant by duct system.
PROTECTIVE SKIN (*Bark*)
GROWING LAYER (*Cambium*)
INNER TISSUE. Circulates food and raw materials; stores food.
GROWING POINTS.
1. Leaves, stems, flowers come from buds.
2. Stems of woody plants increase in girth.
3. Growing tips of roots press on for nutrient elements, water.
SOIL SUSTAINS PLANT.
Plant depends on soil for support, water, nutrients. How well soil sustains plant depends on texture (compacted or open), water-holding capacity, readiness with which it releases needed nutrient elements to the plant, and its population of beneficial soil organisms (chiefly bacteria).
ROOT HAIRS FEED.
Roots draw water and nutrients through hairs behind root tips. These concentrate at outermost limit of root system and in top soil layers.
ROOTS ANCHOR.
Main roots hold plant upright against wind, gravity; convey water, nutrients in solution.
ROOTS STORE.
Some roots store reserve food to carry plant through winter, start it up in spring.
AIR. Needed by soil organisms and root tips.
WATER. Essential to plant; brings nutrients to soil organisms, roots.
ESSENTIAL ELEMENTS
Nitrogen
Potassium
Phosphorus
MINOR ELEMENTS
Boron
Calcium
Copper
Iron
Magnesium
Manganese
Molybdenum
Sulfur
Zinc

A typical plant, shown in cross-section, makes use of sun, air, water, soil, and an assortment of chemical elements.

either by nipping off lateral buds to channel growth energy into the terminal bud (thereby increasing height or length), or by removing terminal growth to promote growth of lateral buds, resulting in more branches and, therefore, a bushier plant.

In some plants, the growth buds may lie dormant in stem or bark for many years. Called *latent buds,* these will begin to grow only after the growth above them is removed by pruning or injury.

A primary function of the stem is to transport water and nutrients absorbed by the root hairs to the plant's growing points—buds, leaves, and flowers—and to return to the roots the sugars manufactured in the leaves. This exchange is carried on by a complex duct system of specialized cells that begins in the roots and leads to the growing points (see illustration above).

In the stems of most trees, shrubs, and herbaceous (soft-stemmed) plants, the tissues that make up the duct

Germination of a Seed

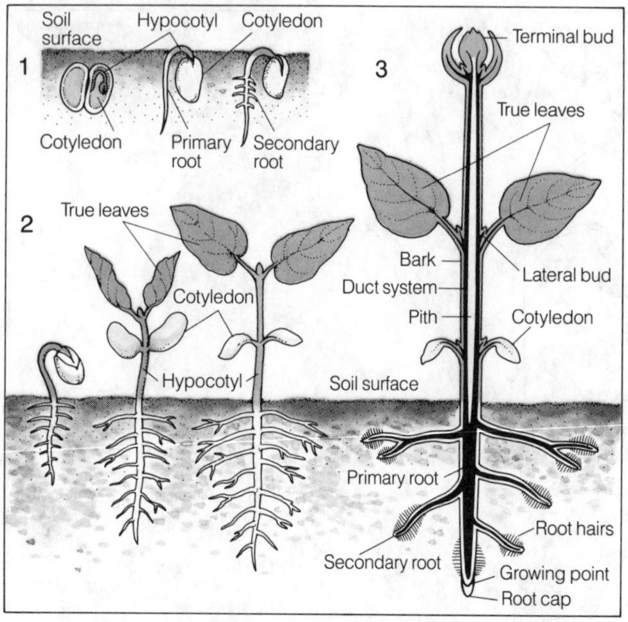

Germinating seed has primary root, hypocotyl, cotyledons. Cotyledons sustain plant until true leaves, roots appear.

system are concentrated on either side of (or very near) the *cambium,* which is a layer of cells usually located just inside a plant's bark or "skin." This cambium layer produces the cells that constitute the duct system, as well as the tissues that increase the plant's girth. If plant ties or the wires that attach labels become too tight, they not only cut off the plant's circulation system but also interfere with the cambium layer. Unless these ties are loosened, they may cause severe damage (usually referred to as *girdling*) or may even kill a plant. Some fungi, insects, and animals can cause similar damage to the cambium layer.

Support of the plant is another important function of the stem. Many plants have quite rigid stems because the walls of their cells are stiffened by cellulose, lignin, and similar substances. In trees and shrubs, the interior dense heartwood serves solely as support, having outlived the functions of conductive or storage tissue. Some plants have stems too long and thin to be held erect even by woody tissue. Vines have developed twining stems, tendrils, coiled leaf stalks, or adhesive disks to carry leaves and flowers up into the sunlight. Because their stems don't form enough woody tissue to stand upright, and they lack the support mechanisms of vines, some annuals and perennials must be staked to keep them from sprawling on the ground.

A third function of the stem is to store food that will tide the plant over through dormancy, start growth in spring, and help seeds develop. Food moves through a plant in the form of plant sugars; when stored, these sugars are changed to starch. In spring, when the plant is ready to resume growth, the stored starch is changed back into sugar and again circulates through the plant.

Many familiar garden plants (such as bulbs, rhizomes, corms, or tubers) lack a woody branch structure but have, instead, underground stems or modified stems. In those specialized underground or modified stems is stored the food (starch) to carry the plant through its dormant period and to provide push for new spring growth.

The Leaves

The basic function of leaves is the manufacture of sugars and other carbohydrates. This manufacture—called *photosynthesis*—is carried out by the green material in leaves known as *chlorophyll,* which, with energy from sunlight, converts carbon dioxide from the air and water from the soil to carbohydrates and oxygen.

Photosynthesis requires large quantities of water, which is drawn up through the stem from the roots and into the leaf tissue. There, the water encounters carbon dioxide, which enters the leaf from the air through minute breathing pores (*stomata*) located most abundantly on the leaves' undersides. Since the interior leaf tissues must be moist but outside air frequently is dry, the stomata are able to close when necessary to prevent dehydration. The leaf is further protected against drying by an outer coat (*epidermis*), which may be waxy, resinous, hairy, or scaly.

In addition to allowing the inflow of carbon dioxide from the air, the stomata also permit the outflow of excess water vapor and oxygen, which are by-products of the photosynthesis process.

Photosynthesis stops in deciduous plants during the dormant season, and slows down greatly in evergreen plants during their modified dormancy in cold weather. Simultaneously, the plant requires less water, and roots no longer strain to keep up with the demands of the leaf system's manufacturing process. As a consequence, we are able to dig up most plants and move them with moderate safety during their dormant period (often from late fall to early spring).

Anything that interferes with photosynthesis and the subsequent transfer of carbohydrates throughout the plant can have harmful consequences. Inadequate nutrient supply, for example, results in poor or slow growth: the plant lacks nutrients it needs to manufacture essential carbohydrates. Likewise, insect infestation, fungus disease, or severe midyear pruning not only slows the manufacture of food and hence impedes growth, but also interferes with the plant's accumulation of winter food. Soot, grime, and dust on leaves can impede free air circulation through pores and reduce the amount of vital light available to the leaves. A smothering mat of leaves on a lawn can likewise halt production of chlorophyll and cause grass to yellow and cease growth.

Flowers & Fruit

Most garden plants form flowers if permitted to do so, but not all flowers are noticeable. Some are green and scarcely distinguishable from leaves without close inspection; others are hidden by leaves or are so small that they escape detection.

The majority of flowering plants bear *perfect* flowers, in which both male and female reproductive parts are contained in a single flower. In the minority are plants that have separate female and male flowers—either on the same plant (for example, corn) or on separate plants (asparagus).

When the female flower parts are fertilized by *pollen* (the male sexual cells), the flower produces a fruit of some sort, which contains seeds. Some fruits become large, fleshy, and conspicuous, as do the peach, tomato, banana, and apple; but many are simply dry, papery enclosures for the seeds. The fruit—seed containers—of some kinds of plants are adapted to distribute seeds far from the parent plants (for example by floating or spinning through the air).

If left on the plant, flowers often are pollinated and form seeds. More plant energy then goes toward seed development than toward vegetative growth or production of additional flowers. For that reason, rather than just for neatness, gardeners remove spent flowers from many annuals, perennials, and some flowering shrubs.

In nature, the seedlings of any single kind of plant tend to vary to some degree. Isolation or carefully controlled breeding can assure uniform seedlings. Such work is done for you by growers when they select the seed that goes into seed packets or from which nursery plants are grown.

Although producing seeds is nature's primary method for starting new plants, many plants can be propagated by other methods and, in the nursery trade, usually are. These methods, collectively called *vegetative propagation,* are discussed on pages 82–87.

Anatomy of a flower. A complete flower contains all the parts needed to reproduce the plant from seed. In some plants, flowers are highly developed and conspicuous like *Hibiscus,* often designed to attract the insects or birds that will accomplish the pollination that leads to seed formation. These are the showy flowers beloved of gardeners. But seemingly flowerless plants like boxwood (*Buxus*) simply produce tiny blossoms inconspicuously, concealed by foliage or their own green coloring.

Among flowering plants, blossom form varies enormously. But this diversity obscures the fact that all flowers share a basic structural plan and that the structural elements always appear in the same order. The illustration at right shows a schematic flower and its parts, which are described below.

- ***Receptacle*** is the point where floral parts are attached to the tip of the specialized stem that bears the flower. Frequently the receptacle is somewhat enlarged.

- ***Sepals*** make up the outer circle or ring of floral parts. Very often sepals are green, though in some flowers (fuchsias and irises, for example) they are brightly colored and petal-like. In *Clematis,* the sepals are petal-like and actual petals are absent. Collectively the sepals are called a *calyx.*

- ***Petals*** form the next circle of flower parts, just inward from the sepals. In showy flowers, it is usually the petals that make the show. Petals may be separate, as in camellias and roses, or united into tubular, cupped, or bell-like shapes, as in rhododendrons and petunias. Collectively the petals are called the *corolla* (and the *calyx* and *corolla* together are known as the *perianth*).

- ***Stamens,*** positioned inward from the petals, contain the male reproductive elements. Typically a stamen consists of a slender stalk (the *filament*) topped by an *anther* (most often a yellow color). The latter contains the grains of pollen, which is the male element needed to fertilize the flower in order to produce seeds (see "Pollination," below).

- ***Pistils,*** found in the center of a flower, bear the female reproductive parts. Each pistil typically consists of an *ovary* at the base (in which seeds will form following pollination) and a stalklike tube called the *style* that rises from the ovary. The style is topped by a *stigma,* the part that receives the pollen.

A *complete flower*—a term that describes most of the flowers we grow—comprises all the parts described above. An *incomplete flower* (such as *Clematis,* referred to under "Sepals") lacks one or more of the floral parts, but those it does contain appear in the order listed. For more information on flowers and flower parts, refer to Glossary entries (beginning on page 571) for *Composite family, Single flower, Semidouble flower,* and *Double flower.*

Pollination. The transfer of pollen from stamens to pistil accomplishes pollination—which leads to seed formation and thus to a new generation of plants. Usually pollination happens by natural means—wind, insects, birds, self-pollination—though the gardener can transfer pollen from one flower to another to ensure fruit or to attempt a hybrid cross.

Some plants produce separate male flowers (with stamens only) and female flowers (with pistils only). These may appear on the same plant (in pecans and walnuts, for example) or on separate plants (as in hollies). In the latter case, you need a male plant nearby to produce fruits on the female plant. To get a crop from some fruit and nut trees, you need to plant two varieties—either because a variety will not set fruit using its own pollen or because its own pollen will not be ripe when its pistils are receptive.

Anatomy of a Complete Flower

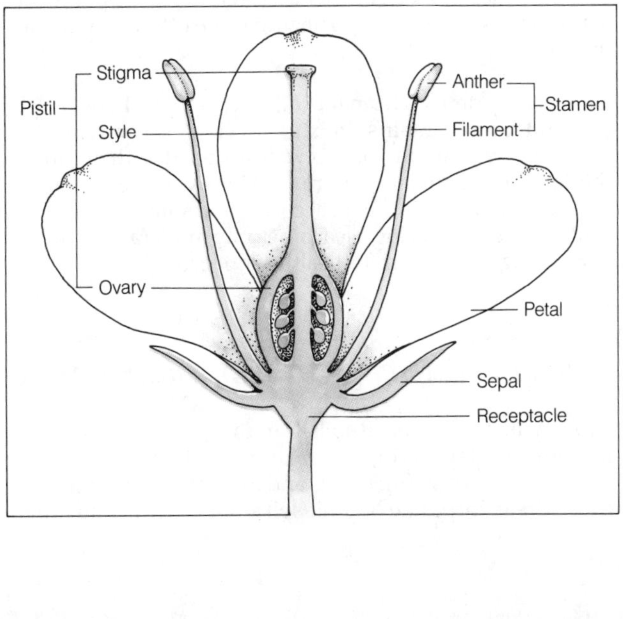

Soils

An understanding of your soil is perhaps the most important aspect of gardening. That understanding will guide you in watering and fertilizing your plants—in other words, in caring for them.

Soil is a mass of mineral particles mixed with air, water, and living and dead organic matter. The size and form of the mineral particles chiefly determine the structure of the soil; the basic soil structure—together with its pH and its content of organic matter, air, and nutrients—determines a soil's quality.

Clay particles are the smallest mineral component, sand particles are the largest, and silt represents the intermediate size. Clay and sand give their names to two soil types. A combination of the three particle sizes forms the basis for the soil called "loam."

Clay soils (also called adobe, gumbo, or just "heavy" soils) are composed of microscopically small mineral particles. These tiny particles are flattened and fit closely together; pore spaces between particles (for air and water) also are small. But because small clay particles offer the greatest surface area per volume of all soil types, clay soils can contain the greatest volume of nutrients in soluble or exchangeable form (see "Fertilizers," pages 73–75). When clay soils get wet, *drainage*—the downward movement of water—is slow. This means that loss of soluble nutrients by leaching also is slow. And because of its high density, clay soil is the slowest to warm in spring.

Sandy soils have comparatively large particles that are rounded rather than flattened. The particle size and shape allow for much larger pore spaces between particles than clay soils have; consequently, sandy soils contain a lot of air, drain well, and warm quickly. In a given volume of sandy soil, the surface area of particles is less than that in the same volume of clay. The volume of soluble and exchangeable nutrients in sandy soil is therefore correspondingly less. And because sandy soil drains quickly, and hence leaches out nutrients faster than clay, plants in sand need watering and fertilizing more often than those in clay.

Loam, a gardener's term for soil intermediate between clay and sand, contains a mixture of clay, silt, and sand particles. In addition, loam is well supplied with organic matter. Thus loam—a compromise between the extremes of clay and sand—is the ideal gardening soil: draining well (but not too fast drying), leaching only moderately, and containing enough air for healthy root growth.

Organic Matter & Soil Amendments

Vital to the fertility of all soils—and particularly needed in sand and clay—is organic matter, the decaying remains of once-living plants and animals. Gardeners therefore incorporate organic soil amendments into their soil to improve or maintain the soil's texture and thereby encourage healthy root growth.

Advantages. Organic soil amendments immediately improve aeration and drainage of clay soils by acting as wedges between particles and particle aggregates. In a sandy soil, organic amendments help hold water and dissolved nutrients in the pore spaces, so the soil will stay moist and hold dissolved nutrients longer.

As organic matter decomposes, it releases nutrients, which add to soil fertility. But the nitrogen released by decaying organic matter isn't immediately available to plants. First it must be converted by soil microorganisms (bacteria, fungi, molds) into *ammonia,* then into *nitrites,* and finally into *nitrates,* which can be absorbed by plant roots (see "Fertilizers," pages 73–75).

The microorganisms that do this converting are living entities themselves and need a certain amount of warmth, air, water, and nitrogen in order to live and carry on their functions. Soil amendments, by improving aeration and water penetration, also improve the efficiency of these organisms in their making nitrogen available.

The final product of the action by soil bacteria and other organisms on organic materials is *humus.* By binding minute clay particles into larger crumbs, this soft, sticky material improves aeration and drainage. And in sandy soil, humus remains in pore spaces and helps hold water and nutrients.

Types of amendments. Because all organic materials are continuously being decomposed by soil organisms, even the best of soils will benefit from periodic applications of organic amendments. Included among organic

Soil Particles & Soil Types

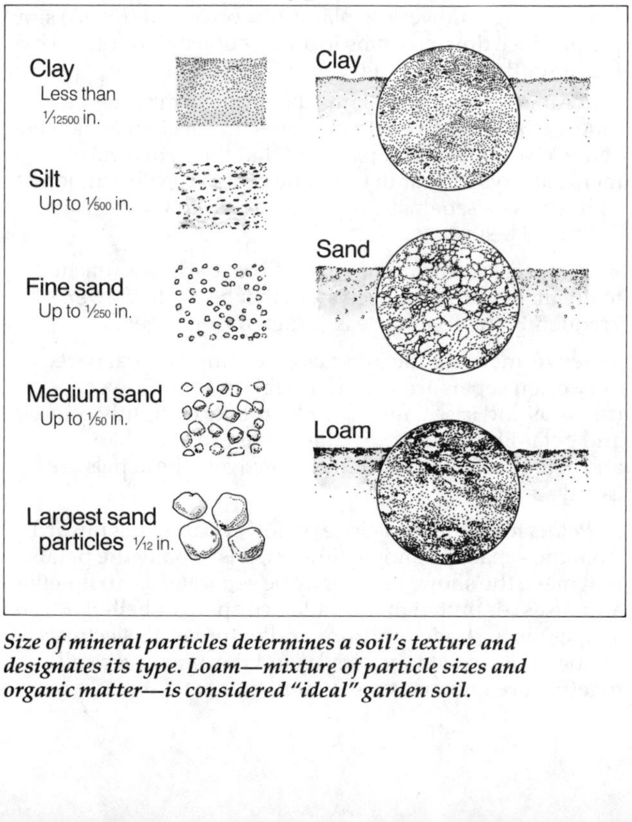

Size of mineral particles determines a soil's texture and designates its type. Loam—mixture of particle sizes and organic matter—is considered "ideal" garden soil.

soil amendments are ground bark, peat moss, leaf mold, sawdust and wood shavings, manure, compost (see page 63), and many other plant remains.

When you add organic amendments to your soil, be generous and mix them deeply and uniformly. For the most marked improvement, add a volume equal to 25 to 50 percent of the total soil volume in the cultivated area. Mix in thoroughly, either by spading and respading or by rotary-tilling. The mixing will add some air to the soil, and the amendments will help to keep it there.

Cautions. Organisms that break down organic materials need nitrogen to sustain their own lives. If they cannot get all the nitrogen they require from the organic material itself, they will draw upon any available nitrogen in the soil. This, in effect, "steals" the nitrogen that is vital to plants' roots; the result can be a temporary nitrogen depletion and reduced plant growth.

Most organic amendments you can buy at a nursery contain enough nitrogen to satisfy the soil organisms. These amendments include peat moss, leaf mold, manure, and wood by-products, such as ground bark, that have been *nitrogen fortified.* Compost and various animal manures that are free from undecomposed litter (such as straw or sawdust) also contain enough nitrogen, as do composted wood by-products. But to *raw* wood shavings, ground bark, straw, or manure containing much litter, you will need to add nitrogen. After application, use 1 pound of ammonium sulfate for each 1-inch-deep layer of raw organic material spread over 100 square feet. A year later, apply half as much ammonium sulfate, and in the third and fourth years, use one-fourth as much.

Liberal and prolonged use of organic matter can significantly lower soil pH—that is, increase its acidity (see next page). Where soil already is neutral or acid, this can result, over a period of time, in an overly acid soil. A simple soil test (see "Soil Problems & Remedies," at right) will reveal your soil's pH and let you know if excess acidity might become a problem. In potential problem soils, a yearly soil pH test will tell you when to take corrective measures (see "Chemical problems" beginning at right and "Acid soil" on page 62).

Inorganic Soil Amendments

Various inorganic soil amendments may be useful in special situations. But because they provide no nourishment for soil microorganisms, they are no substitute for organic amendments. Use inorganic materials only to supplement organic amendments when a specific need arises.

Physical amendments. This group of mineral amendments includes perlite, pumice, and vermiculite. These materials improve the texture of clay soils and increase the capacity of sandy soils to hold water and dissolved nutrients. But their relatively high cost limits use to small-scale projects: amending soil in containers or in small planting beds.

Perlite and pumice are hard, sponge-textured, inert materials (as sand is), but their porosity makes them water-absorbent. Soft-textured vermiculite (expanded mica) can absorb nutrients as well as water and will contribute some potassium and magnesium, which are essential to plant growth. Vermiculite breaks down after several years; perlite and pumice last considerably longer.

A Soil's Water-holding Capacity

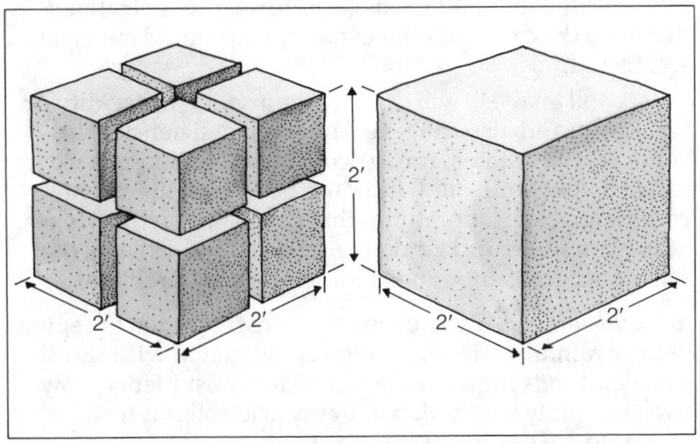

Particle size determines amount of water a soil can hold. Eight 1-foot cubes (representing clay) have 48 square feet of surface to which water can adhere. The 2-foot cube (representing sand) has same outside dimensions as the eight 1-foot cubes but has less surface area—only 24 square feet—to which water can adhere.

Chemical amendments. Included here are lime and gypsum, both sold as fine powder or granules to be scattered over the soil surface and dug or tilled in. Although lime is the traditional remedy for raising the pH of overly acid soils, both lime and gypsum may improve some clay soils by causing the tiny clay particles to group together into larger units or "crumbs." There then will be larger spaces between particle aggregates, with a corresponding improvement in aeration and drainage.

Which material you might use depends on the pH of your soil. Where soil is alkaline and is high in sodium—the "black alkali" soils of low-rainfall Southwest and West—application of gypsum (calcium sulfate) will react with the sodium and clay particles to produce the larger soil "crumbs." If your soil is acid—generally in regions of plentiful rainfall—lime is the material that might be useful. Lime will add calcium to soil, gypsum furnishes both calcium and sulfur; either material may be used as a nutrient supplement in regions (such as parts of the Pacific Northwest) where these minerals sometimes are deficient.

Before using either lime or gypsum, check with your county agricultural agent for advisability and guidelines.

Soil Problems & Remedies

Although an amazing variety of soils support thriving gardens, many were not always so hospitable to the plants they now host. Possible soil problems—aside from those mentioned above—fall into two categories: chemical problems and physical problems.

Chemical problems. These problems—acidity, alkalinity, and related conditions—are invisible to the gardener's eye but are revealed by poor plant performance. If you know little about your soil's chemical nature or suspect that it might be the cause of poor growth, you should have your soil tested.

A soil analysis will disclose your soil's pH (acidity or alkalinity) and also can reveal nutrient deficiencies. In some western states, the agricultural extension service can test your soil; if not, it should be able to direct you to commercial soil laboratories that can make such analyses. Many nurseries and garden centers sell soil-test kits that will be accurate enough to indicate definite problems.

■ ***Acid soil*** (pH 6.9 and lower) is most common in regions where rainfall is heavy; it often is associated with sandy soils and soils high in organic matter. Most plants grow well in mildly acid soil, but highly acid soil is inhospitable.

In the West, overly acid soils are common in western Washington, in western Oregon, and along the north coast of California. Add lime to such soils only if a soil test indicates that it is needed and only in the quantity recommended by your county agricultural agent. If you attempt to raise your soil's pH with lime, be sure that any fertilizers you use thereafter do not have an acid reaction.

■ ***Alkaline soil*** (pH 7.1 and higher), common in regions with light rainfall, is high in calcium carbonate (lime) or certain other minerals, such as sodium. Many plants grow well in moderately alkaline soil; others, notably camellias, rhododendrons, and azaleas, will not thrive there because the alkalinity reduces availability of particular elements necessary for their growth.

Large-scale chemical treatment of highly alkaline soil is expensive and complex. A better bet is to plant in raised beds or containers, using a good prepared soil mix.

Soils that are only slightly alkaline will support many garden plants. They can be made to grow acid-soil plants with liberal additions of peat moss, ground bark, or sawdust; fertilization with acid-type fertilizers; and periodic applications of chelates (see "Chlorosis" below).

Deep watering can help lessen alkalinity but is advisable only if the soil drains quickly.

■ ***Salinity.*** An excess of salts in the soil is a widespread problem in arid parts of the West. These salts may be naturally present in the soil or they may come from water (especially softened water, which has a high sodium content), from fertilizers and chemical amendments, and from manures with high salt content. Where these salts are not leached through the soil by high rainfall or deep irrigation, they reach high concentration in the root zone, inhibiting germination of seeds, stunting growth, and producing "salt burn"—scorched and yellowed leaves or browned and withered leaf margins.

Periodic, thorough leaching of the soil with water will lessen its salts content; but again, to carry out this leaching, drainage must be good.

■ ***Chlorosis.*** A systemic condition in which a plant's newer leaves turn yellow, chlorosis is usually caused by a deficiency of iron (rarely, it results from lack of another mineral, such as zinc). If the deficiency is mild, areas of yellow show up between the veins of the leaves, which remain a dark green. In severe or prolonged cases, the entire leaf turns yellow. Iron deficiency is only occasionally the result of a lack of iron in the soil; more frequently it is the result of some other substance (usually lime) making the iron unavailable to the plant.

To correct chlorosis, treat the soil with iron sulfate or with iron chelate (the latter has the important ability to hold iron in a form that is available to plants). Plants can also be treated with foliar sprays containing iron.

■ ***Nutrient deficiency.*** If soil drains well, has ample water, is neither too acid nor too alkaline, yet still fails to sustain plant growth well, it may be deficient in nutrients, most likely nitrogen (see "Fertilizers," pages 73–75).

Physical problems. The most common physical soil problem—drainage—is touched upon in the discussion of soil types (see page 60). Shallow soil is one cause of poor drainage that requires special treatment.

■ ***Shallow soil (hardpan).*** A tight, impervious layer of soil can cause trouble if it lies at or near the surface. Such a layer can be a natural formation—in the Southwest, the commonest natural hardpan layer is called *caliche*—or it can be manmade, such as when builders spread excavated subsoil over the surface, then drive heavy equipment over it. If the subsoil has a clay content and is damp while construction is going on, it can take on bricklike hardness when it dries. A thin layer of topsoil may conceal hardpan, but roots cannot penetrate the hard layer, and water cannot drain through it. Planting holes may become water tanks: plants will fail to grow, be stunted, or die.

If the hardpan layer is thin, you may be able to improve the soil by having it plowed to a depth of 12 inches or more. If plowing is impractical, you can drill through it with a soil auger when planting. If the layer is too thick, a landscape architect can help you with a drainage system, which might involve sumps and drain tiles. To improve the soil over large planting areas, dig up the area to a depth of 18 inches or so with heavy equipment, then add organic matter and thoroughly mix it in. As a beneficial extra step, you can then grow a crop of some heavy-rooting grass and, after it grows, rotary-till it into the soil as additional organic material.

If drainage problems prove especially difficult or costly to surmount, consider installing raised beds to accommodate most of your garden plantings. Fill a raised bed with good, well-aerated soil, making beds deep enough to allow for root growth.

■ ***Adding new soil.*** If you must bring additional soil into the garden to fill in low spots or raise the level of your soil, don't add it as a single layer on top of existing soil. Instead, add a portion of new soil (up to half, depending on projected new depth) and mix it thoroughly with existing soil by spading or rotary-tilling. Then add the remaining new soil to bring the level up to the desired height and mix it thoroughly into the previously tilled soil. This extra work prevents formation of an *interface*—a dividing-line barrier between the two dissimilar soils that can slow or stop both upward and downward movement of water.

If you purchase topsoil to add to your garden, try to find material that closely approximates your existing soil. Look for crumbly texture, and avoid very fine-textured clays and silts. Try to steer clear of saline soils (if it comes from good cropland, you can assume that salinity is no problem) and soil that contains seeds of noxious weeds or residue from herbicides.

Composting: Simple to Elaborate

Well-made compost is a soft, crumbly, brownish or blackish substance resulting from decomposition of organic material. It has limited value as a nutrient source but great value as an organic soil amendment. Composting takes time, effort, and space. But if you have a ready supply of plant waste or a small garden that could be supplied by a continually maintained compost pile, the time and effort might be well spent. Remember, though, that a poorly maintained compost pile will be slow to yield its reward and also may breed flies and give off an obnoxious odor.

In its simplest and least efficient form, composting consists of piling up grass clippings, leaves, and other garden debris—plus vegetable kitchen refuse—and permitting them to decompose. In 6 weeks to 6 months, depending on temperature, moisture, and size of materials, the compost will have broken down sufficiently so that you can use it.

For the average garden, a better system is to stack the material for composting to a height of 4 to 6 feet inside an enclosure that has openings in its sides for air to penetrate. A slatted bin or a wire mesh cylinder will do the trick. Turn the piled-up material at least once a week to aerate the mass and to relocate pieces in various stages of decomposition (compost decomposes more rapidly in the heat and moisture of the pile's interior than on the outside). Thoroughly moisten the pile as needed; it should be about as wet as a squeezed-out sponge. If you add a few handfuls of complete fertilizer with every sizable load of raw material, the decomposition will proceed more rapidly.

A more sophisticated composting operation uses three receptacles, as shown below. If receptacles are placed side by side, it will be simple to fork or shovel material from bin to bin.

Since large, coarse pieces decompose slowly, you should chop them up before adding to the pile or omit them altogether. A good mixture consists of green and dried materials in about equal proportions.

The serious composter might consider purchasing a compost grinder. Chopping up everything from leaves to thumb-thick branches into uniformly small fragments, these machines are a great aid to people who live beyond the service area of garbage collectors—particularly those who are prevented by ordinance from burning debris.

Simple compost receptacle is cylinder of welded wire. To turn composting material, lift up cylinder, move it to one side, fork material to aerate, then return it to cylinder.

Classic composting setup: three sections hold new material (left), partly decomposed material (center), and finished compost (right). Material is forked from bin to bin as composting progresses. Side boards are spaced for air penetration and slide out for easy turning, removal of compost.

Planting Techniques

An understanding of your soil and the steps needed to prepare it for planting is the foundation of gardening success. Just as important is knowing the correct way to plant your trees, shrubs, perennials, annuals, and vegetables.

Planting Annuals & Perennials

Busy gardeners often forgo the pleasures of seed planting (see "Propagation," page 80) and buy seedlings of annuals, vegetables, and perennials at the nursery. Many of these plants—as well as some ground covers and hedge plants—are sold in plastic packs, individual plastic pots, peat pots, and flats. Some perennials, perennial vegetables, and strawberries may also be sold bare-root during their dormant seasons.

Small, growing plants. You'll get the best results from these small plants in pots and flats if you prepare the soil well, as you would for sowing seeds (see "Seeds in the open ground" on page 80). Be sure you don't let these plants dry out while they're waiting to be planted. For all small plants discussed below, plant so that the tops of their root balls are even with the soil surface.

Plants in plastic packs, with each plant in an individual cube of soil, are easy to remove. Pushing up with your thumb on the bottom of a soil cube, lift out the root ball with the other hand as soil is pushed up and out of its container. If there is a mat of interwoven roots at the bottom of the root ball, tear it off—the plant will benefit from its removal. Otherwise, loosen roots by pulling apart bottom third of root ball.

Plants in individual pots can be dislodged by placing one hand over the top of the container, with the plant stem between index and middle fingers, and then turning the container upside down. The plant and its root ball should slip out of the container into one hand.

If the plant is in a peat pot, plant it pot and all; the roots will grow through the pot. But make sure that the peat pot is moist before you plant it. A dry peat pot takes up moisture slowly from the soil, so roots may be slow in breaking through into the soil. This can stunt the plant's growth or cause roots within the peat pot to dry out completely. Several minutes before transplanting, set the peat pot in a shallow container of water. Also, be sure to cover the top of a peat pot with soil, because exposed peat will act as a wick to draw moisture out of the soil. If covering the peat would bury the plant too deeply, break off the top of the pot down to slightly below the plant's soil level.

For plants in flats, a putty knife or spatula is a handy transplanting tool: separate the plants in the flat by cutting straight down around each one. Many gardeners prefer to separate individual plants out of flats—gently—with their fingers; they lose some soil this way, but keep more roots on the plant. If you work quickly, there will be little transplant shock.

Dormant, bare-root perennials. A number of popular perennials (irises, daylilies, peonies, oriental poppies) and perennial fruits and vegetables (asparagus, rhubarb, and strawberries) are sold as bare-root plants during their particular dormant periods. Many will have their roots packed in loose, dampened material such as sawdust to prevent dehydration, but some (bearded irises, for example) are packed dry. Be sure to keep those that are in moist material moist until planting. In addition, both types will benefit from a several hours' soak in water before you plant them.

Prepare soil well, as recommended under "Seeds in the open ground," on page 80, and be sure you set out each plant at its proper depth; refer to individual entries in the Western Plant Encyclopedia (pages 199–570) for any specific planting information. Be sure to spread roots out well in the soil, gently firm soil around the roots, and then water thoroughly to establish good contact between roots and the soil.

Planting Trees & Shrubs

At all times of the year, you can purchase trees and shrubs for immediate planting: bare-root in the dormant season, balled-and-burlapped generally in the cooler months, and planted in containers the year around.

Bare-root plants. In winter and early spring, you can buy bare-root plants at many retail nurseries and receive them from mail-order nurseries. A great many of the deciduous plants will be available bare-root: fruit and shade trees, deciduous flowering shrubs, roses, grapes, and cane fruits.

Why get out in the cold and wet of winter to buy and set out bare-root plants when you can wait until spring,

The Planting Hole

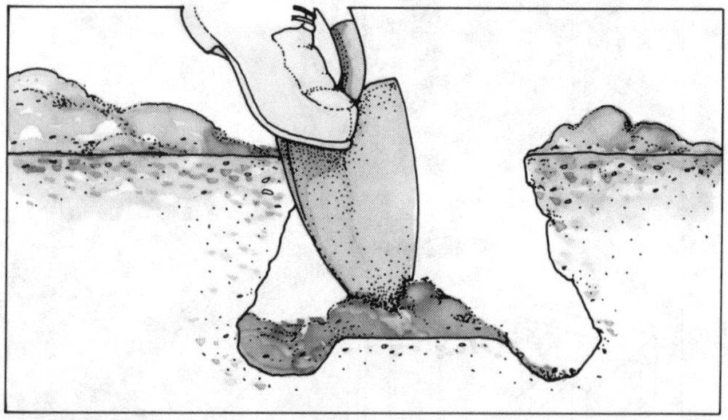

All tree and shrub planting begins with digging a hole. Dig it so that sides taper outward into the soil and are roughened, not smoothly sculpted (use a spading fork to dig, or to roughen shovel-dug sides); this lets roots penetrate more easily into surrounding soil. To prevent or minimize settling of the plant after planting and watering, make the hole a bit shallower than root ball or root system of the plant it will receive, then dig deeper around edges of the hole's bottom. This leaves a firm "plateau" of undug soil to support plant at proper depth.

Bare-root Planting

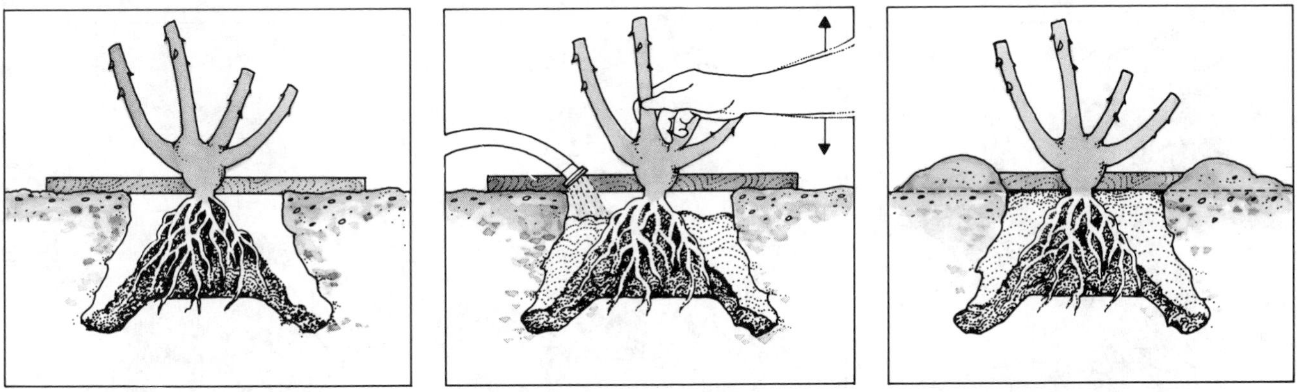

1). Make a firm cone of soil in hole, reaching nearly to the surface. Spread roots over cone, positioning plant at same depth (or slightly higher) as it was in growing field; use stick to check depth.

2) Fill in backfill soil nearly to top of soil, firming it with your fingers as you fill. Then add water. If plant settles, pump it up and down, while soil is saturated, and raise it to proper level.

3) After plant is watered in and correct level has been established, fill in any remaining soil. When growing season begins, make ridge of soil around hole to form a watering basin.

summer, or fall and plant the same plants from containers? There are two valid reasons:

1) You save money. Typically, a bare-root plant costs only 40 to 70 percent of the price of the same plant purchased in a container later in the year.

2) The manner in which a bare-root tree or shrub is planted makes it establish itself faster and often better than it would if set out later from a container.

The advantage of bare-root planting is that when you set out the plant you can refill the planting hole with the *backfill* soil that you dug from the hole: the roots will grow in only one kind of soil. In contrast, when you plant from a container or balled-and-burlapped, you put two soils, usually with different composition and properties, in contact with each other. With two different kinds of soil, it may be difficult to get uniform water penetration into the rooting area.

For successful bare-root planting, the roots should be fresh and plump, not dry and withered. Even if roots appear fresh and plump, it is a good idea to soak the root system overnight in a bucket of water before you plant.

Dig the planting hole broad and deep enough to accommodate roots easily without cramping, bending, or cutting them to fit. But cut back any broken roots to healthy tissue. Set the plant out according to the illustrations above.

After the initial watering, water bare-root plantings conservatively. Dormant plants need less water than actively growing ones, and if you keep the soil too wet, new feeder roots may not form. Check soil periodically for moisture (using a trowel, fingers, soil-sampling tube, or any pointed instrument) and water accordingly: if the root zone soil is damp, the plant doesn't need water.

When weather turns warm and growth becomes active, you will need to water more frequently. *Do not overwater:* check soil for moisture, as mentioned above, before watering. If hot, dry weather follows planting, shade the new plant at least until it begins to grow. And be patient—some bare-root plants are slow to leaf out. Many will not do so until a few warm days break their dormancy.

Plants in containers. Plants grown in containers are popular for many reasons. Most broad-leafed evergreen shrubs and trees—the West's landscaping specialties—are only offered growing in containers, and you can buy these plants in cans in all seasons. Available in a variety of sizes and prices, they are easy to transport and they don't have to be planted immediately. Furthermore, you can buy a container plant in bloom or fruit and see exactly what color or variety you are getting.

When shopping for container-grown plants, look for plants that have a generally healthy, vigorous appearance and good foliage. The root system should be unencumbered—that is, not badly tangled or constricted by the plant's own roots. Two signs of a seriously rootbound plant are roots protruding above the soil level and husky roots growing through the container's drainage holes. Additional indicators of crowded roots: plants that are unusually large for the size of their containers, unusually leggy plants, and dead twigs or branches.

Nurseries sell plants in a variety of containers—metal cans (1-gallon and 5-gallon are standard sizes), plastic, fiber pots, clay pots, and wooden boxes for large specimen shrubs and trees. With straight-sided metal cans, have the cans slit down each side. The best time to cut cans is just before you plant, but you may prefer to have cans cut at the nursery before taking the plants home. Handle cut edges with care. If planting is delayed, keep the plants in a cool place and water often enough to keep roots moist (water gently so that you don't wash out soil). With tapered metal cans and plastic containers, you can easily knock the plants out of their containers; sharp taps on the bottom and sides will loosen the root ball so that the plant will slide out easily. With fiber pots, it's often easier to tear the pots away from the root ball.

First, dig the planting hole, making sure that the plant's soil line will be about 2 inches above the level of the surrounding garden soil. For plants in 2-gallon and larger containers, wash or spray off the outer few inches of the root ball (soak the root ball, if necessary, to loosen roots and soil) and uncoil circling or twisted roots. Cut off any

Planting from a Container

1) Roots of container plants may have become coiled or matted. Spray soil off the outer few inches of root ball, uncoil circling or twisted roots.

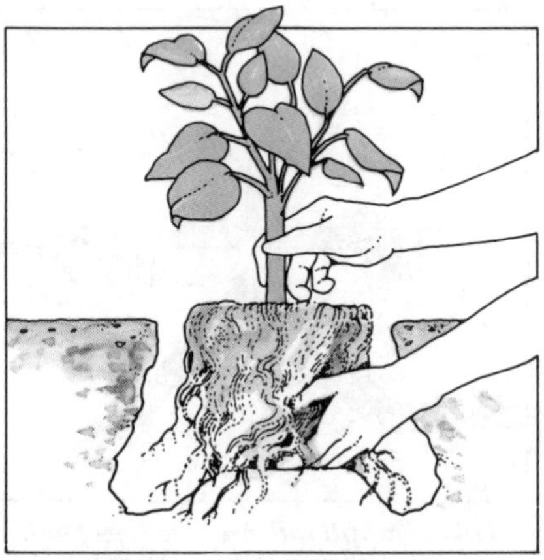

2) Spread roots out over firm plateau of soil, then add unamended backfill soil. Top of root ball should be about 2 inches above surrounding soil.

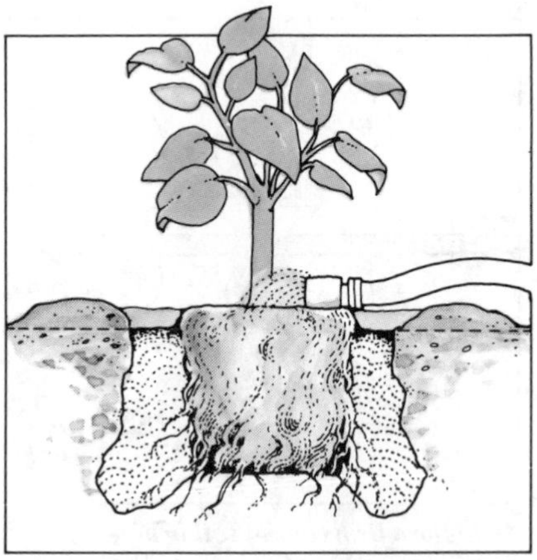

3) Make berm of soil to form watering moat. Irrigate gently—water should remain in moat rather than flood basin; objective is to keep trunk base dry.

roots that seem to be permanently kinked. For 1-gallon-size plants, simply loosen the roots. Place the plant in the hole; spread the roots out. Fill in around the roots with unamended backfill soil, firming it with your fingers, until the hole is about half full. Water thoroughly to eliminate air pockets; then make a ridge of soil around the hole's perimeter to form a watering moat, finish filling in the hole, and water again. Pump the plant up and down slightly to settle wet soil around the roots, and check to see that the top of the root ball remains about 2 inches above soil grade.

Balled-and-burlapped plants. Certain plants have roots that won't survive bare-root transplanting. Instead, they are dug with a ball of soil around their roots, the soil ball is wrapped in burlap (or other sturdy material), and the wrapping is tied with twine to keep the ball intact. These are called balled-and-burlapped (or "B and B") plants. Available in this fashion are some deciduous shrubs and trees, evergreen shrubs such as rhododendrons and azaleas, and various conifers.

Treat B and B plants carefully: don't use the trunk as a handle; and don't drop them, because the root ball could shatter and expose the roots. Cradle the root ball well by supporting the bottom with one or both hands. If it is too heavy for one person to carry, get a friend to help you carry it in a sling of canvas or stout burlap.

Note: Many B and B plants are grown in clay or fairly heavy soil that will hold together well when plants are dug up and burlapped. If your garden soil is medium to heavy in texture (heavier loam to clay), you can plant without amending the soil you return to the planting hole (called *backfill soil*). But when the B and B soil is more dense than the soil of your garden, there can be a problem in establishing the plant: its dense soil will not absorb water as quickly as the lighter garden soil around it. In such situations the soil ball around your B and B plant can be dry even when garden soil is kept moist. To avoid this problem, follow the backfill amendment recommendations in the next paragraph.

To plant a B and B specimen, dig a hole twice as wide as the root ball (as illustrated), and place the plant in the hole. If the root ball is wrapped in burlap or other biodegradable fabric, you can leave it in place. But if a synthetic material encases the root ball, you must carefully remove it so that the roots will be able to grow into the surrounding soil. Then fill the hole half full with backfill soil, firming it with your fingers or a stick. If your soil is light to medium (and your B and B soil is heavier), mix one shovelful of organic amendment to each three shovelfuls of backfill soil. This will improve the water retention of the backfill soil, creating a transition zone between root ball and garden soil. Use peat moss, ground bark, nitrogen-fortified sawdust, or similar organic amendments—but not animal manures.

If you are setting out a B and B plant in a windy location, you should stake it. The root ball can act like a ball-and-socket joint as wind buffets the plant, and such shifting can break new roots that are growing into your garden soil. Drive the stake firmly into the soil beneath the planting hole on the side of the plant that faces the prevailing winds.

After any necessary staking, fill the hole to within 3 to 4 inches from the top. If it is a burlap-wrapped plant, untie the twine that holds the burlap around the trunk, and then spread the burlap open or cut it off down to the backfill soil. Water the plant thoroughly; then add more backfill soil until it reaches the level of soil around the planting hole. After forming a watering basin around the hole's perimeter, water the last soil you added.

During the first couple of years after planting, pay close attention to watering—especially if the root ball is heavier than your garden soil. Keep the surrounding garden soil moist (but never continuously soggy) so that the roots will grow out of the root ball into the surrounding soil as fast as possible.

Note: If a root ball becomes dry, it will shrink, harden, and fail to absorb water. Where there's a great difference between garden soil and root ball soil, you can achieve better water penetration if you carefully punch holes in

Ball-and-burlap Planting

1) Set ball and burlap plant into planting hole, placing root ball on firm plateau of undug soil; top of root ball then should be about 2 inches above surrounding soil.

2) Untie burlap and spread it out to uncover about half of root ball. Drive in stake alongside root ball before hole is filled.

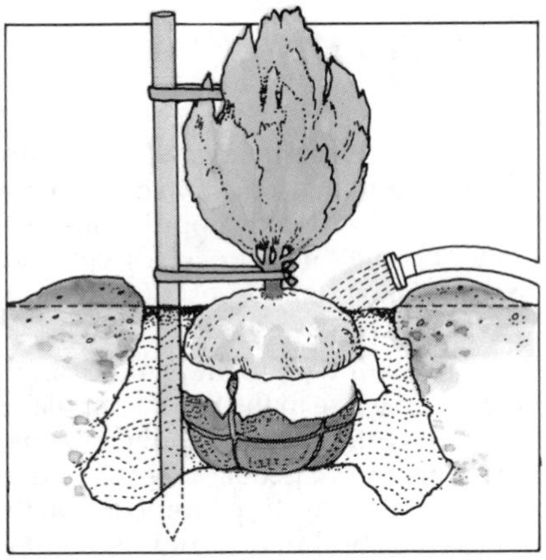

3) After firming in backfill soil, create watering moat as described for container planting. Gently water in plant, then loosely tie plant to stake.

the root ball with a pointed instrument ¼ to ½ inch wide. Or use a root irrigator (see page 70). After several years, when roots have grown out and become established in your garden soil, the difference between soil types won't matter.

Transplanting Shrubs & Small Trees

A time may come when you need or want to move a shrub or small tree from one place to another. With expert care you can do this at any time of year, but with most plants you'll be more assured of success if you transplant in cool weather, while the plant is dormant or semidormant. The inevitable loss of some roots is not as crucial during a plant's dormant season. (Tropical plants, on the other hand, transplant best after the soil has warmed up in spring.)

Dormant deciduous plants, such as roses, can be moved bare-root. Prepare the new planting hole before you dig up the plant to be moved; that way you can accomplish the operation as quickly as possible so that the roots will not dry out.

To move evergreen plants (both broad-leafed and coniferous) or deciduous ones that are in leaf, dig them up with soil around the roots. The bigger the plant, the more difficult and time consuming transplanting becomes. If you plan ahead, you can prepare the plant for moving by partially root-pruning it several months to a year before actual transplanting. Mark a circle around the plant that is ten times (or larger, if practical) the diameter of the plant's trunk at ground level. Then, with a sharp spade, cut around the circle to the spade's depth to encourage the plant to grow a new set of feeder roots. The shock of losing the roots you cut will be minimized by leaving the plant undisturbed for a period of time. When you do transplant, dig outside the circle made by root pruning so that the majority of active roots will be in the root ball.

Several days before the move, thoroughly soak the soil around the plant so that digging will be easy and the root ball will hold together. Particularly in the case of an evergreen, it would be wise to spray the foliage with an antidesiccant spray before moving the plant. The antidesiccant will cut down on the plant's water loss through transpiration during the ensuing months, when new roots will be forming.

To transplant, first prepare a planting hole as shown for balled and burlapped plants. Then, if you pruned the roots months earlier, dig a trench around the plant just outside the circle you cut—or just outside the drip line if you did not. Dig this trench as deep as the root ball is wide, and at least a spade's width wide for easier transplanting. When the trench is completed, you're ready to secure the root ball.

Burlap is the traditional material for wrapping a root ball, but chicken wire is easier to purchase and use. With small-mesh wire (1 inch or less), encircle the root ball tightly, securing the cut ends by wrapping cut wires together or by threading them together with a length of wire. Tighten the wire, then slice under the root ball with a spade. In heavier soils, the wire should help keep the bottom soil intact as you lift or lever the root ball out of the ground. For sandier soils that tend to break up, slide a piece of chicken wire under the root ball and lift the mass from below with this wire.

Set the plant into the planting hole. Next, carefully remove the chicken wire (this is necessary because chicken wire will not degrade in the soil and, in time, may girdle thickening roots that have grown through it). Finally, replant as described and illustrated for balled and burlapped plants.

Small plants will have correspondingly small root balls, so with these you may be able to eliminate the wrapping or wiring process. Any plant whose root ball you can carry in a shovel or in your hands may not need wiring.

Of course, transplanting some very large shrubs and trees is beyond your capability—your hand tools couldn't do the digging job adequately, and the root ball would be too heavy for you to lift. The answer in such cases is to hire a landscape contractor.

Watering

Most western gardeners work in a climate characterized by low rainfall, a long dry season, or both. Well over half the West's gardening population—excluding those living in California's north coast fog belt and in the area north of the Siskiyous and west of the Cascades—spend a good part of each year watering plants.

This annual routine is increasingly affected by the continuing rise in the West's population. Although the overall western water supply remains virtually fixed, more and more people are putting demands on that finite amount of water. Superimposed on this pattern is the unpredictable but recurring drought year, in which so little rain falls during the "wet season" that reservoirs are not filled to capacity to meet needs during the following dry months. Obviously, water management will be a continually increasing challenge.

There are several ways to meet this challenge. Westerners with established gardens can alter their watering practices—convert to drip irrigation systems; upgrade existing permanent systems with water-efficient sprinkler heads; refine watering schedules (perhaps aided by electronic controllers) to eliminate runoff and maximize penetration. Gardeners about to set out a new landscape—and those preparing to revamp an established one—can choose plants that, after they become established, don't need continual watering to survive the hot, dry months (see pages 161–163). And any gardener can employ various water conservation measures (see pages 69–72).

Basic Water Knowledge

"How often shall I water?" is perhaps the question most frequently asked by the novice gardener. No other question is quite so difficult to answer. "Give a plant as much water as it needs for healthy growth"—although accurate— is not really a helpful reply. The variable factors involved are many and complex: the needs of the particular plant, its age, the season, the weather (temperature, humidity, and amount of wind), the nature of the soil (and of the water), the method of application. To ignore these factors and water by calendar or by clock may subject your garden to drought or drowning. But this much we *can* say: frequent light sprinkling and frequent heavy soaking alike are bad. *Water thoroughly—and infrequently.*

To understand this advice, it helps to know how water and soil interact, and what roots need for good health.

How deeply to water. Roots develop and grow in the presence of water, air, and nutrients. Except for naturally shallow-rooted plants (rhododendrons and azaleas, for example), plants will root throughout the depth at which these essentials are found. If only the top foot of soil is kept well watered, roots will develop just in the top foot. Even lawn grasses, frequently thought of as shallow rooted, can run roots from 10 to 24 inches deep. When shallow watering keeps the roots near the surface, plants will be open to severe damage if you go away for a long weekend and the weather turns hot, drying the top inches of soil. There will be no deep reserves of water to tap—and no roots to tap them anyway.

Water penetration. A little water wets only a little soil, so you can't dampen soil to any depth by watering it lightly. Water moves down through the soil by progressively wetting soil particles. Once a particle has acquired its clinging film of water, every additional drop becomes "free" water—free to move and wet other particles. Although water moves primarily downward, it also moves laterally (to a much lesser extent), particularly in claylike soils. This lateral movement allows you to wet as much as a 12- to 18-inch diameter circle of soil (in heavier soils) with one drip emitter, or to water plants 6 to 9 inches on either side of a furrow or soaker tube.

Because you should wet a plant's entire root zone when you water, it's important to understand water movement. You can see that in many soils a small watering basin around a shrub or tree is likely to encourage roots to remain within a small-diameter spread. You also understand that an irrigation ditch 6 inches or more from a row of plants may not water the entire root area. And realizing that water moves primarily downward will affect the length of time you water your plants: taking your soil type into account, allow enough time for water to percolate down and penetrate the root zones.

When you soak your soil, you are wetting each layer, as the water moves downward through it, to a condition known as *field capacity.* In this condition, each soil particle holds the maximum amount of water film it can against the pull of gravity; the amount of air space in the soil then is low. As plant roots and evaporation draw water from the soil, the films of water become thinner, and more space is gained for soil air. The film eventually becomes so thin that its molecular attraction to the soil particle is stronger than the root tips' ability to extract it, and a plant will wilt even though some water remains in the soil. Between the time soil reaches field capacity and the time it dries to the wilting point, the plant has sufficient water for healthy all-over growth.

Field capacity varies by soil type. Clay soils, with many fine particles, have more surface area and thus hold more water than do sandy soils, with their fewer, coarser particles. Loamy soils, with a mixture of particle sizes, have an intermediate field capacity.

How often to water. To maintain a healthy air-to-water ratio for plant roots, you shouldn't keep your garden constantly at field capacity. Water deeply but not too often (depending, of course, upon the various factors mentioned below that influence rate of soil drying). If damp soil continues low in oxygen for any length of time, both root development and nutrient absorption are reduced, so that plant growth is slowed; at the same time, organisms harmful to the roots proliferate. Plants vary in their ability to resist such unfavorable conditions, but all plants (except water plants) need soil air.

If temperature, humidity, wind, and day length never varied, you could water your garden according to a calendar. Weather conditions, however, will upset such a schedule at least part of the time. Under the influence of

Watering to Encourage Deep Roots

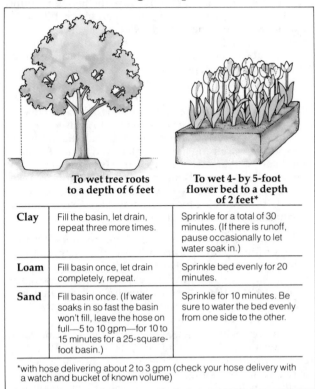

	To wet tree roots to a depth of 6 feet	To wet 4- by 5-foot flower bed to a depth of 2 feet*
Clay	Fill the basin, let drain, repeat three more times.	Sprinkle for a total of 30 minutes. (If there is runoff, pause occasionally to let water soak in.)
Loam	Fill basin once, let drain completely, repeat.	Sprinkle bed evenly for 20 minutes.
Sand	Fill basin once. (If water soaks in so fast the basin won't fill, leave the hose on full—5 to 10 gpm—for 10 to 15 minutes for a 25-square-foot basin.)	Sprinkle for 10 minutes. Be sure to water the bed evenly from one side to the other.

*with hose delivering about 2 to 3 gpm (check your hose delivery with a watch and bucket of known volume)

a hot, dry wind, plants use water so rapidly that shallow-rooted ones sometimes cannot absorb water from the soil fast enough to prevent wilting. In such weather you need to water more frequently than a fixed schedule would call for. Conversely, when coolness or humidity prevail, you should water less frequently. The one watering rule that can be applied safely to all types of soil and climate is this: test the soil. If the top layer (3 to 4 inches) is dry—especially during the growing season—you probably need to water.

In winter, when the days are short and the sun is low on the horizon (diminishing light intensity and lowering plant water use), plants in leaf can exist for days or weeks on much less water than they demand in summer.

How to Apply Water

There are really just two ways to apply water: by sprinkling or by flooding the ground. But there are numerous different sprinklers and soakers available for use. Here we present the basics of sprinkling and soaking, and a water delivery system that can combine both: drip irrigation.

Sprinkling. The simplest way to apply water evenly over a large surface is by sprinkling—essentially, producing artificial rainfall. Many plants, particularly those that like a cool, humid atmosphere, thrive with overhead sprinkling. Plants benefit from having dust rinsed off of their leaves; sprinkling also discourages certain pests, especially spider mites.

But sprinkling has a negative side. It wastes water: wind can carry off a certain amount of water before it reaches the ground; and water sprinkled on, or running off onto, pavement is water thrown away. In areas where humidity is high, sprinkling encourages some foliage diseases (black spot and rust, for example), though you can minimize the risk by sprinkling early in the morning so that leaves will dry quickly as the day warms. Another potential drawback of sprinkling is that some plants with weak stems or heavy flowers will bend and possibly break under a heavy load of water.

■ ***Timing and placement.*** To sprinkle effectively, you need to know the speed at which water penetrates in your soil and the water delivery rate of your sprinklers.

Assume that 1 inch of rainfall (or sprinkling) will penetrate about 12 inches in sandy soil, 7 inches in loam,

Measuring Sprinkler Delivery Rate & Dispersion

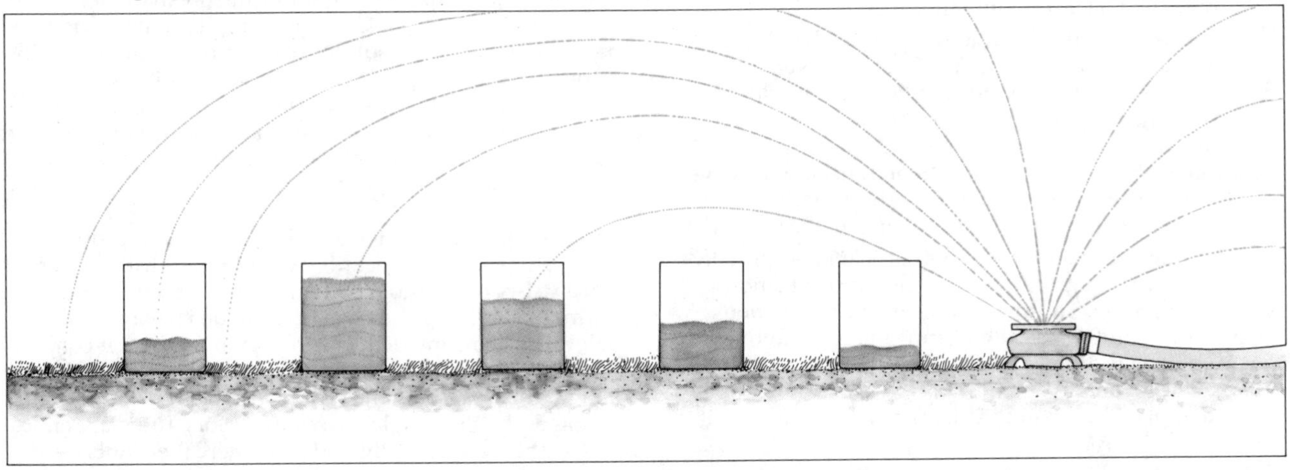

Check sprinkler's delivery rate and dispersal pattern by placing equal-sized containers at varying distances from sprinkler.

and 4 to 5 inches in clay. Therefore, if you want to water to a depth of 12 inches, you will need about an inch of sprinkling if your soil is sandy or 2½ to 3 inches if your soil is clay.

To determine a sprinkler's delivery rate, place a number of same-size containers (such as coffee cans) at regular intervals outward from the sprinkler, and turn on the water. Note the length of time it takes to fill a container with an inch of water. In this process, you'll also learn the sprinkler's delivery pattern. That is, you'll notice that containers fill at an unequal rate.

To achieve fairly even coverage, you'll have to overlap sprinkler coverage so that all areas watered will receive approximately equal amounts.

■ ***Sprinkler types.*** Nurseries, garden supply stores, and hardware stores sell a wide variety of sprinklers, both for attaching to the end of a garden hose and for incorporating into a permanent sprinkler system.

Familiar types are the oscillating fan spray, the fountain of water (or fan of water in those manufactured to cover less than a full circle), the single- or multi-stream rotor sprinklers, and the "machine gun" impact types. Information about delivery rates, which can vary greatly, is available from the retailer or the manufacturer.

Common to all is an uneven distribution pattern, referred to above, though the exact pattern varies from model to model.

■ ***Runoff.*** This may occur in some soils that are unable to absorb water as fast as sprinklers deliver it. Inadequate water penetration results, even when you think you've run the sprinklers long enough. In a clay soil, penetration can be so slow that more than 50 percent of the water is lost by runoff if the ground slopes slightly. In other words, you could easily sprinkle on 6 inches of water and have only 3 enter the soil.

The best way to avoid runoff is to alter your sprinkling procedure or change sprinkler heads—or possibly both. Slow the delivery rate so that the soil can absorb more of the water you deliver. Or water at intervals, each time just to the runoff point, with a period between waterings so that the water will have a chance to soak in. Water as many times as necessary to get the penetration you want. An electronic controller simplifies this operation.

You also can buy low-volume sprinkler heads that will significantly cut the volume of water delivered; the decrease in delivery will more nearly match the slower absorption rate of heavy soils. For the most even coverage, look for matched-precipitation sprinkler heads. These guarantee, for example, that a half-circle head will deliver just half as much water as a full-circle head, rather than deliver the same amount of water over a smaller area.

Another solution to the runoff problem—especially on steeply sloping ground—is to use a drip irrigation setup (see below). The low-volume delivery of various drip emitters and soaker tubing can eliminate runoff without sacrificing thorough penetration. If this approach is not practical, you can enhance water penetration for a particular plant by forming an irrigation basin around it.

Flooding. Flooding, or soaking, is an effective means of supplying sufficient water to the extensive and deep root systems of large shrubs and trees. Make a basin for the plant by forming a ridge of soil several inches high around it at its drip line (see Glossary). To water, simply fill the basin slowly. From the depth of water in a full basin, the length of time it takes to fill it, and knowledge of your soil type and absorption rate, you can calculate the time it will take to achieve the depth you desire.

If you grow vegetables or flowers in rows, the furrow between rows takes the place of basins around individual plants. Broad, shallow furrows are generally better than deep, narrow ones: there is less danger to roots in scooping out shallow furrows, and less likelihood that roots will be exposed by a strong flow of water. And a wide furrow will assure soaking of a wide root area (remember that water in all but clay soils moves primarily downward). Try to do furrowing before root systems have developed and spread; if you wait too long, you may damage roots when you make even a shallow furrow.

■ ***Soil soaker hoses.*** These were the forerunners of drip irrigation and still are particularly useful if you need to water plants in rows. Attached to a hose nozzle, a long tube of canvas (or of perforated or porous plastic) seeps or sprinkles water along its entire length. You also can water trees and shrubs with a soaker, by placing it in a circle around the plant, following the drip line.

Simply position the soaker, attach the hose, and turn on the water for slow and steady water delivery. Plastic tubes perforated with tiny holes were originally designed for overhead sprinkling, but with holes turned to the ground they function as soakers, eliminating water loss from wind evaporation. As with drip irrigation systems, you will need to leave soakers on longer than you would a sprinkler.

Updated versions of soaker hoses are available for use with drip irrigation systems. They include several kinds of porous tubing: drip tubing with laser-drilled holes, double-walled tubing, and soaker tubing that oozes water through its walls.

■ ***Root irrigators.*** Some special hose-end attachments can soak the soil beneath the surface. They are particularly useful for getting water deep into the soil on sloping land, where deep penetration without runoff can be a problem. They also can help trees root more deeply than they would with shallow watering. This can minimize pavement damage and uneven lawn surfaces caused by surface roots. In appearance and in effect, a root irrigator is like a giant hypodermic needle. You attach it to a hose, insert it into the root zone of a tree or shrub, and then turn on the valve: water flows through holes near the irrigator's tip, 12 to 18 inches below ground.

Drip irrigation. The term "drip irrigation" describes application of water not only by controlled-drip emitters but also by soaker tubing and miniature sprayers and sprinklers. What these have in common is that all operate at low pressure and deliver a low volume of water compared with standard sprinklers. The water is applied slowly and near or on the ground: there is no waste from runoff and little or no loss to evaporation. You place emitters so that water is delivered just where the plants need it, and you control penetration by varying the time the system is on or by varying the delivery capacity (in gallons

Components of a Drip Irrigation System

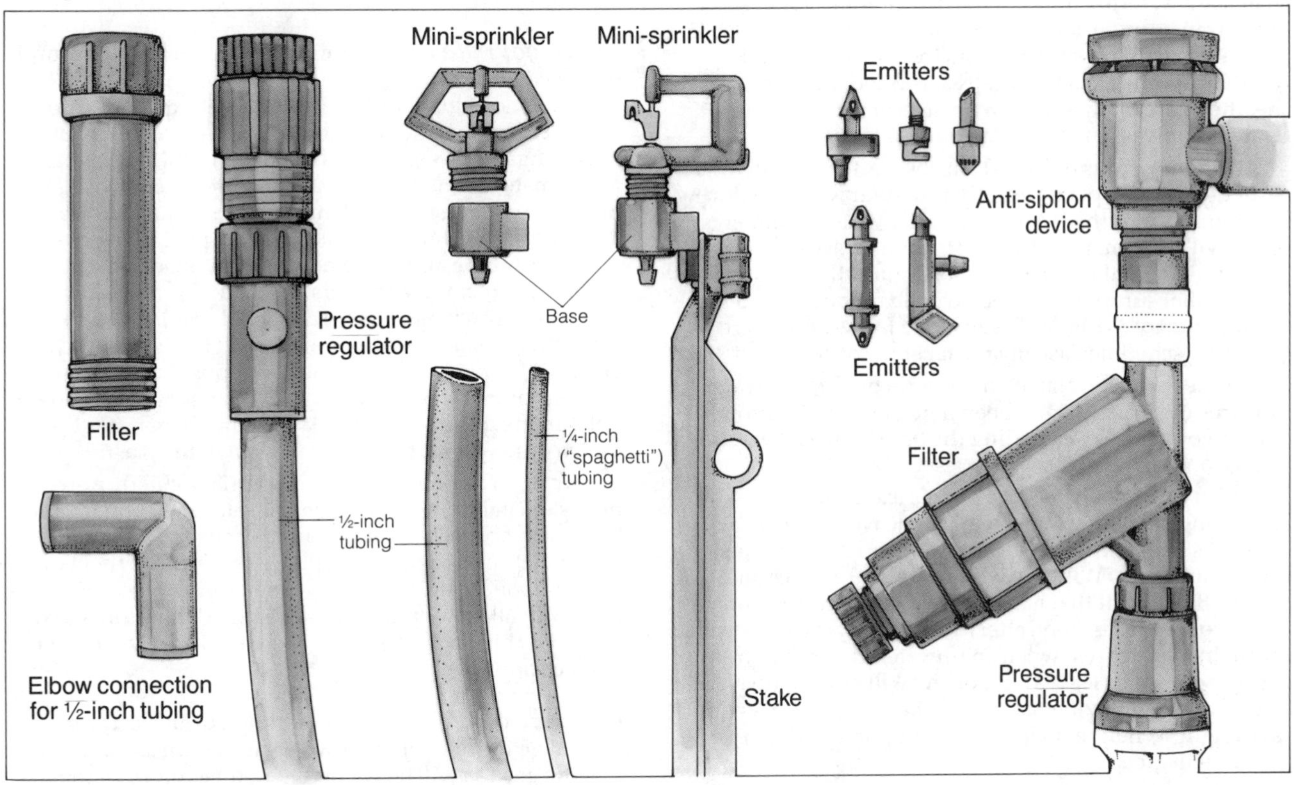

Drip irrigation delivers low volume of water at low pressure. Component parts are easy to assemble with no special tools.

per hour: gph) of the emitters you use. And you can regulate the volume of water to each plant by selecting the type and number of emitters you set for each.

The chief advantage of these systems is their flexibility. You can tailor them to water each plant by its own emitter(s), or you can distribute water over larger areas with microsprayers, minisprinklers, and porous tubing. Because lines are above ground (though they can be concealed by mulch) and are made of limber plastic, you can easily change positioning of lines and layout of systems, adding or subtracting emitters at will. About the only task drip irrigation isn't suited for is watering lawns.

You can set up a drip system to connect to a hose end; or you can make a permanent connection to your main water source, as you would for an underground, rigid-pipe setup. Such a permanent connection can be operated by an electronic controller (see page 72).

■ ***Emitters.*** A great number of different emitters are available, varying in shape, size, and internal mechanism. But all operate on the principle of dispensing water slowly to the soil. You can choose various flow rates, from ½ gph up to about 4 gph. Non–pressure-compensating emitters (the standard kind) work well on flat and relatively level ground, and with lines not exceeding 200 feet in length. But when either gravity or friction (on hillsides or with long lines) will lower water pressure, choose pressure-compensating emitters. These will deliver the same amount of water throughout the system.

In addition to standard emitters that simply drip, you can buy a variety of other specialized emitters. Misters and foggers deliver a fine spray to increase humidity for plants like fuchsias and tuberous begonias. Spitters are favored for watering container plants. Microspray and mini-sprinkler heads offer low-volume equivalents of standard sprinkler-irrigation fixtures, delivering sprays of water over full- and partial-circle areas. These are useful for watering entire beds, as long as plants don't obstruct their flow, preventing even coverage. Just like regular sprinkler heads, they deliver water unevenly over the areas they cover. For even distribution, overlap their coverages by half. Flow rates are greater than those of drip emitters; you can find ones that deliver as little as 3 gph and others that emit as much as 40 gph. Some will operate at the water pressure used for drip emitters, but others require higher pressure. If you want to combine these with standard drip emitters, be sure to check manufacturers' specifications for operating pressure.

Additional Ways to Conserve Water

Throughout this section, we have emphasized the need to use water without wasting it because the West's water supply is both limited and capricious (see also page 68). Here we offer additional tips that will help you cut down on water consumption.

Know your plants. Most annual plants and perennials will need watering through the dry months. For best appearance, many lawns and other ground covers also will need regular watering. And the shallow-rooted garden favorites, such as azaleas, rhododendrons, and heathers, are likely to perish (or at least suffer) if their water supply is cut off.

But numerous trees and shrubs—after they are established—can prosper on less-than-regular watering during the rainless months. Some, especially where summer is cool, will even make it through the entire dry period with no supplemental water. For proof, look at the trees and shrubs that survive in neglected or abandoned gardens, along country roads, and even along freeways, where watering schedules usually fall far short of "regular."

When water is scarce, think twice before you water any tree or shrub that has been in the ground for more than two years. Try extending the time between waterings for as long as the plants look presentable.

You can usually tell by a plant's leaves when it is becoming desperate for water. Most leaves will exhibit a dullness, loss of reflective quality, or curling edges just before they wilt. Wilted leaves, of course, are a certain tipoff. But a plant that has wilted is seriously dry, and you must supply water soon afterward if the plant is to survive at all. In many cases, when an unwatered shrub or tree drops some of its leaves but doesn't wilt or even turn dull, it is simply employing natural mechanisms for surviving a drought. When regular water is supplied again, new leaves will grow.

Some plants, aside from those already mentioned, can't do without water during the dry season. Among these are lawn trees that have grown dependent on summer watering (particularly if their root systems extend only to the depth of the average lawn watering) and plants that are native to cool climates (Monterey pines and cypresses, for example) but are growing in hot inland gardens.

Evaluate your lawn. A lawn uses water at a rate disproportionate to the rest of your garden (see page 190). Reevaluate your need for a lawn, or consider reducing its size. Alternatives to lawns are surfaces of gravel, brick, concrete, and wood decking. You can plant drought-tolerant ground covers, such as juniper, ivy, or *Baccharis.* If you must have a lawn, there are drought-tolerant grasses (see page 365), which require less water than the more familiar types.

Locate plants wisely. You can cut water use if you use care in placing plants that need regular watering. Plant these "thirsty" plants where they will be shielded from drying summer winds, and restrict them to one part of the garden (perhaps close to the house, for easy maintenance). For most areas of your landscape, select drought-tolerant plants.

Schedule your watering. If you water by sprinkling, wind and sun will cause water loss through evaporation even before the water reaches your plants. The best time for sprinkling is when it is windless and cool—during the night or earliest morning, when water pressure also is highest. An electronic controller (below) will schedule such waterings without your having to alter your living schedule.

Mulch your plantings. A mulch placed over the ground occupied by a plant's roots will keep the soil beneath it cool and moist longer than it would be if exposed to hot sun and drying wind. Mulched plants, then, will be able to go longer between waterings than unmulched ones. Many materials have been tried and proven effective as mulches: compost, animal manures, ground bark, leaves, sawdust, straw, hoed or pulled weeds, processing by-products (grape and apple pomace, cottonseed hulls, rice hulls)—even old newspapers. Rocks and gravel will also do the job. Black plastic sheeting, sold in rolls, will conserve moisture and suppress weeds. It is best for strawberries and other low-growing row crops. Lay strips of the plastic along both sides of a row of plants, or cut or punch holes in the plastic for each plant. Water penetrates this mulch only where there's a gap or cut in the plastic.

You can buy rolls of plastic materials (chiefly polypropylene fabric) that are permeable to water and air and have been specially manufactured for use as mulch. Ease of installation is their strong point: you just roll them out onto the soil. Some will last for one year, others are longer-lived. But all are unattractive and should therefore be covered by a thin layer of organic mulch (which also forestalls degradation by sunlight).

Use electronic devices. The addition of an electronic controller, or timer, to your watering system assures you that the garden will be watered whether you're at home or away. But even more important, you can program watering schedules so that your plants receive no less and no more water than they need to thrive.

There are a variety of controllers available for home use, ranging from simple single-program, multiple-station versions to complex and versatile multiple-program, multiple-station sorts that can easily handle large areas containing plants with diverse water needs. Most are designed to operate on normal 110-volt household electrical current. For systems used in places where an electrical hookup would be difficult, there are battery-operated controllers.

By using an electronic controller, you can easily reduce runoff by setting cycles to run for a short period several times a day. With enough repetitions, water can penetrate to the desired depth.

The flaw of automatic controllers is that they operate on a preset schedule regardless of weather: a controller could turn on the water during a rainstorm, or apply amounts of water appropriate for hot summer weather in cooler fall. Besides resetting a controller yourself, according to seasonal weather conditions, two electronic attachments can function as weather sensors to fine-tune the main control.

A *soil moisture sensor,* linked to the controller, will trigger sprinkler operation only when the sensor indicates that soil moisture has dropped to the point where water is needed. And a rain shutoff device accumulates rainwater in a special collector pan, turning off the controller when filled to a prescribed depth, then triggering the controller to resume watering when the collected water has evaporated.

Fertilizers

In addition to light, air, water, and space for roots, growing plants need a supply of nutrients—elements necessary to carry out their life processes. Some of these nutrients, the ones referred to as *trace elements,* are needed in infinitesimal quantities that most soils can supply. But there are three *major nutrients*—nitrogen (chemical symbol N), phosphorus (P), and potassium (K)—that plants need in larger amounts for consistently good growth. These three nutrients are the basis for commercial fertilizers.

Besides the three major nutrients, there are six *minor nutrients* essential to plant health. Where poor growth or soil testing reveals a deficiency in any of these elements, you'll have to supply it in some form of fertilizer.

The Basic Nutrients

The following paragraphs explain the three major and six minor nutrients, their influence on plant performance, and the importance of each in a fertilizing program.

Nitrogen. The most important nutrient, nitrogen, is not a mineral and hence is not present in the minute particles of soil from which plants derive their phosphorus, potassium, and other elements (see below). All nitrogen must come from other sources: organic matter, air, or fertilizers. In nature, nitrogen comes primarily from decomposing organic material, which is generally in very short supply in western soils—especially in the drier regions. Rainfall carries nitrogen from the atmosphere into the soil. In addition, specialized nitrogen-fixing bacteria that live on the roots of certain plants (legumes in particular) extract nitrogen from air between soil particles.

Plants use large quantities of nitrogen to form proteins, chlorophyll, and enzymes needed for plant cells to live and reproduce. When nitrogen is deficient, leaves yellow from their tips toward the stem, the plant yellows from the bottom upward, and growth is stunted.

Nitrogen can be taken up by plants only in its *nitrate* form (see below), which is soluble. Consequently, available nitrogen is easily lost by the leaching action of irrigation and rainfall. Soil organisms also need nitrogen to thrive, and they, too, place demands on the available supply. For these reasons, many plants need supplemental nitrogen from time to time in order to grow as well as we expect them to.

The first of the three numbers shown on a fertilizer label indicates the percentage of nitrogen. In the natural course of events (with no supplemental fertilizer), nitrogen that comes into the soil as dead plant or animal material must undergo several chemical changes before it takes on the nitrate form plant roots can use. If a fertilizer's label says that all or most of the nitrogen contained is in either nitrate or *nitric* form, nitrogen will be released quickly and plants will be able to use it immediately. But if most of the nitrogen is in the *ammonium* form (ammonium sulfate, for example), nitrogen release will be slower—taking anywhere from 2 weeks to 3 months—but should be more sustained once it starts.

Reading a Fertilizer Label

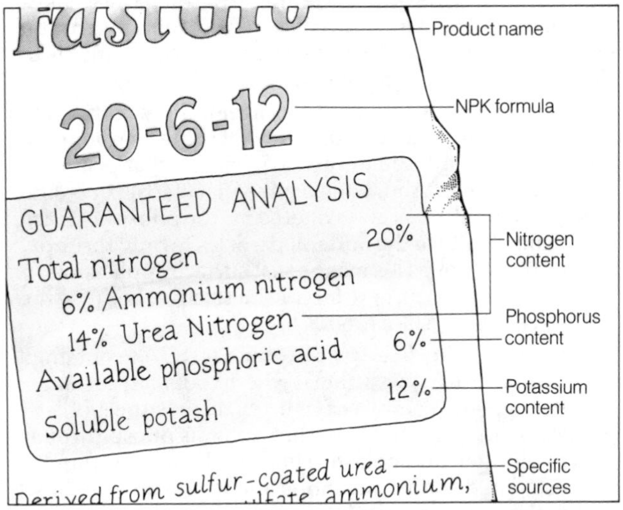

Every fertilizer's label shows, in numbers, the formula of major nutrients; the guaranteed analysis information both specifies the nutrient percentages and mentions their chemical sources.

Ammonium nitrate consists of half ammonium nitrogen and half nitric nitrogen; it therefore yields some of its nitrogen quickly and some slowly. *Organic* nitrogen—as in blood meal, urea, and IBDU (isobutylidene diurea)—first must go through a conversion to ammoniac nitrogen, which then is converted to nitrogen in the nitrate form. These are the slowest acting of the nitrogen sources.

Note: If you add organic matter to your soil as a conditioner, the matter may be high in carbon compared with nitrogen. Soil organisms working to digest the high-carbon material may then compete with plants for the limited amounts of nitrogen available in the soil. For this reason, the high-carbon (high-cellulose) soil conditioners such as sawdust, wood shavings, ground bark, and straw require special handling. One choice is to shop for and buy those materials in fortified form (with nitrogen already added to the material so that the organisms of decomposition will not take any nitrogen from the soil). If you get unfortified material, you should mix a nitrogen fertilizer with it, as directed on page 191.

Phosphorus. The second percentage of the three on a fertilizer label indicates the amount of phosphorus (listed as *available phosphoric acid*) the product contains. Unlike nitrogen, phosphorus does not dissolve and move through the soil for roots to absorb. Soil particles that contain phosphorus ions release them "reluctantly" to the microscopic film of water (soil solution) surrounding them.

As the root tips grow into contact with the soil solution, they absorb the phosphorus that the solution is holding in usable, or available, form. The remaining phosphorus is insufficient to meet the plant's needs until the soil particles release more phosphorus to the solution. The root grows into fresh areas of soil solution, repeating the process.

During periods of rapid growth, the phosphorus absorption-and-renewal cycle around a soil particle takes place continually. But if the concentration of phosphorus in the soil solution is too low, or if the rate of renewal is too slow, plant growth is retarded.

The phosphoric acid in a fertilizer ionizes in the soil to form phosphate compounds. Some of these compounds are useful to plants; others are so insoluble that plants cannot use them. And when a phosphate fertilizer is simply spread on the soil and watered in, the phosphoric acid binds chemically to the mineral particles in only the top inch or two of soil. This means that surface applications of phosphorus fertilizers are largely ineffective, because they will reach only surface roots.

The most effective way to apply a fertilizer containing phosphorus is to concentrate it where roots can get at it. When you plant a new tree or shrub, dig in superphosphate or a complete fertilizer that contains phosphorus as well as nitrogen and potash. Thoroughly mix the amount suggested in the label directions into what you estimate will be the root area for a few years to come. The same advice would apply to planting perennials and annual plants. For seed planting, place the fertilizer beside the seed rows, a couple of inches to one side and a couple of inches below the seed level (following fertilizer label directions for amount per foot of row). For established shrubs and trees, use fertilizer sticks, stakes, or tablets, as explained on page 75.

Potassium. The third percentage on a fertilizer label represents potassium. This element is described in various ways, such as "available or soluble potash" or "water-soluble potash." Plants remove from the soil more potassium than any other nutrient except nitrogen and calcium.

Potassium exists naturally in the soil in several forms. Plants can't use most of the natural soil potassium, even though it may be abundant. But about one percent of the total soil potassium, called *exchangeable* potassium, acts as an important source for plants. Derived from minerals, fertilizers, or crop residues, exchangeable potassium is not soluble until modified by a slow weathering process. However, roots can pick up exchangeable potassium directly from clay or humus particles. Like phosphorus, potassium is effective only if placed near roots, in their anticipated growth routes.

Calcium, magnesium, sulfur. Some fertilizers contain these important elements; others do not. They are usually present in the soil in adequate supply, except that many soils of the high-rainfall areas of the Pacific Northwest have a sulfur deficiency. There, sulfur can be readily leached away, just as nitrogen is. If you live in these areas, apply additional sulfur regularly to annual crops and lawns for optimum performance.

Calcium and sulfur often enter the soil in other kinds of garden products: lime (calcium), lime-sulfur fungicide and soil conditioner (calcium and sulfur), gypsum (calcium and sulfur), superphosphate (sulfur), and soil sulfur used for acidifying alkaline soils.

- ***What they do.*** Calcium plays a fundamental part in cell manufacture and growth—most roots must have some calcium right at the growing tips. Magnesium forms the core of every chlorophyll molecule in the cells of green leaves. And sulfur acts with nitrogen in making new protoplasm for plant cells; it is just as essential as nitrogen, but its deficiency in the soil is not so widespread.

Iron, zinc, manganese. If soil is highly alkaline, as some soils in low-rainfall areas are, plants may not be able to absorb enough iron, zinc, and manganese. Gardeners can buy products to put on soil or spray on leaves to correct the deficiency. Some of these products are *chelated,* meaning that the iron, zinc, or manganese is in a form that can be used by the roots, and is not susceptible to the fixing (a chemical binding process) that makes the native iron, zinc, or manganese unavailable.

- ***What they do.*** Iron is essential to chlorophyll formation. Manganese and zinc seem to function as catalysts, or "triggers," in the utilization of other nutrients.

Types of Fertilizers

A visit to a nursery may reveal a bewildering selection of fertilizers. You'll find fertilizers for a variety of specified uses and with differing formulas; there are granular types packaged in cartons and sacks, and liquid ones in bottles. When you understand the basic fertilizer types, the confusion will clear and you can select for your particular needs.

The first distinction to draw is between dry and liquid forms. There are further differences between *complete, simple, special-purpose* and, *organic* fertilizers and between controlled-release, tablet, and combination products.

Dry fertilizers. These constitute the majority of fertilizers sold. You sprinkle or spread them onto a lawn; sprinkle them onto the soil and scratch, rake, or dig them in; or apply them in subsurface strips. Dissolving when they contact water, the granules begin their fertilizing action quickly. But, depending on the fertilizer, they can last for several months.

Liquid fertilizers. Although the most widely sold fertilizers are the solid types, liquid fertilizers have certain attributes that recommend their use:

- they are easy to use, especially on container plants;
- there is no risk of burning a plant as long as you follow label directions for dilution;
- the nutrients are available to roots immediately.

They are less practical than the solids for large-scale use because they cost more and must be reapplied more often (their nutrients in solution leach through the root zone more rapidly).

Available in a variety of different formulations, liquid fertilizers include complete formulas and special types that offer just one or two of the major nutrients. All are made to be diluted with water: some are concentrated liquids themselves; others are powder or pellets. Growers of container plants often use liquid fertilizers at half the dilution and twice the frequency recommended so that plants receive a more steady supply of nutrients.

Complete fertilizers. Any fertilizer that contains all three of the primary nutrient elements—nitrogen, phosphorus, and potassium—is called a complete fertilizer. Many fertilizer manufacturers put their product's N, P, and K percentages in big numbers on the label, right under the product name—for example, 10-8-6. Without looking at the fine print under *Guaranteed Analysis* (always listed somewhere on a fertilizer label), you know that the fertilizer contains 10 percent total nitrogen, 8 percent phosphoric acid, and 6 percent water-soluble potash.

There are fertilizers with many different nutrient ratios on the market. Even when the percentages are the same on two different products, the formula by which one manufacturer arrived at its ratio can differ from others (see the explanation of different types of nitrogen on page 73). The higher the numbers in the analysis, the stronger or more concentrated is the fertilizer (a 22-6-4 formula contains twice as much nitrogen as does an 11-6-4 fertilizer). And the higher the concentration (of N especially), the less you apply at one time.

Complete fertilizers are most useful when you get them into the soil where active roots can take up the phosphorus and potassium. If you want only the benefits of nitrogen, use a nitrogen-only simple fertilizer.

Simple fertilizers. In contrast to complete fertilizers, the simple kinds contain just one of the three major nutrients. Most familiar are the nitrogen-only types, such as ammonium sulfate (21-0-0), but you can find phosphorus-only and potassium-only fertilizers as well. Falling between the two extremes are "incomplete" types that contain two of the three major elements: N and P, N and K, or P and K.

Special-purpose fertilizers. When shopping for fertilizer, you will find some packaged for specific types of plants—"camellia food," "rhododendron and azalea food," and "rose food," for example. The camellia and rhododendron-azalea fertilizers belong to an old, established group—the acid fertilizers (below). The other fertilizers packaged for certain plants do not have as solid a background of research (compare, for example, the NPK ratios of three different brands of "tomato food").

All chemical fertilizers except calcium nitrate reduce the pH of soil by producing acids as they decompose. Those that are especially acid producing are labeled "acid fertilizers" and are useful on acid-loving plants. They also are good for general purpose fertilizing in alkaline soil regions—to reduce alkalinity.

Organic fertilizers. The word "organic" simply means that the nutrients contained in the product are derived solely from the remains, part of the remains, or a by-product of a once-living organism. Cottonseed meal, blood meal, bone meal, hoof-and-horn meal, and manures are examples of organic fertilizers. (Urea is a *synthetic* organic fertilizer—an organic-like substance manufactured from inorganic materials.) Most of these products packaged as fertilizers will have their NPK ratios stated on the package labels. Usually, an organic fertilizer is high in just one of the three major nutrients and low in the other two, although some are chemically fortified with the other nutrients. In general, the organics release their nutrients over a fairly long period. The potential drawback is that they may not release enough of their principal nutrient at a time to give the plant what it needs for best growth. Because they depend on soil organisms to release the nutrients, most organic fertilizers are effective only when soil is moist and warm enough for the soil organisms to be active.

Although manure is a complete organic fertilizer, it is low in N, P, and K. Nutrient content varies according to the animal species and its diet, but an NPK ratio of 1-1-1 is typical. Rather than as nutrient suppliers, manures are best used as mulches or as soil conditioners.

Controlled-release fertilizers. These beadlike granules are balls of complete fertilizer coated with resin, sulfur, or another permeable substance. When moistened, as in normal watering, some of the fertilizer diffuses through its coating into the surrounding soil—a little bit with each watering until the encapsulated fertilizer is used up. Some products are effective for 3 to 4 months, others for 8 or more months. Scratch or dig the pellets into the soil so that they are covered. These are particularly useful for fertilizing container plants, which need frequent nutrient replenishment because of leaching from frequent watering.

Sticks, stakes, and tablets. These are fertilizers compressed into hard cylinders or tablets; you push or hammer the sticks or stakes into the soil, or drop tablets into holes. Dissolving slowly in the presence of water, they yield nutrients gradually—sometimes for a year or more. These products are convenient for getting phosphorus and potassium down into the regions of active root growth of established shrubs and trees.

Combination products. You can buy fertilizers combined with insecticides (chiefly for roses) or with weed killers, fungicides, or moss killers (all for lawns). These products are appropriate if you need the extra ingredient every time you fertilize; if not, it is more economical to buy it separately.

Calculating Actual Nitrogen

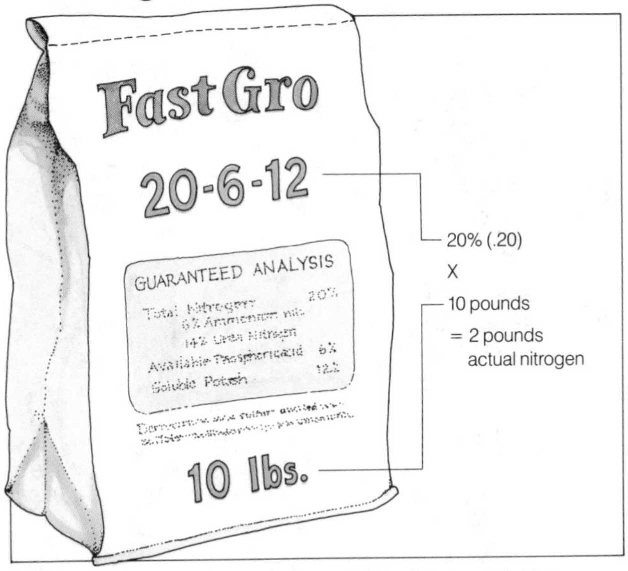

Actual nitrogen is the amount, by weight, of that nutrient in a fertilizer. To calculate the pounds of actual nitrogen, multiply the nitrogen percentage by the fertilizer's total weight.

Pruning

Pruning is both a skill and an art. The skill is in making proper cuts that will heal well. The art is in making cuts in the right places so that the plant will develop its potential beauty or produce an optimum crop.

No matter how much or how little pruning you do on an established plant, the objective is to modify the plant's growth. The modification can be done for any of the following reasons, singly or in combination:

- to maintain plant health by removing dead, diseased, or injured wood
- to control or direct growth
- to increase quality or yield of flowers or fruit

You never should have to cut back a plant continually to keep it in bounds. A plant that seems to require such treatment was the wrong choice for its garden location; the repeated cutting back only destroys the plant's natural beauty. Exceptions are pruning formal hedges, espaliering fruit trees, shaping topiary, and pollarding (see Glossary).

Some of the tools used in pruning are illustrated on pages 93–95.

Plant Growth & Pruning Know-how

To understand how to approach the pruning of any plant, you need to know how growth occurs. And since all growth originates in *buds,* they are the first plant parts to consider.

The *terminal growth bud* develops at the end of a stem or branch. This bud causes the stem to grow in length.

Lateral buds grow along the sides of stems. These buds produce the sideways, or lateral, growth that makes a plant bushy.

In some plants, there may be *latent buds*—buds that lie dormant beneath the bark. These will grow after pruning or injury removes the actively growing part of the stem.

During the season of active growth, terminal buds draw plant energy to themselves and grow, adding length to the stems. This flow of plant energy to a terminal growth bud is caused by hormones, called *auxins,* that are produced within the bud. But if you cut or nip off any growing terminal bud, the stem or branch ceases growing. When you remove the bud, one or more of the buds below it will begin to produce auxins and thus will draw plant energy. All the kinds of pruning cuts, including pinching, should be made just above some growth—a growth bud, stem, or branch. For explanations of how to make proper cuts, see "Pruning cuts" on the next page.

Pinching. The first opportunity you have to control or direct plant growth is to remove—to pinch out—new growth before it elongates into stems. This is especially useful with young plants that you want to make bushier. For example, you can pinch all the terminal buds on every branch of a young fuchsia plant. This will force growth from buds that are at the leaf bases along the stems, creating perhaps two, three, or four new side branches instead of just one lengthening branch. When this happens, you get all-over growth.

Conversely, if you want a plant to gain height, keep side growth pinched back so that the terminal bud on the main stem continues to elongate.

Four Ways to Prune

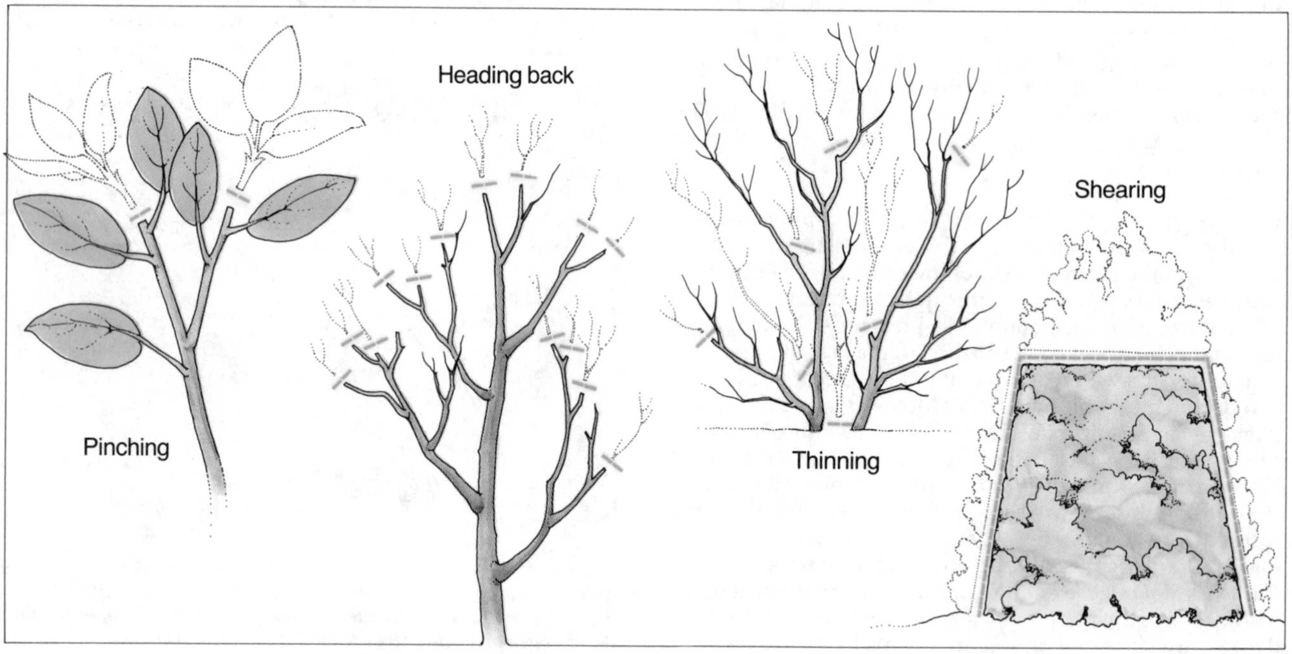

Heading back. This sort of pruning—also called cutting back—takes advantage of the same growth principle: growth elongates in one direction until it is stopped. The difference is that in heading back you cut off lengths of stem already grown rather than removing growth before it forms stems. Cut stems down to promising side branches or to lateral buds that will grow in the desired directions. The annual ritual of rose pruning probably is the most familiar example of heading back.

Heading back may be done for a variety of reasons: to remove weak or unproductive wood; to encourage growth in the direction you want it to take (or prevent growth from continuing in the wrong direction); to stimulate flower or fruit production by encouraging growth of wood that will produce it; to prevent wind or snow damage to very long or heavy branches; and, sometimes, as part of a program to revitalize an old plant.

In heading back, you come to grips with pruning as an artistic exercise, since you will be making decisions about which growth to remove and which to leave. Refer to "Pruning to Shape" on page 78 for some general guidelines on controlling and directing a plant's growth.

Thinning. Think of thinning as an extreme form of heading back: instead of removing parts of stems, you remove entire limbs or branches. Reasons for thinning are essentially the same as for heading back. The operation usually opens up a plant by simplifying its structure and removing old, unattractive, and unproductive growth, weak or excess growth, or limbs that detract from the beauty of the plant's natural shape. Again, a familiar example occurs in rose pruning—removing entire canes to the plant's base.

Shearing. This is the only form of pruning that could be called indiscriminate. You ignore all advice that tells you to cut just above growing points and, instead, clip the surface of densely foliaged plants. Shearing is the process that maintains the even surfaces of formal hedges and topiary work. Because the plants that normally are used for these purposes have buds and branches that are close together on their stems, every cut is close to a growing point.

Pruning Tools

There are specific instruments to perform the various pruning tasks. Pruning shears handle the smallest work, whereas loppers can manage larger limbs—to about broom handle thickness. Pruning saws come into use for branches beyond lopper capability. All of these tools are illustrated and described under "Pruning Tools" on pages 93–95.

Pruning Cuts

After you understand how to approach a pruning job, you need to know how to make good pruning cuts. The first lesson: never leave a stub. Or to put it another way, always make a cut just above some sort of growth (a bud or a stem). To understand why this advice is given, think of a stem or branch as a conveying tube for water and plant nutrients. If you cut a branch some distance beyond its uppermost growing part, you leave nothing in the stub itself to maintain growth. The stub, no longer a part of the plant's active metabolism, withers and dies, though remaining attached to the plant; in time it will decay and drop off, leaving an open patch of dead tissue where it was attached. In contrast, when a cut is made just above a growing point, *callus* tissue will begin to grow inward from the cut edges; in time, this tissue will cover the cut surface.

There is a right way to make pruning cuts—and there are several wrong ways, as the illustrations on this and the next page show. You want to avoid leaving stubs, and you also want to avoid undercutting the bud or branch. Best cuts, as illustrated below, place the lowest part of the cut directly opposite and slightly above the upper side of the bud or branch to which you are cutting back.

When you cut with shears, be sure that the cuts are sharp: clean cuts callus over faster than cuts with ragged edges. Use shears that are strong enough for the job. If you can't get them to cut easily through a branch, the shears are too small, too dull, or both. Switch to a stronger pair of shears or use a pruning saw instead. With hook-and-blade pruning shears, remember to place the blade, not the hook, closer to the branch or stem that will remain on the plant. As the drawings on the next page show, if the position of the shears is reversed, you will leave a small stub.

Pruning saws come in handy when you need to cut limbs that are too thick for shears or loppers, or when a plant's growth won't allow your hand and the shears to get into position to make a good cut.

How to Make a Pruning Cut

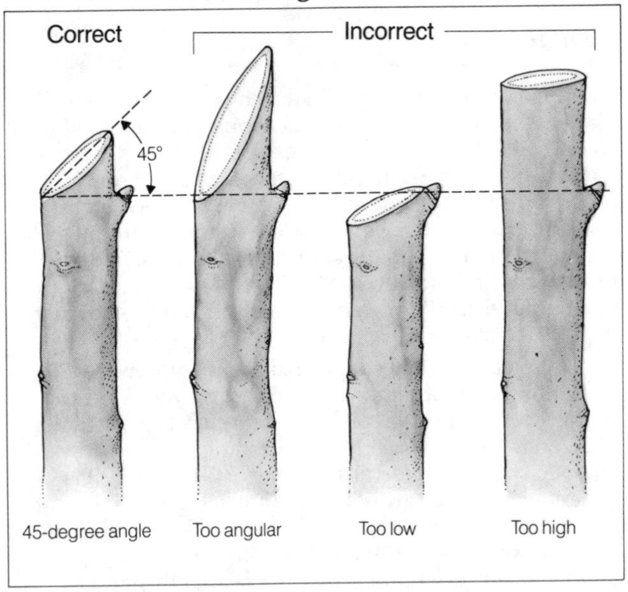

A correct pruning cut has its lowest point even with the top of growth bud, slants upward at about a 45-degree angle.

How to Position Shears

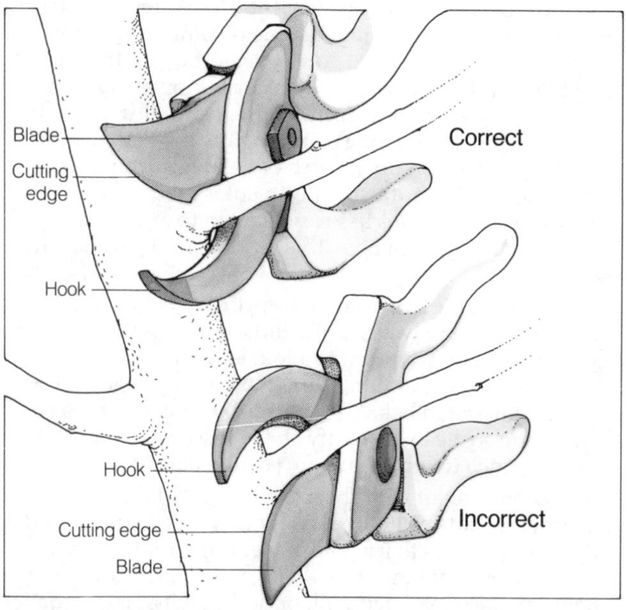

To make a proper close pruning cut, hold pruning shears with the blade closest to the growth that will remain on the plant. A stub results when you reverse the position and place the hook closest to the plant.

Removing a Large Limb

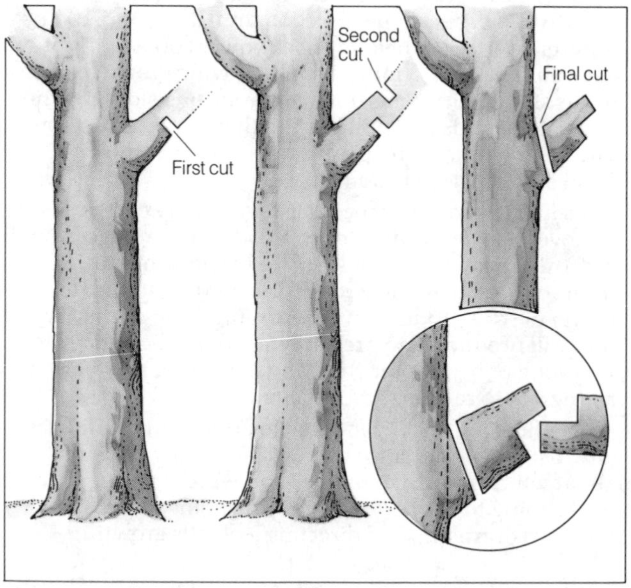

First, cut beneath branch, one-third to one-half through; then cut off limb beyond first cut. Finally, remove limb stub, cutting just outside bark ridges at limb's base (or on a line bisecting top and bottom angles branch makes to trunk).

Larger limbs—from wrist size upward—are heavy and need special care in removal. If you try to cut through one with a single cut, the branch is likely to fracture before you've finished the cut. The limb may fall, tearing wood and bark with it and leaving a large, ugly wound. To cut a larger limb safely, make it a three-step operation, as illustrated.

Pruning to Shape

Shaping is another concept in which your artistic side plays a role in determining what form a particular plant should take. Every plant has a natural shape; its growth tends to conform to a natural pattern, whether round, gumdrop shaped, wide spreading, vase shaped, or arching. Observe what a plant's natural shape is, and then prune the plant in a manner that will allow the natural form to continue to develop. Remove any excess growth that obscures the basic pattern or any errant growth that departs from the natural form.

When pruning to shape, make your cuts above a bud or side branch that points in the direction you'd like the new growth to take. If you have no preference, remember that generally it is better for a new branch to grow toward an open space than toward another branch. Also, it is generally better for growth to be directed toward the outside of the plant than toward its interior. Try to eliminate branches that cross and touch one another. Crossing branches can suffer injury by rubbing together and are usually unattractive, especially in deciduous plants out of leaf.

Special Kinds of Pruning

The general information already presented will guide you through most ordinary pruning situations, but for particular plants and for particular landscape situations, there are additional guidelines.

Pruning for flower production. Flowering shrubs will bloom either from new growth or from old wood, depending on the plant species. Before you prune, determine which sort of growth bears flowers. In this way, you can avoid inadvertently cutting out stems that would give you a flower display.

Most spring-flowering shrubs bloom from wood formed during the previous year. Wait until these plants have finished flowering before pruning them (or do some pruning by cutting flowers while they are in bud or bloom). Growth that the shrubs make after flowering will provide blooms for the next year.

Most summer-flowering shrubs bloom on growth from the spring of the same year. These are the shrubs you can prune during the winter dormant season without sacrificing the next crop of blooms.

A few shrubs bloom twice or throughout the growing season (many roses, for example). Spring flowers grow from old wood, later blooms come both from recent growth and from wood of previous years. During the dormant season, remove weak and unproductive stems, and, if necessary, lightly head back remaining growth. During the growing season, prune as necessary to shape while you remove spent blossoms.

Pruning for specific landscape uses. Many plants are adaptable enough to do landscape jobs not conventionally associated with them. Some sprawling shrubs or vines (climbing roses, *Bougainvillea,* and *Xylosma,* for instance) can easily be made into good ground covers by suppressing vertical growth and pegging down horizontal branches (use pieces of wire bent into hairpin shapes). California pepper (*Schinus molle*), ordinarily considered a tree, makes a very fine clipped hedge. And the sturdily upright Japanese black pine may be trained to cascade.

- ***Espalier training*** (see illustration below) can be the solution if you want greenery, flowers, or fruit in a narrow planting space. To create an espalier, you carefully train a shrub or tree into a framework of branches in a vertical plane. The essential operations are directing branches into this flat pattern and suppressing growth that departs from it. Espaliers usually need frequent pinching, pruning, and tying, and, in addition, they may need sturdy support.
- ***Standards*** are plants shaped to resemble small trees—as in the familiar "tree rose." Sometimes the crown portion of the "tree" is grafted onto the "trunk"; in other cases, careful pruning develops the tree form. Even vines can be staked and pruned, or trained over wire and wood forms to become standards.
- ***Pollarding and pleaching*** are specialized growth training methods. Pollarding is used to keep naturally spreading trees in bounds—yearly drastic cutting eventually forms large knobby stubs from which long, slender shoots grow each spring. Pleaching involves weaving branches together to form a hedge or arbor, resulting in a neat, rather formal pattern.

Pruning conifers. These evergreens fall into two broad classes: those with branches radiating out from the trunk in whorls and those that sprout branches in a random fashion. Spruce, fir, and most pines are examples of the whorl type; arborvitae, hemlock, juniper, and taxus (yew) are examples of random-branching conifers. Pruning guidelines differ for the two groups.

On whorl-branching types, buds appear at the tips of new growth, along the lengthening new growth, and at the bases of new growth. You can cut back the new growth "candles" about halfway to induce more branching, or you can cut them out entirely to force branching from buds at their bases. The point to remember is that you *must* make cuts above potential growth buds or back to existing branches. Cutting back into an old stem—even one that still bears foliage—won't force branching unless you're cutting back to latent buds.

The random-branching conifers can be pruned selectively, headed back, even sheared; new growth will emerge from stems or branches below the cuts. But when you shorten a branch, don't cut into bare wood below green growth: most kinds (yew is an exception) won't develop new growth from bare wood.

Some conifers—chiefly the random-branching kinds, plus deodar cedar and hemlock—can be kept at a controlled size, either as dense specimens or as hedges. When growth reaches within a foot or so of the size you desire, cut back all but about 1 inch of the new growth. This will produce enough small side branchlets to make full, dense foliage. Once this bushy growth forms at the ends of the branches, you can hold the plant to a small size year after year by shortening new growth that develops and cutting out any wild shoots.

Avoid damaging the central *leader* (the central vertical stem) of conifers unless you want to limit the height. If the central leader is damaged, you can stake one of the next lower branches vertically and train it as a new leader.

When a conifer has been damaged by cold or breakage, you may have to remove entire limbs. It's almost impossible to restore the natural shape, but you can often make the most of the situation by trimming or training the damaged plant into an unusual sculptural form.

Popular Espalier Patterns

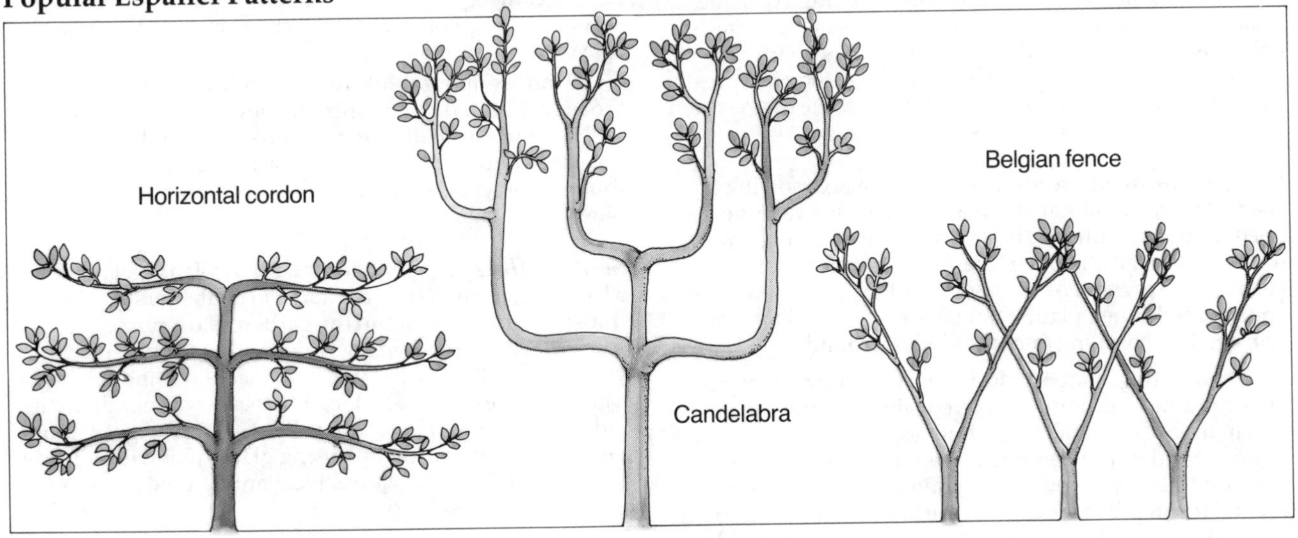

Espalier training can take a number of different forms; for a list of plants that take to this training, see page 132.

Propagating Plants

A gardener speaking of "propagation" refers to the many ways of starting new plants. These methods range from the simplicity of planting seeds to the more complicated arts of budding and grafting.

With the exception of seed sowing, all methods of starting new plants are known as *vegetative propagation:* the new plants that result will be identical to the parent plant. Vegetative propagation therefore maintains uniformity—assuring, for example, that each plant of the rose 'Queen Elizabeth' is like every other.

On the other hand, plants grown from seeds may appear to be identical or nearly so, or they may vary considerably. Seed strains of many annuals, for example, are developed for near-uniform appearance. But despite any illusion of sameness among seedlings, each seed is an individual, unique product of the union of two separate individuals. This combining of parental characteristics is the foundation of plant breeding—whether the breeder is striving for uniformity or for entirely new characteristics from parent plants that differ greatly.

Plants from Seeds

In nature, seeds are scattered randomly from the seed-bearing plant. And scattering, or *broadcasting*, seeds is a common method for planting seeds of lawn grasses and sometimes of wildflowers. For planting seeds of most garden plants, though, the gardener sows seeds more carefully in the open ground or in some sort of container.

You can buy seeds of most ornamental plants in three different forms. The traditional packaging is the seed packet—a picture of the flower, fruit, or plant on the outside, the loose seeds within. You also can buy packets or packages of pelletized seeds: each seed is coated, like a small pill, so that handling and proper spacing are made easier. The third form is seed tapes—strips of biodegradable plastic in which seeds are embedded, properly spaced for growing to maturity. You just unroll the tape in a prepared furrow and cover it with soil. In all three cases, you will find planting instructions on the package.

Seeds in the open ground. One advantage of sowing seeds directly in the earth is that you usually avoid the need for transplanting. The seeds germinate and grow into mature plants in one place. You may need to thin seedlings to prevent overcrowding, filling in a few sparse spots with thinned plants. But most of the seedling plants will need no handling once they break ground.

■ ***Broadcasting.*** Native wildflowers will make a reasonably good show if simply scattered where they are to grow and in time to catch fall rains. But they will do even better if the ground is first cleared of weeds and grasses and prepared a bit by tilling and by adding organic amendments. If you plan to broadcast seeds in drifts or patterned plantings, or if you wish to sow a broad area with tough, easy-to-grow plants (such as sweet alyssum or California poppies), you can achieve a more even distribution by mixing the seed with several times its bulk of fine sand. After you have scattered the seeds—or seed-and-sand mixture—rake lightly and carefully sprinkle the area with water. Then cover the area with a very thin mulch (see page 72) to prevent the soil from crusting and to hide the seeds from predators. (Be prepared, though, for a certain amount of loss to birds and, sometimes, to rodents.)

Most garden annuals and vegetables also can be sown in place, but they will benefit from a bit more attention than simple broadcasting calls for. With a fork, spade, or rotary tiller, prepare the seedbed, working in soil amendments (see "Types of Amendments," pages 60–61) and a complete fertilizer (read the label and apply recommended amount). Smooth the prepared soil with a rake and moisten it well a few days before you intend to plant (if rains don't do the watering for you). Then follow the sowing and covering directions outlined in the preceding paragraph.

■ ***Row planting.*** If you intend to grow vegetables or annuals in rows, prepare the soil as described above. But you can omit the fertilizer and apply it, instead, at seeding time in furrows 1 inch deeper than the seeds and 2 inches on either side of the seed row (again, consult label recommendations for the proper amount of fertilizer per foot of row). Follow the seed packet instructions for optimum planting depth and for best spacing of the rows, and lay them out in a north–south direction so that both sides will receive equal sunlight during the day. Use a hoe, rake, or stick to form the furrow; for perfectly straight rows, use a board or a taut string as a guideline.

■ ***Sowing and thinning.*** To sow seeds or seed pellets from packets, one of two methods will work best. Either tear off a small corner of the packet and tap the seeds out as you move the packet along the furrow or prepared seedbed; or pour a small quantity of seed into your palm, and then scatter pinches of seed as evenly as possible.

When seedlings appear, thin excess plants (if necessary) so that those remaining will be spaced as directed on the seed packet. Bare seeds scattered in furrows almost always come up too thickly; pelletized seeds are easier to sow at the proper spacing, and seed tapes do the spacing for you.

Thin seedlings while they are still small. If you wait too long to thin them, plants will develop poorly, and it will be more difficult to remove one without disturbing the surrounding plants. Work quickly but gently in the thinning process, replanting the surplus seedlings elsewhere as you go.

Seeds in flats and containers. Many plants get off to a better start when they are sown in containers and later transplanted into place in the garden. Most nurseries stock seedling plants in flats or other containers, ready for you to plant. By starting your own seedlings indoors or in a greenhouse—or in any location that is warmer than the out-of-doors and has adequate light—you can get a jump on the planting season by raising plants that will be ready to set out at the earliest possible planting time in spring (see "Greenhouses," page 89).

■ ***Containers.*** Almost anything that will hold soil and has provision for drainage will do for a seed-starting con-

Seed Planting in Containers

Planting seeds in containers offers greatest ease in handling. You can plant in pans, flats, or pots (right), then transplant into individual containers, or you can use small peat, soil, or paper pots (left) to start individual seeds.

tainer. Your choice will be dictated by what you have readily available and by the number of seeds you have to plant.

Plastic or wooden nursery flats will accommodate the largest number of seeds; other choices are clay or plastic pots, peat pots, aluminum foil pans (the sort sold for kitchen use), styrofoam or plastic cups, cut-down milk cartons, or shallow wooden boxes that you can make yourself.

Remember to punch holes for drainage in the bottom of any container that will hold water; if you make your own wooden flats or boxes, leave about a ¼-inch space for drainage between boards that form the container's bottom.

If you use containers that have held plants before, give them a thorough cleaning to avoid the possibility of infection by damping-off fungi, which destroy seedlings. A vigorous scrubbing followed by a few days of drying in the sun usually will suffice.

■ ***Soil.*** Unless you plan a large-scale seed-planting operation, it will be easiest to buy a prepared planting mixture for starting the seeds. Nurseries carry a variety of such mediums—look for labels that say "potting soil." Prepared mixtures are ready to use immediately; they usually have been sterilized to destroy disease organisms. If you prefer, you can prepare your own mixture, using about equal portions of potting soil, peat moss, and vermiculite or perlite: your objective is a soil that will drain easily yet still retain moisture.

You can use good garden soil in your seed planting mixture (equal parts soil, sand, and peat moss or ground bark), but such mixtures introduce the risk of damping-off fungi unless sterilized before use. You can bake soil in the oven at 160° to 180°F in a shallow pan for two hours to kill potentially harmful organisms (the odor during the process is terrible), or you can fumigate the mixture with a commercial soil sterilant according to label directions.

■ ***Sowing.*** Gently firm the mixture into the container and level it off about ¾ inch to 1 inch from the top of the container. If the mixture is powdery dry, water it thoroughly and wait a day or two to plant. Very fine seeds can be broadcast over the surface and covered with sand; larger seeds can either be planted in shallow furrows scratched into the surface or be poked in individually. Always remember that seeds should be planted no deeper than recommended on packet labels; a good general rule is to cover seeds to a depth equal to twice their diameter. Cover seeds with the proper amount of prepared mixture, press down gently but firmly, and then water. In order not to dislodge the seeds by directly watering the soil surface, place the container in a tub, sink, or bucket containing a few inches of water. The planting mix in the container will absorb enough water within a few hours.

Thereafter, keep the seeding mixture moist but not soaking wet. One way to do this is to place the container in a warm, protected spot not exposed to direct sunlight and cover with a pane of glass to conserve moisture and a newspaper to exclude light. As soon as the first seedlings begin to appear (begin checking for them in about 3 days), remove the covering to give them full light but not direct sun.

For slow-sprouting seeds or for plants whose seedlings develop slowly, you can sow seeds in a pot, and then tie a clear plastic bag around it. Place the pot where it receives good light but not direct sunlight. Air can get through the plastic, but water vapor cannot get out; seedlings will have enough water to complete germination without further watering. If you use this technique, be sure that your planting mixture is sterile and that the container has not been used for planting before.

■ ***Transplanting.*** When the new seedlings have developed their second set of true leaves, it will be time to transplant or thin them. If you don't need many plants, you will be able to thin them in place. Give them enough "elbowroom" (1½ to 2 inches between them) to allow them to grow larger before you plant them out in the garden. But if you're going to want most of the plants that have germinated, you will need to transplant them to larger containers for further growth to planting-out size. Preferably, transplant them into individual pots or cups; then when you plant out in the garden, they'll suffer a minimum of root disturbance.

To do the first transplanting, fill a new container with moist planting mix. Loosen the soil around the seedling plants (a kitchen fork is handy for this), and carefully lift out a seedling. Or lift a clump of seedlings and gently tease individual plants apart from the tangled mass of roots. Handle a seedling by its leaves to avoid bruising or crushing its tender stem. With a pencil, poke a hole in the new container's planting mix, place the seedling in the hole, and firm the soil around it. Water the transplant right away. Do this for each seedling plant until all are transplanted. Keep these plants out of direct sunlight for a few days, until they have adjusted to the change.

A few weeks to a month after the initial transplant, the seedlings should be ready to plant in the garden. During that month you can help their development by watering once with a half-strength liquid fertilizer solution or by sprinkling lightly with a slow-acting fertilizer.

Division

If you grow clumping perennials, bulbs, or plants with rhizomes or tubers, you're bound to become involved with division sooner or later. Each year the typical perennial gains in girth by growing new roots and stems, usually around the perimeter of the previous year's growth. Eventually (usually in 2 to 4 years), these clumps get too big for their space in the garden, and growth becomes less vigorous due to crowding and competition. To keep these plants healthy and strong, it's necessary to divide them periodically.

Each rooted segment or division is actually a plant in itself, or is capable of becoming a new plant. Dividing an overgrown clump into its separate parts is a fast and inexpensive way of increasing your supply of favorite perennials.

Division generally is done in autumn or early spring, when plants are dormant. In most climate zones, fall is the best time to divide perennials that bloom in spring or early summer, whereas early spring is better for those that blossom in late summer and autumn. But in the coldest zones, the spring-blooming perennials must be divided in *early* fall so that their roots will have a chance to grow before the coldest weather sets in. Some gardeners in such climates have better luck establishing these perennials if they divide and replant in early spring, even though that year's flowers may be sacrificed.

To divide deciduous and semideciduous perennials, cut the foliage back to about 4 inches from the ground. With evergreen perennials, leave all young, healthy foliage, but remove all dead leaves. (Perennials that form a tap root and grow from a compact crown are best propagated by making stem cuttings (see next page) or by sowing seeds.)

When decline in flower quantity and quality signals overcrowding of bulbs and bulblike plants (see pages 184–186), let foliage ripen thoroughly before you dig and separate the bulbs. Replant in well-prepared soil or store until

Dividing

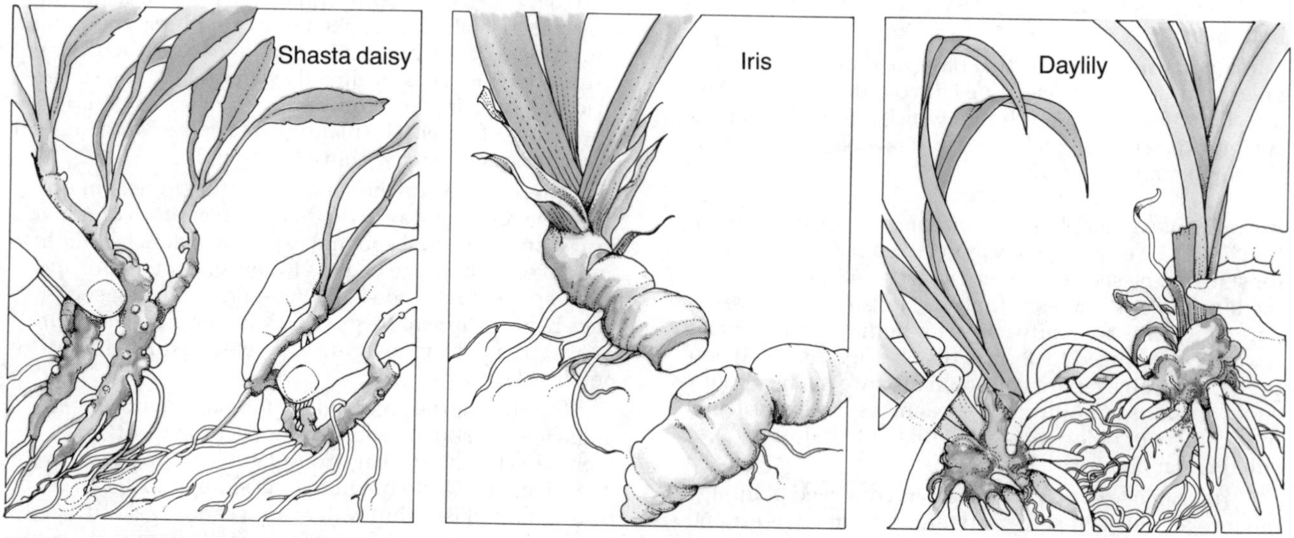

Dividing is an easy way to increase stock of many perennials and bulblike plants. Pull apart individual plants of clump-forming perennials (such as daylilies and Shasta daisies); break or cut apart separate plants of rhizomes (such as iris), some bulbs, and tuberous-rooted plants.

Cuttings: Softwood & Hardwood

Take softwood and semi-hardwood cuttings during the growing season; cut below a leaf, remove lower leaves, dip cut in rooting hormone, then plant.

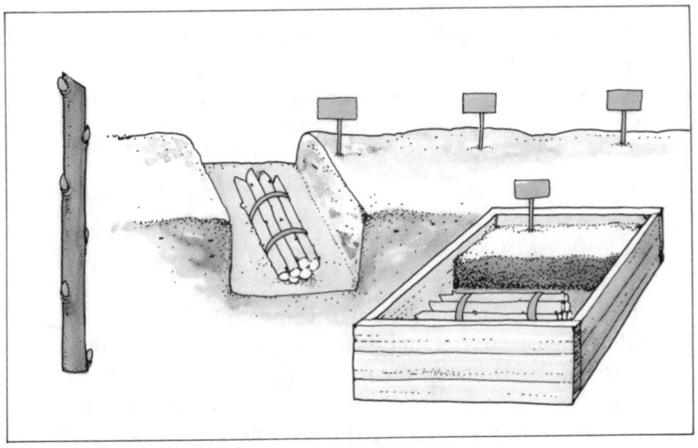

Take hardwood cuttings at onset of dormant season; make cut below a leaf bud, dip cut in rooting hormone. Store over winter in Zones 1–3; plant outdoors immediately in warmer climates.

the appropriate planting time, depending on the bulb's need (see individual descriptions in the Western Plant Encyclopedia, pages 199–568).

Cuttings

Most gardeners who have propagated new plants have started cuttings from plant stems, roots, or leaves. Stem cuttings are of three types—softwood, semihardwood, and hardwood—depending on the maturity of the wood.

Softwood and semihardwood cuttings. Softwood cuttings, taken from spring until late summer, are the easiest and quickest-rooting stem cuttings. You take them during the active growing season from soft, succulent, flexible new growth. You take semihardwood cuttings after the active growing season or after a growth flush, usually in summer or early fall. Growth is then firm enough that a sharply bent twig snaps (if it just bends, the stem is too mature for satisfactory rooting).

In addition to deciduous and evergreen shrubs and trees, many herbaceous or evergreen perennials may be propagated by softwood or semihardwood cuttings.

For both types of cutting, the procedures are the same. You'll have a better percentage of successful rootings if you start cuttings in a container of some sort—pot, flat or box, or can. Be sure the container will drain water; if it has no drainage holes, poke or punch holes in its bottom so that excess water will be able to drain out.

Choices of rooting medium are several, but they all allow for easy water penetration and fast drainage. Pure sand (builder's sand or river sand) is the simplest medium but requires the most frequent watering. Better are half-and-half mixtures of sand and peat moss or of perlite and peat moss, or perlite or vermiculite alone. Fill the container with rooting medium and lightly firm it down so that the surface is about an inch below the top.

For the best cutting material, look for healthy, normal tip growth. Avoid spindly twigs and unusually fat shoots. With a sharp blade (shears or knife), cut a 4- to 5-inch-long stem, making the cut just below a leaf; remove all leaves on the lower half of the cutting. Dip the cut end into rooting hormone powder, tap off the excess powder, and then insert the cutting to about half its length in the rooting medium you have readied. After you have finished one potful of cuttings, thoroughly water them.

Loss of water through the leaves that remain on the cuttings is the greatest threat to softwood and semihardwood cuttings. To minimize this water loss, you can provide a greenhouse atmosphere—high humidity—for the cuttings while they are striking roots. A tried-and-true method is to invert a clear glass jar over a cutting, though with a large pot or flat full of cuttings, this method is clearly impractical. Easiest of all is to place a plastic bag over the cuttings and container, then tie it around the container to confine humid air within the bag. Or, if the container is small, place it in a plastic bag and tie the bag at the top. Ventilate any of these improvised greenhouses for a few minutes every day or two.

Some softwood cuttings—fuchsias and impatiens, for example—root so easily that the glass jar or plastic bag is unnecessary. But whether the cuttings are covered or exposed, you should keep them out of direct sunlight during the rooting period.

When you see new growth forming on the cuttings, you can be fairly sure that they have rooted. Wait until the rooted cuttings appear to be growing well; then move them into individual containers of potting soil to further their development. Loosen the rooting medium around each new plant carefully, so that you can remove it easily without tearing off new roots. Quickly transplant it into its individual container, water it, and move it to a spot where it will receive good light but no direct sun. After you see that new growth is continuing, you can shift sun-loving plants to sunnier locations to prepare them for their ultimate places in the garden.

Hardwood cuttings. Hardwood cuttings are best made during the fall-to-spring dormant season from wood of the previous season's growth. Many deciduous shrubs and trees can be increased from cuttings taken during the dormant season: among well-known plants, some examples are *Deutzia, Forsythia,* grape, *Kolkwitzia, Philadelphus,* rose, and *Weigela.* Without very special treatment, most nut and fruit trees and the large hardwood shade trees (beech, birch, maple, and oak, for example) will not root satisfactorily from cuttings. These are propagated by grafting or budding (see pages 86–87) or from seed.

Hardwood cuttings may take longer to root and start growth than softwood cuttings, so you will want to put your hardwood cuttings where they will remain undisturbed.

For this method, best cuttings are the diameter of a pencil, measure 6 to 9 inches long, and have at least three leaf buds. Take them not from the tips of branches but from farther back on the stems. The top of each cutting should be cut just above a leaf bud, the bottom cut just below one. Be sure to cut the stub that remains on the plant back to a bud.

In all but the coldest climate zones (1, 2, and 3), you can set the cuttings out in the soil to root. Dig a trench as deep as half their length, put an inch of sand (builder's sand or river sand) in the bottom, set the base of each cutting on the sand, and fill in the trench with garden soil mixed with some organic matter, perlite, or sand. Water the cuttings and be sure that the soil does not dry out. To encourage root formation, try dipping the ends of the cuttings in a rooting hormone powder.

In Climate Zones 1, 2, and 3, you have a choice of several propagating methods. One is to take cuttings late in the dormant season, after most cold weather is past, and plant directly in the ground as described above. Or you can take the cuttings earlier, put them in a tightly sealed plastic bag, and place the bag in the refrigerator or in an unheated (but not freezing) room for the winter. When the coldest weather is past, plant out in the garden. A third option is to tie hardwood cuttings of each variety in separate bundles (labeled), and dig a trench in well-drained soil that will be deep enough to bury the bundles, laid on their sides, with 2 to 3 inches of soil. Place the bundles in the trench, cover with soil, and water them. Where the ground is likely to freeze, cover the buried cuttings with enough mulch to keep the ground from freezing. During the winter the lower ends of the cuttings will begin to form calluses from which roots will grow. When weather starts to warm as spring approaches, dig out the cuttings and plant them in the open ground or in containers. Although you should make sure that they receive good light, you also should protect them from direct sun. Cuttings must be planted top side up; to be sure, make the top cut slanted, the bottom cut square.

Root cuttings. Any plant that will produce sprouts from the roots will grow from root cuttings. Familiar examples are Japanese anemone, Oriental poppy, trumpet creeper, blackberry, and raspberry. Actually, the roots you plant will show no visible growth buds; the buds develop after the root cutting is planted.

To make root cuttings, select roots ⅛ to ¼ inch in diameter from vigorous plants, and cut the roots into pieces 1 to 3 inches long. Mix garden soil with an equal amount of potting mix, sand, or perlite. Then fill a flat, box, or other shallow container (with drainage provided) to within an inch of its top with this garden soil mixture. Placing the root cuttings on their sides on top of the soil, cover them with ½ inch of additional soil mixture and water thoroughly. Then cover the container with a pane of glass or piece of cardboard, and set it in the shade. Check every week for moisture and for sprouts; remove the covering when growth shows.

If you have only a few cuttings to root, place them upright in a pot of the rooting medium described above. The thickest end of the root cuttings should be upright, the tops of the cuttings just at soil level. Water the cuttings and place the pot in the shade, covered (if you wish) by glass or cardboard.

Leaf cuttings. Some plants will root successfully from a leaf or portion of a leaf. Begonias, African violets, various succulents, and sansevieria are among the more familiar plants you can propagate from leaves.

To multiply begonias, take a mature leaf, cut several of the main veins on the leaf's underside, and place the leaf flat on a moist rooting medium so that the cut veins

Cuttings: Leaf & Root

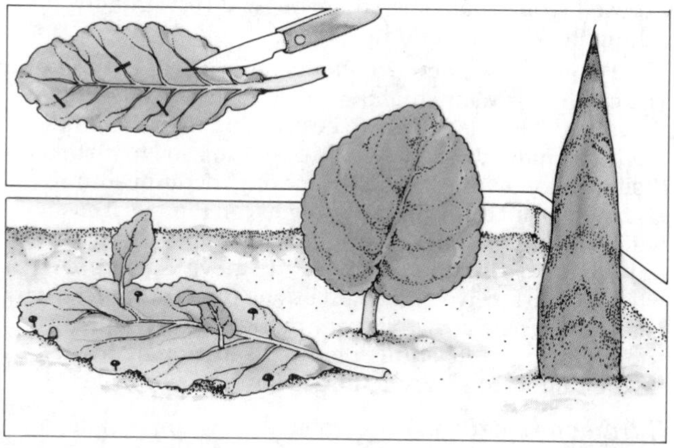

Leaf cuttings will increase many succulents, African violets, **Sansevieria, Begonia,** *and others. With some, cut veins and lay leaf flat on soil; others will grow from part of leaf inserted in soil.*

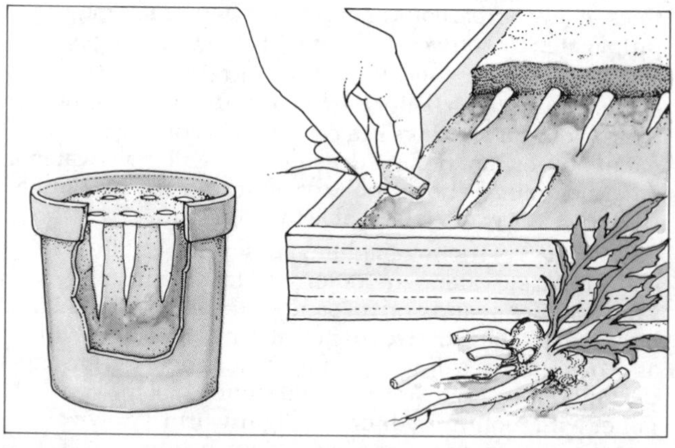

To make root cuttings, cut pencil- to finger-thick sections of roots; place them on their sides and cover with soil, or insert upright in soil with tops just at soil surface.

are in contact with the soil. If necessary, hold the leaf in place with toothpicks. New plants will form on the leaf's upper surface above each cut.

With African violets, leave a bit of leaf stalk (¼ inch to 2 inches) attached to the leaf; insert the leaf stalk upright into the rooting medium and steady the leaf with toothpicks. New plants will grow from the base of the stalk.

Most succulents will send up new plants from the base of a leaf that touches soil—often from a leaf that has fallen onto the ground.

Cut the long leaves of sansevieria into segments about 3 inches long; insert each segment upright about an inch deep into the rooting medium. New plants will sprout from the base of each leaf section and can be transplanted when 2 to 3 inches high.

Air Layering

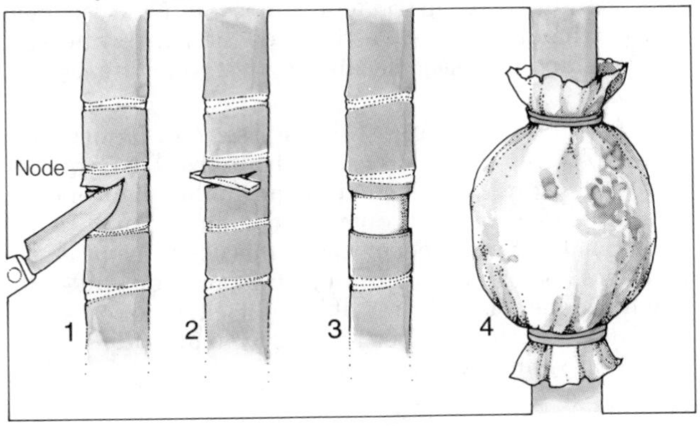

Begin air layering below a node. Make a slanting cut (inserting matchstick to keep it open) or remove ring of bark. Dust cut with rooting hormone, encase in damp moss, and wrap with polyethylene to keep moss moist.

Layering

The two layering methods—ground layering and air layering—tend to be slow to produce results, but with some hard-to-root plants you are more sure of success by these methods than with cuttings. Because you don't remove the branch from the parent plant until it has formed roots, the original plant continues to keep the layer alive.

Ground layering. Select a low-growing branch, about pencil size or slightly smaller, that can be bent easily to the ground. About 8 to 12 inches back from the branch tip, make a notch halfway through the underside of the branch and just below a leaf joint. Dust powdered rooting hormone onto the cut and insert a matchstick or small pebble into the cut to keep it open. Dig a wide hole about 4 inches deep so that you can bend the branch down into the hole, positioning the cut portion toward the bottom and bending the end of the branch up and out of the hole. Then anchor the bent branch in the hole with a wire loop or rock, fill the hole (with garden soil mixed with potting soil, peat moss, or other soil amendment), firm the soil in, and water it. To help hold the layer in place, tie the protruding end of the branch upright to a stake.

Keep the soil around the layer moist, as you would for any cutting. In a few months to a year, you should see new growth—indicating successful rooting—coming from the end of the branch you have tied upright. If not, carefully dig down to see if any roots have formed. (Some plants may take two years or more to form roots.) When you are sure roots have formed, you can cut the new plant free from the parent plant, dig it up, and move it to its intended location.

Air layering. The principle of air layering is the same as that of ground layering; the difference is that air layering is used for branches higher on the plant. It is especially useful with some of the large house plants.

Select a branch from pencil size up to an inch in diameter. Below a leaf joint, make a slanting cut one-third of the way through the stem, inserting a piece of matchstick to keep it spread apart. Alternatively, you can remove a ring of bark about ¾ inch wide, scraping it down to the hard core at the center of a stem or branch. Dust the cut lightly

Ground Layering

Select low, flexible branch that can be bent into shallow hole. Cut halfway through it, put pebble in cut, stake tip upright.

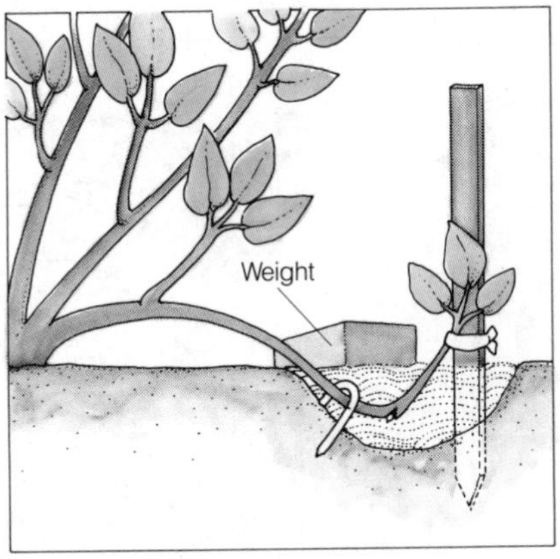

Secure prepared branch in shallow hole, using wire pin if needed. Brick or rock on soil also helps hold branch in place.

When staked branch shows growth, check to see if roots are formed. Cut branch from parent plant when well rooted.

with rooting hormone powder, wrap the area with a generous handful of damp sphagnum moss, and enclose the moss with polyethylene plastic. Above and below the ball of moss, bind the plastic securely with string, wire, or plastic ties.

If the rooting is successful, you'll see roots appearing in the sphagnum moss after several months. Then you can sever the newly rooted stem from the mother plant and pot it or plant it out on its own. At that time it usually is wise to halve the number of leaves; this will prevent excessive loss of moisture through transpiration while the newly independent plant establishes itself. If no roots form, the branch will callus where it was cut, and new bark will eventually grow over the cut area.

Budding & Grafting

Anyone who has ever brought home from the nursery a bare-root rose plant or apple tree has benefited from the arts of budding and grafting. Relatively few home gardeners, however, have tried to propagate plants by either of these methods. Budding and grafting aren't really difficult, but they usually require some practice, a steady hand, and a few special tools.

Commercial propagators have very sound reasons for practicing budding and grafting. Either method uses much less tissue of the plant to be propagated than cuttings would. For plants in short supply—new rose varieties, for example—production is increased greatly by these methods. From a performance standpoint, it makes sense to bud or graft plants to a rootstock that is known to grow well over much of the country. Many dwarf fruit trees, much better adapted to the home garden than are full-sized versions, owe their reduced stature to rootstocks that dwarf the growth of normal-sized varieties grafted onto them. And the novelty offerings, such as three different apples on one tree, come about only through grafting. The standard or "tree" rose is another of these products, comprising three different varieties: one for the roots, another for the sturdy trunk, and a third for the bush that provides the desired flowers.

Budding

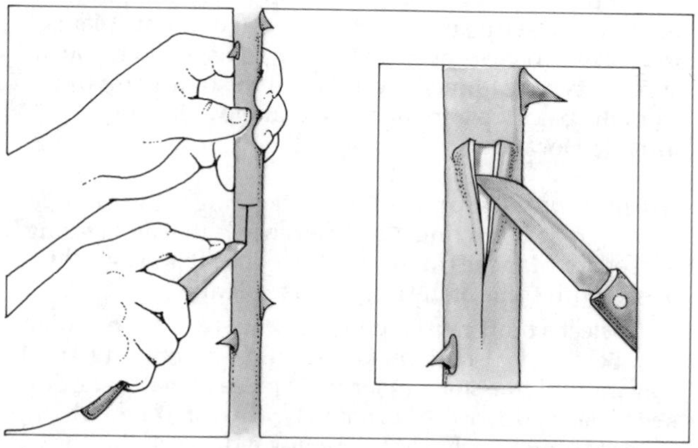

T-budding is fairly easy for the novice. Make T-shaped cut in branch ¼ to ½-inch in diameter; top of T should extend about ⅓ the distance around stem. Gently pry up corners where cuts meet.

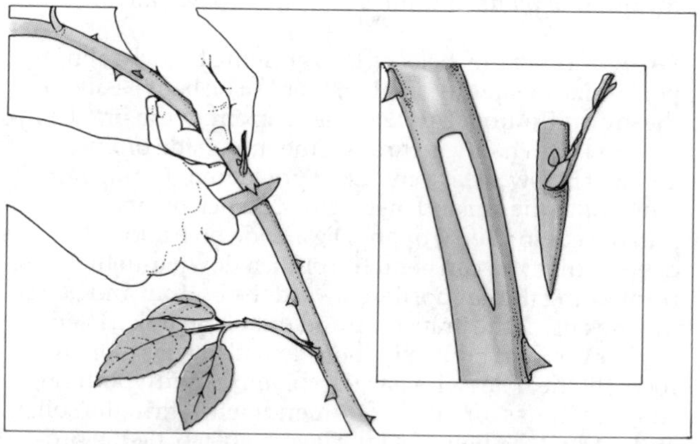

Cut shield-shaped patch containing bud from selected budwood plant. Begin about ½ inch below bud and finish about 1 inch above it; leave a bit of wood attached to back of bud shield.

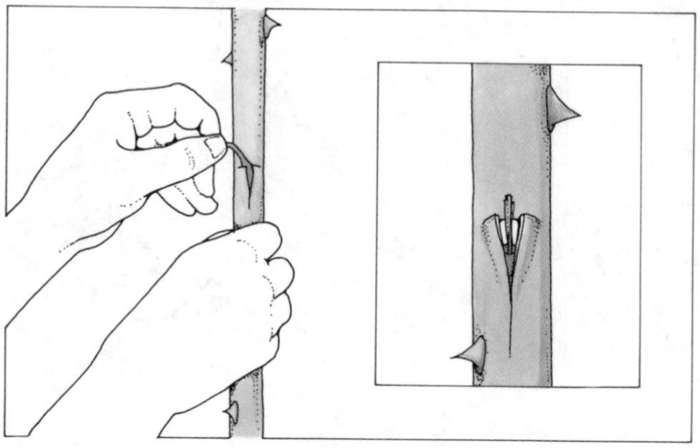

Push bud shield down between flaps of T-cut, being careful not to damage the bud. Cut off top of shield even with horizontal cut of the T; all of shield should fit beneath bark flaps.

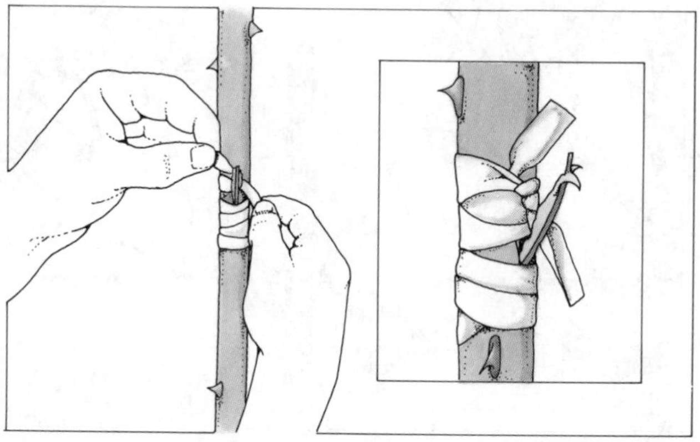

Bind the operation snugly with plastic tape, starting beneath the bud and finishing above it so that tape overlaps in shingle fashion. Only bud itself should be exposed.

Before you read the directions that follow, you'll have to learn a few terms of the trade:

- *stock* or *understock* is the name for the plant onto which you bud or graft; it supplies the root system (or trunk, or both) for the ultimate product
- *bud* is the single growth bud that is placed into the stock in the budding process
- *scion* is the piece of stem that you graft onto the stock
- *cambium* is the layer of cells that lies between the plant's bark and the woody core of a stem; it is the region in which growth takes place

Only when the cambium of the scion or bud unites with that of the stock will a graft or bud be successful.

Budding techniques. Budding accomplishes the same result as grafting, but it is considerably easier to do and, for the novice, is more likely to be successful. In summer or early fall, when plants are actively growing, insert a growth bud from one plant under the bark of another plant of a related kind. If the plants are compatible and if you do the budding carefully, the bud will unite with the stem into which it was inserted. Throughout fall and winter the bud will remain plump but dormant; it will begin to grow in spring when all buds on the plant have a growth spurt. At that time, cut off the stem at a point just above the growing bud you inserted.

Roses and some other flowering shrubs are routinely propagated this way. The rootstock is either a pencil-thick rooted cutting of a sort known to produce a good root system, or a seedling plant of a species grown for that purpose. The bud is inserted into the rootstock close to the ground.

If the bark pulls away easily, you can use the T-bud method with plants (roses, for example) that have thin bark. Or, on thick-barked plants such as walnuts, pecans, and avocados, you can try patch budding (not illustrated).

To do T-budding, the stem from which you take the bud, the *budstick*, should be about the same diameter as the stock you are going to use. You will find the buds on the budstick at the base of leaf stalks. Remove the leaf, but don't cut off the leaf stalk—use it as a handle and also as an indicator: If, when the leaf stalk withers in a week or two after budding, the bud remains plump and green, the operation has succeeded. But if the entire bud shield or patch (the bud and its attached bark and cambium) withers or turns dark, the budding has failed.

Grafting methods. Although many different grafting methods have been devised, all involve uniting a short length of stem—the scion—with the stock. The stock plant may be either a pencil-slim seedling to be grafted near ground level or an old fruit tree to be grafted at the top of its trunk or on its major limbs. Illustrated at right is cleft grafting, popular for converting old fruit and nut trees to new varieties.

With any grafting it is crucial to align scion cambium with stock cambium. When that is done, the two cambiums will unite, the cuts will callus over, and the scion will be ready to grow. Use a very sharp knife for making all cuts; the cleaner the cuts, the better the chance for successful union. When the operation is completed, cover the union with some sort of sealing agent to keep air from getting to the area.

Cleft Grafting

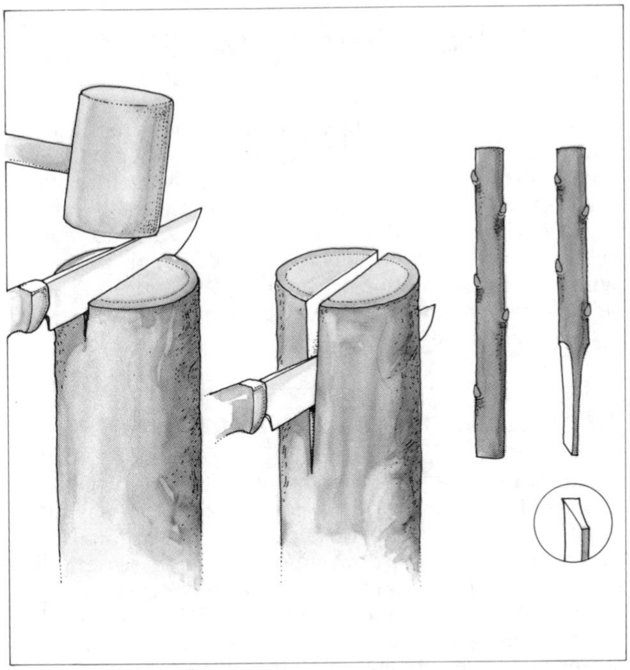

Prepare stock by splitting it several inches through a smooth, straight-grained section (so the split will be even). Shape one end of the scion into a long, gradually tapering wedge; outside edge of wedge should be slightly thicker than the inside (as shown in cross-section diagram).

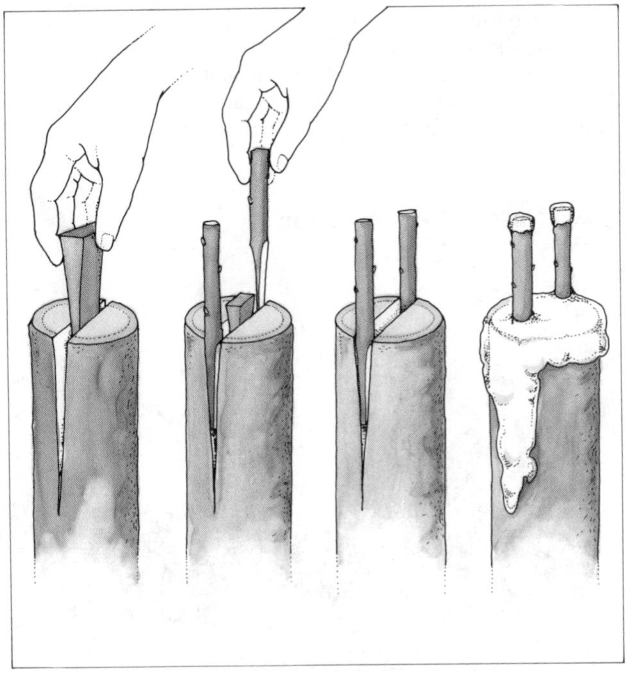

Use a wedge to hold open the split in the stock while you work. Insert the scion (or two, as illustrated) into the stock, carefully placed so that cambium layers of stock and scions match. After the scions are properly placed, cover the entire union with grafting wax.

Climate Modification

Many gardeners restrict their planting choices to those plants that will comfortably endure the weather of their area in all four seasons. Others, tempted by the lure of the exotic or willing to pamper favorite plants native to other regions with different climate conditions, will find themselves wanting to know how to provide frost protection, winter cover, or additional humidity. And for those gardeners who want to outwit the weather completely, there is the greenhouse.

Protection from Occasional Frosts

Virtually no place in the West is completely free from the threat of frost. From the dip below freezing that may hit San Diego once or twice in a decade to the occasional Big Freeze that will sweep down upon Seattle, these periodic deviations from the norm can wreak havoc on a landscape. Established plants that reach the limit of their cold tolerance in a particular zone's typical winter weather may suffer extensive damage—or they may die.

Fortunately, there are ways to prepare for the occasional big chill and thereby avert potential disaster in your garden.

Know your plants. Build your basic landscaping—trees, screen and hedge plants, principal shrubs—with plants that are hardy enough for the extremes of your climate zone. Use the chancy or tender plants as fillers, as summertime display plants, in borders, or in areas of secondary interest. Locate these plants in sheltered sites (see below), or grow them in containers and move them to sheltered sites when the weather turns cold.

Know your garden. Learn your garden's microclimates: discover which areas are warm, which are cool. Most dangerous for marginally hardy plants (and all tender vegetation) are stretches of open ground exposed to the air on all sides, particularly to the north. Hollows and low, enclosed areas that catch cold air as it sinks and hold it motionless also are poor choices. For iffy plants, safest areas are under overhanging eaves (the best protection), lath structures, or branches of evergreen trees. Slopes from which cold air drains freely are safer than hollows and valley or canyon floors. South-facing walls absorb heat during the day and radiate it at night, warming nearby plants. The warmest location of all is a south-facing wall with an overhang. Not only does it give maximum protection against frost, but in cool-summer/mild-winter climates, it also supplies the warmth needed to stimulate buds, blossoms, and fruit of heat-loving plants such as bougainvillea, hibiscus, fig, and evergreen magnolia.

Condition plants and soil for frosts. Feed and water while plants are growing fastest, in late spring and early summer. To discourage production of new growth that would not have time to mature before cold weather hits, taper off nitrogen feeding in late summer. Actively growing plants are more susceptible to cold than are dormant or semidormant plants. Reducing water will help harden growth, but soil around plants should be moist at the onset of the frost season; moist soil holds and releases more heat than dry soil does.

Some hardy plants have early blossoms that are damaged by spring frosts. Try to delay bloom of deciduous magnolias and some early rhododendrons beyond the time of heavy frosts by planting them with a north exposure or in the shade of high-branching deciduous trees.

Be especially watchful for frosts early in fall or in spring after growth is under way. These are much more damaging than frosts that occur while plants are semidormant or dormant. The warning signs are still air (tree branches motionless, smoke going straight up); absence of

Heat Loss & Conservation

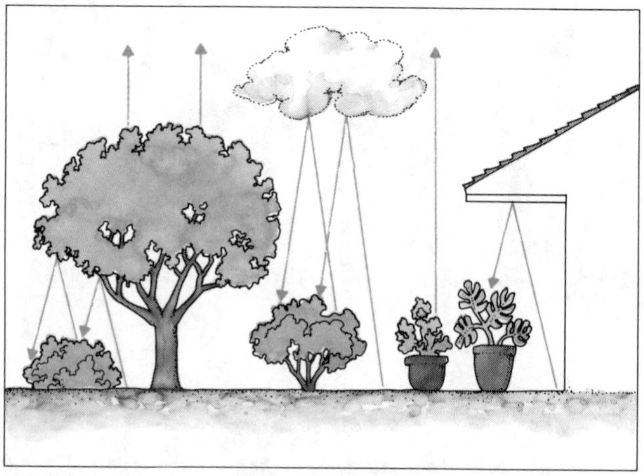

Upward-pointing arrows represent heat loss; downward-deflected arrows represent re-radiated heat from overhead protection. Plants exposed to open sky are more subject to frost damage than are plants under trees or overhangs.

Garden Microclimates

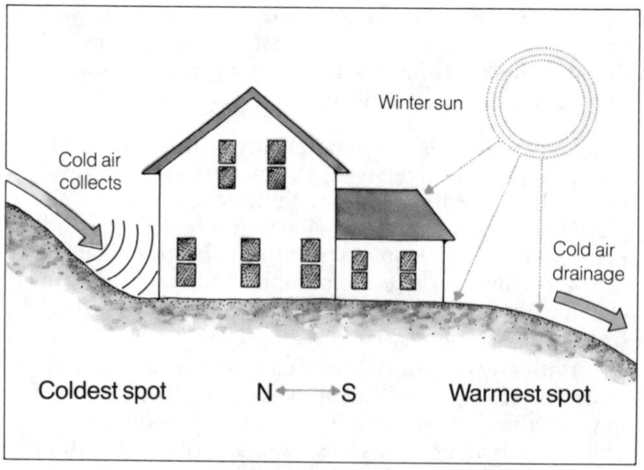

Garden microclimates are influenced by hills and hollows, points of the compass, and structures. Cold air moves downslope to the lowest point but will collect if flow is impeded by fences, walls, or structures.

cloud cover (stars easily visible, very bright); low humidity (windshields and grass dry); and low temperature (45°F or less at 10 P.M.). If you notice these danger signs at bedtime, get any at-risk container plants under a porch roof or eaves, or in a garage. Shelter any such plants that are in the ground: use burlap or plastic film—even evergreen boughs will help—secured over frames or stakes so that the covering material will not touch the plant (freezing is likely where the material touches foliage). Remove coverings during the daytime.

After a frost. If plants have been damaged by frost, don't hurry to prune them. Premature trimming may stimulate new, tender growth that will be nipped by later frosts. And you may cut out more than necessary, mistaking still-alive growth for dead. Wait until new growth begins in spring, then remove only wood that is clearly dead.

Winter-long Protection in Severe Climates

At high elevations where soil freezes hard and temperatures drop below zero, tender plants will not thrive. But many gardeners do grow roses, and a few attempt broad-leafed evergreens—boxwood, *Euonymus,* holly, *Pieris,* and rhododendrons. All these plants will need help to survive the harsh winters.

With roses, which are basically deciduous, your aim—at the very least—is to keep roots and bud union alive, and to preserve as many live canes as possible. For detailed instructions on winter protection for roses, see page 511 in the Western Plant Encyclopedia.

Some broad-leafed evergreens will survive fairly low temperatures but succumb to windburn and sunburn when low temperatures, strong sun, and cold, drying winds combine forces. Greatest damage to these plants comes when they transpire water from their leaves but can't replace moisture because water in the soil is frozen.

Careful selection of garden location will minimize damage to broad-leafed evergreens. Locate these plants where bright sun—especially in early morning—will not strike frozen plants. To avoid rupturing plant tissues, thawing should be gradual. Above all, keep soil moist and unfrozen by means of a thick mulch.

To protect an exposed broad-leafed evergreen, shelter with burlap, lath, plywood, styrofoam, or cardboard secured on its windward side. A palisade of evergreen boughs stuck in the ground around the plant will offer further protection.

Heat, Shade, & Humidity

These three subjects are bound together very closely. Shade-loving plants, such as tuberous begonias, fuchsias, and azaleas, mostly native to forest floors, have shallow roots that seldom penetrate beneath the surface layer of leaf mold. During growth and bloom they use a lot of water, but their leaves are not adapted to store water (as succulent plants do) or to resist evaporation in warm, dry, windy weather (as many waxy or leathery-leafed plants do). In hot sun, in very dry weather, or in warm windy weather, they lose water faster than they can take it up. Sunburn, wilting, or withering results.

Shade plants. To grow shade plants successfully, keep direct sunlight low and humidity high. If you live near the ocean, fog cover and natural humidity may be enough; but even here you'll need to furnish shelter against strong, constant winds. Farther inland, place your shade plants under shelter of high-branching trees, under lath structures, or on the north or east sides of buildings, walls, or fences. Protect from drying winds by fences, louvers, or windbreak plantings. You also increase humidity by mulching (a coarse, moist mulch will evaporate a considerable amount of water into the air), and of course by watering often.

When temperatures are really high or humidity exceptionally low, water with special diligence and supplement surface irrigation with sprinkling or misting.

Newly set plants. Protect newly set plants from strong sun and wind with temporary shelters. These can be as simple as a shingle lean-to on the sunny side of the plant or a small newspaper pup tent held down at the edges by a few handfuls of soil. Or they can be as elaborate as lath or burlap panels supported above the plants on low stakes. Whichever type you choose, the object is to keep strong sun and wind from the young plants until the roots are able to do an efficient job of taking water from the soil to meet the plants' needs.

Greenhouses

The ultimate in climate modification is a greenhouse. In such a structure of glass or plastic, you have the opportunity to exercise complete control over temperature, humidity, and even day length. Not every gardener will feel the need for a growing environment in which the climatic factors are so regulated. But many have discovered the usefulness of a greenhouse for these purposes:

- ***Wintering plants*** that are too tender for the normal outdoor winter low temperatures.
- ***Starting seeds*** of annuals and vegetables early so that plants can be set out in the garden as soon as weather permits.
- ***Starting cuttings and seeds*** that require the growth stimuli a greenhouse can provide.
- ***Raising vegetables and flowers*** out of season (particularly when outside conditions are too cold), or maturing them earlier than would be normal if planted outdoors.
- ***Growing specialty plants*** (orchids and tropical plants, for example) that could not be grown outdoors because temperature or humidity or both are unfavorable.

A greenhouse may be a simple lean-to constructed of plastic, a small bay window attachment on a house window, or a more elaborate separate structure with precise controls for regulation of heat, humidity, ventilation, and water. The size and style of greenhouse you choose will be dictated by your needs and the cost of construction; the variations are numerous.

Garden Tools

Nearly any maintenance work requires the proper tool or tools. In this section we present the many gardeners' helpers and the uses for which they are intended.

Whether garden maintenance is pleasant exercise or just hard work depends, in part, on what tools you use to accomplish the tasks at hand. You needn't buy a multitude of tools for your outdoor work; rather, you should own precisely the tools needed to accomplish the routine work in your garden.

It pays to buy the best quality available, even though this will mean a greater initial expense: a high-quality tool will give you more years of service per dollar spent than will a cheaper model.

Tools for Soil Work

Soil work—whether digging, smoothing, or cultivating—is a basic gardening activity that will occur time and again. Durability is a prime consideration in tool purchase, but so is comfort. When you shop for a hand tool—from shovel to pruning shears—test the feel of it in your hand before you buy. Length and style of handle, for example, partly determine how comfortable a tool will be for you to use.

Shovels and spades. These are the tools for digging holes and trenches and for transplanting. Many styles are available, each designed for a particular purpose. Choice of handle length and shape (D-handle or straight) is personal; choose the one that will be the most comfortable in the type of work you intend to do. For working the soil (as opposed to simply digging), see "Spading Forks" (page 91).

- ***Round-point shovel.*** A versatile tool for digging and scooping. The round-point irrigation shovel pictured here has a straight shank, which gives it more strength and adapts well to digging planting holes or ditches with vertical sides.
- ***Garden shovel.*** Somewhat smaller and lighter than the regular round-point shovel. Use it for digging holes, cultivating, and edging.
- ***Square-point shovel.*** For leveling areas for patios and walks, squaring off the bottoms of ditches, and shoveling snow. When shoveling dirt or gravel, this shovel is especially handy toward the bottom of the pile.
- ***D-handle shovel.*** For jobs such as moving soil, sand, and gravel or for picking up litter. Round-point and square-point models are available.
- ***Square-end spade.*** For edging, digging, and cultivating. It can be used with a chopping motion to break up earth clods. You have a choice of a long handle or the shorter D-handle; both are easy to use.
- ***Transplanting spade.*** A favorite with gardeners for transplanting shrubs and moving perennials.

Shovels & Spades

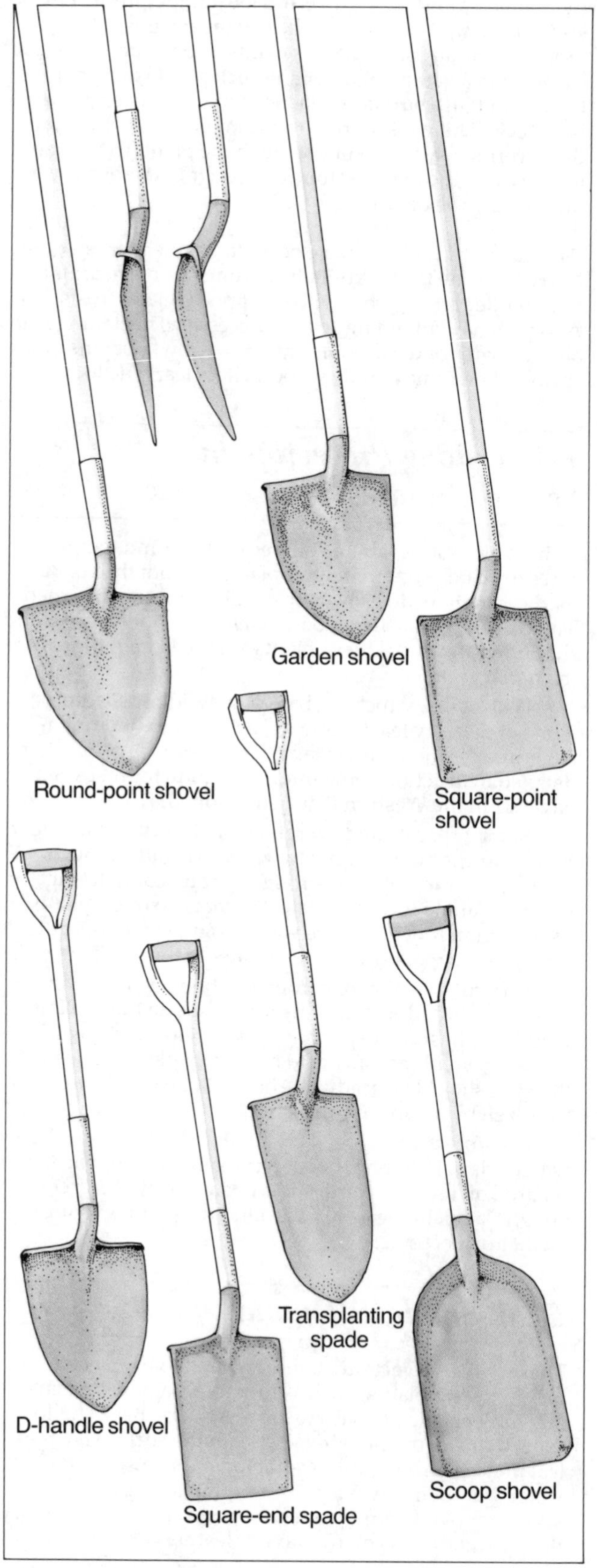

■ ***Scoop shovel.*** For moving sawdust, manure, and other light materials. Use it as a garden dustpan for collecting litter.

Spading forks. These are the tools to use for breaking up the soil; digging in rocky, claylike, or heavy soil; and digging out plants when you want to sever as few roots as possible.

■ ***Long-handled spading fork.*** The long handle gives good leverage when you are working in hard soil. Breaks up adobe clods better than a spade does.

■ ***Short-handled spading fork.*** You have a choice of a number of models. Tines range from 7 to 11 inches long; weight also varies. Generally, short-handled spading forks work best for cultivating crowded planting beds or for lifting clumps of perennials without damaging tubers, rhizomes, or a plant's thickly matted system of roots.

■ ***Barn or manure fork.*** Not for spading; use for moving garden prunings, long weeds, manure, and other materials that hang together. Also good for turning over layers of compost.

Trowels. Use trowels to plant bulbs, annuals, vegetables, and small perennials. You can also use them while on your hands and knees for shallow digging or uprooting weeds. A *straight shank* type is good for bulb planting; the *drop shank* is most popular for general use. Pick a trowel that fits your hand and feels balanced. Buy a sturdy one: working in hard soil will bend and soon break the shanks on all except the best-quality trowels.

Hoes. There are hoes to perform a variety of garden jobs, from cultivating to digging furrows to destroying weeds.

Spading Forks

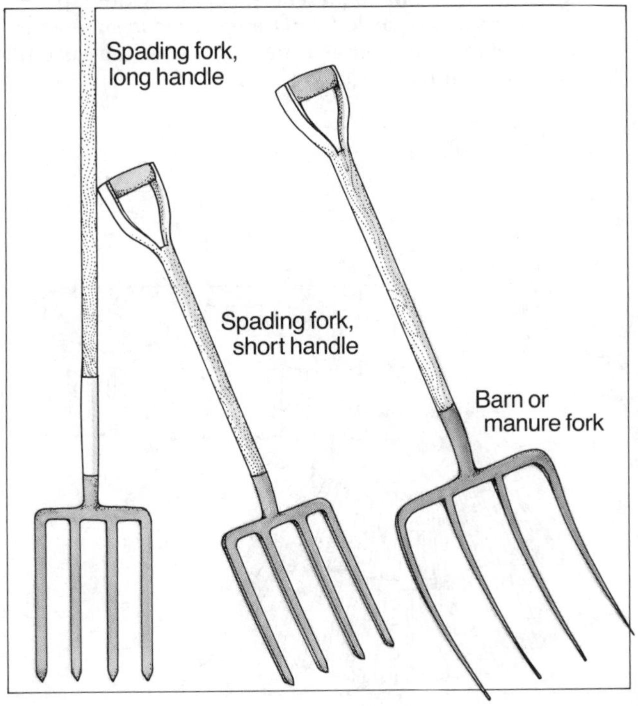

Trowels

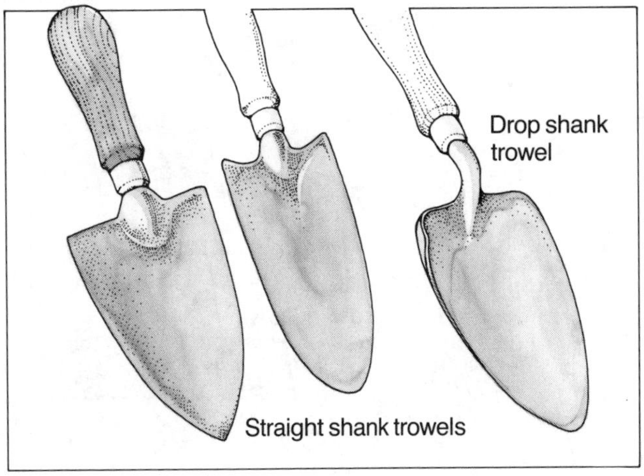

■ ***Garden hoes.*** The 6-inch-wide hoe is the most commonly used. Other types have a 2½-inch-wide blade for light jobs in narrow spots or an 8-inch-wide blade for driveways and walks. Some have names that suggest their use: planter hoe, cotton hoe, square-top onion hoe. The latter, also called a strawberry hoe, has a blade 7 inches wide and about 1¾ inches high; use it around shallow-rooted plants.

To be effective, a hoe should be sharpened each time you take it into the garden. On hard cutting jobs, resharpen about every 2 hours.

Hoes with the conventional design of those illustrated on the next page have flat front edges to cut weeds off at ground level and sharp corners to work like a small pick. Get a hoe that is light enough to be wielded for an hour or two at a time.

When hoeing weeds with a conventional hoe, advance at the unhoed weeds as you work, rather than backing into them and trampling them before they are hoed. Hold the hoe so the blade is at about a 30° angle to the ground, and work with a smooth, horizontal movement, drawing it back toward you so that weeds are deposited in a straight line. Don't chop downward, because chopping jars your arms and shoulders needlessly, makes an uneven surface, and may cut roots of desirable plants.

■ ***Warren hoe.*** For cultivating between plants or for making furrows. You make the furrow with the pointed end, sow seed, and then turn the hoe over and use the "ears" to pull the soil over the seed.

■ ***Weeding hoe.*** This tool is a hoe on one side, a weed puller on the other.

■ ***Grape hoe or eye hoe.*** The wide blade of this tool smashes through hard, root-filled soil. Use it to cut bushy weeds, invasive tree roots, and spreading ground cover.

■ ***Push-pull weeder-cultivator.*** One of many variations on the scuffle hoe. You scrape the surface of a bed, cutting off seedling weeds and breaking the soil crust. This one wobbles as you change direction, so the blade is always at the proper angle. Other varieties have a blade shaped like a flat rectangle, a double disk, or a golf iron.

Hoes

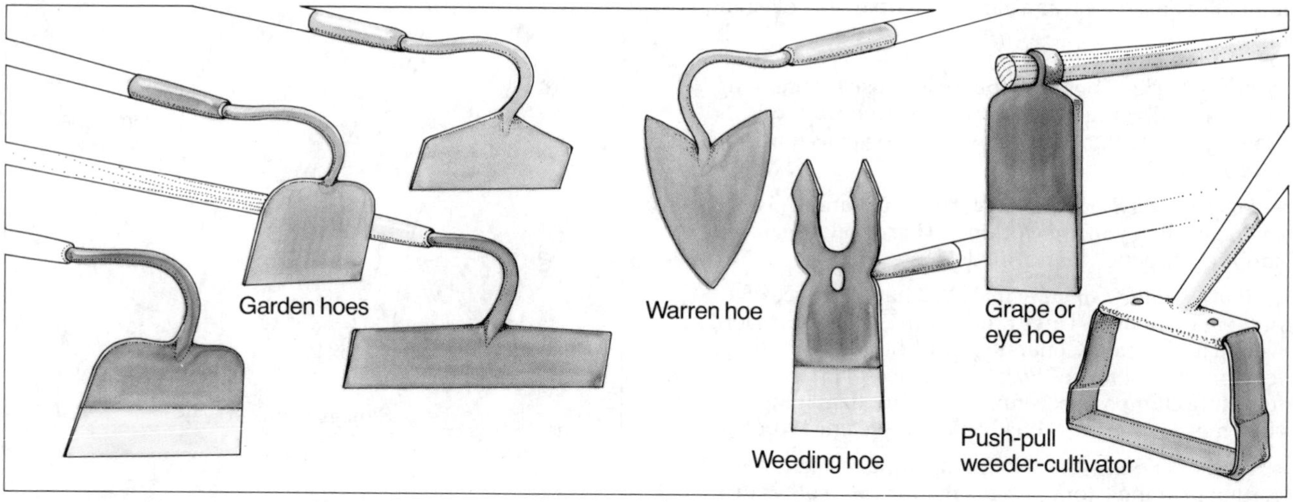

Rakes. Use rakes to smooth seedbeds, gather up debris, and aid in renewing lawns.

- ***Level-head rake.*** Use the flat top to level seed beds and to break up earth clods.
- ***Bow rake.*** The bow acts as a shock absorber, giving the rake springy, resilient action and makes this a good tool for leveling soil or gravel and for breaking up earth clods.
- ***Lawn rakes.*** Indispensable for raking lawn clippings, leaves, and other light matter on both paved and natural surfaces, these come in a wide selection. Some are made of metal, others of bamboo or plastic; some are fan shaped, others rectangular.
- ***Self-cleaning rake.*** This rake, heavier than the other types, is for clearing out lawn thatch and severing long surface runners of certain lawn grasses. You don't lift it from the ground: the pull stroke gathers debris toward the operator; the push stroke clears material from the blades.

Special tools. In addition to the standard garden maintenance tools, a number of other pieces can be highly useful for particular jobs.

- ***Cultivators.*** Although these are good for breaking up hard soil around plants, they won't qualify for deep cultivating. For best results, combine chopping and pulling motions.
- ***Weed and grass cutters.*** The weed cutter is used for rugged weeds and grasses in uncultivated garden areas. It removes top growth but not weed roots, unless you use the blade as a chopper. The grass cutter helps cut grass along the edges of a lawn. Swing it as you would a golf club. Test various models for balance and weight.
- ***Asparagus or dandelion weeders.*** For lifting out taprooted weeds in the garden and for weeding in such tight places as between stepping-stones. These tools are useful, too, for small cultivating jobs.

Rakes

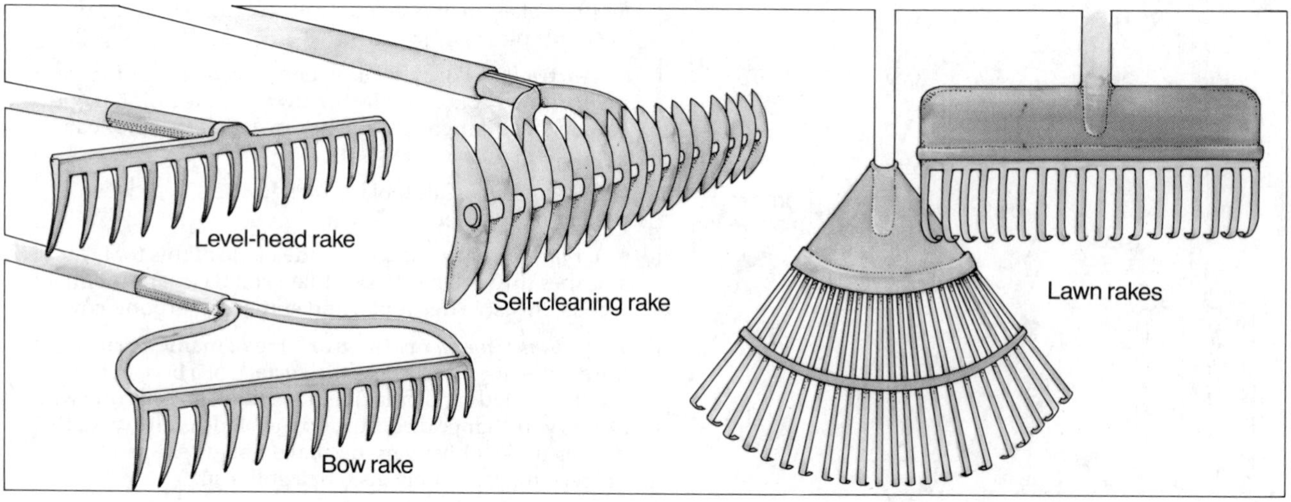

Special Tools

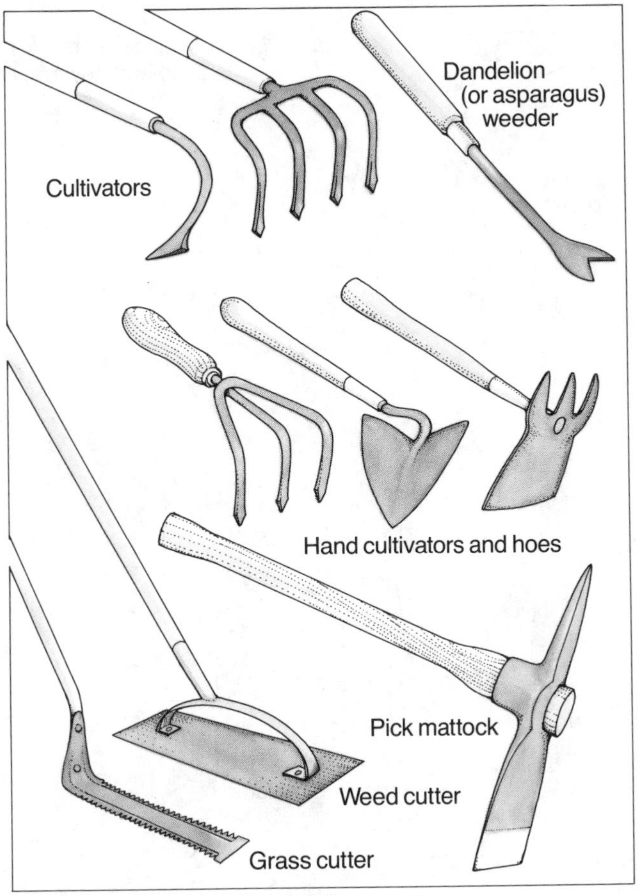

■ ***Small hand cultivators and hoes.*** For close-up kneeling or sitting jobs or for planting on a hillside. The working end is the same shape as that of the regular-sized tools, but these are smaller, with palm-sized handles.

■ ***Pick mattock.*** This is two tools in one. The sharp pick is handy for loosening compacted or rocky soil that is difficult to penetrate with a spading fork or shovel; it will also break up asphalt. The wide mattock blade cuts through root-filled soil.

Pruning Tools

Shears and saws for pruning come in many different forms and sizes, to match the many kinds of pruning operations; each implement is designed to do a certain type of pruning. Most home gardeners can get along with just three basic implements: (1) hand shears, for routine cutting of spent flowers, twigs, and small branches; (2) hand loppers, for cutting finger-sized limbs; and (3) a pruning saw, for removal of larger limbs or for branch removal where shears or loppers can't fit easily to give a proper cut.

If you attempt to use just one kind of pruning instrument for many types of plant cutting, you're bound to

Pruning Shears

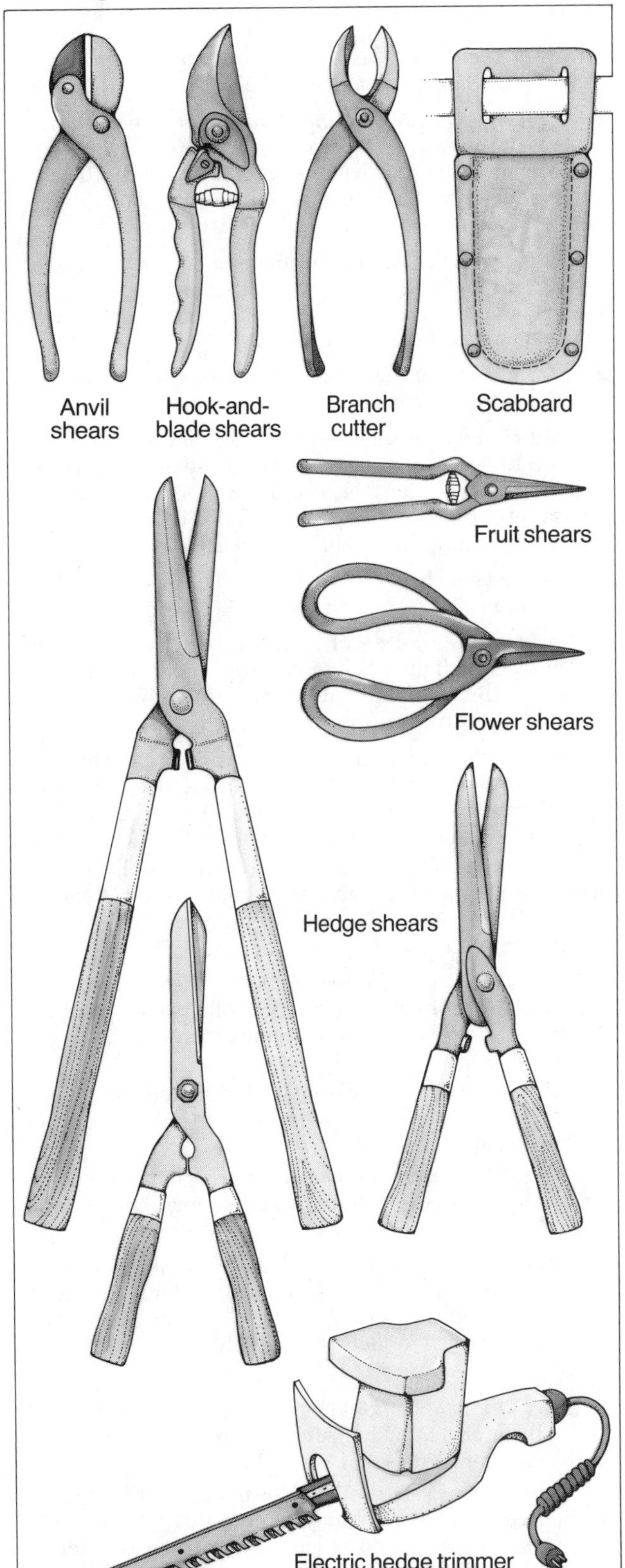

make bad cuts at times—often damaging both the plants and the misused tool.

Pruning shears. At least one of these shears is an essential part of any gardener's tool kit.

- ***Anvil shears and hook-and-blade shears*** are the basic tools for light pruning jobs. The first type cuts with a steel blade against a brass anvil; the second cuts with a hook and blade. Many gardeners use both and find no difference in the quality of cuts made.
- ***The branch cutter*** comes from Japan. When it removes a branch at the base, it leaves a concave depression rather than a flush cut or a stub. Such a cut can heal very fast. Bonsai experts like to prune with it.
- ***A leather scabbard*** has belt slots at the top. You can hang one on your hip to keep your pruning shears handy.
- ***Fruit shears*** come in many models. They are used to cut stems that don't break off—such as those of lemon trees and grape vines. Sharp blade crosses over sharp blade. The same cutting method is employed in other one-hand specialty pruning shears that look like these.
- ***Flower shears*** have blades designed to cut and hold flower stems.
- ***An extension pruner*** with blade-and-anvil cutter at one end of a 4-foot, lightweight pole, and a squeeze handle to work it on the other end is used for cutting flowers and doing light pruning beyond arm's reach.
- ***Lopping shears.*** Use these wherever the added leverage of long handles will give you more cutting strength than you get from one-hand shears and wherever the added reach of the long handles will be needed.

With the *hook-and-blade* style, the hook holds the branch while the blade slices through it. With the *blade-and-anvil* type, a sharp steel blade cuts against a flat plate, or anvil, of brass.

- ***Hedge shears.*** Hand-operated hedge shears are used by gardeners with small hedges and by others who believe that they can do a better job manually than with an electric trimmer.

Most *hedge shears* have one blade serrated and notched. The notch holds bigger twigs to prevent slippage while you cut.

The short-handled shears have 10-inch handles; the long-handled type has 20-inch handles, enabling you to trim tall hedges to about 3 feet beyond your body height.

- ***The electric hedge trimmer*** will do the same job as the hand-operated shears (above) but in less time. Illustrated is one that operates off normal 110-volt current; battery powered, cordless models also are sold.

Pruning saws. You should never try to force pruning shears through a branch. If shears won't cut a branch easily, use a pruning saw.

Pruning saws are designed to cut quickly through fresh, green, wet wood. Many of them, such as the curved types, are also designed to fit into close quarters. Although straight pruning saws cut on the push stroke, curved saws have teeth made in such a way that they cut on the pull stroke. Curved ones therefore are especially

Lopping Shears

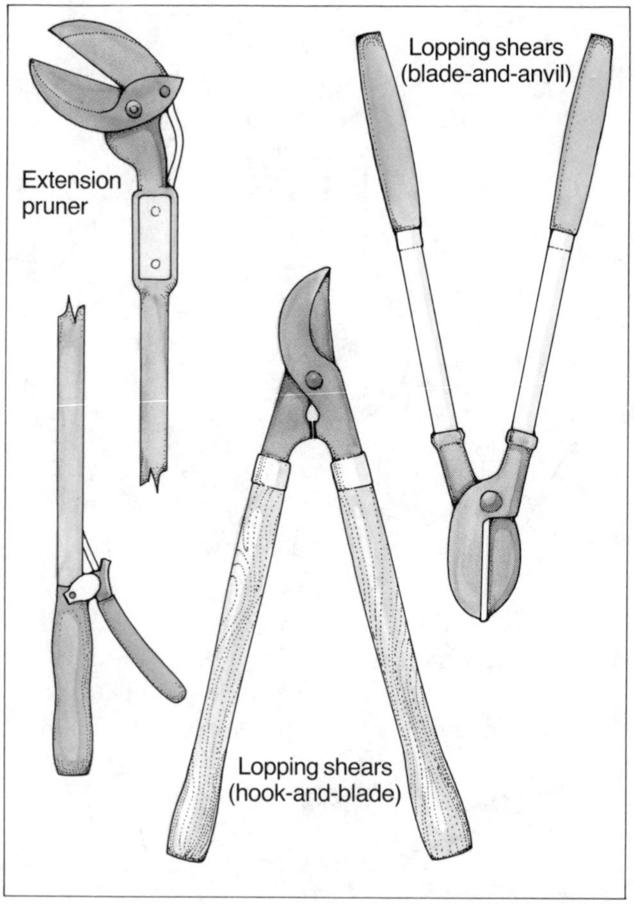

useful for doing overhead work. The curved blade on the folding saw folds into the handle for safe carrying and storage. A hole at the base of the blade, exposed when folded, makes it possible to hang the saw, with a clip, from your belt. The curved blade on the rigid saw is broad and has fewer points to the inch than the folding version, suiting it to heavier work.

The *straight pruning saw* has 6 points to the inch (more than the rigid saw and fewer than the folding saw); and it's designed for the heaviest pruning work.

The *bow-frame saw* is one of several utility saws for pruning and for cutting up logs. Whereas some of them have a full bow frame, this model has a triangular bow frame. The acute-angled end, which points away from you, pushes overhanging branches out of the way as you cut.

Pole pruners and pole saws. You need one of these devices to cut or saw branches high overhead.

The telescoping, lightweight metal tube, shown in the illustration, can be extended from 6 to 12 feet (and, with an accessory unit, to 18 feet). To the wooden cap at the upper end you can attach either of two units.

The first is a combination pruning saw and cord-operated cutting shears (the shears are inside the beak-like hook). After placing the hook over a branch, you pull the cord to draw the blade through the branch. The saw attached to the unit is a regular draw-cut, curved pruning saw.

The second device is simply a saw attachment for the telescoping pole. The hook at the base of the saw pulls off dead branches; the little horn on the outer end of the hook pushes branches.

Instead of a telescoping metal tube, some units use a series of wooden poles that lock together to make any length up to 18 feet. If, in your pruning, there is any chance of contacting electric lines overhead, the wooden units offer the only safe choice.

Lawn-care Tools

Maintaining a lawn requires a mower and shears for trimming the lawn edges. In each category, you have a choice between hand-operated and power-driven tools.

Lawn mowers. Two types are sold—the reel mower and the rotary mower. Reel mowers are either hand operated or power driven; all rotary mowers are power driven.

- ***A typical reel mower*** has five blades, though models may have from four to seven. Six- and seven-blade mowers are for cutting low or wiry grasses (such as Bermuda and bent grasses), which need close mowing. Reel mowers cut only when moving in the forward direction: the blades rotate downward and cut grass with a scissorslike action against a stationary bar. In most power-driven models (unlike rotary mowers), the engine drives the wheels as well as the blades; this makes power reel mowers especially well suited for cutting sloping lawns with the least physical effort. Use any reel mower *only* for mowing a lawn.
- ***The power rotary mower*** cuts with swiftly rotating blades that spin in a horizontal plane. A rotary mower will not cut as low as a reel type, but it can be adjusted to cut considerably higher. This feature, plus the machine's overall ruggedness (rotary blades can eject rocks and sticks without killing the engine), makes a rotary mower the number one choice for cutting tall grass and weedy fields. In contrast to the reel mower, a rotary mower cuts in both forward and backward directions; it also will cut closer to trees and structures. Most rotary mowers, like power reel mowers, are gasoline powered. The electric models—easy to start, quiet, and fumeless—are good for cutting small, unobstructed lawns; few are powerful enough (because electric motors are slower than gasoline motors) to do heavy-duty weed cutting. Furthermore, you are limited by the length of the cord.

Pruning Saws & Pole Saws

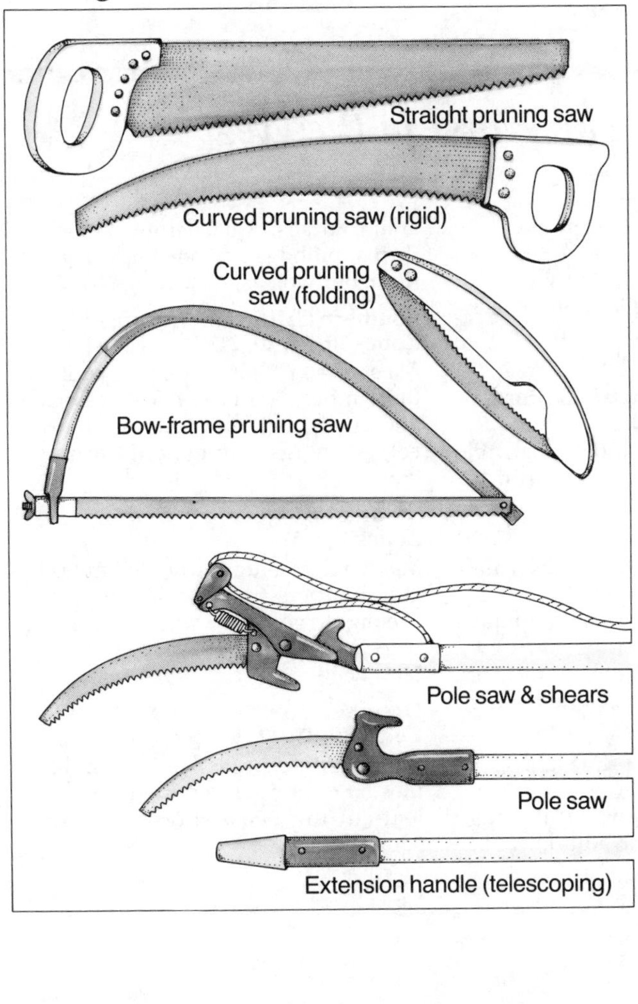

Nylon string trimmer. Powered by gasoline or by electricity, this machine stands midway between mower and edging tool. Nylon filaments are attached to a quickly rotating disk mounted at an angle at the end of a long handle; the spinning filaments cut tall grass and weeds with a whipping action. You can rough-mow a field or hillside with a string trimmer, then rake up the cut material. Other common uses are for edging along fences and around trunks of mature, thick-barked trees. Filaments wear down or break with use—especially when they repeatedly hit hard objects—but are easily replaced.

Lawn-edging shears. There are several different tools you can use to edge lawns and ground cover plantings. All cut by means of scissors action; the differences are in the options of handle length and electric power.

Most basic of these tools are the various short-handled shears. One type operates by vertical squeezing action: one handle is above the other, and each squeeze closes the blades which cut as they pass by one another. In another model, one blade remains in a fixed position while the other blade slices across it: the harder you squeeze on the handles, the more tension you apply to the blades, thereby forcing a cut through tough grass stems and stolons. Still another kind operates by horizontal action; the handles are on the same plane as the blades, but offset so that you don't bruise your knuckles. If you want to make an edging job nearly effortless, you can use cordless electric grass shears that operate by a rechargeable battery.

Long-handled, heavy-duty grass shears let you stand up to cut lawn edges and the margins of thick, spreading ground covers such as ivy and vinca. They will even cut right into the sod. Also available are grass shears with wheels at the base of a 3-foot handle. You stand up and wheel it along, squeezing the handle which operates scissors-action blades that cut the grass.

Pests

In these next pages we present the pest troublemakers most likely to be encountered on a variety of plants in the West. Pests that affect only specific plants (eucalyptus borer, for example) are dealt with under the appropriate entries in the Western Plant Encyclopedia, pages 199–568.

Pest Management

The notion of pest *control*—where control implies eradication—has been superseded by the concept of pest *management*. The management concept acknowledges that many of our perceived "problems" are indeed natural components of gardens: their simple presence doesn't necessarily spell trouble. In a diversified garden, most insect pests are kept in check by natural forces (such as predators and weather); only if the pests reach seriously damaging levels do you have an indication that natural controls are temporarily unbalanced—suggesting temporary intervention by the gardener.

Because of this natural system of checks and balances in a garden, it makes sense to determine which form of intervention will return the situation to a normal balance with the least risk of also destroying the helpful (as well as harmless) organisms that maintain the equilibrium. Your action choices range from doing nothing (giving nature a chance to correct the imbalance), to using restraints (washing plants, or repelling or physically destroying the damagers), to biological controls (improving the helpful side of nature's control system), to chemical controls.

More and more gardeners are turning to restraints and biological controls as a first line of defense against garden pests. Yet almost all horticulturists acknowledge the need for at least occasional treatment with chemical controls. This approach—preferred use of natural and mechanical controls, plus chemicals as a discretionary second choice—is called *integrated pest management* (IPM). Increasingly, IPM is being used in parks (including national parks), city landscapes, public gardens, and greenhouses. The following five points explain how you can implement IPM in your own garden.

Select well-adapted plants. Choose plants that are adapted to your area and that are resistant to pest and disease problems likely to be troublesome in your region (see below). Plants stressed by inhospitable climate or from lack of water or nutrients are more vulnerable to damaging organisms than are their healthy, well cared-for counterparts.

Try mechanical controls. Hand-picking, traps, barriers, or a strong jet of water can reduce or thwart many pests,

Garden Troublemakers: The Worst in the West

The number of different pests—insects, diseases, weeds, and animals—that may harass western gardens numbers in the hundreds if not thousands. But among this horde is a much smaller number that plagues our plants and calls us into combat.

To discover the West's most troublesome pests, and learn their regional distributions, *Sunset* surveyed 56 garden clubs in the eleven western states. From this poll emerged a total of 34 pests of all kinds that earned the unenviable title of "major." Different climates foster different problems: a worst offender in one region might rank far down on the list in another area—or not be noted at all. The summary presented here groups the West's 24 climate zones into seven larger climatic regions. For each of these regions is given the primary pests, listed in order of troublesomeness.

Pacific Northwest (west of the Cascades): Zones 4, 5, 6, 7
Major pests: Slugs, root weevils, aphids, moles, mildew, mites, blackberry, dandelion, cutworms, crows, black spot, deer, gophers.

Northern and Central California–Coastal: Zones 15, 16, 17
Major pests: Slugs and snails, mildew, gophers, earwigs, aphids, whiteflies, oak moths, mites, rust, mealybugs, deer, moles, cutworms.

Northern and Central California–Inland: Zones 7, 8, 9, 14
Major pests: Slugs and snails, aphids, mites, Bermuda grass, mildew, crabgrass, whiteflies, geranium budworms, bindweed, earwigs, scale, oxalis, rust.

Southern California–Coastal: Zones 22, 23, 24
Major pests: Mildew, whiteflies, gophers, slugs and snails, rust, aphids, oxalis, scale, Bermuda grass, thrips, pillbugs and sowbugs, geranium budworms, mealybugs.

Southern California–Inland: Zones 18, 19, 20, 21
Major pests: Grasshoppers, whiteflies, mites, aphids, mildew, slugs and snails, oak root fungus, squirrels, earwigs, moles, cutworms, crows.

Mountain: Zones 1, 2, 3
Major pests: Slugs, aphids, mites, grasshoppers, mildew, leaf rollers, fireblight, gophers, crabgrass, earwigs, cutworms, leaf-cutting bees, bindweed.

Desert: Zones 10, 11, 12, 13
Major pests: Aphids, mites, whiteflies, grasshoppers, spotted spurge, leaf-cutting bees, slugs, mildew, squash bugs.

especially in the early stages of a potential problem. Cleanup of plant debris can remove the environment where certain pests and diseases breed or overwinter.

Accept minor damage. A totally pest-free garden is neither possible nor desirable. Allow natural control methods the major role in maintaining a healthy balance between pests and the beneficial (plus the harmless) insects and creatures that are normal garden components.

Use non-chemical alternatives. Release or encourage beneficial insects; use soaps, horticultural oils, botanical insecticides (such as natural pyrethrins), and one of several packaged forms of *Bacillus thuringiensis;* see page 104 for further explanation of these products. Realize that beneficial insects may take a while to reduce the pests they prey upon, and that you may have to use the non-chemical controls at more frequent intervals than chemical controls.

Use chemical preparations prudently. Occasionally you will need to use a chemical control—especially for management of diseases (pages 105–109). Before you purchase a chemical control and begin applying it, be sure you have correctly identified the problem. If you are at all uncertain, ask at a reputable local nursery or contact the nearest Cooperative Extension agent. Follow label directions *exactly.*

Insects & Their Relatives

Several kinds of creatures can damage garden plants, ranging from true insects (such as aphids, cutworms, scale) and their juvenile forms to arachnids (mites) and mollusks (slugs and snails). In these 8 pages we profile the West's most notable of these pests and recommend management measures.

APHIDS

Aphids are soft, oval, pinhead-to-match-head-sized insects that huddle together on new shoots, buds, and leaves. They come in many colors—including green, pink, red, and black—with and without wings.

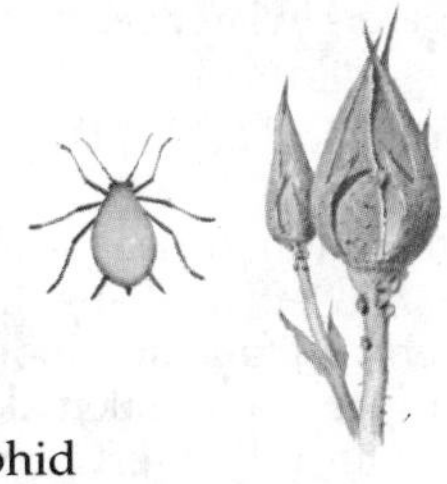

Numerous creatures keep aphid populations in check; often the best tactic is to do nothing and watch natural controls go to work. Lacewings, ladybird beetles, syrphid flies, predatory midges, parasitic wasps, and even lizards and some small birds are among the many natural aphid controls that may live in your garden. If you spray with a toxic insecticide, you risk killing the insect predators along with the problem.

Fortunately, you can get rid of most aphids with a blast of water from the hose. For greater effectiveness, you can wash them off with an insecticidal soap—the soap kills aphids but does not have a residual effect (so won't harm other insects later).

The most troublesome aphids are those that curl leaves around them or stay in protected places (inside a head of cabbage, for example). The best control for these aphids is anticipation: if you had them last year, expect them this year; hose or wash them off when the aphid colony is young and leaves are still open.

If an aphid infestation is severe, spray with insecticidal soap, diazinon, malathion, or (on nonedible plants) Orthene.

Ants often maintain aphid colonies, fighting off parasites and predators in order to feed on the sticky honeydew aphids produce. If you get rid of the ants, natural aphid controls often can reestablish themselves in short order. To keep ants out of plants, encircle trunks with bands of a sticky ant barrier, put out diazinon or Dursban granules, or use poisonous ant baits.

CUTWORMS

A large variety of hairless larvae of night-flying moths make up this diverse group. They feed at night and on overcast days, and most can cut off young plants at the ground—hence their name. In the daytime, they hide in the ground, curled up (as illustrated).

Once you lose seedling plants to cutworms, you should protect that kind of plant thereafter. Put a physical barrier around each seedling the day it sprouts or the day you plant it. One simple barrier is a cutoff milk carton sleeve with 1 inch below soil level, 2 inches above, and at least an inch between the sleeve and the plant. As an extra precaution you can put petroleum jelly or a sticky ant barrier along the upper edge.

Some cutworms crawl up into plants and eat buds, leaves, and fruit. One way to keep them out is to spread a sticky ant barrier around the base of each susceptible plant. If you have too many plants to easily employ barriers, try handpicking cutworms by night. Or try trapping them by placing cardboard, plywood, wide boards, or heavy paper sacks in garden paths. During daylight, lift the traps and destroy the worms that have taken refuge beneath.

Cutworms in lawns are a more difficult matter. Your clue to infestation in grass or dichondra is small bare patches that grow rapidly in size day by day. (If you're not sure the damage is from cutworms, go out several hours after sunset and examine the lawn by flashlight.) You can try to handpick cutworms after dark, though control is bound to be incomplete. To aid handpicking during the day, flood the infested area with water for 5 to 10 minutes; cutworms will then emerge from their burrows.

Chemical controls are not very effective against mature cutworms but can help control young worms. *Bacillus thuringiensis,* however, has been very effective against nearly full-grown individuals of several cutworm species. To control seedling-eating cutworms, try dusting the ground where the cutworms feed with Sevin; for cutworms in lawns, apply diazinon, Dursban, or Sevin.

EARWIGS

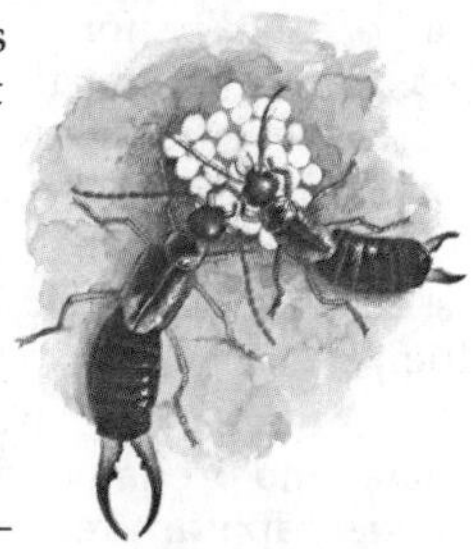

Gardeners in all western climates except the desert complain about earwigs. In the San Francisco Bay Area and along the northern California coast, they are often second only to snails and slugs as a garden damager.

Earwigs will eat almost any soft materials. One common food is insects—such as aphids—which means that earwigs can be an important natural control of plant pests. Unfortunately, earwigs also feed on soft parts of plants, such as flower petals and corn silks. A large earwig population can significantly damage desirable plants.

Earwigs hide during the day, but they are active at night. When dawn comes, they scurry back into tight, cozy places. You can trap earwigs by providing the type of tight-fitting, moist shelter in which they like to spend the day. At night, put moistened rolled-up newspapers, rolls of corrugated cardboard, or short sections of garden hose on the ground; in the morning, dispose of the accumulated insects.

Or you can buy earwig bait, which usually contains Baygon or Sevin as the killing ingredient; around nonedible plants, you can use bendiocarb dust. If the lure in bait is fish oil, it also can attract pets, which may be harmed by the active ingredient.

GERANIUM (TOBACCO) BUDWORMS, CORN EARWORMS

In the 1960s and 1970s, the geranium budworm (properly the tobacco budworm) ballooned from obscurity to first-rank garden pest status in California. More recently it has appeared in damaging numbers in some mountain regions outside California. It is closely related to another familiar garden troublemaker, the corn earworm. Both worms are larvae of stout-bodied, dull-colored, night-flying moths. During the full moon, the moths refrain from mating and laying eggs—the bright light seems to distract them. But right after that, moths start mating at an increased rate; by the time of the new moon, young larvae are numerous. And each such cycle results in a still bigger population.

The typical geranium budworm lives through the winter as a pupa in the soil. Then, in late April or May, a mature gray moth emerges and lays eggs on geranium buds—one egg per bud. From the egg hatches a very small worm, which enters and feeds on the geranium bud (or on a rosebud or petunia bud). As the worm grows, it consumes the initial bud and moves on to the rest of the plant taking on the color of the plant tissue it eats.

Once you see a hole in a bud, pick the bud, squash it, and discard it; this destroys the young worm, which already will have damaged the potential blossom. For heavy geranium budworm infestations—where worms have outgrown the protective covering of flower buds—spray with *Bacillus thuringiensis,* pyrethrins, Sevin, or Orthene. Repeat at weekly intervals until damage ceases.

For control of corn earworm, see "Corn," page 298.

GRASSHOPPERS

During their periodic outbreaks, grasshoppers own much of the West—except areas where coastal weather prevails. By preference, they lay their eggs in dry, undisturbed areas, such as along roadsides and in empty lots, but they also will lay in gardens.

Eggs begin hatching from March to early June, depending on temperature and climate. Newly hatched nymphs resemble adults but are smaller and lack wings; these nymphs feed voraciously, sometimes stripping entire areas bare. When they mature and develop wings, they fly out and find new feeding areas.

When you are cultivating in fall, winter, and early spring, watch for and destroy egg clusters, which contain up to 75 cream or yellow rice-shaped eggs. In spring and early summer, while grasshoppers are still young and wingless, they are most vulnerable to chemicals and baits. Use malathion, diazinon, Orthene, Sevin, Dursban, or bran-and-Sevin bait. Grasshoppers roost at night in hedges, tall weeds, and shrubs: observe their evening behavior to locate roosting sites, then spray in these areas after dark.

Your best defense against large numbers of grasshoppers may be to protect desirable plants with floating row covers (see page 198) or netting.

In summer, when grasshoppers are mature and less vulnerable to chemicals, handpick them in early morning.

The disease-producing organism, *Nosema locustae,* causes grasshoppers to produce fewer eggs. Over large areas—on a ranch, for example—applying this commercially packaged material can help reduce grasshopper problems in later years.

LEAF-CUTTING BEES

Even though the leaf-cutting bee is extremely efficient at pollinating the flowers of alfalfa, it is looked upon as a prime garden troublemaker in some mountain and desert regions. As the bees gather materials for nest building, they cut disks from the foliage or petals of certain plants to line their nests. The bees seem to prefer rose and bougainvillea leaves, although they also cut disks from developing rosebuds.

Although leaf-cutting bees may temporarily disfigure some favorite garden plants, their activity doesn't really damage healthy plants. Be philosophical: knowing that the benefit to agriculture of more pollinating insects offsets the sacrifice of some leaves and flowers.

LEAF ROLLERS

These are yet another group of larval garden pests. The two most common kinds are the fruit tree leaf roller and the oblique-banded leaf roller. As its name suggests, the fruit-tree species feeds almost exclusively on fruit trees. But the other group is less discriminating: it feeds on more than 40 kinds of domestic trees and plants.

In spring, summer, or fall, adult moths can lay egg clusters, which they cover with a waterproof cement. In some species, the eggs hatch early and overwinter in cracks in the bark of their host tree; other species don't hatch until spring. For the first few weeks after hatching, while the green larvae are about the size of long rice grains, they eat day and night. Then, when they are about half grown, they begin to hide during the daytime by folding leaves together, as illustrated; at night they crawl out and feed on the plant. When disturbed, they thrash about violently.

At some point in maturity, a larva pupates. From the pupa—a light brown or green segmented cylinder within the rolled-up leaf—emerges the adult moth. The oblique-banded leaf roller produces one or two generations a year; the fruit tree leaf roller, just one.

A number of parasitic insects usually keeps populations of leaf rollers low. Light infestations are easy to take care of physically: just pick off and destroy rolled leaves, or squash them in place.

Use sprays only when leaf rollers threaten serious damage. The favored control is *Bacillus thuringiensis;* the surest chemical sprays are diazinon, Sevin, and Orthene.

MEALYBUGS

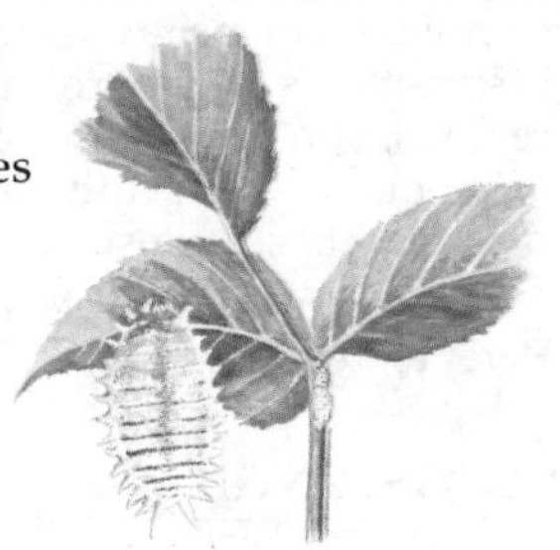

Closely related to scale insects, mealybugs have an oval-shaped body with overlapping soft plates and a white, cottony covering. Unlike scale, a mealybug can move around—at a very slow crawl. These pests suck plant juices, causing stunting or death. Often a black, sooty mold grows on the honeydew excreted by mealybug colonies.

Mealybugs are prime house plant pests everywhere; outdoors, they are especially troublesome in Zones 15–17 and 22–24. For any infestation indoors or for a minor infestation outdoors, daub mealybugs with a cotton swab dipped in rubbing alcohol. Outdoors, hose plants with jets of water (or insecticidal soap) every two to four weeks to remove adult mealybugs, their eggs and young, and the black mold, which deters beneficial insects. Ants have the same symbiotic relationship to mealybugs as to aphids and scale insects; see "Aphids," page 97, for control.

Natural predators, such as ladybird beetles, can help control mealybugs—as can some commercially available predators such as larvae of *Cryptolaemus* beetles and lacewings. Be careful not to confuse *Cryptolaemus* beetle larvae with mealybugs: they look quite similar.

When mealybug infestations are heavy, spray with malathion, diazinon, Orthene, or horticultural oil.

MITES

To the naked eye, mites look like specks of red, yellow, or green; in reality, they are tiny spider relatives (each has eight legs). Especially troublesome in interior regions, spider mites rank among the top 10 home garden pests throughout the West.

The first (and sometimes the only) sign of mite damage is yellow-stippled leaves. But leaves yellow from many causes. To confirm that mites are the problem, hold a piece of white paper beneath the stippled leaves, and sharply rap the stem from which they are growing. If mites are present, the blow will knock some onto the paper—where they will look like moving specks. With some mites on some plants, you also will see fine webbing across the leaves (especially on the undersides) and around the stems.

If the plant is small, you might jet it thoroughly with water to wash off the mites; insecticidal soap added to a water spray will increase the spray's effectiveness. Dust that settles on leaves encourages mites, so continual hosing will help keep mite populations down.

Many natural predators keep mites in check most of the time. Some of these predators—lacewing larvae and five different species of predatory mites—are bred and sold by biological control companies.

If you can't wash off the plant, or if washing is not effective, try spraying with Kelthane (if available). For a severe mite infestation, spray a second time 7 to 10 days after the first application. Light-grade horticultural oils or sulfur are other options.

OAK MOTHS

The pale brown California oak moth can damage oaks in Zones 7–9 and 14–24; it can be a major pest in coastal California, particularly around the San Francisco and Monterey bays.

The tan, inch-wide moths lay eggs in live oak trees twice a year (three times if winters are unseasonably mild). The first generation of larvae hatch in November and overwinter on live oak leaves, growing and eating more as weather warms in spring. About an inch long, full-sized worms have bulbous brown heads and olive green bodies with distinct black and olive or yellow stripes. The moths emerge from their pupae in June and

July, and their offspring larvae eat leaves again from late July to October. The worms aren't a problem every year; populations may become heavy enough to defoliate trees for two or three years in a row and then almost disappear for several years.

In late March or April, look for the telltale little green pellets—the droppings of feeding larvae—falling from live oaks. Even if the worm population is heavy, trees may get by without treatment and suffer no real damage beyond unsightliness. However, if you can't tolerate the loss of shade or the rain of droppings on patios, walks, and people, have the tree sprayed by a professional (it takes a high-pressure rig to reach the top of most oak trees).

Commercial spray operators use three controls: *Bacillus thuringiensis* (*BT*), Sevin, or Orthene. *BT* won't harm natural predators and parasites (and there are many), but it must be applied as soon as worms are large enough to eat completely through leaves. As worms grow larger, they become more difficult to kill with *BT.* Sevin and Orthene, on the other hand, kill all sizes of worms quickly, but both are highly toxic to bees.

PILLBUGS, SOWBUGS

These familiar creatures have sectioned shells and seven pairs of legs. Pillbugs roll up into black balls about the size of a large pea; sowbugs are gray and cannot roll up as tightly. Their principal food is decaying vegetation, but they also will eat very young seedling plants and the skins of melons, cucumbers, squash, and berries—particularly if they are overripe and have a break in the skin.

Mulching and composting encourage pillbugs and sowbugs. If you sprout seeds near a compost pile or in heavily composted soil, you may get some pillbug and sowbug damage. You can apply Sevin to the seedlings or to the ground where the pests are active. Around nonedible plants you also can use bendiocarb dust. To avoid damage to vegetables and berries, keep compost far from these plantings, and let soil surface dry between waterings.

ROOT WEEVILS

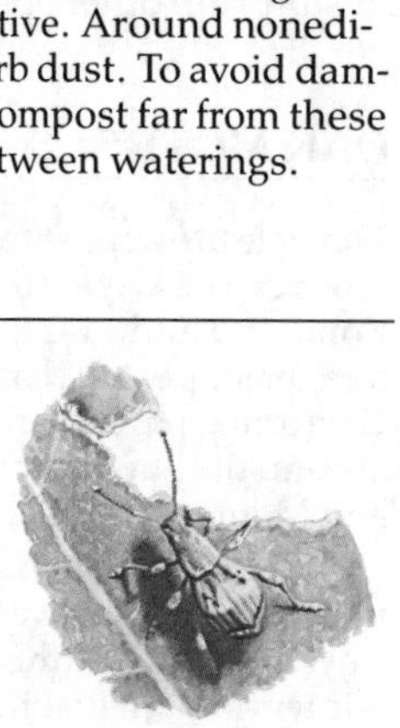

More than a dozen different kinds of root weevil are found in western Washington and Oregon and in northern California. From the moment they emerge in spring through fall, flightless gray or black adult weevils eat notches (as illustrated) from leaf edges of many plants—especially azaleas and rhododendrons, roses, and viburnums. In late summer, the weevils lay eggs on the soil or in folds of leaves. Eggs hatch into larvae with pinkish or whitish bodies and tan heads; these burrow into the soil and eat roots—particularly of strawberry plants.

To control adult weevils (which feed only at night) on nonedible plants, apply bendiocarb or orthene. No home garden chemical can kill root weevil larvae. One biological control of root weevil larvae that shows promise is parasitic nematodes.

SCALE INSECTS

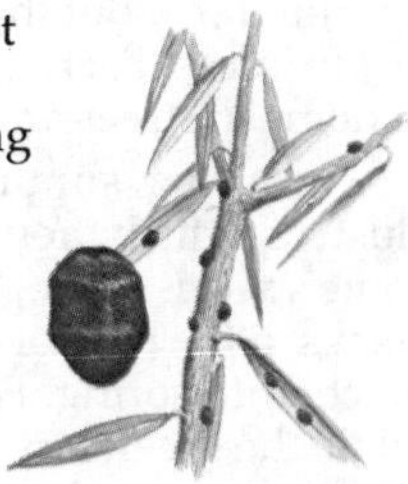

Scale insects can be a garden problem throughout the West in all areas except the desert. Closely related to mealybugs and aphids, scales differ in having a waxy shell-like covering that camouflages them and protects them from many natural enemies (and insecticides). Scales are often classified as being "hard" or "soft"; the latter produce a sticky honeydew during feeding.

An adult scale insect lives under its stationary, waxy shell, which sticks to a plant. Running from the underside of the insect into the plant tissue is a tiny filamentous mouth part, through which the scale sucks plant juices. Scale eggs hatch beneath the stationary shell; then, sometime in spring or summer, the young crawl out from under the protective cover and seek their own feeding sites.

If scale infestation is light, you may control it by picking scales off the plant or scraping them off with a plastic scouring pad. On deciduous plants, you can kill adult scales in winter with a dormant oil spray. Insecticides are effective against scales only during the juvenile "crawler" stage, before waxy shells develop. Effective at this time are summer oil spray, malathion, diazinon, Orthene, and Sevin. (To check for "crawlers," shake infested branches over a piece of paper and look for moving specks.)

Many naturally occurring parasites and predators usually control or limit scale insect populations. Unless a valuable plant is in jeopardy from scale infestation, don't spray with an insecticide: it can also kill the scales' natural enemies. A parasite of some kinds of scale, *Aphytis* wasps, is sometimes sold for release in the home garden. In dry regions, you can help scale-infested plants by hosing them off frequently: dust inhibits the various parasites and predators of scale insects.

Ants tend and protect scale insects as they do aphids. Refer to "Aphids," page 97, for ant control tips.

SLUGS, SNAILS

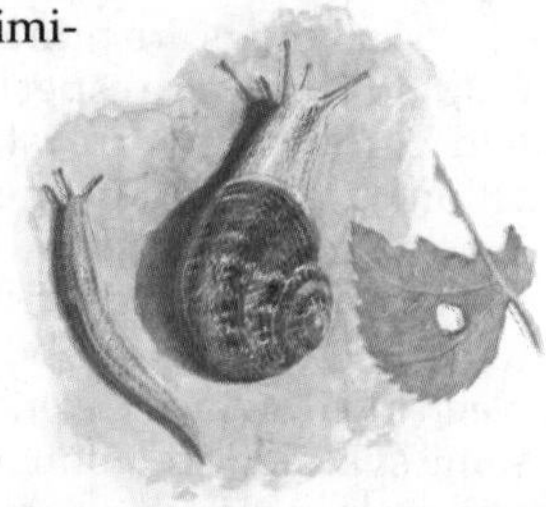

Slugs and snails rank as the West's overall worst garden pests. They are similar creatures (a slug is just a snail without a shell), feeding on many plants by biting tissue with rasping mouths underneath their bodies. Both hide by day and feed at night, though they may be active during daytime hours on very gray, damp days.

Nobody ever gets rid of slugs or snails for good. They always return—from neighbors' lots, on new plants, or even in new soil (often in container-grown plants), as eggs. The eggs look like clusters of ⅛-inch pearls; look for them under rocks, boards, and pots, and destroy those you find.

The most popular controls are packaged baits containing metaldehyde or mesurol in pellets, meal, or emulsion form. Metaldehyde is the most widely used, but its effectiveness is limited during periods of high humidity. Mesurol, commonly used in slug bait, should not be used around fruits and vegetables. If you put out pellets, scatter them so there is space between them rather than making piles. And be careful using baits where dogs live or visit, because the bait can poison dogs, too. Never apply it when dogs are present: it may look as though you're putting out dry dog food.

Handpicking is an easy way to control snails: you simply grab them by their shells and dispose of them however you wish. (Slugs are harder to pick up because they have no shell to grab.) Best hunting time is after 10 P.M.

You can also trap slugs and snails. One easy-to-set trap is a wide plank or piece of plywood elevated about an inch off the ground. Placed in an infested area, it offers a daytime hiding place—from which you can collect and dispatch the pests. Squash a slug or snail on the board's underside; this will attract other slugs and snails. Beer or a solution of sugar water and yeast appeals to slugs' fondness for fermented foods. Put the liquid in a saucer or other shallow container, and set it in the garden so the rim is even with the soil. Slugs will crawl into the dish and drown. Refill the container daily with fresh liquid.

Decollate snails feed on the common brown garden snail but leave most garden plants alone; they are sold only in a number of southern California counties. Check with your county extension agent for sources.

You can prevent snails from damaging such plants as citrus by wrapping copper bands around the tree trunks. Snails and slugs will not cross this barrier.

SQUASH BUGS

These ⅝-inch-long creatures are a problem on many plants of the squash family, particularly in the high desert and mountain areas. Damage is usually greatest on winter squash and pumpkin plants: the bugs can cause leaves to wilt completely and also will damage the fruit. Summer squash, melons, and cucumbers are seldom affected.

In spring, adult bugs lay their eggs on squash leaves. If you find a mass of hard, brown eggs crowded together on a leaf underside, destroy the eggs. Squash bugs spend nights under flat objects, so put out boards in the evening; in early morning, turn over the boards and kill the bugs (they can emit an unpleasant odor).

Sevin is an effective chemical control, but getting it applied to all the leaves is a problem—particularly on older plants with plenty of foliage. For best results, start control when plants are small.

THRIPS

These near-microscopic pests feed by rasping soft flower and leaf tissue and then drinking the juices the plants secrete. In heavy infestations, flowers and leaves fail to open normally, appearing twisted or stuck together and discolored. Look closely and you'll see seersuckerlike puckerings in flower or leaf tissue and small, black fecal pellets that thrips deposit while feeding. Leaves may take on a silvery or tan cast, distinguished from spider mite damage by the absence of webbing. The Cuban laurel thrips, illustrated here, is unusual in two respects: it is darker and larger than the more widespread kinds (which are about half its size), and it causes a noticeable curl in the leaves of its host plant, Indian laurel fig (*Ficus microcarpa nitida*).

Thrips can be a problem starting in May (as early as March in the desert) and breed rapidly, increasing in numbers as the season goes on. Thrips are notoriously fond of white and light pink rose blossoms and of gladiolus leaves and flowers.

The natural enemies of flower thrips are numerous, including ladybird beetles and larvae, green lacewing larvae, and predaceous thrips and mites.

For serious thrips infestations on ornamental plants, try malathion, diazinon, Dursban, Orthene, and Thiodan. On edible plants, use malathion.

WHITEFLIES

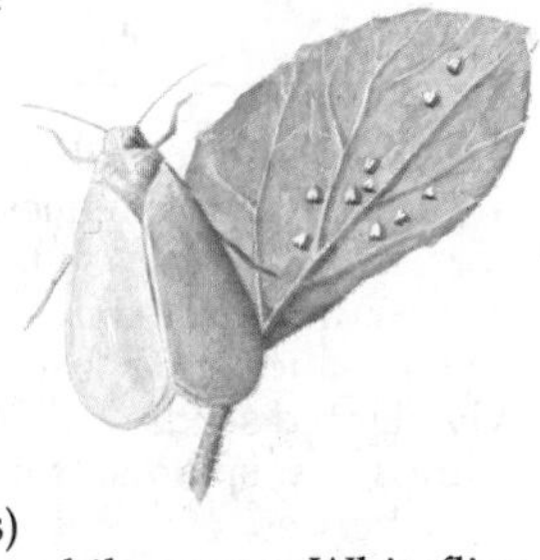

The aptly named whiteflies are those annoying winged creatures (about ⅛ inch long) that fly up from a plant when you brush or touch it. Turn over an infested plant's leaf and you see winged adults, stationary pupae, and nymphs that suck plant juices and exude a sticky substance, and (with sharp eyes or a hand lens) tiny eggs and freshly hatched, mobile young. Whiteflies are on the list of the top 10 pests in every part of the West.

Nature keeps whitefly populations in check most of the time: tiny wasp species are parasites of the nymphs and pupae, and some predatory creatures feed on them. When you spray with a chemical insecticide, you may also kill the parasites and predators—resulting in an increase of whiteflies. So before you decide to use a chemical control, consider these options:

- Eliminate the highly susceptible plants from your garden.
- Hose off the infested plants, hitting both sides of all leaves to wash off and destroy immature crawlers (nymphs); do this every few days. To put more authority into hydraulic control, use a solution of insecticidal soap: it is less harmful than insecticides to natural enemies.

- Place yellow cards or stakes covered with sticky material among infested plants. The color attracts adult whiteflies; the sticky material captures and holds them.
- Buy and release in your garden a commercially reared natural parasite: *Encarsia* wasps. They are parasites of the greenhouse whitefly (the principal species), and will kill them in a greenhouse or outdoors.
- On a plant such as squash, get rid of old, nonproductive yellow leaves in the center of the plant. These leaves carry the most whitefly eggs, pupae, and nymphs.

If you decide to use an insecticide, be sure to spray at 4- to 6-day intervals; every Saturday won't work. On edible plants, use pyrethrins or malathion. On nonedible plants, you can use systemics, Dursban, or horticultural oils. Increase spray effectiveness by spraying at night, while whiteflies are resting.

In cooler climates—including all of Colorado and areas to the north and northwest—whiteflies don't overwinter outdoors; all garden infestations originate from indoor plants. Inspect greenhouse and indoor plants and eliminate any whiteflies you find. When you buy new plants for your garden—particularly bedding plants, which may have started their lives in a greenhouse—carefully examine the undersides of leaves for the nymphs.

Rodents, Birds & Deer

These diverse creatures are sources of great frustration to the gardeners who must deal with them. Unlike most of the pests previously described—which remain in place or move around slowly—these animals are marauders, staging hit-and-run attacks on desirable plants.

BIRDS

Most gardeners see birds as friends rather than enemies, but certain birds (crows in particular) at certain times can be nuisances: they eat newly planted seeds, tender seedlings, transplants, fruits, nuts, or berries.

Reflectors, fluttering objects, and scarecrows may reduce damage briefly, but birds soon become accustomed to them and resume their activities. The only surefire solution to bird depredation is to use screen or nylon or plastic netting material.

Broad-mesh netting (¾ inch) is popular for trees, since it easily lets in air, water, and sunlight. Enclose fruit trees with nets 2 or 3 weeks before fruit ripens; tie nets off where the lowest branches spring from the trunk. Remove netting to harvest.

For protecting sprouting seedlings and maturing vegetables, floating row covers (see page 198) are the easiest to use because they need no supports. Other options—which need to be supported with stakes and string, in tent fashion—are fine-mesh screen and nylon netting. If crows are your problem, you can get protection with chicken wire folded into a tent shape over the rows.

DEER

With their soulful eyes and graceful gait, deer may be pleasant to watch, but they can make a garden ragged in no time by nipping off flower heads and nibbling tender leaves and new shoots. As wild plants dry out, deer spend more time looking for food in gardens on the fringes of suburbia. They develop browsing patterns, visiting tasty gardens regularly—most often in the evening. Fond of a wide array of flowering plants, especially roses, deer will eat foliage or fruit of nearly anything you grow for your table. For a list of plants deer usually ignore, see pages 171–173.

Fencing is the most certain protection. On level ground, a 7-foot woven-wire fence usually will keep deer out, although some determined deer can jump even an 8-foot fence. A horizontal "outrigger" extension on a fence makes it harder for a deer to jump it. On a slope, you may need to erect a 10- to 11-foot fence to guard against deer jumping from higher ground. Because deer can jump high or jump wide—but not simultaneously—some gardeners have had success with a pair of parallel 5-foot fences, with a 5-foot-wide "no-deer's-land" between.

If you don't fancy a fortress garden, you can focus on individual plants (or areas). Put chicken-wire cages around young plants and cylinders of wire fencing around larger specimens. Cover raised beds with mesh, and use floating row covers on vegetables (see page 198). It sometimes helps to keep a zealous (and vocal) watchdog in the yard—particularly during evening and nighttime hours.

Commercial repellents can work if you spray enough to keep new growth covered and to replace what rain and watering wash away (though some repellents may make sticky, unsightly spots on flowers and foliage). Some gardeners repel deer by hanging small cloth bags filled with blood meal among their plants; disadvantages are that blood meal attracts dogs and smells bad when wet.

GROUND SQUIRRELS

Throughout the West, ground squirrels are especially troublesome in gardens that border fields or wild land. The California ground squirrel (illustrated) is the most common kind in California, western Oregon, and southwestern Washington. It lives in burrows, usually 2½ to 4 feet underground, where it stores food, raises young, and hides from its chief predators: foxes, hawks, and owls.

During spring and summer, it scurries around most actively in midmorning or late afternoon (except in very hot weather), nibbling through tomato patches, digging up bulbs, gnawing roots and bark, and sometimes climbing low trees after fruits and nuts.

Methods of control include using a baited, box-type trap placed outside the burrow; anticoagulant types of poison bait—usually grain—placed inside the burrow (these require 5 to 6 days of continuous feeding to be lethal); and gas bombs placed well back in the burrow (make sure all entry holes are plugged). Before you try any of these, check with your county agent or farm advisor: laws in some areas prohibit catching certains kinds of ground squirrel.

Metal guards around tree trunks can keep ground squirrels out of trees. Protect bulb beds with a cover of fine-mesh chicken wire.

MOLES

Notorious pests in good soils throughout the West, moles have short forelegs pointing outward; large, flattened hands; and claws for digging tunnels. Townsend's mole—common in the Pacific states west of the Sierra-Cascades chain of mountains—has velvety blue-black fur and a nearly hairless tail and snout.

Moles are primarily insectivorous, eating earthworms, bugs, and larvae, and only occasionally nibbling greens and roots. Irrigation and rain keep them near the soil surface, where they do the most damage as they tunnel: heaving plants from the ground, severing tender roots, and disfiguring lawns. A mole's main runways, which are used repeatedly, are usually from 6 to 10 inches underground and are frequently punctuated with volcano-shaped mounds of excavated soil. Shallower burrows, created while feeding, are used for short periods and then abandoned.

Trapping is the most efficient control. The spear- or harpoon-type trap is the easiest to set because you simply position the trap above the soil. A scissor-jaw trap must be carefully set into the main runway (probe with a sharp stick to find it); a wily mole will spring, heave out, or go around a faultily set trap.

Moles, because of their feeding habits, are very difficult to control with poison baits. And moles, like gophers, are difficult to control with toxic gas. To be successful with this method, place gas "mole bombs" directly in the main runways and block all holes. Be persistent with follow-up treatments.

You can dispatch a mole with a shovel blade, but you may wait a long time for a mole to appear. Your chances are best at dawn. If you see a mole scuttling along below ground (you'll notice the ground surface heaving), try the two-shovel method: block the runway in front of the mole with one shovel blade, and dig out the creature with the other.

POCKET GOPHERS

Gophers are serious pests in many areas of the West, and in coastal California they rank among the top three garden pests.

Like little bulldozers, these furry creatures dig a network of tunnels —usually 6 to 18 inches below the surface—with strong, clawed forefeet and powerful shoulders. Tunnels near the surface are for gathering food; deeper ones are for sleeping, storing food, and raising young. Gophers eat roots, bulbs, and sometimes entire plants by pulling them down into their burrows. Well suited to burrow life, they have small eyes and ears that don't clog with dirt, and the flexibility needed to turn around in tight spaces.

The first sign of gopher trouble often is a fan-shaped mound of fresh, finely pulverized earth in a lawn or flower bed; this soil is a by-product of burrowing operations, brought to the surface through short side runs opening off the main burrow. You may find a hole in this mound or (more often) a plug of earth blocking the exit.

Trapping is the most efficient method of catching gophers. Avoid the temptation to place a single trap down a hole. Your chances of catching a gopher are much greater when you dig down to the main horizontal runway connecting with the surface hole and place two traps in the runway, one on either side of your excavation. Attach each trap to a stake on the surface with a chain or wire (this prevents a trapped gopher from dragging the trap farther into a burrow). The Macabee trap is the most effective. Box-type traps also work and are easier to set.

When the traps are in place, plug the hole with a ball of carrot tops, fresh grass, or other tender greens; their scent attracts gophers. Next, place a board or soil over the greens and the hole to block all light. Check traps frequently, and clear tunnels if the gopher has pushed soil into the traps. Be persistent: a wily gopher may avoid your first traps.

Poison baits are very effective for the control of trap-wise gophers. Probe for the deep burrows with a rod or sharp stick, insert bait, and close the hole. These baits are hazardous to other living things so be sure not to spill any on the ground. Poisoning of dogs and cats from eating poisoned gophers is rare, but it can happen.

Dispatching a gopher with a shovel can work after the victim has been flushed from his tunnel by flooding. This approach works only where ground is level. Toxic gases will be effective soon after gophers arrive in your garden, before they have had time to construct extensive burrow systems. Before you inject gas into the burrow, water areas around the tunnel to prevent gas from seeping through its sides. Be persistent with follow-up treatments.

If your garden is subject to ongoing invasion by gophers from neighboring fields or orchards—or if all your trapping efforts fail—you can protect roots of young plants by lining sides and bottom of planting holes with light-gauge chicken wire or hardware cloth.

Pest Controls

Biological controls. A number of living organisms can provide some measure of pest control. Many of these occur naturally in gardens (and may be eliminated by unwise pesticide use).

■ ***Bacillus thuringiensis (BT).*** A bacteria that will control caterpillars (including various "worms"). After eating treated leaves, the caterpillar dies within 2 to 3 days. BT can be used on all food crops up to harvest. Sold under several trade names.

■ ***Cryptolaemus beetle larvae.*** A species of ladybird beetle, the larvae of which feed on mealybugs.

■ ***Encarsia (whitefly parasite).*** A small wasp, this develops within developing whiteflies. Control requires average temperatures above 75°.

■ ***Lacewings.*** Commonly found in gardens, the larvae and adults feed on a variety of insects and mites.

■ ***Nosema locustae (grasshopper spore).*** This organism cripples and kills many grasshopper species. Most of its effects occur a year after application.

■ ***Parasitic nematodes.*** The most commonly sold species—*Neoaplectana carpocapsae* and *Heterorhabditis*—control a variety of soil insects. Availability is limited.

■ ***Predator mites.*** Various species of mites feed on spider mites but do no damage to plants.

■ ***Scale parasites.*** *Aphytis* wasps attack and kill certain scale insects.

■ ***Trichogramma wasps.*** These tiny wasps develop within the eggs of caterpillars. Repeated applications usually achieve desired control.

Packaged pesticides. These products carry one or more active ingredients in a liquid, powder, or granular form.* Their availability is continually shifting. New products continue to be developed and marketed. Existing products may be withdrawn from sale for home use if research reveals any possible hazard to health or the environment.

On the label of each product is a list of plants on which the control is registered for use. It is illegal to apply the control to a plant not listed on the label unless the wording specifically condones use on other plants not mentioned by name.

■ ***Baygon (propoxur).*** Common in earwig baits, and wasp and hornet sprays. Do not use on edible crops.

■ ***Bendiocarb.*** A dust to control crawling pests such as earwigs, pillbugs and sowbugs, and some soil pests, including root weevils.

■ ***Diazinon.*** A broad-spectrum insecticide also widely used to control various lawn pests. It is the only control for soil pests in vegetable gardens. Extremely toxic to birds.

■ ***Dursban (chlorpyrifos).*** A control for certain borers in shade trees, for control of lawn insects and many other pests of ornamental plants. Do not use on vegetables.

■ ***Ethion.*** Effective against mites, whiteflies, and some species of scale.

■ ***Kelthane.*** A common control for spider mites; often it is an ingredient in multipurpose insecticides.

■ ***Malathion.*** A broad-spectrum insecticide for use on both edible and ornamental crops; it is toxic to honeybees.

■ ***Mesurol.*** An effective control for slugs and snails—but it also will kill earthworms. Not for use around edible crops.

■ ***Metaldehyde.*** The most common slug and snail control. Usually it is the active ingredient in various baits, is contained in some liquids. It is safe to use around vegetable and fruit crops; it loses effectiveness in moist weather and after waterings.

■ ***Methoxychlor.*** An older insecticide still found in some all-purpose fruit sprays to control various beetles and caterpillars. Also effective against whitefly.

■ ***Oil sprays.*** Special, highly refined oils smother insects and their eggs. "Dormant" oils are used during winter period for control of insects that overwinter on deciduous plants. "Summer oils" can be used after leaves have emerged and on woody evergreen plants such as *Citrus*.

■ ***Pyrethrum/pyrethrins.*** An insecticide derived from *Pyrethrum* daisies. Effective against many insects but will break down within a few hours after exposure to sunlight.

■ ***Rotenone.*** An insecticide derived from South American plants; use is commonly as dust to control chewing insects on vegetables. Fairly toxic to mammals (especially hogs) and extremely toxic to fish.

■ ***Sevin (carbaryl).*** Insecticide commonly used in vegetable gardens. Effective against most chewing insects but generally not effective against sucking insects. It often will increase problems with the latter pests by destroying their natural predators. Highly toxic to honeybees and earthworms.

■ ***Soaps.*** These mixtures of special fatty acids are of low toxicity to humans and beneficial organisms but will control most small insects and mites. Safe for use on edible plants, fast acting, but with no residual effectiveness; some plants are injured by soap.

■ ***Sulfur.*** Finely ground sulfur mixed with clay, talc, and gypsum to be dusted over plants (or sometimes diluted with water and sprayed) to control mites, psyllids, and certain mildews. Never use when temperature will exceed 90°.

■ ***Systemics.*** These pesticides are absorbed by a plant's foliage or roots; insects that pierce the plants' external tissues and ingest the juices or chew the leaves are killed. Sprayed on the foliage, systemics also kill insects on contact. Widely available are Cygon (apply to leaves or soil), Disyston (apply only to soil), and Orthene (apply only to leaves). None can be used on edible crops.

■ ***Thiodan (endosulfan).*** A broad-spectrum insecticide particularly effective against thrips, aphids, borers, fuchsia mites, and whiteflies.

*Packaged pesticides are listed alphabetically by trade name or common name; the generic name, which you will find under "active ingredients" on the product label, appears in parentheses when it differs from the trade name.

Plant Diseases

There are different kinds of organisms that produce diseases. Most leaf and stem diseases result from bacteria, fungi, or viruses, as explained below. The most prevalent soilborne diseases are caused by various fungi.

But sometimes disease results from the plant interacting with unfavorable environmental factors, such as air pollution, a deficiency or excess of nutrients or of sunlight, or the wrong climate (too hot, too cold, too dry, too wet).

For information on symptoms and treatments of the most common results of nutrient deficiency and excess—chlorosis and salt damage, respectively—refer to page 62. Exposure and climate preferences are spelled out for each plant listed in the Western Plant Encyclopedia, which begins on page 199. Here, we discuss the various diseases that are caused by other organisms.

Bacterial diseases. Bacteria are single-celled microorganisms that are unable to manufacture their own food (as green plants do); those bacteria that cause plant diseases must obtain their nutrients from the host plants.

Fungal diseases. Certain multicellular branching, threadlike plants called *fungi* obtain their food parasitically from green plants, causing diseases in the process. Many fungi produce great numbers of tiny reproductive bodies called *spores*, which can be carried by wind or water from leaf to leaf and from plant to plant. Each spore, under the right conditions, will germinate and grow—producing new infections. Fungus diseases are among the most widespread of plant maladies, but many are controllable by good sanitation and cultural practices and with fungicide sprays or dusts.

Viral diseases. Ultramicroscopic viruses are capable of invading plant tissue and reproducing in it, usually at the expense of the host plant. Viruses may produce symptoms such as abnormalities in growth, variegation of foliage, or "breaking" (color distortion, usually streaking) of blossoms.

In agriculture—especially among beans, *Citrus,* sugar beets and cane, grapes, cucumbers, squash, potatoes, and tomatoes (to cite just a few)—virus-induced diseases are a serious threat because they affect vigor and productivity. In the home garden, a viral infection may or may not be detrimental. Undesirable viruses are those that cause an undecorative mottling on leaves or that stunt and yellow foliage; in some diseases, such as rose mosaic, the virus causes a striking foliage variegation but does not significantly reduce plant vigor. Some attractive plants—such as the various tulips that have bizarrely striped flowers, and the variegated-leaf *Abutilon*—owe their variegation to a virus.

There is no home cure at this time for a virus-infected plant. However, you can reduce chances of a virus spreading to other plants in two ways. First, remove from your garden any plants that are severely stunted or mottled. Second, try to control the insects that carry viruses. Aphids are most efficient in spreading different kinds of viruses; leafhoppers and thrips can be vectors, too. And humans may spread viruses by inadvertently propagating virus-infected plants or by handling tobacco while working around plants (thereby spreading tobacco mosaic virus, which affects many plants in addition to tobacco).

Leaf & Stem Diseases

Described below are the principal diseases caused by bacteria and fungi that can attack aboveground plant parts. The causal organism is listed for each disease.

ANTHRACNOSE (fungus). *See* Leaf spot

BLACK SPOT (fungus). *See* Leaf spot

DUTCH ELM DISEASE (fungus)

This devastating disease, for decades confined to the East and Midwest, spread slowly across the United States to reach the West in the early 1970s.

Dutch elm disease (abbreviated DED) is spread primarily by the elm bark beetle, although it also can spread from infected trees to nearby healthy ones by natural root grafting. Normal transmission starts with beetle larvae that overwinter in dead and dying elm trees. When the young beetles emerge in spring, the sticky fungus spores adhere to their bodies; as beetles migrate to healthy new growth on elms to feed, they spread the fungus. The fungus spores begin to grow in feeding wounds, and the fungus moves through the water-conducting system of the tree. The first symptom of infection usually is wilted foliage (because water conductivity is interrupted); then leaves turn yellow and fall, and the tree dies.

DED is incurable at present, but sometimes its progress can be slowed. Removal of trees showing infection may help save other trees. (Do not save wood from infected trees.) If you have an elm you suspect has DED, call your county agricultural agent and report the symptoms. The agent should then advise you on the best course of action to take.

FIREBLIGHT (bacterium)

This disease is troublesome in all of the West but worse at high elevations and along the eastern slope of the Rocky Mountains. It affects only plants in the pome tribe of the rose family. When a flowering shoot of an apple, cotoneaster, crabapple, hawthorn, pear, pyracantha, quince, or toyon dies suddenly and looks as though it has been scorched by fire (as illustrated), fireblight probably was the culprit.

The bacteria that cause fireblight survive in blighted twigs and cankers. During moist weather—especially in early spring, when temperatures are above 60°—the bacteria are carried to blossoms by splashing water, flies, and other insects. Once in the blossoms, the bacteria are spread to other flowers by honeybees. Infection progresses from the blossoms down the shoots into the larger limbs, where dark, sunken cankers form. Infection also can enter a plant through any fresh wound in the bark or foliage, including pruning cuts and hailstone bruises.

Wherever fireblight is a persistent problem, you should avoid growing susceptible plants or, if you continue to grow them, take regular control measures. To protect blossoms from infection, spray at 4- or 5-day intervals during the flowering season with a fixed copper-based spray (or agricultural streptomycin, if available).

To control the disease once it has appeared, prune out and burn diseased twigs and branches. On a small branch, make the cut 4 to 6 inches below the infection; on larger branches, make cuts at least 12 inches below blighted tissue. If you must make more than one cut, disinfect your shears between cuts so you don't spread the bacteria. Dip shears for 20 to 30 seconds in rubbing alcohol or a 10-percent solution of household bleach. If you use bleach, be sure to wash and dry the blades afterward; otherwise, the bleach solution may corrode steel shears.

LEAF SPOT (fungus)

Red, brown, yellow, or black disease spots on leaves and stems may be found on a number of different plants. On some *Prunus* plants, the spots drop out, leaving a "shot-hole" appearance. Sometimes spots enlarge and coalesce, and then infected leaves drop; severe infections can defoliate some plants.

These symptoms represent several different diseases, including anthracnoses, black spot (familiar to rose growers), and scab, which affects some fruits. The fungus spores that cause these diseases are airborne or waterborne. And because the spores need free moisture to germinate, these diseases are far less serious in low-rainfall areas than they are in Zones 4–6 and 17. Some types of leaf-spot fungus, activated by moisture during the winter rainy period, affect evergreen plants in the three coastal states.

The source of these diseases is mainly live infected plants, though some disease-producing organisms can overwinter in plant refuse. Thorough garden cleanup each winter is important if you hope to lessen or eradicate infection. In addition, the following controls can be used as sprays to curtail infections: benomyl, captan, folpet, mancozeb, and maneb.

Three particular leaf-spot diseases are troublesome enough to warrant further explanation.

■ ***Anthracnose*** fungi infect leaves and tender shoots as they emerge in spring; they also infect older leaves, on which they produce large, irregular brown blotches and cause premature dropping of leaves. The fungi also cause twig dieback and canker on small branches, and these blighted twigs and cankers will be a source of infection the following spring. Spores are spread by rain and by sprinkling; hence the disease is most severe in wet springs and is checked by dry weather.

Your first attempt at control should be to eliminate sources of future infection: prune out all infected twigs and branches, if feasible. To prevent infection in spring, use benomyl (on ash trees) or chlorothalonil. Spray when leaves unfold, then 2 or 3 more times, at 2-week intervals.

Some anthracnoses are very difficult to control, and sometimes it is necessary to live with them—especially if the disease affects a large or favorite plant. But the best approach to the problem is to grow plants that resist the disease. Among susceptible trees such as ash, Chinese elm, and sycamore, resistant cultivars are available.

■ ***Black spot*** (pictured at left) thrives where humidity is high and summer rainfall is common. It is especially troublesome on roses in the Northwest and is an increasing problem in California. The disease appears on leaves and stems as roughly circular spots of black with fringed edges, usually circled with yellow. In severe cases, the plant will defoliate; unchecked infestations, with repeated defoliation, can seriously weaken the host plant.

The black spot fungus lives through winter in lesions on canes and on old leaves on the ground. In spring the fungus again becomes active and produces spores, which are then spread by splashing water to new leaves. Preventive control consists of sanitation: clean up and destroy (burn or discard) old leaves in winter. In spring, spray new foliage with triforine (the favorite of most rose growers), benomyl, folpet, or chlorothalonil. Repeat sprayings will be needed as long as weather conditions favor the fungus's development.

■ ***Scab*** produces disfiguring lesions on apple and crabapple fruits and, when severe, can also cause defoliation. Another kind of scab occurs on loquats, pyracanthas, and toyons, while still another infects willows. Scab is most prevalent in high-rainfall regions. The scab fungus (as well as the fungus that causes black spot on roses) differs from other leaf-infesting fungi in that the dark spots on leaves represent fungus growth on the foliage rather than areas of dead tissue.

For control of scab on deciduous trees, spray just before flower buds open with benomyl, captan, mancozeb, or wettable sulfur. Spray again when blossoms show color and again when three quarters of the blossom petals have fallen. Whenever possible, try to avoid the problem by planting scab-resistant varieties of apple and crabapple. Scab on evergreen ornamentals is more difficult to control. Thoroughly spray with benomyl as needed; clean up all infected foliage debris.

PEACH LEAF CURL (fungus)

Named for its most widely grown host plant, this disease also infects nectarines. In early spring the emerging new leaves thicken and pucker along their midribs, producing the characteristic curling. The curled and distorted leaves may be tinged with red, pink, yellow, or white; later in the season, they may become covered with white spores that can be carried by the wind to other leaves or plants. Lodging in and on the buds of next year's growth, these spores become the source of next year's infection. By midsummer the curled leaves usually fall, and trees then produce new leaves. Successive years of infection severely weaken a tree and decrease or eliminate fruit production.

The fungus overwinters on and in buds and on old, infected leaves, developing most rapidly during cool, moist winter or spring weather. Actual infection takes place when the bud scales (protective coverings on growth buds) first crack open—as early as December or as late as March, depending on the year, variety, and the region. If buds swell early, they are susceptible to infection for several months, until active growth starts (once leaf differentiation takes place, plants are resistant to infection).

For best control, protect the buds with fungicide until leaves start to show. Spray with fixed copper (wettable powder) or lime sulfur; make the first application around the first of the year and follow up with two further applications at 3- to 4-week intervals. You also can control infection by covering trees with plastic during rainy weather; this is easiest with genetic dwarf varieties.

POWDERY MILDEW (fungus)

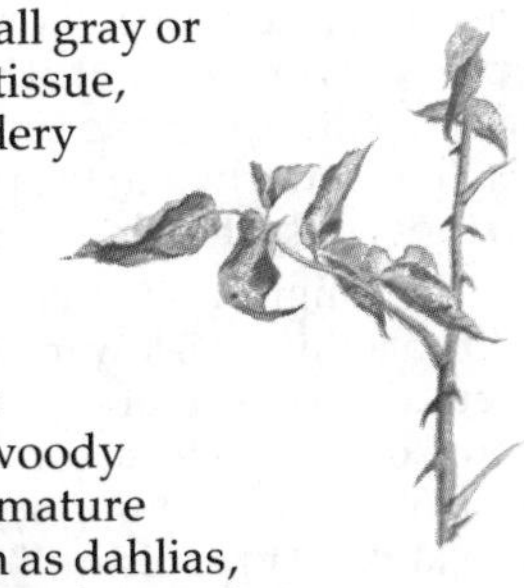

This disease first appears as small gray or white circular patches on plant tissue, spreading rapidly to form powdery areas of fungus filaments and spores. Powdery mildew can infect leaves, buds, and stems, depending on the exact kind of mildew and the host plant. It attacks young growth of some woody plants such as roses but infects mature leaves of nonwoody plants such as dahlias, chrysanthemums, peas, beans, and squash. Infected leaves may become crumpled and distorted.

Powdery mildew spores are unique in that they can cause infection in the absence of moisture: most mildews (there are many kinds) thrive in humid air. But spores need dry leaves on which to become established. You're likely to find powdery mildew when days are warm and nights are cool; it also resurges when days shorten and cool, humid nights lengthen. No climatic region escapes powdery mildew: it occurs in inland gardens, in coastal regions, and in the desert. Areas with summer rainfall generally have less mildew than dry-summer regions.

Some plants are notoriously mildew-prone (*Photinia glabra, Euonymus japonica,* and certain rose varieties, for example). Where powdery mildew is especially troublesome, it is best to exclude such plants from your garden.

Several fungicides are effective at controlling powdery mildew. Triadimefon has been noted by rose growers as the most effective at both preventing and eradicating powdery mildew, although it has a tendency to shorten growth and can be difficult to find. Other helpful chemicals with similar properties are triforine and benomyl. Some rose growers have had good luck controlling powdery mildew by spraying plants with antitranspirant products. For simple protection against powdery mildew, folpet might be effective.

RUST (fungus)

One kind of rust is a notorious plague on rose foliage; other kinds attack hollyhocks, snapdragons, and many other plants. But each type of rust is specific to a certain type of plant: rose rust will not infect hollyhocks, for example, and vice versa. On roses, the disease usually appears in late spring as yellow to orange pustules on undersides of older leaves. (Other rusts may be brownish or even purple.) As the infection progresses, leaf undersides become covered with powdery masses of spores, and upper surfaces display a yellow mottling. In advanced stages, entire leaves may turn yellow and drop.

Warm days, cool nights, and moisture (even heavy dew) will encourage rust development; rain, sprinkling, and wind spread the fungus from plant to plant. Leaf surfaces must be wet for a minimum of 4 hours in order for spores to germinate and infect. Prolonged hot, dry weather will halt rust development. The fungus can survive over winter on both live and dead leaves.

Rust prevention begins in winter. Thoroughly clean up fallen leaves and debris; remove any rust-infected leaves that remain on plants. During the rust season, choose from a number of fungicide sprays that kill the disease: triforine is favored by rose growers; triadimefon also is effective (but see note about growth under "Powdery Mildew") as are chlorathalonil and wettable sulfur. If you water by overhead sprinkling, do it in early morning on sunny days so that leaves will dry quickly.

SCAB (fungus). *See* Leaf spot

SHOT HOLE (fungus). *See* Leaf spot

Soilborne Diseases

These diseases result from infection through plant roots; frequently you don't see symptoms above ground until roots have been severely damaged. Most of the following diseases, which result from infection by fungi, are less treatable than those that occur on leaves and stems.

DAMPING OFF

In the most conspicuous type of this disease (which can be caused by a number of different organisms), the stem of a seedling collapses at or near the soil surface, and the seedling topples. Another type rots the seedling before it emerges from the soil or causes the seed to decay before sprouting. In some woody seedlings, infected plants may remain alive and standing for a while.

Professional horticulturists practice careful sanitation, pasteurizing their soil mixes; a home method is outlined on page 183. But the home gardener can take steps to reduce the occurrence of damping off: (1) buy seeds that have been treated with a fungicide, or dust them with one before planting; (2) provide good air circulation and ventilation (especially if growing seedlings indoors) to keep tops of seedlings dry and standing moisture to a minimum; and (3) sow seeds or root cuttings in an inert (sterile) material rather than in garden soil: vermiculite, perlite, pumice, sand, sphagnum moss, and sterilized commercial mixes all are safe—at least the first time they are used. You also can reduce problems by not planting too deeply or too close together and by avoiding overwatering.

A number of chemical fungicides will help control damping off. Look for products that contain captan, thiram, or zineb. But realize that one product may not be effective against all damping-off organisms. If a particular product doesn't work, switch to another.

OAK ROOT FUNGUS

Especially in low-elevation, non-desert regions of California, oak root fungus (*Armillaria mellea*) infects mainly a variety of woody garden plants. First symptoms may be dull or yellowed leaves and/or sparse foliage. Leaves may wilt and entire branches die; eventually, the affected plant succumbs.

To verify a problem as oak root fungus, check the bark of the stem or trunk (or large roots) at or below ground level: just beneath the bark you'll find a mat of whitish fungus tissue. In late autumn or early winter, clumps of tan mushrooms may appear around infected plants. The fungus kills its host by gradually decaying the roots and moving into the main stem, where it girdles the plant; the aboveground part of the plant shows distress because its supply of water and nutrients is reduced and finally cut off.

You may be able to save lightly infested trees—or at least prolong their lives—if you remove soil from their bases, exposing the juncture of roots and trunk or stems to the air, and cut out all destroyed and infected tissue. More often, though, the disease runs its full course despite remedial action. The fungus will live for many years in root systems of plants it has killed; roots of susceptible plants that contact infected roots will be invaded by the fungus. If you intend to replace a victim with a susceptible tree or shrub you must thoroughly remove all infected roots from the soil. It's better to choose replacement plants from the list of resistant sorts on pages 174–175.

ROOT ROTS, WATER MOLDS

The diseases caused by the water-mold fungi are seldom mentioned as such. But they are indirectly referred to in directions that specify *"infrequent but deep watering," "sharp drainage"* or *"well-drained soil," "good aeration,"* or *"keeping a plant on the dry side."* These phrases are advising you about care required to avoid water molds.

Free water (excess water that fills the air spaces in the soil—see page 60) can suffocate plant roots. But water can pass through the soil continuously without damaging roots *if it carries air with it*. The damage to roots from overwatering is, in almost all cases, not caused by water itself but by water-mold fungi that thrive when free water stands too long around roots—especially when soil is warm.

To offset problems caused by water-mold fungi, take steps to improve soil drainage (if necessary) for susceptible plants; see page 62 for more information. And be sure you don't overwater. The only symptom that almost always indicates a need for more water is wilting. Other signs—such as poor growth, dropping leaves, and yellowing—suggest other problems.

Two chemicals—metalaxyl and aliette—have proven effective against water molds, but they are costly and often hard to find.

TEXAS ROOT ROT

This is a damaging and widespread disease in the semiarid and arid Southwest at elevations below 3,500 feet—from California's Imperial and Coachella valleys through Arizona and New Mexico and eastward. It is caused by a fungus (*Phymatotrichum omnivorum*) that destroys the outer portion of roots, thus cutting off water supply to the upper parts of the plant. The first sign of the disease is a sudden wilting of leaves in summer, with the wilted leaves remaining attached to the plant. When this occurs, at least half the root system has already been damaged.

The fungus is favored by high temperatures and a highly alkaline soil low in organic matter. Fortunately, the fungus does not compete well with other soil-inhabiting organisms. Therefore, control measures focus on lessening alkalinity (by adding soil sulfur) and increasing the population of organisms that "crowd out" the fungus (by adding organic matter that decomposes rapidly).

You can attempt to save a damaged tree or shrub by the following method. First, prune and thin the growth to remove half the foliage; this reduces transpiration stress on the damaged root system. Then, loosen the surrounding soil as far as the plant's drip line. Cover the loosened ground to a depth of 2 inches with composted manure. On top of the manure, scatter ammonium sulfate at the rate of 1 pound to 10 square feet (*do not* use ammonium nitrate or any other nitrate fertilizer). Finally, add soil sulfur at the same rate of application. Make a ridge of soil around the treated area to form a watering basin, and then soak the soil to a depth of 3 to 4 feet by flooding the basin.

Because the fungus will move through the soil from diseased to healthy roots, it is necessary to treat nearby noninfected but susceptible plants. Where the rot has occurred, treat the soil each year in March or April.

Before you plant trees and shrubs where Texas root rot is known to be present, you should make the following special preparations. Dig a hole 2½ feet deep and 4 to 6 feet in diameter. Be prepared to add manure, soil sulfur, and ammonium sulfate to the backfill soil in these amounts: for a 4-foot-diameter hole, use 6 cubic feet of manure, 7½ pounds of soil sulfur, and 1¾ pounds of ammonium sulfate; for a 6-foot-diameter hole, use 12 cubic feet of manure, 17 pounds of soil sulfur, and 4¼ pounds of ammonium sulfate. To refill the hole, first add about 2 inches of composted manure in the bottom of the hole; then scatter sulfur and ammonium sulfate. Mix the materials with 3 inches of soil and repeat until the hole is filled to within 6 inches of the top. Flood the hole to settle the soil, and plant when soil is in good condition. Ideally, you should prepare these holes 1 to 2 months before you intend to plant. When you plant bare-root trees and shrubs in prepared soil, be sure no manure or fertilizer comes in contact with the roots: protect roots with 2 to 3 inches of plain soil.

VERTICILLIUM WILT

This is one of the most widespread and destructive plant diseases—especially in California. The verticillium fungus invades and plugs the water-conducting tissues in the roots and stems. A common symptom is a wilting of one side of the plant. Leaves yellow, starting at their margins and progressing inward, and then turn brown and die upward or outward from the base of the plant or branch. Affected branches die. If you cut one of these branches, you may find that the sapwood (the outer layer of tissue just under the bark) is discolored—it frequently is streaked olive green, dark brown, or black. Development of the fungus is favored by cool, moist soil, but wilting of foliage may not show until days are sunny and warm and the plant is under water stress (the leaves transpiring water faster than the diseased roots and stems can supply).

The fungus can survive in the soil for years in the absence of susceptible plants. Even rotation (the growing of nonsusceptible plants in the infested soil) will not rid the soil of verticillium fungus. Highly susceptible crops—such as tomatoes, potatoes, cotton, strawberries, and various melons—frequently leave soil infested.

Mildly affected plants may recover from an attack. You can aid recovery by deep but infrequent irrigation. If a plant has been neglected, apply fertilizer to stimulate new root growth. However, shrubs and trees showing lush growth should not be fertilized after the disease appears.

No measures will kill the fungus once it has invaded a plant. If you are planting shallow-rooted plants, you can control the fungus *before* you plant by having the soil fumigated. A commercial fumigation specialist will use chloropicrin (tear gas) or methyl bromide. But fumigation has not been successful with deep-rooted shrubs and trees.

The most certain solution to verticillium wilt is to grow wilt-resistant plants. Refer to page 176 for lists of resistant plants.

Disease Controls

With plant diseases, your first line of defense is prevention. Whenever possible, choose disease-resistant plants; make sure that planting locations and conditions don't encourage diseases that could be troublesome in your region.

Numerous packaged products are available for control of diseases.* They can be categorized as *preventatives*—products that prevent diseases from occurring but are ineffective in controlling them once they are established—and *eradicants*—materials that help control diseases (many simply protect new growth) once they are established. The controls described are the ones most useful and commonly available. Several other products—generally less widely sold—are mentioned under the specific diseases they control.

The product descriptions (below) mention the common diseases each product controls, but this usually is just a fraction of the diseases listed on the product labels. (You may find a disease listed on a product label but not mentioned in the description below; this is because other products described for that disease usually are more effective.)

Read product labels carefully to be sure you will apply the product to a plant listed. Some products will control a disease on one plant but not on another; moreover, some products can do damage if applied to inappropriate plants.

- ***Benomyl (Benlate).*** Systemic, wettable powder useful for prevention or eradication of many foliage diseases including powdery mildew and several types of leaf spot.
- ***Captan.*** Dust or wettable powder for prevention or eradication of damping-off, leaf spots, and many other fungal diseases.
- ***Chlorothalonil (Daconil).*** Multipurpose liquid fungicide for prevention of diseases on lawns, fruits, vegetables, and ornamentals.
- ***Copper compounds.*** A group of general purpose fungicides and bactericides, most often used to prevent fireblight, peach leaf curl, and shot hole diseases.
- ***Lime sulfur (calcium polysulfide).*** Liquid preventative for various leaf spots, peach leaf curl, and powdery mildew. Often used as a dormant spray. Also controls some mites, scale insects, and thrips.
- ***Sulfur.*** Dust or wettable powder; one of the oldest and safest fungicides used to prevent powdery mildew, scab, and rust.
- ***Triadimefon (Bayleton).*** Wettable powder; systemic for prevention or eradication of powdery mildew, rust, and some lawn diseases; also effective against azalea petal blight.
- ***Triforine (Funginex).*** Liquid systemic for prevention and eradication of powdery mildew, rust, black spot, and a variety of other diseases. You must wear goggles and face mask when using it.

*Packaged controls are listed alphabetically by generic name (the name you will find on product label under "active ingredients") or common name; trade name (where different from generic name) appears in parentheses.

Weeds

Weed control is more than mere garden housekeeping. A weed-free garden not only is more attractive than a weed-filled one but is healthier as well. Weeds compete with garden plants for water, nutrients, light, and space. In some instances, they harbor insect and pathogen populations you'd rather live without.

Weeds can be controlled in several ways. You can control them biologically, by preventing them from germinating. You can control them physically, by pulling, hoeing, digging, or mowing. Or you can control them chemically, with herbicides. The old slogan "Keep weeds from going to seed" will go far toward holding weed populations in check.

Weed prevention. There are several effective ways to prevent weed seeds from germinating or weed plants from growing. You can plant annuals and vegetables close together so that their growth will shade out weeds. Ground-cover plantings—and ground-hugging plants beneath taller ones in a mixed planting—can blanket the soil so that even when weed seeds sprout, they'll have trouble getting the sunlight necessary to become established. And any sort of mulch (see page 72) will materially cut down on annual weed establishment; any weeds that do appear will be quite easy to remove. Another form of prevention is mentioned below, under "Chemical control."

Physical control. Pulling annual weeds by hand is sometimes necessary, especially when weeds grow among choice, shallow-rooted plants such as cyclamen, rhododendrons, and azaleas. Where damage to surface roots is not a risk, hoeing and cultivating furnish adequate weed control and, in roughing up the soil surface and breaking the crust, will temporarily improve water penetration.

Many tools are available for various types of weeds and plantings, as shown on pages 90–95. Common garden hoes and cultivating forks in a variety of sizes are useful for working among row crops, little garden plants, and shrubs. Scuffle hoes (flat-bladed, disk type, or U-shaped) are easier to use in close quarters or under spreading plants. As you push and pull them, they cut weeds without digging into roots of desirable plants.

For larger areas (orchards, roadsides, vacant lots), rotary-tilling or disking will do the job, especially where there is no summer rain to germinate late weed crops. Either method will not only knock down weeds but also incorporate them into the soil, where they will decay to form humus. Weed-eaters knock down weed growth but leave severed tops on the ground; rotary mowers cut weeds and grind up the refuse in one operation.

Chemical control. The herbicides, or chemical weed killers, were conceived as agricultural aids but years ago were welcomed into the home gardener's realm. These chemicals offer several approaches to weed control. *Preplant herbicides* are for use before you set out vegetables (if so labeled), bedding plants, or ornamentals. *Preemergence herbicides* applied to the soil will kill weed seeds as they germinate. *Contact herbicides* kill weeds onto which they are sprayed or sprinkled. *Translocated herbicides* contain an active ingredient that, when absorbed by a weed, moves to another part of the plant and interferes with its metabolism, causing the weed's death.

Chemical weed killers can, in certain situations, save the home gardener a great amount of time—especially if there is a large weed problem to clear up or if the weeds are in difficult-to-weed areas. They are much more useful in established plantings (shrubs, ground covers, turf grasses) than among bedding plants. No herbicide should be used in a small vegetable garden after planting, though you can safely use a preplant herbicide to prepare the area for vegetables if it is labeled for that purpose.

You must use chemical herbicides with extreme care so that you run no risk of damaging other plants. Begin by identifying the weeds that are present (check with a local nursery, farm advisor, or county agricultural agent for those you cannot identify); then choose the right product for your specific weed situation. Thoroughly read product labels for directions and cautions, and *always follow directions to the letter.* Some of these chemicals are so persistent that traces will remain in a sprayer even after rinsing. Play it safe: keep a separate sprayer just for applying weed killers. And always apply herbicides when there is no wind that could blow the spray onto ornamental or crop plants.

The herbicides listed on page 112 are the most widely available and useful in home gardens. Many other chemicals, such as 2, 4-D, DSMA, MSMA, and pendimethalin are most common in "weed and feed" fertilizer-herbicide combinations or in products for use on lawns. You will find these chemicals mentioned in the individual weed descriptions that follow.

Common Western Weeds

Even though there are literally countless different weeds (a weed being any plant that grows where you don't want it to be), there are select members from among the horde that are troublemakers on a grand scale. From surveys conducted in the western states, the following 7 weeds scored highest in this garden unpopularity contest.

BERMUDA GRASS

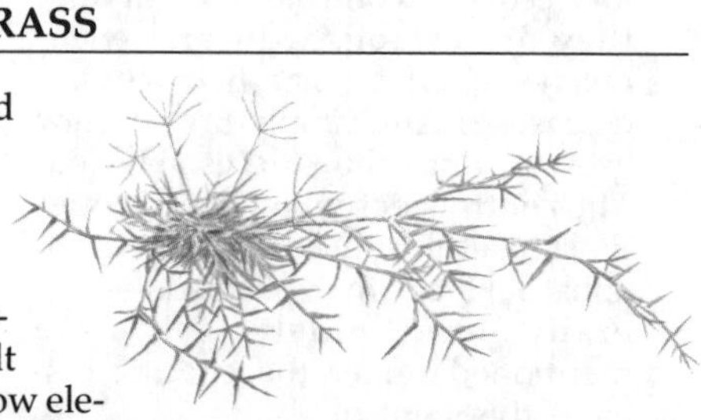

This fine-textured fast-growing perennial is a well-established lawn grass and the second-most difficult garden weed at low elevations in California, Arizona, and New Mexico. Native to warm areas of the Old World, Bermuda grass spreads underground by rhizomes and above ground by seeds and stolons. If not carefully confined, rhizomes and stolons invade shrubbery and flower beds and can be difficult to eradicate once established.

If stray clumps do turn up in flower beds, pull or dig them up before they form sod. Be sure to remove all of the underground stem; otherwise, it can start new shoots. Or spray isolated patches with fluazifop-butyl, sethoxydim, or glyphosate. Where patches are too big to be dug out of a lawn, apply glyphosate in summer or fall, as common Bermuda grass slows its growth (avoid desirable plants nearby). Repeat applications may be necessary.

BINDWEED

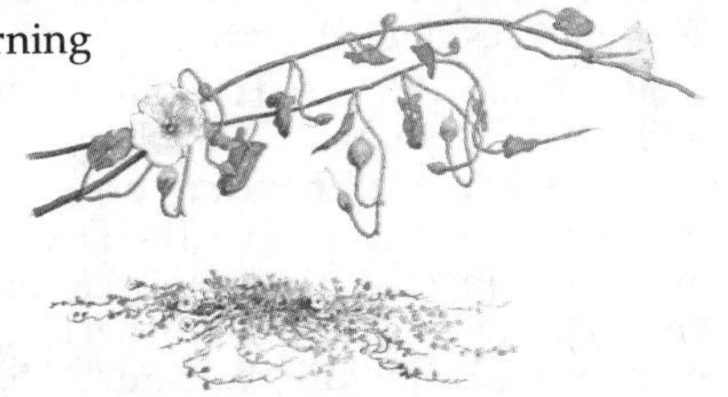

Also called wild morning glory, bindweed grows in open, exposed areas—usually in loam to heavy clay—throughout the West, but it is especially bothersome for gardeners in the Northwest, northern California, and mountain states. Bindweed crawls over the ground and twines over and around other plants, competing with them for nutrients and light. Its white to pale pink funnel-shaped flowers appear in summer or early fall, before the plant goes dormant for winter.

When you pull it, stems break off, but frequently the deep roots and underground stems remain. The more you break it, the more it sprouts. If allowed to go to seed, bindweed becomes nearly impossible to control: its hard-coated seeds can sprout after lying dormant in the soil for years.

In midsummer, at the plant's peak growth but before seeds are set, spray isolated patches with 2,4-D or glyphosate; repeat applications may be needed. If bindweed is intertwined with desirable plants, carefully paint its leaves with herbicides.

BLACKBERRY

Of the three common blackberry varieties in the Northwest, 'Himalaya' is predominant. It grows wild in pastures and along highways, thriving in the mild, moist climates of western Oregon and Washington (where gardeners name it as a top pest). It can turn up in flower beds, gravel paths, or lawns.

The roots are perennial, but the canes are biennial: they grow one year and flower and form fruit the next. Blackberry spreads rapidly by underground runners and seeds; birds eat the ripe, shiny berries in late summer and scatter the seeds willy-nilly across the landscape.

Pull out young plants in spring, before feeder roots develop. Cut back established plants during the summer growing season, when foliage is green (it's easier to dispose of fresh than dry). Wear heavy gloves; use a pick and shovel to dig up as many roots as possible.

Paint fresh shoots with glyphosate when 6 to 12 inches tall (spray only in isolated areas). Retreatment is usually necessary to control plants growing from dormant seeds, old and incompletely killed roots, and root crowns.

CRABGRASS

The infamous summer annual grows well in hot, damp areas. A shallow-rooted weed, it thrives in lawns and flower beds that get frequent surface watering, in underfed lawns, and in poorly drained fields.

Seeds germinate in early spring in southern California, later in northern California. As the plant grows, it branches out at the base; stems can root where they touch the soil. Seed heads form in mid- to late summer. As crabgrass declines in fall, it turns purplish, becoming especially noticeable in lawns.

In flower beds, pull crabgrass before it makes seeds. Keep lawns well fertilized and vigorous to provide tough competition for weeds; to dry out crabgrass roots, water lawns deeply but not frequently. In late winter or early spring, apply a granular preemergent—such as DCPA (Dacthal)—with a fertilizer spreader. Otherwise, apply MSMA (but not to St. Augustine lawns) or DSMA in turfgrass, fluazifop-butyl or sethoxydim in ornamental plantings.

DANDELION

A familiar lawn weed throughout the West, dandelion is particularly troublesome in Northwest and mountain states. It grows from a deep, fleshy taproot that often breaks (and can regrow) when you try to pull the plant out. It spreads by dispersing wind-borne seeds and by sprouting root crowns. Flowering begins in spring and often continues until frost; in mild weather, seeds can germinate year round.

Pull out young plants before the taproot has a chance to grow deep into the soil. On lawns, apply 2,4-D in spring and fall. Spray isolated plants with glyphosate, 2,4-D, or other herbicides for broad-leaved weeds.

OXALIS, YELLOW

This aggressive weed thrives throughout the West in sun or shade; gardeners in central and southern California rate it especially troublesome. It grows mainly in lawns and greenhouses, spreading quickly by seed. Seedlings start out from a single taproot, which soon develops into a shallow, spreading, knitted root system.

Yellow flowers are followed by elongated seed capsules that open like popcorn as they dry, shooting seeds as far as 6 feet. In mowed lawns, clumps generally stay low and tight. In flower beds, they grow rangier and tangle up with desirable plants.

Control is difficult. Dig out small plants, or carefully spot-treat isolated plants with glyphosate. Once you have removed or killed plants, oryzalin is an effective preemergence control. MSMA and DSMA work in both cool-season and warm-season lawns, but repeat applications are necessary. Do not use MSMA on St. Augustine lawns.

A vigorous, well-fertilized lawn provides tough competition for oxalis. Frequent surface watering encourages the shallow-rooted weed; water the lawn less frequently and more deeply.

SPOTTED SPURGE

A demon in hot weather, this aggressive summer annual grows from a shallow taproot in exposed areas such as sparse lawns, garden walks, and flower beds. It spreads fast; in as little as a month, each plant can produce several thousand seeds in clusters of tiny pinkish seed capsules. Oblong, ¼- to ⅜-inch leaves have reddish green undersides. Cut stems exude a milky juice. Plants turn red-orange and decline in fall (especially noticeable in lawns) as temperatures drop. Seeds germinate as early as January in Palm Springs, and seedlings start active growth when temperatures climb in spring.

Control is difficult. Hoe out isolated plants early, before they produce seed, or spray them with glyphosate. On lawns (except dichondra), use a preemergence broad-leaved herbicide such as DCPA (Dacthal) or pendimethalin. Watch for small plants in areas that have been problems in past years. A vigorous, well-fertilized lawn provides tough competition for spurge. For cool-season lawn grasses, mowing the grass higher helps discourage spotted spurge.

Weed Controls

"Caution" is the byword in using any chemical herbicide. Read (and follow) carefully not only label directions for application but also for the plants on which the product may be used (those not harmed by proper application of the product). The herbicide user can be held responsible for damage to neighboring properties that result from use not specified on the product label.

Preemergence. These herbicides work by inhibiting germination of weed seeds or growth of very young seedlings. Apply to weed-free soil; if weeds are already present, thoroughly remove them or kill them with a translocated herbicide (see "Postemergence" at right).

- ***DCPA (Dacthal).*** Controls annual grasses and some broad-leaved weeds. Can be used in a wide variety of ornamental plantings.
- ***EPTC (eptam).*** Controls a number of grasses and broad-leaved weeds among ornamental plants. Must be incorporated into soil immediately to reduce loss through vaporization.
- ***Oryzalin (Surflan).*** Controls annual grasses and many broad-leaved weeds (including spotted spurge and yellow oxalis) in turfgrasses and ornamental plantings.
- ***Simazine.*** Controls a wide variety of broad-leaved and grassy weeds among ornamentals and some crops. Effect is long-lasting—could nearly fit into the last category, "Total Soil Cleanup." Not recommended for desert regions or sandy soils.
- ***Trifluralin.*** Controls many grasses and annual broad-leaved weeds in ornamental plantings; may injure Bermuda grass.

Postemergence. Two types of weed killer act on growing weeds and other unwanted vegetation. The *contact herbicides* are effective as they contact the plant. *Translocated herbicides* must be absorbed by the plant, which they kill by interfering with plant metabolism; these are slower to show effectiveness than the contact kinds.

- ***Fluazifop-butyl (Grass-b-gon).*** Translocated. Controls actively growing grassy weeds; best results when weeds are healthy and you add a surfactant (spreader-sticker) to the mixture. Can be sprayed over many ornamentals; see product label.
- ***Glyphosate.*** Translocated. Controls a great variety of actively growing vegetation: grasses, perennial weeds, woody plants (including poison oak); repeat application sometimes needed on perennial and woody plants. Effectiveness may be enhanced by addition of a surfactant (spreader-sticker).
- ***Sethoxydim (Poast).*** Contact. Controls annual grasses (but not annual bluegrass) in ornamental plantings. Should be applied at particular stage of weed growth; needs addition of surfactant (spreader-sticker) to be effective.

Total soil cleanup (sterilants and fumigants). These chemicals (metham and prometon are most common) have a broader-spectrum toxicity than the previous herbicides and/or a significant longevity in the soil. They are often misused. Follow special application procedures outlined on product label.

*Packaged controls are listed alphabetically by generic name (the name you will find on product label under "active ingredients") or common name; trade name (where different from generic name) appears in parentheses.

Planting for a Purpose— A Plant Selection Guide

The thousands of plants described in the Western Plant Encyclopedia (beginning on page 199) include an almost infinitely varied assortment of sizes, shapes, textures, and colors.

The pleasure of choosing from this rich assortment is available to anyone with a sense of adventure and a bit of earth. But such abundance sometimes can lead to bewilderment. The lists of plants that follow, used with the Western Plant Encyclopedia, will help you select plants for specific landscape functions or effects, or for solutions to garden problems.

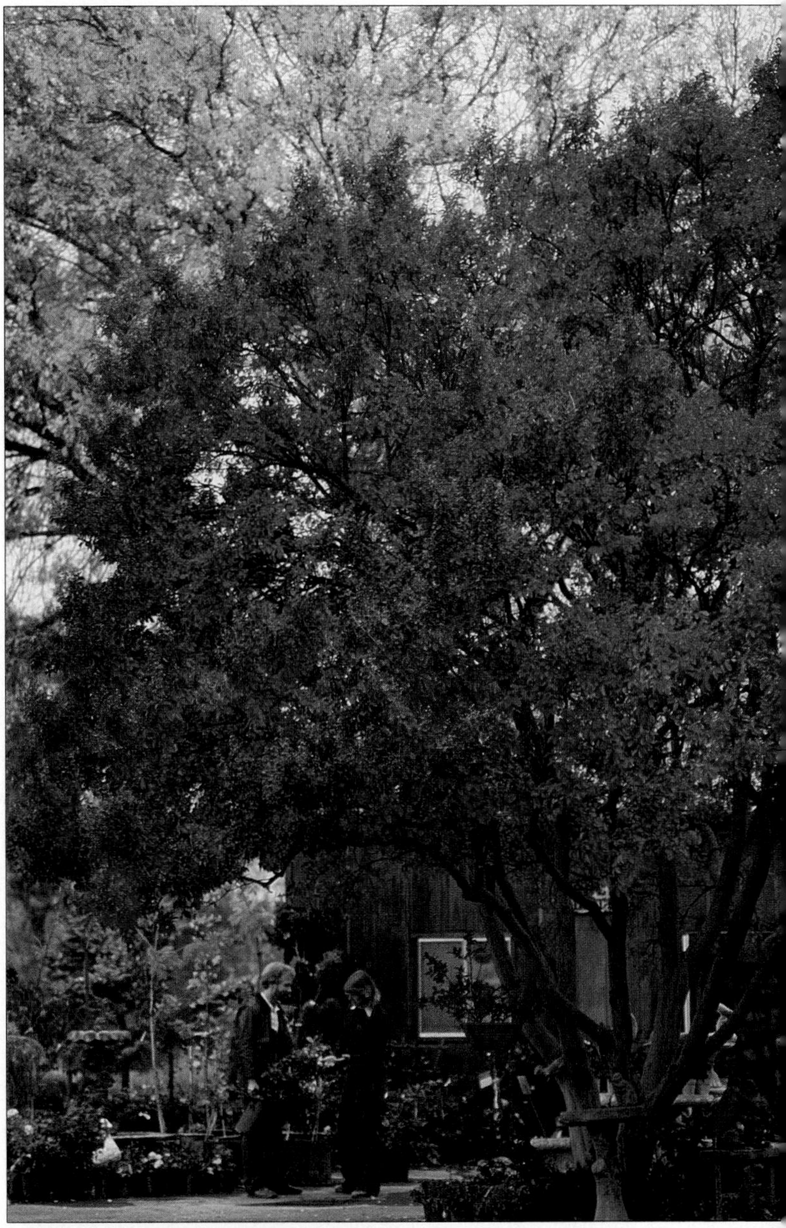

Western gardens begin at nurseries and garden centers. In much of the West, fall is prime planting time.

Trees for Garden & Patio

Patio trees are generally small, as trees go, and look good at close range. Many have showy displays of flowers, fruit, or both; some have striking fall foliage or unusually decorative bark. All are "well mannered": root systems are not likely to crack pavement or greedily take water and nutrients from neighboring plants; branches do not shed annoying quantities of leaves or drop messy fruit to litter or stain patio surfaces.

All patio trees qualify as fine candidates for garden planting, but the list of garden trees contains additional kinds that lack patio qualifications. Some are too large or dense for most patios but can provide needed height or shade in a larger landscape. Others may shed leaves or fruit that would require frequent cleanup on a patio but pose no problem in garden plantings.

For more detailed guidelines on choosing trees, read the "Trees" section, pages 177–178.

Lavish Jacaranda mimosifolia becomes cloud of lavender during its summer flowering period.

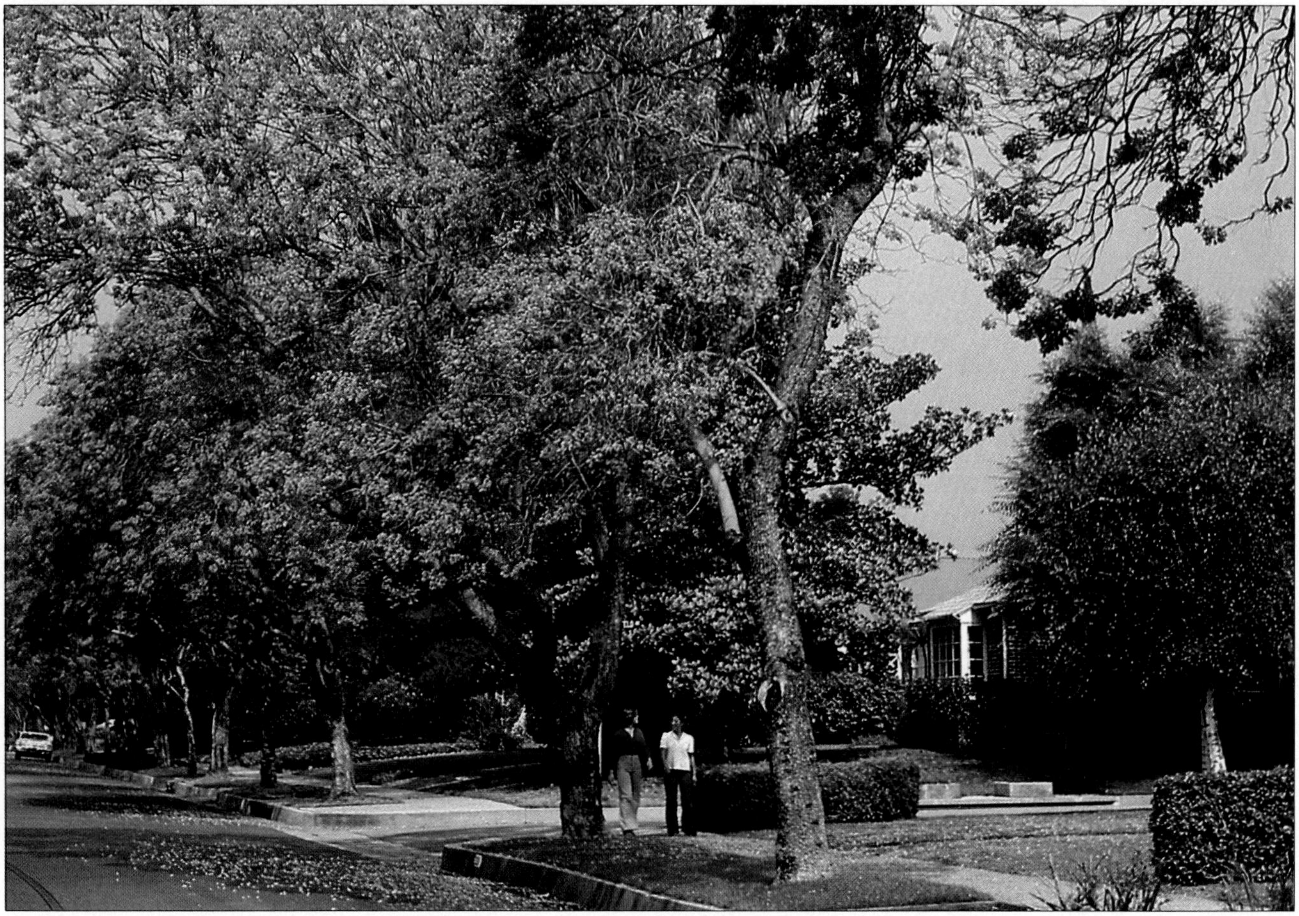

DECIDUOUS

NAME OF PLANT	CLIMATE ZONES	GARDEN	PATIO
Acer buergeranum	4–9, 14–17, 20, 21		■
Acer capillipes	1–9, 14–24	■	
Acer circinatum	1–6, 14–17		■
Acer davidii	1–6, 15–17, 20, 21	■	■
Acer ginnala	1–9, 14–16		■
Acer griseum	1–9, 14–21	■	■
Acer palmatum	1–9, 14–24	■	■
Albizia julibrissin	2–23	■	■
Amelanchier	1–6	■	■
Bauhinia blakeana	19, 21, 23		■
Bauhinia variegata	13, 18–23		■
Betula	Vary	■	
Calodendrum capense	19, 21–24	■	
Carpinus	Vary	■	
Celtis	Vary	■	
Cercidiphyllum japonicum	1–6, 14–16, 18–20	■	
Cercidium	10–14, 18–20	■	■
Cercis	Vary	■	■
Chilopsis linearis	11–13, 18–21	■	■
Chionanthus	Vary		■
Cladrastis lutea	1–9, 14–16	■	■
Cornus florida	1–9, 14–16	■	■
Cornus kousa	3–9, 14, 15, 18, 19		■
Crataegus	1–11, 14–17	■	■
Davidia involucrata	4–9, 14–21	■	■
Erythrina	Vary	■	■
Filbert	2–7	■	■
Firmiana simplex	5, 6, 8, 9, 12–24		■
Franklinia alatamaha	2–6, 14–17	■	■
Fraxinus holotricha	4–24	■	
Fraxinus velutina	8–24	■	
Ginkgo biloba	1–9, 14–24	■	
Gleditsia triacanthos	1–16, 18–20	■	
Gymnocladus dioica	1–3, 7–10, 12–16, 18–21	■	
Halesia	2–9, 14–24	■	■
Idesia polycarpa	4–9, 14–17, 19–24	■	
Jacaranda mimosifolia	12, 13, 15–24	■	
Koelreuteria	Vary	■	■
Laburnum	1–10, 14–17	■	
Lagerstroemia indica	7–9, 12–14, 18–21	■	■
Liquidambar	Vary	■	
Liriodendron tulipifera	1–12, 14–23	■	
Magnolia (many)	Vary	■	■
Malus	1–11, 14–21	■	■
Morus alba	All	■	
Nyssa sylvatica	3–10, 14–21	■	
Oxydendrum arboreum	3–9, 14–17		■
Parkinsonia aculeata	11–24	■	
Parrotia persica	4–6, 15–17		■
Persimmon	Vary	■	■
Pistacia chinensis	4–16, 18–23	■	■
Prosopis glandulosa torreyana	10–13	■	
Prunus mume	2–9, 12–22	■	■
Prunus, flowering cherry	4–6, 15–17	■	■
Prunus, flowering peach	2–24	■	
Prunus, flowering plum	Vary	■	■
Punica granatum	7–24	■	

NAME OF PLANT	CLIMATE ZONES	GARDEN	PATIO
Pyrus	Vary	■	■
Quercus coccinea	All	■	
Quercus douglasii	All	■	
Quercus garryana	4–6, 15–17	■	
Quercus kelloggii	5–7, 15, 16, 18–21	■	
Quercus palustris	All	■	
Quercus phellos	1–4, 6–16, 18–21	■	
Quince	All		■
Robinia ambigua 'Idahoensis'	All	■	
Robinia pseudoacacia	All	■	
Sapium sebiferum	8, 9, 12, 14–16, 18–21	■	■
Sophora japonica	All	■	■
Sorbus aucuparia	1–10, 14–17	■	
Stewartia	4–6, 14–17, 20, 21		■
Styrax	3–10, 14–21	■	■
Tabebuia	15, 16, 20–24	■	■
Tilia cordata	1–17	■	
Tilia euchlora	1–17	■	
Tipuana tipu	12–16, 18–24	■	■
Vitex agnus-castus	4–24	■	
Zelkova serrata	3–21	■	
Ziziphus jujuba	7–16, 18–24	■	

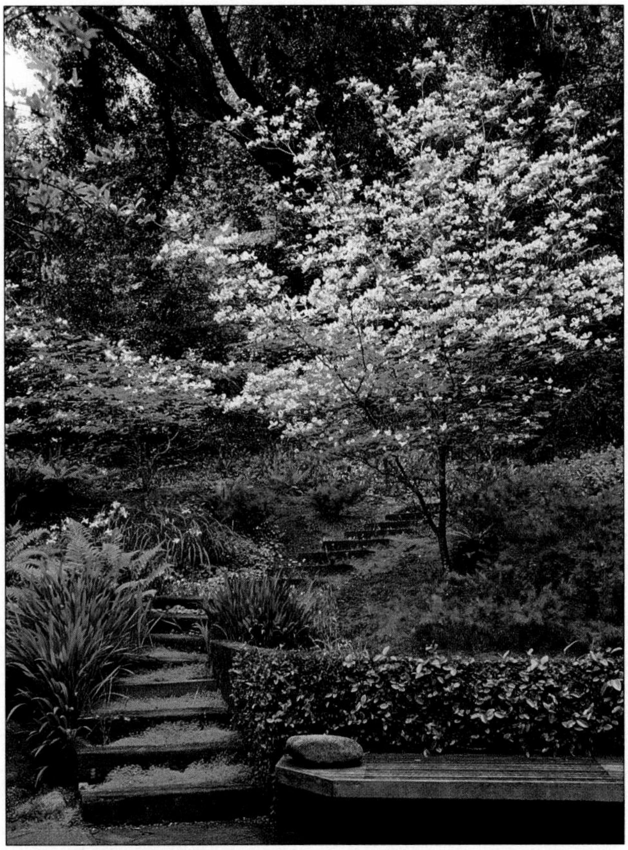

Flowering dogwood (Cornus florida) offers color in two seasons: pink or white flowers in spring, red foliage in fall.

EVERGREEN

NAME OF PLANT	CLIMATE ZONES	GARDEN	PATIO
Acacia baileyana	7–9, 13–24	■	
Acacia pendula	13–24	■	
Acacia podalyriifolia	8, 9, 13–24		■
Acer oblongum	8–10, 12, 14–24	■	
Acer paxii	8, 9, 14–24	■	
Acmena smithii	15–17, 19–24	■	
Agonis	15–17, 20–24	■	
Arbutus unedo	4–24	■	■
Bauhinia forficata	9, 12–23		■
Brugmansia	16–24	■	
Callistemon citrinus	8, 9, 12–24		■
Callistemon viminalis	8, 9, 12–24		■
Cassia leptophylla	21–24	■	■
Castanospermum australe	18–22	■	
Ceanothus 'Ray Hartman'	4–7, 14–24	■	
Citrus	Vary		■
Clethra arborea	15–17, 21–24		■
Cocculus laurifolius	8, 9, 12–24	■	■
Cornus capitata	8, 9, 14–20	■	
Crinodendron patagua	14–24	■	
Cupaniopsis anacardioides	16, 17, 19–24	■	■
Dodonaea viscosa	7–9, 12–24		■
Drimys winteri	8, 9, 14–24	■	■
Eriobotrya deflexa	8–24		■
Eriobotrya japonica	4–24	■	
Eucalyptus calophylla	8–24	■	
Eucalyptus erythrocorys	8–24	■	■
Eucalyptus ficifolia	8–24	■	
Eucalyptus forrestiana	8–24		■
Eucalyptus leucoxylon macrocarpa 'Rosea'	8–24	■	■
Eucalyptus macrandra	8–24	■	■
Eucalyptus nicholii	8–24	■	
Eucalyptus pauciflora	8–24	■	
Eucalyptus polyanthemos	8–24	■	
Eucalyptus pulchella	8–24	■	
Eucalyptus torquata	8–24	■	■
Ficus benjamina	13, 23, 24	■	■
Ficus microcarpa	9, 15–24	■	
Ficus rubiginosa	18–24	■	
Hakea laurina	9, 12–17, 19–24		■
Harpephyllum caffrum	17, 19, 21–24	■	
Heteromeles arbutifolia	5–24	■	■
Hoheria populnea	4–6, 15–17, 21–24	■	
Hymenosporum	8, 9, 14–23	■	
Ilex (many)	Vary	■	
Lagunaria patersonii	13, 15–24	■	
Laurus nobilis	5–9, 12–24		■
Leptospermum laevigatum	14–24		■
Leptospermum petersonii	14–24		■

Sumptuous, fragrant blossoms of southern magnolia (Magnolia grandiflora) appear throughout summer and fall.

Citrus trees bring fragrant flowers and delicious fruits to mild-winter western gardens. This is 'Washington Navel' orange.

Golden trumpet tree (Tabebuia chrysotricha) lights up with flowers during brief mid-spring deciduous period.

The delicacy and grace of a weeping willow are captured in evergreen mayten tree (Maytenus boaria).

EVERGREEN (*cont'd.*)

NAME OF PLANT	CLIMATE ZONES	GARDEN	PATIO
Ligustrum lucidum	5, 6, 8–24	■	■
Lysiloma thornberi	10, 12–24	■	■
Macadamia	9, 16, 17, 19–24	■	
Magnolia (many)	Vary	■	■
Maytenus boaria	8, 9, 14–21	■	■
Melaleuca ericifolia	9, 12–24		■
Melaleuca quinquenervia	9, 13, 16, 17, 20–24	■	■
Melaleuca styphelioides	9, 13–24	■	
Metrosideros	Vary	■	
Michelia doltsopa	14–24		■
Nerium oleander	8–16, 18–23	■	■
Olea europaea (if fruit prevented)	8, 9, 11–24	■	■
Olmediella betschlerana	9, 14–24	■	
Osmanthus fragrans	8, 9, 12–24		■
Palms	Vary	■	■
Photinia fraseri	4–24		■
Pinus contorta	See Encyclopedia	■	
Pinus densiflora	See Encyclopedia	■	
Pinus nigra	See Encyclopedia	■	
Pinus wallichiana	See Encyclopedia	■	
Pittosporum eugenioides	9, 14–17, 19–22	■	■
Pittosporum phillyraeoides	9, 12–24		■
Pittosporum rhombifolium	12–24	■	■
Pittosporum tenuifolium	9, 14–17, 19–24	■	■
Pittosporum tobira	8–24		■

NAME OF PLANT	CLIMATE ZONES	GARDEN	PATIO
Pittosporum undulatum	16, 17, 21–24	■	
Pittosporum viridiflorum	15–17, 20–24	■	■
Podocarpus gracilior	8, 9, 13–24	■	■
Podocarpus macrophyllus	4–9, 12–24	■	■
Prunus caroliniana	7–24	■	
Prunus ilicifolia	7–9, 12–24	■	
Prunus lusitanica	4–9, 14–24	■	
Prunus lyonii	7–9, 12–24	■	
Pyrus	Vary	■	■
Quercus ilex	4–24	■	
Quercus suber	8–16, 18–23	■	
Rhus lancea	8, 9, 12–24		■
Schefflera actinophylla	21–24		■
Schinus terebinthifolius	15–17, 19–24	■	■
Sequoia sempervirens	4–9, 14–24	■	
Sophora secundiflora	8–16, 18–24	■	■
Stenocarpus sinuatus	16, 17, 20–24	■	■
Thevetia thevetioides	22–24	■	■
Tristania conferta	19–24	■	
Tristania laurina	19–24		■
Tsuga canadensis	3–7, 17	■	
Tupidanthus calyptratus	19–24	■	■
Umbellularia californica	4–10, 12–24	■	■
Xylosma congestum	8–24	■	■

Hedges, Screens, Backgrounds & Barriers

All plants on this list have foliage from the ground up and thus are able to provide a dense separation or screen in your landscape. Some are knee-high shrublets, mainly useful for edging a walk or path; at the other extreme are shrubby trees that, grouped closely, can block an objectionable view or direct the eye to a garden focal point. Those plants indicated as being good barriers are impenetrably dense, armed with thorns, or both.

Singled out with double squares (■■) are the plants that will tolerate shearing into formal hedges; those with a single square (■) are best suited for informal hedges.

Clipped hedge of boxwood (Buxus sempervirens) joins forces with Wisteria sinensis to define garden's perimeter.

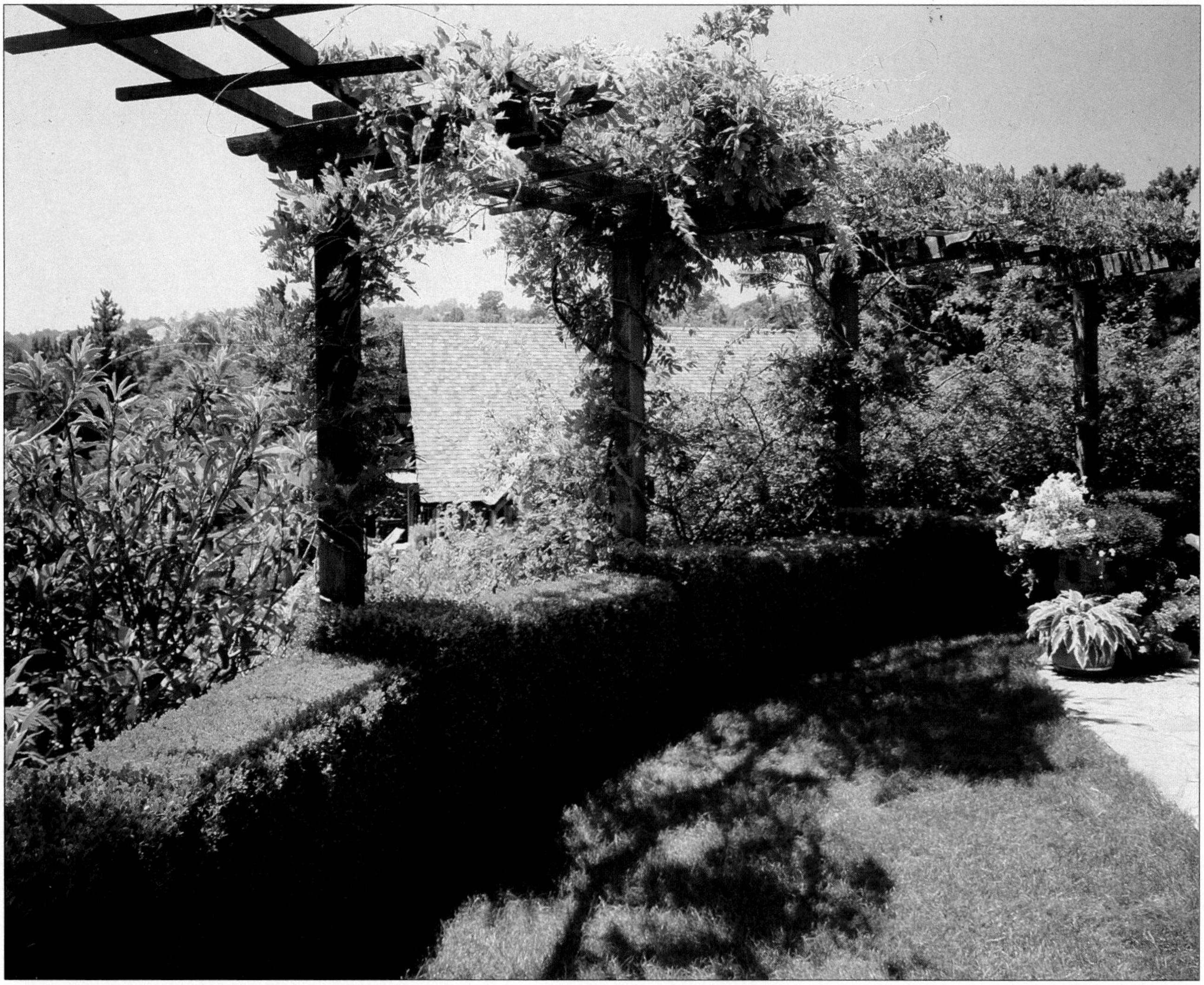

A hedge also can function as architecture. Boxwood (Buxus sempervirens) provides green definition for entryway.

DECIDUOUS

NAME OF PLANT	CLIMATE ZONES	HEDGE	SCREEN	BACKGROUND	BARRIER
Atriplex lentiformis	7–14, 18, 19	■			
Berberis	1–11, 14–17	■	■	■	■
Blueberry	See Encyclopedia	■			
Caesalpinia pulcherrima	12–16, 18–23		■		
Callicarpa bodinieri giraldii	1–6	■			
Caragana arborescens	1–21	■			
Carpinus betulus	3–9, 14–17	■■	■		
Chaenomeles	1–21	■			■
Crataegus monogyna	1–11, 14–17	■■	■	■	■
Elaeagnus angustifolia	1–3, 7–14, 18, 19	■	■	■	■
Fouquieria splendens	10–13, 18–20	■	■		■
Ligustrum	Vary	■■	■		
Liquidambar styraciflua	1–11, 14–24		■		
Lonicera	Vary	■	■	■	
Maclura pomifera	All	■		■	■
Rhamnus frangula 'Columnaris'	1–7, 10–13	■■	■	■	
Rosa eglanteria	All	■	■		■
Rosa hugonis	All		■	■	■
Rosa rugosa	All	■			■
Rosa (Floribunda, Grandiflora, Shrub types)	Vary	■			■
Salix purpurea 'Gracilis'	All	■		■	
Viburnum opulus 'Nanum'	1–9, 14–24	■			
Weigela	1–11, 14–17		■	■	

EVERGREEN

NAME OF PLANT	CLIMATE ZONES	HEDGE	SCREEN	BACKGROUND	BARRIER
Abelia grandiflora	5–24	■	■		
Bamboo (many)	Vary	■	■	■	■
Berberis	1–11, 14–17	■		■	■
Buxus	Vary	■■			
Callistemon citrinus	8, 9, 12–24	■■	■	■	
Callistemon salignus	8, 9, 12–24	■■	■	■	
Calocedrus decurrens	1–12, 14–24		■	■	
Camellia japonica and C. sasanqua	4–9, 14–24	■	■	■	
Carissa	22–24	■■	■		■
Ceratonia siliqua	9, 13–16, 18–24	■	■	■	
Chamaecyparis lawsoniana (several)	4–6, 15–17	■	■	■	
Choisya ternata	7–9, 12–17	■	■		
Cocculus laurifolius	8, 9, 12–24		■	■	
Corynocarpus laevigata	16, 17, 23, 24	■	■	■	
Cotoneaster (some)	Vary	■	■	■	
Crassula argentea	16, 17, 22–24	■			
Cupressocyparis leylandii	3–24		■	■	
Cupressus forbesii	8–14, 18–20	■■	■	■	
Cupressus glabra	5, 8–24	■■	■	■	
Dodonaea viscosa	7–9, 12–24	■	■	■	
Elaeagnus	Vary	■■	■		
Erica (some)	Vary		■	■	

EVERGREEN (*cont'd.*)

NAME OF PLANT	CLIMATE ZONES	HEDGE	SCREEN	BACKGROUND	BARRIER
Escallonia	4–9, 14–17, 20–24	■■	■	■	
Eucalyptus globulus 'Compacta'	8–24		■		
Eucalyptus gunnii	8–24		■		
Eucalyptus lehmannii	8–24		■		
Eucalyptus platypus	8–24		■		
Eucalyptus spathulata	8–24		■		
Eucalyptus stellulata	8–24		■		
Eugenia uniflora	21–24	■			
Euonymus fortunei 'Sarcoxie'	1–17	■■			
Euonymus japonica	2–20	■■	■		
Euonymus kiautschovica	1–13	■■	■		
Feijoa sellowiana	7–9, 12–24	■	■		
Ficus benjamina	13, 23, 24	■	■		
Gardenia jasminoides	7–9, 12–16, 18–23	■			
Garrya elliptica	5–9, 14–21	■	■		
Grevillea robusta	8, 9, 12–24	■	■		
Grevillea rosmarinifolia	8, 9, 12–24	■			
Grewia occidentalis	8, 9, 14–24	■	■		
Griselinia	9, 15–17, 20–24		■		
Hakea suaveolens	9, 12–17, 19–24		■	■	■
Hebe buxifolia	14–24	■			
Heteromeles arbutifolia	5–24		■	■	

NAME OF PLANT	CLIMATE ZONES	HEDGE	SCREEN	BACKGROUND	BARRIER
Hibiscus rosa-sinensis	9, 12, 13, 15, 16, 19–24		■		
Hypericum beanii	4–24	■			
Ilex	Vary	■■	■	■	■
Itea ilicifolia	4–24		■		
Juniperus (columnar types)	All	■■	■	■	■
Juniperus (shrub types)	All				■
Kochia	All	■			
Lagunaria patersonii	13, 15–24		■		
Lantana	See Encyclopedia	■			
Larrea tridentata	10–13, 19	■	■		
Laurus nobilis	5–9, 12–24	■■	■	■	
Leptospermum	14–24	■■	■		
Leucophyllum frutescens	7–24	■			
Ligustrum	Vary	■■	■		
Lonicera (shrub type)	Vary	■	■		
Lysiloma thornberi	10, 12–24			■	
Mahonia aquifolium	1–21	■	■		■
Mahonia nevinii	8–24	■	■		■
Melaleuca armillaris	9, 12–24	■■	■		■
Melaleuca hypericifolia	9, 12–24	■■	■		
Melaleuca nesophylla	9, 13, 16–24	■■	■		
Murraya paniculata	21–24	■			

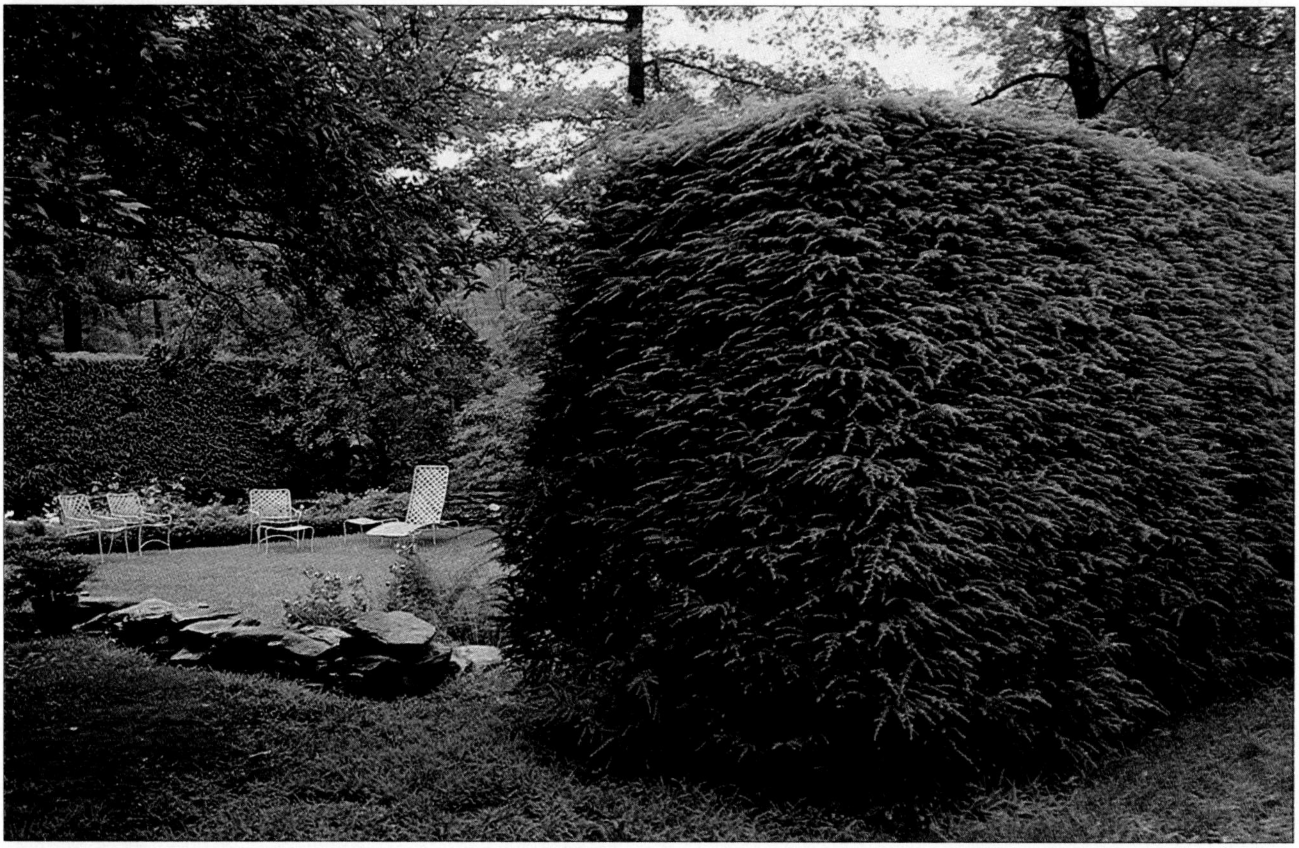

Canadian hemlock (Tsuga canadensis) serves double duty as fence and windbreak. Annual shearing maintains feathery surface.

EVERGREEN (*cont'd.*)

NAME OF PLANT	CLIMATE ZONES	HEDGE	SCREEN	BACKGROUND	BARRIER
Myrica californica	4–6, 14–17, 20–24	■■	■	■	
Myrsine africana	8, 9, 14–24	■■			
Myrtus communis	8–24	■■	■		
Nandina domestica	5–24	■	■		
Nerium oleander	8–16, 18–23	■	■	■	
Olmediella betschlerana	9, 14–24	■	■	■	■
Osmanthus fragrans	8, 9, 12–24	■	■	■	
Osmanthus heterophyllus	3–10, 14–24	■	■	■	
Osmarea burkwoodii	4–9, 14–17	■			
Pernettya mucronata	4–7, 15–17	■			
Photinia	Vary	■	■	■	
Pittosporum eugenioides	9, 14–17, 19–22	■■	■	■	
Pittosporum tenuifolium	9, 14–17, 19–24	■■	■	■	
Pittosporum tobira	8–24		■		
Pittosporum undulatum	16, 17, 21–24		■	■	
Pittosporum viridiflorum	15–17, 20–24		■		
Platycladus orientalis	All	■	■		
Podocarpus	Varies	■	■	■	
Portulacaria afra	13, 16, 17, 22–24	■	■		
Prunus caroliniana	7–24	■■	■	■	
Prunus ilicifolia	7–9, 12–24	■■	■	■	
Prunus laurocerasus	4–9, 14–24	■■	■	■	
Prunus lusitanica	4–9, 14–24	■■	■	■	
Prunus lyonii	7–9, 12–24	■■	■	■	
Pseudotsuga menziesii	1–10, 14–17		■	■	
Psidium cattleianum	9, 15–24	■	■		
Pyracantha	Vary	■	■	■	■
Quillaja saponaria	8, 9, 14–24	■	■		
Rhamnus alaternus	4–24	■■	■	■	
Rhamnus crocea ilicifolia	7–16, 18–21		■		
Rhapiolepis	8–10, 12–24	■		■	
Rhus integrifolia	15–17, 20–24	■■	■	■	
Rhus lancea	8, 9, 12–24	■■	■	■	
Rhus laurina	20–24	■■	■		
Rhus ovata	7–24	■■	■	■	
Ribes speciosum	8, 9, 14–24				■
Rosmarinus officinalis	4–24	■■			
Sedum dendroideum praealtum	8, 9, 12, 14–24	■			
Sequoia sempervirens	4–9, 14–24	■	■	■	
Simmondsia chinensis	10–13, 19–24	■■			
Syzygium paniculatum	16, 17, 19–24	■■	■	■	
Taxus	3–9, 14–24	■■	■	■	
Tecoma stans	12, 13, 21–24		■		
Tecomaria capensis	12, 13, 16, 18–24	■			
Ternstroemia gymnanthera	4–9, 12–24	■			
Teucrium	Vary	■■	■		
Thevetia	Vary	■	■	■	
Thuja	Vary	■■	■	■	
Tsuga canadensis	3–7, 17	■■	■	■	
Tsuga heterophylla	1–7, 14–17	■■	■	■	
Umbellularia californica	4–10, 12–24	■	■	■	
Viburnum cinnamomifolium	5–9, 14–24		■	■	
Viburnum odoratissimum	8, 9, 14–24		■		
Viburnum suspensum	8–10, 13–24	■	■		
Viburnum tinus	14–23	■	■		
Xylosma congestum	8–24	■■	■	■	

Effective barrier hedges are thorny as well as dense. Darwin barberry (Berberis darwinii) also gives showy flower display.

Plants to Use for Windbreaks

Where a wind blows from a predictable direction daily or almost daily through certain seasons, the best plan is to lift the wind gradually. If you have space, plant as many as five rows of shrubs and trees, with rows 16 feet apart; if space is limited, use a row of shrubs on the windward side and trees inside. Even if space allows only one row, some bushy trees will help moderate wind.

Tall specimens of cajeput tree (Melaleuca quinquenervia) diffuse strong winds, shelter outdoor living space.

Trees

EVERGREEN

NAME OF PLANT	CLIMATE ZONES
Acacia melanoxylon	8, 9, 13–24
Calocedrus decurrens	1–12, 14–24
Casuarina stricta	8, 9, 12–24
Chamaecyparis lawsoniana	4–6, 15–17
Cupressocyparis leylandii	3–24
Cupressus glabra	5, 8–24
Cupressus macrocarpa	17
Eucalyptus camaldulensis	8–24
Eucalyptus cinerea	8–24
Eucalyptus cladocalyx	8–24
Eucalyptus cornuta	8–24
Eucalyptus erythronema	8–24
Eucalyptus ficifolia	8–24
Eucalyptus globulus	8–24
Eucalyptus globulus 'Compacta'	8–24
Eucalyptus gunnii	8–24
Eucalyptus lehmannii	8–24
Eucalyptus leucoxylon	8–24
Eucalyptus melliodora	8–24
Eucalyptus microtheca	8–24
Eucalyptus niphophila	8–24
Eucalyptus robusta	8–24
Eucalyptus rudis	8–24
Eucalyptus spathulata	8–24
Lagunaria patersonii	13, 15–24
Ligustrum lucidum	5, 6, 8–24
Melaleuca quinquenervia	9, 13, 16, 17, 20–24
Picea abies	1–6, 14–17
Pinus canariensis	See Encyclopedia
Pinus contorta	See Encyclopedia
Pinus halepensis	See Encyclopedia
Pinus muricata	See Encyclopedia
Pinus nigra	See Encyclopedia
Pinus radiata	See Encyclopedia
Pinus sylvestris	See Encyclopedia
Pinus torreyana	See Encyclopedia
Pittosporum (all but P. phillyraeoides)	Vary
Pseudotsuga menziesii	1–10, 14–17
Schinus molle	8, 9, 12–24
Sequoia sempervirens	4–9, 14–24
Tamarix aphylla	7–24
Thuja plicata	1–9, 14–24

DECIDUOUS

NAME OF PLANT	CLIMATE ZONES
Broussonetia papyrifera	3–24
Elaeagnus angustifolia	1–3, 7–14, 18, 19
Maclura pomifera	All
Populus alba 'Pyramidalis'	All
Populus nigra 'Italica'	All
Prosopis glandulosa torreyana	8–14
Tamarix	Vary
Ulmus pumila	All

Shrubs

EVERGREEN

NAME OF PLANT	CLIMATE ZONES
Acacia cyclopis	8, 9, 13–24
Acacia verticillata	14–24
Bambusa oldhamii	16–24
Callistemon citrinus	8, 9, 12–24
Callistemon phoeniceus	8, 9, 12–24
Callistemon salignus	8, 9, 12–24
Cortaderia selloana	4–24
Dodonaea viscosa	7–9, 12–24
Elaeagnus pungens	4–24
Escallonia	4–9, 14–17, 20–24
Eucalyptus grossa	9, 14–24
*Eucalyptus platypus	9, 14–24
Eucalyptus tetraptera	9, 14–24
Griselinia littoralis	9, 15–17, 20–24
*Hakea suaveolens	9, 12–17, 19–24
*Juniperus (columnar shrubs)	All
Laurus nobilis	5–9, 12–24
Lavatera assurgentiflora	14–24
*Leptospermum laevigatum	14–24
Ligustrum japonicum 'Texanum'	4–24
*Melaleuca	Vary
*Myoporum laetum	8, 9, 14–17, 19–24
Nerium oleander	8–16, 18–23
Photinia	Vary
*Pittosporum (all but *P. napaulense*)	Vary
*Prunus caroliniana	7–24
Prunus ilicifolia	7–9, 12–24
Prunus lusitanica	4–9, 14–24
*Prunus lyonii	7–9, 12–24
Pyracantha (tall-growing ones)	Vary
*Rhamnus alaternus	4–24
*Taxus baccata 'Stricta'	3–9, 14–24
*Taxus cuspidata	3–9, 14–24
*Taxus media	3–9, 14–24
Tecomaria capensis	12, 13, 16, 18–24
*Thuja occidentalis	2–9, 15–17, 21–24

DECIDUOUS

NAME OF PLANT	CLIMATE ZONES
Acer ginnala	1–9, 14–16
Atriplex lentiformis	7–14, 18, 19
*Caragana arborescens	1–21
Lonicera korolkowii	1–9, 14–24
Lonicera tatarica	1–9, 14–21
Punica granatum	7–24
Rhamnus frangula	1–7, 10–13
Syringa vulgaris	1–11
*Tamarix	Vary
Viburnum lentago	1–9, 14–21
Viburnum prunifolium	1–9, 14–21

*Can become small tree.

Fast-growing Plants

In the case of a shrub, tree, or vine, this designation means that it will grow rapidly enough (in both height and width) to begin assuming its mature landscape role in 1 to 4 years. For an annual or perennial, "fast-growing" means that it will reach an impressive size within a year.

Not all fast growers, however, are fault-free. Some grow quickly but soon slide into an unattractive old age. These are best used when planted for quick effect at the same time as slower-growing, choicer plants; remove the fast growers when they lose their beauty. By that time, the slower-growing plants will be large enough to be presentable. Some plants grow fast under almost any conditions; others need specific conditions and care to grow with racehorse speed. To avoid being surprised by any one of these fast growers, read the description of the plant in the Western Plant Encyclopedia (beginning on page 199).

TREES

NAME OF PLANT	CLIMATE ZONES
Acacia	Vary
Acer saccharinum	1–9, 14–24
Ailanthus altissima	All
Albizia distachya	15–17, 22–24
Alnus rhombifolia	1–9, 14–21
Betula nigra	All
Callistemon citrinus	8, 9, 12–24
Cassia excelsa	12, 13, 19–24
Casuarina	8, 9, 12–24
Catalpa	All
Cedrus deodara	2–12, 14–24
Cercidium	10–14, 18–20
Chilopsis linearis	11–13, 18–21
Chorisia speciosa	15–24
Cupressocyparis leylandii	3–24
Cupressus forbesii	8–14, 18–20
Cupressus glabra	5, 8–24
Eriobotrya japonica	4–24
Eucalyptus	8–24
Fraxinus ornus	3–9, 14–17
Fraxinus quadrangulata	1–6
Fraxinus uhdei	9, 12–24
Gleditsia triacanthos	1–16, 18–20
Grevillea robusta	8, 9, 12–24
Harpephyllum caffrum	17, 19, 21–24
Hoheria populnea	4–6, 15–17, 21–24
Ligustrum lucidum	5, 6, 8–24

NAME OF PLANT	CLIMATE ZONES
Liriodendron tulipifera	1–12, 14–23
Maclura pomifera	All
Magnolia veitchii	4–9, 14–24
Melaleuca	Vary
Metasequoia glyptostroboides	3–9, 14–24
Morus alba	All
Myoporum laetum	8, 9, 14–17, 19–24
Olmediella betschlerana	9, 14–24
Parkinsonia aculeata	11–24
Paulownia tomentosa	All
Phyllostachys bambusoides	4–24
Pinus	Vary
Platanus	Vary
Populus	Vary
Pterocarya stenoptera	5–24
Quercus rubra	1–12, 14–24
Robinia pseudoacacia	All
Salix	All
Sapium sebiferum	8, 9, 12, 14–16, 18–21
Schinus molle	8, 9, 12–24
Sequoia sempervirens	4–9, 14–24
Sequoiadendron giganteum	All
Sorbus aucuparia	1–10, 14–17
Taxodium mucronatum	5, 6, 8–10, 12–24
Tecoma	12, 13, 21–24
Tipuana tipu	12–16, 18–24
Ulmus parvifolia	8, 9, 12–24

SHRUBS

NAME OF PLANT	CLIMATE ZONES
Abutilon	13, 15–24
Acacia	Vary
Baccharis pilularis	5–11, 14–24
Buddleia davidii	1–9, 12–24
Caesalpinia	Vary
Callistemon	8, 9, 12–24
Caragana arborescens	1–21
Ceanothus	4–7, 14–24
Cestrum	Vary
Chamelaucium uncinatum	8, 9, 12–24
Choisya ternata	7–9, 12–24
Chorizema	15–17, 19–24
Cistus	4–9, 12–24
Convolvulus cneorum	7–9, 12–24
Cornus stolonifera	1–9, 14–21
Corynabutilon vitifolium	5, 6, 15–17
Cotoneaster lacteus	4–24
Crotalaria agatiflora	13, 15–24
Cytisus	Vary
Dodonea viscosa	7–9, 12–24
Duranta	Vary
Elaeagnus	Vary
Eriobotrya deflexa	8–24
Escallonia	4–9, 14–17, 20–24
Eucalyptus	Vary
Forsythia intermedia	2–11, 14–16, 18, 19
Fremontodendron	7–24
Fuchsia	Vary
Grewia occidentalis	8, 9, 14–24
Griselinia littoralis	9, 15–17, 20–24
Hakea suaveolens	9, 12–17, 19–24
Hebe	Vary
Hibiscus	Vary
Hydrangea	Vary
Hypericum calycinum	2–24
Ilex 'Nellie Stevens'	4–9, 14–24
Lantana	See Encyclopedia
Lavatera assurgentiflora	14–24
Ligustrum japonicum	4–24
Lycianthes rantonnei	15–24
Melaleuca	Vary
Melianthus major	8, 9, 12–24
Nerium oleander	8–16, 18–23
Philadelphus	Vary
Prunus laurocerasus	4–9, 14–24
Pyracantha coccinea	All
Rhamnus alaternus	4–24
Rhus (some)	Vary
Rosa	Vary
Salix	All
Sesbania tripetii	7–9, 12–16, 18–23
Sparmannia africana	17, 21–24
Spartium junceum	5–9, 11–24
Tamarix	Vary
Thevetia	Vary
Tibouchina urvilleana	14–17, 21–24
Weigela florida	1–11, 14–17

PERENNIALS, ANNUALS

NAME OF PLANT	CLIMATE ZONES
Acanthus mollis	4–24
Ajuga reptans	All
Carpobrotus	12–24
Chrysanthemum frutescens	All
Colocasia esculenta	13, 16–24
Cortaderia selloana	4–24
Cyperus papyrus	8, 9, 12–24
Ensete	13, 15–24
Euryops	14–17, 19–24
Felicia amelloides	4–9, 13–24
Grasses, ornamental	Vary
Lavatera trimestris	All
Musa	Vary
Philodendron	Vary
Phormium tenax	7–24
Ricinus communis	All
Romneya coulteri	All
Saxifraga rosacea	1–7, 14–17

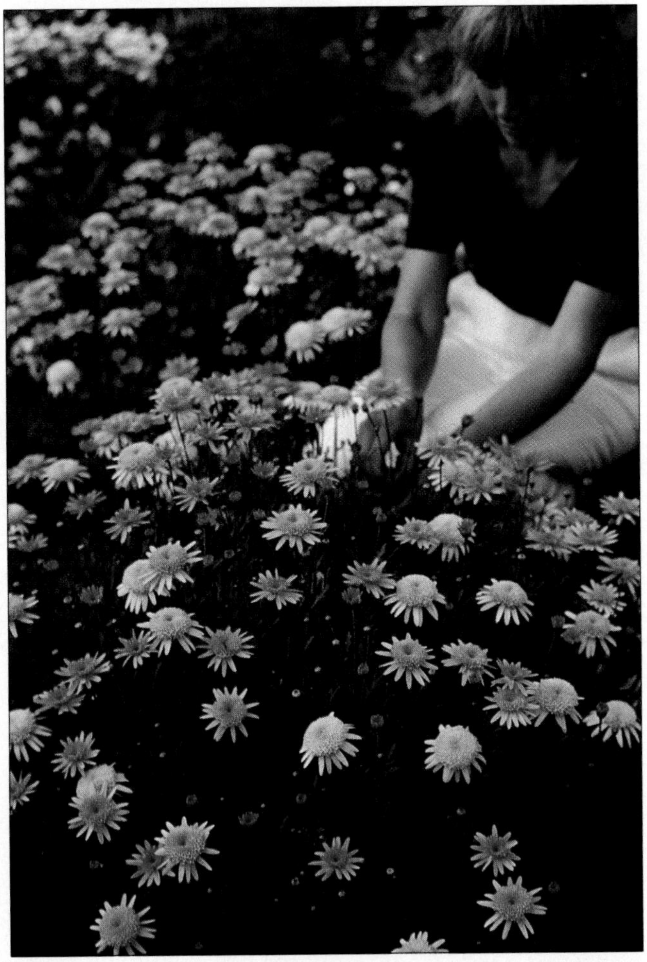

Perennial marguerite (Chrysanthemum frutescens) serves as flowering shrub where winter is mild. Yellow, white are other colors.

Ground Covers & Lawn Substitutes

The best-known ground cover, a lawn (see pages 190–193), is unsurpassed as a surface to walk and play on. But where foot traffic is infrequent or undesirable, many other ground cover plants can offer much of a lawn's neatness and uniformity with considerably less maintenance. Ground covers run the gamut of foliage textures and colors, and many are noted for their colorful flowers. Pattern plantings are possible, using different ground covers to contrast pleasantly with one another. Most of these ground covers function as barriers in a landscape rather than as the green bridge a lawn provides.

Brightly colored gazanias give long season of color but demand little care; trailing kinds spread rapidly to form complete cover.

SHRUBS

NAME OF PLANT	CLIMATE ZONES
Abelia grandiflora 'Prostrata'	5–24
Arctostaphylos edmundsii	6–9, 14–24
Arctostaphylos hookeri	6–9, 14–24
Arctostaphylos hookeri Monterey Carpet'	6–9, 14–24
Arctostaphylos media	4–9, 14–24
Arctostaphylos pumila	17
Arctostaphylos uva-ursi	1–9, 14–24
*Ardisia japonica	5, 6, 15–17
Atriplex semibaccata	8, 9, 12–24
Baccharis pilularis	5–11, 14–24
Bamboo (some)	Vary
Calluna vulgaris (some)	2–6, 15–17
*Camellia sasanqua (some)	4–9, 14–24
Carissa macrocarpa (some)	See Encyclopedia
Ceanothus gloriosus	See Encyclopedia
Ceanothus griseus horizontalis	Vary
Ceanothus maritimus	4–7, 14–24
Chorizema ilicifolium	15–17, 19–24
Cistus salviifolius	7–9, 12–24
Coprosma kirkii	8, 9, 14–17, 21–24
Cornus canadensis	1–7
Correa pulchella	14–24
Cotoneaster (some)	Vary
Cytisus kewensis	4–6, 16, 17
*Daphne blagayana	4–6
Erica (some)	Vary
*Gaultheria ovatifolia	4–7, 14–17
*Gaultheria procumbens	2–7, 14–17
Genista lydia	4–6, 14–17
Genista sagittalis	2–9, 11–22
Hebe menziesii	14–24
*Hypericum calycinum	2–24
Hypericum coris	4–24
Juniperus (ground cover forms)	All
Lantana montevidensis	12, 13, 15–24
Leucothoe fontanesiana	4–7, 15–17
*Lysimachia	1–9, 14–24
*Mahonia nervosa	2–9, 14–17
*Mahonia repens	1–21
*Muehlenbeckia	Vary
Myoporum parvifolium	14–16, 18–24
*Nandina domestica 'Harbour Dwarf'	5–24
*Pachysandra terminalis	1–10, 14–21
Paxistima canbyi	1–10, 14–21
Pyracantha 'Santa Cruz'	4–24
Pyracantha 'Walderi'	4–24
Rhapiolepis (some)	8–10, 12–24
Ribes viburnifolium	8, 9, 14–24
Rosmarinus officinalis 'Collingwood Ingram'	4–24
Rosmarinus officinalis 'Lockwood de Forest'	4–24
Rosmarinus officinalis 'Prostratus'	4–24
*Ruscus hypoglossum	4–24
*Sarcococca hookerana humilis	4–9, 14–24
*Taxus baccata 'Repandens'	3–9, 14–24
Teucrium chamaedrys	All
*Vaccinium vitis-idaea	2–7, 14–17

*Will grow in shade.

VINES

NAME OF PLANT	CLIMATE ZONES
Bougainvillea	See Encyclopedia
*Cissus	Vary
*Euonymus fortunei (and varieties)	1–17
*Fatshedera lizei	4–10, 12–24
Gelsemium sempervirens	8–24
Hardenbergia	Vary
*Hedera	Vary
Hibbertia scandens	16, 17, 21–24
Jasminum nitidum	12, 13, 16, 19–21
Jasminum polyanthum	9, 12–24
Lonicera japonica	2–24
*Muehlenbeckia axillaris	3–9, 14–24
Passiflora	Vary
Pyrostegia venusta	13, 16, 21–24
*Rhoicissus capensis	16, 17, 21–24
Rosa banksiae	4–24
Rosa bracteata 'Mermaid'	4–24
Sollya heterophylla	8, 9, 14–24
Tetrastigma voinieranum	13, 17, 20–24
Thunbergia gregorii	21–24
Trachelospermum	Vary

PERENNIALS

NAME OF PLANT	CLIMATE ZONES
Acaena	4–9, 14–24
Achillea tomentosa	All
*Aegopodium podagraria	1–7
*Ajuga reptans	All
Arabis	Vary
Arctotheca calendula	8, 9, 13–24
Arctotis	7–9, 14–24
*Asarum caudatum	4–6, 14–17, 21
Asparagus densiflorus 'Sprengeri'	12–24
*Brunnera macrophylla	All
Calocephalus brownii	16, 17, 19, 21–24
*Campanula	All
Carpobrotus	12–24
Cephalophyllum 'Red Spike'	8, 9, 11–24
Cerastium tomentosum	See Encyclopedia
Ceratostigma plumbaginoides	2–9, 14–24
*Convallaria majalis	1–7, 14–20
Convolvulus mauritanicus	4–9, 12–24
Coronilla varia	All
*Crassula multicava	16, 17, 22–24
*Cymbalaria muralis	3–24
Dampiera diversifolia	15–24
Delosperma 'Alba'	12–24
Drosanthemum	14–24

*Will grow in shade.

Fast-spreading Ajuga reptans brings bonus of blue flowers to thick foliage carpet. Varieties have bronze, variegated leaves.

PERENNIALS (*cont'd.*)

NAME OF PLANT	CLIMATE ZONES
Dryas	1–6
*Duchesnea indica	All
*Epimedium	1–9, 14–17
Erigeron karvinskianus	8, 9, 12–24
Festuca ovina glauca	All
*Fragaria chiloensis	4–24
*Galax urceolata	1–6
Gazania	8–24
Halimium	7–9, 12–24
Helianthemum	All
*Heterocentron elegans	17, 21–24
Iberis sempervirens	All
Lampranthus	14–24
*Liriope spicata	All
Lotus berthelotii	9, 15–24
*Lysimachia nummularia	1–9, 14–24
Malephora	Vary
*Myosotis	All
Nepeta faassenii	All
*Ophiopogon japonicus	5–10, 12–24
Oscularia	15–24
Osteospermum fruticosum	8, 9, 14–24
*Oxalis oregana	4–9, 14–24
Pelargonium peltatum	8, 9, 12–24
*Pellaea viridis	14–17, 19–24
Polygonum capitatum	8, 9, 12–24
Polygonum cuspidatum compactum	All
Polygonum vacciniifolium	4–7
Potentilla cinerea	1–17
Potentilla tabernaemontanii	All
Santolina	All
Saponaria ocymoides	All
Saxifraga rosacea	1–7, 14–17
*Saxifraga stolonifera	1–9, 14–24
*Saxifraga umbrosa	1–7, 14–17
Sedum (many)	Vary
*Soleirolia soleirolii	8–24
Thymus	All
*Tolmiea menziesii	5–9, 12–24
*Vancouveria	Vary
Verbena	Vary
Vinca	Vary
Viola hederacea	8, 9, 14–24
Viola odorata	All

WALK-ON LAWN SUBSTITUTES

NAME OF PLANT	CLIMATE ZONES
Chamaemelum nobile	All
*Cotula squalida	4–9, 14–24
Dichondra micrantha	8, 9, 12–24
Hippocrepis comosa	8–24
Mazus reptans	1–7, 14–24
Phyla nodiflora	8–24
Sagina subulata	1–11, 14–24
Zoysia tenuifolia	8, 9, 12–24

*Will grow in shade.

Vines & Vinelike Plants

Vines are some of the most tractable plants. Unlike shrubs and trees, which have predictable growth habits, most vines can be guided to grow where you want them to. You can train a vine to grow upward or outward (or both) on a flat, vertical surface; up and around a post or tree trunk; or up and over a pergola. Many will perform alternative duty as a ground cover on a horizontal surface.

Though vines characteristically are flexible and long limbed, they climb in different manners: with tendrils, by twining, by clinging, or—for those that have no means of attachment—by being tied to a support (see "Vines," page 180). The climbing habit of each vine listed on these pages is noted.

Fast-growing black-eyed Susan vine (Thunbergia alata) gives plentiful summer color, will be perennial in mild climates.

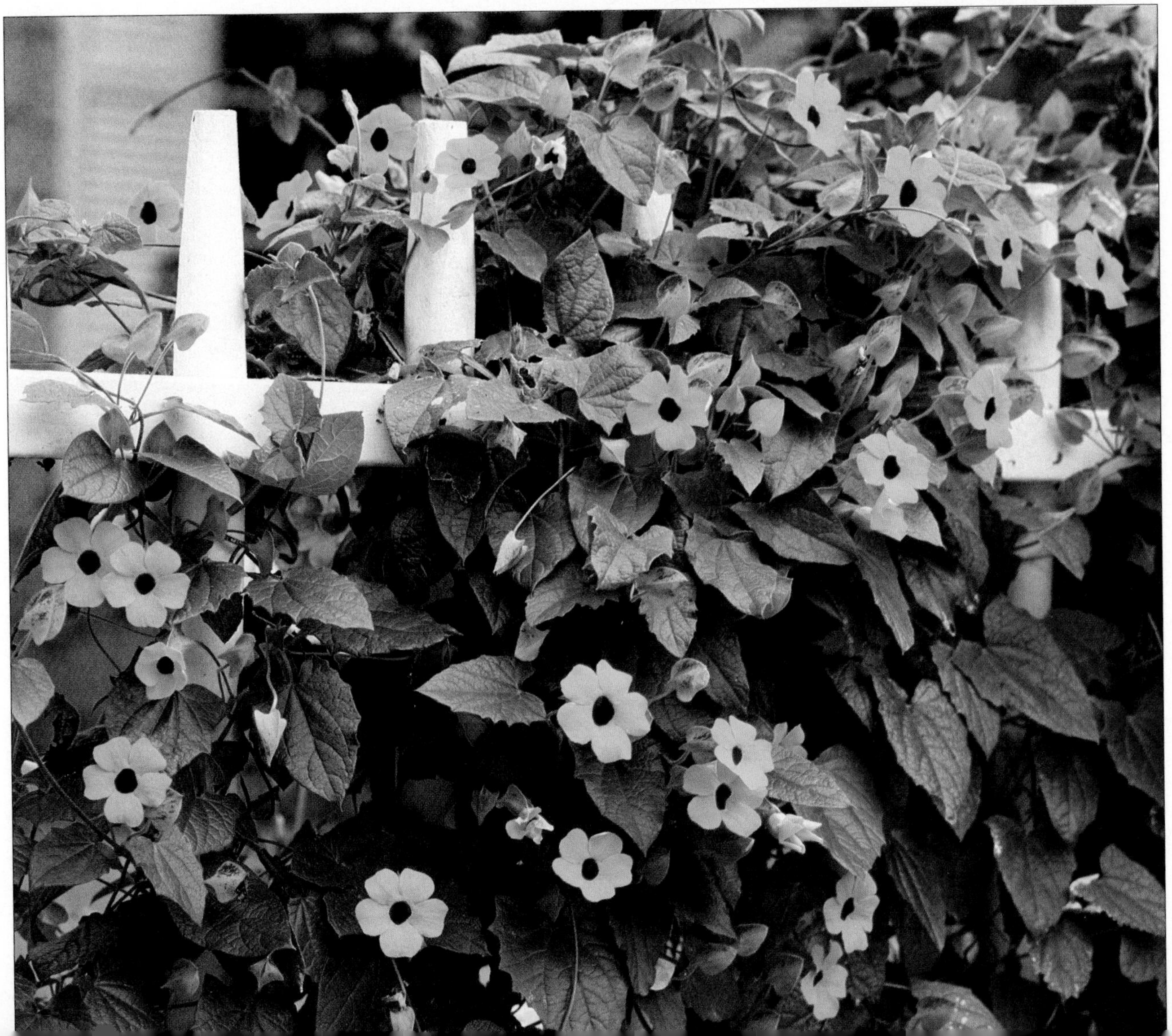

EVERGREEN

NAME OF PLANT	CLIMATE ZONES	HOW IT CLIMBS	GROWTH RATE	FLOWERS	SUITED TO SHADE
Anemopaegma chamberlaynii	15–17, 19, 21–24	Tendrils	Medium	■	
Antigonon leptopus	12, 13, 18–21	Tendrils	Fast	■	
Beaumontia grandiflora	12, 13, 16, 17, 21–24	Twining	Fast	■	
Bougainvillea	See Encyclopedia	Must be tied	Fast	■	
Cissus	Vary	Tendrils	Medium		■
Clematis armandii	4–9, 12–24	Tendrils	Fast	■	■
Clerodendrum thomsoniae	22–24	Twining	Slow	■	
Clytostoma callistegioides	9, 13–24	Tendrils	Fast	■	■
Distictis	Vary	Tendrils	Medium fast	■	■
Euonymus fortunei	1–17	Clinging	Medium		■
Fatshedera lizei	4–10, 12–24	Must be tied	Medium		■
Ficus pumila	8–24	Clinging	Medium fast		■
Gelsemium sempervirens	8–24	Twining	Medium	■	
Hardenbergia comptoniana	15–24	Twining	Medium	■	■
Hardenbergia violacea	9–24	Twining	Fast	■	
Hedera canariensis	8, 9, 12–24	Clinging	Fast		■
Hedera colchica	7–9, 12–24	Clinging	Fast		■
Hedera helix	All	Clinging	Fast		■
Hibbertia scandens	16, 17, 21–24	Twining	Fast	■	■
Hoya carnosa	15–24	Twining, must be tied	Slow	■	■
Jasminum grandiflorum	5–9, 12–24	Must be tied	Fast	■	■
Jasminum nitidum	12, 13, 16, 19–21	Must be tied	Medium	■	■
Jasminum officinale	12–24	Twining	Fast	■	■
Jasminum polyanthum	9, 12–24	Twining	Fast	■	
Lapageria rosea	5, 6, 15–17, 23, 24	Twining	Slow	■	■
Lonicera hildebrandiana	9, 14–17, 19–24	Twining	Fast	■	■
Lonicera japonica	2–24	Twining	Fast	■	■
Lonicera sempervirens	3–24	Twining	Medium	■	■
Macfadyena unguis-cati	8–24	Tendrils	Medium fast	■	
Mandevilla 'Alice du Pont'	21–24	Twining	Medium	■	■
Millettia reticulata	20–24	Twining	Fast	■	
Muehlenbeckia complexa	8, 9, 14–24	Twining	Fast		■
Pandorea	16–24	Twining	Fast	■	■
Passiflora	Vary	Tendrils	Fast	■	
Petrea volubilis	23–24	Twining	Fast	■	
Plumbago auriculata	8, 9, 12–24	Must be tied	Fast	■	
Podranea ricasoliana	9, 12, 13, 19–24	Must be tied	Fast	■	
Polygonum aubertii	8, 9, 13–24	Twining	Fast	■	
Pyrostegia venusta	13, 16, 21–24	Tendrils	Fast	■	■
Rhoicissus capensis	16, 17, 21–24	Tendrils	Slow		■
Rosa (climbing sorts)	Vary	Must be tied	Medium	■	
Senecio confusus	16–24	Twining	Fast	■	
Senecio mikanioides	14–24	Twining	Fast	■	
Solandra maxima	15–24	Must be tied	Fast	■	
Solanum jasminoides	8, 9, 12–24	Twining	Fast	■	■
Sollya heterophylla	8, 9, 14–24	Twining	Medium	■■	
Stephanotis floribunda	23, 24	Twining	Medium	■	■
Stigmaphyllon ciliatum	19–24	Twining	Fast	■	■
Tecomaria capensis	12–16, 18–24	Must be tied	Fast	■	
Tetrastigma	13, 17, 20–24	Tendrils	Fast		
Thunbergia	Vary	Twining	Fast	■	
Trachelospermum	Vary	Twining	Medium	■	■

Bougainvillea 'San Diego Red' brings a touch of the tropics to gardens where winter temperatures seldom dip below freezing.

DECIDUOUS

NAME OF PLANT	CLIMATE ZONES	HOW IT CLIMBS	GROWTH RATE	FLOWERS	SUITED TO SHADE
Actinidia deliciosa	4–9, 14–24	Twining, must be tied	Fast	■	■
Actinidia kolomikta	4–9, 15–17	Twining	Fast		■
Akebia quinata	All	Twining	Fast	■	■
Ampelopsis brevipedunculata	All	Tendrils, twining	Fast		■
Anredera cordifolia	4–24	Twining	Fast	■	
Antigonon leptopus	12, 13, 18–21	Tendrils	Fast	■	
Aristolochia durior	All	Twining	Fast	■	■
Campsis	Vary	Clinging	Fast	■	
Celastrus	See Encyclopedia	Twining	Fast		■
Clematis (all but C. armandii)	Vary	Twining	Fast	■	
Grape	Vary	Tendrils	Fast		
Humulus lupulus	All	Twining	Fast		
Hydrangea anomala	1–21	Clinging	Slow	■	■
Lonicera heckrottii	2–24	Twining	Fast	■	■
Mandevilla laxa	4–9, 14–21	Twining	Medium fast	■	
Parthenocissus	Vary	Tendrils, clinging	Fast		■
Polygonum aubertii	1–7, 10–12	Twining	Fast	■	
Polygonum baldschuanicum	All	Twining	Fast	■	
Rosa (climbing sorts)	Vary	Must be tied	Medium	■	
Solanum wendlandii	16, 21–24	Twining	Fast	■	
Vigna caracalla	12–24	Twining	Fast	■	
Wisteria	All	Twining	Fast	■	■

ANNUALS

NAME OF PLANT	CLIMATE ZONES	HOW IT CLIMBS	GROWTH RATE	FLOWERS	SUITED TO SHADE
Bean, scarlet runner	All	Twining	Fast	■	
Cobaea scandens	All	Tendrils	Fast	■	
Ipomoea	Vary	Twining	Fast	■	
Lathyrus odoratus	All	Tendrils	Fast	■	
Tropaeolum majus	All	Twining	Fast	■	

Plants for Espaliers

The classic espalier is a fruit tree trained so that its branches grow in a flat plane, often in a rigid candelabra arrangement. With this method of training against a sunny wall, crops could be raised early or in marginally warm regions. In today's landscaping, the practice of espaliering has expanded to include purely ornamental plants trained against walls and fences, both in the traditional formal arrangement and in irregular patterns determined by a plant's natural growth habits. Espaliers are well suited to the narrow planting space between a walk and wall and to any wall or fence where you want a tracery of branches, foliage, or flowers. The plants listed below are among the easiest to train on espaliers. Their growth naturally tends toward arrangement in flat surfaces and is strong enough to be self-supporting yet flexible enough to be guided.

NAME OF PLANT	CLIMATE ZONES
Abutilon	13, 15–24
Acer circinatum	1–6, 14–17
Apple	Vary
Apricot	Vary
Azalea (rhododendron)	Vary
Bauhinia punctata	13, 15, 16, 18–23
Calliandra haematocephala	22–24
Callistemon	8, 9, 12–24
Camellia (some)	4–9, 14–24
Carissa macrocarpa 'Fancy'	22–24
Cestrum (some)	Vary
Citrus	Vary
Clianthus puniceus	8, 9, 14–24
Cocculus laurifolius	8, 9, 12–24
Coprosma repens	15–17, 21–24
Cotoneaster 'Hybridus Pendulus'	4–24
Cotoneaster lacteus	4–24
Elaeagnus (evergreen ones)	Vary
Eriobotrya deflexa	8–14
Eriobotrya japonica	4–24
Escallonia exoniensis	4–9, 14–17, 20–24
Eucalyptus caesia	8–24
Eucalyptus orbifolia	8–24
Eucalyptus rhodantha	8–24
Euonymus fortunei (some)	1–17
Feijoa sellowiana	7–9, 12–24
Ficus auriculata	20–24
Ficus benjamina	13, 23, 24
Fig, Edible	4–9, 12–24
Gardenia	Vary
Grewia occidentalis	8, 9, 14–24
Griselinia	9, 15–17, 20–24
Hibiscus rosa-sinensis	9, 12, 13, 15, 16, 19–24
Ilex altaclarensis 'Wilsonii'	3–24
Iochroma cyaneum	16, 17, 19–24
Itea ilicifolia	4–24
Juniperus chinensis 'Torulosa'	All
Laburnum watereri	1–10, 14–17
Magnolia grandiflora	4–12, 14–24
Malus	1–11, 14–21
Michelia figo	9, 14–24
Nectarine	Vary
Ochna serrulata	14–24
Osmanthus fragrans	8, 9, 12–24
Peach	Vary
Pear	1–11, 14–18
Photinia fraseri	4–24
Plum	Vary
Podocarpus gracilior	8, 9, 12–24
Podocarpus macrophyllus	4–9, 12–24
Prunus (deciduous)	Vary
Pyracantha	Vary
Pyrus kawakamii	8, 9, 12–24
Rhododendron 'Else Frye'	See Encyclopedia
Rhododendron 'Fragrantissimum'	See Encyclopedia
Rhus integrifolia	15–17, 20–24
Rhus laurina	20–24
Rhus ovata	7–24
Sarcococca ruscifolia	4–9, 14–24
Sophora secundiflora	8–16, 18–24
Tecomaria capensis	12, 13, 16, 18–24
Viburnum burkwoodii	1–10, 14–24
Viburnum macrocephalum	1–9, 14–24
Viburnum plicatum	1–9, 14–24
Xylosma congestum	8–24

Good Choices for Rock Gardens

Small or tiny shrubs, miniature bulbous plants, annuals and perennials that form low tufts of leaves or creeping mats of foliage—these are the choices listed here for planting in rock gardens. Classic European rock gardens and Alpine landscapes can be re-created in the cool Pacific Northwest; but to produce the same effect in southern California will call for a different assortment of plants. Read carefully the climate zone adaptations and the individual plant descriptions in the Western Plant Encyclopedia (beginning on page 199).

TREES

NAME OF PLANT	CLIMATE ZONES
Abies balsamea 'Nana'	3–7, 15–17
Acer palmatum	1–9, 14–24
Pinus albicaulis	See Encyclopedia
Pinus contorta latifolia	See Encyclopedia
Pinus densiflora 'Umbraculifera'	See Encyclopedia
Pinus edulis	See Encyclopedia
Pinus monophylla	See Encyclopedia
Pinus mugo mugo	See Encyclopedia
Pinus strobus 'Nana'	See Encyclopedia

SHRUBS & SHRUBLETS

NAME OF PLANT	CLIMATE ZONES
Andromeda polifolia	All
Azalea (rhododendron)	Vary
Berberis stenophylla 'Corallina Compacta'	1–11, 14–17
Calluna vulgaris (some)	2–6, 15–17
Calocephalus brownii	16, 17, 19, 21–24
Chamaecyparis (some)	Vary
Cistus	7–9, 12–24
Daboecia (some)	Vary
Daphne (some)	Vary
Erica (some)	Vary
Gaultheria (most species)	Vary
Genista (some)	Vary
Halimiocistus sahucii	4–24
Halimium	7–9, 12–24
Hebe cupressoides 'Nana'	14–24
Helianthemum nummularium	All
Hypericum coris	4–24
Jasminum parkeri	5–9, 12–24
Juniperus	All
Myoporum debile	15–17, 19–24
Penstemon rupicola	1–7
Pimelea prostrata	4–7, 14–17
Polygala chamaebuxus	4–6
Potentilla cinerea	1–17

Mild-winter rock gardens can include succulents in variety; pictured are aeoniums, Kalanchoe, and Senecio serpens.

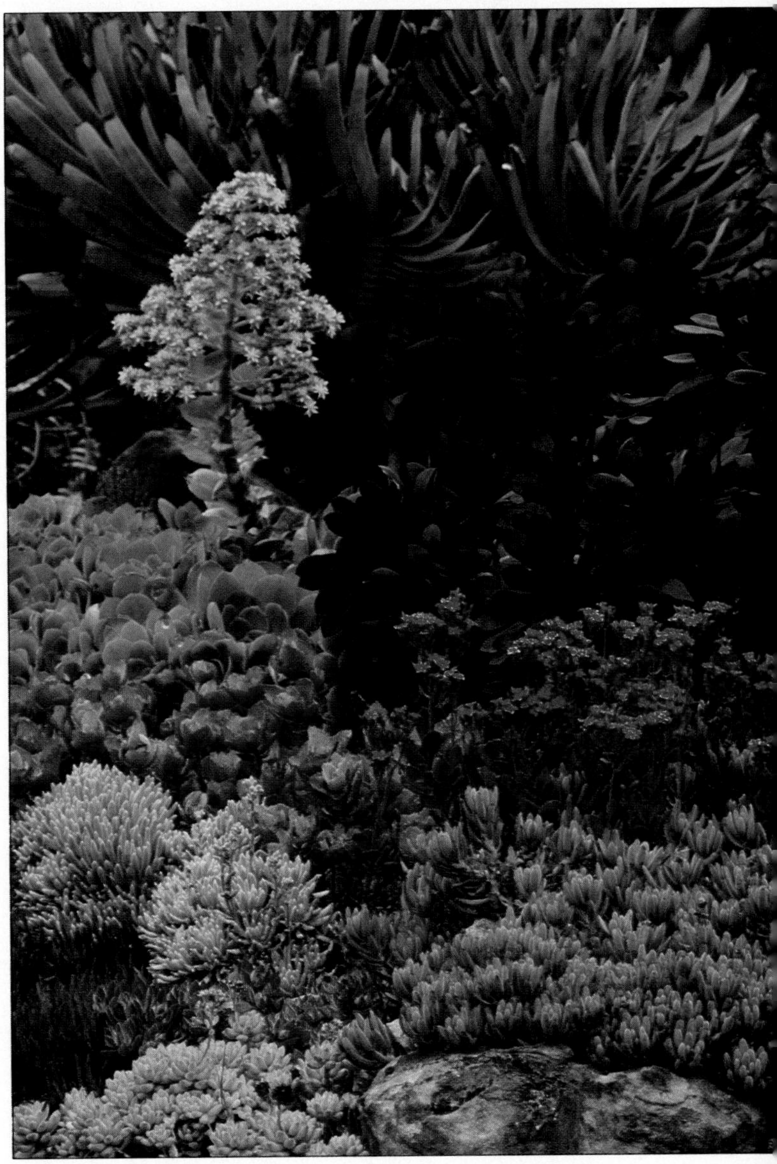

SHRUBS (*cont'd.*)

NAME OF PLANT	CLIMATE ZONES
Rhododendron chryseum	4–6, 15–17
Rhododendron impeditum	4–6, 15–17
Rhododendron keiskei	4–6, 15–17
Rhododendron moupinense	4–6, 15–17
Rhododendron pemakoense	4–6, 15–17
Teucrium	Vary

PERENNIALS

NAME OF PLANT	CLIMATE ZONES
Acaena	4–9, 14–24
Achillea tomentosa	All
Aeonium	15–17, 20–24
Aethionema	1–9, 14–21
Ajuga genevensis	All
Alyssum	All
Anacyclus depressus	All
Anagallis monelli linifolia	All
Androsace	1–6, 14–17
Anemone pulsatilla	1–6, 15–17
Arabis	Vary
Arenaria	2–9, 14–24
Armeria	All
Aubrieta deltoidea	1–9, 14–21
Campanula	Vary
Cerastium tomentosum	All
Crassula lactea	16, 17, 22–24
Crassula schmidtii	16, 17, 22–24
Dianthus (smallest)	All
Dryas	1–6
Echeveria (many)	Vary
Erigeron	Vary
Eriogonum	Vary
Erodium chamaedryoides	7–9, 14–24
Erysimum kotschyanum	1–11, 14–21
Euphorbia myrsinites	All
Gazania (clumping sorts)	8–24
Gentiana	1–6, 14–17
Geranium	Vary
Graptopetalum	8–24
Gypsophila repens	1–11, 14–16, 18–21
Herniaria glabra	All
Heuchera	Vary
Iberis sempervirens	All
Iris cristata	4–9, 14–24
Iris tectorum	4–9, 14–24
Iris, Pacific Coast	4–24
Kalanchoe beharensis	21–24
Leontopodium alpinum	1–9, 14–24
Lewisia	1–7
Lithodora diffusa	5–7, 14–17
Mazus reptans	1–7, 14–24
Oenothera missourensis	All
Onosma tauricum	1–9, 14–17
Origanum dictamnus	8–24
Oxalis adenophylla	4–9, 12–24
Oxalis hirta	8, 9, 14–24
Papaver burseri	All

PERENNIALS (*cont'd.*)

NAME OF PLANT	CLIMATE ZONES
Penstemon davidsonii	1–7
Phlox divaricata	1–17
Phlox nivalis	4–7
Phlox subulata	1–17
Polemonium reptans	1–11, 14–17
Primula (most)	Vary
Raoulia australis	7–9, 13–24
Saxifraga	Vary
Sedum (many)	Vary
Sempervivum	All
Senecio	16, 17, 21–24
Silene acaulis	1–11, 14–16, 18–21
Thymus	All
Veronica	All

BULBS

NAME OF PLANT	CLIMATE ZONES
Allium ostrowskianum 'Zwanenburg'	All
Crocus	All
Cyclamen	Vary
Freesia	8, 9, 12–24
Fritillaria (most)	1–7, 15–17
Galanthus	1–9, 14–17
Iris reticulata	All
Leucocoryne ixioides	13, 16, 19, 21–24
Milla biflora	13, 16–24
Muscari	All
Narcissus (smaller species)	All
Sparaxis tricolor	9, 13–24
Sternbergia lutea	All
Tritonia	9, 13–24
Tulipa (species, not hybrids)	See Encyclopedia
Zephyranthes	1–9, 14–24

Northwest rock garden features tapestry of low shrubs (apricot Helianthemum in foreground), small perennials, and bulbs.

Showy Flowers by Season

Most gardeners eagerly anticipate the flowering of plants in their gardens—whether this means a grandiose display of rhododendrons or a single potful of crocuses. Flowers provide changing interest throughout the year. Listed here, under the seasons in which they flower, are the most widely grown color producers.

Harmonious, fragrant, early spring duo is creamy Freesia and Spanish bluebell (Endymion hispanicus).

Spring

TREES

NAME OF PLANT	CLIMATE ZONES	YELLOW/ORANGE	RED/PINK	BLUE/PURPLE	WHITE	MULTICOLORED
Acacia	Vary	■				
Aesculus carnea	1–9, 14–17		■			
Bauhinia	Vary		■	■	■	
Catalpa	All				■	
Cornus	Vary		■		■	
Crataegus	1–11, 14–17		■		■	
Erythrina	Vary	■	■			
Laburnum	1–10, 14–17	■				
Leptospermum	14–24		■		■	
Magnolia	Vary	■	■	■	■	
Malus	1–11, 14–21		■		■	
Melaleuca	Vary		■	■	■	
Paulownia tomentosa	All			■		
Prunus (flowering types)	Vary		■		■	
Tabebuia chrysotricha	15, 16, 20–24	■				

SHRUBS

NAME OF PLANT	CLIMATE ZONES	Y	R	B	W	M
Abutilon hybridum	13, 15–24	■	■		■	
Acacia	Vary	■				
Azalea (rhododendron)	Vary	■	■	■	■	
Callistemon	8, 9, 12–24		■	■	■	
Camellia	4, 9, 14–24		■		■	
Ceanothus	Vary			■	■	
Choisya ternata	4–9, 12–24				■	
Cistus	4–9, 12–24		■		■	
Deutzia	1–11, 14–17		■		■	
Erythrina	Vary	■	■			
Forsythia	2–11, 14–16, 18, 19	■				
Fremontodendron	7–24	■				
Jasminum	Vary	■			■	
Kolkwitzia amabilis	1–11, 14–20		■			
Leptospermum	14–24		■		■	
Melaleuca	Vary		■	■	■	
Philadelphus	Vary				■	
Rhapiolepis	8–10, 12–24		■		■	
Rhododendron	Vary	■	■	■	■	
Rosa	All	■	■	■	■	
Spiraea	1–11, 14–21		■		■	
Syringa	Vary		■	■	■	
Weigela	1–11, 14–17	■	■		■	

VINES

NAME OF PLANT	CLIMATE ZONES	Y	R	B	W	M
Bougainvillea	See Encyclopedia	■	■	■	■	
Clematis	Vary	■	■	■	■	
Distictis buccinatoria	8, 9, 14–24		■			
Hibbertia scandens	16, 17, 21–24	■				
Jasminum	Vary	■	■		■	
Lonicera	Vary	■	■		■	
Solandra maxima	15–24	■				
Solanum jasminoides	8, 9, 14–24			■	■	
Wisteria	All		■	■	■	

PERENNIALS

NAME OF PLANT	CLIMATE ZONES	YELLOW/ORANGE	RED/PINK	BLUE/PURPLE	WHITE	MULTICOLORED
Aethionema	1–9, 14–21		■			
Alstroemeria	5–9, 14–24	■	■			■
Aquilegia	All	■	■	■	■	
Arabis	Vary		■		■	
Arctotis	7–9, 14–24	■	■	■	■	■
Aster	All		■	■	■	
Aubrieta deltoidea	1–9, 14–21		■	■		
Aurinia saxatilis	All	■				
Bergenia	1–9, 14–24		■		■	
Campanula	Vary		■	■	■	
Convallaria majalis	1–7, 14–20				■	
Cynoglossum amabile	All		■	■	■	
Delphinium	Vary		■	■	■	
Dianthus	All	■	■	■	■	
Dicentra spectabilis	1–9, 14–24		■			
Digitalis	All	■		■	■	
Filipendula	1–9, 14–24		■		■	
Heliotropium arborescens	8–24			■	■	
Helleborus	Vary		■	■	■	
Heuchera sanguinea	All		■		■	
Iberis sempervirens	All				■	
Kniphofia uvaria	1–9, 14–24	■	■		■	
Osteospermum	8, 9, 14–24	■		■	■	
Paeonia (herbaceous)	1–11, 14–16		■		■	
Papaver orientale	1–17	■	■		■	
Phlox subulata	1–17		■	■	■	
Primula (many)	Vary	■	■	■	■	■
Saxifraga	Vary		■		■	
Senecio hybridus	16, 17, 22–24		■	■	■	■
Viola	Vary	■	■	■	■	

BULBS & BULBLIKE PLANTS

NAME OF PLANT	CLIMATE ZONES	Y	R	B	W	M
Anemone coronaria	All		■	■	■	
Babiana	4–24		■	■	■	
Clivia miniata	15–17, 19–24	■				
Crocus	All	■		■	■	■
Cyclamen	Vary		■	■	■	
Dietes	8, 9, 13–24	■			■	
Endymion hispanicus	All		■	■	■	
Freesia	8, 9, 12–24	■	■	■	■	■
Fritillaria	1–7, 15–17	■	■		■	■
Gladiolus	All	■	■	■	■	■
Hippeastrum	12, 13, 19, 21–24	■	■		■	
Hyacinthus orientalis	All	■	■	■	■	
Iris	Vary	■	■	■	■	■
Ixia maculata	5–24	■	■		■	
Muscari	All			■	■	
Narcissus	All	■			■	■
Ranunculus	All	■	■		■	
Sparaxis tricolor	9, 13–24	■	■	■	■	
Tulipa	All	■	■	■	■	■
Watsonia pyramidata	4–9, 12–24	■	■			
Zantedeschia	5, 6, 8, 9, 14–24	■	■		■	

Where Western climate is cool and moist, rhododendrons can be a spring garden feature. This is low-growing 'Bow Bells'.

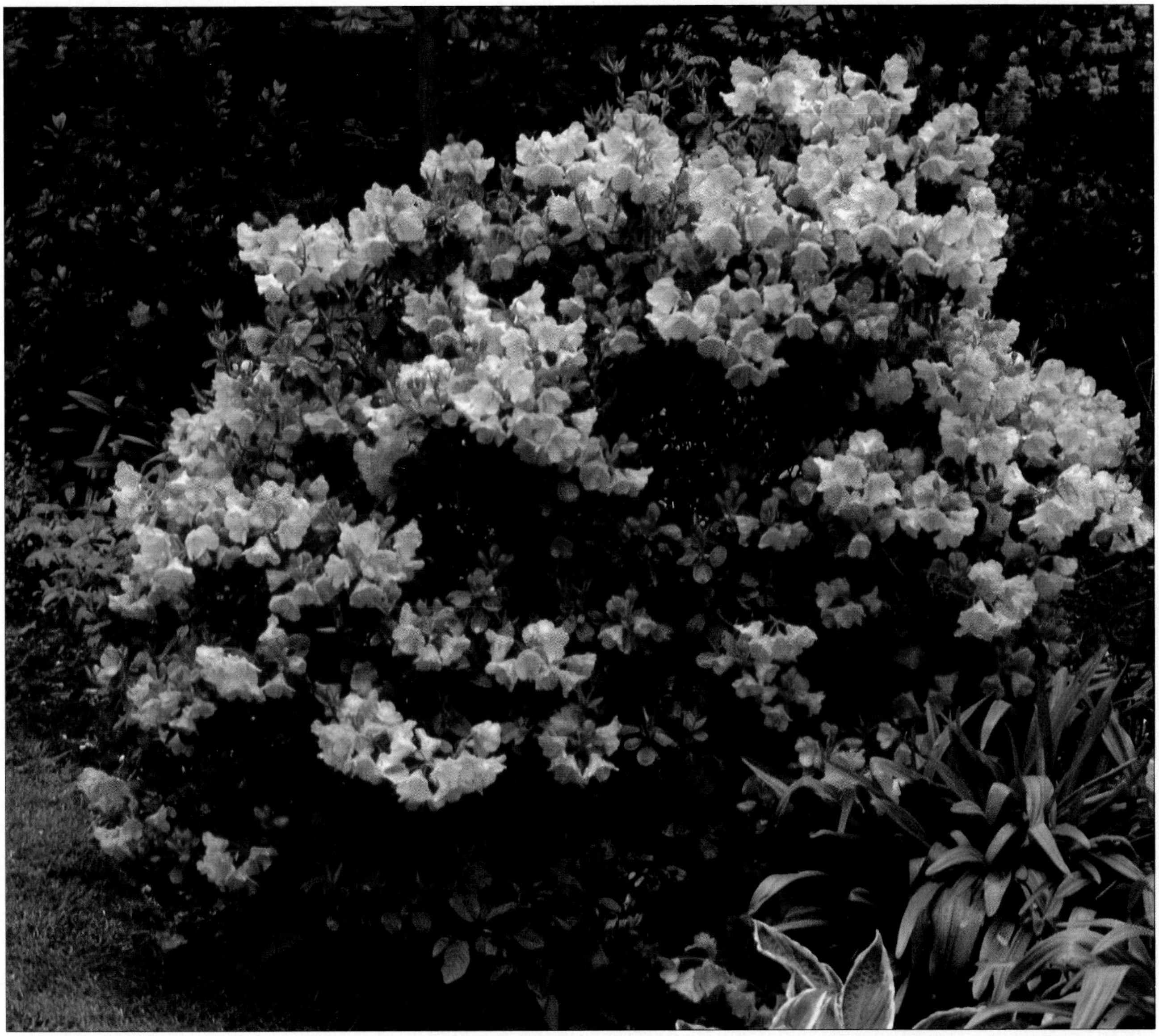

ANNUALS

NAME OF PLANT	CLIMATE ZONES	YELLOW/ORANGE	RED/PINK	BLUE/PURPLE	WHITE	MULTICOLORED
Antirrhinum majus	All	■	■		■	■
Calendula officinalis	All	■	■			
Centaurea cyanus	All		■	■	■	
Clarkia	All	■	■	■	■	■
Consolida ambigua	All		■	■	■	
Dianthus barbatus	All		■	■	■	■
Dimorphotheca	All	■				
Eschscholzia californica	All	■	■		■	
Lathyrus odoratus	All		■	■	■	■
Lobularia maritima	10–24		■	■	■	
Lupinus nanus	8, 9, 14–24			■		
Matthiola incana	All	■	■	■	■	
Mimulus hybridus	All	■	■		■	■
Myosotis sylvatica	All			■		
Nemesia strumosa	15–17, 21–24	■	■	■	■	■
Nemophila menziesii	All			■		
Papaver rhoeas	All	■	■		■	
Viola wittrockiana	All	■	■	■	■	■

Fuchsias, both shrubby and trailing, give nonstop summer color in coastal zones. 'Gartenmeister Bonstedt' is perennial favorite.

Summer

TREES

NAME OF PLANT	CLIMATE ZONES	YELLOW/ORANGE	RED/PINK	BLUE/PURPLE	WHITE	MULTICOLORED
Albizia julibrissin	2–23		■			
Calodendrum capense	19, 21–24		■			
Cassia leptophylla	21–24	■				
Catalpa	All				■	
Erythrina humeana	12, 13, 20–24		■			
Eucalyptus ficifolia	8–24		■			
Jacaranda mimosifolia	12, 13, 15–24			■		
Lagerstroemia indica	7–9, 12–14, 18–21		■	■		
Lagunaria patersonii	13, 15–24		■			
Magnolia grandiflora	4–12, 14–24				■	
Melaleuca	Vary		■	■	■	
Oxydendrum arboreum	3–9, 14–17				■	
Tipuana tipu	12–16, 18–24	■				

SHRUBS

NAME OF PLANT	CLIMATE ZONES	Y	R	B	W	M
Abutilon megapotamicum	13, 15–24	■	■			
Brunfelsia	13–17, 20–24			■		
Callistemon	8, 9, 12–24		■		■	
Caryopteris	1–7, 14–17			■		
Corynabutilon vitifolium	5, 6, 15–17			■	■	
Erythrina (some)	Vary		■			
Fuchsia	Vary		■	■	■	■
Gardenia jasminoides	7–9, 12–16, 18–23	■			■	
Hibiscus mutabilis	4–24		■			
Hibiscus rosa-sinensis	9, 12, 13, 15, 16, 19–24	■	■		■	
Hibiscus syriacus	1–21		■	■	■	
Hydrangea macrophylla	2–24		■	■	■	
Jasminum	Vary	■			■	
Justicia carnea	8, 9, 13–24		■			
Lagerstroemia indica	7–9, 12–14, 18–21		■	■	■	
Melaleuca	Vary		■	■	■	
Nerium oleander	8–16, 18–23	■	■		■	
Philadelphus	Varies				■	
Rosa	All	■	■	■	■	■
Tibouchina urvilleana	16, 17, 21–24			■		

VINES

NAME OF PLANT	CLIMATE ZONES	Y	R	B	W	M
Antigonon leptopus	12, 13, 18–21		■			
Bean, Scarlet Runner	All		■			
Bougainvillea	See Encyclopedia	■	■	■	■	
Clematis	Vary	■	■	■	■	
Hibbertia scandens	16, 17, 21–24	■				
Jasminum	Vary	■			■	
Lonicera (some)	Vary	■	■		■	
Mandevilla	Vary		■			
Passiflora	Vary		■	■	■	
Petrea volubilis	23–24			■		
Podranea ricasoliana	9, 12, 13, 19–24		■			
Polygonum aubertii	All				■	
Trachelospermum jasminoides	8–24				■	

Heat-loving Madagascar periwinkle (Catharanthus roseus) flowers well into fall, until stopped by frost.

PERENNIALS

NAME OF PLANT	CLIMATE ZONES	YELLOW/ORANGE	RED/PINK	BLUE/PURPLE	WHITE	MULTICOLORED
Achillea	All	■	■		■	
Aquilegia	All	■	■	■	■	
Arctotis	7–9, 14–24	■	■	■	■	■
Aster	All		■	■	■	
Astilbe	2–7, 14–17		■		■	
Begonia (semperflorens)	All		■		■	
Bellis perennis	All		■		■	
Calceolaria integrifolia	14–24	■	■			
Campanula	Vary		■	■	■	
Catharanthus roseus	All		■		■	
Ceratostigma plumbaginoides	2–9, 14–24			■		
Chrysanthemum frutescens	All	■	■		■	
Chrysanthemum maximum	All				■	
Chrysanthemum parthenium	All	■			■	
Coreopsis grandiflora	All	■				
Delphinium	Vary		■	■	■	
Dianthus	All	■	■	■	■	■
Digitalis	All	■	■	■	■	■
Echinops exaltatus	All			■		
Eustoma grandiflorum	All		■	■	■	
Gaillardia grandiflora	All	■	■			■

NAME OF PLANT	CLIMATE ZONES	YELLOW/ORANGE	RED/PINK	BLUE/PURPLE	WHITE	MULTICOLORED
Gazania	8–24	■	■		■	■
Gerbera jamesonii	8, 9, 12–24	■	■			
Heliotropium arborescens	8–24			■	■	
Heuchera sanguinea	All		■		■	
Kniphofia uvaria	1–9, 14–24	■	■		■	
Limonium	Vary		■	■	■	
Lobelia cardinalis	1–7, 13–17		■			
Macleaya cordata	All		■			
Malva alcea	All		■			
Mirabilis jalapa	4–24	■	■		■	
Osteospermum	8, 9, 14–24	■		■	■	
Pelargonium domesticum	8, 9, 12–24		■	■	■	■
Pelargonium hortorum	8, 9, 12–24	■	■	■	■	
Penstemon gloxinioides	All		■	■	■	■
Perovskia atriplicifolia	All			■		
Phlox paniculata	1–14, 18–21		■	■	■	
Platycodon grandiflorus	All		■	■	■	
Rodgersia	2–9, 14–17				■	
Romneya coulteri	All				■	
Rudbeckia hirta	All	■				
Trachelium caeruleum	7–9, 14–24			■	■	

Summer (cont'd.)

BULBS & BULBLIKE PLANTS

NAME OF PLANT	CLIMATE ZONES	YELLOW/ORANGE	RED/PINK	BLUE/PURPLE	WHITE	MULTICOLORED
Agapanthus	7–9, 12–24			■	■	
Amaryllis belladonna	4–24		■			
Begonia (tuberous)	4–9, 14–24	■	■		■	
Canna	All	■	■		■	
Cyclamen purpurascens	1–9, 14–24		■			
Dahlia	All	■	■	■	■	
Dietes	8, 9, 13–24	■			■	
Gladiolus	All	■	■	■	■	■
Hemerocallis	All	■	■		■	■
Homeria collina	4–24	■	■			
Lilium	All	■	■	■	■	■
Tigridia pavonia	All	■	■		■	

ANNUALS

NAME OF PLANT	CLIMATE ZONES	Y	R	B	W	M
Ageratum houstonianum	All			■		
Amaranthus	All		■			
Antirrhinum majus	All	■	■		■	■
Calendula officinalis	All	■	■			
Callistephus chinensis	All		■	■	■	
Celosia	All	■	■			
Centaurea cyanus	All		■	■	■	
Clarkia	All	■	■	■	■	■
Coreopsis tinctoria	All	■	■			
Cosmos	All	■	■		■	
Dianthus barbatus	All		■	■	■	■
Gaillardia pulchella	All	■	■			
Gypsophila elegans	All		■		■	
Helianthus annuus	All	■				
Helichrysum bracteatum	All	■	■		■	
Impatiens wallerana	All	■	■	■	■	
Ipomoea (most)	All		■	■	■	
Lathyrus odoratus	All		■	■	■	■
Limonium (some)	All	■		■		
Linum grandiflorum 'Rubrum'	All		■			
Lobelia erinus	All		■	■	■	
Lobularia maritima	10–24		■	■	■	
Mimulus hybridus	All	■	■			■
Nicotiana	All		■	■	■	
Papaver rhoeas	All	■	■		■	■
Petunia hybrida	All	■	■	■	■	■
Phlox drummondii	All	■	■		■	
Portulaca grandiflora	All	■	■		■	
Salvia splendens	All		■	■	■	
Scabiosa atropurpurea	All		■	■	■	
Tagetes	All	■	■			■
Thunbergia alata	All	■			■	
Tropaeolum majus	All	■	■		■	
Verbena (most)	All		■	■	■	■
Zinnia	All	■	■	■	■	

Vibrant marigolds (foreground) and zinnias are favorite summer annuals available in a variety of sizes, heights, and colors.

Sunny, summery gloriosa daisies (Rudbeckia hirta) are tough, easy-to-grow perennials that flower into fall.

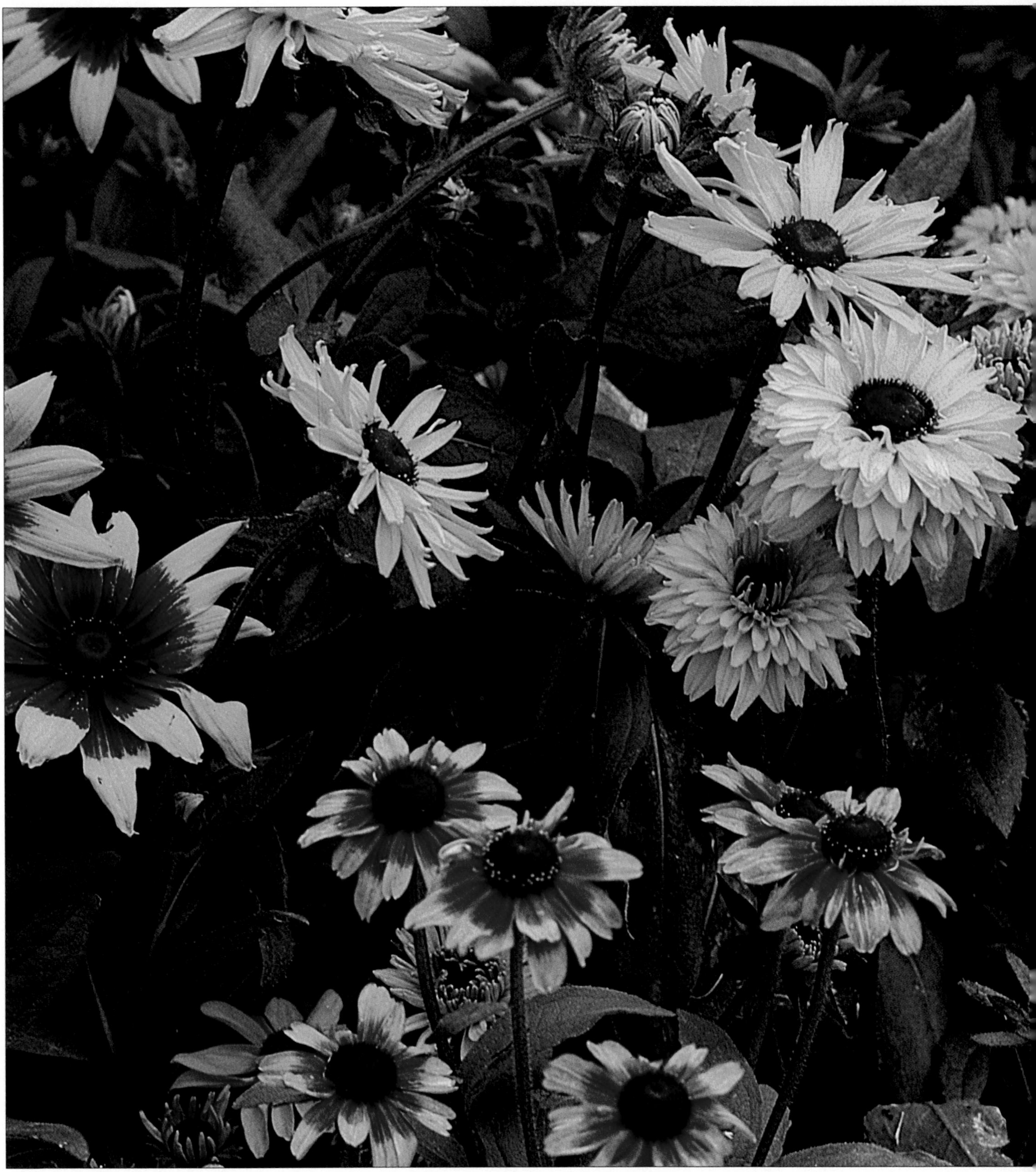

Fall

TREES

NAME OF PLANT	CLIMATE ZONES	YELLOW/ORANGE	RED/PINK	BLUE/PURPLE	WHITE	MULTICOLORED
Bauhinia blakeana	19, 21, 23		■	■		
Erythrina humeana	12, 13, 20–24		■			
Magnolia grandiflora	4–12, 14–24				■	
Melaleuca	Vary		■	■	■	

SHRUBS

NAME OF PLANT	CLIMATE ZONES	Y	R	B	W	M
Brugmansia	16–24		■		■	
Callistemon	8, 9, 12–24		■		■	
Camellia sasanqua	4, 9, 14–24		■		■	■
Cleyera japonica	4–6, 8, 9, 14–24				■	
Erythrina humeana	12, 13, 20–24		■			
Fuchsia magellanica	2–9, 14–24		■	■		
Hydrangea macrophylla	2–24		■	■	■	
Jasminum	Vary	■			■	
Melaleuca (some)	Vary		■	■	■	
Nerium oleander	8–16, 18–23	■	■		■	

VINES

NAME OF PLANT	CLIMATE ZONES	YELLOW/ORANGE	RED/PINK	BLUE/PURPLE	WHITE	MULTICOLORED
Clematis	Vary	■	■	■	■	
Distictis buccinatoria	8, 9, 14–24		■			
Hibbertia scandens	16, 17, 21–24	■				
Mandevilla	Vary		■			

PERENNIALS

NAME OF PLANT	CLIMATE ZONES	Y	R	B	W	M
Anemone hybrida	All		■		■	
Anthemis tinctoria	All	■				
Arctotis	7–9, 14–24	■	■	■	■	■
Aster	All		■	■	■	
Begonia (semperflorens)	All		■		■	
Calceolaria integrifolia	14–24	■	■			
Campanula fragilis	1–7			■	■	
Catharanthus roseus	All		■		■	
Ceratostigma plumbaginoides	2–9, 14–24			■		
Chrysanthemum frutescens	All	■	■		■	
Chrysanthemum maximum	All				■	
Chrysanthemum morifolium	All	■	■	■	■	■
Delphinium	Vary		■	■	■	
Digitalis	All	■	■	■	■	■
Echinops exaltatus	All			■		
Gaillardia grandiflora	All	■	■			■
Gerbera jamesonii	8, 9, 12–24	■	■			
Osteospermum	8, 9, 14–24			■	■	
Sedum spectabile	All		■			
Solidago	All	■				
Stokesia laevis	1–9, 12–24			■	■	

BULBS & BULBLIKE PLANTS

NAME OF PLANT	CLIMATE ZONES	Y	R	B	W	M
Begonia (tuberous)	4–9, 14–24	■	■		■	
Canna	All	■	■		■	
Colchicum autumnale	1–9, 15–24		■	■	■	
Cyclamen (hardy)	1–9, 14–24		■		■	
Dietes	8, 9, 13–24	■			■	
Lycoris	Vary	■	■			
Schizostylis coccinea	5–9, 14–24		■			
Zephyranthes	1–9, 14–24	■	■		■	■

ANNUALS

NAME OF PLANT	CLIMATE ZONES	Y	R	B	W	M
Ageratum houstonianum	All			■		
Calendula officinalis	All	■				
Helianthus	All	■				
Lobularia maritima	10–24		■	■	■	

No flower says "fall" quite as well as chrysanthemum (Chrysanthemum morifolium) in its variety of colors.

Winter

TREES

NAME OF PLANT	CLIMATE ZONES	YELLOW/ORANGE	RED/PINK	BLUE/PURPLE	WHITE	MULTICOLORED
Acacia	Vary	■				
Bauhinia variegata	13, 18–23		■	■		
Erythrina	Vary	■	■			
Melaleuca	Vary		■	■	■	

SHRUBS

NAME OF PLANT	CLIMATE ZONES	Y	R	B	W	M
Acacia	Vary	■				
Camellia	4–9, 14–24		■		■	■
Chaenomeles	1–21		■		■	
Chamelaucium uncinatum	8, 9, 12–24		■			
Erythrina	Vary	■	■			
Euphorbia pulcherrima	13, 16–24		■		■	
Forsythia	2–11, 14–16, 18, 19	■				
Jasminum mesnyi	4–24	■				
Melaleuca	Vary		■	■	■	

PERENNIALS

NAME OF PLANT	CLIMATE ZONES	Y	R	B	W	M
Arctotis	7–9, 14–24	■	■	■	■	■
Bergenia crassifolia	1–9, 14–24		■			
Cymbidium	See Encyclopedia	■	■		■	
Euryops pectinatus	14–17, 19–24	■				
Helleborus	Vary		■	■	■	
Lampranthus	14–24	■	■	■		
Osteospermum	8, 9, 14–24			■	■	
Primula polyantha	1–10, 12–24	■	■	■	■	■
Senecio hybridus	16, 17, 22–24		■	■	■	
Strelitzia reginae	9, 12–24					■
Tulbaghia fragrans	13–24		■	■		

BULBS & BULBLIKE PLANTS

NAME OF PLANT	CLIMATE ZONES	Y	R	B	W	M
Clivia miniata	13–17, 19–24	■	■			
Crocus	All	■		■	■	■
Cyclamen	Vary		■		■	
Eranthis hyemalis	1–9, 14–17	■				
Iris unguicularis	5–24			■		

ANNUALS

NAME OF PLANT	CLIMATE ZONES	Y	R	B	W	M
Antirrhinum majus	All	■	■		■	
Calendula officinalis	All	■				
Dimorphotheca	All	■			■	
Linaria maroccana	10–13	■	■	■		■
Lobularia maritima	10–24		■	■	■	
Matthiola incana	8, 9, 12–24	■	■	■	■	
Papaver nudicaule	All	■	■		■	
Primula malacoides	12–24		■	■	■	
Viola (several)	Vary	■	■	■	■	■

Winter belongs to camellias. Delicate C. japonica 'Magnoliaeflora' has been a favorite for nearly a century.

Cymbidium orchids offer long-lasting flowers in great range of colors throughout winter. This is Tapestry 'Red Duke'.

Fragrant Plants

A garden's fragrance can be as memorable as its appearance; years later, the scent of a particular blossom or leaf can evoke a past experience. Notably aromatic plants are presented here in two groups: those with perfumed flowers and those with fragrant foliage.

Flower fragrance usually is most pronounced on warm and humid days and least noticeable when weather is dry and hot. Many of the aromatic foliage plants release more scent when foliage is moistened, bruised, or brushed against. Note that many of these scented foliage plants also are culinary herbs.

Roses and fragrance seem synonymous; your choice is wide—from the many old rose types to the newest hybrids.

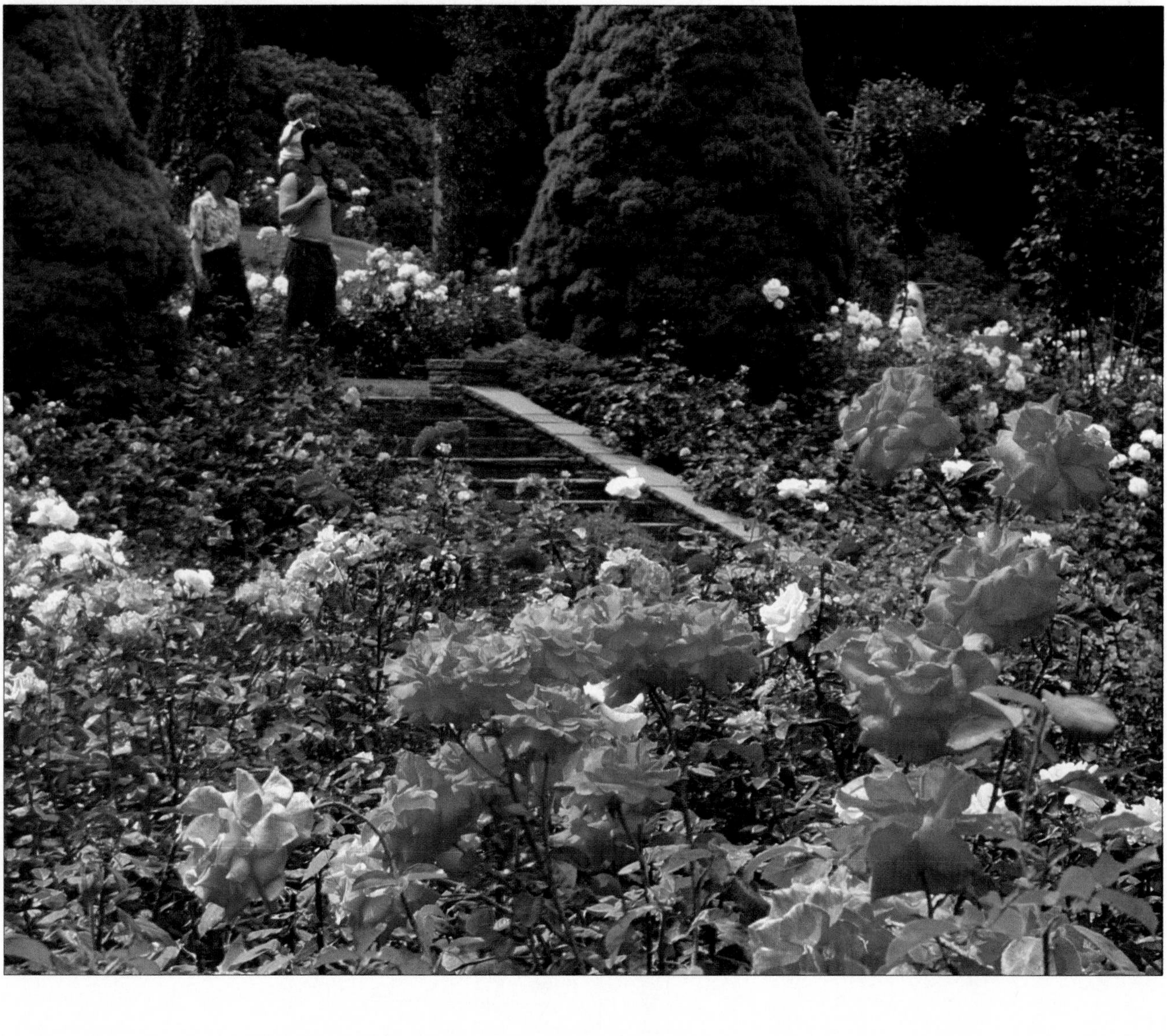

TREES

NAME OF PLANT	CLIMATE ZONES	FLOWERS	FOLIAGE
Calocedrus decurrens	1–12, 14–24		■
Caragana arborescens	1–21	■	
Chionanthus virginicus	1–6, 15–17	■	
Cinnamomum	Vary	■	■
Citrus	Vary	■	
Cryptocarya rubra	14–17, 20–24		■
Cupressus	Vary		■
Dalea spinosa	11–13	■	
Drimys winteri	8, 9, 14–24	■	
Eucalyptus (many)	8–24		■
Hymenosporum flavum	8, 9, 14–23	■	
Idesia polycarpa	4–9, 14–17, 19–24	■	
Laurus nobilis	5–9, 12–24		■
Magnolia grandiflora	4–12, 14–24	■	
Malus	1–11, 14–21	■	
Michelia	Vary	■	
Pinus	Vary		■
Pittosporum eugeniodes	9, 14–17, 19–22	■	
Pittosporum undulatum	16, 17, 21–24	■	
Pittosporum viridiflorum	15–17, 20–24	■	
Prunus blireiana	2–12, 14–22	■	
Robinia pseudoacacia	All	■	
Styrax obassia	3–10, 14–21	■	
Thuja	Vary		■
Tilia	Vary	■	
Umbellularia californica	4–10, 12–24		■
Vitex agnus-castus	4–24		■

SHRUBS

NAME OF PLANT	CLIMATE ZONES	FLOWERS	FOLIAGE
Acacia (several)	Vary	■	
Aloysia triphylla	9, 10, 14–24		■
Artemisia	All		■
Azara (some)	Vary	■	
Boronia megastigma	15–17, 20–24	■	
Bouvardia longiflora 'Albatross'	12, 13, 16, 17, 19–24	■	
Brugmansia candida	16–24	■	
Buddleia	Vary	■	
Calycanthus floridus	1–9, 14–22	■	
Carissa macrocarpa	See encyclopedia	■	
Cestrum nocturnum	13, 16–24	■	
Cestrum parqui	13–24	■	
Chimonanthus praecox	4–9, 14–17	■	
Choisya ternata	4–9, 12–24	■	
Cistus	7–9, 12–24		■
Citrus	Vary	■	
Clerodendrum bungei	5–9, 12–24	■	
Clethra	Varies	■	
Coleonema	7–9, 14–24		■
Corylopsis	4–7, 15–17	■	
Cytisus	Vary	■	
Daphne	Vary	■	
Elaeagnus	Vary	■	

Well-named sweet peas (Lathyrus odoratus) emit penetrating, sweet fragrance from ruffled, silky blossoms.

SHRUBS (*cont'd.*)

NAME OF PLANT	CLIMATE ZONES	FLOWERS	FOLIAGE
Escallonia (some)	4–9, 14–17, 20–24		■
Gardenia	Vary	■	
Hamamelis mollis	4–7, 15–17	■	
Jasminum	Vary	■	
Juniperus	All		■
Lavandula angustifolia	4–24	■	■
Lonicera	Vary	■	
Michelia figo	9, 14–24	■	
Murraya paniculata	21–24	■	
Myrica pensylvanica	4–7		■
Myrtus communis	8–24		■
Origanum	Vary		■
Osmanthus	Vary	■	
Osmarea burkwoodii	4–9, 14–17	■	
Philadelphus (most)	Vary	■	
Pittosporum napaulense	15–17, 20–24	■	
Pittosporum tobira	8–24	■	
Plumeria	Vary	■	
Raphiolepis 'Majestic Beauty'	8–10, 12–24	■	
Rhododendron 'Else Frye'	See Encyclopedia	■	
Rhododendron 'Fragrantissimum'	See Encyclopedia	■	
Rhus aromatica	1–3, 10		■
Ribes viburnifolium	8, 9, 14–24		■
Rosa (many)	All	■	
Rosa eglanteria	All		■
Rosmarinus	4–24		■
Salvia	Vary		■
Sarcococca	4–9, 14–24	■	
Spartium junceum	5–9, 11–24	■	
Styrax officinalis californicus	8, 9, 14–24	■	
Syringa vulgaris	1–12, 14–16, 18–22	■	
Ternstroemia gymnanthera	4–9, 12–24	■	
Viburnum (many)	Vary	■	

VINES

NAME OF PLANT	CLIMATE ZONES	FLOWERS	FOLIAGE
Anredera cordifolia	4–24	■	
Beaumontia grandiflora	12, 13, 16, 17, 21–24	■	
Clematis armandii	4–9, 12–24	■	
Clematis dioscoreifolia	1–6, 15–17	■	
Distictis laxiflora	16, 22–24	■	
Hoya carnosa	15–24	■	
Ipomoea alba	See Encyclopedia	■	
Jasminum	Vary	■	
Lonicera	Vary	■	
Mandevilla laxa	4–9, 14–21	■	
Passiflora alatocaerulea	5–9, 12–24	■	
Stephanotis floribunda	23, 24	■	
Trachelospermum	Vary	■	
Wisteria	All	■	

PERENNIALS, ANNUALS, BULBS

NAME OF PLANT	CLIMATE ZONES	FLOWERS	FOLIAGE
Achillea	All		■
Alpinia zerumbet	15–17, 22–24	■	
Amaryllis belladonna	4–24	■	
Anethum graveolens	All		■
Anthemis	All		■
Chamaemelum nobile	All		■
Cheiranthus cheiri	4–6, 14–17, 22, 23	■	
Chrysanthemum balsamita	All		■
Convallaria majalis	1–7, 14–20	■	
Crinum	12–24	■	
Crocus chrysanthus	All	■	
Dianthus	All	■	
Dictamnus albus	1–9		■
Foeniculum vulgare	All		■
Freesia	8, 9, 12–24	■	
Galium odoratum	1–6, 15–17		■
Hedychium	17, 22–24	■	
Heliotropium arborescens	8–24	■	
Hemerocallis lilioasphodelus	All	■	
Hosta plantaginea	1–10, 12–21	■	
Hyacinthus	All	■	
Hymenocallis	5, 6, 8, 9, 14–24	■	
Hyssopus officinalis	All		■
Iberis amara	All	■	
Iris (bearded)	All	■	
Lathyrus odoratus	All	■	
Leucocoryn ixioides	13, 16, 19, 21–24	■	
Lilium	All	■	
Lobularia maritima	All	■	
Marrubium vulgare	All		■
Matthiola	All	■	
Melissa officinalis	All		■
Mentha	Vary		■
Milla biflora	13, 16–24	■	
Monarda	All		■
Narcissus (many)	All	■	
Nelumbo	All	■	
Nepeta	All		■
Nicotiana	All	■	
Paeonia	Vary	■	
Pelargonium (several)	8, 9, 12–24		■
Polianthes tuberosa	24	■	
Primula alpicola	1–6, 17	■	
Reseda odorata	All	■	
Ruta graveolens	All		■
Salvia	Vary		■
Satureja	Vary		■
Tanacetum vulgare	All		■
Tagetes	All		■
Thymus	All		■
Tropaeolum majus	See Encyclopedia	■	
Viola odorata	All	■	

Autumn Foliage Color

Plants that change leaf color in fall do so in varying degrees, depending on the nature of the plant and the kind of climate it grows in (generally, the change is less noticeable in mild-winter areas than in cold-winter regions). The plants listed below display an autumnal foliage change that will attract attention; many are worth planting for that reason alone.

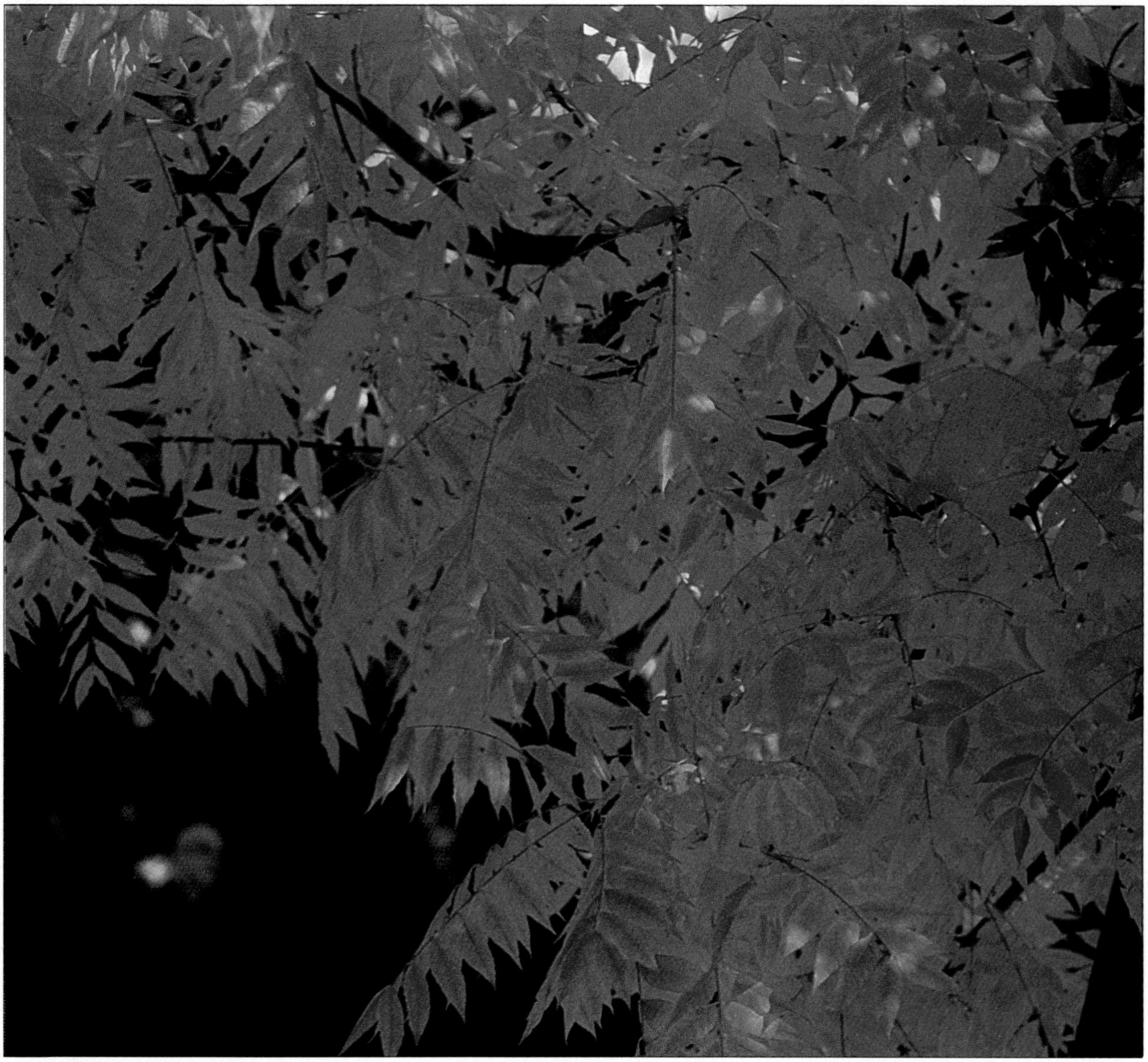

Fall foliage color isn't limited to cold-winter regions. Mild zones can enjoy Chinese pistache (Pistacia chinensis).

TREES

NAME OF PLANT	CLIMATE ZONES
Acer (many)	Vary
Amelanchier	1–6
Betula occidentalis	1–3, 10
Betula pendula	1–11, 14–24
Cercidiphyllum japonicum	1–6, 14–16, 18–20
Cercis	Vary
Cladrastis lutea	1–9, 14–16
Cornus	Vary
Crataegus	1–11, 14–17
Fagus sylvatica	1–9, 14–24
Franklinia alatamaha	2–6, 14–17
Fraxinus (deciduous species)	Vary
Ginkgo biloba	1–9, 14–24
Gleditsia triacanthos	1–16, 18–20
Gymnocladus dioica	1–3, 7–10, 12–16, 18–21
Halesia	2–9, 14–24
Hamamelis mollis	4–7, 15–17
Koelreuteria bipinnata	8–24
Lagerstroemia indica	4–9, 12–14, 18–21
Larix	Vary
Liquidambar	Vary
Liriodendron tulipifera	1–11, 14–23
Malus	1–11, 14–21
Nyssa sylvatica	3–10, 14–21
Oxydendrum arboreum	3–9, 14–17
Pear	1–11, 14–18
Persimmon	Vary
Pistacia chinensis	4–16, 18–23
Populus	Vary
Prunus (deciduous)	Vary
Pyrus (deciduous)	Vary
Quercus coccinea	All
Quercus kelloggii	5–7, 15, 16, 18–21
Quercus palustris	All
Quercus phellos	1–4, 6–16, 18–21
Quercus rubra	1–12, 14–24
Salix	All
Sapium sebiferum	8, 9, 12, 14–16, 18–21
Sassafras albidum	4–6, 10, 12, 14–17
Sorbus aucuparia	1–10, 14–17
Styrax japonicus	3–10, 14–21
Taxodium distichum	1–9, 14–24
Zelkova serrata	3–21

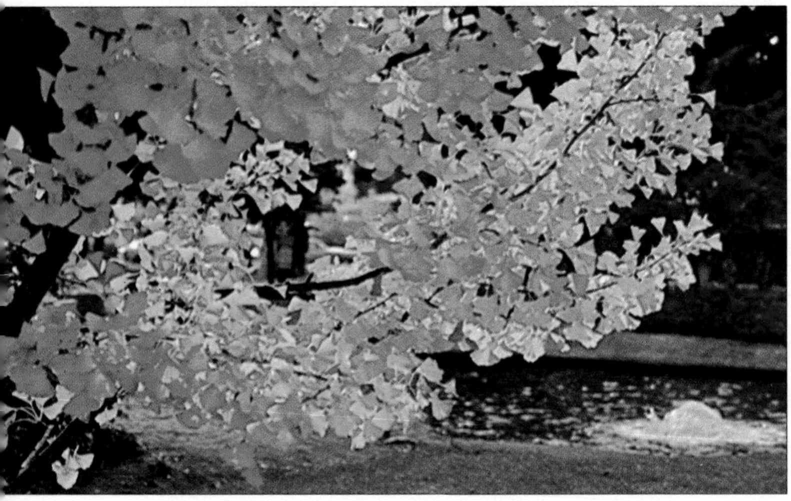

Maidenhair tree (Ginkgo biloba) is renowned for its annual display of luminous yellow fall foliage.

SHRUBS

NAME OF PLANT	CLIMATE ZONES
Amelanchier	1–6
Aronia arbutifolia	1–7
Berberis thunbergii	1–11, 14–17
Blueberry	2–9, 14–17
Cercis	Vary
Cornus	Vary
*Cotinus coggygria	All
Cotoneaster divaricatus	All
Cotoneaster horizontalis	1–11, 14–24
Crataegus	1–11, 14–17
Cryptomeria japonica 'Elegans'	4–9, 14–24
Enkianthus	2–9, 14–21
Euonymus alata	1–9, 14–16
Fothergilla	3–9, 14–17
Hamamelis virginiana	1–9, 14–16, 18–21
Hydrangea quercifolia	1–22
Kerria japonica	1–21
Lagerstroemia indica	4–9, 12–14, 18–21
*Magnolia salicifolia	2–9, 14–21
*Malus (some)	1–11, 14–21
Nandina domestica	5–24
*Parrotia persica	4–6, 15–17
Photinia villosa	1–6
*Punica granatum	7–24
*Rhamnus purshiana	1–9, 14–17
Rhododendron (deciduous azalea hybrids)	4–7, 14–17
Rhododendron schlippenbachii	4–6, 14–17
*Rhus glabra	1–10, 14–17
*Rhus typhina	1–10, 14–17
Salix	Vary
Spiraea (several)	1–11, 14–21
Stachyurus praecox	4–6, 14–17
*Stewartia	4–6, 14–17, 20, 21
Viburnum (many)	Vary

*Can become small tree.

PERENNIALS, ANNUALS, VINES

NAME OF PLANT	CLIMATE ZONES
Grape	Vary
Kochia scoparia trichophylla	All
Parthenocissus	Vary
Saxifraga rosacea	1–7, 14–17
Sedum sieboldii	All
Wisteria	All

Colorful Fruits & Berries

These plants offer garden color in the form of colorful fruit or seed capsules. Some produce this color in addition to flower display; others, as a surprise following an inconspicuous blossoming.

Even in the black-and-white of winter, Cotoneaster horizontalis will continue to add its touch of red fruits.

TREES

NAME OF PLANT	CLIMATE ZONES
Acmena smithii	15–17, 19–24
Citrus	Vary
Cornus nuttallii	2–9, 14–20
Crataegus	1–11, 14–17
Ilex	Vary
Koelreuteria	Vary
Malus	1–11, 14–21
Persimmon	Vary
Pittosporum rhombifolium	12–24
Schinus	Vary
Sorbus	1–10, 14–17
Syzygium paniculatum	16, 17, 19–24

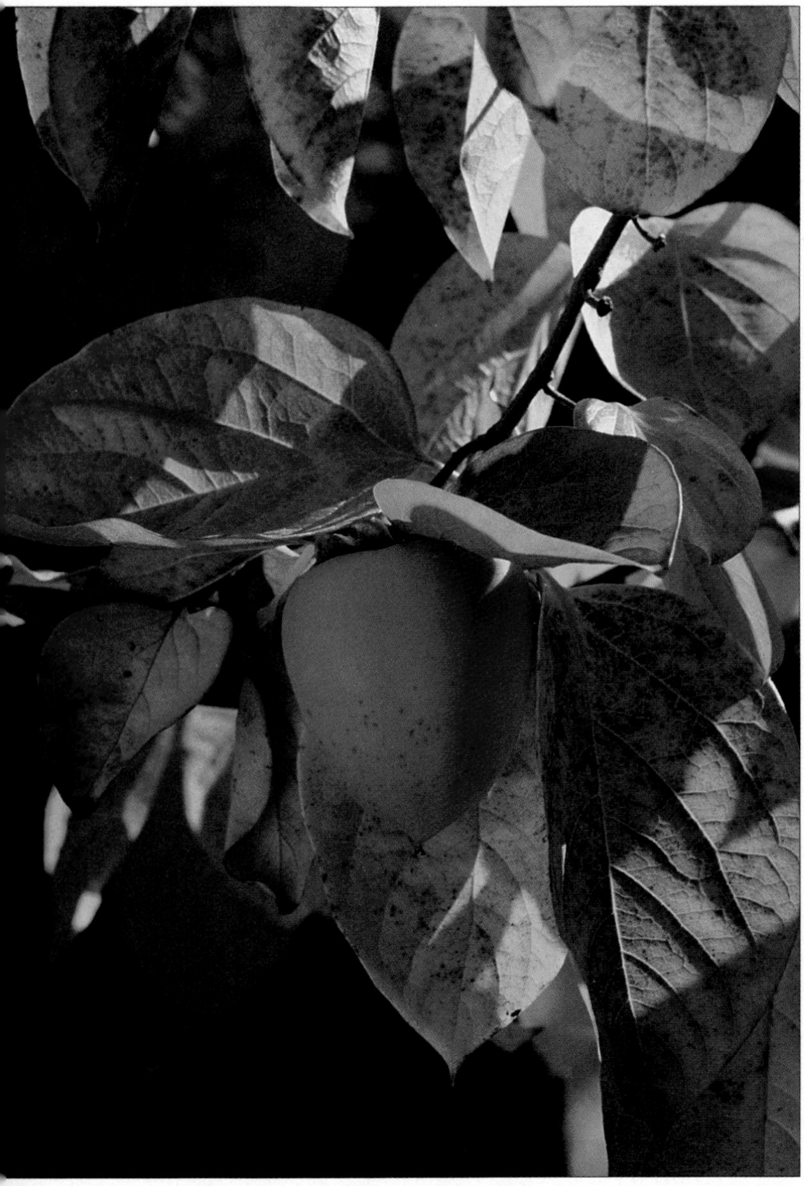

SHRUBS

NAME OF PLANT	CLIMATE ZONES
*Arbutus unedo	4–24
Aronia arbutifolia	1–7
Berberis darwinii	1–11, 14–17
Berberis thunbergii	1–11, 14–17
Berberis wilsoniae	1–11, 14–17
Callicarpa bodinieri giraldii	1–6
Carissa macrocarpa	22–24
Cestrum	Vary
*Clerodendrum trichotomum	15–17, 20–24
*Cornus kousa	3–9, 14, 15, 18, 19
*Cornus mas	1–6
Corokia cotoneaster	4–24
*Corylus	1–9, 14–20
Cotoneaster	Vary
Daphne mezereum	1–7, 14–17
Duranta	Vary
Elaeagnus	Vary
Euonymus alata	1–9, 14–16
Euonymus fortunei 'Carrierei', 'Vegeta'	1–17
Euonymus kiautschovica	1–13
*Heteromeles arbutifolia	5–24
Ilex	Vary
Kolkwitzia amabilis	1–11, 14–20
Lonicera (most shrubby types)	Vary
Mahonia	Vary
Malus	1–11, 14–21
Nandina domestica	5–24
Ochna serrulata	14–24
Pernettya mucronata	4–7, 15–17
*Photinia serrulata	4–16, 18–22
Photinia villosa	1–6
*Punica granatum	5–24
Pyracantha	Vary
Rhapiolepis	8–10, 12–24
Sarcococca ruscifolia	4–9, 14–24
Skimmia	4–9, 14–22
Solanum pseudocapsicum	23, 24
*Stranvaesia davidiana	4–11, 14–17
Symphoricarpos	Vary
*Taxus	3–9, 14–24
Ugni molinae	14–24
Vaccinium	Vary
Viburnum (many)	Vary

*Can become small tree.

PERENNIALS, VINES

NAME OF PLANT	CLIMATE ZONES
Ampelopsis brevipedunculata	All
Arum italicum	4–6, 8–24
Celastrus	1–7
Dianella tasmanica	8, 9, 14–24
Ophiopogon jaburan	5–10, 12–24

Persimmons provide fall foliage color as well as colorful, edible fruits which remain on the tree after leaves drop.

Plants with Colored Foliage

Not all color comes from flowers or fruit. Here are candidates for long-term garden accents in the form of colored leaves: gray, red or bronze, yellow, blue, and variegated. They can be used to enliven the basic green of other garden foliage, to form contrasting combinations (such as gray and red) with one another, and to complement flower colors in season.

Gray

TREES

NAME OF PLANT	CLIMATE ZONES
Cupressus glabra	5, 8–24
Eucalyptus baueriana	8–24
Eucalyptus caesia	8–24
Eucalyptus globulus 'Compacta'	8–24
Eucalyptus kruseana	8–24
Eucalyptus leucoxylon	8–24
Eucalyptus macrocarpa	8–24
Eucalyptus pulverulenta	8–24
Eucalyptus rhodantha	8–24
Juniperus scopulorum (some)	All

SHRUBS

NAME OF PLANT	CLIMATE ZONES
Artemisia	All
Atriplex	Vary
Convolvulus cneorum	7–9, 12–24
Elaeagnus 'Coral Silver'	All
Juniperus (some)	All
Leucodendron argenteum	16, 17, 20–24
Leucophyllum frutescens	7–24
Mahonia nevinii	8–24
Pimelea prostrata	4–7, 14–17
Salvia leucophylla	10–24
Santolina chamaecyparissus	All
Teucrium fruticans	4–24
Zauschneria cana	2–10, 12–24

PERENNIALS, ANNUALS

NAME OF PLANT	CLIMATE ZONES
Achillea	All
Artemisia	All
Artichoke	8, 9, 14–24
Calocephalus brownii	16, 17, 19, 21–24
Centaurea (perennial kinds)	8–24
Cerastium tomentosum	All
Cotyledon orbiculata	16, 17, 21–24

As colorful as flowers are burgundy leaves of Acer palmatum 'Ornatum' and green-and-white Hosta undulata 'Variegata'.

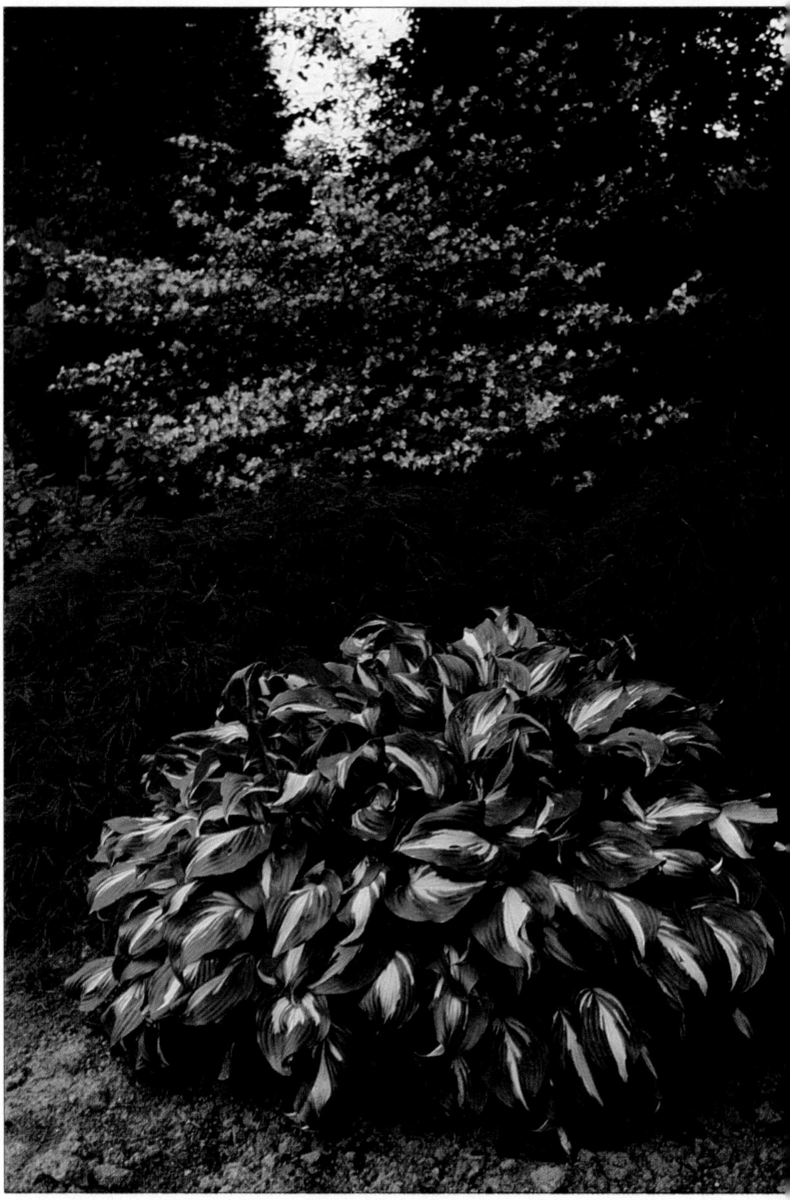

Silvery gray to white foliage is feature of many Artemisia species; this is A. ludoviciana albula.

PERENNIALS (*cont'd.*)

NAME OF PLANT	CLIMATE ZONES
Dudleya	16, 17, 21–24
Echeveria (many)	Vary
Euryops	14–17, 19–24
Graptopetalum	8–24
Kalanchoe beharensis	21–24
Lavandula (most)	Vary
Leontopodium alpinum	1–9, 14–24
Lotus berthelotii	9, 15–24
Lychnis coronaria	All
Origanum dictamnus	8–24
Sempervivum	All
Senecio cineraria	All
Senecio vira-vira	All
Stachys byzantina	All

Bronze, Red

TREES

NAME OF PLANT	CLIMATE ZONES
Acer palmatum (some)	1–9, 14–24
Acer platanoides (some)	1–9, 14–17
Cercis canadensis 'Forest Pansy'	1–3, 7–20
Cordyline australis 'Atropurpurea'	5, 8–11, 14–24
Corylus maxima 'Purpurea'	1–9, 14–20
Cotinus coggygria (some)	All
Fagus sylvatica (some)	1–9, 14–24
Prunus blireiana	2–12, 14–22
Prunus cerasifera (some)	2–22

SHRUBS

NAME OF PLANT	CLIMATE ZONES
Acokanthera	21, 23, 24
Cordyline terminalis (some)	21–24
Corylus avellana 'Fusco-Rubra'	1–9, 14–20
Dodonaea viscosa 'Purpurea', 'Saratoga'	7–9, 12–24
Prunus cistena	2–12, 14–22
Pseudopanax crassifolius	16, 17, 21–24

PERENNIALS

NAME OF PLANT	CLIMATE ZONES
Aechmea hybrids	22–24
Aeonium arboreum 'Atropurpureum'	15–17, 20–24
Ajuga reptans varieties	All
Astilbe 'Fanal'	2–7, 14–17
Caladium bicolor	See Encyclopedia
Canna (some)	All
Crassula corymbulosa	16, 17, 22–24
Kalanchoe laciniata	17, 21–24
Pennisetum setaceum 'Cupreum'	All
Phormium tenax varieties	7–24
Sedum spathulifolium 'Purpureum'	All
Sedum spurium 'Dragon's Blood'	All

Yellow, Golden

TREES

NAME OF PLANT	CLIMATE ZONES
Acer japonicum 'Aureum'	1–6, 14–16
Chamaecyparis lawsoniana	4–6, 15–17
Gleditsia triacanthos 'Sunburst'	1–16, 18–20
Robinia pseudoacacia 'Frisia'	All
Thuja plicata 'Aurea'	1–9, 14–24

SHRUBS, PERENNIALS

NAME OF PLANT	CLIMATE ZONES
Chamaecyparis lawsoniana (some)	4–6, 15–17
Chrysanthemum parthenium 'Aureum'	All
Juniperus (several)	All
Ligustrum 'Vicaryi'	All
Milium effusum 'Aureum'	All
Platycladus orientalis (several)	All
Taxus baccata (several)	3–9, 14–24
Thuja occidentalis 'Rheingold'	2–9, 15–17, 21–24

Blue

TREES

NAME OF PLANT	CLIMATE ZONES
Chamaecyparis lawsoniana (some)	4–6, 15–17
Cunninghamia lanceolata 'Glauca'	4–6, 14–21
Eucalyptus niphophila	8–24
Juniperus deppeana pachyphlaea	All
Juniperus occidentalis	All
Picea pungens (some)	1–10, 14–17

SHRUBS, PERENNIALS

NAME OF PLANT	CLIMATE ZONES
Chamaecyparis lawsoniana (some)	4–6, 15–17
Eucalyptus macrocarpa	8–24
Eucalyptus rhodantha	8–24
Festuca ovina glauca	All

Variegated

TREES

NAME OF PLANT	CLIMATE ZONES
Acer negundo 'Variegatum'	1–10, 12–24
Cornus florida 'Welchii'	1–9, 14–16
Cornus nuttallii 'Goldspot'	2–9, 14–20
Fagus sylvatica 'Tricolor'	1–9, 14–24
Ilex (various)	Vary

SHRUBS

NAME OF PLANT	CLIMATE ZONES
Aucuba japonica (several)	4–24
Bougainvillea 'Brilliant Variegated'	12, 13, 15–17, 19, 21–24
Buxus sempervirens 'Aureo-Variegata'	3–6, 15–17
Coprosma repens 'Argentea', 'Variegata'	15–17, 21–24
Cotoneaster horizontalis 'Variegatus'	1–11, 14–24
Daphne odora (some)	4–9, 14–24
Elaeagnus pungens (some)	4–24
Euonymus (some)	Vary
Fatsia japonica 'Variegata'	4–9, 13–24
Griselinia littoralis 'Variegata'	9, 15–17, 20–24
Griselinia lucida 'Variegata'	9, 15–17, 20–24
Hydrangea macrophylla 'Tricolor'	2–24
Ilex (various)	Vary
Juniperus (various)	All
Leucothoe fontanesiana 'Rainbow'	4–7, 15–17
Myrtus communis 'Compacta Variegata', 'Variegata'	8–24
Osmanthus heterophyllus 'Variegatus'	3–10, 14–24
Pieris japonica 'Variegata'	1–9, 14–17
Pittosporum tobira 'Variegata'	8–24
Rhamnus alaternus 'Variegata'	4–24
Salvia officinalis 'Tricolor'	All
Taxus baccata 'Stricta Variegata'	3–9, 14–24
Viburnum tinus 'Variegatum'	4–9, 14–23
Weigela florida 'Variegata'	1–11, 14–17

VINES

NAME OF PLANT	CLIMATE ZONES
Actinidia kolomikta	4–9, 15–17
Euonymus fortunei (some)	1–17
Fatshedera lizei 'Variegata'	4–10, 12–24
Hedera (some)	Vary
Lonicera japonica 'Aureoreticulata'	2–24

PERENNIALS, ANNUALS

NAME OF PLANT	CLIMATE ZONES
Aegopodium podagraria 'Variegatum'	1–7
Aloe saponaria	8, 9, 12–24
Aloe variegata	8, 9, 12–24
Arabis caucasica 'Variegata'	All
Caladium bicolor	See Encyclopedia
Coleus hybridus	All
Euphorbia marginata	All

PERENNIALS, ANNUALS (*cont'd.*)

NAME OF PLANT	CLIMATE ZONES
Hakonechloa macra 'Aureola'	All
Hosta (various)	1–10, 12–21
Houttuynia cordata 'Variegata'	4–9, 14–24
Ligularia tussilaginea 'Argentea', 'Aureo-maculata'	4–10, 14–24
Liriope muscari 'Silvery Sunproof', 'Variegata'	5–10, 12–24
Pachysandra terminalis 'Variegata'	1–10, 14–21
Pelargonium hortorum (several)	8, 9, 12–24
Pelargonium peltatum (several)	8, 9, 12–24
Phormium tenax 'Variegatum'	7–24
Portulacaria afra 'Foliis Variegatis', 'Variegata'	13, 16, 17, 22–24
Sansevieria trifasciata	12–24
Sedum sieboldii 'Variegatum'	All
Thymus citriodorus 'Argenteus', 'Aureus'	All
Thymus vulgaris 'Argenteus'	All
Tradescantia fluminensis 'Variegata'	12–24
Tulbaghia violacea (some)	13–24
Vinca major (variegated form)	5–24
Vinca minor (variegated form)	All
Zantedeschia albomaculata	5, 6, 8, 9, 14–24
Zantedeschia elliottiana	5, 6, 8, 9, 14–24

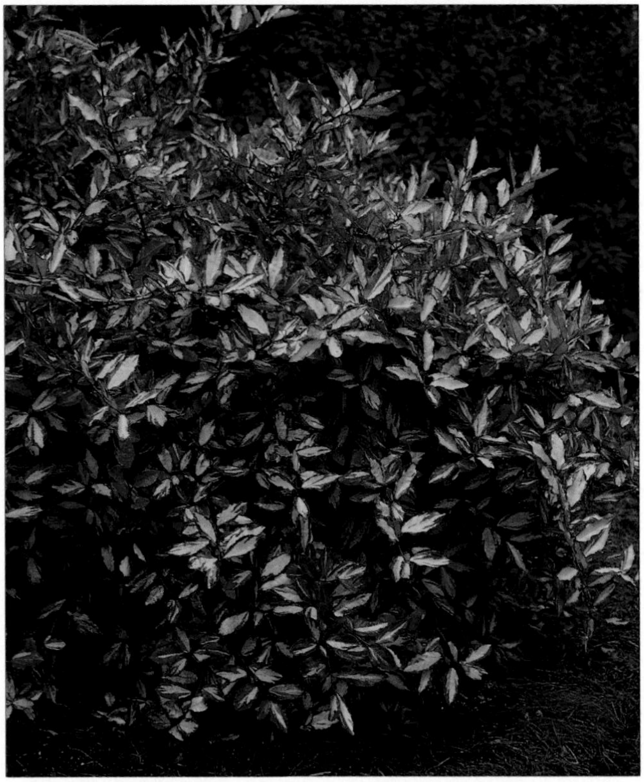

Each leaf prominently marked with yellow, Elaeagnus pungens 'Maculata' serves as an all-year accent shrub.

Plants that Attract Birds

If you like to have birds in your garden, you can include some of these plants in your landscaping. Remember, though, that if your attempt to lure birds succeeds, you probably won't get full enjoyment from plants that produce enticing fruit: birds will eat them just when they become colorful.

Most plants with flowers listed as attractants are ones that hummingbirds visit in their search for flower nectar.

Fruit

TREES

NAME OF PLANT	CLIMATE ZONES
Amelanchier laevis	1–6
Arbutus	Vary
Carpinus caroliniana	1–9, 14–17
Celtis	Vary
Cornus	Vary
Crataegus	1–11, 14–17
Eriobotrya japonica	4–24
Fig (edible)	4–9, 12–24
Malus	1–11, 14–21
Morus	Vary
Persimmon	Vary
Prunus	Vary
Sambucus	Vary
Schinus	Vary
Sorbus	1–10, 14–17

SHRUBS

NAME OF PLANT	CLIMATE ZONES
*Arbutus unedo	4–24
Arctostaphylos	Vary
Aronia arbutifolia	1–7
Blackberry	Vary
Callicarpa bodinieri ginaldii	1–6
Carissa macrocarpa	22–24
Cestrum	Vary
Cornus	Vary
Cotoneaster	Vary
Elaeagnus	Vary
Euonymus	Vary
Garrya	Vary
Gaultheria	4–7, 14–17
Grape	Vary
*Heteromeles arbutifolia	5–24
*Ilex	Vary
Lantana	8–10, 12, 24

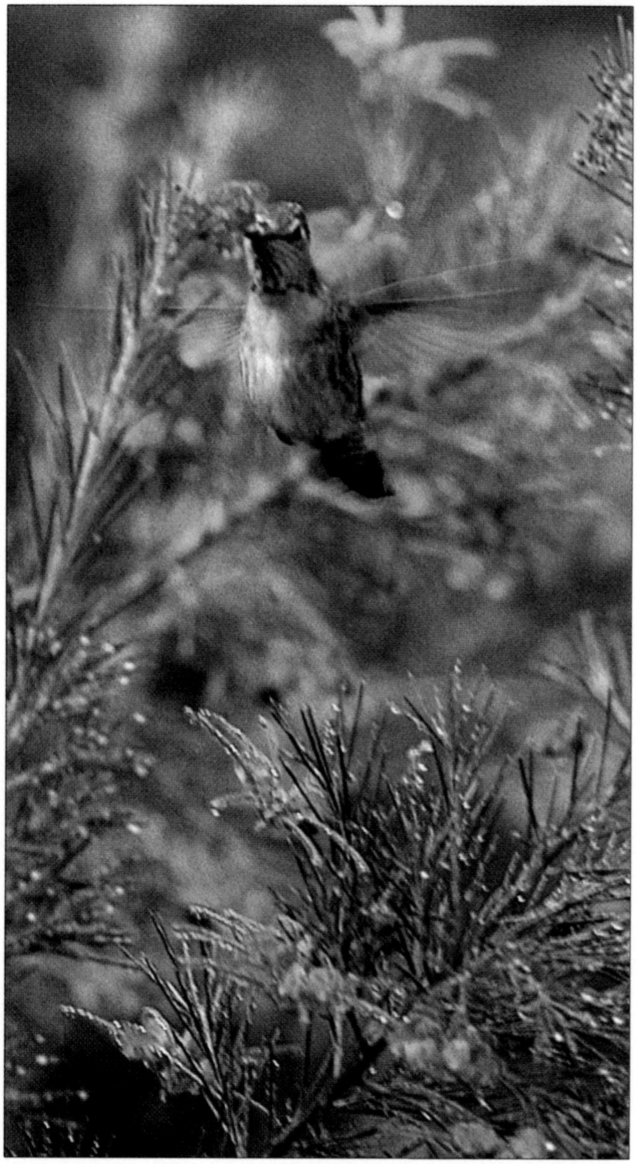
Hummingbird proves that blossoms of Grevillea are attractive nectar sources: G. 'Canberra' entices this hummer.

SHRUBS (*cont'd.*)

NAME OF PLANT	CLIMATE ZONES
Ligustrum	Vary
Lonicera	Vary
Mahonia	Vary
*Myrica	Vary
*Photinia	Vary
*Prunus	Vary
Pyracantha	Vary
*Rhamnus purshiana	1–9, 14–17
Rhus laurina	20–24
Ribes	Vary
Rosa multiflora	All
Rubus deliciosus	1–5, 10
Symphoricarpos	Vary
Vaccinium	Vary
Viburnum	Vary

*Can become small tree.

PERENNIALS, VINES

NAME OF PLANT	CLIMATE ZONES
Ampelopsis brevipedunculata	All
Duchesnea indica	All
Fragaria	4–24
Lonicera	Vary
Parthenocissus	Vary

Seeds

TREES

NAME OF PLANT	CLIMATE ZONES
Abies	Vary
Alnus	Vary
Betula	Vary
Cercidium	10–14, 18–20
Fagus sylvatica	1–9, 14–24
Larix	Vary
Picea	Vary
Pinus	Vary
Quercus	Vary
Ulmus	Vary

SHRUBS, PERENNIALS, ANNUALS

NAME OF PLANT	CLIMATE ZONES
Ageratum houstonianum	All
Atriplex	Vary
Coreopsis	Vary
Cosmos	All
Helianthus annuus	All
Lonicera	Vary
Rosmarinus officinalis	4–24
Solidago	All
Tagetes	All

Flowers

TREES

NAME OF PLANT	CLIMATE ZONES
Acacia	Vary
Albizia	Vary
Cercidium	10–14, 18–20
Citrus	8, 9, 12–24
Eriobotrya	Vary
Eucalyptus platypus	8–24
Melia azedarach	6, 8–24

SHRUBS

NAME OF PLANT	CLIMATE ZONES
Abutilon	13, 15–24
Acacia	Vary
Buddleia	Vary
Caesalpinia gilliesii	8–16, 18–23
Callistemon	8, 9, 12–24
Ceanothus	4–7, 14–24
Cestrum	Vary
Chaenomeles	1–21
Chilopsis linearis	11–13, 18–21
Feijoa sellowiana	7–9, 12–24
Fuchsia	Vary
Grevillea lanigera	15–24
Holodiscus discolor	1–7, 14–17
Justicia brandegeana	12, 13, 15–17, 21–24
Kolkwitzia amabilis	1–11, 14–20
Lonicera	Vary
Melaleuca	Vary
Ribes	Vary
Rosmarinus officinalis	4–24
Weigela	1–11, 14–17

PERENNIALS, VINES

NAME OF PLANT	CLIMATE ZONES
Alcea rosea	All
Aloe	8, 9, 12–24
Antirrhinum	All
Aquilegia	All
Campsis radicans	1–21
Delphinium	Vary
Digitalis	All
Heuchera	Vary
Impatiens	Vary
Kniphofia uvaria	1–9, 14–24
Lobelia cardinalis	1–7, 13–17
Lonicera	Vary
Mimulus	Vary
Monarda didyma	All
Nicotiana	All
Penstemon	Vary
Phlox	Vary
Tecomaria capensis	12–16, 18–24
Zauschneria	2–10, 12–24

Shade-tolerant Plants

Shade, whether cast by leafy trees, north-facing walls, or an overhead, is characterized by lower light intensity and cooler atmosphere than are nearby sunny locations. Many plants that thrive on sunlight and warmth fail to perform in the different environment that shade provides. In these lists are trees, shrubs, vines, perennials, and annuals that tolerate shade; many prefer *it.*

High shade, cool atmosphere, and moist soil combine to create near-ideal environment for mass planting of candelabra primroses.

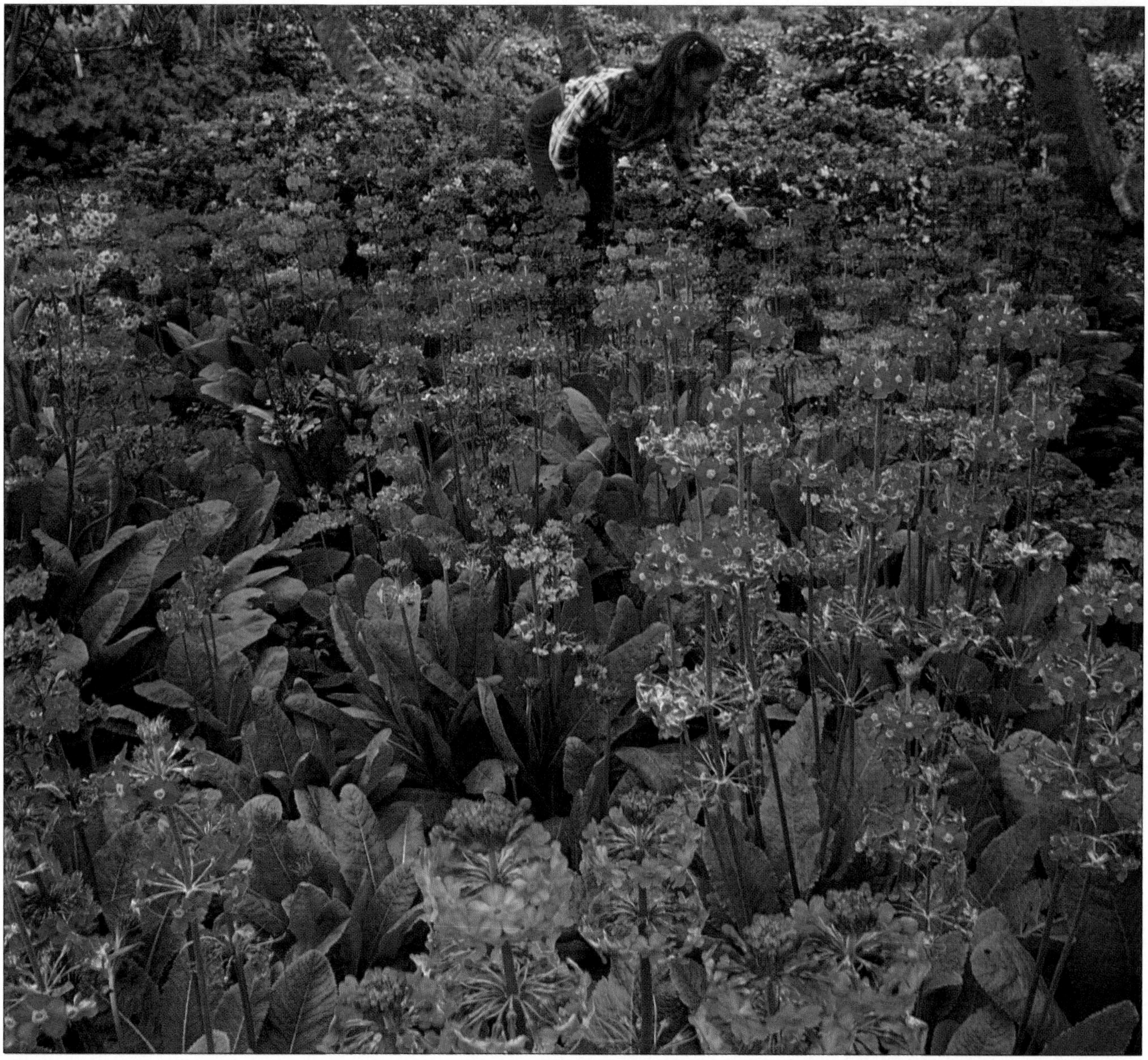

TREES

NAME OF PLANT	CLIMATE ZONES
Acer circinatum	1–6, 14–17
Acer palmatum	1–9, 14–24
Arbutus unedo	4–24
Corynocarpus laevigata	16, 17, 23, 24
Ficus	Vary
Ilex	Vary
Laurus nobilis	5–9, 12–24
Lithocarpus densiflorus	4–7, 14–24
Olmediella betschlerana	9, 14–24
Palms	Vary
Podocarpus	Vary
Pseudopanax lessonii	17, 20–24
Schefflera	Vary
Stenocarpus sinuatus	16, 17, 20–24
Strelitzia nicolai	22–24
Tree ferns	Vary
Tupidanthus calyptratus	19–24
Umbellularia californica	4–10, 12–24

SHRUBS

NAME OF PLANT	CLIMATE ZONES
Abutilon	13, 15–24
Ardisia japonica	5, 6, 15–17
Aucuba japonica	4–24
Azalea (rhododendron)	Vary
Azara	Vary
Brunfelsia pauciflora calycina	13–17, 20–24
Buxus	Vary
Calycanthus	Vary
Camellia	4–9, 14–24
Cantua buxifolia	16–24
Carpenteria californica	5–9, 14–24
Cleyera japonica	4–6, 8, 9, 14–24
Cocculus laurifolius	8, 9, 12–24
Coprosma repens	15–17, 21–24
Cordyline stricta	16, 17, 20–24
Cycads	Vary
Daphne odora	4–9, 14–24
Dizygotheca elegantissima	16, 17, 22–24
Enkianthus	2–9, 14–21
Euonymus fortunei	1–17
Fatsia japonica	4–9, 13–24
Fuchsia	Vary
Gardenia jasminoides	7–9, 12–16, 18–23
Gaultheria	Vary
Griselinia lucida	9, 15–17, 20–24
Hydrangea	Vary
Ilex	Vary
Itea ilicifolia	4–24
Juniperus	All
Kalmia	1–7, 16, 17
Kalmiopsis leachiana	4–6, 14–17
Leucothoe	Vary
Loropetalum chinense	6–9, 14–24
Mahonia nervosa	2–9, 14–17
Nandina domestica	5–24

SHRUBS (*cont'd.*)

NAME OF PLANT	CLIMATE ZONES
Olmediella betschlerana	9, 14–24
Osmanthus	Vary
Pernettya mucronata	4–7, 15–17
Philodendron selloum	8, 9, 12–24
Pieris	Vary
Pittosporum	Vary
Rhamnus purshiana	1–9, 14–17
Rhapis	Vary
Rhododendron	Vary
Ruscus	4–24
Sarcococca	4–9, 14–24
Skimmia	4–9, 14–22
Stachyurus praecox	4–6, 14–17
Symphoricarpos	Vary
Taxus	3–9, 14–24
Ternstroemia gymnanthera	4–9, 12–24
Vaccinium	Vary
Viburnum davidii	4–9, 14–24
Viburnum suspensum	8–10, 13–24

VINES

NAME OF PLANT	CLIMATE ZONES
Cissus	Vary
Fatshedera lizei	4–10, 12–24
Hedera	Vary
Hoya carnosa	15–24
Monstera deliciosa	21–24
Parthenocissus	Vary
Rhoicissus capensis	16, 17, 21–24
Trachelospermum jasminoides	8–24

PERENNIALS, BULBS, ANNUALS

NAME OF PLANT	CLIMATE ZONES
Acanthus mollis	4–24
Aconitum	1–9, 14–21
Aegopodium podagraria	1–7
Ajuga	All
Alpinia zerumbet	15–17, 22–24
Anemone hybrids	All
Aquilegia	All
Arum	4–6, 8–24
Asarum caudatum	4–6, 14–17, 21
Aspidistra elatior	4–9, 12–24
Astilbe	2–7, 14–17
Begonia	Vary
Bergenia	1–9, 14–24
Billbergia	16–24
Browallia	All
Caladium bicolor	See Encyclopedia
Calceolaria crenatiflora	14–24
Calceolaria 'John Innes'	All
Campanula	Vary
Clivia miniata	13–17, 19–24
Coleus hybridus	See Encyclopedia
Colocasia esculenta	See Encyclopedia

All Impatiens can add spark to shady gardens; some New Guinea hybrids, such as 'Osage', also contribute variegated foliage.

PERENNIALS, BULBS, ANNUALS (*cont'd.*)

NAME OF PLANT	CLIMATE ZONES
Convallaria majalis	1–7, 14–20
Cotula squalida	4–9, 14–24
Crassula	8, 9, 12–24
Cymbalaria muralis	3–24
Cymbidium	See Encyclopedia
Dianella tasmanica	8, 9, 14–24
Dicentra	1–9, 14–24
Digitalis	All
Doronicum	1–7, 14–17
Duchesnea indica	All
Epimedium	1–9, 14–17
Erythronium	1–7, 15–17
Ferns	Vary
Galax urceolata	1–6
Haemanthus katherinae	See Encyclopedia
Hedychium	17, 22–24
Helleborus	Vary
Hosta	1–10, 12–21
Houttuynia cordata	4–9, 14–24
Impatiens oliveri	15–17, 21–24
Impatiens wallerana	All
Iris foetidissima	All
Iris (crested)	Vary
Kalanchoe beharensis	21–24
Ligularia tussilaginea	4–10, 14–24
Lilium	All
Liriope	Vary
Lysimachia nummularia	1–9, 14–24
Maianthemum dilatatum	1–9, 14–17
Meconopsis betonicifolia	1–7, 17
Mertensia	1–21
Mimulus hybridus	All
Monarda	All
Myosotis	All
Narcissus	All
Ophiopogon	5–10, 12–24
Oxalis oregana	4–9, 14–24
Pachysandra terminalis	1–10, 14–21
Phlox divaricata	1–17
Polemonium	1–11, 14–17
Polygonatum	1–7, 15–17
Primula	Vary
Pulmonaria	1–9, 14–17
Ranunculus repens 'Pleniflorus'	All
Rehmannia elata	7–10, 12–24
Rohdea japonica	4–9, 14–24
Sanguinaria canadensis	1–6
Sansevieria trifasciata	12–24
Saxifraga stolonifera	1–9, 14–24
Saxifraga umbrosa	1–7, 14–17
Schizanthus pinnatus	1–6, 15–17, 21–24
Scilla	Vary
Sedum morganianum	13–24
Senecio hybridus	All
Shortia	1–7
Smilacina racemosa	1–7, 15–17
Soleirolia soleirolii	8–24
Strelitzia	Vary
Streptocarpus	17, 22–24
Thalictrum	All
Tolmiea menziesii	5–9, 12–24
Tradescantia	Vary
Tricyrtis	1–9, 14–17
Trillium	Vary
Trollius	All
Vancouveria	Vary
Vinca	Vary
Viola	Vary
Zantedeschia	5, 6, 8, 9, 14–24

Plants that Grow in Wet Soil

Water must pass through the root area quickly or plants will suffer from lack of oxygen (see "How Often to Water," page 68). Even so, some plants grow very well in wet soils where excess water limits but does not exclude oxygen. Some of these plants are listed below. Don't expect heroic swamp-plant tolerance; most simply offer better-than-average performance under poor drainage conditions. Check descriptions in the Western Plant Encyclopedia (beginning on page 199) for the degree of moisture tolerance of each.

Feathery Astilbe—in colors from white through pink to dark red—revels in organic-enriched, damp soil.

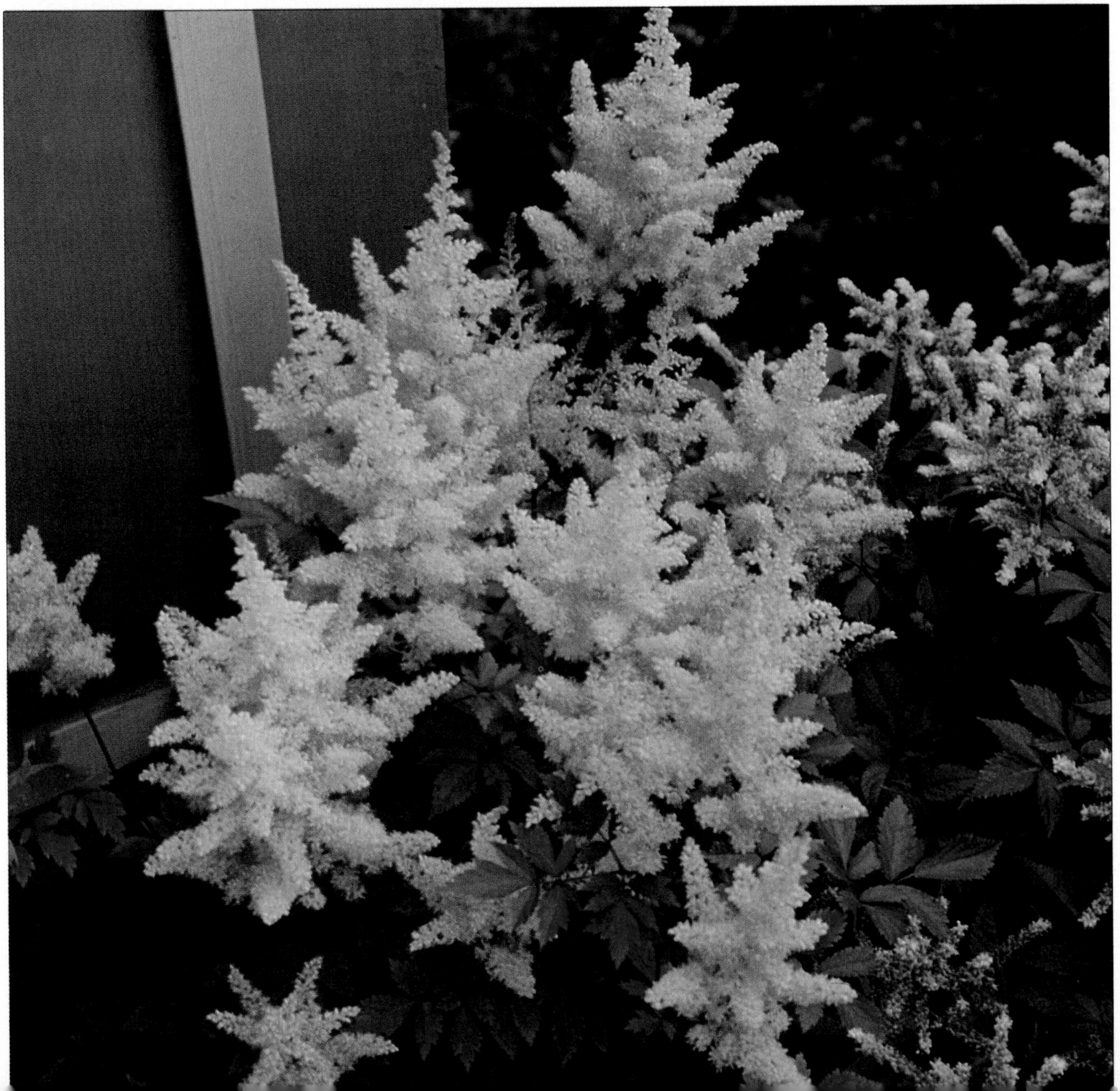

TREES

NAME OF PLANT	CLIMATE ZONES
Acer rubrum	1–9, 14–17
Alnus	Vary
Betula	Vary
Casuarina	8, 9, 12–24
Clethra arborea	15–17, 21–24
Eucalyptus citriodora	8–24
Eucalyptus erythrocorys	8–24
Fraxinus latifolia	4–24
Fraxinus pennsylvanica	1–6
Liquidambar styraciflua	1–11, 14–24
Magnolia grandiflora	4–12, 14–24
Magnolia virginiana	4–9, 14–24
Melaleuca quinquenervia	9, 13, 16, 17, 20–24
Myoporum laetum	8, 9, 14–17, 19–24
Nyssa sylvatica	3–10, 14–21
Pear	1–11, 14–18
Picea sitchensis	4–6, 14–17
Platanus	Vary
Populus	Vary
Pterocarya stenoptera	5–24
Quercus bicolor	1–3, 10
Salix	Vary
Sambucus caerulea	1–17
Sambucus callicarpa	4–7, 14–17
Sequoia sempervirens	4–9, 14–24
Taxodium	Vary
Thuja occidentalis	2–9, 15–17, 21–24
Umbellularia californica	4–10, 12–24

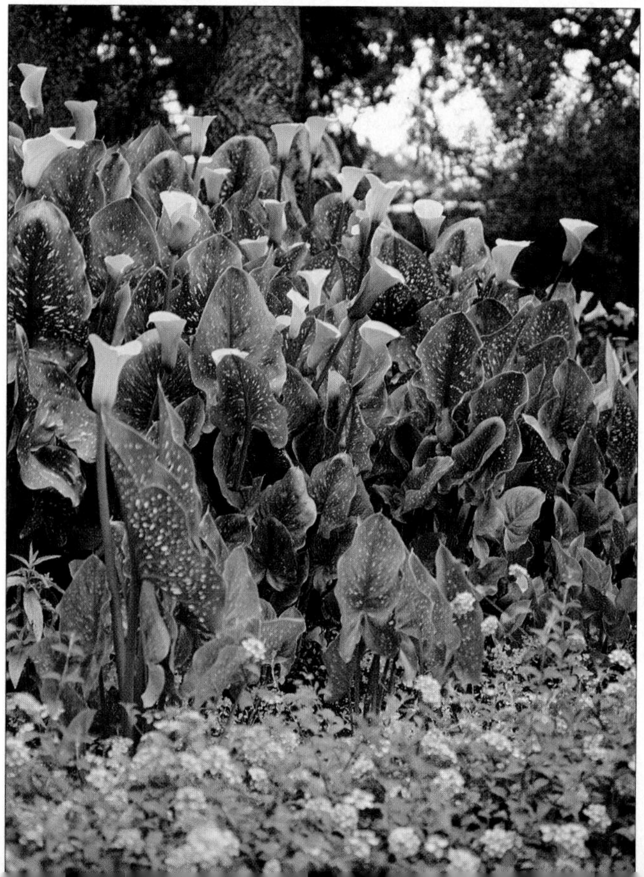

SHRUBS

NAME OF PLANT	CLIMATE ZONES
Andromeda polifolia	All
Aronia arbutifolia	1–7
Calycanthus	Vary
Clethra alnifolia	2–6
Cornus stolonifera	1–9, 14–21
Gaultheria shallon	4–7, 14–17
Itea ilicifolia	4–24
Kalmia microphylla	1–7, 16, 17
Leucothoe	Vary
Myrica	Vary
Salix	All
Thuja occidentalis	2–9, 15–17, 21–24
Vaccinium	Vary
Zenobia pulverulenta	4–7, 14–17

PERENNIALS

NAME OF PLANT	CLIMATE ZONES
Aconitum	1–9, 14–21
Alocasia	22–24
Arundo donax	All
Aster novae-angliae	All
Astilbe	2–7, 14–17
Bambusa (most)	Vary
Caltha palustris	All
Colocasia esculenta	See Encyclopedia
Cortaderia selloana	4–24
Cyperus	8, 9, 12–24
Eichhornia crassipes	8, 9, 13–24
Equisetum hyemale	All
Ferns (many)	Vary
Galium odoratum	1–6, 15–17
Hibiscus moscheutos	1–21
Iris ensata	All
Iris pseudacorus	All
Iris, Louisiana hybrids	2–24
Iris, Siberian hybrids	All
Lobelia cardinalis	1–7, 13–17
Lysimachia nummularia	1–9, 14–24
Lythrum salicaria	All
Mentha	Vary
Mimulus	Vary
Monarda didyma	All
Myosotis scorpioides	All
Phyllostachys (most)	Vary
Primula (sections Candelabra, Sikkimensis)	Vary
Rodgersia	2–9, 14–17
Sanguinaria canadensis	1–6
Sisyrinchium californicum	4–24
Soleirolia soleirolii	8–24
Tolmiea menziesii	5–9, 12–24
Trollius	All
Zantedeschia	5, 6, 8, 9, 14–24

Golden calla (Zantedeschia elliottiana) tolerates much moisture or moderate watering during the growth and flowering period.

Drought-tolerant Plants

Much of the West is characterized by a short annual rainy season followed by many dry months in which plants receive no water except what is artificially supplied. And in periodically recurring drought years, in which rainfall is far below normal, water available for gardens may be severely limited or completely cut off. Fortunately, many fine plants will thrive with little or no water during the normal dry season once they are established in the garden. Here are some proven performers.

Congenial dry-soil trio is French lavender (*Lavandula dentata*, left), Russian sage (*Perovskia atriciplifolia*, top), and lavender cotton (*Santolina chamaecyparissus*, right).

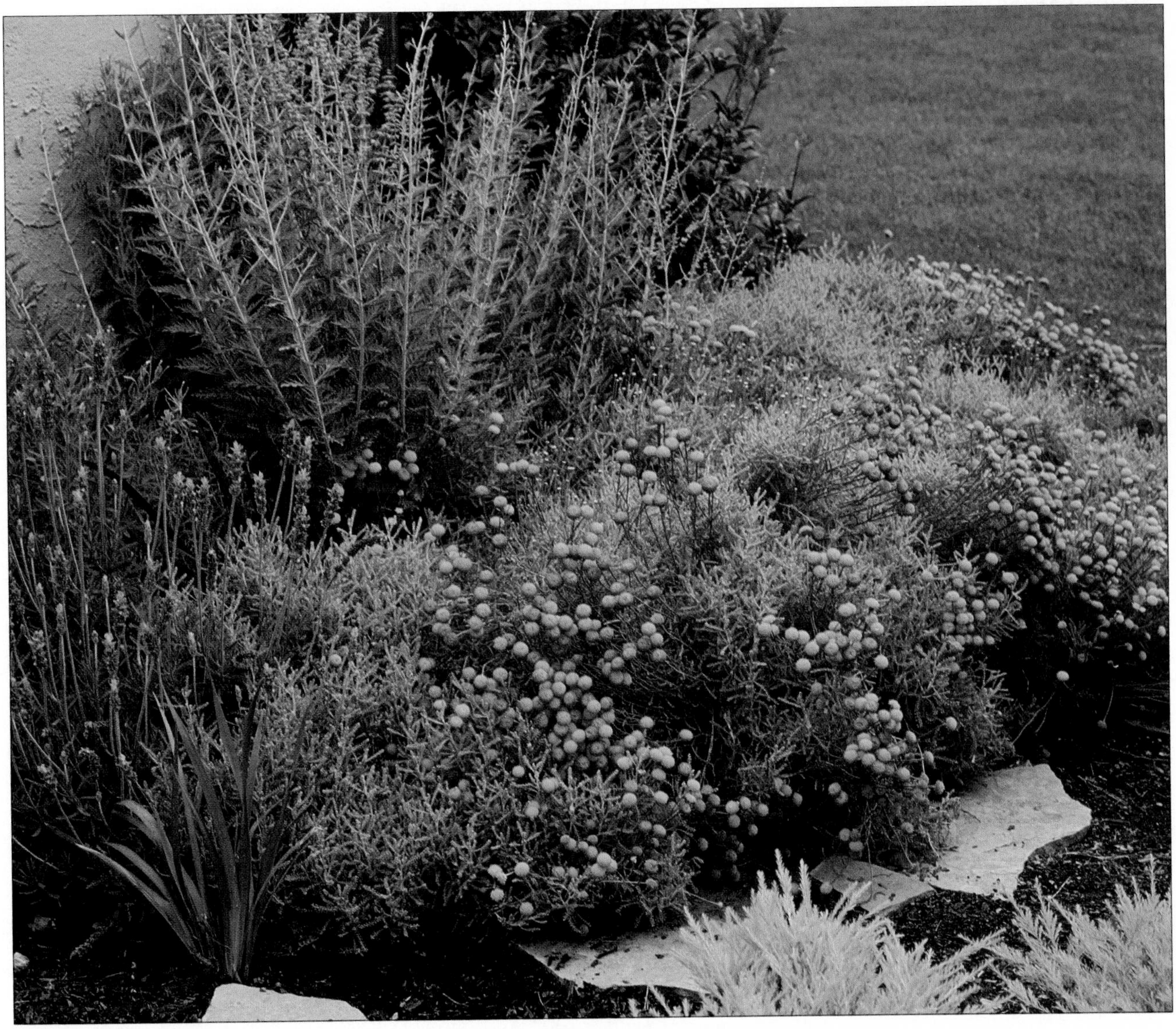

TREES

NAME OF PLANT	CLIMATE ZONES
Acacia (many)	Vary
Aesculus californica	4–7, 14–19
Ailanthus altissima	All
Albizia julibrissin	2–23
Brahea armata	12–17, 19–24
Calocedrus decurrens	1–12, 14–24
Casuarina	8, 9, 12–24
Cedrus deodara	2–12, 14–24
Celtis	Vary
Ceratonia siliqua	9, 13–16, 18–24
Cercidium	10–14, 18–20
Eriobotrya japonica	4–24
Eucalyptus (most)	8–24
Fig (edible)	4–9, 12–24
Geijera parviflora	8, 9, 13–24
Grevillea	Vary
Koelreuteria paniculata	2–21
Lyonothamnus floribundus	15–17, 19–24
Maclura pomifera	All
Melia azedarach	6, 8–24
Olea europaea	8, 9, 11–24
Parkinsonia aculeata	11–24
Pinus (many)	Vary
Pistacia	Vary
Populus fremontii	7–24
Quercus (many)	Vary
Rhus lancea	8, 9, 12–24
Robinia	All
Schinus molle	8, 9, 12–24
Schinus terebinthifolius	13–17, 19–24
Sequoiadendron giganteum	3–24
Tilia tomentosa	1–21
Tristania conferta	19–24
Ulmus pumila	All
Walnut	Vary
Ziziphus jujuba	7–16, 18–24

SHRUBS

NAME OF PLANT	CLIMATE ZONES
Acacia (many)	Vary
*Arbutus unedo	4–24
Arctostaphylos	Vary
Artemisia	All
Atriplex	Vary
Baccharis pilularis	5–11, 14–24
Caesalpinia gilliesii	8–16, 18–23
*Callistemon citrinus	8, 9, 12–24
Capparis spinosa	8, 9, 12–24
*Caragana arborescens	1–21
Cassia artemisioides	8, 9, 12–16, 18–23
Catha edulis	13, 16–24
Ceanothus	Vary
*Cercis occidentalis	2–24
*Cercocarpus	Vary
*Chamaerops humilis	4–24
Chamelaucium uncinatum	8, 9, 12–24

*Can become small tree.

SHRUBS (*cont'd.*)

NAME OF PLANT	CLIMATE ZONES
Cistus	7–9, 12–24
Convolvulus cneorum	7–9, 12–24
Coprosma kirkii	8, 9, 14–17, 21–24
*Cotinus coggygria	All
Cotoneaster	Vary
Crassula argentea	8, 9, 12–24
Crassula falcata	8, 9, 12–24
*Cupressus glabra	5, 8–24
Cytisus	Vary
*Dalea spinosa	11–13
Dendromecon	5–8, 14–24
*Dodonaea viscosa	7–9, 12–24
Echium	Vary
Elaeagnus	Vary
Escallonia	4–9, 14–17, 20–24
Fallugia paradoxa	2–23
Fremontodendron	7–24
Garrya	Vary
Genista	Vary
Grevillea	Vary
*Hakea	9, 12–17, 19–24
*Heteromeles arbutifolia	5–24
Hypericum calycinum	2–24
*Lagerstroemia indica	4–9, 12–14, 18–21
Lantana	8–10, 12–24
Lavandula	Vary
Lavatera assurgentiflora	14–24
Leucophyllum frutescens	7–24
*Lysiloma thornberi	10, 12–24
Mahonia	Vary
*Melaleuca (most species)	Vary
Myoporum debile	15–17, 19–24
*Nerium oleander	8–16, 18–23
*Photinia serrulata	4–16, 18–22
*Pinus edulis	See Encyclopedia
*Pinus monophylla	See Encyclopedia
*Pittosporum	Vary
Plumbago auriculata	8, 9, 12–24
Portulacaria afra	13, 16, 17, 22–24
*Prosopis glandulosa torreyana	10–14
*Prunus caroliniana	7–24
*Prunus ilicifolia	7–9, 12–24
*Prunus lyonii	7–9, 12–24
*Punica granatum	7–24
Pyracantha	Vary
*Rhamnus alaternus	4–24
Rhamnus californica	4–24
*Rhamnus crocea ilicifolia	7–16, 18–21
Rhus ovata	7–24
Rosa rugosa	All
Rosmarinus officinalis	4–24
Salvia clevelandii	10–24
Salvia leucantha	10–24
Santolina chamaecyparissus	All
Simmondsia chinensis	10–13, 19–24
Sollya heterophylla	8, 9, 14–24
Spartium junceum	5–9, 11–24

*Can become small tree.

SHRUBS *(cont'd.)*

NAME OF PLANT	CLIMATE ZONES
*Tamarix	Vary
Taxus	3–9, 14–24
Teucrium	Vary
Trichostema lanatum	14–24
*Xylosma congestum	8–24

*Can become small tree.

VINES

NAME OF PLANT	CLIMATE ZONES
Bougainvillea	See Encyclopedia
Cissus trifoliata	12, 13
Tecomaria capensis	12–16, 18–24
Wisteria	All

PERENNIALS, BULBS, ANNUALS

NAME OF PLANT	CLIMATE ZONES
Achillea	All
Agave	Vary
Aloe arborescens	8, 9, 12–24
Amaryllis belladonna	4–24
Anacyclus depressus	All
Arctotheca calendula	8, 9, 13–24
Baccharis pilularis	5–11, 14–24
Baptisia australis	All
Carpobrotus	12–24
Centranthus ruber	7–9, 14–24
Cleome spinosa	All
Coreopsis	Vary
Cortaderia selloana	4–24
Dietes vegeta	8, 9, 13–24
Dudleya brittonii	16, 17, 21–24
Echeveria (most)	Vary
Eriogonum	Vary
Euphorbia (most)	Vary
Euryops	14–17, 19–24
Gaillardia	All
Hippocrepis comosa	8–24
Iris, bearded	All
Iris (Pacific Coast natives)	Vary
Kniphofia uvaria	1–9, 14–24
Leonotis leonurus	8–24
Leucocoryne ixioides	13, 16, 19, 21–24
Liatris	1–3, 7–10, 14–24
Limonium perezii	13, 15–17, 20–24
Linum	All
Marrubium vulgare	All
Mimulus	7–9, 14–24
Narcissus	All
Oenothera berlandieri	All
Pennisetum setaceum	All
Perovskia atriplicifolia	All
Phlomis fruticosa	All
Phormium	7–24
Polygonum cuspidatum compactum	All

PERENNIALS, BULBS, ANNUALS *(cont'd.)*

NAME OF PLANT	CLIMATE ZONES
Portulaca grandiflora	All
Puya berteroniana	9, 13–17, 19–24
Romneya coulteri	All
Sedum (many)	Vary
Sisyrinchium bellum	4–24
Tithonia rotundifolia	All
Verbena	Vary
Yucca (most)	Vary
Zauschneria	4–10, 12–24

Golden flowered flannel bush (Fremontodendron californicum) demands complete summer drought once it is established.

Heat-resistant Plants for South & West Exposures

One of the most troublesome garden locations is the south- or west-facing wall or fence, against which the sun shines for the longest—or hottest—part of the day. It is an especially tough plant that can grow under conditions of intense solar heat, plus heat reflected from a fence or wall. Here are the most successful and widely available plants that are well suited to a south or west exposure.

NAME OF PLANT	KIND	CLIMATE ZONES
Antigonon	Vine	12, 13, 18–21
Bamboo	Perennial	Vary
Bauhinia punctata	Shrub	13, 15, 16, 18–23
Beaumontia grandiflora	Vine	12, 13, 16, 17, 21–24
Bougainvillea	Vine	See Encyclopedia
Caesalpinia	Shrub, tree	Vary
Calliandra	Shrub	Vary
Callistemon	Shrub	8, 9, 12–24
Citrus	Shrub, tree	Vary
Coprosma kirkii	Shrub	8, 9, 14–17, 21–24
Cotoneaster horizontalis perpusillus	Shrub	1–11, 14–24
Dais cotinifolia	Shrub, tree	16–24
Distictis buccinatoria	Vine	8, 9, 14–24
Elaeagnus	Shrub	Vary
Exochorda macrantha	Shrub	3–9, 14–18
Fig (edible)	Tree	4–9, 12–24
Grevillea	Shrub	Vary
Grewia occidentalis	Shrub, tree	8, 9, 14–24
Hibbertia scandens	Vine	16, 17, 21–24
Hibiscus rosa-sinensis	Shrub	9, 12, 13, 15, 16, 19–24
Juniperus	Shrub, tree	All
Lantana	Shrub	See Encyclopedia
Ligustrum ovalifolium	Shrub	4–24
Lonicera hildebrandiana	Vine	9, 14–17, 19–24
Macfadyena unguis-cati	Vine	8–24
Magnolia grandiflora	Tree	4–12, 14–24
Malus	Tree	1–11, 14–21
Nerium oleander	Shrub	8–16, 18–23
Olea europaea	Tree	8, 9, 11–24
Photinia fraseri	Shrub	4–24
Pittosporum	Shrub, tree	Vary
Prunus caroliniana	Shrub, tree	7–24
Punica granatum	Shrub	7–24
Pyracantha	Shrub	Vary
Pyrostegia venusta	Vine	13, 16, 21–24
Pyrus	Tree	Vary
Rosa (climbing)	Vine	Vary
Solandra maxima	Vine	15–24
Tecomaria capensis	Vine	12, 13, 16, 18–24
Thevetia peruviana	Tree	13–14, 21–24
Thunbergia grandiflora	Vine	16, 21–24
Wisteria	Vine	All
Xylosma congestum	Shrub	8–24
Yucca	Shrub, tree	Vary

Reflected heat fails to daunt planting of dwarf pomegranate (Punica granatum 'Nana') and potted Aloe.

Plants to Use near Swimming Pools

Plants chosen to landscape swimming pool areas must meet two requirements. Branches, foliage, and flowers should be smooth—not bristly, prickly, sharp, or thorny so as to annoy or injure pool users. And plants should be as litter-free as possible; what litter they produce should be too large to pass into the pool's filter. The plants listed here will meet these specifications.

Simple planting of low-litter juniper dominates this poolside planting. Clump of swordlike foliage is Dietes vegeta.

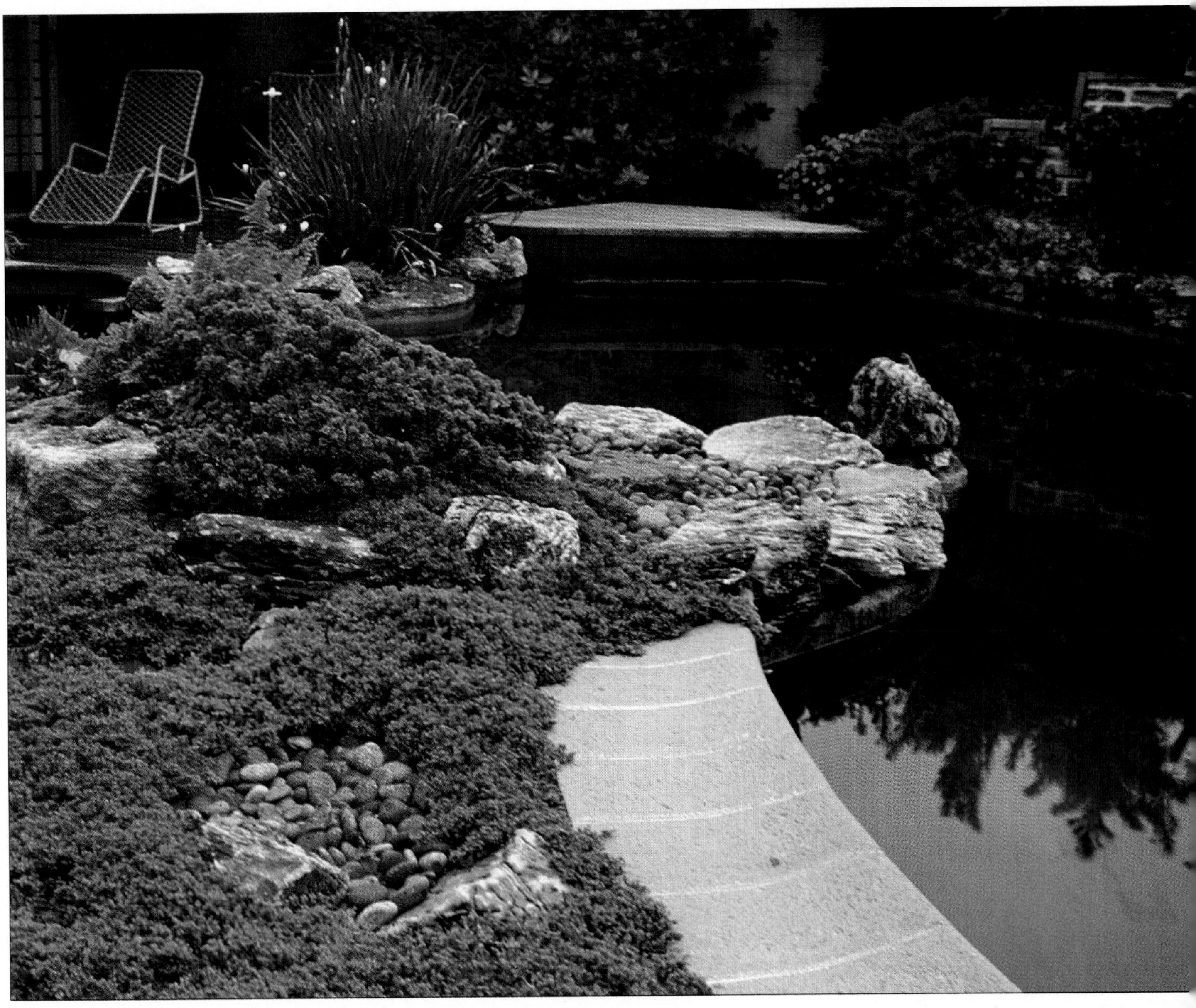

TREES

NAME OF PLANT	CLIMATE ZONES
Cordyline	Vary
Cupaniopsis anacardioides	16, 17, 19–24
Dracaena	Vary
Ensete	13, 15–24
Ficus auriculata	20–24
Ficus lyrata	22–24
Firmiana simplex	5, 6, 8, 9, 12–24
Montanoa arborescens	16, 17, 20–24
Musa	Vary
Palms	Vary
Schefflera	Vary
Stenocarpus sinuatus	16, 17, 20–24
Strelitzia	22–24
Tree ferns	Vary
Trevesia	21–24
Tupidanthus calyptratus	19–24

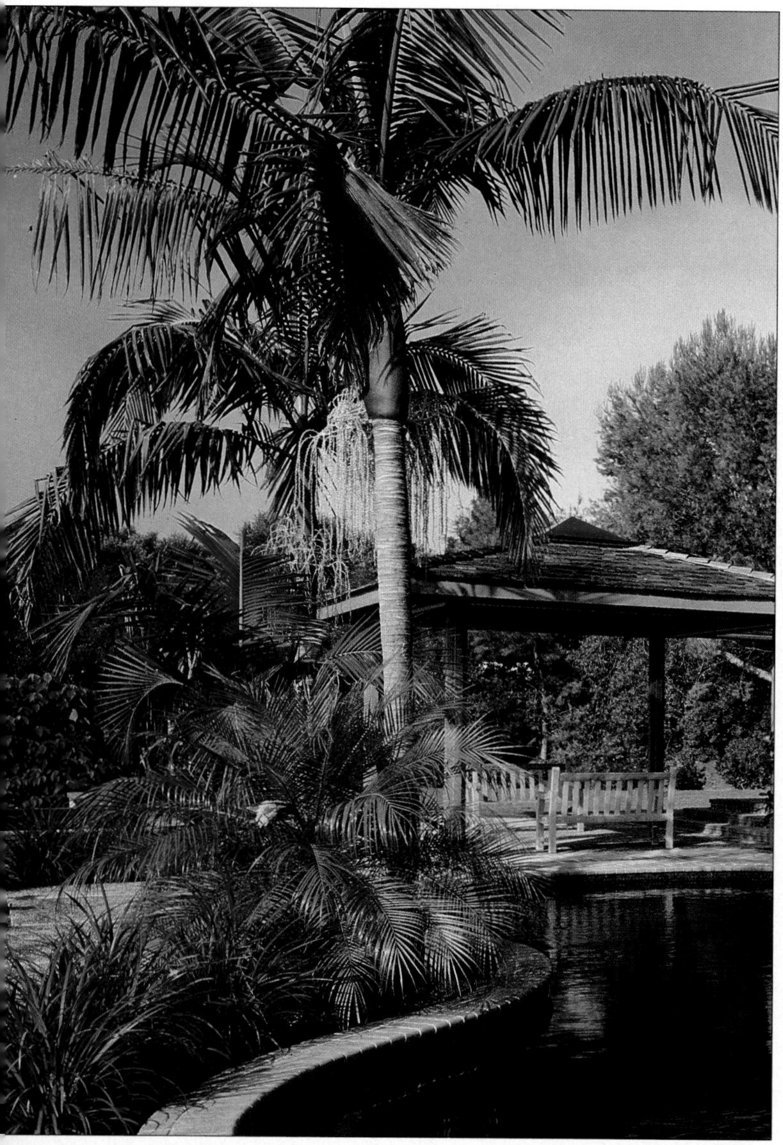

Palms beside pool create at-home oasis. Dominant specimen is king palm (Archontophoenix cunninghamiana).

SHRUBS

NAME OF PLANT	CLIMATE ZONES
Camellia	4–9, 14–24
Crassula argentea	16, 17, 22–24
Fatsia japonica	4–9, 13–24
Griselinia	9, 15–17, 20–24
Juniperus	All
Pittosporum tobira 'Wheeler's Dwarf'	8–24
Rhapiolepis	8–10, 12–24
Sparmannia africana	17, 21–24
Ternstroemia gymnanthera	4–9, 12–24
Viburnum davidii	4–9, 14–24

VINES

NAME OF PLANT	CLIMATE ZONES
Beaumontia grandiflora	12, 13, 16, 17, 21–24
Cissus	Vary
Fatshedera lizei	4–10, 12–24
Solandra maxima	15–24
Tetrastigma voinieranum	13, 17, 20–24

PERENNIALS

NAME OF PLANT	CLIMATE ZONES
Agapanthus	7–9, 12–24
Agave attenuata	20–24
Aloe saponaria	8, 9, 12–24
Alpinia zerumbet	15–17, 22–24
Artichoke	8, 9, 14–24
Aspidistra elatior	4–9, 12–24
Canna	All
Clivia miniata	13–17, 19–24
Colocasia esculenta	See Encyclopedia
Cyperus	8, 9, 12–24
Dianella tasmanica	8, 9, 14–24
Dietes	8, 9, 13–24
Gazania	8–24
Hedychium	17, 22–24
Hemerocallis	All
Kniphofia uvaria	1–9, 14–24
Liriope	Vary
Ophiopogon	5–10, 12–24
Philodendron (treelike types)	Vary
Phormium	7–24
Sedum	Vary
Strelitzia	22–24
Succulents	Vary
Yucca	Vary
Zoysia tenuifolia	8, 9, 12–24

Plants for Hillsides & for Erosion Control

Hillsides generally offer a less hospitable plant environment than do level gardens. Soil may be shallow, poor, or—where the bank is the result of a grading cut—virtually nonexistent. Hillsides also are more difficult to water thoroughly, unless you form watering basins around each new plant or set up a drip-irrigation system that will apply water slowly (see page 70).

Fortunately, many plants will cope successfully with less-than-ideal conditions and provide good-looking cover for slopes. In addition, plants with stars (*) have dense, strong root systems that will help prevent soil erosion.

Multicolored froth of heath (Erica) tumbles down hillside. Many species, varieties are sold that vary in color and bloom season.

SHRUBS

NAME OF PLANT	CLIMATE ZONES
Abelia	Vary
Acacia cultriformis	13–24
Acacia longifolia	8, 9, 14–24
Acacia saligna	8, 9, 13–24
Arctostaphylos densiflora	7–9, 14–21
Arctostaphylos edmundsii	6–9, 14–24
Arctostaphylos hookeri	6–9, 14–24
Arctostaphylos uva-ursi	1–9, 14–24
Atriplex	Vary
Baccharis pilularis	5–11, 14–24
Bamboo (Group I kinds)	Vary
Calluna vulgaris	2–6, 15–17
Carissa macrocarpa	See Encyclopedia
*Ceanothus	Vary
Cercis occidentalis	2–24
Chaenomeles	1–21
Chamelaucium uncinatum	8, 9, 12–24
Chorizema	15–17, 19–24
*Cistus	Vary
Coleonema	7–9, 14–24
Convolvulus cneorum	7–9, 12–24
*Coprosma kirkii	8, 9, 14–17, 21–24
Correa	14–24
*Cotoneaster	Vary
Cytisus kewensis	4–6, 16, 17
Daboecia azorica	8, 9, 14–24
Daboecia cantabrica	3–9, 14–24
Dendromecon	5–8, 14–24
*Echium fastuosum	14–24
Elaeagnus	Vary
Erica (some)	Vary
*Eriogonum fasciculatum	8, 9, 14–24
Eucalyptus (smallest species)	8–24
*Fallugia paradoxa	2–23

Sweep of daylilies (Hemerocallis hybrids) blankets slope with color over long period, attractive foliage when flowers are past.

SHRUBS (*cont'd.*)

NAME OF PLANT	CLIMATE ZONES
Forsythia suspensa	2–11, 14–16, 18, 19
Fremontodendron	7–24
Gaultheria shallon	4–7, 14–17
Genista (some)	Vary
Grevillea lanigera	15–24
Grewia occidentalis	8, 9, 14–24
Halimiocistus sahuchii	4–24
Halimium	7–9, 12–24
Heteromeles arbutifolia	5–24
*Hypericum calycinum	2–24
*Jasminum mesnyi	4–24
Jasminum nudiflorum	3–21
*Juniperus (ground covers)	All
Lagerstroemia indica (shrub types)	7–9, 12–14, 18–21
*Lantana	8–10, 12–17, 23, 24
Lonicera pileata	2–9, 14–24
*Mahonia repens	1–21
Myoporum debile	15–17, 19–24
Plumbago auriculata	8, 9, 12–24
Prunus laurocerasus 'Zabeliana'	3–9, 14–21
Pyracantha 'Santa Cruz'	4–24
Pyracantha 'Walderi'	4–24
*Rhamnus crocea ilicifolia	7–16, 18–21
*Rhus aromatica	1–3, 10
*Rhus integrifolia	15–17, 20–24
*Rhus laurina	20–24
*Rhus trilobata	1–3, 10
*Ribes viburnifolium	8, 9, 14–24
*Rosa multiflora	All
*Rosa rugosa	All
*Rosmarinus officinalis	4–24
Salvia	Vary
Santolina	All
Sollya heterophylla	8, 9, 14–24
Sophora secundiflora	8–16, 18–24
*Symphoricarpos	Vary
Taxus baccata 'Repandens'	3–9, 14–24
Trichostema lanatum	14–24
Westringia rosmariniformis	15–17, 19–24
Xylosma congestum	8–24

*Will control erosion.

VINES

NAME OF PLANT	CLIMATE ZONES
Bougainvillea	See Encyclopedia
*Cissus antarctica	16–24
*Cissus hypoglauca	13–24
*Euonymus fortunei (prostrate forms)	1–17
*Hedera	Vary
Ipomoea acuminata	8, 9, 12–24
Lathyrus latifolius	All
*Lonicera japonica	2–24
*Parthenocissus quinquefolia	All
Passiflora	Vary
Polygonum aubertii	All
*Rhoicissus capensis	16, 17, 21–24
*Rosa banksiae	4–24
Senecio confusus	13, 16–24
Solandra maxima	17, 21–24
Tecomaria capensis	12, 13, 16, 18–24
*Tetrastigma voinieranum	13, 17, 20–24
*Trachelospermum jasminoides	8–24
Tropaeolum majus	All
*Vinca	Vary

*Will control erosion.

PERENNIALS

NAME OF PLANT	CLIMATE ZONES
Arctotheca calendula	8, 9, 13–24
*Bamboo (Group I kinds)	Vary
Centranthus ruber	7–9, 14–24
Cerastium tomentosum	All
Convolvulus cneorum	7–9, 12–24
Convolvulus mauritanicus	4–9, 12–24
*Coronilla varia	All
Delosperma 'Alba'	12–24
*Drosanthemum floribundum	14–24
Gazania rigens leucolaena	8–24
Hemerocallis	All
Hippocrepis comosa	8–24
Lampranthus	14–24
*Malephora	Vary
Osteospermum fruticosum	8, 9, 14–24
Pelargonium peltatum	15–17, 22–24
Phlomis fruticosa	All
*Polygonum cuspidatum compactum	All
Polygonum vacciniifolium	4–7
*Romneya coulteri	All
Sedum	Vary

*Will control erosion.

Seacoast Plantings

Salt-laden winds, fog and humid air, sandy soil, and low sun intensity are among the special conditions seacoast gardens impose on plants. These conditions prevail whether you live along the cool coast of Washington or in subtropical Zone 24. For gardens directly or largely influenced by the ocean, these plants are proven performers.

Mild-winter coastal gardens can experience the full range of lantana's palette—from chili-pepper bright to soft pinks and cream.

TREES

NAME OF PLANT	CLIMATE ZONES
Albizia distachya	15–17, 22–24
Casuarina stricta	8–9, 12–24
Cordyline australis	5, 8–11, 14–24
Cordyline indivisa	16, 17, 20–24
Corynocarpus laevigata	16, 17, 23, 24
Cupaniopsis anacardioides	16, 17, 19–24
Cupressus macrocarpa	17
Eucalyptus (some)	8–24
Ficus rubiginosa	18–24
Melaleuca quinquenervia	9, 13, 16, 17, 20–24
Metrosideros	Vary
Myoporum laetum	8, 9, 14–17, 19–24
Pinus (some)	Vary
Quercus ilex	4–24
Vitex lucens	16, 17, 22–24

SHRUBS

NAME OF PLANT	CLIMATE ZONES
Acacia longifolia	8, 9, 14–24
Acacia verticillata	14–24
Acokanthera	21, 23, 24
*Arbutus unedo	4–24
Atriplex	Vary
Calothamnus	8–9, 12–24
Carissa	22–24
Cistus	7–9, 12–24
Coprosma	Vary
Corokia cotoneaster	4–24
Correa	14–24
Cytisus	Vary
*Dodonaea viscosa	7–9, 12–24
Echium	Vary
Elaeagnus	Vary
Escallonia	4–9, 14–17, 20–24
Euonymus japonica	5–20
Garrya elliptica	5–9, 14–21
Gaultheria shallon	4–9, 14–17
Genista	Vary
Griselinia	9, 15–17, 20–24
*Hakea	9, 12–17, 19–24
Halimium	7–9, 12–24
Hebe	14–24
Juniperus	All
*Lagunaria patersonii	13, 15–24
*Laurus nobilis	5–9, 12–24
Lavatera assurgentiflora	14–24
Leptospermum	14–24
*Leucodendron argenteum	17, 20–24
Lonicera nitida	4–9, 14–24
Lonicera pileata	2–9, 14–24
Melaleuca (most species)	Vary
*Myoporum (some)	Vary
Myrica	Vary
*Pittosporum crassifolium	9, 14–17, 19–24
*Rhamnus alaternus	4–24
Rhapiolepis	8–10, 14–24

*Can become small tree.

SHRUBS (*cont'd.*)

NAME OF PLANT	CLIMATE ZONES
Rhus integrifolia	15–17, 20–24
Rosa rugosa	All
Rosmarinus officinalis	4–24
Spartium junceum	5–9, 11–24
Tamarix	Vary
Westringia rosmariniformis	15–17, 19–24

*Can become small tree.

VINES, GROUND COVERS

NAME OF PLANT	CLIMATE ZONES
Abronia	5, 17, 24
Arctostaphylos uva-ursi	1–9, 14–24
Arctotheca calendula	8, 9, 13–24
Atriplex semibaccata	8, 9, 12–24
Baccharis pilularis	5–11, 14–24
Bougainvillea	22–24
Carissa	22–24
Carpobrotus	12–24
Ceanothus gloriosus	Vary
Ceanothus griseus	Vary
Delosperma	Vary
Drosanthemum	14–24
Juniperus conferta	All
Lampranthus	14–24
Muehlenbeckia complexa	8, 9, 14–24
Osteospermum fruticosum	8, 9, 14–24
Polygonum aubertii	All
Solandra maxima	17, 21–24
Tecomaria capensis	12, 13, 16, 18–24

PERENNIALS, ANNUALS

NAME OF PLANT	CLIMATE ZONES
Aloe arborescens	8, 9, 12–24
Aurinia saxatilis	All
Calocephalus brownii	16, 17, 19, 21–24
Centaurea cyanus	All
Cerastium tomentosum	All
Chrysanthemum carinatum	All
Chrysanthemum frutescens	All
Cortaderia selloana	4–24
Erigeron glaucus	4–6, 15–17, 22–24
Erigeron speciosus	All
Eriogonum	Vary
Eschscholzia californica	All
Euryops	14–17, 19–24
Felicia amelloides	4–9, 13–24
Impatiens oliveri	15–17, 21–24
Lavandula angustifolia	4–24
Limonium perezii	13, 15–17, 20–24
Lonas annua	All
Pelargonium	15, 16, 22–24
Phormium	7–24
Santolina chamaecyparissus	All
Tropaeolum majus	15–24

Deerproof Plants

Browsing deer are charming to watch, but they can do considerable damage to gardens in country areas and in suburban fringes. Various ways to discourage or repel deer are presented on page 102; another solution is to grow plants that deer will leave untouched. But deer in different areas seem to have somewhat different tastes. To further complicate the picture, plants untouched in spring may be eaten in fall, when wild vegetation is dry or scarce. And as a final frustration, tastes sometimes change: what deer pass by one year they may find irresistible the next.

Despite these variables, gardeners in the West have identified a number of plants that can be considered "best bets" in deer country. The list below contains those plants that are deerproof—or close to it.

TREES

NAME OF PLANT	CLIMATE ZONES
Abies	Vary
Acacia	Vary
Acer circinatum	1–6, 14–17
Acer negundo	1–10, 12–24
Acer palmatum	1–9, 14–24
Albizia	Vary
Araucaria	Vary
Arbutus menziesii	3–7, 14–19
Brachychiton populneus	12–24
Callistemon	8, 9, 12–24
Cordyline australis	5, 8–11, 14–24
Eucalyptus	8–24
Fraxinus	Vary
Ilex	Vary
Liquidambar styraciflua	1–9, 14–24
Lithocarpus densiflorus	4–7, 14–24
Melia azedarach	6, 8–24
Myoporum laetum	8, 9, 14–17, 19–24
Palms	Vary
Picea	Vary
Pinus	Vary
Podocarpus	Vary
Umbellularia californica	4–10, 12–24

SHRUBS

NAME OF PLANT	CLIMATE ZONES
Arbutus unedo	4–24
Baccharis pilularis	5–11, 14–24
Berberis	1–11, 14–17
Brugmansia	16–24
Buddleia davidii	1–9, 12–24

SHRUBS (*cont'd.*)

NAME OF PLANT	CLIMATE ZONES
Buxus	Vary
Callistemon	8, 9, 12–24
Calycanthus occidentalis	4–9, 14–22
Ceanothus 'Blue Jeans'	4–7, 14–24
Ceanothus gloriosus	4–7, 14–24
Chamaerops humilis	4–24
Choisya ternata	7–9, 12–17
Cistus	7–9, 12–24
Coprosma repens	15–17, 21–24
Corokia cotoneaster	4–24
Correa	14–24
Corylus cornuta californica	1–9, 14–20
Cotinus coggygria	All
Cotoneaster buxifolius	4–24
Cycas revoluta	8–24
Cytisus scoparius	4–9, 14–22
Daphne	Vary
Dodonaea viscosa	7–9, 12–24
Elaeagnus pungens	4–24
Erica	Vary
Euonymus japonica	4–20
Gaultheria shallon	4–7, 14–17
Genista monosperma	16, 17, 22–24
Grevillea	Vary
Griselinia lucida	9, 15–17, 20–24
Hakea suaveolens	9, 12–17, 19–24
Heteromeles arbutifolia	5–24
Hypericum	4–24
Ilex	Vary
Iochroma cyaneum	16, 17, 19–24
Jasminum	Vary

SHRUBS (*cont'd.*)

NAME OF PLANT	CLIMATE ZONES
Juniperus	All
Kerria japonica	1–21
Lantana	8–10, 12–24
Leptospermum	14–24
Mahonia	Vary
Melianthus major	8, 9, 12–24
Michelia figo	9, 14–24
Myrica californica	4–6, 14–17, 20–24
Myrtus communis	8–24
Nandina domestica	5–24
Nerium oleander	8–16, 18–23
Paeonia (tree peonies)	2–12, 14–21
Plumbago auriculata	8, 9, 12–24
Potentilla (deciduous types)	1–21
Prunus caroliniana	7–24
Punica granatum 'Nana'	7–24
Rhododendron (not azaleas)	Vary
Rhus ovata	7–24
Ribes	Vary
Rosmarinus officinalis	4–24
Ruscus aculeatus	4–24
Salvia	Vary
Santolina	All
Solanum	Vary
Spartium junceum	5–9, 11–24
Syzygium paniculatum	16, 17, 19–24
Taxus	3–9, 14–24
Teucrium fruticans	4–24

VINES, GROUND COVERS

NAME OF PLANT	CLIMATE ZONES
Arctostaphylos uva-ursi	1–9, 14–24
Asparagus falcatus	12–24
Clematis	Vary
Fatshedera lizei	4–10, 12–24
Fragaria chiloensis	4–24
Gelsemium sempervirens	8–24
Hedera helix	All
Hibbertia scandens	16, 17, 21–24
Hypericum calycinum	2–24
Jasminum	Vary
Laurentia fluviatilis	4, 5, 8, 9, 14–24
Osteospermum fruticosum	8, 9, 14–24
Pandorea pandorana	16–24
Solanum jasminoides	8, 9, 12–24
Solanum wendlandii	16, 21–24
Tecomaria capensis	12–16, 18–24
Trachelospermum jasminoides	8–24
Vinca major	5–24

PERENNIALS, BULBS

NAME OF PLANT	CLIMATE ZONES
Acanthus mollis	4–24
Achillea	All

PERENNIALS (*cont'd.*)

NAME OF PLANT	CLIMATE ZONES
Aconitum	1–9, 14–21
Agapanthus	7–9, 12–24
Agave	Vary
Aloe	8, 9, 12–24
Amaryllis belladonna	4–24
Anemone hybrida	All
Artemisia	All
Artichoke	8, 9, 14–24
Arum	4–6, 8–24
Asarum caudatum	4–6, 14–17, 21
Aster alpinus	All
Bamboo	Vary
Begonia (tuberous)	4–9, 14–24
Brodiaea	All
Cactus	Vary
Cerastium tomentosum	All
Chives	All
Chrysanthemum frutescens	14–24
Chrysanthemum maximum	All
Clivia miniata	13–17, 19–24
Coreopsis grandiflora	All
Cortaderia selloana	2–24
Crinum	12–24
Crocosmia	5–24
Cyclamen	Vary
Cymbalaria muralis	3–24
Cyperus	8, 9, 12–24
Dicentra formosa	1–9, 14–24
Dicentra spectabilis	1–9, 14–24
Dietes vegeta	8, 9, 13–24
Digitalis	All
Echium fastuosum	14–24
Epimedium	1–9, 14–17
Eriogonum	Vary
Eschscholzia californica	All
Euphorbia	Vary
Euryops	14–17, 19–24
Ferns	Vary
Filipendula rubra	1–9, 14–24
Freesia	8, 9, 12–24
Gaillardia grandiflora	All
Galium odoratum	1–6, 15–17
Grasses, ornamental	Vary
Gunnera	4–6, 14–17, 20–24
Helichrysum petiolatum	16, 17, 22–24
Helleborus	Vary
Hemerocallis	All
Hosta	1–10, 12–21
Iris	Vary
Ixia	5–24
Kniphofia uvaria	1–9, 14–24
Lamium maculatum	All
Lavandula	Vary
Leonotis leonuris	8–24
Leucojum	Vary
Liriope	Vary
Lupinus	Vary

PERENNIALS *(cont'd.)*

NAME OF PLANT	CLIMATE ZONES
Mirabilis jalapa	4–24
Monarda	All
Myosotis scorpioides	All
Narcissus	All
Nepeta	All
Ophiopogon japonicus	5–10, 12–24
Oxalis	Vary
Papaver orientale	1–17
Penstemon	Vary
Phlomis fruticosa	All
Phormium tenax	7–24
Raoulia australis	7–9, 13–24
Romneya coulteri	All
Rudbeckia hirta	All
Scabiosa	Vary
Scilla peruviana	14–17, 19–24
Senecio cineraria	All
Silene acaulis	1–11, 14–16, 18–21
Sisyrinchium	4–24
Sparaxis tricolor	9, 13–24
Stachys byzantina	All
Strelitzia reginae	9, 12–24
Trillium	Vary
Tulipa	All
Vallota speciosa	16, 17, 23, 24
Zantedeschia	5, 6, 8, 9, 14–24
Zauschneria	2–10, 12–24

ANNUALS

NAME OF PLANT	CLIMATE ZONES
Ageratum houstonianum	All
Calendula officinalis	All
Campanula medium	1–9, 14–24
Catharanthus roseus	All
Impatiens wallerana	All
Lupinus	Vary
Moluccella laevis	All
Myosotis sylvatica	All
Papaver nudicaule	All
Papaver rhoeas	All
Ricinus communis	All
Scabiosa	All
Zinnia	All

Vivid orchid rockrose (Cistus purpureus) gives summer flower display on plant that grows in variety of climates.

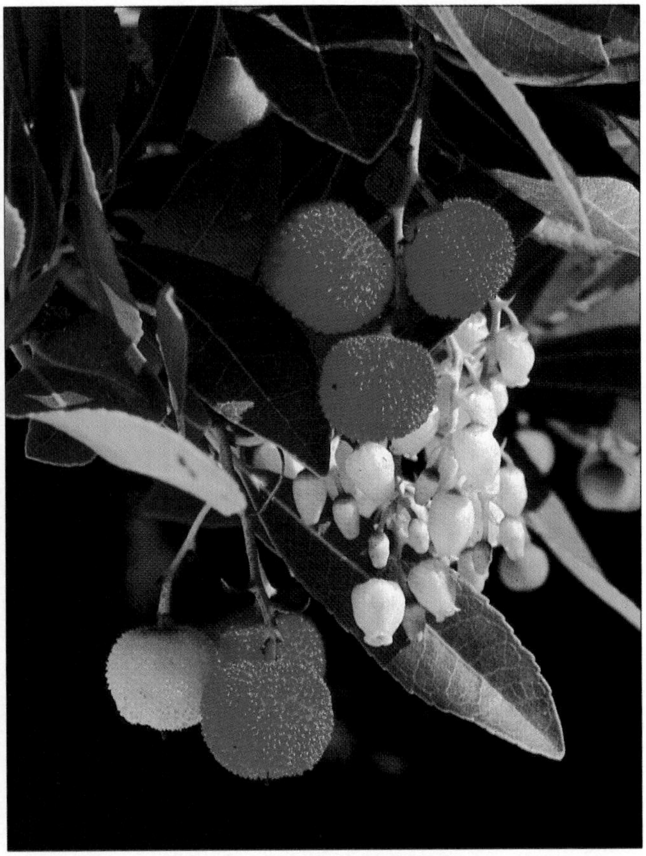

Handsome, drought-tolerant strawberry tree (Arbutus unedo) flowers in fall at the same time that fruits ripen.

Plants that Resist Oak Root Fungus

Oak root fungus (Armillaria mellea) *infects the soil in many parts of the world, but for various reasons it is more of a problem in California than elsewhere in the West. The fungus organism sustains itself on buried wood, mostly dead roots, but it also gets into the tissues of living plants—and often kills them (see page 108). Some plants resist this fungus infection; gardeners in armillaria-infested neighborhoods can play it safe by planting known resistant plants such as these.*

Fig tree (Ficus carica) thrives in armillaria-infested soil, offering attractiveness plus tasty fruits.

TREES

NAME OF PLANT	CLIMATE ZONES
Abies concolor	1–9, 14–24
Acacia longifolia	8, 9, 14–24
Acer ginnala	1–9, 14–16
Acer macrophyllum	4–17
Acer palmatum	1–9, 14–24
Ailanthus altissima	All
Angophora costata	16, 17, 21–24
Arbutus menziesii	3–7, 14–19
Avocado	Vary
Brachychiton populneus	12–24
Broussonetia papyrifera	3–24
Calocedrus decurrens	1–12, 14–24
Carya illinoensis	4–9, 12–16, 18–23
Castanea sativa	2–9, 14–17
Catalpa bignonioides	All
Celtis australis	8–16, 18–20
Celtis occidentalis	All
Ceratonia siliqua	9, 13–16, 18–24
Cercis occidentalis	2–24
Cercis siliquastrum	2–19
Cryptomeria japonica	4–9, 14–24
Cupaniopsis anacardioides	16, 17, 19–24
Cupressocyparis leylandii	3–24
Cupressus glabra	5, 8–24
Elaeagnus angustifolia	1–3, 7–14, 18, 19
Eucalyptus camaldulensis	8–24
Eucalyptus cinerea	8–24
Fig (edible) 'Kadota', 'Mission'	4–9, 12–24
Fraxinus oxycarpa	3–9, 14–24
Fraxinus uhdei	9, 12–24
Fraxinus velutina 'Modesto'	3–24
Geijera parviflora	8, 9, 13–24
Ginkgo biloba	1–9, 14–24
Gleditsia triacanthos inermis 'Shademaster'	1–16, 18–20
Gymnocladus dioica	1–3, 7–10, 12–16, 18–21
Ilex aquifolium	4–9, 14–24
Ilex opaca	2–9, 15, 16, 19–23
Jacaranda mimosifolia	12, 13, 15–24
Liquidambar orientalis	5–9, 14–24
Liquidambar styraciflua	1–11, 14–24
Liriodendron tulipifera	1–12, 14–23
Macadamia	9, 16, 17, 19–24
Maclura pomifera	All
Magnolia	Vary
Malus	1–11, 14–21
Maytenus boaria	8, 9, 14–21
Melaleuca styphelioides	9, 13–24
Metasequoia glyptostroboides	3–9, 14–24
Pear	1–11, 14–18
Persimmon	Vary
Pinus canariensis	5–24
Pinus monticola	See Encyclopedia
Pinus nigra	See Encyclopedia
Pinus patula	See Encyclopedia
Pinus radiata	See Encyclopedia
Pinus sylvestris	See Encyclopedia
Pinus torreyana	See Encyclopedia
Pistacia chinensis	8–16, 18–23
Pittosporum rhombifolium	12–24
Plum, Japanese	Vary
Prunus cerasifera	2–22
Pseudotsuga menziesii	1–10, 14–17
Pyrus calleryana	2–9, 14–21
Quercus ilex	4–24
Quercus lobata	1–3, 6–16, 18–21
Quillaja saponaria	8, 9, 14–24
Sapium sebiferum	8, 9, 12, 14–16, 18–21
Sequoia sempervirens	4–9, 14–24
Sophora japonica	All
Taxodium distichum	1–9, 14–24
Ulmus parvifolia	8, 9, 12–24
Walnut, California black (Juglans hindsii)	5–9, 14–20

SHRUBS

NAME OF PLANT	CLIMATE ZONES
Acacia verticillata	14–24
Brugmansia suaveolens	16–24
Buxus sempervirens	3–6, 15–17
Calycanthus occidentalis	4–9, 14–22
Carpenteria californica	5–9, 14–24
Chamaecyparis lawsoniana 'Ellwoodii'	4–6, 15–17
Clerodendrum bungei	5–9, 12–24
Corynabutilon vitifolium	5, 6, 15–17
Cotinus coggygria	All
Dais cotinifolia	16–24
Erica arborea	15–17, 21–24
Exochorda racemosa	3–9, 14–18
Hibiscus syriacus	1–21
Hypericum beanii	4–24
Ilex aquipernyi	4–9, 14–24
Lonicera nitida	4–9, 14–24
Mahonia aquifolium	1–21
Mahonia nevinii	8–24
Myrica pensylvanica	4–7
Nandina domestica	5–24
Phlomis fruticosa	All
Prunus caroliniana	7–24
Prunus ilicifolia	7–9, 12–24
Prunus lyonii	7–9, 12–24
Psidium cattleianum	9, 15–24
Rhus aromatica	1–3, 10
Sambucus canadensis	1–7, 14–17
Shepherdia argentea	1–3, 10
Vitex agnus-castus	4–24

VINES

NAME OF PLANT	CLIMATE ZONES
Hedera helix	All
Wisteria sinensis	All

Plants that Resist Verticillium Wilt

The fungi that cause verticillium wilt can persist in the soil for many years. Fumigation of the soil may make it safe for growing shallow-rooted plants, but wilt-susceptible deeper-rooted shrubs and trees still will be at risk. In regions where verticillium wilt is a problem, your safest landscape selections will come from the list of wilt-resistant plants below.

TREES

NAME OF PLANT	CLIMATE ZONES
Betula	Vary
Carpinus	Vary
Cedrus	Vary
Cercidiphyllum japonicum	1–6, 14–16, 18–20
Citrus	Vary
Cornus	Vary
Crataegus	1–11, 14–17
Eucalyptus	Vary
Fagus	1–9, 14–24
Fig (edible)	4–9, 12–24
Gleditsia triacanthos	1–16, 18–20
Ilex	Vary
Juglans (see Walnut)	Vary
Liquidambar styraciflua	1–9, 14–24
Malus	Vary
Morus	Vary
Pinus	Vary
Platanus	Vary
Pyrus	Vary
Quercus	Vary
Salix	All
Sorbus aucuparia	1–10, 14–17
Tilia	Vary
Umbellularia californica	2–10, 14–24

SHRUBS

NAME OF PLANT	CLIMATE ZONES
Arctostaphylos	Vary
Buxus	Vary
Ceanothus	4–7, 14–24
Cistus corbariensis	7–9, 12–24
Cistus salviifolius	7–9, 12–24
Cornus	Vary
Hebe menziesii	14–24
Ilex	Vary
Lantana	12, 13, 15–24
Nerium oleander	8–16, 18–23
Pyracantha	Vary

PERENNIALS, BULBS

NAME OF PLANT	CLIMATE ZONES
Alcea rosea	All
Alyssum	All
Anemone	Vary
Aquilegia	All
Begonia (semperflorens)	All
Cheiranthus cheiri	4–6, 14–17, 22, 23
Dianthus	All
Gaillardia grandiflora	All
Geum	All
Gypsophila paniculata	1–10, 14–16, 18–21
Helianthemum nummularium	All
Helleborus niger	1–7, 14–17
Heuchera sanguinea	All
Iberis sempervirens	All
Mimulus	Vary
Nierembergia hippomanica violacea	8–24
Oenothera	All
Penstemon	Vary
Platycodon grandiflorum	All
Potentilla	Vary
Primula	Vary
Ranunculus asiaticus	All
Vinca minor	All
Viola	Vary

ANNUALS

NAME OF PLANT	CLIMATE ZONES
Ageratum houstonianum	All
Calendula officinalis	All
Dianthus barbatus	All
Gaillardia pulchella	All
Iberis	All
Impatiens wallerana	All
Nemesia strumosa	All
Portulaca grandiflora	All
Scabiosa atropurpurea	All
Tropaeolum majus	All
Verbena hybrida	All
Zinnia	All

Basic Plant Care

Trees

No distinct line separates plants known as trees from those called shrubs. There are trees that reach 15 feet at maturity, but some shrubs reach up to 20 feet. And some of these shrubs will serve as small trees, particularly if the lower branches are removed.

Think of a tree as having a trunk topped by a foliage canopy. Some trees assume that aspect readily; others go through a prolonged, shrubby youth during which they maintain branches down to ground level. In time, though, most develop a canopy high enough to walk under.

Tips for Selecting a Tree

Because trees are the largest plants in the landscape, it is no surprise that they require more years to reach mature height, or even to begin to fulfill your expectations, than other garden plants do. That fact underscores the importance of selecting just the right trees for your needs and desires.

Consider these seven points:

- ***Climate adaptability.*** First be sure that any tree you consider is noted as being successful in your climate zone.
- ***Garden adaptability.*** If a tree will grow in your climate zone, read its cultural requirements and decide how well your garden can satisfy them.
- ***Growth rate.*** Different trees grow at different rates, and their speed, or lack of it, can be a crucial factor when you are choosing a tree to solve some garden problems. If, for example, you need a tree to screen hot sun from south-facing windows, or to block an objectionable view, you may want one that will grow fast to do the job in a hurry. On the other hand, if you are choosing a tree only for the beauty of its flowers, you may be willing to wait a number of years before the plant assumes mature proportions.
- ***Root system.*** A tree with a network of greedy surface roots is a poor candidate for sharing a lawn or garden area; the tree will take most of the water and nutrients. But the same tree planted at the garden's edge or along a country drive may be an outstanding choice. Some trees grow surface roots that can lift and crack nearby pavement, a point to check out if you're choosing a tree for patio, entryway, or parking strip.
- ***Maintenance.*** Notice words like "messy" or "litter" in a tree's description. Those words may refer to foliage, flower, or fruit drop; they may spell work if the litter gathers in a place that you want to keep neat, such as a lawn or a patio. But the same tree may pose no problem if grown toward the back of a garden or in a naturalistic setting so that litter can remain where it falls.

  In a region that receives regular high winds or consistent annual snowfall, avoid trees described as having weak or brittle wood or weak crotches. Such a tree's beauty may be ruined by the necessary removal of broken limbs.
- ***Pest and disease problems.*** Some trees may be plagued by particular insects or diseases in part of the region to which they are adapted. Often damage may be trivial. But if the action of a particular pest or disease will spoil your enjoyment of a tree (or compel you to wage eternal battle), you would be wise to plant a less troublesome one.
- ***Longevity.*** There are trees you can plant for your grandchildren to enjoy, and others that will grow quickly but slide into unattractive old age while the rest of your garden is still maturing. The short-lived trees are not necessarily less desirable, but they should be planted only where their removal won't be difficult or be a blow to your overall garden design. Many attractive flowering trees will run their course in about 20 years but can be replaced by another of the same kind to fill the gap again within a few years. But if you want to screen out the neighboring high rise for a long time, look for a tree that's likely to last as long as you will.

Planting & Caring for Young Trees

Some trees are sold with roots bare (no soil) during the dormant season, from late fall through early spring. Many of these trees, and others as well, are sold in containers or as balled-and-burlapped plants all year. Refer to planting guidelines on pages 64–67.

For all trees, follow a regular watering schedule during the first several years. Even a drought-tolerant tree needs routine watering for the first year or two after planting so the roots can grow enough to carry the tree through dry periods. See watering advice on pages 68–72 for frequency, based upon your climate and soil type.

A newly planted tree's trunk benefits from protection during at least the first year after planting. Drying winds, scorching sun, freezes, and physical damage by chewing dogs, scratching cats, gnawing wild animals (rabbits, deer, rodents), and careless lawn mowers can injure tender bark, resulting in anything from slowed growth to death. As a simple precaution, wrap the trunk with burlap (loosely tied) or a manufactured trunk wrapping. If animals are likely to be a problem, you can also encircle the lower portion of the trunk with a cylinder of woven wire.

Whenever you encircle a trunk or limb with a non-expandable tie (for staking or for protection), be sure to check the tie several times each growing season. Before you might expect it, a tree can grow enough that the tie will constrict and damage the trunk.

If possible, it is better to leave a newly planted tree unstaked; the trunk will strengthen and thicken faster without additional support. But if a new tree is top-heavy enough to topple in a strong wind, staking by the method shown at right was proven best in University of California experiments. This technique strengthens the trunk by permitting some flexibility in wind—but not so much flexibility that the tree would fall or tilt.

Young trees increase in trunk girth faster if lower branches are allowed to remain on the trunk for several years. Cut back low branches only if they show signs of growing at the expense of higher branches that you intend for the tree's permanent framework. Then, in 3 to 5 years, remove the unwanted lower branches from the trunk.

Fertilizing. You may want to include young trees in a regular, annual fertilizer program for several years after you plant them. Assuring a nitrogen supply (see page 73) for the springtime growth surge will encourage the young trees to establish themselves as quickly as possible.

After a tree has become established, it may grow satisfactorily with no further nutrient assistance. If it continues to put out healthy, vigorous new growth, fertilizer applications may be a waste of time, effort, and materials. (Exceptions are fruit and nut trees that are fertilized to ensure or enhance productivity; for specific guidelines, see Sunset's *Fruits, Nuts & Berries*.) But if new growth appears weak, sparse, or unusually pale, or if the tree has much dieback (and you know that soil and watering practices are appropriate), supplemental nutrients are in order. Other times of need are following periods of stress: a severe insect or disease attack (especially one that partially or entirely defoliates the tree) or damage to the tree that requires heavy pruning.

In the coldest zones (where snow covers the ground during winter), apply fertilizer either in fall or in earliest spring. With a fall application, nutrients will become available as soon as the soil warms and growth begins—even during winter, if soil isn't frozen deeply.

In the rest of the West, where winter is warmer and rainy to some extent, nitrogen applied in fall or winter may be leached out of the root zone. In these areas, it's better to apply fertilizer about a month before the expected flush of late-winter to spring growth.

A tree that displays the poor growth symptoms mentioned above should benefit from the application of nitrogen (see page 73). One application may suffice, or you may need to extend treatment over several years; the tree's growth will be your guide. For a moderate application, measure the trunk diameter at 4 feet above ground, then multiply that number by 0.1; this gives you the pounds of *actual nitrogen* (see page 75) to apply.

Apply fertilizer in a circular area roughly 1⅓ times the diameter of the canopy. For a tree growing in uncovered sandy soil, you can simply broadcast the fertilizer over the prescribed area, then water it in. But for trees growing in lawn, heavy ground cover, and in other-than-sandy soil, you will have to get the fertilizer into the soil by one of the two following methods.

To apply dry fertilizer, bore holes in the soil beneath the tree, using a soil-sampling tube or soil auger. Remove plugs of soil 6 to 12 inches deep. Holes should be at an angle (so nutrients will leach into a wider area), 2 to 3 feet apart, and in concentric rings around the tree trunk, each ring 4 feet wider than the previous one. Mix the dry fertilizer with an equal amount of dry sand, soil, peat moss, or a combination of these materials, and then distribute the mixture as evenly as possible among the holes. Water each hole thoroughly after filling.

To apply fertilizer in liquid form, you can use a special root feeder like the root irrigator described on page 70 but with a chamber that holds soluble fertilizer. Inject the root feeder 6 to 12 inches into the soil in the concentric rings described above, but in each ring space injections 4 to 6 feet apart. Fertilize for about 5 minutes in each setting.

How to Stake a Tree

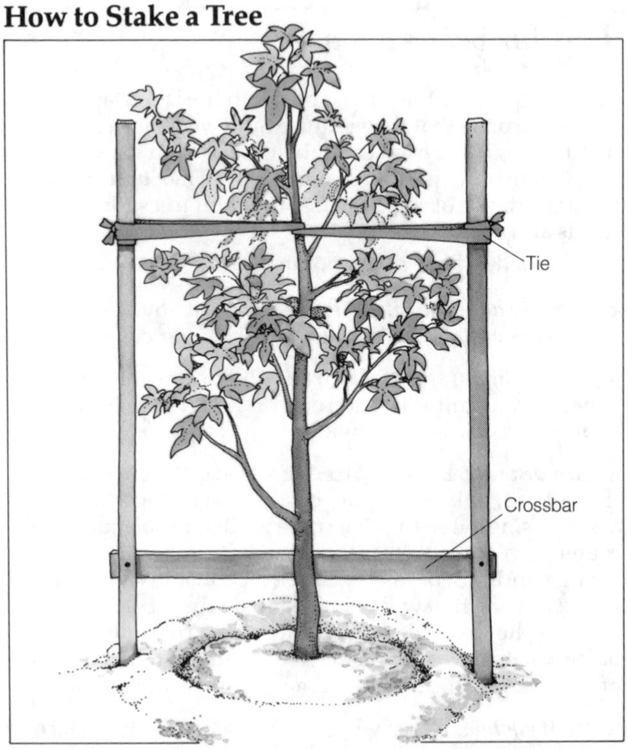

Drive two 2-by-2 stakes a foot from opposite sides of trunk and in line with prevailing winds. Attach firm brace between stakes close to the ground. Tie tree to each stake with a flexible loop of plastic tree tie or cord; tie loosely enough so that trunk is not rigid, will move a bit in wind.

Shrubs

A shrub is a woody plant that usually increases in size by growing new wood from older wood, as well as new stems from the plant's base. Unless specially trained, a shrub will have many stems that rise from ground level or close to it (in contrast to most trees, which grow a single trunk and branch higher up). Shrubs range from ankle-height dwarfs to multistemmed giants you can walk under; forms run from spreading to upright, from stiff to vinelike.

Many shrubs produce colorful flowers, fruits, or both, but some seem to do neither. Among the latter type are the familiar junipers and their coniferous relatives. On the other hand, roses, camellias, and rhododendrons have been cultivated so long for their beautiful blossoms that—though they are indisputably shrubby—one automatically thinks of them as "flowers" in the same sense as petunias and marigolds.

Whether a foot-high shrublet or a 15-foot shrub-tree, a shrub is planted to occupy a more or less permanent place in the garden. This permanence is perhaps a shrub's greatest virtue: after planting, you can expect years of enjoyment with no more effort than routine garden care and occasional shaping or guidance. That is not to say you must never move or discard a shrub. But it does mean that you have no *need* to replant each year, as with annuals, or to dig up and rejuvenate periodically, as with perennials.

Choosing Shrubs

In times past, homeowners sought out bulky shrubs for "foundation plantings," to provide transition from house to garden by hiding the unattractive house foundation. But with the disappearance of high foundations in many modern homes, shrubs have taken on new roles. Because they encompass such a diversity of sizes, shapes, and appearances, shrubs naturally can perform a great range of landscape functions well.

Some shrubs grow slowly, taking many years to achieve the beauty of maturity; their attractiveness makes them worth waiting for, but wait you must. Others can be found that will grow rapidly to a satisfying size and beauty but will pass into a less attractive old age (or even die) in 10 to 15 years. The wise garden planner can take advantage of both sorts. While the slower shrubs are building their bulk and character, the faster but less permanent ones can fill in the blank spaces with their own worthwhile forms and colors. Then, when the fast-maturing shrubs begin their decline, the slower growers will be well on their way to playing their intended roles. And the short-lived ones can always be counted on to function as long-term perennials whenever there is garden space for them.

When you set out to choose shrubs for your garden, don't be guided solely by flashy color or sentimental attachment. Keep in mind the following basic points:

■ ***Adaptability.*** No shrub will satisfy you unless it is suited to your climate, your soil, and your garden environment. First, then, be sure that the shrubs you're considering are recommended for the climate zone in which you live. Next, check the plant description to learn if your garden can meet the plant's additional requirements.

■ ***Plant size.*** If you have a space for a 4- by 4-foot plant but install one that will reach 12 feet in all directions, you're bound to be unhappy in time. The overgrown plant will crowd its neighbors. Then you'll probably try cutting it back to fit, usually destroying much of its natural beauty and possibly interfering with its potential flower or fruit display. Remember that the most attractive shrubs (except those intended for sheared hedges) are those that are allowed to reach their natural size without severe restriction.

■ ***Growth rate.*** Hand in hand with knowledge of a plant's ultimate size should go the realization of how fast it will get there. Slow growth is the price you will have to pay for some of the most desirable shrubs, so place those plants where their slowness will be no detriment to your plans.

■ ***Texture.*** The texture of individual leaves, as well as the texture of many leaves in mass, varies almost as much as do shrubs themselves—from the minute needles and scales of junipers or tiny boxwood leaves to the foot-and-a-half fans of Japanese aralias. Shiny, dull, hairy or fuzzy, smooth, quilted—these qualities, combined with the size and shape of a leaf, give a plant its character.

You can do much to highlight a shrub's inherent beauty if you consider how its foliage texture will complement that of its neighboring plants and how it will relate to any nearby structure. Many bold-leafed plants of different kinds grouped together fight with one another for visual dominance. As is the case with a combination of many different bold-patterned fabrics, the effect is assertive but confused: no one plant is displayed to full advantage. Conversely, a grouping of finely textured, small-leafed shrubs produces an indistinct landscape where nothing is highlighted. If you capitalize on *differences* in texture—whether large leaves against small (or vice versa) or fine-textured against broad and stiff—the individual plants will have a chance to show off.

■ ***Color.*** Though many shrubs are planted for the floral display they will make, foliage colors are just as important in the landscape picture. Just consider the different greens—from the bright yellowish green of *Xylosma* to the dark green of *Osmanthus* or *Rhapiolepis,* from the bronzed green of *Abelia* to the grayed green of *Elaeagnus pungens.* There also are many departures from green: gray or silver, bronze to wine red, blue, yellow, and variegated combinations. See pages 151–153 for lists of shrubs with leaves of different colors.

Much of the advice under "Texture," above, also applies to choosing and combining foliage colors. Visualize the combinations and juxtapositions, remembering that too much of a good thing—color, in this case—produces not an artistic statement but a jumble.

Planting Shrubs

Nurseries sell shrubs in containers, in bare-root form (during the dormant season), and sometimes balled and burlapped. Full planting instructions for all three sorts appear under "Planting Techniques" on pages 64–67.

Vines & Ground Covers

Although the plants in this category are as diverse an assortment as you could imagine, they share common features. These are special-purpose plants with fairly well-defined landscape roles, and these roles can be summarized in one word: covering. Ground covers, of course, are plants that you use to blanket a more or less horizontal surface. Vines, on the other hand, are generally thought of as plants for vertical surfaces—to cover or decorate walls and fences, or to ascend posts and tree trunks. But many vines have a horizontal life, too. Consider the wisteria or bougainvillea atop a pergola, and the ivy or star jasmine performing alternative duty as ground cover.

Vines

A vine is a more or less flexible shrub that doesn't stop growing in height or length (depending on whether you grow it vertically or horizontally). Most need some sort of support if they are to be anything more than a sprawling mass or a ground cover. But therein lies their usefulness: with their ability to "wander" and their willingness to be guided, they can find employment as decorative garden frosting, as emphasizers (or maskers) of architectural lines, or as sunscreens, windscreens, or view screens.

Choosing a vine. You've heard of "a clinging vine," but not all vines cling in the same manner—and some don't cling at all. Vines fall into four general climbing types. When you select a vine for a particular location or purpose, be sure to choose one whose mode of climbing suits the situation (see "Vines & Vinelike Plants," pages 129–131).

■ ***Twining vines.*** New growth twists or spirals as it grows. It will twist around other growth, new or old, or around itself (and around nearby plants as well), requiring some thinning and guidance. Most have too small a turn circumference to encircle a large post; the best support is a cord or wire.

■ ***Vines with twining tendrils.*** Specialized growths along the stems or at the ends of leaves reach out and wrap around whatever is handy—wire or rope, another stem of the vine, or another plant. Tendrils grow out straight until they make contact, then they contract into a spiral. A few vines (such as *Clematis*) have twining leaf stalks instead of special tendrils.

■ ***Clinging vines.*** Special growths along the stems attach to a flat surface. Some clingers have tendrils with suction cup discs at the ends; others have hooklike claws or tips on tendrils that hook into small irregularities or crevices of a flat surface. Still others possess small roots along the stems; these roots cling fast even to vertical surfaces.

■ ***Vines that require tying.*** These vines have no means of attachment and must, therefore, be tied to a support. Some of these plants—climbing roses, for example—can anchor or stabilize themselves in adjacent shrubs or trees by means of their thorns. Others, such as *Fatshedera lizei*, are naturally sprawling and somewhat shrubby but will grow reasonably flat as long as you tie and train them.

Four Types of Vine Attachments

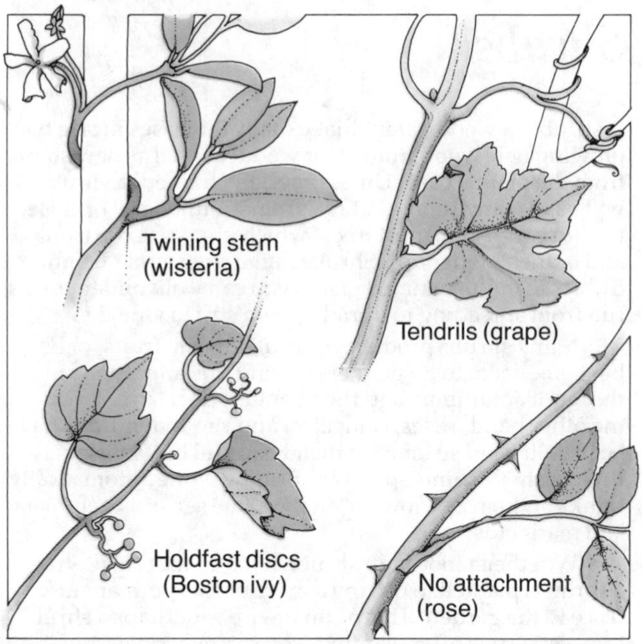

Vines climb by means of various natural devices. How a vine climbs will influence your choice of supports, ultimate training.

Planting and care. Most vines are sold in containers (1 gallon or larger); a few are offered in small pots, and some deciduous kinds (roses and grapes, for example) are available bare-root. See pages 66–67 for container and bare-root planting guidelines.

Care after planting will depend on the particular vine you plant but almost certainly will involve some thinning, pruning, and training. Consult descriptions of individual vines in the Western Plant Encyclopedia, pages 199–568, for particulars of care.

Ground Covers

A gardener selects a ground cover to blanket a prescribed area of soil and present a uniform appearance. The area may be just a 4- by 4-foot patch beneath a tree, or it may run to an acre or more. The best-known ground cover is, of course, grass; you'll find information on choosing and installing a lawn on pages 190–193. Other ground covers include perennials, shrubs, and vines—particular types that will produce a relatively even surface (which may be as low as turf or as tall as 3 feet). Some matlike plants can be walked upon, though none will take the amount of foot traffic a lawn will tolerate.

Choosing a ground cover. Is the ground you want covered level or sloping, sunny or shady, small or large in extent? Do you want a cover that will act as a barrier, or do you want to be able to walk across it? Will the ground cover have the space all to itself, or will it flow around shrubs, landscape boulders, or trees? And what of appearance: do you prefer foliage alone or green punctuated by colorful flowers or fruits? Answers to these questions will help you select the ground cover you need. Consider also the relationships that will exist between the ground cover and the adjacent landscape; take into account foliage textures and colors, as presented under "Shrubs" on page 179. And the lists on pages 126–127 serve as a guide to more than 150 of the West's most popular ground-cover plants.

Planting and care. As was mentioned above, you'll find ground-cover plants among perennials, shrubs, and vines. General guidelines for planting and care differ a bit from one group to another.

■ ***Perennials.*** Many of these plants root as they spread, in time forming dense, interlacing carpets; examples are *Vinca minor* and *Arctotheca calendula*. Others spread much more slowly as they increase from clumps (*Liriope, Convallaria majalis*). Still another sort behaves more as a nonwoody shrub, sending spreading branches out from the plant's base (*Nepeta faassenii, Iberis sempervirens*).

For all perennial ground covers, prepare the soil as recommended on page 187 for perennials. Those that root as they spread may be sold in flats of rooted cuttings or in packs of small plants; those that spread from clumps generally appear in individual small pots or in 1-gallon containers. Consult individual plant entries in the Western Plant Encyclopedia, pages 199–568, for appropriate spacing. Mulch plantings to conserve moisture, suppress weeds, and present a neat appearance while young plants develop. As plantings mature, some may need periodic shearing or light cutting back for neatness.

■ ***Shrubs.*** Among the low-growing shrubs used for ground covers, you'll find three types: those that send out horizontal branches from a central point; those that begin at a central point but root from branches as they spread; and those—typified by *Hypericum calycinum*—that increase their territory by underground runners. Plants are sold in 1-gallon cans, small pots, or flats of rooted cuttings. Set out plants at recommended spacing (see individual plant descriptions in the Western Plant Encyclopedia). If you plant rooted cuttings or plants from small pots, prepare soil as directed in "Perennials," page 187; for 1-gallon container plants, follow container planting guidelines on page 182. Mulch new plantings, as for "Perennials," above. As plantings mature, you may have to head back branches that grow above the desired foliage surface or that spread too far; you may also need to restrict spread of those that increase by underground runners.

■ ***Vines.*** Among vines used for ground cover are some that spread by rooting branches, such as ivy and euonymus, but most will spread far and wide by extending branches from a central point. Those vines that root as they spread may be sold in flats as rooted cuttings; most vines, however, are available in 1-gallon (or larger) containers. Refer to planting and mulching directions under "Shrubs," above. As plants grow, you may need to do some untangling, thinning, or directing of growth to achieve even coverage, and mature plants may call for periodic heading back or shearing to maintain evenness and limit spread.

Guidelines for planting & care on a slope. Sloping land frequently is prime territory for ground cover planting: it is too steep to mow or to cultivate easily, and it is prone to erosion in the rainy season. The lists on pages 167–168 recommend ground cover plants that are well adapted to life on an incline; those that also control erosion are indicated.

■ ***Planting technique.*** On a gentle slope, follow the directions on page 65 for planting from containers or on page 64 for setting out young plants. On more steeply sloping land, however, the simplest method is to create a terrace for each plant as shown in the illustration. Such terraces create individual watering basins, but the high planting keeps a plant's crown from becoming saturated during waterings and from becoming buried if soil gradually washes downslope into the basin.

■ ***Care and training.*** Applying water is the most important aspect of care, at least when plants are young and becoming established. And for sloping land, a drip irrigation setup (see page 70) will provide the most thorough watering of each plant while it minimizes or eliminates any problem with water runoff or soil erosion that can result from watering with sprinklers.

After ground cover is planted and watered in, and a drip system is in place, you should mulch the entire area. The mulch will conserve moisture (thus encouraging better and faster rooting) and will suppress weed growth.

If you have planted vining plants to cover a bare slope, you may need to periodically untangle the growing stems and, more important at first, train some stems to grow upslope to achieve faster cover. To pin stems in place, use short lengths of wire bent into a "U" like a croquet wicket.

Planting on a Slope

On steep slope, set out plants on individual terraces with crowns high and watering basins behind the plants.

Container Plants—Indoors & Out

Container plants generally require more attention than plants growing in the ground, but their potential advantages may make the extra care worthwhile. For the gardener with only a balcony or a paved patio, plants in containers are the only way to have a garden at all. And even those who have a garden can use container plants to bring seasonal flowers on stage when colorful and remove them to an unobtrusive area when past their prime. Other plants have such handsome foliage that they deserve to be grown in containers so they can be appreciated at close range throughout the year.

Container culture also offers you a chance to enjoy plants that aren't entirely suited to your garden conditions. You can grow acid-soil plants in regions where native soil is alkaline and plants that demand fast drainage when your garden soil is clay. Plants too tender for your climate can be moved to shelter when cold weather comes; and plants sensitive to winter cold or summer heat may function well as container subjects indoors.

Basic Container Care

The routine extra attention container plants need can be directed into three categories: soil preparation, watering, and fertilizing. They will require periodic transplanting and replanting as well.

Soil mixes for containers. A container plant needs soil that is porous and well drained but that retains moisture. The soil must allow roots to grow easily, and it must drain fast enough that roots don't become suffocated in soggy soil. Yet the soil should retain enough moisture so that you won't have to water the plants continually.

Even the best garden soils fail to satisfy container soil requirements: in containers, garden soil inevitably forms a dense mass that roots can't penetrate easily, and it remains soggy for too long after watering. For these reasons, gardeners growing container plants turn to potting mixes.

You can purchase packaged potting mixes that are ready to use directly out of the bag. Formulations (listed on the bags) will vary somewhat from brand to brand, but none will contain actual soil. Look for a mix high in bark, forest materials, or sphagnum peat plus vermiculite. A 2-cubic-foot bag of potting mix will suffice to fill a planter box 36 by 8 by 10 inches, or to transplant 8 to 10 plants from 1-gallon nursery containers to separate 10- or 12-inch pots.

Packaged potting mixes vary greatly in their content of soluble salts, which, in high concentrations, can be detrimental to plant growth. To be on the safe side, thoroughly leach any packaged potting soil three or four times before planting in it. And because such leaching will remove nutrients as well as salts, you should apply a soluble fertilizer within 2 weeks after planting.

If you prefer to mix your own potting soil—or if you are planning a large-scale operation that would be too costly using packaged mixes—you can purchase the basic component materials and combine them yourself. There are countless possible formulations, but they all combine organic material (bark, peat moss, leaf mold, compost) and mineral matter (soil, sand, perlite, vermiculite) in proportions that will produce the desired porosity, drainage, and moisture retention.

One time-honored basic container mixture consists of 1 part good garden soil (not clay), 1 part sand (river or builder's sand) or perlite, and 1 part peat moss or nitrogen-stabilized bark. For plants that prefer acid soil (such as rhododendrons, azaleas, and heather), alter the above mix to 2 parts peat moss or nitrogen-stabilized bark.

The use of soil-less mixes lessens the danger from soil-borne diseases. But they dry faster than mixes containing soil, and they will need fertilizer applications more often because of the frequent leaching from frequent watering. For a quantity of soil-less mix, combine ⅔ cubic yard of nitrogen-stabilized bark (or peat moss) and ⅓ cubic yard washed 20-grit sand; add to this 6 pounds of 0-10-10 dry fertilizer and 10 pounds dolomite or dolomitic limestone.

Superabsorbent polymers are a recent development that can increase water retention of a container soil mix. These gel-like polymers absorb hundreds of times their weight in water; in potting soil, the gel holds both water and dissolved nutrients for plant roots to use. Because the gel retains water that normally drains from the soil, plants still have a source of moisture when potting soil becomes dry. This lets you stretch intervals between waterings. And plants grow better because the gel eliminates the wide fluctuations of moisture that can occur between waterings. Polyacrylamide gel is the longest-lasting kind. Mix the dry material with water to expand the particles; then add to potting mix in the proportion recommended by the manufacturer—usually about 1 pint gel to 6 pints potting mix.

Watering. When watering container plants, be guided not by a calendar but by an inspection of the soil. Unlike plants in the ground, which can survive a short drought because their roots penetrate deep into the soil, container plants have dense, compact root systems and are wholly dependent for moisture on watering (unless they are placed outdoors, where they receive rainfall).

In hot, dry, windy weather you may need to water actively growing plants more than once a day; when weather is cool, still, and overcast, or if plants are semidormant, you may get by with weekly (or even less frequent) watering. Test with your fingers: it's time to water if the soil is dry beneath the surface.

To water thoroughly, be sure to apply water on the entire soil surface until you see it flowing out the drainage holes. This will guarantee moistening the entire soil mass and also will prevent any potentially harmful salts from accumulating in the soil.

Note: If water comes out the drainage hole too fast, check to see if water is just running down the inside surface of the container and not through the soil. A root ball that has become too dry can shrink away from the sides of the container; when that happens, water will run around the root ball without penetrating it. To correct the problem, set the container in a tub of water and soak the plant until bubbles stop rising. If that method isn't practical, cork the container's drainage holes and then water the plant. Remove corks after the soil is soaked.

Fertilizing. Heavy and thorough watering leaches out plant nutrients from container soils, so regular fertilizer applications are required for best plant growth. Use either liquid or dry fertilizer according to label directions. The slow-release, dry fertilizers, which release nutrients steadily over a period of time, don't need to be applied as often as other fertilizers. With other types of fertilizers, light and frequent applications will give best results. But again, let the plant, not a fixed schedule, be your guide. Observe its growth rate, bloom period, season of new growth, and dormant season; then give fertilizer only when the plant needs it for growth and bloom.

Transplanting. Shift a plant to a larger container when its root system fills the container in which it is growing; usually the first sign of this is roots protruding from drainage holes. Generally speaking, container plants should be shifted to a slightly larger container rather than to a much larger one, since you want to keep the soil mass fairly well filled with roots (unused soil in a container can stagnate and become a haven for potentially harmful organisms). With fast-growing plants, you can safely shift to a definitely larger container. And you can always put a number of small plants in a large container—their combined root systems will occupy the total soil mass.

When moving a plant to a larger container, select a new container that will allow an inch or two of fresh soil on all sides of the root mass. If the plant's root ball appears compacted, cut it vertically with a sharp knife to encourage roots to move out into new soil in the larger container. Make at least four equally spaced cuts about ¼ to 1 inch deep, depending on root ball size.

If you have an older plant in a large container and want to keep it in that container indefinitely, you can periodically root-prune the plant. During the plant's dormant period, gently turn it out of the container. Shave off an inch or two of the outer root mass on all sides and on the bottom with a sharp knife; then replant in the same container with fresh soil mix around and underneath the roots.

House Plants

Plants that you keep indoors need careful attention to soil preparation, watering, and fertilizer application as outlined above, for container plants in general, and as amended in paragraphs that follow. In addition, you should pay special attention to light and humidity.

Soil. Container soil for house plants should be composed *entirely* of sterile materials—such as a prepared potting soil mix or a soil-less mix you make yourself. Potentially harmful organisms in garden soils pose a great threat to plant health when confined with roots in a limited soil mass and in the warmth and low light level of a home. If you wish to include garden soil in a potting medium for house plants, you'll have to sterilize it with heat or a chemical soil sterilizer.

To heat-treat a batch of container soil, follow these steps. (1) Mix soil ingredients thoroughly. (2) Moisten mix slightly, then spread it (no deeper than 4 inches) in a shallow, ovenproof pan. (3) Place filled pan in a 180° oven and bake for 2 hours minimum (the baking process produces a very unpleasant, but short-lived, odor). (4) Remove sterilized soil from the oven and let it air for a few days indoors (for example, in a garage); store it in sturdy plastic bags or plastic buckets.

Water. The best water for house plants is rainwater, but most people rely instead on water from the tap—which is usually satisfactory unless it contains quantities of harmful salts or is artificially softened with sodium. If you have a water softener, draw water for your house plants from an outside tap. If you must use softened water (or water that is high in alkaline salts), give your house plants complete leachings about once a month. Thoroughly flush water through the soil several times, or set each plant in the sink or tub and let a trickle run through it for a while.

Light. Give house plants good light, but avoid the searing sun that comes through south and west windows. Unless you set plants back from such windows or moderate sunlight with thin curtains, stick to a northern or eastern exposure. Plants grown for their flower display generally need more light than plants grown for foliage alone.

Humidity. Low humidity is the bane of most house plants, and low humidity goes hand in hand with heated rooms. Best places for plants are the cooler (but adequately lit) spots around the house; the higher humidity in bathrooms and kitchens favors growth. Avoid at all costs locating plants near hot-air registers.

Pebble-filled, waterproof tray holds water below pot; evaporation raises humidity around plant.

Bulbs

Bulbs are a very specialized group of perennial plants. Following popular usage, we call a number of plants that are not true bulbs—corms, rhizomes, tubers, and tuberous roots—by the same name (see next page). But whether true bulbs or bulblike plants, they all hold a reserve of nutrients in a thickened underground storage organ. This reserve almost guarantees that the bulb you purchase in summer or fall will bloom next spring: all the nutrients the plant needs to complete its life cycle are in storage, waiting for the right combination of moisture and soil temperature to trigger the cycle's beginning phase.

Planting & Care

Although the bulb you purchase from a nursery or commercial specialist is likely to be a sure first-season performer, performance in subsequent years will depend on the care you give it. Proper care—as always—begins with the soil.

Most bulbs prefer soil that drains well yet retains a certain amount of water. These requirements may sound mutually exclusive, but they are not. The ideal soil will hold enough water to keep roots healthy without retaining so much that it stays saturated (see "Soils," page 60). By adding organic matter to your soil, you achieve this balance: organic matter will improve drainage in a heavy soil, but will increase water retention in lighter soils. Any soil in which annuals or vegetables thrive also should be good for bulbs.

In planting true bulbs and most corms, the rule of thumb is to dig a hole about three times as deep as the bulb's greatest diameter. (To determine planting depths for the other "bulbs," see individual plant descriptions in the Western Plant Encyclopedia, pages 199–568.) If you will be planting many bulbs in one bed, it may be easier to dig a trench or to excavate the bed to the desirable planting depth than to dig numerous individual holes.

This is the time to add fertilizer high in phosphorus and potassium—two nutrients especially important to the formation of healthy bulbs. If you plant bulbs in individual holes, dig up to a tablespoonful of fertilizer into the soil at the bottom of each hole, then cover with about 2 inches of soil and plant the bulb. Otherwise, dig fertilizer into the bottom of the trench or excavated bed.

When all the bulbs are set in place and covered with soil, soak the area thoroughly. In some regions this initial watering, along with subsequent rain, will supply all the moisture bulbs will need until their leaves poke above the soil surface. But if you live in an arid climate or have an unusually dry winter, you will need to soak the bulbs periodically throughout the winter and into the blooming season. Summer-flowering bulbs will need watering at least until they finish blooming.

The roots of bulbs grow below the depth at which you planted, so that water, to do them any good, must penetrate deep into the soil. (See "Watering" on pages 68–72 for more specific advice on watering practices.) A mulch will help conserve soil moisture and in hot, dry regions will also hold down soil temperature. In addition, it will suppress weeds, even after the bulb foliage has disappeared.

Bulb plantings established for a year or more may benefit from application of a nitrogen fertilizer at the start of the growing season (as recommended for perennials, page 187). But the crucial moment for applying fertilizer comes after the blooms have faded.

When a bulb has finished flowering, much of its supply of stored nutrients is depleted. It must replenish those nutrients if it is to perform well the next year. For this reason, it is essential to leave the foliage on the plant, even if it begins to look unsightly, until it has yellowed and can be pulled off easily. The leaves continue to manufacture food for the plant (see "The Leaves," page 58); cutting them off prematurely amounts to removing the next year's blossoms—or at least reducing their quantity and quality.

Furthermore, fertilizer application at this time helps bulbs form not only the next year's flowers but also new bulbs that will increase the planting. Phosphorus and potassium—the nutrients emphasized in "bulb food"—are most useful now, though they must reach the root zone in order to be fully effective (see pages 73–74). In an established planting, you may be able only to scatter fertilizer over the soil surface, scratch it in, and hope that some phosphorus and potassium will reach the roots. You can improve your chances in alkaline soil by using an acid fertilizer (see page 75). Where bulbs are spaced far enough apart, or in rows, you may be able to get fertilizer deep into the soil by digging narrow trenches or holes 8 inches deep, placing fertilizer at the bottom, and then filling with soil.

Container Culture

Most bulbs are quite easy to grow in containers, which furnish great flexibility in changing garden color schemes and flower placement. Not only can you change the scene by shifting pots of blooming bulbs, you also can take them off stage when bloom is finished.

A number of bulbs will grow permanently in containers with occasional repotting and soil rejuvenation, including applications of fertilizer. The general advice under "Container Plants" (pages 182–183), plus tips under individual plant names in the Western Plant Encyclopedia, will cover container culture over a long period of time.

In addition, many gardeners plant favorite spring-flowering sorts—daffodils, tulips, crocuses, Dutch irises, hyacinths, scillas, and freesias—in pots for their first bloom season; afterward, they plant them out in the garden. For spring-flowering bulbs, a suitable container soil mixture contains equal parts of good garden soil (loam), coarse sand, and organic matter such as peat moss, leaf mold, compost, or ground bark. Select top-quality bulbs for container culture. They will give the best flower display and will recuperate fastest when planted out in the garden after their debut season in containers.

Plant spring-flowering bulbs so that they nearly touch one another, their tips level with the soil surface (which

The Five Bulb Types

True bulb & bulblet

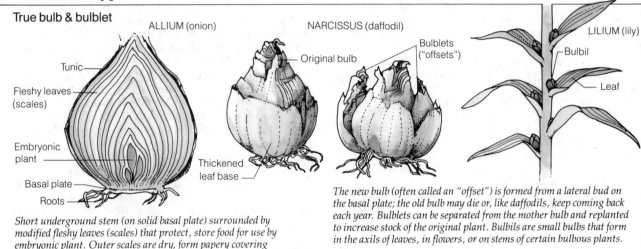

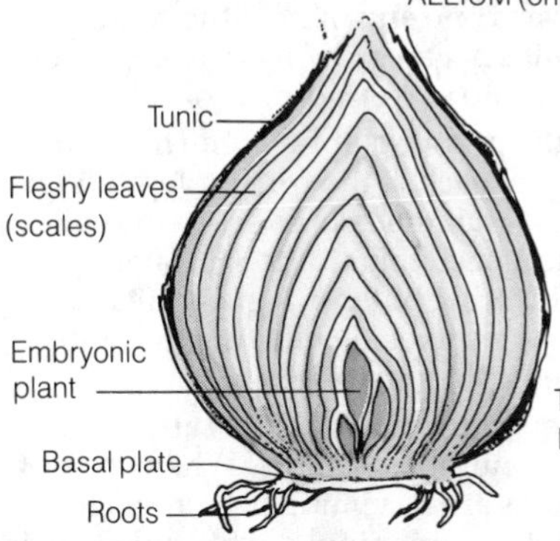

Short underground stem (on solid basal plate) surrounded by modified fleshy leaves (scales) that protect, store food for use by embryonic plant. Outer scales are dry, form papery covering (tunic).

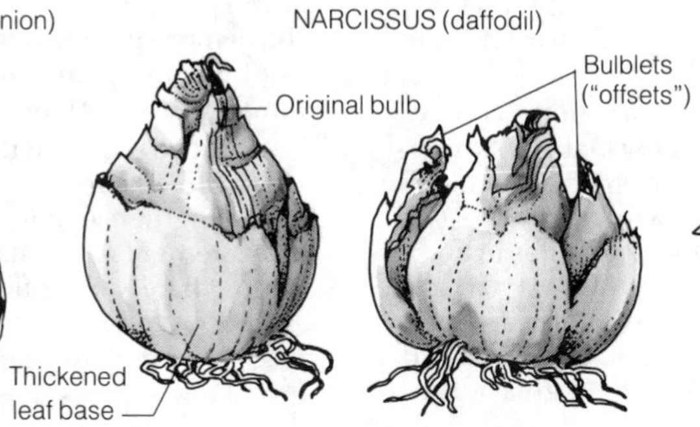

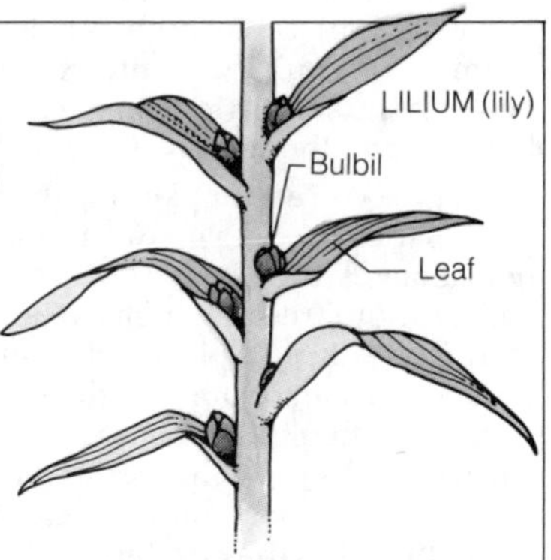

The new bulb (often called an "offset") is formed from a lateral bud on the basal plate; the old bulb may die or, like daffodils, keep coming back each year. Bulblets can be separated from the mother bulb and replanted to increase stock of the original plant. Bulbils are small bulbs that form in the axils of leaves, in flowers, or on stems of certain bulbous plants.

Corm & cormel

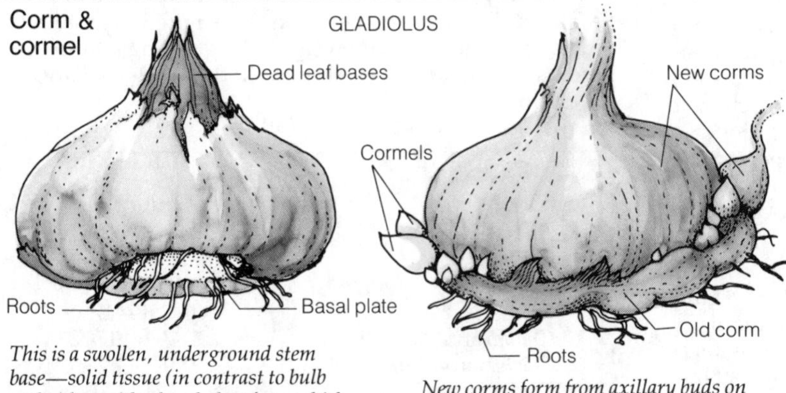

This is a swollen, underground stem base—solid tissue (in contrast to bulb scales) but with a basal plate from which roots grow. Growth point is on the corm's top; many corms have tunics that consist of dried bases of previous season's leaves. An individual corm lasts just one year (see right).

New corms form from axillary buds on the top of an old corm as it completes its growth cycle. Fingernail-size cormels will take two to three years to flower; larger corms should bloom in the following year.

Tuber

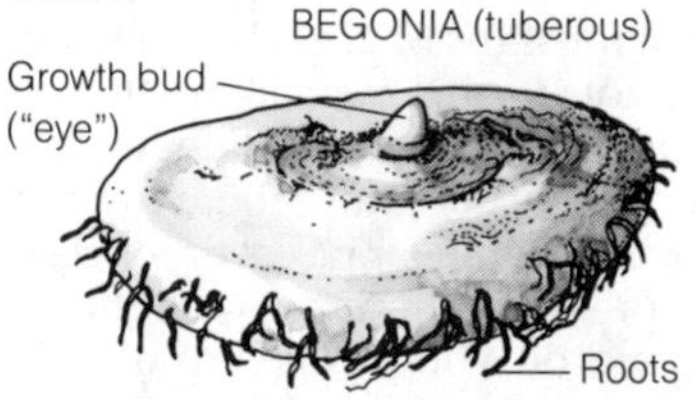

Like a corm, a tuber is a swollen, underground stem base, but it lacks the corm's distinct organization. There is no basal plate, so roots can grow from all sides; multiple growth points are distributed over the upper surface—each is a scalelike leaf with a growth bud in its axil. Divide by cutting into sections that have growth buds.

Tuberous roots

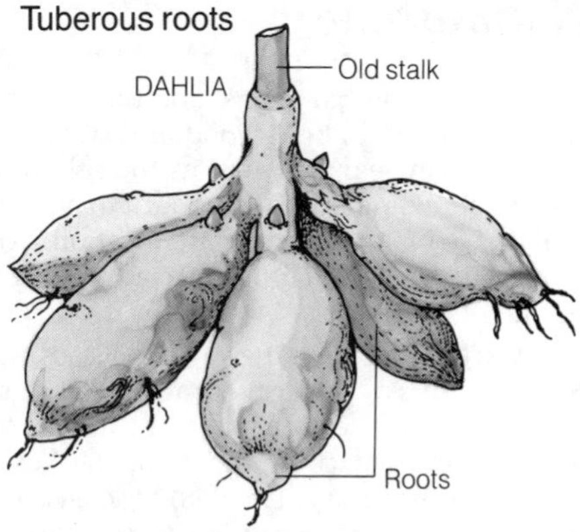

These are actual roots (rather than stems) that are specialized to store nutrients. Growth buds are at the bases of old stems rather than on the tuberous roots. To divide, cut apart so that each division will contain both roots and part of the stem's base with one or more growth buds.

Rhizome

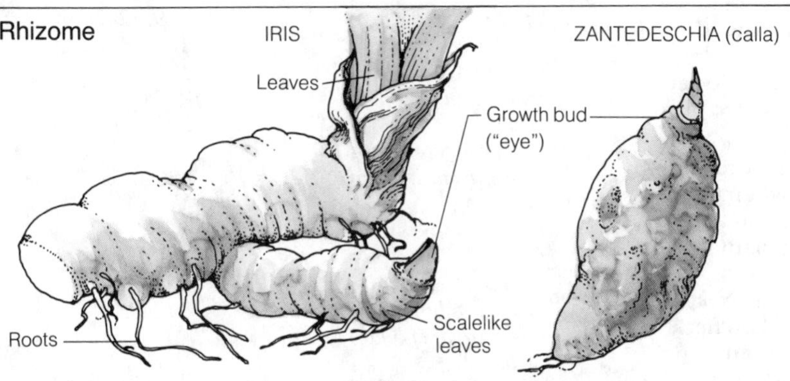

This is a thickened stem that grows partially or entirely beneath the ground. Roots generally grow from the underside; the principal growing point is at the tip, though additional growing points will form along the rhizome's length. To divide, cut into sections that have visible growing points.

should be about an inch below the container's rim to facilitate watering). Small bulbs—crocuses and scillas, for example—should be planted slightly deeper, with tips just beneath the soil. After you have filled soil in around the bulbs, water them thoroughly.

Since you aren't planting these bulbs in the cool soil depths they prefer, you must somehow make up for this deficiency. The objective is to give the bulbs a good winter chill without freezing them. Where winters are cool (Climate Zones 1 to 7), placing the pots full of bulbs in an unheated room or burying them to the pots' rims in soil covered with mulch on the north side of a house may be sufficient. Where winters are warm (Climate Zones 8 to 24), you can choose among these options to give bulbs the winter chill they prefer:

- Bury pots in a foot-deep trench and cover with 6 to 8 inches of moist wood shavings, sawdust, sand, peat moss, or even earth.
- Place pots in a shaded cold frame and bury as above.
- Set pots in a deep basket or box, cover as above, and place in the shadiest garden spot; keep the covering moist to maintain coolness.

After 8 to 10 weeks, carefully uncover a pot or two and check for signs of growth—roots emerging from the drainage hole or shoots breaking through the potting soil. When you see such signs, lift pots from their trench, cold frame, or basket and move them to a shaded location. Shoots will be white or palest green; leave the pots in the shady spot—without direct sunlight—until the shoots begin to take on a normal green color. Then move them into the chosen garden location.

When potted bulbs have finished blooming, continue watering and fertilizing until foliage turns yellow. At that time, you can remove bulbs from their pots and plant them out in the garden. Bloom the following spring usually will not be up to par but should return to normal in following years, with good soil and fertilizer.

Naturalizing

A number of bulbs, corms, and tubers can be planted in meadow, field, or light woodland situations where they will perform year after year as though they were wildflowers. By choosing bulbs that adapt to naturalizing and that will thrive in your climate and location, you can enjoy an annual display with little more effort than it takes to plant them.

Careful choice is the key to success with naturalizing. Refer to the list of easy naturalizers (at right) when making a preliminary selection for your climate zone. Then read descriptions of each candidate in the Western Plant Encyclopedia (pages 199–568) to see if your choices will thrive under the conditions you can provide. Note especially the requirements for sun or shade; also check moisture needs: Will the selected bulbs go without supplemental water, or will you have to provide water during the dry months?

Planting. To achieve a naturalistic effect—as though the bulbs had not been deliberately planted—many gardeners broadcast handfuls of bulbs over the desired area, and then plant each bulb where it has landed. For the most realistic effect, broadcast the bulbs so that their density varies over the planting area. Each drift of bulbs should have more plants toward one end or near the center, to look as though the bulbs began growing in one location and spread from there into surrounding ground.

Set out bulbs at the proper planting time for your zone, being sure to plant each at the correct depth. Water them in, then let natural rainfall take over (unless cultural requirements indicate a need for additional watering). If you plant spring-flowering bulbs in a grassy field or meadow you will mow, try to delay mowing the bulbs' area until bulb foliage has begun to yellow.

Flower size and quantity may decrease after bulbs have been in place for a number of years. When you notice this, you know the bulbs are becoming overcrowded. After flowering and foliage ripening, dig the bulbs, divide if needed, and replant when the time is right.

Good naturalizing choices. The following bulbs will naturalize successfully within their zones of adaptability, as long as your garden satisfies their cultural needs. Make preliminary choices from those noted as growing in your climate zone, then check the growing requirements in individual descriptions in the Western Plant Encyclopedia.

Name	***Zones***
Anemone blanda	1–9, 14–23
Brodiaea	All
Calochortus	All
Camassia	1–9, 14–17
Chionodoxa	1–7, 14, 17–20
Colchicum autumnale	1–9, 14–24
Convallaria majalis	1–7, 14–20
Crocosmia	5–24
Crocus	All
Cyclamen	1–9, 14–24
Dichelostemma	All
Endymion	All
Eranthis hyemalis	1–9, 14–17
Erythronium	1–7, 15–17
Freesia	8, 9, 12–24
Fritillaria	1–7, 15–17
Galanthus	1–9, 14–17
Ipheion uniflorum	4–24
Ixia	5–24
Ixiolirion tataricum	5–24
Leucocoryne ixioides	13, 16, 19, 21–24
Leucojum	Varies
Lilium (some species)	Varies
Muscari	All
Narcissus	All
Ornithogalum umbellatum	5–24
Puschkinia scilloides	All
Scilla	Varies
Sparaxis tricolor	9, 13–24
Sternbergia lutea	All
Triteleia	All
Tulipa (some species)	All

Perennials

Perennials are as diverse an assortment of plants as you'll find under one collective heading, yet all have two traits in common: unlike shrubs, they are not woody; and unlike annuals, they live from year to year. Typically, a perennial has one blooming season each year, from only a week to more than a month long. After blooming, the plant may put on new growth for the next year; it may die down and virtually disappear until the time is right, some months later, for growth to resume; or it may retain much the same appearance throughout the year.

Some perennials store reserve food for the next season in specialized underground tissues. These plants, which form a cohesive and distinct group, are discussed separately under "Bulbs" on pages 184–186.

Many of the popular perennials are grown for the beauty of their flowers, and any attractive foliage is merely an added bonus. Conversely, a smaller group of perennials—artemisias, for example—are grown for foliage alone, the flowers being inconsequential or even unattractive. Some perennials have evergreen foliage and are attractive throughout the year.

Garden Uses

At one time, perennials were considered plants to be grouped together in the perennial border, a garden fashion legacy from Edwardian England. Perennial borders *can* be beautiful, but they require careful planning and a great deal of maintenance. More and more, gardeners are using perennials as individuals combined with other kinds of plants in the landscape.

Like annuals, perennials provide color masses, but unlike annuals, they will bloom several years in a row without having to be dug up and replanted. Perennials are thus more permanent than annuals but less permanent than flowering shrubs. In fact, their semipermanence is a definite selling point. You can leave perennials in place for several years with little maintenance beyond annual cleanup, some fertilizing, and routine watering; but if you want to change the landscape, perennials are easy to dig up and replant—much more so than the average flowering shrub.

Planting & Care

Most perennials—like other plants—perform best in good soil. Because you expect them to remain in place for several years after planting, it pays to prepare the soil well before you set them out. Dig liberal amounts of organic material into the soil; use about 25 percent by volume of amendments such as ground bark, peat moss, compost, or aged manure. At the same time, you can incorporate a fertilizer that is high in phosphorus and potash into the planting area. These nutrients must be dug into the anticipated root zone in order to be effective (see pages 73–74). If you can, prepare the soil at least a few weeks prior to planting so that it will have a chance to settle.

Care of established perennials. Most perennials begin their yearly growth cycle in spring, following a winter dormant period, and will benefit from fertilizer application at that time. A fertilizer that contains 10 to 17 percent nitrogen will provide a boost to get the plants going through the bloom season. Then—to replace soluble nitrogen that will be leached through the soil (see page 73)—give plants another application just after flowering. They will then put on good new growth, which will produce the next year's flowers. Use amounts of fertilizer specified on the product label.

For perennials that are periodically dug up, divided, and replanted, you can renew phosphorus and potassium when you prepare the soil for replanting. But even the "permanent" perennials, such as peonies, may appreciate replenishment of these nutrients from time to time. The best way to apply them is to use a complete fertilizer high in phosphorus and potassium: carefully dig it in, apply it in deep trenches, or use fertilizer stakes or tablets (see page 75).

Routine watering during the growth and bloom period will satisfy most perennials. Exceptions are noted in the Western Plant Encyclopedia as preferring dry or unusually wet soil.

After a perennial has finished blooming, remove the old blossoms to prevent the plant's energy from going into seed production. Remove only old flowers and stems; leaving most of the foliage will help the plant manufacture food to store for the next year's growth.

Later in the season (usually in fall), when old leaves and flower stalks have dried, you should clean up the area. Removing dead growth minimizes the carry-over from year to year of certain diseases and eliminates hiding and breeding places for various insects, snails, and slugs.

In cold-winter regions (Zones 1 to 3), many gardeners routinely mulch their perennials to protect them from alternate freezing and thawing. Where soil is reliably frozen all winter and a good snow cover is virtually guaranteed, mulching is not as necessary because plants will remain dormant until spring arrives. But where cold snowy days alternate with sunny and warmer ones during winter, a mulch is necessary to ensure that plants stay cold and inactive. After the ground first freezes, apply a lightweight mulch that won't pack down into a sodden mass. Straw is one popular choice; evergreen boughs are good where available.

Digging, dividing, & replanting. As was mentioned above, some perennials—peonies, for example—will thrive almost indefinitely in one location. But more typically, a perennial will grow over time into such a thick clump that performance declines because plants are crowded. When this happens, dig up the clump during its dormant period (sometime after bloom season or in earliest spring; see "Division" on page 82), separate it into smaller clumps or individual plants, and replant in soil that you have prepared by adding organic matter and fertilizer. If you plan to replant in the same soil, *heel in* (see Glossary) the clumps while you get the soil into shape.

Annuals

Think of annuals as the real workhorses of the garden. Their lives are short—within one growing season, they germinate from seed, grow and bloom, form seeds, and die—but that brief lifetime is almost incredibly productive. The majority of flowering shrubs and perennials have one flowering period during a few weeks of the year, then are without blooms for the remainder. Annuals, on the other hand, can bloom literally for months, from the moment the plants are mature enough to bear flowers until they are cut down by frost. And in areas of no frosts or mild frosts (Zones 8 to 24), certain annuals can brighten even a winter garden with blossoms.

Preparing the Soil

Good soil, the foundation on which a successful annual planting is built, requires some advance preparation. Unlike trees, shrubs, and some perennials—around which you can continue to improve soil years after planting—annuals must make do with the soil they are planted in during their months in your garden. For growing annuals in containers (see next page), you'll find information about container soil on page 182.

Essential soil properties are good drainage and porosity. Organic soil amendments such as ground bark, peat moss, aged animal manures, and compost dug into the soil prior to planting will help create a good environment for annuals' roots. These amendments improve moisture retention, help prevent rapid leaching of nutrients, and improve soil structure, so that roots will grow freely. Whether you plan to sow seeds or set out small plants, first refer to soil preparation advice on page 80 under "Seeds in the Open Ground."

If you can, prepare your soil a month or more before you intend to sow seeds or set out plants. This gives soil time to "mellow" after addition of amendments and gives the gardener a chance to eliminate weeds that will germinate before the annuals are set out.

Planting & Timing

Annuals begin their year as seedlings emerging from the soil. Many gardeners prefer to sow their own annual seeds—to try out new strains sold by seed firms, to get a jump on the season by starting plants indoors while it is still too cold outside to plant, or to save money. But one of the greatest benefits of planting seeds is the simple pleasure of watching seedlings grow. You'll find guidelines for seed sowing on pages 80–81.

If you have neither the time nor the desire to raise annuals from seed, you'll find it easy to buy a wide selection of popular types and varieties already started at nurseries. They may be sold in small individual containers, in packs of four or six, or in flats. The handling of these plants is discussed on page 64.

In the mild-winter zones (8 to 24), there are two principal times of year for planting annuals: early spring, for those that bloom in late spring, summer, and fall; and late summer or fall, for the winter and early spring bloomers. Both are periods of moderately cool temperatures preceding the sort of weather that favors development of annuals. Gardeners in cold-winter zones (1 to 7) can plant only in early spring.

The summer-flowering annuals need to establish roots before really warm days come along to hasten growth. If planted when weather is already warm, the plants that result rarely attain full size or productivity. Nor do you gain an advantage by setting out plants too early. At best, annuals planted too early will simply sit there in cold soil and air without growing until the days begin to get longer and warmer. At worst, they can be damaged by a late frost.

Winter-blooming annuals should be set out while days are still warm enough for good plant growth but nights are lengthening. Winter annuals set out while days are longer than nights may perish or rush to maturity as stunted, poorly established plants.

In the charts on pages 135–143, you will find favorite annuals listed according to their seasons of bloom. For specific planting information on each annual, refer to individual entries in the Western Plant Encyclopedia, pages 199–568.

Care After Planting

For any annual, the secret to success after planting is to keep the plant growing steadily. The keys to plant growth are watering, fertilizing, and grooming.

Watering. By itself, watering will ensure steady growth if you attend to it faithfully. The objective is to supply water before plants show they need it by wilting, yet not to overwater: soggy soil restricts root development. Let the top inch (less for very small and newly planted annuals) of soil dry before you water, and then apply enough water to penetrate deeply.

Sprinkling is an effective way to water annuals, though the spray of water may topple tall or weak-stemmed plants. An economical and thorough way to water annuals grown in rows or in block beds is to irrigate in furrows between rows. With a small bed of annuals, you may be able to hoe up a shallow dike around the bed and irrigate by flooding. Drip irrigation, with the various sorts of emitters available, offers a range of watering options. Refer to pages 69–71 for detailed information on watering techniques.

But no matter how you water, a mulch of some sort of organic material will prolong intervals between waterings by slowing the drying of the soil. In addition, mulches will prevent the soil surface from crusting, thus improving water and air penetration.

Fertilizing. If you mixed a complete fertilizer into the soil before planting your annuals (as recommended on page 80), you probably supplied enough nutrients to last at least half the growing season. In cold-winter zones

(1 to 7), an application of fertilizer after bloom is under way will tide annuals through their season. Where winters are warmer, and the growing season for annuals is correspondingly longer, give plants another fertilizer application in late summer.

If you didn't add fertilizer to your soil before planting annuals, give plants an application of a high-nitrogen complete fertilizer about 2 weeks after planting; then follow with a second application about 6 weeks after the first. In warmest zones, where growing seasons are longest, a third application may be in order 6 to 8 weeks after the second.

For information on the various fertilizer types, see pages 74–75. Controlled-release fertilizers—though costlier than traditional granular types—are popular with many gardeners because they release nitrogen, in particular, over a period of time. Their longevity and sustained yield let you stretch periods between applications. In the cold-winter zones, one application, at planting time, usually is sufficient.

Liquid fertilizers may be convenient for a small number of plants. Monthly applications of regular-strength dilution or applications every 2 weeks at half strength will keep plants growing steadily.

Grooming. An annual plant's life work is to produce seeds that perpetuate the species. Once seed is set, the plant hardens into maturity and produces fewer and fewer flowers. To keep blooms coming all season long, you have to interrupt nature's seed-producing process by removing old blossoms before they can begin seed formation. This grooming need be no more than a weekly removal of faded blossoms. Some hybrid strains of certain annuals (triploid marigolds, for example) are sterile and so will not set seeds. With these plants, grooming serves only to keep them tidy.

Ordinarily, removing flowers will prolong bloom—as long as you have given your annuals regular attention. If, however, they appear to have slowed flower production too soon, the cause may be any one or more of these factors: inadequate water during hot weather, depletion of nutrients, or cold or frosty nights, which signal to the plant the end of the growing season.

Annuals in Containers

Most of the annuals popular for flower beds also excel as showy container subjects. Basic information for container plants (pages 182–183) apply to annuals as well.

Either in pots and tubs or in hanging baskets, annuals lend themselves to mass plantings. You can group plants of one kind together for color impact or let your imagination run wild by combining different annuals in one container. There are no real guidelines for combinations other than personal preference and trial and error. You may want to use annuals in combination with perennials to lengthen the container garden's flowering period; some annuals also are effective as underplantings for container plantings of shrubs and trees. The lists at right suggest various annuals and annual combinations for these purposes.

Mixed bouquet plantings. Riotous combinations of annuals (or annuals and perennials) in large containers are easy successes if you follow the guidelines below.

- ***Containers.*** It takes pots, tubs, or other containers that are at least 18 inches across to give the plants ample root space and to be in the right scale for the volume of plants. Experience has shown that four types are best for mixed bouquet plantings; in decreasing order of cost, they are clay pots, wooden half barrels, simulated clay pots made of terra-cotta–colored plastic, and paper pulp pots.
- ***Potting soil.*** You can mix your own, as described on page 182, but most growers choose the convenience of packaged potting soils, which can be used directly from the bag or doctored up to suit you.
- ***Planting.*** To achieve the overflowing look, place plants much closer together than you would if planting in garden beds. For most combinations, a distance of about 4 inches apart is good. With such close spacing, plants grow up and out, intermingling much like cut flowers in a bouquet; and if a few plants fail to grow, there's little likelihood of the gaps showing.
- ***Water and fertilizer.*** Success depends on a continual supply of moisture and nutrients. Water faithfully, never allowing the planting to dry to the wilting point. Frequent watering leaches nutrients, so you will need to apply fertilizer several times during the growing season. A proven regime is to apply controlled-release granules at planting time, then apply a liquid fertilizer (approximately 20-20-20) every three weeks after growth is under way.
- ***Grooming.*** To keep plants producing flowers, remove faded blossoms before they divert the plant's energies into forming seed. Do this at least every other day. With some plants, judicious cutting back or pinching will result in more bloom, because it increases the number of stems.
- ***Choices.*** Mixed bouquet plantings lend themselves to experimentation with planting combinations. Simply be sure that you place the tallest growers in the center of each container, the medium height and short growers toward the outside. And, of course, be sure that all your choices are likely to grow well not only in your climate zone but also in the container's garden location.

A number of annuals and perennials usually treated as annuals are proven performers in these mixed container plantings. Arranged according to height, they are:

Low-growing: ageratum, alyssum (*Lobularia maritima*), *Campanula portenschlagiana*, dwarf morning glory (*Convolvulus tricolor*), ivy geranium (*Pelargonium peltatum*), lobelia, *Lotus berthelotii*, marigold (*Tagetes*), nasturtium (*Tropaeolum majus*), petunia, *Phlox drummondii*, Swan River daisy (*Brachycome iberidifolia*), verbena

Medium-height: Achillea taygetea, basil 'Dark Opal' (*Ocimum*), begonia (semperflorens kinds), *Calceolaria integrifolia* 'Golden Nugget', celosia, coreopsis, dusty miller (*Centaurea cineraria, C. gymnocarpa, Senecio cineraria*), dahlia (bedding kinds), impatiens, snapdragon (*Antirrhinum majus*), zinnia

Tall-growing: calliopsis (*Coreopsis tinctoria*), cosmos, geranium (*Pelargonium hortorum*), gloriosa daisy (*Rudbeckia hirta*), marguerite (*Chrysanthemum frutescens*), marigold (*Tagetes*), *Nicotiana, Salpiglossis sinuata, Salvia farinacea*, snapdragon (*Antirrhinum majus*), zinnia

Lawns

The irrigated, mowed lawn became a basic part of landscaping for the arid West during the early part of the twentieth century, when dams, pipelines, and electric pumps began to make water abundant. Now a burgeoning population has caught up to the limited water supply and, in much of the West, has reached the limit of that supply. Water conservation has assumed a sense of urgency. And as a result, attention has focused on water needs of lawns, revealing that our favored turf grasses (Kentucky bluegrass, ryegrass, fescues, bentgrasses) require more water per square foot than any other kind of garden plant. Further research also has revealed that as much as half the water used by a typical single-family residence goes outdoors—mostly on lawns—and that most homeowners apply at least twice as much water as their lawns actually need.

These startling facts have led many western communities to concentrate outdoor water conservation programs on providing more precise lawn-watering guidelines. Founded on *evapotranspiration* (ET)—a weather-based, localized measurement of how much water a plant uses and how much evaporates from the soil—these guidelines give you the average amount of water your lawn needs on a daily, weekly, or seasonal basis. For lawn-watering guidelines for your area, contact your local water department or cooperative extension office.

Various alternatives to lawns are presented on page 72 (see "Evaluate Your Lawn"). If, however, a lawn is a necessary component of your landscape (as a play surface, for example), you should consider these options: minimizing lawn size; choosing a grass adapted to your climate; installing a sprinkler system tailored to your lawn; and automating the watering (with an electronic controller and moisture sensor—see page 72) so that the turf will receive no more than the minimum amount of water needed for good appearance.

Any good lawn—even if it is of drought-tolerant grasses—consumes a great amount of labor in preparation and subsequent care. You must prepare soil well, carefully sow seeds or plant live plants (sod, plugs, stolons), and then pamper the young lawn while it becomes established. Thereafter, routine maintenance involves mowing, watering, fertilizing, and controlling weeds and pests. On these pages we touch upon selecting grass type and installing the lawn; material on watering appears on pages 68–72. Further information on the various grasses appears in the Western Plant Encyclopedia, pages 199–568; see the listing under Grasses, page 365, for the individual entries. For detailed information on lawn care—watering, mowing, fertilizing, weed and pest control—consult the *Sunset* book *Lawns and Ground Covers.*

Lawn Grasses

Your choice of a lawn grass should be dictated by your climate in two ways. First is water. If water supply is sufficient (especially in areas where summer rain is common), you can consider one of the high water consumers such as bluegrass, ryegrass, bentgrass, or fine-textured fescue. Where water is scarce or supply is unpredictable, choose from among the drought-tolerant kinds.

The second climate factor to consider is temperature. Your summer heat and winter cold will direct you to either cool-season or subtropical grass types, as explained below.

Cool-season grasses withstand winter cold, but most types languish in hot, dry summers. They are best adapted to the Northwest, to regions where marine influence tempers summer heat, and to the Rocky Mountain area where they can get plenty of water.

Subtropical grasses, unlike the cool-season types, grow vigorously during hot weather and go dormant in cool or cold winters. But even in their brown or straw-colored winter phase, they maintain a thick carpet that keeps mud from being tracked into the house. If you find their winter brownness offensive, they can be either dyed green or overseeded with certain annual cool-season grasses that will provide green during mild winters.

Drought-tolerant grasses fall into one or the other of the two following groups:

- Certain ones are among the hardy, cool-season grasses that you grow from seeds sown in October. Most of these will stay green all year.
- Others belong to the group of warm-season grasses that you start in spring from stolons, sprigs, plugs, or sod. In most climates, all of these turn brown in winter (hybrid Bermuda often stays green in Southern California's mild coastal climates).

Cool-season grasses. These grasses are started from seeds sold either in blends of several different grasses or as individual types. Lawns made of a single grass type will be the most uniform in appearance, giving you the maximum expression of whatever characteristic you desire (fine texture or toughness, for example). The chief disadvantage of homogeneous lawns is that they may be wiped out by a pest infestation or disease to which they are susceptible or by extreme weather (drought or unusually high temperatures, for example). A blend of several kinds of grasses is safer. Those that survive to maturity will be the one, two, or three that do best given your soil conditions, climate, and maintenance practices.

Buy your seed considering both the kind of lawn you want and the cost required to cover your area. Don't be fooled by the cost per pound. Choice, fine-leafed blends contain many more seeds per pound than do coarse, fast-growing blends; therefore, seeds of fine-textured grasses will cover a greater area per pound.

In general, grasses that stand up to drought and can be started from seed in the fall look somewhat more coarse than the familiar Kentucky bluegrass. There are two basic kinds: the tall fescues, which are used mostly at low elevations (they can't take subzero temperatures), and several specialties of the Rocky Mountains and high plains—wheat grass (*Agropyron*), blue grama grass (*Bouteloua*), and buffalo grass (*Buchloe*)—that are almost untried in milder winter regions.

Subtropical grasses. The better subtropical grasses are grown from stolons, sprigs, plugs, or sod. Common Bermuda, hybrid Bermuda, and *Zoysia japonica* may be available in seed form, but results of seeding are unsatisfactory and hence the seeds are not widely offered. The hybrid Bermudas and St. Augustine grass cover quickly from runners; most zoysias are relatively slow. (Faster-growing zoysias are now becoming available as sod.) All can crowd out broad-leaved weeds. Hybrid Bermudas require frequent, close mowing and thatch removal.

Soil Preparation

A good lawn begins with a good environment for roots: the soil should be (1) of a texture easily permeable by water and roots to a depth of at least 8 to 12 inches, (2) well furnished with nutrients, and (3) neither highly acid nor overly alkaline.

If you're replacing an existing lawn (even a dead one), first remove the old sod. Digging sod into the soil makes for poor rooting, erratic water penetration, and irregular settling. Use a power-driven lawn edger (more satisfactory than a power sod cutter) to make parallel slices a spade's width apart across the lawn; then push a sharp spade under the sod and between the slice marks to peel the old sod from the soil beneath. If you must then add topsoil to raise the grade, buy the best you can find and blend it carefully with existing soil to avoid an interface—a plane where two unlike soils meet (see page 62).

■ ***Soil pH.*** Overly acid soils typically are found in high-rainfall regions, while highly alkaline soils are associated with arid lands. But before you do any guesswork and start tampering with the acidity or alkalinity of your soil, have the soil tested. Contact your county agricultural agent, or look in the index to your telephone book's yellow pages under "Soil Testing" for the names of laboratories that perform such testing. In some areas, the county agricultural agencies will test your soil.

If tests indicate a highly acid soil (pH below 5.5), add lime (calcium carbonate is best) at the rate of 50 to 75 pounds per 1,000 square feet. Apply it with a spreader (for even distribution) to dry soil, being careful to keep lime away from roots of acid-loving plants. Thoroughly incorporate any additives required for pH correction into the top 6 inches of soil.

If the soil is highly alkaline (pH above 8.0), add iron sulfate at 20 pounds per 1,000 square feet. Iron sulfate is fast acting and will supply the iron that is lacking in alkaline soils. A pH higher than 8.5 may indicate an alkaline soil problem caused by excessive sodium. Consult your county agricultural agent or a commercial soil laboratory for assistance in correcting this soil problem.

■ ***Add organic soil amendments.*** Few soils are naturally capable of taking up water easily, without runoff, and holding it so that watering intervals can be lengthened during a long dry season. To get this kind of soil, blend in organic soil amendments to supply air spaces in the soil and improve water penetration.

Nitrogen-stabilized soil amendments derived from sawdust and ground bark are available at most garden supply stores. Though costlier, these materials are easier to use than raw sawdust or bark products, which need the treatment outlined in the next two paragraphs. Use plenty of organic material in the seedbed: 1 cubic yard per 1,000 square feet of surface.

If you use raw sawdust or bark, provide extra nitrogen for soil organisms that will work to decompose them. Mix in 55 pounds of ammonium sulfate or 35 pounds of ammonium nitrate for each 1,000 square feet of sawdust or bark laid 3 inches deep.

When adding nitrogen to raw materials to hasten their breakdown, keep the seedbed moist for at least 30 days prior to seeding. Failure to do so will produce a temporary salinity, which could slow or prevent germination and subsequent growth.

Blend in the amendment and nutrients thoroughly with a rotary tiller, making repeated passes until the mixture is completely uniform.

■ ***Mix nutrients into rooting area.*** Although you can't possibly add enough nitrogen to last the lifetime of your lawn, you should add enough nitrogen to sustain the grass right after it sprouts. This either can be added along with organic materials or spread on the finished seedbed. But you should add phosphorus during the preparatory stages; tilling it in is the only way to get it into the rooting area. Before cultivating, add 40 pounds of single superphosphate per 1,000 square feet.

In some areas of the West, especially where rainfall is high, you might need potash. Check with your county agricultural agent or other local expert. If you do need it, cultivate in 10 pounds of muriate of potash per 1,000 square feet. This is a good time to add iron, in the form of sulfate or chelate, to prevent iron-deficiency chlorosis. Use 5 to 10 pounds of iron sulfate per 1,000 square feet, being careful to avoid scattering any on concrete—which it will stain red. Follow label directions for chelates.

■ ***Smooth the seedbed.*** Rake and drag the seedbed until it is smooth and flat, free of clods and high and low spots. Usually you'll have to conform to surrounding paving, but if you have a choice, try to have a slight pitch away from the house—a fall of 6 to 12 inches per 100 feet will provide good drainage. After raking and leveling, firm the seedbed with a full roller, making passes in two directions. Rolling sometimes brings unnoticed low spots to light; if such low spots show up, rake or drag the seedbed and roll it again.

Soak the area and keep it moist (sprinkle daily) for 24 to 30 days; in warm weather, you may not have to wait so long. To test the soil's readiness, sow a few radish seeds, which will sprout in a few days. If they begin to form true leaves, soil is safe for sowing grass seed.

Seed Sowing

Although cool-season grasses may be sown in almost any month of the year in mild climates and from spring through fall in colder areas, fall and spring are usually best. Fall seeding reduces danger of heat injury. But to give grass a good start before heavy frosts come and soil turns cold, allow 6 weeks of 50° to 70° weather. Fall seeding saves water, since fall and winter rains help germinate the seed and establish the roots. Spring seeding gives grass a long growing season in which to get established. On the other hand, late spring and summer heat calls for frequent hand watering during germination and careful irrigation and weeding later.

Pick a windless day for sowing, and sow seed as evenly as possible; a spreader or mechanical seeder will help. After sowing, rake in seed very lightly to ensure contact with seedbed. If you expect hot, dry weather or drying winds, put down a thin, moisture-holding mulch. Use ⅛ to 3/16 inch of peat moss or screened, aged sawdust. To keep peat moss from blowing away (and to overcome its reluctance, when dry, to take up water), soak, knead, and pulverize it. After mulching, roll with an empty roller to press seed into contact with soil.

Water thoroughly, taking care not to wash out seed, and then keep seedbed dark with moisture until all the grass is sprouted. This may mean watering 5 to 10 minutes each day (sometimes two or three times a day, depending on weather) for up to 3 weeks if your seed mixture contains slow-germinating kinds. Although a well-designed underground system may do the job without causing flooding or washouts, hand sprinkling is best.

Mow most grasses for the first time when blades are about 2 inches high, or when they begin to take on a noticeable curvature. Mow bentgrasses when they reach 1 inch. Be sure mower blades are sharp, and let sod dry out enough so that mower wheels will not skid or tear the turf.

The drought-tolerant, cool-season grasses differ somewhat in their post-sowing needs. Their particular mowing and watering requirements are mentioned in the Western Plant Encyclopedia under individual entries for *Agropyron, Bouteloua gracilis, Buchloe dactyloides,* and *Festuca elatior.*

Planting a Lawn from Seed

1) Add to the seedbed organic soil amendments, commercial fertilizer, and any materials necessary to adjust soil's pH.

2) Thoroughly incorporate the amendments and fertilizers into the soil, using a rotary-tiller (which is easier) or spading fork.

3) Remove all weeds and surface rocks with a rake or by hand; make sure seedbed is free of all such foreign matter.

4) Rake or drag the seedbed to establish a level, to smooth out soil, and to reveal any high or low spots that will need correcting.

Sod, Sprigs, Stolons & Plugs

Western turf farms offer ready-made lawns in the form of sod. Compared with the cost of seeds, sod is expensive, but the saving in time and labor is considerable. Prepare a seedbed as for seeds, but make the surface about ¾ inch lower than the surrounding paving. Spread a layer of complete fertilizer (the amount that the label suggests for new lawns), and then unroll sod on the prepared seedbed. Lay strips parallel, with strip ends pressed against each other, and with these seams staggered. Roll with a half-filled roller, and then water carefully until roots have penetrated deeply into the seedbed.

For sprigging—used to establish hybrid Bermudas and some bentgrasses—prepare the seedbed as for seeds. To make the seedbed moist but of a good working consistency, presoak it. Make a series of parallel trenches 3 inches deep and 10 inches apart, take sprigs from plastic bags or tear from flats or sod, lay in trenches, and press soil back into trenches. Keep soil evenly moist until the sprigs root and begin to grow.

To plant stolons, broadcast them over the prepared seedbed at the rate of 3 to 5 bushels per 1,000 square feet. With a half-filled lawn roller, roll the broadcast stolons into the soil; then mulch with ½ inch of topsoil, peat moss, sawdust, or ground bark. Roll again, water thoroughly, and keep evenly moist until grass begins to grow.

To plant plugs of grass from flats, first cut the grass with a sharp knife into equal-sized 2-inch squares. Then plant the plugs in prepared soil, spacing them evenly in all directions, about 12 to 15 inches apart.

5) After raking and leveling, firm the seedbed with a full lawn roller; make passes in two directions.

6) Sow grass seed on a still, windless day; broadcast by hand or use mechanical seed sower. Then rake in seed lightly.

7) Apply mulch; keep seedbed moist until grass has germinated. Leave barrier around lawn until 8 weeks after first mowing.

8) A week after grass is up, begin pulling weeds (kneel on board to avoid denting lawn).

Vegetables

Raising your own vegetables can be fun, fulfilling, and economical. But for the experience to be all three, you will need to invest some time in planning and, afterward, in maintenance.

Before you take a shovel to the soil, stop to evaluate your needs. How many people do you hope to feed from your vegetable plot? It is all too easy to overplant and then work too hard to maintain a garden that ends up producing a larger crop than you can use.

Make a list of vegetables you really like and choose your plants from that list. Especially if you have a limited garden area, raise only those that will give you a satisfactory return from the space they occupy. Melons, some squashes, and corn, for example, require large land areas relative to their edible yield; beans, tomatoes, and zucchini, on the other hand, can overwhelm you with their bounty from a postage-stamp–size plot.

Location, Planting & Care

Success with vegetables begins with choosing the right location for your garden. Vegetables need plenty of sunshine for steady growth, so be sure to plant them where they will receive at least 6 hours of sunlight each day. To avoid not only shade but also any possible root competition, try to plant your vegetable patch at a distance from trees and large shrubs. If possible, choose a spot that is sheltered from regular high winds, which can dehydrate plants and may therefore necessitate frequent watering. And avoid planting vegetables in low-lying areas that

Plant These Vegetables for Summer-Fall Harvest

Plant	Planted as	Planting time by climate zone 1–3	4–7	8, 9	10, 11	12, 13	14–17	18, 19	20, 21	22–24	Approx. days to harvest
Beans (lima)	Seeds*	June	May–June	Apr.–June	May–July	July–Aug.	Apr.–July	Mar.–Aug.	Mar.–Aug.	Mar.–Aug.	65–95**
Beans (snap)	Seeds*	June	May–June	Apr.–June	May–June	July–Aug.	Apr.–July	Mar.–Aug.	Mar.–Aug.	Mar.–Aug.	50–70**
Beets	Seeds*	May–June	Apr.–June	Apr.–June	Mar.–May	Sept.	Apr.–Sept.	Apr.–Sept.	Apr.–Sept.	Apr.–Sept.	46–65
Broccoli	Plants	Apr.–June	Apr.–May	Mar., Aug.	Apr.–July	Sept.	Mar., Aug.				50–90
Brussels sprouts	Plants	May–June	Mar.–May	Aug.	July–Aug.						80–90
Cabbage	Plants	May–June	Mar.–May	Jan.–Feb.	Mar.–May	Sept.					60–120
Carrots	Seeds	May–July	May–July	May–June	Mar.–May Aug.–Sept.	Sept.	Mar.–Apr. Sept.	Mar.–Aug.	Mar.–Aug.	Mar.–Aug.	65–75
Cauliflower	Plants	May–June	Mar.–May	July–Aug.	Mar.–May	Sept.					60–100
Celery	Plants	June–July	May		May–June						100–135
Chard	Seeds	Mar.–June	Mar.–June	Mar.–Apr., Aug.	July–Sept.	Sept.	Aug.–Sept.	Aug.–Oct.	Aug.–Oct.	Aug.–Oct.	45–60
Corn	Seeds	June	May–June	May–June	May–July	Mar.–Apr.	Mar.–July	Mar.–July	Mar.–July	Mar.–July	60–90**
Cucumbers	Seeds	Mid-May–June	May–June	May–June	May–June	Aug.–Sept.	Apr.–June	Mar.–July	Mar.–July	Mar.–July	55–65
Eggplant	Plants	Mid May–June	May–June	May–June	May–June	Apr.–May	Apr.–June	Mar.–June	Mar.–June	Mar.–June	65–80
Endive	Seeds	Apr.–June	Apr.–May	Apr.–May		Sept.	Mar.–Apr.	Apr.–June	Apr.–June	Apr.–June	65–90
Kohlrabi	Seeds	Apr.–May	Apr.–May	Apr.–May		Sept.	Mar.–Apr.				55–65
Lettuce	Seeds*	Mar.–Aug.	Mar.–Apr. Aug.	Mar.–Apr. Aug.	July–Aug.	Sept.–Nov.	Mar. Aug.–Sept.	Sept.	Sept.	Apr., Sept.	40–95**

can become winter "frost pockets"—you want to aim for the longest possible growing season for the greatest productivity.

Level ground makes vegetable growing easier. You can run rows in north-south alignment so that plants receive an even amount of sunlight during the day; and level ground also gives you a choice among watering options—irrigation, sprinkling, drip irrigation—with the least risk of runoff. (For detailed watering information, see pages 68–72.)

If you have to plant on sloping land, try to select a slope that faces south or southeast for maximum sunlight; plant the tallest vegetables on the north side of the plot to avoid shading shorter ones. Lay out rows along the slope's contours to minimize water runoff and erosion.

Most of the commonly grown vegetables are annual plants. Prepare your vegetable garden soil as described under "Annuals" on page 188.

In planting vegetables, you usually have two options: planting seeds or setting out young plants sold by a nursery. Seed planting is far more economical if you compute price per plant, but for a small garden the purchase of young plants will not represent any great outlay. Realize that the earliest crops usually will come on plants set out as early as possible in the growing season (see "Planting and Timing," page 188, and "Extending the Season," page 198). If you prefer to start from scratch, remember that seeds started indoors just before garden soil warms up enough to plant outdoors will be ready to set out at the very beginning of the growing season; see pages 80–81 for seed-planting information. Otherwise, nurseries and garden centers often have young plants available at the earliest moment that it is advisable to plant outdoors.

For the best possible crop, remember this one tip: keep plants growing. Be sure vegetable plants receive steady amounts of both water and nutrients; any check in growth detracts from productivity, quality, or both.

Plant	Planted as	Planting time by climate zone 1–3	4–7	8, 9	10, 11	12, 13	14–17	18, 19	20, 21	22–24	Approx. days to harvest
Melons	Seeds	May–June	May–June	May–June	May–June	Apr.–June	Apr.–June	Apr.–July	Apr.–July	June–July	80–95
Onions (bunching)	Seeds*	Apr.–May	Apr.–May	Mar.–Apr. Sept.	Apr.	Sept.	Mar.–Apr. Sept.				60–75
Onions (bulbing)	Sets, Seeds	Apr.–May Mar.	Mar.–May Mar.	Feb.–Apr. Nov.–Feb.		Oct.–Apr. Nov.–Feb.	Oct.–Apr. Feb.–Mar.	Oct.–Apr. Nov.–Feb.	Oct.–Apr. Nov.–Feb.	Oct.–Apr. Nov.–Feb.	100–120 130–180
Parsley	Seeds	Apr.–May	Apr.–May	Apr.–May	May–June		Apr.–June	Apr.–June	Apr.–June	Apr.–June	70–90
Parsnip	Seeds	Apr.–May	Apr.–May	Apr.–May	Mar.–Apr.		Apr.–May	Mar.–May	Mar.–May	Mar.–May	100–120
Peas	Seeds	Mid Feb.–May	Mid Feb.–May	Feb.–Apr. Sept.	July–Aug.	Aug.–Sept.	Mar.–Apr. Sept.	Sept.	Sept.	Sept.	60–70
Peppers	Plants	May	May	May–June	May–June	Mar.–May	Mar.–June	Mar.–July	Mar.–July	June–July	60–80
Potatoes	Sets	May	Apr.–May	Dec.–Mar.	Mar.–July	Nov.–Jan.	Mar. June	Mar.–Apr.	Mar.–May	Mar.–May	90–105
Pumpkins	Seeds	June	June	Apr.–June	May–June	Apr.–Aug.	Apr.–June	Apr.–June	Apr.–June	Apr.–June	100–120
Radishes	Seeds*	Apr.–June	Apr.–June	Mar.–May, Sept.–Oct.	July–Sept.	Sept.–Oct.	Mar.–May Sept.–Oct.	May–Oct.	May–Oct.	May–Oct.	20–50**
Rutabagas	Seeds	Apr.–May	Mar.	Mar.	Mar.		Mar.				90
Spinach	Seeds*	Apr.–May	Apr.–May	Apr.–May	July–Aug.	Sept.–Oct.	May	Sept.	Sept.	Sept.	40–50
Squash	Seeds	May–June	Apr.–June	Mar.–June	May–July	May–Aug.	Mar.–June	Mar.–July	Mar.–July	Mar.–July	50–60
Tomatoes	Plants	May–early June	May–June	Apr.–July	May–June	Mar.	Apr.–July	Apr.–July	Apr.–July	June–July	55–90**
Turnips	Seeds*	Apr.–May	Mar.–May	Mar.–May		Aug.–Sept.	Mar.–Apr.	Apr.–Sept.	Apr.–Sept.	Apr.–Sept.	35–60

*For continuous crop, sow seeds at 2–3 week intervals.
**Depends on variety planted.

Six Ways to Support Vegetables

Tomatoes benefit from some sort of support: production is heavier, fewer fruits rot, and picking is easy. Simplest is wood stake for each plant. Cylinder of welded wire fencing gives plenty of support with minimum of tying for single plant. For row of plants, use crossed pairs of bamboo poles tied together at crosspole.

Plant These Vegetables for Winter-Spring Harvest

Plant	Planted as	Planting time by climate zone									Approx. days to harvest
		1–3	4–7	8, 9	10, 11	12, 13	14–17	18, 19	20, 21	22–24	
Artichokes	Plants or roots			Sept.–May			Oct.–May	Oct.–May	Oct.–May	Oct.–May	1 year
Asparagus	Roots	Apr.–May	Apr.	Nov.–Mar.	Feb.–Apr.		Nov.–Mar.	Oct.–Feb.	Oct.–Feb.	Oct.–Feb.	2 years
Beets	Seeds*					Oct.–Mar.		Oct.–Mar.	Oct.–Mar.	Oct.–Mar.	46–65
Broccoli	Plants					Oct.–Dec.	Sept.–Feb.	Oct.–Feb.	Oct.–Feb.	Oct.–Feb.	50–90
Brussels sprouts	Plants			Aug.–Oct.		Sept.–Dec.	Sept.–Oct.	Oct.–Feb.	Oct.–Feb.	Oct.–Feb.	80–90
Cabbage	Plants			July		Oct.–Dec.	Sept.–Oct.	Oct.–Jan.	Oct.–Jan.	Oct.–Jan.	60–120
Carrots	Seeds*					Oct.–Mar.	Oct. Mar.–June	Sept.–Feb.	Sept.–Feb.	Sept.–Feb.	65–75
Cauliflower	Plants			Aug.–Nov.		Oct.–Dec.	Sept.–Oct.	Sept.–Feb.	Sept.–Feb.	Sept.–Feb.	60–100
Celery	Plants			June–Aug.		Aug.–Oct.	Sept.	Aug.–Oct.	Aug.–Oct.	Aug.–Oct.	100–135
Chard	Seeds				Feb.–Apr.	Oct.–Mar.	Mar.	Oct.–Mar.	Oct.–Mar.	Oct.–Mar.	45–60
Cucumbers	Seeds					Dec.–Mar.					55–65
Eggplant	Plants					Feb.–Mar.					65–80
Endive	Seeds				Feb.–Mar.	Oct.–Feb.		Oct.–Jan.	Oct.–Jan.	Oct.–Jan.	65–90
Kohlrabi	Seeds				Feb.–Mar.	Oct.–Feb.		Oct.–Jan.	Oct.–Jan.	Oct.–Jan.	55–65
Lettuce	Seeds*				Feb.–Mar.	Oct.–Apr.	Sept.–Mar.	Oct.–Mar.	Oct.–Mar.	Oct.–Mar.	40–95**

Pole beans and peas will eagerly climb strings stretched over wooden A-frame support as well as bamboo poles tied into teepee formation. To support cucumbers and squash, as well as pole beans and peas, drive in row of metal fencing stakes 4 to 6 feet apart and attach broad-mesh plastic netting to hooks in the fenceposts.

Plant	Planted as	Planting time by climate zone 1–3	4–7	8, 9	10, 11	12, 13	14–17	18, 19	20, 21	22–24	Approx. days to harvest
Melons	Seeds					Feb.–Mar.					80–95
Onions (bunching)	Seeds				Feb.–Mar.	Oct.–Feb.	Oct.–Feb.	Oct.–Jan.	Oct.–Jan.	Oct.–Jan.	60–75
Onions (bulbing)	Sets				Nov.–Apr.	Nov.–Feb.					100–120
Parsley	Seeds					Sept.–Jan.		Oct.–Jan.	Oct.–Jan.	Oct.–Jan.	70–90
Parsnip	Seeds					Sept.–Jan.		Jan.	Jan.	Jan.	100–120
Peas	Seeds				Feb.–Mar.	Oct.–Mar.	Oct.	Oct.–Jan.	Oct.–Jan.	Oct.–Jan.	60–70
Peppers	Plants					Feb.					60–80
Potato	Sets					July–Aug.	Feb.–Mar.		July–Aug.	July–Aug.	90–105
Radishes	Seeds*			Mar.–Apr.	Mar.–Apr.	Nov.–Apr.	Mar.–Apr.	Nov.–Apr.	Nov.–Apr.	Nov.–Apr.	20–50**
Rhubarb	Roots	Mar.–Apr.	Mar.–Apr.		Mar.–Apr.		Jan.	Nov.–Feb.	Nov.–Feb.	Nov.–Feb.	1 year
Rutabagas	Seeds					Sept.–Feb.	Sept.–Oct.	Oct.–Nov.	Oct.–Nov.	Oct.–Nov.	90 days
Spinach	Seeds*				Feb.–Mar.	Nov.–Mar.	Sept.–Nov.	Oct.–Feb.	Oct.–Feb.	Oct.–Feb.	40–50
Squash	Seeds					Dec.–Mar.					50–60
Tomatoes	Plants					Jan.–Mar.					55–90
Turnips	Seeds*				Mar.	Oct.–Mar.	Sept.–Oct.	Oct.–Mar.	Oct.–Mar.	Oct.–Mar.	35–60

*For continuous crop, sow seeds at 2–3 week intervals.
**Depends on variety planted.

The basic advice provided in "Care After Planting," page 188, covers vegetables as well. The one difference is that whereas you groom annuals to prolong flower production, you *harvest* vegetables to prolong production.

Extending the Season

Traditionally, gardeners wanting to extend nature's vegetable season have used glass or plastic covers to shelter young transplants from late frosts and, in the process, warm the soil. By planting earlier than their climate normally allowed, then protecting and warming the young plants, they brought vegetables to bearing size earlier.

Now gardeners can use plastic row covers—made of polyethylene, polyester, or polypropylene—both to get a jump on the growing season and to extend it into the chill of autumn. Sold in rolls, these fabriclike covers are designed to be laid over vegetables at planting time (or over bearing plants toward the season's end), where they serve as miniature greenhouses—trapping heat, warming soil, and boosting growth. The various materials are extremely lightweight, transmit 80 to 95 percent of sunlight, and let both water and air pass through. If the cover's edges are buried in soil or held securely against it, it will seal off plants from outside pests (though any insect pests already present on plants will proliferate under such protection).

To use row covers, just lay the material over rows of plants 1 to 3 feet wide, and secure the edges by burying them in the soil or holding them in place with 2 by 4s. Covers float on top of the plants without restricting or distorting growth.

Most gardeners who use row covers put them up for 4 to 6 weeks in early spring. As weather turns warm, the covers come off: when the air temperature climbs into the 80s, it can be 30° warmer under the covers. But where frost can occur anytime during the growing season, gardeners cover plants on dangerous nights and days, and then remove covers on warm days. In cool-summer climates, they can use covers to mature warm-season vegetables that normally wouldn't receive enough heat to produce. And, at the end of a growing season, row covers can ripen the last crop of tomatoes, for example, that otherwise would remain green.

Because all materials used to make row covers are permeable to water, you can water covered plants by sprinkling—and rainfall gets through too. Young plants will be somewhat weighted down after a sprinkling but will pop back up once the material dries. The simplest method for applying water to row-covered vegetables, however, is drip irrigation (as presented on pages 70–71).

Using Plastic Row Covers

Plastic row covers let you get the jump on vegetable season or prolong it into fall. Cover traps heat, thus warming soil; light and water penetrate it but insect pests and birds are excluded.

Warm-season versus Cool-season Vegetables

A distinct difference in heat requirements for growth separates warm-season from cool-season vegetables and determines which of each are best adapted to your particular climate.

Warm-season vegetables, the summer crops, need warmth both to germinate and to form and ripen fruit. With nearly all of these vegetables, the fruit (rather than the leaves, roots, or stems) is the object of the harvest. The basic need of warm-weather vegetables is for enough growing heat—without significant cooling at night—both to keep plants growing steadily and to ripen the edible portions of the plants.

Cool-season vegetables grow steadily at average temperatures 10 to 15 degrees below those needed by warm-season crops. Many of them will endure some frost. But the most important difference is that you do not grow cool-season vegetables for their fruit or seeds: most of them are leaf or root crops. The exceptions are peas and broad beans (grown for edible seeds) and artichokes, broccoli, and cauliflower (grown for edible flowers).

Success with cool-season crops depends on bringing plants to maturity in the kind of weather that favors vegetative growth rather than flowering. In general, you plant in very early spring so that the crop will mature before summer heat settles in, or in late summer so that the crop matures during fall or even winter. In the warmer regions —Zones 12 to 24—many cool-season vegetables can be planted in fall to harvest either in winter or in early spring.

Part of the care for some vegetables is providing support for the vining or sprawling plants. Pole beans and peas, tomatoes, cucumbers, and melons, for example, benefit from support that raises them off the ground; plants will produce larger crops, and the fruit won't rot from being in contact with the soil. Six ideas for supporting vegetable plants are illustrated on pages 196 and 197. In regions with hot summers, avoid metal and wire construction: metal can heat up enough to burn plant parts that touch it.

Occasionally, technical words are used; these are defined in the Glossary at the end of the book.

Western Plant Encyclopedia

The plant descriptions in this encyclopedia appear in alphabetical order under each plant's scientific name (genus and species), except for common fruits and vegetables, which are described under their common names (apple, eggplant, tomato). If you only know a plant's common name, look for it in its alphabetical place, where you will find a cross-reference to its scientific name. Scientific names are based on *Hortus Third* (New York: Macmillan Publishing Company, 1976); in rare instances, names based on more recent publications have been used. Some of these names may be unfamiliar to you, but they represent the latest research and their use will make it easier for gardeners everywhere to speak a common language. For the convenience of plant shoppers, former (and perhaps more familiar) scientific names are listed as cross-references.

After the scientific name come any former scientific names (in parentheses) and the plant's family name (in italics). Next comes the plant's common name, then a few words describing the kind of plant it is (bulb, shrub, tree). The terms *family, genus,* and *species* are explained in the Glossary (page 569), under Plant classification.

Plant families are also included in the alphabetical listings, though a family name may be omitted if only one member of the family is given in the plant encyclopedia. (In these instances, the plant listed provides adequate illustration of family characteristics.)

Climate adaptability is noted for each plant except summer annuals and some house plants. "All Zones" means that the plant is recommended for the entire West. Other than that, Zones are indicated by numbers which are explained and mapped on pages 33–55. Where two Zone numbers are joined by a dash, as in "Zones 1–6, 15–17," the plant is recommended for the Zones specified and all the Zones between them. Microclimates (the varying climates of small areas within a larger region) are discussed on page 34; any garden may contain favored sites where plants of borderline hardiness stand a fairly good chance of survival.

The drawings are intended to give a general idea of the appearance of one or more members of a group; not all members of the group necessarily look alike. Read the individual descriptions.

All plants described here are sold in the West or have been sold within recent years. Many are rare; others may be rare in one region, common elsewhere. If you can't find a plant you want, ask your best local nurseryman for help in finding it or recommending a specialist supplier.

Sample Entry

Scientific name (genus and species); or common name of familiar fruit or vegetable.

Plant family.

Former scientific name(s), if any.

FATSIA japonica *(Aralia sieboldii, A. japonica).* *Araliaceae.* JAPANESE ARALIA. Evergreen shrub. Zones 4–9, 13–24.

Type of plant.

Climate adaptability.

Common name.

CLIMATE ZONES, PAGES 33–55

A

AARON'S BEARD. See *Hypericum calycinum*.

ABELIA. *Caprifoliaceae.* Evergreen, partially evergreen, or deciduous shrubs. Graceful, arching branches densely clothed with oval, usually glossy leaves ½–1½ in. long; bronzy new growth. Tubular or bell-shaped flowers in clusters at ends of branches or among leaves. Though small, blossoms are plentiful enough to be showy mostly during summer and early fall. When blooms drop, they usually leave purplish or copper-colored sepals which provide color into the fall months. Leaves also may take on bronzy tints in fall.

Abelia grandiflora

To keep the shrub's graceful form, prune selectively; don't shear. The more stems you cut to the ground in winter or early spring, the more open and arching next year's growth will be. Abelias grow and flower best in sun, but they will take some shade. These are adaptable plants, useful in shrub borders, as space dividers and visual barriers, and near house walls; lower kinds are good bank or ground covers. They need average watering.

A. floribunda. MEXICAN ABELIA. Evergreen. Zones 8, 9, 12–24. Severely damaged at 20°F. Usually 3–6 ft. tall, sometimes 10 ft. Arching, reddish stems are downy or hairy. Pendulous tubular flowers, 1½ in. long, reddish purple, single or in clusters. Usually summer blooming, but often in full bloom in January. Needs partial shade in hot-summer areas.

A. grandiflora. GLOSSY ABELIA. Evergreen to partially deciduous. Zones 5–24. Hybrid of 2 species from China. Best known and most popular of the abelias. Grows to 8 ft. tall or taller; spreads to 5 ft. or more. Flowers white or faintly tinged pink, June–October.

A. g. 'Edward Goucher' (*A. gaucheri*). Like *A. grandiflora*, evergreen in milder climates to nearly deciduous at 15°F. Lower growing (to 3–5 ft.) and lacier than *A. grandiflora*. Small lilac pink flowers with orange throats make a showy display, June–October.

At 0°F., both *A. grandiflora* and *A. g.* 'Edward Goucher' freeze to the ground, but usually recover to bloom the same year, making graceful border plants 10–15 in. tall.

A. g. 'Francis Mason'. Low, densely branched shrub with pink flowers; leaves variegated with yellow. Blooms June–October.

A. g. 'Prostrata'. Occasionally partially deciduous even in mildest climates. Low-growing (1½–2 ft.), spreading variety useful as ground cover, bank planting, low foreground shrub. For massing, set 3–4 ft. apart. Blooms June–October.

A. g. 'Sherwoodii'. Smaller than *A. grandiflora*, more compact; grows 3–4 ft. tall, 5 ft. wide. Blooms June–October.

ABELIOPHYLLUM distichum. *Oleaceae.* WHITE FORSYTHIA. Deciduous shrub. Zones 3–6. Native to Korea. Not a forsythia but resembles it in growth habit and profusion of fragrant bloom in February—but flowers are dazzling white, not yellow. Lower and slower growing than most forsythias, to 3–4 ft. and as wide. Leaves bluish green, opposite, 1–2 in. long. Attractive purple buds in fall and winter on brown or black new wood. Buds open pink, flowers quickly turn white. Budded branches will bloom in winter when brought indoors. Easy to grow in sun or light shade. Routine garden care. Prune in bloom or immediately after. Cut some of oldest branches at base to keep new flowering wood coming.

Abeliophyllum distichum

ABELMOSCHUS moschatus. *Malvaceae.* SILK FLOWER. Annual. Bushy plant about 1½ ft. tall and wide, with deep green, deeply cut leaves. Five-petaled, 3–4½-in. flowers, cherry red or pink with white centers, resemble tropical hibiscus. Likes good average garden soil, heat, and full sun, but will bloom in shade.

Grow from seed; flowering begins 100 days after sowing and continues up to frost or cold weather. Can be grown as house plant in a 6-in. pot.

Abelmoschus moschatus

ABIES. *Pinaceae.* FIR. Evergreen trees. In nature, firs are tall, erect, symmetrical trees with uniformly spaced branch whorls. Large cones are held erect; they shatter after ripening, leaving a spiky stalk. Most (but not all) native firs are high mountain plants which grow best in or near their natural environment. They grow slowly if at all in hot, dry, windy areas at low elevations, though firs from some other parts of the world do well in warm, dry climates.

Abies concolor

Christmas tree farms grow native firs for cutting, and nurseries in the Northwest and northern California grow a few species for the living Christmas tree trade. Licensed collectors in the Northwest dig picturesque, contorted firs at high elevations near the timberline and market them through nurseries as "alpine conifers." Use these in rock gardens; small specimens are good container or bonsai subjects.

Birds are attracted by fir seeds.

A. amabilis. SILVER FIR, CASCADE FIR. Zones 1–7, 15–17. Native to southern Alaska south through Coast Ranges and Cascades of Washington and Oregon. Tall tree in the wilds, smaller (20–50 ft.) in lowland gardens in the Pacific Northwest. Dark green needles, silvery beneath, curve upward along the branches. Give it room to grow.

A. balsamea. BALSAM FIR. Zones 3–7, 15–17. Native to eastern American mountains. Only the dwarf variety 'Nana' is occasionally sold in the West. Interesting rock garden subject. Slow-growing, dense, dark green cushion; give partial shade, ample water.

A. bracteata *(A. venusta).* SANTA LUCIA FIR, BRISTLECONE FIR. Zones 8, 9, 14–21. From steep, rocky slopes on the seaward side of the Santa Lucia Mountains, Monterey County, California. A tall tree (70 ft. in 50 years), with spreading (15–20 ft.) lower branches and slender steeplelike crown. Stiff, 1½–2½-in.-long needles are dark green above, with white lines beneath; needle points are unusually sharp. Roundish cones are unique—about 4 in. long, with a long, slender, pointed bract on each cone scale. Exceptionally tolerant of heat and drought.

A. concolor. WHITE FIR. Zones 1–9, 14–24. Native to mountains of southern Oregon, California, southern Rocky Mountains, Baja California. One of the big five in the timber belt of the Sierra Nevada, along with ponderosa pine, sugar pine, incense cedar, and Douglas fir. It's a popular Christmas tree and one of the most commonly grown native firs in western gardens.

Large, very symmetrical tree in its native range and in the Northwest. Slower growing in California gardens; has reached 30 ft. in as many years in lowland California. Best as container plant in southern California. Bluish green, 1–2-in.-long needles. Variety 'Candicans' has bluish white foliage. Some consider it the "bluest" of all conifers.

A. grandis. LOWLAND FIR, GRAND FIR. Zones 1–9, 14–17. From British Columbia inland to Montana, southward to Sonoma County, California. In California it grows near the ocean along Highway 1.

Many Northwest gardeners live and garden successfully under this fir; they prune it high. It's one of the largest firs, reaching to 300 ft.; lower in cultivation. Handsome, deep green, 1–1½-in.-long needles in 2 rows along branches; glossy above, white lines beneath.

A. koreana. KOREAN FIR. Zones 3–9, 14–24. Native to Korea. Slow-growing, compact, pyramidal tree seldom over 30 ft. Shiny, short green needles. Sets cones on young, small trees. Variety 'Aurea', with gold green foliage, is even smaller, slower growing.

A. lasiocarpa. ALPINE FIR. Zones 1–9, 14–17. Native to Alaska, south through the high Cascades of Washington and Oregon; nearly throughout the Rocky Mountains. Narrow, steeple-shaped tree, 60–90 ft. tall in good soil in moist areas. Bluish green, 1–1½-in.-long needles.

Best known in gardens as an "alpine conifer" dug near timberline and sold in nurseries. Extremely slow growing in California gardens. Allow 15–20-ft. spread in Northwest gardens, as it usually doesn't hold its narrow shape in cultivation.

A. l. arizonica. CORK FIR. Zones 1–9, 14–17. Native to San Francisco Peaks, Arizona, at 8,500 ft. elevation. Interesting creamy white, thick, corky bark. Very handsome as a youngster. Good bonsai.

A. magnifica. RED FIR. Zones 1–7. Native to the mountains of southern Oregon, California's Sierra Nevada south to Kern County, and the Coast Ranges south to Lake County. This is the "silver tip" fir of the California cut Christmas tree trade. Tall and stately, with symmetrical, horizontal, rather short branches. New growth silvery gray. Mature needles blue green, 1 in. long; curve upward on upper limbs, in 2 rows on lower branches.

Hard to grow at low elevations.

A. nordmanniana. NORDMANN FIR. Zones 1–11, 14–24. Native to the Caucasus, Asia Minor, Greece. Vigorous, densely foliaged fir; 30–50 ft. tall and 20 ft. wide in cultivation. Dark green, shiny, ¾–1½-in.-long needles, with whitish bands beneath, densely cover branches.

More adaptable to California gardens than native firs, becoming a symmetrical, densely branched cone. Needs adequate water; will submit to long-term container growing.

A. pinsapo. SPANISH FIR. Zones 5–11, 14–24. Native to Spain. Very slow growing, to 25 ft. in 40 years. In southern California, good dwarf effect for years. Dense, symmetrical form; it's sometimes taken for a spruce. Stiff, deep green, ½–¾-in.-long needles are set uniformly around branches. Variety 'Glauca' is blue gray.

A. procera *(A. nobilis).* NOBLE FIR. Zones 1–7, 15–17. Native to the Siskiyou Mountains of California, northern mountains of Oregon and Washington. Similar to California's red fir in appearance; grown in Northwest nurseries as a live Christmas tree. Grows 90–200 ft. tall in wilds, almost as tall in Northwest gardens. Short, stiff branches; blue green, 1-in.-long needles. Large cones with extended bracts as in *A. bracteata*.

ABRONIA. *Nyctaginaceae.* SAND VERBENA. Zones 4, 5, 17, 24. Not a true verbena. Oval to roundish, very thick, fleshy leaves. Small, tubular, fragrant flowers in headlike clusters. *A. latifolia* and *A. umbellata* are naturally suited for holding sand in beach gardens. They are not hardy in severe climates.

Abronia latifolia

Grow all species from seed. Seeds are hard to find; you may be able to buy them from wildflower specialists.

A. latifolia. YELLOW SAND VERBENA. Perennial. Native to seacoast, British Columbia to Santa Barbara. Thick leaves 1½ in. long and as wide; under ideal conditions, plants form leafy mats up to 3 ft. across. The whole plant is gummy enough to become encrusted with sand or dust. Bright yellow flowers from May–October. Sow seeds in flats, in pots, or in light, well-drained, sandy soil. Scrapping or peeling off each seed's papery covering should facilitate germination.

A. umbellata. PINK SAND VERBENA. Perennial. Native to coasts, British Columbia to Baja California. Creeping, rather slender, fleshy, often reddish stems 1 ft. or more long. Leaves 1–2 in. long, not quite as wide. Rosy pink flowers bloom almost all year. Grow as *A. latifolia*.

A. villosa. Annual. Resembles *A. umbellata*, but plant is hairy and somewhat sticky. Desert native that thrives in heat, drought. Sow fall or spring. Will tolerate summer water.

ABUTILON. *Malvaceae.* FLOWERING MAPLE, CHINESE BELLFLOWER, CHINESE LANTERN. Evergreen viny shrubs. Zones 13, 15–24. Mostly native to South America. Planted primarily for the pleasure provided by flowers. Growth rapid, coarse, and rangy; control by pinching out branch tips.

Abutilon hybridum

Can be trained as standards or espaliers, but best as loose, informal espalier. Abutilon enjoys moist soil. Give full sun on coast, partial shade inland; will not bloom in deep shade. In cold climates, it can be used as container plant indoors in winter, out on terrace in summer. Gets whitefly and scale insects; control both with malathion or light oil spray.

A. hybridum. The best-known flowering maple. Upright, arching growth to 8–10 ft., with equal spread. Broad maplelike leaves. Drooping bell-like flowers in white, yellow, pink, and red. Main blooming season April–June, but white and yellow forms seem to bloom almost continuously.

A. megapotamicum. Vigorous growth to 10 ft. and as wide. Leaves are arrowlike, 1½–3 in. long. Flowers resembling red and yellow lanterns gaily decorate the long, rangy branches, May–September. This vine-shrub is more graceful in detail than in entirety, but can be trained to an interesting pattern. Good hanging basket plant. 'Marianne' has superior form; 'Variegata' has leaves mottled with yellow.

A. pictum 'Thompsonii'. Similar to *A. hybridum*, but foliage strikingly variegated with creamy yellow. Blooms almost continuously, bearing pale orange bells veined with red.

A. vitifolium. See *Corynabutilon.*

ABYSSINIAN BANANA. See *Ensete ventricosum.*

ABYSSINIAN SWORD LILY. See *Gladiolus callianthus.*

ACACIA. *Leguminosae.* Evergreen or deciduous shrubs or trees. Native to the tropics or warm regions of the world, notably Australia, Mexico, and our southwestern states. Of the many species tested over the last 150 years, nearly 30 serve beautifully and functionally in California and Arizona landscapes; new species are continually under test.

Acacia baileyana

Of species in use today, several offer fountains of clear yellow flowers in January and February. Some are quite fragrant when in bloom. Many decorate and protect hillsides, banks, freeway landscapes. Some serve well in beach plantings. All are attractive to birds.

Most nurseries sell only a few of the hundreds of acacia species, but you can easily grow acacias from seed you collect yourself or order from a specialist. Sow individually in peat pots; set out, pot and all, when well established.

Acacia melanoxylon

The acacias differ widely in foliage and growth habit. Some have feathery, much divided leaves; others have flattened leaf stalks that fulfill the function of leaves. Many start life with feathery leaves and later develop leathery ones.

Larger-growing acacia species may end up as shrubs or trees, depending on how they are pruned in youth. Remove the lead shoot and the plant grows as a shrub; remove the lower branches and it will be treelike. Stake the tree types until they are deeply anchored; deep, infrequent watering encourages deep rooting and better anchorage.

(Continued on page 204)

CLIMATE ZONES, PAGES 33–55

A

Acacia

NAME	ZONES	HEIGHT	SPREAD	LEAVES	FLOWERS	COMMENTS
Acacia abyssinica	13–24	20–25 ft.	20–25 ft.	Finely divided, feathery. Evergreen in mildest climates.	Yellow puff balls on short stems. Spring.	Slow growth to spreading, flat-topped silhouette. Grow as single- or multitrunked tree or big shrub.
A. aneura MULGA	8, 9, 12–24	To 20 ft.	To 12 ft.	Small, silvery gray, undivided.	Yellow rods. Spring.	Evergreen small patio tree. Definitely gray. Clean, hardy, trouble free under desert conditions. Avoid needle-leafed forms.
A. armata KANGAROO THORN	13–24	10–15 ft.	10–12 ft.	Light green, waxy, 1-in.-long leaves on thorny branches.	Yellow, single, ¼-in.-wide balls. Feb.–Mar.	Blooms when young. Used as pot plant in cold areas. Thorniness makes it a real barrier.
A. baileyana BAILEY ACACIA (Often called MIMOSA as cut flowers.)	7–9, 13–24. Borderline Zone 6.	20–30 ft.	20–40 ft.	Feathery, finely cut, blue gray.	Yellow, in clusters. Fragrant. Profuse in Jan.–Feb.	Most commonly planted and one of hardiest. Wonderful tree on banks when grown as multitrunked tree-shrub.
A. b. 'Purpurea' PURPLE-LEAF ACACIA	8, 9, 14–24	20–30 ft.	20–30 ft.	Same, except for lavender to purple new growth.	Same.	Cut back to encourage new growth, prolong foliage color.
A. constricta WHITE THORN MESCAT ACACIA	10–24	10–18 ft.	To 18 ft.	Tiny, feathery.	Yellow, fragrant. Summer.	Open, spiny, deciduous shrub. Valuable in natural desert landscape for texture, size, summer flowers.
A. craspedocarpa	8, 9, 12–24	To 18 ft.	To 10 ft.	Roundish, thick, gray.	Yellow rods. Late winter, spring.	Tolerates desert soils, drought, neglect. Dense foliage makes good screen.
A. cultriformis KNIFE ACACIA	13–24	10–15 ft.	10–15 ft.	Silvery gray, shaped like 1-in.-long paring knife blades.	Yellow, in clusters. Mar.	Naturally a multistemmed tree. Barrier or screen. Useful on banks, slopes.
A. cyanophylla (See *A. saligna*)						
A. cyclopis	8, 9, 13–24	10–15 ft.	15–20 ft.	Dark green, narrow, to 3½ in. long.	Bright yellow, single or clustered; inconspicuous. Spring.	Screening plant along highways. Very drought resistant. Good for hedges. Unusual seeds—black with red rings.
A. dealbata (*A. decurrens dealbata*)	8, 9, 14–24. Borderline Zone 6.	To 50 ft.	40–50 ft.	Feathery, silvery gray.	Similar to *A. baileyana*.	Twigs and young branches also silvery gray; attractive. Very fast growing.
A. decora GRACEFUL WATTLE	13–24	6–8 ft.	6–8 ft.	Rather narrow, 2 in. long, curved, bluish.	Yellow balls in 2-in.-long clusters. Mass display in spring.	Screening. Can be used as trimmed hedge 5 ft. high. Drought resistant.
A. decurrens (*A. decurrens mollis*) (Plants offered are often the similar *A. mearnsii*.) GREEN WATTLE	8, 9, 14–24. Borderline Zone 6.	To 50 ft.	40–50 ft.	Feathery, dark green.	Yellow, in clusters. Feb.–Mar.	Longer lived than *A. baileyana;* more tolerant of wind and water. Invasive roots, litter rule it out of small gardens.
A. farnesiana SWEET ACACIA (See also *A. smallii.*)	13–24 (See Comments)	To 20 ft.	15–25 ft.	Deciduous. Feathery, finely divided. Branches thorny.	Deep yellow, fragrant balls most of the year. May freeze in cold snaps.	Needs frost-free location in Zone 13. Can freeze to stump in Zone 12. Better for desert is similar *A. smallii,* often sold as *A. farnesiana.*
A. longifolia (Often sold as *A. latifolia.*) SYDNEY GOLDEN WATTLE	8, 9, 14–24	To 20 ft.	To 20 ft.	Bright green, 3–6 in. long.	Golden yellow, loose 2½-in.-long spikes along branches in late winter, early spring.	Usually big, rounded, billowy shrub. Very fast growing; very tolerant. Used as road screening against dust, headlights. Good soil binder near beach (winds make it prostrate). Short lived (20–30 years).

A

NAME	ZONES	HEIGHT	SPREAD	LEAVES	FLOWERS	COMMENTS
A. melanoxylon BLACKWOOD ACACIA, BLACK ACACIA	8, 9, 13–24	To 40 ft.	To 20 ft.	Dark green, 2–4 in. long.	Creamy to straw color, in short clusters. Mar.–Apr.	Fast, dense, upright growth. Can be pruned as ball or standard. Roots, litter, brittle branches a problem in confined areas. Thrives in California's Central Valley.
A. minuta (See *A. smallii*)						
A. notabilis	12–24	To 10 ft.	To 10 ft.	Leathery, blue green, 2–5 in. long.	Bright yellow balls. Spring.	Clean, sharp lines, blue green color, flower display make this a good dense screen in desert.
A. pendula WEEPING ACACIA, WEEPING MYALL	13–24	To 25 ft.	To 15 ft.	Blue gray, to 4 in. long, on long weeping branches.	Yellow, in pairs or clusters. Blooms erratically in Apr., May.	Beautiful weeping tree. Perfect for cascading from behind wall. Interesting structural form as mature individual. Makes graceful espalier. Slow grower, seldom looks good in container.
A. podalyriifolia PEARL ACACIA	8, 9, 13–24	10–20 ft.	12–15 ft.	Roundish, 1½ in. long, silvery gray, soft and satiny to touch.	Light yellow, fluffy, in long clusters. Nov.–Mar.	Shrub or can be trained as rounded, open-headed tree. Excellent for patio use. Good winter color. Won't tolerate summer watering.
A. redolens (*A. ongerup*)	8, 9, 12–24	1–2 ft.	15 ft.	Narrow, gray green, leathery.	Puffy yellow balls. Spring.	Ground cover for banks, large areas of poor soil. Endures drought, heat. 'Ongerup' and *A. melanoxylon* 'Ongerup' similar or identical.
A. retinodes (Often sold as *A. floribunda*.) WATER WATTLE, FLORIBUNDA ACACIA	8, 9, 13–24. Borderline Zones 5, 6.	To 20 ft.	To 20 ft.	Yellow green, to 5 in. long.	Yellow, small heads in clusters. Blooms most of year near coast.	Quick screen. Can be a pendulous, see-through tree. Tends to get leggy. The only acacia with chance of survival in Seattle if mild winters come 4 in a row.
A. salicina WILLOW ACACIA, AUSTRALIAN WILLOW	8, 9, 12–24	20–40 ft.	To 15 ft.	Dark green, narrow, to 3 in. long.	Cream-colored balls. Blooms most of year; heaviest in fall and winter.	Fast-growing tree with semiweeping habit. Water moderately to control growth; prune to keep open, prevent wind damage. Don't overwater. Best with one side of tree always dry.
A. saligna (*A. cyanophylla*) BLUE-LEAF WATTLE	8, 9, 13–24	20–30 ft.	15–20 ft.	Narrow, blue green, 6–12 in. long.	Nearly orange balls in clusters. Heavy bloom Mar., Apr.	Screen for privacy or wind control. Multitrunked big shrub or tree.
A. schaffneri	8, 9, 12–24	To 18 ft.	To 20 ft.	Finely divided, deciduous, closely set along branches.	Yellow balls, fragrant. Spring.	Exotic form with curving branches like green tentacles. Prune to form trunk and shape branches. Short thorns hidden in leaves.
A. smallii (*A. minuta*)	8, 9, 12–24	Variable. Can reach 30–35 ft.	15–25 ft.	Finely divided, deciduous. Thorny branches.	Yellow, fragrant puff balls. Spring.	Often sold as *A. farnesiana*, which is cold-tender. Plant *A. smallii* where frost occurs.
A. stenophylla SHOESTRING ACACIA	8, 9, 12–24	To 30 ft.	To 20 ft.	Long (to 16 in.), narrow, drooping pale leaves contrast with maroon new bark.	Creamy, ½-in. balls. Late winter, spring.	Fast-growing, open, weeping tree. Makes wonderful shadows on walls, provides lightest shade for flowers.
A. subporosa BOWER WATTLE, RIVER WATTLE	8, 9, 13–24	20–30 ft.	20–30 ft.	Narrow, drooping.	Paired yellow puffs. Spring.	Graceful, weeping, 20–30-ft. tree. 'Emerald Cascade', 'Emerald Showers' are selections. Needs good drainage, protection from ocean wind or hot inland sun.
A. verticillata	14–24	To 15 ft.	To 15 ft.	Dark green, needlelike leaves, ¾ in. long, in whorls. Looks like an airy conifer.	Pale yellow in 1-in.-long spikes. Apr.–May.	Good low hedge in wind. Unpruned, it develops open form with many spreading, twisting trunks. Sheared, it grows dense and full. Good at beach; resists oak root fungus.

A

Prune large trees to open interiors to reduce dieback of shaded branches and prevent wind damage. Thin by removing branches entirely to the trunk.

Many acacias are relatively short lived—20–30 years. But if a tree grows to 20 ft. high in 3 years, the short life can be accepted.

Many acacias become chlorotic where water is bad and salts accumulate, as do many other plants in such soil.

The blackwood acacia (*A. melanoxylon*) has aggressive roots, lifts sidewalks, splits easily, and suckers. In shallow soil or where roots compete, it is a bad actor. Yet in the right place it is well behaved and beautiful, vigorous and dependable under difficult conditions of poor soil, wind, and drought.

ACAENA. *Rosaceae.* SHEEP BUR. Perennials. Zones 4–9, 14–24. The 2 New Zealand natives described below form large, loose mats of attractive gray green or pale green leaves that are divided into leaflets. Grow from seed or divisions in spring. Rather slow to establish. Plant 6–12 in. apart in sun or part shade. They burn in hot sun. Need ample water. Use in areas where a gray green, loose, fine-textured mat is wanted—beside paths, in filtered shade beneath trees, in rock gardens. Can take some foot traffic. Remove burrs, which look messy, stick to clothing and pets.

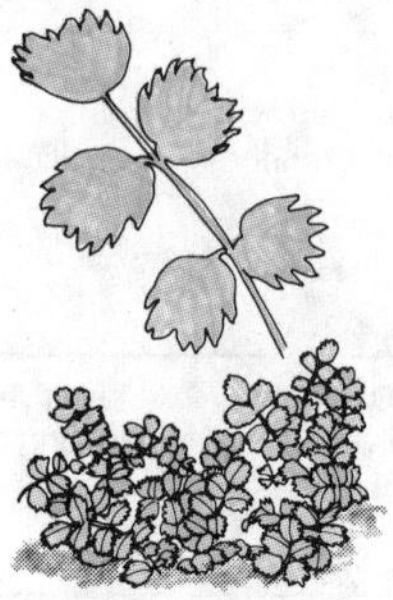

Acaena microphylla

A. buchananii. Has dense, silky, whitish green leaves, each with 11–13 round, small leaflets with scalloped edges.

A. microphylla. NEW ZEALAND BUR. Pale green leaves similar to above, but larger and almost without hairs; 7–13 leaflets per leaf.

ACALYPHA. *Euphorbiaceae.* Evergreen tropical shrubs. Zones 21–23. Both species described below are quite tender; *A. wilkesiana* can be used as an annual.

A. hispida. CHENILLE PLANT. Native to the East Indies. Needs tropical climate. Best grown in plastic-covered outdoor rooms. Control size by pinching and pruning; can grow to a bulky 10 ft. Heavy, rich green leaves to 8 in. wide. Flowers hang in 1½-ft.-long clusters resembling tassels of crimson chenille. Blooms most heavily in June; scattered bloom throughout year. With heavy pruning, a good house plant.

Acalypha hispida

A. wilkesiana (*A. tricolor*). COPPER LEAF. Native to South Pacific islands. Foliage more colorful than many flowers. Used as an annual, substituting for flowers from September to frost. Leaves to 8 in.; may be bronzy green mottled with shades of red and purple; red with crimson and bronze; or green edged with crimson and stippled with orange and red. In a warm, sheltered spot, it can grow as a shrub to 6 ft. or more if winter appearance is not important. Best in container with fast-draining potting mix, kept slightly dry through winter.

Acanthaceae. The acanthus family consists of herbs and shrubs, generally from warm or tropical areas. Many have showy flowers or foliage. Examples are *Acanthus, Aphelandra,* and *Thunbergia.*

ACANTHUS mollis. *Acanthaceae.* BEAR'S BREECH. Perennial. Zones 4–24. Native to southern Europe. Fast-growing, spreading plant with basal clusters of handsome, deeply lobed and cut, shining dark green leaves to 2 ft. long. Rigid 1½-ft. spikes of tubular whitish, lilac, or rose flowers with spiny green or purplish bracts top 2–3-ft. stems. Blooms late spring or early summer. Variety 'Latifolius' has larger leaves, is hardier.

Requires light shade but will take sun in coastal areas. Cut back after flowering. If you grow it for the foliage alone, cut off flower stalks before they bloom. Bait for slugs and snails. Divide clumps between October and March. Plant where it can be confined; roots travel underground, make plant difficult to eradicate. Effective with bamboo, large-leafed ferns. Best in moist, shady situations, but will also grow in dry, sunny areas—even in parking strips.

Acanthus mollis

ACER. *Aceraceae.* MAPLE. Deciduous or evergreen trees or large shrubs. When you talk about maples, you're talking about many trees—large and medium-sized deciduous shade trees, smaller evergreen and deciduous trees, and dainty, picturesque shrub-trees. In general, maples are highly favored in the Pacific Northwest, in the intermountain areas, and to a lesser extent in northern California; with a few exceptions, they are not adapted to southern California or the Southwest's desert areas. Practically all maples in southern California show marginal leaf burn after mid-June and lack the fall color of maples in colder areas.

The larger maples have extensive fibrous root systems that take water and nutrients from the topsoil. The great canopy of leaves calls for a steady, constant supply of water—not necessarily frequent watering, but constantly available water throughout the root zone. Ample deep watering and periodic feeding will help keep roots down.

Acer palmatum

A. buergeranum. TRIDENT MAPLE. Deciduous tree. Zones 4–9, 14–17, 20, 21. Native to China, Japan. Grows 20–25 ft. high. Roundish crown of 3-in.-wide, glossy, 3-lobed leaves that are pale beneath. Fall color usually red, varies to orange or yellow. Low, spreading growth; stake and prune to make it branch high. A decorative, useful patio tree and favorite bonsai subject.

A. campestre. HEDGE MAPLE. Deciduous tree. Zones 1–9, 14. Native to Europe, western Asia. Slow growing to 70 ft., seldom over 30 ft. in cultivation. Forms an especially dense, compact, rounded head in the Northwest; thinner in California. Leaves 3–5 lobed, 2–4 in. wide, dull green above; turn yellow in fall. Rated high in the Northwest. 'Queen Elizabeth' has glossier foliage, more erect habit.

A. capillipes. Deciduous tree. Zones 1–9, 14–24. Native to Japan. Moderate growth rate to 30 ft. Young branches red, turning brown with white stripes with age. Young leaves red, leaf stalks and midribs red. Leaves shallowly 3 lobed, 3–5 in. long; turn scarlet in fall.

A. cappadocicum. COLISEUM MAPLE. Deciduous tree. Zones 1–6. Native to western Asia. Known here in its variety 'Rubrum', RED COLISEUM MAPLE. Grows to 35 ft.; forms compact, rounded crown. Leaves 5–7 lobed, 5½ in. wide. Bright red spring foliage turns rich, dark green.

A. circinatum. VINE MAPLE. Deciduous shrub or small tree. Zones 1–6, 14–17. Native to moist woods, stream banks in coastal mountains of British Columbia south to northern California. Crooked, sprawling, and vinelike in the forest shade, with many stems from the base; single-trunked small tree 5–35 ft. high in full sun. Loses its vinelike characteristics in open situations. Leaves 5–11 lobed, 2–6 in. wide and as long, light green turning orange, scarlet, or yellow in the fall. New spring foliage usually has reddish tints. Tiny reddish purple flowers in clusters, April–May, followed by paired winged seeds which look like little red bow ties among the green leaves. One of the most airy and delicate western natives. The rare variety 'Monroe' has finely cut leaves.

Let it go untrimmed to make natural bowers, ideal settings for ferns and woodland flowers. Use under a canopy of tall conifers where its blazing fall color offers brilliant contrast. Can be espaliered against shady side of a wall. Its contorted leafless branches make an intricate pattern in winter. Select in fall to get best forms for autumn color.

A. davidii. DAVID'S MAPLE. Deciduous tree. Zones 1–6, 15–17, 20, 21. Native to central China. This 20–35-ft.-high maple is distinctive on several counts. Bark is shiny green striped with silvery white, particularly striking in winter. Leaves are glossy green, oval or lobed, 2–7 in. long, 1½–4 in. wide, deeply veined. New foliage bronze tinted; fall color of bright yellow, red orange, and purple. Clustered greenish yellow flowers showy in April or May.

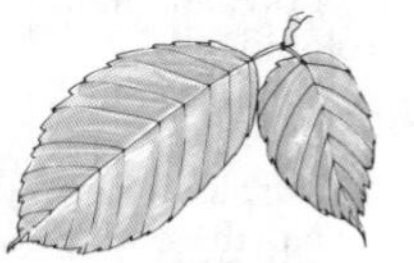

Acer davidii

A. ginnala. AMUR MAPLE. Deciduous shrub or small tree. Zones 1–9, 14–16. Native to Manchuria, north China, Japan. To 20 ft. high. Three-lobed, toothed leaves to 3 in. long, 2 in. wide. Striking red fall color. Clusters of small, fragrant yellowish flowers in early spring are followed by handsome bright red, winged fruit. Comes into its own in the coldest areas of the West. Grown as staked, trained single tree or multiple-trunked tall shrub. 'Flame', 15–20 ft. tall, shows fiery red fall color.

A. glabrum. ROCKY MOUNTAIN MAPLE. Deciduous shrub or small tree. Zones 1–3, 10. Leaves 2–5 in. wide, 3–5 lobed or divided into 3 leaflets; borne on dark red twigs. Fruit tinged red. Fall foliage yellow. Multitrunked clumps may be only 6 ft. tall or up to 30 ft. under ideal conditions. Needs well-drained soil and ample moisture.

A. griseum. PAPERBARK MAPLE. Deciduous tree. Zones 1–9, 14–21. Native to China. Grows to 25 ft. or higher with narrow to rounded crown. In winter it makes a striking silhouette with bare branches angling out and up from main trunk and reddish bark peeling away in paper-thin sheets. Late to leaf out in spring; leaves are divided into 3 coarsely toothed leaflets 1½–2½ in. long, dark green above, silvery below. Inconspicuous red flowers in spring develop into showy winged seeds. Foliage turns brilliant red in fall.

A. japonicum. FULLMOON MAPLE. Deciduous shrub or small tree. Zones 1–6, 14–16. Native to Japan. To 20–30 ft. Nearly round, 2–5-in.-long leaves cut into 7–11 lobes. Practically unknown in western gardens, but 2 varieties are obtainable; both are small, slow growing, and best placed as shrubs.

A. j. 'Aconitifolium'. FERNLEAF FULLMOON MAPLE. Leaves are deeply cut, almost to leaf stalk; each lobe is also cut and toothed. Fine fall color where adapted.

A. j. 'Aureum'. GOLDEN FULLMOON MAPLE. Leaves open pale gold in spring and remain a pale chartreuse yellow all summer.

A. macrophyllum. BIGLEAF MAPLE. Deciduous tree. Zones 4–17. Native to streambanks, moist canyons, Alaska to foothills of California. Broad-topped, dense shade tree 30–95 ft. high—too big for a small garden or a street tree. Large 3–5-lobed leaves are 6–15 in. wide, sometimes bigger on young, vigorous sapling growth; leaves turn from medium green to yellow in fall. Small greenish yellow flowers in drooping clusters, April–May, followed by clusters of paired winged seeds which look rather like tawny, drooping butterflies. Yellow fall color spectacular in cool areas. Resistant to oak root fungus.

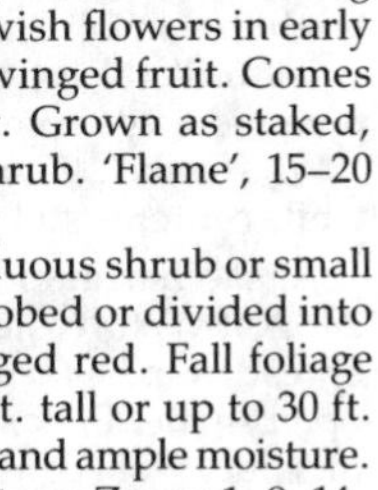

Acer macrophyllum

A. morrisonense. FORMOSAN MAPLE, MT. MORRISON MAPLE. Deciduous tree. Zones 4–6, 15–17. Native to Taiwan (Formosa). Fast, upright growth rounding with age; probably 30–40 ft. Greenish bark striped white. New growth red in early spring, fall foliage red. Summer foliage light green, red leaf stalks; leaves 3 lobed, 5 in. long, 4 in. wide. Needs ample water, good soil; not for areas where summers are hot, dry, and windy.

A. negundo. BOX ELDER. Deciduous tree. Zones 1–10, 12–24. Native to most of U.S. Where you can grow other maples of your choice, this is a weed tree of many faults—it seeds readily, hosts box elder bugs, suckers badly, and is subject to breakage. Fast growing to 60 ft., usually less. Leaves divided into 3–5 (or 7–9) oval, 2–5-in.-long leaflets with toothed margins; yellow in fall.

A. n. 'Variegatum'. VARIEGATED BOX ELDER. Not as large or weedy as the species. Combination of green and creamy white leaves stands out in any situation. Large, pendant clusters of white fruit are spectacular. Highly regarded in the Northwest; occasionally planted in northern California.

A. nigrum. BLACK MAPLE. Similar to sugar maple (*A. saccharum*), but more resistant to heat and drought. Light green leaves turn yellow in fall. 'Greencolumn' can reach 65 ft. tall, 25 ft. wide.

A. oblongum. EVERGREEN MAPLE. Evergreen or partially evergreen tree. Zones 8–10, 12, 14–24. Native to the Himalayas and China. Reaches 20–25 ft. high and almost as wide; branches tend to sweep outward and upward. Slender, shiny, deep green leaves, no lobes. New growth attractive bronzy pink in spring. Loses all leaves in sharp cold.

A. o. biauritum. See *A. paxii*.

A. palmatum. JAPANESE MAPLE. Deciduous shrub or tree. Zones 1–9, 14–24. Native to Japan and Korea. Slow growing to 20 ft.; normally many stemmed. Most airy and delicate of all maples. Leaves 2–4 in. long, deeply cut into 5–9 toothed lobes. All-year interest: young spring growth is glowing red; summer's leaves are soft green; fall foliage scarlet, orange, or yellow. Slender leafless branches in greens and reds provide winter pattern. Resistant to oak root fungus.

Grafted garden varieties are popular (the list below includes only the best known of dozens available), but common seedlings have uncommon grace and usefulness. They are more rugged, faster growing, more drought tolerant, and stand more sun and wind than named forms. Japanese maples thrive everywhere in the Northwest, where they make good small street trees. They can be grown with success in California if given shelter from hot, dry, or constant winds. Filtered shade is best but full sun is satisfactory. In California consider the local soil and water; wherever azaleas are difficult and suffer from salt buildup in the soil, Japanese maples will show burn on leaf edges. Give same watering treatment as azaleas—flood occasionally to leach out salts.

Used effectively on north and east walls, in patios and entryways, as small lawn trees. Attractive in groves (like birches) as woodland planting; for natural effect, set out plants of different sizes with varying spacing. Good under oaks, as background for ferns and azaleas, alongside pools. Invaluable in tubs and for bonsai. Japanese maple is inclined to grow in planed surfaces, so pruning to accentuate this growth habit is easy. Prune to plane downward when given a water foreground.

The grafted garden forms are usually smaller than seedlings, more weeping and spreading, brighter in foliage color, and more finely cut in leaf. In California, it seems that the more finely cut the leaf, the greater the leaf burn problem. Since these kinds make good tub plants, it's easy to give them special placement and watering attention. Some of the best are:

'Atropurpureum'. RED JAPANESE MAPLE. Purplish or bronze to bronzy green leaves, brighter in sun. Holds color all summer.

'Bloodgood'. Vigorous, upright growth to 15 ft. Deep red spring and summer foliage, scarlet in fall. Bark blackish red.

'Bonfire'. Orange pink spring and fall foliage; twisted trunk, short branches, drooping branchlets.

'Burgundy Lace'. Leaves more deeply cut than those of 'Atropurpureum'; branchlets bright green.

'Butterfly'. Small (to 7-ft.) shrub with small bluish green leaves edged in white. Cut out growth that reverts to plain green.

'Crimson Queen'. Small, shrubby, with finely cut leaves that hold color all summer, turn scarlet before dropping off in fall.

'Crimson Sentry'. More erect, narrower than 'Crimson Queen', with closely spaced leaves. Good where space is limited.

'Dissectum' ('Dissectum Viridis'). LACELEAF JAPANESE MAPLE. Small shrub with drooping branches, green bark; pale green, finely divided leaves turn gold in autumn.

'Ever Red' ('Dissectum Atropurpureum'). Small mounding shrub with weeping branches. Finely divided, purple-tinged, lacy foliage turns crimson in fall.

'Garnet'. Similar to 'Crimson Queen' and 'Ever Red'; somewhat more vigorous grower.

(Continued on next page)

'Heptalobum Osakazuki'. Vigorous (to 10 ft. or more) plant with large green leaves that turn fiery scarlet in autumn.

'Koshimino' ('Sessilifolium'). Upright, narrowish to 12 ft. Small leaves without leaf stalks sit right on branches. Green leaves turn red in fall.

'Linearilobum' ('Scolopendriifolium'). To 8 ft., with green leaves divided into extremely long, narrow segments. Fall color yellow.

'Ornatum' ('Dissectum Atropurpureum'). RED LACELEAF JAPANESE MAPLE. Like 'Dissectum', but with red leaves turning brighter red in autumn.

'Oshio Beni'. Like 'Atropurpureum' but more vigorous; has long, arching branches.

'Roseo-marginatum'. Small. Pale green leaves are edged with pink. Cut out growth that reverts to green.

'Sango Kaku' ('Senkaki'). Vigorous, upright, treelike. Fall foliage yellow, tinted rose. Twigs, branches striking coral red.

A. paxii *(A. oblongum biauritum).* Zones 8, 9, 14–24. Evergreen tree to 30 ft. Leaves usually 3 lobed, occasionally oval or mitten shaped. Slow growth; compact head of dense foliage.

A. platanoides. NORWAY MAPLE. Deciduous tree. Zones 1–9, 14–17. Native to Europe, western Asia. Broad-crowned, densely foliaged tree to 50–60 ft. Leaves 5 lobed, 3–5 in. wide, deep green above, paler beneath; turn yellow in fall. Showy clusters of small, greenish yellow flowers in early spring. Very adaptable, tolerating many soil and climate conditions, but performs poorly in southern California and desert. Once a widely recommended street tree but now objected to where aphids cause honeydew drip and sooty mold. Voracious root system deep down and at surface also a problem. Here are some of the best horticultural varieties (purple-leafed forms perform poorly in alkaline soils unless soil is conditioned):

'Cavalier'. Compact, round headed, to 30 ft.

'Cleveland' and 'Cleveland II'. Shapely, compact, well-formed trees about 50 ft. tall.

'Columnare'. Slower grower, narrower form than the species.

'Crimson King'. Holds purple foliage color until leaves drop. Slower growing than the species. Fine in Northwest and California foothills.

'Deborah'. Like 'Schwedler', but faster growing, straighter.

'Drummondii'. Leaves are edged with silvery white; unusual and striking.

'Faassen's Black'. Pyramidal in shape, with dark purple leaves.

'Globe'. Slow growing with dense, round crown; eventual height 20–25 ft.

'Green Lace'. Finely cut, dark green leaves; moderate growth rate to 40 ft.

'Jade Glen'. Vigorous, straight-growing form with bright yellow fall color.

'Parkway'. Essentially a broader tree than 'Columnare', with a dense canopy.

'Royal Red Leaf'. Another good red- or purple-leafed form.

'Schwedler' or 'Schwedleri'. Purplish red leaves in spring turn to dark bronzy green, gold in autumn.

'Summershade'. Fast-growing, upright, heat-resistant selection.

A. pseudoplatanus. SYCAMORE MAPLE. Deciduous tree. Zones 1–9, 14–20. Native to Europe, western Asia. Moderate growth to 40 ft. or more. Leaves 3–5 in. wide, 5 lobed, thick, prominently veined, dark green above, pale below. No particular fall color. The variety 'Atropurpureum' ('Spaethii') has leaves that are rich purple underneath.

A. rubrum. SCARLET MAPLE, RED MAPLE. Deciduous tree. Zones 1–9, 14–17. Native to eastern U.S. Fairly fast growth to 40 ft. or more, with 20-ft. spread. Faster growing than Norway or sycamore maples. Red twigs, branchlets, and buds; quite showy flowers. Fruit dull red. Leaves 2–4 in. long, 3–5 lobed, shiny green above, pale beneath; brilliant scarlet fall color in frosty areas. Rates high in Pacific Northwest where several selected forms are available. Needs ample moisture in Zone 14.

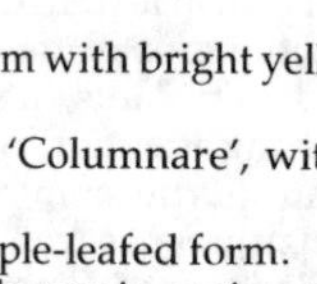

Acer rubrum

'Armstrong' and 'Armstrong II'. Tall, very narrow trees with good red fall color.

'Autumn Radiance'. Broad oval form, orange red fall color.

'Bowhall'. Tall, narrow, cone shaped, with orange red foliage color in fall.

'Columnare'. Tall, broadly columnar.

'Gerling'. Broadly pyramidal, to 35 ft. with 20-ft. spread.

'Karpick'. Narrow grower with red twigs, yellow to red fall color.

'Northwood'. Rounded form. Extremely cold hardy.

'October Glory'. Tall, round-headed tree; last to turn color in fall.

'Red Sunset'. Upright, vigorous branching pattern.

'Scarlet Sentinel'. Columnar, fast-growing form.

'Schlesingeri'. Tall, broad, fast growing, with regular form; orange red fall color.

'Shade King'. Very fast grower to 50 ft. Pale green foliage turns bright red in fall.

'Tilford'. Nearly globe-shaped crown if grown in the open; pyramidal when crowded.

'V.J. Drake'. Unusual fall color; leaf borders turn red and violet while center is still green. Leaves eventually turn completely red.

A. saccharinum. SILVER MAPLE. Deciduous tree. Zones 1–9, 14–24. Native to eastern U.S. Grows fast to 40–100 ft. with equal spread. Open form, with semipendulous branches; casts fairly open shade. Bark silvery gray except on oldest wood. Leaves 3–6 in. wide, 5 lobed, light green above, silvery beneath. In Northwest, fall color is a mixture of scarlet, orange, and yellow—often in same leaf.

You pay a penalty for the advantage of fast growth: weak wood and narrow crotch angles make this tree break easily. Many rate it the least desirable of maples. Unusually susceptible to aphids and cottony scale. Suffers from chlorosis in alkaline soils. Nevertheless, it is often planted for fast growth and graceful habit.

A. s. 'Silver Queen'. Fast growing, more upright than the species, seedless. Bright gold fall color.

A. s. 'Wieri' (**A. s.** 'Laciniatum'). WIER MAPLE, CUTLEAF SILVER MAPLE. Same as species, but leaves are much more finely cut; provides open shade.

A. saccharum. SUGAR MAPLE. Deciduous tree. Zones 1–10, 14–20. From eastern U.S.; in the Northeast, it's the source of maple sugar. Moderate growth to 60 ft. and more. Stout branches with upward sweep form fairly compact crown. Leaves 3–6 in. wide, 3–5 lobed, green above, pale below. Spectacular fall color in cold-winter areas—yellow and orange to deep red and scarlet. Varieties include: 'Arrowhead' (erect pyramid); 'Bonfire' (tall, spreading, bright red fall color); 'Commemoration' (heavy leaf texture; orange, yellow, red fall color); 'Green Mountain' (tolerant of heat and drought); 'Legacy' (fast growing, multihued in fall); 'Monumentale' (narrow, erect); and 'Seneca Chief' (narrow form, orange to yellow fall color).

A. s. grandidentatum *(A. grandidentatum).* WASATCH MAPLE, BIG-TOOTH MAPLE, ROCKY MOUNTAIN SUGAR MAPLE. Leaves 3–5 lobed, with large blunt teeth. Grows as shrub or 20–30-ft.-tree. Brilliant fall color in tones of yellow, orange, rose red. In nature, it grows in canyons and on streambanks. In gardens, requires well-drained soil on dry side.

A. tataricum. TATARIAN MAPLE. Zones 1–6, 14–16. Resembles *A. ginnala* in size and habit. Leaves toothed, lobed only on young plants, 2–3½ in. long. Winged seeds red in summer, showy; fall color yellow to reddish brown. Extremely hardy.

A. truncatum. Deciduous tree. Zones 1–9, 14–23. Native to China. Grows fairly rapidly to 25 ft. Like a small Norway maple with more deeply lobed leaves to 4 in. wide. Expanding leaves are purplish red, summer leaves green, autumn leaves dark purplish red. A good lawn or patio tree.

Aceraceae. The maple family consists of deciduous (rarely evergreen) trees and shrubs with paired opposite leaves and paired, winged seeds.

ACHILLEA. *Compositae.* YARROW. Perennials. All Zones. Yarrows are among the most carefree and generously blooming perennials for summer and early fall, several being equally useful in the garden and as cut flowers (taller kinds may be cut and dried for winter bouquets). Leaves are gray or green, bitter-aromatic, usually finely divided (some with toothed edges). Flower heads usually in flattish clusters. Yarrows thrive in sun, need only routine care: moderate watering (though they endure drought once established), cutting back after bloom, dividing when clumps get crowded. Fire retardant.

Achillea tomentosa

A. ageratifolia. GREEK YARROW. Native to Balkan region. Low mats of silvery leaves, toothed or nearly smooth edged. White flower clusters ½–1 in. across on stems 4–10 in. tall.

A. clavennae (often sold as *A. argentea*). SILVERY YARROW. Mats of silvery gray, silky leaves, lobed somewhat like chrysanthemum leaves. Loose, flat-topped clusters of ½–¾-in.-wide, ivory white flower heads on 5–10-in.-high stems. Combines beautifully with *Festuca ovina glauca,* yellow sunroses *(Helianthemum),* creeping yellow-flowered sedums.

A. filipendulina. FERNLEAF YARROW. Native to the Orient. Tall, erect plants 4–5 ft. high, with deep green, fernlike leaves. Bright yellow flower heads in large flat-topped clusters. Dried or fresh, they are good for flower arrangements. Several horticultural varieties are available. 'Gold Plate', a tall plant, has flower clusters up to 6 in. wide; 'Coronation Gold', to about 3 ft., also has large flower clusters. Combine these tall yarrows in borders with clumps of delphiniums, red-hot poker (*Kniphofia uvaria*), and Shasta daisies (*Chrysanthemum maximum*).

A. millefolium. COMMON YARROW, MILFOIL. This species may spread a bit or grow erect to 3 ft. Narrow, fernlike, green or gray green leaves on 3-ft. stems. White flower clusters grow on long stems. *A. m.* 'Rosea' has rosy flower heads. One of the more successful garden varieties is 'Fire King'. It grows to about 3 ft., has gray foliage and dark reddish flowers, and is good for dry, hot situations. 'Cerise Queen' has brighter red flowers.

A. ptarmica. Erect plant up to 2 ft. high. Narrow leaves with finely toothed edges. White flower heads in rather open, flattish clusters. 'The Pearl' has double flowers.

A. serbica. Like *A. ageratifolia* but more mounding in habit, with clustered rather than single flower heads.

A. taygetea. Native to the Levant. Grows to 1½ ft. Gray green, divided leaves 3–4 in. long. Dense clusters of bright yellow flower heads fade to primrose yellow—excellent contrast in color shades until it's time to shear off old stalks. Good cut flowers.

A. tomentosa. WOOLLY YARROW. Native to Europe and the Orient. Makes a flat, spreading mat of fernlike, deep green, hairy leaves. Golden flower heads in flat clusters top 6–10-in. stems in summer. 'Primrose Beauty' has pale yellow flowers; 'King George' has cream flowers. A good edging and a neat ground cover for sunny or partly shaded small areas; used in rock gardens. Shear off dead flowers to leave attractive green mat of low-growing foliage.

ACHIMENES. *Gesneriaceae.* Tender perennial with very small, irregular, conelike rhizomes. Native to tropical America. Related to African violet and gloxinia, and requires similar treatment. Plants 1–2 ft. high, some trailing. Slender stems; roundish, crisp, bright to dark green, hairy leaves. Flaring tubular flowers, 1–3 in. across, in pink, blue, lavender, orchid, purple.

Achimenes

Grow as house plant, in greenhouse or lathhouse, or on patio protected from direct sun and wind. Plant rhizomes March–April, placing ½–1 in. deep in moist peat moss and sand. Keep in light shade at 60°F. with even moisture. When 3 in. high, set 6–12 plants in 6–7-in. fern pot or hanging basket, in potting mix of equal parts peat moss, perlite, leaf mold. In fall, cure and dry rhizomes. Store in cool, dry place over winter; repot in spring.

ACIDANTHERA bicolor. See *Gladiolus callianthus*.

ACMENA smithii *(Eugenia smithii).* *Myrtaceae.* LILLY-PILLY TREE. Evergreen large shrub or small tree. Zones 15–17, 19–24. Australia. Big feature is its dramatic show of clustered white, lavender, or lavender pink, ¼–½-in.-wide, edible berries in winter; they last a long time. If trained, can grow as tree to 10–25 ft. high. Awkward in growth unless trained. Shiny, pinkish green to green, 3-in.-long leaves. Many small white flowers in clusters at branch tips. Takes normal good garden care but is at its best with deep, rich soil and ample water.

Acmena smithii

ACOELORRHAPHE wrightii *(Paurotis wrightii).* *Palmae.* Outdoors Zones 19–24; house plant anywhere. Native to Florida, West Indies. Fan palm with several slender trunks that grow stiffly and somewhat slowly to 10–15 ft. Leaves 2–3 ft. across, green above, silvery below. Very hardy (to 20°F.) but somewhat difficult to establish. Does best in partial shade with ample feeding and plenty of water. Subject to chlorosis; prepare soil carefully with organic amendments and iron where salts in soil or water are a problem. Treat with iron if leaves turn yellow green. Large plants are among the most beautiful of palms—but because they take so long to reach a substantial size, they're rare and expensive.

Acoelorrhaphe wrightii

ACOKANTHERA. *Apocynaceae.* Evergreen shrub. Zones 21, 23, 24. Native of South Africa. Distinguished, rather slow growing, to 10 ft. and as wide (keep smaller and more dense by cutting back long branches and removing weak ones). Most admired for leaf color—glossy dark green to deep plum purple—against a framework of very dark brown stems and branches. Flowers, white or tinged pink and very fragrant, appear throughout the year, but the big show is in early spring. Flowers are followed by blackish purple, olive-sized fruit which is very poisonous (to prevent formation of fruit, remove blooms as they fade).

Acokanthera oblongifolia

Especially tolerant of wind and salt. Best in full sun. Needs plenty of water in summer. Useful in hedges, foundation plantings, and as an espalier.

A. oblongifolia *(A. spectabilis).* AFRICAN WINTERSWEET. Narrow leaves, 3–5 in. long. Flowers about 1 in. long. Many plants sold under this name belong to the next species.

A. oppositifolia *(A. venenata).* BUSHMAN'S POISON. Flowers smaller than above. Leaves broader, relatively shorter, tinged red, purplish, or bronze.

ACONITUM. *Ranunculaceae.* ACONITE, MONKSHOOD. Perennial. Zones 1–9, 14–21. Leaves, usually lobed, in basal clusters. Flowers shaped like hoods or helmets, along tall spikes. Monkshood has a definite place in rich soil under trees, at the back of flower beds, or even at the edge of a shaded bog garden. Substitute for delphinium in shade. Combines effectively with ferns, thalictrum, Japanese

A

anemone (*Anemone hybrida*), astilbe, hosta, and francoa.

Hard to establish in warm, dry climates. Needs ample water; never let dry out. Sow seeds in spring; or sow in late summer and early fall for bloom the next year. Divide in early spring or late fall, or leave undivided for years. Completely dormant in winter; mark site.

Aconitum napellus

Caution: all parts of the plant are poisonous.

A. carmichaelii *(A. fischeri).* Native to central China. Densely leafy stems 2–4 ft. high. Leaves leathery, dark green, lobed and coarsely toothed. Blooms in fall; deep purple blue flowers form dense, branching clusters 4–8 in. long. Variety 'Wilsonii' grows 6–8 ft. high, has more open flower clusters 10–18 in. long.

A. napellus. GARDEN MONKSHOOD. Native to Europe. Upright leafy plants 2–5 ft. high. Leaves 2–5 in. wide, divided into narrow lobes. Flowers usually blue or violet, in spikelike clusters.

ACORUS gramineus. *Araceae.* Perennial. All Zones. Native to Japan, northern Asia. Related to callas, but fans of grasslike leaves more nearly resemble miniature tufts of iris. Flowers are inconspicuous. Two varieties are better known than species. 'Pusillus' is tiny, its leaves seldom more than 1 in. long. It is used in planting miniature landscapes and dish gardens. 'Variegatus', with white-edged, ¼-in.-wide leaves to 1½ ft. long, can be planted in bog gardens or at pool edges. 'Variegatus' is also useful in dry landscapes—collections of grasses, bamboos, or sword-leafed plants among gravel and boulders.

Acorus gramineus

ACROCARPUS fraxinifolius. *Leguminosae.* PINK CEDAR. Deciduous to nearly evergreen tree. Zones 21–24. Native to India, Burma. Despite the common name, not a cedar but a relative of the cassias. In Zones indicated, it fills a definite need for a tall, slender tree. Fast growing, with a clean, green trunk and striking foliage: long, 2-ft.-wide leaves, divided into many leaflets, are red on expanding, green at maturity. Small scarlet blossoms in dense clusters bloom in great profusion on bare branches in late winter, early spring. Only does its best where protected from strong winds. Although successful street plantings exist, pink cedar has never been common; nurseries fail to follow up on early sales with continuing supply of plants.

Acrocarpus fraxinifolius

ACROCOMIA. *Palmae.* GRU-GRU PALM. Slow-growing feather palms from Mexico, West Indies, South America. Long, black spines grow on the single or multiple trunks. Fruit sweet and edible. Needs ample water.

A. mexicana. Zone 24. Mexican palm 15–20 ft. tall, with olive to dark green, 8–12-ft., feathery leaves on mature plants. Takes little or no frost.

A. totai. Zones 23, 24. Native to Paraguay and Argentina. To 20 ft., with 6–9-ft.-long, feathery, medium to dark green leaves. Hardier than *A. mexicana.*

Acrocomia mexicana

ACTINIDIA. *Actinidiaceae.* Deciduous vines. Native to east Asia. Handsome foliage. Plant in rich soil. Give ample water and feed often. Supply sturdy supports for them to twine upon—such as a trellis, arbor, or patio overhead. You can also train them to cover walls and fences; guide and tie vines to the support as necessary. Thin occasionally to shape or to control pattern.

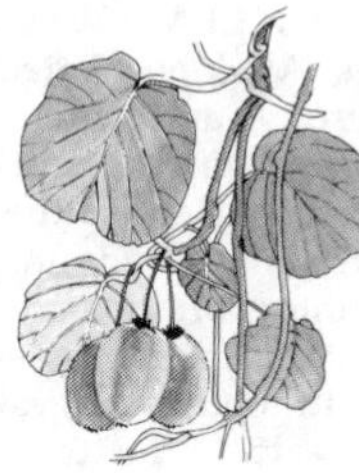

Actinidia deliciosa

In winter, prune and shape plant for form and fruit production. Shape to 1 or 2 main trunks; cut out closely parallel or crossing branches. Fruit is borne on shoots from year-old or older wood; cut out shoots that have fruited for 3 years and shorten younger shoots to 3–7 buds beyond previous summer's fruit.

In summer, shorten overlong shoots and unwind shoots that twine around main branches.

A. arguta. HARDY KIWI. Zones 1–9, 14–24. Much like *A. chinensis* but with smaller leaves, flowers; fruit 1–1½ in. long, fuzzless (eat skin and all). Female varieties 'Ananasnaja' and 'Hood River' need male varieties for pollen. The rare variety 'Issai' is self-fertile. Winter chill requirement not determined.

A. deliciosa *(A. chinensis).* KIWI, CHINESE GOOSEBERRY VINE. Zones 4–9, 14–24. Twines and leans to 30 ft. if not curbed. Leaves 5–8 in. long, roundish, rich dark green above, velvety white below. New growth often has rich red fuzz. Flowers (May) 1–1½ in. wide, opening creamy and fading to buff. Fruit egg sized, roughly egg shaped, covered with brown fuzz. Green flesh edible and delicious, with hints of melon, strawberry, banana. Although single plants are ornamental, you need both a male and a female plant for fruit. The best female (fruiting) varieties are 'Chico' and 'Hayward' (similar, possibly identical varieties); 'Vincent' needs little winter chill, is a good variety for mildest winter climates.

Harvest fruit in latest October or November. Store at refrigerator temperature in plastic bags. Ripen fruit at room temperature as needed.

A. kolomikta. Zones 4–9, 15–17. Rapid growth to 15 ft. or more to produce a wondrous foliage mass made up of heart-shaped, 3–5-in.-long, variegated leaves. Some leaves all white, some green splashed with white, others have rose, pink, or even red variegation.

ADENIUM obesum. *Apocynaceae.* Shrub, usually grown in container indoors. Can be kept outdoors in Zones 23, 24. Twisted branches grow from huge, fleshy, half-buried trunk or rootstock. Leaves sparse; plant leafless for long periods. Clustered saucer-shaped blossoms are deep pink, 2 in. or more across. Cannot take frost or winter chill and cold soil. Needs heat, light, good drainage, infrequent watering in summer, even less in winter; in short, this is a plant for careful enthusiasts and collectors. In bloom, extremely showy; in eastern tropical Africa, where it is native, it is known as desert rose or desert azalea. Milky sap is poisonous.

Adenium obesum

ADIANTUM. *Polypodiaceae.* MAIDENHAIR FERN. Mostly native to tropics; some are western natives. Stems thin, wiry, and dark; fronds finely cut, the leaflets mostly fan shaped, bright green, thin textured. Plants need shade, steady moisture, and soil rich in organic matter. Leaves of even hardy varieties die back in hard frosts. Kinds listed as tender or indoor plants sometimes succeed in sheltered places or lanais in mild-winter areas. Protect from snails and slugs.

A. capillus-veneris. SOUTHERN MAIDENHAIR. Zones 5–9, 14–24. Native to North America. To 1½ in. tall, fronds twice divided but not forked. Needs leaf mold or peat moss.

A. hispidulum. ROSY MAIDENHAIR. Tropics of Asia, Africa. Indoor or greenhouse plant. To 1 ft. tall. Young fronds rosy brown, turning medium green, shaped somewhat like five-finger fern (*A. pedatum*).

Adiantum pedatum

A. jordanii. CALIFORNIA MAIDENHAIR. Zones 5–9, 14–24. Native to California, southern Oregon. Twice-divided fronds to 2 ft. tall.

A. pedatum. FIVE-FINGER FERN, WESTERN MAIDENHAIR. Zones 1–9, 14–21. North America. Fronds fork to make a fingerlike pattern atop slender 1–2½-ft. stems. General effect airy and fresh; excellent in containers or shaded ground beds.

A. peruvianum. SILVER DOLLAR MAIDENHAIR. Peru. Indoor or greenhouse plant. To 1½ ft. or more in height. Segments of leaves quite large, to 2 in. wide.

A. raddianum *(A. cuneatum, A. decorum)*. Brazil. Tender fern for indoors or greenhouse. Fronds cut 3 or 4 times, 15–18 in. long. Many named varieties differing in texture and compactness. Grow in pots; move outdoors to a sheltered, shaded patio in summer. Varieties commonly sold are 'Fritz-Luthii', 'Gracillimum' (most finely cut), and 'Pacific Maid'.

A. tenerum. (Plant sold as *A. t.* 'Wrightii' is similar or identical.) New World tropics. Indoors or greenhouse. Long, broad fronds arch gracefully, are finely divided into many deeply cut segments ½–¾ in. wide.

ADROMISCHUS. *Crassulaceae.* Succulents. Zones 15–24; indoor plants anywhere. Native to South Africa. Short-stemmed plants grown for their fleshy, often interestingly marked leaves; flowers not important. All need sun, warmth, and good drainage, but leaves will burn in full summer desert sun.

Adromischus festivus

A. cristatus. Leaves fleshy and light green, to 2 in. long, 1 in. wide. Leaf tips are squared off and have a wavy margin.

A. festivus. PLOVER EGGS. Leaves fleshy, somewhat flattened, gray green with purplish mottling.

AECHMEA. *Bromeliaceae.* Outdoors Zones 22–24. Elsewhere, greenhouse or indoor plants. In frost-free areas, grow in pots, in hanging baskets, or in moss fastened in crotches of trees—always in shaded places with good air circulation. Indoors or outdoors, soil should be fast draining but moisture retentive. Apply water every 1–2 weeks into cups within leaves. Put water on soil when it's really dry to the touch. Bromeliad specialists list dozens of species and varieties, and new hybrids appear frequently.

Aechmea fasciata

A. chantinii. Rosettes of leaves 1–3 ft. long, green to gray green branded with silver or darker green. Tall flower clusters have orange, pink, or red bracts, yellow and red flowers; white or blue fruit.

A. fasciata. Gray green leaves, cross banded with silvery white. From the center grows a cluster of rosy pink flower bracts in which nestle pale blue flowers that change to deep rose. 'Silver King' has unusually silvery leaves; leaves of 'Marginata' are edged with creamy white bands.

A. 'Foster's Favorite'. Hybrid with bright wine red, lacquered leaves about 1 ft. long. Drooping spikelike clusters of coral red and blue flowers. 'Royal Wine', another hybrid, forms an open rosette of somewhat leathery, glossy, light green leaves, that are burgundy red beneath. Orange-and-blue flowers are borne in drooping clusters.

A

A. fulgens. Green leaves dusted with gray, 12–16 in. long, 2–3 in. wide. Flower cluster usually above the leaves; blossoms red, blue, and blue violet. Variety *A. f. discolor* has brownish red or violet red leaves, usually faintly striped. Many hybrids.

A. pectinata. Stiff rosettes up to 3 ft.; leaves to 3 in. wide, strongly marked pink or red at bloom time. Flowers whitish and green.

A. weilbachii. Shiny leaves, green or suffused with red tones, in 2–3-ft.-wide rosettes. Dull red, 1½-ft. flower stalk has orange red berries tipped with lilac.

AEGOPODIUM podagraria. *Umbelliferae.* BISHOP'S WEED, GOUT-WEED. Deciduous perennial. Zones 1–7. Very vigorous ground cover, best in semishade or shade with moderate water. Many light green, divided leaves make a low (to 6 in.), dense mass; leaflets are ½–3 in. long. To keep it low and even, mow it 2 or 3 times a year. Spreads by creeping underground rootstocks, may become invasive; best if contained behind underground barrier of wood, concrete, or heavy tarpaper.

Aegopodium podagraria 'Variegatum'

A. p. 'Variegatum'. The most widely planted form. Leaflets are edged white, giving a luminous effect in shade. Pull plants that revert to solid green leaves.

AEONIUM. *Crassulaceae.* Succulents. Zones 15–17, 20–24. Among the most useful succulents for decorative effects, in pots or in the ground. Especially good in full sun near ocean; give part shade inland.

A. arboreum. Branched stems to 3 ft. tall, each branch with a 6–8-in.-wide rosette of light green, lightly fringed, fleshy leaves. Yellow flowers in long clusters. Variety 'Atropurpureum' has dark purple rosettes, is more striking and more widely grown than the green one. Rosettes of 'Zwartkop' are nearly black.

Aeonium arboreum

A. decorum. Bushy, rounded, many-branched plants to 10 in., each branch ending in a 2-in. rosette. Fleshy, reddish-tinted leaves with red edges. Neat, compact. Pink flowers.

A. floribundum. Hybrid between *A. simsii* and *A. spathulatum*; 1-ft. cushion with 2–3-in. rosettes of medium green, fleshy leaves streaked with darker green. Abundant yellow flowers in spring.

A. haworthii. Free branching, shrubby, to 2 ft., with blue green, red-edged rosettes 2–3 in. wide. White flowers.

A. 'Pseudotabulaeforme'. Smooth, flat, light green rosettes to 10 in. wide. Makes offsets freely.

A. simsii *(A. caespitosum)*. Low, dense, spreading, very leafy, 6 in. tall. Bright green leaf rosettes. Yellow flowers.

A. urbicum. "Dinner platter" rosettes to 8–10 in. wide. Long, narrow, light green leaves, loosely arranged, have reddish edges. Similar plants may be sold under the same name.

AESCHYNANTHUS *(Trichosporum)*. *Gesneriaceae.* Trailing indoor plants and greenhouse plants. Related to African violets, but you wouldn't guess it. Shiny leaves, usually in pairs along stems; bright tubular flowers. Good in hanging pots. Need high temperatures, high humidity, and much light. Plant in loose, open, fibrous potting mix.

Aeschynanthus radicans

A. 'Black Pagoda'. Dark green leaves marbled with blackish purple; good display of clustered deep orange flowers at the branch tips.

(Continued on next page)

A

A. marmoratus. ZEBRA BASKET VINE. Grown for its green leaves mottled with maroon rather than for its inconspicuous greenish flowers.

A. pulcher. Resembles *A. radicans,* but has shorter, greenish flower tubes.

A. radicans (*A. lobbianus*). LIPSTICK PLANT. Tubular, red, 2-in. flowers emerge from tubular, purplish black flower tubes like lipsticks from their cases.

A. speciosus. Bright yellow and orange flowers up to 4 in. long.

A. splendidus. Yellow orange to orange, 4-in. flowers in clusters of 6–20 at ends of trailing stems.

AESCULUS. *Hippocastanaceae.* HORSECHESTNUT. Deciduous trees or large shrubs. Leaves are divided fanwise into large, toothed leaflets. Flowers, in long, dense, showy clusters at the ends of branches, attract hummingbirds. Leathery fruit capsules enclose glossy seeds.

Aesculus carnea

A. californica. CALIFORNIA BUCKEYE. Zones 4–7, 14–19. Native to dry slopes and canyons below 4,000 ft. elevation in Coast Ranges and Sierra Nevada foothills.

Shrublike or small tree, often with several stems to 10–20 ft. or taller. Very wide spreading (give it room). New foliage pale apple green; mature leaves have 5–7 rich green, 3–6-in.-long leaflets. Striking sight in April or May when fragrant, creamy flower plumes make it a giant candelabrum. Large, pear-shaped fruits, with green covering splitting to reveal large, brown, shiny seeds, are favorites for fall flower arrangements. Seeds sprout freely and seedlings make unusual bonsai subjects.

In drought conditions, *A. californica* drops its leaves very early—by July—but if given plenty of water will hold them until fall. After leaf drop, the tree presents an interesting silhouette—silvery trunk, branches, branchlets.

A. carnea. RED HORSECHESTNUT. Zones 1–9, 14–17. Hybrid between *A. hippocastanum* and *A. pavia*. To 40 ft. high and 30 ft. wide. Round headed with large, dark green leaves, each divided fanwise into 5 leaflets; casts dense shade. In April–May, bears hundreds of 8-in.-long plumes of soft pink to red flowers. 'Briotii' has rosy crimson flowers; 'O'Neill' ('O'Neill Red') has single flowers of bright red.

Members of *A. carnea* are smaller than *A. hippocastanum* and easier to accommodate in small gardens; they need summer water.

A. hippocastanum. COMMON HORSECHESTNUT. Zones 1–9, 14–17. To 60 ft. high with a 40-ft. spread; bulky, densely foliaged tree giving heavy shade. Needs summer water. Leaves divided fanwise into 5–7-toothed, 4–10-in.-long leaflets. Spectacular spring flower show: ivory blooms with pink markings in 1-ft.-long plumes. Invasive roots can break up walks. Seeds are slightly toxic. 'Baumannii' has double flowers, sets no seeds.

AETHIONEMA. *Cruciferae.* STONECRESS. Perennials. Zones 1–9, 14–21. Native to Mediterranean region and Asia Minor. Choice little shrublets, attractive in or out of bloom, best adapted to colder climates; a favorite among rock gardeners. Need full sun, grow best in a light, porous soil with considerable lime. Bloom late spring to summer. When flowering stops, cut back dead flower stems.

Aethionema warleyense

A. schistosum. Erect, unbranched stems 5–10 in. high, densely clothed with narrow, slate blue, ½-in.-long leaves. Fragrant, rose-colored flowers; petals about ¼ in. long.

A. warleyense (*A.* 'Warley Rose'). Hybrid form; neat, compact plant to 8 in. high. Pink flowers in dense clusters. Widely used; only one planted to any extent in warmer climates.

AFRICAN BOXWOOD. See *Myrsine africana.*

AFRICAN CORN LILY. See *Ixia maculata.*

AFRICAN DAISY. See *Arctotis, Dimorphotheca, Osteospermum.*

AFRICAN IRIS. See *Dietes.*

AFRICAN LINDEN. See *Sparmannia africana.*

AFRICAN RED ALDER. See *Cunonia capensis.*

AFRICAN VIOLET. See *Saintpaulia.*

AGAPANTHUS. *Amaryllidaceae.* LILY-OF-THE-NILE. Evergreen or deciduous perennials with thick rootstocks and fleshy roots. Outdoor plants in Zones 7–9, 12–24; indoor/outdoor tub or pot plants where winters are cold.

Agapanthus orientalis

Adaptable. Grow in full sun or as little as 3 hours sun a day. Best in loamy soil but will grow in heavy soils; thrives with ample water during growing season, but established plants can endure drought. Divide infrequently; every 5 or 6 years is usually sufficient. In cold-winter areas, lift and store over winter, replant in spring. Superb container plant. Good near pools.

A. africanus. (Often sold as *A. umbellatus.*) Evergreen. Leaves shorter, narrower than those of *A. orientalis;* flower stalks shorter (to 1½ ft. tall), fewer flowered (20–50 to a cluster). Blue flowers midsummer to early fall.

A. Headbourne Hybrids. Deciduous, 2–2½ ft. tall, cold hardy (with mulching) in western Washington and Oregon.

A. 'Henryi'. Resembles 'Peter Pan' but has white flowers.

A. inapertus. Deciduous. Deep blue tubular flowers droop from a 4–5-ft. stalk.

A. orientalis. (Often sold as *A. africanus, A. umbellatus.*) Evergreen. Most commonly planted. Broad, arching leaves in big clumps. Stems to 4–5 ft. tall bear up to 100 blue flowers. There are white ('Albus'), double ('Flore Pleno'), and giant blue varieties.

A. 'Peter Pan'. Evergreen. Outstanding free-blooming dwarf variety. Foliage clumps are 8–12 in. tall; clustered blue flowers top 1–1½-ft. stems.

A. 'Queen Anne'. Evergreen. Foliage clump 12–15 in. tall; leaves narrow. Flower stalks 2 ft. tall; flowers medium blue over a long summer season.

A. 'Rancho White'. Evergreen. Foliage clump 1–1½ ft. tall; leaves broad. Flower stalks 1½–2 ft. tall carry heavy clusters of white flowers. Also known as 'Dwarf White' and 'Rancho'. 'Peter Pan Albus' is similar or identical.

AGAPETES serpens (*Pentapterygium serpens*). *Ericaceae.* Evergreen shrub. Zones 15–17, 23, 24, or greenhouse. Arching, drooping branches to 3 ft. or more rise from a swollen, tuberlike base. Narrow leaves ½–1 in. long crowd in 2 rows along branches. Lanternlike, inch-long flowers, red marked with deeper red chevrons, hang under the branches in spring. A blueberry relative, it needs acid planting mix, some shade, and liberal watering. Odd, showy hanging basket plant. Also attractive planted above retaining wall or on high bank where viewers can see stripings on flowers. Native to moderate elevations in Himalayas, it merits trial in mildest Northwest gardens; try planting it in a rotten stump where it can root and trail.

Agapetes serpens

AGATHAEA coelestis. See *Felicia amelloides*.

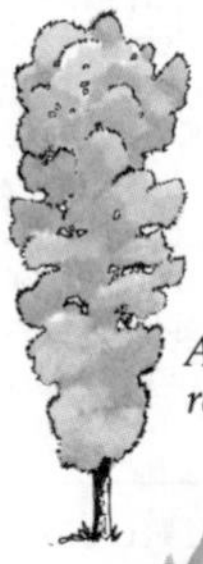

Agathis robusta

AGATHIS robusta. *Araucariaceae.* QUEENSLAND KAURI. Evergreen tree. Zones 15, 16, 20–23. Here's a dramatic strong skyline tree. Handsome in youth in containers. Moderate growth to an eventual 75 ft. in 80 years. Typically narrow and columnar. Open spaces between clumped branches present a striking layered effect. Leaves are broad, leathery, 2–4 in. long, and exceptionally glossy; light green to pinkish copper in new growth, dark green when mature. The foliage mass shines in the sun, sparkles in the rain, and ripples brightly in the breeze. A moisture-loving tree—be generous with water and fertilizer. Sometimes confused with *Podocarpus nagi* in nurseries. Rare.

Agavaceae. The agave family contains rosette-forming, sometimes treelike plants generally from dry regions. Flower clusters are spikes or spikelike; leaves often contain tough fibers.

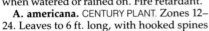

Agave attenuata

AGAVE. *Agavaceae.* Succulents, mostly gigantic, with large clumps of fleshy, strap-shaped leaves. The flower clusters are big, but not colorful. After flowering—which may not occur for years—the foliage clump dies, usually leaving behind suckers which make new plants. Drought resistant; they shrivel from serious drought but plump up again when watered or rained on. Fire retardant.

A. americana. CENTURY PLANT. Zones 12–24. Leaves to 6 ft. long, with hooked spines along the edges and a wicked spine at the tip; blue green in color. Be sure you really want one before planting it: the bulk and spines make it formidable to remove. After 10 years or more, the plant produces a branched, 15–40-ft. flower stalk bearing yellowish green flowers. There are several varieties with yellow- or white-striped leaves.

A. attenuata. Zones 20–24. Leaves 2½ ft. long, soft green or gray green, fleshy, somewhat translucent, no spines. Makes clumps to 5 ft. across; older plants develop a stout trunk to 5 ft. tall. Greenish yellow flowers dense on arching spikes to 12–14 ft. long. Will take poor soil but does best in rich soil with ample water. Protect from frost and hot sun. Statuesque container plant. Good near ocean or pool.

A. filifera. Zones 12–24. Rosettes less than 2 ft. wide; leaves are narrow, dark green, lined with white and edged with long white threads.

A. parryi huachucensis. Zones 12–24. Gray green, 2–3-ft.-wide rosettes resemble giant artichokes. Tips of leaves fiercely spined. Makes offsets freely.

A. victoriae-reginae. Zones 12, 13, 15–17, 21–24. Clumps only a foot or so across. The many dark green leaves are 6 in. long., 2 in. wide, stiff, thick, with narrow white lines. Slow growing; will stand in pot or ground 20 years before flowering (greenish flowers on tall stalks), then dying.

A. vilmoriniana *(A. mayoensis).* OCTOPUS AGAVE. Zones 12–24. Pale green or yellowish green rosettes up to 3 ft. wide. Leaves 3–4 in. wide, fleshy, deeply channeled above, with a single long spine at the end. Arching, twisted leaves give plant look of an octopus or huge spider. Very handsome in containers.

AGERATUM houstonianum. *Compositae.* FLOSS FLOWER. Annual. All Zones, if planting times followed. Reliable favorite for summer and fall color in borders and containers. The lavender blue–flowered varieties combine with flowers of almost any color or shape. Leaves roundish, usually heart shaped at the base, soft green, hairy. Tiny lavender blue, white, or pink tassel-like flowers in dense clusters. Dwarf varieties make excellent edgings or pattern plantings with other low-growing annuals.

Ageratum houstonianum

Plant in sun except in hot-summer climates, where filtered shade is better. Rich, moist soil is best. In mild-winter areas, plant in late summer for fall color. Easy to transplant, even when in bloom. Effective combinations: lavender blue ageratum with salmon pink annual phlox, Madagascar periwinkle (*Catharanthus*, formerly known as *Vinca rosea*) in pink shades, or dwarf yellow marigolds (*Tagetes*).

Dwarf lavender blue varieties (4–6 in. tall) include 'Blue Blazer', 'Blue Danube' ('Blue Puffs'), 'Blue Surf', and 'Royal Delft'. 'Blue Mink' and 'North Sea' are somewhat taller (9–12 in.). Pink-flowered 'Pink Powderpuffs' is 9 in. tall; 'Summer Snow', also 9 in. tall, has white blooms.

Aglaomorpha coronans

AGLAOMORPHA. *Polypodiaceae.* Tropical epiphytic ferns. Zones 15–17, 19–24. Grown in hanging baskets, on plaques, rarely in the ground. Well-established plants can take an occasional very light frost but do best in a humid, sheltered environment. Fronds resemble coarse conventional ferns but often broaden toward the base into brown shield-like organs that recall shields of staghorn ferns (*Platycerium*).

A. coronans *(Polypodium coronans).* Plant has 2–4-ft.-long fronds.

A. heraclea *(Polypodium heracleum).* Fronds are 3–6 ft. long.

Aglaonema modestum

AGLAONEMA. *Araceae.* Perennials. Tropical plants valued mostly for their ornamental foliage, usually grown in greenhouses or as indoor plants. Flowers resemble small, greenish white callas. Need a rich, porous potting mix; thrive with lots of water but will get along with small amounts. Cut stems will grow a long time in a glass of water. Exudation from leaf tips, especially of *A. modestum*, spots wood finishes (as on table tops).

Among the best plants for poorly lighted situations. In fact, few plants can get by on as little light as aglaonema; *A. modestum* is especially tolerant of low light.

A. commutatum. Grows to 2 ft. Deep green leaves to 6 in. long, 2 in. across, with pale green markings on veins. Flowers followed by inch-long clusters of yellow to red berries. *A. c. maculatum*, with many irregular, gray green stripes on leaves, is the most common. 'Pseudobracteatum', 1–2 ft. tall, has white leaf stalks and deep green leaves marked with pale green and creamy yellow. 'Treubii' has narrow leaves heavily marked with silvery gray.

A. costatum. Slow-growing, low plant with broad, deep green leaves spotted white and a broad white stripe along the midrib. *A. c.* 'Foxii' is similar or identical.

A. crispum *(A. roebelenii).* Robust plant with leathery leaves to 10 in. long, 5 in. wide, dark green with pale green markings. Sometimes sold as *A.* 'Pewter'.

A. modestum (often sold as *A. simplex*). CHINESE EVERGREEN. A serviceable, easily grown plant, in time forming substantial clumps with several stems 2–3 ft. high. Shiny dark green leaves to 1½ ft. long, 5 in. across.

A. 'Silver King' and **'Silver Queen'.** Both are heavy producers of narrow, dark green leaves strongly marked with silver. Both grow to 2 ft. 'Silver King' has larger leaves than 'Silver Queen'.

A

AGONIS. *Myrtaceae.* Evergreen tree. Zones 15–17, 20–24. Native to Australia.

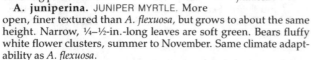

Agonis flexuosa

A. flexuosa. PEPPERMINT TREE, AUSTRALIAN WILLOW MYRTLE. One of the best small trees for California gardens where temperatures stay above 27°F. Will freeze to the ground at 25°F.; in the Sacramento Valley, it has come back from the stump. Spreading, medium fast growing to 25–35 ft., or a big shrub. Narrow, willowlike leaves to 6 in. long densely clothe the weeping branches. Leaves smell like peppermint when crushed. Small white flowers carried abundantly in June. Use it in a lawn, trained as an espalier, or as a tub plant. Very tolerant of soil types, watering practices.

A. juniperina. JUNIPER MYRTLE. More open, finer textured than *A. flexuosa,* but grows to about the same height. Narrow, ¼–½-in.-long leaves are soft green. Bears fluffy white flower clusters, summer to November. Same climate adaptability as *A. flexuosa.*

AGROPYRON. *Gramineae.* WHEATGRASS. Zones 1–3, 10. Two kinds of wheatgrass, both basically pasture grasses, make reasonably attractive lawns in Rocky Mountains and high plains. They can survive with 8–18 in. of rainfall per year, but when planted close and mowed at 2 in. they should be soaked to 18–20 in. every 30 days. Plant 2 lbs. per 1,000 sq. ft.

Agropyron smithii

A. cristatum. CRESTED WHEATGRASS. Bunching rather than sod-forming grass. Fairway strain, used for low-maintenance, low-irrigation lawns, is shorter, denser, and finer than common kind.

A. smithii. WESTERN WHEATGRASS. Forms sod, but slowly. Tolerates great heat, cold, moderate alkali.

AGROSTEMMA githago. *Caryophyllaceae.* CORN COCKLE. Annual. All Zones. The species is an attractive weed of roadside and grain field. Variety 'Milas' is a superior plant with 3-in. flowers of deep purplish pink, lined and spotted with deep purple and centered with a white eye. Stems 6–12 in. long make it a good cut flower. Plants wispy but sturdy, 2–3 ft. tall. Sow seed in spring or early summer for summer and fall bloom in most climates; sow in fall for winter–spring bloom in warmest climates. Full sun, ordinary soil suit it. Mass at rear of border, among shrubs, in front of fence or hedge for cut flowers.

Agrostemma githago

AGROSTIS. *Gramineae.* BENT, BENT GRASS. Lawn grasses. All Zones. All except redtop make beautiful velvety lawns under proper conditions and with constant care. They need frequent close mowing, frequent feeding, occasional topdressing, and much water. In hot weather they succumb to fungus diseases. In San Francisco Bay Area, bent grasses (planted intentionally or distributed by birds) tend to dominate bluegrasses and fescues. Best putting greens are of bent grass.

Agrostis stolonifera

A. gigantea. REDTOP. Coarser than other bents, not generally used in lawns. Has been used as quick-sprouting nurse grass in mixtures or for winter overseeding of Bermuda or other winter-dormant grasses.

A. stolonifera. CREEPING BENT. Premium lawn, but requires most care, including frequent mowing to ½ in. tall with special mower. Seed-grown strains include Emerald, Penncross, and Seaside. In some areas you can buy sprigs or sod of choice strains named Congressional and Old Orchard.

A. tenuis. COLONIAL BENT. More erect than creeping bent; somewhat easier to care for, but still fussy. Astoria and Highland are best-known strains; the latter is tougher, hardier, more disease resistant. Mow at ¾ in.

AILANTHUS altissima *(A. glandulosa).* *Simaroubaceae.* TREE-OF-HEAVEN. Deciduous tree. All Zones. Native to China. Planted in the 1800s in California's gold country, where it now runs wild. Fast growth to 50 ft. Leaves 1–3 ft. long are divided into 13–25 leaflets 3–5 in. long. Inconspicuous greenish flowers are usually followed by handsome clusters of red brown, winged fruit in late summer and fall; great for dried arrangements. Often condemned as a weed tree because it suckers profusely and self-seeds, but it must be praised for its ability to create beauty and shade under adverse conditions—drought, hot winds, extreme air pollution, and every type of difficult soil.

Ailanthus altissima

AIR PLANT. See *Kalanchoe pinnata.*

Aizoaceae. This family of succulent plants includes all the ice plants and most of the so-called living stones.

AJUGA. *Labiatae.* CARPET BUGLE. Perennial. All Zones. One species is a rock garden plant; the others, better known, are ground covers.

Ajuga reptans

A. genevensis. Rock garden plant 5–14 in. high, no runners. Grayish, hairy stems and coarse-toothed leaves to 3 in. long. Flowers in blue spikes; rose and white forms are also sold. Full sun.

A. pyramidalis. Erect plants 2–10 in. high; do not spread by runners. Stems, with long grayish hairs, have many roundish 1½–4-in.-long leaves. Violet blue flowers are not obvious among the large leaves. Variety 'Metallica Crispa' has reddish brown leaves with a metallic glint.

A. reptans. The popular ground cover ajuga. Spreads quickly by runners, making a mat of dark green leaves that grow 2–3 in. wide in full sun, 3–4 in. wide in part shade. Bears mostly blue flowers in 4–6-in.-high spikes. Many varieties are available; some are sold under several names.

All the varieties of *A. reptans* (listed below) make thick carpets of lustrous leaves, enhanced from spring to early summer with spikes of showy flowers. Plant in spring or early fall 6–12 in. apart, 1½ ft. for the big ones. Give full sun to part shade; those with bronze or metallic tints keep color best in full sun. Feed in spring or late summer. Water every 7–10 days in summer. Mow or trim off old flower spikes. Subject to root-knot nematodes; also subject to rot and fungus diseases where drainage or air circulation is poor.

Varieties listed below as giant and jungle ajugas are sold under many names: green ones as 'Crispa' and purplish or bronzy ones as 'Metallica Crispa', 'Bronze Ripple', or 'Rubra'. (These are not the same as *A. pyramidalis* 'Metallica Crispa'.) All have blue flowers.

'Burgundy Lace' ('Burgundy Glow'). Variety of *A. reptans* with reddish purple foliage variegated with white and pink.

'Giant Bronze'. Deep metallic bronze leaves larger, more vigorous, and crisper than those of *A. reptans.* To 6 in. tall in sun, 9 in. tall in shade.

'Giant Green'. Like 'Giant Bronze', but leaves are bright green.

'Jungle Bronze'. Large, rounded, wavy-edged leaves of bronzy tone, in clumps; tall growing. Flowers on 8–10-in.-high spikes.

'Jungle Green'. Largest leafed ajuga—rounded, crisp edged, and green. Less mounding than 'Jungle Bronze'.

'Purpurea'. (Often sold as 'Atropurpurea'.) Similar to *A. reptans* but with bronze or purple tint in leaves. Leaves often slightly larger.

'Variegata'. Leaves edged and splotched with creamy yellow.

AKEBIA quinata. *Lardizabalaceae.* FIVELEAF AKEBIA. Deciduous vine, evergreen in mild winters. All Zones. Native to Japan, China, and Korea. Twines to 15–20 ft. Grows fast in mild regions, slower where winters are cold. Dainty leaves on 3–5-in. stalks, each divided into 5 deep green leaflets 2–3 in. long, notched at tip. Clusters of quaint dull purple flowers in spring are more a surprise than a show. The edible fruit, if produced, looks like a thick, 2½–4-in.-long, purplish sausage.

Akebia quinata

Plant in sun or shade. Give support for climbing; keep under control. Benefits from annual pruning. Recovers quickly when cut to the ground. For a tracery effect on post or column, prune out all but 2 or 3 basal stems.

A. trifoliata. THREELEAF AKEBIA. Like the above, but with 3 instead of 5 leaflets per leaf.

ALASKA YELLOW CEDAR. See *Chamaecyparis nootkatensis.*

ALBIZIA (formerly *Albizzia*). *Leguminosae.* Deciduous to semievergreen trees. Birds are attracted to flowers.

Albizia julibrissin

A. distachya *(A. lophantha).* PLUME ALBIZIA. Semievergreen. Zones 15–17, 22–24. Native to Australia. Not as hardy as the better-known *A. julibrissin.* In California coastal areas it often naturalizes. Drought tolerant; will grow in pure sand at beach. Many mass plantings in Golden Gate Park, San Francisco. Fast growing to 20 ft. Foliage is dark velvety green compared to the light yellowish green of *A. julibrissin,* but also fernlike. The flowers in late spring are greenish yellow in fluffy, 2-in.-long spikes. Best as a temporary screen at beach while slower permanent planting develops. Gets shabby-looking inland.

A. julibrissin. SILK TREE (this is the MIMOSA of eastern U.S.). Deciduous. Zones 2–23. Native to Asia from Iran to Japan. Rapid growth to 40 ft. with wider spread. Can be headed back to make a 10–20-ft. umbrella. Pink, fluffy flowers like pincushions on ferny-leafed branches in summer. Light-sensitive leaves fold at night. The variety 'Rosea' has richer pink flowers and is considered hardier.

Does best with high summer heat. One of the best sellers in inland valleys of southern California. Attractive in both high and low deserts of the Southwest. It's sufficiently hardy in the mild areas of the Pacific Northwest. With ample water grows fast; on skimpy irrigation usually survives, but grows slowly, looks yellowish.

Silk tree is an excellent small shade tree with unique flat-topped shape making a true canopy for a patio. Because of its undulating form and flowers held above the foliage, it's especially beautiful when viewed from above, as from a deck or hilltop. Somewhat of a problem to get started as a high-headed tree. Must be staked and trained by rubbing out buds which start too low. Best planted from containers established at least 1 year; bare-root plants need skillful planting, watering.

Silk tree is most attractive in its natural growth habit—as a multiple-stemmed tree. Filtered shade permits growth of lawn and shrubs beneath. However, for patio use, litter of fallen leaves, flowers, and pods must be considered.

ALCEA rosea *(Althaea rosea).* *Malvaceae.* HOLLYHOCK. Biennial or short-lived perennial. All Zones. This old-fashioned favorite has its place against a fence or wall or at the back of a border. Old single varieties can reach 9 ft.; newer strains and selections are shorter. Big, rough, roundish heart-shaped leaves more or less lobed; single, semidouble, or double flowers 3–6 in. wide in white, pink, rose, red, purple, creamy yellow, apricot. Summer bloom. Chater's Double is a fine perennial strain; 6-ft. spires have 5–6-in. flowers. So-called annual strains bloom first year from seed sown in early spring; Summer Carnival strain is 5–6 ft. tall with double 4-in. flowers, Majorette strain 2½ ft. tall with 3–4-in. flowers. Pinafore strain (mixed colors) branches freely from base, has 5–8 bloom stalks per plant.

Alcea rosea

Destroy rust-infected leaves as soon as disease appears. Bait to protect from snails and slugs.

ALDER. See *Alnus.*

ALDER BUCKTHORN. See *Rhamnus frangula.*

ALEXANDRA PALM. See *Archontophoenix alexandrae.*

ALGERIAN IVY. See *Hedera canariensis.*

ALLIUM. *Liliaceae.* ORNAMENTAL ALLIUM. Bulbs. All Zones except as noted below. About 500 species, all from the Northern Hemisphere, many from mountains of the West. Relatives of the edible onion, peerless as cut flowers (fresh or dried) and useful in borders; smaller kinds are effective in rock gardens. Most ornamental alliums are hardy, sun loving, easy to grow. Thrive in deep, rich, sandy loam; need ample moisture when growing. Plant bulbs in fall. Lift and divide only after they become crowded. Alliums bear small flowers in compact or loose roundish clusters at ends of leafless stems 6 in.–5 ft. or more tall. Many are delightfully fragrant; those with onion odor must be bruised or cut to give it off. Flowers from late spring through summer, in white and shades of pink, rose, violet, red, blue, yellow.

Allium giganteum

A. aflatunense. Round clusters of lilac flowers on stems 2½–5 ft. tall. Resembles *A. giganteum* but with smaller (2–3-in.) flower clusters; blooms late May.

A. albopilosum. See *A. christophii.*

A. atropurpureum. Stems to 2½ ft. tall carry 2-in. clusters of dark purple to nearly black flowers in May or June.

A. caeruleum *(A. azureum).* BLUE ALLIUM. Cornflower blue flowers in dense, round clusters 2 in. across on 1-ft. stems. June bloom.

A. carinatum pulchellum *(A. pulchellum).* Tight clusters of reddish purple flowers on 2-ft. stems, May or June.

A. cepa. See Onion.

A. christophii *(A. albopilosum).* STAR OF PERSIA. Distinctive. Very large clusters (6–12 in. across) of lavender to deep lilac, starlike flowers with metallic sheen; June bloom. Stems 12–15 in. tall. Leaves to 1½ ft. long, white and hairy beneath. Dried flower cluster looks like an elegant ornament.

A. giganteum. GIANT ALLIUM. Spectacular ball-like clusters of bright lilac flowers on stems 5 ft. or more tall. Leaves 1½ ft. long, 2 in. wide. July bloom.

A

A. karataviense. TURKESTAN ALLIUM. Large, dense, round flower clusters in May, varying in color from pinkish to beige to reddish lilac. Broad, flat, recurving leaves, 2–5 in. across.

A. moly. GOLDEN GARLIC. Bright, shining, yellow flowers in open clusters on 9–18-in.-tall stems; June bloom. Flat leaves 2 in. wide, almost as long as flower stems.

A. narcissiflorum. Foot-tall stems with loose clusters of ½-in., bell-shaped bright rose flowers, May or June.

A. neapolitanum. Spreading clusters of large white flowers on 1-ft. stems bloom in May. Leaves 1 in. wide. Variety 'Grandiflorum' is larger, blooms earlier. A form of 'Grandiflorum' listed as 'Cowanii' is considered superior. Grown commercially as cut flowers; pot plant in cold climates.

A. ostrowskianum *(A. oreophilum ostrowskianum).* Large, loose clusters of rose-colored flowers in June on 8–12-in. stems; 2–3 narrow, gray green leaves. Variety 'Zwanenburg' has deep carmine red flowers, 6-in. stems. Rock gardens, cutting.

A. porrum. See Leek.

A. pulchellum. See *A. carinatum pulchellum.*

A. rosenbachianum. Similar to *A. giganteum* but slightly smaller; blooms earlier.

A. sativum. See Garlic.

A. schoenoprasum. See Chives.

A. scorodoprasum. See Garlic.

A. sphaerocephalum. DRUMSTICKS, ROUND-HEADED GARLIC. Tight, dense, spherical red purple flower clusters on 2-ft. stems, May or June. Spreads freely.

A. tuberosum. CHINESE CHIVES, GARLIC CHIVES, ORIENTAL GARLIC. Spreads by tuberous rootstocks and by seeds. Clumps of gray green, flat leaves ¼ in. wide, 1 ft. or less long. Abundance of 1–1½-ft.-tall stalks bear clusters of white flowers in summer. Flowers have scent of violets, are excellent for fresh or dry arrangements. Leaves have mild garlic flavor, are useful in salads, cooked dishes. Grow like chives. Dormant in winter.

A. unifolium. California native with extremely handsome, satiny, lavender pink flowers on 1–2-ft. stems; June bloom.

ALLOPLECTUS nummularia *(Hypocyrta nummularia).* *Gesneriaceae.* GOLDFISH PLANT. Related to African violet, with similar cultural needs. Foot-long, arching branches closely set with shiny oval or roundish leaves to 2½ in. long. Flowers about 1 in. long, orange, puffy and roundish, pinched at tip into pursed mouth like that of goldfish.

Alloplectus nummularia

With ample warmth and humidity, this plant will bloom the year around. Easy to root from tip cuttings; stems may root when in contact with damp soil mix. Because of arching, trailing growth, best in hanging pot.

ALLSPICE, CAROLINA. See *Calycanthus floridus.*

ALMOND. *Rosaceae.* Deciduous tree. For ornamental relatives, see *Prunus.* Zones 8–10, 12, 14–16, 19–21. As trees, almonds are nearly as hardy as peaches, but as nut producers they are more exacting in climate adaptation. Zones listed are for best nut production. Frost during the trees' early blooming period cuts the crop, and if they escape that a late (April) frost will destroy small fruits that are forming. Nuts will not develop properly in areas with cool summers and high humidity. To experiment in areas where frost is a hazard, choose late-blooming varieties.

Almond

Tree grows to 20–30 ft. high, erect when young, spreading and dome shaped in age. Leaves 3–5 in. long, pale green with gray tinge. Flowers 1–2 in. across, palest pink or white. Fruit looks like a leathery, flattened, undersized green peach. The hull splits to reveal the pit, which is the almond that you harvest.

Harvest almonds when hulls split. At this stage, you may need to knock nuts from trees or pick them off ground. Remove leathery hull and spread hulled nuts in sun for day or two to dry. To test for adequate dryness, shake nuts—kernels should rattle in shells. Store dried nuts indoors.

Almonds do well in any type of soil except heavy, poorly drained soil, where they are subject to root rot. Need deep soil—at least 6 ft. Will exist on less water than most fruit trees. Water deeply but infrequently. Almonds need spraying to control mites, which cause premature yellowing and falling of leaves and may also cause weakening or eventual death. Brown rot makes fruit rot and harden; it also attacks twigs, killing them back and forming cankers on main trunk and branches.

Unless you choose a self-fertile strain, 2 varieties must be planted for pollination. (If you don't have room, plant 2 or 3 in one hole.) These are the varieties you may find in nurseries:

'All-in-One'. Semidwarf tree blooms with 'Texas' and 'Nonpareil'. Medium to large sweet, soft-shell nuts, September–October. Self-fertile.

'Carmel'. A regular heavy bearer of small nuts with good flavor. Pollinates 'Nonpareil' and 'Texas'.

'Garden Prince'. Dwarf tree with showy pink bloom, medium-sized soft-shell nuts. Self-fertile.

'Hall' ('Hall's Hardy'). Hard-shell nut of good size and quality. Pink bloom comes late—an advantage in late frost regions. Tree is as hardy as a peach. Partially self-fertile, but better with 'Jordanolo' or 'Texas' as pollinators.

'Jordanolo'. High-quality nut, but subject to bud failure in areas of extreme summer heat. 'Ne Plus Ultra' and 'Nonpareil' are pollinators.

'Kapareil'. Small, soft-shell nuts. Pollinator for 'Nonpareil'.

'Ne Plus Ultra'. Large kernels in attractive soft shells. Pollinator for 'Nonpareil'.

'Nonpareil'. Best all-around variety. Easily shelled by hand. Some bud failure in very-hot-summer regions. Pollinate with 'Jordanolo', 'Ne Plus Ultra', 'Kapareil'.

'Texas' ('Mission'). Small, semihard-shell nut. Regular, heavy producer. Late bloomer, one of safest for cold-winter, late frost areas. Use 'Nonpareil' or 'Hall' as pollinators.

ALMOND, FLOWERING. See *Prunus.*

ALNUS. *Betulaceae.* ALDER. Deciduous tree. Moisture loving; of remarkably rapid growth. All give interesting display of tassel-like, greenish yellow male flower catkins (in clusters) before leaves. Female flowers develop into small woody cones that decorate bare branches in winter; these delight flower arrangers. Seeds attract birds. Roots are invasive—less troublesome if deep watering practices are followed.

Alnus rhombifolia

A. cordata. ITALIAN ALDER. Zones 8, 9, 14–24. Native to Italy, Corsica. Young growth vertical; older trees to 40 ft., spreading to 25 ft. Heart-shaped, 4-in. leaves, glossy rich green above, paler beneath. Short deciduous period. More restrained than *A. rhombifolia.* Favored in Southwest, except high desert.

A. glutinosa. BLACK ALDER. Zones 1–10, 14–24. Native to Europe, North Africa, Asia. Not as fast growing as *A. rhombifolia.* Probably best as multistemmed tree. Grows to 70 ft. Roundish, 2–4-in., coarsely toothed leaves, dark lustrous green. Makes dense mass from ground up. Good for screen.

A. oregona *(A. rubra).* RED ALDER. Zones 4–6, 15–17. Native to streambanks and marshy places. Most common alder of lowlands in Pacific Northwest. Ranges from Alaska south to Santa Cruz

County, California; rarely found more than 10 miles from coast in California. Grows to 90 ft. high, but usually 45–50 ft. Attractive smooth, light gray bark. Dark green, 2–4-in. leaves, rust colored and hairy beneath; coarsely toothed margins are rolled under. Can take surprising amount of brackish water and is useful wherever underground water is somewhat saline. Generally disliked in Northwest because it's a favorite of tent caterpillars.

A. rhombifolia. WHITE ALDER. Zones 1–9, 14–21. Native along streams throughout most of California's foothills except along coast; mountains of Oregon, Washington, north to British Columbia, east to Idaho. Very fast growing to 50–90 ft., with 40-ft. spread. Very tolerant of heat and wind. Spreading or ascending branches often pendulous at tips. Coarsely toothed, 2½–4½-in. leaves dark green above, paler green beneath. In its native areas, it's susceptible to tent caterpillars.

A. tenuifolia. MOUNTAIN ALDER, THINLEAF ALDER. Zones 1–3, 10. Shrub or small tree to 20–25 ft. Extremely hardy to cold.

ALOCASIA. *Araceae*. ELEPHANT'S EAR. Perennials. Outdoors in Zones 22–24; indoor/outdoor plants anywhere. Native to tropical Asia. Handsome, lush plants for tropical effects. Flowers like those of calla (*Zantedeschia*). Plant in filtered sunlight, in wind-protected places. Provide ample organic matter in soil, lots of water and light, frequent feedings. Tropical plant specialists sell many kinds with leaves in coppery and purplish tones, often with striking white veins.

Alocasia macrorrhiza

A. amazonica. AFRICAN MASK. House plant. Leathery, deep bronzy green leaves to 16 in. long have wavy edges, heavy white main veins.

A. macrorrhiza. Evergreen at 29°F.; loses leaves at lower temperatures but comes back in spring if frosts not too severe. Large, arrow-shaped leaves to 2 ft. or longer, on stalks to 5 ft. tall, form a dome-shaped plant 4 ft. across. Tiny flowers on spike surrounded by greenish white bract. Flowers followed by reddish fruit, giving spike the look of corn on the cob.

A. odora. Similar to above, but not quite as hardy. Flowers fragrant.

ALOE. *Liliaceae*. Succulents. Zones 8, 9, 12–24. Aloes range from 6-inch miniatures to trees; all form clumps of fleshy, pointed leaves and bear branched or unbranched clusters of orange, yellow, cream, or red flowers. Most are South African. Showy, easy to grow, and drought tolerant, they rate among southern California's most valuable ornamentals. Most kinds make outstanding container plants. Some species in bloom every month; biggest show February–September. Leaves may be green or gray green, often strikingly banded or streaked with contrasting colors. Aloes grow easily in well-drained soil in reasonably frost-free areas. Sun or light shade in hot-summer areas. Where winters are cooler, grow in pots and shelter from frosts. Aloes listed here are only a few of the many kinds.

Aloe arborescens

A. arborescens. TREE ALOE. Older clumps may reach 18 ft. Branching stems carry big clumps of gray green, spiny-edged leaves. Flowers (December–February) in long, spiky clusters, bright vermilion to clear yellow. Withstands drought, sun, salt spray. Tolerates shade. Foliage damaged at 29°F., but plants have survived 17°F.

A. aristata. Dwarf species for pots, edging, ground covers. Reaches 8–12 in. tall and wide. Rosettes densely packed with 4-in.-long, ¾-in.-wide leaves ending in whiplike threads. Flowers orange red in 1–1½-ft.-tall clusters, winter.

A. bainesii. Slow-growing tree with heavy, forking trunk and branches. Rosettes of 2–3-ft. leaves, spikes of rose pink flowers on 1½–2-ft. stalks. Used for stately, sculpturesque pattern in landscape. Hard to find in nurseries.

A. barbadensis. See *A. vera*.

A. brevifolia. Low clumps of blunt, thick, gray green, spiny-edged leaves 3 in. long. Clusters of red flowers, 20 in. tall, intermittent all year.

A. ciliaris. Climbing, sprawling, with pencil-thick stems to 10 ft. long. Leaves small, thick, soft green. Long-stalked, 3–6-in. flower clusters with 20–30 green- or yellow-tipped scarlet flowers, intermittent all year. Takes some shade, little frost.

A. distans. JEWELED ALOE. Running, rooting, branching stems make clumps of 6-in., fleshy, blue green leaves with scattered whitish spots and white teeth along edges. Forked flower stems 1½–2 ft. tall carry clusters of red flowers.

A. marlothii. When small, use in pots or dish gardens. When mature, a tree type with 2½-ft.-long, spiny leaves and red flowers in large candelabra.

A. nobilis. Dark green leaves edged with small hooked teeth grow in rosettes to 1 ft. across and about as tall. Clustered orange red flowers appear on 2-ft. stalks in June, last for 6 weeks. Good container subject—takes limited root space.

A. plicatilis. Slow growing, with thick, forking trunks crowned with fans (not rosettes) of smooth, gray green, foot-long leaves. Clusters of scarlet flowers 1½ ft. tall. Sculpturesque container plant when young; reaches 3–5 ft. in 10 years.

A. saponaria. Short-stemmed, broad clumps. Broad, thick, 8-in.-long leaves variegated with white spots. Clumps spread rapidly and may become bound together—take up too-thick clumps and separate them. Branched flower stalk 1½–2½ ft. tall. Orange red to shrimp pink flowers over long period.

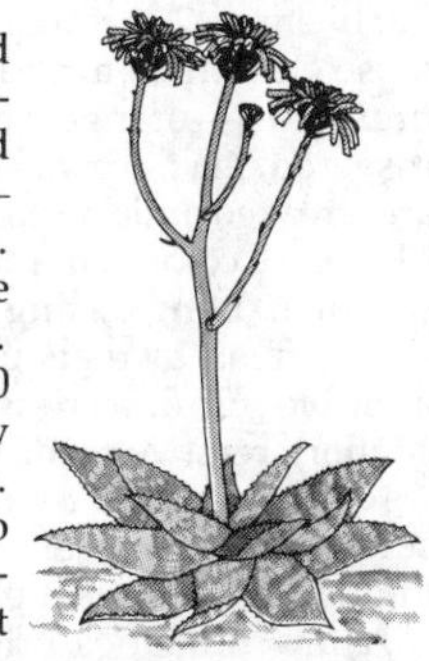
Aloe saponaria

A. striata. CORAL ALOE. Leaves broad, 20 in. long, spineless, gray green, with narrow pinkish red edge. They grow in rosettes 2 ft. wide on short trunk. Brilliant coral pink to orange flowers in branched clusters, February–May. Handsome, tailored plant. Keep it from hottest sun in desert areas.

A. variegata. PARTRIDGE-BREAST ALOE, TIGER ALOE. Foot-high, triangular rosette of fleshy, triangular, dark green, 5-in.-long leaves strikingly banded and edged with white. Loose flower clusters of pink to dull red flowers, intermittent all year.

A. vera *(A. barbadensis)*. MEDICINAL ALOE, BARBADOS ALOE. Clustering rosettes of narrow, fleshy, stiffly upright leaves 1–2 ft. long. Yellow flowers in dense spike atop 3-ft. stalk. Favorite folk medicine plant used to treat burns, bites, inflammation, and a host of other ills. One of best for Zones 12, 13. Survives without extra water, but needs some to look good.

ALOYSIA triphylla *(Lippia citriodora)*. *Verbenaceae*. LEMON VERBENA. Deciduous or partially evergreen herb-shrub. Zones 9, 10, 14–24. Borderline hardy as far north as Seattle if planted against warm wall. Legginess is the natural state of this plant; it's the herb that grew like a gangling shrub in grandmother's garden. Prized for its lemon-scented leaves. Used in potpourri, iced drinks; leaf put in bottom of jar when making apple jelly. Grows to 6 ft. or taller; narrow leaves to 3 in. long are arranged in whorls of 3 or 4 along branches. Bears open clusters of very small lilac or whitish flowers in summer. By pinch-pruning, you can shape to give interesting tracery against wall. Or let it grow among lower plants to hide its legginess. Give full sun, good drainage, average water.

Aloysia triphylla

A

ALPINIA. *Zingiberaceae.* Perennials with rhizomes. Evergreen in Zones 22–24; die down in winter in Zones 15–17. Roots hardy to about 15°F. Give lightly shaded, wind-free exposure, good soil. In order to bloom, must be established at least 2 years and have lots of water. Remove flowered canes yearly.

Alpinia zerumbet

A. sanderae. VARIEGATED GINGER. To 3–4 ft. tall, with 8-in.-long leaves striped with white. Rarely flowers. Good in containers.

A. zerumbet *(A. nutans, A. speciosa).* SHELL GINGER, SHELL FLOWER. Native to tropical Asia and Polynesia. Grandest of gingers, best all-year appearance. To 8–9 ft. tall. Leaves shiny, 2 ft. long, 5 in. wide, with distinct parallel veins; grow on stems that are maroon at maturity. Waxy white or pinkish, shell-like, fragrant flowers marked red, purple, brown, in pendant clusters on arching stems in late summer.

ALSOPHILA australis, A. cooperi. See *Cyathea.*

ALSTROEMERIA. *Liliaceae.* Perennials. Zones 5–9, 14–24. South American natives. Leafy stems 2–5 ft. tall, topped with broad, loose clusters of azalealike flowers in beautiful colors—orange, yellow, shades of pink, rose, red, lilac, creamy white to white; many are streaked and speckled with darker colors. Masses of color in borders from May to midsummer. Long-lasting cut flowers. Plants spread freely by roots and seeds. Tops wither after bloom (flowerless shoots dry up even sooner); remove seeds to limit their spread.

Alstroemeria aurantiaca

Nurseries differ as to what names they sell them by, but you're sure to get vibrant colors whether you buy them as Chilean hybrids, Ligtu hybrids, or just plain alstroemeria.

A few nurseries offer 3–4-ft.-tall PERUVIAN LILY (*A. aurea, A. aurantiaca*), with orange yellow, brown-spotted flowers ('Orange King'); 'Lutea' is yellow, 'Splendens' red. *A. psittacina (A. pulchella)* is 1–1½ ft. tall, more or less evergreen, with dark red flowers tipped green and spotted deep purple. It can be invasive.

Best in cool, moist, deep, sandy to medium loam. Plant roots in fall; if you buy alstroemeria in gallon cans, you can plant it out any time in mild-winter climates. Set roots 6–8 in. deep, 1 ft. apart; handle brittle roots gently. Leave clumps undisturbed for many years because they reestablish slowly after transplanting. Alstroemerias are easily started from seed sown where plants are to grow or sown in individual pots for transplanting. Sow in fall, winter, or earliest spring. All are hardy in cold-winter climates if planted at proper depth and kept mulched in winter. Give them ample water in spring and summer; taper off in late summer, fall. Give partial shade in warm-summer areas, sun along coast.

ALTERNANTHERA ficoidea (often sold as *A. bettzickiana*). *Amaranthaceae.* Perennial grown in most Zones as annual for colorful foliage, which somewhat resembles that of coleus. Plants grow 6–12 in. tall and should be planted 4–10 in. apart for colorful effect. Plant in full sun; where winters are cold, plant only after soil warms up. Average water. Keep low and compact by shearing. Grow from cuttings. 'Aurea Nana' is low grower with yellow-splotched foliage. 'Bettzickiana' has spoon-shaped leaves with red and yellow markings. 'Magnifica' is a red bronze dwarf. 'Parrot Feather' and 'Versicolor' have broad green leaves with yellow markings and pink veins.

Alternanthera ficoidea 'Bettzickiana'

ALTHAEA rosea. See *Alcea rosea.*

ALUMINUM PLANT. See *Pilea cadierei.*

ALUMROOT. See *Heuchera.*

ALYOGYNE huegelii *(Hibiscus huegelii).* *Malvaceae.* BLUE HIBISCUS. Evergreen shrub. Zones 15–17, 20–24. Upright growth to 5–8 ft. Foliage deeply cut, dark green, rough textured. Flowers 4–5 in. across, lilac blue with glossy petals. Blooms off and on throughout year; individual flowers last 2–3 days. Hardy to about 23°F. Pinch or prune occasionally to keep it compact. Best in dry, warm location, full sun. Variable from seed. 'Santa Cruz' is good deep blue selection. 'Monterey Bay' is even bluer.

Alyogyne huegelii

ALYSSUM. *Cruciferae.* Perennials. All Zones. Mostly native to Mediterranean region. Mounding plants or shrublets that brighten spring borders and rock gardens with their cheerful bloom. Best in full sun or just a little shade. Fairly drought tolerant.

Alyssum montanum

A. montanum. Stems up to 8 in. high; leaves gray, hairy (denser on underside); flowers yellow, fragrant, in dense short clusters.

A. saxatile. See *Aurinia.*

A. wulfenianum. Prostrate and trailing, with fleshy, silvery leaves and sheets of pale yellow flowers.

ALYSSUM, SWEET. See *Lobularia.*

AMARACUS dictamnus. See *Origanum dictamnus.*

Amaranthaceae. The amaranth family consists largely of herbaceous plants, many of them weedy. Flowers are small and chaffy, and often effective when massed.

AMARANTHUS. *Amaranthaceae.* AMARANTH. Annuals. All Zones. Coarse, sometimes weedy plants; a few ornamental kinds are grown for their brightly colored foliage or flowers. Grow in full sun or part shade; give average soil and water. Sow seed in early summer—soil temperature must be above 70°F. for germination.

Amaranthus caudatus

Picked when young and tender, leaves and stems of many species (even some of the weedy ones) can be cooked like spinach, and can take its place in hot weather. Seeds, which look like sesame seeds, have been used as grain in Central and South America and are coming into use in this country. They have a high protein content.

A. caudatus. LOVE-LIES-BLEEDING, TASSEL FLOWER. Sturdy, branching plant 3–8 ft. high; leaves 2–10 in. long, ½–4 in. wide. Red flowers in drooping, tassel-like clusters. A curiosity rather than a pretty plant. One of the amaranths which produce grain.

A. hybridus erythrostachys. PRINCE'S FEATHER. To 5 ft. high with leaves 1–6 in. long, ½–3 in. wide, usually reddish. Flowers red or brownish red in many-branched clusters. Some strains grown as "spinach" or for grain.

A. tricolor. JOSEPH'S COAT. Branching plant 1–4 ft. high. Leaves 2½–6 in. long, 2–4 in. wide, blotched in shades of red and green.

Newer selections such as 'Early Splendor', 'Flaming Fountain', and 'Molten Fire' bear masses of yellow to scarlet foliage at tops of main stems and principal branches. Green-leafed strains used as "spinach" under the name of TAMPALA.

AMARCRINUM memoria-corsii (A. 'Howardii'). *Amaryllidaceae.* Bulb. Zones 8, 9, 12–24. Indoor/outdoor or houseplant elsewhere. Hybrid between *Crinum moorei* and belladonna lily (*Amaryllis belladonna*). Flowering stems to 4 ft. carry very large clusters of soft pink, funnel-shaped, very fragrant, long-lasting flowers resembling belladonna lily. Sun or partial shade, ample water. With year-round water, plant stays evergreen in mild climates. If no water is available, it simply endures until water comes, then starts growth and bloom. Scarce in nurseries; get offset bulbs from a friend. Be especially careful to protect from snails and slugs.

Amarcrinum memoria-corsii

Amaryllidaceae. The amaryllis family consists of herbaceous plants with strap-shaped leaves, bulbous or rhizomatous rootstocks, and clustered flowers (rarely a single flower) on top of a leafless stem.

AMARYLLIS belladonna *(Brunsvigia rosea).* *Amaryllidaceae.* BELLADONNA LILY, NAKED LADY. Bulb. Zones 4–24. Hardy in mild-winter areas; needs protected south exposure and warm, dry summer to bloom in western Oregon and Washington. Native to South Africa. Bold, straplike leaves in clumps 2–3 ft. across in fall and winter; dormant late spring and early summer. In August, clusters of 4–12 trumpet-shaped, rosy pink, fragrant flowers bloom on top of bare, reddish brown stalks 2–3 ft. tall. Will grow in almost any soil; drought resistant, very long lived. Plant right after bloom; set bulb top even with ground level. Lift and divide clumps infrequently; may not bloom for several years if disturbed at wrong time. For plants with common name AMARYLLIS, see *Hippeastrum*.

Amaryllis belladonna

A. hallii. See *Lycoris squamigera*.

AMELANCHIER. *Rosaceae.* JUNEBERRY, SHADBLOW, SERVICEBERRY (often pronounced *sarvisberry*). Deciduous shrubs, small trees. Zones 1–6. Drooping clusters of white or pinkish flowers in early spring are showy but short lived. Purplish new foliage turns deep green, then yellow and red in fall. Small dark blue fruits, popular with birds, taste like blueberries. Roots not aggressive, shade not dense. Plant against dark background to show off flowers, form, fall color. Give sun, ordinary good soil, moderate water.

Amelanchier laevis

A. alnifolia. SASKATOON. Shrub or small tree to 20 ft., spreading by rhizomes. Native to western Canada and mountainous parts of the West.

A. canadensis. Narrowish big shrub or small tree to 25 ft., with short, erect flower clusters.

A. laevis. Narrow shrub or small tree to 40 ft., with nodding or drooping flower clusters. 'Cumulus' has regular form, yellow orange to red fall color.

AMERICAN SWEET GUM. See *Liquidambar styraciflua*.

AMETHYST FLOWER. See *Browallia*.

AMPELOPSIS brevipedunculata. *Vitaceae.* BLUEBERRY CLIMBER. Deciduous vine. All Zones. Strong, rampant climber with twining tendrils. To 20 ft. Large, handsome, 3-lobed, 2½–5-in.-wide leaves are dark green. In warm climates, leaves turn red and partially drop in fall; more leaves come out, redden, and drop all winter. Many clusters of small grapelike berries turn from greenish ivory to brilliant metallic blue in late summer and fall. Sun or shade. Average water. Needs strong support. Superb on concrete and rock walls, or to shade arbors. Attracts birds. The variety 'Elegans' has leaves variegated with white and pink. Smaller, less vigorous, and less hardy than the species, it is a splendid hanging basket plant.

Ampelopsis brevipedunculata

Boston ivy and Virginia creeper, formerly included in genus *Ampelopsis*, are now placed under genus *Parthenocissus* because, unlike *Ampelopsis*, both have disks at ends of their tendrils.

AMUR CHOKECHERRY. See *Prunus maackii*.

Anacardiaceae. The cashew family includes evergreen or deciduous trees, shrubs, and vines with small, unshowy, but often profuse flowers. Foliage is attractive, fruits sometimes showy or edible. Many have poisonous or irritating sap. Mango and poison oak indicate the diversity of the family.

ANACYCLUS depressus. *Compositae.* Perennial. All Zones. Slowly forms dense, spreading mat somewhat like chamomile. Grayish leaves finely divided. Single daisylike flowers to 2 in. across, with yellow center disks and white ray-type petals (red on reverse side). Blooms in summer. Good in sunny, dry, hot rock gardens. Generally hardy, but may freeze in extremely severe winters or rot in cold, wet, heavy soil.

Anacyclus depressus

ANAGALLIS. *Primulaceae.* PIMPERNEL. Annuals or perennials. All Zones. Two species sometimes seen, one a weed. Like warm soil, full sun, much or little water; less aggressive kinds attractive in rock gardens with sunroses (*Helianthemum*), sedums, snow-in-summer (*Cerastium*).

A. arvensis. SCARLET PIMPERNEL. Annual. Low-growing weed with ¼-in. flowers of brick red. *A. a. caerulea* has somewhat larger flowers of deep, pure blue and is attractive enough to plant.

Anagallis monelli linifolia

A. monelli. Perennial or biennial to 1½ ft., with ¾-in. flowers of bright blue. *A. m.* 'Phillipsii' is compact 1-ft.-tall selection; *A. m. linifolia* has narrower leaves.

ANCHUSA. *Boraginaceae.* Annuals, biennials, or perennials. All Zones. Related to forget-me-not (*Myosotis*) but larger and showier, anchusas are worth growing for vibrant blue color. Prefer sun, dry soil.

A. azurea *(A. italica).* Perennial. All Zones. Coarse, open, spreading, 3–5 ft. tall. Leaves 6 in. or longer, covered with bristly hairs. Clusters of bright blue blossoms ½–¾ in. across bloom in summer and fall. Horticultural forms include 'Dropmore', gentian blue;

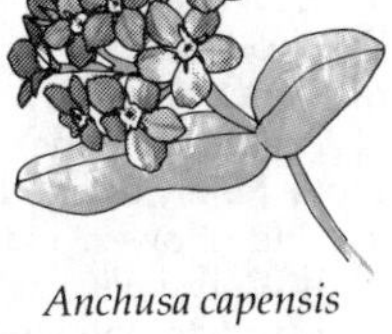

Anchusa capensis

'Opal', sky blue; and 'Loddon Royalist' (more recent), bearing rich blue flowers. Not for small areas. Once established, difficult to eradicate.

A. capensis. CAPE FORGET-ME-NOT, SUMMER FORGET-ME-NOT. Zones 7–24. Native of South Africa. Hairy annual or biennial, 1½ ft. high; leaves narrow, to 5 in. long, ½ in. wide. Flowers bright blue, white throated, ¼ in. across, in clusters 2 in. long. Use for vivid clean blue in summer borders with marigolds (*Tagetes*), petunias.

ANDROMEDA polifolia. *Ericaceae.* BOG ROSEMARY. Evergreen shrublet. All Zones. Not adapted in areas with alkaline soil or water. Grows to 1 ft., spreading by creeping rootstocks. Leathery, narrow, 1½-in.-long leaves, somewhat like those of rosemary; gray green above, gray beneath. Attractive clusters of pale pink, ¼-in., globe-shaped flowers at branch tips in April. Sun or part shade; ample water. Choice rock garden plant in Zones 4–6, where it combines well with other acid-loving plants. Inconsistent in northern California. Varieties 'Nana' and 'Nana Compacta' are lower growing and more compact.

Andromeda polifolia

A. floribunda, A. japonica. See *Pieris floribunda, P. japonica.*

A. speciosa. See *Zenobia pulverulenta.*

ANDROSACE. *Primulaceae.* ROCK JASMINE. Perennials. Most frequently used Zones 1–6, 14–17. Choice rock garden miniatures grown mostly by alpine plant specialists. All types require sun, moderate watering, and perfect drainage, and best adapted to gravelly banks in rock gardens. Protect from more aggressive rockery plants such as alyssum, arabis, aubrieta. Rarely succeed in warm-winter areas.

Androsace lanuginosa

A. lanuginosa. Trailing plant forms mats 3 ft. across. Silvery leaves to ¾ in. long, covered with silky white hairs. Pink flowers in dense clusters on 2-in. stems. *A. l. leichtlinii* has white flowers with crimson eyes.

A. primuloides. Trailing; forms 4-in.-long runners. Leaves ½–2 in. long in rosettes covered with silvery hairs. Flowers pink, to ½ in. across, in clusters on 5-in. stems.

A. sarmentosa. Spreads by runners. Leaves to 1½ in. long, in rosettes, covered with silvery hairs when young. Flowers rose colored, ¼ in. across, in clusters on stems 5 in. tall. Variety *chumbyi* forms dense clump, has woolly leaves.

ANEMONE. *Ranunculaceae.* WINDFLOWER, ANEMONE. Perennials with tuberous or fibrous roots. All Zones (but see notes under *A. fulgens* below). A rich and varied group of plants ranging in size from alpine rock garden miniatures to tall Japanese anemones grown in borders; bloom extends from very early spring to fall, depending on species. First 3 species described below (*A. blanda, A. coronaria, A. fulgens*) can be grown from tubers. Directions for planting all of them are given in the 2 paragraphs that follow description of *A. fulgens*. Remaining 2 species (*A. hybrida, A. pulsatilla*) are treated as hardy perennials.

Anemone blanda

A. blanda. Zones 1–9, 14–23. Stems rise 2–8 in. from tuberous roots. Finely divided leaves covered with soft hairs. In spring, one sky blue flower, 1–1½ in. across, on each stem. Often confused with *A. apennina,* which has more pointed leaf segments. Grow with and among Japanese maples, azaleas, and other light shrubbery. Associate with miniature daffodils, tulips, scillas; or grow in pots. Newer selections have larger (2-in.) flowers on larger (10–12-in.) plants. 'Blue Star' is blue, 'Pink Star' pink, 'Radar' purplish red, and 'White Splendor' white.

A. coronaria. POPPY-FLOWERED ANEMONE. All Zones. Common large-flowered, showy anemone valued for cutting and for spectacular color in spring borders. Finely divided green leaves. Flowers red, blue, and white, 1½–2½ in. across, borne singly on 6–18-in. stems. Tuberous rooted. Flowers blue, red, tones and mixtures of these colors, and white. Most popular strain is Tecolote Giants, with 2½–5-in. flowers borne singly on 6–18 in. stems; available as De Caen (single) and St. Brigid (semidouble to double).

Anemone coronaria

A. fulgens. SCARLET WINDFLOWER. Zones 1–9, 14–24. To 1 ft. from tuberous roots. Leaves entirely or slightly divided. Flowers 2½ in. across, brilliant scarlet with black stamens. St. Bavo strain comes in unusual color range including pink and rusty coral.

All 3 of the species above perform best in a location receiving some shade every day. Set out tubers October or November; in cold-winter areas, wait until spring to set out *A. coronaria* and *A. fulgens*. (Or, if planted in November, mulch with 6–8 in. of leaf mold or peat moss after first hard frost.)

Plant 1–2 in. deep, 8–12 in. apart, in rich, light, well-drained garden loam. Or start in flats of damp sand; set out in garden when leaves are a few inches tall. Protect from birds until leaves toughen. In warmer climates, some soak tubers of poppy-flowered anemones for a few hours before planting. In high-rainfall areas, excess moisture induces rot.

A. hybrida *(A. japonica, A. hupehensis japonica).* JAPANESE ANEMONE. All Zones. A long-lived, fibrous-rooted perennial indispensable for fall color in partial shade. Graceful, branching stems 2–4 ft. high rise from clump of dark green, 3–5-lobed leaves covered with soft hairs. Flowers semidouble, in white, silvery pink, or rose. Many named varieties. Slow to establish, but once started spreads readily if roots not disturbed. Mulch in fall where winters are extremely severe. Increase by divisions in fall or early spring, or by root cuttings in spring. May need staking. Effective in clumps in front of tall shrubbery, or under high-branching trees.

A. pulsatilla. EUROPEAN PASQUE FLOWER. Zones 1–6, 15–17. Attractive alpine plant forming 9–12-in.-high clumps. Fernlike, silky-hairy leaves, 4–6 in. long, appear after flowers. Blossoms in April and May: bell shaped, to 2½ in. across, blue to reddish purple, with golden stamens. Handsome seed clusters like feathery, smoky gray pompons. This hardy plant is best adapted to cool, moist climates, rarely succeeds in warm, dry areas. Sun or partial shade. Sow seed or make divisions in spring.

ANEMOPAEGMA chamberlaynii *(Bignonia chamberlaynii).* *Bignoniaceae.* YELLOW TRUMPET VINE. Evergreen vine. Zones 15–17, 19, 21–24. Climbs by unbranched tendrils. Leaves divided into 2 leaflets to 7 in. long. Flowers yellow, trumpet shaped, 3 in. long, in clusters longer than the leaves. Summer blooming. Often confused with *Macfadyena (Doxantha) unguis-cati; Anemopaegma* has larger leaflets (7 in. against 2 in.), paler yellow flowers with purple or white markings in the throat, and unbranched tendrils that coil instead of branched tendrils with little hooks (like cat's claws) at the end. *Macfadyena* can fasten itself to nearly any surface, clinging by its claws; *Anemopaegma* needs something to cling to. Give full sun or partial shade, average water.

Anemopaegma chamberlaynii

ANETHUM graveolens. *Umbelliferae.* DILL. Annual herb. All Zones. To 3–4 ft. Soft, feathery leaves; umbrellalike 6-in.-wide clusters of small yellow flowers. Seeds and leaves have pungent fragrance. Sow seed where plants are to be grown, in full sun; sow several times during spring and summer for constant supply. Thin seedlings to 1½ ft. apart. Sprouts and grows better in spring than summer. An easy way to grow it in a casual garden is to let a few plants go to seed. Seedlings appear here and there at odd times and can be pulled and chopped as "dill weed." Use seeds in pickling and vinegar; fresh or dried leaves on lamb chops, in salads, stews, sauces.

Anethum graveolens

ANGELICA archangelica. *Umbelliferae.* ANGELICA. Biennial. All Zones. To 6 ft. Tropical-looking plant with divided and toothed, yellow green leaves 2–3 ft. long. Greenish white flowers in large umbrellalike clusters. Grow in moist, rich, slightly acid soil in part shade. Cut flowers before buds open to prolong plant's life. Propagate from seed sown as soon as ripe in fall. Use to flavor wines; hollow stems may be candied.

Angelica archangelica

ANGEL'S HAIR. See *Artemisia schmidtiana.*

ANGEL'S TEARS. See *Narcissus triandrus, Soleirolia soleirolii.*

ANGOPHORA costata *(A. lanceolata).* *Myrtaceae.* GUM MYRTLE. Evergreen tree. Zones 16, 17, 21–24. Native to eastern Australia. Highly praised by those who have planted it and seen it. Mature trees may reach 40–50 ft. high and almost as broad.

Beautiful smooth trunk in tones of cream, rose, and mauve. Has thick, glossy, 3–5-in.-long, eucalyptuslike leaves with a prominent midrib. New growth is shiny red, turning to rich green. White flowers are carried in clusters at branch ends in summer, followed by fruit with prickly spines. Appears to adapt to variety of soils, watering treatments. As tough and tolerant as its eucalyptus relatives. Skyline tree where it has room.

Angophora costata

ANIGOZANTHOS. *Haemodoraceae.* KANGAROO PAW. Evergreen perennials. Zones 12, 13, 15–24, hardy to about 25°F. Native to open eucalyptus forests in western Australia. From thick rootstocks grow clumps of dark green, smooth, swordlike leaves to 3 ft. or taller. Striking tubular flowers in red, purple, green, or yellow, curved at tips like kangaroo paws (tips split into 6 segments); borne in woolly one-sided spikes on 3–6-ft. stems. Flowers attract hummingbirds. Intriguing in flower, otherwise not outstanding. Blooms from late spring to fall if spent flowering spikes are cut to ground. Light sandy soil, or heavier soil with good drainage and careful watering; sunny exposure.

A. flavidus *(A. flavida).* Branching stems to 5 ft. Tubular, curved, hairy flowers 1–1½ in. long, yellow green tinged with red. Variations occur, with colors ranging from deep rust red to pure yellow, with many shades of orange and buff between. Heavy flower producer.

Anigozanthos flavidus

A. manglesii. Unbranched green stems to 3 ft., thickly covered with red hairs. Flowers brilliant deep green, red at base, woolly on outside, 3 in. long.

ANISACANTHUS thurberi. *Acanthaceae.* DESERT HONEYSUCKLE. Evergreen or deciduous shrub. Zones 8–13, 18, 19. Native to Arizona, New Mexico, Texas, northern Mexico. In mild-winter areas grows to 3–5 ft. with stout branches. Looks best when treated as perennial, cut to ground in winter either by frost or by pruning shears. Plant in sun. Drought tolerant. Valued for its long, spring–summer season of color. Tubular, 1½-in.-long, yellow orange flowers in spikes; light green leaves, 1½–2 in. long and ½ in. wide. Plants sold under this name may be *Justicia leonardii;* these have bright red flowers and leaves to 6 in. long.

Anisacanthus thurberi

ANISE. See *Pimpinella anisum.*

Annonaceae. The annona family consists primarily of tropical trees and shrubs; many have edible fruit, but only a very few are hardy in the West.

ANNONA cherimola. *Annonaceae.* CHERIMOYA. Briefly deciduous large shrub or small tree. Zones 21–24. Hardy to about 25°F. Ample water. Grows fast first 3–4 years, then slows to make 15-ft. tree with 15–20-ft. spread. After tree has developed for 4–5 years, prune annually to produce bearing wood. Leaves dull green above, velvety-hairy beneath, 4–10 in. long; leaves drop in late spring. Thick, fleshy, 1-in., brownish or yellow, hairy flowers with a fruity fragrance begin opening about time of leaf fall and continue forming for 3–4 months. Pleasant near terrace.

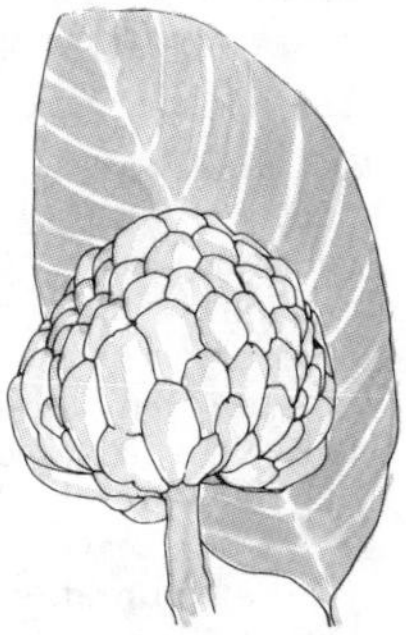

Annona cherimola

To insure fruit set, gather pollen on a brush and transfer it to the stigma of a freshly opened flower.

Large green fruits weigh ½–1½ lbs. Skin of most varieties looks like short overlapping leaves; some show knobby warts. Pick when fruit turns to yellowish green, then store in refrigerator until skin turns brownish green to brown. Skin is tender and thin. Handle fruit carefully. Creamy white flesh contains large black seeds. Flesh is almost custardlike; eat it with a spoon.

ANNUAL MALLOW. See *Lavatera trimestris.*

ANREDERA cordifolia *(Boussingaultia baselloides, B. gracilis pseudo-baselloides).* *Basellaceae.* MADEIRA VINE. Perennial vine. Zones 4–24. In Zones 4–10, treat as you would dahlias: dig in fall and store tubers over winter. Heart-shaped green leaves 1–3 in. long. Fragrant white flowers in foot-long spikes in late summer, fall. Climbs by twining; may reach 20 ft. in one season. Sun; average water. Small tubers form where leaves join stems. Old-fashioned plant useful for summer screening of decks or other sitting areas. Can run rampant in mildest coastal climates.

Anredera cordifolia

ANTHEMIS. *Compositae.* Evergreen perennials. All Zones. Aromatic foliage, especially when bruised. Leaves divided into many segments. Flowers daisylike or buttonlike.

A. marschalliana *(A. biebersteiniana).* Rounded plant 1 ft. tall and as wide, with finely cut, fernlike, silvery leaves and 1-in., brilliant yellow, daisylike blooms.

A. nobilis. See *Chamaemelum.*

A. tinctoria. GOLDEN MARGUERITE. Erect, shrubby. Grows to 2–3 ft. Angular stems. Light green, much-divided leaves. Golden yellow, daisylike flowers to 2 in. across bloom in summer and fall. Plant in full sun. Average water. Grow from seed, stem cuttings, or divisions in fall or spring. Summer border plant. Varieties are: 'Beauty of Grallagh', golden orange flowers; 'E. C. Buxton', white with yellow centers; 'Kelwayi', golden yellow; 'Moonlight', soft, pale yellow.

Anthemis tinctoria

ANTHRISCUS cerefolium. *Umbelliferae.* CHERVIL. Annual culinary herb. All Zones. Grows 1–2 ft. Finely cut, fernlike leaves resembling parsley; white flowers. Use like parsley, fresh or dried; flavor milder than parsley. Grow from seed in raised bed near kitchen door, in box near barbecue, or in vegetable garden. Part shade best; give ordinary garden soil, moisture. Goes to seed quickly in hot weather. Keep flower clusters cut to encourage vegetative growth.

Anthriscus cerefolium

ANTHURIUM. *Araceae.* Perennial greenhouse or house plants. Native to tropical American jungles. Exotic anthuriums with handsome dark green leaves and lustrous flower bracts in vivid red, luscious pinks, or white are no more difficult to grow as house plants than are some orchids.

The higher the humidity, the better. Anthurium leaves lose shiny texture and may die if humidity drops below 50 percent for more than a few days. Keep pots on trays of moist gravel, in bathroom, or under polyethylene cover. Sponge or spray leaves several times daily. For good bloom, plant by window with good light but no direct sun. Generally grow best in 80°–90°F. temperatures, but will get along in normal house temperature (low 70s). Growth stops below 65°F., is damaged below 50°F. Protect from drafts. Pot anthuriums in coarse, porous mix of leaf mold, sandy soil, and shredded osmunda. Give light feeding every 4 weeks.

Anthurium andraeanum

A. andraeanum. Dark green, oblong leaves to 1 ft. long and 6 in. wide, heart shaped at base. Flower bracts spreading, heart shaped, to 6 in. long, surrounding yellow, callalike flower spike. Flower bracts in shades of red, rose, pink, and white shine as though lacquered. Bloom more or less continuously—plant may have 4–6 flowers during the year. Flowers last 6 weeks on plant, 4 weeks after cut.

A. crystallinum. Leaves up to 1½ ft. long, 1 ft. wide are deep green with striking white veining. Flowers unexciting, with small, narrow, greenish bracts. Many similar anthuriums exist in florist trade; plants offered as *A. crystallinum* may be *A. clarinervium, A. magnificum,* or some other species.

A. scandens. Climbing or trailing plant to 2 ft., with 3-in.-long tapered oval leaves and small, fragrant greenish flowers, translucent lilac berries.

A. scherzeranum. Slow-growing, compact plant to 2 ft. Dark green leaves 8 in. long, 2 in. wide. Flower bracts broad, 3 in. long, deep red varying to rose, salmon, white. Yellow flower spikes spirally coiled. Easier to handle than *A. andraeanum* and often thrives under ordinary good house plant conditions.

ANTIGONON leptopus. *Polygonaceae.* ROSA DE MONTANA, QUEEN'S WREATH, CORAL VINE (must have been loved by many to earn so many nice common names). Deciduous vine, evergreen in warmest winter areas. Zones 12, 13, 18–21; in sheltered locations in Zones 22–24. Native to Mexico. Revels in high summer heat, sun, ample water. Fast growing, climbing by tendrils to 40 ft. Foliage—dark green, 3–5-in.-long, heart-shaped or arrow-shaped leaves—is open and airy. Small rose pink flowers to 1½ in. long are carried in long, trailing sprays from midsummer to fall. In cold winters, leaves fall and most of top dies. Recovers quickly. Treat as perennial. Where winter temperatures drop below 25°F. protect roots with mulch. There is a rare white variety 'Album', and a hot rose pink—nearly red—variety named 'Baja Red'; from seed the color of the latter is variable, but the best forms are as red as 'Barbara Karst' bougainvillea.

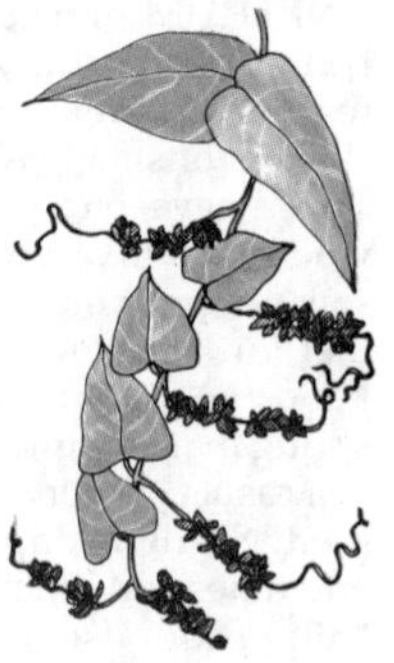

Antigonon leptopus

A wonderful vine in the low deserts of California and Arizona. In those climates it can grow without irrigation, but it may die back to ground in summer. Elsewhere give it hottest spot in garden. Let it shade patio or terrace; drape its foliage and blossom sprays along eaves, fence, or garden wall.

ANTIRRHINUM majus. *Scrophulariaceae.* SNAPDRAGON. Perennial usually treated as annual. All Zones. Among best flowers for sunny borders and cutting, reaching greatest perfection in spring and early summer—in winter and spring in warm-winter, hot-summer regions. Individual flower of basic snapdragon has 5 lobes, which are divided into unequal upper and lower "jaws"; slight pinch at side of flower will make dragon open his jaws. Later developments include double flowers; the bell-shaped flower, with round, open flowers; and the azalea-shaped flower, which is a doubled bellflower.

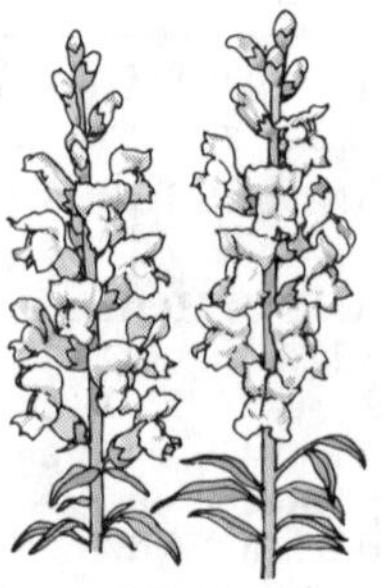

Antirrhinum majus

Snapping snapdragons in tall (2½–3-ft.) range include Pocket and Topper strains (single flowers) and Double Supreme. Intermediate (12–20 in.) are Cinderella, Coronette, Minaret, 'Princess White with Purple Eye', Sprite, and Tahiti. Dwarfs (6–8 in.) include Dwarf Bedding Floral Carpet, Kim, Kolibri, and Royal Carpet.

Bell-flowered or penstemon-flowered strains include Bright Butterflies and Wedding Bells (both 2½ ft.); Little Darling and Liberty Bell (both 15 in.); and Pixie (6–8 in.). Azalea-flowered (double bell-shaped) strains are Madame Butterfly (2½ ft.) and Sweetheart (1 ft.).

Sow seed in flats from late summer to early spring for later transplanting, or buy flat-grown plants at nursery. Set out plants in early fall in mild-winter areas, spring in colder sections. If snapdragons set out in early fall reach bud stage before night temperatures drop below 50°F., they will start blooming in winter and continue until weather gets hot. Rust is most serious handicap; start with rust-resistant varieties and keep plants in vigorous growth, watered and fed regularly. Avoid overhead watering, which helps spread rust spores, but don't let plants go dry. If necessary, change snapdragon planting locations from one year to another in order to avoid rust.

Valuable cut flowers. Tall and intermediate forms are splendid vertical accents in borders with delphinium, iris, daylily (*Hemerocallis*), peach-leafed bluebell (*Campanula persicifolia*), Oriental poppy. Dwarf kinds effective as edgings, in rock gardens, raised beds, or pots.

APACHE PLUME. See *Fallugia paradoxa.*

A

APHELANDRA squarrosa. *Acanthaceae.* Evergreen house plant. Native to Mexico, South America. Popular for leaves and flowers. Large, 8–12-in.-long, dark green leaves strikingly veined with white. Green-tipped yellow flowers and waxy, golden yellow flower bracts make colorful upright spikes at tips of stems. Variety 'Louisae' is best known, but newer varieties 'Apollo White' and 'Dania' are more compact and show more white venation. To make plants bushy, cut stems back to 1–2 pairs of leaves after flowering. Give plant routine house plant culture. Place it where it gets morning (or filtered) sun. Occasionally used outdoors in protected spots in southern California gardens.

Aphelandra squarrosa

Apocynaceae. The dogbane family contains shrubs, trees, and vines with milky, often poisonous sap. Flowers are often showy and fragrant, as in frangipani (*Plumeria rubra*) and oleander (*Nerium oleander*).

Aponogetonaceae. Only the following genus is of importance in this small family of aquatic plants.

APONOGETON distachyus. *Aponogetonaceae.* CAPE PONDWEED, WATER HAWTHORN. Aquatic plant. All Zones. Native to South Africa. Like miniature water lily, it produces floating leaves from submerged tuber. Leaves are long and narrow; ⅓-in.-long, white, fragrant flowers stand above water in 2-branched clusters. In hot-summer climates, blooms in cool weather and is dormant in hottest weather; where winters are cold, blooms in summer and is dormant in winter. Same culture as waterlily (*Nymphaea*); will bloom in considerable shade.

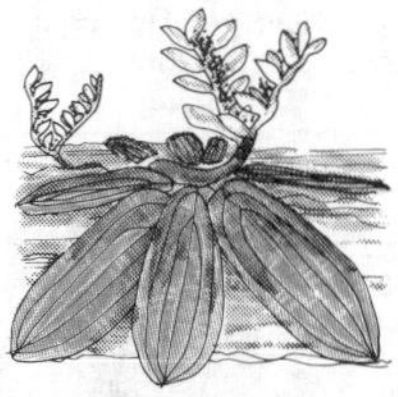
Aponogeton distachyus

APPLE. *Rosaceae.* Deciduous fruit tree. For ornamental relatives, see *Malus*. Most widely adapted deciduous fruit, grown in every western climate—even in low deserts of California and Arizona. Mild winters of the low desert and the marine and coastal climates of southern California do not provide enough winter cold for most standard varieties. Since nursery customers often insist on the popular varieties they see on fruit stands, varieties are sold in areas unfavorable to best performance. In southern California, Phoenix, and Tucson, nurseries often offer varieties for customers who live in nearby higher elevations. For this reason, the apple chart indicates where some varieties perform best, as well as where they are sold.

Apple

All apples require pollination. Most will set adequate fruit on their own pollen, but will set more fruit if pollinated by another variety. Certain varieties (triploids) do not produce fertile pollen and will not fertilize either their own flowers or those of other apples. If a pollinating variety grows in your neighborhood, you need not plant one yourself.

If you have a tree that is not bearing, graft a branch of another variety onto it; or place fresh flower bouquets from another variety (in can of water) at base of tree. Don't use 'Gravenstein', 'Winesap', or any other triploid (pollen-sterile) tree to pollinate other self-unfruitful varieties.

The apple needs sun and has moderate water requirements. Don't crowd it into partially shaded places. To have more than one variety in limited space, buy multiple-variety trees or dwarf trees.

Multiple-variety trees have 3–5 varieties grafted onto a single trunk and rootstock; they may be standard, dwarf, or semidwarf. You get not only variety but also pollination, if needed.

In selecting varieties, remember that all good apples are not red. Skin color is not an indicator of quality or taste. Red varieties are widely sold only because red apples have sales appeal. Make sure that eye appeal alone or slight preference of taste or name doesn't influence you to choose a difficult-to-grow variety. For example, if

(Continued on page 224)

Apple

VARIETY	CLIMATE ADAPTATION	RIPENING DATE	FRUIT	REMARKS
'Akane'	Zones 1–9, 14–16.	September.	Medium sized, bright red; firm, white, juicy flesh. Fine flavor. Hangs well on tree, stores well.	Productive tree; resists scab and mildew. Thin fruit for good size.
'Anna'	Zones 8–24.	Early summer. Sometimes a later, light crop.	Large, pale green blushed red. Sweet with some acid. Crisp, stores well.	Produces at young age. Needs very little winter chill to bear. Use 'Ein Shemer' or 'Dorsett Golden' as pollinator. Good annual bearer.
'Apple Babe'	Zones 2–9, 14–16.	September.	Red blush over pale green; waxy. Medium sized, crisp, moderately sweet.	Spur-type genetic dwarf to 8 ft. tall and wide. Needs pollinator such as 'Garden Delicious'.
'Arkansas Black'	Zones 1–3, 10–11.	October, November.	Medium sized. Dark, deep red. Hard-crisp.	'Arkansas Black Spur' is spurred variation.
'Bellflower'	Zones 14–16, 18–22.	September–October.	Medium to large. Greenish to yellow. Semifirm, fine texture, good quality.	Big, spreading form makes good shade tree.
'Beverly Hills'	Zones 18–24. One of best for southern California coast.	Early.	Small to medium, yellow, splashed and striped red. Tender, somewhat tart. Fair quality. Somewhat resembles 'McIntosh'.	Definitely for cool areas. Will not develop good quality in hot interiors.

(Continued on next page)

A

VARIETY	CLIMATE ADAPTATION	RIPENING DATE	FRUIT	REMARKS
'Chehalis'	Zones 4–6.	Mid-September–early October.	Large, yellow green. Soft, but bakes well. Mild flavor, melting flesh; good in salads.	Like 'Golden Delicious' but resists scab in western Washington, Oregon.
'Cortland'	Zones 1–6.	Fall.	Medium sized, pale red, fine texture, mild flavor. Flesh stays white when cut for salads.	Related to 'McIntosh' but lacking its quality. Can be too soft when ripe.
'Cox Orange Pippin'	Zones 7, 14–16.	Late September.	Medium sized, dull orange red. Flesh yellow, firm, juicy. Flavor superb. English dessert favorite.	Susceptible to scab and cracking. Dense growth, profits from thinning out branches. Dislikes extreme cold, heat, low humidity.
'Criterion'	Zones 2, 3, 6, 7, 15, 16.	Late midseason.	Large, bright yellow with pink blush on one cheek. Pointed shape of 'Delicious'.	Firm, sweet, juicy. Use for dessert and cooking. Vigorous tree, biennial bearer.
'Delicious' ('Red Delicious')	Sold wherever apples will grow. Best in Zones 2, 3, 7.	Midseason to late.	Everybody recognizes pointed blossom end with 5 knobs. Color varies with strain and garden climate; best where days are bright and warm, nights cool. Often older, striped kinds have better flavor than highly colored commercial strains.	Many strains that vary in ripening season, depth and uniformity of coloring. 'Crimson Spur' popular home variety. Highly susceptible to scab, this apple is difficult for home gardeners in Zones 4–6. Needs pollinator; 'Golden Delicious' good.
'Dorsett Golden'	Zones 13, 17–24.	Early summer.	Medium to large. Yellow or greenish yellow skin. Sweet. Keeps a few weeks.	Seedling of 'Golden Delicious' from Bermuda. Needs no winter chill. Good pollinator for 'Anna'.
'Earligold'	Zones 4–9.	Early July.	Light yellow, medium sized. Tart, juicy, crisp.	One of best very early apples. Long season for summer apple.
'Early Crimson'	Zones 8, 9, 14–17.	Late June, early July.	Large red apple with white flesh; good dessert quality.	One of the earliest apples. Keeps well after harvest.
'Ein Shemer'	Zones 13, 17–24.	Early summer.	Yellow to greenish yellow. Medium sized. Juicy, crisp, mildly acid.	Needs very little winter chill. Pollinates 'Anna'.
'Empire'	Zones 2, 3, 6, 7, 14–16.	Late midseason.	'McIntosh'-'Delicious' cross. Medium sized, roundish, dark red. Flesh creamy white, juicy, crisp, aromatic, subacid. Stores well.	Good tree structure, annual bearer.
'Fuji'	Zones 7–9, 14–16.	Late October.	Tapered form, red stripes. Large, firm, very sweet, excellent flavor, good keeper.	Heavy bearer. Needs long season.
'Gala'	Zones 4–9, 14–16.	Early midseason.	Medium sized; beautiful red on yellow color. Firm, crisp, yellow flesh. Juicy, very sweet. Stores well.	Vigorous, heavy bearer with long, supple branches.
'Garden Delicious'	Zones 1–3, 6–9, 14–20.	Late summer.	Medium to large, golden green, red blush.	Genetic dwarf 6–8 ft. tall and as wide.
'Golden Delicious' ('Yellow Delicious')	Zones 1–3, 7–11, 14–24.	Midseason to late.	Clear yellow; similar in shape to 'Delicious', with less prominent knobs. Highly aromatic, crisp, excellent for eating and cooking.	Not yellow-colored 'Red Delicious'; different taste, habit. Spurred types available: 'Goldspur', 'Yelospur'. 'Prime Gold' is rust-resistant variety. Excellent pollinator for many other varieties.
'Gordon'	Zones 18–24.	July–October.	Large, greenish yellow blushed red. Sweet-tart. Long blooming, bearing periods.	Tree vigorous, upright, semidwarf. Many closely spaced spurs.
'Granny Smith'	Zones 6–11, 14–16. Late ripening and scab limit use Zones 4–6.	Late August, mid-September; much later in cool-summer areas.	Large, bright to yellowish green, firm fleshed, tart.	Australian favorite before it came to U.S. Stores well, makes good pies, sauce.
'Gravenstein'	Widely sold Zones 4–11, 14–24. Best in 15–17.	Early to midseason.	Brilliant red stripes over deep yellow. Crisp, aromatic, juicy. Excellent for eating; makes applesauce with character.	Justly famous variety of California's north coast apple district. 'Red Gravenstein' is more highly colored. Needs pollinator and will not pollinate other apple varieties. Susceptible to mildew Zones 4–6.

VARIETY	CLIMATE ADAPTATION	RIPENING DATE	FRUIT	REMARKS
'Holland' ('Summer Champion')	Zones 20–24.	Early to mid-October.	Very large; dark strawberry red. Firm, smooth, juicy. Stores well.	Bears at early age.
'Idared'	Zones 4–6, 15–17.	October.	Bright red apple with firm white flesh, tart at picking time.	Stores well and flavor sweetens in storage. Early, annual heavy bearer.
'Jonagold'	Zones 2–9, 14–16.	Mid-September–early October.	Large; heavy red striping over yellow. Firm, subacid, juicy, fine flavor, resembles 'Jonathan'. Stores well. A frequent taste-test favorite.	Productive, medium-sized tree. Heavy bearer. Needs pollinator; will not pollinate other varieties.
'Jonathan'	Sold everywhere. Best Zones 2, 3, 7.	Early fall. Midseason.	Medium to large, round-oblong. High-colored red. Juicy, moderately tart, crackling crisp, sprightly.	All-purpose apple. Subject to mildew, scab.
'King'	Zones 4–6.	Midseason to late.	Large, waxy yellow with red striping. Crisp, sweet. Good for baking, eating. Keeps very well.	Large, rangy, sparsely branched tree. Needs pollinator, and will not pollinate other varieties.
'Liberty'	Zones 4–9, 14–16.	Late September, early October.	Medium sized, elongated, heavy red blush. Fine sweet-tart flavor. Crisp, dessert quality.	Productive annual bearer. Immune to scab; can get mildew west of Cascades. Resists rust, fireblight.
'Lodi'	Zones 1–6, 8, 9.	Early.	Large, pale yellow, crisp and tart. Must be picked early; soon gets overripe.	Resembles 'Yellow Transparent', but larger, firmer, less mealy.
'Macoun'	Zones 1–7, 15, 16.	Mid-October.	Medium sized, red striped on green ground. Sweet, crisp and juicy. Tasty for dessert and good cooking. A taste-test winner.	Large, upright trees fairly resistant to mildew, scab. Thin for good fruit size. Drops badly when ripe.
'McIntosh' ('Red McIntosh')	Zones 2–6, 14–16.	Late midseason.	Medium to large. Bright red, nearly round. Snowy white, tender flesh. Tart, excellent.	Excellent apple for garden if given good care. 'Double Red McIntosh' and 'Nured McIntosh' have high color. Drops badly when ripe.
'Melrose'	Zones 1–7, 15, 16.	Late October.	Medium to large, roundish, red striped deeper red. Flesh white, mildly subacid, aromatic.	Cross between 'Jonathan' and 'Delicious'. Exceptional storage, good dessert apple. Somewhat mildew resistant.
'Mollie's Delicious'	Zones 8, 9, 14–20.	August.	Large, light yellow blushed red. Light yellow flesh, aromatic, juicy, sweet. Stores well.	Bears early, needs little winter chill.
'Mutsu'	Zones 4–9, 15, 16.	Late October.	Large, greenish yellow to yellow blushed red. Flesh white, very crisp, somewhat more tart than 'Golden Delicious'. Frequent taste-test winner in Northwest.	Good dessert and cooking apple with long storage life. Tree exceptionally large and vigorous. Needs pollinator. Tends to get bitter pit.
'Newtown Pippin' ('Yellow Newtown', 'Yellow Pippin')	Zones 1–11, 13–22. Susceptible to mildew Zones 4–6.	Late.	Large, green. Crisp and tart, fair for eating, excellent for cooking.	Large, vigorous tree.
'Northern Spy' ('Red Spy')	Zones 1–3, 6, 7. Best in cold-winter areas.	Late.	Large, red. Tender, fine-grained flesh. Apple epicure's delight for sprightly flavor.	Slow to reach bearing age. Needs pollinator.
'Paulared'	Zones 4–9, 15–17.	Early September.	Average size, yellow turning red. White, firm flesh, juicy, subacid.	Medium-sized tree with good structure, regular bearer on spurs and on tip buds.
'Pettingill'	Zones 23, 24.	Midseason to late.	Large, red-blushed green to red, thick skinned. Firm, white, tasty, moderately acid flesh.	Large, upright, productive tree with very low chilling requirement. Regular bearer.
'Red Fireside' ('Connelred')	Zones 1–3, 6, 7.	Late.	Large, striped dark red over medium red. Flesh yellowish, juicy, mildly acid.	Tree vigorous, very hardy.
'Redfree'	Zones 4–9, 14–17.	Late August.	Red, firm, crisp, medium sized, good flavor.	Heavy bearer, immune to scab.
'Red Gold'	Zones 2, 3, 7–9, 14–17.	Early fall.	Medium-sized, slightly oblong, glossy red apple with yellowish, mild flesh. Juicy. Keeps well.	Vigorous hybrid between 'Red Delicious' and 'Golden Delicious'.

(Continued on next page)

CLIMATE ZONES, PAGES 33–55

A

VARIETY	CLIMATE ADAPTATION	RIPENING DATE	FRUIT	REMARKS
'Red Melba'	Zones 6, 7, 15, 16.	Very early summer.	Pale green blushed red to all-over red. Medium to large. Crisp, white flesh.	Tree productive, bears young. Bears every other year.
'Rome Beauty' ('Red Rome')	Zones 3, 7, 10, 11.	Late midseason.	Large, round, smooth, red. Greenish white flesh. Outstanding baking apple.	Early bearer. 'Red Rome' is all-over red kind most frequently sold. Blooms late, escapes frost.
'Sierra Beauty'	Zones 2, 3, 6–9, 14–16.	Early October.	Large, yellow with red stripes. Firm, sweet-tart. Keeps well.	Needs little winter chill.
'Spartan'	Zones 4–7, 15, 16.	Midseason to late.	Small to medium, dark red with purplish bloom. Crisp flesh, excellent flavor. Frequent taste-test winner.	Equals 'McIntosh' in flavor. Tree habit good; heavy bearing necessitates thinning.
'Spitzenberg' ('Esopus Spitzenberg')	Zones 1–7.	Late.	Medium to large, red-dotted yellow. Crisp, fine grained, tangy, spicy.	Old favorite, best in cold-winter areas. Subject to fireblight, mildew.
'Spur Criterion'	Zones 4–7, 15–17.	Midseason.	Same as 'Criterion'.	Smaller tree than 'Criterion' and ripens 10–14 days ahead of 'Criterion'.
'Stayman Winesap' (and 'Winesap')	Zones 1–7, 10, 11. Susceptible to scab Zones 4–6.	Latest.	Medium to large, round. Lively flavor. Fine grained, firm, juicy. 'Stayman Winesap' is large, red with green and russet dots. 'Winesap' is smaller, all red.	Old-timers that remain top favorites. Most 'Winesap' trees sold at nurseries are really 'Stayman Winesap'. Poor pollinators.
'Summerred'	Zones 4–7, 15, 16.	Late August.	Medium sized, bright red; tart and good chiefly for cooking until fully ripe, then good dessert quality too.	Consistent annual bearer for western Oregon and Washington. Goes overripe too fast in hot-summer climates.
'Tydeman's Red' ('Tydeman's Early Worcester')	Zones 4–7, 15, 16.	Late August, early September.	Medium, round, bright red. Resembles 'McIntosh'. Good for cooking, tart but good eating. 'Gala' is more attractive substitute.	Long, sprawling branches need control; tip-prune to encourage branching or grow as espalier. Scab resistant. Tends to drop early.
'Valmore'	Zones 8, 9, 18–24.	August.	Large, red blushed yellow. Flesh yellowish white, aromatic, good for cooking, eating.	Will fruit in warm areas with little winter chill.
'Wealthy' ('Red Wealthy', 'Double Red Wealthy')	Zones 1–7.	Midseason.	Large, rough, red. Flesh white veined pink, firm, tart, juicy. Good cooking variety.	Small, cold-hardy tree that tends to alternate bearing.
'Winter Banana'	Zones 4–9, 14–24.	Midseason.	Large, attractive, pale yellow blushed pink, waxy finish. Tender, tangy, aromatic.	One of few standard varieties that will accept mild winters. Needs pollinator. There is a 'Spur Winter Banana'.
'Winter Pearmain' ('White Winter Pearmain')	Zones 20–24.	Midseason.	Medium to large. Pale greenish yellow skin with pink blush. Excellent flavor, tender flesh, fine grained. All-purpose.	Performs better than standard cold-winter varieties in southern California. Needs pollinator.
'Yellow Transparent' ('Transparent')	Zones 1–9, 14, 15, 19, 20.	Early.	Medium to large, greenish or whitish yellow, lightly blushed on one side. Soft, sour, good for cooking.	Ripens mid-June to mid-July in Sacramento Valley. Doesn't keep. Very short season.

to your taste 'Golden Delicious' and 'Red Delicious' are nearly equal, consider differences in growing them. 'Golden Delicious' produces fruit without pollinator and comes into bearing earlier. It keeps well, while 'Red Delicious' becomes mealy if not stored at 50°F. or lower. And it can be used for cooking, while 'Red Delicious' is strictly an eating apple.

The apple tree will need much care if you want perfect fruit. However, as an ornamental tree it has more character, better form, and longer life than most deciduous fruit trees. It does best in deep soil but gets by in many imperfect situations, including heavy soils. Codling moth is the universal insect pest of apples; to control it, spray with diazinon, malathion, or sevin as soon as petals have fallen and repeat according to label instructions or recommendations of local farm advisors. Apple maggot is a serious pest in some areas and is spreading; check with local authorities to find out if it is a problem where you live. If so, spray in midsummer, with later sprays at 2-week intervals until 2 weeks before harvest.

Dwarf and Spur Apples

True dwarf apples (5–8 ft. in height and spread) are made by grafting standard apples on dwarfing rootstocks named M (or EM) IX or X. Such trees take up little room but have shallow roots; they need the support of a fence, wall, or sturdy trellis to stand against wind and rain. They also need good soil and extra care in feeding and watering. Genetic dwarf apples are naturally small (5–8 ft.) even when grafted on standard, nondwarfing rootstocks. 'Apple

Babe' and 'Garden Delicious' are examples.

Semidwarf trees are larger than true dwarfs but smaller than standard trees. They bear bigger crops than dwarfs and take up less space than standards. Many commercial orchards get high yields by using semidwarf trees and planting them close together. Semidwarf rootstocks reduce tree size by approximately the following factors: EM 26 and EM VIIA are about half normal size; they may be espaliered or trellised if planted 12–16 ft. apart and allowed to grow 10–12 ft. tall. Trees on MM 106 are approximately 65% of normal height, those on MM 111 75% of normal height.

Rarely, growers offer trees dwarfed by double-working—grafting a piece of M IX trunk on vigorous rootstock, then grafting a bearing variety on this "interstock." The resulting dwarf is somewhat larger than a true dwarf tree and has much more vigorous roots.

Apples bear flowers and fruit on spurs—short branches which grow from 2-year or older wood. Spurs normally begin to appear only after tree has grown in place 3–5 years. On spur-type apples, spurs form earlier (within 2 years after planting) and grow closer together on shorter branches, giving more apples per foot of branch. Spur apples are natural or genetic semidwarfs about ⅔ the size of normal apple trees when grafted on ordinary rootstocks. They can be further dwarfed by grafting onto dwarfing rootstocks; M VIIA and M 26 give smallest trees, MM 106 and MM 111 somewhat larger ones.

Training and Pruning Apple Trees

Careful early training and some annual pruning and shaping are necessary to make apple trees manageable in size, healthy, and productive. Most home and orchard apples grow on vase-shaped trees—broad, spreading, with 3 (sometimes more) main scaffold branches arising from trunk 2½–3 ft. tall. These branches should not arise at the same point; select ones that are evenly spaced around trunk and at least 8 or 9 in. apart. As tree grows, prune out crossing branches and overvigorous branches growing toward center of tree.

Spur apples and apples on semidwarfing rootstocks are often trained as central-leader or pyramidal trees. Side branches grow outward from central trunk to form symmetrical pyramid, with tiers of branches that grow shorter toward top of plant. Keep branches from growing directly above and close to lower branches; upper ones will shade lower ones out. Keep side branches from outgrowing the leader and secondary side branches from outstripping primary branches. If branches grow at a narrow angle to leader, spread them to a 45° angle by heavy wire or wood-and-nail spreaders.

Dwarf trees can grow as pyramids, as single-stem trees with fruiting spurs along main trunk, or as espaliers tied to wood or wire frames, fences, or other supports.

Apples' fruiting spurs remain productive for up to 20 years. Pruning of mature trees consists of removing weak, dead, or poorly placed branches and twigs to encourage development of strong new growth and to permit sunlight to reach into tree, where it will encourage spur growth and discourage mildew.

APRICOT. *Rosaceae.* Deciduous fruit tree. For ornamental relatives, see *Prunus*. Apricots can be grown throughout the West, with these limitations: because they bloom early in the season, they will not fruit in regions with late frosts; in cool, humid coastal areas, tree and fruit are unusually subject to brown rot and blight; in mild-winter areas of southern California, only varieties with low requirements for winter chill will do well. Apricots are good dual-purpose fruit and shade trees, easy to maintain. They can also be trained as espaliers. Your county agent or farm advisor can give you a local timetable and directions for spraying apricots (essential dates: during dormant season, before and after flowering, and at red-bud stage). To get big apricots, do this: in midspring, thin excess fruit from branches, leaving 2–4 in. between individual apricots.

Apricot

Apricots bear most fruit on short fruit spurs which form on last year's growth and remain fruitful for about 4 years. Pruning should be directed toward conserving enough new growth (which will produce spurs) to replace old, exhausted spurs, which should be cut out.

Here's a list of varieties sold at nurseries. Many are available on dwarf and semidwarf rootstocks. Some varieties need a pollinator, as indicated.

'Aprigold'. Zones 2, 3, 6–9, 12–16, 18–23. Good quality, full-sized fruit. Genetic (natural) dwarf 4–6 ft. tall, 6–8 ft. wide.

'Autumn Royal'. Zones 2, 3, 6–9, 12–16, 18–23. Resembles 'Royal' but ripens fruit in September; only autumn-ripening apricot tree.

'Blenril'. Zones 2, 3, 6. Like 'Royal' in quality. Needs pollinator (any variety except 'Riland').

'Chinese' ('Mormon'). Zones 1–3, 6. Late bloom, hardy tree; good production in late-frost and cold-winter regions.

'Early Gold'. ('Early Golden', 'Earligold'). Zones 8–12, 14–23. Early-fruiting variety that needs little winter chill.

'Floragold'. Zones 2, 3, 6–24. Early-ripening, full-sized fruit grows on genetic (natural) semidwarf tree (about half size of normal apricot tree).

'Golden Amber'. Zones 2, 3, 6–9, 12–16, 18–23. Resembles 'Royal', but tree blooms over month-long period; fruit ripens over similar period from mid-June to mid-July.

'Goldrich'. Zones 2–6. Good-quality fruit on hardy, cold-resistant tree. Needs pollinator.

'King'. Zones 8–9, 12–16, 18–23. Early ripening, very large, very highly colored. Hard to pollinate; 'Perfection' does best job.

'Moongold'. Zones 1–3. Plum-sized, golden, sweet, sprightly fruit. Developed for coldest winter climates.

'Moorpark'. Zones 2, 3, 6–11, 14–16. Very large fruit, fine flavor. Color develops unevenly. Good home dessert or drying variety, poor canner.

'Newcastle'. Zones 10–12, 20–23. Good southern California variety; needs little winter chilling.

'Nugget'. Zones 18–23. Large fruit with good flavor and color. Low chilling requirement. Ripens very early, before extreme summer heat.

'Perfection' ('Goldbeck'). Zones 2–9, 12–16, 18–23. Fruit very large but flavor only mediocre. Chilling requirement low, tree hardy. Needs pollinator (any variety except 'Reeves').

'Puget Gold'. Zones 4–6. Consistent bearer in Puget Sound area, fairly tolerant of apricot diseases. Medium-sized fruit in early August. Flavor good, low in acid.

'Redsweet'. Zones 12–16, 18–23. Highly colored, very early-ripening fruit. Needs early-blooming pollinator ('Nugget' or 'Perfection').

'Reeves'. Zones 12, 13, 18–24. Medium-sized yellow orange fruit. Ripens early. Needs pollinator. Largely supplanted by newer varieties.

'Riland'. Zones 2, 3, 6. Early-ripening, highly colored, roundish fruit. Needs pollinator.

'Rival'. Zones 2–6. Large, oval orange fruit blushed red. Needs early-flowering pollinator ('Perfection').

'Royal', 'Blenheim'. Zones 2, 3, 6–23. Regardless of how labeled in nurseries, these are either 2 identical varieties or one variety under 2 names. Standard variety in California's apricot regions. Good for canning or drying.

'Royalty'. Zones 2, 3, 6–9, 12–23. Extra-large fruit on heavy, wind-resistant spurs. Early bearing.

'Snowball'. Zones 14–16, 18–23. Early ripening; white skin with pink blush, white flesh.

'Southern Giant'. Zones 8–9, 14–24. Fine-quality fruit with very low chilling requirement.

'Sun-Glow'. Zones 2–6. Highly colored, early fruit. Hardy tree with extra-hardy fruit buds.

'Sungold'. Zones 1–3. Plum-sized, slightly flattened, bright orange, sweet, mild fruit. Developed for coldest winter climates.

(Continued on next page)

'Tilton'. Zones 1–8, 10, 11, 18, 20. Higher chilling requirement than 'Royal', but less subject to brown rot and sunburn.

'Valnur'. Zones 2, 3, 6. Very early, medium-large fruit. Good pollinator.

'Wenatchee' ('Wenatchee Moorpark'). Zones 2, 3, 6. Large fruit, excellent flavor.

APTENIA cordifolia *(Mesembryanthemum cordifolium)*. *Aizoaceae.* Shrubby perennial. Zones 17, 21–24. Sun. Needs little water. Ice plant relative with trailing stems to 2 ft. long and profusion of inch-wide, heart-shaped or oval, bright green, fleshy leaves. Purplish red, inch-wide ice plant flowers in spring and summer. Though fleshy, looks less like ice plant than most. Use as trailer in rock garden, on slope or wall, or in hanging pot. *A.* c. 'Variegata' has white-bordered leaves.

Aptenia cordifolia

Aquifoliaceae. The holly family contains evergreen trees or shrubs with berrylike fruit. *Ilex* (holly) is the only important genus.

AQUILEGIA. *Ranunculaceae.* COLUMBINE. Perennials. All Zones. Columbines have fairylike, woodland quality with their lacy foliage and beautifully posed flowers in exquisite pastels, deeper shades, or white. Erect, branching, 2 in.–4 ft. high. Fresh green, divided leaves reminiscent of maidenhair fern. Bloom in spring, early summer. Flowers to 3 in. across, erect or nodding, often with sepals and petals in contrasting colors; usually have backward-projecting, nectar-bearing spurs. Some kinds have large flowers and very long spurs; these have an airier look than short-spurred kinds or double-flowered strains, although the latter make bolder color mass.

Aquilegia
McKana Giant

Preferred tall hybrid strains are graceful, long-spurred McKana Giants and double-flowering Spring Song. Lower-growing strains are Biedermeier and Dragonfly (1 ft.), long-spurred Music (1½ ft.) and single to double, upward-facing Fairyland (15 in.).

All columbines are hardy. They tolerate filtered shade but will take full sunlight, especially along coast. Cut back old stems for second crop of flowers; leave some seed if you want plants to self-sow. All kinds of columbines attract hummingbirds. Subject to leaf miners, aphids, and red spider mites but usually require only routine care, water. Replace old plants about every 3 years.

A. alpina. ALPINE COLUMBINE. Native of the Alps. Grows 12–16 in. high. Flowers blue, to 2 in. across, with straight or curved spurs 1 in. long.

A. caerulea. ROCKY MOUNTAIN COLUMBINE. State flower of Colorado. 1½–3 ft. high. Flowers erect, 2 in. or more across, blue and white. Spurs straight or spreading, to 2 in. long. This species hybridized with *A. chrysantha* and others to produce many long-spurred hybrids. Best in filtered shade and moist soil.

A. chrysantha. GOLDEN or GOLDEN-SPURRED COLUMBINE. Native to Arizona, New Mexico, and adjacent Mexico. Large, many-branched plant to 3–4 ft. One of showiest species. Leaflets densely covered with soft hairs beneath. Flowers erect, 1½–3 in. across, clear yellow; spurs slender, 2–2½ in. long.

A. flabellata. Native to Japan. Stocky 9-inch plant with lilac blue and creamy white flowers in early spring. Good rock garden plant. *A. f.* 'Nana' is even shorter.

A. formosa. WESTERN COLUMBINE. Native to Utah and California to Alaska. Grows 1½–3 ft. high. Flowers nodding, 1½–2 in. across, red and yellow; spurs stout and straight, red. Good in woodland garden; allow to form seeds which are relished by song sparrows, juncos, and other small birds. *A. f. truncata* is sometimes sold as *A. californica;* it is a tall columbine with red spurs, orange petals, and yellow sepals.

A. longissima. Native to southwest Texas and northern Mexico; 2½–3 ft. tall. Similar to *A. chrysantha.* Flowers numerous, erect, pale yellow; spurs very narrow, drooping, 4–6 in. long.

A. vulgaris. EUROPEAN COLUMBINE. Naturalized in eastern U.S. Grows to 1–2½ ft. Flowers nodding, up to 2 in. across, blue, purple, or white; short, knobby spurs about ¾ in. long.

ARABIS. *Cruciferae.* ROCKCRESS. Perennials. All Zones, except as noted. Low-growing, spreading plants for edgings, rock gardens, ground covers, pattern plantings. All kinds have attractive year-round foliage and clusters of white, pink, or rose purple flowers in spring. Sun. Moderate water.

Arabis caucasica

A. alpina. MOUNTAIN ROCKCRESS. Zones 1–7. Low, tufted plant, rough-hairy, with leafy stems 4–10 in. high and basal leaves in clusters. White flowers in dense, short clusters. Variety 'Rosea', 6 in. high, has pink flowers; 'Variegata' has variegated leaves. Plants sold as *A. alpina* are often really *A. caucasica.*

A. blepharophylla. CALIFORNIA ROCKCRESS, ROSE CRESS. Zones 5, 6, 15–17. Native to rocky hillsides and ridges near sea, Marin County to Monterey County, California. Tufted perennial 4–8 in. high. Basal leaves 1–2¾ in. long. Rose purple flowers, fragrant, ½–¾ in. wide, in short, dense clusters. Blooms March and April. Rock plant in nature, equally adapted to well-drained spot in rock garden. Also good container plant.

A. caucasica *(A. albida)*. WALL ROCKCRESS. Native Mediterranean region to Iran. Dependable old favorite. Forms mat of gray leaves to 6 in. high. White, ½-in. flowers almost cover plants in early spring. Excellent ground cover and base planting for spring-flowering bulbs such as daffodils and paper-white narcissus. Companion for *Aurinia saxatilis* and aubrieta.

A. c. 'Variegata'. Has gray leaves with creamy white margins. 'Floreplena' has double flowers; 'Rosabella' and 'Pink Charm' have pink blooms. Latter 2 are popular rock garden plants in colder climates. Start plants from cuttings or sow seeds in spring or fall. Provide some shade in hot, dry areas. Short lived where winters are warm.

A. sturii. Dense, fist-sized cushions of small bright green leaves eventually grow into small mats. Clusters of white flowers on 2–3-in. stems in early spring. Some consider it one of 50 finest rock garden plants.

Araceae. The arum family contains plants ranging from tuberous or rhizomatous perennials to shrubby or climbing tropical foliage plants. Leaves are often highly ornamental; variable in shape, but tend to be arrowlike. Inconspicuous flowers cluster tightly on a club-shaped spadix within an often showy leaflike bract (spathe). Examples are anthurium, calla (*Zantedeschia*), and philodendron. Sap of many is highly irritating to mouth and throat.

ARALIA. *Araliaceae.* Deciduous shrub-trees. Zones 2–24. Striking bold-leafed plants that may eventually grow to 25–30 ft. under ideal conditions. Often shrublike, especially in colder areas where they may grow as multi-stemmed (because of suckering habit) shrubs to 10 ft. Branches are nearly vertical or slightly spreading, usually very spiny. Huge leaves, clustered at ends of branches, are divided into many leaflets, have effective pattern value. White flowers are small but in such large, branched clusters they are showy in midsummer; followed by purplish berrylike fruit.

Aralia chinensis

Not good near swimming pools because of spines; even leaf stalks are sometimes prickly. Protect plants from wind to avoid burning foliage. Give sun or light shade, moderate water.

A. chinensis. CHINESE ANGELICA. Only moderately spiny. Leaves 2–3 ft. long, divided into 2–6-in.-long, toothed leaflets without stalks. Flower clusters grow 1–2 ft. wide.

A. elata. JAPANESE ANGELICA TREE. Native to northeast Asia. Similar to *A. chinensis* but leaflets are narrower, have fewer teeth. *A. e.* 'Variegata' has leaflets strikingly bordered with creamy white.

A. elegantissima. See *Dizygotheca*.

A. papyrifera. See *Tetrapanax*.

A. sieboldii. JAPANESE ARALIA. See *Fatsia*.

Araliaceae. The aralia family of herbaceous and woody plants is marked by leaves that are divided fanwise into leaflets or veined in pattern like the fingers of a hand. Individually tiny flowers are in round clusters or in large compound clusters. Examples are English ivy, Japanese aralia (*Fatsia*), and schefflera.

ARAUCARIA. *Araucariaceae.* Evergreen trees. These strange-looking conifers provide definite silhouette with their evenly spread tiers of stiff branches. Prominent skyline trees in many parks and old estates in California. Most have stiff, closely overlapping, dark to bright green leaves. These are not trees to sit under—in age they bear large, spiny, 10–15-lb. cones that fall with a crash.

Araucaria araucana

All do well in wide range of soils with adequate drainage and abundance of moisture. They become so towering that they should be given park space. Can serve well as skyline trees. They thrive in containers for several years, even in desert areas.

A. araucana *(A. imbricata)*. MONKEY PUZZLE TREE. Zones 4–9, 14–24. Native to Chile. Arboreal oddity with heavy, spreading branches and ropelike branchlets closely set with sharp-pointed dark green leaves. Hardiest of araucarias. Slow growing in youth, it eventually reaches 70–90 ft. Hardy west of Cascades in Northwest.

A. bidwillii. BUNYA-BUNYA. Zones 7–9, 12–24. Native to Australia. Probably most widely planted araucaria both in coastal and valley areas of California. Moderate growth to 80 ft.; broadly rounded crown supplies dense shade. Two kinds of leaves: juvenile are glossy, rather narrow, ¾–2 in. long, stiff, more or less spreading in 2 rows; mature leaves are oval, ½ in. long, rather woody, spirally arranged and overlapping along branches. Unusual house plant; very tough and tolerant of low light.

Araucaria heterophylla

A. cunninghamii. HOOP PINE. Zones 17, 21–24. Native to Australia. Unusual silhouette of long horizontal or upswept branches with foliage tufted at tips. Eventual height of 100 ft. Juvenile leaves needlelike and flattened, ½ in. long, with spiny recurved points; adult leaves broader, overlapping, points incurved.

A. heterophylla *(A. excelsa)*. NORFOLK ISLAND PINE. Zones 17, 21–24. Moderate growth rate to 100 ft., of pyramidal shape. Juvenile leaves rather narrow, ½ in. long, curved and with sharp points; mature leaves somewhat triangular and densely overlapping. Can be held in containers for many years—outdoors in mild climates, house plant anywhere.

Araucariaceae. Coniferous trees with symmetrical branching habit and leaves that vary from needlelike to broad and leathery. *Agathis* and *Araucaria* are the only representatives.

ARAUJIA sericofera. *Asclepiadaceae.* WHITE BLADDER FLOWER. Evergreen or partially deciduous vine. Zones 8, 9, 14–24. Native to Brazil. Woody vine that sometimes pops up spontaneously in gardens from wind-borne, silky-tufted seeds. Becomes weedy, massive tangle in year or two. Leaves tend to drop at base. Twines 20–30 ft. in one season. Leaves 2–4 in. long, glossy dark green above, whitish beneath. White or pinkish, bell-shaped flowers, 1–1½ in. wide, followed by long, flat, leathery fruit. Not first-class vine. Used for quick temporary screen in poor soil, windy places. Sun or partial shade, much or little water.

Araujia sericofera

ARBORVITAE. See *Thuja, Platycladus*.

ARBUTUS. *Ericaceae.* Evergreen trees and shrub-trees. *A. menziesii* is a western native; *A. unedo* comes from the Mediterranean. *A.* 'Marina' is of uncertain origin. Resistant to oak root fungus.

A. 'Marina'. Evergreen tree to 40 ft., usually less. Zones 8, 9, 14–24. Hybrid of uncertain parentage. Resembles *A. unedo* but has larger leaves, rosy pink flowers in the fall. Good garden substitute for madrone.

A. menziesii. MADRONE, MADROÑO. Evergreen tree or large shrub. Zones 3–7, 14–19. Native from British Columbia to southern California in Coast Ranges, occasionally in middle elevations of Sierra Nevada. Mature height varies from 20–100 ft. Forms broad, round head almost as wide as tall. In groves, plants are more slender.

Arbutus unedo

Main feature is smooth, reddish brown bark that peels in thin flakes. Leathery, 3–6-in.-long leaves are shiny dark green on top, dull gray green beneath. In spring, large clusters of white to pinkish, bell-shaped flowers at branch ends. These are followed in early fall by clusters of brilliant red and orange, rough-coated berries that remain on tree most of winter if birds don't get them.

If you live in madrone country and have a tree in your garden, treasure it. It is exacting in requirements in gardens outside of its native area. Must have fast drainage and nonalkaline water. Water just enough to keep plants going until they are established, and then give only infrequent and deep watering.

A. unedo. STRAWBERRY TREE. Evergreen shrub-tree. Zones 4–24. Native to southern Europe, Ireland. Damaged in severe winters in Zones 4–7, but worth risk. Remarkably good performance in both climate and soil extremes from desert (in shade) to seashore. Needs little water once established; tolerates much water if planted in well-drained soil.

In California, one of the best lawn or raised-bed trees. It tolerates wind at the beach and thrives even on water of indifferent quality.

Slow to moderate growth to 8–35 ft. with equal spread. Normally has basal suckers, stem sprouts. Can be pruned, not sheared, to make open-crowned tree. Or plant several and leave unpruned to make screen. Trunk and branches have rich red brown, shreddy bark; tend to become somewhat twisted and gnarled in age. Dark green, handsome, red-stemmed leaves are oblong and 2–3 in. long. Clusters of small, white or greenish white, urn-shaped flowers and round, red and yellow, ¾-in. fruit, somewhat strawberry-like in texture, appear at the same time in fall and winter; fruit is edible but mealy and nearly tasteless.

A. u. 'Compacta' is a smaller shrub, but still larger than *A. u.* 'Elfin King', a picturesque, contorted true dwarf form (not over 5 ft. tall at 10 years of age) which flowers and fruits nearly continuously. 'Elfin King' is splendid container plant or show plant for small entry garden.

A

ARCHONTOPHOENIX. *Palmae.* Outdoors in Zones 21–24, house plant anywhere. Called BANGALOW or PICCABEEN palms in Australia. They grow to 50 ft. or more, with 10–15-ft. spread. Handsome, stately, difficult to transplant when large. Where winds are strong, plant in lee of buildings to prevent damage. Young trees can't take frost; mature plants may stand 28°F. They tolerate shade and can grow many years grouped under tall trees. Moderate water requirements. Old leaves shed cleanly, leaving smooth green trunks. Feathery leaves on mature trees 8–10 ft. long, green above, gray green beneath.

Archontophoenix cunninghamiana

A. alexandrae. ALEXANDRA PALM. Trunk enlarged toward base.

A. cunninghamiana *(Seaforthia elegans)*. KING PALM. More common than the above. Trunk not prominently enlarged at base. Clustered amethyst flowers are handsome. Highly recommended for nearly frost-free areas.

ARCTOSTAPHYLOS. *Ericaceae.* MANZANITA. Evergreen shrubs. Large group of western natives ranging in size from creepers to full-sized shrubs to small trees. Waxy, bell-like flowers and fruit like tiny apples. Most are characterized by (and admired for) crooked branches with smooth red to purple bark. Shrubs attract birds.

Arctostaphylos densiflora

Low-growing ground cover manzanitas do best in loose soils that drain rapidly. They tolerate heavier soils. Taller ground covers (especially those that spread by rooting branches) and most shrub and tree forms *must* have loose, well-drained soil.

First summer after planting, water every 4–7 days, depending on weather. In warm-summer areas, established plants in well-drained soil generally thrive on once-a-month watering; in heavy soil, water less frequently. You may be able to stretch intervals to once or twice a summer. Control growth by frequent pinching during growing season. Plants feeble in heavy shade.

Blooming season is not noted in the following list unless it differs from general February-March-April sequence.

A. bakeri 'Louis Edmunds'. Zones 4–9, 14–17. Upright shrub to 5–6 ft. tall. Gray green foliage. Pink flowers in hanging clusters. Good garden tolerance.

A. columbiana. HAIRY MANZANITA. Zones 4–6, 15–17. Native to low coastal mountains, central California to British Columbia. Form propagated and sold in northwestern nurseries is called 'Oregon Hybrid'. Low-growing, compact shrub with reddish bark, gray green leaves 3 in. long, white flowers, and red-cheeked summer fruit. Useful plant, tough enough for highway landscaping in western Oregon and Washington.

A. densiflora. VINE HILL MANZANITA. Zones 7–9, 14–21. Native to Sonoma County, California. All varieties except 'Sentinel' grow low and spreading; outer branches take root when they touch soil. Main stems slender and crooked. Bark of trunks and branches smooth, reddish black. Leaves light or dark green, glossy, small, in ½–1 in. range. Flowers white or pink. In bank planting, low types do best on east- or northeast-facing slopes, in loose soil with good drainage.

A. d. 'Harmony'. Very similar to 'Howard McMinn' (below) but somewhat taller and broader. Less well known, but considered best form by some specialists. Pinkish white flowers.

A. d. 'Howard McMinn'. Grows in mound to 5–6 ft. tall (usually much less); spreads as much as 7 ft. in 5 years. If tip-pruned after flowering, plant becomes as dense as sheared Kurume azalea. (Don't prune tips of prostrate branches.) Flowers whitish pink.

A. d. 'Sentinel'. An upright form to 6 ft. or more and spreading to 8 ft. Light green, downy leaves. Full sun. Can be trained as small tree by selecting dominant stem or stems and removing others. Sensitive to salt burn, root rots.

A. edmundsii. LITTLE SUR MANZANITA. Zones 6–9, 14–24. Low-growing manzanitas from coastal Monterey County, California. Three varieties are grown from cuttings. 'Danville' is 4–24 in. tall, to 12 ft. wide, with roundish, light green, inch-long leaves on red stems and pink flowers in December and January. 'Carmel Sur' has exceptionally good form—gray green, neat-looking foliage, soft pink flowers; is fast growing, very garden tolerant. 'Little Sur' has dense, flat growth, bronzy new growth, pointed leaves with reddish margins, slow growth rate, and soft pink flowers in March–April. Good hillside planting.

A. 'Emerald Carpet'. Zones 6–9, 14–24. Dense, uniform carpet 9–14 in. tall, mounding slightly higher after many years. Leaves roundish oval, ½ in. long, bright green in hottest, driest weather. Small pink flowers in March–April, not showy. In hot interior valleys needs deep irrigation every 2–3 weeks. One of greenest, most uniform manzanitas.

A. franciscana. Zones 6–9, 14–24. Grows to 2½ ft., spreads slowly to 7 ft. (in 15 years). Native to San Francisco but nearly extinct there. White flowers.

A. hookeri. MONTEREY MANZANITA. Zones 6–9, 14–24. Native to Monterey Peninsula. Slow growing to form dense mounds 1½–4 ft. high, spreading to 6 ft. and more. Oval, ¾-in.-long, bright green, glossy leaves. Flowers white to pinkish; fruit bright red, shiny; bark red brown, smooth. Good on hillsides.

A. h. 'Monterey Carpet'. Compact growth to make foot-high ground cover spreading by rooting branches to 12 ft.

A. h. 'Wayside'. Taller growing, to 4 ft., while spreading to 8 ft. and more. Trailing branches take root. May be slow to fill in; eventually dense, attractive mound.

A. manzanita. COMMON MANZANITA. Tall shrub or treelike shrub. Zones 4–9, 14–24. Native to inner Coast Ranges, Sierra Nevada foothills. Widely adapted. Grows 6–20 ft. high, spreads 4–10 ft. wide. Crooked picturesque branching habit; purplish red bark. Shiny bright green to dull green, broadly oval leaves, ¾–1½ in. long. Flowers white to pink in open, drooping clusters. Fruit white turning to deep red.

A. m. 'Dr. Hurd'. Treelike form to 15 ft. tall, as wide or wider. Mahogany bark; large, light green leaves; white flowers January–March. Good garden tolerance; subject to salt burn.

A. media. Zones 4–9, 14–24. May be a natural hybrid of *A. uva-ursi* and *A. columbiana.* As far as gardener is concerned, it's a higher-growing *A. uva-ursi* (to 2 ft.) with brighter red branches and leathery dark green leaves. Spreads faster than *A. uva-ursi.*

A. nummularia. FORT BRAGG MANZANITA. Zones 14–24. Low-growing (6–18 in., rarely taller), densely foliaged shrub with small bright green leaves, small white flowers. Attractive, but considered difficult outside its native north coastal California forests. Needs good drainage, acid soil, and shade except near coast.

A. pumila. DUNE MANZANITA. Zone 17. Native to dunes around Monterey Bay, California. Spreading, prostrate habit, to 1–2½ ft. high. Roots freely where branches touch ground. Leaves dull green, narrowish, ½–1 in. long. Short, dense clusters of small white to pink flowers. Good ground cover in sandy soil near coast.

A. 'Sunset'. Zones 6–9, 14–24. Natural hybrid between *A. hookeri* and *A. pajaroensis* from Monterey County, California. New foliage coppery red, turning bright green. Makes mound 4–5 ft. tall by 4–6 ft. wide. Pinkish white flowers in March–April.

A. uva-ursi. BEARBERRY, KINNIKINNICK. Zones 1–9, 14–24. Native from San Mateo County, California, north to Alaska. Also widespread in other northern latitudes. Long a popular ground cover in Pacific Northwest and intermountain areas. Prostrate, spreading and rooting as it creeps to 15 ft. wide; glossy, bright green, leathery leaves to 1 in., turning red in winter. Flowers white or pinkish. Fruit bright red or pink. A most useful plant in Northwest: for slopes too steep for lawn, as trailing mat atop wall, combining with mugho pines, yews. Slowness in starting causes weed problems. Mulch with peat moss or sawdust to keep down weeds, and keep soil moist for root growth and rooting of branches. Good on hillsides, near coast.

A. u. 'Alaska'. Flat grower with small, round, dark green leaves.

A. u. 'Massachusetts'. Like 'Alaska', this is small leafed, flat growing. Good resistance to leaf spot and leaf gall in Northwest.

A. u. 'Point Reyes'. Dark green leaves are closely set along branches. More tolerant of heat and drought than *A. u.* 'Radiant'.

A. u. 'Radiant'. Leaves lighter green than those of *A. u.* 'Point Reyes', more widely spaced. Heavy crop of large bright red fruit in autumn, lasting into winter; sometimes fails to fruit if pollinating insects not active at bloom time.

ARCTOTHECA calendula. *Compositae.* CAPE WEED. Evergreen perennial. Zones 8, 9, 13–24. Rapid running ground cover, less than 1 ft. tall, with yellow daisy flowers 2 in. across most of year, peaking March through June. Gray green, deeply divided leaves. Full sun; not fussy about soil or irrigation practices. Needs little water once established. Space 1½ ft. apart for fast cover. Some frost damage in high 20s, but quick recovery. Not for small areas; good on hillsides.

Arctotheca calendula

ARCTOTIS. *Compositae.* AFRICAN DAISY. Annuals and perennials, the latter usually grown as annuals but hardy Zones 7–9, 14–24. "African daisy" can refer to any of several plants; names and identities of the plants are often confused, even by seedsmen and nurserymen. African daisies in *Arctotis* have lobed leaves that are rough, hairy, or woolly; their flower heads usually have contrasting ring of color around central eye. African daisies in *Dimorphotheca* (common for winter mass flower color) are annuals with smooth green foliage and flowers in the yellow-orange-salmon range, or white. Trailing ground cover African daisies and woody, shrubby white, yellow, or purple African daisies are *Osteospermum.* All do best with full sun and light soil; need little water except when in active growth.

Arctotis acaulis

A. acaulis. Perennial. Spreading, stemless clumps of leaves; flower heads to 3½ in. wide on 6-in.-long stalks are yellow with purplish black centers.

A. breviscapa. Annual, somewhat smaller than *A. acaulis,* with orange yellow, brown-centered flowers.

A. hybrids. Most garden plants are hybrids 1–1½ ft. tall. Three-inch flowers come in white, pink, red, purplish, cream, yellow, and orange, usually with dark ring around nearly black eye spot. In mild climates plants make growth in winter and early spring, bloom from spring into early summer, with scattered bloom later. They will self-sow, but tend to revert to orange. You can perpetuate colors you like by taking cuttings. Plants survive as perennials in mildest climates, but bloom best in their first year.

A. stoechadifolia grandis. Bushy annual to 2 ft., with gray green, slightly hairy leaves and 3-in. white daisies in which yellow ring surrounds deep blue central eye.

ARDISIA. *Myrsinaceae.* Evergreen shrubs or shrublets.

A. crenata (A. crenulata, A. crispa). Usually grown indoors. Most familiar as 1½-ft. single-stemmed pot plant. In large tub it can reach 4 ft. with nearly equal spread. In spring, spirelike clusters of tiny (¼-in.) white or pinkish flowers are carried above shiny, wavy-edged, 3-in.-long leaves. Flowers are followed by brilliant scarlet fruit in autumn and usually through winter. Routine house plant care.

Ardisia japonica

A. japonica. Zones 5, 6, 15–17. Low shrub that spreads as ground cover by rhizomes to produce succession of upright branches 6–18 in. high. Leathery, bright green leaves (4 in. long) are clustered at tips of branches. White, ¼-in. flowers, 2–6 in cluster, appear in fall, followed by small (¼-in.), round, bright red fruits that last into winter. Makes quality ground cover in shade. Needs ample water.

ARECA lutescens. See *Chrysalidocarpus lutescens.*

ARECASTRUM romanzoffianum. (Often sold as *Cocos plumosa.*) *Palmae.* QUEEN PALM. Zones 12, 13, 15–17, 19–24. South America. Exceptionally straight trunk to 50 ft. tall; arching, bright green, glossy, feather-type leaves 10–15 ft. long are subject to breakage in high wind. Fast grower, responding quickly to water and fertilizer. Very subject to mites; wash frequently. Damaged at 25°F., but has recovered from 16°F. freeze.

Arecastrum romanzoffianum

ARENARIA. *Caryophyllaceae.* SANDWORT. Perennial ground covers. Zones 2–9, 14–24. Low evergreen plants carpet ground with dense mats of mosslike foliage, have small white flowers in late spring and summer. They are often used as lawn substitutes, between stepping stones, or for velvety green patches in rock gardens. Can be invasive, hard to eradicate in well-watered gardens.

Arenaria montana

A. balearica. CORSICAN SANDWORT. Forms dense mat to 3 in. high. Leaves oval, thick, glossy, to ⅛ in. long. Grows best in shade with lots of water. Adapted to planting in small areas such as carpet at base of container-grown tree.

A. montana. Grows 2–4 in. high, with weak stems up to 1 ft. long usually covered with soft hairs. Leaves grayish, ½–¾ in. long. White flowers, 1 in. across, profuse in June. Good plant to let trail over sunny rock or tumble over low wall. Moderate water requirements.

A. verna (A. caespitosa). See *Sagina subulata.*

ARGEMONE. *Papaveraceae.* PRICKLY POPPY. Annuals or biennials. All Zones. Prickly-leafed, prickly-stemmed plants with large, showy poppy flowers. Native to desert or dry areas, Wyoming to Mexico and west to California. Grow easily from seed sown where plants are to bloom, or from seed sown in pots for gentle transplanting. Need sun and good drainage. Bloom mostly in summer. To 3 ft. Extremely drought tolerant.

Argemone mexicana

A. intermedia. See *A. polyanthemos.*

A. mexicana. Annual. Yellow to orange flowers.

A. platyceras. Annual. White flowers. Most common kind.

A. polyanthemos (A. intermedia). Annual or biennial. White flowers.

ARISTOLOCHIA. *Aristolochiaceae.* Deciduous or evergreen vines. Curiously shaped flowers in rather sober colors resemble curved pipes with flared bowls.

A. californica. CALIFORNIA DUTCHMAN'S PIPE. Deciduous. Zones 7–9, 14–24. Native to Coast Ranges and Sierra Nevada foothills of northern California. Will cover 8- by 12-ft. screen with some training, or climb by long thin shoots 10–16 ft. into nearby tree. Flower display before leaves, late January to April. Pendulous, 1-in.-long flowers are cream colored with red purple veins at maturity. Bright green, heart-shaped leaves to 5 in. long. Grows from seed or from

A

rooted shoots around base of vine. Interesting and useful where many less hardy vines would freeze. Accepts any soil, but needs partial shade and ample moisture.

Aristolochia elegans

A. durior. DUTCHMAN'S PIPE. Deciduous. All Zones. Native to eastern United States. Will cover 15 by 20 ft. in one season. Easily grown from seed. Large, 6–14-in.-long, kidney-shaped, deep green glossy leaves are carried in shinglelike pattern to form dense cover on trellis. June and July flowers, with yellowish green, 3-in., curved tube, flare into 3 brownish purple lobes about 1 in. wide; flowers almost hidden by leaves. Thrives in full sun or heavy shade. No special care. Generous feeding and watering will speed growth. Cut back in winter if too heavy. Short lived in warm-winter areas. Will not stand strong winds.

A. elegans. CALICO FLOWER. Outdoors in Zones 23, 24; house or greenhouse plant elsewhere. Twining evergreen vine to 6 ft. or more. Wiry, slender stems; heart-shaped leaves 3 in. long. Whitish buds shaped like little pelicans open to 3-in.-wide, heart-shaped flowers of deep purple veined creamy white. Needs rich soil, moisture, partial shade.

Aristolochiaceae. This family includes the previous plants and *Asarum,* the wild gingers. All display odd-shaped flowers in low-key colors.

ARMERIA. *Plumbaginaceae.* THRIFT, SEA PINK. Hardy evergreen perennials. All Zones. Narrow, stiff leaves grow in compact tufts or basal rosettes; small white, pink, rose or red flowers in dense globular heads from early spring to late fall. Sturdy, dependable plants for edging walks or borders and for tidy mounds in rock gardens, raised beds. Attractive in containers. Need full sun; not fussy about water if drainage is excellent. Shear flowers after bloom. Feed once a year with slow-acting fertilizer. Propagate by divisions or from seeds in spring or fall.

Armeria maritima

A. juniperifolia *(A. caespitosa).* Native to mountains of Spain. Stiff, needle-shaped leaves ½ in. long in low, extremely compact rosettes. Flowers rose pink or white in dense, round clusters on 2-in. stems. This little mountain native is very touchy about drainage; apply mulch of fine gravel around plants to prevent basal stem rot, especially in summer.

A. maritima *(Statice armeria, Armeria vulgaris).* COMMON THRIFT. Tufted mounds spreading to 1 ft. with 6-in.-long, stiff, grasslike leaves. Small white to rose pink flowers in tight, round clusters at top of 6–10-in. stalks. Blooms almost all year along coast; flowers profusely in spring in other areas.

ARONIA. *Rosaceae.* CHOKEBERRY. Deciduous shrubs. Zones 1–7. Native to eastern U.S. and Canada. Spreading, suckering habit to 10 ft. Extremely tolerant of cold, heat, wind, damp soil. Leaves narrow ovals to 3 in. long, half as wide, dark green above, whitish beneath. White- or pink-tinged, ½-in.-wide flowers in 2-in. clusters, April or May. Fruit showy, long lasting, appealing to birds. Foliage is attractive in summer, spectacular in fall. Increase by seeds, cuttings, or division.

Aronia arbutifolia

A. arbutifolia. RED CHOKEBERRY. Bright red, ¼-in. fruits ripen in September, matching red fall leaf color.

A. melanocarpa. BLACK CHOKEBERRY. Glossy black fruits, somewhat larger than those of red chokeberry.

ARTEMISIA. *Compositae.* Evergreen or deciduous shrubs or woody perennials. All Zones. Several species are valuable for interesting leaf patterns and silvery gray or white aromatic foliage; others are aromatic herbs. Plant in full sun. Drought resistant. Keep on dry side. Divide in spring and fall. Most kinds excellent for use in mixed border where white or silvery leaves soften harsh reds or oranges and blend beautifully with blues, lavenders, and pinks.

Artemisia dracunculus

A. abrotanum. SOUTHERNWOOD, OLD MAN. Deciduous shrub. To 3–5 ft. Beautiful lemon-scented, green, feathery foliage; yellowish white flower heads. Use for pleasantly scented foliage in shrub border. Hang sprigs in closet to discourage moths. Burn a few leaves on stove to kill cooking odors.

A. absinthium. COMMON WORMWOOD. Evergreen woody perennial. To 2–4 ft. Silvery gray, finely divided leaves with bitter taste, pungent odor. Minute yellow flowers. Keep pruned to get better-shaped plant. Divide every 3 years. Background shrub. Good gray feature in flower border, particularly fine with delphiniums. Leaves used to flavor wine, season poultry; also for medicinal uses.

Artemisia abrotanum

A. californica. CALIFORNIA SAGEBRUSH. Native to coast, northern California to Baja California. Finely divided grayish white leaves on stems 1½–5 ft. tall. Drought tolerant once established; loses leaves in extreme drought. 'Canyon Gray' is a compact, silvery white selection.

A. cana. Native east of the Sierra-Cascade divide. Evergreen shrub 1½–3 ft. tall with narrow, silvery green leaves. Extremely hardy to drought, cold.

A. caucasica. SILVER SPREADER. Evergreen shrublet 3–6 in. tall, spreading to 2 ft. in width. Silky, silvery green foliage; small yellow flowers. Bank or ground cover. Needs good drainage, requires little, if any, summer water. Takes extremes of heat and cold, is fire retardant. Plant 1–2 ft. apart.

A. dracunculus. FRENCH TARRAGON, TRUE TARRAGON. Perennial. To 1–2 ft.; spreads slowly by creeping rhizomes. Creeping habit. Shiny dark green, narrow leaves—very aromatic. Woody stems. Flowers greenish white in branched clusters. Dies to ground in winter. Attractive container plant. Cut sprigs in June for seasoning vinegar. Use fresh or dried leaves to season salads, egg and cheese dishes, fish. Divide plant every 3 or 4 years to keep it vigorous. Propagate by divisions or by cuttings. Plants grown from seed are not true culinary tarragon.

A. frigida. FRINGED WORMWOOD. Perennial. To 1–1½ ft. with white, finely cut leaves. Small yellow flowers in late August. Young plants compact. Cut back when they become rangy.

A. lactiflora. WHITE MUGWORT. Border perennial. Tall, straight column to 4–5 ft. One of few artemisias with attractive flowers: creamy white in large, branched, 1½-ft. sprays, August–September. Leaves dark green with broad, tooth-edged lobes.

A. ludoviciana albula *(A. albula).* SILVER KING ARTEMISIA. Bushy perennial. To 2–3½ ft., with slender, spreading branches. Silvery white, 2-in. leaves, the lower ones with 3–5 lobes, upper ones narrow, unlobed. Cut foliage useful in arrangements.

A. pontica. ROMAN WORMWOOD. Shrub. To 4 ft. Feathery, silver gray leaves. Heads of nodding, whitish yellow flowers in long, open, branched clusters. Leaves used in sachets.

A. pycnocephala. SANDHILL SAGE. Shrubby perennial. Native to beaches of northern California. Erect, rounded, somewhat spreading; 1–2 ft. tall. Soft, silvery white or gray leaves, crowded, divided into narrow lobes. Very small yellow flowers. Remove flower spikes as they open to keep plants compact. Becomes unkempt with age. Replace every 2 years.

A. schmidtiana. ANGEL'S HAIR. Perennial. Forms dome, 2 ft. high

A

and 1 ft. wide, of woolly, silvery white, finely cut leaves. Flowers insignificant. Variety 'Silver Mound' is 1 ft. high.

A. stellerana. BEACH WORMWOOD, OLD WOMAN, DUSTY MILLER. Woody perennial. Dense, silvery gray plant to 2½ ft. with 1–4-in., lobed leaves. Hardier than *Senecio cineraria* (another dusty miller), this artemisia is often used in its place in colder climates. Yellow flowers in spikelike clusters.

A. tridentata. BIG SAGEBRUSH. Evergreen shrub. Native to Great Basin region of the West. Grows 1½–15 ft. high. Many branches. Narrow, hairy gray leaves ¾ in. long, usually 3 toothed at tip, very aromatic. Insignificant flowers. Sagebrush that gives pungent fragrance for which western deserts are known. Of limited landscape use, but grows easily in any sunny, well-drained spot.

ARTICHOKE. *Compositae.* Perennial vegetable with landscape value. Grow as dependable perennial crop in Zones 8, 9, 14–24. Anywhere else, plant in spring when offered and hope for the best—you'll get foliage, maybe flowers, and a crop if you're lucky. A big ferny-looking plant with irregular, somewhat fountainlike form—to 4 ft. high, 6–8 ft. wide. Leaves are silvery green. Big flower buds form at tops of stalks: they are the artichokes you cook and eat. If not cut, buds open into spectacular purple blue, 6-in. thistlelike flowers which can be cut for arrangements.

Artichoke

In California's cool-summer coast (Zone 17), where it is grown commercially, artichoke can be both handsome ornamental plant and a producer of fine, tender artichokes from September to May or all year. In climate Zones 8, 9, 14–16, 18–24, plant grows luxuriantly at least from spring through fall, and edible buds come as extra dividend in early summer only. In colder winter climates artichoke is rarity and must be protected through winter to keep roots and shoots alive.

Plant dormant roots or plants from containers in winter or early spring, setting root shanks vertically with buds or shoots just above soil line. Space plants 4–6 ft. apart in full sun. After growth starts, water thoroughly once a week, wetting entire root system. If grown only for ornamental value, can tolerate much drought, going dormant in summer heat. Spray to control aphids; after buds start to form use just strong jet sprays of water to blast off aphids (no insecticides then). Bait to control snails and slugs. For gopher control, plant in raised beds with wire-mesh bottoms or in large containers. Harvest buds while they are still tight and plump. Cut off old stalks near ground level when leaves begin to yellow. In cold-winter areas, cut tops to 1 ft. in fall, tie them over root crown and mulch heavily to protect from frost.

ARTILLERY PLANT. See *Pilea microphylla.*

ARUM. *Araceae.* Perennials with tuberous roots. Zones 4–24. Arrow-shaped or heart-shaped leaves. Curious callalike blossoms on short stalks. Flower bract half encloses thick, fleshy spike which bears tiny flowers. Require shade, rich soil, ample moisture. Use in flower borders where hardy; as indoor plants in cold-winter climates.

A. cornutum. See *Sauromatum.*

A. italicum. ITALIAN ARUM. Arrow-shaped leaves, 8 in. long and wide, veined with white. Very short stem; white or greenish white (sometimes purple-spotted) flowers in spring and early summer. Bract first stands erect, then folds over and conceals short yellow spike. Dense clusters of bright red fruit follow. These last long after leaves have faded and are the most conspicuous feature of the plant. They resemble small, bright red ears of shucked corn.

Arum italicum

A. palaestinum. BLACK CALLA. Leaves 6–8 in. long. Also has arrow-shaped flower bract about same length, greenish outside, blackish purple within, curved back, revealing the blackish purple spike; spring and early summer.

A. pictum. Light green, heart-shaped, 10-in.-long leaves on 10-in. stalks appear in spring. Flower bract is violet, green at base. Spike purplish black.

ARUNDINARIA. See *Bamboo.*

ARUNDO donax. *Gramineae.* GIANT REED. Perennial. All Zones. One of largest grasses, planted for bold effects in garden fringe areas or by watersides. Also planted in hot-summer climates as quick windbreak or erosion control. Often called a bamboo. Strong, somewhat woody stems, 6–20 ft. high. Leaves to 2 ft. long, flat, 3 in. wide. Flowers in rather narrow, erect clusters to 2 ft. high. *A. d.* 'Versicolor' (*A. d.* 'Variegata') has leaves with white or yellowish stripes. Needs rich, moist soil. Protect roots with mulch in cold-winter areas. Cut out dead stems and thin occasionally to get look-through quality. Extremely invasive; plant only where you can control it. Can become a pest in irrigation ditches. Stems have some utility as plant stakes or, if woven together with wire, as fencing or shade canopy.

Arundo donax

ASARUM caudatum. *Aristolochiaceae.* WILD GINGER. Perennial. Zones 4–6, 14–24. Native to woods of Coast Ranges, mainly in redwood belt from Santa Cruz Mountains to Del Norte County, north to British Columbia. Remarkably handsome ground cover for shade, forming a lush, lustrous dark green carpet of heart-shaped leaves 2–7 in. across, 7–10 in. high. Reddish brown flowers, bell shaped with long tails, produced close to ground under leaves; bloom in spring.

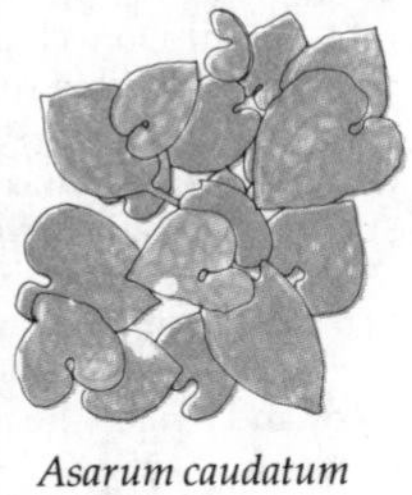

Asarum caudatum

Grows in average soil with heavy watering but spreads faster, is more luxuriant in rich soil with ample humus. Start from divisions or from container-grown plants. Protect from slugs and snails.

Asclepiadaceae. Best-known family members are the milkweeds (*Asclepias*), but other garden plants also belong to this group, among them many succulents and some perennials and vines, including stephanotis.

ASCLEPIAS. *Asclepiadaceae.* Perennials or shrubs. Milkweeds are best-known representatives. Just a few are grown as garden plants. Full sun, average soil and water.

A. fruticosa ***(Gomphocarpus fruticosus)*** and **A. physocarpa** ***(G. physocarpus).*** SWAN PLANT, GOOSE PLANT. Shrubby perennials. Zones 14–24. These 2 very similar plants sometimes volunteer in gardens. Plants are occasionally sold for fat, puffy, pale green inflated seed pods with curving stems like swans' necks. Fruits have covering of soft, fleshy prickles. Stripped of leaves and dried, stems make striking arrangements. Plants are narrowly upright, 3–6 ft. tall, and the many stems are clothed with gray green, willowlike leaves. Flowers are not showy.

Asclepias fruticosa

A. tuberosa. BUTTERFLY WEED. All Zones. Many stems to 3 ft. rise every year from perennial root. Broad clusters of bright orange flowers appear in midsummer, attract swarms of butterflies. Hardy anywhere; prefers good drainage and little summer water. Native to eastern U.S.

ASH. See *Fraxinus.*

ASH, MOUNTAIN. See *Sorbus.*

ASPARAGUS, EDIBLE. *Liliaceae.* Perennial vegetable. All Zones. One of most permanent and dependable of home garden vegetables. Plants take 2–3 years to come into full production, but then furnish delicious spears every spring for 10–15 years. They take up considerable space, but do so in the grand manner; plants are tall, feathery, graceful, highly ornamental. Use asparagus along sunny fence or as background for flowers or vegetables.

Edible Asparagus

Seeds grow into strong young plants in one season (sow in spring), but roots are far more widely used. Set out seedlings or roots (not wilted, no smaller than man's hand) in fall or winter (mild climates), or early spring (cold winters). Make trenches 1 ft. wide and 8–10 in. deep. Space trenches 4–6 ft. apart. Heap loose, manure-enriched soil at bottom of trenches and soak. Set roots so that tops are 6–8 in. below surface. Space them 1 ft. apart. Spread roots out evenly. Cover with 2 in. of soil and water again.

As young plants grow, gradually fill in trench, taking care not to cover growing tips. Soak deeply whenever soil begins to dry out at root depth. Don't harvest any spears the first year; object at this time is to build big root mass. When plants turn brown in late fall or early winter, cut stems to ground. In cold-winter areas, permit dead stalks to stand until spring; they will help trap and hold snow, which will furnish protection to root crowns.

The following spring you can cut your first spears; cut only for 4–6 weeks, or until appearance of thin spears indicates that roots are nearing exhaustion. Then permit plants to grow. Cultivate, feed, and irrigate heavily. The third year you should be able to cut spears for 8–10 weeks. Spears are ready to cut when they are 5–8 in. long. Thrust knife down at 45° angle to soil; flat cutting may injure adjacent developing spears. If asparagus beetle appears during cutting season, control with rotenone or (carefully noting label precautions) malathion. After cutting season, spray with any all-purpose insecticide. Use bait to control snails and slugs; use sevin, dibrom, or diazinon for earwigs or cutworms.

ASPARAGUS, ORNAMENTAL. *Liliaceae.* Perennials. Outdoors in Zones 12–24, house plants anywhere. There are about 150 kinds of asparagus besides edible one—all members of lily family. Best known of ornamental kinds is the fern asparagus (*A. setaceus*)—not a true fern. Although valued mostly for their handsome foliage of unusual textural quality, some have small but fragrant flowers and colorful berries. Green foliage sprays are made up of what look like leaves (needle-like or broader). Actually they are short branches called cladodes. True leaves are inconspicuous dry scales.

Asparagus densiflorus 'Sprengeri'

Most ornamental asparagus look greenest in part shade, but thrive in sun near coast. Leaves turn yellow in dense shade. Plant in well-drained soil to which peat moss or ground bark has been added. Because of fleshy roots, plants can withstand some drought, but grow better with ample water. Feed in spring with complete fertilizer. Trim out old shoots to make room for new growth. Will survive light frosts but may be killed to ground by severe cold. Frosted plants often come back from roots.

A. asparagoides. SMILAX ASPARAGUS. Much-branched vine with spineless stems to 20 ft. or more. Often seen in older gardens. Leaves to 1 in. long, sharp pointed, stiffish, glossy grass green. Small, fragrant white flowers in spring, followed by blue berries. Birds feed on berries, drop seeds which sprout at random about the garden. (Plant also self-sows readily.) Roots are clusters of fleshy thongs and are nearly immortal, surviving long drought and sprouting when rains come. Foliage sprays prized for table decoration. If it gets little water, plant dies back in summer, revives with fall rains. Becomes tangled mass unless trained. Variety 'Myrtifolius', commonly called baby smilax, is a more graceful form with smaller leaves.

A. crispus (often sold as *A. scandens* 'Deflexus'). BASKET ASPARAGUS. Airy, graceful plant for hanging baskets. Drooping, zigzag stems have bright green, 3-angled leaves in whorls of three.

A. densiflorus 'Myers' (sometimes sold as *A. meyeri* or *A. myersii*). MYERS ASPARAGUS. Plants send up several to many stiffly upright stems to 2 ft. or more, densely clothed with needlelike deep green leaves. Plants have fluffy look. Good in containers. A little less hardy than Sprenger asparagus.

A. d. 'Sprengeri' (sometimes sold as *A. sprengeri*). SPRENGER ASPARAGUS. Arching or drooping stems 3–6 ft. long. Shiny, bright green needlelike leaves, 1 in. long, in bundles. Bright red berries. Popular for hanging baskets or containers, indoors and out. Train on trellis; climbs by means of small hooked prickles. Used as billowy ground cover where temperatures stay above 24°F. Takes full sun as well as part shade; grows in ordinary or even poor soil. Will tolerate dryness of indoors but needs bright light. Form sold as *A. d.* 'Sprengeri Compacta' or *A. sarmentosus* 'Compacta' is denser with shorter stems.

A. falcatus. SICKLE-THORN ASPARAGUS. Derives common name from curved thorns along stems by which it climbs to 40 ft. in its native area (in gardens usually grows to 10 ft.). Leaves 2–3 in. long in clusters of 3–5 at ends of branches. Tiny, white, fragrant flowers in loose clusters. Brown berries. Rapid growing. Excellent foliage mass to cover fence or wall, or provide shade for a pergola or lathhouse. Foliage resembles that of *Podocarpus macrophyllus.*

A. meyeri, A. myersii. See *A. densiflorus* 'Myers'.

A. officinalis. See Asparagus, Edible.

A. plumosus. See *A. setaceus.*

A. retrofractus. Erect, shrubby, slightly climbing, very tender. Slender, silvery gray stems grow slowly to 8–10 ft. high. Leaves threadlike, 1 in. long, in fluffy, rich green tufts. Clusters of small white flowers. Handsome in containers; useful in flower arrangements. Cut foliage lasts 10 days out of water, several weeks in water. *A. myriocladus* and *A. macowanii* are either similar or identical.

A. sarmentosus. See *A. densiflorus* 'Sprengeri Compacta'.

A. scandens. BASKET ASPARAGUS. Slender, branching vine climbing to 6 ft. Deep green needlelike leaves on zigzag, drooping stems. Greenish white flowers ⅛ in. long. Scarlet berries.

A. scandens 'Deflexus'. See *A. crispus.*

A. setaceus *(A. plumosus).* FERN ASPARAGUS. Sometimes called EMERALD FEATHER. Branching woody vine climbs by wiry, spiny stems to 10–20 ft. Tiny threadlike leaves form feathery dark green sprays that resemble fern fronds. Tiny white flowers. Berries purple black. Dense, fine-textured foliage mass useful as screen against walls, fences. Florists use foliage as fillers in bouquets; holds up better than delicate ferns. Dwarf variety 'Nanus' is good in containers. 'Pyramidalis' has upswept, windblown look, is less vigorous than common fern asparagus.

A. sprengeri. See *A. densiflorus* 'Sprengeri'.

ASPEN. See *Populus.*

ASPEN DAISY. See *Erigeron speciosus macranthus.*

ASPERULA odorata. See *Galium odoratum.*

ASPIDISTRA elatior ***(A. lurida).*** *Liliaceae.* CAST-IRON PLANT. Evergreen perennial. Zones 4–9, 12–24, also house plant. Sturdy, long-lived foliage plant remarkable for its ability to thrive under conditions unacceptable to most kinds of plants. Leaf blades 1–2½ ft. long, 3–4 in. wide, tough, glossy dark green and arching, with distinct parallel veins; each blade supported by a 6–8-in.-long, grooved leaf stalk. Inconspicuous brownish flowers bloom in spring close to ground. Although extremely tolerant, requiring minimal care, aspidistra grows best in porous soil enriched with organic matter, and responds to feeding in spring and summer. Will grow in dark, shaded areas (under decks or stairs) anywhere, as well as in filtered sun—except in Zones 12 and 13, where it takes full shade only. Keep leaves dust free and glossy by hosing them off, or clean with soft brush or cloth. Average water best; tolerates some drought.

Aspidistra elatior

Variegated form (*A. elatior* 'Variegata') has leaves striped with white, loses its variegation if planted in soil that's too rich.

ASPIDIUM capense. See *Rumohra adiantiformis.*

ASPLENIUM. *Polypodiaceae.* Ferns. Widespread and variable group. Need shade, liberal watering.

A. bulbiferum. MOTHER FERN. Outdoors Zones 14 (protected), 15–17, 20–24; house plant elsewhere. From New Zealand. Graceful, very finely cut light green fronds to 4 ft. tall. Fronds produce plantlets which can be removed and planted. Heavy or medium shade. Hardy to 26°F. Watch for snails and slugs.

Asplenium bulbiferum

A. daucifolium ***(A. viviparum).*** House plant. Similar to *A. bulbiferum* but smaller (to 2 ft.), with more finely divided fronds. Also makes plantlets.

A. nidus ***(A. nidus-avis).*** BIRD'S NEST FERN. House plant. Tender fern with showy, apple green, undivided fronds to 4 ft. long, 8 in. wide, growing upright in cluster. Striking foliage plant; best as container plant to be grown indoors in winter, on shady patio in summer. One snail or slug can ruin a frond.

Asplenium nidus

ASTER. *Compositae.* Perennials. All Zones. (For the common annual or China aster, sold in flats at nurseries, see *Callistephus.*) There are over 600 species of true asters, ranging from alpine kinds forming compact mounds 6 in. high to open-branching plants 6 ft. tall. Flowers come in white or shades of blue, red, pink, lavender, or purple, mostly with yellow centers. Most asters bloom in summer and fall; some hybrids start flowering in spring. Taller asters are invaluable for abundant color in large borders or among shrubs. Large sprays effective in arrangements. Compact dwarf or cushion types make tidy edgings, mounds of color in rock gardens, good container plants.

Aster frikartii

Plant in full sun. Adapted to most soils. Need routine care, although more luxuriant in fertile soil with regular watering. Resistant to insects and diseases, except for mildew on leaves in late fall. Strong-growing asters have invasive roots, need control. Divide clumps yearly in late fall or early spring. Replant vigorous young divisions from outside of clump; discard old center. Divide smaller, tufted, less vigorously growing kinds every 2 years.

A. alpinus. Mounding plant 6–12 in. tall. Leaves ½–5 in. long, mostly in basal tuft. Several stems grow from basal clump, each carrying one violet blue flower 1½–2 in. across; May–June bloom. Best in cold-winter areas.

A. amellus. ITALIAN ASTER. Sturdy, drought-resistant, hairy plant to 2 ft. Branching stems with violet, yellow-centered flowers 2 in. across.

A. dumosus. BUSHY ASTER. To 2–3 ft. Narrow leaves 3 in. long. Blue or white flowers ½ in. across. Widely used in developing lower-growing varieties, commonly called dwarf Michaelmas daisies, invaluable as low border plants.

A. frikartii. One of the finest, most useful and widely adapted perennials. Hybrid between *A. amellus* and *A. thomsonii,* a hairy-leafed, lilac-flowered, 3-ft. species native to the Himalayas. Abundant clear lavender to violet blue single flowers are 2½ in. across. Open, spreading growth to 2 ft. high. Blooms May–October—almost all year in mild-winter areas if dead flowers are removed regularly. 'Wonder of Stafa' is most common variety; scarce 'Mönch' is better.

A. fruticosus. See *Felicia fruticosa.*

A. novae-angliae. NEW ENGLAND ASTER. Stout-stemmed plant to 3–5 ft. with hairy leaves to 5 in. long. Flowers deep purple, 2 in. across. Good in wet areas.

A. novi-belgii. NEW YORK ASTER. To 3 ft., similar to New England aster, but with smooth leaves. Full clusters of bright blue violet flowers.

Michaelmas daisy is the name applied to hybrids of *A. novae-angliae* and *A. novi-belgii.* They are tall (3–4-ft.), graceful, branching plants. Many horticultural varieties with flowers in white, pale to deep pink, rose, red, and many shades of blue, violet, and purple.

Oregon-Pacific asters, hybrids between a dwarf species native to the West and some well-known Michaelmas daisies, are splendid garden plants. Dwarf, intermediate, taller forms range in height from under 1 ft. to 2½ ft. Compact, floriferous, blooming late spring to fall. Many named varieties available in white, blue, lavender, purple, rose, pink, cream.

A. yunnanensis 'Napsbury'. An improved garden variety of this Chinese species. Leaves dark green in basal tufts. Stems to 1½ ft., each bearing a single lavender blue, orange-centered flower. Blooms in summer.

ASTILBE. *Saxifragaceae.* FALSE SPIRAEA, MEADOW SWEET. Perennials. Zones 2–7, 14–17 (short lived in Zones 8, 9, 18–24). Valued for light, airy quality of plumelike flower clusters and attractive foliage, ability to provide color from May through July. Leaves divided, with toothed or cut leaflets; leaves in some species simply lobed with cut margins. Small white, pink, or red flowers in graceful, branching clusters held on slender, wiry stems from 6 in. to 3 ft. or higher.

Astilbe Hybrid

Most astilbes sold in nurseries are hybrids. There are many varieties, but most nurseries stock only a few. Some of best are: 'Avalanche', 2 ft., white flowers; 'Betsy Cuperus', 2½ ft., pale pink flowers; 'Deutschland', 2 ft., creamy white flowers; 'Fanal', 2 ft., bronzy foliage, garnet red flowers; 'Glow', 2 ft., ruby red flowers; 'Rheinland', 2 ft., bright pink flowers; 'Straussenfeder', 2½ ft., drooping, arching, coral pink flowers.

Plant in sun or shade depending on light intensity of climate zone. Needs cool, moist soil, rich in humus. Cut back after flowering. Divide clumps every 4–5 years. Combine in shade gardens with columbine, meadow rue, plantain lily, bergenia; in sunnier situations with peonies, delphiniums, iris. Often planted at edge of pools. Good in pots and tubs.

A. chinensis 'Pumila'. Low mats of leaves make 4-in.-deep ground cover. In summer, lilac pink flower clusters to 12–15 in.

A. taquetii. To 4 ft. tall, with pinkish purple flowers in erect, dense clusters. Blooms late summer. 'Superba' is best form.

ATHEL TREE. See *Tamarix aphylla.*

A

ATHYRIUM. *Polypodiaceae.* Ferns. Zones 1–9, 14–24. Evergreen in mildest areas, these ferns turn brown after repeated frosts. Leave dead fronds on plant as mulch and to shelter emerging fronds in early spring, then cut back. Prefer rich, damp soil, shade. Propagate by dividing old clumps in early spring.

Athyrium filix-femina

A. filix-femina. LADY FERN. Grows to 4 ft. or more. Rootstock rises up on older plants to make short trunk. Vertical effect, narrow at bottom, spreading at top. Thin fronds, finely divided. Vigorous; can be invasive. Specialists stock many varieties with oddly cut and feathered fronds.

A. nipponicum 'Pictum' (***A. goeringianum*** 'Pictum'). JAPANESE PAINTED FERN. Fronds grow to 1½ ft. long, making a tight, slowly spreading clump. Leaflets are purplish at base, then lavender, then silvery greenish gray toward ends.

ATRIPLEX. *Chenopodiaceae.* SALTBUSH. Evergreen or deciduous shrubs. Unusually tolerant of direct seashore conditions or highly alkaline desert soils. Saltbushes are mostly grown for their gray or silvery foliage; flowers and seeds attract birds. Many species useful as fire-retardant plants on arid hillsides of California. Plants char but come back. Because of their fire retardance, drought tolerance, and erosion control, new kinds are likely to appear in desert nurseries.

Atriplex hymenelytra

A. canescens. FOUR-WING SALTBUSH. Evergreen. Zones 2–24. Native throughout much of arid section of West. Fire retardant. Dense growth 3–6 ft. high, spreading to 4–8 ft. Narrow gray leaves ½–2 in. long.

A. hymenelytra. DESERT HOLLY. Evergreen (everwhitish). Zones 3, 7–14, 18, 19. Native to deserts of southern California, western Arizona, southern Nevada, southwestern Utah. Compact shrub 1–3 ft. high with whitish branches and silvery, deeply toothed roundish leaves, to 1½ in. long. Has Christmas holly look—in white. Much used for decorations. Outside its native range, needs very fast soil drainage. Water heavily only February–May.

A. lentiformis. QUAIL BUSH. Deciduous. Zones 7–14, 18, 19. Native to alkali wastes in California valleys and deserts and east to Nevada, Utah, and New Mexico. Densely branched, sometimes spiny shrub, 3–10 ft. high, 6–12 ft. wide. Oval, bluish gray leaves ½–2 in. long. Useful as salt-tolerant hedge or windbreak.

A. l. breweri. BREWER SALTBUSH. Almost evergreen. Zones 8, 9, 14–24. Native to California coast south of San Francisco Bay, inland to Riverside County. Fire retardant. Like quail bush but not spiny. Grows 5–7 ft. high, 6–8 ft. wide; can be hedge sheared. Useful gray plant on ocean front. Will grow in reclaimed marine soil.

A. semibaccata. AUSTRALIAN SALTBUSH. Evergreen. Zones 8, 9, 12–24. Fire retardant. Excellent gray green ground cover spreading to 1–6 ft. and more. Forms dense, foot-tall mat of ½–1½-in.-long leaves. Deep rooted. Plant 3 ft. apart for solid cover.

AUBRIETA deltoidea. *Cruciferae.* COMMON AUBRIETA. Perennial. Zones 1–9, 14–21. Native from east Mediterranean region to Iran. Low, spreading, mat-forming perennial—familiar sight in Northwest and high-elevation rock gardens where it is often seen in bloom in early spring, with basket-of-gold, rockcress (*Arabis*), perennial candytuft (*Iberis*), and *Phlox subulata.* Ideal for chinks in dry stone walls or between patio flagstones. Grows 2–6 in. high, 1–1½ ft. across. Small gray green leaves with a few teeth at top. Tiny rose to deep red, pale to deep lilac, or purple flowers.

Aubrieta deltoidea

Plant in full sun except in hot areas, where light shade is recommended. Needs water before and during bloom. Takes some drought later on. After bloom, shear off flowers before they set seed. Don't cut back more than half—always keep some foliage. After trimming, topdress with mixture of gritty soil and bone meal. Sow seeds in late spring for blooms the following spring. Difficult to divide clumps; make cuttings in late summer.

AUCUBA japonica. *Cornaceae.* JAPANESE AUCUBA. Evergreen shrub. Zones 4–24. Native from Himalayas to Japan. Important shrub to western gardeners. Performs well in deep shade. Seedlings vary in leaf form and variegations; many varieties offered. Standard green-leafed aucuba grows at moderate rate to 6–10 (sometimes 15) ft. and almost as wide. Can be kept lower by pruning. Buxom shrub, densely clothed with polished, dark green, toothed leaves 3–8 in. long, 1½–3 in. wide.

Aucuba japonica

Minute, dark maroon flowers in March are followed by clusters of bright red, ¾-in. berries from October to February. Both sexes must be planted to insure fruit crop.

Green-leafed varieties are: 'Longifolia' ('Salicifolia'), narrow willowlike leaves (female); 'Nana', dwarf female form to about 3 ft.; 'Serratifolia', long leaves, coarsely toothed edges (female).

Variegated varieties (usually slower growing) are: 'Crotonifolia' (male), leaves heavily spotted or splashed with white and gold; 'Fructu Albo' (female), leaves variegated with white, berries pale pinkish buff; 'Picturata' ('Aureo-maculata') (female), leaves centered with golden yellow, edged with dark green dotted yellow; 'Sulphur' (female), green leaves with broad yellow edge; 'Variegata', GOLD DUST PLANT (male or female), dark green leaves spotted with yellow (best-known aucuba).

Tolerant of wide range of soil, but will grow better and look better if poor or heavy soils are improved. Requires shade from hot sun, accepts deep shade. Tolerates low light level under trees, competes successfully with tree roots. Gets mealybug and mites. Prune to control height or form by cutting back to a leaf joint (node). Drought tolerant once established.

All aucubas make choice tub plants for shady patio or in the house. Use variegated forms to light up dark corners. Associate with ferns, hydrangeas.

AURICULA. See *Primula auricula.*

AURINIA saxatilis *(Alyssum saxatile).* *Cruciferae.* BASKET-OF-GOLD. Perennial. All Zones. Stems 8–12 in. high; leaves gray, 2–5 in. long. Dense clusters of tiny golden yellow flowers in spring and early summer. Use as foreground plant in borders, in rock gardens, atop walls. Full sun or light shade, moderate water. Shear lightly (not more than half) right after bloom. Generally hardy, but may be killed in extremely cold winters. Self-sows readily. Varieties include: 'Citrina' ('Lutea'), with pale yellow flowers; 'Compacta', dwarf, tight growing; 'Plena' ('Flore Pleno'), double flowered; 'Silver Queen', compact, with pale yellow flowers.

Aurinia saxatilis

AUSTRALIAN BLUEBELL CREEPER. See *Sollya heterophylla.*

AUSTRALIAN FLAME TREE. See *Brachychiton acerifolius.*

AUSTRALIAN FUCHSIA. See *Correa.*

AUSTRALIAN TEA TREE. See *Leptospermum laevigatum.*

AUSTRALIAN TREE FERN. See *Cyathea cooperi.*

AUSTRALIAN WILLOW. See *Geijera parviflora.*

AUSTRIAN BRIER. See *Rosa foetida.*

AVOCADO. *Lauraceae.* Evergreen trees. In California, 2 races of avocados are grown: Mexican and Guatemalan. (Widely planted 'Fuerte' is thought to be hybrid of the 2.) Guatemalan varieties find ideal climate protected from direct wind in Zones 19, 21, 23, and 24. Mexican varieties, bearing smaller, less attractive fruit, are hardier and grow in Zones 9, 16–24. Although avocados are hardy to 20°–24°F., flowers form in winter and temperatures much below freezing destroy crop. Resistant to oak root fungus.

Avocado

Avocados tend to bear crops in cycles, producing heavy crop one year, light crop the next. (Light crop is generally enough for homeowner.) Consistent bearing varieties are noted below.

When using in landscape, remember that most varieties will grow to 30 ft. and spread wider (tree size can be controlled by pruning). Tree should have best of protection from winds. It drops leaves quite heavily all year. Wide-spreading branches with heavy foliage make dense shade beneath—good garden area for potted plants that need shade. St. Augustine grass will grow beneath avocado trees.

The all-important factor in growing avocados is good drainage. High water table in winter rainy season is often fatal, even in well-drained soils. Build wide basin for watering, let fallen leaves build up there to provide mulch. Most roots are in top 2 ft. of soil, so water lightly and frequently enough to keep that layer moist but not wet (fast drainage is important). Give heavy irrigation every third or fourth time to wash out any excess accumulated salts. This will minimize salt burn. Fertilize lightly. Control chlorosis with iron sulfate or iron chelate.

Fruit of all varieties in following list has thin, pliable, smooth skin unless otherwise noted.

'Bacon'. Mexican. Zones 9, 16, 17, 19–24. Upright grower. Medium-sized green fruit of good quality, November–March. Regular annual crop. Produces when young.

'Duke'. Mexican. Zones 16–22. Large tree. Medium to large green fruit, September–November.

'Fuerte'. Hybrid. Zones 20–24. Large tree; best-known avocado. Early flowers subject to frost in borderline areas. Medium-sized green fruit of high quality, November–June.

'Gwen'. Guatemalan. Zones 19–24. Tree to 20 ft. tall, narrow. Black-skinned fruit ripens February–November.

'Hass'. Guatemalan. Zones 16, 17, 19, 21, 23, 24. Large, spreading tree. Medium to large dark purple (almost black) fruit, April–October. Pebbly skin, thick but pliable.

'Jim'. Mexican. Zones 19–24. Upright growth. Medium-sized fruit with thin green skin. Bears young and regularly, October–January.

'Mexicola'. Mexican. Zones 9, 16–22. Good garden avocado but fruit too small for commercial market. Probably hardiest. Consistent bearer of small, dark purple fruit with thin, tender skin and outstanding nutty flavor, August–October.

'Pinkerton'. Guatemalan. Zones 19–24. Large tree with heavy annual production of large green fruit. Main crop January–April.

'Reed'. Guatemalan. Zones 21–24. Slender upright grower. Medium to large, round, rough-skinned fruit. Bears most years, July–September.

'Rincon'. Guatemalan. Zones 19–24. Low-growing tree. Small green fruit with large seed, ripens January–April. Smooth skin, medium thick, pliable.

'Santana'. Mexican. Zones 9, 19–24. Resembles 'Zutano' but slightly larger; heavy bearer winter–early spring.

'Whitsell'. Guatemalan. Zones 19–24. Tree 10–12 ft. tall. Large black-skinned fruit February–November. Tends to bear in alternate seasons.

'Wurtz'. (Often sold as 'Dwarf', 'Littlecado', and 'Minicado'.) Guatemalan. Small tree (8–10 ft. tall) with slender weeping branches. Medium-sized green fruit in summer; bears young, but not an annual bearer. For small garden or large containers.

'Zutano'. Mexican. Zones 9, 19–24. Upright grower. Pear-shaped fruits, 'Fuerte' size, green, good quality, October–February. In southern California, tends to get "end spot" (brown scaly area at tip of fruit).

AZALEA. See *Rhododendron.*

AZARA. *Flacourtiaceae.* Evergreen shrubs. Most appreciated in Zones 14–17. Best known species is *A. microphylla.* Its flat-branching habit and neatly arranged leaves make it natural for espaliers or as free-standing silhouettes against walls. Other 3 species are quite different, but all 4 have sweetly fragrant yellow flowers that smell like chocolate to some, vanilla to others.

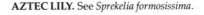

All azaras need protection from hot afternoon sun. All need fast-draining soil, ample water, and regular fertilizing.

Azara microphylla

A. dentata. Zones 15–17. Large shrub or small tree to 15 ft. Inch-wide, toothed, rounded shiny leaves. Dense branching, rounded shape make it useful for screen or hedge. Fluffy yellow spring flowers highly fragrant. Tolerates considerable shade.

A. lanceolata. LANCELEAF AZARA. Zones 15–17. Large, spreading shrub to 20 ft. Equal to *A. microphylla* in pattern value but with much larger leaves, more lush effect. Leaves mostly 2½ in. long, rather narrow. Foliage bright yellowish green. April flowers pale yellow, in short clusters.

A. microphylla. BOXLEAF AZARA. Zones 5–9, 14–24. Slow growing when small, fast when established; to 12–18 ft., spreading 8–12 ft. When old, treelike to 30 ft.

Arching branches spread fanlike to give definite 2-dimensional effect. May become leggy and awkward unless controlled by tipping young branches. Shiny dark green leaves, roundish, ½–¾ in. long. Flowers yellow, fragrant, in short clusters from February to March.

A. petiolaris *(A. gilliesii).* Zones 15–17. Large shrub to 15–20 ft., but easily trained into single-stemmed tree. Deep green, lustrous, oval to roundish leaves, 1½–3 in. long, look somewhat like holly leaves and hang from branches like aspen. Nodding, 1-in.-long clusters of bright yellow, tiny flowers February–March.

AZTEC LILY. See *Sprekelia formosissima.*

BABACO. See *Carica heilbornii.*

BABIANA. *Iridaceae.* BABOON FLOWER. Corms. With care, outdoors in Zones 4–24. Native to South Africa. Spikes of freesialike flowers in blue, lavender, red, cream, and white bloom in March (California) to June (Northwest). Leaves are strongly ribbed, usually hairy, set edgewise to stem. Full sun or very light shade. Plant corms 4 in. deep, 3 in. apart. Plant along border edge, paths, in rock gardens; also in deep pots. Ample water during growth, less after leaves turn yellow. In mild climates leave in ground several years, but never in cold, wet, heavy ground. In coldest areas, lift and store corms like gladiolus.

Babiana stricta

(Continued on next page)

B

B. rubrocyanea. Spikes to 5–6 in. with 6 or 7 flowers to a spike. Bottom half of each flower deep red, upper half royal blue.

B. stricta. Very attractive. Royal blue flowers on 1-ft. stems. Leaves 6 in. high. Varieties in purple, lavender, white, and blue-and-white.

BABOON FLOWER. See *Babiana.*

BABY BLUE EYES. See *Nemophila menziesii.*

BABY'S BREATH. See *Gypsophila paniculata.*

BABY SNAPDRAGON. See *Linaria maroccana.*

BABY'S TEARS. See *Soleirolia soleirolii.*

BACCHARIS. *Compositae.* Evergreen shrubs. All grow in difficult growing conditions. Some are useful landscape plants.

Baccharis pilularis

B. 'Centennial'. Zones 10–13. Hybrid between *B. pilularis* and *B. sarothroides.* Grows 5 ft. wide, half as tall, with narrow leaves and tufted tan seed capsules in spring. Tolerates desert heat, resists root rot caused by water molds.

B. pilularis. COYOTE BRUSH, DWARF CHAPARRAL BROOM. Zones 5–11, 14–24. Native to California coast, Sonoma to Monterey counties. Remarkable climate and soil adaptation. Thrives in almost swampy situations or without summer water along coast. Most dependable of all ground covers in California's high desert.

Makes dense, rather billowy, bright green mat, 8–24 in. high and spreading to 6 ft. or more. Small, ½-in., toothed leaves are closely set on many branches.

Very valuable, very dependable bank cover for minimum maintenance areas in sun. Needs pruning once a year before new growth starts. Cut out old arching branches and thin to rejuvenate. Male and female flowers, borne on different plants, are of no interest. Female plants produce cottony seeds which can make a mess when blown by wind. Plants available in most nurseries are cutting-grown from male plants. 'Twin Peaks' ('Twin Peaks #2') has small, dark green leaves and moderate growth rate. 'Pigeon Point' has larger, lighter green leaves, grows faster (9 ft. wide in 4 years); untrimmed, makes a 2–3-ft. hedge.

B. sarothroides. DESERT BROOM. Zones 10–12. Nearly leafless, but with bright green branches throughout year. Grows 6–7 ft. tall, but can be clipped to 2–3 ft. Female plants covered with cottony fluff of seeds in late fall and winter. Can take good or poor drainage. Useful for erosion control, replanting disturbed land, or natural landscape in desert regions.

BACHELOR'S BUTTON. See *Centaurea cyanus.*

BAILEYA multiradiata. *Compositae.* DESERT MARIGOLD. Annual. Western desert native displays inch-wide, bright yellow flower heads above gray foliage on 1–1½-ft. plants. Basic bloom period spring through fall, but in low desert, year-round bloom from self-sown seedlings is possible. Sow seed fall or spring, rake in, and water thoroughly. Keep moist until seeds sprout, then reduce watering to 1 or 2 times a week. Thin to 1½ ft. apart. To prolong bloom, water every week or two if rains fail.

Baileya multiradiata

BALD CYPRESS. See *Taxodium distichum.*

BALLOON FLOWER. See *Platycodon grandiflorum.*

BALSAM. See *Impatiens balsamina.*

Balsaminaceae. The touch-me-not family embraces herbaceous or shrubby plants with juicy stems, irregular flowers with spurs, and explosive seed capsules. *Impatiens* is the only important member.

BALSAM PEAR. See *Momordica.*

BAMBOO. *Gramineae.* Giant grasses with large, woody stems known as *culms* divided into sections (called *internodes*) by obvious joints (*nodes*). Upper nodes produce buds which develop into branches; these, in larger bamboos, divide into secondary branches which bear leaves. Bamboos spread by underground stems (rhizomes) which, like the aboveground culms, are jointed and carry buds. Manner in which rhizomes grow explains difference between running and clump bamboos.

Bambusa multiplex

In running bamboos (*Arundinaria, Chimonobambusa, Phyllostachys, Pseudosasa, Sasa, Semiarundinaria,* and *Shibataea*), underground stems grow rapidly to varying distances from parent plant before sending up new vertical shoots. These bamboos eventually form large patches or groves unless spread is curbed. They are generally fairly hardy plants from temperate regions in China and Japan.

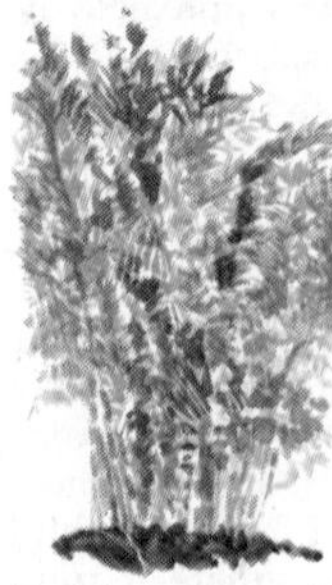

Bambusa oldhamii

In clump bamboos (*Bambusa, Chusquea, Otatea, Sinarundinaria, Thamnocalamus*), underground stems grow only a short distance before sending up new stems. These form clumps that expand slowly around the edges. Most are tropical or subtropical.

Plant container-grown bamboos at any time of year. Best time to propagate from existing clumps is just before growth begins in spring; divide hardy kinds in March or early April, tropical ones in May or early June. (Transplanting at other times is possible, but risk of losing divisions is high in summer heat or winter chill and wet soil.) Cut or saw out divisions with roots and at least 3 connected culms. If divisions are large, cut back tops to balance loss of roots and rhizomes. Foliage may wilt or wither, but culms will send out new leaves.

Phyllostachys aurea

Rhizome cuttings are another means of propagation. In clumping bamboos, this cutting consists of rooted base of culm; in running bamboos, it is a foot-long length of rhizome with roots and buds. Plant in rich mix with ample organic material added.

Culms of all bamboos have already attained their maximum diameter when they poke through ground; in mature plants, they usually reach their maximum height within a month. Many do become increasingly leafy in subsequent years, but not taller. Plants are evergreen, but there is considerable dropping of older leaves; old plantings develop nearly weedproof mulch of dead leaves. Individual canes live for several years, but eventually die and should be cut out.

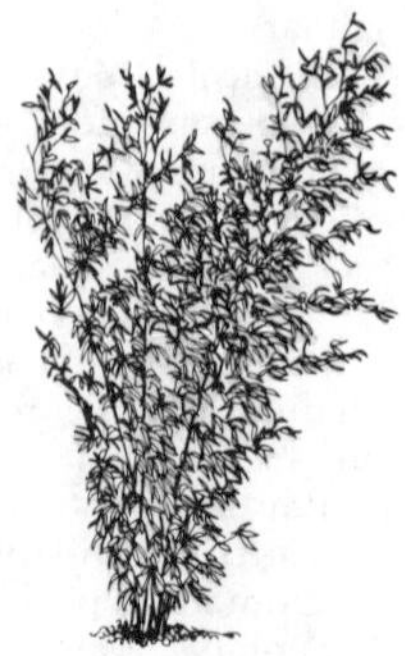

Phyllostachys nigra

(Continued on page 239)

B

Bamboo

(*Synonyms* refers to alternate names under which these bamboos may be sold. For explanation of Controlled and Uncontrolled Height, see page 239; for Roman numerals I, II, III, and IV, see pages 239–240.)

NAME	SYNONYMS	CONTROLLED HEIGHT (UNCONTROLLED HEIGHT) AND GROWTH HABIT	STEM DIAMETER	HARDINESS	COMMENTS (GROWTH HABIT, CHARACTERISTICS, USES)
Arundinaria argenteostriata		2–3 ft. (3–4 ft.) Running.	¼ in.	10°F.	I. Good light-colored ground cover for shade. Looks best cut back every year. White stripes on leaves.
A. chino vaginata 'Variegata'		2–3 ft. (3–4 ft.) Running.	⅜ in.	10°F.	I. Graceful, densely foliaged. Slender leaves striped white. Sun or light shade.
A. disticha DWARF FERNLEAF BAMBOO	*Sasa disticha, Pleioblastus distichus.*	1–2 ft. (2–3 ft.) Running.	⅛ in.	10°F.	I. Delicate in appearance. Tiny, 2-ranked ferny leaves. Rampant; cut back to ground if rank or stemmy.
A. pygmaea	*Sasa pygmaea.*	½–1 ft. (1–1½ ft.) Running.	⅛ in.	0°F.	I. Aggressive spreader; good bank holder and erosion control. Can be mowed every few years to keep it from growing stemmy and unattractive.
A. simonii SIMON BAMBOO, MEDAKE	*Pleioblastus simonii.*	10 ft. (20 ft.) Running.	1½ in.	0°F.	III. Vertical growth pattern, moderate spreader. Screens, hedges; garden stakes.
A. s. variegata		10 ft. (20 ft.) Running.	1½ in.	0°F.	III. Like above, but some leaves have white striping.
A. variegata DWARF WHITESTRIPE BAMBOO	*Sasa variegata, S. fortunei.*	1–2 ft. (2–3 ft.) Running.	¼ in.	–10°F.	I. Fast spreader; curb rhizomes. Use in tubs or as deep ground cover. Sun or light shade.
A. viridistriata	*A. auricoma.*	1–2 ft. (2½ ft.) Running.	¼ in.	0°F.	I. Leaves 8 in. long, 1½ in. wide are strikingly variegated green and gold.
Bambusa beecheyana BEECHEY BAMBOO	*Sinocalamus beecheyanus.*	12–20 ft. (20–40 ft.) Clump.	4–5 in.	15°F.	IV. Culms arch strongly for broad, graceful effect. Tropical looking. Scarce.
B. multiplex	*B. glaucescens.*	8–10 ft. (15–25 ft.) Clump.	1½ in.	15°F.	II. Branches from base to top. Dense growth. Hedges, screens. Less common than its varieties described below.
B. m. 'Alphonse Karr' ALPHONSE KARR BAMBOO		8–10 ft. (15–35 ft.) Clump.	½–1 in.	15°F.	II. Similar to above, but culms are brilliantly striped green on yellow. New culms pinkish and green.
B. m. 'Fernleaf' FERNLEAF BAMBOO	*B. nana, B. disticha.*	6–10 ft. (10–20 ft.) Clump.	½ in.	15°F.	II. Closely spaced leaves, 10–20 to twig, give ferny look. Loses this look, grows coarser with rich soil, ample water.
B. m. 'Golden Goddess' GOLDEN GODDESS BAMBOO	Sometimes sold as *B. falcata.*	6–8 ft. (6–10 ft.) Clump.	½ in.	15°F.	II. Graceful, dense, arching growth. Good container or screen plant. Give tops room to spread.
B. m. riviereorum CHINESE GODDESS BAMBOO		4–6 ft. (6–8 ft.) Clump.	¼ in.	15°F.	II. Solid culms arch gracefully. Tiny leaves in lacy, ferny sprays.
B. m. 'Silverstripe'		20 ft. (40 ft.) Clump.	1½ in.	15°F.	II. Most vigorous of hedge bamboo varieties. Leaves have white stripes; occasional white stripes on culms.
B. oldhamii OLDHAM BAMBOO, CLUMPING GIANT TIMBER BAMBOO	*Sinocalamus oldhamii.*	15–25 ft. (20–55 ft.) Clump.	4 in.	15°F.	IV. Densely foliaged, erect clumps make it good plant for big, dense screens. Or use single plant for imposing vertical mass. Commonest big bamboo in southern California.
B. textilis		15–20 ft. (20–40 ft.) Clump.	2 in.	13°F.	II or IV. Handsome, erect, reasonably hardy, rare. New culms blue green, sheaths green to orange.

(Continued on next page)

B

NAME	SYNONYMS	CONTROLLED HEIGHT (UNCONTROLLED HEIGHT) AND GROWTH HABIT	STEM DIAMETER	HARDINESS	COMMENTS (GROWTH HABIT, CHARACTERISTICS, USES)
B. tuldoides PUNTING POLE BAMBOO		15–20 ft. (20–55 ft.) Clump.	2 in.	15°F.	IV. Prolific producer of slender, erect culms. Best as single plant.
B. ventricosa BUDDHA'S BELLY BAMBOO		3–6 ft. (15–30 ft.) Clump.	2 in.	20°F.	II or IV. Stays small, produces swollen culms that give it its name only when confined in tubs or grown in poor, dryish soil. Otherwise a giant bamboo with straight culms.
B. vulgaris vittata		15–25 ft. (to 50 ft.) Clump.	4 in.	30°F.	IV. Yellow culms have vertical green stripes. Used in well-lit interiors and mildest coastal areas. Striking color. Rare.
Chimonobambusa marmorea MARBLED BAMBOO (sometimes sold as "dwarf black bamboo")	*Arundinaria marmorea.*	2–4 ft. (4–6 ft.) Running.	¼ in.	20°F.	III. New culm sheaths marbled cream and purplish. Older culms nearly black. Densely leafy; makes first-class hedge plant if roots are curbed.
C. quadrangularis SQUARE-STEM BAMBOO	*Bambusa quadrangularis.*	10–15 ft. (20–30 ft.) Running.	1 in.	15°F.	III. Squarish culms have prominent joints, carry heavy whorls of branches. Valued for vertical effect.
Chusquea coronalis		8–12 ft. (12–15 ft.) Clump.	¾ in.	28°F.	IV. Arching culms bear masses of tiny leaves on short whorled branches. Exceptionally attractive. Sun or light shade. Rare.
Otatea acuminata aztecorum MEXICAN WEEPING BAMBOO	*Yushania aztecorum, Arthrostylidium longifolium.*	8–10 ft. (20 ft.) Clump.	1½ in.	15°F.	II. Extremely narrow leaves (6 in. by ⅛ in.) give lacy look. Foliage masses bend nearly to ground. Fairly drought resistant when established. Rare.
Phyllostachys aurea GOLDEN BAMBOO		6–10 ft. (10–20 ft.) Running.	2 in.	0°F.	III. Erect, stiff culms, usually with crowded joints at base—good identifying mark. Dense foliage makes it good screen or hedge. Can take much drought, but looks better with ample water. Good choice for growing in tubs.
P. aureosulcata YELLOW GROOVE BAMBOO		12–15 ft. (15–25 ft.) Running.	1½ in.	–20°F.	III. Like more slender, more open golden bamboo. Young culms green with pronounced yellowish groove. One of 2 hardiest bamboos.
P. bambusoides GIANT TIMBER BAMBOO, JAPANESE TIMBER BAMBOO	*P. reticulata.*	15–35 ft. (25–45 ft.) Running.	6 in.	0°F.	IV. Once commonest of large, hardy timber bamboos. Most perished during blooming period in 1960s–1970s. New plants from seed will eventually become available. Makes beautiful groves if lowest branches are trimmed off.
P. b. 'Castillon'	*P. castillonis.*	10–15 ft. (15–20 ft.) Running.	2 in.	0°F.	III. Yellow culms show green stripe above each branch cluster. Rare.
P. heterocycla pubescens MOSO BAMBOO	*P. edulis.*	20–40 ft. (40–60 ft.) Running.	8 in.	5°F.	IV. Largest of running timber bamboos. Gray green, heavy culms; small, feathery leaves. Rare and hard to establish.
P. meyeri		10–20 ft. (20–30 ft.) Running.	2 in.	–4°F.	III. Somewhat like *P. aurea*, but lacks crowded basal joints. Hardy to cold.
P. nigra BLACK BAMBOO		4–8 ft. (10–15 ft.) Running.	1½ in.	0°F.	III. New culms green, turning black in second year (rarely olive green dotted black). Best in afternoon shade where summers are hot.
P. n. 'Henon'		50 ft. (to 54 ft.) Running.	3½ in.	0°F.	III. Much larger than black bamboo. Culms whitish green, not changing to black, rough to touch.

NAME	SYNONYMS	CONTROLLED HEIGHT (UNCONTROLLED HEIGHT) AND GROWTH HABIT	STEM DIAMETER	HARD-INESS	COMMENTS (GROWTH HABIT, CHARACTERISTICS, USES)
Pseudosasa japonica ARROW BAMBOO	*Arundinaria japonica.*	6–10 ft. (10–18 ft.) Running.	¾ in.	0°F.	III. Stiffly erect culms with one branch at each joint. Leaves large, with long pointed tails. Rampant thick hedge in mild-winter climates; slow spreader where winters are cold, making dense, erect clumps.
Sasa palmata PALMATE BAMBOO	Sometimes sold as *S. senanensis.*	4–5 ft. (8–12 ft.) Running.	⅜ in.	0°F.	In class by itself. Grows bigger in Zones 4–6 and 15–17 than in 18–24. Broad, handsome leaves (to 15 in. long by 4 in. wide) spread fingerlike from stem and branch tips. Rampant spreader; curb it.
S. tessellata	*Arundinaria ragamowskii.*	2–3 ft. (3–6 ft.) Running.	¼ in.	0°F.	Resembles *S. palmata*, but much lower growth, much longer leaves (to 2 ft.). Slow spreader, best in shade. Rare.
S. veitchii		2–3 ft. (2–3 ft.) Running.	¼ in.	0°F.	I. Rampant spreader with large (7 in. by 1 in.) dark green leaves that turn whitish buff all around edges in autumn for variegated effect. Appropriate in Japanese gardens if curbed.
Semiarundinaria fastuosa NARIHIRA BAMBOO		8–10 ft. (12–25 ft.) Running.	1¼ in.	−4°F.	II or III. Rigidly upright growth. Slow spreader easily kept to a clump. Planted closely makes tall, narrow, dense hedge or windbreak.
Shibataea kumasaca		2–3 ft. (5–6 ft.) Running.	¼ in.	10°F.	III. Slow spreading, makes compact clumps of unbamboolike appearance. Leaves are short and broad (4 in. by 1 in.), distinctly stalked. Needs acid soil.
Sinarundinaria nitida FOUNTAIN BAMBOO		6–8 ft. (15–20 ft.) Clump.	¾ in.	0°F.	II. Light, airy, graceful, narrow clump, arching and drooping at top. Greenish purple culms mature to deep purplish black. Needs shade to look its best. Rare.
Thamnocalamus spathaceus	*Sinarundinaria murielae.*	6–8 ft. (15 ft.) Clump.	¾ in.	−20°F.	II. One of 2 hardiest bamboos for U.S. Light, airy, narrow clump, arching and drooping at top. Rare.

Mature bamboos grow phenomenally rapidly during their brief growth period—culms of giant types may increase in length by several feet a day. Don't expect such fast growth the first year after transplanting, though. Giant timber bamboo, for example, needs 3–5 years to build up a rhizome system capable of supporting culms that grow several feet a day; growth during early years will be less impressive. To get fast growth and great size, water frequently and feed once a month with high-nitrogen or lawn fertilizer; to restrict size and spread, water and feed less. Once established, plants tolerate considerable drought, but rhizomes will not spread into dry soil (or into water). The accompanying chart lists 2 heights for each bamboo. Controlled Height means average height under dry conditions with little feeding, or with rhizome spread controlled by barriers. Uncontrolled Height refers to plants growing under best conditions and unconfined by barriers.

Difficult to mass-produce and little known, most bamboos are hard to find in nurseries. Inquire about specialists in your area. The American Bamboo Society has chapters in the Northwest, in northern California, and in southern California. Society members often propagate rare varieties for sales in connection with their meetings. Arboretum and botanic garden sales are another source.

In the case of bamboo, disregard the rule of never buying rootbound plants. The more crowded the plant is in the container, the faster its growth when planted out. Both running and clumping types grow well when roots are confined. Spread of running kinds can be controlled by planting in stout boxes, above or in ground. In large areas, control with soil barriers of 1½-ft.-deep strips of galvanized sheet metal or poured concrete, or by planting in bottomless oil drums or long flue tiles. You can limit lateral spread by running a spade to its full depth around circumference of clump. New shoots are tender and break off easily; they do not resprout. Another way to limit spread of large running bamboos: dig foot-deep trench around plant and sever any rhizomes that grow into it; trench will fill with loose mulch of bamboo leaves. Sift through leaves with gloved hands to find roving rhizomes.

Scale, mealybugs, and aphids are occasionally found on bamboo but seldom do any harm; if they secrete honeydew in bothersome amounts, spray with malathion.

The chart classes each bamboo by habit of growth, which, of course, determines its use in the garden. In **Group I** are the dwarf or low-growing ground cover types. These can be used for erosion control or (carefully confined in a long section of flue tile) as small clumps for border or rock garden. **Group II** includes clump bamboos with fountainlike habit of growth. These have widest use in landscaping. They require no more space than average strong-growing shrub. Clipped, they make hedges or screens that won't spread much into surrounding soil; unclipped, they line up as informal screens or grow singly to show off their graceful form.

(Continued on next page)

B

Bamboos in **Group III** are running bamboos of moderate size and more or less vertical growth. Use them as screens, hedges, or (if curbed) alone. **Group IV** includes the giant bamboos. Use running kinds for groves or for Oriental effects on a grand scale. Clumping kinds have a tropical look, especially if they are used with broad-leafed tropical plants. All may be thinned and clipped to show off culms. Thin clumps or groves by cutting out old or dead culms at the base.

Some of the smaller bamboos bloom on some of their stalks every year and continue to grow. Some bloom partially and at erratic intervals. Some have never been known to bloom. Others bloom heavily, set seed, and die. Giant timber bamboo (*Phyllostachys bambusoides*) and other species of *Phyllostachys* bloom at rare intervals of 30–60 years, produce flowers for a long period, and become enfeebled. They may recover very slowly or die. There is evidence that very heavy feeding and watering may speed their recovery.

Bamboos are not recommended for year-round indoor culture, but container-grown plants can spend extended periods indoors if located in cool, bright rooms. You can revive plants by taking them outdoors, but it is important to avoid sudden changes in temperature and light.

There are several ways to eliminate unwanted bamboo. Digging it out with mattock and spade is the surest method, though sometimes difficult. Rhizomes are generally not deep, but they may be widespread. Remove them all or regrowth will occur. Starve out roots by cutting off all shoots before they exceed 2 ft. in height; repeat as needed—probably many times over the course of a year. Contact foliage sprays that kill leaves have the same effect as removing culms. Translocation weed killers have only a temporary effect on bamboo. Soil sterilants will kill them; repeat treatments may be necessary. Avoid damaging roots of nearby plants and beware of runoff to other parts of the garden.

BAMBURANTA. See *Ctenanthe compressa.*

BAMBUSA. See Bamboo.

BANANA. See *Musa, Ensete.*

BANANA SHRUB. See *Michelia figo.*

BAPTISIA australis. *Leguminosae.* FALSE INDIGO, WILD INDIGO. Perennial. All Zones. Native to eastern and southern U.S. Somewhat like bush lupine in habit. Grows 3–6 ft. tall, with bluish green, deeply cut leaves. Spikes of small, indigo blue, sweet pea–shaped flowers appear in early summer, followed by inflated seed pods; both flowers and pods are interesting in arrangements. Cut back spent flowers for repeat bloom. Give full sun and ordinary soil. Plant is tap rooted, so can withstand drought. Specialists carry seed.

Baptisia australis

BARBADOS PRIDE. See *Caesalpinia pulcherrima.*

BARBERRY. See *Berberis.*

BARREL CACTUS. See *Echinocactus, Ferocactus.*

BASEBALL PLANT. See *Euphorbia obesa.*

BASIL. See *Ocimum.*

BASKET FLOWER. See *Hymenocallis narcissiflora, Centaurea americana.*

BASKET-OF-GOLD. See *Aurinia saxatilis.*

BASSWOOD. See *Tilia americana.*

BAUHINIA. *Leguminosae.* Evergreen or deciduous trees or half-climbing shrubs. These flamboyant flowering plants have a very special place in Hawaii, mild-winter areas of California, and Arizona. They vary greatly by species and climate. Common to all garden bauhinias are twin "leaves" (actually twin lobes). Need sun, warmth, moderate water.

Bauhinia forficata

B. blakeana. HONG KONG ORCHID TREE. Partially deciduous for short period. Zones 19, 21, 23. Native to southern China. Flowers are shaped like some orchids; colors range from cranberry maroon through purple and rose to orchid pink, often in same blossom. Flowers are much larger (5½–6 in. wide) than those of other bauhinias; also unlike others, they appear in autumn and early winter. Gray green leaves tend to drop off around bloom time but not completely. Umbrella-type growth habit. To 20 ft. high.

B. forficata. (Often sold as *B. corniculata* or *B. candicans.*) Evergreen to deciduous large shrub or tree. Zones 9, 12–23. Native to Brazil. Probably hardiest bauhinia. In spring and through summer, bears narrow-petaled, creamy white flowers to 3 in. wide. Deep green leaves, more pointed lobes than others. Grows to 20 ft., often with twisting, leaning trunk, picturesque angled branches. Short, sharp thorns at branch joints. Good canopy patio tree. In hot, dry weather, give some afternoon shade; if unshaded, blooms tend to shrivel during day.

B. punctata *(B. galpinii).* RED BAUHINIA. Evergreen to semideciduous shrub. Zones 13, 15, 16, 18–23. Native to South and tropical Africa. Brick red to orange flowers, as spectacular as bougainvillea where adapted. Sprawling, half climbing, with 15-ft. spread. Best as espalier on warm wall. With hard pruning, can make splendid flowering bonsai for large pot or box.

B. variegata. (Commonly sold as *B. purpurea.*) PURPLE ORCHID TREE. Partially to wholly deciduous. Zones 13, 18–23. Native to India, China. Most frequently planted. Hardy to 22°F. Spectacular street trees where spring is warm and stays warm. Wonderful show of light pink to orchid purple, broad-petaled, 2–3-in.-wide flowers, usually January to April. Light green, broad-lobed leaves generally drop in midwinter. Produces huge crop of beans after blooming; messy looking. Trim beans off if you wish—trimming brings new growth earlier. Inclined to grow as shrub with many stems. Staked and pruned, becomes attractive 20–35-ft. tree.

B. v. 'Candida'. WHITE ORCHID TREE. Like *B. variegata,* but with white flowers.

BAY. See *Laurus, Umbellularia californica.*

BAYBERRY. See *Myrica pensylvanica.*

BEACH ASTER. See *Erigeron glaucus.*

BEACH WORMWOOD. See *Artemisia stellerana.*

BEAD PLANT. See *Nertera granadensis.*

BEAN, BROAD. *Leguminosae.* Also called "fava bean" or "horse bean." All Zones (but see climate restrictions below). This bean (actually a giant vetch) was known in ancient and medieval times; it is a Mediterranean plant, while all other familiar beans are New World plants. It is an annual of bushy growth to 2–4 ft. Best known in coastal climates. You can cook and eat immature pods like edible-pod peas; prepare immature and mature seeds in same way as green or dry limas.

Unlike true beans, this is a cool-season plant. In cold-winter areas, plant as early in spring as soil can be worked. In mild coastal climates, plant in fall for late winter or early spring ripening. Matures in 120–150 days, depending on temperature. Space rows 1½–2½ ft. apart. Plant seeds 1 in. deep, 4–5 in. apart; thin to 8–10 in. apart. Spray or dust for aphids.

Most people can safely eat fava beans, though a very few (principally of Mediterranean ancestry) have an enzyme deficiency that can cause severe reactions to the beans and even the pollen.

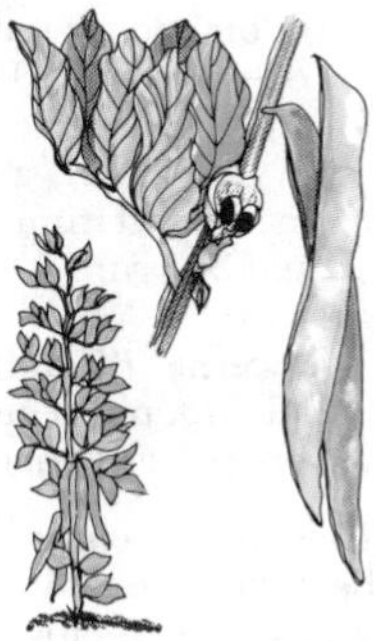

Fava Bean

BEAN, DRY. *Leguminosae.* Annual. All Zones. Same culture as bush form of snap bean. Let pods remain on bush until they turn dry or begin to shatter; thresh beans from pods, dry, store to soak and cook later. 'Pinto', 'Red Kidney', and 'White Marrowfat' belong to this group.

Dry Bean

BEAN, LIMA. *Leguminosae.* Annual. All Zones. Like snap or string beans (which they resemble), limas come either in bush or vine (pole) form. They develop slower than string beans—bush types require 65–75 days, pole kinds 78–95 days—and do not produce as reliably in extremely dry, hot weather. They must be shelled before cooking—a tedious chore, but worth it if you like fresh limas. Among bush types, 'Burpee's Improved Bush', 'Henderson Bush', and 'Fordhook 242' are outstanding; the last 2 are especially useful in hot-summer areas. 'Prizetaker' and 'King of the Garden' are fine large-seeded climbing forms; 'Small White Lima' or 'Sieva', usually grown for drying, gives heavy yields of shelled beans. Grow like snap beans.

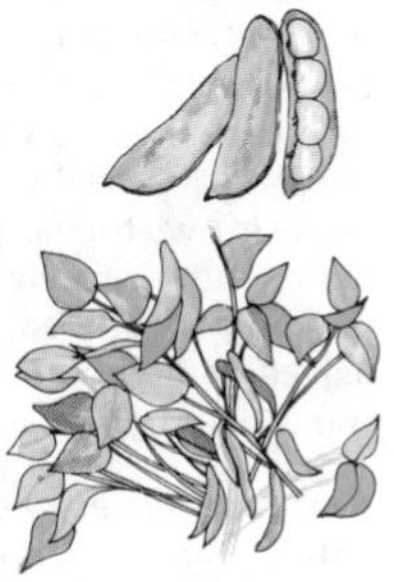

Lima Bean

BEAN, SCARLET RUNNER. *Leguminosae.* Annual twining vines. All Zones. Showy and ornamental with bright scarlet flowers in slender clusters, and with bright green leaves divided into 3 roundish, 3–5-in.-long leaflets. Use to cover fences, arbors, outbuildings; for quick shade on porches, summer cottages.

Flowers are followed by flattened, very dark green pods which are edible and tasty when young, but which toughen as they reach full size. Beans can be shelled from older pods for cooking like green limas. Culture is same as for snap beans.

Scarlet Runner Bean

BEAN, SNAP. *Leguminosae.* Annual. All Zones. Of all beans, the snap (string, green) bean is most widely planted and most useful for home gardens. They have tender, fleshy pods with little fiber; they may be green, yellow (wax beans), or purple ('Royalty'). Purple kinds turn green in cooking. Plants grow as self-supporting bushes or as climbing vines (pole beans). Bush types bear earlier, but vines are more productive. Plants resemble scarlet runner bean, but white or purple flowers are not showy.

Plant seeds as soon as soil is warm, in full sun and good soil. These seeds must push heavy seed leaves through soil, so see that it is reasonably loose and open. Plant seeds of bush types an inch deep and 1–3 in. apart in rows, with 2–3 ft. between rows. Pole beans can be managed in a number of ways: set 3 or 4 poles in the ground and tie together at top in wigwam fashion; or set single poles 3 or 4 ft. apart and sow 6 or 8 beans around each, thinning to 3 or 4 strongest seedlings; or insert poles 1 or 2 ft. apart in rows and sow seeds as you would bush beans; or sow along sunny wall, fence, or trellis and train vines on web of light string supported by wire or heavy twine. Moisten ground thoroughly before planting; do not water again until seedlings have emerged.

Once growth starts, keep soil moist. Occasional deep soaking is preferable to frequent light sprinklings which may encourage mildew. Feed after plants are in active growth and again when pods start to form. Pods are ready in 50–70 days, according to variety. Pick every 5–7 days; if pods mature, plants will stop bearing. Control aphids and diabrotica (spotted cucumber beetle) with rotenone or all-purpose vegetable garden dust. Check whiteflies with malathion spray, following precautions on label concerning harvest date.

Snap Bean

BEARBERRY. See *Arctostaphylos uva-ursi.*

BEARD TONGUE. See *Penstemon.*

BEAR'S BREECH. See *Acanthus mollis.*

BEAR'S FOOT FERN. See *Humata tyermannii.*

BEAUCARNEA recurvata. *Agavaceae.* PONYTAIL, BOTTLE PALM. Succulent shrub or tree. House plant anywhere, hardy Zones 13, 16–24 (but note cautions below). Base of stem is greatly swollen. In young plants, it resembles a big onion sitting on soil; on old trees in the ground, it can be a woody mass several feet across. Trunk is at first single, later sparsely branched. Leaves cluster at ends of branches in dense tufts; arching and drooping, they measure 3 ft. or more in length, ¾ inch wide. Very old trees may produce inconspicuous clusters of creamy white flowers.

Outdoors, give plants sun, well-drained soil, and infrequent deep watering. They do exceptionally well as house plants when given good light and not overwatered. Mature plants have endured temperatures to 18°F.; young plants in containers freeze to death in the low 20s. Plants moved from indoors to permanent garden locations outdoors should have gradually increasing exposure to sun and low temperatures.

Beaucarnea recurvata

BEAUMONTIA grandiflora. *Apocynaceae.* HERALD'S TRUMPET, EASTER LILY VINE. Evergreen vine. Zones 12, 13, 16, 17, 21–24. Climbs by arching, semitwining branches to as much as 30 ft., and spreads as wide. Large, dark green, 6–9-in., oval to roundish leaves, smooth and shiny above, slightly downy beneath, furnish lush tropical look. From April until September, bears fragrant, trumpet-shaped, 5-in.-long, green-veined white flowers which look like Easter lilies.

Needs deep, rich soil, ample water, and heavy feeding. Prune after flowering to keep

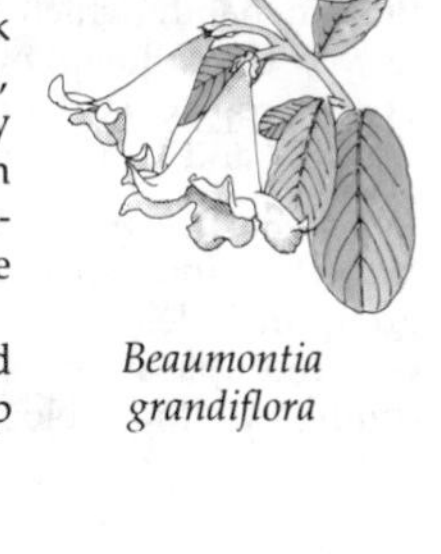

Beaumontia grandiflora

it in scale, but preserve good proportion of 2- and 3-year-old wood; flowers are not borne on new growth. Makes big espalier on warm wall, sheltered from wind. Or train along eaves of house; give it a sturdy support. Good near swimming pools. Hardy to 28°F.

BEAUTYBERRY. See *Callicarpa bodinieri giraldii.*

BEAUTY BUSH. See *Kolkwitzia amabilis.*

BEE BALM. See *Monarda.*

BEECH. See *Fagus.*

BEEFWOOD. See *Casuarina.*

BEET. *Chenopodiaceae.* Biennial grown as annual. All Zones. To have fresh beets all summer, plant seeds in short rows at monthly intervals, starting as soon as soil can be worked in spring. Best in sun; where summers are very hot, plant to mature before or after extreme summer heat. Cover seeds with ¼ in. of compost, sand, or vermiculite to prevent caking. Sow seeds 1 in. apart; thin to 2 in. while plants are small, using thinnings—tops and roots—for food. To keep roots tender, water often in dry weather. Feed plants at 3–4-week intervals for speedy growth. Begin harvesting when beets are 1 in. wide; complete harvesting before beets exceed 3 in.—larger ones are woody.

Beet

Round red varieties include 'Detroit Dark Red' and 'Crosby's Egyptian' (old favorites) and many newer varieties. Novelties include 'Cylindra' and 'Forma Nova' (long cylindrical roots); there are golden yellow and white varieties.

BEGONIA. *Begoniaceae.* Perennials, sometimes shrubby, grown for textured, multicolored foliage, saucer-sized flowers, and/or lacy clusters of smaller flowers. Outdoors, most grow best in pots in the ground, or in hanging baskets in filtered shade with rich, porous, fast-draining soil, consistent but light feeding, and enough water to keep soil moist but not soggy. Most thrive as indoor plants, in greenhouse, or under lath. Some prefer terrarium conditions. Almost all require at least moderate humidity. (During hot, dry summers, misting may be necessary.)

Most can be propagated easily from leaf, stem, or rhizome cuttings. They also grow from dust-fine seed. Of the many hundreds of species and varieties, relatively few are sold widely. In the list below, you'll find the most widely grown begonias. Enthusiasts obtain others from specialty dealers, at American Begonia Society sales, and from the ABS seed fund.

Tuberous begonia

The society classifies begonias by grouping them according to growth habit, which coincidentally groups them by their care needs. The following list uses a version of the society's classifications to replace such outdated misnomers as "fibrous," "tuberous-rooted," and "wax begonias."

Cane-type begonias. They get their name from their stems, which grow tall and woody, with prominent bamboolike joints. The group includes so-called "angel-wing" begonias. Plants are erect with multiple stems, some reaching 5 ft. or more under the right conditions. Most bloom profusely with large clusters of white, pink, orange, or red flowers early spring through autumn. Some are everblooming. When roots fill 4-inch pots, plants can be placed in large containers or in the ground where they will get plenty of light, some sun, and no wind. They may require staking or a trellis. Protect from heavy frosts. Old canes that have grown barren should be pruned to 2 leaf joints in early spring to stimulate new growth.

'Lucerna' ('Corallina de Lucerna', 'Lucerne'). Tall plant with broad, drooping clusters of rose red flowers in spring and summer. Silver-spotted "angel-wing" leaves. Old-fashioned, still popular.

Hiemalis begonias. Some members of this group are called "Rieger begonias." Bushy, compact; profuse bloomers and outstanding house plants. Flowers average about 2 in. across and appear over a long season that includes winter. On well-grown plants, green leaves and stems are all but invisible underneath a blanket of bloom. Give plenty of light in winter. In summer, keep out of hot noonday sun. Water thoroughly when top inch of soil is dry. Don't sprinkle leaves. If powdery mildew appears, control with benomyl. Plant may get rangy, an indication of approaching dormancy. In this case, cut stems to 4-in. stubs.

Rex begonias. With their bold, multicolored leaves, these are probably the most striking of all foliage begonias. While many named varieties are grown by collectors, easier-to-find unnamed seedling plants are almost as decorative. The leaves grow from a rhizome; see "Rhizomatous begonias" for care. In addition, rex begonias should get high humidity (at least 50 percent) to do their best. Provide it by misting with a spray bottle, placing pot on wet pebbles in a tray, or keeping plants in greenhouse. When rhizome grows too far past edge of pot for your taste, either repot into slightly larger container or cut off rhizome end inside pot edge. Old rhizome will branch and grow new leaves. Make rhizome cuttings of the piece you remove and root in mixture of half peat moss, half perlite.

Rex begonia

Rhizomatous begonias. Like rex begonias, these grow from a rhizome, a usually creeping stem-type structure at or near soil level. Although some have handsome flowers, they are grown primarily for foliage, which varies in color and texture among species and varieties. The group includes so-called "star begonias," named for their leaf shape. Rhizomatous begonias perform well as house plants when given bright light through a window and watered only when the top inch or so of soil is dry. Plant them in wide, shallow pots. They flower from winter through summer, the season varying among specific plants. White to pink flowers appear in clusters on erect stems above the foliage. Rhizomes will grow over edge of pot, eventually forming a ball-shaped plant; if you wish, cut rhizomes back to pot. The old rhizome will branch and grow new leaves. Root the pieces of rhizome in mixture of half peat moss, half perlite.

B. 'Erythrophylla'. BEEFSTEAK BEGONIA. Widely grown plant with roundish leaves that are dark green on top, deep red beneath. Plant can grow to several feet across. Flowers pink. Variety 'Helix' has spiraled leaves. Variety 'Bunchii' has lettucelike frills and ruffles on leaf edges.

B. masoniana. IRON CROSS BEGONIA. Large puckered leaves known for chocolate brown pattern resembling Maltese cross on green background. Flowers insignificant.

Semperflorens begonias. BEDDING BEGONIAS. These tough plants used to be called "wax begonias." Grown in garden beds or containers as if annuals, they produce lots of small flowers spring through fall in a white-through-red range. In mild climates, can overwinter, live for years. Foliage can be green, red, bronze, or variegated. Very useful western garden plant. Thrives in full sun along coast. Prefers broken shade inland, but dark-foliaged kinds will take sun if well watered. Dwarf strains (6–8 in.) include

Cocktail (bronze foliage), Hot Tip, Olympic, Prelude, and Vision. Taller (10–12-in.) strains: Glamour, Partyfun, Pizzazz. Double Ruffles strain has 2-in. fully double flowers on 1-ft. plants.

B. 'Calla King' and **B. 'Calla Lily'.** Varieties with variegated green and white leaves. First has pink-and-white flowers, second red flowers. Choice house plants; too delicate for outdoor use.

Shrublike begonias. This large class is marked by multiple stems which are soft and green rather than bamboolike as in the cane-type group. They are grown for both foliage and flowers. Leaves are very interesting—some are heavily textured; others grow white or red "hairs"; still others develop a soft, feltlike coating. Most grow upright and bushy, but others are less erect and make suitable hanging basket subjects. Flowers in shades of pink, red, white, and peach can come any time, depending on species or variety. Care consists of repotting into larger container as the plant outgrows its pot. Some shrublike begonias can get very large—as tall as 8 ft. They require ample moisture—water when soil begins to dry on surface. Prune to shape; pinch tips to encourage branching.

B. foliosa. Inch-long leaves packed tightly on twiggy plant give fernlike look. Stems arch or droop to 3 ft. Flowers are small, white to red.

B. 'Richmondensis'. Exceeds 2 ft. tall with arching stems carrying deep green, shiny, crisp leaves with red undersides. Salmon pink flowers develop from darker buds. Big and sturdy. Good for narrow space with limited light.

Trailing or climbing begonias. These have stems that trail or climb, depending on how you train them. They are suited to hanging basket culture or planting in the ground where well protected.

B. solananthera. Glossy light green leaves; fragrant white flowers with red centers.

Tuberous begonias. Among the best-known begonias in the West are these magnificent large-flowered hybrids that grow from a tuber. Types range from plants with saucer-sized blooms and a few upright stems to multistemmed hanging basket types covered with flowers. Except for some rare kinds, they are summer- and fall-blooming in almost any flower color except blue.

In early February, buy dormant tubers, the bigger the better. Place in shallow flats and cover ½–1 in. deep with coarse organic matter such as leaf mold. Water regularly and keep in broken shade or under lights indoors. As each plant reaches 3 in. high, repot into 8–10-in. pot with rich, humusy, fast-draining potting mix. For upright types, insert a stake or two at that time, being careful not to pierce the tuber. Water to keep soil moist, but not soggy; if leaves turn yellow, you are overwatering. Fertilize weekly with quarter-strength high-nitrogen fertilizer until mid-May, when you should switch to a program alternating bloom fertilizer with complete fertilizer. Grow in filtered shade, such as under lath or in the open with eastern exposure. For best bloom, mist with water several times a day unless you live in foggy coastal area. Watch for fuzzy white spots on leaves which signal powdery mildew. Control with karathane; prevent with benomyl. In fall, when leaves begin to yellow and wilt, reduce watering. When stems have fallen off the plant on their own, lift tuber, shake off dirt, dry tuber in the sun for 3 days, and store in cool, dry place with its label until spring, when little pink buds will become visible. Then begin the process again. In April and May, you can buy small seedling plants and plant them directly in pots.

Older strains are sold as hanging or upright. The former bloom more profusely; the latter have larger flowers. Colors are white, red, pink, yellow, and peach; shapes are frilly (carnation), formal double (camellia), and tight-centered (rose). Some have petal edges in contrasting colors (picotee). Newer strains are Double Trumpet (improved rose form), Prima Donna (improved camellia), and Hanging Sensation.

Multiflora begonias. Bushy, compact plants 1–1½ ft. tall. Profuse bloom in carmine, scarlet, orange, yellow, apricot, salmon, pink. Includes Clips and Nonstop.

Bertinii hybrids. Similar in form to multifloras, with flowers of pink, red, coral, orange. Good in southern California.

BELAMCANDA chinensis. *Iridaceae.* BLACKBERRY LILY. Perennial with rhizome. All Zones. Common name derives from cluster of shining black seeds exposed when capsules split. Sword-shaped, irislike leaves 1 in. wide. Flowers 1½–2 in. across, orange dotted with red, on 2–3-ft. branching stems; bloom over long period in August, September. Sun or part shade, average water. Plant rhizomes 1 in. deep in porous soil. Effective in clumps in border. Seed capsules make unique arrangements.

Belamcanda chinensis

BELLADONNA LILY. See *Amaryllis belladonna.*

BELLFLOWER. See *Campanula.*

BELL-FRUITED MALLEE. See *Eucalyptus preissiana.*

BELLIS perennis. *Compositae.* ENGLISH DAISY. Perennial, often treated as an annual for winter-spring bloom in hot-summer areas. All Zones. Native to Europe and Mediterranean region. The original English daisies are the kind you often see growing in lawns. Plump, fully double ones sold in nurseries are horticultural varieties. Rosettes of dark green leaves 1–2 in. long. Pink, rose, red, or white double flowers on 3–6-in. stems, in spring and early summer. Meadow plant; needs good soil, much moisture, light shade in warm areas, full sun near coast. Edging or bedding plant; effective with bulbs.

Bellis perennis

BELLS-OF-IRELAND. See *Moluccella laevis.*

BELOPERONE. See *Justicia.*

BENT, BENT GRASS. See *Agrostis.*

Berberidaceae. The barberry family contains both shrubs and herbaceous perennials. Barberry and nandina are typical of the former; *Epimedium* and *Vancouveria* typify the latter.

BERBERIS. *Berberidaceae.* BARBERRY. Deciduous and evergreen shrubs. Zones 1–11, 14–17. Approximate hardiness for each species, deciduous and evergreen, is given in descriptions below. Ability of barberries, especially the deciduous species, to take punishment in climate and soil extremes makes them worth attention in all "hard" climates. Barberries require no more than ordinary garden care. Give sun or light shade, average water. Vigorous growers can take a lot of cutting back for growth renewal; if plants are left to their own devices, some of inner branches die and plants becomes ratty. In list below, details on bloom time, flower color, and spines are omitted unless plant lacks the typical yellow spring flowers and spiny branches.

Berberis darwinii

B. buxifolia. MAGELLAN BARBERRY. Evergreen. Hardy to 0°F. Rather rigid upright growth to 6 ft. and as wide. Leaves small, leathery, to 1 in. long. Flowers orange yellow. Berries dark purple, 1 or 2 at each leaf cluster.

B. b. nana. To 1½ ft. high and 2 ft. wide. Use as traffic regulator or where yellow bloom in evergreen is important. (There is an even lower-growing variety, 'Pygmaea'.)

(Continued on next page)

B

B. chenaultii. Evergreen. Hardy to 0°F. Slow growing, low (to 4 ft.), with arching branches. Leaves dark green, spine toothed, 1–1½ in. long. Flowers bright yellow. Low barrier hedge, foreground planting.

B. darwinii. DARWIN BARBERRY. Evergreen. Hardy to 10°F. Showiest barberry. Fountainlike growth to 5–10 ft. high and 4–7 ft. wide. Leaves small (1 in.), crisp, dark green, hollylike. Orange yellow flowers are so thick along branches that it's difficult to see foliage. Berries dark blue and numerous—popular with birds. Wonderful as background for Oregon grape (*Mahonia aquifolium*). Spreads by underground runners.

B. gladwynensis 'William Penn'. Evergreen, partially deciduous around 0°–10°F. Resembles *B. julianae* in size and general effect, but with broader, glossier leaves; faster growing. Good show of bright yellow flowers.

B. irwinii *(B. stenophylla irwinii)*. Hybrid. Evergreen. Hardy to 0°F. Graceful, fountainlike growth habit to 1½ ft. high. Attractive foliage: narrow, dark green, 1-in.-long leaves.

B. julianae. WINTERGREEN BARBERRY. Evergreen or semideciduous. Hardy to 0°F., but foliage damaged by winter cold. Dense, upright, to 6 ft., with slightly angled branches. Very leathery, spine-toothed, 3-in.-long, dark green leaves. Fruit bluish black. Reddish fall color. One of thorniest—formidable as barrier hedge.

B. mentorensis. Hybrid. Evergreen to about −5°F. Semideciduous to deciduous in colder weather. Hardy to −20°F. Stands hot, dry weather. Rather compact growth to 7 ft. and as wide. Easy to maintain as hedge at any height. Leaves dark green, 1 in. long; beautiful red fall color in cold climates. Berries dull dark red.

B. stenophylla. ROSEMARY BARBERRY. Evergreen garden hybrids. Hardy to 0°F. Leaves narrow, ½–1 in. long, with inrolled edges, spiny tip. Of many varieties, best known is 'Corallina Compacta', CORAL BARBERRY, 1½ ft. tall, with nodding clusters of bright orange flowers. Rock garden, foreground.

B. thunbergii. JAPANESE BARBERRY. Deciduous. Hardy to −20°F. Graceful growth habit with slender, arching, spiny branches; if not sheared, usually reaches 4–6 ft. tall with equal spread. Densely foliaged with roundish, ½–1½-in.-long leaves, deep green above, paler beneath, turning to yellow, orange, and red before they fall. Beadlike, bright red berries stud branches in fall and through winter. Hedge, barrier planting, or single shrub.

B. t. 'Atropurpurea'. RED-LEAF JAPANESE BARBERRY. Foliage bronzy red to purplish red all summer. Must have sun to develop color.

B. t. 'Aurea'. Bright golden yellow foliage, best in full sun. Will tolerate light shade. Slow growing to 1½–2 ft.

B. t. 'Crimson Pygmy' (*B. t.* 'Atropurpurea Nana'). Hardy to −10°F. Selected miniature form, generally less than 1½ ft. high and 2½ ft. wide as 10-year-old. Mature leaves bronzy blood red, new leaves bright red. Must have sun to develop color.

B. t. 'Kobold'. Extra-dwarf bright green variety of Japanese barberry. Like 'Crimson Pygmy' in habit, but fuller and rounder.

B. t. 'Rose Glow'. New foliage marbled bronzy red and pinkish white, deepening to rose and bronze. Colors best in full sun or lightest shade.

B. verruculosa. WARTY BARBERRY. Evergreen. Hardy to 0°F. Neat, tailored shrub with informal elegance. Can reach 3–4 ft. tall, but can be held to 1½ ft. without becoming clumpy. Perky, glossy dark green, 1-in.-long leaves are whitish beneath. In fall and winter, a red leaf develops as highlight here and there in green foliage. Berries black with purplish bloom. Very choice and easy to use on banks, in foreground of shrubbery, or in front of leggy rhododendrons or azaleas.

B. wilsoniae. WILSON BARBERRY. Deciduous to nearly evergreen in mild climates. Hardy to 5°F. Moderate growth to 6 ft. high and as wide, but can be held to 3–4-ft. hedge. Fine-textured foliage, with light green, roundish, ½–1-in. leaves. Small yellow flowers in dense clusters. Beautiful coral to salmon red berries. Handsome barrier hedge.

BERCKMAN DWARF ARBORVITAE. See *Platycladus orientalis*.

BERGENIA. *Saxifragaceae.* Perennials. Evergreen except in coldest areas. Zones 1–9, 14–24. Native to Himalayas and mountains of China. Thick rootstocks; large, glossy green leaves. Thick leafless stalks, 1–1½ ft. high, bear graceful nodding clusters of small white, pink, or rose flowers. Ornamental foliage an all-year asset. Strong, substantial textural quality in borders, under trees, as bold-patterned ground cover. Effective with ferns, hellebores, hostas, and as foreground planting for *Fatsia japonica*, aucubas, rhododendrons.

Bergenia crassifolia

Best performance in partial shade but will take full sun in cool coastal climates. *B. cordifolia* and *B. crassifolia* endure neglect, poor soil, cold, but respond to good soil, regular watering, grooming. Established plants in shade fairly drought tolerant. Cut back yearly to prevent legginess. Divide crowded clumps, replant vigorous divisions. Bait for snails and slugs.

B. ciliata *(B. ligulata)*. Choicest, most elegant. To 1 ft. Lustrous, light green leaves to 1 ft. long and wide, smooth on edges but fringed with soft hairs; young leaves bronzy. Flowers white, rose, or purplish, bloom late spring, summer. Slightly tender; leaves burn in severe frost. Plants sold under this name may be garden hybrids.

B. cordifolia. HEARTLEAF BERGENIA. Leaves glossy, roundish, heart shaped at base, with wavy, toothed edges. In spring, rose or lilac flowers in pendulous clusters partially hidden by large leaves. Plant grows to 20 in.

B. crassifolia. WINTER-BLOOMING BERGENIA. Best-known bergenia. Leaves dark green, 8 in. or more across, with wavy, sparsely toothed edges. Flowers rose, lilac, or purple, in dense clusters on erect stems standing well above leaves. Plants 20 in. high. Blooms January, February.

B. hybrids. With searching, connoisseurs may find named hybrids like 'Ballawley' (purple crimson flowers, 9-in. leaves); 'Evening Glow' and 'Sunningdale' (magenta flowers, maroon winter foliage); or 'Silver Light' (white flowers, hardier than *B. ciliata*).

BERMUDA, BERMUDA GRASS. See *Cynodon*.

BERMUDA BUTTERCUP. See *Oxalis pes-caprae*.

BETHLEHEM SAGE. See *Pulmonaria saccharata*.

BETULA. *Betulaceae.* BIRCH. Deciduous trees. The white-barked European white birch has relatives that resemble it in graceful habit and small-scale, finely toothed leaves, but which vary in size and bark color. All birches need ample water at all times and a regular feeding program. All are susceptible to aphids that drip honeydew; for that reason, these are not trees for a patio or to park a car under. Bronze birch borer can be a problem in the northern Rocky Mountain states; leafminers can be a problem in Oregon. Generally too greedy for lawns. Poor tolerance of drought. On all birches, small conelike fruit hangs on branches through the winter.

Betula pendula

B. albo-sinensis. Zones 1–11, 14–24. Western China. Tall tree (to 100 ft.) grown chiefly for beautiful pinkish brown to coppery bark covered with gray powdery bloom. Leaves 3 in. long. Variety *B. a. septentrionalis* has flaking bark that is orange to orange brown. Rare.

B. jacquemontii. Zones 3–11, 14–17. Northern India. Tall, narrow tree with brilliant white bark. Grows about 2 ft. a year to 40 ft., then more slowly to an eventual 60 ft. Seedlings vary in bark color; buy grafted trees. Somewhat resistant to leaf miners.

B. maximowicziana. MONARCH BIRCH. Zones 3–9, 14–24. Native to Japan. Fast growing; open growth when young. Can reach 80–100 ft. Bark flaking, orange brown, eventually gray or white. Leaves large (up to 6 in. long), turning bright yellow in fall. Resistant to bronze birch borer.

B. nigra. RIVER BIRCH, RED BIRCH. All Zones. Native to eastern half of U.S. Very fast growth in first years; eventually reaches 50–90 ft. Pyramidal form. Trunk often forks near ground, but tree can be trained to single stem. Young bark is pinkish, very smooth and shiny. On older trees it flakes and curls in cinnamon brown to blackish sheets. Diamond-shaped leaves, 1–3 in. long, are bright glossy green above, silvery below. Needs ample moisture. Resistant to bronze birch borer. 'Heritage' is more erect, has tan bark.

B. occidentalis *(B. fontinalis).* Zones 1–3, 10. Large shrub or clumping small tree to 12–15 ft. Bark smooth, shiny, cinnamon brown. Leaves 2 in. long, turning pale clear yellow in fall. A native streamside tree, it likes moisture but needs good drainage as well.

B. papyrifera. CANOE BIRCH, PAPER BIRCH. Zones 1–6. Native to northern part of North America. Similar to *B. pendula*, but taller (to 100 ft.), more open, less weeping. Trunk creamy white. Bark peels off in papery layers. Leaves are larger (to 4 in. long), more sparse.

B. pendula. EUROPEAN WHITE BIRCH. Zones 1–11, 14–24. Native from Europe to Asia Minor. Probably most frequently planted deciduous tree in West. Delicate and lacy. Upright branching with weeping side branches. Average mature tree 30–40 ft. high, spreading to half its height. Bark on twigs and young branches is golden brown. Bark on trunk and main limbs becomes white, marked with black clefts; oldest bark at base is blackish gray. Rich green, glossy leaves to 2½ in. long, diamond shaped, with slender tapered point. Often sold as weeping birch, although trees vary somewhat in habit, and young trees show little inclination to weep.

European white birch has many uses. Its form and color are enhanced by dark background of pines. Dramatic when night-lighted. Lends itself to planting in grove formation, some single, some grouped. Trees of unequal sizes, planted with unequal spacing, look more natural. Trees grown in clumps of several trunks are available.

B. p. 'Dalecarlica' ***(B. p.* 'Laciniata').** CUTLEAF WEEPING BIRCH. Leaves deeply cut. Branches strongly weeping; graceful open tree. Weeping forms are more affected by dry, hot weather than species. Foliage shows stress by late summer.

B. p. 'Fastigiata' ***(B. alba* 'Fastigiata').** PYRAMIDAL WHITE BIRCH. Branches upright; habit somewhat like Lombardy poplar. Excellent screening tree.

B. p. 'Purpurea' ***(B. alba* 'Purpurea').** PURPLE BIRCH. Twigs purple black. New foliage rich purple maroon, fading to purplish green in summer; striking effect against white bark. Best in cool to cold climates.

B. p. 'Trost's Dwarf'. True 3 ft. by 3 ft. dwarf for bonsai, container, rock garden. Needs excellent drainage.

B. p. 'Youngii'. YOUNG'S WEEPING BIRCH. Slender branches hang straight down. Form like weeping mulberry, but tree is more graceful. Decorative display tree. Trunk must be staked to desired height. Same climate limitations as *B. p.* 'Dalecarlica'.

B. platyphylla japonica. JAPANESE WHITE BIRCH. Zones 1–11, 14–24. Native to Japan. Fast growth to 40–50 ft.; narrow, open habit. Glossy green leaves to 3 in. long turn yellow in fall. Bark white. Resistant to bronze birch borer.

Betulaceae. The birch family includes deciduous trees and shrubs with inconspicuous flowers in tight clusters (catkins). Representatives are alder, birch, filbert, and hornbeam.

Bignoniaceae. The bignonia family includes vines (mostly), trees, shrubs, and (rarely) perennials or annuals—all with trumpet-shaped, often 2-lipped flowers. The family gets its name from the genus *Bignonia*, which once included most of the trumpet vines; though most of these have been reclassified, they are often still sold as *Bignonia*. Listed below are the older names, followed by the new:

B. chamberlaynii. See *Anemopaegma chamberlaynii*.
B. cherere. See *Distictis buccinatoria*.
B. chinensis. See *Campsis grandiflora*.
B. jasminoides. See *Pandorea jasminoides*.
B. radicans. See *Campsis radicans*.
B. speciosa. See *Clytostoma callistegioides*.
B. tweediana. See *Macfadyena unguis-cati*.
B. venusta. See *Pyrostegia venusta*.
B. violacea. See *Clytostoma callistegioides*.

BIG SAGEBRUSH. See *Artemisia tridentata*.

BIG TREE. See *Sequoiadendron giganteum*.

BILLBERGIA. *Bromeliaceae*. Evergreen perennials. Zones 16–24. Indoor/outdoor plants anywhere. Relative of pineapple, native to Brazil, where the plants grow as epiphytes on trees. Stiff, spiny-toothed leaves in basal clusters. Showy bracts and tubular flowers in drooping clusters. Usually grown in containers for display indoors or on patios. In southern California, often grown as an easy ground cover under trees; in borders; or on limbs of trees or bark slabs, with roots wrapped in sphagnum moss and leaf mold. Excellent cut flowers.

Billbergia nutans

Best in filtered shade. Pot in light, porous mixture of sand, ground bark, or leaf mold. Need little water in winter when growth is slow, large amounts during active growth in warm weather. Usually hold water in funnel-like center of leaf rosette, which acts as reservoir. When grown as house plants, give plenty of light and sun. Increase by cutting off suckers from base of plant. Specialists in bromeliads list dozens of varieties.

B. nutans. QUEEN'S TEARS. Most commonly grown. Spiny green leaves to 1½ ft. long. Long spikes of rosy red bracts; drooping flowers with green petals edged deep blue. Vigorous. Makes offsets freely; easy to grow, propagate.

B. pyramidalis. Leaves to 3 ft. long, 2½ in. wide, with spiny-toothed margins. Flowers with red, violet-tipped petals and bright red bracts in dense spikes 4 in. long.

B. sanderana. Leaves leathery, to 1 ft. long, spiny toothed, dotted with white. Loose, nodding, 10-in.-long clusters of flowers with blue petals, yellowish green at the base; blue-tipped sepals, rose-colored bracts.

BIRCH. See *Betula*.

BIRCH BARK CHERRY. See *Prunus serrula*.

BIRD OF PARADISE. See *Strelitzia*, *Caesalpinia mexicana*.

BIRD OF PARADISE BUSH. See *Caesalpinia gilliesii*.

BIRD'S-EYE BUSH. See *Ochna serrulata*.

BIRD'S-EYES. See *Gilia tricolor*.

BIRD'S FOOT FERN. See *Pellaea mucronata*.

BIRD'S FOOT TREFOIL. See *Lotus corniculatus*.

BIRD'S NEST FERN. See *Asplenium nidus*.

B

BISHOP'S HAT. See *Epimedium grandiflorum.*

BISHOP'S WEED. See *Aegopodium podagraria.*

BITTER MELON. See *Momordica.*

BITTERROOT. See *Lewisia rediviva.*

BITTERSWEET. See *Celastrus.*

BLACKBERRY. *Rosaceae.* For ornamental relatives see *Rubus.* The West has its own special kinds of blackberries. Most are trailing types as compared to the hardy, upright, stiff-caned kinds of the Midwest and East. The wild blackberry of the Pacific Northwest and northern California has contributed its rich, sprightly flavor to several varieties. Each has its own pattern of climate adaptation. Leaves are divided fanwise, often with thorny stalks and midribs.

Blackberry

All blackberries require deep soil, full sun, and ample water through growing season. Trailing types are best grown on some kind of trellis.

Pruning must follow growth habit. Roots are perennial but canes are biennial, appearing and growing one year, flowering and fruiting the second. Where grown on trellis, train only 1-year-old canes on trellis, and remove all canes that have fruited in August after harvest (cut canes to the ground). Train canes of current season (growing beneath trellis) on trellis and prune to 6–8 ft. Thin out all but 12–16 canes. These will produce side branches during remainder of growing season. Cut side branches back to 1 ft. in early spring. With new spring growth, small branches grow from the side branches. These bear fruit.

Thin out semiupright varieties to 4–8 canes, prune at 5–6 ft., and spread fanwise on trellis. Upright varieties need no trellis but are easier to handle tied to a wire about 2½ ft. above ground. Select 3 or 4 canes and tip them at 2½–3 ft. to force side growth. Tie where canes cross wire.

Red-berry mite (mostly in the 'Himalaya' and 'Evergreen' varieties), spider mites, and whitefly are sometimes a problem. To control, spray in winter and again as buds are about to break, with a dormant spray containing lime sulfur. Spray with malathion as leaves unfold and again a month later.

Fertilize established plantings with commercial fertilizer according to manufacturer's label. In Northwest, feed at blossom time. Best results in California if you split yearly amount into 3 applications: before new growth starts, again in midspring, and again in midsummer. Keep down weeds. Pull out suckers. Above all, don't let plants get away from you.

These varieties are available in western nurseries (all are trailing types except where noted otherwise):

'Boysen' and 'Thornless Boysen'. All Zones. Not reliably hardy in Zone 1 but come through winter if canes are left on ground and covered with snow or with straw mulch. Popular for high yield and flavor—eaten fresh, cooked, or frozen. Berries are reddish, large (1¼ in. long, 1 in. thick), soft, sweet-tart, and have a delightful aroma. Berries carry dusty bloom, are not shiny.

'Cascade'. Best in Zones 4–6, 16, 17. Some grown Zones 20–24. Not adapted Zones 10–13. Not reliably hardy Zones 1–3. Berries bright, deep red, almost black (red when cooked), about 1 in. long, ½ in. thick, with classic wild blackberry flavor. Tender and very juicy; a poor shipper but an excellent garden variety.

'Evergreen' and 'Thornless Evergreen'. Strong canes, semierect growth. This is *the* commercial blackberry in Zones 4–6. Not reliably hardy Zones 1–3. Grown in Zones 15–17 where quantity is important. Bushes vigorous with heavy crops of large (1½-in.-long, ¾-in.-thick), exceptionally firm, black, sweet berries. Seeds large.

'Himalaya'. Seldom sold but has escaped and grows wild wherever adapted. Can be prodigious, spreading pest. Grown in Zones 14–17 for long harvest season—mid-July to October. Extremely vigorous, semierect canes grow 20–30 ft. in one season. Berries shiny jet black, medium sized (1 in. long, ¾ in. thick). Seeds medium large.

'Logan' and 'Thornless Logan'. Same climate adaptation as 'Boysen'. Berries (1¼ in. long, ¾ in. thick) are light reddish, not darkening when ripe, with fine hairs that dull color. Flavor tarter than 'Boysen'; excellent for canning and pies.

'Marion'. Similar to 'Olallie' in berry size and quality but better adapted Zones 4–6. Climate adaptation same as 'Cascade'.

'Nectar'. Identical to 'Boysen'.

'Olallie'. Better adapted in California than in its Oregon homeland. Zones 7–9, 14–24. Berries large (1½ in. long, ¾ in. thick), shiny black, firm, sweeter than 'Cascade' but with some wild blackberry sprightliness.

'Smoothstem'. Zones 4–9, 14–17. Semierect canes 8–10 ft. long. Fruit large, blunt, jet black. Productive; poor shipper but good home variety. Thornless.

'Tay' or 'Tayberry'. Zones 4–9, 14–17. Hybrid between blackberry and raspberry. Long, trailing, thorny vines. Heavy bearer of mild-flavored dark red to purple black, 1½-in. fruit. Bears earlier than other blackberries.

'Thornfree'. Zones 4–9, 14–17. Semierect thornless canes 7–8 ft. long. Tart, shiny black berries are medium large. Heavy bearing.

'Young' and 'Thornless Young'. Climate adaptation similar to 'Boysen' berry, but not as productive in all climates. Berry same size and color as 'Boysen' but shiny and somewhat sweeter.

BLACKBERRY LILY. See *Belamcanda chinensis.*

BLACK CALLA. See *Arum palaestinum.*

BLACK-EYED SUSAN. See *Rudbeckia hirta.*

BLACK-EYED SUSAN VINE. See *Thunbergia alata.*

BLACKFOOT DAISY. See *Melampodium.*

BLACK SALLY. See *Eucalyptus stellulata.*

BLACK SNAKEROOT. See *Cimicifuga racemosa.*

BLANKET FLOWER. See *Gaillardia grandiflora.*

BLAZING STAR. See *Mentzelia.*

BLECHNUM *(Lomaria).* *Polypodiaceae.* Evergreen ferns of symmetrical, formal appearance.

B. brasiliense. Zones 19, 21–24. Dwarf tree fern reaching only 4 ft. in height. Nearly erect fronds in compact clusters. Variety 'Crispum' has elegantly ruffled fronds, reddish when young. Shade, ample water.

B. gibbum. Zones 19, 21–24. Dwarf tree fern with wide-spreading crown of fronds atop slender trunk eventually 3 ft. high. 'Moorei' has wider, more leathery leaflets, is more attractive in winter. Needs moist soil and shade, but avoid overhead water.

Blechnum spicant

B. penna-marina. Zones 15–17, 20–24; with protection Zones 4–6. Spreads slowly to make patches of refined 4–8-in. fronds in cool, moist, sheltered places; can be used as house plant.

B. spicant. DEER FERN, DEER TONGUE FERN. Zones 1–9, 14–24. Native to northern California and Northwest. Produces fronds of

2 kinds. Sterile fronds are narrow, dark glossy green, spreading or angled, 1–3 ft. tall; fertile fronds are stiffly erect, very narrow, with narrow, widely spaced leaflets. Deep shade, moisture, woodsy soil. Difficult to grow in southern California's mild winters.

BLEEDING HEART. See *Dicentra.*

BLETILLA striata *(B. hyacinthina).* *Orchidaceae.* CHINESE GROUND ORCHID. All Zones except in conditions noted below. A terrestrial orchid native to China and Japan. Lavender, cattleya-like, 1–2-in. flowers, up to a dozen on 1½–2-ft. stem, produced for about 6 weeks beginning in May or June. Pale green, plaited leaves, 3–6 to a plant. *B. s.* 'Alba' is a white-flowered form.

Bletilla striata

Plant the tuberlike roots outdoors in fall or in all but coldest areas of West for spring and early summer bloom. Hardy to about 20° F. (to 10°F. if roots are protected). Dies back to ground each winter. Mulch with straw in cold climates. In time will develop large clumps if grown in light shade and in a moist soil, rich in humus. Can be divided in early spring before growth starts, but don't do it too often; blooms best when crowded.

Locate plants (potted or in ground) under high-branching trees or under lath.

BLISTER CRESS. See *Erysimum.*

BLOOD-LEAF. See *Iresine herbstii.*

BLOOD LILY. See *Haemanthus katharinae.*

BLOOD-RED TRUMPET VINE. See *Distictis buccinatoria.*

BLOODROOT. See *Sanguinaria canadensis.*

BLUEBEARD. See *Caryopteris.*

BLUEBELL. See *Endymion, Scilla.*

BLUEBERRY. *Ericaceae.* For ornamental relatives, see *Vaccinium.* Deciduous shrub. Best in Zones 4–6. Hardy in Zones 2, 3, but needs special acid soil preparation there. Grown successfully in northern California coastal area (Zone 17) and by gardeners willing to give it special attention in Zones 7–9, 14–16. Native to eastern U.S. Blueberries thrive under conditions that suit rhododendrons and azaleas, to which they are related. They need sun and cool, moist, acid soil that drains well. In California, if soil is at all alkaline, grow them in straight peat moss or ground bark.

Blueberry

Blueberries contribute more than fruit to garden. They are handsome plants for hedge or shrub border. Most varieties are upright growers to 6 ft. or more; a few are rather sprawling and under 5 ft. Leaves, to 3 in. long, are bronze when new, then dark green, turning scarlet or yellow in fall. Spring flowers tiny, white to pinkish, urn shaped. Fruit very decorative in summer. Plant 3 ft. apart as informal hedge; in larger plantings, as shrubs, space 4–5 ft. apart. Commercial growers allow 6–8 ft. or even more between plants.

Plant 2 varieties for better pollination. Shallow roots benefit from 4–6-in.-thick mulch of sawdust, ground bark, or the like. Water frequently. Use acid-forming fertilizers. In California you may need to use iron sulfate or iron chelate to correct chlorosis.

Prune to prevent overbearing. Plants shape themselves, but often produce so many fruit buds that fruit is undersized and growth of plants slows down. Keep first-year plants from bearing by stripping off flowers. On older plants, cut back ends of twigs to point where fruit buds are widely spaced. Or, simply remove some of oldest branches each year. Remove all weak shoots.

The following varieties have proved themselves in home gardens. Choose for long harvest season. Plant at least 2 for each season ("early" means ripening early to mid-June; "midseason" means early to mid-July; "late" means late July into August). Allow 2 plants for each member of your family. Although all varieties are sold in Northwest and northern California, growers especially recommend these for California: 'Berkeley', 'Bluecrop', 'Dixi', 'Earliblue', 'Jersey'.

'Atlantic'. Late. Sprawling habit. Large light blue berries.

'Berkeley'. Midseason to late. Open, spreading, tall. Very large light blue berries.

'Bluecrop'. Midseason. Erect, tall growth. Large berries. Excellent flavor. Attractive shrub.

'Blueray'. Midseason. Vigorous, tall. Large, highly flavored, crisp berries. Attractive shrub.

'Collins'. Early to midseason. Erect, attractive bush. Small clusters of large, very tasty fruit.

'Concord'. Midseason. Upright to spreading growth. Attractive. Large berry, tart flavored until fully ripe.

'Coville'. Late. Tall, open, spreading. Unusually large leaves. Very attractive. Long clusters of very large light blue berries.

'Dixi'. Late. Not attractive plant—tall and open. Needs heavy pruning. Berries, among largest and tastiest, are medium blue, firm and sweet.

'Earliblue'. Early to midseason. Tall, erect. Large, heavy leaves. Large berries of excellent flavor.

'Ivanhoe'. Early to midseason. Very large dark blue berries—firm, crisp, tart.

'Jersey'. Midseason to late. Tall, erect growing. Large light blue berries. Very bland. Yellow fall and winter color.

'Pemberton'. Very vigorous, tall. Berries large, dark blue, of good dessert quality.

'Rancocas'. Early to midseason. Tall, erect, open, arching habit. Excellent shrub. Leaves smaller than most. Needs heavy pruning. Berries mild and sweet. Dependable old-timer.

'Rubel'. Early to late. Erect, tall growth. Berries firm and tart. Needs pruning to produce large berries.

'Stanley'. Early to midseason. Erect, medium tall. Attractive foliage. One of tastiest—firm, aromatic berries with spicy flavor.

'Weymouth'. Very early. Ripens all berries quickly. Erect, medium height. Large dark blue berries of fair quality; lack aroma.

Dwarf varieties include 'Northblue' (3 ft.), 'North Country' (2 ft.), and 'Northsky' (1½ ft.); all are extremely hardy.

Rabbiteye blueberries are selections of *Vaccinium ashei,* a native of the Southeast. Plants tolerate heat better than the previously mentioned selections of *V. corymbosum,* but have the same need for acid soil; they can be grown in southern California. 'Sharpblue', bearing in April or May, is the only self-fertile kind; others need cross-pollination.

'Aliceblue' and 'Beckyblue' ripen in late May and June; 'Bluegem', 'Briteblue', 'Delite', 'Southland', and 'Woodward' ripen in April and May, with some fruit lingering into July.

BLUE BLOSSOM. See *Ceanothus thyrsiflorus.*

BLUE-EYED GRASS. See *Sisyrinchium bellum.*

BLUE FESCUE. See *Festuca ovina glauca.*

BLUE GINGER. See *Dichorisandra thyrsiflora.*

B

BLUE GRAMA GRASS. See *Bouteloua gracilis.*

BLUEGRASS. See *Poa.*

BLUE GUM. See *Eucalyptus globulus.*

BLUE HIBISCUS. See *Alyogyne huegelii.*

BLUE LACE FLOWER. See *Trachymene coerulea.*

BLUE MARGUERITE. See *Felicia amelloides.*

BLUE MIST. See *Caryopteris clandonensis.*

BLUE SPIRAEA. See *Caryopteris incana.*

BLUE STAR CREEPER. See *Laurentia fluviatilis.*

BLUE THIMBLE FLOWER. See *Gilia capitata.*

BOCCONIA cordata. See *Macleaya cordata.*

BOG ROSEMARY. See *Andromeda polifolia.*

Bombacaceae. This tropical family of trees and shrubs contains 3 plants grown in the mild-winter West: *Chiranthodendron, Chorisia,* and *Fremontodendron.* All have showy flowers.

Boraginaceae. The borage family consists of annuals and perennials (rarely shrubs or trees), most of which have small flowers in coiled clusters which straighten as bloom progresses. Forget-me-not (*Myosotis*) is a familiar example.

BORAGO officinalis. *Boraginaceae.* BORAGE. Annual herb. All Zones. Grows 1–3 ft. high. Bristly, gray green leaves up to 4–6 in. long are edible, with a cucumberlike flavor. Blue, saucer-shaped, nodding flowers in leafy clusters on branched stems. Sun or shade, medium watering; tolerates poor soil. Grows large, needs lots of room. Seeds itself freely but doesn't transplant easily. Good drought-resistant ground cover, soil binder. Use small tender leaves in salads, for pickling, or cooked as greens. Cut flowers for arrangements or use as an attractive garnish.

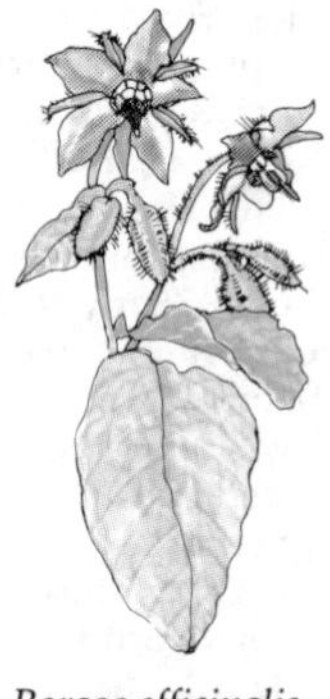

Borago officinalis

BORONIA. *Rutaceae.* Evergreen shrubs. Small shrubs from Australia. Finely divided leaves with needlelike leaflets give plants a wispy look. Attractive but relatively short lived. They need sun or light shade, well-drained, slightly acid, sandy or light loamy soil, and careful watering; they can never go completely dry or stay wet at root for any length of time and survive.

B. denticulata. Zones 15–17. Grows 3–4 ft. high. Fragrant, narrow leaves. Starlike light pink flowers. Easier to grow than following 2 species.

B. elatior. PINK BORONIA, TALL BORONIA. Zones 15–17. Grows to 4–6 ft. Clouds of ¼-in., bell-shaped, pink to rose flowers in spring. Cut back severely after flowering.

Boronia megastigma

B. megastigma. BROWN BORONIA. Zones 15–17, 20–24. Only 1–2 ft. tall, with nodding, ½-in., bell-shaped flowers, brown lined with yellow. Powerful, pleasant scent combines freesia, orange blossom, and other fragrances; blooms February–March. Count on replacing it every 2 or 3 years from seed or cuttings. Will last longer if grown in light potting mix in containers.

BOSTON FERN. See *Nephrolepis exaltata* 'Bostoniensis'.

BOSTON IVY. See *Parthenocissus tricuspidata.*

BO-TREE. See *Ficus religiosa.*

BOTTLEBRUSH. See *Callistemon, Melaleuca.*

BOTTLE PALM. See *Beaucarnea recurvata.*

BOTTLE TREE. See *Brachychiton populneus.*

BOUGAINVILLEA. *Nyctaginaceae.* Evergreen shrubby vines. Reliably hardy in nearest we have to tropical climate (Zones 22–24), yet widely and satisfyingly grown in Zones 12, 13, 15–17, 19, 21. Use has even extended into Zones 5, 6 of Northwest, thanks to low-growing shrubby types which can be purchased in full bloom in gallon cans and grown as container plants. They are used on terrace or patio as summer annual or moved into protected area over winter. Where frost is expected, vines should be given protected warm wall or warmest spot in garden. If vines get by first winter or two they will be big enough to take winter damage and recover. In any case, flower production comes so quickly that replacement is not a real deterrent.

Bougainvillea 'San Diego Red'

Bougainvilleas' vibrant colors come not from the small inconspicuous flowers, but from the 3 large bracts that surround them. Vines make dense cover of medium-sized, medium green leaves. Vigor and growth habit vary by species and variety. Plant in sun, or light shade in hottest areas—in early spring (after frosts) to give longest possible growing time before next frost.

Caution: Bougainvillea roots don't knit soil together in firm root ball in container, and roots are highly sensitive to disturbance. If you knock plant from container roughly, you may fatally damage roots. For plastic container, cut out bottom, place container in planting hole, then cut container from top to bottom and remove sides; fill in with soil. For metal container, poke 6–8 holes in sides and bottom of can before setting it in hole. Fill in around can with soil; metal will rust.

Supply sturdy supports and keep shoots tied up so that they won't whip in wind, and so strong gusts won't shred leaves against sharp thorns along stems.

Fertilize in spring and summer. Water normally while plants are growing fast, then ease off temporarily in midsummer to promote better flowering. Don't be afraid to prune—to renew plant, shape, or direct growth. Prune heavily in spring after frost. On wall-grown plants, nip back long stems during growing season to produce more flowering wood. Shrubby kinds or heavily pruned plants make good self-supporting container shrubs for terrace or patio. Without support and with occasional corrective pruning, bougainvillea can make broad, sprawling shrub, bank and ground cover, or hanging basket plant.

Double-flowering kinds can look messy because they hold faded flowers for a long time.

All of the following are tall-growing vines except those noted as shrubs.

'Afterglow'. Yellow orange; heavy bloom. Open growth, sparse foliage.

'Barbara Karst'. Bright red in sun, bluish crimson in shade; blooms young and for long period. Vigorous growth. Likes heat of desert. Fast comeback after frost.

'Betty Hendry' ('Indian Maid'). Basically red, but with touches of yellow and purple. Blooms young and for a long period.

B. brasiliensis. See *B. spectabilis.*

'Brilliant Variegated'. Spreading, mounding shrub. Leaves variegated with gray green and silver. Brick red flowers. Often used in hanging baskets, pots.

'California Gold' ('Sunset'). Close to pale yellow. Blooms young.

'Camarillo Festival'. Hot pink to gold blend.

'Cherry Blossom'. Double-flowered rose pink, with white to pale green centers.

'Crimson Jewel'. Vigorous shrubby, sprawling plant. Good in containers, as shrub, sunny bank cover. Lower growth, better color than 'Temple Fire'. Heavy bloom, long season.

'Crimson Lake'. See 'Mrs. Butt'.

'Don Mario'. Large, vigorous vine with huge clusters of deep purple red blooms.

'Hawaii'. ('Raspberry Ice'). Shrubby, mounding, spreading. Leaves have golden yellow margins. New leaves tinged red. Flowers red. Good hanging basket plant. Regardless of its tropical name, it's one of the hardiest.

'Isabel Greensmith'. Flowers variously described as orange, red orange, or red with yellow tinting.

'Jamaica White'. Bracts white, veined light green. Blooms young. Moderately vigorous.

'James Walker'. Big reddish purple flowers on big vine.

'La Jolla'. Bright red bracts, compact, shrubby habit. Good shrub, container plant.

'Lavender Queen'. An improved *B. spectabilis,* with bigger bracts, heavier bloom.

'Manila Red'. Many rows of magenta red bracts make heavy clusters of double-looking bloom.

'Mary Palmer's Enchantment'. Very vigorous, large-growing vine with pure white bracts.

'Mrs. Butt' ('Crimson Lake'). Old-fashioned variety with good crimson color. Needs lots of heat for bloom. Moderately vigorous.

'Orange King'. Bronzy orange. Open growth. Needs long summer, no frost.

'Pink Tiara'. Abundant pale pink to rose flowers over long season.

'Raspberry Ice'. See 'Hawaii'.

'Rosea'. Large rose red bracts on large vine.

'Rosenka'. Can be held to shrub proportions if occasional wild shoot is pruned out. Gold flowers age pink.

'San Diego Red' ('San Diego', 'Scarlett O'Hara'). One of best on all counts: large, deep green leaves that hold well in cold winters; deep red bracts over long season; hardiness equal to old-fashioned purple kind. Vigorous, high climbing. Can be trained to tree form by staking and pruning.

'Southern Rose'. Lavender rose to pink.

B. spectabilis (B. brasiliensis). Hardy and vigorous. Blooms well in cool summers. Purple flowers. Best for Zones 16, 17.

'Tahitian Dawn'. Big vine with gold bracts aging to rosy purple.

'Tahitian Maid'. Extra rows of bracts give double effect to blush pink clusters.

'Temple Fire'. Shrublike growth to 4 ft. high, 6 ft. wide. Partially deciduous. Bronze red.

'Texas Dawn'. Choice, vigorous pink. Purplish pink bracts in large sprays.

'Torch Glow' is an oddity, an erect, multistemmed plant to 6 ft. It needs no support. Reddish pink flowers close to stems are partially hidden by foliage.

'White Madonna'. Pure white bracts.

BOULDER RASPBERRY. See *Rubus deliciosus.*

BOUSSINGAULTIA. See *Anredera.*

BOUTELOUA gracilis. *Gramineae.* BLUE GRAMA GRASS. Pasture grass used for low-maintenance, low-water-use lawns in sunny, arid, alkaline regions of Rocky Mountains and high plains. Hardy throughout this area, but little tested elsewhere. Bunching rather than sod forming, it nevertheless makes fair lawn if sown at 1 lb. per 1,000 sq. ft. Sow in fall to take advantage of winter rain, snow. Water to depth of 1 ft. while it is becoming established; thereafter it can get along with virtually no irrigation. Mow at 1½ in.

Bouteloua gracilis

BOUVARDIA. *Rubiaceae.* Evergreen shrubs. Native to Arizona, New Mexico, Mexico, and Central America. Loose, often straggling growth habit. Showy clusters of tubular flowers; *B. longiflora* 'Albatross' has fragrant blossoms, but is also the most tender and looks poorest after flowers are gone. The nonfragrant red-flowered types are hardier, easier to grow.

Bouvardia longiflora

B. glaberrima. Zones 8–10, 14–24. Native to mountain canyons in southern Arizona, New Mexico. To 3 ft. tall, shrubby but dying back at tops in cold weather. Smooth green leaves 1–3 in. long. Clustered inch-long, tubular, red (rarely pink or white) flowers. Tolerates drought, likes part shade.

B. longiflora 'Albatross' ***(B. humboldtii* 'Albatross').** Zones 12, 13, 16, 17, 19–24. Fragrant, snow white, 3-in.-long, tubular flowers in loose clusters on a weak-stemmed shrub, 2–3 ft. high with paired 2-in. leaves. Blossoms appear at almost any time. Pinch out stem tips to make bushier. Cut back flowering branches from time to time to stimulate new growth. Grow in tubs or boxes in rich, fast-draining soil mix. Ample water.

B. ternifolia *(B. jacquinii).* Zones 8–10, 14–24. A 6-ft.-tall shrub with 2-in. leaves in whorls of 3 or 4. Red, 1-in.-long, tubular flowers in loose clusters at ends of branches. Selected forms are pink, rose, coral, red. Same requirements as *B. glaberrima.*

BOWER VINE. See *Pandorea jasminoides.*

BOWLES' GOLDEN GRASS. See *Milium effusum* 'Aureum'.

BOX, BOXWOOD. See *Buxus.*

BOX ELDER. See *Acer negundo.*

BOYSENBERRY. See Blackberry.

BRACHYCHITON *(Sterculia).* *Sterculiaceae.* Evergreen to partly or wholly deciduous trees. Native to Australia. All have woody, canoe-shaped fruits that delight flower arrangers but are merely litter to some gardeners. Drought tolerant.

Brachychiton populneus

B. acerifolius *(Sterculia acerifolia).* FLAME TREE, AUSTRALIAN FLAME TREE. Deciduous for brief period. Zones 16–21, 23. When at its best, a most spectacular red-flowering tree reaching 60 ft. or more. Hardy to 25°F. Strong, heavy, smooth trunk, usually green. Leaves are handsome, glossy, bright green, 10-in.-wide fans, deeply lobed. Showiest flowering season usually May to June. Tree wholly or partially covered with great clusters of small, ¾-in., tubular, red or orange red bells. Leaves drop before flowers appear in portion of tree that blooms.

(Continued on next page)

B. populneus *(Sterculia diversifolia).* BOTTLE TREE. Evergreen. Zones 12–24. Moderate growth to 30–50 ft., 30-ft. spread. Common name from very heavy trunk, broad at base, tapering quickly. Leaves (2–3 in. long) give general effect of poplar. They shimmer in breeze like aspen's. Clusters of small, bell-shaped, white flowers in May and June noticeable close up; 2½–3-in. woody fruits that follow are noticeable in litter they produce. Appreciated in low and intermediate deserts, where they are frequently used as screens or high, wide windbreaks. Susceptible to Texas root rot.

BRACHYCOME. *Compositae.* SWAN RIVER DAISY. Annuals and perennials. Neat, charming Australian daisies make mounds 1 ft. tall, 1½ ft. across, with finely divided leaves and a profusion of inch-wide daisies in spring and summer. Need sun or lightest shade, good drainage. Use in rock garden, front of border, in containers or raised beds.

Brachycome iberidifolia

B. iberidifolia. Annual. All Zones. Flowers are blue, white, or pink. Sow seed where plants are to grow.

B. multifida. Perennial. Zones 14–24. Very similar to *B. iberidifolia,* but perennial. Blue most common color. Propagate by cuttings.

BRACHYSEMA lanceolatum. *Leguminosae.* SCIMITAR SHRUB, SWAN RIVER PEA SHRUB. Evergreen. Zones 8, 9, 12–24. Unusual flowers have earned it its common names and place in gardens. Blooms are bright red and shaped like sweet peas, but with inch-long pairs of petals (keels) shaped like a scimitar. Never makes great show of flowers, but it's rarely out of bloom. To 3 ft. or more, loosely formed, erect in growth, spreading in age. Leaves narrow, to 4 in. long, dark green above, silvery beneath. Prune by thinning out old, straggly stems. Best in full sun, with fast drainage, in sandy soil. Takes drought. Don't pamper. Go light with fertilizers.

Brachysema lanceolatum

BRACKEN. See *Pteridium aquilinum.*

BRAHEA *(Erythea).* *Palmae.* These fan palms from Mexico are somewhat like the more familiar washingtonias in appearance, but with important differences. All tolerate drought.

B. armata. MEXICAN BLUE PALM. Zones 12–17, 19–24. Grows slowly to 40 ft., top spreading 6–8 ft. Leaves silvery blue, almost white. Conspicuous creamy flowers. Hardy to 18°F. and takes drought, heat, and wind.

Brahea armata

B. brandegeei. SAN JOSE HESPER PALM. Zones 19, 21–24. Slow grower with slender, flexible trunk. Eventually tall; reaches 125 ft. in its native Baja California. Trunk sheds leaves when old. Three-ft. leaves are light gray green. Hardy to 26°F.

B. edulis. GUADALUPE PALM. Zones 13–24. From Guadalupe Island off Baja California. Like *B. armata* but leaves are light green, flowers less conspicuous. Slow grower to 30 ft., stout trunked. Old leaves drop, leaving the naked, elephant hide trunk ringed with scars. Hardy to below 20°F.; takes beach and desert conditions.

B. elegans. FRANCESCHI PALM. Zones 13–17, 19–24. Slowest growing of braheas; develops a trunk very slowly and reaches only 15 ft. Leaves gray green. From northern Mexico; hardy to 22°F.

BRAKE. See *Pteris.*

BRAMBLE. See *Rubus.*

BRASSAIA actinophylla. See *Schefflera actinophylla.*

BRASSAVOLA. *Orchidaceae.* Epiphytic orchids native to tropical America. House or greenhouse plants. Large, spiderlike, white or greenish white flowers with large lip and narrow sepals and petals. Flowers grow singly or in short-stemmed clusters. Tough, leathery leaves grow from small pseudobulbs. Plants similar to laelias. Grow in any orchid soil mix. Need 60°–65°F. night temperature, 5°–10°F. higher in day. Water liberally and give plenty of sun during growing season. Reduce humidity during dormant period.

Brassavola nodosa

B. cucullata. Fragrant, 2-in. flowers in summer or fall. Grasslike leaves to 1 ft. long with pseudobulb included. Hardy enough to grow outdoors through winter in warm climate areas in southern California.

B. digbyana *(Laelia digbyana).* Fragrant 4–6-in. flowers notable for huge, fringed, white to cream lip. Petals pale green tinted lavender. Summer bloom. Tough, leathery, gray green leaves. Transmits big fringed lip to its hybrids and is famous orchid parent.

B. nodosa. LADY-OF-THE-NIGHT. In fall, 3-in. flowers appear, 2–6 on a stem; sweetly fragrant at night. Fleshy, 6-in.-long leaves. Hardy outdoors in winter where temperatures are mild.

BRAZILIAN FLAME BUSH. See *Calliandra tweedii.*

BRAZILIAN PLUME FLOWER. See *Justicia carnea.*

BRAZILIAN SKY FLOWER. See *Duranta stenostachya.*

BREATH OF HEAVEN. See *Coleonema and Diosma.*

BRIDAL VEIL. See *Tripogandra multiflora.*

BRIDAL VEIL BROOM. See *Genista monosperma.*

BRIMEURA amethystina *(Hyacinthus amethystinus).* *Liliaceae.* Bulb. All Zones. Bulbs, leaf rosettes exactly resemble small hyacinths. For rock gardens or naturalizing. Plants bloom in spring bearing loose spikes of clear blue bells with paler blue streaks on 6–8-in.-tall stems. Plant in mid to late autumn, 2 in. deep, 3 in. apart. Mulch in areas where winters are very cold.

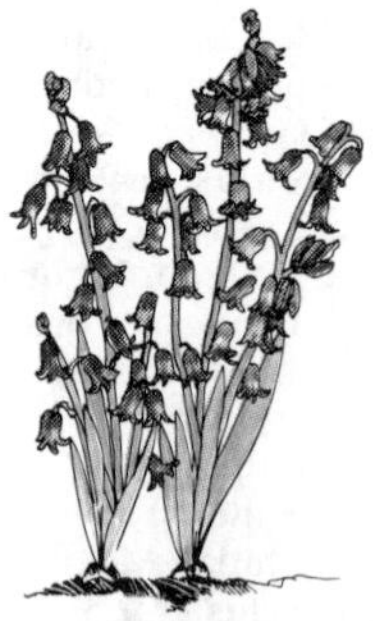

Brimeura amethystina

BRISBANE BOX. See *Tristania conferta.*

BRIZA maxima. *Gramineae.* RATTLESNAKE GRASS, QUAKING GRASS. Annual. All Zones. Native to Mediterranean region. Ornamental grass of delicate, graceful form; used effectively in dry arrangements and bouquets. Grows 1–2 ft. high. Leaves are ¼ in. wide, to 6 in. long. Clusters of nodding, seed-bearing spikelets, ½ in. long (or longer), papery and straw colored when dry, dangle on threadlike stems. Spikelets resemble rattlesnake rattles. Scatter seed where plants are to grow; thin seedlings to 1 ft. apart. Often grows wild along roadsides, in fields.

Briza maxima

BROCCOLI. *Cruciferae.* Biennials grown as annuals. All Zones in conditions noted below. Best all-round cole crop (cabbage and its close relatives) for home gardener; bears over long season, is not difficult to grow. Grows to 4 ft. and has branching habit. Central stalk bears cluster of green flower buds that may reach 6 in. in diameter. When central cluster is removed, side branches will lengthen and produce smaller clusters. Good varieties are 'Calabrese', 'Cleopatra', 'De Cicco', 'Italian Green Sprouting'.

Broccoli

Broccoli is a cool-season plant which tends to bolt into flower when temperatures are high, so plant it to mature during cool weather. In mild climates, plant in late summer, fall, or winter for winter or early spring crops. In cold-winter areas, set out young plants about 2 weeks before last frost.

Young plants resist frost but not hard freezes. Good guide to planting time is appearance of young plants in nurseries. You can raise young plants from seed sown 4–6 weeks ahead of planting time. One pack of seed will produce far more plants than even the largest home garden could handle, so save surplus seed for later plantings. A dozen plants at each planting will supply a family.

Choose a sunny location; space plants 1½–2 ft. apart in rows and leave 3 ft. between rows. Keep plants growing vigorously with regular deep irrigation and 1–2 feedings of commercial fertilizer before heads start to form. Cut heads before clustered buds begin to open. Include 5–6 in. of edible stalk and leaves. Control aphids and cabbage worm with malathion *before heads form,* or use all-purpose vegetable dust.

BRODIAEA. *Liliaceae.* Corms. All Zones (but note conditions below). Many are natives of the Pacific Coast, where they bloom in sunny fields and meadows, spring and early summer. Few grasslike leaves; clusters of funnel-shaped or tubular, ½–2-in.-long flowers atop the stem. In nature often found in adobe soil, in areas where it rains heavily in winter and early spring and corms completely dry out in summer. In gardens, give similar conditions (no dry-season watering). Where plants must take summer watering, plant in sandy or gritty soil. Plant corms 2–3 in. deep. In cold-winter areas, grow in containers or mulch to protect from freezing and thawing.

Brodiaea elegans

Brodiaea includes many plants now listed under different names. Cross-references below will guide you to appropriate entries under *Dichelostemma* and *Triteleia.*

B. capitata. See *Dichelostemma pulchellum.*

B. coronaria *(B. grandiflora).* HARVEST BRODIAEA. Clusters of dark blue, inch-long flowers on 6–10-in. stems. Late spring, early summer bloom.

B. elegans (often seen as *B. grandiflora* or *B. coronaria*). HARVEST BRODIAEA. Similar to *B. coronaria,* but taller (to 16 in.).

B. grandiflora. See *B. coronaria.* Another plant known by same name is *Triteleia grandiflora.*

B. hyacinthina. See *Triteleia hyacinthina.*

B. ida-maia. See *Dichelostemma ida-maia.*

B. ixioides. See *Triteleia ixioides.*

B. lactea. See *Triteleia hyacinthina.*

B. laxa. See *Triteleia laxa.*

B. lilacina. See *Triteleia hyacinthina lilacina.*

B. lutea. See *Triteleia ixioides.*

B. minor. Dark blue flowers on stems that may be 3–4 in. long, rarely 1 ft.

B. peduncularis. See *Triteleia peduncularis.*

B. 'Queen Fabiola'. See *Triteleia* 'Queen Fabiola'.

B. tubergenii. See *Triteleia tubergenii.*

B. uniflora. See *Ipheion uniflorum.*

BROMELIA balansae. *Bromeliaceae.* HEART OF FLAME. Zones 19–24. Pineapple relative. Forms impressive cluster of 30–50 arching, saw-toothed leaves, glossy dark green above, whitish beneath. To 4 ft. tall, 4–6 ft. across. Center leaves turn bright scarlet in spring or early summer. From this center rises a stalk bearing a spike of rose-colored flowers margined with white. Needs warm nights to perform satisfactorily. Almost any soil if drainage is good. Grows best in sun, in porous soil with plenty of organic matter. Water occasionally; feed lightly once or twice in summer.

Bromelia balansae

Bromeliaceae. The bromelia or pineapple family; all its members are called bromeliads. Most bromeliads are stemless perennials with clustered leaves and showy flowers in unbranched or branched clusters. Leaves of many kinds are handsomely marked, and the flower clusters gain beauty from colorful bracts. Pineapple, the best known example, is sometimes grown as a houseplant.

In most areas of the West, bromeliads are considered choice house plants. Kinds most often grown indoors are, in their native homes, epiphytes: plants that perch on trees or rocks and gain their sustenance from rain and from whatever leaf mold gathers around their roots. These often have cupped leaf bases that hold water between rains. In mildest areas of the West, many of these epiphytes grow well outdoors in sheltered places. Fanciers often fasten them to tree branches, packing sphagnum moss around the roots to hold moisture and encourage root growth. More often they are grown in pots of loose, fast-draining, highly organic growing mix. Feed lightly but frequently, and keep central cups filled with water.

A few bromeliads (*Puya* is the best known) are desert plants that resemble yuccas and thrive in the same conditions.

BRONZE DRACAENA. See *Cordyline australis* 'Atropurpurea'.

BROOM. See *Cytisus, Genista, Spartium.*

BROUSSONETIA papyrifera. *Moraceae.* (Has been sold as *Morus papyrifera.*) PAPER MULBERRY. Deciduous tree. Zones 3–24. Valuable as shade tree where soil and climate limit choice. Takes stony, sterile, or alkaline soils, strong winds, desert heat, drought. Hardy in all but coldest areas. Moderate growth to 50 ft., with dense, broad crown to 40 ft. across. Smooth, gray bark. Heart-shaped, 4–8-in., rough leaves, gray and velvety beneath; edges toothed, often lobed when young. Male flowers, catkins; female, rounded heads. Suckering habit can be problem in highly cultivated gardens. Seldom suckers in desert. Good in rough bank plantings. Common name comes from inner bark, used for making paper and Polynesian tapa cloth.

Broussonetia papyrifera

BROWALLIA. *Solanaceae.* AMETHYST FLOWER. Annuals, sometimes living over as perennials. All Zones in conditions noted below. Choice plant for connoisseur of blue flowers. Bears one-sided clusters of lobelialike blooms ½–2 in. long and just as wide in brilliant blue, violet, or white; blue flowers are more striking because of contrasting white eye or throat. Blooms profusely in warm shade or filtered sunlight. Graceful in hanging basket or pots. Fine cut flower.

Browallia speciosa

(Continued on next page)

B

Sow seeds in early spring for summer bloom, in fall for winter color indoors or in greenhouses. Plants need warmth, regular moisture. You can lift vigorous plants in fall, cut back and pot; new growth will produce flowers through winter in warm spot. Rarely sold as plants in nurseries; get seeds from specialists.

B. americana. Branching, 1–2 ft. high; roundish leaves. Violet or blue flowers ½ in. long, ½ in. across, borne among leaves. 'Sapphire', dwarf compact variety, dark blue with white eye, is very free blooming. This species and its variety often listed in catalogs as *B. elata* and *B. elata* 'Sapphire'.

B. speciosa. Lives over as perennial in mild-winter climates. Sprawling, to 1–2 ft. high. Flowers dark purple above, pale lilac beneath, 1½–2 in. across. 'Blue Bells Improved', lavender blue, grows 10 in. tall, needs no pinching to make it branch. 'Marine Bells' has deep indigo flowers, 'Silver Bells' white flowers.

BRUGMANSIA ***(Datura).*** *Solanaceae.* Evergreen shrubs. Zones 16–24. Related to the annual or perennial jimsonweeds or thorn apples (*Datura*). All kinds sold have tubular flowers and are known as "angel's trumpet." Flowers and seeds poisonous if eaten.

Brugmansia candida

All are large shrubs that can be trained as small trees. Garden care is same for all: plant in wind-sheltered location in sun or shade. Give ample water during growth and bloom season. Expect frost damage and unattractive winter appearance. Prune in early spring after last frost. Cut back branchlets to 1 or 2 buds. (Tubbed plants can be wintered indoors with a little light and very little water.)

Large of leaf and flower, these are dominating shrubs and should be brought into garden with that in mind. White-flowered angel's trumpet is showy in moonlight.

B. arborea. Plants usually offered under this name are either *B. candida* or *B. suaveolens*. The true *B. arborea* has smaller flowers.

B. candida. Native to Peru. Fast and rank growing with soft, pulpy growth to 10–15 ft. (6 ft. or more in one season). Dull green, large leaves in the 8–12-in. range. Heavy, single or double white trumpets, 8 in. or more long, are fragrant, especially at night. They appear in summer and fall, often as late as November or December in warm, sheltered gardens.

B. sanguinea. Native to Peru. Fast growing to 12–15 ft. Leaves bright green to 8 in. long. Trumpets, orange red with yellow veinings, about 10 in. long, hang straight down bell fashion from new growth. Rare.

B. suaveolens. Native to Brazil. Similar to *B. candida,* but leaves and flowers are somewhat larger and flowers less fragrant.

B. versicolor. To 15 ft. tall. Flowers white or peach colored. Named versions of uncertain origin include 'Charles Grimaldi' (pale orange yellow) and 'Frosty Pink' (cream deepening to pink).

BRUNFELSIA pauciflora calycina ***(B. calycina).*** *Solanaceae.* Evergreen shrubs. Zones 13–17, 20–24. In all but warmest locations, these shrubs lose most of their foliage for short period. Upright or spreading, to about 3 ft. Oval, 3–4-in.-long leaves dark green above, pale green below. Tubular, rich dark purple flowers, several in a cluster, flare to 2 in. wide; bloom comes in spring, early summer.

Brunfelsia pauciflora 'Floribunda'

Brunfelsias are handsome plants that deserve extra attention. Give them rich, well-drained soil mix on acid side. Give iron in Zone 13 to prevent chlorosis. Protect from full sun for very best in foliage and flower. Provide constant supply of water; feed through growing season. Prune in spring to remove scraggly growth and to shape. Use where you can admire spectacular flower show. Brunfelsias grow well in containers.

B. p. 'Eximia' ***(B. c. eximia).*** Somewhat dwarfed, compact version of the following, more widely planted variety. Flowers are a bit smaller but more generously produced.

B. p. 'Floribunda'. YESTERDAY-TODAY-AND-TOMORROW. Common name comes from quick color change of blossoms: purple ("yesterday"), lavender ("today"), white ("tomorrow"). Flowers profusely displayed all over plant. In partial shade, will reach 10 ft. or more with several stems from base. (May be held to 3 ft. by pruning.)

B. p. 'Macrantha' ***(B. floribunda*** **'Lindeniana', B. grandiflora).** Differs markedly from above. The most tender. More slender growing; larger leaves, often 8 in. long, 2½ in. wide. Flowers 2–4 in. across, deep purple with lavender zone bordering white throat. Treat with iron if foliage yellows.

BRUNNERA macrophylla. *Boraginaceae.* BRUNNERA. Perennial. All Zones. Charming in filtered shade in warm areas, sun or light shade on coast. Reaches 1½ ft. tall; leaves heart shaped, dark green, 3–4 in. wide. There is also a rare variety with white-edged leaves. In spring, airy clusters of tiny, clear blue, forget-me-not flowers with yellow centers. Uses: Informal ground cover under high-branching deciduous trees; among spring-flowering shrubs such as forsythia, deciduous magnolias; filler between newly planted evergreen shrubs. Once established, self-sows freely. Planted seeds often difficult to germinate (try freezing them before sowing). Increase by dividing clumps in fall.

Brunnera macrophylla

BRUNSVIGIA rosea. See *Amaryllis belladonna.*

BRUSH CHERRY, AUSTRALIAN BRUSH CHERRY. See *Syzygium paniculatum.*

BRUSSELS SPROUTS. *Cruciferae.* Annual. All Zones except in conditions noted below. A cabbage relative of unusual appearance. Mature plant has crown of fairly large leaves and its tall stem is completely covered with tiny sprouts. Fairly easy to grow where summers are not too hot, long, or dry. 'Jade Cross Hybrid' is easiest to grow and most heat tolerant; 'Long Island Improved' ('Catskill') is standard market variety. You may have to grow your own from seed. Sow outdoors or in flats in April, transplant young plants in June or early July to sunny place where they will grow and bear in fall. In mild climates plant in fall or winter for winter and spring use.

Brussels sprouts

Treat the same as broccoli. When big leaves start to turn yellow, begin picking. Snap off little sprouts from bottom first—best when slightly smaller than golf ball. Leave little sprouts on upper stem to mature. After picking, remove only leaves below harvested sprouts. A single plant will yield from 50–100 sprouts.

BUCHLOE dactyloides. *Gramineae.* BUFFALO GRASS. Pasture grass often used as low-maintenance, drought-tolerant lawn in Rocky Mountains and high plains. Slow to sprout and fill in, it spreads rapidly by surface runners once established and makes matted, reasonably dense turf that takes hard wear and looks fairly good with very little summer water. Needs sun. Gray green from late spring to hard frost, straw colored through late fall and winter. Runners can invade surrounding garden beds. Given minimum

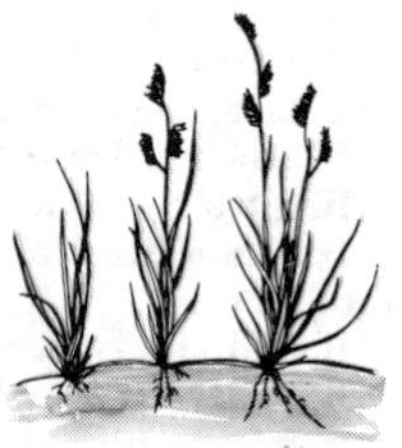

Buchloe dactyloides

water, it grows to 4 in. tall and requires little or no mowing. More water means higher growth, some mowing. Sow 2 lbs. per 1,000 sq. ft. Soak occasionally to 1 ft. while grass is getting started. To start from sod, in spring, plant 4-in.-wide plugs 3–4 ft. apart on prepared soil; cover should be complete in 2 seasons.

BUCKEYE. See *Aesculus californica.*

BUCKTHORN. See *Rhamnus cathartica.*

BUCKWHEAT. See *Eriogonum.*

BUDDLEIA. *Loganiaceae.* BUTTERFLY BUSH. Evergreen or deciduous shrubs or small trees. Many species known; all have some charm in either flower color or fragrance, but only 2 species are readily available. Sun or light shade, average water.

Buddleia davidii

B. alternifolia. FOUNTAIN BUTTERFLY BUSH. Deciduous shrub or small tree. All Zones. It can reach 12 ft. or more, with arching, willowlike branches rather thinly clothed with 1–4-in.-long leaves, dark dull green above, gray and hairy beneath. Blooms in spring from previous year's growth; profuse small clusters of mildly fragrant, lilac purple flowers make sweeping wands of color. Tolerates many soils; does very well in poor, dry gravels. Prune after bloom: remove some of oldest wood down to within few inches of ground. Or train up into small single or multiple-trunked tree. So trained, it somewhat resembles a small weeping willow.

B. davidii. COMMON BUTTERFLY BUSH, SUMMER LILAC. Deciduous or semievergreen shrub. Zones 1–9, 12–24. Fast, rank growth each spring and summer to 3, 4, or even 10 ft. Leaves tapering, 4–12 in. long, dark green above, white and felted beneath. In midsummer, small fragrant flowers (lilac with orange eye) appear in dense, arching, spikelike, slender clusters 6–12 in. or more long, at branch ends. Butterflies often visit flowers.

Needs good drainage and enough water to maintain growth, but little else. In cold climates, the soft wood freezes nearly to ground but roots are hardy. Whether plants are deciduous in cold-winter areas or semievergreen in mild winters, for best appearance cut plants back to within a few inches of ground—do this after fall flowering in Zones 4–9, 12–24; or in spring in Zones 1–3, 10, 11. Susceptible to red spider mites in hot, dry areas.

Many varieties are obtainable, differing mostly in flower color; colors include pink, lilac, blue, purple, and white.

BUFFALO GRASS. See *Buchloe dactyloides.*

BUGBANE. See *Cimicifuga.*

BULBINELLA floribunda *(B. robusta, B. setosa).* *Liliaceae.* Perennial, tuberous rootstock. Zones 14–24. Native to South Africa. Valuable for winter color, forming large clump of 20–26-in., narrow, floppy leaves topped in January–February with 4-in.-long spikes of clear yellow flowers. Similar to poker plant (*Kniphofia*) but spikes are shorter and less pointed, and individual flowers are bell shaped, not tubular. Splendid cut flower. Low-maintenance borders—makes colonies in rather short time. Sun; part shade in hot-summer areas. Any soil, if well drained. Ample water in winter, spring; keep on dry side in summer. Pull off old, dry foliage after bloom. Divide crowded clumps. Easy to grow from seed sown in spring.

Bulbinella floribunda

BULL BAY. See *Magnolia grandiflora.*

BUNCHBERRY. See *Cornus canadensis.*

BUNNY EARS. See *Opuntia microdasys.*

BUNYA-BUNYA. See *Araucaria bidwillii.*

BURMESE PLUMBAGO. See *Ceratostigma griffithii.*

BURRO TAIL. See *Sedum morganianum.*

BUSH ANEMONE. See *Carpenteria californica.*

BUSHMAN'S POISON. See *Acokanthera oppositifolia.*

BUSH MORNING GLORY. See *Convolvulus cneorum.*

BUSH POPPY. See *Dendromecon.*

BUSHY YATE. See *Eucalyptus lehmannii.*

BUTCHER'S BROOM. See *Ruscus aculeatus.*

BUTIA capitata. *Palmae.* PINDO PALM. Zones 7–9, 12–24. Native to Brazil, Uruguay, Argentina. Slow-growing, very hardy palm to 10–20 ft. Trunk heavy, strongly patterned with stubs of old leaves: attractive if these are trimmed to same length. Feathery, gray green, arching leaves. Very small flowers, yellow to red. Hardy to 15°F. Slow growth. Sun or light shade, average water.

Butia capitata

BUTTERFLY BUSH. See *Buddleia.*

BUTTERFLY FLOWER. See *Schizanthus pinnatus.*

BUTTERFLY WEED. See *Asclepias tuberosa.*

BUTTERNUT. See *Juglans cinerea* under Walnut.

BUTTONWOOD. See *Platanus occidentalis.*

Buxaceae. The boxwood family comprises principally evergreen shrubs with inconspicuous flowers (fragrant in *Sarcococca*). Members include *Buxus, Pachysandra,* and *Sarcococca.*

BUXUS. *Buxaceae.* BOXWOOD, BOX. Evergreen shrubs, small trees. Widely used for edging and hedging. When not clipped, most grow soft and billowing. All grow in full sun or shade. All are easy to grow where adapted, and are therefore often neglected. Extra care with watering, feeding, and spraying in summer for mites and scale will pay off in better color and greater vigor. Flowers quite inconspicuous.

B. harlandii. Zones 8–24. The boxwood sold by this name in California, commonly called Korean boxwood, does not fit description of the true species *B. harlandii* and differs from both Japanese boxwood and true Korean boxwood. Leaves are narrower and

Buxus microphylla japonica

brighter green than those of Japanese boxwood and plant appears better suited to colder areas of California.

B. microphylla. This species is rarely planted. Its widely planted varieties include:

B. m. japonica. JAPANESE BOXWOOD. Zones 8–24. Hardy to 0°F. but poor winter appearance in cold areas. It takes California's dry heat and alkaline soil—conditions that rule out English boxwood. Compact foliage (small, ⅓–1-in., round-tipped leaves) is lively bright green in summer, brown or bronze in winter in many areas. Grows slowly to 4–6 ft. if not pruned, making a pleasing informal green shrub. Most often clipped as low or medium hedge or shaped into globes, tiers, pyramids in containers. Can be held to 6-in. height as a hedge or border edging.

B. m. j. 'Compacta'. Extra-dwarf plant with tiny leaves. Slow growing; good rock garden plant.

B. m. j. 'Green Beauty'. Zones 3–24. Hardier than common Japanese boxwood (to −10°F.), holds its deep green color in coldest weather, and is considerably greener than *B. m. japonica* in summer heat.

B. m. j. 'Richardii'. Zones 4–24. Hardy to 0°F. Tall growing (6 ft. or more), more vigorous than Japanese boxwood. Leaves deeper green, larger, and usually notched at tip.

B. m. j. 'Winter Gem'. Zones 2–24. Hardiest of Japanese boxwoods.

B. m. koreana. KOREAN BOXWOOD. All Zones. Hardy to −18°F. Slower and lower growing than Japanese boxwood. Leaves smaller (¼–½ in.). This should not be confused with "Korean boxwood" or "*Buxus harlandii*" commonly sold in California. *B. m. koreana* is noted for its hardiness and will live where others freeze out. It is slower growing and smaller in leaf than the plant sold as *B. harlandii*.

B. sempervirens. COMMON BOXWOOD, ENGLISH BOXWOOD. Zones 3–6, 15–17. Dies out in alkaline soils, hot-summer areas. Will grow to height of 15–20 ft. with equal spread. Dense foliage of medium-sized, lustrous, dark green, oval leaves. Dwarf form *B. s.* 'Suffruticosa' is best known; the taller-growing varieties are used in Northwest.

B. s. 'Arborescens'. Slow growing. Becomes beautiful small tree to 18 ft. More open than *B. sempervirens*.

B. s. 'Aureo-variegata'. Leaves yellow or marked with yellow.

B. s. 'Inglis'. Densely branched, cone-shaped shrub with dark green foliage. Holds color well in winter. Hardy to −20°F.

B. s. 'Rotundifolia'. Dwarf, slow-growing plant with nearly round leaves.

B. s. 'Suffruticosa'. TRUE DWARF BOXWOOD. Slower growing than others, to 4–5 ft. but generally clipped lower. Small leaves, dense form and texture. There's a silver-edged variegated form.

Byttneriaceae. This family of tropical trees and shrubs has only *Dombeya* and *Hermannia* as representatives in western gardens.

CABBAGE. *Cruciferae.* For ornamental relatives, see Cabbage, Flowering. Annual or biennial grown as annual. All Zones in conditions noted below. There are early varieties that mature in 7–8 weeks from transplanting into garden and late varieties that require 3–4 months. In addition to green cabbage, you can also get red and curly-leafed (Savoy) varieties. To avoid overproduction, set out a few plants every week or two; or plant both early and late kinds. Time plantings so heads will form either before or after hot summer months. In cold-winter areas, set out late varieties in midsummer for late fall and early winter crops. In mild-winter areas, plant in fall or winter. To avoid pest buildup, plant in different site each year. Sow seeds ½ in. deep about 6 weeks before planting-out time. Transplant to rich, moist soil, spacing plants 2–2½ ft. apart. Give frequent light applications of nitrogen fertilizer and never let plants wilt. Mulch helps keep soil moist and cool. Best in sun; tolerates light shade in hot climates. Control aphids with soapy water spray, rotenone, or malathion. Control green cabbage worm with vegetable dust, *Bacillus thuringiensis*, or rotenone. Light frost doesn't hurt cabbage, but harvest and store before heavy freezes occur.

Cabbage

CABBAGE, FLOWERING. *Cruciferae.* Annual or biennial grown as annual. All Zones in conditions noted below. Flowering cabbage and flowering kale are grown for their highly ornamental, highly colored leaf rosettes, which look like giant peonies in deep blue green marbled and edged with white, cream, rose, or purple. Kale differs from cabbage in being slightly looser in the head, more heavily fringed at leaf edges. It appreciates same soil, care, and timing as conventional cabbage, and its 10-in. "flowers" are spectacular in cool-season garden, either 15–18 in. apart in open-ground beds, potted singly in 8-in. pots, or potted several plants to a large container. Colors are strongest after first frosts touch plants. Single rosette cut and placed on spike holder in bowl makes striking harvest arrangement. Foliage is sold as salad savory; it is edible raw or cooked, and is highly decorative as a salad garnish.

Flowering Cabbage

CABBAGE PALM. See *Sabal palmetto*.

Cactaceae. The cactus family contains a huge number of succulent plants (see also Succulent). Generally leafless, they have stems modified into cylinders, pads, or joints which store water in times of drought. Thick skin reduces evaporation, and most species have spines to protect plants against browsing animals. Flowers are usually large and brightly colored; fruit may also be colorful and is sometimes edible.

All (with one doubtful exception) are native to the Americas—from Canada to Argentina, from sea level into high mountains, in deserts or in dripping jungles. Many are native to drier parts of the West.

Cacti range in height from a few inches to 50 ft. Larger species are used to create desert landscapes. Smaller species are grown in pots or, if sufficiently hardy, in rock gardens. Many are easy-care, showy house or greenhouse plants. Large types for landscaping require full sun, well-drained soil. Water newly planted cacti very little; roots are subject to rot before they begin active growth. In 4–6 weeks, when new roots are active, water thoroughly, then let soil dry before watering again. Reduce watering in fall to allow plants to go dormant. Feed monthly in spring, summer. For some larger kinds for garden use, see *Carnegiea, Cephalocereus, Cereus, Echinocactus, Espostoa, Ferocactus, Lemaireocereus, Opuntia.*

Smaller cacti for pot or rock garden culture usually have interesting form and brightly colored flowers. Feed and water plants well during warm weather for good display; taper off on fertilizer to encourage winter dormancy. Use fast-draining soil mix. See *Chamaecereus, Coryphantha, Echinopsis, Gymnocalycium, Lobivia, Lobivopsis, Mammillaria.*

Showiest in flower are jungle cacti that grow as epiphytes on trees or rocks. These need rich soil with much humus, frequent feeding and watering, partial shade, and protection from frost. Grow in lathhouse or greenhouse, or handle as outdoor/indoor plants. See *Epiphyllum, Rhipsalidopsis, Schlumbergera.*

CAESALPINIA *(Poinciana).* *Leguminosae.* Evergreen and deciduous shrubs, small trees. (Tropical royal poinciana is *Delonix regia.*) They grow quickly and easily in hot sun with light, well-drained soil and infrequent, deep watering.

C. gilliesii *(Poinciana gilliesii).* BIRD OF PARADISE BUSH. Deciduous or evergreen shrub or small tree. Zones 8–16, 18–23. Occasionally seen Zones 6, 7. Tough, interesting, fast growing to 10 ft., with finely cut, filmy foliage on rather open, angular branch structure. Drops leaves in cold winters. Blooms all summer; clusters of yellow flowers adorned with protruding, bright red, 4–5-in.-long stamens. Flowers attract hummingbirds.

C. mexicana. MEXICAN BIRD OF PARADISE. Zones 12–16, 18–23. Evergreen shrub or small tree. Moderately fast growth to 10–12 ft.; may be pruned to 6–8 ft. Foliage coarser than that of *C. pulcherrima.* Blooms year round except in coldest months, bearing lemon yellow flower clusters 6 in. long, 4 in. thick.

Caesalpinia gilliesii

C. pulcherrima *(Poinciana pulcherrima).* DWARF POINCIANA, BARBADOS PRIDE. Deciduous shrub. Zones 12–16, 18–23. Fast, dense growth to 10 ft. tall, 10 ft. wide. Dark green leaves with many ¾-in.-long leaflets. Blooms throughout warm weather; flowers orange or red (rarely yellow), clustered, with long red stamens. May be evergreen in mild winters. Useful for quick screening. Freezes to ground in colder areas but rebounds quickly in spring. Even if it doesn't freeze back, you can cut it back to ground in early spring to make more compact mound.

CAJEPUT TREE. See *Melaleuca quinquenervia.*

CALADIUM bicolor. *Araceae.* FANCY-LEAFED CALADIUM. Tuberous-rooted perennial. Best adapted Zones 23, 24; in protected gardens Zones 12, 13, 16, 17, 22; elsewhere as indoor or greenhouse plant in winter, outdoors in summer. Native to tropical America.

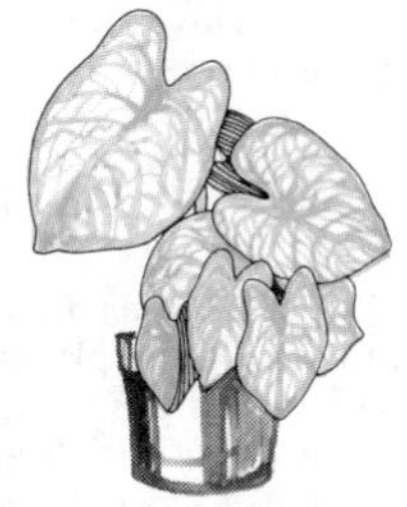

Caladium bicolor

Not grown for flowers. Instead, entire show comes from large, arrow-shaped, long-stalked, almost translucent leaves colored in bands and blotches of red, rose, pink, white, silver, bronze, and green. Most varieties sold in nurseries derived from *C. bicolor*—usually 2 ft. tall, occasionally 4 ft. Caladiums need warm shade, daytime temperature of 70°F.; they're best adapted as summer pot plant in sheltered patios or plunged in borders. Combine with ferns, coleus, alocasias, colocasias, and tuberous begonias.

Same pot culture as tuberous begonias. Start tubers indoors in March, outdoors in May. Pot in mix of equal parts coarse sand, leaf mold, and ground bark or peat moss. Use 5-in. pot for 2½-in. tuber, 7-in. pot for 1 larger or 2 smaller tubers. Fill pot halfway with mix, stir in heaping teaspoon of fish meal. Add 1 in. mix, set tuber with knobby side up, cover with 2 in. of mix. Water thoroughly.

To plant in ground, replace top 6 in. of existing soil with same mix as for pots. Place 1 tablespoon of fish meal in bottom of each hole; proceed as described above. Keep soil moist, not wet. Provide more moisture as leaves develop. Syringe overhead every day or two during active growth. Feed with liquid fish fertilizer once a week, starting when leaves appear. Bait for slugs and snails. Gradually withhold water when leaves start to die down. In about a month, lift tubers, remove most of soil, dry in semishade for 10 days. Dust tubers with insecticide-fungicide preparation; store for winter in dry peat moss or vermiculite at temperature between 50°–60°F.

C. esculentum. See *Colocasia esculenta.*

CALAMONDIN. See *Citrus,* Sour-Acid Mandarin Oranges.

CALATHEA. *Marantaceae.* Indoor or greenhouse plants. Native to tropical America or Africa. Calatheas are usually called marantas, to which they are closely related and from which they differ only in technical aspects. Interesting plants for indoor decoration in winter, outdoor use in summer. Ornamental leaves, beautifully marked in various shades of green, white, and pink, arranged in basal tufts. Flowers of most are inconspicuous and of no consequence. Need warm atmosphere (not under 55°F.) and shade, although good light necessary for rich leaf color. Porous potting mix, perfect drainage; stagnant conditions harmful. Wet leaves frequently. Repot as often as necessary to avoid rootbound condition.

Calathea zebrina

C. crocata. ETERNAL FLAME. Leaves 6 in. long, 1–1½ in. wide, dark green above, purple beneath. Two-in. spikes of bright orange flower bracts look like little torches. Clump has several shoots; each shoot dies after blooming, but new ones appear to keep up the show. Variable performance as house plant; subject to mites in low humidity. Does better in greenhouse.

C. insignis. Striking, 3–7 ft. in native jungle, lower in cultivation, with 1–1½-ft.-long, yellow green leaves striped olive green.

C. lancifolia (usually sold as *C. insignis*). Long (1–1½-ft.), narrow, wavy-edged leaves are yellow green banded with dark olive green.

C. louisae. To 3 ft. Foot-long dark green leaves heavily feathered with gray green along midrib.

C. makoyana. Showy, 2–4 ft. high. Leaves with areas of olive green or cream above; pink blotches beneath. Silver featherings on rest of upper surface, with corresponding cream-colored area underneath.

C. ornata. Sturdy, 1½–3 ft. high. Leaves 2–3 ft. long, rich green above, purplish red beneath. Juvenile leaves usually pink striped between veins; intermediate foliage striped white. Variety 'Roseolineata' has pink and white stripes at angle to midrib.

C. zebrina. ZEBRA PLANT. Compact plant to 1–3 ft. high. Ellipse-shaped leaves reach 1–2 ft. long, almost half as wide. Upper surfaces are velvety green with alternating bars of pale yellow green and olive green extending outward from midrib; under sides are purplish red.

CALCEOLARIA. *Scrophulariaceae.* Perennials. Native Mexico to Chile. Loose clusters of small pouchlike or slipperlike flowers, usually yellow; sometimes red bronze or spotted with red or orange brown. Blooms in spring and summer. Plants much branched, often woody stemmed and shrubby, 8 in.–6 ft. high, with dark green, crinkly leaves.

Calceolaria integrifolia

C. crenatiflora. Zones 14–24 as bedding plant or pot plant for outdoor use in shade; house plant elsewhere. Usually grown from seed sown in spring or summer in light, porous soil, with plants ready for final potting or planting out in fall. Average water. This is florists' calceolaria, with masses of inch-long yellow to velvety red flowers, often spotted and marbled. Can reach a height of 2½ ft., but the most popular strains are the lower-growing Multiflora Nana and Multiflora, which grow 9–15 in. tall. Plants are usually discarded after flowering but sometimes live over. Strain called Anytime tolerates high temperatures better than other strains; start it indoors in late winter for summer bloom.

C. integrifolia. Zones 14–24. Shrubby plant 1½–6 ft. high. Leaves about 3 in. long and 1 in. wide. Clusters of yellow to red brown, unspotted flowers ½ in. across. Will grow in full sun, take heat, light frost. Average water. Borders, pots, hanging baskets. Best bloom when rootbound. Good cut flower. Variety 'Golden Nugget' most commonly sold; vigorous, 1½–2 ft., clear golden yellow flowers spring to fall. 'Russet' and 'Kentish Hero' have orange red to brown flowers.

C. 'John Innes'. All Zones. Bedding and rock garden plant to 8 in. high, with 3-in.-long leaves and large, purple-spotted golden yellow flowers in June, July. Spreading growth habit in some instances; stems tend to take root in contact with soil. Needs rich, moist soil and shade.

C

CALENDULA officinalis. *Compositae.* CALENDULA, POT MARIGOLD. Annual. All Zones in conditions noted below. Sure, easy color from late fall through spring in mild-winter areas; spring to midsummer in colder climates. Besides familiar orange and bright yellow double, daisylike blooms 2½–4½ in. across, calendulas come in more subtle shades of apricot, cream, and soft yellow. Plants somewhat branching, 1–2 ft. high. Leaves are long, narrow, round on ends, slightly sticky, and aromatic. Plants effective in masses of single colors in borders, parking strips, along drives, in containers. Long-lasting cut flowers.

Calendula officinalis

Sow seed in place or in flats in late summer or early fall in mild-winter climates; spring elsewhere. Or buy seedlings at nurseries. Needs sun. Adapts to most soils, ample or little water, if drainage is fast. Remove spent flowers to prolong bloom. Although an excellent pot plant, the common name is actually derived from the plant's earlier use as a "pot herb"—a vegetable to be used in the cooking pot.

Dwarf strains (12–15 in.) include Bon Bon (earliest), Dwarf Gem, and Fiesta (Fiesta Gitana). Taller (1½–2 ft.) are Kablouna (pompon centers with looser edges), Pacific Beauty, and Radio (quilled, "cactus" blooms).

CALIFORNIA BAY. See *Umbellularia californica.*

CALIFORNIA FAN PALM. See *Washingtonia filifera.*

CALIFORNIA FUCHSIA. See *Zauschneria.*

CALIFORNIA GERANIUM. See *Senecio petasitis.*

CALIFORNIA LAUREL. See *Umbellularia californica.*

CALIFORNIA NUTMEG. See *Torreya californica.*

CALIFORNIA POPPY. See *Eschscholzia californica.*

CALLA. See *Zantedeschia.*

CALLIANDRA. *Leguminosae.* Evergreen shrubs. Group of 250 or more species represented here by a flame bush, a pink powder puff, and fairy dusters. All are showy, spreading shrubs that need sun and warmth.

C. californica. Zones 10–24. Similar to *C. eriophylla,* but foliage is more luxuriant. Blooms through warm part of year if given some supplemental summer water.

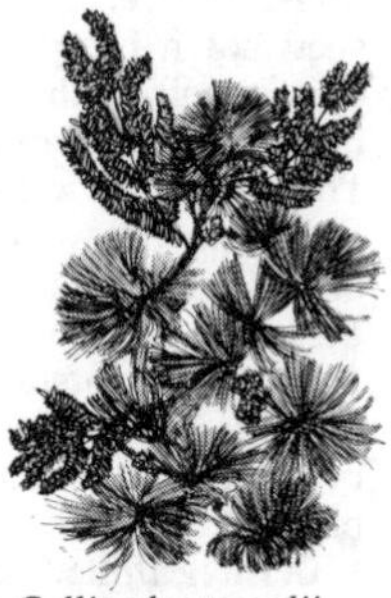

Calliandra tweedii

C. eriophylla. FAIRY DUSTER, FALSE MESQUITE. Zones 10–24. Native from California's Imperial and eastern San Diego counties east to Texas; and Baja California. Open growth to 3 ft. tall, 4–5 ft. wide. Leaves finely cut into tiny leaflets. Flower clusters show pink to red stamens in fluffy balls to 1½ in. across, February or March. Very drought resistant.

C. haematocephala *(C. inaequilatera).* PINK POWDER PUFF. Zones 22–24. Native to Bolivia. Grows fast to 10 ft. or more, equal spread. Its beauty has carried it into harsher areas than Zones 22–24: into 13, 16–21 where it is given special protection of overhang or warm sunny wall. (In form, it's a natural espalier.) Foliage not as feathery as that of *C. tweedii;* leaflets longer, broader, and darker—glossy copper when new, turning to dark metallic green. Big puffs (2–3 in. across) of silky stamens, watermelon pink, are produced October–March. There is a rare white-flowered form. Needs plenty of water and light soil.

C. tweedii (often sold as *C. guildingii*). TRINIDAD FLAME BUSH, BRAZILIAN FLAME BUSH. Best in Zones 22–24; satisfactory 15–21; freezes back but recovers in Zones 7–9, 12–14.

Graceful, picturesque structure to 6–8 ft. tall, 5–8 ft. wide. Leaves, lacy and fernlike, divided into many tiny leaflets, scarcely hide branches. Flower clusters show as bright crimson pompons at branch ends, February to fall. Not fussy about soil. Once established, it's quite drought resistant. Prune to thin and also to retain interesting branch pattern.

CALLICARPA bodinieri giraldii *(C. giraldiana).* *Verbenaceae.* BEAUTYBERRY. Deciduous shrub. Zones 1–6. This species seems to be the only one in cultivation in the West. To 6–10 ft., with gracefully recurving branches. Leaves narrow, to 4 in. long, something like peach leaves in form; turn pink to purple before falling. Small lilac flowers in 1-in.-wide clusters followed by small violet fruit that lasts well into fall. Freezes to ground in cold winters, comes back quickly from stump sprouts. Sun, average water.

Callicarpa bodinieri giraldii

CALLIOPSIS. See *Coreopsis tinctoria.*

CALLISIA. *Commelinaceae.* House plants or indoor/outdoor plants for hanging pots. They look like, and are related to, wandering Jews (*Tradescantia* and *Zebrina*). For care, see *Tradescantia* description.

C. elegans. Stems spread or reach upward instead of drooping, usually much less than maximum of 2 ft. Leaves thick, semisucculent, 3 in. long by 1 in. wide. Upper surfaces dark olive green with white pinstripes running lengthwise; undersides purple. Small flowers, not often seen.

Callisia elegans

C. fragrans. Leaves to 10 in. long make big rosettes that resemble loose-knit hen and chicks (*Echeveria*). Long runners produce miniatures of parent at tips. Makes massive hanging basket plant that is impressive rather than attractive. Branched clusters of fragrant flowers seldom produced. Offsets can be detached and set in shallow trays of water, the rosettes resting on pebbles or other support. They will root and grow for several months with no further attention, tolerating low light, dryness.

C. repens. This creeping, trailing plant is often sold as *Tradescantia* or as 'Little Jewel'. Closely spaced, thick, fleshy, shiny, bright green leaves an inch long or less make it attractive hanging pot plant. Small flowers bloom infrequently.

CALLISTEMON. *Myrtaceae.* BOTTLEBRUSH. Evergreen shrubs or trees. Zones 8, 9, 12–24, but borderline—often severely damaged—at 20°F. Native to Australia. Colorful flowers in dense spikes or round clusters consisting principally of long, bristlelike stamens—hence the common name. Flowers followed by woody capsules that persist for years and sometimes look like bands of beads pressed into bark. Thrive in full sun. Drought tolerant but grow best in moist, well-drained soils. Generally tolerant of saline-alkaline soils but sometimes suffer from chlorosis. Fast growing, easy to train. Quick wall cover as informal espaliers.

Callistemon citrinus

Several can be trained as small trees. Some can be used in formal clipped hedges or as informal screens or windbreaks. A few can be trained as ground covers.

Many kinds are being sold under names whose identification is uncertain. Closely related to melaleuca, and some plants sold as *Callistemon* may be melaleucas.

C. citrinus *(C. lanceolatus).* LEMON BOTTLEBRUSH. Best-selling bottlebrush, most tolerant of heat, cold, and adverse soils (can be troubled with chlorosis in Zones 12 and 13). Massive shrub to 10–15 ft., but with staking and pruning in youth easily trained into narrowish, round-headed, 20–25-ft. tree. Nurseries offer it as shrub, espalier, or tree. Narrow, 3-in.-long leaves coppery in new growth, then vivid green. Bright red, 6-in.-long brushes appear in cycles throughout year. Hummingbirds love flowers.

Variable plant when grown from seed. Cutting-grown selections with good flower size and color are *C. c.* 'Improved' and *C. c.* 'Splendens'. *C. c.* 'Compacta' is smaller (4 ft. by 4 ft. at 3 years), with smaller spikes. *C. c.* 'Jeffersii' is smaller (to 6 ft. tall, 4 ft. wide), stiffer in branching, with narrower, shorter leaves and reddish purple flowers fading to lavender.

C. cupressifolius. The plant sold under this name may be a melaleuca or variety of some other species of *Callistemon*. Shrubby, 4–5 ft. high, 4–6 ft. wide. Growth is spreading, with drooping branchlets. Foliage gray green; new foliage pink. Red flower clusters to 3 in. long in June–July.

C. 'Jeffersii'. See *C. citrinus* 'Jeffersii'.

C. linearis. NARROW-LEAFED BOTTLEBRUSH. Shrubby, 6–8 ft. tall (sometimes to 15 ft.), 5 ft. wide, with narrow, 2–5-in.-long leaves. Bright crimson brushes 5 in. long in summer.

C. pachyphyllus viridis. Stiff-branched, spreading shrub to 6–7 ft. Leaves nearly as narrow and stiff as pine needles. Flower spikes are bright apple green against dark green foliage.

C. rigidus. STIFF BOTTLEBRUSH. Erect, sparse, rigid shrub or small tree to 20 ft. with 10-ft. spread. Leaves sharp pointed, gray green (sometimes purplish). Red flower brushes 2½–4½ in. long, spring and summer. Seed capsules prominent. Least graceful bottlebrush, but drought tolerant.

C. 'Rosea'. Plants sold under this name are similar to *C. citrinus* 'Jeffersii', but grow taller and bear rose pink flowers.

C. salignus. WHITE BOTTLEBRUSH. Shrub or tree to 20–25 ft. Dense crown of foliage. New growth bright pink to copper. Willowy leaves 2–3 in. long. Flowers pale yellow to cream colored in 1½–3-in. clusters. Train as small shade tree or plant 4–5 ft. apart as hedge.

C. viminalis. WEEPING BOTTLEBRUSH. Shrub or small tree with pendulous branches. Fast growing to 20–30 ft. with 15-ft. spread. Leaves narrow, light green, 6 in. long. Bright red brushes May–July, and scattered bloom throughout the year. Needs ample water. Not for windy, dry areas. May be damaged by cold winters in Zones 8, 9, 12, 13. As tree, needs staking, thinning of surplus branches to prevent tangled, topheavy growth. Inclined toward sparseness because leaves tend to grow only at ends of long, hanging branches. 'Captain Cook' is dwarf variety useful as border, low hedge, or screen plant. 'McCaskillii' is denser in habit than others, more vigorous, and better in flower color and form. Variety sold as 'Dwarf' resembles 'McCaskillii'.

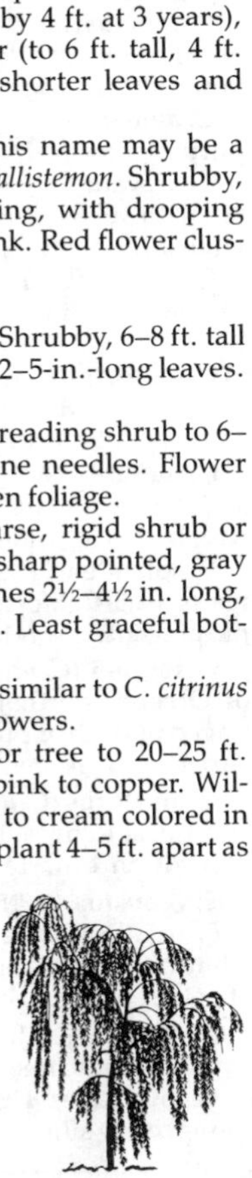

Callistemon viminalis

CALLISTEPHUS chinensis. *Compositae.* CHINA ASTER. Annual. All Zones in conditions noted below. Splendid cut flower and effective bedding plant when well grown and free of disease. Plants 1–3 ft. high, some kinds branching, others (developed mainly for florists) with strong stems and no side shoots. Leaves deeply toothed or lobed. Summer is bloom season. Many different flower forms: quilled, curled, incurved, ribbonlike, or interlaced rays; some with crested centers. Varieties offered as pompon, peony-flowered, anemone-flowered, ostrich feather. Colors range from white to pastel pink, rose pink, lavender, lavender blue, violet, purple, crimson, wine, and scarlet.

Callistephus chinensis

Plant in rich, loamy or sandy soil in full sun. Sow seed in place after frosts or set out plants from flats. Keep growth steady; sudden checks in growth are harmful. Subject to aster yellows, a virus disease carried by leafhoppers. Remove and burn infected plants. Spray or dust to control leafhoppers. All but wilt-resistant types are subject to aster wilt or stem rot, caused by parasitic fungus which lives in soil and is transmitted through roots into plants. Overwatering produces ideal condition for diseases, especially in heavy soil. Never plant in same location in successive years.

CALLUNA vulgaris. *Ericaceae.* SCOTCH HEATHER. Evergreen shrub. Zones 2–6, 15–17. This, the true and only Scotch heather, has crowded tiny, scalelike, dark green leaves and one-sided spikes of bell-shaped, rosy pink flowers. Garden varieties (far more common than wild kind) include dwarf ground cover and rock garden plants 2–4 in. tall and robust 2–3-footers. Flower colors include white, pale to deep pink, lavender, and purple. Foliage can vary to paler and deeper greens, yellow, chartreuse, gray, or russet, often changing color in winter. Most bloom in mid to late summer; a few bloom into late fall. To prune, shear off faded flowers and branch tips immediately after bloom (with latest varieties, delay pruning until March).

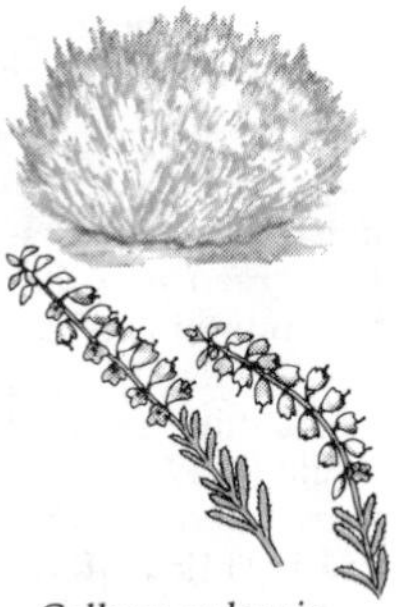

Calluna vulgaris

Heathers thrive in full sun (light shade in hot interior valleys) in sandy, peaty, fast-draining soil. In Northwest, where they are best adapted, they require little or no fertilizing. Where watering must be frequent, light feeding with acid plant food—once in February or March, a second time in June—will encourage good growth and bloom.

Lower kinds make good rock garden or ground cover plants; taller varieties make good backgrounds for lower kinds and are attractive cut flowers. Good hobby plants, they come in stimulating variety of colors and textures; by carefully choosing varieties, you can have bloom from June–November. Combine them with heaths (*Erica*) for year-round bloom, or use with other acid-loving plants (rhododendron, pieris, huckleberry) for contrasting texture. Here are a few of the scores of varieties obtainable from specialists:

'Alba Plena'. Loose, medium green mound to 1 ft. Double white flowers August–September. Fast growing.

'Aurea'. Spreading, twiggy, 8–12-in. plant with gold foliage turning russet in winter. Sparse purple bloom August–September.

'Aureafolia'. Upright, to 1½–2 ft. Chartreuse foliage, tinged gold in summer. White flowers August–September.

'County Wicklow'. Mounding, 9–18 in., medium green. Pink double flowers from white buds August–October.

'Dainty Bess'. Tiny gray leaves form mat 2–4 in. tall. Lavender flowers August–September; shapes itself to rocks, crevices.

'David Eason'. Spreading mound, 1–1½ ft. Light green foliage; reddish purple flowers October–November.

'Else Frye'. Erect plant to 2 ft. Medium green foliage; double white flowers July–August.

'Foxii Nana'. Small mound to 6 in. Dark green foliage; purple flowers August–September. A dwarf pincushion.

'Goldsworth Crimson'. Mounding, 1½–2 ft. Dark or smoky green foliage; crimson flowers October–November.

'H. E. Beale'. Loose mound to 2 ft. Dark green foliage; soft pink double flowers from August–October. Long spikes are good for cutting.

(Continued on next page)

'J. H. Hamilton'. Prostrate, bushy, to 9 in. Deep green foliage; profuse double pink bloom August–September.

'Mair's Variety'. Erect, 2–3 ft. Medium green foliage; white flowers July–September. Easy to grow, good background.

'Mrs. Pat'. Bushy, to 8 in. Light green foliage; pink new growth. Light purple flowers July–September.

'Mrs. Ronald Gray'. Creeping mound, to 3 in. Dark green foliage; reddish purple flowers August–September. Excellent ground cover.

'Mullion'. Tight mound to 9 in. Dark green foliage, rosy purple flowers August–September. Fine ground cover.

'Nana'. Low, spreading, to 4 in. Dark green foliage; purple flowers July–September. Often called carpet heather.

'Nana Compacta'. Tight mound to 4 in. Medium green. Purple flowers July–September. Pincushion heather for rockery.

'Roma'. Compact, to 9 in. Dark green foliage; deep pink flowers August–October.

'Searlei'. Bushy, 1–1½ ft. Yellow green feathery foliage. White flowers August–October.

'Tib'. Rounded, bushy, to 1–1½ ft. Medium green foliage; deepest rosy purple double flowers August–September.

CALOCEDRUS decurrens *(Libocedrus decurrens).* *Cupressaceae.* INCENSE CEDAR. Evergreen tree. Zones 1–12, 14–24. Native to mountains of southern Oregon, California, western Nevada; northern Baja California. Unlike most of its native associates—white fir, Douglas fir, sugar pine—it adapts to many western climates. Symmetrical tree to 75–90 ft. with dense, narrow, pyramidal crown; trunk with reddish brown bark. Rich green foliage in flat sprays. Tree gives pungent fragrance to garden in warm weather. Small, yellowish brown to reddish brown cones which, when open, look like ducks' bills.

Calocedrus decurrens

Although slow growing at first, it may grow 2 ft. per year when established. Deep but infrequent watering in youth will make it unusually drought tolerant when mature. Takes blazing summer heat. Tolerates poor soils. Good tree to make green wall, high screen, windbreak. Common on the Yosemite Valley floor, this tree has been seen by millions.

CALOCEPHALUS brownii. *Compositae.* CUSHION BUSH. Evergreen shrubby perennial. Zones 16, 17, 19, 21–24. Best adapted Zones 17, 24. Native to Australia, Tasmania. An unusual mounding plant, silvery white throughout; at its best when buffeted by winds and exposed to salt air and spray. Wiry, branching stems; tiny threadlike leaves, ⅛ in. long, pressed tightly against slender stems. Grows 3 ft. tall, equally broad. Flower heads button shaped, ½ in. across, in clusters. Stunning high ground cover or rock garden plant. Effective in large planters with succulents. Fresh or dried foliage attractive in arrangements. Full sun, sandy or gravelly soil, fast drainage. Sensitive to excess water, severe cold. Cut out dead wood on older plants.

Calocephalus brownii

CALOCHORTUS. *Liliaceae.* Bulbs. Western natives, most numerous in California. Of most interest to hobbyists willing to devote more than ordinary care to beautiful group of plants. It's best to plant kinds native to your area or similar climate. All kinds should be kept moist in winter and spring, allowed to go dry in summer. You may grow them in cans or boxes, plunge into ground in fall, then lift after bloom to dry out in summer.

Flower forms divide into 3 groups. Globe tulips or fairy lanterns have 3–5 nodding flowers to a stalk, and petals turn inward to form a globe. Star tulips have erect, cup-shaped flowers, often with tips of petals rolled outwards; some have long, straight hairs on inner flower surfaces and are called cat's ears or pussy ears. Most striking are mariposa lilies, whose erect, branching, 10–24-in. stems hold big, colorful, cup-shaped flowers. Leaves scanty, long, grasslike. Here are kinds most often available for sale:

Calochortus venustus

C. albus. WHITE GLOBE LILY, FAIRY LANTERN. Sierra foothills, Coast Ranges. Two-ft. stems; white, 1¼-in. flowers March–May.

C. amabilis. GOLDEN FAIRY LANTERN. Northern Coast Ranges. Stems 15 in. tall; flowers 1¼ in. long, deep yellow often tinged brown, March–May.

C. amoenus. PURPLE GLOBE TULIP. Sierra Nevada foothills. Rosy purple lanterns, 1¼ in. long, on 8–16-in. stems; April–June.

C. clavatus. Coast Ranges, Sierra Nevada foothills. Mariposa lily with yellow flowers sometimes marked brownish red, 2–3 in. wide on stems to 3 ft. Blooms April–June.

C. luteus *(C. luteus citrinus).* Coast Ranges or Sierra Nevada foothills. Yellow, 2½-in. mariposa lilies on 1–1½ ft. stems April–June.

C. maweanus. See *C. tolmiei.*

C. nudus. Mountains of northern California. White to lavender star tulips, 1–1½ in. wide, on 4–10-in. stems.

C. nuttallii. SEGO LILY. Eastern Montana, south to New Mexico and Arizona. State flower of Utah. Flowers white, marked lilac or purple, 2–3 in. wide; stems 1½ ft. tall. Early summer bloom.

C. splendens. LILAC MARIPOSA. Coast Ranges, northern California to Baja California. Deep lilac, 2-in. flowers, sometimes with purple centers, on 1–2 ft. stems. Early summer bloom.

C. tolmiei *(C. maweanus).* CAT'S EARS, PUSSY EARS. Mountains of Oregon, northern California. White to cream flowers often tinged pinkish or purplish, 1½ in. wide, fringed and furry on inner surfaces. Weak stems to 16 in. Spring blooming.

C. uniflorus *(C. lilacinus).* STAR TULIP. Northern California coast and Coast Ranges, southern Oregon. Lilac flowers 1 in. long, 1½ in. wide on 4-in. stems. Spring.

C. venustus. WHITE MARIPOSA LILY. Central and southern California Coast Ranges, central Sierra Nevada. Flowers 3–3½ in. wide, white or yellow to purple, dark red, often with peacock eye at base of petals. Stems 10 in. tall, often much taller. May–July bloom.

C. vestae. Northern California Coast Ranges. White through pink and lilac to rose, centered with red brown peacock eye banded in yellow. Lilies 1½ in. wide, carried on 1–1½-ft. stems in late spring, early summer.

CALODENDRUM capense. *Rutaceae.* CAPE CHESTNUT. Briefly deciduous tree. Zones 19, 21–24; worth risking Zones 15, 16. Native to South Africa. Broad crowned, 25–40 ft. Noteworthy for profuse display of spikes of rosy lilac, 1½-in.-long flowers. Whole flower cluster measures 10–12 in. high by as much across and extends well above foliage, giving effect of candelabrum. Generally blooms from May into July. Seldom flowers when young. Slow growing. Leaves are light to medium green, oval, to 6 in. Time of flowering and deciduous period varies by location and season. Plant it out of prevailing wind. Average water requirement; plant should never be allowed to go completely dry at roots. Light, sandy soils are not to its liking.

Calodendrum capense

CALONYCTION aculeatum. See *Ipomoea alba.*

CALOTHAMNUS. *Myrtaceae.* NET BUSH. Evergreen shrubs. Native to western Australia. Zones 8–9, 12–24. Related to bottlebrush (*Callistemon*) and probably adapted to same climates. Fairly drought resistant; take sun, heat, wind, salt breeze, and poor soil if it drains well (expect root rot if drainage is poor). Needlelike leaves densely clothe rather spreading branches. Flowers, somewhat resembling one-sided bottle brushes, grow along branches, rather close to wood. Sporadic bloom throughout year.

Calothamnus quadrifidus

Prune hard after flowering to keep plants from getting straggly. Generally not attractive in age, showing more wood than foliage.

Of many species introduced, these 2 are being grown by nurseries:

C. quadrifidus. Grows 6–8 ft. high. Dark green leaves, ½–1 in. long. Short clusters of dark red flowers.

C. villosus ***(C. villosus prostratus).*** To 4 ft. Leaves ½ in. long, covered with soft hairs. Long, deep red flower clusters.

CALTHA palustris. *Ranunculaceae.* MARSH-MARIGOLD. Perennial. All Zones. Native to eastern U.S., Europe, Asia. Bog or marsh plant up to 2 ft. tall, well adapted to edges of pools, ponds, streams, other moist situations. With sufficient water, can be grown in borders, but must not dry out in summer. Sun or shade. Good with bog irises, moisture-loving ferns. Green leaves 2–7 in. across; vivid yellow flowers are 2 in. across, in clusters. Lush, glossy foliage gives an almost tropical effect. Plant is vigorous; increase by divisions or sow seed in boggy soil. There is a double-flowered form.

Caltha palustris

Calycanthaceae. The calycanthus family contains shrubs with paired opposite leaves and flowers that somewhat resemble small water lilies—each bloom has an indefinite number of segments not easily defined as petals or sepals. *Calycanthus* and *Chimonanthus* are typical.

CALYCANTHUS. *Calycanthaceae.* Deciduous shrubs, represented in western gardens by a western and eastern native. Average water needs.

C. floridus. CAROLINA ALLSPICE. Hardy Zones 1–9, 14–22. Native Virginia to Florida. Stiffly branched shrub to 10 ft. tall, 5–8 ft. wide. Leaves oval to 5 in., glossy dark green above, grayish green beneath. Flowers, 2 in. wide, maroon brown, with strawberrylike fragrance, carried at ends of leafy branchlets May–July, depending on climate and exposure. Blooms followed by brownish, pear-shaped capsules, fragrant when crushed. Grows in shade or sun, any soil. Rare; plants are usually obtainable only from mail-order nurseries in eastern U.S.

Calycanthus occidentalis

C. occidentalis. SPICE BUSH. Zones 4–9, 14–22. Native along streams, moist slopes, California Coast Ranges, Sierra Nevada foothills. To 4–12 ft. high. Leaves 2–6 in. long, 1–2 in. wide, bright green, turning yellow in fall. Reddish brown flowers to 2 in. across, resembling small water lilies, appear April–August depending on climate. Both flowers and bruised leaves have fragrance of old wine barrel. Takes sun or part shade, ordinary garden care. Can be trained into multistemmed small tree, but is most useful as a background shrub or medium-tall screen. Easily grown from seed.

CALYPSO bulbosa. *Orchidaceae.* Terrestrial orchid. Zones 4–6, 15–17. Native to northern hemisphere and fairly common in heavily forested areas of Northwest, where it grows on decayed logs or in leaf mold. Needs shade, moist (not constantly wet) soil.

Solitary, pendant, pink flowers an inch or more across have brown spots in lines and purple and yellow markings in pouchlike lip. Flower stalk to 9 in. tall; solitary roundish leaf 3 in. across. Grow in leaf mold or forest duff and protect from birds and slugs. Will take subzero temperatures.

Calypso bulbosa

CAMASS. See *Camassia.*

CAMASSIA. *Liliaceae.* CAMASS. Bulbs. Zones 1–9, 14–17. Most species native to moist meadows, marshes, fields in northern California and Northwest. Starlike, slender-petaled blossoms are carried on spikes in late spring, early summer; grasslike basal leaves dry quickly after bloom. Plant in moist situation, fairly heavy soil, where bulbs can remain undisturbed for many years. Set bulbs 4 in. deep, 6 in. apart. To avoid premature rooting, plant after weather cools in fall. Need lots of water while growing.

C. cusickii. Dense clusters of pale blue flowers on stems 2–3 ft. tall.

C. leichtlinii. Large, handsome clusters of creamy white flowers on stems 2–4 ft. tall. *C. l. suksdorfii* is attractive blue variety. 'Alba' has whiter flowers than species, and 'Plena' has double greenish yellow blooms.

Camassia quamash

C. quamash ***(C. esculenta).*** Loose clusters of deep blue flowers on 1–2-ft. stems; flowers of 'Orion' are deeper blue, those of 'San Juan Form' deeper still.

CAMELLIA. *Theaceae.* Evergreen shrubs and small trees. Zones 4–9, 14–24. Native to eastern and southern Asia. There are over 3,000 named kinds, and range in color, size, and form is remarkable. But camellia breeding is still in its infancy, and what is yet to come stirs the imagination—blue and purple camellias, yellow and orange camellias, fragrant camellias. All are possible.

In these few pages, we treat briefly the cultural requirements of camellias and describe some of the lesser-known species as well as the widely distributed old favorites and new varieties. Where a certain type of camellia has a specific cultural need, that need is given in the description. General cultural requirements appear below.

Camellias need well-drained soil rich in organic material. Never plant camellias so trunk base is below soil line, and never permit soil to wash over and cover this base. Keep roots cool with 2-in.-thick mulch.

Camellias make outstanding container plants—especially in wooden tubs and half-barrels. As a general rule, plant gallon-can camellias into 12–14-in.-wide tubs, 5-gallon ones into 16–18-in. tubs. Fill with a planting mix containing 50 percent or more organic material.

Camellias thrive and bloom best when sheltered from strong, hot sun and drying winds, though some species and varieties are more sun tolerant than others. Tall old plants in old gardens prove that camellias can thrive in full sun when mature enough to have roots shaded by heavy canopy of leaves. Young plants will grow better and bear more attractive flowers if grown under partial shade of tall trees, under lath cover, or on north side of a building. A few camellias, like *C. japonica* 'Lotus', need shade at any age.

Established plants (over 3 years old and vigorous) can survive on natural rainfall. If your water is high in salts and you irrigate your camellias, leach accumulated salts with deep soaking—twice in summer—to dissolve harmful salts and carry them deep below the root zone.

Fertilize with a commercial acid plant food. Generally, time to feed is in weeks and months following bloom; read fertilizer label for complete instructions. Don't use more than called for. Better to cut amounts in half and feed twice as frequently. Don't feed sick plants. Poor drainage, water or soil with excess salts are the main troublemakers. Best cure is to move plant into above-ground bed of pure ground bark or peat moss until it recovers.

Scorched or yellowed areas in center of leaves are usually due to sunburn. Burned leaf edges, excessive leaf drop, or corky spots usually indicate overfertilizing. Yellow leaves with green veins are signs of chlorosis. Check drainage, leach, and treat with iron or iron chelates.

One disease may be serious: camellia petal blight. Flowers rapidly turn ugly brown. Browning at edges of petals (especially whites and pale pinks) may be caused by sun or wind, but if brown rapidly runs into center of flower, suspect petal blight. Sanitation is the best control. Pick up and burn (or place in covered garbage can) all fallen flowers and petals, and pick off all infected flowers from plants; encourage neighbors to do the same. Remove mulch (if you use one), haul it away, and replace with fresh one; a deep mulch (4–5 in.) helps keep spores of fungus from reaching the air. Spraying ground under plants with PCNB several weeks before flowers open will lessen chance of infection; benomyl will prevent infestation if present on flowers when spores alight.

Some flower bud dropping may be natural phenomenon; many camellias set more buds than they can open. Some bud drop can be caused by overwatering, more by underwatering, especially during summer. It can also be caused by spells of very low humidity.

Some varieties bear too many flowers. To get nicest display from them, remove buds in midsummer like this: from branch-end clusters, remove all but one or two round flower buds (leaf buds are slender); along stems, remove enough to leave single flower bud for each 2–4 in. of branch.

Prune right after flowering or during summer and fall. Remove dead or weak wood and thin when growth is so dense that flowers have no room to open properly. Prune at will to get form you want. Shorten lower branches to encourage upright growth. Lanky shrubs can be fattened by cutting back top growth. Make cut just above scar that terminates previous year's growth (it is usually slightly thickened, somewhat rough area where bark texture and color change slightly). A cut just above this point will usually force 3 or 4 dormant buds into growth.

C. chrysantha. GOLDEN CAMELLIA. Tall, vigorous, open grower with large (6 in. or longer), glossy, heavily net-veined leaves and 2–2½-in. golden yellow flowers. Hybridizers use it to enlarge the camellia color palette. Rare.

C. granthamiana. Becomes a big shrub or small tree of rather open growth with leathery, glossy, heavily veined and crinkled leaves 2–6 in. long. Flowers large (to 6 in. or more across), white, single, often with fluted or folded ("rabbit-ear") petals and a heavy central tuft of bright yellow stamens. Flowers open in October, November, and December from large, brown, scaly, silky-haired buds. A cross between this one and *C. reticulata* produced 'China Lady', which looks like big pink *C. granthamiana.* This species has been the parent of several other remarkable seedling camellias. Needs excellent drainage; avoid overwatering.

C. hiemalis. Includes number of varieties formerly listed as Sasanquas but differing in their later and longer bloom and heavier-textured flowers. Four good examples:

'Chansonette'. Vigorous, spreading growth. Large, bright pink, formal double flowers with frilled petals.

'Shishi-Gashira'. One of most useful and ornamental shrubs. Low growing with arching branches that in time pile up tier on tier to make compact, dark green, glossy-leafed plant. Leaves rather small for camellia, giving medium-fine foliage texture. Flowers rose red, semidouble to double, 2–2½ in. wide, heavily borne over long season—October–March in good year. Full sun or shade.

Camellia hiemalis

'Showa-No-Sakae'. Faster growing, more open than 'Shishi-Gashira'; willowy, arching branches. Semidouble to double flowers of soft pink, occasionally marked with white. Try this as espalier or in hanging basket.

'Showa Supreme' is very similar to above, but has somewhat larger flowers of peony form.

Higo camellias. These camellias, bred for 200 years in Japan but only now attracting attention in the U.S., are probably varieties of *C. japonica.* They are generally compact plants with dense, heavy foliage and thick-petaled single flowers with broad, full brush of stamens in the center. In ideal Higo camellia, mass of stamens should be at least half the diameter of flower. Colors include white, pink, red, and variegated. Many named varieties are already available in this country, and more are likely to appear.

C. japonica. To most gardeners, this is *the* camellia. Naturally a large shrub or small tree, but variable in size, growth rate, and habit. Hundred-year-old plants in California reach 20 ft. high and equally wide, and larger plants exist, but most gardeners can consider camellias 6–12-ft. shrubs. Many are lower growing.

Here are 16 varieties that are old standbys with western gardeners. Easily obtainable, inexpensive, and handsome even in comparison with some of the newest introductions, they are plants for the beginner—but not only for the beginner.

In the list, season of bloom is noted by "E," "M," or "L." In California "early" means October–January; "midseason," January–March; "late," March–May. In the Northwest, it's December–February for "early"; March and April, "midseason"; May, "late."

Flower size is also noted for each variety. A "very large" flower is over 5 in. across. "Large" is 4–5 in., "medium large" 3½–4 in., "medium" 3–3½ in., "small" 2½–3 in., "miniature" 2½ in. or less.

'Adolphe Audusson'. M. Very large, dark red, semidouble flowers, heavily borne on a medium-sized, symmetrical, vigorous shrub. Hardy. 'Adolphe Audusson Variegated' is identical, but heavily marbled white on red.

'Alba Plena.' E. Brought from China in 1792, and still a favorite large, white, formal double. Slow, bushy growth. Early bloom a disadvantage in cold or rainy areas. Protect flowers from rain and wind.

'Berenice Boddy'. M. Medium semidouble, light pink with deeper shading. Vigorous upright growth. One of the most cold hardy.

'Debutante'. E–M. Medium-large, peony-form flowers of light pink. Profusely blooming. Vigorous upright growth.

'Donckelarii'. M. Red marbled white; amount of marbling varies, even on same plant. Large semidouble flowers. Slow, bushy growth. Hardy.

'Elegans' ('Chandler'). Also known as 'Chandleri Elegans'. E–M. Very large anemone-form camellia with rose pink petals and smaller petals called petaloids, the latter often marked white. Slow growth and spreading, arching branches make it a natural for espalier. Stake to provide height, and don't remove main shoot; it may be very slow to resume upward growth. A 100-year-old-plus variety that remains a favorite. Its offspring resemble it in every way except flower color: 'C. M. Wilson', pale pink; 'Shiro Chan', white, sometimes faintly marked with pink; and 'Elegans (Chandler) Variegated', heavily marbled rose pink and white. A solid rose pink form is called 'Francine'. 'Elegans Champagne' has creamy-centered white flowers. 'Elegans Splendor' is blush pink edged white.

'Glen 40' ('Coquetti'). M–L. Large formal double of deep red. One of best reds for corsages. Slow, compact, upright growth. Handsome even out of flower. Hardy; very good in containers.

'Herme' ('Jordan's Pride'). M. Medium-large, semidouble flowers are pink, irregularly bordered white and streaked deep pink. Sometimes has all solid pink flowers on certain branches. Free blooming, dependable.

'Kramer's Supreme'. M. Very large, deep, full peony-form flowers of deep, clear red. Some people can detect a faint fragrance. Unusually vigorous, compact, upright. Takes some sun.

'Kumasaka'. M–L. Medium large, rose form to peony form, rose pink. Vigorous, compact, upright growth and remarkably heavy flower production make it choice landscape plant. Hardy. Takes morning sun.

'Magnoliaeflora'. M. Medium semidouble flowers of pale pink. Many blossoms, good cut flower. Medium grower of compact yet spreading form. Hardy.

'Mathotiana'. M–L. Very large rose form to formal double of deep crimson, sometimes with purplish cast. Vigorous upright grower. Takes cold and stands up well in hot summer areas. Does not grow very well along the southern California coast.

'Mrs. Charles Cobb'. M. Large semidouble to peony-form flowers in deep red. Freely flowering. Compact plant with dense foliage. Best in warmer areas.

'Pope Pius IX' ('Prince Eugene Napoleon'). M. A cherry red, medium-large formal double. Medium, compact, upright growth.

'Purity'. L. White, medium rose form to formal double, usually showing a few stamens. Vigorous upright plant. Late bloom often escapes rain damage.

'Wildfire'. E–M. Medium semidouble orange red flowers. Vigorous, upright plant.

The preceding 16 are the old classics in the camellia world. The following, all introduced since 1950, may supplant them in time:

'Betty Sheffield Supreme'. M. Unique flower markings: petals white with deep pink to red border. Flower form variable, from semidouble through peony form to formal double. Large flowers on medium, compact shrubs.

'Carter's Sunburst'. E–L. Large to very large pale pink flowers striped deeper pink. Semidouble to peony form to formal double flowers on medium, compact plants.

'Drama Girl'. M. Huge semidouble flowers of deep salmon rose pink. Vigorous, open, pendulous growth.

'Grand Slam'. M. Large to very large flowers in glowing deep red. Semidouble to peony form. There is a variegated form.

'Guilio Nuccio'. M. Coral rose, very large semidouble flowers with inner petals fluted in "rabbit-ear" effect. Unusual depth and substance. Vigorous upright growth. This variety is considered by many to be the world's finest camellia. Variegated, fringed forms are available.

'Mrs. D. W. Davis'. M. Spectacular, very large, somewhat cup-shaped flowers of palest blush pink open from egg-sized buds. Vigorous, upright, compact plant with very handsome broad leaves.

'Nuccio's Gem'. E–M. Medium to large full formal double, white. Strong, full, upright grower.

'Reg Ragland'. E–L. Large, semidouble red flowers with smaller, upright center petals surrounding mass of yellow stamens. Medium, compact growth.

'Swan Lake'. M–L. Very large, white, formal double to peony-form flower. Vigorous upright growth.

'Tiffany'. M–L. Very large, warm pink flowers. Rose form to loose, irregular semidouble. Vigorous, upright shrub.

'Tomorrow'. E–M. Very large semidouble to peony-form flower of strawberry red. Vigorous, open, somewhat pendulous growth.

C. lutchuensis. Limber-branched shrub to 10 ft. with tiny (1½ in. long, ½ in. wide) leaves and profusion of tiny white flowers with strong, pleasant fragrance. Is being used as parent to introduce fragrance to larger camellias. Long, pliant branches make it an easily trained espalier.

C. reticulata. Some of the biggest and most spectacular camellia flowers occur in this species, and likely as not they appear on some of the lankiest and least graceful plants.

Camellia reticulata

Plants differ somewhat according to variety, but generally speaking, they are rather gaunt and open shrubs which eventually become trees of considerable size—possibly 35–50 ft. tall. For gardens, consider them 10-ft.-tall shrubs, 8 ft. wide. Leaves also variable, but tend to be dull green, leathery, and strongly net-veined.

Culture is quite similar to that of other camellias, except that the plants seem intolerant of heavy pruning. This, added to their natural lankiness and size, makes them difficult to place in garden. They are at their best in light shade of old oaks, where they should stand alone with plenty of room to develop. They are good container subjects while young, but are not handsome out of bloom. They develop better form and heavier foliage in open ground. In Zones 4–6, grow them in containers so you can move them into winter protection, or plant beneath overhang or near wall for protection.

Best-known varieties have very large, semidouble flowers with the inner petals deeply fluted and curled. These inner petals give great depth to flower. All bloom January–May in California, March–May in Northwest. The following varieties are the best choices for garden use:

'Buddha'. Rose pink flower of very large size; inner petals unusually erect and wavy. Gaunt, open; fast growth.

'Butterfly Wings'. Loose, semidouble, of great size (reported up to 9 in. across), rose pink; petals broad and wavy. Growth open, rather narrow.

'Captain Rawes'. Reddish rose pink semidouble flowers of large size. Vigorous bushy plant with good foliage. Hardiest of Reticulatas.

'Chang's Temple'. True variety is large, open-centered, deep rose flower, with center petals notched and fluted. 'Cornelian' (see below) is sometimes sold as 'Chang's Temple'.

'Cornelian'. Rosy pink to red, heavily variegated with white. Large, deep, irregular peony-form flowers with wavy petals. Vigorous plant with big leaves; leaves are usually marked with white. This variety is often sold as 'Chang's Temple' (see description above) or as 'Lion Head'. The true 'Lion Head' is not found in American gardens.

'Crimson Robe'. Very large, bright red, semidouble flowers. Petals firm textured and wavy. Vigorous plant of better appearance than most Reticulatas.

'Purple Gown'. Large, purplish red, peony-form to formal double flowers. Compact plant with best growth habit and foliage in the group.

'Shot Silk'. Large, loose, semidouble flowers of brilliant pink with iridescent finish that sparkles in sunlight. Fast, rather open growth.

(Continued on next page)

Flower forms of **Camellia japonica**; *formal double is the most familiar, but others are gaining in popularity.*

'Tali Queen'. Very large, deep reddish pink flowers of loose semidouble form with heavily crinkled petals. Plant form and foliage very good. This plant is often sold as 'Noble Pearl'; true 'Noble Pearl' is not available in this country.

C. rusticana. SNOW CAMELLIA. A race of small-flowered camellias from a cold and extremely snowy part of Japan. Flowers may be white, pink, or red, and single to double in form. Plants tend to be spreading and branches are remarkably supple. They are not any hardier than *C. japonica* and are generally considered to be a subspecies—*C. j. rusticana*.

C. saluenensis. Shrub of densely leafy growth to 10–15 ft. tall. Leaves elliptic, rather narrow, pointed, thick textured, 1½–2½ in. long and half as wide. Flowers are bell shaped and rather small, and vary in color from white to fairly deep pink. Flowering is in early spring. Not of great value in itself, it has brought floriferousness, hardiness, and graceful appearance to a large group of its hybrids.

C. sasanqua. Sasanquas are useful broad-leafed evergreens for espaliers, ground covers, informal hedges, screening, containers, and bonsai. They vary in form from upright and densely bushy to spreading and vinelike. Leaves dark green, shiny, 1½–3½ in. long, a third as wide. Flowers very heavily produced in autumn and early winter, short lived, rather flimsy, but so numerous that plants make a show for months. Some are lightly fragrant.

Most Sasanquas tolerate much sun, and some thrive in full hot sun if soil is right and watering ample. They take drought very well. The Sasanquas are perfectly hardy in camellia areas of Pacific Northwest, but flowers are too often damaged by fall and winter rains and frost to call them successful.

'Apple Blossom'. Single white flowers blushed with pink, from pink buds. Spreading plant.

'Cleopatra'. Rose pink semidouble flowers with narrow, curving petals. Growth is erect, fairly compact. Takes clipping well.

'Hana Jiman'. Large semidouble flowers white, edged pink. Fast, open growth; good espalier.

'Jean May'. Large double shell pink. Compact, upright grower with exceptionally glossy foliage.

'Mine-No-Yuki' ('White Doves'). Large white peony-form double. Drops many buds. Spreading, willowy growth; effective espalier.

'Momozono-Nishiki'. Large semidouble flowers are rose, shaded white. Twisted petals.

'Narumigata'. Large single, cupped flowers, white tinged pink.

'Setsugekka'. Large white semidouble flowers with fluted petals. Considerable substance to flowers; cut sprays hold well in water. Shrub's growth is upright and rather bushy.

'Sparkling Burgundy'. Large peony-form flowers of ruby rose. Vigorous upright growth. Excellent espalier.

'Tanya'. Deep rose pink single flowers. Tolerates much sun. Good ground cover.

'White Frills'. Semidouble, frilled white flowers on a spreading, willowy plant. Outstanding in Zones 23, 24.

'Yuletide'. Profusion of small single bright red flowers on dense, compact, upright plant. Late fall, winter bloom.

C. sinensis *(Thea sinensis)*. TEA. In the West, the tea plant grows as dense round shrub to 15 ft. with leathery dull dark green leaves to 5 in. long. Fall flowers are white, small (1½ in. across), and fragrant. Takes well to pruning. Can be trimmed as hedge. Tea can be grown in California but has never been a major crop for economic reasons.

C. vernalis. Certain camellias once classed as Sasanquas have been placed here because they bloom later than Sasanquas, are denser in growth, shinier in leaf, and have firmer-textured flowers. They are generally sold as Sasanquas. Best-known varieties are:

'Dawn'. Small single to semidouble white flowers blushed pink. Dense, upright shrub of unusual hardiness.

'Hiryu'. Deep red, small, rose form. Dense, upright plant. 'Hiryu Nishiki' has white markings on flowers.

Hybrid camellias. The term as used here refers to camellias that are hybrids between 2 or more species. Several hundred of these hybrids have been introduced, and a few can be found with a little looking. The first wave of hybridizing utilized *C. japonica* and *C. saluenensis;* this cross gave plants of generally good garden form, resembling *C. japonica* in foliage and with a profusion of medium-sized flowers. Although some of these are still around, the big effort now is in crosses involving *C. reticulata*. These hybrids are more spectacular in flower and should be considered separately. (The E-M-L code for bloom season and the terms used for flower size are explained under *C. japonica*.)

Hybrids involving *C. saluenensis* or other small-flowered species and varieties:

'Donation'. M. Large semidouble flowers of orchid pink borne all along stems. Blooms young and heavily, on vigorous, upright, compact plant with slightly pendulous branches. Quite resistant to cold and sun. Appreciates a little shade in hot, dry areas. There is a variegated form.

'E. G. Waterhouse'. M–L. Medium, full, formal double of excellent form. Light pink flowers heavily produced on vigorous, upright shrub.

'Fragrant Pink'. M. Cross between *C. j. rusticana* and *C. lutchuensis* has loose peony-form flowers on spreading bush. Flowers small, deep pink, very fragrant.

'J. C. Williams'. E–L. Medium single, cup-shaped flowers of phlox pink over very long season. Vigorous upright shrub with rather pendulous branches. This and the similar 'Mary Christian' and 'St. Ewe' are good plants for the Northwest.

Hybrids involving *C. reticulata:*

'Flower Girl'. E–M. Large to very large semidouble to peony-form flowers of bright pink. Vigorous upright growth. Profuse flowering and small leaves come from its Sasanqua parent, big flowers from its Reticulata ancestor.

'Francie L.' M–L. Very large semidouble flowers with upright, wavy petals. Deep rose pink.

'Valentine Day'. M. Large to very large salmon pink formal double flowers. Fast, upright grower.

'Valley Knudsen'. M–L. Large to very large deep orchid pink semidouble to loose peony form. Compact upright growth.

CAMPANULA. *Campanulaceae.* BELLFLOWER. Mostly perennial, some biennial, a few annual. All Zones, but see Uses, Remarks in chart on facing page. Majority best adapted in Zones 1–7, but several thrive in Zones 8, 9, 14–24. Vast and varied group (nearly 300 species) including creeping or tufted miniatures, trailers, and erect kinds 1–6 ft. tall. Flowers generally bell shaped, but some star shaped, cup shaped, or round and flat. Usually blue, lavender, violet, purple, or white; some pink. Bloom period from spring to fall.

Campanula isophylla

Uses for campanulas are as varied as the plants. Gemlike miniatures deserve special settings—close-up situations in rock gardens, niches in dry walls, in raised beds, or containers. Trailing kinds are ideal for hanging pots or baskets, wall crevices; vigorous spreading growers serve well as ground covers. Upright growers are valuable in borders, for cutting, occasionally in containers.

In general, campanulas grow best in good, well-drained soil that's kept moist through the dry months; plant in filtered shade in warmer climates, full sun near coast. Exceptions are noted in chart. Most species fairly easy to grow from seed sown in flats in spring or early summer, transplanted to garden in fall for bloom the following year; also increased by cuttings or divisions. Divide clumps in fall every 3–4 years; some may need yearly division. Low-growing kinds especially attractive to snails, slugs.

Campanulaceae. The campanula or bellflower family contains perennials or biennials, typically with bell-shaped or saucer-shaped flowers in shades of blue to purple, lilac, and white.

Campanula

NAME	GROWTH HABIT, SIZE	FOLIAGE	FLOWERS	USES, REMARKS
Campanula barbata Short-lived perennial or biennial	Clumps of erect stems 4–18 in. high.	Leaves mostly at base of stem, 2–5 in. long, narrow, hairy.	Bell shaped, lilac blue, bearded inside, 1 in. long, nodding, few near top of each stem. Summer.	Foreground in borders, rock gardens. Tap rooted and needs good drainage. White forms may appear from seed.
C. carpatica *(C. turbinata)* TUSSOCK BELLFLOWER Perennial	Compact leafy tufts, stems branching and spreading. Usually about 8 in. tall, may reach 12–18 in.	Leaves smooth, bright green, wavy, toothed, 1–1½ in. long.	Open bell or cup shaped, blue or white, 1–2 in. across, single and erect on stems above foliage. Late spring.	Rock garden, foreground in borders, edging. Variable in flower size and color. 'Blue Chips' and 'White Chips' good dwarf varieties. Easily grown from seed; sometimes sold as 'Blue Clips', 'White Clips'.
C. elatines garganica *(C. garganica)* Perennial	Low (3–6 in. high), with outward spreading stems.	Small, gray or green, sharply toothed, heart-shaped leaves.	Flat, star shaped, violet blue, borne few or singly at tops of stems. June to fall.	Rock gardens, Usually sold as *C. garganica*. Somewhat like a miniature, prostrate *C. poscharskyana*.
C. fragilis Perennial	Vinelike, trailing flower stems 12–16 in. long. Dies back to a tight basal rosette of leaves.	Glossy oval leaves 1 in. across.	Star shaped, blue with white centers, 1½ in. across, in leaf joints at ends of branches. Late summer and fall.	Choice spots in rock gardens or walls. Hanging containers. A plant for collectors, specialists.
C. glomerata Perennial	Upright, with erect side branches to 1–2 ft.	Basal leaves broad, wavy edged. Stem leaves broad, toothed. Both somewhat hairy.	Narrow, bell shaped, flaring at the mouth, 1 in. long, blue violet, tightly clustered at tops of stems. June–July.	For shaded borders or large rock gardens. Plants have proportionately more foliage than flowers. Seed-grown strains Superba and Alba are deepest purple and white respectively.
C. isophylla ITALIAN BELLFLOWER, STAR OF BETHLEHEM Perennial	Trailing or hanging stems to 2 ft. long.	Leaves heart shaped, light green, toothed, 1–1½ in. long and wide.	Pale blue, star shaped, 1 in. wide, profuse in late summer and fall. Variety 'Alba' most popular, has white flowers, larger than the above. Variety 'Mayi' has gray, soft-hairy leaves, large lavender blue flowers.	Hanging baskets, wall pots, on top of walls, rock garden. Choice ground cover for small areas on slopes, in mild-winter climates. Filtered shade. Hardy San Francisco and south; in southern California, best near coast; indoor/outdoor plant in cold-winter areas. Grow from cuttings or from seed of Kristal strain, which blooms first year from winter sowing indoors.
C. lactiflora Perennial	Erect, branching, leafy, 3½–5 ft. tall.	Oblong, pointed, toothed leaves 2–3 in. long.	Broadly bell shaped to star shaped, 1 in. long, white to pale blue in drooping clusters at ends of branches. June–September.	Rear of borders in sun or partial shade. Quite drought resistant. Endures even dry shade and is long lived.
C. medium CANTERBURY BELL, CUP-AND-SAUCER Biennial or annual	Sturdy, hairy, leafy, with erect stems 2½–4 ft. tall.	Basal leaves 6–10 in., stem leaves 3–5 in., wavy margined.	Bell shaped or urn shaped, 1–2 in. across, single or double, held upright in long, loose open clusters. Purple, violet, blue, lavender, pink, white. May–July.	Sow seed in May or June for bloom next year, or set out plants from nursery 15–18 in. apart. Good for cutting. 'Calycanthema', commonly called cup-and-saucer, very popular. Annual variety with bell-shaped flowers (not cup-and-saucer) blooms in 6 months from seed.
C. persicifolia PEACH-LEAFED BLUEBELL Perennial	Strong-growing, slender, erect stems 2–3 ft. tall. Plants leafy at base.	Basal leaves smooth edged, green, 4–8 in. long. Stem leaves 2–4 in. long, shaped like leaves of peach tree.	Open, cup shaped, about 1 in. across, held erect on short side shoots on sturdy stems. Blue, pink, or white. June–August.	Choice plant for borders. Easy to grow from seed sown in late spring. 'Telham Beauty', old but still popular, has 3-in. blue flowers. 'Blue Gardenia' and 'White Pearl' have double flowers.
C. portenschlagiana *(C. muralis)* DALMATIAN BELLFLOWER Perennial	Low, leafy, mounding mats 4–7 in. high.	Roundish, heart-shaped, deep green leaves with deeply toothed, slightly wavy edges.	Flaring bell-shaped, violet blue flowers to 1 in. long; 2 or 3 on each semierect stem. May–August, sometimes blooming again in fall.	Fine plant for edging or as small-scale ground cover. In warm regions best in partial shade. Spreads moderately fast, is sturdy, permanent, and not invasive. Easily increased by dividing.
C. poscharskyana SERBIAN BELLFLOWER Perennial	Spreading, many branched, leafy, with semiupright flowering stems 1 ft. tall or taller.	Long heart-shaped, irregularly toothed, slightly hairy leaves 1–3½ in. long, ¾–3 in. wide.	Star shaped, ½–1 in. across, blue lilac or lavender. Spring to early summer.	Very vigorous. Shaded border near pools, shaded rock gardens, with fuchsias and begonias. Stands some drought; takes sun near coast. Small area ground cover.

(Continued on next page)

C

NAME	GROWTH HABIT, SIZE	FOLIAGE	FLOWERS	USES, REMARKS
C. pyramidalis CHIMNEY BELLFLOWER Biennial or short-lived perennial	Sturdy upright stems, unbranched or branched at base, 4–6 ft. tall.	Leaves nearly heart shaped, about 2 in. long, with long stalks.	Flat, saucer-shaped blue or white flowers, over 1 in. long, in dense spikes. July–September.	For back of perennial borders or for bays in big shrubbery borders, or in containers. Stake early to keep stems straight. In cold-winter climates, mulch around plants.
C. rapunculoides ROVER BELLFLOWER Perennial	Clumps of long-stemmed leaves send up 3-ft. spires of blue purple bells.	Medium green, large, heart shaped at base.	Funnel-shaped flowers 1 in. long. Sometimes pale blue or white.	Tough, invasive plant, useful in difficult soils, climates. Don't plant near delicate subjects.
C. rotundifolia BLUEBELL OF SCOTLAND, HAREBELL Perennial	Upright or spreading, simple or many branched, 6–20 in. tall.	Leaves green or sometimes slightly grayish. Basal leaves roundish, long stalked, 1 in. across. Stem leaves grasslike, 2–3 in. long. May dry up before blooming time.	Broad bell shaped, bright blue, 1 in. across, one or a few nodding in open clusters. July–August.	Flower color variable, sometimes in lavender, purple, or white shades. Rock gardens, borders, naturalized under deciduous trees. Self-sows in favorable situations.

CAMPHOR TREE. See *Cinnamomum camphora.*

CAMPSIS. *Bignoniaceae.* TRUMPET CREEPER, TRUMPET VINE. Deciduous vines. Vigorous climbers that cling to wood, brick, and stucco surfaces with aerial rootlets. Old plants sometimes become topheavy and pull away from supporting surface unless thinned. Will spread through garden and into neighbor's by suckering roots. If you try to dig suckers up, any piece of root left will grow another plant. Can be trained as big shrub, flowering hedge if branches are shortened after first year's growth. Use for large-scale effects—quick summer screen. All produce open, arching sprays of trumpet-shaped flowers in August and September. Sun, average water.

Campsis radicans

C. grandiflora *(Bignonia chinensis).* CHINESE TRUMPET CREEPER. Zones 2–12, 14–21. Not as vigorous, large, or hardy as the American native *C. radicans* (common trumpet creeper), but with slightly larger, more open scarlet flowers. Leaves divided into 7–9 leaflets, each 2½ in. long.

C. radicans *(Bignonia radicans).* COMMON TRUMPET CREEPER. Zones 1–21. Native to eastern United States. Most used in cold-winter areas. Deep freeze will kill to ground but new stems grow quickly. Leaves divided into 9–11 toothed leaflets, each 2½ in. long. Flowers, growing in clusters of 6–12, are 3-in.-long orange tubes with scarlet lobes that flare to 2 in. wide. Grows fast to 40 ft. or more, bursting with health and vigor. There is a rare, yellow-flowered variety, 'Flava'.

C. tagliabuana. All Zones. Hybrid between the 2 above species. 'Mme. Galen', best-known variety, has attractive salmon red flowers. 'Crimson Trumpet' bears pure red blooms.

CANARY BIRD BUSH. See *Crotalaria agatiflora.*

CANARY BIRD FLOWER. See *Tropaeolum peregrinum.*

CANDLE BUSH. See *Cassia alata.*

CANDOLLEA cuneiformis. See *Hibbertia cuneiformis.*

CANDYTUFT. See *Iberis.*

CANNA. *Cannaceae.* Tuberous rootstocks. All Zones. Native to tropics and subtropics. Best adapted to warm-summer climates; in Zones 1–3, lift and store the roots over winter. An old favorite that can add a tropical touch in the right place. Large, rich green to bronzy red leaves resemble those of banana or ti plants. Flowers reminiscent of ginger lilies (*Hedychium*) bloom on 3–6-ft. stalks in summer, fall. A dozen or more varieties of varying sizes and shapes available, in white, ivory, shades of yellow, orange, pink, apricot, coral, salmon, and red. Bicolors include 'Cleopatra', with flowers strikingly streaked and spotted red on yellow. Low-growing strains are Grand Opera (26 in.), Pfitzer's Dwarf (2½–3 ft.), and Seven Dwarfs (1½ ft.); grow the last from seed.

Canna

Needs full sun. Most effective in groups of single colors against plain background. Grow in borders, near poolside (with good drainage), in large pots or tubs on terrace or patio. Leaves useful in arrangements; cut flowers do not keep well. Plant rootstocks in spring after frosts, in rich, loose soil. Set 5 in. deep, 10 in. apart. Water heavily during flowering season; remove faded flowers after bloom. After all flower clusters have bloomed, cut stalk to ground.

CANTALOUPE. See Melon.

CANTERBURY BELL. See *Campanula medium.*

CANTUA buxifolia. *Polemoniaceae.* MAGIC FLOWER, SACRED FLOWER OF THE INCAS. Evergreen shrub. Zones 16–24. Native of Peru, Bolivia, and northern Chile. Scraggly open growth to 6–10 ft. Small leaves 1 in. or less in length. Magnificent blossoms come sporadically through year; 4-in., tubular, rose or cerise red flowers with yellow stripes appear in terminal clusters, bending branches with their weight.

Give light soil, partial shade. Drought tolerant. Needs support of stake or trellis. Young plants effective in hanging baskets. Or grow in tub and hide plant when it's out of bloom. Prune after flowering.

Cantua buxifolia

CAPE CHESTNUT. See *Calodendrum capense.*

CAPE COWSLIP. See *Lachenalia.*

CAPE FORGET-ME-NOT. See *Anchusa capensis.*

CAPE FUCHSIA. See *Phygelius capensis.*

CAPE HONEYSUCKLE. See *Tecomaria capensis.*

CAPE MARIGOLD. See *Dimorphotheca, Osteospermum.*

CAPE PONDWEED. See *Aponogeton distachyus.*

CAPE PRIMROSE. See *Streptocarpus.*

CAPER. See *Capparis spinosa.*

CAPE WEED. See *Arctotheca calendula.*

Capparaceae. The caper family includes *Capparis,* the caper plant, and the spider flower (*Cleome*).

CAPPARIS spinosa. *Capparaceae.* CAPER. Deciduous shrub. Zones 8, 9, 12–24. Native to Mediterranean. Habit varies from sprawling semivine to dense, rounded shrub to 5 ft. Leaves deep green, nearly round, up to 2 in. across (usually less) on sprawling, vinelike, sometimes spiny branches. White, 2–3-in. flowers with showy brushes of lavender stamens rise on long stalks from every leaf base, open at dawn and close in late afternoon. Unopened buds are pickled as commercial capers.

Capparis spinosa

Propagate from cuttings or seed (slow to sprout and grow). Needs good drainage. Tolerates poor soil, heat; needs little water. Grow as ground cover, wall spiller, or garden curiosity.

Caprifoliaceae. The honeysuckle family of shrubs and vines contains many ornamentals in addition to honeysuckle (*Lonicera*); among them are *Abelia, Viburnum,* and *Weigela.*

CARAGANA. *Leguminosae.* PEASHRUB. Deciduous shrubs or small trees from Russia, Manchuria, Siberia. Zones 1–21. Leaves divided into small leaflets. Spring flowers sweet pea–shaped, bright yellow. Useful where choice is limited by cold, heat, wind, bright sun; nearly indestructible in desert, mountain climates. Use as windbreak, clipped hedge, cover for wildlife.

C. arborescens. SIBERIAN PEASHRUB. Fast growing to 20 ft., with 15-ft. spread. Leaves to 3 in. long, each with 4–6 pairs of leaflets.

C. frutex. RUSSIAN PEASHRUB. To 10 ft.; leaves have 1 or 2 pairs of 1-in. leaflets.

Caragana arborescens

CARAWAY. See *Carum carvi.*

CARDINAL CLIMBER. See *Ipomoea quamoclit.*

CARDINAL FLOWER. See *Lobelia cardinalis.*

CARDOON. *Compositae.* Perennial. Zones 8, 9, 14–24. Vegetable closely related to artichoke, but grown for edible leaf stalks rather than for flower buds. For climate, soil, and other requirements, see Artichoke. To prepare leaves for harvest, blanch them by gathering them together, tying them up, and wrapping with paper to exclude light. Allow 1 month's blanching before harvest. To cook, cut heavy leaf midribs into 3–4-in. lengths, parboil until tender, then fry; or serve boiled with butter or other sauce.

Cardoon

As ornamental, makes large (to 8 ft. or more), striking, gray green plant that naturalizes in mild-winter climates. Size, spininess rule it out in small gardens. Purple artichoke flowers attractive cut and dried. Can escape and become weed.

CAREX. *Cyperaceae.* SEDGE. Zones 4–9, 14–24. Grasslike, clumping perennial plants grown for foliage effect in borders, rock gardens, containers, water gardens. Long, narrow evergreen leaves are often striped or oddly colored. Specialists offer many varieties.

Carex buchananii

C. buchananii. FOX RED CURLY SEDGE, LEATHERLEAF SEDGE. Curly-tipped, arching blades 2–3 ft. tall make clumps of striking reddish bronze. Use with gray foliage or with deep greens.

C. morrowii expallida (*C. m.* 'Variegata'). VARIEGATED JAPANESE SEDGE. Drooping leaves striped with green and white make a 1-ft. mound. Give moist to boggy soil, full sun near coast to light shade inland. Edging plant; single clumps attractive among rocks. *C. m.* 'Aurea-variegata' has gold-striped leaves.

CARICA. *Caricaceae.* Evergreen big shrubs or small trees. All need sun or light shade, excellent drainage, warmth. The key to success is choosing the right location. Root rot in cold, wet soil is the principal cause of failure, so locate plants on south slope or south side of house where winter sun can heat soil. The more reflected heat in winter, the better.

C. heilbornii. BABACO, BUSH MELON OF THE ANDES. Zones 19, 21–24. Native to higher elevations in the Andes. Resembles a dwarfish (5–8-ft.-tall) papaya. Foot-long, seedless fruits have been described as having flavor of honeydew and lime. Plants are costly; propagation by rooting shoots from decapitated plants is slow.

Carica pubescens

C. papaya. PAPAYA. Outdoors Zones 21, 23, 24; or a greenhouse plant. Native to tropical America.

Grow 3–5 trees in a group; you need male and female trees for fruit production. Tree grows 20–25 ft. tall, with a straight trunk topped by crown of broad (to 2 ft.), fanlike, deeply lobed leaves on 2-ft.-long stems. Cream-colored flowers are inconspicuous; trees bear fruit when young. To get most fruit, don't attempt to grow papaya as permanent tree. Keep a few plants coming along each year and destroy old ones. Give plants ample water and fertilizer in warm weather. Grow from seeds saved from fruit, or start with purchased plants.

C. pubescens. MOUNTAIN PAPAYA. Zones 21–24. Native to mountains of Colombia and Ecuador. Generally grown as a shrub, though it resembles a many-trunked, upright tree to 10–12 ft. Foliage borne in dense clusters at tops of trunks. Elaborately lobed, foot-wide leaves are fanlike, veined, sandpapery, dark green above, lighter beneath. Inconspicuous cream-colored flowers. Fruit small, edible when cooked. Male and female plants needed for fruit set.

C

CARISSA. *Apocynaceae.* Evergreen shrubs. Their rightful climates are Zones 22–24, but so many gardeners find carissa appealing that these shrubs are grown in Zones 12, 13, 16–21—far beyond safe limits. Excellent in ocean wind, salt spray. Easy to grow. Accept variety of soils, exposures. Fairly drought tolerant near coast; need water in hot inland summers. Bloom and fruit best in full sun but will take fairly heavy shade. Prune to control erratic growth.

C. edulis. Native to Africa. Differs from widely grown *C. grandiflora* in several ways. Shrubby or somewhat vinelike to 10 ft. (Will grow to 30 ft. high and as wide.) Foliage of glossy, bright green, red-tinged leaves to 2 in. long. Bears large clusters of pure white, fragrant flowers, opening from pink buds. Cherry-sized fruit changes from green to red to purplish black as it ripens.

C. macrocarpa *(C. grandiflora).* NATAL PLUM. Native to South Africa. Fast-growing, strong, upright, rounding shrub of rather loose habit to 5–7 ft. (occasionally to 18 ft.). Lustrous, leathery, rich green, 3-in., oval leaves. Spines along branches and at end of each twig. White flowers, almost as fragrant as star jasmine and of same 5-petaled star shape but larger (to 2 in. wide), appear throughout year, followed by red, plum-shaped, 1–2-in. fruit. Flowers, green fruit, and ripe fruit often appear together. Fruit varies in sweetness, but generally has quality of rather sweet cranberry and makes good sauce. You can eat it fresh; harvest when scarlet.

Carissa macrocarpa

Use as screen or hedge. Prune heavily for formal hedges, lightly for informal screen. Strong growth, spines discourage trespassers. Don't plant near walkways, where spines can be annoying to passersby.

If you grow Natal plum outside Zones 22–24, give it same favorite spot you'd give bougainvillea—warm south- or west-facing wall, preferably with overhang to keep off frost. It may also be grown as an indoor plant in good light.

C. m. 'Boxwood Beauty'. Exceptionally compact growth to 2 ft. and as wide. Deep green leaves, like a large-leafed boxwood. Excellent for hedging and shaping. No thorns.

C. m. 'Fancy'. Upright grower to 6 ft. Unusually large fruit, good show of flowers. Use as lightly pruned screen.

C. m. 'Green Carpet'. Low growing to 1–1½ ft., spreading to 4 ft. or more. Smaller leaves than *C. macrocarpa.* Excellent ground cover.

C. m. 'Horizontalis'. To 1½–2 ft., spreading, trailing. Dense foliage.

C. m. 'Minima'. Slow growth to 1–1½ ft. tall, 2 ft. wide. Leaves and flowers both tiny.

C. m. 'Prostrata'. Vigorous, to about 2 ft. and spreading. Good ground cover. Prune out any growth that tends toward upright. Can be trained as espalier.

C. m. 'Ruby Point'. Upright grower to 6 ft. New leaves hold their red color through the growing season.

C. m. 'Tomlinson'. Dwarf, compact growth to 2–2½ ft. high, 3 ft. wide. Shiny mahogany-tinted foliage, large flowers, wine-colored fruit. No thorns. Slow growing. Tub plant, foundation plantings.

C. m. 'Tuttle' ***(C. m.* 'Nana Compacta Tuttlei').** To 2–3 ft. high, 3–5 ft. wide. Compact, dense foliage. Heavy producer of flowers and fruit. Used as ground cover.

CARMEL CREEPER. See *Ceanothus griseus horizontalis.*

CARNATION. See *Dianthus caryophyllus.*

CARNEGIEA gigantea. *Cactaceae.* SAGUARO. Giant cactus. Zones 12, 13, 18–21. Native to northern Mexico, Arizona, California. Columnar and branching, with prominent ribs that give it fluted appearance. Grows very slowly to 50 ft. Spines light brown, ½–3 in. long.

Mature plants bloom in May, bearing white, single flowers 4–5 in. long (state flower of Arizona). Night blooming. Oval, edible fruit splits open to show red pulp within; sometimes mistaken for flowers. Slow growing; stays pot size or garden size for many years.

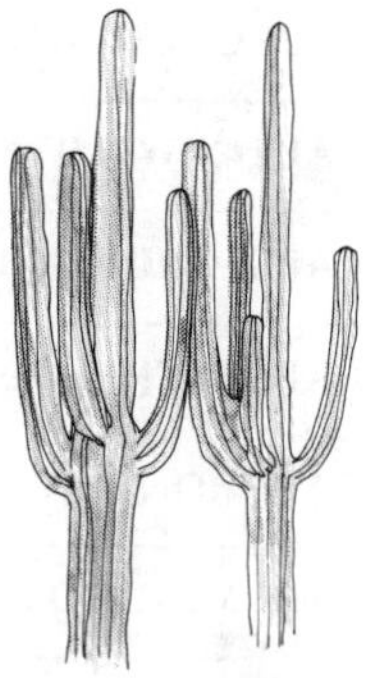

Carnegiea gigantea

CAROB. See *Ceratonia siliqua.*

CAROLINA ALLSPICE. See *Calycanthus floridus.*

CAROLINA JESSAMINE. See *Gelsemium.*

CAROLINA LAUREL CHERRY. See *Prunus caroliniana.*

CARPENTERIA californica. *Saxifragaceae.* BUSH ANEMONE. Evergreen shrub. Zones 5–9, 14–24. Native to California, localized in Sierra Nevada foothills between Kings and San Joaquin rivers in Fresno County. Slow growing to 3–6 ft., with many stems arising from base. Older bark light colored and peeling, new shoots purplish. Leaves thick, narrow, dark green above and whitish beneath, 2–4½ in. long. Flowers white, anemonelike, 1½–3 in. wide, with a slight, pleasant fragrance. Blooms May–August. Resistant to oak root fungus.

Carpenteria californica

This attractive native with rather formal look accepts ordinary garden conditions. Grows in shade or sun, but looks best in light shade. Takes much drought once established. Inspect new growth occasionally and wash off aphids that could disfigure plants. Spray as new leaves form. Prune after flowering to restrain growth or shape.

CARPET BUGLE. See *Ajuga.*

CARPINUS. *Betulaceae.* HORNBEAM. Deciduous trees. Hardy, well-behaved, relatively small shade trees. Long life and good habits as street trees (not recommended for southern California and desert). Retain leaves well into winter. Fruit—small, hard nutlets in leaflike bracts—is carried in attractive drooping clusters. Give ordinary garden watering.

C. betulus. EUROPEAN HORNBEAM. Zones 3–9, 14–17. Moderate growth to 40 ft. Dense pyramidal form, eventually becoming broad with drooping outer branches. Dark green, toothed leaves, 2–5 in. long. Fall color yellow or dark red in cold winters. Fruit clusters to 5 in. long. Subject to scale insect infestations. Can be clipped into hedge or screen. Variety 'Fastigiata' is narrow column in youth, dense pyramid in maturity; it is the variety commonly sold.

Carpinus betulus

C. caroliniana. AMERICAN HORNBEAM. Zones 1–9, 14–17. Native from Florida to Texas, north to Virginia, southern Illinois. Moderate growth to round-headed, 25–30-ft. tree. Bark is smooth and gray. Dark green leaves, 1–3 in. long, edges toothed. In fall, leaves turn mottled yellow and red. Fruit clusters 1½–4 in. long.

CARPOBROTUS. *Aizoaceae.* ICE PLANT. Succulent perennials or subshrubs. Zones 12–24. Coarse-leafed, trailing plants useful for binding sand at the beach and for covering sunny banks (but not steep banks, where their weight when waterlogged could cause them to slide). Drought resistant; moderately fire retardant. Can develop patches of dieback if severely stressed by lack of water or nitrogen during growth season. Scale can be a problem; control with malathion or acephate (orthene).

Carpobrotus chilensis

C. chilensis *(Mesembryanthemum aequilaterale).* Native along coast, Oregon to Baja California. The straight 3-sided fleshy leaves are 2 in. long; flowers lightly fragrant, rosy purple. Summer bloom.

C. edulis *(Mesembryanthemum edule).* From South Africa. Leaves curved, 4–5 in. long. Flowers pale yellow to rose. Fruit edible, but not very good.

CARRION FLOWER. See *Stapelia.*

CARROT. *Umbelliferae.* Biennial grown as annual. All Zones in conditions noted below. The variety to plant depends on the soil condition: carrots reach smooth perfection only in good-textured soil free of stones and clods. Plant long market kinds only if you can give them a foot of this ideal, light soil. If you can provide only a few inches, plant half-long varieties such as 'Nantes' and 'Chantenay', or miniatures such as 'Amstel', 'Lady Finger', or 'Short and Sweet'.

Carrot

Grow in sun. Sow thickly in rows at least 1 ft. apart. Soil should be fine enough for root development and loose enough so crusting can't check sprouting of seeds. If crust should form, keep soil soft by sprinkling. Too much nitrogen or a lot of manure will make excessive top growth and cause forking of roots. Maintain even soil moisture: alternating dry and wet conditions cause split roots.

Make successive plantings when first planting is up and growing; in cold-winter climates, make last sowing 70 days before anticipated killing frost. When tops are 2 in. high, thin plants to 1½ in. apart; thin again if roots begin to crowd. Tiny carrots removed in thinnings are good for butter-steaming. After first thinning, apply narrow band of commercial fertilizer 2 in. out from the row. Begin harvest when carrots reach finger size. In mild-winter climates, carrots store well in the ground; dig as needed. Diseases, insects, and mites not a problem in most home gardens.

CARROT WOOD. See *Cupaniopsis anacardioides.*

CARTHAMUS tinctorius. *Compositae.* SAFFLOWER, FALSE SAFFRON. Annual. All Zones in conditions noted below. A relative of the thistles that is ornamental as well as economically useful. Erect, spiny-leafed stems, 1–3 ft. tall, branching above, bearing orange yellow flower heads above leafy bracts; inner bracts are spiny. Durable cut flower, fresh or dried. (An ornamental spineless safflower is also available.) Grown commercially for oil extracted from the seeds. The dried flowers from the flower heads have been used for seasoning in place of true saffron, which they strongly resemble in color and flavor. Sow seeds in place in spring after frosts. Full sun. Once established, plants need little water.

Carthamus tinctorius

CARUM carvi. *Umbelliferae.* CARAWAY. Biennial herb. All Zones in conditions noted below. Mound of carrotlike leaves, 1–2 ft. high, first year. Umbrellalike clusters of white flowers rise above foliage second year. Plant dies after seeds ripen in midsummer. Start from seed sown in place in fall or spring. Thrives in well-drained soil in full sun. Average water. Thin seedlings to 1½ ft. To harvest seed, pick dry heads and rub off seeds. Sift to remove chaff, dry thoroughly, and store in jars or canisters. Use dried seeds for flavoring pickles, vegetables, cookies, rye bread.

Carum carvi

CARYA illinoensis *(Carya pecan).* *Juglandaceae.* PECAN. Deciduous tree. Zones 4–9, 12–16, 18–23 as ornamental; Zones 8–9, 12–14, 18–20 to produce good nut crop. Native to southern and central U.S. Graceful, shapely tree to 70 ft. tall and equally wide. Foliage like that of English walnut but prettier, with more (11–17) leaflets that are narrower and longer (4–7 in.); foliage pattern finer textured, shade lighter. Resistant to oak root fungus.

Carya illinoensis

Needs well-drained, deep soils (6–10 ft. deep). Won't stand salinity. In zinc-deficient desert soils, prevent (or cure) pecan rosette (abnormal clumps of twigs) with zinc sulfate sprays or soil treatment. Needs occasional deep watering in hot-summer climates. Prune to shape or to remove dead wood. Select varieties by climate: 'F. W. Anderson' (self-fertile) is good for San Joaquin Valley; 'Mahan' (self-fertile) thrives in low desert; 'Western Schley' fruits over wide range of climates, needs pollinator. 'Wichita' is good pollinator for 'Western Schley', bears good nuts very young. 'Barton', 'Burkett', 'Choctaw', 'Mohawk', 'Stuart', 'Success', and many others also sold. Of these, 'Burkett' needs pollinator.

To plant, set out bare-root trees in winter. Dig deep holes to accommodate the long tap root; position bud union above soil level and about an inch deeper than it was in the nursery. Firm soil about roots, water thoroughly, and irrigate every 1–2 weeks the first year.

Caryophyllaceae. The pink family includes many garden annuals and perennials, as well as a few weeds. Leaves are borne in opposite pairs at joints that are often swollen; leaves are often joined together at their bases. Pinks and carnations are typical representatives, along with *Cerastium* and *Lychnis.*

CARYOPTERIS. *Verbenaceae.* BLUEBEARD. Deciduous shrubs. Zones 1–7, 14–17. Valued for contribution of cool blue to flower border from August to frost. Generally grown as shrubby perennial. If not frozen back in winter, cut back nearly to ground in spring. Light soil. Full sun. Takes considerable drought. If you cut it back after each wave of bloom, it may flower repeatedly July to frosts.

Caryopteris clandonensis

C. clandonensis. BLUE MIST. A hybrid. Low growing to 2- by 2-ft. mound of narrow, 3-in.-long leaves. Clusters of small blue flowers top the upper parts of stems. Selected forms 'Azure' and 'Heavenly Blue' both have deep blue flowers.

C. incana *(C. mastacanthus).* COMMON BLUEBEARD, BLUE SPIRAEA. Taller growing than above, to 3–4 ft., with lavender blue flowers.

C

CARYOTA. *Palmae.* FISHTAIL PALM. Outdoors in Zones 23, 24; house plant anywhere. Feather palms with finely divided leaves, the leaflets flattened and split at the tips like fish tails. Tender. Native to southeast Asia, where they grow in full sun. In California, they need partial shade, protected site. Indoors, give them as much light as possible.

Caryota ochlandra

C. mitis. CLUSTERED FISHTAIL PALM. Slow grower to 20–25 ft. Basal offshoots eventually form clustered trunks. Foliage light green. Very tender; thrives only in ideal environment. Not for novices.

C. ochlandra. CANTON FISHTAIL PALM. In time, will probably reach 25 ft. Medium dark green leaves. Hardiest of the caryotas, it has survived to 26°F.

C. urens. FISHTAIL WINE PALM. Single-stemmed palm to 100 ft. in Asia, to 15–20 ft. here with careful protection. If temperatures go below 32°F., it's certain to die. Dark green leaves. Avoid handling fruit with bare hands; invisible crystals can cause severe itching.

CASCARA sagrada. See *Rhamnus purshiana.*

CASHMERE BOUQUET. See *Clerodendrum bungei.*

CASIMIROA edulis. *Rutaceae.* WHITE SAPOTE. Evergreen, or erratically behaves as deciduous tree. Zones 15, 16, 22–24. Beautiful tropical tree that will withstand more cold than most avocados and seems to do well wherever lemons are grown. To 50 ft. Keep it to almost any height by pinching out terminal bud if wide umbrella type is wanted. Prune off lower branches. Luxuriant, glossy green leaves divided fanwise into 3–7 oval, 3–5-in.-long leaflets.

Casimiroa edulis

Tree bears heavy crop of 3–4-in., round, pale green to yellow fruits. Flavor is described in many ways—similar to peach but more bland, like banana but sweeter, ripe pear in rich syrup, custard with banana-peach flavor. Consistency of custard. Fruit ripens August through November. Overripe fruit becomes slightly bitter. Pick when firm ripe; allow yellowish flesh to become mellow and sweet. Mature tree may produce several hundred pounds of fruit, far more than any one family can use. Cleanup becomes a chore, so plant where dropping fruit can be raked up or get lost in a ground cover. Goes deciduous for short time—when hit by frost or in June, when tree "moults" or becomes completely bare for brief period.

Not particular about soil; needs ample water and consistent feeding. Budded trees give best fruit, and are grown in limited quantities; 'Coleman', 'Pike', 'Wilson', and 'Suebelle' are all good.

CASSIA. *Leguminosae.* SENNA. Evergreen, partially evergreen, or deciduous shrubs and trees from many lands, providing a great number of landscaping choices for southern California and Arizona. "Yellow" and "golden" are the words for cassia. Flowers may be yellow, bright yellow, egg-yolk yellow, deep yellow, gold. As a group, cassias bloom better and live longer in fast-draining soil with infrequent but deep watering. Some of the tree forms, *C. excelsa* and *C. leptophylla,* will grow in lawns where drainage is fast. All need sun.

Cassia artemisioides

Flowering dates in the following list are approximate. Many species will bloom almost any time or scatter bloom over a long period.

C. alata. CANDLE BUSH. Deciduous shrub. Zone 23. Native to tropics. Grows 8–12 ft. tall and spreads wider. Golden yellow flowers (1 in. wide) in big spikelike clusters, November–January. Leaves divided into 12–28 2½-in.-long leaflets. Prune hard after bloom.

C. artemisioides. FEATHERY CASSIA. Evergreen shrub. Zones 8, 9, 12–16, 18–23. Native to Australia. Attractive, light and airy structure to 3–5 ft. Leaves are gray, divided into 6–8 needlelike, 1-in.-long leaflets. Flowers (¾ in.) sulfur yellow, 5–8 in a cluster, January–April, often into summer. Prune lightly after flowering to eliminate heavy setting of seed. Drought resistant.

C. bicapsularis. Evergreen shrub. Zones 13, 22–24. Native to tropics. To 10 ft. Recovers after killed to ground by frost. Yellow, ½-in.-wide flowers in spikelike clusters, October–February if not cut short by frost. Prune severely after flowering. Leaflets roundish, rather thick, 6–10 to a leaf.

C. candolleana. Zones 12–24. Evergreen shrub. To 5–6 ft. Showy golden yellow flowers in fall.

C. corymbosa. FLOWERY SENNA. Large evergreen shrub. Zones 13, 21–24. Native to Argentina. To 10 ft. Yellow flowers in rounded clusters, spring to fall. Dark green leaves with 6 narrow, oblong, 1–2 in. leaflets. Prune severely after flowering. (For small garden, less rank-growing *C. tomentosa* is better.) Naturalized here and there in Santa Barbara.

C. didymobotrya (also sold as *C. nairobensis*). Evergreen shrub. Zones 13, 22–24. Native to east Africa. Often escapes, naturalizes. Rangy grower to 10 ft. Leaflets 2 in. long, 8–16 pairs per leaf. Yellow, 1½-in.-wide flowers in upright, dense clusters (to 1 ft.), December–April. Thrives in heat. Stands some drought when established. Smelly but attractive plant for large wild gardens.

C. excelsa *(C. carnaval).* CROWN OF GOLD TREE. Partially evergreen tree. Zones 12, 13, 19–24. Native to Argentina. Grows fast to 25–30 ft. Leaves divided into 10–20 pairs of 1-in.-long leaflets. Large bright yellow flowers in 12–16-in.-long clusters, late summer, early fall. Prune hard after flowering. Needs moisture in growing season.

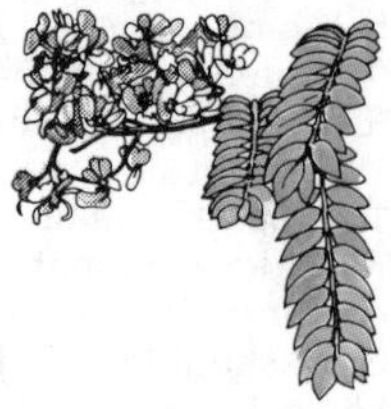

Cassia excelsa

C. leptophylla. GOLD MEDALLION TREE. Near-evergreen tree. Zones 21–24. Native to Brazil. Most shapely and graceful of the cassias. Fast growing to 20–25 ft.; open headed, low spreading, tending to weep. Leaves with up to 12 pairs of narrow leaflets. Deep yellow flowers to 3 in. wide, in 6–8-in.-long spikes through July–August; scattered blooms later. Prune as for *C. excelsa.*

C. multijuga. Evergreen tree. Zones 22–24. Native to Brazil. Heavy-foliaged, much-branched tree to 15–20 ft. Somewhat brittle. Yellow, 2-in.-wide flowers in clusters in late summer and fall. Leaves have 18–40 pairs of rather narrow leaflets that grow to ¾ in. long. Prune as for *C. excelsa.*

C. nemophila *(C. eremophila).* Zones 12–24. Resembles *C. artemisioides* but has green rather than gray foliage and takes cold somewhat better.

C. phyllodenia. Zones 11–24. Grows rapidly to 5–6 ft. tall. Leaves are narrow, curved, silvery gray. Sulfur yellow flowers appear over a long season—December through April in Phoenix. Needs no watering when established, but looks better with a little summer irrigation. Needs no feeding. Prune only to shape or remove dead wood.

C. splendida. GOLDEN WONDER SENNA. Evergreen shrub. Zones 12, 13, 21–24. Native to Brazil. This name has been applied to a number of cassias of varying growth habits. Those in Los Angeles State and County Arboretum are 10–12 ft. high, and about as wide.

Orange yellow, 1½-in.-wide flowers in loose clusters at branch ends, November–January. Other plantings of cassias with this name, with bright yellow flowers, are strongly horizontal in branch pattern, 5–8 ft. high, spreading to 12 ft. wide. All must be severely pruned after flowering.

C. sturtii. Evergreen shrub. Zones 12–14. Native to Australia. Leaves with 2–5 pairs of narrow, inch-long leaflets. Bushy, 3–6-ft., gray green shrub with clustered bright yellow flowers. Longer bloom than *C. artemisioides,* neater plant.

C. surattensis *(C. glauca)*. Evergreen shrub. Zones 19–24. Grows fast to 6–8 ft. and spreads wider. Bright yellow flowers (¾ in. wide) in small clusters at branch ends, nearly all year. Roundish, 1½-in.-long leaflets, 12–20 to each leaf. Does not need to be pruned heavily. This shrub is one of best for small gardens.

C. tomentosa. WOOLLY SENNA. Evergreen shrub. Zones 13, 17, 22–24. Native to Mexico and South America. Vigorous, rank growth to 8 ft. (or 12–15 ft.). Leaves divided into 12–16 leaflets, each 2½ in. long, that are green above, white and hairy beneath. Deep yellow flowers in upright clusters at ends of branches in winter, early spring. Prune hard after flowering.

CASTANEA. *Fagaceae.* CHESTNUT. Deciduous trees. Zones 2–9, 14–17. The American chestnut (*C. dentata*) is nearing extinction as a result of a fungus disease. However, 2 other chestnuts are available in the West. They have handsome dark to bright green foliage. Creamy white, small flowers in long (8–10-in.), slim catkins make quite a display in June or July. The large edible nuts are enclosed in prickly burrs. Wonderful dense shade trees where there is space to accommodate them, as at large country places. Need occasional deep watering.

Castanea mollissima

C. mollissima. CHINESE CHESTNUT. Native to China, Korea. Grows to 60 ft. with rounded crown that may spread to 40 ft. Leaves 3–7 in. long, with coarsely toothed edges. Most nursery trees are grown from seed, not cuttings; hence, nuts are variable, but generally of good quality. Single trees bear lightly or not at all. Plant 2 or more to insure cross-pollination and you'll get a substantial crop. Intolerant of alkaline soil conditions.

C. sativa. SPANISH CHESTNUT. Native to southern Europe, north Africa, western Asia. Larger, broader tree than Chinese chestnut. Can reach 100 ft. in height with greater spread, but usually a 40–60-ft. tree in gardens. Leaves 4–9 in. long, with sharply toothed edges. Produces large chestnuts of excellent quality; these are the nuts usually sold in markets. Size, litter, and disagreeable odor of pollen make it a tree for wide-open spaces. Resistant to oak root fungus.

Dunstan Hybrid Chestnuts. Zones 2–9, 14–24. These are offspring of American and Chinese chestnut parents, with characteristics intermediate between the 2 (the American chestnut is—or was—a tall, broad timber tree with small but very sweet nuts). The hybrids seem resistant to the blight and produce nuts equal to Spanish chestnuts in size and sweeter in flavor. Rare.

CASTANOSPERMUM australe. *Leguminosae.* MORETON BAY CHESTNUT. Evergreen tree. Zones 18–22. Native to Australia. Beautiful in foliage; spectacular in flower. To 50–60 ft. tall, nearly as wide. Large, shiny, dark green leaves are divided into 11–15 leaflets about 1½ by 5 in. Flowers bright red and yellow, in stiff spikes about 8 in. long. They grow from twigs, branches, and main trunk in summer. Seeds like chestnuts are occasionally roasted and eaten, but are considered unwholesome. Moderate water requirements.

Castanospermum australe

CAST-IRON PLANT. See *Aspidistra elatior.*

CASTOR BEAN. See *Ricinus communis.*

CASUARINA. *Casuarinaceae.* BEEFWOOD, SHE-OAK. Evergreen trees. Zones 8, 9, 12–24. Native mostly to Australia. Sometimes called Australian pine—but it's not a pine, despite slight resemblance in its form and woody, conelike fruits. Long, thin, jointed, green branches look like long pine needles; true leaves are inconspicuous. Tolerates many tough conditions: dry or wet soil, salinity, heat, wind. Particularly useful in desert areas. Hardy to 15°F. In desert, it is often confused with Athel tamarisk (*Tamarix aphylla*) because of similar foliage. Distinctive difference: the casuarina's conelike fruit.

Casuarina stricta

C. cunninghamiana. RIVER SHE-OAK. Tallest and largest. To 70 ft. Finest texture, with dark green branches.

C. equisetifolia. HORSETAIL TREE. Fast grower to 40–60 ft., 20 ft. wide. Has pendulous, gray green branches. Plant sold under this name may be *C. cunninghamiana* or hybrid between it and *C. glauca*.

C. stricta. MOUNTAIN or DROOPING SHE-OAK, COAST BEEFWOOD. Fast grower to 20–35 ft. Darkest green foliage and largest cones (1 in.). Makes beautiful silhouette against sky. Properly watered and shaped, is attractive street tree. Good at seashore.

CATALINA CHERRY. See *Prunus lyonii.*

CATALINA IRONWOOD. See *Lyonothamnus floribundus.*

CATALINA PERFUME. See *Ribes viburnifolium.*

CATALPA. *Bignoniaceae.* Deciduous trees. All Zones. One of the few truly hardy deciduous trees that can compete in flower and leaf with subtropicals of southern California. Large, upright clusters of trumpet-shaped, 2-in.-wide flowers, pure white, striped and marked with yellow and soft brown, displayed in late spring and summer above large, bold, heart-shaped leaves. Flowers are followed by long, bean-shaped seed capsules, sometimes called Indian beans or Indian stogies.

Catalpa speciosa

Unusually well adapted to extremes of heat and cold and to soils throughout the West. Moderate water. Where winds are strong, should be planted in lee of taller trees or buildings to protect leaves from wind damage. Some gardeners object to litter of fallen flowers in summer and seed capsules in autumn. Plants need attention to shaping while young, seldom develop a well-established dominant shoot. Shorten side branches as tree grows. When branching begins at the desired height, remove lower branches.

For the tree sometimes called DESERT CATALPA, see *Chilopsis.* Another tree sometimes mistakenly called catalpa is the very similar *Paulownia* or EMPRESS TREE, with lavender flowers. *Paulownia* shows flower buds in winter; catalpa does not.

C. bignonioides. COMMON CATALPA, INDIAN BEAN. Native to southeastern United States. Generally smaller than *C. speciosa*, 20–50 ft. according to climate or soil, with somewhat smaller spread. Leaves 5–8 in. long, often in whorls, give odd odor when crushed. The variety 'Aurea' has yellow leaves. Resistant to oak root fungus.

C. b. 'Nana'. (Almost always sold as *C. bungei.*) UMBRELLA CATALPA. A dense globe form usually grafted high on *C. bignonioides*. It never blooms. Cut it back to keep it in scale.

C. erubescens 'Purpurea'. Young leaves and branchlets of this catalpa are deep blackish purple, turning purple-toned green in summer.

C. speciosa. WESTERN CATALPA. Native southern Illinois to Arkansas. Round headed; 40–70 ft. tall. Leaves 6–12 in. long; no odor when crushed. Fewer flowers per cluster than for *C. bignonioides*. Most widely distributed in the West. Early training and pruning will give tall trunk and umbrella-shaped crown.

CATANANCHE caerulea. *Compositae.* CUPID'S DART. Perennial. All Zones. Sturdy, free-flowering plant for summer borders and arrangements. Leaves gray green, 8–12 in. long, mostly at base of stem. Lavender blue, 2-in. flower heads reminiscent of cornflowers are surrounded by strawlike, shining bracts. Stems 2 ft. tall. Flowers may be dried for use in bouquets. Remove faded flowers to prolong bloom. Plant in full sun. Drought resistant. 'Alba' is a white variety.

Catananche caerulea

CATHA edulis. *Celastraceae.* KHAT. Evergreen shrub. Zones 13, 16–24. Valued for all-year foliage beauty. Bronzy green, shiny, oval, 2–4-in.-long, slightly toothed leaves take on reddish tints through fall and winter. Grown as spreading shrub to 8 ft. tall; old plants in parks are more than 20 ft. tall. Pinch or prune to keep compact. Effective as espalier. Red stems and bark add interest. Medium-sized leaves make good transition between small-scale foliage and large leaves such as loquat. Very small white flowers. Needs fast drainage but not rich soil. Does well in poor soil, dry situations, or coastal winds.

Catha edulis

CATHARANTHUS roseus *(Vinca rosea).* *Apocynaceae.* MADAGASCAR PERIWINKLE. Perennial, usually grown as annual. All Zones in conditions noted below. Invaluable for summer–fall color in hot climates. Showiest summer flower in desert gardens. Glossy leaves 1–3 in. long cover bushy plant 1–2 ft. high. Phloxlike flowers 1½ in. wide in pure white, white with rose or red eye, blush pink, or bright rose. The Little series grows a compact 8–10 in. Creeping strains, including the Carpet series, grow 4–8 in. tall, 1½ ft. wide. Will bloom first season from seed sown early indoors, in greenhouse or coldframe. Nurseries sell plants in flats in late spring. Plant in full sun or partial shade. Requires little water, ordinary soil. Self-sows readily.

Catharanthus roseus

Continues to flower after zinnias and marigolds have gone, until Thanksgiving if weather stays mild. Lives over in frostless areas, but may look ragged in winter. In coastal areas, blooms in late summer after heat builds up.

CATMINT. See *Nepeta faassenii.*

CATNIP. See *Nepeta cataria.*

CAT'S CLAW. See *Macfadyena unguis-cati.*

CAT'S EARS. See *Calochortus tolmiei.*

CATTLEYA. *Orchidaceae.* Epiphytic orchids. Native to tropical America. Most popular and best known of orchids. For house and greenhouse primarily. Showy flowers are used for corsages.

Species, varieties, and hybrids are too numerous to list here. All have pseudobulbs 1–3 in. thick bearing leathery leaves and a stem topped with 1–4 or more flowers. Plants range from a few inches tall to 2 ft. or more. Commercial growers offer wide range of flower colors: lavender and purple; white; semi-albas (white with colored lip); novelties—yellow, orange, red, green, bronze (many of these are crosses between *Cattleya* and other genera). Newest hybrid forms are the miniature cattleyas and the bifoliates or multifloras. The latter are standard-sized plants with leaves in pairs. These plants produce large clusters of 3–5-in. flowers and, best of all, many bloom more than once a year.

All cattleyas grow best in greenhouse where temperature, humidity, and light can be readily controlled. However, you can also grow them as house plants. Main requirements: (1) warm temperature (60°F. at night, 70°F. or higher during the day); (2) relatively high humidity—50–60 percent or better; (3) good light—20–40 percent of outside light with protection from hot midday sun. (Color of orchid foliage should be light green and leaves should be erect. When light intensity is too low, leaves turn dark green and new growth becomes soft.) Also see *Orchidaceae.*

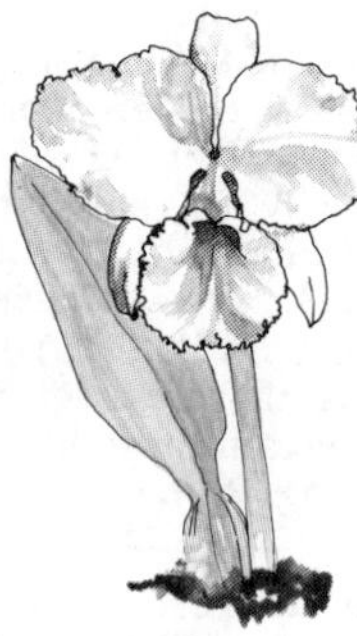

Cattleya

CAULIFLOWER. *Cruciferae.* Annual or biennial grown as annual. All Zones in conditions noted below. Related to broccoli and cabbage with similar cultural requirements, but more difficult to grow. Easiest in cool, humid coastal regions; where summers are dry and hot, grow it to harvest well before or well after midsummer. Home gardeners usually plant one of the several 'Snowball' varieties, or hybrids such as 'Early White Hybrid' and 'Snow Crown Hybrid'. An unusual variety is 'Purple Head', which has large plants with heads of deep purple color, turning green in cooking.

Cauliflower

Grow cauliflower like broccoli. Start with small plants. Space them 18–20 in. apart in rows 3 ft. apart. Be sure to keep plants actively growing; any check during transplanting or later growth is likely to cause premature setting of undersized heads. When heads first appear, tie up the large leaves around them to keep them white. Harvest heads as soon as they reach full size.

CEANOTHUS. *Rhamnaceae.* WILD LILAC. Mostly evergreen shrubs, small trees, or ground covers. Zones 4–7, 14–24. In Zones 1–3, stay with varieties locally tested and sold. Some species grow in eastern U.S., Rocky Mountains, the Northwest, and Mexico, but most are native to California. They range in flower color from white through all shades of blue to deep violet blue. They all flower in spring, mostly in March or April. In descriptions on chart, time of flowering is not indicated unless it is unusual. New varieties (most of them propagated from selected wild plants) appear frequently, and old varieties disappear from nurseries. For the widest choice, deal with a specialist in western natives.

Ceanothus griseus horizontalis

Ceanothus sometimes get aphids and whitefly, but these are easy to control. As a group, ceanothus plants don't live very long; 5–10 years is typical.

Almost all ceanothus can succumb to root rot caused by water mold organisms. In the wild, this doesn't happen because the plants grow on rocky slopes and generally go without water all summer. But in the garden, it's a major factor. If possible, plant ceanothus beyond reach of sprinklers, and water them by hose through the first dry season only. In subsequent years they can grow on whatever water they get during the rainy season or from the subsoil during the dry season.

Ceanothus gloriosus

Ceanothus

SPECIES OR VARIETY	SIZE	FOLIAGE	FLOWERS	COMMENTS
Ceanothus 'Blue Jeans'	7–9 ft. tall, 7–9 ft. wide.	Dark green, leathery leaves.	Profuse, pale powder blue clusters.	Tolerates heavy soil, drought, summer water. Shear after bloom for low-water-use hedge.
C. 'Concha'	6–7 ft. tall, 6–8 ft. wide.	Densely clad in dark green 1-in. leaves.	Dark blue 1-in. clusters.	One of the best. Tolerates summer water. Hardy to 15°F.
C. 'Dark Star'	5–6 ft. tall, 8–10 ft. wide.	Tiny (¼-in.), dark green leaves.	Dark cobalt blue 1½-in. clusters.	Similar to 'Julia Phelps', maybe better. Deerproof.
C. 'Frosty Blue'	6–9 ft. tall, 8–10 ft. wide.	Dark green ½-in. leaves. Dense.	Deep blue, white-frosted 2½–3-in. spikelike clusters.	Flowers shimmer with white. Sturdy stems. Can be shaped as small tree.
C. 'Gentian Plume'	10–20 ft. tall, 12–20 ft. wide.	Dark green 2½-in. leaves.	Dark blue 10-in. spikelike clusters.	Leggy when young; pinching helps. If stems get so long that plants "fall apart," prune them.
C. gloriosus POINT REYES CEANOTHUS	1–1½ ft. tall, 12–16 ft. wide.	Dark green, oval 1-in. leaves, tough and spiny.	Mostly light blue 1-in. clusters.	Much used in Zones 4–6. Does not do well in summer heat of Zones 7, 14, 18–21.
C. g. 'Anchor Bay'	1–1½ ft. tall, 6–8 ft. wide.	Very dense.	Somewhat deeper blue than above.	Dense foliage holds down weeds.
C. g. exaltatus 'Emily Brown'	2–3 ft. tall, 8–12 ft. wide.	Dark green, hollylike 1-in. leaves.	Dark violet blue 1-in. clusters.	Stands heavy soil, water near coast.
C. g. porrectus	3–4 ft. tall, 6–8 ft. wide.	Dark green, hollylike ½-in. leaves.	Medium dark blue 1-in. clusters.	Dense growth but sparse bloom.
C. griseus horizontalis CARMEL CREEPER	1½–2½ ft. tall, 5–15 ft. wide.	Glossy, oval, 2-in., bright green leaves.	Light blue 1-in. clusters.	Some sold under this name may be 'Hurricane Point'. Sometimes winter-damaged in Zones 4–7, 14.
C. g. h. 'Hurricane Point'	2–3 ft. tall, to 36 ft. wide.	Glossy, oval 2-in. leaves.	Pale blue 1-in. clusters.	Very fast, somewhat rank grower. Deer love this and the other forms of *C. griseus*.
C. g. h. 'Yankee Point'	3–5 ft. tall, 8–10 ft. wide.	Glossy, dark green 1½-in. leaves.	Medium blue 1-in. clusters.	One of best ground-covering kinds. Looks refined.
C. g. 'Louis Edmunds'	5–6 ft. tall, 9–20 ft. wide.	Bright glossy green 1-in. leaves.	Medium sea blue 1-in. clusters.	Stands heavy soil, water.
C. g. 'Santa Ana'	4–5 ft. tall, 10–15 ft. wide.	Rich dark green ½-in. leaves.	Dark midnight blue 1-in. clusters.	Small leaves, somewhat brushy stems, but beautiful flowers.
C. hearstiorum	6 in. tall, 6–8 ft. wide.	Bumpy 1½-in. leaves.	Medium blue 1-in. clusters.	One of flattest, but lets in weeds. Spreads from center like a star. Variable performance; not dependable.
C. impressus SANTA BARBARA CEANOTHUS	6–9 ft. tall, 10–15 ft. wide.	Dense mass of dark green ½-in. leaves.	Lovely dark blue 1-in. clusters.	Temperamental; does best near coast.
C. 'Joyce Coulter'	2–5 ft. tall, 10–12 ft. wide.	Medium green 1-in. leaves.	Medium blue 3–5-in. spikelike clusters.	Grows as mound rather than ground cover.
C. 'Julia Phelps'	4½–7 ft. tall, 7–9 ft. wide.	Small (½-in.), dark green leaves.	Dark indigo blue 1-in. clusters.	One of best colors, best bloomers.
C. maritimus	1–3 ft. tall, 3–8 ft. wide.	Blue green to grayish ½-in. leaves, typically gray or white beneath.	White to pale lavender ½-in. clusters.	Height and color vary greatly.
C. 'Owlswood Blue'	8–10 ft. tall, 10–12 ft. wide.	Dark green, oval 2½-in. leaves.	Dark blue 4–6-in. spikelike clusters.	Reliable, heavy bloom.
C. prostratus SQUAW CARPET, MAHALA MATS	Prostrate; to 8 ft. wide.	Leathery, toothed, light green leaves, ½–1 in. long.	Deep to light blue clusters.	Blooms April–June. Useful in native range (higher elevations in northern Sierra Nevada), nearly impossible elsewhere. *C. p. occidentalis* from northern Coast Ranges has promise in lowland gardens.

(Continued on next page)

C

SPECIES OR VARIETY	SIZE	FOLIAGE	FLOWERS	COMMENTS
C. 'Ray Hartman'	12–20 ft. tall, 15–20 ft. wide.	Big (2–3-in.), dark green leaves.	Medium blue 3–5-in. spikelike clusters.	Can be trained as small tree.
C. rigidus 'Snowball'	6 ft. tall, 12–16 ft. wide.	Dark green ½-in. leaves.	White puffs, ¾ in. wide.	Handsome, dense, mounding.
C. 'Sierra Blue'	10–12 ft. tall, 8–10 ft. wide.	Glossy, medium green 1½-in. leaves.	Bright medium blue 6–8-in. spikelike clusters.	Very fast grower; weedy first few years.
C. thyrsiflorus BLUE BLOSSOM	6–21 ft. tall, 8–30 ft. wide.	Green, glossy leaves to 2 in.	Light to dark blue 3-in. spikelike clusters.	One of the hardiest evergreen ceanothus.
C. t. 'Skylark'	3–6 ft. tall, 5 ft. wide.	Glossy, medium green 2-in. leaves.	Dark blue clusters; profuse bloom over a long season.	Tolerates summer water.
C. t. 'Snow Flurry'	6–10 ft. tall, 8–12 ft. wide.	Rich green 2-in. leaves.	Profuse pure white clusters.	

CEDAR. See *Cedrus.*

CEDAR, INCENSE. See *Calocedrus decurrens.*

CEDAR OF LEBANON. See *Cedrus libani.*

CEDAR, WESTERN RED. See *Thuja plicata.*

CEDRELA. *Meliaceae.* Deciduous or evergreen trees. Flower in spring. Leaves with many leaflets, somewhat like those of tree of heaven (*Ailanthus*). Average water needs.

C. fissilis. Evergreen in tropical areas, deciduous in mildest California climates. Zones 16, 17, 22–24. Native to Central and South America. Smooth-trunked, round-headed tree grows to 50 ft. or more. Beautiful old street trees in Santa Barbara. Yellowish, velvety flowers in dense, drooping clusters followed by star-shaped, woody capsules containing winged seeds; much prized for dry arrangements.

Cedrela sinensis

C. sinensis. Deciduous. Zones 2–9, 14–24. Native to China. Slow to medium growth to 50 ft. Long, pendulous clusters of white flowers appear in April and May, followed by capsules similar to those of *C. fissilis.* Prized for beauty of new growth—tinted in shades of cream, soft pink, and rose. Suckers freely.

CEDRUS. *Pinaceae.* CEDAR. Evergreen trees. These conifers are the true cedars, and among the most widely grown conifers in the West. Cedars bear needles in tufted clusters. Cone scales, like those of firs, fall from tree, leaving a spiky core behind. Male catkins produce prodigious amounts of pollen that may cover you with yellow dust on a windy day. All are deep rooted and drought tolerant once established.

Cedrus atlantica

C. atlantica. ATLAS CEDAR. Zones 2–23. Native to Algeria. Slow to moderate growth to 60 ft. and more. Open, angular growth in youth. Branches usually get too long and heavy on young trees unless tips are pinched out or cut back. In Zones 4–7, branches of any age tend to break in heavy snows. Growth naturally less open with age. Less spreading than other true cedars, but still needs 30-ft. circle. Needles, less than 1 in. long, are bluish green. Varieties: *C. a.* 'Aurea', needles with yellowish tint; *C. a.* 'Glauca', silvery blue; *C. a.* 'Pendula', vertically drooping branches. Untrained, spreading, informally branching plants are sold as "rustics."

C. brevifolia. CYPRUS (or CYPRIAN) CEDAR. Zones 5–24. Native to island of Cyprus. Resembles *C. libani* but is a smaller tree (to 50 ft.) with shorter needles (¼–½ in.) and smaller cones. Sometimes considered variety of *C. libani.* Very slow growing.

Cedrus deodara

C. deodara. DEODAR CEDAR. Zones 2–12, 14–24. Native to the Himalayas. Fast growing to 80 ft., with 40-ft. spread at ground level. Lower branches sweep down to ground, then upwards. Upper branches openly spaced, graceful. Nodding tip identifies it in skyline. Softer, lighter texture than other cedars. Planted as living Christmas tree in small lawn, it soon overpowers area. However, you can control spread of tree by cutting new growth of side branches halfway back in late spring. This pruning also makes tree more dense. Very drought resistant once established.

Although deodars sold by nurseries are very similar in form, many variations occur in a group of seedlings—from scarecrows to compact low shrubs. Following 3 variations are propagated by cuttings or grafting: 'Aurea', with yellow new foliage turning golden green in summer; 'Descanso Dwarf' ('Compacta'), a slow-growing form reaching 15 ft. in 20 years; and 'Pendula' ('Prostrata'), which grows flat on ground or will drape over rock or wall. Deodar cedar can be pruned to grow as spreading low or high shrub. Annual late spring pruning will keep it in the shape you want.

C. libani. CEDAR OF LEBANON. Zones 2–24. Native to Asia Minor. To 80 ft., but slow growing—to 15 ft. in 15 years. Variable in growth habit. Usually a dense, narrow pyramid in youth. Needles, less than 1 in. long, are brightest green of the cedars in young trees, dark gray green in old trees. Spreads picturesquely as it matures to become majestic skyline tree with long horizontal arms and irregular crown. Rather scarce and expensive because of time to reach salable size. Routine garden care. No pruning needed. 'Sargentii' or 'Pendula Sargentii' grows even more slowly than the species, has a short trunk and crowded, weeping branches; choice container or rock garden plant.

Celastraceae. This family of evergreen or deciduous woody plants has undistinguished flowers, but fruit is often brightly colored. *Celastrus* and *Euonymus* are examples.

CELASTRUS. *Celastraceae.* BITTERSWEET. Deciduous vines. Hardy all Zones, best 1–7 where winters are cold. Grown principally for clusters of handsome fruit—yellow to orange capsules which split open to display brilliant red-coated seeds inside. Branches bearing fruit are much prized for indoor arrangements. Since birds seem uninterested in fruit, display is prolonged into winter.

Celastrus scandens

Vigorous and twining with ropelike branches; needs support. Will become tangled mass of intertwining branches unless pruned constantly. Cut out fruiting branches in winter; pinch out tips of vigorous branches in summer. Routine feeding, watering.

C. orbiculatus. To 30–40 ft. Leaves roundish, toothed, to 4 in. Fruit on short side shoots is partially obscured until leaves fall.

C. rosthornianus *(C. loeseneri).* CHINESE BITTERSWEET. To 20 ft. with dark green, oval leaves to 5 in. long. Fruit heavily borne.

C. scandens. AMERICAN BITTERSWEET. Native to eastern U.S. To 10–20 ft. Leaves very light green, oval, toothed, to 4 in. Fruit in scattered dense clusters is held above leaves, looks showy before foliage falls. Male and female flowers on different plants. To get fruit, plant one male plant with the female plants.

CELERIAC. *Umbelliferae.* Biennial grown as annual. All Zones in conditions noted for celery below. Celeriac is a form of celery grown for its large, rounded, edible roots rather than for its leaf stalks; it is usually displayed in markets as "celery root." Roots are peeled, then cooked or used raw in salads.

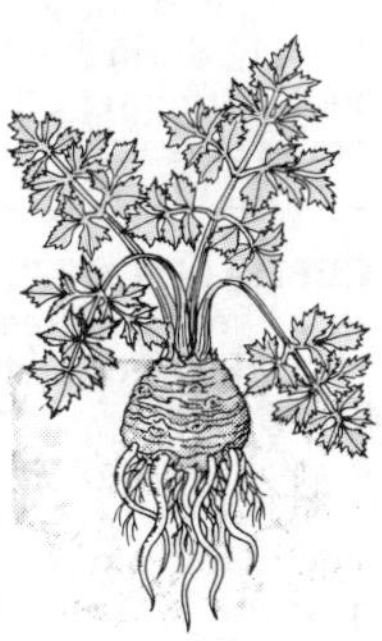
Celeriac

Growth requirements are same as for celery. Grow plants 6–8 in. apart in rows spaced 1½–2 ft. apart. Harvest when roots are 3 in. across or larger—in about 120 days. 'Giant Prague' is the recommended variety.

CELERY. *Umbelliferae.* Biennial grown as annual. All Zones in conditions noted below. Plant seeds in flats in early spring. Where winters are mild, start in summer and grow as winter crop. Seedlings are slow to reach planting size (save time by purchasing seedlings). Plant seedlings 6 in. apart in rows 2 ft. apart. Enrich planting soil with fertilizer. Soak ground around plants thoroughly and often. Every 2–3 weeks, apply liquid fertilizer with irrigation water. Work some soil up around plants as they grow to keep them upright and whiten stalks. Or blanch by setting bottomless milk carton, tar paper cylinder, or similar device over plants to exclude light from stalks (leaves must have sunlight). Or use unblanched (green). Bait to control snails and slugs; use fungicide to control blight.

Celery

CELERY ROOT. See Celeriac.

CELOSIA. *Amaranthaceae.* COCKSCOMB, CHINESE WOOLFLOWER. Annuals. All Zones in conditions noted below. Grow best in hot-summer climates, including desert. Richly colored tropical plants, some with flower clusters in bizarre shapes. Although attractive in cut arrangements with other flowers, in gardens celosias are most effective by themselves. Cut blooms can be dried for winter bouquets. Sow seed in place in late spring or early summer, or set out plants from flats. Succeed with little summer water in Zones 4–9, 14–24. Need full sun.

Celosia cristata

There are 2 kinds of cockscombs, both derived from a silvery white–flowered species, *C. argentea,* which has narrow leaves 2 in. or more long. One group, the plume cockscombs (often sold as C. 'Plumosa'), has plumy flower clusters. Some of these, like Chinese woolflower (sometimes sold as C. 'Childsii'), have plumy flower clusters that look like tangled masses of yarn. Flowers come in brilliant shades of pink, orange red, crimson, gold. You can get 2½–3-ft.-high forms or dwarf, more compact varieties. The latter grow about 1 ft. high and bear heavily branched plumes.

The other group is the crested cockscombs (often sold as C. 'Cristata'). These have velvety, fan-shaped flower clusters, often much contorted and fluted. Flowers are yellow, orange, crimson, purple, and red. Tall kinds grow to 3 ft., dwarf varieties to 10 in. high.

CELTIS. *Ulmaceae.* HACKBERRY. Deciduous trees. Related to elms and similar to them in most details, but smaller. All have virtue of deep rooting; old trees in narrow planting strips expand in trunk diameter and nearly fill strips—but without a surface root or any sign of heaving the sidewalk or curb. Bare-root plants, especially in larger sizes, sometimes fail to leaf out. Safer to buy in containers. Or try for small bare-root trees with big root systems. Especially good in windy locations, though young trees should be staked until well established. When established, trees will take wind, desert heat, much drought, and alkaline soil.

Celtis occidentalis

Street or lawn trees, even near buildings or paving; will take overhead shade. All have inconspicuous flowers. Only pest problem of note seems to be occasional aphid attack. In Zones 1–3, 10–13, insects cause leaf gall on hackberry trees. Attractive to birds.

C. australis. EUROPEAN HACKBERRY. Zones 8–16, 18–20. Moderate grower to 40 ft. in 14–15 years. In youth, branches are more upright than other hackberries. Never as wide-spreading as common hackberry. Dark green leaves 2–5 in. long, more coarsely toothed and more sharply pointed than common hackberry (*C. occidentalis*). Has shorter deciduous period than common hackberry.

C. occidentalis. COMMON HACKBERRY. All Zones. Native to eastern U.S. Grows to form rounded crown 50 ft. high or more and nearly as wide. Branches are spreading and sometimes pendulous. Leaves oval, bright green, 2–5 in. long, finely toothed on edges. Tree does not leaf out until April or later. In Zones 10–13, it lives longer than and is superior to commonly planted so-called Chinese elm (actually the Siberian elm—*Ulmus pumila*). Resistant to oak root fungus. Tolerates high plains heat, wind, alkaline soil, urban pollution.

C. pallida. DESERT HACKBERRY, GRANJENO. Shrub or small tree to 18 ft. Zones 10–13. Evergreen (deciduous in cold-winter areas). Dense, spiny growth; leaves 1 in. or less in length. Small orange berries. Useful in desert regions as honey source or bird food, for screen or barrier planting, or for erosion control.

C. reticulata *(C. douglasii).* WESTERN HACKBERRY. Zones 1–3, 10–12. Native to eastern Washington and through intermountain area to Utah, and in desert mountains of Arizona and southern California. Worthwhile ornamental tree in that area. Grows 25–30 ft. high with similar spread. Has somewhat pendulous branches. Oval leaves to 2½ in. long, margins toothed, pale beneath, strongly veined. Tiny red or brown berries eaten by birds.

C. sinensis. CHINESE HACKBERRY, YUNNAN HACKBERRY. Zones 8–16, 18–20. Similar in growth habit to common hackberry, but smaller. Leaves to 4 in. long, smoother and glossier than those of other hackberries, with scallop-toothed edges.

CENTAUREA. *Compositae.* Annuals and perennials. Perennial kinds hardy Zones 8–24. Out of some 500 species, only dozen or so widely cultivated. Of these, annuals (cornflower and sweet sultan) grown mainly for cut flowers; perennial kinds used principally for soft, silvery white or gray foliage. All centaureas are relatively easy to grow. For best performance, they need full sun and light, neutral soils; add lime to acid soils. Sow seeds of annuals in spring or fall. Set out plants of perennial kinds any time, preferably in spring or fall; also sow seed, make cuttings in summer. Generally moderate water users, but *C. gymnocarpa* is drought tolerant.

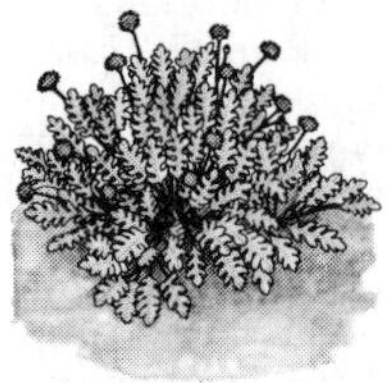
Centaurea cineraria

C. americana. BASKET FLOWER. Annual to 5–6 ft., native to central and southwestern U.S. Leaves rather rough, oval, to 4 in. long. Flower heads to 4 in. wide are rose pink, paler toward center. Good in arrangements, fresh or dried.

C. cineraria *(C. candidissima).* DUSTY MILLER. (This common name applied to many plants with whitish foliage. Also see *C. gymnocarpa, Senecio cineraria.*) Compact perennial to 1 ft. or more. Velvety white leaves, mostly in basal clump, are strap shaped, with broad, roundish lobes. Solitary 1-in. flower heads (purple, occasionally yellow) in summer. Trim back after flowering. Most popular of dusty millers in California. Attracts bees.

C. cyanus. CORNFLOWER, BACHELOR'S BUTTON. Annual. To 1–2½ ft., branching if given sufficient space. Narrow, gray green leaves, 2–3 in. long. Flower heads 1–1½ in. across, blue, pink, rose, wine red, and white. Blue varieties are traditional favorites for boutonnieres. 'Jubilee Gem' is bushy, compact, 1 ft. tall, with deep blue flowers; Polka Dot strain has all cornflower colors on 16-in. plants. Sow seed in early spring in cold-winter areas, late summer or fall where winters are mild.

C. gymnocarpa. VELVET CENTAUREA. (Often called dusty miller.) Perennial. 1–3-ft. plant; white, feltlike leaves, somewhat resembling those of *C. cineraria* but more finely divided. Usually 2 or 3 purple flower heads at ends of leafy branches. Trim plants after bloom. Drought tolerant.

C. hypoleuca 'John Coutts'. Resembles *C. montana,* but has deeply lobed leaves and deep rose flower heads.

C. montana. Perennial. Clumps 1½–2 ft. tall and as wide, with grayish green leaves to 7 in. long. Flowers resembling ragged 3-in. blue cornflowers top the stems. Use in perennial borders. Average soil, water. Protect from snails. Divide every other year.

C. moschata. SWEET SULTAN. Annual. Erect, branching at base, to 2 ft.; Imperialis strain to 3 ft. Green, deeply toothed leaves; thistlelike, 2-in. flower heads mostly in shades of lilac through rose, sometimes white or yellow. Musklike fragrance. Splendid cut flower. Sow seed directly on soil in spring or set out as transplants. Needs lots of heat; no overhead water.

CENTIPEDE PLANT. See *Homalocladium platycladum.*

CENTRANTHUS ruber *(Valeriana rubra).* *Valerianaceae.* JUPITER'S BEARD, RED VALERIAN. Perennial. Zones 7–9, 14–24. Rank, invasive, and much maligned. Used correctly, it's hard to beat for long, showy bloom in difficult situations. Very drought tolerant. Bushy, to 3 ft. high. Bluish green leaves 4 in. long. Small, deep crimson to pale pink flowers about ½ in. long, in dense terminal clusters. Blooms late spring, early summer. Variety 'Albus' is white.

Centranthus ruber

Use in fringe areas of garden, on rough slopes, banks, walls, streetside areas far from hose. Naturalized in many parts of West. White variety especially attractive with large beds of daylilies. Good cut flower. Plant in sun or partial shade. Will grow in poor, dry soil, accepts almost any condition except damp shade. Self-sows prolifically because of small dandelionlike parachutes on seeds. Cut off old flowering stems to shape plant and prolong bloom.

CENTURY PLANT. See *Agave americana.*

CEPHALOCEREUS senilis. *Cactaceae.* OLD MAN CACTUS. Zones 21–24. Native to Mexico. Slender, columnar cactus growing slowly to 40 ft., usually much less. Covered with long, grayish white hairs. Yellow, 1½-in. spines. Old plants have 2-in.-long, rose-colored flowers in April. Night blooming. Protect from hard frosts. Good pot plant; older plants striking in cactus garden. Indoors, give it south light.

Cephalocereus senilis

CEPHALOPHYLLUM 'Red Spike'. (Often sold as *Cylindrophyllum speciosum.*) *Aizoaceae.* RED SPIKE ICE PLANT. Succulent perennial. Zones 8, 9, 11–24. Clumping plant 3–5 in. high, slowly spreading to 15–18 in. wide. Spiky, bronzy red leaves point straight up. Bright cerise red, 2-in.-wide flowers in winter, with scattering of bloom at other seasons. Needs sun, tolerates drought. Plant 6–12 in. apart for ground cover. Water infrequently during summer in Zones 11–13 to avoid damping off. Can be fire retardant; draws bees.

Cephalophyllum 'Red Spike'

CEPHALOTAXUS. *Cephalotaxaceae.* PLUM YEW. Evergreen trees or shrubs. Zones 4–9, 14–17. Related to yews (*Taxus*), differing in larger, brighter green needles and (on female plants only) larger fruit that resembles small green or brown plums. Plum yews grow slowly, tolerate shade (require it where summers are hot), and like acid to neutral soil, average water.

Cephalotaxus harringtonia

C. fortunei. CHINESE PLUM YEW. Big shrub or small tree to 10 ft. tall (rarely more) with soft, needlelike leaves up to 3½ in. long, ⅛ in. wide.

C. harringtonia. Spreading shrub or small tree with needles 1–2½ in. long. The variety 'Fastigiata' is the only one available in the West; narrow and erect, it resembles Irish yew (*Taxus baccata* 'Stricta').

CERASTIUM tomentosum. *Caryophyllaceae.* SNOW-IN-SUMMER. Perennial. All Zones. Low-growing plant that performs equally well in mild and cold climates, coastal or desert areas. Spreading, dense, tufty mats of silvery gray, ¾-in.-long leaves. Masses of snow white flowers, ½–¾ in. across, in early summer. Plant grows to about 6–8 in. high, spreads 2–3 ft. in 1 year.

Cerastium tomentosum

Use as ground cover on sunny bank or on level ground. (Avoid extensive planting in prominent situations; not as long lived as some ground covers.) Effective in patterns with other low perennials; in rock gardens; cascading from top of walls; edging paths or driveways; between stepping stones or bulbs; as filler between low shrubs.

Plant in full sun; in warmest areas, give light shade. Any soil as long as drainage is good: standing water causes root rot. Set divisions or plants 1–1½ ft. apart, or sow seed. Once established, needs only occasional watering; for fast growth, water regularly and feed 2 or 3 times a year. Shear off faded flower clusters. May look a bit shabby in cold winters, but revives rapidly in spring. Divide in fall or early spring.

CERATONIA siliqua. *Leguminosae.* CAROB, ST. JOHN'S BREAD. Evergreen large shrub or tree. Zones 9, 13–16, 18–24. Native to eastern Mediterranean region. Allowed to grow naturally, it maintains bushy form with branches to ground, often multistemmed. Use this way as big hedge, informal or trimmed. Trained as tree, with lower branches removed, it grows at moderate rate to become dense and round headed, up to 30–40 ft. tall and as wide. Will reach 20 ft. in 10 years. As street tree, it needs more than normal space, since roots will break sidewalks.

Foliage is unusually dense, dark green with a sparkle. Individual leaves are divided into 4–10 round leaflets averaging about 2 in. long. Small red flowers in spring. Female trees offer problem of pod pick-up: flattened, dark brown, leathery pods, 1 ft. long, grow abundantly. Rich in sugar, the pods are milled to a fine powder and sold in health food stores as substitute for chocolate.

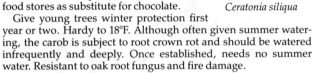

Ceratonia siliqua

Give young trees winter protection first year or two. Hardy to 18°F. Although often given summer watering, the carob is subject to root crown rot and should be watered infrequently and deeply. Once established, needs no summer water. Resistant to oak root fungus and fire damage.

CERATOSTIGMA. *Plumbaginaceae.* Technically evergreen or semievergreen subshrubs or perennials, but all are best treated as perennials, cut back each winter regardless of frost. Valued for clusters of rich deep blue, phloxlike flowers that bloom in summer to late fall, when garden needs cool hues. Tolerant of varying soils, water schedules, sun or part shade.

Ceratostigma plumbaginoides

C. griffithii. BURMESE PLUMBAGO. Zones 4–9, 14–24. Similar to *C. willmottianum* in hardiness and appearance, but more compact and lower growing (2½–3 ft.). Displays its brilliant blue flowers somewhat later, from July into late fall.

C. plumbaginoides. (Often sold as *Plumbago larpentae.*) DWARF PLUMBAGO. Zones 2–9, 14–24. A perennial wiry-stemmed ground cover 6–12 in. high. In loose soil and where growing season is long, spreads rapidly by underground stems, eventually covering large areas. Bronzy green to dark green leaves, 3 in. long, turn reddish brown with frosts. Intense blue, ½-in.-wide flowers from July until first frosts. When plants show signs of aging, remove old crowns, replace with rooted stems. Although hardy to extreme cold and fluctuating winter temperatures, it will not bloom well unless it has a long growing season. Most effective in early or mid-autumn, when blue flowers contrast with red autumn foliage.

C. willmottianum. CHINESE PLUMBAGO. Zones 4–9, 14–24. Grows as airy mass of wiry stems to 2–4 ft. high and as wide. Deep green leaves, roundish to oval, 2 in. long; turn yellow or red and drop quickly after frost. Bright blue, ½-in.-wide flowers, June–November. In coldest winters, stems die back to ground and are replaced by new ones. In milder winters, stems survive and should be cut back hard in early spring. Very similar to *C. griffithii,* but with larger, more diamond-shaped leaves with tapering tips.

For pale blue–flowered CAPE PLUMBAGO, see *Plumbago auriculata*.

CERATOZAMIA mexicana. *Zamiaceae.* Cycad. Zones 21–24. Related to *Cycas revoluta,* similar in appearance. Trunk usually a foot high, 4–6 ft. in great age, a foot thick. Very slow growing. Leaves in whorl, 3–6 ft. long, divided featherwise into 15–20 pairs of foot-long, inch-wide leaflets. Striking in containers or protected place in open ground. Part shade. Protect from frosts. Give ample water.

Ceratozamia mexicana

CERCIDIPHYLLUM japonicum. *Cercidiphyllaceae.* KATSURA TREE. Deciduous tree. Zones 1–6; under high-branching trees in Zones 14–16, 18–20. Native to Japan. A tree of many virtues where adapted. Light and dainty branch and leaf pattern. Foliage, always fresh looking, shows tints of red throughout growing season. Beautifully colored brilliant red or yellow in fall, especially if watered infrequently at end of summer.

Rather slow growing, eventually to 40 ft. or more. Varying growth habits: some have single trunk; most have multiple trunks angled upward and outward. Nearly round, 2–4-in. leaves neatly spaced in pairs along arching branches. Mature leaves are dark blue green above, grayish beneath. Flowers inconspicuous. There is a weeping form, known as 'Pendulum' or 'Pendula'.

Cercidiphyllum japonicum

Needs special protection from hot sun and dry winds; needs plenty of moisture during growing season in interior climates.

CERCIDIUM. *Leguminosae.* PALO VERDE. Deciduous trees. Zones 10–14, 18–20. The common name palo verde covers 4 desert trees—Mexican palo verde (see *Parkinsonia*), blue palo verde, littleleaf palo verde, and Sonoran palo verde. All attract birds.

C. floridum *(C. torreyanum).* BLUE PALO VERDE. Native to deserts of southern California, Arizona, Sonora, Baja California. It belongs to and beautifies desert and the garden oases that have been planted there. In gardens, grows fast to 30 ft. and as wide. In spring, 2–4½-in.-long clusters of small, bright yellow flowers almost hide the branches. When out of bloom, shows intricate pattern of bluish green, spiny branches, branchlets, and leaf stalks. (Leaves—each with 1–3 pairs of smooth, tiny leaflets—are shed early, leaving leaf stalks for lightly filtered shade.)

Cercidium floridum

Will survive much drought, but is denser, more attractive, and faster growing with water and fertilizer.

C. microphyllum. LITTLELEAF PALO VERDE, FOOTHILLS PALO VERDE. Native to eastern San Bernardino County, California; Arizona; Sonora; Baja California. Similar to blue palo verde, but bark and leaves (with 4–12 pairs of hairy leaflets) are yellowish green; flowers are paler yellow, in 1-in.-long clusters.

C. praecox *(C. plurifoliolatum).* SONORAN PALO VERDE. Native to Sonora and Baja California. The handsomest palo verde in form and trunk color (lime green). Develops beautiful umbrella top.

CERCIS. *Leguminosae.* REDBUD. Deciduous shrubs or trees. Five redbuds are grown in the West: 2 western natives, one eastern native, one from Europe, one from China. Early spring flowers are sweet pea–shaped, small, in clusters; where tree is adapted, blossoms are borne in great profusion on bare twigs, branches, sometimes even on main trunk. Flowers are followed by clusters of flat pods. Attractive broad, rounded leaves are heart shaped at base. All give fall color with first frosts. Average water needs (except for drought-tolerant *C. occidentalis*).

Cercis occidentalis

C. canadensis. EASTERN REDBUD. Zones 1–3, 7–20. Native of eastern U.S. Largest and fastest growing of available species where adapted. To 25–35 ft. tall. Most apt to take tree form. Round headed but with horizontally tiered branches in age. Rich green, 3–6-in.-long leaves have pointed tips. Small (½-in.-long), rosy pink flowers clothe bare brown branches in early spring. Valuable for filling the gap between the early-flowering fruit trees (flowering peach, flowering plum) and the crabapples and late-flowering cherries.

Garden varieties include: 'Alba' ('White Texas'), white flowers, choice; 'Forest Pansy', purple foliage and reddish branches; 'Oklahoma', wine red flowers; 'Plena' ('Flame'), double flowers like rosebuds; 'Rubye Atkinson', pure pink flowers.

C. chinensis. CHINESE REDBUD. Zones 4–20. Native to China, Japan. Seen mostly as light, open shrub to 10–12 ft. Flower clusters (3–5 in. long) are deep rose, almost rosy purple. Leaves are sometimes glossier and brighter green than those of *C. canadensis,* with transparent line around the edge. Spectacular tree in high deserts of Arizona.

C. occidentalis. WESTERN REDBUD. Zones 2–24. Native to California, Arizona, Utah, but predominantly in California foothills below 4,000 ft.

A shrub or small tree 10–18 ft. in height and spread. Usually grows several trunks from base. All-year interest. In spring it delivers 3-week display of brilliant magenta flowers, ½ in. long. Summer foliage of handsome blue green, 3-in. leaves, notched or rounded at tip; interspersed are brilliant magenta newly forming seed pods. In fall, whole plant turns light yellow or red. In winter, bare branches in picturesque pattern hold reddish brown seed pods.

Excellent for dry, seldom watered banks. Water regularly in first year or two to speed growth. Profuse flower production only where winter temperatures drop to 28°F. or lower. Resistant to oak root fungus.

C. reniformis. Zones 2–9, 14–24. Native to Southwest. Leaves leathery, blue green, 2–3 in. wide, with rounded or notched tips. Flowers as in *C. canadensis;* variety 'Alba', with white flowers, is sold in West.

C. siliquastrum. JUDAS TREE. Zones 2–19. Native to Europe and western Asia. Generally of shrubby habit to 25 ft., occasionally a taller, slender tree with single trunk. Flowers are purplish rose, ½ in. long. Large 3–5-in. leaves, deeply heart shaped at base, rounded or notched at tip. Occasionally damaged by late frosts in Northwest. Resistant to oak root fungus.

CERCOCARPUS. *Rosaceae.* MOUNTAIN MAHOGANY. Evergreen or deciduous tall shrubs or small trees. Natives of western mountains and foothills. Very drought tolerant. Several have a most attractive open structure and branching pattern. Distinguished in fall by long-lasting small fruit topped by a long, twisted, feathery, tail-like plume that sparkles in sunlight. Sun or light shade. About 20 kinds are native to the West, but these 3 are most widespread:

Cercocarpus betuloides

C. betuloides. HARDTACK, MOUNTAIN IRONWOOD, SWEET BRUSH. Zones 6–24. Evergreen, native to dry slopes and foothills below 6,000 ft. elevation, southwestern Oregon, California, northern Baja California. Generally a shrub 5–12 ft. high. Can form small tree to 20 ft. with wide-spreading crown of arching branches. Wedge-shaped, ½–1-in. leaves clustered on short spurs; leaves are dark green above, pale beneath, with feathery veining and toothed edges.

C. ledifolius. CURL-LEAF MOUNTAIN MAHOGANY. All Zones. Evergreen, native to dry mountain slopes, 4,000–9,000 ft. elevation, throughout the western states from eastern slopes of Sierra-Cascades divide to Rockies. In warmer western part of its range about the same size as *C. betuloides;* in highest, coldest part of range, very slow growing and an excellent hedge or small tree of character. Leaves leathery, ½–1 in. long, resinous, dark green above, white beneath, with inrolled edges.

C. montanus. All Zones; most useful 1–2, 10. Deciduous shrub, usually 4–6 ft. tall and as wide, rarely to 8–9 ft. Leaves 1–2 in. long, white beneath. Useful in dry places, coldest climates.

CEREUS peruvianus. *Cactaceae.* Cactus. Zones 16, 17, 21–24. Tall, branching, treelike cactus eventually reaching 30–50 ft. Striking bluish green, especially when young; ribbed with scattered spines. Flowers white, 6–7 in. long, 5 in. across, in June. Night blooming. Variety 'Monstrosus' is smaller, slower growing, with ribs irregularly broken up into knobs and crests. Striking outline; effective in large containers. Protect from hard frosts.

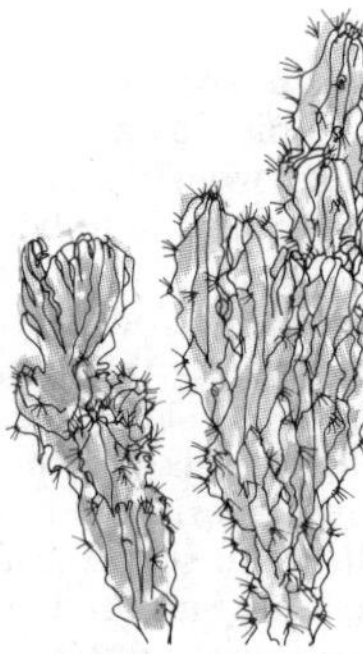

Cereus peruvianus 'Monstrosus'

CEROPEGIA woodii. *Asclepiadaceae.* ROSARY VINE. Succulent. Outdoors in Zones 21–24, house plant anywhere. From South Africa. Little vine with hanging or trailing thin stems growing from tuberous base. Paired heart-shaped leaves—thick and succulent, ⅔ in. long, dark green marbled white. Little tubers that form on stems can be used to start new plants. Flowers small, dull pink or purplish, not showy but interesting in structure. Best in pots; stems may trail in thin curtain or be trained on small trellis. Give some shade and regular watering.

Other ceropegias are available from specialists: some are shrubby, some vining, some stiffly succulent, but all have fascinating flower structure.

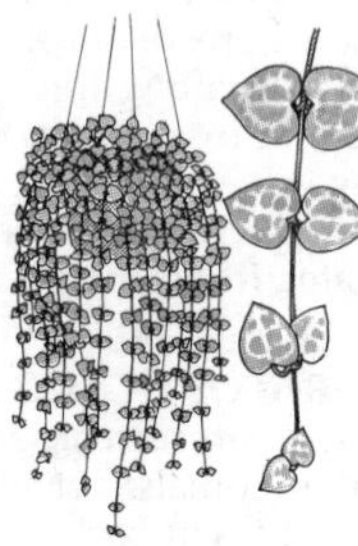

Ceropegia woodii

CESTRUM. *Solanaceae.* Evergreen shrubs. Native to American tropics. All kinds have showy, tubular flowers. Flowers and fruit attract birds. Fast growing, inclined to be rangy and top-heavy unless consistently pruned. Best in warm, sheltered spot in part shade. Feed and water generously. Add organic soil amendments before planting. Nip back consistently for compactness and cut back severely after flowering or fruiting. In climates specified below, plants may freeze back in heavy frosts but will recover quickly.

Cestrum elegans

C. aurantiacum. ORANGE CESTRUM. Zones 16, 17, 21–24. Native to Guatemala. Rare and handsome. To 8 ft. Brilliant show of clustered 1-in.-long, orange flowers in late spring, summer, followed by white berries. Deep green, oval, 4-in. leaves. Tall growing; best used as vine or espalier.

C. elegans *(C. purpureum).* RED CESTRUM. Zones 13, 17, 19–24. Shrub or semiclimber to 10 ft. or higher, with arching branches, deep green 4-in. leaves. Masses of purplish red, 1-in.-long flowers in spring and summer, followed by red berries. Good espalier.

C. nocturnum. NIGHT JESSAMINE. Zones 13, 16–24. Native to West Indies. Evergreen shrub to 12 ft. with 4–8-in.-long leaves and clusters of creamy white flowers in summer, white berries. Powerfully fragrant at night—too powerful for some people.

C. parqui. WILLOW-LEAFED JESSAMINE. Zones 13–24. Native to Chile. To 6–10 ft. tall with many branches from base. Dense foliage of willowlike leaves, 3–6 in. long. Greenish yellow, 1-in.-long summer flowers in clusters. Berries dark violet brown. Not as attractive as other species in form, flowers, or fruit, but its perfume is potent. Leaves blacken in light frost. Best used where winter appearance is unimportant. In cold-winter areas, protect roots with mulch and use as perennial.

CHAENOMELES. (Some formerly called *Cydonia.*) *Rosaceae.* FLOWERING QUINCE. Deciduous shrubs. Zones 1–21. Flowering quinces are among first shrubs to bloom each year. As early as January, you can take a budded stem or two indoors, place it in water in warm window, and watch buds break into bloom. The plants themselves are picturesque, practically indestructible shrubs of varying growth habit. Shiny green leaves are red tinged when young. Branches are attractive when out of leaf—strong in line, with an Oriental feeling. Some flowering quinces grow to 10 ft. and spread wider; some are compact and low growing. Most are thorny; a few are thornless. Some of them bear small quincelike fruit. All are useful grown as hedges and barriers.

Chaenomeles

All are easy to grow in sun with average garden watering. Tolerant of extremes in cold and heat, light to heavy soil. May suffer from chlorosis in alkaline soils (use iron chelate or iron sulfate). May bloom reluctantly in warm-winter areas. Prune any time to shape, limit growth, or gain special effects. Good time to prune is in bud and bloom season. (Use cut branches for indoor arrangements.) New growth that follows will bear next year's flowers. Flowers attract birds.

In the following list of choice varieties, we have noted both height and flower color. Tall types are in the 6-ft. and over class; low varieties are in the 2–3-ft. range. All are garden hybrids; specialists can furnish even more varieties.

'Apple Blossom'. Tall. White and pink.
'Cameo'. Low, compact. Double, soft apricot pink.
'Contorta'. Low. White to pink; twisted branches. Good as bonsai.
'Corallina' ('Coral Glow'). Tall. Reddish orange.
'Coral Sea'. Tall. Large, coral pink.
'Enchantress'. Tall. Large, shell pink.
'Falconet Charlot'. Tall, thornless. Double salmon pink.
'Hollandia'. Tall. Large red flowers, reblooms in fall.
'Jet Trail'. Low. Pure white.
'Low-n-White'. Low, spreading. White.
'Minerva'. Low, spreading. Cherry red.
'Nivalis'. Tall. Large, pure white.
'Orange Delight' ('Maulei'). Low, spreading. Orange to orange red.
'Pink Beauty'. Tall. Purplish pink.
'Pink Lady'. Low. Rose pink blooms from deeper-colored buds.
'Red Ruffles'. Tall. Almost thornless. Large, ruffled, red.
'Snow'. Tall. Large, pure white.
'Stanford Red'. Low, almost thornless. Tomato red.
'Super Red'. Tall, upright. Large, bright red.
'Texas Scarlet'. Low. Tomato red.
'Toyo Nishiki'. Tall. Pink, white, pink and white, solid red all on same branch.

CHAIN FERN. See *Woodwardia.*

CHAMAECEREUS sylvestri. *Cactaceae.* PEANUT CACTUS. Zones 16, 17, 19–24. Native to Argentina. Dwarf cactus with cylindrical, ribbed, spiny, 2–3-in. joints that fall off easily and root just as easily. Likes sun, average water during growth and bloom cycle. Profusely blooming in spring and early summer; even tiny rooted joints bloom. Flowers bright scarlet, almost 3 in. long. Great favorite with children.

Chamaecereus sylvestri

CHAMAECYPARIS. *Cupressaceae.* FALSE CYPRESS. Evergreen trees, shrubs, and shrublets. All produce cones ½ in. long. Take average water.

Many varieties, but all sold are forms of 5 kinds—2 western natives, one from the eastern U.S., and 2 from Japan. These are the basic 5 (they and their many varieties are charted for size, shape, texture, and performance on pages 278–279).

Chamaecyparis lawsoniana

Chamaecyparis is rich source of bonsai material. For this use, there are many interesting dwarf forms and climate restrictions are less limiting; container-grown plants can be sheltered against extreme cold and wind in coldframe or similar shelter. The variety list on pages 278–279 is not exhaustive; new varieties appear nearly every year. In purchasing, be aware that many of these garden varieties are very similar and are frequently mislabeled.

Chamaecyparis lawsoniana

In growing chamaecyparis, be sure to provide fast drainage. They are susceptible to root rot in heavy, slow-draining soils. Many forms develop dead foliage on the inner parts. Some of this is normal aging; an excess may indicate spider mite infestation or too much shade. A strong jet from hose will clear out most of the mites and the dead foliage as well.

C. lawsoniana. An important timber tree in coastal Oregon (also native to extreme northern California). It and its varieties are probably the most adaptable in mild western climates. Its yellow-leafed varieties seem to burn in California. Best in Zones 4–6. Foliage burns in dry cold or hot sun in Zones 2, 3. Good performance in Zones 15–17 and poor to satisfactory in Zones 7–9, 14, 18–21 (best in partial shade there). Can be used as hedge, screen, or background plant.

C. nootkatensis. The hardy timber tree of Alaska and mountains of Oregon and Washington. It and its varieties do not thrive in cold, dry winds or high summer heat. Use in Zones 4–6, 15–17.

C. obtusa. Japanese species of tree best known for its dwarf and compact varieties. Best adapted Zones 4–6, 15–17.

C. pisifera. Japanese species of tree with many forms. Best adapted Zones 4–6, 15–17; will grow in favored sites Zones 1–3.

C. thyoides. Eastern American tree represented by a few garden varieties. Zones as for *C. pisifera.*

CHAMAEDOREA. *Palmae.* Palms. House plants; outdoors Zones 16, 17, 22–24. Small, shade-tolerant feather type. Generally slow growing, they are good in containers indoors or on shaded patio. All need ample water along with good drainage. Some have single trunks, others clustered trunks. Leaves variable in shape.

Chamaedorea elegans

C. cataractarum. Single-stemmed palm growing slowly to 4–5 ft.; trunk speckled. Older plants take some frost.

C. costaricana. Develops fairly fast into bamboolike clumps of 8–10-ft. trunks if well fed and liberally watered. Good pot palm; will eventually need good-sized container. Lacy, feathery leaves 3–4 ft. long.

C. elegans. (Widely sold as *Neanthe bella.*) Often called parlor palm. The best indoor chamaedorea, tolerating crowded roots, poor light. Single stemmed; grows very slowly to eventual 3–4 ft. Douse potted plants with water occasionally; feed regularly. Groom by removing old leaf stalks. Repot every 2–3 years, carefully washing off old soil and replacing with good potting mix. Effective potted 3 or more to container.

C. ernesti-augustii. Slow growing to 5 ft., with dark green leaves shaped like a fish's tail. Needs shade and protected location.

C. erumpens. Cluster-forming, bamboolike dwarf with drooping leaves. Slow grower to 4–5 ft. Needs shade or part shade, no frost.

C. geonomiformis. Fine palm for pots. Grows slowly to 4 ft. Broad oblong leaves are not feathery, but are deeply split at tips like fish tails.

C. glaucifolia. Slow growing to 8 ft. or more. Fine-textured, feathery leaves, 4–6 ft. long, with bluish green tint on both sides (most marked on underside).

C. klotzschiana. Single-trunk palm, growing slowly to 4–5 ft. Handsome, dark green, feathery leaves. Hardy to 28°F.

C. microspadix. Cluster palm with slender, ringed stems to 8 ft. Feathery leaves. One of hardier kinds, it takes very light frost.

(Continued on page 280)

C

Chamaecyparis

SPECIES OR VARIETY	HEIGHT	SPREAD	COLOR	FORM, TEXTURE	REMARKS
Chamaecyparis lawsoniana PORT ORFORD CEDAR, LAWSON CYPRESS	To 60 ft. or higher.	To 30 ft. at base.	Blue green, variable.	Pyramidal or columnar form with lacy, drooping, flat foliage sprays and conical crown.	Can be planted as close as 3 ft. apart without becoming thin or straggly, and topped at 10 ft. or more for windbreak or sun screen.
C. l. 'Allumii' SCARAB CYPRESS, BLUE LAWSON CYPRESS	To 30 ft.	Narrow.	Blue green; new foliage metallic blue.	Compact, narrow pyramidal form. Scalelike leaves are carried in regular vertical planes.	A widely adapted, slow-growing tree. Planted 2–3 ft. apart, makes narrow, formal hedge.
C. l. 'Azurea'	To 6 ft.	To 3 ft.	Silvery gray blue.	Broad pyramidal form. Soft-textured, drooping.	Avoid crowding for shapely plants.
C. l. 'Ellwoodii' ELLWOOD CYPRESS	Slowly to 6–8 ft., higher with age.	2–3 ft.	Silvery blue.	Dense, compact columnar form. Light textured with soft, prickly, needlelike leaves.	One of most widely planted and widely adapted trees. 'Ellwoodii Improved' is slower growing, bluer.
C. l. 'Fletcheri' FLETCHER CYPRESS	6–8 ft., higher with age.	3–4 ft.	Blue gray; purplish or brown in winter.	Dense pyramidal form. Soft, prickly foliage.	Somewhat like 'Ellwoodii' but taller, broader, and faster growing.
C. l. 'Forsteckensis' (*C. l.* 'Forsteckiana') FORSTECK CYPRESS	4 ft.	To 6 ft.	Dark green.	Dense, compact form. Mosslike texture; densely tufted branches.	A rock garden or container plant. Makes a dense, informal hedge.
C. l. 'Lutea' GOLDEN LAWSON CYPRESS	To 30 ft. or more.	10–12 ft.	New growth yellow, old growth blue gray.	Soft fronds.	Probably best of the taller yellow false cypresses. Susceptible to sunburn.
C. l. 'Minima Glauca' LITTLE BLUE CYPRESS	To 3 ft.	To 2½ ft.	Blue green.	Compact, nearly globular form. Dense foliage; soft texture.	A shrub well suited for pots, boxes, rock gardens, low uniform landscape plantings.
C. l. 'Nidiformis' (*C. nidiformis, C. l.* 'Nestoides', *C. nidifera)* BIRD NEST CYPRESS	To 5 ft. or more in 10 years.	3–5 ft.	Dark green.	Spreading, flat-topped form with outward-spraying branches, often with depressed "nest" in center of top.	Good for informal screening, hedge, as showy isolated plant. 'Grandi' ('Tamariscifolia') similar, with bluish foliage.
C. l. 'Stewartii' STEWART GOLDEN CYPRESS	To 30 ft.	10–12 ft. at 18-ft. height.	New growth yellow, old growth dark green.	Upright, slender, pyramidal form. Soft texture; drooping branchlets.	Handsome and widely planted. Needs room for good growth. Used in parks, public playgrounds.
C. l. 'Wisselii' WISSEL CYPRESS	To 15–18 ft., higher in 15–20 years.	4–5 ft.	Dark blue green.	Slender, upright form with twisted foliage; irregular branches, somewhat like those of *Juniperus chinensis* 'Torulosa'.	Subject to insects and diseases, especially in hot, dry climates. Keep sprayed for red spider mites.
C. nootkatensis NOOTKA CYPRESS, ALASKA YELLOW CEDAR	80 ft.	20–30 ft.	Bluish green.	Pyramidal form, with dense, fine-textured foliage. Often has pendulous branches. Coarser than Lawson cypress.	Slow growing, it will stand greater cold and poorer soil than Lawson cypress, though latter can probably stand more heat.
C. n. 'Compacta'	To 3–5 ft.	2–2½ ft.	Blue green.	Narrow, pyramidal form.	Handsome in containers—a miniature tree rather than shrub.
C. n. 'Pendula'	10 ft. in 10 years, eventually 30 ft.	3–10 ft.	Yellowish green.	Weeping branch tips, nodding top.	Like *C. nootkatensis*, takes damp soil conditions better than Lawson cypress.
C. obtusa HINOKI FALSE CYPRESS	40–50 ft., higher with great age.	15–30 ft.	Dark glossy green.	Spreading, irregular, open form.	Very slow growing and suited principally to a large Oriental garden. Splendid bonsai subject.
C. o. 'Aurea' GOLDEN HINOKI CYPRESS	30–40 ft.	10–15 ft.	Dark green. Young growth is golden.	Foliage is bunched, flattened in horizontal plane.	Slow growing. For Oriental garden, woodland edge. Color hard to blend. Useful with dark greens. Subject to sunburn.
C. o. 'Crippsii' CRIPPS GOLDEN CYPRESS	To 30 ft. Can be kept smaller.	To 10 ft.	Yellow when young, dark green later.	Somewhat open, pyramidal habit.	Use for line and pattern in Oriental gardens or against fence, screen, wall. Can be pruned attractively by spacing branches.

SPECIES OR VARIETY	HEIGHT	SPREAD	COLOR	FORM, TEXTURE	REMARKS
C. o. 'Filicoides' FERNSPRAY CYPRESS	To 15 ft.	To 6 ft.	Medium green.	Dense foliage; branchlets short, crowded, frondlike.	Slow growing, with gracefully curved limbs. For Oriental gardens, entryways, large planting boxes.
C. o. 'Gracilis' (Often sold as *C. obtusa*) SLENDER HINOKI CYPRESS	Slow to 20 ft.	4–5 ft.	Very dark, glossy green.	Slender, somewhat weeping form. Soft and dense, with nodding top and branch ends.	Choice plant that is slow to outgrow its place. Good entryway plant or container subject.
C. o. 'Kosteri'	To 2½ ft. in 10 years.	To 2½ ft.	Dark glossy green.	Like a more dwarf, denser *C. o.* 'Nana Gracilis'.	One of best for rock garden, small container, Japanese garden.
C. o. 'Nana' DWARF HINOKI CYPRESS	Very slow to 3 ft.	2 ft. or more	Dark green.	Dense foliage in flat, stratified planes.	A 60-year-old plant may be 3 ft. tall, 2 ft. across. Rock gardens, mass plantings on slopes.
C. o. 'Nana Aurea' GOLDEN DWARF HINOKI CYPRESS	To 4 ft.	To 3 ft.	New foliage yellow. Old foliage dark green.	Dense foliage in flat-sided sprays.	Useful where touch of yellow is needed; Oriental and rock gardens.
C. o. 'Nana Gracilis' (Usually sold as *C. o.* 'Nana') DWARF HINOKI CYPRESS	To 4 ft.	To 3 ft.	Dark green.	Dense foliage; flattened, cupped fronds.	Most commonly used dwarf hinoki cypress; Oriental and rock gardens.
C. pisifera (*Retinispora pisifera*) SAWARA FALSE CYPRESS	20–30 ft. or more.	To 20 ft.	Dark green above, lighter beneath.	Spine-tipped, scalelike leaves; rather loose, open growth.	Good in large Oriental gardens. Prune heavily to force new growth, hide dead foliage on inner branches.
C. p. 'Cyano-Viridis' (*C. p.* 'Boulevard')	Rather slow to 5–8 ft.	3–4 ft.	Light, silvery blue green.	Good, dense form; soft, fine-textured, fluffy-looking foliage.	Good for color and texture contrast with other evergreens.
C. p. 'Filifera' THREAD CYPRESS, THREADBRANCH CYPRESS	To 8 ft. or higher.	To 6 ft.	Dark green.	Loose mound, attractive when young. Too open in old age. Weeping, threadlike twigs.	Oriental and rock gardens. Contrast with dense, solid shrubs. Prune to keep in bounds. *C. p.* 'Filifera Aurea', GOLDEN THREAD CYPRESS, has yellow foliage.
C. p. 'Plumosa' PLUME FALSE CYPRESS	20–30 ft.	10–12 ft.	Bright green.	Upright branches; compact, cone-shaped tree. Short, soft needles. Frondlike, feathery twig structure.	Carefully pruned, a big shrub. Unpruned, a tree. Slow growing at first.
C. p. 'Plumosa Aurea'	20–30 ft.	10–12 ft.	New growth golden yellow; old growth green.	Like *C. p.* 'Plumosa'.	Prune hard by pinching tips to restrain growth, promote density. Like variety 'Plumosa', tends to lose lower branches as it ages.
C. p. 'Squarrosa' MOSS CYPRESS	20–30 ft. or much higher.	10–30 ft.	Silvery gray green.	Soft, feathery, with long, needlelike leaves.	Attractive while young. As it ages, thin it out for greater character, picturesqueness. Big background plantings, massive yet soft-textured area cover.
C. p. 'Squarrosa Minima' (*C. p.* 'Pygmaea', *C. p.* 'Squarrosa Pygmaea')	Dwarf (see Remarks).	(See Remarks.)	Gray green to dark green, depending on form.	Sharp-pointed leaves.	Several forms go under this name. One is a very compact, very slow growing globe form to 6 by 6 in. in 5 years, with dark green, very short needles. Another is gray green, lacy foliaged, grows to 1½ ft. high and spreads much wider.
C. p. 'Squarrosa Veitchii'	To 20–30 ft.	10–30 ft.	Blue green.	Lighter, airier than variety 'Squarrosa'.	An improvement in color and texture over variety 'Squarrosa'.
C. thyoides WHITE CEDAR	To 90 ft.	20–25 ft.	Light green to gray green. Turns bronzy in winter.	Narrow, tall, cone-shaped tree.	Needs soil moisture, winter chill for good growth.
C. t. 'Andelyensis'	To 3 ft. at 10 years, eventually 10 ft.	1 ft. at 10 years, eventually 3 ft.	Gray green.	Dense cone.	Used as miniature columnar evergreen in bonsai, rock gardens.

C

C. radicalis. Slow-growing, single-stemmed plant to 4 ft. tall. Strong-patterned dark green leaves. Interesting, colorful seed formation. Will take temperatures down to a range of 22°–28°F.

C. seifrizii. Cluster palm of dense, compact growth to 8–10 ft. Feathery leaves with narrow leaflets. Takes 28°F. and can be used outdoors in protected areas in part shade. Needs ample moisture.

C. tenella. Single trunk to 3–4 ft. Dark bluish green leaves are exceptionally strong, large, and broad; undivided but deeply cleft at ends.

C. tepejilote. Single trunk ringed with swollen joints like bamboo. Moderate growth to 10 ft.; leaves 4 ft. long, feathery. Grows well inland in shady areas protected from frost.

CHAMAEMELUM nobile *(Anthemis nobilis).* *Compositae.* CHAMOMILE. Evergreen perennial. All Zones. Forms soft-textured, spreading, 3–12-in. mat of bright light green, finely cut, aromatic leaves. Most commonly grown form has summer-blooming flower heads resembling small yellow buttons; some forms have little daisylike flower heads. Makes lawn substitute if mowed or sheared occasionally. 'Treneague' is a nonflowering variety which needs no mowing. Also used between stepping stones. Plant divisions 1 ft. apart in full sun or very light shade. Water moderately. Chamomile tea is made from dried flower heads, but sweeter, more flavorful tea comes from flowers of *Matricaria recutita* (*M. chamomilla*).

Chamaemelum nobile

CHAMAEROPS humilis. *Palmae.* MEDITERRANEAN FAN PALM. Zones 4–24. Probably hardiest palm; has survived 6°F. Clumps develop slowly from offshoots, curve to height of 20 ft.; may also reach 20 ft. wide. Growth extremely slow in Portland and Seattle. Leaves green to bluish green. Versatile: Use in containers, mass under trees, grow as impenetrable hedge. Drought and wind resistant. Feed and water in summer to speed growth.

Chamaerops humilis

CHAMELAUCIUM uncinatum. (Sometimes sold as *C. ciliatum.*) *Myrtaceae.* GERALDTON WAXFLOWER. Evergreen shrub. Zones 8, 9, 12–24. Native to Australia. Bright green, needlelike leaves and showy sprays of winter-blooming, pale pink or rosy, ½-in. flowers are cherished for flower arrangements of long-lasting beauty. Light and airy, loose and sprawling, fast growth to 6–8 ft. (10–12 ft. when staked) with equal spread. Looks somewhat like loose-growing heather. Very old plants have interesting twisted trunks and shaggy bark.

Plant on dry, sunny bank or in cutting garden in fast-draining soil; water deeply but infrequently in summer. Or combine with plants that don't require regular summer watering, such as *Cassia artemisioides* or rosemary. Prune freely for arrangements or cut back after flowering. Seedling plants vary. Select in bloom to get color you want. Variety 'Vista' has large pink flowers.

Chamelaucium uncinatum

CHAMOMILE. See *Chamaemelum nobile, Matricaria recutita.*

CHAPARRAL BROOM. See *Baccharis pilularis.*

CHARD. See Swiss Chard.

CHASMANTHIUM latifolium *(Uniola latifolia).* *Gramineae.* SEA OATS, BAMBOO GRASS. Perennial. All Zones. Ornamental grass making broad clumps of broad, bamboolike leaves topped with arching flowering stems, 2–5 ft. tall, carrying showers of silvery green flower spikelets that resemble flattened clusters of oats (or flattened armadillos). Flowering stems dry to an attractive greenish straw color and look good in dried arrangements. Clumps broaden slowly and are not aggressive like bamboo. Leaves turn brown in winter, when plants should be cut back near the ground. Give full sun in cool-climate areas, partial shade where summers are hot. Average soil, average garden watering. Divide clumps when they become overgrown and bloom drops off. Stake if flowering stems sprawl too far.

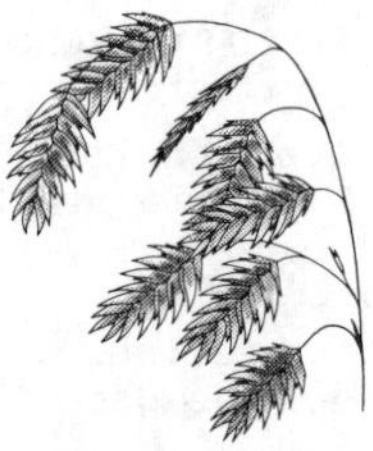
Chasmanthium latifolium

CHASTE TREE. See *Vitex.*

CHAYOTE. *Cucurbitaceae.* Vine with edible fruit, climbing by tendrils. Related to squash. Perennial in Zones 14–16, 19–24, annual elsewhere. Vine and leaves resemble those of squash. Flowers inconspicuous. Fruit is principal crop—3–8 in. long, green or yellow green, irregularly oval, grooved, with a large seed surrounded by solid, meaty flesh. When boiled or baked, both flesh and seed taste something like summer squash. Well-grown plant should produce 200 or more fruits. Large, fleshy roots are also edible.

Chayote

Needs full sun; warm, rich soil; ample water; and fence or trellis to climb. Buy fruit at store in fall and allow to sprout; plant whole fruit edgewise, sprouted end at lowest point, narrow end exposed. If shoot is long, cut it back to 1–2 in. Plant 2 or more vines to assure pollination. Plant in February or March; in area where roots might freeze, plant in 5-gallon can or tub and store plant until after frost. Plants can produce 20–30 ft. of vine in first year, 40–50 ft. in second. Tops die down in frost. Bloom starts when day length shortens in fall; fruit is ready in a month.

CHECKERBERRY. See *Gaultheria procumbens.*

CHECKERED LILY. See *Fritillaria meleagris.*

CHECKER LILY. See *Fritillaria lanceolata.*

CHEIRANTHUS allionii. See *Erysimum hieraciifolium.*

CHEIRANTHUS cheiri. *Cruciferae.* WALLFLOWER. Perennial or biennial. Zones 4–6, 14–17, 22, 23. Old-timers esteemed for sweet fragrance and rich flower colors. Erect, bushy plants to 1–2½ ft.; narrow, bright green leaves 3 in. long. Half-inch-wide flowers bloom in spring and early summer, in velvety tones of yellow, orange, brown, red, pink, rose, burgundy, in dense clusters at tops of leafy stems. Excellent with tulips in yellow, orange, or lilac shades, or beneath lilacs, which bloom at same time.

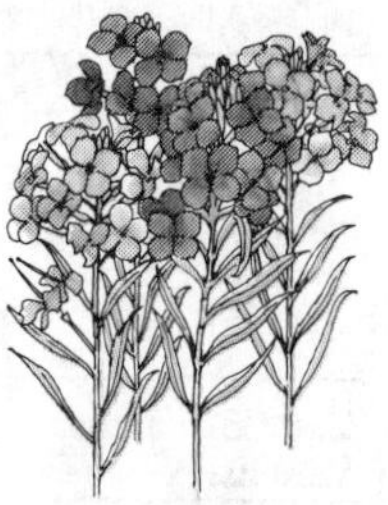
Cheiranthus cheiri

Locate in full sun, or in light shade if spring sun is bright. Likes moist soil. Plant in mounded or raised beds to provide best possible drainage. Sow seeds in spring for bloom following year, or set out nursery transplants in fall or early spring. Young plants need long period to develop vegetative growth.

For Siberian wallflower, see *Erysimum hieraciifolium.*

CHEIRANTHUS linifolius. See *Erysimum linifolium.*

CHENILLE PLANT. See *Acalypha hispida.*

Chenopodiaceae. The goosefoot family contains many annuals and perennials (some of them weeds) and a few shrubs. Flowers are inconspicuous. Many will tolerate salty or alkaline soil, and some are useful food plants, notably beet and spinach.

CHENOPODIUM. *Chenopodiaceae.* Annuals or perennials. All Zones, except as noted. Most are weeds; some have use as food.

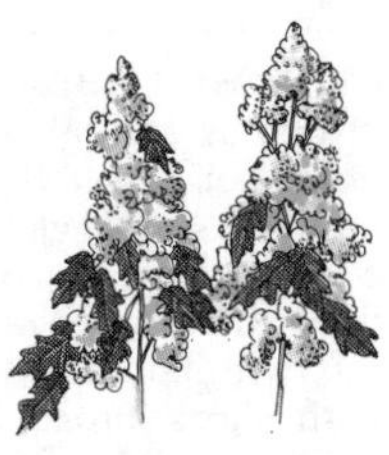

Chenopodium quinoa

C. album. PIGWEED, LAMB'S QUARTERS. Tall weed. Leaves to 4 in. long; whitish underneath, smooth pale green above. Leaves can be cooked like spinach.

C. ambrosioides. EPAZOTE, MEXICAN TEA. Annual everywhere, perennial in Zones 8, 9, 14–24. Strongly scented leaves to 5 in. long, deeply cut or toothed. Sometimes grown in gardens or collected from the roadside as seasoning for Mexican dishes.

C. quinoa. QUINOA. Annual. To 5 ft. tall, with dense flower and seed clusters. A traditional grain of the Andes. Individual seeds look like sesame seeds; they are rinsed to remove surface bitterness, then cooked like rice. Protein content is high. Needs lots of light but cannot tolerate high temperatures at blooming or seed-setting. Needs short days to bloom; can tolerate light frost. Thrives on 10 inches of water during the growing season. Plant in May or June and harvest in fall. Excellent production in high mountain valleys in the Rocky Mountains. Strains that yield at sea level are obtainable but scarce.

CHERIMOYA. See *Annona cherimola.*

CHERRY. *Rosaceae.* Here we consider the sweet and sour cherries. Both types require well-drained soil and regular deep watering.

Fruiting Cherry

Sweet Cherries

Most common market type and most widely known in the West. Trees 30–35 ft. tall, as broad in some varieties; at their best in deep, well-drained soil in Zones 2, 6, 7, 14, 15. They have high chilling requirement (need many winter hours below 45°F.), and are therefore not adapted to mild-winter areas of southern California or low desert.

Two trees are usually needed to produce fruit, and second tree must be chosen with care. No combination of these will produce fruit: 'Bing', 'Lambert', 'Royal Ann'. These varieties will pollinate any other cherry: 'Black Tartarian', 'Corum', 'Deacon', 'Republican', 'Sam', 'Stella', and 'Van'. However, because 'Lambert' blooms late, it is pollinated best by 'Republican'.

'Stella' and 'Sunburst' are self-fertile.

Fruiting spurs are long lived, do not need to be renewed by pruning. Prune trees only to maintain good structure and shape. Fruit appears in late spring in warm areas, early summer in Northwest.

Birds everywhere like sweet cherries. Protect with manufactured netting over tree.

For control of brown rot and blossom blight, spray with a copper spray just as leaves fall in autumn, then with a fungicide when first blooms appear and weekly during bloom. To control mites, spray with a miticide in spring before buds open.

Varieties:

'Berryessa'. Resembles 'Royal Ann', but larger, less tendency to produce double fruit in hot weather.

'Bing'. Top quality. Large, dark red, meaty, fruit of fine flavor. Midseason.

'Black Tartarian'. Smaller than 'Bing', purplish black, firm, sweet fruit. Ripens early.

'Chinook'. Resembles 'Bing', ripens 4–10 days earlier.

'Corum'. Light-colored fruit with colorless juice, whitish flesh. Excellent flavor. Ripens 7 days before 'Royal Ann'.

'Deacon'. Large tree. Large to medium-sized, firm, black fruit. Sweet, pleasant flavor. Ripens 7 days before 'Bing'.

'Early Burlat'. Like 'Bing'; ripens 2 weeks earlier.

'Early Ruby'. Dark red, purple-fleshed early cherry that performs well in all sweet cherry areas. Needs pollinator (see list above); 'Black Tartarian', 'Royal Ann', 'Van' are all good.

'Hardy Giant'. Dark red fruit resembles 'Bing'. Good pollinator, especially for 'Lambert'.

'Jubilee'. Resembles 'Bing', but fruit larger. Fewer double fruits.

'Kansas Sweet' ('Hansen'). Large red cherry with semisweet flavor. Late ripening.

'Lambert'. Very large, black, late-ripening fruit, very firm. Flavor more sprightly than 'Bing'.

'Mona'. Resembles 'Black Tartarian' but larger. Ripens very early.

'Rainier'. Has yellow skin with pink blush; ripens a few days before 'Bing'.

'Republican' ('Black Republican', 'Black Oregon'). Large, spreading tree. Small, round, purplish black fruit; dark juice, tender yet crisp texture. Good flavor. Late season.

'Royal Ann' ('Napoleon'). Large, spreading tree, very productive. Light yellow fruit with pink blush; tender, crisp. Sprightly flavor. Midseason.

'Sam'. Vigorous tree. Large, firm, black fruit. Excellent flavor.

'Stella'. Dark red fruit like 'Lambert'; ripens a few days later. Self-fertile and good pollinator for other cherries.

'Sunburst'. Self-fertile cross between 'Stella' and 'Van'. Early ripening. Large black fruit, good tree structure.

'Sunset'. Very late dark red cherry; late ripening lessens danger of cracking in late spring rains.

'Utah Giant'. Ripens with 'Bing' but is larger, sweeter; develops sweetness even before fully ripe. Holds color when processed. Pollinate with 'Van' or 'Stella'.

'Van'. Heavy-bearing tree. Shiny black fruit, firmer and slightly smaller than 'Bing'. Good flavor. Ripens earlier than 'Bing' in Northwest, right with it in California.

Sour Cherries

Sour cherry is a spreading, irregular-growing, garden-sized tree to 20 ft. You can prune to increase irregularity if you want an ornamental tree, or force more regular, upright pattern by pruning out drooping side branches. Sour cherries are self-fertile, and are reasonably good pollinators for sweet cherries. 'Montmorency' and 'Early Richmond' are preferred varieties with small, bright red, soft, juicy, sweet-tart fruit. 'English Morello' is darker, with tarter fruit and red juice. 'Meteor' has fruit like 'Montmorency', but it's a smaller tree. 'North Star', with red to dark red skin and yellow, sour flesh, is a small, very hardy tree.

CHERRY, FLOWERING. See *Prunus.*

CHERRY PLUM. See *Prunus cerasifera.*

CHERVIL. See *Anthriscus cerefolium.*

CHESTNUT. See *Castanea.*

CHICORY. *Compositae.* All Zones, but difficult in hot-summer areas. Botanically known as *Cichorium intybus.* Dried ground roots can be roasted and used as substitute for coffee. Wild form grows as 3–6-ft. perennial roadside weed in much of West and is recognized by its pretty sky blue flowers. Grown for its leaves, known as chicory, endive, or curly endive; or for its bleached sprouts,

C

known as Belgian or French endive, endive hearts, or witloof ("white leaf"). For culture, see Endive.

Chicory

Radicchio is the name given to a number of red-leafed chicories grown for salads. 'Rossa de Verona' or 'Rouge de Verone' is the best known. It makes lettucelike heads that color to a deep rosy red as weather grows cold in autumn or winter. Slight bitterness lessens as color deepens. Sow in early summer to mature in cold weather. Sow seeds of the similar 'Giulio' in spring to harvest in summer, 'Cesare' in midsummer for fall, winter harvest.

CHILEAN BELLFLOWER. See *Lapageria rosea.*

CHILEAN GUAVA. See *Ugni molinae.*

CHILEAN JASMINE. See *Mandevilla laxa.*

CHILEAN WINE PALM. See *Jubaea chilensis.*

CHILOPSIS linearis. *Bignoniaceae.* DESERT WILLOW, DESERT CATALPA. Deciduous large shrub or small tree. Zones 11–13, 18–21. Native to desert washes and stream beds below 5,000 ft.

Open and airy when trained as small tree. Grows fast (to 3 ft. in a season) at first, then slows down, levels off at about 25 ft. In age, develops shaggy bark and twisting trunks somewhat like Australian tea tree (*Leptospermum laevigatum*). Drops leaves early, holds a heavy crop of catalpalike fruit through winter, and can look shaggy. But pruning can make it very handsome. .

Chilopsis linearis

Long, narrow, 2–5-in. leaves. Flowers look somewhat like catalpa's, trumpet shaped with crimped lobes—pink, white, rose, or lavender, marked with purple. Flower color varies among seedlings. Nurseries select most colorful. Flowers appear in spring and often through fall, borne first year from gallon cans; attract birds.

CHIMONANTHUS praecox *(C. fragrans, Meratia praecox).* *Calycanthaceae.* WINTERSWEET. Deciduous shrub. Zones 4–7 (where it blooms February–March), 8, 9, 14–17 (where it blooms December–May). Native to China and Japan. Needs some winter cold.

Tall, open, growing slowly to 10–15 ft. high and 6–8 ft. wide, having many basal stems. Keep lower by pruning while in flower. Or prune as small tree by removing excess stems. Leaves medium green, tapering, 3–6 in. long and half as wide. Flowers on leafless stems, 1 in. across, outer sepals pale yellow, inner sepals chocolate colored, smaller. Plant where its winter fragrance can be enjoyed. Some possible locations: near a much-used service entrance or path, near a bedroom window. In hot-summer areas, it grows best if shaded from afternoon sun. Needs occasional deep watering in summer.

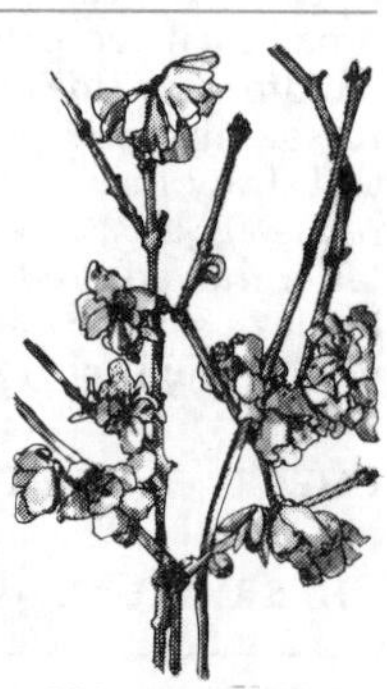
Chimonanthus praecox

CHIMONOBAMBUSA. See Bamboo.

CHINA ASTER. See *Callistephus chinensis.*

CHINABERRY. See *Melia azedarach.*

CHINA FIR. See *Cunninghamia lanceolata.*

CHIN CACTUS. See *Gymnocalycium.*

CHINCHERINCHEE. See *Ornithogalum thyrsoides.*

CHINESE BELLFLOWER. See *Abutilon.*

CHINESE CABBAGE. *Cruciferae.* Biennial grown as annual. All Zones in conditions noted below. Makes head somewhat looser than usual cabbage; sometimes called "celery cabbage." Raw or cooked, has more delicate flavor than cabbage. There are 2 kinds: *pe-tsai,* with tall, narrow heads, and *wong bok,* with short, broad heads. Favored pe-tsai variety is 'Michihli'; wong bok varieties include 'Springtime', 'Summertime', and 'Wintertime' (early to late maturing). Definitely cool-season crop; very prone to bolt to seed in hot weather or in long days of spring and early summer. Plant seeds directly in open ground in July in Zones 1–6, 10, 11; in August or September in other areas. Sow seeds thinly in rows 2–2½ ft. apart and thin plants to 1½–2 ft. apart. Heads should be ready in 70–80 days.

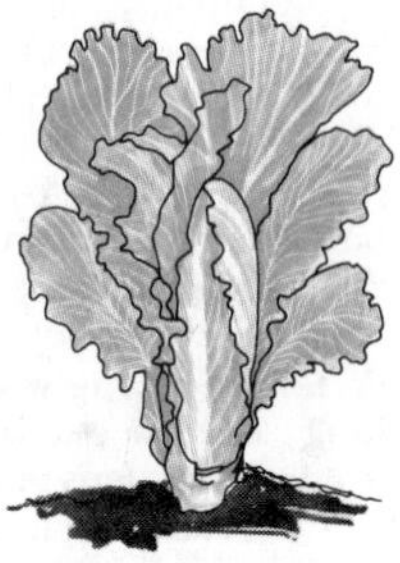
Chinese Cabbage

CHINESE CHIVES. See *Allium tuberosum.*

CHINESE ELM. See *Ulmus parvifolia.*

CHINESE EVERGREEN. See *Aglaonema modestum.*

CHINESE FLAME TREE. See *Koelreuteria bipinnata.*

CHINESE FORGET-ME-NOT. See *Cynoglossum amabile.*

CHINESE GROUND ORCHID. See *Bletilla striata.*

CHINESE HOUSES. See *Collinsia heterophylla.*

CHINESE LANTERN. See *Abutilon.*

CHINESE LANTERN PLANT. See *Physalis alkekengi.*

CHINESE PARASOL TREE. See *Firmiana simplex.*

CHINESE PARSLEY. See *Coriandrum sativum.*

CHINESE PLUMBAGO. See *Ceratostigma willmottianum.*

CHINESE REDBUD. See *Cercis chinensis.*

CHINESE SCHOLAR TREE. See *Sophora japonica.*

CHINESE SWEET GUM. See *Liquidambar formosana.*

CHINESE TALLOW TREE. See *Sapium sebiferum.*

CHINESE WINGNUT. See *Pterocarya stenoptera.*

CHINESE WOOLFLOWER. See *Celosia.*

CHIONANTHUS. *Oleaceae.* FRINGE TREE. Deciduous trees. Earn common name from narrow, fringelike, white petals on flowers that are borne in impressive, ample lacy clusters. There are male and female trees. If both are present, female plants produce fruit like small dark olives in clusters. Male trees have larger flowers. Broad leaves turn deep yellow in fall. Water requirement moderate.

C. retusus. CHINESE FRINGE TREE. Zones 2–9, 14–24. Generally smaller growing than *C. virginicus*—to 20 ft. Leaves 2–4 in. long. Flower clusters to 4 in. long in June and July. In bloom, this is a magnificent tree, something like a tremendous white lilac.

Chionanthus retusus

C. virginicus. FRINGE TREE. Zones 1–6, 15–17. Native Pennsylvania to Florida and Texas. Grows to 30 ft. where well adapted. Leaves and flower clusters are twice as big as those of *C. retusus,* and it blooms earlier (May). Fragrant.

In Zones 1–6, the most you can hope for is 12 ft. in 10 years; the plant is best used as a very slow-growing, airy shrub (it blooms profusely when only 2–3 ft. tall). In these Zones, it is one of last deciduous plants to leaf out in spring; flowers are more greenish than white.

Chionanthus virginicus

CHIONODOXA. *Liliaceae.* GLORY-OF-THE-SNOW. Bulbs. Zones 1–7, 14, 17–20. Native to alpine meadows in Asia Minor. Charming small bulbous plants 4–6 in. high; among first to bloom in spring. Narrow basal leaves, 2 or 3 to each flower stalk. Blue or white, short, tubular, open flowers in loose spikes. Plant bulbs 3 in. deep in September or October in half shade; keep moist. Under favorable conditions, plants self-sow freely.

C. luciliae. Most generally available. About 10 brilliant blue, white-centered, starlike flowers on 6-in. stalks. 'Alba' offers larger white flowers; 'Gigantea' has larger leaves, larger flowers of violet blue with white throat.

C. sardensis. Deep true gentian blue flowers with very small white eye.

Chionodoxa luciliae

CHIRANTHODENDRON pentadactylon ***(C. platanoides).*** *Bombacaceae.* MONKEY HAND TREE. Evergreen tree. Zones 16, 17, 20–24. Fast growing to 40–50 ft. with spread of 20–30 ft. Leaves 8–10 in. long, shaped like sycamore leaves, medium green with rusty underside. Odd flowers somewhat resemble waxy, deep red, smallish tulips, covered on outside with soft fuzz. Projecting from flower is fantastic structure that resembles tiny red hand, complete with fingernails. Blooms appear near ends of branches from March–October; leaves almost cover them. Flowers are followed by woody, 4-inch capsules which split into 5 sections, revealing seeds surrounded by golden wool. Tree has survived temperatures in low 20s.

Chiranthodendron pentadactylon

Continual leaf-drop in summer and strong surface rooting rule it out as patio or street tree. Best in deep soil with infrequent but deep watering.

Native to southern Mexico and Central America. It was revered by the Aztecs for its peculiar flowers and for supposed medicinal qualities.

CHIVES. *Liliaceae.* Small, clump-forming, perennial onion (*Allium*) relative. For garlic chives (Chinese chives), see *Allium tuberosum.* All Zones in conditions noted below. Leaves are grasslike in general appearance but round and hollow in cross-section. Clumps may reach 2 ft. in height but are usually shorter. Cloverlike, rose purple spring flowers are carried in clusters atop thin stems. Plant is pretty enough to use as edging for sunny or lightly shaded flower border or herb garden. Does best in moist, fairly rich soil. May be increased by divisions or grown from seed. Evergreen (or nearly so) in mild regions; goes dormant where winters are severe, but small divisions may be potted in rich soil and grown on kitchen window sill. Chop or snip leaves; use as garnish or add to salads, cream cheese, cottage cheese, egg dishes, gravies, and soups for delicate onionlike flavor.

Chives

Garlic Chives

CHLOROPHYTUM. *Liliaceae.* Lily relatives with clumps of attractive evergreen foliage and small white or greenish flowers in long clusters.

C. bichetii. House plant. Slow growing to an eventual 8–10 in. tall, 1½ ft. across. Leaves dark green with white stripes, shorter and relatively broader than those of spider plant (below), gracefully recurved. Small white flowers on 8-in. stalks. Does not make runners. Light to heavy shade. Water only when dry; feed occasionally to maintain good leaf color.

C. comosum (often sold as *C. capense*). SPIDER PLANT. Evergreen perennial. House plant; outdoor ground cover in Zones 15–17, 19–24. Native to Africa. Shade-loving plant forms 1–3-ft.-high clumps of soft, curving leaves like long, broad grass blades. 'Variegatum' and 'Vittatum', striped white, are popular. Flowers white, ½ in. long, in loose, leafy-tipped spikes standing above foliage. Greatest attraction: miniature duplicates of mother plant, complete with root, at end of curved stems (as with strawberry plant offsets); these offsets can be cut off, potted individually. Excellent, easily grown house plant for fully lighted window, greenhouse. Ground cover or hanging basket plant in partial shade. As ground cover, set 2 ft. apart in diamond pattern. Plants will fill in same year.

Chlorophytum comosum

CHOISYA ternata. *Rutaceae.* MEXICAN ORANGE. Evergreen shrub. Borderline Zones 4–6; good in 7–9, 12–17; good but often suffers from pests and soil problems in Zones 18–24. Hardy to 15°F. Fast growing to 6–8 ft. high and as wide. Lustrous yellow green leaves held toward end of branches are divided into fans of 3 leaflets (to 3 in. long); fans give shrub dense, massive look but with highlights and shadows. Clusters of fragrant white flowers, somewhat like small orange blossoms, open in very early spring and bloom continuously into April, intermittently through summer. Appealing to bees.

Choisya ternata

Use as attractive informal hedge or screen. Mass to fill large spaces. Prune throughout growing season to shape and thin out branches, forcing replacement wood from inside plant. Cut freely for decoration when in bloom.

(Continued on next page)

C

Grows in full sun in cool-summer areas, in light shade elsewhere. Gets straggly and bears few flowers when in too much shade. It's touchy about soil conditions. Difficult in alkaline soils or where water is high in salts. Under such conditions, prepare special soil mix as for azaleas. Subject to root rot and crown rot if drainage is not fast. Water infrequently but deeply. Subject to damage from sucking insects and mites.

CHOKEBERRY. See *Aronia.*

CHOKECHERRY. See *Prunus virginiana.*

CHORISIA. *Bombacaceae.* FLOSS SILK TREE. Evergreen to briefly deciduous trees with heavy trunks studded with thick, heavy spines. Native to South America. Young trunks are green, becoming gray with age. Leaves divided into leaflets like fingers of a hand; leaves fall during autumn flowering or whenever winter temperatures drop below 27°F. Reduce water in late summer (on blooming-sized trees) to encourage more flowers.

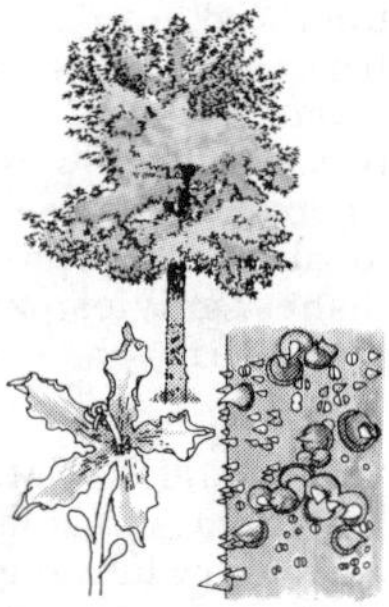

Chorisia speciosa

Flowers large and showy, somewhat resembling narrow-petaled hibiscus. Fast drainage and controlled watering are keys to success. Water established trees once a month.

C. insignis. WHITE FLOSS SILK TREE. Zones 19–24. To 50 ft. tall. Flowers white to pale yellow, 5–6 in. across. Blooms from fall into winter; flowering stopped by frost.

C. speciosa. Zones 15–24. Grows 3–5 ft. a year for first few years, then slowly to 30–60 ft. tall. Flowers are pink, purplish rose, or burgundy. Two grafted kinds are obtainable: 'Los Angeles Beautiful' has wine red flowers and 'Majestic Beauty' has rich pink flowers. In Zone 15 and sheltered areas in Zone 14, *C. speciosa* survived the heavy frosts of 1972, although trees lost major limbs and tops of trunks.

CHORIZEMA. *Leguminosae.* FLAME PEA. Evergreen shrubs. Zones 15–17, 19–24. Native to Australia. Hardy to about 24°F. Both species present riotous, gaudy display of clustered, sweet pea–shaped flowers in blended orange and purplish red, February–June. Fast growing, with slender, graceful branches.

Chorizema cordatum

Flame peas take sun, but flower color is more intense in part shade. Average water requirements. Left to go their own way, they are attractive spilling over wall, on banks, in containers, or hanging baskets. Pruned, pinched, and cut back severely after flowering, they make compact 2-ft. shrubs for ground cover, edging, or flower border. Source of late winter color.

C. cordatum. (Sometimes erroneously sold as *C. ilicifolium.*) HEART-LEAF FLAME PEA. Grows 3–5 ft. high, sometimes more under ideal conditions. Dark green leaves 1–2 in. long, with small prickly teeth along the edges.

C. ilicifolium. HOLLY FLAME PEA. Low, spreading shrub grows to 2–3 ft. high. Oval, ¾–1-in. leaves are similar to *C. cordatum,* but edges are wavy and have long, prickly teeth; vaguely resemble holly leaves.

CHRISTMAS BERRY. See *Heteromeles arbutifolia.*

CHRISTMAS CACTUS. See *Schlumbergera bridgesii.*

CHRISTMAS ROSE. See *Helleborus niger.*

CHRYSALIDOCARPUS lutescens. *Palmae.* (Often sold as *Areca lutescens.*) Zone 24; can grow in pots or in shady sheltered spot in frost-free areas, Zone 23. House plant anywhere. Clumping feather palm of slow growth to 10–15 ft. Graceful plant with smooth trunks and yellowish green leaves. Takes sun near coast; average water. Gets spider mites when grown indoors. Tricky to maintain, but a lovely palm.

Chrysalidocarpus lutescens

CHRYSANTHEMUM. *Compositae.* Annuals, perennials. All Zones. There are about 160 species of chrysanthemum, mostly native to China, Japan, and Europe. Included are some of most popular and useful of garden plants—top favorite being *C. morifolium,* whose modern descendants are known as florists' chrysanthemums. But there are many other worthwhile species in cultivation, capable of producing summer and fall color in borders, containers, or (widest use) as cut flowers. Water during dry spells.

Botanists have recently split *Chrysanthemum* into 4 genera, a decision not universally accepted or welcomed. Under the reclassification, *C. morifolium* becomes *Dendrathema morifolium, C. maximum* becomes *Leucanthemum maximum, C. frutescens* becomes *Argyranthemum frutescens,* and *C. coccineum* becomes *Tanacetum coccineum.*

Chrysanthemum morifolium

C. arcticum. ARCTIC CHRYSANTHEMUM. Very hardy autumn-blooming perennial, forming clump with stems 6–12 in. high. Spoon-shaped leaves, usually 3 lobed, 1–3 in. long, leathery in texture. White or pinkish flower heads 1–2 in. across. From this species have been developed group of hybrids known as Northland daisies with single flowers 3 in. or more across, in shades of pink, rose, rosy purple, and yellow. *C. arcticum* itself is primarily rock garden plant. Taller-growing varieties serve best in borders.

C. balsamita. COSTMARY. Weedy 2–4-ft. perennial with sweet-scented foliage that justifies its presence in herb garden (use leaves in salads and sachets). If leggy stems are cut back, gray green basal leaves with tiny scalloped margins can make herb garden edging. Divide clumps and reset divisions in late summer or fall.

C. carinatum. SUMMER CHRYSANTHEMUM, TRICOLOR CHRYSANTHEMUM. Summer- and fall-blooming annual, growing 1–3 ft. high, about 3 ft. wide. In mild-winter climates, blooms winter and spring. Deeply cut foliage; showy, single, daisylike, 2-in.-wide flower heads in purple, orange, scarlet, salmon, rose, yellow, and white, with contrasting bands around dark center. Satisfactory, long-lasting cut flowers. Sow seeds in spring either in flats or in open ground. Where winters are mild, sow in fall. Court Jesters is an excellent strain. Full sun. Light or heavy soil; grows wild in sand dunes along sections of southern California coast.

C. coccineum *(Pyrethrum roseum).* PAINTED DAISY, PYRETHRUM. Bushy perennial to 2–3 ft. with very finely divided, bright green leaves and single, daisylike, long-stemmed flowers in pink, red, and white. Also available in double and anemone-flowered forms. Starts blooming in April in mild-winter climates, in May or June in colder areas; if cut back, blooms again in late summer. Excellent for cutting, borders; combine with *Campanula persicifolia,* columbine, delphinium, dianthus. Best in full sun. Needs summer heat to perform well. Divide clumps or sow seeds in spring. Double forms may not come true from seed; they may revert to single flowers.

C. frutescens. MARGUERITE, PARIS DAISY. Zones 14–24. Short-lived perennial grown as annual in cold climates. Bright green, coarsely divided leaves; abundant daisylike flowers, 1½–2½ in. across, in white, yellow, or pink. 'Snow White', double anemone type, has pure white flowers, more restrained growth habit; 'White Lady' and 'Pink Lady' have buttonlike flower heads; 'Silver Leaf' has gray green leaves and masses of white flowers that are much smaller than those of regular marguerite. All kinds, but particularly familiar white and yellow marguerites, are splendid for containers and for quick effects in borders, mass displays in new gardens.

Small plants set out in spring will grow 4 ft. across by summer. In buying plants, avoid large, vigorous-looking ones with large leaves—they will bloom sparsely. Also avoid plants showing signs of fasciation (flattening or widening of stems) near crown.

Chrysanthemum frutescens

Plant in full sun, light soil. Marguerites grow exceptionally well near coast; with sufficient water and good drainage, also succeed inland, but may freeze in cold winters. For continued bloom, prune lightly at frequent intervals. Do not prune older plants severely—they seldom produce new growth from hardened wood. Replace every 2–3 years with new plants. Few pests, but subject to leaf miner, to thrips (which reduce flower quality), and—on old plants—to root galls and nematodes.

C. maximum. SHASTA DAISY. Hardy, sturdy perennial, valuable for summer and fall bloom in all climates. Original 2–4-ft.-tall Shasta daisy, with coarse, leathery leaves and white, gold-centered flower heads 2–4 in. across, has been largely superseded by varieties with larger, better-formed, longer-blooming flowers. They are available in single, double, quilled, and shaggy-flowered forms. All are white, but two show a touch of yellow. Some bloom May–October. Shasta daisies are splendid in borders and cut arrangements.

Following are some of the varieties available in nurseries:

'Esther Read', most popular double white, longest bloom; 'Marconi', large frilly double; 'Aglaya', similar to 'Marconi', longest blooming season; 'Alaska', big, old-fashioned single; 'Horace Read', 4-in.-wide, dahlialike flower; 'Majestic', large yellow-centered flower; 'Thomas Killin', 6-in.-wide (largest) yellow-centered flower.

'Cobham's Gold' has distinctive flowers in yellow-tinted, off-white shade. 'Canarybird', another yellow, is dwarf, with attractive dark green foliage.

Most popular varieties for cut flowers are 'Esther Read', 'Majestic', 'Aglaya', and 'Thomas Killin'.

Shasta daisies are easy to grow from seed. Catalogues offer many strains, including Roggli Super Giant (single) and Diener's Strain (double). 'Marconi' (double), also available in seed, nearly always blooms double. 'Silver Princess' (also called 'Little Princess' and 'Little Miss Muffet') is 12–15-in. dwarf single. 'Snow Lady' (single), an All-America winner, grows 10–12 in. tall, begins to bloom in 5 months from seed, then blooms nearly continuously.

Set out divisions of Shasta daisies in fall or early spring, container-grown plants at any time. Thrive in fairly rich, moist, well-drained soil. Prefer sun, but do well in partial shade in hot-summer climates; double-flowered kinds hold up better in very light shade. In coldest regions, mulch around plants, but do not smother foliage. Divide clumps every 2–3 years in early spring (or in fall in mild-winter areas). Shasta daisies are generally easy to grow, but have a few problems. Disease called "gall" causes root crown to split into many weak, poorly rooted growing points that soon die. Dig and burn affected plants; sterilize soil before planting in same spot. Bait to control snails and slugs.

Shasta daisies in well-drained soils can take plenty of water, especially before and during bloom; at this time, apply liquid fertilizer to encourage large flowers.

C. morifolium. FLORISTS' CHRYSANTHEMUM. The most useful of all autumn-blooming perennials for borders, containers, and cutting, and the most versatile and varied of all chrysanthemum species, available in many flower forms, colors, plant and flower sizes, and growth habits. Colors include yellow, red, pink, orange, bronze, purple, lavender, and multicolors. Following are flower forms as designated by chrysanthemum hobbyists:

Anemone. One or more rows of rays with large raised center disk or cushion, same color as rays or different. (Disbud for very large flowers.)

Brush. Narrow, rolled rays give brush or soft cactus dahlia effect.

Decorative. Long, broad rays overlap in shingle effect to give broad, full flower.

Incurve. Big double flowers with broad rays curving upward and inward.

Irregular curve. Like above, but with looser, more softly curving rays.

Laciniated. Fully double, with rays fringed and cut at tips in carnation effect.

Pompon. Globular, neat, compact flowers with flat, fluted, or quilled rays. Usually small, they can reach 5 in. with disbudding.

Quill. Long, narrow rolled rays; like spider, but less droopy.

Reflex. Big double flowers with rays that curl in, out, and sideways, creating shaggy effect.

Semidouble. Somewhat like single or daisy, but with 2, 3, or 4 rows of rays around a yellow center.

Single or *daisy.* Single row of rays around a yellow center. May be large or small, with broad or narrow rays.

Spider. Long, curling, tubular rays ending in fish-hook curved tips.

Spoon. Tubular rays flatten at tip to make little disks, sometimes in colors that contrast with body of flower.

Garden culture. It's easy to grow chrysanthemums, not so easy to grow prize-winning chrysanthemums. The latter need more water, feeding, pinching, pruning, grooming, and pest control than most perennials.

Plant in good, well-drained garden soil improved by organic matter and a complete fertilizer dug in 2 or 3 weeks before planting. In most areas, chrysanthemums do best in full sun; in hot climates, provide shade from afternoon sun. Don't plant near large trees or hedges with invasive roots.

Set out young plants (rooted cuttings or vigorous, single-stem divisions) in early spring. When dividing clumps, take divisions from outside; discard woody centers. Water deeply at intervals determined by your soil structure—frequently in porous soils, less often in heavy soils. Too little water causes woody stems and loss of lower leaves; overwatering causes leaves to yellow, then blacken and drop. Stems are attacked by borers in desert areas. Aphids are the only notable pest in all areas. Good way to avoid them is to feed plants with systemic insecticide/fertilizer combination.

Feed plants in ground 2 or 3 times during the growing season; make last application with low-nitrogen fertilizer not less than 2 weeks before bloom.

Sturdy plants and big flowers are result of frequent pinching, which should begin at planting time with removal of tip of new plant. Lateral shoots will form; select 1–4 of these for continued growth. Continue this pinching all summer, nipping top pair of leaves on every shoot that reaches 5 in. in length. On some early-blooming cushion varieties, or in coldest regions, pinching should be stopped earlier. Stake plants to keep them upright. To produce huge blooms, remove all flower buds except for 1 or 2 in each cluster—this is called *disbudding*.

Pot culture. Pot rooted cuttings February–April, using porous, fibrous, moisture-holding planting mix. Move plants to larger pots as growth requires—don't let them become rootbound. Pinch as directed above; stake as required. Plants need water daily in warm weather, every other day in cool conditions. Feed with liquid fertilizer every 7–10 days until buds show color.

Care after bloom. Cut back plants to within 8 in. of ground. Check labels; renew if necessary. Where soils are heavy and likely to remain wet in winter, dig clumps with soil intact, and set on top of ground in inconspicuous place. Cover with sand or sawdust if you wish. Take cuttings from early to late spring (up until May for some varieties), or when shoots are 3–4 in. long. As new shoots develop, you can make additional cuttings. In cold-winter areas, store in coldframe or mulch with light, noncompacting material like excelsior.

(Continued on next page)

Off-season, potted chrysanthemums. Florists and stores sell potted chrysanthemums in bloom every day of the year, even though by nature a chrysanthemum blooms in late summer or fall. Growers force these plants to bloom out of season by subjecting them to artificial day lengths, using lights and dark cloths. You can plunge the potted flowering plants right into a garden bed or border as an immediate (but expensive) display of chrysanthemums. Or you can enjoy them in the house while flowers remain fresh, and then plant them out. Either way, they will not bloom again at the same off-season time the next year. Instead, they will revert to their natural inclinations and commence fall bloom once again.

Cut off flowers when they fade, leaving stems about 6–8 in. long. Remove soil clump from pot and break apart the several individual plants that were grown in the pot. Plant these individual plants. When new growth shows from the roots, cut off remainder of old flower stems.

C. multicaule. Annual. Broad-rayed, buttery yellow daisies 2½ in. across rise above 6–8-in.-wide mats of bright green, fleshy foliage. Blooms best in cool weather; usually sold in fall, winter, early spring from flats or pots. Plants may live over a second year in cool coastal climates. Give them sun, average soil, water.

C. paludosum. Annual, sometimes living over for a second bloom season. Flowers look something like miniature Shasta daisies. White daisy flower heads 1–1½ in. wide appear on 8–10-in. stems above dark green, deeply toothed leaves. For care, see *C. multicaule*.

C. parthenium. FEVERFEW. Compact, leafy, aggressive perennial, once favored in Victorian gardens. The old-fashioned single, white-flowered forms self-sow freely, grow as weeds in some areas. Leaves have strong odor, offensive to some. Named varieties range from 1–3 ft. tall. 'Golden Ball' has bright yellow flower heads and no rays; 'Silver Ball' is completely double with only the white rays showing. In 'Aureum', commonly sold in flats as 'Golden Feather', chartreuse-colored foliage is principal attraction. Sow seeds in spring for bloom by midsummer, or divide in fall or spring (in cold climates). Can also grow from cuttings. Full sun or light shade.

C. ptarmiciflorum. DUSTY MILLER, SILVER LACE. Perennial Zones 16, 17, 19–24; grown as annual elsewhere. To 6–10 in. tall, 8–10 in. wide. Very finely cut, silvery white leaves. Where hardy, produces white daisy flowers on 1½-ft. stems.

CHRYSOLARIX amabilis, C. kaempferi. See *Pseudolarix kaempferi*.

CHUPAROSA. See *Justicia californica*.

CIBOTIUM. *Dicksoniaceae*. Tree ferns. One fairly common, one quite rare.

Cibotium glaucum

C. glaucum. (Usually sold as *C. chamissoi*.) HAWAIIAN TREE FERN. Zones 17, 24. Grows to 6 ft. high, 8 ft. wide, and has feathery, golden green fronds (apple green if shaded). Bare trunks imported from Hawaii; these trunks can be potted up in loose, fast-draining soil rich in organic material. If temperatures and humidity are kept high and soil is not too wet, plants will root and grow. Give good light, but not hot sun; average water. Leaf crowns can become very broad. Hardy to 32°F.

C. schiedei. MEXICAN TREE FERN. Zones 16, 17, 21–24. Can reach 15 ft. tall with wide-spreading, lacy, arching and drooping, chartreuse fronds. Hardy to 24°F. when mature. Shade. Rare.

CIDER GUM. See *Eucalyptus gunnii*.

CIGAR PLANT. See *Cuphea ignea*.

CILANTRO. See *Coriandrum sativum*.

CIMICIFUGA. *Ranunculaceae*. BUGBANE. Perennials. Zones 1–7, 17. Stately, upright, slim spikes of small white flowers grow from clumps of shiny, dark green leaves divided into many 1½–3-in.-long, deeply toothed leaflets. Flowers late summer to fall. Handsome among large ferns in woodland garden. Best in partial shade and rich, well-drained, moist soil. Will take considerable sun with ample water. Clumps can remain undisturbed for many years. Divide in fall or (in cold areas) in early spring before growth starts. Dried seed clusters useful in flower arrangements.

Cimicifuga racemosa

C. racemosa. BLACK SNAKEROOT. Flower spikes grow to 7 ft.

C. simplex. KAMCHATKA BUGBANE. Flower spikes to 3–5 ft.

CINERARIA. See *Senecio hybridus*.

CINNAMOMUM. *Lauraceae*. Evergreen trees. Slow to moderate growth rate; trees eventually reach considerable size. Both species have aromatic leaves that smell like camphor when crushed. Good for large lawns but competitive root system makes them poor choice for garden beds. Thrive in hot-summer areas where winter temperatures stay above 20°F.

Cinnamomum camphora

Not much bothered by pests, but subject to a root rot—verticillium wilt. Symptoms: wilting and dying of twigs, branches, entire center of tree, or entire tree. Wood in twigs or branches shows brownish discoloration. Trees most susceptible after wet winters or if planted in poorly drained soil. No cure is known, though trees often outgrow the problem. To treat, cut out damaged branches. Fertilize trees with nitrogen fertilizer and water deeply.

C. camphora. CAMPHOR TREE. Zones 8, 9, 12–24. Native to China, Japan. A delight to the eye in every season. Winter foliage is shiny yellow green. In early spring, new foliage may be pink, red, or bronze, depending on tree. Usually strong structure, heavy trunk, and heavy, upright, spreading limbs. Beautiful in rain when trunks look black. Grows slowly to 50 ft. or more with wider spread. Leaves 2½–5 in. long. Drops leaves quite heavily in March; flowers, fruits, and twigs drop later. Clusters of tiny, fragrant, yellow flowers in profusion in May, followed by small blackish fruits.

C. glanduliferum. NEPAL CAMPHOR TREE. Zones 15–17, 19–24. Native to Himalayas. Differs in having larger, richer green, more leathery leaves. Nepal camphor tree is more upright in branching habit than the common camphor tree, slightly more tender, and apparently faster growing.

CINQUEFOIL. See *Potentilla*.

CISSUS. *Vitaceae*. Evergreen vines distinguished for their foliage. Most climb by tendrils. Related to Virginia creeper, Boston ivy, and grape. Easy to grow. Not fussy about soil, water, or fertilizer. Flowers inconspicuous. Useful near swimming pools.

C. antarctica. KANGAROO TREEBINE. Zones 16–24. Native to Australia. A graceful vine, vigorous once established. To 10 ft. Medium green, shiny leaves, 2–3½ in. long and almost as wide, with toothed edges. Good tub plant indoors or out, in sun or shade, for climbing up or tumbling down, for trellis, wall, or hillside.

Cissus antarctica

C. capensis. See *Rhoicissus capensis.*

C. discolor. House or greenhouse plant. Climbing, but usually grown in hanging pots. Leaves 4–6 in. long, oval, toothed, with showy pink and silver markings; maroon on lower surface. Resemble leaves of rex begonia in color and texture. Needs warmth, semishade, humidity, ample water.

C. hypoglauca. Zones 13–24. Native to Australia. Rapid growth to 15 ft. in one season. Eventually climbs to 30–50 ft. Leaves highly polished, divided into 5 roundish, leathery leaflets 3 in. long; foliage strong in texture with bronzy color tones. New growth covered with rust-colored fuzz. Use in same way as *C. antarctica.* Makes good bank cover in sun or light shade; will control erosion.

C. quadrangula *(C. quadrangularis).* House or greenhouse plant. Succulent vine, usually grown in hanging baskets. Generally leafless, with fleshy, jointed, thick, 4-angled or winged stems that climb or trail several feet. Occasional leaves oval or 3 lobed, 2 in. long. Odd rather than pretty, but easy to grow with good light, good drainage.

C. rhombifolia. GRAPE IVY. Zones 13, 15, 16, 21–24 (needs all-year warmth). Native to South America. To 20 ft. Beautiful dark green foliage. Leaves divided into diamond-shaped leaflets 1–4 in. long, with sharp-toothed edges; show bronze overtones because of reddish hairs on veins beneath. Widely used indoors. Outdoors, it grows to good size and can be trained on trellis, pergola, or driftwood branches. Grows in sun or fairly deep shade, tolerating low light intensity indoors. The variety 'Mandaiana' is more upright and compact, with larger, more substantial leaflets. 'Ellen Danica' has leaflets shallowly lobed like an oak leaf; it grows more compactly than grape ivy and has darker green, less lustrous leaves.

C. striata. Zones 13–24. Native to South America. To 20 ft. In effect a miniature Virginia creeper, with small, leathery leaves divided into 3–5 leaflets, each 1–3 in. long. Stems reddish. Use to make long traceries against plain surfaces, as ground or wall cover, or to spill over wall. Sun or shade. Useful and beautiful.

C. trifoliata. Zones 12, 13. Hardy deciduous vine with small, almost succulent, ivy-shaped leaves, 1–2 in. wide. Very fast growing. Good on trellis or rough wall, or scrambling over rocks. Looks woodsy and cool even though it's quite drought resistant.

C. voinieriana. See *Tetrastigma.*

C. vomerensis. See *Tetrastigma.*

Cistaceae. Members of the rockrose family grown in the West are evergreen shrubs with flowers that look something like single roses—small in *Helianthemum*, large in *Cistus*. Individual flowers are short lived, but appear over a long season.

CISTUS. ROCKROSE. Evergreen shrubs. Borderline in Zones 4–6; satisfactory in Zones 7–9, 12–15, 18–22; best in Zones 16, 17, 23, 24. Native to Mediterranean region. Hardy to 15°F. Producers of showy spring flowers, rockroses are also sun loving, fast growing, drought resistant, recommended for planting in fire-hazard areas, and tolerant of poor, dry soil. Will take cold ocean winds, salt spray, or desert heat. Rockroses should have well-drained soil if they are to be watered frequently. To keep plants vigorous and neat, cut out a few old stems from time to time. Tip-pinch young plants to thicken growth, or give a light overall shearing to new growth.

Cistus purpureus

When planting in area that will be neglected—no water once plant is established—don't plant rootbound plants. Cut circling roots and spread out the mass so plant will have chance to root down to lower soil levels.

Use as dry-bank cover, massed by themselves, or interplanted with ceanothus, wild buckwheat (*Eriogonum*), or sunroses (*Helianthemum*). Taller kinds make good informal screens or low dividers. Useful in big rock gardens, in rough areas along drives and roads, or for sunny wild areas. They can control erosion.

C. corbariensis. See *C. hybridus.*

C. 'Doris Hibberson'. Compact, to 3 ft. tall and as wide. Gray green foliage. Leaves 1–2 in. long, oval. Clear pink, 3-in.-wide flowers with crinkled silky petals in June, July. Flowers blend with other flower colors better than do blooms of commonly grown *C. purpureus.*

C. hybridus *(C. corbariensis).* WHITE ROCKROSE. Spreading growth to 2–5 ft. high and almost as wide. Leaves to 2 in. long, gray green, crinkly; fragrant on warm days. Flowers 1½ in. across, white with yellow centers, in late spring. Widely grown.

C. incanus *(C. villosus).* Bushy plant 3–5 ft. tall and equally wide. Oval 1–3-in.-long leaves densely covered with down. Flowers purplish pink, 2–2½ in. across, in late spring and early summer. Used in fire-hazard areas. *C. i. creticus* (*C. creticus*) is similar, but with wavy-edged leaves.

C. ladanifer *(C. ladaniferus maculatus).* CRIMSON-SPOT ROCKROSE. Compact, to 3–5 ft. high, with equal spread. Leaves to 4 in. long, dark green above, lighter green beneath, fragrant. White, 3-in.-wide flowers with dark crimson spot at base of each petal, June–July.

C. palhinhae. Low, spreading plant to 2 ft. tall and wide, with dark green leaves and big (3–4-in.) flowers in late spring. Rare. Parent of several equally rare hybrids with large white flowers.

C. purpureus. ORCHID ROCKROSE. Compact grower to 4 ft. tall and wide, often shorter and wider where constant ocean winds keep plants low. Leaves 1–2 in. long, dark green above, gray and hairy beneath. Reddish purple, 3-in.-wide flowers with red spot at base of each petal, June–July. Very fine where cool winds and salt spray limit choice of plants.

C. salviifolius (usually sold as *C. villosus* 'Prostratus'). SAGELEAF ROCKROSE. Wide-spreading shrub to 2 ft. high and 6 ft. across. Leaves light gray green, about 1 in. long, crinkly, veined, crisp looking. Flowers 1½ in. wide, white with yellow spots at base of petals, very profuse in late spring. Good bank or ground cover for rough situations.

C. skanbergii. Low, broad bush 1–1½ ft. tall and wide. Gray green leaves; pure pink, 1-in. flowers in great profusion in late spring.

C. villosus. See *C. incanus.*

C. villosus 'Prostratus'. See *C. salviifolius.*

CITRON. See *Citrus*, Miscellaneous.

CITRUS. *Rutaceae.* Evergreen trees and shrubs highly valued for fruit and as landscaping plants. Most can be grown outdoors in Zones 8, 9, 12–24; indoor/outdoor container plants anywhere. As landscaping plants, they offer year-round attractive form and glossy deep green foliage, fragrant flowers, and decorative fruit in season. If you want quality fruit, your choice of varieties will depend on the total amount of heat available through the fruit-developing period (need varies according to type) and on the winter cold in your Zone. Choice and use are also determined by whether plants are standard trees or dwarfs. Citrus flowers draw bees.

Orange

Heat requirements. Lemons and limes need the least heat, and will produce usable fruit in cool-summer areas (where winter temperatures are not too low). 'Valencia' orange has higher heat requirement and greater frost tolerance. Navel oranges need even more heat, but their fruit development period is shorter than that of 'Valencia' and a tree will produce palatable fruit between winter frosts if summer heat is high. Navel, therefore, is a good selection for Zones 8, 9, 12, 13. Mandarin oranges (tangerine group) need high heat for top flavor. Grapefruit develops full flavor only in areas of prolonged high heat.

(Continued on next page)

C

Hardiness. Citrus of one kind or another are grown in every Arizona and California climate where winter temperatures do not fall much below 20°F. From least hardy to hardiest, they rank generally in this order: 'Mexican' lime (28°F.), limequat, grapefruit, pummelo, regular lemon, tangelo and tangor, 'Bearss' lime, sweet orange, most mandarin oranges (tangerines), 'Rangpur' lime and 'Improved Meyer' lemon, 'Owari' mandarin, sour orange, orangequat, kumquat, calamondin (20°F.).

Standard or dwarf. Practically all citrus sold have been budded or grafted on an understock. Standard trees (20–30 ft. tall and as wide) are grown on a variety of understocks. Dwarf trees are grown on understocks of trifoliate orange (*Poncirus trifoliata*) or Hiryu (Flying Dragon); the latter is a naturally dwarf, contorted, spiny form of trifoliate orange (variety *P.t.* 'Monstrosa'). Trifoliate orange understocks produce trees 4–10 ft. tall (some may eventually reach 15–20 ft.); Hiryu produces even smaller trees (5–7 ft. at 13 years old).

Check citrus periodically for suckers (branches that arise below the graft line) and remove them before they compete with (or overwhelm) the desired variety.

Drainage. First requirement is fast drainage. If soil drains slowly, don't attempt to plant citrus in it regardless of how you condition planting soil. In poorly drained soil, plant above soil level in raised beds or by mounding up soil around plant. Drainage in average soil, and water retention in very light soil, will be improved by digging in a 4–6 in. layer of peat moss, sawdust, or ground bark to depth of 1 ft.

Watering. Citrus needs moist soil, but never free-standing water. It needs air in the soil. Danger from overwatering is greatest in clay soil where air spaces are minute. In soil with proper drainage, water newly planted trees almost as frequently as trees in containers—twice a week in normal summer weather, more frequently during hot spells. Water established trees every other week. In clay soils, space watering intervals so top part of soil dries between irrigations. Don't let tree reach wilting point.

If you build basins, make them wider than spread of branches. Citrus roots extend out twice as far as the distance from the trunk to branch ends. Keep trunk dry by starting basin 6 in. or more from trunk. When you water, be sure to wet entire root zone (that is, wet to depth of 4 ft.).

Mulching. Since citrus roots grow near surface as well as deeper, a mulch over soil is beneficial. Use a 2–3-in.-deep layer of sawdust or the like, or large pebbles or gravel.

Fertilizing. Universities recommend from 1½–2 lbs. of actual nitrogen for mature trees each year. (To get pounds of "actual nitrogen," multiply percentage of total nitrogen, as stated on label, times weight of fertilizer.) It's best to apply ⅓ in late winter, ⅓ in June, and ⅓ in August. Spread fertilizer beneath and well beyond branch spread of tree, and water in deeply. Use a high-nitrogen formula.

Citrus may suffer from iron chlorosis or zinc deficiency. Chlorosis (yellowing leaves with dark green veins) may also be caused by excess water, so check your irrigation practice. Treat with chelated iron or iron sulfate. Zinc deficiency shows up as a yellowish blotch or mottle between leaf veins. Control with zinc foliar sprays. Commercial products are available as sprays containing both iron chelates and zinc.

Pests and diseases. Citrus can get aphids, mites, scale insects, and mealybugs. If these pests' natural enemies fail to handle the infestations, and if jets of water fail to keep the pests in check, spray with appropriate chemicals (see "Pest Controls," page 104). If scale remains troublesome, spray with light oil in early spring. Bait or spray for snails and slugs whenever necessary, especially during warm-night spells of winter and spring.

Copper bands, available in some areas, will keep snails out of trees. Where it is legal to do so (in southern California), colonize citrus groves with decollate snails, which prey on the garden snail.

Weirdly deformed fruit (especially lemons) is caused by the citrus bud mite. Control by a light summer oil spray in spring and in fall; in hot-summer areas, spray only in fall. Reduce harmful insect populations by keeping ants out of trees with sticky bands on trunks. (Ants prey on natural insect predators of the mites.)

The few fungus ailments of citrus occur in poorly drained soil. Water molds, causing root rot, show up in yellowing and dropping foliage. Best control is to correct your watering schedule.

Brown rot gummosis usually occurs in older trees at base of trunk. Keep base of trunk dry; trim and clean the oozing wounds, removing decayed bark to a point where discolored wood does not show. Paint areas with Bordeaux paste mixture.

Sunburn. Citrus bark sunburns in hot-sun areas. Trunks should be wrapped (commercial paper trunk band is available). When exposing trunks or limbs by heavy pruning, protect bark with whitewash or cold-water paint. Common cold-water wall paint in tan or brown, similar to bark color, is satisfactory.

Pruning. Commercial trees are allowed to carry branches right to ground. Production is heaviest on lower branches. Growers prune only to remove twiggy growth and weak branches or, in young plant, to nip back wild growth and balance plant. You can prune garden trees to shape as desired; espaliers of citrus are traditional. Lemons and sour oranges are often planted close and pruned as hedges. Many citrus are thorny. Pruners and pickers should wear gloves and long-sleeved shirts.

Citrus in containers. Daily watering may be necessary in hot weather. Containers should have diameter of at least 1½ ft.

Citrus indoors. Gardeners in cold-winter, warm-summer areas can store plants indoors for winter protection. A cool greenhouse is best, but a basement area with good bright light is satisfactory. Use very little water.

Grapefruit

'Marsh' seedless. The West's main commercial type. Large light yellow fruit. Ripens 18 months after bloom—late November to June in desert areas. Needs highest, most prolonged summer heat for top quality. Even out of best climate it's a beautiful tree. Standard tree grows to 30 ft. or more; on dwarf rootstock, less than half as high. Large glossy leaves.

'Oro Blanco'. Large light yellow fruit with thick skin. Yellow flesh has grapefruit flavor but is sweeter, less astringent. Extends season in southern California, bearing November–February ('Marsh' November–February in the same region).

'Ruby' ('Redblush', 'Ruby Red'). Pink grapefruit. Red-blushed skin and pinkish flesh. Does not color well except in desert.

'Star Ruby'. Resembles 'Ruby', with deeper color in peel and flesh. Needs less heat to ripen.

Lemons

Lemon

'Eureka'. The standard lemon of markets. Bears throughout year. Not as vigorous as 'Lisbon' lemon. Somewhat open growth, branches with few thorns. As a dwarf, it's dense with large dark leaves. New growth is bronzy purple. Height 20 ft.; less as dwarf.

'Improved Meyer'. This strain supposedly has more resistance to infection and virus diseases than older 'Meyer' lemons; it has been propagated from stock that is free of disease that the older strain harbored and could pass on to other citrus. Other than that, it should be like the original. Fruit is quite different from commercial lemon—rounder, thin skinned, more orange in color. Tangy aroma, very juicy, but less acid than standard lemon. Bears fruit all year round, at early age. Tree is not a dwarf on its own roots. Will grow to 12 ft. with a 15-ft. spread. On dwarf rootstock it's half that size.

'Lisbon'. Vigorous growth, thorny, upright, denser than 'Eureka', to 20–25 ft. Can be trimmed up into highly decorative small tree. Fruit practically identical to 'Eureka'. Ripens mostly in fall, but some ripening all year. More resistant to cold than 'Eureka' and better adapted to high heat. Best lemon for Arizona.

'Ponderosa'. A novelty. Bears huge, rough lemons with thick, coarse skin. Two-lb. fruits not unusual. Mild lemon flavor. Bears at early age, frequently in gallon-can size. Main crop winter with some fruit through year. Tree angular branched, open; large leaves widely spaced. To 8–10 ft.; dwarf size, 4–6 ft.

'Sungold'. Attractive semidwarf (to 14 ft. tall, 8 ft. wide) lemon with green-striped yellow fruit and leaves mottled with white and cream.

'Villa Franca'. Generally similar to 'Eureka' but tree is larger, more vigorous, and has denser foliage and thornier branches. Fruit is similar to 'Eureka'. Sold in Arizona to grow in Zones 12 and 13; not common in California.

Limes

'Bearss'. Best lime for California gardens. Succeeds where oranges are successful. Tree is quite angular and open when young, but forms dense round crown to 15–20 ft. when mature (half that size on dwarf rootstock). It's thorny and inclined to drop many leaves in winter. Young fruit green, light yellow when ripe, almost size of lemon. When fully ripe it is especially juicy. Seedless. Main crop winter to late spring, some fruit all year.

'Mexican'. The standard bartender's lime—small, green to yellow green. Grow it in Zones 21–23. Grows to 12–15 ft. with upright twiggy branches.

Limequat

'Eustis'. Hybrid of 'Mexican' lime and kumquat. Fruit is the shape and size of a jumbo olive, light yellow when ripe. Flavor and aroma of lime; provides fresh lime flavor in regions too frosty for true limes. Rind edible. Ripens late fall and winter. Some fruit all year. Tree is shrublike, angular branching, twiggy, and rather open. Dwarf plant excellent in container.

'Tavares'. Plant is more compact, fuller, shapelier than 'Eustis'. Fruit is larger, long oval in shape, heavily borne. Lime flavor weak in overripe fruit.

Mandarin Oranges (Tangerines)

'Clementine'. Algerian tangerine. Fruit a little larger than 'Dancy', fewer seeds, ripens November–December. Fruit remains on tree, juicy and sweet, for months. Grows to 12 ft., semiopen with vertical, spreading, somewhat willowy branches. Seems to develop full flavor in areas too cool for a good 'Dancy'. 'Clementine' usually bears light crops unless planted with another variety for pollination.

'Dancy'. The standard tangerine in markets before Christmas. Fruit smaller and seedier than other mandarins. Best flavor in Zones 12 and 13 but good in Zones 21–23. Ripens December–January. Holds well on tree. Upright tree with erect branches. Dwarf tree handsome in container or as espalier.

'Encore'. Light orange, thin-skinned fruit ripens in summer, holds until fall. Quality good. Erect tree with slender branches and narrow leaves.

'Fairchild'. Hybrid between 'Clementine' mandarin and 'Orlando' tangelo. Medium-sized, deep orange fruit peels easily, is juicy and tasty, has many seeds. Ripens November–December. Small, compact tree bears every year. Needs another variety nearby for pollination.

'Fremont'. Hybrid between 'Clementine' and an Oriental mandarin called Ponkan. Medium-sized, bright orange fruit ripens December–January. Flavor good. Tree tends to bear in alternate years; thin fruit when unusually heavy.

'Honey'. Hybrid between 'King' and 'Willow' mandarin. Small, seedy fruit with rich, sweet flavor. Tends to bear heavily in alternate years. Vigorous tree. Not the same as 'Murcott', a Florida variety often sold in markets as 'Honey'.

'Kara'. Hybrid between 'King' and 'Owari'. Fruit large (2½ in.) for mandarin. Tart-sweet, aromatic flavor when ripened in warm interior climates. Ripens January and February in Zones 12, 13; March to May and June in Zones 8, 9, 14, 15, 18–23. From one season to another, may be very seedy or nearly seedless. Tree form resembles 'Owari'. Spreading, often drooping branches with large leaves. Grows to a rounded 15–20 ft., half that size as dwarf.

'Kinnow'. Hybrid between 'King' and 'Willow' mandarin. Medium-sized fruit has rich, aromatic flavor. Stores well on tree. Ripens January–May. Handsome tree–columnar, dense, very symmetrical to 20 ft. (dwarf will reach 10 ft.). Densely foliaged with slender leaves. Good in any citrus climate.

'Mediterranean' ('Willow Leaf'). The important mandarin of the Mediterranean region. Sweet, aromatic fruit ripens in spring. Tree spreading, with thin, willowy branches and narrow leaves.

'Owari'. Owari Satsuma. Source of imported canned mandarins. Sweet, delicate flavor; nearly seedless, medium to large fruit. Loose skin. Earliest mandarin to ripen—October to Christmas. Gets overripe soon if left on tree, but keeps well in cool storage. Standard trees are spreading, to 10–15 ft. high. Dwarf trees can be used as 6-ft. shrubs. Open, angular growth in early age; then more compact. Not suited to desert.

'Wilking'. From same parents as 'Honey' and 'Kinnow'. Small to medium-sized fruit with relatively thin rind; very juicy with rich, distinctive flavor. Fruit stores well on tree. Tree is rounded, medium height, and nearly thornless; tends to bear heavily in alternate years.

Oranges

The commercial oranges of the West are typified by the 'Washington' navel and the 'Valencia'. Listed here are first 'Washington' and the other navel varieties, then 'Valencia' and its counterparts, and finally the other, lesser-known oranges.

'Washington' navel. Widely adapted except in desert regions; best in warm interiors. Standard tree is 20–25-ft. globe. On dwarf stock it becomes 8-ft. mound. Bears December–February.

'Robertson' navel. Variant of 'Washington' navel. Fruit identical but earlier by 2–3 weeks. Tends to carry fruit in clusters. Tree generally smaller in size than 'Washington'. Has same climate adaptation. Dwarf trees produce amazing amounts of fruit.

'Skaggs Bonanza'. Another variant of 'Washington'. Fruit colors and ripens earlier; tree comes into bearing younger. Very heavy bearing.

'Summernavel'. Fruit much like 'Washington'. Sometimes fails to color as well, but flavor is good. Later ripening—well into summer months. Tree is more openly branched, with much larger leaves than 'Washington'. A dwarf tree will cover area bigger than 8 ft. square quite rapidly.

In some seasons, navel oranges are subject to split navels. This seems unrelated to culture, generally occurring when weather conditions favor fast fruit development. However, it's best to keep tree in even growth by avoiding excess fertilizer. Watch leaf color: yellowish leaves are signs of nitrogen need; dark green, lush leaves with burning tips or edges indicate too much nitrogen.

'Valencia'. The juice orange of stores. Most widely planted orange in the world, widely adapted in California. Poor risk in Arizona; if planted there, select a warm location or provide some protection to fruit, which must winter on tree. One of Arizona Sweets (see below) would be safer selection. Fruit matures in summer and stores on tree for months, improving in sweetness. Tree vigorous and fuller growing than 'Washington' navel, both as standard and dwarf.

'Seedless Valencia'. Variant of 'Valencia'. Fruit size, quality, and season are same. May not bear as prolifically.

Arizona Sweets. These are a group of varieties grown in Arizona. 'Diller', 'Hamlin', 'Marrs', and 'Pineapple' are the principal ones.

'Diller'. Small to medium-sized oranges with few seeds, high-quality juice. Ripen November–December (before heavy frost). Vigorous, large, dense tree with large leaves.

'Hamlin'. Similar to 'Diller', with medium-sized fruit; not as hardy.

'Marrs'. Early-ripening, tasty, low-acid fruit on a naturally semi-dwarf tree. Bears young.

'Pineapple'. Early-ripening, medium-sized fruit of excellent flavor.

'Shamouti' ('Palestine Jaffa'). Originated in Palestine and considered there to be finest orange. Large, seedless, no navel. Not a commercial orange in California because not sufficiently superior to 'Washington' navel. Grown on dwarf rootstock for home gardeners because of beauty in form and foliage. It's wider than tall. Leaves larger than navel. Heavy crop of fruit in early spring.

'Trovita'. Originated from seedling of 'Washington' navel. Thin skinned and about navel size, but without navel. Ripens in early spring. Apparently requires less heat than other sweet oranges and develops good-quality fruit near—not on—coast. Nevertheless, it tolerates heat well enough to pass as one of the Arizona Sweets. Dwarf tree has 'Washington' navel look with handsome dark green leaves.

Blood Oranges. These are characterized by red pigmentation in flesh, juice, and (to a lesser degree) rind. Flavor is excellent, with raspberry overtones. Generally speaking, they thrive wherever oranges produce good fruit. Pigmentation varies with local microclimates and weather.

'Moro'. Deep red flesh with touch of red on rind. No rind pigmentation near coast. Bears January–April.

'Sanguinelli'. Red-skinned fruit with red-streaked flesh. Bears February–May.

'Tarocco'. Red or red-suffused pulp, pink to red juice. Color varies. The less heat, the more color. Good quality in cooler areas. Ripens late spring. Tree is very vigorous and open growing, with long, willowy, vinelike branches. Dwarf tree makes ideal espalier.

Kumquat (Fortunella)

Very hardy. May not flower or fruit in cold-winter citrus climates, but always worthwhile for form and foliage. Leaves bright green, 3 in. long, oval, pointed. White flowers have rich orange blossom perfume. Edible rind is sweet; flesh is tart. Fruit is candied, preserved whole, or used in marmalade or jelly. Expect regular fruit production only in warm-summer areas. Plant size variable (6–25 ft.) when grown on its own roots. On dwarf rootstock, a compact, dense shrub-tree to 4 ft. In pots or tubs, admirably suited for patio or garden.

F. crassifolia. MEIWA KUMQUAT. Fruit round; larger, somewhat sweeter than Nagami. Tree less hardy.

F. margarita. NAGAMI KUMQUAT. Fruit oval, bright orange, about 1 in. in diameter.

Sour-Acid Mandarin Oranges

Calamondin. Fruit looks like tiny (¾–1½-in.) orange. Hundreds hang from tall (8–10-ft. even as dwarf), columnar plant. Most attractive in containers. Flesh is tender, juicy, sour, with a few small seeds. Primary use is as an ornamental; not a fruit to eat fresh. Skin and flesh good in marmalades.

'Otaheite' orange. Natural dwarf only a few feet tall. Usually grown indoors as decorative pot plant. Not true orange. Will bear very young. Fruit is orange to reddish orange, small, round, rough skinned, insipid in flavor. About as hardy as lemon.

'Rangpur' (commonly called Rangpur lime). Probably not lime at all. Fruit looks and peels like a mandarin, does not have lime taste. Less acid than lemon but with other flavors that make it a rich, interesting base for ades and mixed drinks. Good landscape tree, vigorous, sturdy, bushy. Fast growth to 15 ft. and as wide (as dwarf, to 8 ft.). Dense when pruned, open otherwise. Fruits colorful as ornaments, hang on tree throughout year. Has wide climate tolerance.

Tangelos

'Minneola'. Hybrid of 'Dancy' tangerine and grapefruit. Fruit is bright orange red, smooth, large. Flavor similar to tangerine. Few seeds. Ripens February–March. Stores well on tree for 2 months. Tree is not as large or dense as grapefruit. Leaves 3½–5 in. long and pointed. Thrives in all citrus districts.

'Orlando'. Fruit medium large, looks like a flattened orange. Rind is orange, adheres to orange-colored flesh. Very juicy, mildly sweet, matures early in season. Tree is similar to 'Minneola' but with distinctively cupped leaves. Less vigorous than 'Minneola' but more resistant to cold.

'Sampson'. Hybrid of tangerine and grapefruit, but fruit more like small, golden grapefruit with orange red pulp. Best for juice and marmalades. Ripens February–April. Standard tree is vigorous, fast growing to 30 ft. Form similar to grapefruit. Most decorative as dwarf tree. Dark green, oval, 2–3-in. leaves. Best in Zones 14–16, 20–23. Subject to sunburn in desert areas.

Tangor

'Temple'. Tangerine-orange hybrid. High-quality fruit in Zone 13. Flattened, deep bright orange fruit is loose skinned and easy to peel. Pulp tender textured, orange, juicy; "different" but good flavor (not too sweet). Ripens in early spring. Tree to 12 ft. high with greater spread; bushy and thorny. To a wide 6 ft. on dwarf stock. Leaves are similar to mandarin, smaller and narrower than orange.

Miscellaneous

Sour orange, Seville orange (*Citrus aurantium*). Makes large hedges, street trees, lawn trees. Fragrant flowers. Spectacular orange red, 3-in. fruits in clusters. Fruit is bitter and makes excellent bitter marmalade. Tree grows to 20–30 ft. with 15–20-ft. spread, dense foliage. Plant 6–10 ft. apart for tall screen, 3–4 ft. (prune heavily) for hedge.

'Bouquet', 'Bouquet des Fleurs' (commonly called Bouquet orange). Another very hardy sour orange. Big shrub or small tree to 8–10 ft. Graceful foliage, dark green. Used as hedge or windbreak. Flowers unusually large and extremely fragrant. Fruit small, bitter, used only in marmalades.

'Chinotto' orange (often sold as myrtle-leaf orange). Smaller in all dimensions than other sour oranges. Dense, bushy, round headed, with closely set, small, almost myrtlelike leaves. Very slow growing to 7–10 ft. tall. Formal appearance, often rounded high on stem and clipped. Makes an ideal tub plant. Fruit is ornamental, small, round, bright orange; it is used in Europe for candying.

'Etrog' citron. Attractive foliage. Fruit is small, oblong, yellow, fragrant, and unusually lumpy on the surface. Peel usually candied.

'Nippon' orangequat. Hybrid between kumquat and 'Owari' mandarin. Fruit larger than kumquat, with sweet rind and mild-flavored pulp; can be eaten whole. Winter-spring fruit holds well, makes plant a fine tubbed ornamental.

'Chandler' pummelo. The pummelo (pomelo, shaddock) is probably one parent of the grapefruit. The fruit is huge and thick skinned, with firm, relatively dry pulp; it has not proven popular in this country. 'Chandler', with pinkish flesh, is flavorful, moderately juicy. To eat: peel fruit, separate segments, then remove membrane surrounding segments.

Trifoliate orange (*Poncirus trifoliata*). Deciduous shrub or small tree to 15 ft., with spiny branches, typically fragrant flowers, and hard, bitter, yellow fruit. Fruit is inedible, but plant is useful as dwarfing understock and a parent in breeding hardy citrus. Rarely grown as an ornamental oddity or as an impenetrable hedge.

CLADRASTIS lutea. *Leguminosae.* YELLOW WOOD. Deciduous tree. Zones 1–9, 14–16. Native to Kentucky, Tennessee, and North Carolina. Slow growing to 30–35 ft. with broad, rounded head half as wide as tree is high. Divided 8–12-in.-wide leaves—bright green in summer, brilliant yellow in fall—look somewhat like those of English walnut.

Cladrastis lutea

May not flower until 10 years old, and may skip bloom some years, but spectacular when it does bloom. In May or early June, it produces long (6–10-in.) clusters of white, very fragrant flowers that resemble wisteria blossoms. Blooms followed by flat, 3–4-in.-long seed pods. Useful and attractive as terrace, patio, or lawn tree even if it never blooms. Average water and soil.

Prune when young to shorten side branches. Remove lower branches entirely when tree has height you want.

CLARKIA (includes *Godetia*). *Onagraceae*. Annuals. All Zones in conditions noted below. Native to western South and North America; especially numerous in California. They grow in the cool season, bloom in spring and early summer. Attractive in mixed borders or in mass displays, alone or with love-in-a-mist (*Nigella*), cornflower (*Centaurea*), violas, sweet alyssum (*Lobularia*). Cut branches keep for several days; cut when top bud opens (others open successively).

Clarkia amoena

Sow seed in place in fall (in mild-winter areas) or spring. Seedlings difficult to transplant but volunteer seedlings grow very well. Keep soil moist during and after germination and until flowering. Best in sandy soil without added fertilizer. Sun.

C. amoena *(Godetia amoena, G. grandiflora)*. GODETIA, FAREWELL-TO-SPRING. Native California to British Columbia. Two wild forms: coarse stemmed and sprawling, 4–5 in. high; slender stemmed, 1½–2½ ft. high. Tapered leaves, ½–2 in. long. On both forms, upright buds open into cup-shaped, slightly flaring, pink or lavender flowers, 2 in. across, usually blotched or penciled crimson. Although seeds of named varieties are rarely sold in United States (more available in England), strains of mixed colors are easy to find. Dwarf Gem grows 10 in. tall; Tall Upright reaches 2–3 ft.

C. concinna. RED-RIBBONS. California native. To 1½ ft. tall. Deep pink to lavender flowers with 3-lobed, fan-shaped petals. Leaves rounded, ½–2 in. long. May be found in wildflower seed mixes.

C. pulchella. Native to Pacific Northwest. Slender, upright, mostly unbranched, 1–1½ ft. high. Stems reddish; leaves narrow, 1–2 in. long, sparse. Flowers single, 4 petaled; petals taper to clawlike base, are 3 lobed at tip. There are semidouble and dwarf forms. Some garden clarkias probably hybrids between *C. pulchella* and *C. unguiculata*.

C. unguiculata *(C. elegans)*. CLARKIA, MOUNTAIN GARLAND. Erect, to 1–4 ft. Reddish stems, 1–1¾-in.-long leaves, 1-in.-wide flowers in rose, purple, white. Some varieties have double white, orange, salmon, crimson, purple, rose, pink, and creamy yellow flowers. Double-flowered kinds are ones usually sold in seed packets.

CLEMATIS. *Ranunculaceae*. Most of the 200-odd species are deciduous vines; exceptions are the evergreen *C. armandii* and a few interesting free-standing or sprawling perennials or small shrubs. All have attractive flowers, and most are spectacular. The flowers are followed by fluffy clusters of seeds with tails, often quite effective in flower arrangements. Leaves of deciduous kinds are dark green, usually divided into leaflets; leaf stalks twist and curl to hold plant to its support. Although the deciduous clematis are hardy in all western climates and are enjoyed in most, they are truly glorious in the intermountain West and the Pacific Northwest (Zones 1–6) and coastal northern California (Zones 15–17).

Clematis armandii

Clematis are not demanding, but their few specific requirements should be met. Plant vine types next to trellis, tree trunk, or open framework to give stems support for twining. Plant so that roots are cool while tops are in sun—either 5–6 hours of full sun daily or all-day filtered sun. Give them rich, loose, fast-draining soil; add generous quantities of peat moss, ground bark, and the like. Add lime only where soil tests indicate calcium deficiency.

To provide cool area for roots, add mulch, place large flat rock over soil, plant shallow-rooted ground cover over the root area, or plant in shade of small shrub or evergreen vine and stake so the top can catch sun. Put in support when planting and tie up stems at once. Stems are easily broken, so protect them with wire netting if child or dog traffic is heavy. Clematis need constant moisture and nutrients to make their great rush of growth; apply a complete liquid fertilizer monthly during the growing season.

Pruning clematis sounds complicated, but it need not be; plants are forgiving and will quickly repair mistakes. Do remember that dormant wood can look dead, and take care not to make accidental cuts. Watch for healthy buds at leaf bases and preserve them. The basic objective is to get the greatest number of flowers on the shapeliest plant.

The type of pruning you will do depends on when your plants flower. If you don't know what kind you have, watch them for a year to see when they bloom; then prune accordingly.

Clematis that bloom in spring bloom only on the previous year's wood. Cut back a month after flowering to restrict sprawl and tangle, preserving main branches.

Summer- and fall-blooming clematis bloom on wood produced in the spring. Cut back in late fall after flowering, or in early spring as buds swell. For the first 2–3 years, cut to within 6–12 in. of the ground, or to 2–3 buds; cut to 2 ft. or less on older plants.

Clematis that bloom in spring and again in summer or fall bloom on old wood in spring, new wood later. Do only light, corrective pruning in fall or early spring; pinch or lightly shape portions which have bloomed to stimulate low branching and avoid a bare base.

Cut flowers are choice for indoors (float in bowl). Burn cut stems with match to make flowers last longer. Unless otherwise specified, flowers are 4–6 in. across.

C. armandii. EVERGREEN CLEMATIS. Hardy Zones 4–9, 12–24, but best adapted Zones 4–6, 15–17. Native to China. Leaves burn badly at tips where soil or water contains excess salts. Fast growing to 20 ft. Leaves divided into 3 glossy dark green leaflets, 3–5 in. long; they droop downward to create strongly textured pattern. Glistening white, 2½-in.-wide, fragrant flowers in large, branched clusters in March–April.

Slow to start; races when established. Needs constant pruning after flowering to prevent tangling and build-up of dead thatch on inner parts of vine. Keep and tie up stems you want, and cut out all others. Frequent pinching will hold foliage to eye level.

Train along fence tops or rails, roof gables. Allow to climb tall trees. Trained on substantial frame, makes privacy screen if not allowed to become bare at base.

There is a light pink–flowered form, *C. a.* 'Hendersoni Rubra'.

C. chrysocoma. Deciduous vine. Native to western China. To 6–8 ft. or more in height; fairly open. Young branches, leaves, and flower stalks covered with yellow down. Flowers long stalked, white, shaded pink, 2 in. wide, in clusters from old wood in spring, with later flowers following from new wood. Will take considerable shade.

C. davidiana. See *C. heracleifolia davidiana*.

C. dioscoreifolia *(C. paniculata)*. SWEET AUTUMN CLEMATIS. Native to Japan. Tall, vigorous, forming billowy masses of 1-in-wide, creamy white, fragrant flowers in late summer and fall. Dark green, glossy leaves divided into 3–5 oval, 1–2½-in.-long leaflets. After bloom or in early spring, prune year's growth to 1 or 2 buds. Good privacy screen, arbor cover.

C. heracleifolia davidiana *(C. davidiana)*. Native to China. Half-woody perennial to 4 ft. high. Deep green leaves divided into 3 broad, oval, 3–6-in.-long leaflets. Dense clusters of 1-in.-long, tubular, medium to deep blue, fragrant flowers July–August. Use in perennial or shrub border.

C. integrifolia. Native to Europe and Asia. Semishrubby perennial to 3 ft. with dark green, undivided, 2–4-in.-long leaves and nodding, urn-shaped, 1½-in.-long blue flowers in June–July. Prune after bloom.

C. jackmanii. Series of hybrids between forms of *C. lanuginosa* and *C. viticella*. All are vigorous plants of rapid growth to 10 ft. or more in one season. The best known of the older large-flowered hybrids is known simply as *C. jackmanii*. It has a profusion of 4–5-in., rich purple flowers with 4 sepals. Blooms heavily from June–July on. Later hybrids have larger flowers with more sepals, but none blooms as profusely. *C. j.* 'Comtesse de Bouchaud' has silvery rose pink flowers, *C. j.* 'Mme. Edouard Andre' purplish red blossoms. All flower on new wood; all do best with severe pruning in early spring as buds begin to swell. Freezes to ground in cold-winter areas. (For more on large-flowered hybrid clematis, see below.)

C. lanuginosa. Native to China. A parent of many of the finest large-flowered hybrids. Grows only to about 6–9 ft. but produces magnificent display of large (6-in.), lilac to white flowers May–July. Best known for its variety *C. l.* 'Candida', with 8-in. white flowers and light yellow stamens. Blooms on new and old wood. In favorable climates will bloom in March–April. Prune only to remove dead or weak growth in early spring. Then after first flush of flowers, cut back flowered portions promptly for another crop later in the summer.

C. lawsoniana. Thought to be hybrid of *C. lanuginosa* and *C. patens*. To 6–10 ft. Large (6–9-in.) flowers, rosy purple and dark veined. Its best-known form is *C. l.* 'Henryi', which bears tremendous 8-in. flowers, white with dark stamens, June–August.

C. ligusticifolia. Native to much of the West. High-climbing (to 20 ft. or more), deciduous vine much like *C. dioscoreifolia* in habit and flowering. Slightly fragrant flowers in spring, summer; attractive seed heads.

C. macropetala. DOWNY CLEMATIS. Native to China, Siberia. Variable in size, may be 6–10 ft. high. In early spring, produces 4-in. lavender to powder blue flowers that look double; they resemble ballet skirts. Blooms are followed by showy bronzy pink, silvery-tailed seed clusters. *C. m.* 'Markham Pink' has lavender pink flowers. Prune lightly in February to remove weak shoots and limit vigorous growth to sound wood.

C. montana. ANEMONE CLEMATIS. Native to Himalayas, China. Vigorous to 20 ft. or more. Extremely hardy, easy to grow. Massive early spring display of 2–2½-in., anemonelike flowers, opening white, turning pink. Flowers on old wood, so can be heavily thinned or pruned immediately after flowering to rejuvenate or reduce size.

Clematis montana

C. m. 'Rubens'. To 15–25 ft. Foliage is bronzy green, new growth crimson. Fragrant flowers, rose red changing to pink, are carried throughout vine fabric.

C. m. 'Tetrarose'. Considered more vigorous than *C. m.* 'Rubens'.

C. 'Nelly Moser'. Mauve sepals marked by dark red stripe in center of each.

C. paniculata. See *C. dioscoreifolia*.

C. 'Ramona'. Lavender blue; classic for planting with yellow or coppery climbing roses.

C. tangutica. GOLDEN CLEMATIS. Native to Mongolia, northern China. To 10–15 ft., with gray green, finely divided leaves. Bright yellow, 2–4-in., nodding, lantern-shaped flowers in great profusion from July to fall. They are followed by handsome, silvery-tailed seed clusters. Prune like *C. dioscoreifolia*. Uncommon.

C. texensis. SCARLET CLEMATIS. Native to Texas. Fast growing to 6–10 ft. Dense bluish green foliage. Bright scarlet, urn-shaped flowers to 1 in. long, in July–August. Has not done well in Seattle, but flourishes in Reno. More tolerant of dry soils than most clematis.

C. viticella. Native to southern Europe, western Asia. To 12–15 ft. Purple or rose purple, 2-in. flowers, June–August. Very hardy. Named varieties include 'Purpurea Plena Elegans' (double violet purple), 'Rubra' (deep crimson), and 'Venosa Violacea' (purple with purple-veined white center).

Large-Flowered Hybrid Clematis

Although well over a hundred varieties of large-flowered hybrid clematis are being grown today, your local nursery is not likely to offer more than a dozen—usually fewer—of the old favorites. Mail-order catalogues remain the best source for collectors seeking the newest. Flowers on some of these may reach 10 in. in width.

Here are varieties to choose from—old favorites first, then newer offerings:

White. 'Henryi' and *C. l.* 'Candida' are standard. 'Marie Boisselot' or 'Mme. Le Coultre' (large, flat, round flowers) and 'Gillian Blades' (huge, star-shaped flowers) are newer.

Pink. 'Comtesse de Bouchaud', the standard pink, has these rivals: 'Charissima' (veined pink with deeper bars), 'Hagley Hybrid' ('Pink Chiffon'), shell pink with pointed sepals, and 'Lincoln Star' (pink with paler edges).

Red. Red clematis have deep purplish red flowers that are best displayed where the sun can shine through them, as on the top of a fence. 'Mme. Edouard Andre', 'Ernest Markham', and 'Red Cardinal' are standards. 'Ville de Lyon' has full, rounded, velvety flowers; 'Niobe' is the darkest red of all.

Blue violet. Mid-blue 'Ramona' is still popular. Newer varieties are: 'Edo Murasaki' (deep blue), 'General Sikorski' (huge, with faint red bar), 'Lady Betty Balfour' (late dark blue), 'Mrs. Cholmondeley' (big, veined sky blue), 'Piccadilly' (purplish blue), 'Prince Philip' (huge purplish blue with ruffled edges), and 'Will Goodwin' (lavender to sky blue).

Purple. *C. jackmanii* is still the popular purple. Others are 'Gypsy Queen' (deepest purple), 'Jackmanii Superba' (larger, somewhat redder than *C. jackmanii*), 'Mrs. N. Thompson' (deep bluish purple with red bar), and 'Richard Pennell' (rosy purple).

Bicolor. 'Nelly Moser' (pink with reddish bar) is deservedly one of the most popular clematis. 'Carnaby' (white with a red bar) and 'Dr. Ruppel' (pink with red bar) are newer, splashier.

Double. Fully double, roselike blooms in early summer on old wood are usually followed later by single or semidouble flowers on new wood. 'Belle of Woking' is silvery blue, 'Duchess of Edinburgh' white, 'Mrs. P.T. James' deep blue, 'Teshio' lavender, and 'Vyvyan Pennell' deep blue with lavender blue center.

CLEOME spinosa. *Capparaceae.* SPIDER FLOWER. Summer annual. Shrubby, branching plant topped in late summer and fall with many open, fluffy clusters of pink or white flowers with extremely long, protruding stamens. Slender seed capsules follow blossoms. Short, strong spines on stems; lower leaves divided, upper ones undivided. Leaves and stems feel clammy to the touch and smell strong, but not unpleasant. Plants grow 4–6 ft. tall, 4–5 ft. wide; especially vigorous in warm, dry inland areas. Grow in background, as summer hedge, against walls or fences, in large containers; or naturalize in fringe areas of garden. Flowers and dry capsules useful in arrangements.

Cleome spinosa

Sow seeds in place in full sun; seeds sprout rapidly in warm soil. Keep plants on dry side or they will become too rank. A number of varieties can be grown from seed. In most cases color is indicated by variety name: 'Cherry Queen', 'Mauve Queen', 'Pink Queen', 'Purple Queen', 'Rose Queen', and 'Ruby Queen'. 'Helen Campbell' is snow white.

CLERODENDRUM. *Verbenaceae.* GLORYBOWER. Evergreen and deciduous; shrubs, trees, or vinelike shrubs. Some outdoor; some house plants. Average water.

C. bungei ***(C. foetidum).*** CASHMERE BOUQUET. Evergreen shrub. Zones 5–9, 12–24. Native to China. Grows rapidly to 6 ft. tall; soft wooded. Prune severely in spring and pinch back through growing season to make 2–3-ft. compact shrub. Spreads by suckers, eventually forming thicket if not restrained. Big leaves (to 1 ft.), broadly oval with toothed edges, dark green above, with rusty fuzz beneath; ill smelling when crushed. Delight-

Clerodendrum thomsoniae

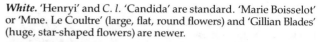

fully fragrant flowers in summer: ¾ in. wide, rosy red, in loose clusters to 8 in. across. Plant in part shade where its appearance, except in flowering season, is not important. It is resistant to oak root fungus.

C. fragrans pleniflorum. Evergreen to partly deciduous shrub. Zones 8, 9, 12–24. Coarse shrub spreading freely by root suckers unless confined. To 5–8 ft. (much less in containers), with 10-in. leaves like those of *C. bungei*. Flowers pale pink, double, in broad clusters that resemble florist's hydrangea; they have sweet, clean fragrance. Shade.

C. thomsoniae *(C. balfouri).* BLEEDING HEART GLORYBOWER. Evergreen shrubby vine. Outdoors in most protected spots of Zones 22–24; elsewhere, indoor/outdoor pot plant. Native to west Africa. Leaves oval, 4–7 in. long, dark green, shiny, distinctly ribbed. Flowers are a study in color contrast—scarlet 1-in. tubes surrounded by large (¾-in.-long) white calyces, carried in flattish 5-in.-wide clusters August–October. Will flower in 6-in. pot. Does well as indoor/outdoor tubbed vine. Can grow to 6 ft. or more if left untrimmed. Give support for twining. Needs rich, loose soil mix, plenty of water with good drainage. Prune after flowering.

C. trichotomum. HARLEQUIN GLORYBOWER. Deciduous shrub-tree. May freeze to ground in Zones 5, 6 and come back from roots; adapted Zones 15–17, 20–24. Native to Japan. Grows with many stems from base to 10–15 ft. or more. Leaves oval, to 5 in. long, dark green, soft, hairy. Fragrant clusters of white, tubular flowers almost twice as long as prominent, fleshy, ½-in.-long scarlet calyces. Late summer bloom. Calyces hang on and contrast pleasingly with turquoise or blue green, metallic-looking fruit. Variety *C. t. fargesii*, from China, is somewhat hardier and smaller; it has smooth leaves and green calyces that later turn pink. Grow in sun or partial shade. Routine care. Give room to spread at top and plant under it to hide its legginess.

C. ugandense. Evergreen shrub. Zones 9, 14–24. To 10 ft. (usually much less), with glossy dark green, 4-in.-long leaves and 1-in.-long flowers with one violet blue petal and 4 pale blue ones. Pistil and stamens arch outward and upward. Sun near coast, shade inland.

CLETHRA. *Clethraceae.* Deciduous shrub and evergreen tree. Distinctive plants with definite climate and soil preferences.

Clethra arborea

C. alnifolia. SUMMERSWEET, SWEET PEPPERBUSH. Deciduous shrub. Zones 2–6. Native to eastern U.S. To 10 ft. high with thin, strong branches forming vertical pattern. Spreads slowly by suckers into broad clumps. Dark green leaves, 2–4 in. long and half as wide, have toothed edges. Leafs out very late, in mid-May. Blooms in late summer: each branch tip carries several 4–6-in.-long spires of tiny, gleaming white flowers, spicily perfumed. Grows best in soils where rhododendrons thrive. Full sun in cool gardens, some shade where summers are warm. *C. a.* 'Pinkspire' has deep pink flowers; *C. a.* 'Rosea' bears pale pink blooms.

C. arborea. LILY-OF-THE-VALLEY TREE. Evergreen tree. Zones 15–17, 21–24. Native to Madeira. (For another lily-of-the-valley tree, see *Crinodendron*.) Beautiful small tree. Grows at moderate rate to 20 ft., rather stiffly upright with 10-ft. spread. Densely clothed with glossy, bronzy green, 4-in.-long leaves. White flowers in upright, branched clusters resemble lily-of-the-valley, even to their fragrance. They appear in late summer.

Leaf tips burn with frost, but plant comes back from old wood or from roots when damaged.

Easy to grow in soils where azaleas or rhododendrons thrive. Where salts build up, condition soil with peat moss or ground bark and make sure drainage is fast. Needs abundant moisture. If necessary, spray for red spider mites in summer.

CLEYERA japonica *(Eurya ochnacea).* *Theaceae.* Evergreen shrub. Zones 4–6, 8, 9, 14–24. Native to Japan and southeast Asia. Handsome foliage shrub related to camellia. Similar in character to ternstroemia. Grows at moderate rate to 15 ft. tall and as wide, with graceful, spreading, arching branches. New leaves are beautiful deep brownish red. Mature leaves, 3–6 in. long, are glossy dark green with reddish midrib. Small clusters of fragrant, creamy white flowers in September–October are followed by small, dark red, puffy berries which last through winter. Flowers and berries are attractive but not showy, don't form on young plants. 'Tricolor' (*C. fortunei*) has yellow and rose variegation on its foliage. Same soil and care as camellias.

Cleyera japonica

CLIANTHUS puniceus. *Leguminosae.* PARROT-BEAK. Evergreen shrublike vine. Zones 8, 9, 14–24. Native to New Zealand. Moderate growth to 12 ft. Foliage hangs gracefully in open pattern made up of sprays of glistening, dark green, 3–6-in. leaves divided into many narrow leaflets. Blooms in June: rose scarlet (rarely pink or white), sweet pea–shaped flowers with 3-in. parrot-beak keels swung downward between leaves. Pods that follow are 3 in. long. Full sun on coast; part shade inland. Train as espalier or on support to bring out full beauty of leaves and flowers. Routine garden care with ample water through blooming season. If soil is heavy, mix in organic soil amendment. Watch for snails and spider mites.

Clianthus puniceus

CLIFF-BRAKE. See *Pellaea*.

CLIFF ROSE. See *Cowania mexicana stansburiana*.

CLIMBING FERN. See *Lygodium japonicum*.

CLIMBING LILY. See *Gloriosa rothschildiana*.

CLIVIA miniata. *Amaryllidaceae.* KAFFIR LILY. Evergreen perennial with tuberous roots. Zones 13–17, 19–24. Native to South Africa. Striking member of amaryllis family with brilliant clusters of orange, funnel-shaped flowers rising from dense clumps of dark green, strap-shaped, 1½-ft.-long leaves. Blooming period is December–April; most bloom March–April. Ornamental red berries follow flowers. French and Belgian hybrids have very wide, dark green leaves and yellow to deep red orange blooms on thick, rigid stalks.

Clivia miniata

In frostless areas or well-protected parts of garden, clivias are handsome in shaded borders with ferns, azaleas, other shade plants. Superb in containers; grow indoors in cold climates. For best growth, clivia needs ample light, no direct sun. Plant with top of tuber just above soil line. Let clumps grow undisturbed for years. Container plants bloom best with regular fertilizing, crowded roots.

CLOVE PINK. See *Dianthus caryophyllus*.

CLOVER. See *Trifolium*.

C

CLYTOSTOMA callistegioides *(Bignonia violacea, B. speciosa).* *Bignoniaceae.* VIOLET TRUMPET VINE. Evergreen. Permanent in Zones 9, 13–24; perennial elsewhere. Tops hardy to 20°F., roots to 10°F. Strong growing; will clamber over anything by tendrils. Needs support on walls. Extended terminal shoots hang down in curtain effect. Leaves divided into 2 glossy, dark green leaflets with wavy margins. Trumpet-shaped flowers in violet, lavender, or pale purple; 3 in. long and nearly as wide at the top, in sprays at end of shoots, late spring to fall. Full sun or shade, average water. Prune in late winter to discipline growth, prevent tangling. At other times of year, remove unwanted long runners and spent flower sprays.

Clytostoma callistegioides

COARSE-FLOWERED MALLEE. See *Eucalyptus grossa.*

COBAEA scandens. *Polemoniaceae.* CUP-AND-SAUCER VINE. Tender perennial grown as annual in all Zones. Native of Mexico. Extremely vigorous growth to 25 ft. Bell-shaped flowers are first greenish, then violet or rose purple; there is also a white-flowered form. Called cup-and-saucer vine because 2-in.-long cup of petals sits in large, green, saucerlike calyx. Leaves divided into 2 or 3 pairs of oval, 4-in. leaflets. At ends of leaves are curling tendrils that enable vine to climb rough surfaces without support.

Cobaea scandens

The hard-coated seeds may rot if sown out of doors in cool weather. Start seeds indoors in 4-in. pots; notch seeds with knife and press edgewise into moistened potting mix. Barely cover seeds. Keep moist but not wet; transplant to warm, sunny location when weather warms up. Blooms first year from seed. In mild winters it lives from year to year, eventually reaching more than 40 ft. in length and blooming heavily from May until October. When growing it near the coast, plant out of ocean wind.

COBRA LILY. See *Darlingtonia californica.*

COCCULUS laurifolius. *Menispermaceae.* Evergreen shrub or small tree. Zones 8, 9, 12–24. Native to Himalayas. Grows slowly at first, then moderately rapidly to 25 ft. or more. Can be kept lower by pruning or trained as espalier. Usually multistemmed shrub with arching, spreading growth as wide as high. Staked and trained as tree, it takes on umbrella shape. Leaves shiny, leathery, oblong to 6 in., with 3 strongly marked veins running from base to tip. Will grow in sun or dense shade; likes moisture, tolerates many soil types. Useful as screen or background plant. Long, willowy branches are as easily led and trained as vines; fastened to a trellis, they make an effective screen.

Cocculus laurifolius

COCKSCOMB. See *Celosia.*

COCKSPUR CORAL TREE. See *Erythrina crista-galli.*

COCKSPUR THORN. See *Crataegus crus-galli.*

COCOS plumosa. See *Arecastrum romanzoffianum.*

CODIAEUM variegatum. *Euphorbiaceae.* CROTON. Greenhouse or house plant; outdoor annual in Zone 24. Grown principally for coloring of large, leathery, glossy leaves, which may be green, yellow, red, purple, bronze, pink, or almost any combination of these. Leaves may be oval, lance shaped, or very narrow; straight edged or lobed. Dozens of named forms combine these differing features. Can reach 6 ft. or more, but is usually seen as single-stemmed plant 6–24 in. tall. It performs best in a warm, bright, humid greenhouse.

Codiaeum variegatum

COELOGYNE. *Orchidaceae.* Epiphytic orchids. Greenhouse plants. Native to the eastern hemisphere. Close to 60 species varying widely in growth habit, but most are not sold. Grow like cattleyas: regular feeding during the growing season, partial shade. Osmunda, firmly packed, is one of the best potting media for these orchids. To prevent rot, keep water out of new growth where flower cluster forms.

Coelogyne cristata

C. cristata. Probably most popular species in collections. Light green, 1–3-in. pseudobulbs topped by 6–9-in. leaves. Large, showy, 3–4-in. white flowers with yellow throats; 3–8 pendulous flowers to a stem. Bloom winter to spring. Can be grown outdoors all winter in mildest climate areas. Keep plant on dry side from the time growth has matured (in October or November) until after flowers have faded. Slight shriveling of pseudobulbs is not harmful.

COFFEA arabica. *Rubiaceae.* COFFEE. House or patio plant (outdoor shrub Zones 21–24). Native to east Africa. The coffee tree of commerce is sold as a handsome container plant for patio, lanai, and large well-lit rooms. It's an upright shrub to 15 ft. with evenly spaced tiers of branches, clothed with shining, dark green, oval leaves to 6 in. long. Small (¾-in.), fragrant white flowers are clustered near leaf bases. They are followed by ½-in. fruits that start green and finally turn purple or red. Each contains 2 seeds—coffee beans. Grow in container, using same potting mixes and culture as for camellias. Needs shade outdoors; must be protected from frosts.

Coffea arabica

COFFEEBERRY. See *Rhamnus californica.*

COFFEE FERN. See *Pellaea andromedifolia.*

COIX lacryma-jobi. *Gramineae.* JOB'S TEARS. Perennial grass grown as annual in colder climates. A curiosity grown for its ornamental "beads." Loose growing with smooth, prominently jointed stems to 6 ft. Sword-shaped leaves to 2 ft. long, 1½ in. wide. Outside covering of female flower hardens as seed ripens; becomes shiny, ¼–1½-in. bead in pearly white, gray, or violet. String beads in bracelets, rosaries, other articles. Cut stems for winter arrangements before seeds dry and shatter. Sun or shade; ordinary soil.

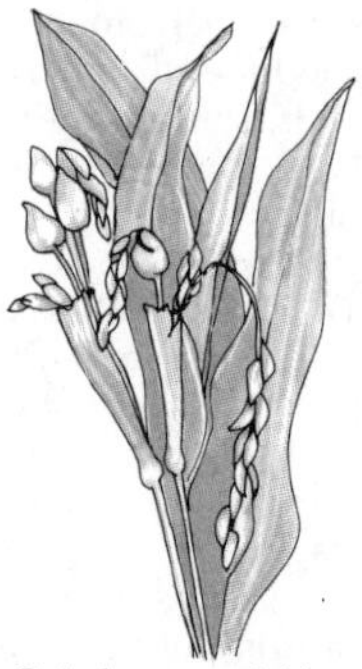

Coix lacryma-jobi

COLCHICUM autumnale. *Liliaceae.* MEADOW SAFFRON. Corm. Zones 1–9, 14–24. Mediterranean plant; sometimes called autumn crocus, but not a true crocus. Shining, brown-skinned, thick-

Colchicum autumnale

scaled corms send up clusters of long-tubed, flaring, lavender pink, rose purple, or white flowers to 4 in. across in late summer, whether corms are sitting in dish on window sill or planted in soil. When planted out, broad, 6–12-in.-long leaves show in spring and then die long before flower cluster rises from ground. Best planted in sun in average soil, in location where they need not be disturbed more often than every 3 years or so. Corms available during brief dormant period in July–August. The 2 best varieties are 'The Giant', single lavender, and 'Waterlily', double violet. Plant with tips 3–4 in. under soil surface. To plant in bowls, set upright on 1–2 in. of pebbles, or in special fiber sold for this purpose, and fill with water to base of corms.

Corms are highly poisonous; they are the source of colchicine, a drug used to control gout. Colchicine can also alter gene structure and is used in plant breeding.

COLEONEMA and DIOSMA. *Rutaceae.* BREATH OF HEAVEN. Evergreen shrubs. Zones 7–9, 14–24. Native to South Africa. Plants of filmy appearance and delicate character, with slender branches and narrow, heathlike leaves, fragrant when brushed or bruised. Flowers tiny, freely carried over long season in winter and spring, with scattered bloom to be expected at any time. You will find plants in nurseries under either *Coleonema* or *Diosma*. Actually, your choice amounts to a white- or a pink-flowering breath of heaven.

Coleonema pulchrum

Plant in light soil and full sun. Plants can take some shade, but are likely to grow rather taller there than expected. Fast drainage is a must. Average water; don't overwater. To control size and promote compactness, shear lightly after main bloom is over. For even more filmy look, thin out some interior stems.

Good on banks or hillsides, along paths where you can break off and bruise a twig to enjoy foliage fragrance. Frequently used next to buildings, though a little wispy for such use.

C. album. (Almost universally sold as either *Diosma reevesii* or *D. alba.*) WHITE BREATH OF HEAVEN. Grows to 5 ft. or more and as wide. White flowers.

C. pulchrum. (Often sold as *Diosma pulchra.*) PINK BREATH OF HEAVEN, PINK DIOSMA. Usually grows to 5 ft., occasionally to 10 ft. Flowers pink.

Diosma ericoides. BREATH OF HEAVEN. Introduced into California in 1890. However, most plants sold under this name now are *Coleonema album*. Has similar form and white flowers.

COLEUS hybridus (often sold as *C. blumei*). *Labiatae.* COLEUS. Perennial treated as annual, winter greenhouse or house plant. Native to tropics. Grown for brilliantly colored leaves; blue flower spikes are attractive, but spoil shape of plant and are best pinched out in bud. Leaves may be 3–6 in. long in large-leafed strains (1½–2 ft. tall), 1–1½ in. long in newer dwarf (1-ft.) strains. Colors include green, chartreuse, yellow, buff, salmon, orange, red, purple, brown, often with many colors on one leaf.

Coleus hybridus

Giant Exhibition and Oriental Splendor are large-leafed strains. Carefree is dwarf, self-branching, with deeply lobed and ruffled 1–1½-in. leaves. Salicifolius has crowded, long, narrow leaves; plant resembles foot-high feather duster. Named cutting-grown varieties exist, but most plants are grown from seed.

Useful for summer borders and as outdoor/indoor container and hanging basket plants. Plant from flats or pots in spring. Easy from seed sown indoors or, with protection, out of doors in warm weather. Easy from cuttings, which root in water as well as other media. Best in strong, indirect light or thin shade—color less vivid in too much shade or too much sun. Needs rich, loose, well-drained soil, warmth, ample water. Feed regularly with high-nitrogen fertilizer. Pinch stems often to encourage branching and compact habit; remove flower buds to ensure vigorous growth.

COLLARDS. See Kale.

COLLINSIA heterophylla *(C. bicolor)*. *Scrophulariaceae.* CHINESE HOUSES. Annual. Native to California. Rather uncommon plant; blooms spring to early summer, with snapdragonlike flowers to 1 in. long held in tiers at top of 1–2-ft.-tall, somewhat hairy stems. Upper lip of flower white, lower one rose or violet. Leaves oblong, to 2 in. long. Gives light, dainty effect in front of borders, scattered under deciduous trees, or as ground cover for bulbs. Sow seed in place in fall or spring in rich, moist soil. Self-sows under favorable conditions.

Collinsia heterophylla

COLOCASIA esculenta *(Caladium esculentum)*. *Araceae.* TARO, ELEPHANT'S EAR. Perennial with tuberous roots. Evergreen only in Zones 23, 24 (tops freeze at 30°F.); grows as herbaceous perennial in Zones 13, 16–22 where tubers may be left in ground. In Zones 1–12, 14, 15, grow in containers or lift and store tubers over winter. Native to tropical Asia and Polynesia. Fast growing to 6 ft. Mammoth, heart-shaped, gray green leaves add lush effect to any tropical planting within one season. Flowers resemble giant callas but are seldom seen. Effective with tree ferns, araliads, ginger, strelitzia. Handsome in large tub, raised beds, near swimming pools.

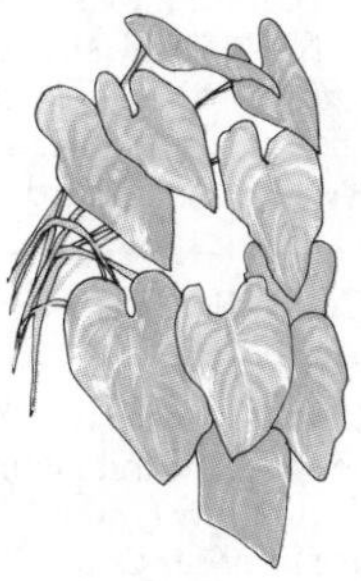

Colocasia esculenta

Thrives in warm filtered shade with protection from wind, which tears leaves. Plant tubers in spring in rich, moist soil. Give lots of water; feed lightly once a month in growing season.

The starchy roots are a staple food in Hawaii and the Pacific area in general, and taro is occasionally grown for food production by Polynesian people in California.

COLONIAL BENT. See *Agrostis tenuis.*

COLUMBINE. See *Aquilegia.*

COLUMNEA. *Gesneriaceae.* House plants. Some shrubby, but most arching or trailing. Attractive foliage and showy flowers in shades of red, orange, and yellow. Related to African violets although they don't look it; require similar care, although they prefer slightly cooler temperatures and aren't as touchy about water. Paired, shiny leaves; long, tubular flowers with flared mouths.

There are many named varieties, all good looking, and many species from Central and South America. Easiest to find is:

C. 'Stavanger'. NORSE FIRE PLANT. Trailing stems can reach several feet if plant is grown in hanging basket. Neat pairs of rounded, shiny leaves, ½ in. across; 3–4-in.-long red flowers.

Columnea 'Stavanger'

C

COMAROSTAPHYLIS diversifolia. *Ericaceae.* SUMMER HOLLY. Evergreen shrub or small tree. Zones 7–9, 14–24. Native to coastal southern California and Baja California. A handsome plant that deserves wider use. Related to manzanita. Rather formal growth to 6 ft. as shrub, 18 ft. as small tree. Gray bark. Leathery, 1–3-in.-long leaves, shiny dark green above, white and hairy beneath, margins inrolled. (Variety *C. d. planifolia* has flat leaves.) Small, white, manzanitalike flowers in April–May, followed by clusters of red, warty berries similar to those of madrone. Adaptable to many situations, but grows best in half shade with some moisture, good drainage.

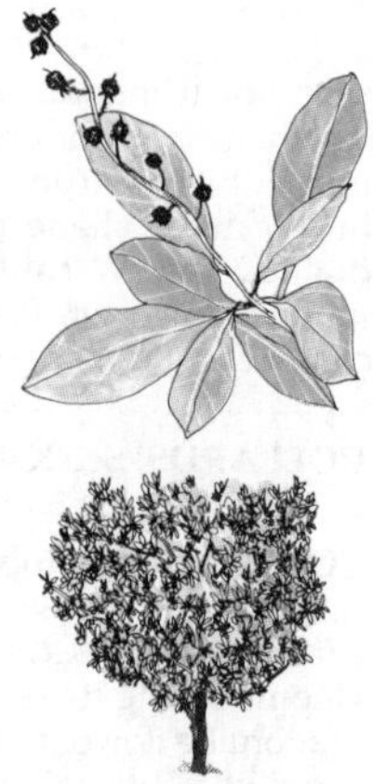

Comarostaphylis diversifolia

COMBRETUM fruticosum. *Combretaceae.* Zones 15–24. Evergreen vine. Moderate to slow growth to 10 ft. tall, 15 ft. wide in 10 years. Can be pinched to form a shrub, or staked to form a small tree. Paired, drooping, bright green, oval leaves 2–4 in. long. Flowers are bottlebrush clusters 4 in. long, up to 2 in. wide; they open greenish yellow and gradually turn bright orange. All colors are present during 6-week bloom period in September, October.

Needs full sun and average soil, water, and feeding. Tie stems to wall or weave through a trellis. Hardy to 26°F., but may lose leaves in hard frost.

Combretum fruticosum

COMFREY. See *Symphytum officinale.*

Commelinaceae. The spiderwort family is composed of herbaceous perennials, often fleshy, mostly tropical or subtropical. Wandering Jew (*Tradescantia* and *Zebrina*) and spiderwort (*Trandescantia*) are familiar examples. Flowers generally have 3 rounded petals.

COMPASS BARREL CACTUS. See *Ferocactus acanthodes.*

Compositae. The sunflower or daisy family, one of the largest plant families, is characterized by flowers borne in tight clusters (heads). In the most familiar form, these heads contain 2 types of flowers—small, tightly clustered *disk flowers* in the center of the head, and larger, strap-shaped *ray flowers* around the edge. The sunflower is a familiar example. The family is often called *Asteraceae.*

CONFEDERATE ROSE. See *Hibiscus mutabilis.*

CONSOLIDA ambigua *(Delphinium ajacis).* *Ranunculaceae.* LARKSPUR, ANNUAL DELPHINIUM. All Zones. Native to southern Europe. Upright, 1–5 ft. tall, with deeply cut leaves; blossom spikes densely set with 1–1½-in.-wide flowers (most are double) in white, blue-and-white, or shades of blue, lilac, pink, rose, salmon, carmine. Best bloom in cooler spring and early summer months. Giant Imperial strain has many 4–5-ft. vertical stalks compactly placed. Regal strain has 4–5-ft., base-branching stems, thick spikes of large flowers similar to perennial delphiniums. Super Imperial strain is base branching, has large flowers in 1½-ft., cone-shaped spikes. Steeplechase is base branching, has biggest double flowers on 4–5-ft. spikes; heat resistant. Sow seed where plants are to grow; fall planting is best except in heavy, slow-draining soils. Cover seed with ⅛ in. soil; thin plants to avoid crowding, get biggest flowers.

Consolida ambigua

CONVALLARIA majalis. *Liliaceae.* LILY-OF-THE-VALLEY. Perennial grown from pip (upright small rootstock). Zones 1–7, 14–20. Small, fragrant, drooping, waxy white, bell-shaped, spring-blooming flowers on 6–8-in. stems rising above 2 broad basal leaves. Ground cover in partial shade; carpet between camellias, rhododendrons, pieris, under deciduous trees or high-branching, not-too-dense evergreen trees.

Convallaria majalis

Plant clumps or single pips in November, December in Zones 4–7, 14–20; in September, October in Zones 1–3. Give rich soil with ample humus. Average water. Set clumps 1–2 ft. apart, single pips 4–5 in. apart, 1½ in. deep. Cover yearly with leaf mold, peat moss, or ground bark. Large, prechilled forcing pips, available in December, January (even in mild-climate areas), can be potted for bloom indoors. After bloom, plunge pots in ground in cool, shaded area. When dormant, either remove plants from pots and plant in garden, or wash soil off pips, place in plastic bags, and store in vegetable compartment of refrigerator until December or January; at this time, either pot (as before, for bloom indoors) or plant out in permanent spot in garden. All parts of the plant are poisonous.

Convolvulaceae. The morning glory family contains climbing or trailing plants, usually with funnel-shaped flowers. Morning glories (*Convolvulus* and *Ipomoea*) are typical examples.

CONVOLVULUS. *Convolvulaceae.* Evergreen shrub, evergreen perennial, and annual. All have funnel-shaped flowers much like morning glories. In fact, common vining morning glories (*Ipomoea*) are sometimes sold as *Convolvulus.*

Convolvulus cneorum

C. cneorum. BUSH MORNING GLORY. Evergreen shrub. Marginal Zones 5, 6; best Zones 7–9, 12–24. Native to southern Europe. Rapid growing to 2–4 ft. and as wide. Silky-smooth, silvery gray, lance-shaped leaves 1–2½ in. long. White or pink-tinted morning glories with yellow throats open from pink buds, May–September. Compact and fully flowered if grown in full sun; looser habit with more scattered flowers in light shade. Give light soil and fast drainage. Avoid planting where it will get frequent sprinklings. Prune severely to renew plant; can get leggy if left alone. Fire retardant if flourishing.

C. mauritanicus. GROUND MORNING GLORY. Evergreen perennial. Zones 4–9, 12–24. Native to Africa. Grows 1–2 ft. high with branches trailing to spread of 3 ft. or more. Soft, hairy, gray green, roundish leaves ½–1½ in. long. Flowers lavender blue, 1–2 in. wide, June–November. Grows well in light, gravelly soil with good drainage, but will take clay soil if not overwatered. Full sun. Tends to become woody; prevent by trimming in late winter. Use on dry banks as ground cover (plant 3 ft. apart), or group with sunroses (*Helianthemum*) or cerastium.

C. tricolor. DWARF MORNING GLORY. Summer annual. Native to southern Europe. Bushy, branching, somewhat trailing plants to 1 ft. high and 2 ft. wide. Small, narrow leaves. Flowers, 1½ in. across, variable in color but usually blue with yellow throat. Nick tough seed coats with knife and plant in place when soil has warmed up. Needs sun and warmth; blooms best when kept on dry side. Use as edging, against low trellis, or at top of wall. 'Blue Flash' and Rainbow Flash (mixed colors) grow 6 in. tall.

COPPER LEAF. See *Acalypha wilkesiana.*

COPROSMA. *Rubiaceae.* Evergreen shrubs. Native to New Zealand. Drought tolerant once established.

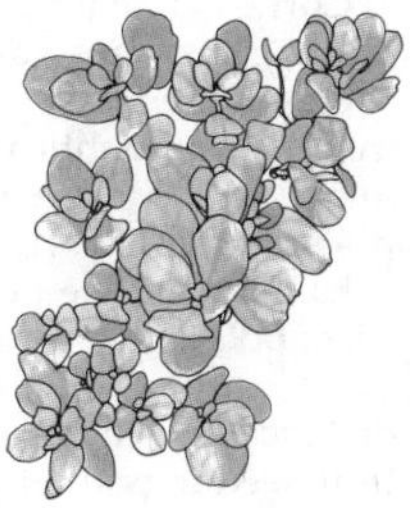

Coprosma repens

C. 'Coppershine'. Zones 8, 9, 14–17, 21–24. Rounded shrub to 6 ft. with equal spread; fast growing while young. Leaves 1–1¾ in. long, half as wide, leathery, polished bright green heavily shaded coppery brown; new growth even more heavily tinted, and entire plant bright copper in winter. Good medium-sized hedge, screen.

C. kirkii. Zones 8, 9, 14–17, 21–24. Spreading shrub to 2–3 ft. high or nearly prostrate, with long, straight stems slanting outward from base. Leaves, closely set on stems, are yellow green, small (½–1 in. long), narrow. Tolerant of sun or partial shade; grows in wide range of soils. Prune regularly to keep plants dense. Tough, medium-height ground cover or bank cover. Tolerates sea wind, salt spray. Will control erosion.

C. pumila. Zones 8, 9, 14–24. Spreading, mounding shrub to 2–2½ ft. tall, eventually 8 ft. wide. Leaves bright shining green, roundish oval, to ¾ in. long. Plant 2–2½ ft. apart for ground cover in 3 years. Prune out upwardly growing branches. Tolerates most soils, much drought or heavy watering. 'Verde Vista' is best cutting-grown selection.

C. repens *(C. baueri).* MIRROR PLANT. Zones 15–17, 21–24. Rapid growth to 10 ft. with 6-ft. spread. Open, straggly shrub if neglected but beautiful plant when cared for. You can't imagine shinier, glossier leaves: they're dark to light green, 3 in. long, oval or oblong. Inconspicuous greenish or white flowers often followed by small yellow or orange fruit. Variety 'Variegata' has leaves blotched with yellowish green. Variety 'Argentea' is blotched with white.

Two prunings a year will keep it dense and at any height desired. Where shrub receives ocean wind, no pruning is necessary. Except in beach areas, give it part shade; water generously. Use as hedge, screen, wall shrub, informal espalier.

'Marble Queen' grows only 2–3 ft. tall, has striking white variegation.

CORAL BELLS. See *Heuchera sanguinea.*

CORAL BERRY. See *Symphoricarpos orbiculatus.*

CORAL GUM. See *Eucalyptus torquata.*

CORAL TREE. See *Erythrina.*

CORAL VINE. See *Antigonon leptopus.*

CORDIA boissieri. *Boraginaceae.* Zones 8–24. Evergreen shrub or small tree. Native to Texas and Mexico; adapted to the heat and drought of low and intermediate deserts. Hardy to 20°F., but loses leaves in severe frost. Oval, grayish green, rough-surfaced leaves to 5 in. long. White flowers with yellow throats, 2½ in. wide, in clusters April–May and continuing over long season. May rebloom in fall.

Cordia boissieri

Can be kept pruned as a low (3–5-ft.) shrub or allowed to reach 8–10 ft. With training, can be made into a small tree. Grow in sun or light shade. Give deep watering every 7–10 days in summer.

CORDYLINE. *Agavaceae.* Evergreen palmlike shrubs or trees. (Often sold as *Dracaena;* for true *Dracaena,* see that entry.) Woody plants with swordlike leaves, related to yuccas and agaves but usually ranked with palms in nurseries and in landscape. Like moisture. Good next to swimming pools.

Cordyline australis

C. australis *(Dracaena australis).* Zones 5, 8–11, 14–24. In youth, fountain of 3-ft.-long, narrow (2–5-in.-wide), swordlike leaves. Upper leaves are erect; lower leaves arch and droop. In maturity, 20–30-ft. tree, branching high on trunk, rather stiff (like Joshua tree). Fragrant, ¼-in. flowers in late spring are carried in long, branching clusters.

For more graceful plant, cut back when young to force multiple trunks. Or plant in clumps of 6–8; each year, cut a few back to ground until all develop multiple trunks. Hardiest of cordylines, to 15°F. or lower. Takes almost any soil but grows fastest in soil deep enough for big, carrotlike root. Drought tolerant. Used for tropical effects; with boulders and gravel for desert look; on patio or terrace where there's room for it. Useful near seashore.

C. a. 'Atropurpurea'. BRONZE DRACAENA. Like the above, but with bronzy red foliage. Slower growth. Combine with gray or warm yellowish green to bring out color.

C. indivisa. BLUE DRACAENA. Zones 16, 17, 20–24. Trunk to 25 ft., topped with crown of rather stiff, huge leaves (6 ft. long, 6 in. wide). White flowers in 4-ft.-long clusters. Plant in groups of varying heights. Hardy to 26°F. Tolerates drought and seaside conditions.

C. stricta. Zones 13, 16, 17, 20–24. Slender stems clustered at base or branching low with branches quite erect. Swordlike, 2-ft.-long leaves are dark green with hint of purple. Lavender flowers in large, branched clusters, very decorative in spring. Will grow to 15 ft., but can be kept lower by cutting tall canes to ground. New canes replace them. Long cuttings stuck in ground will root quickly. Hardy to 26°F. Needs shade except near coast. Takes desert heat with ample water in shade. Fine container plant indoors or out; good for tall, tropical-looking background in narrow, shaded areas, lanais, or side gardens.

C. terminalis. TI. Outdoors Zones 21–24, house plant elsewhere. Plants are usually started from "logs"—sections of stem imported from Hawaii. Lay short lengths in peat moss–sand mixture, covering about ½ their diameter. Keep moist. When shoots grow out and root, cut them off and pot them. Take ordinary indoor care; tolerate low light intensity. Plant has many named forms with red, yellow, or variegated leaves. White, foot-long flower clusters. Outdoors in Hawaii, it's 10-ft. plant with 2½-ft.-long, 5-in.-wide leaves; usually much smaller when grown indoors. Outdoors in southern California, reaches 6–8 ft. in special, frost-free locations where soil stays warm.

COREOPSIS. *Compositae.* Annuals and perennials. Easily grown members of sunflower family yielding profusion of yellow, orange, maroon, or reddish flowers from late spring to fall. Remove old flowers from all types to prolong bloom. Both annual and perennial kinds are easy to propagate—annuals from seed sown in place (full sun) or in flats, perennials from seed or division of root crown. Tend to self-sow; seeds attract birds. Established plants can thrive on very little water.

Coreopsis tinctoria

C. auriculata 'Nana'. Perennial. Evergreen to semievergreen in Zones 17–24; deciduous in Zones 1–16. Makes 5–6-in.-high mat of 2–5-in.-long leaves. Under ideal conditions, it will spread by stolons to form 2-ft.-broad clump in a year. Bright orange yellow flower heads, 1–2½ in. wide, rise well above foliage. Long and profuse blooming season from spring to fall if you remove faded flowers. Best used in foreground of taller plants, in border, or as edging.

(Continued on next page)

C. gigantea. Perennial. Zones 16, 17, 21–24. Native to coastal southern California, Baja California. Thick, succulent trunks 3 ft. tall (rarely to 10 ft.) hold a few branches tipped with clusters of fernlike leaves. Clusters of 3-in. yellow daisies appear in spring. Showy in seaside plant collection; rarely sold in nurseries.

C. grandiflora. COREOPSIS. Perennial. All Zones. Grows 1–2 ft. high, spreading to 3 ft.; leaves narrow, dark green, 3–5 lobed. Bright yellow, 2½–3-in.-wide flowers bloom all summer, carried on long slender stems high above foliage. Variety 'Sunburst' has large, semidouble flowers; it will bloom the first year from seed sown early in spring, then spread by self-sowing.

C. lanceolata. COREOPSIS. Perennial. All Zones. Grows 1–2 ft. high. Leaves somewhat hairy, narrow, mostly in tuft near base. Flower heads 1½–2 in. across, yellow, on pale green stems. Some leaves on lower stem have a few lobes. When well established, will persist year after year. Excellent cut flower.

C. maritima. Perennial. Zones 14–24. Native to coast of southern California. Sometimes called sea dahlia. Grows 1–3 ft. high from tuberous tap root. Stems hollow. Leaves somewhat succulent, divided into very narrow lobes. Clear yellow, 2½–4-in. flower heads on 9–12-in.-long stems bloom in spring. Borders, naturalizing, striking cut flowers.

C. tinctoria. ANNUAL COREOPSIS, CALLIOPSIS. Annual. All Zones. Slender, upright, 1½– 3 ft. tall with wiry stems; much like cosmos in growth habit. Leaves and stems smooth. Flowers similar to perennial coreopsis, in yellow, orange, maroon, bronze, and reddish, banded with contrasting colors; purple brown centers. Dwarf and double varieties. Sow seed in place in full sun and dryish soil.

C. verticillata. Perennial. Zones 14–24. Plant is 2½–3 ft. tall, half as broad. Many erect or slightly leaning stems carry many whorls of finely divided, very narrow leaves. At top are 2-in., bright yellow daisies, freely borne over long summer and autumn season. One of the most tolerant of drought, neglect. 'Moonbeam', 1½–2 ft. tall, has pale yellow flowers; 'Zagreb', 1 ft. tall, has golden yellow flowers.

CORIANDER. See *Coriandrum sativum*.

CORIANDRUM sativum. *Umbelliferae.* CORIANDER, CHINESE PARSLEY, CILANTRO. Annual herb. All Zones in conditions noted below. Grows 12–15 in. high. Delicate fernlike foliage; flat clusters of pinkish white flowers. Aromatic seeds crushed before use as seasoning for sausage, beans, stews, cookies, wines. Young leaves used in salads, soups, poultry recipes, and variety of Mexican and Chinese dishes. Grow in good, well-drained soil, full sun. Start from seed (including coriander seed sold in grocery stores); grows quickly, self-sows.

Coriandrum sativum

CORN. *Gramineae.* Annual. All Zones in conditions noted below. Sweet corn is the one cereal crop that home gardeners are likely to grow; it requires considerable space, but is still well worth growing. Once most sweet corn is picked, its sugar changes to starch very quickly; only by rushing ears from garden direct to boiling water can you capture full sweetness. Supersweet varieties of corn are actually sweeter than standard kinds, and maintain their sweetness longer after harvest because of a gene that increases the quantity of sugar and slows its conversion to starch. A very few people find these varieties too sweet.

Sweet Corn

Corn needs heat, but suitable early hybrid varieties will grow even in cool-summer areas of the Northwest.

Corn is widely adapted but grows best in deep, rich soils; good drainage is important. Give full sun. Sow seed 2 weeks after average date of last frost, and make 3 or 4 more plantings at 2-week intervals; or plant early, midseason, and late varieties. Plant corn in blocks of short rows rather than stringing out single long rows; pollination is by wind, and unless good supply of pollen falls on silks, ears will be poorly filled. Don't plant popcorn near sweet corn; pollen of one kind can affect characteristics of other. For the same reason, some supersweet varieties have to be grown at a distance from other varieties. Plant either in rows 3 ft. apart and thin seedlings to stand 1 ft. apart, or plant in "hills" (actually clumps) 3 ft. apart each way. Place 6 or 7 seeds in each hill and thin to 3 strongest plants. Give plants ample water and one feeding when stalks are 7–8 in. tall. Make certain that you apply good deep watering that thoroughly wets entire root zone just as tassel emerges from stalk; repeat again when silk forms. Don't remove suckers that appear. Check carefully when ears are plump and silk has withered; pull back husks and try popping a grain with your thumb. Generally, corn is ready to eat 3 weeks after silks first appear. Kernels should squirt milky juice; watery juice means that corn is immature. Doughy consistency indicates overmaturity. Elderly home-grown sweet corn is no better than market sweet corn.

Corn earworm is principal insect pest. Control it by spraying or dusting sevin directly on silk clusters when silks first become visible. Or squirt silks with mixture of 1 teaspoon malathion in ½ pint mineral oil, applying about ½ teaspoon of the mixture on each cluster of silks with a medicine dropper or oil can. Make 3 or 4 applications at 3–4-day intervals.

Ornamental Corn

Ornamental corn. Annual. Some kinds of corn are grown for beauty of shelled ears rather than for eating qualities. Calico, Indian, Squaw, and rainbow corn are among names given to strains which have brightly colored grains—red, brown, blue, gray, black, yellow, and many mixtures of these colors. Grow like sweet corn, but let ears ripen fully; silks will be withered, husks turning straw color, and kernels firm. Cut ear from plant, including 1½ in. of stalk below ear; pull back husks (leave attached to ears) and dry thoroughly. Grow well away from late sweet corn; pollen can affect flavor of the latter.

Zea mays japonica includes several kinds of corn grown for ornamental foliage; one occasionally sold is 'Gracilis', a dwarf corn with bright green leaves striped white.

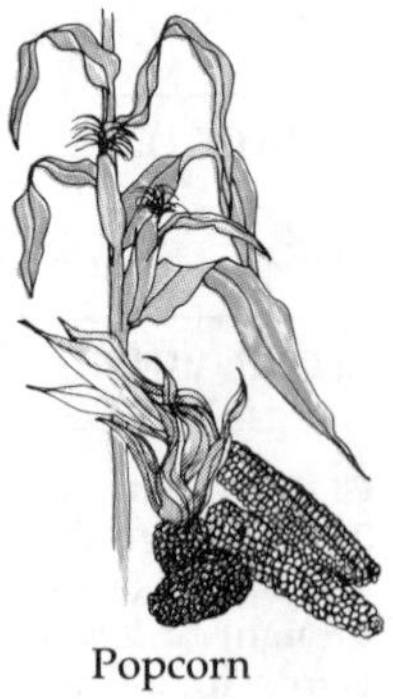

Popcorn

Popcorn. Annual. Grow and harvest popcorn just like ornamental corn described above. When ears are thoroughly dry, rub kernels off cobs and store in dry place. White and yellow popcorn resemble other corn in appearance. Strawberry popcorn, grown either for popping or for its ornamental value, has stubby, fat ears packed with red, strawberrylike kernels.

Cornaceae. The dogwood family consists of trees and shrubs with clustered inconspicuous flowers (sometimes surrounded by showy bracts) and berrylike fruit. *Aucuba* and *Cornus* are examples.

CORNELIAN CHERRY. See *Cornus mas*.

CORNFLOWER. See *Centaurea cyanus*.

CORN PLANT. See *Dracaena fragrans*.

CORNUS. *Cornaceae.* DOGWOOD. Deciduous (except where noted) shrubs or trees (one's a ground cover perennial). All offer attractive foliage and flowers; some are spectacular in fruit and winter bark. Need ample water.

Cornus florida

C. alba. TATARIAN DOGWOOD. Shrub. Zones 1–9, 14–24. In cold-winter areas, its bare, blood red twigs are colorful against snow. Upright to about 10 ft. high; wide spreading, eventually producing thicket of many stems. Branches densely clothed with 2½–5-in.-long leaves to 2½ in. wide, deep, rich green above, lighter beneath; red in fall. Small, fragrant, creamy white flowers in 1–2-in.-wide, flattish clusters in April, May. Bluish white to whitish small fruits. Variety 'Argenteomarginata' (C. 'Elegantissima') has showy green and white leaves on red stems. Best in shade.

C. a. 'Sibirica'. SIBERIAN DOGWOOD. Less rampant than species; grows to about 7 ft. high with 5-ft. spread. Gleaming coral red branches in winter. Tolerates shade.

In both *C. alba* and *C. a.* 'Sibirica', new wood is brightest; cut back in spring to force new growth.

C. alternifolia. PAGODA DOGWOOD. Shrub or small tree. Zones 1–6. Multitrunked, to 20 ft. high. Strong horizontal branching pattern makes attractive winter silhouette. Light green leaves turn red in fall. Small clusters of creamy spring flowers are not showy. Blue black fruit follows. Tolerates shade.

C. canadensis. BUNCHBERRY. Deciduous carpet plant. Zones 1–7. Difficult but possible in Zones 8, 9, 14–16. Native northern California to Alaska and eastward. It's difficult to believe this 6–9-in. perennial is related to dogwoods when you see it under trees by lakes and streams in Northwest. Creeping rootstocks send up stems topped by whorls of 4–6 oval or roundish, 1–2-in.-long leaves; deep rich green, they turn yellow in fall, die down in winter.

Plants bloom in May or June, bearing small, compact clusters of tiny flowers surrounded by (usually) 4 oval, ½–¾-in.-long, pure white bracts. Clusters of small, shiny, bright red fruit in August and September.

For cool, moist climates, in acid soil with generous amounts of humus or rotten wood. Considered hard to establish, but when transplanted with piece of rotten log with bark attached, it establishes readily. Excellent companion plant for rhododendrons, ferns, trilliums, lilies.

C. capitata. EVERGREEN DOGWOOD. Big shrub or small tree. Zones 8, 9, 14–20. From Himalayas. Hardy to 15°F. Not reliably evergreen in cold weather. In mild winters, it often loses half its leaves. Moderate growth to 20–30 ft. high, eventually with equal spread. Green to grayish green, 2–4-in.-long by ¾–1¾-in.-wide leaves; some turn red or purplish in fall.

Unless grown from cuttings, trees don't flower until about 8–10 years old, but when they do they are delightful. Small flower cluster is surrounded by 4–6 creamy to pale yellow, 1½–2-in.-long bracts in May and June. Large, fleshy, reddish purple fruit in October and November can be a litter problem, though birds may do some cleaning up for you.

C. controversa. GIANT DOGWOOD. Tree. Zones 3–9, 14, 18, 19. From the Orient. Hardy to 5°F. Resembles big shrubby dogwoods in leaves, flowers, and fruit, but grows rapidly into magnificent 40–60-ft. tree with picturesque horizontal branches. Luxuriant 3–6-in.-long, oval leaves, 2–3 in. wide, are dark green above, silvery green beneath, glowing red in fall. Creamy white flowers are not spectacular, but so abundant in May they give good show. They form in fluffy, flattish clusters 3–7 in. wide. Shiny, bluish black, ½-in.-wide fruit, enjoyed by birds, ripens in August and September.

Locate plants in full sun for most flowers and best autumn color. Keep soil moist.

C. 'Eddie's White Wonder'. Tree. Zones 2–9, 14–20. Hybrid between *C. florida* and *C. nuttallii;* taller, more erect than former, twiggier than latter. Blooms in May, with 4- or 5-bracted flower clusters. Easier to transplant than western native *C. nuttallii.*

C. florida. FLOWERING DOGWOOD, EASTERN DOGWOOD. Tree. Zones 1–9, 14–16. Sometimes succeeds in southern California if given azalea conditions. Native to eastern U.S. To 20 ft. high. Most commonly planted flowering dogwood in Northwest and mountain areas, where it's easy to grow and much a part of spring flower display. Generally performs best in high shade; screen from western sun.

In its horizontal branching pattern, it somewhat resembles our western native, *C. nuttallii,* but gray twigs at branch ends tend to be upright. It usually has shorter trunk. Small flower clusters are surrounded by 4 roundish, 2–4-in.-wide, white bracts with notched tips. Bracts form in autumn; in harsh, dry winters, tips may wither, preventing inflorescence from opening fully. Flowers almost cover tree in May before leaves expand. Oval, 2–6-in.-long by 2½-in.-wide leaves are bright green above, lighter beneath; they turn glowing red before they fall. Clusters of small, oval, scarlet fruit last into winter or until birds eat them.

C. f. 'Cherokee Chief'. Deep rosy red bracts that are paler at base.

C. f. 'Cherokee Princess'. Gives unusually heavy display of white blooms.

C. f. 'Cloud Nine'. Blooms young and heavily. Tolerates southern California heat and lack of winter chill better than other varieties. Blooms better in cold climates than other kinds of *C. florida.*

C. f. 'Pendula'. Drooping branches give it weeping look.

C. f. 'Pink Flame'. Leaves green and cream, deepening to dark green and red. Bracts pink.

C. f. 'Rainbow'. Leaves strongly marked bright yellow on green. Heavy bloomer, large bracts.

C. f. 'Rubra'. Long-time favorite for its pink or rose bracts.

C. f. 'Welchii'. TRICOLOR DOGWOOD. Best known for its variegated, 4-in.-long leaves of creamy white, pink, deep rose, and green throughout spring and summer; leaves turn deep rose to almost red in fall. Rather inconspicuous pinkish to white bracts are not profuse. Does best with some shade.

C. kousa. KOUSA DOGWOOD. Big shrub or small tree. Zones 3–9, 14, 15, 18, 19. Native to Japan and Korea. Later blooming (June–July) than other flowering dogwoods. Big multistemmed shrub or (with training) small tree to 20 ft. or higher. Delicate limb structure and spreading, dense horizontal growth habit. Lustrous, medium green leaves, 4 in. long, have rusty brown hairs at base of veins on undersurface. Yellow and scarlet fall color.

Cornus kousa

Flowers along tops of branches show above leaves. Creamy white, slender-pointed, 2–3-in.-long, rather narrow bracts surround flower cluster, turn pink along edges. In October, red fruit hangs below branches like big strawberries. 'Milky Way' is more floriferous and has pure white bracts.

C. k. chinensis. Native to China, has larger leaves and larger bracts.

C. mas. CORNELIAN CHERRY. Shrub or tree. Zones 1–6. Native to southern Europe and Orient. One of earliest dogwoods to bloom, it shows mass of clustered small yellow blossoms on bare twigs in February and March. It's usually an airy, twiggy shrub but can be trained as 15–20-ft. small tree. Oval leaves, 2–4 in. long, shiny green turning to yellow; some forms turn red in fall. Autumn color is enhanced by clusters of bright scarlet, ¾-in.-long fruit which hangs on from September until birds get it. Fruit is edible and is used in making preserves. Withstands subzero temperatures. Tolerates alkaline soils.

C. nuttallii. PACIFIC DOGWOOD, WESTERN DOGWOOD. Tree. Zones 2–9, 14–20. Native to Pacific Northwest and northern California. One of our most spectacular natives when it wears its gleaming white bracts on bare branches in April or May. Often there's a second flowering with leaves in September. Unfortunately, it's not as easy to grow in gardens as Eastern dogwood (*C. florida*). It reacts unfavorably to routine garden watering, fertilizing, pruning; injury to its tender bark provides entrance for insects and diseases. But if you give plants exceptionally good drainage, infrequent summer watering, and plant under high-branching trees so bark will not sunburn, you have a chance of success.

Anthracnose causes blotched leaves. Prevention is best treatment; prune out cankered twigs and rake up and destroy infected fallen leaves. Spraying with benomyl in spring and throughout wet weather can help.

Where adapted, this tree will grow to 50 ft. or taller with 20-ft. spread, with one trunk or several. Gray-barked branches grow in pleasing horizontal pattern, attractive in winter. Oval, 3–5-in.-long leaves are rich green above, grayish green beneath; they turn to beautiful yellows, pinks, and reds in fall. The 4–8 bracts are 2–3 in. long, roundish, rounded or pointed at tips, white or tinged with pink. Decorative red to orange red fruit in buttonlike clusters forms in fall.

C. n. 'Colrigo Giant' (often sold as 'Corigo Giant'). Low-branching but erect habit, vigorous, heavy trunked, with profusion of 6-in. flower heads. Named for Columbia River Gorge, where parent plant was found.

C. n. 'Goldspot'. Leaves splashed with creamy yellow. Blooms when only 2 ft. tall. Bracts are larger than those of species. Long (2-month) flowering season, often with some fall bloom.

C. sanguinea. BLOODTWIG DOGWOOD. Shrub. Zones 1–7. Big show comes in fall with dark blood red foliage and in winter with bare, purplish to dark red twigs and branches. Prune severely in spring to produce new branches and twigs for winter color. Grows as big multistemmed shrub to 12 ft. high, about 8 ft. wide. Dark green leaves 1½–3 in. long. June flowers are greenish white in 2-in.-wide clusters. Black fruit.

C. stolonifera *(C. sericea).* REDTWIG DOGWOOD, RED-OSIER DOGWOOD. Shrub. Zones 1–9, 14–21. Native to moist places, northern California to Alaska and eastward. Another dogwood with brilliant show of red fall color and bright red winter twigs. Not only thrives in coldest mountain areas of West, but throughout California—even intermediate valleys of southern California if given frequent watering. Grows rapidly as big multistemmed shrub to 15 ft. or more high. Spreads widely by creeping underground stems and rooting branches. Tolerates shade. To control, use a spade to cut off roots that have gone too far. Cut off branches that touch ground. Small, creamy white flowers in 2-in.-wide clusters appear among leaves (oval, 1½–2½ in. long, fresh deep green in color) throughout the summer months and into fall. Fruit is white or bluish.

Use this adaptable native as a space filler on moist ground or plant along property line as a screen.

C. s. baileyi. Grows 6–8 ft. tall; exceptionally bright red twigs in winter. *C. s. coloradensis*, COLORADO REDTWIG, is shorter (5–6 ft.) and twigs are not such a bright red.

C. s. 'Flaviramea'. YELLOWTWIG DOGWOOD. Has yellow twigs and branches.

C. s. 'Kelseyi' (*C. s.* 'Nana'). Dwarf seldom over 1½ ft. tall. Bright red stems.

COROKIA cotoneaster. *Cornaceae.* Evergreen shrub. Zones 4–24. Native to New Zealand. Slow growing to 10 ft., but usually seen as 2–4-ft. plant in container. Intricate branch pattern made up of many slim, contorted, interlaced, nearly black branches. Sparse foliage; leaves ¾ in. long, dark glossy green above, white underneath. Tiny, starlike, ½-in., yellow flowers in spring, followed by small orange fruits on older plants. Sun or part shade, average water. Tolerates alkaline soil, seaside conditions. Thrives in container with fast-draining mix. Night lighting from beneath emphasizes bizarre zigzag branch pattern, which can be further emphasized by pruning.

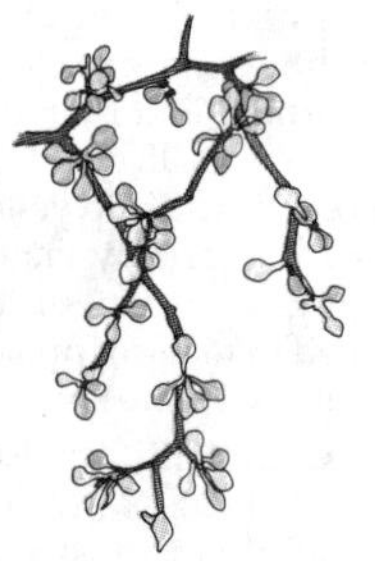

Corokia cotoneaster

CORONILLA varia. *Leguminosae.* CROWN VETCH. Perennial. All Zones. Related to peas, beans, and clovers. Creeping roots and rhizomes make it tenacious ground cover with straggling stems to 2 ft. Leaves made up of 11–25 oval leaflets, ½–¾ in. long. Lavender pink flowers in 1-in. clusters soon become bundles of brown, slender, fingerlike seed pods. Goes dormant and looks ratty during coldest weather. Tolerates shade; thrives in full sun. In spring, mow it, feed and water several times, and it will make a lush green summer cover. Too invasive and rank for flower beds. Use for covering cut banks and remote places, controlling erosion. Once established, difficult to eliminate. Variety 'Penngift' is widely sold in cold-winter climates.

Coronilla varia

CORREA. *Rutaceae.* AUSTRALIAN FUCHSIA. Evergreen shrubs. Successful in Zones 5, 6 when winters aren't too cold (hardy to about 20°F.); generally successful Zones 14–24. Flower form may suggest fuchsia, but in all other ways, these plants are far from fuchsialike. Low to medium height, usually dense and spreading. Leaves small (to 1 in.), roundish, densely felted underneath; shrubs have a gray or gray green color that contrasts subtly with other grays and distinctly with dark greens. All except summer-flowering *C. alba* are valued for their long winter flowering season, normally November–April. Small (½–¾-in.) flowers are individually handsome but not showy; they hang down along branches like small bells.

Correa pulchella

Correas do well in poor, even rocky soil, but must have fast drainage. Easy to kill with kindness—overwatering and overfeeding. Use as ground covers on banks or slopes. Attractive in large containers placed where flowers can be enjoyed close up. Generally thought to do best in full sun in coastal areas, partial shade inland, but many can be seen in full sun, all climates. Should not get reflected heat from wall or paving.

C. alba. To 4 ft., with arching branches. White flowers bloom in summer.

C. backhousiana. (Often sold as *C. magnifica.*) More successful in southern California than *C. pulchella.* Growth habit upright and rather sprawling to 4–5 ft. and as wide. Flowers chartreuse.

C. 'Carmine Bells'. Low-growing (2-ft.), broad plant with deep red flowers.

C. harrisii. To 2½ ft. high and more compact than other correas. Flowers beautiful clear red.

C. 'Ivory Bells'. Resembles 'Carmine Bells' but with creamy white flowers.

C. pulchella. Most widely grown correa in northern California. To 2–2½ ft. high, spreading as wide as 8 ft. Leaves green above, gray green below. Light pink flowers.

CORTADERIA selloana. *Gramineae.* PAMPAS GRASS. Evergreen giant ornamental grass. Zones 4–24. Deciduous (roots hardy) in Zones 2, 3. Native to Argentina. Very fast growing in rich soil in mild climates; from gallon-can size to 8 ft. in one season. Established, may reach 20 ft. in height. Each plant is a fountain of saw-toothed, grassy leaves above which, in late summer, rise long stalks bearing 1–3-ft., white to chamois or pink flower plumes.

Will grow in any soil from driest to wettest, acid to alkaline. Takes hot dry winds of deserts and fog winds of coast. Its willingness to grow under rough conditions gives it value in large bank planting and as first

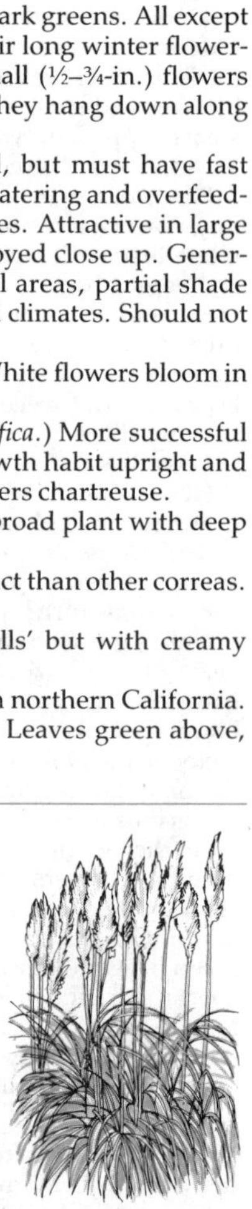

Cortaderia selloana

line of defense in wide windbreak. But sheer bulk of plant can become problem in small gardens, and it's not easy to reduce in size. Roots and stems are tough and woody, and leaf edges are like sharp saws.

Note: A similar grass, *C. jubata,* can become a serious weed in areas where winters are mild. It seeds itself freely and resists summer drought well enough to crowd out many native plants. Leaves are much shorter than those of *C. selloana,* increasing distance between foliage mass and flowering plumes, and plant bears fewer plumes than *C. selloana.* Still, it looks enough like pampas grass to tempt amateur flower arrangers to gather plumes; seeds from these might establish plants in the neighborhood. Best bet: grub out volunteer pampas grass seedlings when they appear.

CORYDALIS. *Fumariaceae.* Perennials. Zones 4–9, 14–24. Handsome clumps of dainty divided leaves similar to those of bleeding heart (to which it is closely related) or maidenhair fern. Clusters of small, spurred flowers, usually yellow. Plant in rich, moist soil, partial shade. Effective in rock crevices, in open woodland, near pool or streamside. Combine with ferns, columbine, bleeding heart, primroses. Divide clumps or sow seed in spring or fall. Plants self-sow in garden.

Corydalis lutea

C. cheilanthifolia. Hardy Chinese native, 8–10 in. high with fernlike green foliage. Clusters of yellow, ½-in.-long flowers in May and June.

C. lutea. Native to southern Europe. To 15 in. tall. Masses of gray green foliage on many stems. Golden yellow, ¾-in.-long, short-spurred flowers throughout summer.

CORYLOPSIS. *Hamamelidaceae.* WINTER HAZEL. Deciduous shrubs. Zones 4–7, 15–17. Valued for show of soft yellow, fragrant flowers that come on bare branches in March or earlier. New leaves that follow bloom are often tinged pink before they turn bright green; they're roundish, somewhat resembling filbert (hazelnut) leaves. Slow growing to 8–10 ft. and as wide. Makes rather open structure with attractive, delicate branching pattern.

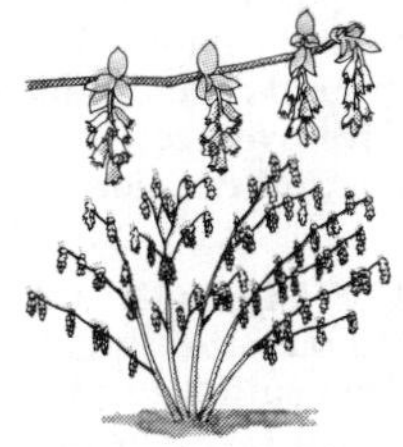

Corylopsis spicata

Plant in sheltered location in sun or partial shade. Give average water, same type soil as rhododendrons. Use in shrub border, edge of woodland.

C. pauciflora. BUTTERCUP WINTER HAZEL. Flowers are primrose yellow, ¾ in., bell shaped, in drooping clusters of 2 or 3. Leaves 1–3 in. long, with sharply toothed edges.

C. spicata. SPIKE WINTER HAZEL. Flowers are pale yellow, ½ in., bell shaped, in 1½-in.-long drooping clusters of 6–12. Leaves to 4 in. long, with toothed edges.

CORYLUS. *Betulaceae.* FILBERT, HAZELNUT. Deciduous shrubs or trees. Zones 1–9, 14–20. Filberts are usually thought of as trees grown for their edible nuts (see Filbert), but the following types are grown as ornamentals; one is a western native. Give average water unless noted otherwise.

C. avellana. EUROPEAN FILBERT. Shrub. Not as widely grown as its 2 varieties described below. To 10–15 ft. high and wide; leaves broad, roundish, 3–4 in. long, turning yellow in fall. Ornamental greenish yellow male flower catkins hang on all winter, turn yellow in earliest spring before leaves appear. Roundish nuts of good flavor enclosed by 2 irregularly lobed bracts.

Corylus avellana
'Fusco-rubra'

C. a. 'Contorta'. HARRY LAUDER'S WALKING STICK. Fantastically gnarled and twisted branches and twigs. Takes well to container culture and lends itself to display as curiosity. Will grow to 8–10 ft. Leaves smaller than those of species.

C. a. 'Fusco-rubra' **(*C. a.* 'Atropurpurea').** Identical to species except for its handsome purple leaf color.

C. colurna. TURKISH HAZEL. Tree. To 75 ft. tall, 30 ft. wide, with 5-in. leaves and clustered nuts smaller than filberts. Extremely cold hardy. Attractive tree in its own right, and a parent of hybrids (with *C. avellana*) called trazels.

C. cornuta californica. WESTERN HAZELNUT. Shrub. Native to damp slopes below 7,000 ft. elevation, northern Coast Ranges and Sierra Nevada of California, north to British Columbia. Open, spreading, multistemmed; 5–12 ft. high. Roundish, somewhat hairy, 1½–3-in.-long leaves with coarsely toothed edges turn bright yellow in fall. Like *C. avellana,* has decorative male flower catkins. Nuts small, kernels flavorful; enveloped in leafy husk with long, drawn-out beak.

C. maxima. See Filbert.

C. m. 'Purpurea'. Tree or shrub. Makes handsome, well-structured, small tree to 20 ft. or suckering shrub to 12–15 ft. Roundish leaves 2–6 in. long, dark purple in spring and summer. Burns quite badly in southern California's hot-summer areas.

CORYNABUTILON vitifolium *(Abutilon vitifolium).* *Malvaceae.* Tall evergreen shrub or small tree. Zones 5, 6, 15–17. To 15–20 ft., usually less. Leaves gray green, maplelike in shape, 6 in. long or longer. Summer flowers lilac blue to white, 2½–3 in. across, borne singly or clustered on long stalks. Likes sun or partial shade, cool summers, high humidity, ample water, good drainage.

Corynabutilon
vitifolium

CORYNOCARPUS laevigata. *Corynocarpaceae.* NEW ZEALAND LAUREL. Evergreen shrub or small tree. Good in Zones 16, 23; best in Zones 17, 24. Handsome, upright, to 20–40 ft. high. Beautiful dark green, very glossy, leathery leaves, oblong to 7 in. by 2 in. wide. Flowers noticeable but of no importance—tiny, whitish, in 3–8-in.-long upright clusters. Fruit orange, oblong, 1 in. long, extremely poisonous.

Easy to grow in sun or part shade. Requires moist conditions. Good in containers. Slow growing; keeps attractive form for years. Use as screen or large hedge, background. Good in sheltered areas, entryways, under overhangs.

Corynocarpus
laevigata

Can be grown indoors; takes low light and humidity, grows slowly, needs even soil moisture, light feedings.

CORYPHANTHA vivipara (usually sold as *Mammillaria vivipara*). *Cactaceae.* Little cactus. All Zones. Native Alberta to north Texas. Has single or clustered globular, 2-in. bodies covered with little knobs bearing white spines. Flowers purple, showy, to 2 in. long. One of hardiest forms of cactus, taking temperatures far below zero. Grow plant in full sun; it will tolerate much to little water in growing season.

Coryphantha
vivipara

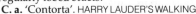

COSMOS. *Compositae.* Annuals. All Zones in conditions noted below. Native to tropical America, mostly Mexico. Showy summer- and fall-blooming plants, open and branching in habit, with bright green divided leaves and daisylike flowers in many colors and forms (single, double, crested, and frilled). Heights vary from 2½–8 ft. Use for mass color in borders, background, or as filler among shrubs. Useful in arrangements if flowers are cut when freshly opened and placed immediately in deep cool water. Sow seed in open ground from spring to summer, or set out transplants from flats. Plant in full sun in not-too-rich soil. Drought resistant. Plants self-sow freely, attract birds.

Cosmos bipinnatus

C. bipinnatus. Flowers in white and shades of pink, rose, lavender, purple, or crimson, with tufted yellow centers. Heights up to 8 ft. Modern improved cosmos include Sensation strain, 3–6 ft. tall, earlier blooming than old-fashioned tall kinds. Sensation varieties are 'Dazzler' (crimson) and 'Radiance' (rose with red center); white and pink are also available. 'Candystripe' has smaller (3-in.) white and rose flowers; blooms even earlier on smaller plants. Seashell strain has rolled, quilled ray florets like long, narrow cones.

C. sulphureus. YELLOW COSMOS. Grows to 7 ft., with yellow or golden yellow flowers with yellow centers. Tends to become weedy looking at end of season. Klondike strain grows 3–4 ft. tall, with 2-in. semidouble flowers ranging from scarlet orange to yellow. Dwarf Klondike or Sunny strain is 1½ ft. tall, with 1½-in. flowers.

COSTA RICAN HOLLY. See *Olmediella betschlerana*.

COSTMARY. See *Chrysanthemum balsamita*.

COTINUS coggygria (*Rhus cotinus*). *Anacardiaceae*. SMOKE TREE. Deciduous tree. All Zones; especially valuable in 1–3, 10, 11. (For another smoke tree, see *Dalea spinosa*.) Unusual shrub-tree creating broad, urn-shaped mass usually as wide as high—eventually to 25 ft. Roundish leaves 1½–3 in. long; bluish green in summer, yellow to orange red in fall. Dramatic puffs of purple to lavender "smoke" come from large, loose clusters of fading flowers: as tiny greenish blossoms fade, stalks of sterile flowers elongate and become clothed with fuzzy purple hairs. Grow in full sun.

Cotinus coggygria

C. c. 'Purpureus' has purple leaves which gradually turn to green, and richer purple smoke puffs. *C. c.* 'Royal Purple' retains purple leaves through the summer.

At its best under stress in poor or rocky soil. When grown in highly cultivated gardens, must have fast drainage and infrequent watering to avoid root rot. Resistant to oak root fungus.

COTONEASTER. *Rosaceae*. Evergreen, semideciduous, and deciduous shrubs. They range from ground covers to stiffly upright, small shrubs to tall-growing (20-ft.) shrubs of fountainlike growth with graceful, arching branches. All grow vigorously and thrive with little or no maintenance. In fact, they look better and produce better crops of fall and winter berries if planted on dry slopes—where they will control erosion—or in poor soil rather than rich, moist garden soil. All do well in full sun except in desert climates, where they should have an eastern exposure. Spring bloom; flowers white or pinkish, resembling tiny single roses, not showy but pretty because of their abundance.

Cotoneaster buxifolius

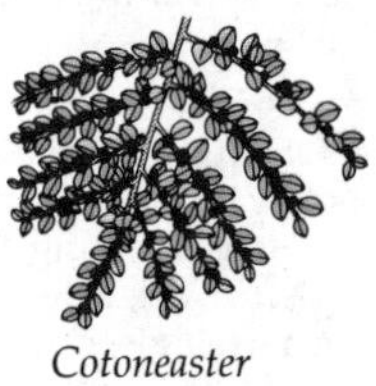

Cotoneaster horizontalis

Sudden wilting and blackening of twigs or branches indicates fireblight (a bacterial disease) or mealybugs. To control fireblight, cut out and destroy damaged wood, making cuts well below damaged tissue and sterilizing pruning tools between each cut with household disinfectant. Treat mealybugs with predatory mealybug destroyer beetles or with a spray.

Cotoneaster horizontalis

While some medium and tall growers can be sheared, they look best when allowed to maintain natural fountain shapes. Prune only to enhance graceful arch of branches. Keep medium growers looking young by pruning out portion of oldest wood each year. Prune ground covers to remove dead or awkward branches. Give flat growers room to spread. Don't plant near walk or drive where branch ends will need shearing, since stubbed branches are unattractive.

Cotoneaster lacteus

Cotoneasters are useful, if not striking shrubs, and can be attractive in the proper setting. Some are especially attractive in form and branching pattern (*C. congestus*, *C. horizontalis*), while others are notable for colorful, long-lasting fruit (*C. lacteus*, *C. microphyllus*). Trailing varieties make excellent ground cover plants and.

COTTONWOOD. See *Populus*.

COTULA squalida. *Compositae*. NEW ZEALAND BRASS BUTTONS. Evergreen perennial. Zones 4–9, 14–24. Grows only a few inches high, but branches creep to 1 ft. or more. Leaves are soft, hairy, fernlike, bronzy green. Flowers are like yellow brass buttons about ¼ in. across. Calyxlike bracts below heads fit tightly against "buttons." Can be used as ground cover in full sun to medium shade. Give average water. Can be increased by planting divisions.

Cotula squalida

COTYLEDON. *Crassulaceae*. Succulents. Various sizes and appearances. Easily grown from cuttings and handsome in containers, raised beds, or open ground beds. Plants are drought tolerant and will grow in full sun, but do best in light shade.

Cotyledon orbiculata

C. orbiculata. Zones 16, 17, 21–24. Shrubby, compact, to 3 ft. tall. Opposing pairs of fleshy leaves are 2–3 in. long, rounded, gray green to nearly white, narrowly edged red. Green-leafed forms are available. Flower stems rise above plant and carry clusters of orange, bell-shaped, drooping flowers in summer. Good landscaping shrub in mild climates and well-drained soils. Splendid container plant.

C. undulata. Zones 17, 23, 24. Striking 1½-ft. plant with broad, thick leaves thickly dusted with pure white powder. Leaf edges wavy. Flowers (spring and early summer) orange, drooping, clustered. Overhead watering washes off powder.

COWANIA mexicana stansburiana. *Rosaceae*. CLIFF ROSE. Evergreen shrub. Zones 1–3, 10–13. Native to California's Mojave Desert, Nevada, Arizona, Utah, Colorado, New Mexico, and Mexico. Much-branched, straggly shrub to 6 ft. high and as wide. Tiny, ½-in., deeply toothed leaves. Flowers like miniature single roses, just ½ in. wide; creamy or sulfur yellow, rarely white, in April–June. Moment of glory comes after bloom, when many very tiny fruits with long, plumy tails soften shrub to feathery

Cowania mexicana stansburiana

(Continued on page 305)

Cotoneaster

SPECIES OR VARIETY	HARDINESS	SIZE, HABIT	LEAVES	FRUIT	USES, COMMENTS
Cotoneaster acutifolius PEKING COTONEASTER	Deciduous. All Zones, best 1–3.	To 10 ft. tall, nearly as wide.	Glossy green when mature, 1–2 in. long. Orange red in fall.	Black, ⅜ in. long.	Useful as 10-ft. screen or 3–5-ft. hedge in coldest, most difficult climates. Tolerates part shade.
C. adpressus CREEPING COTONEASTER	Deciduous. All Zones.	Slow growing, eventually to 1 ft. with 6-ft. spread.	Dark green, nearly smooth, to ½ in. long. Reddish fall color.	Good show of ¼-in. bright red fruit.	Bank or ground cover. Will follow contours of ground or rocks, drape down wall. Tolerates part shade.
C. a. praecox (*C. praecox*)	Deciduous. All Zones.	More vigorous than species; to 1–1½ ft. high, wider spread.	Oval, to 1 in. long, with wavy margins. Maroon red fall color.	Fruit larger than that of species—to ½ in., bright red.	Same as *C. adpressus*.
C. apiculatus CRANBERRY COTONEASTER	Deciduous. All Zones.	To 4 ft. high and spreading wider. Growth similar to *C. horizontalis*.	Roundish, less than ½ in. long, shiny bright green above. Maroon red fall color.	Large (cranberry-sized) bright red fruit in clusters.	Hedge, background. Berries color early, hold long. Tolerates part shade.
C. buxifolius (Often sold as *C. glaucophyllus*, *C. pannosus*, or *C. pannosus* 'Nanus')	Semi-evergreen or evergreen. Zones 4–24.	1–2 ft. and spreading; or to 6 ft. and stiffly arching.	Tiny, oval, dull green above, with white or tan fuzz underneath. Overall look gray.	Bright deep red fruit borne singly on short branchlets.	Mislabeled in nursery trade. Taller plants sold as *C. glaucophyllus*, shorter as *C. pannosus* 'Nanus'. Good contrast with dark green.
C. congestus (*C. microphylla glacialis*)	Evergreen. Zones 2–24.	Grows 8 in. a year to an eventual 3 ft.; dense, rounded form with branches curving downward.	Small (⅓ in.), rounded, dark green above, whitish underneath.	Fruit small (¼ in.), bright red.	Rock hugging, attractive in containers, foreground. Equally good Zone 2 and desert. 'Likiang' is especially fine variety.
C. dammeri (*C. humifusus*) BEARBERRY COTONEASTER	Evergreen. All Zones.	Prostrate branches to 10 ft. long, 3–6 in. tall; branches root freely, grow fast.	Oval, 1 in. long, bright green above, whitish below. *C. dammeri radicans* has blunt, often notched leaves.	Fruit ½ in. across, brilliant red, showy.	Ground cover in sun or part shade, cascades over wall or rocks. 'Coral Beauty' has coral fruit, 'Royal Beauty' deep red fruit. 'Skogsholmen' is taller (1–1½ ft.), looser in growth habit, faster (2 ft. a year spread), a little stiffer in branching, hardy Zones 3–24. Flat-growing 'Eichholz' has carmine fruit, touches of gold and red foliage in fall.
C. divaricatus SPREADING COTONEASTER	Deciduous. All Zones.	To 6 ft. high with many stiff branches spreading out from center.	Oval, ¾ in. long, dark green above, pale beneath; thickly set on branches. Orange to red fall color.	Great show of ⅓-in.-long, egg-shaped red fruit.	Use as boundary, informal hedge or screen, or large bank planting.
C. glaucophyllus	See *C. buxifolius*.				
C. henryanus	Semi-evergreen. Zones 4–24.	Arching, spreading growth to 8–12 ft.	Large (to 5 in.), narrow, willowlike, deeply veined; green above, tawny and hairy beneath.	Fruit showy, red, in dense clusters.	Useful for Christmas greens—fruit is long lasting. Beautiful as individual shrub-tree.
C. horizontalis ROCK COTONEASTER	Deciduous, but out of leaf very short time. Zones 1–11, 14–24.	Low growing (2–3 ft.), wide spreading (to 15 ft.), with stiffly angled branches; secondary branching in herringbone pattern.	Small (½ in. or less), roundish, glossy bright green above, pale beneath. Hold late, turn orange and red before falling.	Shiny bright red fruit makes fine display.	Give it room to spread; don't plant where branch ends must be pruned. Bank cover, filler, low traffic barrier. *C. h. perpusillus* is flatter, more compact, with ¼-in. leaves. 'Variegatus' has leaves edged with white.

(Continued on next page)

C

SPECIES OR VARIETY	HARDINESS	SIZE, HABIT	LEAVES	FRUIT	USES, COMMENTS
C. 'Hybridus Pendulus' (*C.* 'Pendula')	Evergreen or semi-deciduous. Zones 4–24.	To 6 ft., spreading wider. Vertical main branches, curving weeping branchlets.	Deep green, to 2 in. long. Closely set on branches.	Red, ¼-in. diameter.	Use singly in border or as espalier. Often grafted high on treelike understock to make small, spreading, weeping patio tree.
C. lacteus (*C. parneyi*) PARNEY COTONEASTER, RED CLUSTERBERRY	Evergreen. Zones 4–24.	Arching growth to 6–8 ft. or more. Foliage growth to base of plant.	Leathery, to 2 in. long, heavily veined, deep green above, white beneath.	Long-lasting red fruit in clusters 2–3 in. wide.	Beautiful shrub growing free, thinned, or espaliered. Not at its best when clipped formally. Can be used as tall bank cover, trained as small tree.
C. 'Lowfast'	Evergreen. Zones 2–24.	Very vigorous, prostrate, rooting from trailing branches; to 1 ft. high and spreading to 10–15 ft.	Oval, ¾ in. long, dark green above, gray green beneath; somewhat like leaves of *C. dammeri* but not as closely set along branches.	Red fruit.	Fast ground cover; spreads as much as 2 ft. a year. Other uses same as *C. dammeri*. Fireblight a serious problem in southern California.
C. microphyllus ROCKSPRAY COTONEASTER	Evergreen. Zones 2–9, 14–24.	Main branches usually trailing and rooting, secondary branches upright; 2–3 ft. tall, spreading 6 ft. or more.	Small (⅓ in.), dark green above, gray and hairy on lower surface.	Rosy red, ¼ in. across, but seems larger contrasted with small leaves.	Good bank cover if not overfed and overwatered. Prune out upright branches or not, depending on desired effect. Use in big rock gardens, above walls.
C. m. thymifolius	Evergreen. Hardy to −5°F. Zones 2–9, 14–24.	More compact than *C. microphyllus*, but with stiff, upright branches.	Narrower than leaves of *C. microphyllus*, rolled under at edges.	As in *C. microphyllus* but somewhat smaller, sometimes in clusters.	Like other varieties, may tend to become woody, with foliage at ends of stems. Prune to thin and shorten.
C. multiflorus	Deciduous. All Zones.	Spreading shrub 6–8 ft. tall or small tree 10–12 ft. tall.	Oval to nearly round, to 2½ in. long, 1½ in. wide. Dark above, pale beneath.	Clustered red fruit ¼–⅜ in. long.	Clustered white flowers fairly showy in spring. Big shrub for screening.
C. pannosus, C. pannosus 'Nanus'	See *C. buxifolius*.				
C. parneyi	See *C. lacteus*.				
C. salicifolius WILLOWLEAF COTONEASTER	Evergreen or semi-evergreen. Zones 2–24.	Vigorous upright growth to 15 ft. high, arching branches spreading to 15–18 ft.	Narrow, willowlike (1–3½ in. long), wrinkled dark green above, grayish green beneath. *C. s. floccosus* has leaves glossy green above.	Bright red fruit ¼ in. wide, borne in 2-in. clusters.	Useful for big-scale screening, backgrounds. Or use as single or multistemmed small tree. Can be invasive.
C. s. 'Herbstfeuer' ('Autumn Fire')	Same as *C. salicifolius*.	Prostrate, to 6 in. high, spreading to 8 ft.	Same as *C. salicifolius*.	Same as *C. salicifolius*.	Plant 4–6 ft. apart for bank, ground cover.
C. s. 'Repens' (*C. s.* 'Repandens')	Same as *C. salicifolius*.	Trailing or weeping branches with eventual 8-ft. spread.	Like those of *C. salicifolius* but somewhat narrower.	Same as *C. salicifolius*.	Effective in hanging pot, grafted high on treelike stem as small weeping tree, or arching over slope. 'Emerald Carpet' is more compact. 'Shangri-La' is a dense form with cranberry-sized berries.
C. watereri	Evergreen Zones 4–7, 14–17. Deciduous Zones 2–3.	Vigorous, erect, then arching, to 15–20 ft. tall and as wide.	Dark green, 4–5 in. long.	Dark red fruit in 1½–2-in. clusters.	Group of garden hybrids. 'John Waterer' is often trained as short or tall standard tree. 'Cornubia' bears heavy crop of largest fruit in entire group.

haze. Pruning and infrequent watering make cowania acceptable subject in desert gardens.

COWBERRY. See *Vaccinium vitis-idaea.*

COWSLIP. See *Primula veris.*

COYOTE BRUSH. See *Baccharis pilularis.*

CRABAPPLE. *Rosaceae.* Deciduous fruit tree. Zones 1–9, 11–21. Crabapple is a small, usually tart apple. Many kinds are valued more for their springtime flowers than for their fruit; these are flowering crabapples, described under *Malus.* Crabapple varieties grown mostly for fruit (used for jelly making and pickling) are infrequently sold at western nurseries. Of several that may be sold, most popular is 'Transcendent', with red-cheeked yellow apples to 2 in. wide. Ripens in late summer. For culture, see Apple.

Crabapple

CRAB CACTUS. See *Schlumbergera truncata.*

CRANBERRY BUSH. See *Viburnum trilobum.*

CRANESBILL. See *Geranium, Erodium chamaedryoides.*

CRAPE MYRTLE. See *Lagerstroemia indica.*

CRASSULA. *Crassulaceae.* Succulents. Zones 16, 17, 22–24; with overhead protection Zones 8, 9, 12–15, 18–21; house plants anywhere. Mostly from South Africa. Most soils; drought tolerant. Sun or shade, but flowers can be counted on only when plants grown outdoors in some sunshine.

Crassula argentea

C. arborescens. A shrubby, heavy-branched plant very like jade plant, but with gray green, red-edged, red-dotted leaves. Flowers (usually seen only on old plants) are star shaped, white fading to pink. Good change of pace from jade plant; smaller and slower growing.

C. argentea. (Sometimes sold as *C. portulacea.*) JADE PLANT. Top-notch house plant, large container plant, landscaping shrub in mildest climates. Stout trunk, sturdy limbs even on small plants—and plant will stay small in small container. Can reach 9 ft. in time, but is usually less. Leaves are thick, oblong, fleshy pads 1–2 in. long, glossy bright green, sometimes with red-tinged edges. Clusters of pink, star-shaped flowers form in profusion, November–April. Good near swimming pools. Can be grown as hedge.

C. corymbulosa. Low growing—to 6–30 in. Slightly branched, with rosettes of long, triangular, fleshy leaves; leaves are dark red when plant is grown in full sun and poor soil. Tiny white flowers.

C. falcata. Full-grown plants reach 4 ft., with equal spread. Leaves fleshy, sickle shaped, gray green, vertically arranged in opposite rows on stems. Dense, branched clusters of scarlet flowers in late summer.

Crassula falcata

C. lactea. Spreading, semishrubby plant 1–2 ft. tall. Fleshy dark green leaves; white flowers in 4–6-in. clusters, October–December. Grows in shade—even dense shade. Fine rock garden plant.

C. lycopodioides. Leafy, branching, erect stems to 1 ft. high, closely packed with tiny green leaves in 4 rows; effect is that of braided watch chain or of some strange green coral. Very small greenish flowers. Easy and useful in miniature and dish gardens.

C. 'Morgan's Pink'. Fine miniature hybrid. Densely packed, fleshy leaves in tight cluster to 4 in. tall. Big, brushlike clusters of pink flowers are nearly as big as the plant. Spring bloom.

C. multicava. Dark green, spreading ground cover or hanging plant. Light pink, mosquitolike flowers in loose clusters late winter, spring. Rampant grower in sun or shade, in any soil.

C. pyramidalis. Interesting oddity to 3–4 in. high; flat, triangular leaves closely packed in 4 rows give plant squarish cross section. Flowers are insignificant.

C. schmidtii. Mat-forming, spreading plant to 4 in. tall with long, slender, rich green leaves. Winter-spring flowers small, heavily borne, clustered, dark rose or purplish. Good pot or rock garden plant.

C. tetragona. Upright plants with treelike habit, 1–2 ft. high. Leaves narrow, 1 inch long. Flowers white. Widely used in dish gardens to suggest miniature pine trees.

Crassulaceae. This large family of usually herbaceous (rarely shrubby) plants is familiar through sedums, sempervivums, and a host of other familiar succulents. Leaves are often in rosettes, as in the familiar hen and chicks (*Echeveria*).

CRATAEGUS. *Rosaceae.* HAWTHORN. Deciduous trees. Zones 1–11, 14–17. These trees, members of the rose family, are known for their pretty spring flowers and showy fruit in summer, fall. They have thorny branches and need some pruning to thin out excess twiggy growth. Grow plants on dry side to avoid rank, succulent growth.

Keep aphids in check. Fireblight makes entire branches die back quickly; cut out blighted branches well below dead part and wash pruning tools with disinfectant after each cut. Attract bees, birds.

Crataegus laevigata

C. ambigua. RUSSIAN HAWTHORN. Moderate growth to 15–25 ft. Vase form, twisting branches give attractive silhouette. Leaves small (to 2½ in. long), deeply cut. White flowers, heavy crop of small red fruit. Extremely winter hardy.

C. 'Autumn Glory'. Hybrid origin. Vigorous growth to 25 ft. with 15-ft. spread. Twiggy, dense. Dark green leaves similar to those of *C. laevigata* but more leathery. Clusters of single white flowers in spring. Very large, glossy, bright red fruit, autumn into winter. Type most susceptible to fireblight.

C. crus-galli. COCKSPUR THORN. Wide-spreading tree to 30 ft. Stiff thorns to 3 in. long. Smooth, glossy, dark green, toothed leaves. White flowers. Dull orange red fruit. Good red and yellow fall color.

C. laevigata *(C. oxyacantha).* ENGLISH HAWTHORN. Native to Europe and North Africa. Moderate growth to 18–25 ft. with 15–20-ft. spread. Leaves similar to those of *C. monogyna* but lobes are toothed. Best known through its varieties: 'Paul's Scarlet', clusters of double rose to red flowers; 'Double White'; 'Double Pink'. Doubles set little fruit. 'Crimson Cloud' ('Superba') has bright red single flowers with white centers, bright red fruit.

C. lavallei *(C. carrierei).* CARRIERE HAWTHORN. Hybrid origin. To 25 ft. with 15–20-ft. spread. More erect and open branching than other hawthorns, with less twiggy growth. Very handsome. Leaves dark green, leathery, 2–4 in. long, toothed; turn bronze red after first sharp frost and hang on well into winter. White flowers in spring followed by loose clusters of very large orange to red fruit that persist all winter. Fruit is messy on walks, patios.

C. mollis. DOWNY HAWTHORN. Big, broad tree to 30 ft.; looks like mature apple tree. Leaves to 4 in. long, lobed, toothed, covered with down. Flowers white, 1 in. wide. Red fruit 1 in. across, also downy; fruit doesn't last on tree as long as that of other species, but has value in jelly making.

(Continued on next page)

CLIMATE ZONES, PAGES 33–55

C. monogyna. Native to Europe, North Africa, and western Asia. Classic hawthorn of English countryside for hedges and boundary plantings. Represented in western nurseries by variety 'Stricta'. Narrow growth habit to 30 ft. tall and 8 ft. wide. Plant 5 ft. apart for dense, narrow screen or barrier. Leaves 2 in. long, with 3–7 deep, smooth-edged lobes. Flowers white. Small red fruit in clusters, rather difficult to see.

C. oxyacantha. See *C. laevigata*.

C. phaenopyrum *(C. cordata)*. WASHINGTON THORN. Native to southeastern United States. Moderate growth to 25 ft. with 20-ft. spread. Light and open limb structure. Glossy leaves 2–3 in. long with 3–5 sharp-pointed lobes (like some maples); foliage turns beautiful orange and red in fall. Small white flowers in broad clusters in late spring or early summer. Shiny red fruit in autumn hangs on well into winter. More graceful and delicate than other hawthorns, and preferred street or lawn tree. Least susceptible to fireblight.

C. pinnatifida. Native to northeastern Asia. To 20 ft. high, 10–12 ft. wide. Leaves lobed like those of *C. laevigata* but bigger and thicker; they turn red in fall. Tree has more open, upright habit than *C. laevigata*. Flowers white, ¾ in. wide, in 3-in. clusters. Fruit slightly smaller than that of *C. lavallei*.

C. 'Toba'. Canadian hybrid of great cold tolerance. To 20 ft. Leaves similar to those of *C. lavallei*. White flowers age to pink. Sets few large fruit.

C. viridis. GREEN HAWTHORN. Moderate growth to 25–30 ft., with broad, spreading crown. Leaves yellowish in fall, not showy. Clustered white flowers followed by red fruit.

CREAM BUSH. See *Holodiscus discolor*.

CREEPING BENT. See *Agrostis stolonifera*.

CREEPING BUTTERCUP. See *Ranunculus repens* 'Pleniflorus'.

CREEPING CHARLIE. See *Pilea nummulariifolia*.

CREEPING JENNIE. See *Lysimachia nummularia*.

CREEPING ZINNIA. See *Sanvitalia procumbens*.

CREOSOTE BUSH. See *Larrea tridentata*.

CRESS, GARDEN. *Cruciferae*. Summer annual. It is sometimes called PEPPER GRASS and tastes like watercress. Easy to grow as long as weather is cool. Sow seed as early in spring as possible. Plant in rich, moist soil. Make rows 1 ft. apart; thin plants to 3 in. apart (eat thinnings). Cress matures fast; make successive sowings every 2 weeks up to middle of May. Where frosts are mild, sow through fall and winter. Try growing garden cress in shallow pots of soil or planting mix in sunny kitchen window. It sprouts in a few days, can be harvested (with scissors) in 2–3 weeks. Or grow it by sprinkling seeds on pads of wet cheesecloth; keep damp until harvest in 2 weeks.

Garden Cress

CRETE DITTANY. See *Origanum dictamnus*.

CRINODENDRON patagua *(C. dependens, Tricuspidaria dependens)*. *Elaeocarpaceae*. LILY-OF-THE-VALLEY TREE. Evergreen tree. Zones 14–24. Native to Chile. (For another lily-of-the-valley tree, see *Clethra*.) Somewhat like evergreen oak in general appearance; sometimes called flowering oak. Grows at moderate rate to 25 ft. and almost as wide, with upright branching and a rounded crown. Leaves 2½ in. long, ½–1 in. wide, dark green above, gray green beneath, with irregularly toothed edges.

In June and July, sometimes into October, it wears hundreds of ¾-in.-long, white, bell-shaped flowers. These are followed by numerous attractive cream and red seed capsules which drop and can be messy on paving. Tends to grow in shrublike fashion; or some branches turn down, while others stick up. Early staking and pruning important. Prune out brushy growth toward center; remove branches that tend to hang down.

Crinodendron patagua

Does well in wet spots and thrives on lawn watering. In lawn, water deeply once a month to discourage surface rooting.

C. hookeranum. Zones 5, 6, 16, 17. Big shrub or small tree to 25 ft. Stiff branches clothed with narrow, sharply toothed leaves; drooping red flowers 1 in. long open from buds resembling cherries. Rare. Easy to propagate from cuttings, but hard to grow. Needs good drainage, cool summers, high humidity. Spider mites are a constant problem.

CRINUM. *Liliaceae*. Bulbs. Zones 23, 24; or in sheltered, sunny garden situations in Zones 12–22; other areas in containers. Distinguished from its near relative amaryllis by long, slender flower tube that is longer than flower segments. Long-stalked cluster of lily-shaped, 4–6-in.-long, fragrant flowers rises in spring or summer from persistent clump of long, strap-shaped or sword-shaped leaves. Bulbs large, rather slender, tapering to stemlike neck; thick, fleshy roots. Bulbs generally available (from specialists) all year, but spring or fall planting is preferred.

Crinum powellii

Plant in sun or a little shade. Provide soil with plenty of humus. Set bulbs 6 in. under surface; give ample water, space to develop. Divide infrequently. Bait for snails. In colder sections, mulch heavily in winter; move plants in containers into frostproof place.

Plantings of crinum are excellent for tropical effects. Mail-order nurseries offer a wide selection. Here are 2 of the more common species:

C. moorei. Large bulbs with 6–8-in. diameter and stemlike neck 1 ft. or more long. Long, thin, wavy-edged, bright green leaves. Bell-shaped pinkish red flowers.

C. powellii. Resembles *C. moorei* (which is one of its parents), but has dark rose-colored flowers. The variety 'Album' is a good pure white form, vigorous enough to serve as a tall ground cover in shade.

CROCOSMIA. *Iridaceae*. Corms. Zones 5–24, but need sheltered location and winter mulch in colder Zones. Native to tropical and South Africa. Formerly called tritonia, and related to freesia, ixia, sparaxis. Sword-shaped leaves in basal clumps. Small orange, red, yellow flowers bloom in summer on branched stems. Useful for splashes of garden color and for cutting. Plant in full sun near coast and in coastal valleys, part shade inland. Drought-tolerant plants.

C. crocosmiiflora *(Tritonia crocosmiiflora)*. MONTBRETIA. A favorite for generations, montbretias can still be seen in older gardens where they have spread freely, as though native, producing orange crimson

Crocosmia crocosmiiflora

flowers 1½–2 in. across on 3–4-ft. stems. Sword-shaped leaves to 3 ft., ½–1 in. wide. Many once-common named forms in yellow, orange, cream, and near-scarlet are making a comeback. Good for naturalizing on slopes or in fringe areas.

C. masoniorum. From South Africa. Leaves 2½ ft. long, 2 in. wide. Flowers flaming orange to orange scarlet, 1½ in. across, borne in dense, one-sided clusters on 2½–3-ft. stems which arch over at the top. Buds open slowly from base to tip of clusters and old flowers drop cleanly from stems. Flowers last about 2 weeks when cut.

Crocosmia masoniorum

CROCUS. *Iridaceae.* Corms. All Zones, but most species best adapted to colder climates. Leaves are basal and grasslike—often with silvery midrib—and appear before, with, or after flowers, depending on species. Flowers with long stemlike tubes and flaring or cup-shaped petals are 1½–3 in. long; short (true) stems are hidden underground.

Most crocus bloom in earliest spring or late winter, but some species bloom August–November, flowers rising from bare earth weeks or days after planting. All thrive in sun or light shade; mass them for best effect. Attractive in rock gardens, between stepping stones, in containers. Set corms 2–3 in. deep in light, porous soil. Protect from gophers. Divide every 3–4 years.

Crocus vernus

C. ancyrensis. Flowers golden yellow, small, very early.

C. angustifolius (formerly *C. susianus*). CLOTH OF GOLD CROCUS. Orange gold, starlike flowers with dark brown center stripe. January–February bloom, March in cold climates.

C. chrysanthus. Orange yellow, sweet scented. Hybrids and selections of this plant range from white and cream through the yellows and blues, often marked with deeper color. Usually even more freely flowering than Dutch crocus, but with smaller flowers. Spring bloom. Popular varieties are 'Blue Pearl', palest blue; 'Cream Beauty', pale yellow; 'E. P. Bowles', yellow with purple featherings; 'Ladykiller', outside purple edged white, inside white feathered purple; 'Princess Beatrix', blue with yellow center; and 'Snow Bunting', pure white.

C. imperati. Bright lilac inside, buff veined purple outside, saucer shaped. Early spring.

C. kotschyanus (formerly *C. zonatus*). Pinkish lavender or lilac. September bloom.

C. sativus. SAFFRON CROCUS. Lilac. Orange red stigma is true saffron of commerce. Interesting rather than showy. Autumn. To harvest saffron, pluck the stigmas as soon as flowers open, dry them, and store them in glass or plastic vials. Stigmas from a dozen flowers will season a good-sized paella or similar dish. To get continued good yield of saffron, divide corms as soon as leaves turn brown; replant in fresh or improved soil. Mark planting site with low-growing ground cover so you won't dig up dormant bulbs.

C. sieberi. Delicate lavender blue with golden throat. One of earliest.

C. speciosus. Showy blue violet flowers in October. Lavender and mauve varieties available. Fast increase by seed and division. Showiest autumn-flowering crocus.

C. tomasinianus. Slender buds, star-shaped, silvery lavender blue flowers, sometimes with dark blotch at tips of segments. Very early—January or February in milder climates.

C. vernus. DUTCH CROCUS. Familiar crocus in shades of white, yellow, lavender, and purple, often penciled and streaked. February–April (depending on climate). Most vigorous crocus, and only one widely sold in all areas.

CROSSANDRA infundibuliformis. *Acanthaceae.* Evergreen greenhouse or house plant. Native to India. Grow it in 4–5-in. pot as 1–1½-ft. plant. Its glossy, very dark green, gardenialike leaves are attractive all year, and short, full spikes of scarlet orange or coral orange flowers are showy for long period in summer. Grow in warmest spot with good light, as for African violet. Give average water and feed with liquid fertilizer once a month. Buy plants from florist or nurseryman, or raise from seed. Blooms in 6–9 months from seed.

Crossandra infundibuliformis

CROTALARIA agatiflora. *Leguminosae.* CANARY BIRD BUSH. Evergreen shrub. Zones 13, 15–24. Native to east Africa. Recovers quickly after frost damage. Fast, rank growth to 12 ft. and as wide unless frequently pruned (which it should be). Common name is well-earned: unique 1½-in. flowers are strung along flower spike (to 14 in. long) like so many chartreuse birds. Heaviest bloom in summer or fall, but in frost-free areas, blooms intermittently for 10 months. Foliage is pleasing gray green, with leaves divided into 3-in.-long leaflets.

Yellow green flowers harmonize with most colors. Try with red geraniums, zinnias, or coral tree (*Erythrina*), or with yellow-flowered shrubs for long succession of bloom. Almost any soil, sun or part shade, average water. Prune 2 or 3 times a year to correct open, weak-stemmed growth, condense and improve outline, and control size.

Crotalaria agatiflora

CROTON. See *Codiaeum variegatum.*

CROWN IMPERIAL. See *Fritillaria imperialis.*

CROWN OF GOLD TREE. See *Cassia excelsa.*

CROWN-OF-THORNS. See *Euphorbia milii.*

CROWN VETCH. See *Coronilla varia.*

Cruciferae. The mustard or cress family contains many food plants and ornamentals as well as a number of weeds. The notable characteristic is a 4-petaled flower resembling a cross. Familiar members include all the cabbage group, radishes, turnips, stocks, and sweet alyssum (*Lobularia*).

CRYPTANTHUS zonatus. *Bromeliaceae.* Perennial used as house plant; outdoors Zones 17, 23, 24. Native to Brazil. Grown for showy leaves in spreading, low-growing clusters to 1½ ft. wide, usually less. Individual leaves wavy, dark brownish red, banded crosswise with green, brown, or white. Unimportant little white flowers grow among leaves. Pot in equal parts coarse sand, ground bark or peat moss, and shredded osmunda. Shade, average water. These are forest-floor bromeliads and thrive in rather heavy shade, maintaining their colored bands and stripes. They are most effective in mass or mixed plantings, terrariums.

Cryptanthus bivittatus

C. bivittatus is similar to the above in cultural needs and general appearance, but has green leaves with lengthwise stripes of creamy white. Many other striped and banded species and hybrids are available from specialists.

C

CRYPTOCARYA rubra. *Lauraceae.* Evergreen tree. Zones 14–17, 20–24. Native to Chile. Slow to moderate growth to 30–40 ft. Dense, slightly spreading crown. Distinguished by rich brown bark and beautiful coppery red new foliage. When mature, the 2–3-in.-long, roundish, thick-textured leaves are very glossy dark green above, bluish green beneath. Leaves are spicily fragrant when crushed. Stake and prune unless multiple trunk is desired. Occasional frost damage in Zones 14–16. Needs moderate watering.

Cryptocarya rubra

CRYPTOMERIA japonica. *Taxodiaceae.* JAPANESE CRYPTOMERIA. Evergreen tree. Zones 4–9, 14–24. Graceful conifer, fast growing (3–4 ft. a year) in youth. Eventually skyline tree with straight columnar trunk; thin red brown bark peeling in strips. Foliage soft bright green to bluish green in growing season, brownish purple in cold weather. Branches, slightly pendulous, are clothed with ½–1-in.-long needlelike leaves. Roundish, red brown cones ¾–1 in. wide. These trees are sometimes used in closely planted groves for a Japanese garden effect.

Deep soil, ample water (except in Zones 5, 17, 24). Resistant to oak root fungus.

Cryptomeria japonica

C. j. 'Elegans'. PLUME CEDAR, PLUME CRYPTOMERIA. Quite unlike species. Feathery, grayish green, soft-textured foliage. Turns rich coppery red or purplish in winter. Grows slowly into broad-based, dense pyramid, 20–25 ft. high. For Oriental effect, prune out some branches to give tiered look. For most effective display, give it space.

C. j. 'Lobbii Nana' (*C. j.* 'Lobbii'). Upright, dwarf, very slow to 4 ft. Foliage dark green.

C. j. 'Pygmaea' (*C. j.* 'Nana'). DWARF CRYPTOMERIA. Bushy dwarf 1½–2 ft. high, 2½ ft. wide. Dark green, needlelike leaves, twisted branches.

C. j. 'Vilmoriniana'. Slow-growing dwarf to about 1–2 ft. Fluffy gray green summer foliage turns bronze during late fall and winter. Rock garden or container plant.

CTENANTHE. *Marantaceae.* House plants; foliage plants for patio containers or gardens in Zones 23, 24. Leaves are big feature; they may be short stalked, set along stem, or long stalked, rising from base only. Insignificant white flowers form under bracts in spikes at ends of branches. Use with other tropical foliage plants such as philodendron, alocasia, tree ferns. Plant in partial shade in rich, moist soil; feed with liquid fertilizer.

C. 'Burle Marx'. Grows to 15 in. Leaves gray green above, feathered with dark green; maroon underneath. Leaf stalks maroon. Tender; best grown as house plant, even in mild Zones 23, 24.

Ctenanthe compressa

C. compressa (often sold as *Bamburanta arnoldiana*). BAMBURANTA. Plants to 2–3 ft. high. Leathery leaves are oblong, lopsided, to about 15 in. long; waxy green on top, gray green beneath, held at angle on top of wiry stems.

C. lubbersiana *(Maranta lubbersiana).* To 2 ft. Yellow, 8-in. leaves with green markings.

C. oppenheimiana. GIANT BAMBURANTA. Compact, branching, 3–5 ft. high. Narrow, leathery leaves, dark green banded with silver above, purple beneath, set at angle on downy stalks. *C. o.* 'Tricolor' has showy cream patches with its other colors.

CTENITIS pentangularis. *Polypodiaceae.* Fern. Zones 17, 21–24. Native to New Zealand. This low-growing fern makes dense clumps of triangular, finely cut fronds. Will take moderately dry conditions and temperatures down to 26°F.

Ctenitis pentangularis

CUCUMBER. *Cucurbitaceae.* All Zones in conditions noted below. Vines need at least 25 sq. ft. per hill, but you can grow them on fence or trellis to conserve space. A warm-weather, sun-requiring vegetable needing warm soil to sprout seeds and warmth for pollination. Principal types are long, smooth, green, slicing cucumbers; numerous small pickling cucumbers; and roundish, yellow, mild-flavored lemon cucumbers. Novelties include Oriental varieties (long, slim, very mild), Armenian cucumber (actually long, curving, pale green, ribbed melon with cucumber look and mild cucumber flavor), and English greenhouse cucumber. English greenhouse cucumbers must be grown in greenhouse to avoid pollination by bees, with subsequent loss of form and flavor; when well grown, they are mildest of all cucumbers.

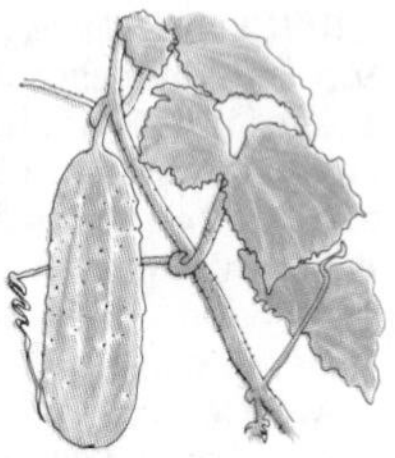

Cucumber

Bush cucumbers—varieties with compact vines—take up little garden space. Burpless varieties resemble hothouse cucumbers in shape and mild flavor, but can be grown out of doors. Pickling cucumbers should be picked as soon as they have reached the proper size—tiny for sweet pickles (gherkins), larger for dills or pickle slices. They grow too large very quickly. For a gourmet pickle, get seed of French cornichons from a dealer in specialty vegetable seeds.

'Sweet Success' has greenhouse cucumber quality but can be grown outdoors. Flowers are all female, but plants need no pollinator. Grow on trellis for long, straight cucumbers.

Plant seeds in sunny spot 1 or 2 weeks after average date of last frost and keep soil evenly moist. To grow cucumbers on trellis, plant seeds 1 in. deep and 1–3 ft. apart and permit main stem to reach top of support. Pick while young to ensure continued production.

CUCUMBER TREE. See *Magnolia acuminata*.

Cucurbitaceae. The gourd family as seen in Western gardens consists of annual vines with yellow or white flowers and large, fleshy, seedy fruits—cucumbers, gourds, melons, pumpkins, and squash.

CUNNINGHAMIA lanceolata. *Taxodiaceae.* CHINA FIR. Evergreen tree. Zones 4–6, 14–21. Native to China. Picturesque conifer with heavy trunk, stout, whorled branches, and drooping branchlets. Grows at moderate rate to 30 ft. with 20-ft. spread. Stiff, needlelike, sharp-pointed leaves are 1½–2½ in. long, green above, whitish beneath. Brown cones (1–2 in.) interesting, but not profuse. Among palest of needled evergreens in spring and summer; turns red bronze in cold winters. Needs protection from hot, dry wind in summer and cold winds in winter. Requires average water. Becomes less attractive as it ages. Prune out dead branchlets.

C. l. 'Glauca' is more widely grown and hardier than *C. lanceolata.* Its foliage is striking gray blue.

Cunninghamia lanceolata

CUNONIA capensis. *Cunoniaceae.* AFRICAN RED ALDER. Evergreen large shrub or small tree. Zones 9, 12–24. Native to South Africa. Small tree with single or multiple trunks, or large shrub.

Slow to moderate growth to 25–35 ft. as tree. Good large tub plant. Foliage effective at close range. Twigs are wine red; new growth is bronzy red, turning dark green. Leaves divided into 5–9 narrowish, toothed leaflets 3 in. long, 1 in. wide. Dense, spiky clusters of small white flowers in late summer. Hardy to 20°F. Severely damaged at 16°F. Average water.

Cunonia capensis

CUP-AND-SAUCER. See *Campanula medium.*

CUP-AND-SAUCER VINE. See *Cobaea scandens.*

CUPANIOPSIS anacardioides. *Sapindaceae.* CARROT WOOD. Evergreen tree. Zones 16–24. Native to Australia. Slow to moderate growth to 40 ft.; glossy dark green leaves divided into 6–10 leathery, 4-in.-long leaflets. Tolerates wet or salt-laden soil, salt winds at the coast, and hot, dry winds inland. Generally neat, never chlorotic in appearance. As they approach maturity, trees may produce marble-sized, leathery, yellow to orange fruit that splits but does not squash or stain. Some trees fruit heavily enough to be an annoyance, while others never fruit, for reasons not understood. Some feel that young trees selected for unusual vigor and broader than usual leaflets will produce less fruit than others; another theory is that trees under stress tend to develop more female flowers, hence more fruit. It is also believed that thinning out the tree every 2 years or so will result in production of young, nonfruiting wood. For several years, at least, an attractive, well-behaved tree. Consider underplanting with a ground cover deep enough to swallow the fruit drop. If you do so, be prepared to pull volunteer seedlings when they appear.

Cupaniopsis anacardioides

Many landscape architects feel that the tree's virtues outweigh its faults, and will continue to use it.

CUP FLOWER. See *Nierembergia.*

CUPHEA. *Lythraceae.* Shrubby perennials or dwarf shrubs. Outdoors all year in Zones 16, 17, 21–24; summer bedding or indoor/outdoor pot plant elsewhere. Native Mexico and Guatemala. Interesting for summer color in small beds, as formal edging for border, along paths. Take ordinary soil, sun or part shade (potted plants best in light shade); lots of moisture. Pinch tips for compact growth; cut back older plants severely in late fall or early spring. Easy from cuttings.

Cuphea ignea

C. hyssopifolia. FALSE HEATHER. Compact shrublet 6 in.–2 ft. tall, with flexible, leafy branchlets. Leaves evergreen, ½–¾ in. long, very narrow. Tiny summer flowers in pink, purple, or white are scarcely half as long as leaves. White form most useful.

C. ignea. CIGAR PLANT. Leafy, compact, 1 ft. high and wide. Leaves narrow, dark green, 1–1½ in. long. Flowers tubular, ¾ in. long, bright red with white tip and dark ring at end (hence name cigar plant). Blooms summer and fall.

CUPID'S DART. See *Catananche caerulea.*

CUP-OF-GOLD-VINE. See *Solandra maxima.*

Cupressaceae. The cypress family differs from the pine and yew families in having leaves that are usually reduced to scales and cones with few scales. Cones may even be berrylike, as in junipers.

CUPRESSOCYPARIS leylandii. *Cupressaceae.* Evergreen tree. Zones 3–24. Hybrid between *Chamaecyparis nootkatensis* and *Cupressus macrocarpa.* Grows extremely fast (from cuttings to 15–20 ft. in 5 years). Most planted as quick screening. However, some 10-year-old plantings have become open and floppy with age. Long, slender, upright branches of flattened, gray green foliage sprays give youthful tree narrow pyramidal form. Produces small cones composed of scales. Accepts wide variety of soil and climate, average water, strong wind; in warm-summer climates, loses stiff, upright habit and is subject to coryneum canker fungus.

Cupressocyparis leylandii

'Naylor's Blue' has grayish blue foliage; 'Castlewellan' has golden yellow new growth and a narrow, erect habit.

CUPRESSUS. *Cupressaceae.* CYPRESS. Evergreen trees. These conifers have tiny scale-like leaves closely set on cordlike branches, and interesting globular, golfball-sized cones made up of shield-shaped scales. All are drought tolerant once established.

C. forbesii. TECATE CYPRESS. Zones 8–14, 18–20. Native to Santa Ana Mountains, Orange County, and mountains of San Diego County, California. Low-branching tree to 20 ft., with cherry red bark and green foliage. Very fast growing—in fact, it may get too top heavy for size of root system. Needs to be kept on dry side for wind resistance. Useful as hedge or screen.

Cupressus glabra

C. glabra (often sold as *C. arizonica*). SMOOTH ARIZONA CYPRESS. Grown in Zones 5, 8–24 but at its best in high desert and hot interiors, where it's valued as fast-growing windbreak tree, tall screen. Native to central Arizona. Unusually drought resistant when established. Seedlings vary in form and foliage color. Usually to 40 ft., spreading to 20 ft. Smooth, cherry red bark; green to blue green to gray foliage. If you want uniformity in growth habit and color, look for selected forms: *C. g.* 'Gareei', rich, silvery, blue green foliage; *C. g.* 'Pyramidalis', compact and symmetrical.

Cupressus sempervirens

C. macrocarpa. MONTEREY CYPRESS. Zone 17. Native to California's Monterey Peninsula. Beautiful tree to 40 ft. or more, with rich bright green foliage. Narrow and pyramidal in youth, spreading and picturesque in age or in windy coastal conditions. Away from cool coastal winds is very subject to coryneum canker fungus, for which there is no cure. Look for foliage that first turns yellow, then deep reddish brown, and falls off slowly. Destroy infected trees. Fast-growing windbreak tree in coastal conditions.

'Golden Pillar' is a slow-growing, large, pyramidal shrub. Foliage is golden yellow in sun, yellow green in partial shade.

C. sempervirens. ITALIAN CYPRESS. Zones 4–24; best in 8–15, 18–20. Native to southern Europe, western Asia. Species itself, with

C

horizontal branches and dark green foliage, is seldom sold. *C. s.* 'Stricta' (*C. s.* 'Fastigiata'), COLUMNAR ITALIAN CYPRESS, and *C. s.* 'Glauca', BLUE ITALIAN CYPRESS (really blue green), are classic Mediterranean cypresses. They eventually grow into dense, narrow, columnar trees to 60 ft. *C. s.* 'Swane's Golden' (narrowly columnar) has golden yellow new growth.

CURRANT. *Saxifragaceae.* For ornamental relatives, see *Ribes*. Deciduous shrub. Best in Zones 1–6, 17, but grown in all Zones except where irrigation water or soil is high in sodium. Grow in shade in hot-summer areas, full sun in coastal areas. Average water. Many-stemmed shrub to 3–5 ft. high and equally broad, depending on vigor and variety. Attractive foliage of lobed and toothed leaves to 3 in. wide.

Currant

Flowers, yellowish in drooping clusters, are followed by clusters of red or white fruit in early summer. Leaves drop rather early in fall. Currants bear at base of year-old wood and on spurs on 2- and 3-year wood. Prune so that you keep balance of 1-, 2-, and 3-year canes; prune out older canes and weak growth. 'Red Lake', 'Perfection', and 'Cherry' are preferred varieties.

In some areas, it is illegal to plant currants, which might be hosts to white pine blister rust. Ask nurseryman or county agent about requirements in your area.

Black currant, formerly illegal as the favored host of the pine rust, is now available in a rust-resistant hybrid named 'Consort'. Fruit production is heavy; fruit is blackish purple and has a distinctive flavor with a suggestion of blackberry. It may be used in preserves or sauces.

CUSHION BUSH. See *Calocephalus brownii.*

CUSHION PINK. See *Silene acaulis.*

CUSSONIA spicata. *Araliaceae.* SPIKED CABBAGE TREE. Evergreen tree. Zones 16, 17, 19–24. Native to South Africa. Known chiefly for its lobed, toothed, and cut leaves—something like giant dark green snowflakes. Leaves grow on 6–10-in. stalks, are 4–7 in. long, divided into 5–9 leaflets. Foliage displayed on 10–20-ft., smooth-trunked tree, with branches in rounded crown. Under best conditions, tree blooms: small flowers, yellowish, in dense spikes 3–9 in. long, stand above leaves. Hardy to about 20°F. Full sun, much summer water (with fast drainage).

Cussonia spicata

CYANOTIS. *Commelinaceae.* Evergreen perennials used as house plants. Related to wandering Jews (*Tradescantia* and *Zebrina*), they resemble them, but have shorter stems, fleshier, more succulent leaves, and noticeable covering of soft "fur." Give them fairly rich, loose planting mix, moderate water, and bright light. Reduce watering in dull winter weather. Propagate by cuttings.

Cyanotis somaliensis

C. kewensis. TEDDY BEAR. Leaves 1–1½ in. long, coated with brown "fur." Small 3-petaled flowers are purplish red.

C. somaliensis. PUSSY-EARS. Stems somewhat longer than above (to 9–10 in.), leaves covered with white "fur," flowers blue.

CYATHEA cooperi *(Alsophila cooperi, Sphaeropteris cooperi;* often sold as ***Alsophila australis).*** *Cyatheaceae.* AUSTRALIAN TREE FERN. Zones 15–24. Fastest growing of the fairly hardy tree ferns; can grow from 1-ft. to 6-ft. spread in a year. Eventually 20 ft. tall. Broad fronds are finely cut, bright green, to a spread of 12 ft. Old fronds drop off cleanly, leaving smooth scars and a smooth trunk (unlike the shaggy trunk of Tasmanian tree fern). Brownish hair on leaf stalks and leaf undersurfaces can be irritating to skin; wear long sleeves, hat, and neckcloth when grooming plants.

Hardy to possibly 20°F., but with damage to fronds. Reasonably safe in sheltered places along the coast and in warm coastal valleys. Established plants will stand full sun in the fog belt, need part shade elsewhere.

Cyathea cooperi

Cycadaceae. This is the best-known family in Cycadales, an order of slow-growing evergreen plants with large, firm, palmlike or fernlike leaves and conelike fruit. Most people think of them as a kind of palm.

Most are native to tropical regions. Some are subtropical, and among these, some are hardy enough to grow out of doors in mild-winter climates. Extremely long lived. Average water. All are choice house plants—tough leaves, slow growth, and smallish root system make them adapted to pot culture indoors.

In addition to *Cycas* (below), other cycads include *Ceratozamia*, *Dioon*, and *Zamia* (members of another, related family, *Zamiaceae*).

CYCAS revoluta. *Cycadaceae.* SAGO PALM. Zones 8–24. In youth (2–3 ft. tall), has airy, lacy appearance of ferns; with age (grows very slowly to as high as 10 ft.), looks more like palm. But it is neither—it is a primitive, cone-bearing plant related to conifers. From central point at top of single trunk (sometimes several trunks), featherlike leaves grow out in rosettes. Leaves are 2–3 ft. long (larger on very old plants), divided into many narrow, leathery, dark glossy green segments. Makes offsets (new plants attached to parent).

Cycas revoluta

Choice container or bonsai plant; useful for tropical look. Tough, tolerant house or patio plant that looks best in partial shade. Average water. Hardiest (to 15°F.), most widely grown cycad.

CYCLAMEN. *Primulaceae.* Tuberous-rooted perennials. Grown for pretty white, pink, rose, or red flowers that resemble shooting stars. Attractive leaves in basal clumps. Zones and uses for large-flowered florists' cyclamen (*C. persicum*) are given under that name.

All other types are small flowered, hardy, best adapted Zones 1–9, 14–24. They bloom as described in listing below, and all lose leaves during part of year. Leaves may appear before or with flowers. Use hardy types in rock gardens, in naturalized clumps under trees, as carpets under camellias, rhododendrons, and large, noninvasive ferns. Or grow them in pots out of direct sun.

Cyclamen persicum

All kinds of cyclamen grow best in fairly rich, porous soil with lots of humus. Plant tubers 6–10 in. apart; cover with ½ in. soil. (Florists' cyclamen is an exception; upper half of tuber should protrude above soil level.) Best planting time is dormant period, June–August—except for florists' cyclamen, which is always sold as a potted plant rather than a tuber and is available in most seasons (although most are sold in late fall or during the winter-spring blooming period). Keep soil moist; topdress annually with light application of potting soil with complete fertilizer added, being careful not to cover top of tuber. Do not cultivate around roots.

The smaller hardy cyclamen grow well under native oaks; they can tolerate a summer resting period.

Cyclamen grow readily from seed; small-flowered hardy species take several years to bloom. Older strains of florists' cyclamen needed 15–18 months from seed to bloom; newer strains can bloom in as little as 7 months. Grown out of doors in open ground, cyclamen often self-sow.

C. atkinsii. Crimson flowers on 4–6-in. stems; deep green, silver-mottled leaves. Also pink, white varieties. January–March.

C. cilicium. Pale pink, purple-blotched, fragrant flowers on 2–6-in. stems; mottled leaves. September–January. There is a white-flowered variety, 'Album'.

C. coum. Deep crimson rose flowers on 4–6-in. stems; round, deep green leaves. White, pink varieties. January–March.

C. europaeum. See *C. purpurascens.*

C. hederifolium *(C. neapolitanum).* Large light green leaves marbled silver and white. Rose pink flowers on 3–4-in. stems, August–September. Also white variety. One of most vigorous and easiest to grow; very reliable in cold-winter climates. Set tubers a foot apart.

C. persicum. Wild ancestor of florists' cyclamen. Original species has deep to pale pink or white, 2-in. fragrant flowers on 6-in. stems. Selective breeding has given large-flowered florists' cyclamen (the old favorites) and, more recently, smaller strains. Fragrance has disappeared, with rare exceptions.

Florists' cyclamen grows outdoors Zones 16–24. Blooms late fall to spring: crimson, red, salmon, purple, or white, on 6–8-in. stems. Kidney-shaped dark green leaves. Good choice for color in places occupied by tuberous begonias in summer. Must have shade in warm summer climates. Plants will lose leaves and go dormant in hot weather, but usually survive if drainage is good and soil not waterlogged.

Dwarf or miniature florists' cyclamens are popular; they are half- or three-quarter-size replicas of standards. Careful gardeners can get these to bloom in 7–8 months from seed. Miniature strains (profuse show of 1½-in. flowers on 6–8-in. plants) include fragrant Dwarf Fragrance and Mirabelle strains.

C. purpurascens *(C. europaeum).* Distinctly fragrant crimson flowers, July–August, on 5–6-in. stems. Bright green leaves mottled silvery white; almost evergreen.

C. repandum. Bright crimson flowers with long, narrow petals on 5–6-in. stems; rich green, ivy-shaped leaves, marbled silver, toothed on edges. Spring.

CYDONIA. See *Chaenomeles.*

CYDONIA oblonga. See Quince, Fruiting.

CYMBALARIA. *Scrophulariaceae.* Small creeping perennial plants. Zones 3–24. Related to snapdragons. Unshowy, but they have their uses as small-scale ground covers in cool, shady places or as decorations for terrarium or hanging basket. In ground, can be invasive.

Cymbalaria muralis

C. aequitriloba. Inch-deep mat that looks like small-scale dichondra. Leaves have 3–5 slight lobes. Purple, snapdragon-shaped flowers are pretty but too tiny to make a show. Shade, good soil, ample water. Use as moss substitute.

C. muralis *(Linaria cymbalaria).* KENILWORTH IVY. Perennial usually growing as annual. Dainty creeper which may appear uninvited in shadier parts of garden, sometimes even sprouting in chinks of stone or brick wall. Trailing stems root at joints. Leaves 1 in. wide or less, smooth, with 3–7 toothlike lobes. Small lilac blue flowers carried singly on stalks a little longer than leaves.

CYMBIDIUM. *Orchidaceae.* Terrestrial orchids. Native to high altitudes in southeast Asia, where rainfall is heavy and nights cool. Very popular because of their relatively easy culture.

Miniature *Cymbidium*

Except in frost-free areas, grow plants in containers in lathhouse, greenhouse, or under overhang or high-branching tree. For added enjoyment bring indoors when in flower. Excellent cut flower.

Long, narrow, grasslike foliage forms sheath around short, stout, oval pseudobulbs. Long-lasting flowers grow on erect or arching spikes, usually from February to early May. There are a few new crosses that bloom in December, a few late-blooming ones to prolong flowering period.

For best bloom, give as much light as possible without burning foliage. In general, plants do well with 50 percent shade—under plastic cloth shading or under lath. Let leaf color be your guide: plants with yellow green leaves generally flower best; dark green foliage means too much shade. (During flowering period, give plants shade to prolong bloom life, keep flowers from fading.)

Plants prefer 45°–55°F. night temperature, rising to as high as 80°–90°F. during day. They'll stand temperatures as low as 28°F. for short time only; therefore, where there's danger of harder frosts, protect plants with covering of polyethylene film. Flower spikes are more tender than other plant tissues.

Keep potting medium moist when new growth is developing and maturing—usually March–September. In winter, water just enough to keep bulbs from shriveling. On hot summer days, syringe foliage early in day.

Good soil mix for cymbidiums is 2 parts redwood bark or sawdust, 2 parts peat moss, 1 part sand. Add 4-in. pot of complete fertilizer to each wheelbarrow of mix. Ready-blended mixes are excellent. Whatever the medium, it should drain fast and still retain moisture.

Feed with complete liquid fertilizer high in nitrogen every 10 days to 2 weeks, January–July. Use low-nitrogen fertilizer August–December.

Transplant potted plants when bulbs fill pots. When dividing plants, keep minimum of 3 healthy bulbs (with foliage) in each division. Dust cuts with sulfur or paint them with tree seal to discourage rot. Watch for slugs and snails at all times.

Most cymbidium growers list only hybrids in their catalogs—large-flowered varieties with white, pink, yellow, green, or bronze blooms. Most have yellow throat, dark red markings on lip. Large-flowered forms produce dozen or more 4½–5-in. flowers per stem. Miniature varieties, about a quarter the size of large-flowered forms, are popular for their size, free-blooming qualities, flower color.

CYNODON dactylon. *Gramineae.* BERMUDA GRASS, BERMUDA. Lawn grass. Subtropical fine-textured grass that spreads rapidly by surface and underground runners. Tolerates heat, needs less water than most lawn grasses, and looks good if well maintained. It turns brown in winter; some varieties stay green longer than others, and most stay green longer if well fed. Bermuda grass can be overseeded with cool-season grasses or dyed green for winter color. Needs sun and should be cut low; ½ in. is desirable. Needs thatching—removal of matted layer of old stems and stolons beneath the leaves—to look its best.

Cynodon dactylon

Common Bermuda is good minimum-maintenance lawn for large area. Needs feeding, careful and frequent mowing to remove seed spikes. Roots invade shrubbery and flower beds if not carefully confined. Can become extremely difficult to eradicate. Plant from hulled seed or sprigs.

Hybrid Bermudas are finer in texture and better in color than common kind. They crowd out common Bermuda in time but are

C

harder to overseed with rye, bluegrass, or red fescue. Help them stay green in winter by feeding in September and October and by removing thatch, which insulates grass from warm soil. Useful in areas with short dormant season. Grow from sprigs (stolons), plugs, or sod.

'Santa Ana'. Deep green, coarse, holds color late, smog resistant. Takes hard wear.

'Tifdwarf'. Extremely low and dense; takes very close mowing Slower to establish than others, but slower to spread where it's not wanted. Useful as small-scale ground cover on banks, among rocks, near garden steps.

'Tifgreen'. Fine textured, deep blue green, dense. Few seed spikes, sterile seeds. Takes close mowing, preferred for putting greens. Outstanding for home lawns.

'Tifway'. Low growth, fine texture, stiff blades, dark green, dense, wear resistant. Slow to start. Sterile (no seeds).

'U-3'. Finer textured than common Bermuda, but with obvious and unattractive seed spikes. Very tough. Grow from sprigs; not dependable from seed, tending to revert to mixture of many types. Not up to other hybrids in quality.

CYNOGLOSSUM. *Boraginaceae.* Biennials, usually treated as annuals; or perennials. Bedding, border, or wild garden plants with blue, white, or pink flowers like forget-me-nots.

Cynoglossum amabile

C. amabile. CHINESE FORGET-ME-NOT. Biennial grown as annual. All Zones. Plant is 1½–2 ft. tall. Leaves grayish green, soft, hairy, lance shaped. Loose sprays of rich blue, pink, or white flowers, larger than forget-me-nots, appear in spring, into summer where weather is cool. 'Firmament', widely available, most popular variety, has rich blue flowers on compact, 1½-ft.-high plants. Combine with snapdragons, godetias, candytuft, clarkia, violas; especially effective with white, yellow, pink, salmon, or coral flowers.

Blooms first year from seed sown (preferably where plants are to grow) in fall or early spring. Hardy except in most severe winters. Sun, regular watering.

C. grande. WESTERN HOUND'S TONGUE. Perennial. Zones 4–9, 14–24. Native to Coast Ranges and Sierra Nevada slopes below 4,000 ft. Leaves hairy, mostly basal, spreading, 6–12 in. long. Blooms March–June. Flowers blue, ⅓–½ in. across, white in center. Plants 1–2½ ft. tall; die back in summer to heavy underground root. Choose woodsy site with cool soil and little or no summer water.

Cyperaceae. Members of the sedge family superficially resemble grasses, but have 3-sided (usually) stems and leaves arranged in 3 ranks. They usually grow in wet places; *Carex* and *Cyperus* are examples.

CYPERUS. *Cyperaceae.* Perennials. Zones 8, 9, 12–24. Belongs to the sedges—grasslike plants distinguished from true grasses by 3-angled, solid stems and very different flowering parts. Valued for striking form, interesting silhouette or shadow pattern.

Most cyperus are bog plants by nature; they grow in rich, moist soil or with roots submerged in water, in sun or shade. Groom plants by removing dead or broken stems; divide and replant vigorous ones when clump becomes too large, saving smaller, outside divisions and discarding overgrown centers. In cold climates, pot up divisions and keep them over the winter as house plants.

C. albostriatus *(C. diffusus).* Resembles *C. alternifolius* (below), but tends to be shorter (to 20 in.), with broader leaves and lusher, softer appearance. Vigorous, invasive, best used in contained space.

Cyperus papyrus

C. alternifolius. UMBRELLA PLANT. Narrow, firm, spreading leaves arranged like ribs of umbrella at tops of 2–4-ft. stems. Flowers in dry, greenish brown clusters. Dwarf form is *C. a.* 'Gracilis' (*C. a.* 'Nanus'). Grows in or out of water. Effective near pools, in pots or planters, or in dry stream beds or small rock gardens. Self-sows. Can become weedy. Can take over a small pool.

C. isocladus *(C. haspan).* DWARF PAPYRUS. Flowers and long, thin leaves combine to make filmy brown and green clusters on slender stems about 1½ ft. high. Sink in pots in water gardens where slender leafless stems will not lose delicately shaped design among larger and coarser plants. Use in Oriental gardens.

C. papyrus. PAPYRUS. Tall, graceful, dark green stems 6–10 ft. high, topped with clusters of green threadlike parts to 1½ ft. long (longer than small leaves at base of cluster). Will grow quickly in 2 in. of water in shallow pool, or can be potted and placed on bricks or inverted pot in deeper water. Protect from strong wind. Also grows well in rich, moist soil out of water. Used by flower arrangers.

CYPHOMANDRA betacea. *Solanaceae.* TREE TOMATO. Evergreen or partially evergreen shrub. Zones 16, 17, 22–24; with overhead protection in 14, 15, 18–21; elsewhere, indoor/outdoor or greenhouse plant. Fast growth to 10–12 ft. Treelike habit.

Cyphomandra betacea

Leaves 4–10 in. long, pointed oval. Summer and fall flowers small, pinkish. Winter fruit is red, 2–3 in. long, egg shaped, edible, with acid, slightly tomatolike flavor. If you find the fruit too tart, try stewing it with a little sugar, as the Australians do. Grow from seed like tomato. Shelter from frost and spray to control sucking insects. Give average water, sun or part shade.

CYPRESS. See *Cupressus.* True cypresses are all *Cupressus;* many plants erroneously called cypress will be found under *Chamaecyparis* and *Taxodium.*

CYPRESS VINE. See *Ipomoea quamoclit.*

CYPRIPEDIUM. For tropical and subtropical orchids sold under this name, see *Paphiopedilum.* True cypripediums, the hardy lady's slipper orchids, are rare or endangered in the wild and extremely difficult to maintain in gardens. Most are collected from wild stands and seldom survive.

CYRTANTHUS mackenii. *Amaryllidaceae.* Bulb. Zones 23, 24; sheltered situations in Zones 16–22; elsewhere, container plant. South African native. Foot-long, narrow (⅓-in.-wide) leaves have somewhat wavy edges. Tubular, curved, 2-in.-long white flowers nod in loose clusters at ends of stems. Blooms in spring. There are also cream- and yellow-flowered forms and hybrids in coral, orange, and red shades. Plants grow actively throughout year, produce numerous offsets. Grow them in partial shade, in well-drained acid soil; keep soil moist. If grown in pots, plants will need annual repotting. At this time, remove small bulblets and pot them up for bloom in 1½–2 years.

Cyrtanthus mackenii

C. purpureus. See *Vallota.*

CYRTOMIUM falcatum. *Polypodiaceae.* HOLLY FERN. Zones 16, 17, 22–24. Coarse-textured but handsome fern, 2–3 ft. tall, sometimes taller. Leaflets large, dark green, glossy, leathery. Takes indoor conditions well and thrives outside in milder areas. Ample water. Hardy to 25°F. Take care not to plant too deeply. Forms with fringed leaflets available.

Cyrtomium falcatum

CYTISUS. *Leguminosae.* BROOM. Most widely planted brooms belong here, but look for Spanish broom under *Spartium,* other choice shrubs under *Genista.* Deciduous or evergreen shrubs (many nearly leafless, but with green or gray green stems). Sweet pea-shaped flowers, often fragrant. Drought tolerant—so much so that they have become weeds in northern California and northwestern park and range lands—but better looking with a little summer water. They need sun and good drainage, tolerate wind, seashore conditions, and rocky, infertile soil. Where soil is highly alkaline, give them iron sulfate. Prune after bloom to keep to reasonable size and form, lessen production of unsightly seed pods.

Cytisus battandieri

C. battandieri. ATLAS BROOM. Semievergreen or deciduous. Zones 5, 6. Fast growth to 12–15 ft. high and as wide. Can be trained as small tree. Leaves divided into 3 roundish leaflets to 3½ in. long, 1½ in. wide, covered with silvery, silky hairs. Fragrant, clear yellow flowers in spikelike 5-in. clusters at branch ends, June–September.

C. canariensis *(Genista canariensis).* CANARY ISLAND BROOM. Evergreen. Zones 8, 9, 12–24. Damaged at 15°F. but recovers quickly. Many-branched, upright shrub to 6–8 ft. high, 5–6 ft. wide. Bright green leaves divided into ½-in. leaflets. Bright yellow, fragrant flowers in short clusters at ends of branches, spring and summer. Genista of florists. Grows like a weed and spreads by seedlings.

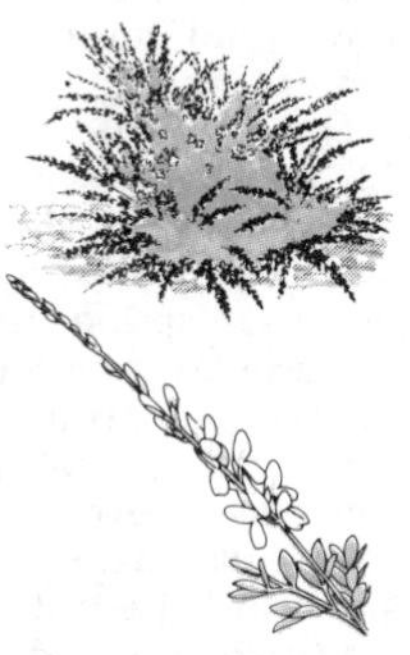
Cytisus spachianus

C. kewensis. KEW BROOM. Dwarf shrublet. Best in Zones 4–6; less vigorous but satisfactory in 16, 17. Low (less than 1 ft. high), spreading with trailing branches to 4 ft. or more. Creamy white, ½-in. flowers in April–May. Tiny leaves. Branches will cascade in open pattern over wall or steep bank. One of best prostrate forms.

C. lydia. See *Genista lydia.*

C. praecox. WARMINSTER BROOM. Zones 2–9, 12–22. Deciduous. Compact growth with many slender stems to 3–5 ft. high and 4–6 ft. wide. Mounding mass of pale yellow to creamy white flowers March–April in south, April–May in north. Small leaves fall early. Effective as informal screen or hedge, along drives, paths, garden steps. 'Allgold', slightly taller, has bright yellow flowers; 'Hollandia', pink ones. 'Moonlight', formerly considered *C. praecox* variety, is now thought to be form of *C. scoparius.*

C. purgans. PROVENCE BROOM. Zones 4–6. Deciduous. Dense, mounding growth to 3 ft. high with equal spread. Silky, hairy leaves roundish, ¼–½ in. long. Fragrant, chrome yellow flowers, May–July.

C. racemosus. See *C. spachianus.*

C. scoparius. SCOTCH BROOM. Evergreen. Zones 4–9, 14–22. This one has given all brooms a bad name. Has spread like weed over thousands of acres of open land in northern California and Northwest. Upright growing mass of wandlike green stems (often leafless or nearly so) may reach 10 ft. Golden yellow, ¾-in. flowers, spring and early summer.

Much less aggressive are lower-growing, more colorful forms. Most of these grow 5–8 ft. tall: 'Burkwoodii', red touched yellow; 'Carla', pink and crimson lined white; 'Dorothy Walpole', rose pink and crimson; 'Lena', lemon yellow and red; 'Lilac Time', lilac pink, compact; 'Lord Lambourne', scarlet and cream; 'Minstead', white flushed lilac and deep purple; 'Moonlight', pale yellow, compact; 'Pomona', orange and apricot; 'St. Mary's', white; 'San Francisco' and 'Stanford', red.

C. spachianus *(C. racemosus, Genista racemosa;* often sold as ***G. fragrans).*** Zones 7–9, 11–24. Similar in growth habit to *C. canariensis,* but with larger leaflets and longer, looser spikes of yellow, fragrant flowers in late spring. Naturalizes where adapted.

DABOECIA. *Ericaceae.* Small evergreen shrubs of heather family. Give them acid, fast-draining soil and partial shade except near coast, where they can tolerate full sun. Most useful on hillsides, in rock gardens or wild gardens. Water dependent but less so than rhododendrons and azaleas.

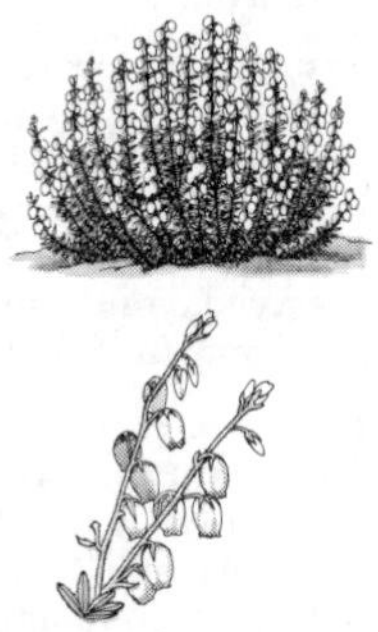
Daboecia cantabrica

D. azorica. Zones 8, 9, 14–24. Mounds to 6–10 in. Closely set, bright green leaves ¼ in. long, broader than those of other heaths and heathers. Egg-shaped, rosy red flowers ½ in. long on spikelike clusters. April–May, occasionally in fall.

D. cantabrica. Zones 3–9, 14–24. Erect stems make slightly spreading plant 1½–2 ft. tall. Larger leaves than those of *D. azorica.* Pinkish purple, ½-in., egg-shaped flowers in narrow 3–5-in. clusters, June–October (April–October warmer areas). Cut back in fall to keep compact. 'Alba' has white flowers, 'Praegerae' pure pink blooms, and 'Rosea' deep pink blooms.

DAFFODIL. See *Narcissus.*

DAHLBERG DAISY. See *Dyssodia tenuiloba.*

DAHLIA. *Compositae.* Perennials grown from tuberous roots. All Zones. Native to Mexico, Guatemala. Except for tree dahlia (*D. imperialis,* described at end of this section), dahlias are represented today exclusively by hybrids and strains—hundreds of them—of bush and bedding dahlias. Through centuries of hybridizing and selection, these dahlias have become tremendously diversified, with numerous flower types in all colors but true blue. Sketches illustrate type based on flower form as classified by American Dahlia Society.

Dahlia hybrid

Bush and bedding dahlias grow from 15 in. to over 6 ft. high. Taller bush forms make summer hedges, screens, fillers among shrubs; lower kinds give mass color in borders and containers. Modern dahlias with strong stems, long-lasting blooms that face outward or upward, and substantial, attractive foliage have become useful as cut flowers. Leaves are generally divided into many large, deep green leaflets.

Planting. Most dahlias are started from tubers. Plant them after frost is past and soil is warm. Full sun; light afternoon shade in hottest areas. Several weeks before planting, dig soil 1 ft. deep and work in ground bark, composted redwood sawdust, or peat moss; also add coarse sand to heavy soils.

Make holes 1 ft. deep and 3 ft. apart for most varieties; space largest kinds 4–5 ft. apart, smaller ones 1–2 ft. If you use fertilizer at planting time, thoroughly incorporate ¼ cup of complete fertilizer in bottom of hole, then add 4 in. of plain soil. Drive 5-ft. stake into hole; place tuber horizontally with eye pointing toward stake and 2 in. from it. Cover tuber with 3 in. of soil. Water thoroughly if no rains are expected. As shoots grow, gradually fill hole with soil.

For tall dahlias, plant seeds early indoors; transplant seedlings to garden position after frosts are over. The following fall and thereafter, dig and store tubers as described below in climates where ground freezes in winter. In other regions, tubers may remain in place as long as drainage is excellent and ground does not freeze deeply. Plants will survive in most of California and the Northwest west of the Cascades; elsewhere in the Northwest, mulch with 4 in. of straw or similar material.

For dwarf dahlias, sow seed in place after soil is warm, or buy and plant started seedlings from the nursery. Dwarf dahlias are best replaced each year (grow them from seed or buy nursery plants), but you may dig and store tubers or overwinter them as for tall dahlias.

Thinning, pinching. On tall-growing types, thin to strongest shoot or 2 shoots (you can make cuttings of removed shoots). When remaining shoots have 3 sets of leaves, pinch off tips just above top set; 2 side shoots develop from each pair of leaves. For large flowers, remove all but terminal buds on side shoots. Smaller flowered dahlias such as miniatures, pompons, singles, or dwarfs need only first pinching.

Watering. Start watering regularly after shoots are above ground. Throughout active growth, keep soil moist to depth of 1 ft. Dahlias planted in enriched soil don't need additional food. If soil lacks nutrients, sidedress plants with fertilizer high in phosphates and potash when first flower buds appear. Avoid high-nitrogen fertilizers: they result in soft growth, weak stems, tubers liable to rot in storage. Mulch to keep down weeds and to eliminate cultivating which may injure feeder roots.

Cut flowers. Pick nearly mature flowers in early morning or evening. Place cut stems immediately in 2–3 in. of hot water; let stand in gradually cooling water for several hours or overnight.

Lifting, storing. After tops turn yellow or are frosted, cut stalks to 4 in. above ground. Dig around plant 1 ft. from center, carefully pry up clump with spading fork, shake off loose soil, and let clump dry in sun for several hours. From that point, follow either of 2 methods:

(1) Divide clumps immediately (as described under method 2 below). This saves storage space. Freshly dug tubers are easy to cut; it is easy to recognize eyes or growth buds at this time. Dust cut surfaces with sulfur to prevent rot, bury tubers in sand, sawdust, or vermiculite, and store through winter in cool (40°–45°F.), dry place.

(2) Leave clumps intact, cover them with dry sand, sawdust, peat moss, perlite, or vermiculite; store in cool, dry place. There is less danger of shrinking with this storage method. About 2–4 weeks before planting in spring, separate tubers by cutting from stalk with sharp knife; leave 1 in. of stalk attached to each tuber, which must have eye or bud in order to produce new plant. Place tubers in moist sand to encourage development of sprouts.

D. imperialis. TREE DAHLIA. Zones 4–6, 8, 9, 14–24. A 10–20-ft. multistemmed tree grows each year from permanent roots; in late fall, 4–8-in., lavender, daisy-type flowers with yellow centers are produced at branch ends. Leaves composed of many leaflets. Frosts kill tops completely; cut back to ground afterward. If tree dahlia bloomed longer or remained evergreen, it would be a valued landscape plant, but annual live-and-die cycle relegates it to tall novelty class. Seldom sold in nurseries. Grow from cuttings taken near tops of stems (or from side shoots) in fall; root in containers of moist sand kept in protected place over winter. Or dig root clump and divide in fall. Full sun or half shade. *D. excelsa, D. maxonii* are similar.

DAIS cotinifolia. *Thymelaeaceae.* POMPON TREE. Briefly deciduous. Zones 16–24. Native to South Africa. Worthwhile flowering shrub or small tree, somewhat like crape myrtle in size and shape. Slow growing to 12 ft. with 10-ft. spread. Flower clusters resemble 1½-in. balls of pink shredded coconut; carried at ends of twigs in June and July. Flowers remain after fading and are then rather unsightly. Bluish green leaves to 2½ in. long drop in sharp frosts. By nature a multi-trunked shrub-tree, it looks best trained to single trunk. Unusually tolerant of heat. Will stand reflected light and heat of pavement and walls. Needs sun, average soil and watering.

Dais cotinifolia

DAISY TREE. See *Montanoa*.

DALEA. *Leguminosae.* Evergreen or deciduous shrubs or trees with finely divided leaves and clusters of sweet pea–shaped flowers.

D. greggii. TRAILING INDIGO BUSH. Zones 12, 13. Fast-growing (to 3 ft. wide in 1½ years), prostrate shrub with pearl gray foliage, clusters of tiny (less than ½-in.), purple flowers in spring and early summer. Excellent ground cover for desert; tolerates heat, desert soil, drought when established. Unappealing to rabbits. To get fast growth, water deeply every 2 weeks.

D. oaxacana. Zones 12, 13. Deciduous shrub to 1–1½ ft. tall. Tiny, finely divided gray green leaves drop in fall, just after tiny purple flowers fade. Useful in furnishing some shade to such heat-sensitive ground covers as red spike ice plant (*Cephalophyllum*).

Dalea spinosa

D. spinosa. SMOKE TREE. Deciduous. Zones 11–13. Native to desert washes below 1,500 ft. in southern California, Arizona, Baja California. The few small leaves drop early. When tree is out of leaf, intricate network of gray, spiny branches resembles cloud of smoke. Good show of fragrant violet blue flowers, April–June (flower branches make choice dry arrangements).

Useful in natural desert gardens. Seems happy at edge of irrigation. Usually grows to 12 ft., but with water in summer grows in

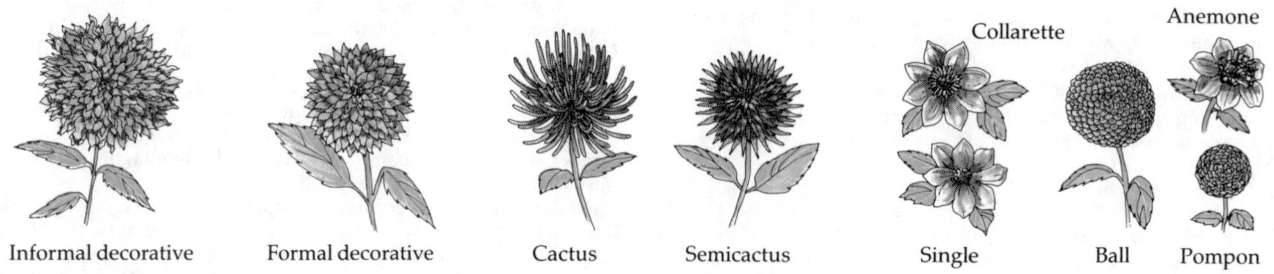

Decorative and cactus dahlias reach impressive sizes; many reach or exceed 1 ft. in diameter. Other kinds shown are equally good for cutting and easier to arrange.

bursts to as much as 30 ft. Easily grown from seed sown in warm weather. Sow in place or in small container and plant out.

DAMPIERA diversifolia. *Goodeniaceae.* Perennial ground cover. Zones 15–24. Prostrate plant spreading by suckers and rooting from trailing stems. Leaves evergreen, narrowly oval, up to 1 in. long. In spring and summer, many small, dark blue flowers appear at end of new growth to produce circle effect. Spreads steadily in loose, well-drained soil, but not invasive or weedy. Best in full sun, average water.

Dampiera diversifolia

DANCING LADY. See *Oncidium varicosum.*

DANDELION *(Taraxacum officinale).* *Compositae.* Perennial. All Zones. It's a weed in lawns and flower beds, but it can also be a cultivated edible-leaf crop. Seeds sold in packets. Cultivated forms have been selected for larger, thicker leaves than those of common weed form.

Tie leaves together to bleach interiors; eat like endive. Add tender leaves to mixed green salads; boil thick leaves like collards or other greens.

Cultivated Dandelion

DAPHNE. *Thymelaeaceae.* Evergreen and deciduous shrubs. Of the many kinds, 3 (*D. burkwoodii, D. cneorum, D. odora*) are widely grown in West; most of the others are choice rock garden subjects with limited distribution in nursery trade.

Although some daphnes are easier to grow than others, all require fast-draining soil and careful hand with summer watering. They are far more temperamental in California than in Northwest. All parts of daphne plants are poisonous, especially the fruits—which, fortunately, are rarely seen.

Daphne odora 'Marginata'

D. bholua. Evergreen or deciduous. Zones 14–17. Variable shrub native to Himalayas and western China. Can be deciduous or evergreen. Sweet-scented flowers from tightly clustered buds may be white or purplish pink with white interiors. Winter blooming. Tends to grow erect and bare based, to 6 ft. or more. Rare.

D. blagayana. Evergreen. Zones 4–6. Spreading, almost prostrate (to 6 in. high), rooting along trailing branches. Oval leaves 1–1½ in. long, half as wide. Fragrant white flowers at ends of leafy twigs from March through April. Use in rock gardens or as small-area ground cover in part shade.

D. burkwoodii. Evergreen or semievergreen to deciduous. Zones 3–6, 14–17. Erect, compact growth to 3–4 ft.; closely set, narrow leaves and numerous small clusters of fragrant flowers (white fading to pink) around branch ends in late spring and again in late summer. Sun or light shade. Use in shrub borders, at woodland edge, as foundation planting.

D. b. 'Carol Mackie'. Resembles the above, but has gold-edged leaves. White flowers open from white buds.

D. b. 'Somerset'. Similar to species, but larger (4–5 ft.), with pink flowers in May–June.

D. cneorum. GARLAND DAPHNE. Evergreen. Zones 2–9, 14–17. Matting and spreading; less than 1 ft. high and 3 ft. wide. Good container plant. Trailing branches covered with narrow, 1-in.-long, dark green leaves. Clusters of fragrant rosy pink flowers in April and May. Choice rock garden plant; give it partial shade in warm areas, full sun in cool-summer areas. After bloom, topdress with mix of peat moss and sand to keep roots cool and induce additional rooting of trailing stems. A noted rock garden authority recommends throwing rocks at your *D. cneorum:* the rock bruises the stem and holds it against the soil in a layering process.

Varieties include 'Eximia', lower growing than the species and with larger flowers; 'Pygmaea Alba', 3 in. tall, 1 ft. wide, with white flowers; 'Ruby Glow', with larger, more deeply colored flowers and with late summer rebloom; and 'Variegata', with gold-edged leaves.

D. collina. Evergreen. Zones 15–17; 5, 6 with protection; 14 in partial shade. Neat, dense mound to 2 ft. high and wide. Small (2-in.-long), dark green leaves, paler beneath. Fragrant deep rose flowers in clusters at branch tips, April–May. Sometimes reblooms in summer and fall.

D. c. neapolitana. Smaller-growing than species, more open and spreading, and perhaps easier to grow.

D. genkwa. LILAC DAPHNE. Deciduous. Best in Zones 4–6, 16, 17. Erect, open growth to 3–4 ft. high and as wide. Before leaves expand, clusters of lilac blue, scentless flowers wreathe branches, making foot-long blossom wands. White fruit follows flowers. Leaves are oval, 2 in. long. Use in rock garden, shrub border. Full sun or partial shade.

D. mantensiana. Evergreen. Zones 4–6, 15–17. Grows slowly to 1½ ft., spreading to 3 ft. Clusters of perfumed purple flowers at branch tips, May–June (and often through summer). Densely branched and well foliaged, it can be used in same way as low-growing azaleas. Leaves narrow, to 1¼ in. long.

D. mezereum. FEBRUARY DAPHNE. Deciduous. Zones 1–7, 14–17. Rather gawky, stiffly twigged, erect growth to 4 ft. with roundish, 2–3-in.-long, thin leaves. Should be planted in groups. Sun to partial shade. Fragrant reddish purple flowers in short stalkless clusters are carried along branches in February before leaf-out, and continue until April. May go dormant by late July or August. Clusters of red fruit follow flowers.

D. m. 'Alba'. Same as above but with white flowers, yellow fruit; not as rangy in growth.

D. odora. WINTER DAPHNE. Evergreen. Zones 4–9, 14–24. So much loved, so prized for its pervasive, pre-spring fragrance that it continues to be widely planted in spite of its unpredictable behavior. Very neat, handsome plant usually to about 4 ft. high and spreading wider; occasionally grows 8–10 ft. high. Rather narrow, 3-in.-long leaves are thick and glossy. Flowers—pink to deep red on outside, with creamy pink throats—appear in nosegay clusters at ends of branches, February–March.

D. odora needs much air around its roots, so plant in porous soil. Otherwise, water molds attack. Dig planting hole twice as wide as root ball and 1½ times as deep. Refill with 1 part soil, 1 part fine sand, 2 parts ground bark. To create ideal drainage: before refilling hole, drill through bottom until you hit a better-draining soil layer. Refill that chimney with mixture, too. Set top of root ball higher than soil surface. Fill containers with same mix.

In Zones 18–24, transplanting an existing *D. odora* often fails; digging cuts roots, plant suffers, water molds get at it. Transplanting works in Zones 4–9, 14–17.

Plant this daphne where it can get at least 3 hours of shade a day. If possible, shade soil around roots with living ground cover. A pH of 7.0 is right for it (important in Zones 4–6). Feed right after bloom with complete fertilizer but not acid plant food.

During dry season, water as infrequently as plant will allow. Little or no water in summer increases flowering next spring and helps prevent death from water molds.

Shape plants by cutting at bloom season; cut flowering twigs back to good bud, small shoot, or large branch.

D. o. 'Marginata'. More widely grown than species. Leaves are edged with band of yellow.

D. retusa. Evergreen. Zones 5, 6, 15–17. Sturdy, compact growth to 1–2 ft. high and as broad. Leaves to 3 in. long; tips broad, sometimes notched. Lilac-scented flowers in 3-in. clusters, white tinged with pink or rose, in May–June, are followed by red fruit. Combines well with dwarf rhododendrons. Takes sun (but not reflected heat) and partial shade.

D

DARLINGTONIA californica. *Sarraceniaceae.* CALIFORNIA PITCHER PLANT, COBRA LILY. Novelty perennial. Zones 4–7, 14–17. Native to bogs in mountains of northern California and Oregon. Grow in containers in sunny spot indoors or in greenhouse. Interesting for its unusual leaves and habit of digesting insects. Plant grows in clumps of 1–2-ft., tubelike, yellow green, veiny leaves, hooded at top. Hood has translucent spots. At mouth opening are 2 flared lobes, often reddish in color. Insects are lured into this leafy trap by sticky glands. Once insects are inside, downward pointing hairs prevent escape. Insects fall to base of leaf and decay; when they reach a soluble state, they become protein food absorbed by plant's cells.

Darlingtonia californica

Striking flowers, nodding at ends of 2½–4-ft. stems, appear April–June. Long, slender, pale green sepals, shorter dark purple petals. Blooms followed by mahogany brown seed capsules.

Pot in live sphagnum moss; keep moist at all times. Water overhead. Dry fertilizer, saline water are harmful. Collected plants are packaged and sold in a few nurseries and specialty shops, generally from October through June. They rarely thrive beyond a season or two.

DASYLIRION wheeleri. *Agavaceae.* DESERT SPOON, SOTOL. Evergreen shrub. Zones 14–24; most widely used in 12, 13. Native to deserts and mountains of the Southwest. A fountain of spiky, bluish gray leaves up to 3 ft. long and less than an inch wide slowly builds a trunk to 3 ft. tall, covered with dried, drooping shag of old leaves. Base of each leaf broadens where it joins the trunk to form a long-handled spoon prized in arrangements. Eventually produces a tall, slender spike (9–15 ft. tall) with myriad tiny, greenish white flowers.

Dasylirion wheeleri

DATE PALM. See *Phoenix.*

DATURA. For cultivated plants known as *Datura,* see *Brugmansia.*

DAUBENTONIA tripetii. See *Sesbania tripetii.*

DAVALLIA trichomanoides. *Polypodiaceae.* SQUIRREL'S FOOT FERN. Outdoors in Zones 17, 23, 24; elsewhere, indoor or greenhouse plant. Very finely divided fronds to 1 ft. long, 6 in. wide rise from light reddish brown, furry rhizomes (like squirrel's feet) that creep over soil surface. Hardy to 30°F.; can be used in mild-winter areas as small-scale ground cover in partly shaded areas. Best use in any climate is as hanging basket plant. Use light, fast-draining soil mix. Needs less water than other ferns. Feed occasionally. (For similar fern, see *Humata.*)

Davallia trichomanoides

DAVIDIA involucrata. *Nyssaceae.* DOVE TREE. Deciduous. Zones 4–9, 14–21. Native to China. Tree to 35 ft. in Pacific Northwest (higher in California), with rounded crown and strong branching pattern. Has clean look in and out of leaf. When it flowers in May, general effect is that of white doves resting among green leaves—or as some say, like handkerchiefs drying on branches. Because leaves are already out at bloom time, blossoms aren't as showy as smaller flowers of deciduous fruit trees.

Leaves are vivid green, 3–6 in. long, roundish to heart shaped. Small, clustered, red-anthered flowers are carried between 2 large, unequal, white or creamy white bracts; one 6 in. long, other about 4 in. Brown fruit about the size of a golf ball hangs on tree well into winter.

Davidia involucrata

In Zones 7–9, 14, 18–21, give partial or afternoon shade. Average water. Plant it by itself; it should not compete with other flowering trees. Nice in front of dark conifers where vivid green and white stand out.

DAWN REDWOOD. See *Metasequoia glyptostroboides.*

DAYLILY. See *Hemerocallis.*

DEAD NETTLE. See *Lamium maculatum.*

DEER FERN. See *Blechnum spicant.*

DEERHORN CEDAR. See *Thujopsis dolabrata.*

DEER TONGUE FERN. See *Blechnum spicant.*

DELOSPERMA. *Aizoaceae.* ICE PLANT. *Delosperma* is a huge group which includes a useful ground cover and 2 of the hardiest ice plants. All thrive in full sun, with good drainage and just enough water to keep them looking bright and fresh.

D. 'Alba'. WHITE TRAILING ICE PLANT. Zones 12–24. Dwarf, spreading, rooting freely from stems. Good ground and bank cover with lively green, fleshy, roundish leaves, small white flowers that attract bees. Plant 1 ft. apart for quick cover. In some climates, no summer water is needed once plants are established. Good near coast. Can be fire retardant if groomed.

Delosperma 'Alba'

D. cooperi. All Zones. One of the 2 hardiest ice plants yet introduced. Grows 5 in. tall, 2 ft. wide. Brilliant, shining purple flowers bloom all summer long. Tolerates 0°F. if protected by snow or mulch.

D. nubigenum. All Zones. Hardiest of all ice plants, it has withstood −25°F. Barely 1 in. high, spreading to 3 ft. Fleshy, cylindrical, bright green leaves turn red in fall, green up again in spring. Bright golden yellow flowers, 1–1½ in. wide, blanket plants in spring. Effective rock garden plant in mountain climates.

DELPHINIUM. *Ranunculaceae.* Perennials, some short lived and treated as annuals. Most people associate delphiniums with blue flowers, but color range also includes white and shades of red, pink, lavender, purple, and yellow. Leaves are lobed or fanlike, variously cut and divided. Taller hybrids offer rich colors in elegant spirelike form. All kinds are effective in borders and make good cut flowers; lower-growing kinds serve well as container plants. Blossoms attract birds. For annual delphiniums (LARKSPURS), see *Consolida.*

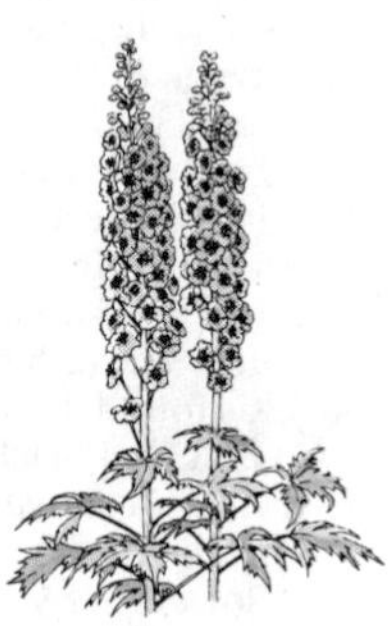
Delphinium elatum

All kinds are easy to grow from seed. Sow fresh seed in flats of light soil mix in July–August in mild-winter areas; set out transplants in October for bloom in late spring and early summer. (In mild-winter climates, most perennial forms are short lived, often treated as annuals.) In cold climates, refrigerate summer-harvested seed in airtight containers until time to sow. Sow seed in March–April, set out transplants in June–July for first bloom by September (and more bloom the following summer).

Delphiniums need full sun, rich, porous soil, and regular watering and fertilizing. Improve poor or heavy soils by blending in soil conditioners. Add lime to strongly acid soils. Work small handful of bonemeal or superphosphate into bottom of each hole before setting out plant. Be careful not to cover root crown.

Here is how to grow close-to-perfect plants: when new shoots develop in spring, remove all but 2 or 3 strongest and apply complete fertilizer alongside plants. Bait for slugs and snails. Stake flower stalks early. After bloom, cut back flower spikes, leaving foliage at bottom; after new shoots are several inches high, cut old stalks to ground. Fertilize to encourage good second bloom in late summer, early fall.

D. ajacis. See *Consolida.*

D. belladonna. Sturdy, bushy perennial. Zones 1–9, 14–24. To 3–4 ft. Deeply cut leaves; short-stemmed, airy flower clusters. Varieties: 'Belladonna', light blue; 'Bellamosum', dark blue; 'Casa Blanca', white; 'Cliveden Beauty', deep turquoise blue. All have flowers 1½–2 in. across, are longer lived than tall hybrids listed under *D. elatum.*

D. cardinale. SCARLET LARKSPUR. Perennial. Zones 14–24. Native to California coastal mountains, Monterey County south. Erect stems grow 3–6 ft. tall from deep, thick, woody roots. Leaves 3–9 in. wide, with deep, narrow lobes. Flowers 1 in. across, with scarlet calyx and spur and yellow, scarlet-tipped petals; May–June bloom. Sow seed early for first-year bloom.

D. elatum. CANDLE DELPHINIUM, CANDLE LARKSPUR. Perennial. Zones 1–9, 14–24. Together with *D. cheilanthum* and others, this 3–6-ft. Siberian species, with small dark or dull purple flowers, is parent of modern tall-growing delphinium strains such as spectacular Pacific strain.

Pacific strain delphinium hybrids (also called Giant Pacific, Pacific Hybrids, and Pacific Coast Hybrids) grow up to 8 ft. tall, come in selected color series such as 'Summer Skies', light blue; 'Blue Bird', medium blue; 'Blue Jay', medium to dark blue; 'Galahad', clear white with white center; 'Percival', white with black center. Other purple, lavender, pink named varieties also sold.

Like Pacific strain but shorter (2–2½ ft. tall) are the Blue Fountains, Blue Springs, and Magic Fountains strains. Even shorter is the Stand Up strain (15–20 in.). These shorter strains seldom require staking.

Other strains have flowers in shades of lilac pink to deep raspberry rose, clear lilac, lavender, royal purple, and darkest violet. Wrexham strain, tall growing with large spikes, was developed in England.

D. grandiflorum *(D. chinense).* CHINESE or BOUQUET DELPHINIUM. Short-lived perennial treated as biennial or annual. All Zones. Bushy, branching, 1 ft. tall or less. Varieties include 'Dwarf Blue Mirror', 1 ft., upward-facing flowers of deep blue; and 'Tom Thumb', 8 in. tall, pure gentian blue flowers.

D. nudicaule. SCARLET LARKSPUR. Perennial. Zones 5–7, 14–24. Native of northern California, southwestern Oregon. Slender plant to 1–3 ft. tall. Leaves long stalked, mostly basal, broadly divided. Flowers few, long spurred, red. Sun or half shade; best in woodland situations.

DENDROBIUM. *Orchidaceae.* Epiphytic orchid. Native to east and southeast Asia. Distributed over wide range of climates; many species differ in cultural needs.

Dendrobium nobile

D. nobile hybrids are best for novice. They vary in color from white through pink to rosy purple. Leathery leaves 5–6 in. long. Flowers grow in clusters all along well-ripened stems. Well-grown plants may have hundreds of 3-in. flowers. Grow under same conditions as cattleyas until new growth matures in fall. Then move plants into cool, bright greenhouse; give little water and no feeding. Resume normal cattleya treatment after flower buds form. Splendid orchids for greenhouse, they seldom get enough light to bloom well in living rooms or sun porches.

DENDROMECON. *Papaveraceae.* BUSH POPPY. Evergreen shrubs. Zones 5–8, 14–24. Has been grown as south-wall shrub in Zone 5. Both species below are sun loving, give showy display of bright yellow, 2-in.-wide, poppylike flowers. Thrive in dry, well-drained soil; good for banks, roadsides, with other native shrubs.

Dendromecon harfordii

D. harfordii *(D. rigida harfordii).* ISLAND BUSH POPPY. Native to Santa Cruz and Santa Rosa islands off coast of southern California. Rounded or spreading large shrub or small tree to 20 ft. Leaves deep green, to 3 in. long, half as wide. Free flowering April–July; scattered bloom throughout year. Prune to thin or shape after bloom.

D. rigida. BUSH POPPY. Native to dry chaparral in lower elevations in California. Untidy growing wild. Freely branched shrub 2–8 ft. tall, with shredding, yellowish gray or white bark. Thick, veiny, gray green leaves 1–4 in. long. Flowers March–June. Prune back to 2 ft. after flowering.

DEODAR CEDAR. See *Cedrus deodara.*

DESERT BROOM. See *Baccharis sarothroides.*

DESERT HOLLY. See *Atriplex hymenelytra.*

DESERT HONEYSUCKLE. See *Anisacanthus thurberi.*

DESERT IRONWOOD. See *Olneya tesota.*

DESERT MARIGOLD. See *Baileya multiradiata.*

DESERT OLIVE. See *Forestiera neomexicana.*

DESERT WILLOW. See *Chilopsis linearis.*

DEUTZIA. *Saxifragaceae.* Deciduous flowering shrubs. Zones 1–11, 14–17. They are best used among evergreens, where they can make a show when in flower, then blend back in with other greenery during the rest of the year. Their May flowering coincides with that of late spring bulbs such as tulips and Dutch iris.

Deutzia rosea

Plant in sun or light shade. Prune after flowering. With low- or medium-growing kinds, cut some of oldest stems to ground every other year. Prune tall-growing kinds severely by cutting back wood that has flowered. Cut to outward-facing side branches. Need average garden water.

D. crenata. Native to Japan. Similar to *D. scabra,* but with white flowers. Deep purple red fall foliage color. The variety *D. c. nakaiana* is dwarf and spreading, with double flowers.

D. elegantissima. Bears pink flowers on a 6-ft. shrub. The variety *D. e.* 'Rosealind', 4–5 ft. tall and spreading, has deep rose flowers.

D. gracilis. SLENDER DEUTZIA. Native to Japan. To 6 ft. or less. Many slender stems arch gracefully, carry bright green, 2½-in., sharply toothed leaves and clusters of snowy white flowers. The variety 'Nikko' grows only 1–2 ft. tall by 5 ft. wide and can be used as a ground cover.

D. rosea. Hybrid. Low-growing shrub (to 3–4 ft.), with finely toothed, 1–3-in.-long leaves. Flowers pinkish outside, white inside, in short clusters.

D. scabra. Native to Japan, China. This plant and its varieties are robust shrubs 7–10 ft. tall. Leaves oval, 3 in. long, dull green, roughish to touch, with scallop-toothed edges. May–June flowers white or pinkish, in narrow, upright clusters. Best-known variety is *D. s.* 'Pride of Rochester', with large clusters of small, double, frilled flowers, rosy purple outside.

DIANELLA tasmanica. *Liliaceae.* Perennial. Zones 8, 9, 14–24. Fibrous-rooted plant with sturdy, swordlike leaves to 4–5 ft. Small, pale blue, summer-blooming flowers in loose clusters on straight, slender stalks, followed by glistening turquoise blue berries lasting 2 months or longer. Grow in partial shade (full sun along coast). Provide rich, porous soil and routine feeding. Plants need ample water to fruit well, but tolerate drought once established. Attractive near swimming pools.

Dianella tasmanica

DIANTHUS. *Caryophyllaceae.* PINK. Perennials, biennials, annuals. All Zones. Over 300 species, many with high garden value, and extremely large number of hybrids. Most kinds form attractive evergreen mats or tufts of grasslike green, gray green, blue green, or blue gray leaves. Single or double flowers in white and shades of pink, rose, red, yellow, and orange bloom in spring or summer, sometimes until frost. Many have rich, spicy fragrance.

Dianthus caryophyllus

Among dianthus are appealing border favorites such as cottage pink and sweet William, highly prized cut flowers such as carnation (clove pink), and rock garden miniatures.

All kinds of dianthus thrive in full sun (light afternoon shade in hot areas) and in light, fast-draining soil. Carnations, sweet William, and cottage pinks need fairly rich soil; rock garden or alpine types require gritty growing medium, with added lime if soil is acid. Avoid overwatering. Shear off faded blooms. Sow seed of annual kinds in flats or directly in garden. Propagate perennial kinds by cuttings made from tips of growing shoots, or by division, layering (see page 85), or seed.

Carnations and sweet William are subject to rust and fusarium wilt. Control rust by spraying foliage weekly with benlate; remove and destroy plants infected by wilt. Replant only in clean or sterilized soil. Take cuttings only from disease-free plants.

D. barbatus. SWEET WILLIAM. Vigorous biennial often grown as annual. Sturdy stems 10–20 in. high; leaves are flat, light to dark green, 1½–3 in. long. Dense clusters of white, pink, rose, red, purplish, or bicolored flowers, about ½ in. across, set among leafy bracts; not very fragrant. Sow seed in late spring for bloom following year. Double-flowered and dwarf (8–10-in.-tall) strains are obtainable from seed. Roundabout and Summer Beauty strains (1 ft.) bloom the first year from seed. Indian Carpet is only 6 in. tall.

D. caryophyllus. CARNATION, CLOVE PINK. Perennial. There are 2 distinct categories of carnations: florists' and border types. Both have double flowers, bluish green leaves, and branching, leafy stems often becoming woody at base.

Border carnations. Bushier, more compact than florist type, 12–14 in. high. Flowers 2–2½ in. wide, fragrant, borne in profusion. Effective as shrub border edgings, in mixed flower border, and in containers. New hybrid carnations grown from seed are usually treated as annuals, but often live over. 'Juliet' makes compact, foot-tall clumps with long production of 2½-in. scarlet flowers; 'Luminette', 2 ft. tall, is similar. Pixie Delight strain also is similar, but includes full range of carnation colors. Knight series has strong stems, blooms in 5 months from seed; Bambino strain is a little slower to bloom. There is also a strain called simply Hanging Mixed, with pink- or red-flowered plants that sprawl or hang from pot or window box.

Florists' carnations. Grown commercially in greenhouses, outdoors in gardens in mild-winter areas. Greenhouse-grown plants reach 4 ft., have fragrant flowers 3 in. wide in many colors—white, pink and red shades, orange, purple, yellow, and variegated. For large flowers, leave only terminal bloom on each stem and pinch out all other buds down to fifth joint, below which new flowering stems will develop. Stake to prevent sprawling. Start with strong cuttings taken from most vigorous plants of selected named varieties. Sturdy plants conceal supports, look quite tidy.

D. chinensis. CHINESE PINK, RAINBOW PINK. Biennial or short-lived perennial; most varieties grown as annuals. Erect, 6–30 in. high; stems branch only at top. Stem leaves narrow, 1–3 in. long, ½ in. wide, hairy on margins. Basal leaves usually gone by flowering time. Flowers about 1 in. across, rose lilac with deeper colored eye; lack fragrance. Modern strains are compact (1 ft. tall or less) domes covered with bright flowers in white, pink, red, and all variations and combinations of these colors. 'Fire Carpet' is a brilliant solid red, 'Snowfire' white with a red eye. Telstar is an extra dwarf (6–8-in.) strain. Petals are deeply fringed on some, smooth edged on others. Some flowers have intricately marked eyes. Sow directly in ground in spring, in full sun, for summer bloom. Pick off faded flowers with their bases to prolong bloom.

D. deltoides. MAIDEN PINK. Hardy perennial forming loose mats. Flowering stems 8–12 in. high, with short leaves. Flowers about ¾ in. across, borne at end of forked stems; petals sharp toothed, light or dark rose to purple or white, spotted with lighter colors. Blooms in summer, sometimes again in fall.

Named varieties are: 'Vampire', deep red; 'Zing', bright scarlet; 'Zing Rose', rose red. Microchip is a mixture including pinks, reds, and whites, often with contrasting eyes. Although these bloom in just a few weeks from seed, they are still hardy perennials.

D. gratianopolitanus *(D. caesius)*. CHEDDAR PINK. Perennial. Neat, compact mounds of blue gray foliage on weak, branching stems up to 1 ft. long. Flowering stems erect, 3–12 in. high. Very fragrant pink blooms with toothed petals, May–June.

D. 'Little Joe'. Perennial. Irresistible little plant forming clump of deep blue gray foliage 4–6 in. high and about 6 in. across. Crimson single flowers bloom from May to November if dead blooms are removed. Especially effective with rock garden campanulas.

D. plumarius. COTTAGE PINK. Perennial. Charming, almost legendary plant, cultivated for hundreds of years, used in developing many hybrids. Typically has loosely matted gray green foliage. Flowering stems 10–18 in. tall; flowers spicily fragrant, single or double, with petals more or less fringed, in rose, pink, or white with dark centers. Highly prized are old laced pinks, with spicy-scented white flowers in which each petal is outlined in red or pink. Blooms from June to October. Indispensable edging for borders or for peony or rose beds. Perfect in small arrangements and old-fashioned bouquets.

D. 'Rose Bowl'. Perennial. Gray green, very narrow leaves form tight mat 2–3 in. high. Richly fragrant, cerise rose flowers 1 in. across on 6-in. stems. Blooms almost continuously if spent blooms are removed regularly.

D. 'Spotty'. Resembles the above, but the pink flowers are heavily spotted with white.

D. 'Tiny Rubies'. Perennial. Tufts of gray foliage to 3 in. high, spreading to 4 in. Small, double, fragrant ruby red flowers in early summer. This and other dwarf kinds of dianthus are among longest lived and most attractive rock garden subjects and small-scale ground covers, with fresh-looking foliage at all seasons.

Diapensiaceae. The diapensia family contains a few perennials and tiny shrubs native to northern parts of the globe. Some, such as *Galax* and *Shortia*, are useful in shady gardens or rock gardens.

DIASCIA. *Scrophulariaceae.* TWINSPUR. Annual, perennial. South African natives with rich salmon to coral pink flowers, each with 2 prominent spurs on back. Flowers in spikelike clusters at ends of stems. Use in rock gardens, borders, pots. Perennial sorts may die in winter if planted in heavy, wet soil.

Diascia barberae

D. barberae. Annual. All Zones. Slender stems 6–12 in. tall. Sow seed directly in ground in full sun (partial shade in hot-summer areas).

D. cordata. Perennial. Zones 7–9, 14–24. Low green mat with 10-in. sprays of salmon pink. Summer blooming.

D. rigescens. Perennial. Zones 7–9, 14–24. Sprawling stems make 2-ft.-wide clumps, turn up at ends to display 6–8-in. spikes of rich pink. Spring and summer bloom. Cut out old stems.

D. 'Ruby Field'. Perennial. Similar to *D. cordata*, with longer bloom season. May be a perennial selection of *D. barberae*.

DICENTRA. *Fumariaceae.* BLEEDING HEART. Perennials. Zones 1–9, 14–24. Short lived in mild-winter areas. Graceful, divided, fern-like foliage. Dainty flowers, usually heart shaped, pink, rose, or white on leafless stems. Most kinds need shade, combine handsomely with ferns, begonias, primroses, fuchsias, bergenias, hellebores. In general, dicentras need rich, light, moist, porous soil. Never let water stand around roots. Since foliage dies down in winter, mark clumps to avoid digging into roots in dormant season.

Dicentra spectabilis

D. chrysantha. GOLDEN EARDROPS. Native to inner Coast Ranges and Sierra Nevada foothills of California. Erect perennial with sparse, blue gray, divided leaves on stout, hollow, 4–5-ft. stems. Flowers golden yellow, short spurred, held upright in large clusters. Requires warmth, good drainage, not-too-rich soil. Has deep tap root, needs no water during flowering in spring and summer. Seed available from wildflower specialists.

D. eximia. FRINGED BLEEDING HEART. Native of northeastern U.S. Forms tidy, nonspreading clumps 1–1½ ft. high. Leaves at base of plant; blue gray, more finely divided than those of western bleeding heart. Deep rose pink flowers with short, rounded spurs bloom May–August. Cut back in July or August for second growth and sometimes repeat bloom. Variety 'Alba' has white flowers. 'Bountiful' has deep blue green foliage and fuchsia-red flowers.

D. formosa. WESTERN BLEEDING HEART. Native to moist woods along Pacific Coast. Leafless flower stalks 8–18 in. high, with clusters of pendulous pale or deep rose flowers on reddish stems, April–June. Blue green foliage. Variety 'Sweetheart', beautiful white flowers, light green leaves, blooms May–October. *D. f. oregana*, native of Siskiyou Mountains in southern Oregon and northern California, grows about 8 in. high, has translucent blue green leaves, cream-colored flowers with rosy-tipped petals.

D. 'Luxuriant'. Hybrid of *D. eximia* and *D. peregrina*. Extremely vigorous. Dark blue green foliage. Flowers are as dark as those of *D. eximia* 'Bountiful', even in full sun. Foliage mass 10 in. tall, flower spikes 18–20 in. high.

D. spectabilis. COMMON BLEEDING HEART. Native of Japan. Old garden favorite, showiest of bleeding hearts. Leafy-stemmed plants 2–3 ft. high. Leaves soft green, largest of all dicentras. Rose pink, pendulous, heart-shaped flowers, 1 in. or more long, with white petals protruding, borne on one side of arching stems in late spring. 'Alba' ('Pantaloons') is a lovely pure white form. Beautiful with maidenhair ferns and in arrangements with tulips and lilacs. In Southwest, you can sometimes establish bleeding heart permanently in cool moist spot in foothill canyons, but usual practice is to plant or pot up new roots each year and discard plants in early summer after blooming. These dormant roots—fleshy and sometimes even woody—are available in late fall, winter, and earliest spring. Plant as soon as they become available in your area.

DICHELOSTEMMA. *Amaryllidaceae.* Corms. All Zones. Western natives usually sold as species of *Brodiaea*, and still considered brodiaeas by many botanists. See *Brodiaea* for culture. All have few narrow, grassy leaves.

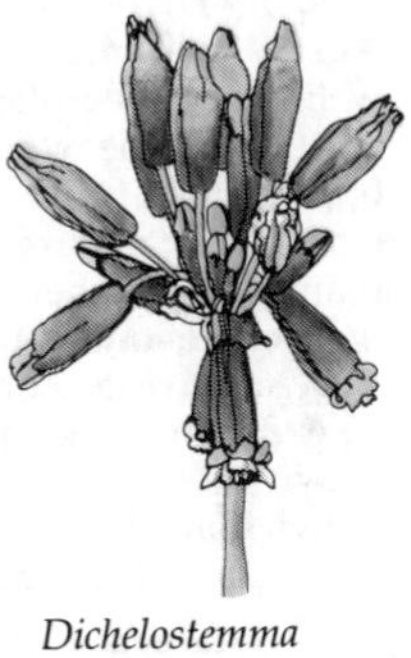

Dichelostemma ida-maia

D. ida-maia *(Brevoortia* or *Brodiaea ida-maia).* FIRECRACKER FLOWER. Clusters of 6–20 or more pendulous, tubular, scarlet flowers tipped green. Blooms May–July. To 3 ft. Good summer-dry woodland plant. Takes some shade.

D. pulchellum *(D. capitatum, B. capitata).* BLUE DICKS, WILD HYACINTH. Deep blue or violet blue flowers in tight, headlike cluster surrounded with purplish bracts. Blooms March–May. To 2 ft. Thrives in poor soils, summer-baked locations. Pretty spring flowers for sunny banks.

DICHONDRA micrantha (often sold as *D. carolinensis* or *D. repens*). *Convolvulaceae.* DICHONDRA. Perennial lawn plant or ground cover plant. Zones 8, 9, 12–24. Ground-hugging plant that spreads by rooting surface runners. Small, round leaves look like miniature water lily pads. In shade and with heavy feeding and watering, it can grow to 6 in. tall and needs frequent mowing. In sun and in areas subject to foot traffic—as between stepping stones—it stays low and seldom, if ever, needs mowing.

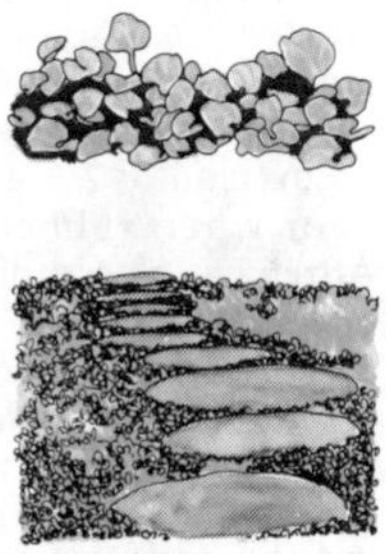

Dichondra micrantha

To plant, prepare soil as for a lawn. Sow seed in April or May. Two lbs. per 1,000 sq. ft. will give fast coverage (lesser amounts bring slower coverage with increased weed problems). Or plant from plugs cut from flats of dichondra. Place 1-in.-sq. or (preferably) 2-in.-sq. pieces at 6–12-in. intervals. Set runners on plugs at soil level or slightly below.

Dichondra requires ample fertilizer and water to look its best. Dichondra flea beetle can devastate lawn. First signs are browning leaves with engraved lines where tissue has been gnawed. Control at once with diazinon. Don't walk on dichondra when it's frozen; leaves will blacken on thawing.

DICHORISANDRA. *Commelinaceae.* Perennials usually grown as house plants. Relatives of wandering Jews (*Tradescantia* and *Zebrina*). Like them in foliage (although leaves are much larger), but have erect, fleshy stems rising from fleshy rootstocks, flowers in dense clusters. They need rich house plant soil mix, ample water and feeding during warm weather. They slow down or even go dormant in cool, dull weather and need partial drying off at that time.

Dichorisandra reginae

D. reginae. To 2 ft. Leaves to 6 in. long, purple beneath, dark green marked with silver above. Blue flowers in dense spikes at ends of stems. Showy plant; subject to leaf burn if overfed or overwatered. Don't discard if top dies; new stems often appear from roots.

D. thyrsiflora. BLUE GINGER. To 3 ft. in 8-in. pot, much taller in open ground or large tub. Stems erect, occasionally with a branch or two. Deep green leaves to 6 in. or more. In greenhouse or other favorable situation, may produce narrow, 6-in.-long clusters of bright blue flowers.

DICKSONIA. *Dicksoniaceae.* Tree ferns. Hardy, slow growing, from southern hemisphere. See Ferns for culture.

Dicksonia antarctica

D. antarctica. TASMANIAN TREE FERN. Zones 8, 9, 14–17, 19–24. Native to southeastern Australia, Tasmania. Hardiest of tree ferns; well-established plants tolerate 20°F. Thick, red brown, fuzzy trunks grow slowly to 15 ft. From top of trunk grow many arching, 3–6-ft. fronds; mature fronds are darker green than those of either Hawaiian tree fern (*Cibotium*) or Australian tree fern (*Cyathea*).

D. squarrosa. Zones 17, 23, 24. Native to New Zealand. Slender, dark trunk grows slowly to 20 ft. tall. Flat crown of 8-ft.-long, stiff, leathery fronds. Much less frequently grown than *D. antarctica*.

Dicksoniaceae. The dicksonia family of tree ferns differs from the other tree fern family, *Cyatheaceae*, only in technical details. Two representatives are *Cibotium* and *Dicksonia*.

DICTAMNUS albus. *Rutaceae.* GAS PLANT, FRAXINELLA. Perennial. Zones 1–9. Sturdy, long lived, extremely permanent in colder climates. Needs little care once established. Forms clumps 2½–4 ft. high. Strong lemony odor when rubbed or brushed against. Attractive, glossy, olive green leaves with 9–11 leaflets, each 1–3 in. long. Spikelike clusters of white flowers about 1 in. long with prominent greenish stamens, June–July. There are varieties with pink and rosy purple flowers and darker green leaves, growing taller and more robust than species. Never common, but worth looking for or growing from seed (a slow process).

Dictamnus albus

Effective in borders; combine white-flowered kind with yellow daylily, Siberian iris, taller campanulas. Good cut flower. Plant in sun or part shade in good soil. Average water. Divide infrequently; divisions take 2–3 years before making a show. Propagate from seed sown in fall or spring or from root cuttings in spring. Common name, gas plant, derives from this phenomenon: if lighted match is held near flowers on warm, still evenings, volatile oil exuded from glands on that part of plant will ignite and burn briefly.

DIDISCUS coeruleus. See *Trachymene coerulea*.

DIEFFENBACHIA. *Araceae.* DUMB CANE. Evergreen indoor foliage plant (you can move it into sheltered patio or lanai in summer). Striking variegated leaves. Colors vary from dark green to yellow green and chartreuse, with variegations in white or pale cream. Small plants generally have single stems; older plants may develop multiple stems. Flowers—like odd, narrow callas—form on mature plants. Common name reflects fact that acrid sap will burn mouth and throat, and may paralyze vocal cords.

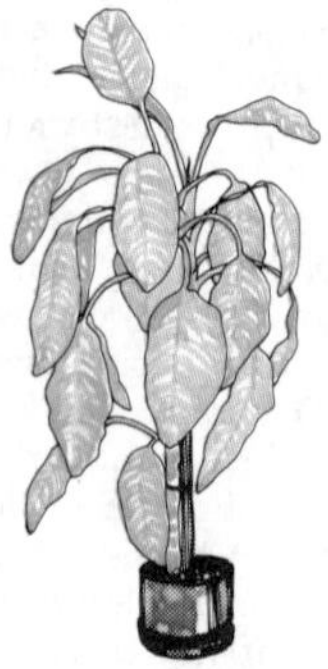
Dieffenbachia amoena

Give ample north light; turn occasionally. Water only when soil surface feels dry. If plant gets leggy, air-layer it (see page 85) or root cuttings in water. Old, leggy plants, cut back to 6 in. from soil line, usually resprout with multiple stems. Repot when roots begin pushing plant up in pot. Once repotted, plant usually sends out new basal shoots. Potting soil should drain freely. Feed bimonthly in spring and summer with half-strength liquid fertilizer. Underfed, underwatered plants show amazingly strong hold on life, recovering from severe wilting when better conditions come. They will not withstand constant overwatering, and sudden change from low to high light level will burn leaves.

D. amoena. To 6 ft. or more. Broad, dark green, 1½-ft.-long leaves with narrow, white, slanting stripes on either side of midrib.

D. bausei. Grows to 3 ft. or more in height, with 1-ft., greenish yellow leaves with deep green blotches and white flecks.

D. 'Exotica'. More compact than others, with smaller leaves. Leaves have dull green edges and much creamy white variegation. Midrib is creamy white.

D. maculata *(D. picta)*. To 6 ft. or taller. Wide, oval, green leaves, 10 in. or more in length, have greenish white dots and patches.

D. m. 'Rudolph Roehrs'. To 6 ft., with 10-in. leaves of pale chartreuse, blotched with ivory and edged with green.

D. m. 'Superba'. Foliage thicker and slightly more durable than that of species; more creamy white dots and patches.

DIERAMA. *Iridaceae.* FAIRY WAND. Corms. Zones 4–24. Native to South Africa. Swordlike 2-ft. leaves; slender, tough, arching stems 4–7 ft. tall, topped with pendulous, bell-shaped, mauve, purple, or white flowers. Effective against background of dark green shrubs or at edge of pool where graceful form can be displayed. Plant in sun, moist soil. When dividing clumps, include several corms in each division.

Dierama pulcherrimum

D. pendulum. Flowers white, lavender pink, or mauve, 1 in. long, March or April.

D. pulcherrimum. Leaves very stiff. Flowers bright purple to almost white, 1½ in. long, May–June.

DIETES *(Moraea)*. *Iridaceae.* FORTNIGHT LILY, AFRICAN IRIS. Evergreen perennials growing from rhizomes. Zones 8, 9, 13–24. Fan-shaped clumps of narrow, stiff, irislike leaves. Flowers like miniature Japanese iris appear on branched stalks throughout spring, summer, and fall, sometimes well into winter in mild areas. Each flower lasts only a day, but is quickly replaced by another. Bloom bursts seem to come at 2-week intervals—hence the name fortnight lily. Break off forming seed pods to increase flower production and prevent volunteer plants. Effective near swimming pools.

Dietes vegeta

Give plants full sun or light shade in any fairly good soil. Established plants tolerate drought but bloom more freely with regular watering. Divide overgrown clumps in autumn or winter. *Moraea* differs from *Dietes* in that corms are dormant for part of the year.

D. bicolor. To 2 ft. Flowers light yellow, about 2 in. wide, with maroon blotches. Cut flower stems to ground after blossoms fade.

D. hybrids. 'Lemon Drops' and 'Orange Drops' are occasionally seen. These resemble *D. vegeta*, but flowers are creamy, with conspicuous yellow or orange blotches.

D. vegeta *(D. iridioides, Moraea iridioides)*. To 4 ft., with 3-in.-wide, waxy white flowers with orange and brown blotch, purple stippling. 'Johnsonii' is robust variety with large leaves and flowers. Break off old blossoms individually to prevent self-sowing and prolong bloom, but don't cut off long, branching flower stems (these last from year to year). Instead, cut back to lower leaf joint near base of plant. Excellent in permanent landscape plantings with pebbles, rocks, substantial shrubs. Very drought tolerant.

DIGITALIS. *Scrophulariaceae.* FOXGLOVE. Biennials or perennials. All Zones. Erect plants 2–8 ft. high with tubular flowers shaped like fingers of glove in purple, yellow, white, pastels. Hairy, gray green leaves grow in clumps at base of plant. Use foxgloves for vertical display among shrubs or with ferns, taller campanulas, meadow rue. Bloom May–September; hummingbirds like the flowers.

Digitalis purpurea

Plant in full, partial, or light shade in rich, moist soil. Set out plants in fall for bloom following spring, summer. Sow seed in spring. Bait for snails, slugs. After first flowering, cut main spike; side shoots develop, bloom until September. Plants self-sow freely.

D. ferruginea. RUSTY FOXGLOVE. Biennial or perennial with very leafy stems to 6 ft. Leaves deeply veined. Flowers ¾–1¼ in. long, yellowish, netted with rusty red, in long, dense spikes.

D. grandiflora ***(D. ambigua).*** YELLOW FOXGLOVE. Biennial or perennial. Hairy-leafed plant 2–3 ft. high. Toothed leaves wrap around stem. Large flowers, 2–3 in. long, yellowish marked with brown.

D. mertonensis. True perennial with 2–3-ft. spikes of odd yet attractive coppery rose blooms. Though hybrid between 2 species, it comes true from seed.

D. purpurea. COMMON FOXGLOVE. Biennial, sometimes perennial. Naturalizes in shaded places. Variable, appears in many garden forms. Bold, erect, to 4 ft. or more high. Clumps of large, rough, woolly, light green leaves. Stem leaves short stalked, becoming smaller toward top of plant; these leaves are source of digitalis, valued but highly poisonous medicinal drug. Flowers 2–3 in. long, pendulous, purple, spotted on lower, paler side, borne in one-sided, 1–2-ft.-long spikes. Several garden strains: Excelsior, 5 ft., has fuller spikes, with flowers more horizontally held to show off interior spotting; Foxy, 3 ft., performs as annual, blooming in 5 months from seed; Gloxiniiflora, 4 ft., has flowers that are individually larger and open wider than common foxglove; Monstrosa, 3 ft., has topmost flower of each spike open or bowl shaped and 3 in. wide. Shirley is tall (6-ft.), robust strain in full range of colors. Volunteer foxglove seedlings are frequently white.

DILL. See *Anethum graveolens.*

DIMORPHOTHECA. *Compositae.* CAPE MARIGOLD, AFRICAN DAISY. (For other plants known as African daisy, see *Arctotis, Osteospermum.*) Annuals. All Zones. Gay, free-blooming, daisy-flowered plants, unsurpassed for winter and spring color in dry, warm-winter areas. Not as well adapted in cool, moist coastal climate. Broadcast seed in late summer or early fall where plants are to grow. Best in light soil, with moderate watering. Need full sun; flowers close when shaded, during heavy overcast, and at night. Use in broad masses as ground cover, in borders, parking strips, along rural roadsides, as filler among low shrubs.

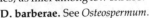

Dimorphotheca sinuata

D. barberae. See *Osteospermum.*

D. ecklonis. See *Osteospermum.*

D. fruticosa. See *Osteospermum.*

D. pluvialis ***(D. annua).*** Branched stems 4–16 in. high. Leaves to 3½ in. long, 1 in. wide, coarsely toothed. Flower heads 1–2 in. across; rays white above, violet or purple beneath; yellow center. Variety 'Glistening White', dwarf form with flower heads 4 in. across, is especially desirable.

D. sinuata (usually sold as *D. aurantiaca*). Best known of annual African daisies. Plants 4–12 in. high. Leaves narrow, 2–3 in. long, with a few teeth or shallow indentations. Flower heads 1½ in. across, with orange yellow rays, sometimes deep violet at base; yellow center. Hybrids between this species and *D. pluvialis* come in white and shades of yellow, orange, apricot, and salmon, often with contrasting dark centers.

Excellent for winter–spring color in Zones 10–13: reseeds yearly. Needs some supplemental water October–March if winter rains don't come. Leave area dry over summer.

DIOON. *Zamiaceae.* In general, resemble *Cycas revoluta* and take same culture. Dioons are more tender and less frequently sold.

Dioon edule

D. edule. Zones 13, 17, 19–24. Very slow. Eventually forms cylindrical trunk 6–10 in. wide, 3 ft. high. Leaves spreading, slightly arching, 3–5 ft. long, made of many leaflets toothed at tips or smooth edged. Leaves dusty blue green, soft, feathery on young plants; darker green, more rigid, hard, shiny on mature plants.

D. spinulosum. Zones 21–24. Slow growth to 12 ft. Leaves to 5 ft. long, with up to 100 narrow, spine-toothed, dark green, 6–8-in.-long leaflets. Protect from frosts.

DIOSMA. See *Coleonema and Diosma.*

DIOSPYROS. See Persimmon.

DIPLACUS. See *Mimulus.*

DIPLADENIA amoena, D. splendens. See *Mandevilla* 'Alice du Pont'.

DIPLOPAPPUS fruticosus. See *Felicia fruticosa.*

DISTICTIS. *Bignoniaceae.* Evergreen vines. Climb by tendrils and have trumpet-shaped flowers. To 20–30 ft. tall. Hardy to 24°F. Sun or part shade.

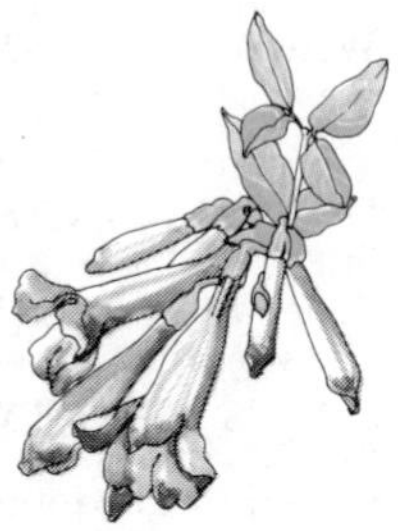

Distictis buccinatoria

D. buccinatoria ***(Bignonia cherere, Phaedranthus buccinatorius).*** BLOOD-RED TRUMPET VINE. Zones 8, 9, 14–24. Leaves have 2 oblong to oval leaflets 2–4 in. long. Clusters of 4-in.-long, trumpet-shaped flowers stand out well from vine. Color is orange red fading to bluish red, with yellow throat. Flowers appear in bursts throughout year when weather warms. Effective on fence, high wall, arbor. Prune yearly to keep under control. Give protected site in interior valleys. Feed and water young plants generously until established.

D. laxiflora ***(D. lactiflora, D. cinerea).*** VANILLA TRUMPET VINE. Zones 16, 22–24. Native to Mexico. More restrained than most trumpet vines and requires less pruning. Leaves, with 2 or 3 deep green, oblong, 2½-in.-long leaflets, make attractive pattern all year. The 3½-in.-long, vanilla-scented trumpets, violet at first, fading to lavender and white, appear in generous clusters throughout warmer months, sometimes giving 8 months of bloom. Average water.

Distictis 'Rivers'

D. 'Rivers' (sometimes labeled *D. riversii*). ROYAL TRUMPET VINE. Zones 16, 22–24. Plants sold under this name have larger leaves and flowers than other kinds and are much more vigorous. Substantial, glossy deep green leaves give them better winter appearance. Purple trumpets (to 5 in.) marked orange inside. Average water. Grows a little more slowly than blood-red trumpet vine; easier to keep neat.

D

DIZYGOTHECA elegantissima (often sold as *Aralia elegantissima*). *Araliaceae*. THREAD-LEAF FALSE ARALIA. House plant (juvenile stage); evergreen garden shrub (mature form) for Zones 16, 17, 22–24. Leaves on juvenile plants are lacy—divided like fans into very narrow (⅜-in.), 4–9-in.-long leaflets with notched edges—shiny dark green above, reddish beneath. As plants mature, leaves become bigger, with coarsely notched leaflets to 1 ft. long and 3 in. wide. Rarely flowers as house plant.

As house plant, give it ample light but no direct sunshine. Needs fast-draining, moisture-retentive soil mix (waterlogged or dry soil will make leaves drop). Feed monthly. Subject to pests indoors, not outdoors.

Dizygotheca elegantissima

In mild climates, plant in sheltered areas. Can become 5–12-ft. shrub, small tree. As single plant, makes lacy pattern on wall.

DODECATHEON. *Primulaceae*. SHOOTING STAR. Perennial. All Zones—adaptability varies with species. Mostly native to West. Spring flowers somewhat like small cyclamen, few to many in cluster on leafless stem ranging from a few inches to 2 ft. tall. Colors of many species range from white to pink, lavender, or magenta. Pale green leaves in basal rosettes dry up in summer heat. Needs porous, rich, well-drained soil, ample water while growing or blooming. Let soil dry out after bloom.

Rarely available in nurseries. Buy seed from native plant seed specialists or gather from wild plants. Grow species native to your area; not all are hardy everywhere. Western *D. hendersonii* has leaves to 6 in., 3–15 white to magenta flowers on 1½-ft. stalks.

Dodecatheon hendersonii

DODONAEA viscosa. *Sapindaceae*. HOP BUSH, HOPSEED BUSH. Evergreen shrub. Zones 7–9, 12–24. Native to Arizona and elsewhere in warmer parts of the world. Fast growing, with many upright stems to 12–15 ft. high, spreading almost as wide (can be trained to tree form by cutting out all but single stem). Willowlike green leaves to 4 in. long.

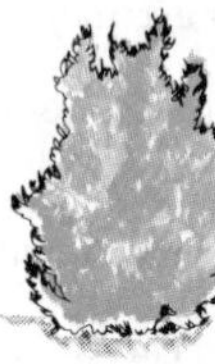

Most popular variety is 'Purpurea', PURPLE HOP BUSH, selected form with rich bronzy green leaves that turn deeper in winter. Seedlings vary greatly in color; variety 'Saratoga' (grown from cuttings) is uniformly rich purple. Plant purple-leafed kinds in full sun to retain rich coloration; they will turn green in shade. Clusters of flowers are insignificant. Creamy to pinkish winged fruit attractive in late summer.

Dodonaea viscosa

Can be pruned as hedge or espalier, or planted 6–8 ft. apart and left unpruned to become big informal screen. Its biggest asset is probably its wide cultural tolerance: it takes any kind of soil, ocean winds, dry desert heat. It's quite drought resistant when established, but will also take ample water (grows well in flower beds).

Native Arizona green form is useful and attractive plant for the desert—hardier to cold and deeper rooted than the purple-leafed form. Pinkish orange, papery seeds stand out better against green foliage. With little water, stays a compact 6–8-ft. shrub; with more water, quickly grows to 15 ft.

DOG-TOOTH VIOLET. See *Erythronium dens-canis*.

DOGWOOD. See *Cornus*.

DOLICHOS. *Leguminosae*. Perennial twining vines which produce dense cover of light green leaves divided like fans into 3 leaflets. Give average watering.

D. lablab. HYACINTH BEAN. Perennial vine usually grown as annual. All Zones in conditions noted below. Fast to 10 ft. Broad, oval leaflets to 3–6 in. long. Sweet pea–shaped purple or white flowers in loose clusters on long stems stand out from foliage. Flowers followed by velvety, beanlike pods to 2½ in. long. Grow plants like string beans for quick screening. Sun, good drainage.

Dolichos lablab

D. lignosus (*Dipogon australis*). AUSTRALIAN PEA VINE. Zones 16, 17, 21–24. Somewhat woody vine with small, triangular, 1½-in.-long leaflets and small rose purple flowers clustered at ends of long stalks. Evergreen in mild winters. Grow from seed and train on trellis or frame for summer screen. Grows to 10 ft. or more. Sun.

DOMBEYA. *Byttneriaceae*. Evergreen shrubs. Zones 21–24. Tender to frost, but make quick comebacks. Some have big, tropical-looking, toothed leaves and large, dense, hydrangealike flower clusters that droop from branches. Dombeyas need only sun, warmth, reasonably good soil, and ample water. Faded flower clusters hang on and look untidy unless removed. Can be espaliered or trained over arbors to display flowers. Mix with trees for jungle background.

D. cacuminum. Slender, erect tree to 30 ft. Three-lobed leaves, 4 in. wide. Blooms in late winter, early spring: bell-shaped, rose red flowers, 2 in. across, in loose clusters near branch tips.

Dombeya cayeuxii

D. cayeuxii. PINK BALL DOMBEYA. To 10 ft. Pink flowers in dense, heavy, drooping clusters. Winter bloom.

D. wallichii. To 30 ft., but usually seen as big, rounded shrub 12–15 ft. high, with big leaves to 6–10 in. long and as wide. Big, ball-shaped flower clusters in coral pink to red. Blooms late August into winter.

DONKEY TAIL. See *Sedum morganianum*.

DORONICUM. *Compositae*. LEOPARD'S BANE. Perennials. Zones 1–7, 14–17. Showy, bright yellow, daisylike flowers on long stems rise from mounds of dense, dark green, usually heart-shaped leaves. Blooms in early spring. Grow in partial shade, good soil. Divide clumps every 2–3 years; young plants bloom best. Average water.

Use in groups under high-branching deciduous trees; combine with white, purple, or lavender tulips, blue violas or forget-me-nots; use in front of purple lilacs or with hellebores at edge of woodland or shade border. Good cut flower.

Doronicum cordatum

D. cordatum *(D. caucasicum)*. Flower heads 2 in. across, borne singly on 1–1½-ft. stems. Increases by stolons. Variety 'Magnificum' more robust, with larger flowers; 'Finesse' has 3-in. flowers.

D. plantagineum. PLANTAIN LEOPARD'S BANE. Grows from tuberous rhizomes. Stout stems 2–5 ft. tall; rather coarse foliage.

Early blooming; flowers 2–4 in. across, few to a stem. Best in wild garden.

Dorotheanthus bellidiformis

DOROTHEANTHUS bellidiformis. *Aizoaceae.* LIVINGSTONE DAISY. Succulent annual. All Zones. Ice plant, but unlike most others, an annual. Pretty and useful temporary carpet in poor, dry soil, full sun. Trailing, a few inches high, with fleshy, bright green leaves and daisylike, 2-in. flowers in white, pink, orange, red. Sow seed in warm weather. Comes into bloom quickly. Fire retardant if well watered. Draws bees.

Doryanthes excelsa

DORYANTHES palmeri. *Agavaceae.* SPEAR LILY. Enormous succulent. Zones 15–17, 19–24. Native to Australia. Gigantic cluster of 100 or so 6-in.-wide leaves which may reach 8 ft. in length. Blooms in summer. Flower stalk 6–15 ft. high; clustered flowers reddish brown, in an elongated cluster up to 6 ft. long. Striking in big gardens. Give about same care as century plant, but remember that spear lily tolerates more shade and requires more water to look good; and unlike century plant, it does not die after blooming. Also striking subject for patio containers. *D. excelsa,* sometimes offered, has shorter leaves and crimson flowers in a tight, globular head.

DOUGLAS FIR. See *Pseudotsuga menziesii.*

DOVE TREE. See *Davidia involucrata.*

DOXANTHA unguis-cati. See *Macfadyena unguis-cati.*

Dracaena draco

DRACAENA. *Agavaceae.* (For other plants often called dracaena, see *Cordyline.*) Evergreen plants (small palmlike trees). Essentially foliage plants, grown in house or on lanais; certain kinds can be grown outdoors, as noted below. Some show graceful fountain forms with broad, curved, ribbonlike leaves, occasionally striped with chartreuse or white. Some have very stiff, swordlike leaves. Almost never flower as house plants. Fairly drought resistant. In containers, water only when top ½–1 in. of soil is dry. Plants take sun outdoors, shade indoors.

D. australis. See *Cordyline australis.*

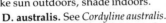

Dracaena marginata

D. deremensis. Outdoors, out of wind, in Zone 24; house plant anywhere. Native to tropical Africa. Most commonly sold is variety 'Warneckii': erect, slow growing to an eventual 15 ft., with 2-ft.-long, 2-in.-wide leaves in rich green striped white and gray. Others are: 'Bausei', green with white center stripe; 'Longii', with broader white center stripe; 'Janet Craig', with broad, dark green leaves. Compact versions of 'Janet Craig' and 'Warneckii' exist.

D. draco. DRAGON TREE. Outdoors in Zones 16, 17, 21–24; house plant anywhere. Native to Canary Islands. Stout trunk with upward-reaching or spreading branches topped by clusters of heavy, 2-ft.-long, sword-shaped leaves. Grows slowly to 20 ft. high and as wide. Makes odd but interesting silhouette. Clusters of greenish white flowers form at branch ends. After blossoms drop, stemmy clusters remain. Trim them off to keep plants neat.

D. fragrans. CORN PLANT. Outdoors, out of wind, in Zones 21, 23, 24; other than that, house plant. Native to west Africa. Upright, eventually to 20 ft. high, but slow growing. Heavy, ribbonlike, blue green leaves to 3 ft. long, 4 in. wide. (Typical plant in 8-in. pot will bear leaves about 1½ ft. long.) Tolerates darker position in house than other dracaenas. Variety 'Massangeana' has broad yellow stripe in center of leaf. Other striped varieties are 'Lindenii' and 'Victoriae'.

D. marginata. Outdoors, out of wind, Zones 21, 23, 24. House plant anywhere. Very easy to grow, very popular. Slender, erect, smooth gray stems to an eventual 12 ft. carry chevron markings where old leaves have fallen. Stems topped by crowns of narrow, leathery leaves to 2 ft. long, ½ in. wide. Leaves are deep glossy green with narrow margin of purplish red. If plant grows too tall, cut off crown and re-root it. New crowns will appear on old stem. 'Tricolor' ('Candy Cane') adds narrow gold stripe to green and red.

D. sanderana. Outdoors, out of wind, Zones 21, 23, 24; house plant anywhere. Native to west Africa. Neat and upright, to a possible 6–10 ft., somewhat resembling young corn plant. Strap-shaped, 9-in.-long leaves striped with white.

D. surculosa *(D. godseffiana).* House plant. Native to west Africa. Slow grower, smaller than other dracaenas. Slender, erect or spreading stems set with pairs or trios of 5-in.-long, 2-in.-wide, dark green leaves spotted with white. 'Kelleri' and 'Florida Beauty' are more heavily spotted.

DRAGON TREE. See *Dracaena draco.*

Drimys winteri

DRIMYS winteri. *Winteraceae.* WINTER'S BARK. Small evergreen tree. Zones 8, 9, 14–24. Native to southern Chile and Argentina. Slender, to 25 ft. Distinguished chiefly for clean foliage and dignified presence. Stems and branches, which tend to droop gracefully, are mahogany red with aromatic bark. Bright green, leathery, fragrant leaves are elliptical, 5–10 in. long. Blooms in winter and spring: jasmine-scented, creamy white flowers about 1 in. wide, in small clusters. Usually multistemmed, but easily trained to single trunk. May require pruning from time to time to maintain outline of pleasing symmetry. Give plenty of water with good drainage. Takes some sun near coast; shade inland.

Drosanthemum floribundum

DROSANTHEMUM. *Aizoaceae.* Succulent perennials. Zones 14–24. Two ice plants described here are often confused with each other, although quite different. In both, leaves are covered with glistening dots that look like tiny ice crystals; both have typical ice plant flowers with many narrow petals. Both are sun loving, will endure poor soil and live with little or no irrigation once established, especially near ocean. Can be fire retardant.

D. floribundum. ROSEA ICE PLANT. Grows to 6 in. tall, but stems trail to considerable length or drape over rocks, walls. Best ice plant for controlling erosion on steep slopes. Pale pink, ¾-in.-wide flowers make sheets of color in late spring, early summer. Bees are fond of them.

D. hispidum. To 2 ft. tall, 3 ft. wide, less inclined to stem-root than *D. floribundum.* Showy, 1-in. purple flowers in late spring, early summer. *D. floribundum* is often sold as *D. hispidum.*

DRUMSTICKS. See *Allium sphaerocephalum.*

DRYAS. *Rosaceae.* Perennials. Zones 1–6. Choice plants for rock gardens. Evergreen or partially so; somewhat shrubby at base, forming carpet of leafy creeping stems. Shiny white or yellow

D

strawberrylike flowers May–July; ornamental seed capsules with silvery white tails. Sun, average soil. Needs less water than most perennials.

Dryas octopetala

D. drummondii. To 4 in. high. Leaves oblong, 1½ in. long, white and woolly beneath. Flowers nodding, bright yellow, ¾ in. across.

D. octopetala. Leaves 1 in. long. Flowers white, 1½ in. across, erect. Mats up to 2–3 ft. high.

D. suendermannii. Hybrid between 2 species above. Leaves oblong, 1–1½ in. long, thick textured, similar to oak leaves. Flowers yellowish in bud, white in full bloom, nodding.

DRYOPTERIS. *Polypodiaceae.* WOOD FERN. Native to many parts of world. Two natives of western U.S. and one exotic species are sometimes sold. Definitely drought tolerant. Grow in part shade.

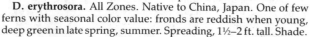

Dryopteris dilatata

D. arguta. COASTAL or CALIFORNIA WOOD FERN. Zones 4–9, 14–24. Native Washington to southern California. Dark green, finely cut, airy fronds to 2½ ft. tall. Not easy to grow in gardens; best naturalized in woods. Avoid overwatering.

D. dilatata. SPREADING WOOD FERN. Zones 4–9, 14–24. Native to much of northern hemisphere, including western U.S. Fronds 1–3 ft. tall, even more finely cut than those of *D. arguta.* Named varieties sometimes seen in northwestern nurseries. In southern California, best in pots. Plant in shade.

D. erythrosora. All Zones. Native to China, Japan. One of few ferns with seasonal color value: fronds are reddish when young, deep green in late spring, summer. Spreading, 1½–2 ft. tall. Shade.

DUCHESNEA indica. *Rosaceae.* INDIAN MOCK STRAWBERRY. Perennial. All Zones. Grows like strawberry, with trailing stems that root firmly along ground. Bright green, long-stalked leaves with 3 leaflets. Yellow, ½-in. flowers are followed by red, ½-in., insipid-tasting fruit that stands above foliage rather than under leaves as in true strawberry. Grows readily in sun or shade without much care. Needs only moderate watering. Best used as ground cover among open shrubs or small trees. Plant 1–1½ ft. apart. In well-watered garden, can become rampant invader. Attracts birds.

Duchesnea indica

DUDLEYA. *Crassulaceae.* Rosette-forming succulents. Zones 16, 17, 21–24. Native to California, Arizona, Baja California and other parts of Mexico. About 40 species are known and some of these are common on California's coastal cliffs or inland hills. Best known in cultivation is *D. brittonii* (from Baja California), with 1½-ft.-wide leaf rosettes on stems that gradually lengthen into 1–2-ft. trunks. Leaves fleshy, covered with heavy coat of chalky powder which can be rubbed off. Striking plant when well-grown; needs bright light and shelter from rain, hail, and frost. Best under glass or plastic roof. Others are also valued for use in containers, rock gardens, low borders. *D. caespitosa* (southern California) and *D. farinosa* (northern California) are familiar sea cliff plants; both are sometimes called cliff lettuce. Very drought resistant. Full sun.

Dudleya brittonii

DUMB CANE. See *Dieffenbachia.*

DURANTA. *Verbenaceae.* Evergreen shrubs. Glossy green leaves arranged in pairs or whorls along stem. Attractive blue flowers in clusters attract butterflies in summer, are followed by bunches of yellow berrylike fruit. Many plants sold as *D. stenostachya* are actually *D. repens.* Distinguishing characteristics described below.

Valued for summer flowers and fruit. Use as quick, tall screen. Thrive in hot-summer areas but require constant level of moisture. Prefer sun. Need continual thinning and pruning to stay under control.

Duranta repens

D. repens *(D. erecta, D. plumieri).* SKY FLOWER, GOLDEN DEWDROP, PIGEON BERRY. Zones 13, 16, 17, 21–24. Native to southern Florida, West Indies, Mexico to Brazil. Fast growing to 10–25 ft. Tends to form multi-stemmed clumps; branches often drooping and vinelike. Stems may or may not have sharp spines. Oval to roundish leaves are 1–2 in. long, rounded or pointed at tip. Tubular, violet blue flowers flare to less than ½ in. wide. Fruit clusters 1–6 in. long.

D. stenostachya. BRAZILIAN SKY FLOWER. Not as hardy as *D. repens;* seems to require more heat, and is not at its best in Zones 17, 24. Makes neater, more compact shrub than *D. repens,* usually growing to about 4–6 ft. (under ideal conditions, 15 ft.). Stems are spineless. Leaves are larger (3–8 in. long) than those of *D. repens* and taper to long, slender point. Lavender blue flowers are also somewhat larger; fruit clusters grow to 1 ft. long.

DUSTY MILLER. This name is given to a number of plants with gray foliage. The dusty miller of one region may be unknown in another. Among many dusty millers are: *Artemisia stellerana, Centaurea cineraria, C. gymnocarpa, Chrysanthemum ptarmiciflorum, Lychnis coronaria,* and *Senecio cineraria.*

DUTCHMAN'S PIPE. See *Aristolochia durior.*

DYMONDIA margaretae. *Compositae.* Zones 15–24. Ground cover. Native to South Africa. Evergreen perennial resembling miniature gazania. Grows in tight mats 2–3 in. deep; spreads slowly by offsets. Narrow (⅛-in.) leaves are 2–3 in. long, deep grayish green above and rolled at the edges to show cottony white undersides. Summer flowers are yellow, 1–1½-in.-wide daisies half buried in the foliage. Deep roots give established plants considerable drought tolerance, but they can take any amount of water and spread the faster for it. Use between paving blocks, stepping stones, in rock gardens; can take light foot traffic.

Dymondia margaretae

DYSSODIA tenuiloba *(Thymophylla tenuiloba).* *Compositae.* DAHLBERG DAISY, GOLDEN FLEECE. Summer annual; may live over as perennial where winters are mild. Southwest native. To 1 ft. high. Divided, threadlike leaves make dark green background for yellow flower heads, which look much like miniature golden marguerites. Use for massed display or pockets of color. Start in flats or plant in place, in full sun and preferably in sandy soil. Needs less water than most annuals. Blooms early summer to fall, or to early winter in warm climates. Pull out plants that get ragged with age.

Dyssodia tenuiloba

EASTER CACTUS. See *Rhipsalidopsis gaertneri.*

EASTER LILY CACTUS. See *Echinopsis.*

EASTER LILY VINE. See *Beaumontia grandiflora.*

ECHEVERIA. *Crassulaceae.* Succulents. All form rosettes of fleshy, green or gray green leaves, often marked or overlaid with deeper colors. Bell-shaped, nodding flowers, usually pink, red, or yellow, on long, slender, sometimes branched clusters. Quite drought tolerant. Good in rock gardens.

Echeveria agavoides

E. agavoides *(Urbinia agavoides).* Zones 8, 9, 13–24. Rosettes 6–8 in. across, with stiff, fleshy, smooth, bright green, sharp-pointed leaves which may be marked deep reddish brown at tips and edges. Flower stalks to 1½ ft. bear small red and yellow blooms.

Echeveria imbricata

E. crenulata. Zones 17, 21–24. Loose rosettes on short, thick stems. Pale green or white-powdered leaves to 1 ft. long and 6 in. wide, with wavy, crimped, purplish red edges. Flower clusters to 3 ft. high, with a few yellow and red flowers. Striking plant. Shelter from hottest sun; water frequently in summer.

E. derenbergii. Zones 17, 20–24. Small, tight rosettes spreading to form mats. The 1½-in.-long, sharp-tipped leaves are grayish white with red edges. Flowers reddish and yellow, in one-sided clusters to 2½ in. long.

E. elegans. HEN AND CHICKS. Zones 8, 9, 12–24. Tight, grayish white rosettes to 4 in. across, spreading freely by offsets. Flowers pink, lined yellow, in clusters to 8 in. long. Common, useful for pattern planting, edging, containers. Can burn in hot summer sun.

E. gibbiflora. Zones 17, 21–24. Striking succulent to 3 ft. tall. Broad, gray green leaves in rosettes to 2½ ft. wide. Slender flowering stems to 5 ft. tall; flowers not especially showy. Variety 'Metallica' has purplish lilac to bronzy leaves; a number of varieties and hybrids have warted, crested, and wavy-edged leaves.

E. hybrids. Generally have large, loose rosettes of big leaves on single or branched stems. Some have leaves crimped, waved, wattled, or heavily shaded with red, bronze, or purple. All are splendid pot plants; they do well in open ground in mild coastal gardens. Among them are: 'Arlie Wright', with large, open rosettes of wavy-edged, pinkish leaves; 'Cameo', with large blue gray leaves, each centered with a large raised lump of the same color; and 'Perle von Nürnberg', with pearly lavender blue foliage. Smaller, with short, close-set leaves, is 'Doris Taylor'; its leaves are densely covered with short hairs. Showy, nodding flowers are red and yellow.

E. imbricata. HEN AND CHICKS. Zones 8, 9, 12–24. Rosettes 4–6 in. across, saucer shaped, gray green. Loose clusters of small, bell-shaped, orange red flowers. Makes offsets very freely. Probably most common hen and chicks in California gardens.

E. pulvinata. Zones 16, 17, 21–24. Small, loose rosettes of very thick leaves, covered with silvery down which later turns red or brownish. Early spring flowers are bright red.

E. secunda. HEN AND CHICKS. Zones 8, 9, 14–24. Rosettes gray green or blue green, to 4 in. across. Makes offsets freely. *E. s. glauca (E. glauca),* its leaves faintly bordered purple red, forms purple-toned blue green rosettes.

E. 'Set-oliver'. Zones 16, 17, 21–24. Rosettes looser than in *E. setosa.* Flowers profuse, red and yellow, very showy in mass plantings.

E. setosa. Zones 17, 23, 24. Dense rosettes to 4 in. across are dark green, densely covered with white, stiff hairs. Flowers red, tipped with yellow. Good choice for rock gardens, shallow containers. Very tender.

ECHINACEA purpurea *(Rudbeckia purpurea).* *Compositae.* PURPLE CONEFLOWER. Perennial. All Zones. Coarse, stiff plant, forming large clumps of erect stems 4–5 ft. tall. Leaves oblong, 3–8 in. long. Showy flower heads with drooping purple rays and dark purple centers bloom over long period in late summer. Coral, crimson, and white varieties exist. Use on outskirts of garden or in wide borders with other robust perennials such as Shasta daisies, sunflowers, Michaelmas daisies. Plant in full sun; give average soil, watering. Divide clumps in spring or fall.

Echinacea purpurea

ECHINOCACTUS. *Cactaceae.* BARREL CACTUS. Zones 12–24. Numerous kinds of large, cylindrical cacti with prominent ribs and stout thorns. Many native to Southwest. Best known in gardens is *E. grusonii,* GOLDEN BARREL, a Mexican cactus of slow growth to 4 ft. high, 2½ ft. in diameter, with showy, stiff, yellow, 3-in. spines and yellow, 1½–2-in. flowers at top of plant in April–May. It needs protection from hard frosts and, in hottest desert climates, some summer shade. Provide frost protection with improvised canopies of branches. Water every 2 weeks during summer.

Echinocactus grusonii

ECHINOPS exaltatus. *Compositae.* GLOBE THISTLE. Perennial. All Zones. Rugged-looking, erect, rigidly branched plants 3–4 ft. high. Coarse, prickly, deeply cut, gray green leaves. Small steel blue flowers in round heads 2 in. across, midsummer to late fall. 'Taplow Blue' is desirable selected form. Flowers are long lasting when cut and hold color when dry. Plants often mistakenly sold under names of *E. ritro* and *E. sphaerocephalus.*

Plant in full sun, ordinary soil with good drainage. Established plants tolerate dry periods; moderate watering makes them look better. Grow from divisions in spring or fall, or sow seed in flats or open ground in spring. Color and interesting form complement yellow and orange rudbeckias, heleniums; combine well with Michaelmas daisies and phlox.

Echinops exaltatus

ECHINOPSIS. *Cactaceae.* EASTER LILY CACTUS, SEA URCHIN CACTUS. Outdoors Zones 16, 17, 21–24; indoors in sunny windows elsewhere. Small (6–10-in.-high), cylindrical or globular cactus from South America, generally grown in pots. Big, long-tubed, many-petaled flowers in shades of white, yellow, pink, and red can reach 6–8 in. long. Free blooming in summer if given good light, frequent feeding, fast-draining soil. Many kinds, all showy and easy to grow. Water every 1–2 weeks from spring through fall; give little or no water in winter.

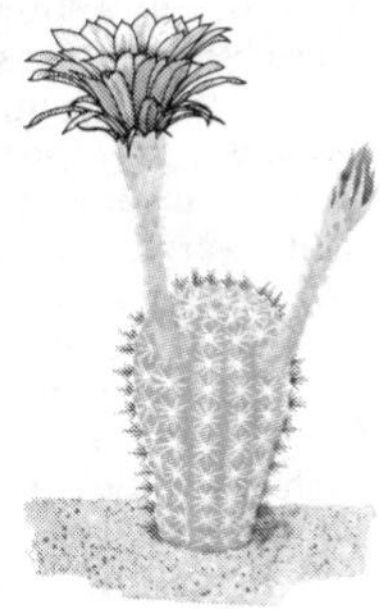

Echinopsis

ECHIUM. *Boraginaceae.* Biennials or shrubby perennials. Striking form and flower clusters. All take full sun, do well in dry, poor soil, but need good drainage. All are excellent for seacoast gardens. Very drought resistant in Zones 15–17, 22–24; need weekly summer watering in Zones 14, 18–21. Attract bees.

E. fastuosum. PRIDE OF MADEIRA. Shrubby perennial. Zones 14–24. Large, picturesque plant with many coarse, heavy branches 3–

6 ft. high. Hairy, gray green, narrow leaves form roundish, irregular mounds at ends of stems. Great spikelike clusters of bluish purple, ½-in.-long flowers stand out dramatically, well above foliage, in May–June. Branch tips and developing flower spikes may be killed by March frosts in inland areas. Use for bold effects against walls, at back of wide flower border, and on slopes. Will control erosion. Very effective with *Limonium perezii.* Prune lightly to keep plant bushy. Cut off faded flower spikes.

Echium fastuosum

E. pininana. Short-lived shrubby perennial. Zones 16, 17, 22–24. Tall (to 18 ft.), sparsely branched. Stems packed with long, narrow, bristly gray green leaves and topped with long spikelike clusters of blue flowers. Rarely sold, but occasionally seen in old gardens near coast.

E. vulgare. Biennial grown as an annual, blooming first year if sown early autumn, winter, or earliest spring. Grows 1–3 ft. tall. Leaves covered with stiff white bristles; blue, white, or pink flowers in spikelike clusters. Endures drought, poor soil. Seeds freely and can become a pest if seedlings are not hoed out.

E. wildpretii. TOWER OF JEWELS. Biennial. Zones 1–17, 21–24. Striking plant from 4–10 ft. high. Spends its first year as attractive, roundish mass of long, narrow leaves covered with silvery gray hairs. In its second year it starts to grow. By mid or late spring, it will form thick column of rose to rose red flowers, 6–10 ft. high and a foot or more thick. When all the countless little flowers have faded, the plant dies, leaving behind a vast amount of seed. If resulting seedlings are not hoed out, these may be grown to flower the next year. An interesting oddity.

EDELWEISS. See *Leontopodium alpinum.*

EGGPLANT. *Solanaceae.* For ornamental relatives, see *Solanum.* Annual vegetable. All Zones in conditions noted below. Few vegetable plants are handsomer than eggplant. Bushes resemble little trees 2–3 ft. high and equally wide. Big leaves (usually lobed) are purple tinged; drooping violet flowers are 1½ in. across. And of course, big purple fruit is spectacular. Plants are effective in large containers or raised beds; a well-spaced row of them makes distinguished border between vegetable and flower garden. Most people plant large roundish or oval varieties such as 'Black Beauty', 'Burpee Hybrid', or 'Early Beauty'; the Japanese, who prefer their eggplant small and very tender, prefer long, slender variety usually sold as 'Japanese'. Specialists in imported vegetable seeds offer numerous colored varieties, including the full-sized 'White Beauty' and a host of smaller varieties in a range of sizes (down to ½ in.) and colors—yellow, red, green. Some of the smaller ones genuinely resemble eggs. All are edible as well as attractive.

Eggplant 'Black Beauty'

Can be grown from seed (sow indoors 8–10 weeks before date of last expected frost), but starting from nursery-grown plants is much easier. Set plants out in sun in spring when frosts are over and soil is warm. Space 3 ft. apart in loose, fertile soil. Feed once every 6 weeks with commercial fertilizer; water when soil at roots is dry. Keep weeds out. Prevent too much fruit setting by pinching out some terminal growth and some blossoms; 3–6 large fruits per plant will result. If you enjoy tiny whole eggplants, allow plants to produce freely. Harvest fruits after they develop some color, but never wait until they lose their glossy shine. Dust or spray to control aphids and whiteflies.

EGLANTINE. See *Rosa eglanteria.*

EICHHORNIA crassipes. *Pontederiaceae.* WATER HYACINTH. Aquatic plant. Zones 8, 9, 13–24. Native to tropical America. Floating leaves and feathery roots. Leaves ½–5 in. wide, nearly circular in shape; leaf stems inflated. Blooms showy, lilac blue, about 2 in. long. Upper petals with yellow spot in center, in many-flowered spikes. Attractive in small pools, ponds, but can become pest. Do not turn it loose in natural or large bodies of water. Needs warmth to flower profusely.

Eichhornia crassipes

Elaeagnaceae. This family contains trees and shrubs with a coating of tiny silvery or brown scales on leaves (and sometimes on flowers) and with small, tart-tasting, single-seeded fruits. Most are tough plants from arid or semiarid climates.

ELAEAGNUS. *Elaeagnaceae.* Deciduous and evergreen large shrubs or small trees. Best in full sun or part shade. All are splendid screen plants. All grow fast when young, becoming dense, full, firm, and tough—and they do it with little upkeep. All tolerate seashore conditions, heat, wind, and average to low watering. Established plants tolerate drought. Plant 10–12 ft. apart for screening.

Elaeagnus pungens

Foliage is distinguished in evergreen forms by silvery (sometimes brown) dots that cover leaves, reflecting sunlight to give plants a special sparkle. Deciduous kinds have silvery gray leaves. Small, insignificant, but usually fragrant flowers are followed by decorative fruit, usually red with silvery flecks. Evergreen kinds bloom in fall; in addition to their prime role as screen plants, they are useful as natural espaliers, clipped hedges, or high bank covers.

E. angustifolia. RUSSIAN OLIVE. Small deciduous tree. Zones 1–3, 7–14, 18, 19. To 20 ft. high, but can be clipped as medium-height hedge. Angular trunk and branches (sometimes thorny) are covered with shredding dark brown bark that is picturesque in winter. Bark contrasts with willowlike, 2-in.-long, silvery gray leaves. Small, very fragrant greenish yellow flowers in early summer are followed by berrylike fruit that resembles miniature olives. Can take almost any amount of punishment in interior. Does poorly and is out of character in mild-winter, cool-summer climates. Resistant to oak root fungus. Good background plant, barrier.

E. commutata. SILVERBERRY. Deciduous shrub. Most useful Zones 1–3. Native to Canada, northern plains, and Rocky Mountains. To 12 ft. with slender, open form, red brown branches, silvery leaves. Tiny, fragrant flowers followed by dry, silvery berries that are good bird food.

E. 'Coral Silver'. Large evergreen or deciduous shrub. All Zones. Has unusually bright gray foliage, coral red berries in fall. Evergreen in Zones 19–24, deciduous or partially deciduous elsewhere.

E. ebbingei (*E. macrophylla* 'Ebbingei'). Evergreen shrub. Zones 5–24. More upright (to 10–12 ft.) than *E. pungens* (see below), with thornless branches. Leaves 2–4 in. long, silvery on both sides when young, later dark green above, silvery beneath. Tiny, fragrant, silvery flowers. Red fruit makes good jelly. 'Gilt Edge' has striking yellow margins on its leaves.

E. multiflora. Deciduous shrub. Zones 2–24. To 6 ft.; leaves silvery green above, silvery and brown below. Small, fragrant flowers followed by attractive, ½-in.-long, bright orange red berries on 1-in. stalks. Fruit is edible but tart, much loved by birds.

E. philippinensis. Evergreen shrub. Zones 15–17, 19–24. More open and erect (to 10 ft.) than other evergreen forms, with somewhat spreading and drooping branches. The 3-in.-long, olive green leaves with silvery cast are quite silvery beneath. Red fruit.

E. pungens. SILVERBERRY. Large evergreen shrub. Zones 4–24. Has rather rigid, sprawling, angular habit of growth to height of 6–15 ft.; can be kept lower and denser by pruning. Grayish green, 1–3-in.-long leaves have wavy edges and brown tinting from rusty dots. Branches are spiny, also covered with rusty dots. Overall color of shrub is olive drab. Oval fruit, ½ in. long, red with silver dust. Tough container plant in reflected heat, wind. Variegated forms listed below are more widespread than the plain olive drab variety and have a brighter, lighter look in the landscape. Both kinds make effective barrier plantings: growth is dense and twiggy, and spininess is a help, yet plant is not aggressively spiny.

E. p. 'Fruitlandii'. Zones 5–24. Leaves larger, more silvery than those of other varieties.

E. p. 'Maculata'. GOLDEN ELAEAGNUS. Leaves have gold blotch in center.

E. p. 'Marginata'. SILVER-EDGE ELAEAGNUS. Leaves have silvery white margins.

E. p. 'Variegata'. YELLOW-EDGE ELAEAGNUS. Leaves have yellowish white margins.

ELDERBERRY. See *Sambucus.*

ELEPHANT'S EAR. See *Alocasia, Colocasia esculenta.*

ELEPHANT'S FOOD. See *Portulacaria afra.*

ELM. See *Ulmus.*

EMERALD RIPPLE. See *Peperomia caperata.*

EMPRESS TREE. See *Paulownia tomentosa.*

ENDIVE. *Compositae.* Fall or late-summer annual vegetable. All Zones in conditions noted below. Botanically known as *Cichorium endivia.* This species includes curly endive and broad-leafed endive (escarole). Forms rosette of leaves. Tolerates more heat than lettuce, grows faster in cold weather. Sow in sun in late summer for maturity during rainy season (in cold-winter areas, sow seed June to August). Endive matures in 90–95 days. Space plants 10–12 in. apart in rows 15–18 in. apart. When plants have reached full size, pull outer leaves over center and tie them up; center leaves will blanch to yellow or white. 'Green Curled' is standard curly endive; 'Broad-leaved Batavian' is best broad-leafed kind.

Endive

Belgian or French endives are the blanched sprouts from roots of a kind of chicory. Roots are dug after a summer's growth, then stored in the dark to sprout. See Chicory.

ENDYMION *(Scilla).* *Liliaceae.* ENGLISH and SPANISH BLUEBELLS, WOOD HYACINTH. Bulbs. All Zones. They resemble hyacinths, but are taller, with looser flower clusters and fewer, narrower leaves. Most dealers still sell them as *Scilla.* Full sun or part shade. Plant informal drifts among tall shrubs, under deciduous trees, among low-growing perennials. In dry-winter areas, supply water from October on. Anywhere, let dry out through summer. They thrive in pots and are good for cutting.

Endymion non-scriptus

E. hispanicus *(Scilla campanulata, S. hispanica).* SPANISH BLUEBELL. Most widely planted. Prolific, vigorous, with sturdy 20-in. stems bearing 12 or more nodding bells about ¾ in. long. Blue is most popular color, 'Excelsior' (deep blue) most popular variety. There are also white, pink, rose forms. Plant in fall—3 in. deep in mild climates, to 6 in. deep where winters are severe. Flowers appear in spring.

E. non-scriptus *(Scilla nonscripta).* ENGLISH BLUEBELL, WOOD HYACINTH. Flowers narrower and smaller than those of Spanish bluebell, on 1-ft. spikes. Culture same as for Spanish bluebell.

ENGLISH DAISY. See *Bellis perennis.*

ENGLISH LAUREL. See *Prunus laurocerasus.*

ENKIANTHUS. *Ericaceae.* Deciduous shrubs. Zones 2–9, 14–21. Native to Japan. Upright stems with tiers of nearly horizontal branches, narrow in youth, broad in age, but always good looking. Leaves, whorled or crowded at branch ends, turn orange or red in autumn. Nodding, bell-shaped flowers in clusters. Grow in light shade, in well-drained soil to which plenty of peat moss or ground bark has been added. Keep soil moist. Prune only to remove dead or broken branches. Plant with other acid-loving plants, in location where silhouette and fall color can be effective.

Enkianthus campanulatus

E. campanulatus. Slow-growing, handsome shrub to 20 ft. in 20 years (10 ft. by 4 ft. wide in 10 years). Bluish green leaves, 1½–3 in. long, turn brilliant red in fall. In May, pendulous clusters of yellow green, red-veined, ½-in.-long bells hang below leaves. *E. c. palibinii* has deep red flowers; its variety 'Albiflorus' has white blooms.

E. cernuus. Seldom over 10 ft. tall, with 1–2-in.-long leaves. White flowers. Not as well-known as its variety *rubens,* which has translucent deep red flowers in May.

E. perulatus. Grows to 6–8 ft. high. Roundish, 1–2-in.-long leaves; exceptionally good scarlet fall color. Nodding clusters of small white flowers open before leaves emerge.

ENSETE. *Musaceae.* Big, palmlike perennials. Evergreen in Zones 17, 19–24; die back each cold winter, regrow in spring in Zones 13, 15, 16, 18. Elsewhere, a container plant to grow outdoors in summer, indoors or in greenhouse over winter. Good near swimming pools.

E. ventricosum *(Musa ensete).* ABYSSINIAN BANANA. Lush, tropical-looking, dark green leaves 10–20 ft. long, 2–4 ft. wide, with stout midrib, grow out in arching form from single vertical stem, 6–20 ft. high. Fast growing. Leaves easily shredded by winds, so plant in wind-sheltered place. Sun or part shade. Needs more water than most shrubs or trees. Flowers typically form 2–5 years after planting; plant dies to roots after flowering. Possible then to grow new plants from shoots at crown, but easier to discard, replace with new nursery plants. Flowers (inconspicuous) form within cylinder of bronze red bracts at end of stem.

Ensete ventricosum

E. v. 'Maurelii'. Similar to *E. ventricosum,* but leaves are tinged with red on upper surface, especially along edges. Leaf stalks are dark red. Stems grow 12–15 ft. high. 'Montbeliardii' is less squat than 'Maurelii'.

EPAULETTE TREE. See *Pterostyrax hispidus.*

EPAZOTE. See *Chenopodium ambrosioides.*

EPIDENDRUM. *Orchidaceae.* Epiphytic or terrestrial orchids. All are easy to grow. Most species bear large clusters of blooms. On the whole, they take same culture as cattleya. Those with hard,

E

round pseudobulbs and thick, leathery leaves are tolerant of sun and drought and need a rest period. These grow in ground bark or other orchid media. Softer-textured (reed-stemmed) plants with thin, stemlike pseudobulbs do best with more shade and year-round moisture.

Epidendrum obrienianum

Reed-stemmed types need abundance of sun to flower, but coolness and shade at roots. Mulch plants in ground beds. If sun is too hot, foliage turns bright red and burns. Grow outdoors in Zones 17, 21–24. Tip growth will burn at 28°F.; plants are killed to ground at about 22°F. In cold-winter areas, grow reed-stemmed plants in pots and move them indoors in winter.

Feed regularly with mild liquid fertilizer during growing season. In pure ground bark, feed at every other watering with high-nitrogen liquid fertilizer. Feed plants grown in other media monthly. When blooms fade, cut flower stem back to within 1 or 2 joints of ground.

E. cochleatum. Native to tropical America. Pear-shaped pseudobulbs 2–5 in. high, with one or more leaves as long as or longer than pseudobulb. Erect flower stem bears 5–10 flowers, 2–3 in. across. Narrow, twisted, yellow green sepals and petals; purplish black lip (shaped like cockleshell) with lighter veins. Blooms at various times. Hardy to 25°F.; grows outdoors in mildest winter climates.

E. ibaguense *(E. radicans).* Native to Colombia. Erect, 2–4-ft., reedlike leafy stems. Dense, globular clusters of 1–1½-in., orange yellow flowers with fringed lip are held at tips of slender stems well above foliage. Bloom season varies. Numerous hybrids in shades of yellow, orange, pink, red, lavender, and white, generally sold by color rather than by name.

E. obrienianum. Best known of reed-stemmed hybrids. Dense clusters of vivid red flowers, each the shape of miniature cattleya orchid, carried on slender stems 1–2 ft. above foliage.

EPIGAEA repens. *Ericaceae.* TRAILING ARBUTUS. Evergreen low shrublet. Zones 1–7. Native to eastern North America. Difficult to grow except under ideal conditions: acid soil, well fortified with leaf mold, pine needles, or peat moss; excellent drainage; shade from summer sun. Choice woodland ground cover. Do not fertilize. Mulch with leaf mold or peat moss when weather warms; keep plants moist all summer. Bait for slugs. Will take any amount of cold.

Epigaea repens

Each plant can cover a patch 1–2 ft. wide, stems rooting as they grow. Oval to roundish leaves 1–3 in. long. In April or May, waxy pink or white, ½-in.-wide, delightfully fragrant flowers cluster at tips of branches.

Another species, *E. asiatica,* occasionally sold, is quite similar to the above but considered easier to grow.

EPIMEDIUM. *Berberidaceae.* Perennials. Zones 1–9, 14–17. Low-growing evergreen or nearly evergreen plant with creeping underground stems. Leathery, divided leaves on thin, wiry stems. Heart-shaped leaflets up to 3 in. long are bronzy pink in spring, green in summer, bronzy in fall. Loose spikes of small, waxy-textured pink, red, creamy yellow, or white flowers in spring. Use as ground cover under trees, among rhododendrons, azaleas, camellias; good in larger rock gardens. Needs modest amount of water. Adaptable to containers. Foliage, flowers long lasting in arrangements. Divide large clumps in spring or fall by cutting through tough roots with sharp spade.

Epimedium grandiflorum

E. grandiflorum. BISHOP'S HAT, LONGSPUR EPIMEDIUM. About 1 ft. high. Flowers 1–2 in. across, shaped like bishop's hat; outer sepals red, inner sepals pale violet, petals white with long spurs. Varieties have white, pinkish, or violet flowers. 'Rose Queen', bearing crimson flowers with white-tipped spurs, is outstanding variety.

E. pinnatum. Grows 12–15 in. high. Yellow flowers are ⅔ in. across, with red petals and protruding stamens. *E. p. colchicum* (often sold as *E. p. elegans*) is larger, with showier flowers.

E. rubrum. To 1 ft. Flowers, borne in showy clusters, have bright crimson sepals, pale yellow or white, slipperlike petals, upcurved spurs. Rosy pink 'Pink Queen' and white 'Snow Queen' are desirable varieties offered in specialty nurseries.

EPIPACTIS gigantea. *Orchidaceae.* STREAM ORCHID. Hardy terrestrial orchid. Zones 1–9, 14–24. Native from Washington to southern California, east to southern Utah and west Texas. Oval or lance-shaped leaves with plaited veins. Creeping rootstocks. Stems 1–3 ft. tall. Flowers grow 3–10 to a stalk; greenish, purple veined, and about 1 in. wide, they somewhat resemble birds in flight. Blooms June–July. Grows near brooks and is probably easiest native orchid to grow. Give it rich, moist soil in sun or partial shade.

Epipactis gigantea

EPIPHYLLUM. *Cactaceae.* ORCHID CACTUS. House plants anywhere; lathhouse, shade, and shelter plants in Zones 8, 9, 14–24. Growers use *Epiphyllum* to cover wide range of plants including epiphyllum itself and a number of crosses with related plants—*Heliocereus, Nopalxochia, Selenicereus, Disocactus (Chiapasia), Aporocactus.* All are similar in being jungle (not desert) cacti, and most grow on tree branches as epiphytes, like some orchids. Grow them in pots. They need rich, quick-draining soil with plenty of sand and leaf mold, peat moss, or ground bark. Cuttings are easy to root in spring or summer. Permit the base of the cutting to dry for a day or two before potting it up. Overwatering and poor drainage cause bud drop. As a rule, water 1 or 2 times a week in summer, very little in winter.

Epiphyllum hybrid

During summer, epiphyllums do best in broken shade under trees or lath; in winter, they need protection from frost. Most have arching (to 2 ft. high), trailing stems and look best in hanging pots, tubs, or baskets. Stems are long, flat, smooth, and usually notched along edges, and are quite spineless. Flowers range from medium sized to very large (up to 10 in. across); color range includes white, cream, yellow, pink, rose, lavender, scarlet, and orange. Many varieties have blends of 2 or more colors. Bloom season April–June. Feed with low-nitrogen fertilizer before and after bloom. Bait for snails and slugs. Control aphids, scale, and mealybugs.

EPIPREMNUM aureum *(Pothos aureus, Raphidophora aurea, Scindapsus aureus).* *Araceae.* POTHOS. Evergreen climbing perennial grown as house plant. Related to philodendron and similar in appearance. Takes same treatment as climbing philodendrons. Flowers are inconspicuous. Oval, leathery leaves 2–4 in. long, bright green splashed or marbled with yellow. (In greenhouse and with plenty of root room, becomes big vine with deeply cut, 2–2½-ft.-long leaves.) Attractive trailer for pots, window boxes, large terrariums.

Epipremnum aureum

EPISCIA. *Gesneriaceae.* FLAME VIOLET. House plants related to African violet. Low-growing plants spread by strawberrylike runners with new plants at tips; excellent display in hanging pots. Leaves 2–5 in. long, 1–3 in. wide; typically oval, velvety, beautifully colored. Flowers somewhat resemble African violets, appear at scattered intervals through the year. Plants bloom best in high humidity of greenhouse, but will grow as house plants with bright light, no direct sun, lots of water.

Episcia cupreata

E. cupreata. Red flowers. Variety *viridifolia* has green leaves with creamy veins; 'Metallica', olive green leaves with pale stripes, red edges; 'Chocolate Soldier', chocolate brown, silver-veined leaves; and 'Silver Sheen', silver leaves with darker margins.

EQUISETUM hyemale. *Equisetaceae.* HORSETAIL. Perennial. All Zones. Rushlike survivor of carboniferous age. Slender, hollow, 4-ft. stems are bright green with black and ash-colored ring at each joint. Spores borne in conelike spikes at end of stem. Several species, but *E. hyemale* most common. Called horsetail because many of the species have bushy look from many whorls of slender, jointed green stems that radiate out from joints of main stem.

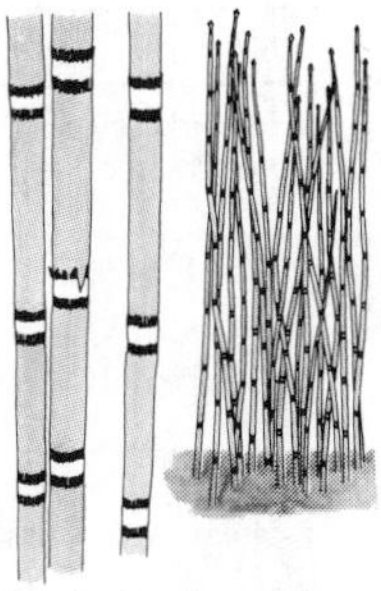

Equisetum hyemale

Although horsetail is effective in sunny or partly shaded garden situations, especially near water, use it with caution: it is extremely invasive and difficult to get rid of. Best confined to containers. Useful in marshy areas, pools, roadside ditches. In open ground, root-prune rigorously, constantly cutting back unwanted shoots.

ERANTHEMUM pulchellum *(E. nervosum).* *Acanthaceae.* Evergreen shrub. Outdoors Zones 23, 24; elsewhere, greenhouse plant. Native to India. Grows rapidly to 2–4 ft. high. Handsome, 4-in-long, long-stalked leaves in pairs—dark green, oval, with prominent veins and somewhat scallop-toothed edges.

Eranthemum pulchellum

From January to April, deep blue (sometimes rose), tubular flowers protrude from prominent overlapping bracts in 3-in.-long solitary or branching spikes at ends of branches and among leaves.

Best grown as container plant, or in ground bed on shady patio or terrace sheltered from wind. Give plants loose, well-drained soil, rich in humus material. Keep moist at all times. Pinch back stem tips 2 or 3 times early in growing season to keep plants compact and encourage more flower production. Cut to ground to stimulate fresh new growth and overcome legginess.

ERANTHIS hyemalis. *Ranunculaceae.* WINTER ACONITE. Tuber. Zones 1–9, 14–17. Charming buttercuplike plant 2–8 in. high, blooming in early spring. Single yellow flowers up to 1½ in. wide, with 5–9 petal-like sepals; each bloom sits on a single, deeply lobed, bright green leaf that looks like a ruff. Round basal leaves divided into narrow lobes appear immediately after flowers. Ideal companions for other small bulbs or bulblike plants that bloom at same time, such as snowdrop (*Galanthus nivalis*) and Siberian squill (*Scilla sibirica*). Plant tubers in August or early September before they shrivel. If tubers are dry, plump up in wet sand before planting. When dividing, separate into small clumps rather than single tubers. Plant tubers 3 in. deep, 4 in. apart, in moist, porous soil in part shade.

Eranthis hyemalis

EREMURUS. *Liliaceae.* FOXTAIL LILY, DESERT CANDLE. Perennials. Zones 1–9. Imposing lily relatives with spirelike flowering stems 4–9 ft. tall. Bell-shaped white, pink, or yellow flowers, ½–1 in. wide, massed closely in graceful, pointed spikes. Plants bloom in late spring, early summer. Strap-shaped basal leaves in rosettes appear in early spring, fade away after bloom in summer. Magnificent in large borders against background of dark green foliage, wall, or solid fence. Fairly drought tolerant. Dramatic in arrangements; cut when lowest flowers on spike open. Plant in sun in rich, fast-draining soil. Handle thick, brittle roots carefully; they tend to rot when bruised or broken. When leaves die down, mark spot; don't disturb roots.

Eremurus himalaicus

E. himalaicus. Leaves bright green, to 1½ ft. long. Flowers white, about 1 in. across, in 2-ft. spikes on tall stems to 3 ft. or more.

E. robustus. Leaves about 2 ft. long, in dense basal rosettes. Stems 8–9 ft. high, topped with 2–3-ft. spikes of clear pink flowers lightly veined with brown.

E. Shelford Hybrids. To 4–5 ft. tall; flowers in white and shades of buff, pink, yellow, and orange.

ERICA. *Ericaceae.* HEATH. Evergreen shrubs with small, needlelike leaves and abundant bell-shaped, urn-shaped, or tubular flowers, usually small. Hardiest kinds, native to northern and western Europe, are widely used as shrubs or ground cover plants in cool-summer, humid regions of California and Northwest. Good on slopes. South African species are tender to frost; where temperatures dip below 28°F., they are safest grown in containers and given shelter. One expert considers them about as hardy as fuchsias. A third group of heaths, native to Mediterranean and southern Europe, is intermediate in hardiness. All attract bees. Taller ones can be used as screens.

Erica carnea 'Springwood'

All need excellent drainage and most need acid soil (exceptions noted in chart on pages 330–332). Sandy soil with peat moss and compost added is ideal; heavy clay is usually fatal. They are not heavy feeders; annual sifting of compost may be enough. If plants lose color, give light feeding of acid plant food in early spring or apply iron sulfate. Water supply should be steady, with no standing water on roots and no absolute drought. Near coast where air is moist, watering intervals are longer than in inland areas and plants like full sun. Inland, give them light shade or afternoon shade. Prune after bloom by cutting back wood that has flowered; don't cut back into leafless wood.

In suitable climates (as in Zones 4–6), fanciers may plant heather gardens for a Persian-carpet ground cover effect. By choosing varieties carefully, it is possible to have color from flowers and foliage the year round. Both *Erica* and *Calluna* are used.

Ericaceae. The heath family contains shrubs or trees with rounded, bell-shaped, tubular, or irregular flowers, often showy, and fruits which are either capsules or berries. All share a preference, if not always a need, for acid soil with ample water and excellent aeration (a few plants from dry-summer climates are exceptions). Many are fine garden plants; azalea and rhododendron (*Rhododendron*), blueberry, heath (*Erica*), and heather (*Calluna*) are examples.

E

Erica

NAME AND ZONES	GROWTH HABIT, SIZE	LEAVES	FLOWER COLOR, SEASON	COMMENTS
Erica arborea TREE HEATH Zones 15–17, 21–24. Southern Europe, north Africa.	Dense shrub or tree to 10–20 ft., with one or many trunks, often with heavy burl at base.	Bright green, ¼ in. long. New growth lighter.	White, fragrant. March–May.	Slow growing. Performs well enough in Zones 4–6 in years between big freezes. Burls are the "briar" used for making pipes.
E. a. alpina	Dense, upright, fluffy-looking shrub to 6 ft.	As above.	White. March–May.	Slow to reach blooming age, but free blooming. Slightly hardier than above.
E. australis SOUTHERN HEATH. Zones 5–9, 14–24. Spain, Portugal.	Upright, spired, 6–10 ft. high.	Dark green.	Rosy or red. Clustered at ends of shoots. March–June.	Needs protection in Northwest. There is a white form, 'Mr. Robert'.
E. blanda	See *E. doliiformis*.			
E. canaliculata (Usually sold as *E. melanthera* and often called Scotch heather, which it is not.) Zones 15–17, 20–24.	Bushy, spreading, but with general spired effect. To 6 ft.	Dark green above, white beneath.	Pink to rosy purple. Fall, winter.	Pink-flowered form is sold as 'Rosea', reddish purple form as 'Rubra'. Excellent winter bloom in California. Sometimes called Christmas heather. One of best choices for Zones 20–24. Good source of cut flowers, which last for weeks, in water or out.
E. c. 'Boscaweniana' (Sometimes sold as *E. melanthera* 'Rosea'.)	Upright bush or small tree to 18 ft.	As above.	Pale lilac pink to nearly white. Winter, spring.	Like *E. canaliculata*, good source of cut flowers.
E. carnea (*E. herbacea*) Zones 2–9, 14–24. European Alps.	Dwarf, 6–16 in. high. Upright branchlets rise from prostrate main branches.	Medium green.	Rosy red. Dec.–June.	Unsightly unless pruned every year. This and its varieties tolerate neutral or slightly alkaline soil. Takes part shade in hot-summer areas.
E. c. 'Ruby Glow'	To 8 in. high.	Dark green.	Deep ruby red. Jan.–June.	One of richest in color.
E. c. 'Springwood' ('Springwood White')	Spreading, to 8 in.	Light green.	White; creamy buds. Jan.–April.	Toughest, fastest growing heather; one of neatest.
E. c. 'Springwood Pink'	Spreading mound, to 10 in.	Bright green.	Pure pink. Jan.–April.	Pinkish rust new growth.
E. c. 'Vivellii'	Spreading mound, to 1 ft.	Dark green; bronzy red in winter.	Carmine red. Feb.–March.	Relatively tidy. Interesting for seasonal change in foliage color as well as for bloom.
E. c. 'Winter Beauty' ('King George')	Bushy, spreading, compact, to 15 in.	Dark green.	Deep, rich pink. Dec.–April.	Often in bloom at Christmas.
E. ciliaris DORSET HEATH. Zones 4–6, 15–17. England, Ireland.	Trailing, 6–12 in.	Pale green.	Rosy red. July–Sept.	Good for massing.
E. c. 'Mrs. C. H. Gill'	Spreading, to 1 ft.	Dark green.	Deep red. July–Oct.	Showy, bell-like flowers.
E. c. 'Stoborough'	As above, but taller, to 1½ ft.	Medium green.	White. July–Oct.	Free blooming, showy.
E. cinerea TWISTED HEATH. Zones 4–6, 15–17. British Isles, northern Europe.	Spreading mound, to 1 ft.	Dark green, dainty.	Purple. June–Sept.	Forms low mat; good ground cover.
E. c. 'Atrosanguinea'	Low, spreading, bushy, to 9 in.	Dark green, dainty.	Scarlet. June–Oct.	Dwarf, slow growing.
E. c. 'C. D. Eason'	Compact, to 10 in.	Dark green.	Red. May–Aug.	Outstanding; good summer flower display.
E. c. 'P. S. Patrick'	Bushy, to 15 in.	Dark green.	Purple. June–Aug.	Long, sturdy spikes, large flowers in summer.

NAME AND ZONES	GROWTH HABIT, SIZE	LEAVES	FLOWER COLOR, SEASON	COMMENTS
E. darleyensis 'Darley Dale' (*E. mediterranea hybrida*, *E. purpurascens* 'Darleyensis') Zones 4–9, 14–24.	Bushy grower, to 1 ft. tall.	Medium green.	Light rosy purple. Nov.–May.	Tough, hardy plant that takes both heat and cold surprisingly well. Tolerates neutral soils. In northern California, most foolproof heath.
E. d. 'Furzey'	Bushy, 14–18 in. tall.	Dark green.	Deep rose pink. Dec.–April.	Spreading, vigorous plant.
E. d. 'George Rendall'	Bushy, 1 ft. tall.	Medium bluish green.	Deeper purple than 'Darley Dale'. Nov.–April.	New growth gold tinted.
E. d. 'Silberschmelze' ('Molten Silver', *E. d.* 'Alba', 'Mediterranea Hybrid White')	Vigorous, 1½–2 ft. tall.	Medium green.	White, fragrant. Winter, spring.	Easy to maintain.
E. 'Dawn' Zones 4–9, 14–24.	Spreading mound, 1 ft. tall.	Green; new growth golden.	Deep pink. June–Oct.	Excellent ground cover. Easy to grow. Hybrid between *E. ciliaris* and *E. tetralix*.
E. doliiformis (*E. blanda*, *E. verticillata*) Zones 15–17, 20–24.	Low-growing, spiky plant to 1 ft. tall.	Rich green, needlelike.	Long, tubular, rosy red. June–Oct.	Blooms better if old blossoms are picked off as they fade.
E. 'Felix Faure' FRENCH HEATHER. Zones 15–17, 20–24.	Low, compact, to 1 ft.	Bright green.	Inch-long, tubular, lilac pink tipped white. Winter.	Often used as potted plant.
E. hyemalis Zones 15–17, 20–24. South Africa.	Upright, spiky, to 2–3 ft.	Bright green.	Inch-long, tubular, pink and white to coral or orange. Winter.	Sometimes sold as potted plant. Orange coral color form often sold as *E. hieliana*, *E. hyalina*, or orange French heath.
E. 'John McLaren'	See *E. mammosa*.			
E. lusitanica (*E. codonodes*) SPANISH HEATH. Zones 5–9, 14–24. Spain, Portugal.	Upright feathery shrub, to 6–12 ft.	Light green.	Pinkish white, slightly fragrant. Jan.–March.	Remarkably profuse bloom. Needs sheltered spot in Northwest. One of best in Zones 20–24.
E. mammosa Zones 15–17, 20–24. South Africa.	Stiff, erect, to 1–3 ft. tall.	Bright green.	Variable, shades of pink. Early spring, repeating through autumn.	Many varieties. 'Jubilee', a salmon pink, is commonly sold as 'John McLaren'.
E. mediterranea BISCAY HEATH. Zones 4–9, 14–24. Ireland, France, Spain.	Loose, upright, 4–7 ft.	Deep green.	Lilac pink. Jan.–April.	Good background. Tolerates neutral soil. 'W. T. Rackliff' is pure white form with brown anthers.
E. m. hybrida	See *E. darleyensis* 'Darley Dale'.			
E. melanthera	See *E. canaliculata*.			
E. persoluta Zones 15–17, 20–24. South Africa.	Stiff, upright shrub, to 2 ft. tall.	Bright green.	Tiny, rose or white. Late winter, early spring.	Offered as pot plants or sold as cut branches.
E. regia Zones 15–17, 20–24.	To 2–3 ft.	Needlelike, dull green.	Tubular, somewhat swollen, to ¾ in. long, sticky, shiny in appearance, red. Spring.	*E. r.* 'Variegata', with white flowers tipped red, is showier.
E. speciosa Zones 15–17, 20–24.	To 3–4 ft. tall.	Bright green, needlelike.	Long, tubular, slightly curved, bright red with greenish tips. Sept.–June.	Nearly everblooming under ideal conditions.
E. tetralix CROSS-LEAFED HEATH. Zones 4–6, 15–17. England, northern Europe.	Upright, to 1 ft.	Dark green, silvery beneath.	Rosy pink. June–Oct.	Very hardy plant. New growth yellow, orange, or red. Best in moist, peaty soil, afternoon shade.

(Continued on next page)

E

NAME AND ZONES	GROWTH HABIT, SIZE	LEAVES	FLOWER COLOR, SEASON	COMMENTS
E. t. 'Alba Mollis'	Upright, slightly spreading, to 1 ft.	Silvery gray.	Clear white. June–Oct.	Foliage sheen pronounced in spring, summer.
E. t. 'Darleyensis'	Spreading, open growth, to 8 in.	Gray green.	Salmon pink. June–Sept.	Good color. Do not confuse with winter-flowering *E. darleyensis* (*E. purpurascens* 'Darleyensis').
E. vagans CORNISH HEATH. Zones 3–6, 15–17, 20–24. Cornwall, Ireland.	Bushy, open, to 2–3 ft. tall.	Bright green.	Purplish pink. July–Sept.	Robust and hardy.
E. v. 'Lyonesse'	Bushy, rounded, to 1½ ft.	Bright, glossy green.	White. July–Oct.	Best white Cornish heath.
E. v. 'Mrs. D. F. Maxwell'	Bushy, rounded, to 1½ ft.	Dark green.	Cherry pink or red. July–Oct.	Outstanding for color and heavy bloom; widely grown.
E. v. 'St. Keverne'	Bushy, rounded, to 1½ ft.	Light green.	Rose pink. July–Oct.	Heavy bloom. Compact if pruned annually.
E. ventricosa Zones 15–17, 20–24.	To 6 ft., usually much less.	Medium green, needlelike.	Heavy spikes at tips of branches. Pale to medium pink, shiny, solid looking. May–July.	Occasionally sold as small pot plant in spring.

ERIGERON. *Compositae.* FLEABANE. Perennials. Free-blooming plants with daisylike flowers; similar to closely related Michaelmas daisy (*Aster*), except that erigeron's flower heads have threadlike rays in 2 or more rows rather than broader rays in a single row. White, pink, lavender, or violet flowers, usually with yellow centers, early summer into fall. Sun or light shade. Sandy soil; moderate watering. Cut back after flowering to prolong bloom. Rock garden species need especially fast drainage.

Erigeron speciosus

E. glaucus. BEACH ASTER, SEASIDE DAISY. Zones 4–6, 15–17, 22–24. Native of California, Oregon coast. Burns in hot sun inland. Basal leaves in clumps. Stout, hairy stems 10–12 in. high, topped by lavender flower heads 1½–2 in. across in spring, summer. Blue green stems and foliage. Use in rock garden, border, beside path. Sun or part shade. 'Arthur Menzies' is unusually compact, mat-forming selection with lavender pink flower heads.

E. karvinskianus (often called *Vittadinia*). MEXICAN DAISY, SANTA BARBARA DAISY. Zones 8, 9, 12–24. Native to Mexico. Graceful, trailing plant 10–20 in. high. Leaves 1 in. long, often toothed at tips. Dainty flower heads ¾ in. across with numerous white or pinkish rays. Drought tolerant. Use as ground cover in garden beds or large containers, in rock gardens, hanging baskets, on dry walls. Naturalizes easily. Stands root competition well; invasive unless controlled.

E. speciosus. All Zones. Native to coast, Pacific Northwest. Erect, leafy stemmed, 2 ft. high. Flower heads 1–1½ in. across, with dark violet or lavender rays; summer bloom. *E. s. macranthus,* ASPEN DAISY, is widespread through Rocky Mountain area. It has 3–5 flower heads to a stalk; stalks nod near top. Hybrids between *E. speciosus* and other species are available; these named sorts have larger flower heads and come in white and pink as well as the blue lavender of wild kinds.

ERIOBOTRYA. *Rosaceae.* LOQUAT. Evergreen trees or big shrubs. Both kinds have large, prominently veined, sharply toothed leaves. One bears edible fruit. Attractive to birds.

E. deflexa. BRONZE LOQUAT. Zones 8–24. Shrubby, but easily trained into small tree form. New leaves have bright coppery color which they hold for a long time before turning green. Leaves aren't as leathery or as deeply veined as those of *E. japonica,* and are shinier and more pointed. Garlands of creamy white flowers attractive in spring. No edible fruit. Good for espaliers (not on hot wall), patio planting, containers in full sun or part shade. Not drought tolerant. Fast growing.

Eriobotrya japonica

E. japonica. LOQUAT. Zones 4–24. Grows 15–30 ft. tall, equally broad in sun, slimmer in shade. Big, leathery, crisp leaves, stoutly veined and netted, 6–12 in. long, 2–4 in. wide, sharply toothed. They are glossy deep green above and show rust-colored wool beneath. New branches woolly; small, dull white flowers in woolly 3–6-in. clusters borne in fall. These are fragrant, but not showy. Fruit 1–2 in. long, orange to yellow, with seeds (usually big) in center; flesh sweet, aromatic, and acid. Hardy to 20°F.; has survived 12°F., but fruit often injured by low temperatures.

Plant in well-drained soil; will thrive in drought when established, but grows better with some moisture. Prune to shape; if you like the fruit, thin branches somewhat to let light into tree's interior. If tree sets fruit heavily, remove some while it's small to increase size of remaining fruit and to prevent limb breakage. Fireblight is a danger; if leaves and stems blacken from top downward, prune back 1 ft. or more into healthy wood. Burn prunings and sterilize shears between cuts. Use as lawn tree for sunny or shady spots; espalier on fence or trellis, but not in reflected heat. Can be held in container for several years. Cut foliage good for indoor decorating. Plants draw bees.

Most trees sold are seedlings, good ornamental plants with unpredictable fruit quality; if you definitely want fruit, look for a grafted variety. 'Champagne' (March–May), best in warm areas, has yellow-skinned, white-fleshed, juicy, tart fruit. 'Gold Nugget' (May–June), best near coast, has sweeter fruit with orange skin, flesh. 'MacBeth' (April–May) has exceptionally large fruit with yellow skin, cream flesh. 'Thales' is a late yellow-fleshed variety.

ERIOGONUM. *Polygonaceae.* WILD BUCKWHEAT. Annuals, perennials, shrubs. Native to most areas of West (the few sold at nurseries are mostly native to California coast). Grow best in full sun in well-drained, loose, gravelly soil. Once established, they need little water—none near coast. Useful to cover dry banks, mass among rocks, or use in rock gardens. Most available kinds withstand wind and heat well.

Individual blossoms are tiny, but flowers grow in long-stemmed or branched clusters—domed, flattish, or ball-like—popular among flower arrangers for dried bouquets. Clusters turn to shades of tan or rust as seeds ripen. If you leave clusters on plants, seeds will drop and produce volunteer seedlings. Transplant when they're small to extend planting or replace overgrown plants. Shrubby kinds get leggy after several years. You can do some pruning to shape if you start when plants are young, but if they've had no attention, it's better to replace them.

Eriogonum arborescens

E. arborescens. SANTA CRUZ ISLAND BUCKWHEAT. Shrub. Zones 14–24. Native to Santa Cruz, Santa Rosa, and Anacapa islands, southern California. Grows 3–4 (sometimes 8) ft. high, spreading to 4–5 ft. or more. Trunk and branches with shredding gray to reddish bark make attractive open pattern. Rather narrow, ½–1½-in.-long, gray green leaves cluster at ends of branches. Long-stalked, flat clusters of pale pink to rose flowers, May–September.

E. cinereum. ASHYLEAF BUCKWHEAT. Shrub. Zones 14–24. Native to coastal bluffs and canyons of southern California. Grows 2–5 ft. tall, with ash-colored, 1-in. leaves and pale pink flowers in ball-shaped clusters, July–September. Best planted in groups and given occasional summer water in hottest locations.

E. crocatum. SAFFRON BUCKWHEAT. Perennial. Zones 14–24. Native to Ventura County, California. Low, compact (to 1½ ft. high) stems and roundish, 1-in.-long leaves are covered with white wool. Sulfur yellow flowers in broad, flattish clusters, April–August.

E. fasciculatum. CALIFORNIA BUCKWHEAT. Shrub. Zones 8, 9, 14–24. Native to foothills of California (Santa Clara to San Diego counties) and desert mountain slopes of southern California. Forms a clump 1–3 ft. high, spreading to 4 ft. Leaves narrow, ½–¾ in. long; may be dark green above, white and woolly beneath, or gray and hairy. White or pinkish flowers in headlike clusters, May–October. Good erosion control plant. 'Theodore Payne', lower growing, makes attractive green ground cover.

E. giganteum. ST. CATHERINE'S LACE. Shrub. Zones 14–24. Native to Santa Catalina and San Clemente islands. Differs from *E. arborescens* in its more freely branching habit; grayish white, broadly oval, 1–2½-in.-long leaves; and longer period of bloom.

E. grande rubescens *(E. rubescens, E. latifolium rubescens)*. RED BUCKWHEAT. Perennial. Zones 14–24. Native to San Miguel, Santa Rosa, and Santa Cruz islands, southern California. Woody based; branches tend to lie on ground, spreading to 1–1½ ft., with upright tips about 10–12 in. high. Gray green, oval leaves 1–3½ in. long. Branch tips and sturdy upright branchlets are topped by headlike clusters of rosy red flowers in summer.

E. umbellatum. SULFUR FLOWER. Perennial. All Zones; plants grow to timberline and above. Low, broad mats of woody stems set with 1-in. green leaves, white-felted beneath. In summer, 4–12-in. stalks carry clusters of tiny yellow flowers that age to rust.

ERODIUM chamaedryoides. *Geraniaceae.* CRANE'S BILL. Perennial. Zones 7–9, 14–24. Native to Balearic Islands and Corsica. Dainty-looking but tough plant, forming dense foliage tuft 3–6 in. high, 1 ft. across. Long-stalked, roundish, dark green leaves ⅓ in. long with scalloped edges. Profuse, cup-shaped, ½-in.-wide flowers with white or rose pink, rosy-veined petals notched at tips, April–October. Good small-scale ground cover, rock garden plant. Plant in sun or part shade in porous soil; give ample moisture. Rather slow growing.

Erodium chamaedryoides

ERYNGIUM amethystinum. *Umbelliferae.* SEA HOLLY, AMETHYST ERYNGIUM. Perennial. All Zones. Erect, stiff-branched, thistlelike plant 2–3 ft. high, blooming July–September. Striking oval, steel blue or amethyst, ½-in.-long flower heads surrounded by spiny blue bracts; upper stems also blue (flowers last long when cut, fresh or dried). Leaves sparse, dark green, deeply cut, spiny toothed. Plant in borders or fringe areas, full sun, deep sandy soil. Drought tolerant. Tap rooted; difficult to divide. Make root cuttings; or sow seed in place, then thin seedlings to 1 ft. apart. Often self-sows.

Eryngium amethystinum

ERYSIMUM. *Cruciferae.* BLISTER CRESS, WALLFLOWER. Perennial or annual. Closely related to wallflower (*Cheiranthus*), with similar 4-petaled flowers, mostly yellow or orange, generally quite fragrant. Most prefer full sun and can take considerable drought.

E. hieraciifolium (usually sold as *Cheiranthus allionii* or *E. asperum*). SIBERIAN WALLFLOWER. Perennial, usually grown as annual. All Zones. Branching plants 1–1½ ft. high, smothered with rich orange flowers in spring. Leaves firm, narrow, 2–4 in. long. Combine with yellow, orange, or bronze tulips, blue forget-me-not (*Myosotis*) or Chinese forget-me-not (*Cynoglossum*). Sow seed in fall in mild climates; elsewhere, sow in summer for well-established plants by fall. Thin seedlings to 1 ft. apart.

Erysimum hieraciifolium

E. kotschyanum. Perennial treated as annual in warm climates. Zones 1–11, 14–21. Forms attractive mats 6 in. high. Leaves pale green, finely toothed, crowded. Deep yellow flowers on 2-in. stems. Plant in sun. Use in rock gardens, rock crevices, between paving stones, or in small pattern plantings with mat-forming perennials such as aubrieta, dwarf candytuft (*Iberis*). If plants hump up, cut out raised portion.

E. linifolium *(Cheiranthus linifolius)*. Shrubby perennial. Zones 14–24. Much confusion surrounds this plant's name and origin; it is probably a hybrid between *E. linifolium* and one of several species of *Cheiranthus*. The plant usually seen is sold as *E. linifolium* 'Variegatum'. It is rounded, freely branching, 1–2 ft. tall, with narrow, white-bordered, 3-in.-long leaves and narrow, spikelike clusters of flowers which open bronzy buff and age to pale purple. Blooms constantly from spring through fall. Needs sun, average soil and water, good drainage, protection from heavy frosts, and grooming to remove spent flowers.

ERYTHEA. See *Brahea*.

ERYTHRINA. *Leguminosae.* CORAL TREE. Mostly deciduous (some nearly evergreen) trees or shrubs. Many kinds; known and used chiefly in southern California. Brilliant flowers from greenish white through yellow, light orange, and light red to orange and red. Thorny plants have strong structural value, in or out of leaf. Leaves divided into 3 leaflets. Unless otherwise noted, plants do best in full sun and well-drained soil (of almost any type), with regular, deep, infrequent watering in dry season. To eliminate too-rapid, succulent growth and limb breakage in larger species (*E. caffra, E. lysistemon, E. sykesii*), give little or no summer irrigation and prune after flowering.

Erythrina caffra

E. americana. Deciduous tree (but may be evergreen in mildest

E

areas near coast). Zones 12, 13, 19–24. Native to Mexico; widely used as street tree in Mexico City. To 25 ft. tall. Resembles *E. coralloides* in habit and flowers.

E. bidwillii. Large deciduous shrub. Zones 8, 9, 12–24. To 8 ft., sometimes treelike to 20 ft. or more, wide spreading. Hybrid origin. Spectacular display—2-ft.-long clusters of pure red flowers on long, willowy stalks from spring until winter; main show in summer. Cut back flowering wood when flowers are spent. Very thorny, so plant away from paths and prune with long-handled shears. Best in hot sun.

E. caffra *(E. constantiana).* KAFFIRBOOM CORAL TREE. Briefly deciduous tree. Zones 21–24. Native to South Africa. Grows 24–40 ft. high, spreads to 40–60 ft. wide. Drops leaves in January; then angular bare branches produce big clusters of deep red orange, tubular flowers that drip nectar. In March or earlier, flowers give way to fresh, light green foliage.

E. coralloides (sometimes sold as *E. poianthes*). NAKED CORAL TREE. Deciduous tree. Zones 12, 13, 19–24. Native to Mexico (some doubt about place of origin). To 30 ft. high and as wide or wider, but easily contained by pruning. Fiery red blossoms like fat candles or pine cones bloom at tips of naked, twisted, black-thorned branches, March–May. At end of flowering season, 8–10-in. leaves develop, give shade in summer, turn yellow in late fall before dropping. Bizarre form of branch structure when tree is out of leaf is almost as valuable as spring flower display.

E. crista-galli. COCKSPUR CORAL TREE. Deciduous shrub or tree. Native to rainy sections of Brazil. Zones 7–9, 12–17, 19–24. Unusual plant with habit all its own. In frost-free areas, becomes many-stemmed, rough-barked tree to 15–20 ft. high and as wide. In colder climates, dies to ground in winter but comes back in spring like perennial (cut back dead growth). First flowers form after leaves come in spring—at each branch tip a big, loose, spikelike cluster of velvety, birdlike blossoms in warm pink to wine red (plants vary). Depending on environment, there can be as many as 3 distinct flowering periods, spring through fall. Cut back old flower stems and dead branch ends after each wave of bloom. Leaves 6 in. long, leaflets 2–3 in. long.

Erythrina crista-galli

E. falcata. Nearly evergreen tree. Zones 19–24. Native to Brazil and Peru. Grows upright to 30–40 ft. high. Must be in ground several years before it flowers (may take 10–12 years). Rich deep red (occasionally orange red), sickle-shaped flowers in hanging, spikelike clusters at branch ends in late winter, early spring. Some leaves fall at flowering time.

E. humeana. NATAL CORAL TREE. Normally deciduous shrub or tree (sometimes almost evergreen). Zones 12, 13, 20–24. Native to South Africa. May grow to 30 ft. but begins to wear its bright orange red flowers when only 3 ft. high. Blooms continuously from late August to late November, carrying flowers in long-stalked clusters at branch ends well above foliage (unlike many other types). Dark green leaves. *E. h.* 'Raja' is shrubbier and has leaflets with long, pointed "tails."

Erythrina humeana

E. lysistemon (sometimes erroneously sold as *E. princeps*). Deciduous tree. Zones 13, 21–24. Native to South Africa. Similar to *E. caffra* in size, but slower growing. Light orange (sometimes shrimp-colored) flowers. Time of bloom varies greatly; may bloom intermittently October–May, occasionally in summer. Many handsome black thorns. A magnificent tree of great landscape value. Very sensitive to wet soil.

E. sykesii. Deciduous tree. Zones 19–24. Hybrid from Australia. Grows 24–30 ft.; spreading habit. Showy red flowers before leaves, January–March. Unlike preceding species, does not form pods.

ERYTHRONIUM. *Liliaceae.* Corms. Zones 1–7, 15–17. Most are native to West. Dainty spring-blooming, nodding, lily-shaped flowers 1–1½ in. across, on stems usually 1 ft. or less high. All have 2 (rarely 3) broad, tongue-shaped, basal leaves, mottled in many species. Plant in shade or partial shade (except *E. dens-canis*), in groups under trees, in rock gardens, beside pools or streams. Set out corms in fall, 2–3 in. deep, 4–5 in. apart, in rich, porous soil; plant corms as soon as you receive them, and don't let them dry out. Growing plants need summer moisture.

Erythronium tuolumnense

E. californicum. FAWN LILY. Leaves mottled with brown. Flowers creamy white or yellow with deeper yellow band at base.

E. dens-canis. DOG-TOOTH VIOLET. European species with purple or rose flowers 1 in. long; stems 6 in. high. Leaves mottled with reddish brown. Needs more sun than others. Specialists can supply named varieties in white, pink, rose, and violet.

E. hendersonii. Flowers deeply curled back at tips, 1½ in. across, light to deep lavender, deep maroon at base surrounded by white band. Leaves mottled.

E. revolutum. Similar to *E. californicum,* with mottled leaves, large rose pink or lavender flowers, banded yellow at base. 'Rose Beauty' and 'White Beauty' are choice varieties.

E. tuolumnense. Solid green leaves. Flowers golden yellow, greenish yellow at base. Robust, with stems 12–15 in. tall. 'Kondo' and 'Pagoda' are extra-vigorous selections.

ESCALLONIA. *Saxifragaceae.* Evergreen shrubs. Zones 4–9, 14–17, 20–24. Native to South America, principally Chile. Wind-hardy, clean looking, with glossy leaves. Clusters of flowers in summer and fall (nearly year round in mild climates). May freeze badly at 10°–15°F., but recover quickly. Will take direct coastal conditions and coastal winds. Grow in full sun near coast, part shade in hot interior valleys. Can take some drought once established, but look better with ample water. Tolerant of most soils, but damaged by high alkalinity. Prune taller ones by removing ⅓ of old wood each year, cutting to the base; or shape into multitrunked trees. Prune after flowers fade. Tip-pinch smaller kinds to keep them compact. Can be sheared as hedges, but this may sacrifice some bloom. Fast growing; good screen plants; attractive to bees. Foliage of some exudes resinous fragrance.

Escallonia rubra

E. 'Apple Blossom'. See *E. langleyensis.*

E. 'Balfouri'. See *E. exoniensis.*

E. bifida *(E. montevidensis).* WHITE ESCALLONIA. Tall, broad shrub to 8–10 ft., useful as big screening plant, or multitrunked small tree to 25 ft. Leaves dark green, glossy, 3–4 in. long. White flowers in large, rounded clusters at branch ends, late summer, fall. Many plants sold under this name are *E. illinita,* a smaller plant to 10 ft. tall with smaller flower clusters and pronounced resinous odor.

E. 'C. F. Ball'. See *E. rubra.*

E. 'Compakta'. To 3 ft. high. Rose red flowers.

E. exoniensis. Name given to hybrids between *E. rosea* and *E. rubra.* Best selections are 'Balfouri', graceful plant to 10 ft. with drooping branchlets, narrow clusters of white, pink-tinted flowers; and 'Frades' (*E.* 'Fradesii'), compact growth to 5–6 ft. (lower with pinching). 'Frades' resembles *E. laevis,* but has smaller, glossy green leaves and prolific show of clear pink to rose flowers nearly year round. Good as espalier.

E. 'Fradesii'. See *E. exoniensis.*

E. 'Ingramii'. See *E. rubra macrantha.*

E. 'Jubilee'. Compact 6-ft. shrub, densely leafy right to ground. Clustered pinkish to rose flowers bloom at intervals throughout year. Foliage inferior to that of *E. exoniensis*. Set 4 ft. apart for informal hedge or low screen.

E. laevis (*E. organensis*). PINK ESCALLONIA. Leafy, dense-growing shrub to 12–15 ft. Leaves bronzy green. Pink to red buds open into white to pink flowers in short, broad clusters. Early summer bloom. Use like *E. bifida*. Leaves burn in beach plantings and in high heat of interior.

E. langleyensis. Name given to hybrids between *E. rubra* and *E. virgata*. Best-known selection is 'Apple Blossom', a dense-growing shrub to 5 ft., sprawling unless pinched back. Pinkish white flowers open from pink buds. Blooms all summer with peaks in late spring, early fall.

E. montevidensis. See *E. bifida*.

E. organensis. See *E. laevis*.

E. 'Pride of Donard'. Dense, rounded shrub wider than tall. Many stems end in clusters of rose pink flowers (plant blooms almost all year). Dark green, glossy leaves.

E. rosea. Shrub to 7 ft. with shiny, oval, 1½-in. leaves. Clustered white to red flowers in summer. Many closely related plants sold under this name; commonest, probably a selection of *E. franciscana*, is 10 ft. tall with tendency to throw out long, uneven branches. It has chocolate-colored bark and dark green leaves ½–1 in. long. Rosy pink flowers all summer long.

E. rubra. Upright, compact shrub 6–15 ft. tall. Leaves smooth, very glossy dark green. Red or crimson flowers in 1–3-in. clusters throughout warmer months. Much used as screen or hedge, especially near coast. Compact varieties are 'C. F. Ball' (to 3 ft. with some pinching) and 'William Watson', to 4 ft., with ruddy cerise flowers, spindly habit unless pruned. *E. r. macrantha* ('Ingramii') is large-flowered variety.

E. virgata. Partially deciduous shrub to 6 ft., with ¾-in. leaves and short clusters of pale rose or white flowers. 'Gwendolyn Anley' has flesh pink flowers. These are hardiest escallonias in frostiest parts of their hardiness range.

ESCHSCHOLZIA californica. *Papaveraceae*. CALIFORNIA POPPY. Perennial usually grown as annual. All Zones. Native to California, Oregon. State flower of California. Free branching from base; stems 8–24 in. long. Leaves blue green, finely divided. Single flowers about 2 in. wide, with satiny petals; color varies from pale yellow to deep orange. Blooms close at night and on gray days.

Eschscholzia californica

California poppy is not the best choice for important, close-in garden beds: unless you trim off dead flowers regularly, plants go to seed and all parts turn straw color. But it can't be surpassed for naturalizing on sunny hillsides, along drives, or in dry fields, vacant lots, parking strips, or country gardens. Sow seed where plants are to grow; California poppies do not transplant well. Broadcast seed in fall on cultivated, well-drained soil in full sun; if rains are late, water to keep ground moist until seeds germinate. Summer watering not necessary but forces more bloom. For large-scale sowing, use 3–4 lbs. of seed per acre. Reseeds freely if not crowded out by weeds. Birds attracted to seeds.

There are also garden forms available in yellow, pink, rose, flame orange, red, cream, and white; Sunset strain has single flowers, Mission Bells semidouble flowers, and Ballerina semidouble flowers with frilled and fluted petals. The Silk strain has bronze-tinted foliage, semidouble flowers in the full color range. Single-color varieties are often available through seed catalogs. Among these are 'Cherry Ripe', 'Milky White', and 'Purple-Violet'.

E. caespitosa. Annual. Smaller than *E. californica;* garden variety 'Sundew' has densely tufted growth to 6 in. Bright yellow, 1-in. flowers. Edging, containers.

E. lobbii. Rarely cultivated species, with a few 1½-in. leaves and yellow, 1–1½-in. flowers on 3–9-in. stems. This and the preceding species are small enough for rock garden use.

ESPOSTOA lanata. *Cactaceae*. PERUVIAN OLD MAN CACTUS. Zones 12–24. Columnar cactus branching with age. Slow growing in pots, fairly fast to 8 ft. in open ground. Grow in full sun or light afternoon shade. Drought tolerant. Plant has light brown, bristly, ½–2-in.-long thorns, usually concealed in long, white hair that covers plant. Hair is especially long and dense near summit. Tubular, pink, 2-in.-long flowers, May–June. Protect from hard frosts.

Espostoa lanata

EUCALYPTUS. *Myrtaceae*. Evergreen trees and shrubs. Zones 8–24 (occasionally and experimentally Zones 5, 6). With few exceptions, native to Australia. Most widely planted non-native trees in California and Arizona; for several hundred miles in parts of California, you never lose sight of a eucalypt. First ones were planted in California in 1856. From 1870 on, they were widely planted for windbreaks, firewood, shade, and beauty. From 1904 to 1912, thousands of acres were planted in an ill-advised hardwood timber scheme. Over the years, eucalyptus proved themselves well in these climates, and remain popular landscaping subjects today. Reasons:

Eucalyptus ficifolia

Great beauty. Some kinds are basically landscape structure trees or shrubs, with unimportant flowers. These kinds are grown for their attractive and functional form and texture. Others bear flowers as striking as roses or rhododendrons, or have foliage so handsome that florists sell it. Some species serve basic landscaping functions and produce pretty flowers, too. The chart on pages 336–342 indicates noteworthy features of over 50 different eucalyptus species.

Climate tolerance. Much of Australia has either a desert, Mediterranean, or subtropical climate, as do sections of California and Arizona. Dozens of eucalyptus species are naturally adapted to our coast, coastal hills, valleys, and deserts—with or without irrigation. Drought tolerance is common to most of these plants.

Eucalyptus sideroxylon

Few pests. Eucalyptus was a pest-free tree until 1984, when the eucalyptus longhorn beetle—one of the tree's native attackers in Australia—was observed in southern California. Without its native predators to keep it in check, the beetle is becoming a serious pest, especially on stressed trees. Signs of infestation include oval holes made by beetles, leaving plant and branches dying with leaves still attached.

For now, the best way to deal with the problem is good management. Avoid pruning from May to October. If any pruning cuts are absolutely necessary, seal them well to prevent sap flow, which attracts beetles. (Freshly cut wood is a lure.) Eliminate eucalyptus firewood with underbark feeding galleries by burning or burying. Remove dead or dying trees; bury logs or cover tightly with tarpaulins for at least 6 months. Keep eucalyptus firewood tightly covered, and do not transport it. Best hope for eventual control will come from introduced predatory insects.

Fast growth. Some tree types grow as fast as 10–15 ft. a year in early stages. Such growth rate is typically associated with short-lived trees, but not in this case; fast-growing tree eucalypts can live for at least a century if planted right.

Eucalypts are influenced through their lives by their condition at planting time and the kind of planting they get. Select the most

E

vigorous-looking plants, not the biggest ones. Avoid those with many leafless twigs or evidence of having been pruned hard. If possible, do not buy plants with canbound roots. If such plants are all that you can get, do this: wash soil off roots, then spread roots out as straight and fanlike as possible in premoistened planting hole (with stem's old soil line ½–1 in. below grade level). At once, fill in thoroughly around fanned-out roots with moistened soil and irrigate heavily. If plants are topheavy, cut back and stake (chart specifically prescribes staking for certain species).

Some descriptions in the chart recommend cutting plants back to make them bushier or stouter. Do this between March and August (where eucalyptus beetle is not a problem), preferably when tree has been in ground at least a year. If possible, cut back to just above side branch or bud. If you can't find such a growth point, cut right into smooth trunk; if plant is established, new growth will break out beneath cut. Later, come back and remove all excess new branches—keep only those that are well-placed.

Best way to plant eucalyptus is directly from seed flats. Seeding is as easy as with many annuals and perennials. Sow seed on flat of prepared soil in spring or summer. Keep flat shaded and water sparingly. When seedlings are 2–3 in. high, lift gently, separate, and plant into another flat of prepared soil, spacing 3 in. apart. Or transplant into gallon cans or cleaned 1-quart oil cans (puncture at bottom for drainage). Plant seedlings in 2–3 months when 6–12 in. high.

A eucalyptus tree in a suitable climate, properly planted and irrigated, is a vigorous, strong, and durable plant. Complete fertilizer is seldom needed, although iron often is required for eucalypts that chronically form yellow leaves. In the desert, eucalypts are especially subject to chlorosis in dense or shallow soils. Iron chelates added during the spring and fall growth flushes are helpful in young trees. Chlorosis can be brought on by overwatering; established trees can get by with infrequent watering. Newly planted trees may need water every day for their first week if the weather is hot and dry; thereafter, you may taper off to 1 or 2 waterings a week for the rest of the first growing season.

The chart gives approximate hardiness for each eucalyptus species listed, but it is important to remember that these temperatures are not absolute. In addition to air temperature, you must take into consideration: age of plant (generally, the older, the hardier); condition of plant; date of frost (24°F. in November is more damaging than 24°F. in January, after weeks of frosts); duration of frost. As a guide: if temperatures in your area are likely to fall within frost-damage range for certain species, plant it as a risk. If they regularly fall below given range, don't plant it. Occasional deep or prolonged freezes may apparently kill even large trees. Do not be too hasty to remove them; they can sprout new growth from trunk or large branches, though heavy freeze damage may alter the tree's appearance. Delay removal or heavy pruning until summer (in areas where eucalyptus beetle is a problem, do not prune heavily May–October; prune in earliest spring or late fall).

Most eucalypts have 2 conspicuously different kinds of foliage: soft, variously shaped juvenile leaves, found on seedlings, saplings, and new branches that grow from stumps; and usually tougher adult or mature foliage. Where a species' juvenile foliage is significant, it is mentioned in the chart. Almost all eucalyptus leaves, juvenile and adult, have distinguishing pungent fragrance. Sometimes you must crush leaves to smell it. There is a common denominator to fragrance of all types, but various ones are additionally spiked with peppermint, lemon, medicinal aromas, or other scents.

Several Australian words are used repeatedly in common names for various eucalypts. Here are their meanings as applied to eucalyptus: *gum,* a name generally applied to any eucalypt, specifically to any of various smooth-barked (often peeling) species; *ironbark,* any with hard, rough bark; *mallee,* originally native term for eucalyptus thicket; here, refers to any shrubby species with round, swollen rootstock from which grow several slender stems; *marlock,* dwarf species; *messmate,* interesting name of no particular significance, applied to several stringy-bark species; *peppermint,* any with peppermint odor in crushed leaves, usually with finely fibrous bark; *yate,* native word applied to certain species.

More than 500 kinds of eucalyptus have been recorded in Australia. About 150 have been grown in California and Arizona (many as solitary representatives in arboretums). A few have been grown in Oregon and Washington.

Eucalyptus

NAME	HARDINESS	FORM AND SIZE	LEAVES AND BARK	FLOWERS AND FRUIT	BEST FEATURES AND HOW TO ENCOURAGE THEM
Eucalyptus albens WHITE BOX	22°F.	Straight trunk, wide crown, fairly dense shade. To 30–80 ft.	Pale gray green leaves. Pale bark.	Clusters of small white flowers from whitish buds. Small fruits.	Like *E. polyanthemos* but stronger growth in desert. Needs little water.
E. baueriana BLUE BOX	10°–18°F.	Fuller-bodied substitute for *E. polyanthemos.*	Leaves broader and rougher than those of *E. polyanthemos.*	Same as *E. polyanthemos.*	Attractive round tree when young; becomes tall and straight with age.
E. caesia (*caesia* means "bluish gray")	22°–25°F.	Graceful, weeping, open habit as mallee or small, weak-structured tree. To 15–20 ft.	Gray green, small leaves contrast with red stems. Bark white and mottled when young, curling when older.	Outstanding dusty pink to deep rose flowers in loose clusters, blooming heavily late winter to early spring. Flowering scattered rest of year. Lavender gray seed capsules shaped like bells, ¾ in. long.	Not good in wind or in heavy soil. Use as thin screen in protected place. Or, with pruning and training, use as espalier, shrub, or multitrunked tree. Prune and stake to give body.
E. calophylla (*calophylla* means "beautiful leaf")	25°–28°F.	Medium to large round-headed tree—90–150 ft. high in Australia, has reached 50 ft. in California.	Broad, oval, dark green leaves, 4–7 in. long. Rough, fissured bark.	Showy flowers in 1-ft. clusters—white, rose, or red, on and off all year. Bulbous seed capsules, 1½ in. wide. Light pink-flowered form often sold as *E. c.* 'Rosea'; rose pink kind is *E. c.* 'Hawkeyi'.	Sturdy, drought tolerant, easy to grow—and it produces showy flowers against nice leaves as part of the package. Similar to *E. ficifolia* in many ways (also hybridizes frequently with it).

NAME	HARD-INESS	FORM AND SIZE	LEAVES AND BARK	FLOWERS AND FRUIT	BEST FEATURES AND HOW TO ENCOURAGE THEM
E. camaldulensis (*E. rostrata*) RED GUM, RIVER RED GUM	12°–15°F.	Ultimately 80–120 ft. Form varies; typically has curved trunk, spreading crown, gracefully weeping branches.	Long, slender, lance-shaped, medium green leaves, pendulous in varying degrees. Tan, mottled trunk.	Unimportant white to pale yellow flowers in drooping clusters, summer. Followed by many rounded, pea-sized seed capsules in long clusters. Not grown for flowers; structural tree.	One of most widely planted eucalypts around world. Mighty tree for highways, broad streets, parks, skylines. Fine desert tree but gets chlorotic in lawns there. OK in lawns elsewhere. Takes more heat and cold than *E. globulus;* has resprouted after 11°F. freeze. Endures alkaline soils.
E. campaspe SILVER-TOPPED GIMLET	18°F.	Slender tree to 25–35 ft.	Silvery gray leaves. Copper brown, polished-looking mature bark.	Flowers and fruit inconspicuous.	Thrives under a wide variety of irrigation conditions. Can grow on 7-in. annual rainfall.
E. cinerea (*cinerea* means "ash colored")	14°–17°F.	Medium-sized tree, 20–50 ft. high, almost as wide. Irregular outline. Can be scrawny.	Juvenile leaves gray green, roundish, 1–2 in. long, in pairs. Mature leaves long. Furrowed bark.	Small white flowers near stems in winter and spring, followed by small conical seed capsules. Flowers are incidental—decorative juvenile foliage is main reason for growing this species.	Inclined to grow snakelike. Corrective pruning yields and encourages juvenile gray-foliaged branches used for indoor decorating. Fast growing. Withstands wind. Best in dry site or with fast drainage.
E. citriodora LEMON-SCENTED GUM	24°–28°F.	One of most graceful of trees—slender, tall (75–100 ft.). Trunk usually straight, sometimes curved.	Leaves long (3–7 in.), narrow, golden green, lemon scented. Trunk and branches powder white to pinkish.	Once tree gets up in the air, you'd need telescope to see flowers (lower ½ to ⅔ of tree is bare trunk). Blooms whitish, not distinctive, in clusters, mostly during winter. Seed capsules that follow are urn shaped, ⅜ in. wide.	Designer's tree. Enhances any architecture. Can grow close to walls, walks. Perfect for groves. Very fast growing. Weak-trunked when young; stake stoutly. Cut back and thin often to strengthen trunk. Tolerates much or little water. Tenderness to frosts is only real drawback.
E. cladocalyx (*E. corynocalyx*) SUGAR GUM	23°–28°F.	Large, upright, graceful, round topped, very open, 75–100 ft. high. Straight trunk.	Oval or variably shaped leaves, 3–5 in. long, shiny, reddish. Tan bark peels to show cream patches.	Creamy white flowers of little significance, in dense 3-in. clusters, bloom June–August. Oval seed capsules (⅜ in. wide) in clusters. Not planted for flowers; used for structure.	Dramatic skyline tree on southern California coast. Puffy clouds of leaves separated by open spaces —a Japanese print in its mature silhouette. Tough, drought resistant. Variety 'Nana' to 20–25 ft.
E. cornuta (*cornuta* means "horn shaped") YATE	22°–25°F.	Large-headed, spreading tree, to 35–60 ft. high. Attractive dense crown gives shade.	Lance-shaped, shiny leaves, 3–6 in. long (young leaves round, gray). Bark peels in strips.	Flower buds have interesting fingerlike buff caps pushed off by opening flowers. Greenish yellow flowers make round, fuzzy clusters, 3 in. wide, summer. Clusters of round seed capsules with short horns.	Appreciated for its flowers, form, and landscape uses. Grows under many kinds of soil, water, and climate conditions. Does well even when neglected. Not subject to wind breakage. Good shade tree.
E. deglupta MINDANAO GUM	24°–26°F.	Erect, clean-trunked tree to 80 ft. or more.	Dark green foliage. Bark flaking, strikingly colored in blue, green, yellow, red, purple.	Flowers, fruit inconspicuous.	Spectacular trunk the feature. This jungle tree from the Philippines and New Guinea grows fast, endures light frost. Needs water.
E. eremophila TALL SAND MALLEE	17°–22°F.	Multitrunked, small, bushy tree, 25 ft.	Dark green, narrow, lance-shaped, shiny leaves. Scaly bark.	Round, yellow, fuzzy 1–2-in. flowers in clusters, June. Opening flowers push off long pointed caps. Capsules slightly cylindrical, about ¼ in. wide.	Very drought-tolerant tree for banks, hillsides, beach areas. No good in lawns. Better liked in southern than in northern California. Good desert plant.
E. erythrocorys RED-CAP GUM	23°–26°F.	Small tree, 10–30 ft., best with multiple trunk; sprawling but attractive bush.	Thick, shiny, 4–7-in., lance-shaped leaves, greener than most eucalyptus leaves. White trunk.	Spectacular. Bright red caps tilt up and drop off to reveal yellow flowers in clusters that look like shaving brushes. Blooms any time, but heaviest bloom comes fall to early spring. Cone-shaped seed capsules follow flowers.	Takes much water if drainage is good. Can be grown in lawn. To make dense multitrunked bush or tree, head back main shoots several times. Attractive in desert.

(Continued on next page)

NAME	HARDINESS	FORM AND SIZE	LEAVES AND BARK	FLOWERS AND FRUIT	BEST FEATURES AND HOW TO ENCOURAGE THEM
E. erythronema RED-FLOWERED MALLEE	17°–22°F.	Mallee or small, bushy, crooked or sinuous tree, 10–25 ft.	Narrow, dull green leaves 1½–3 in. long. Smooth bark in patches of pink, white, tan, pale green.	Watermelon to deep red flowers, 1 in. wide, open from conical, pointed buds, 1 in. long, pinkish green to red. Conical, square-sided seed capsules, ½ in. wide.	Trunk and flowers are its best features. You may have to thin some to make it presentable tree. Resists wind and drought. Good near ocean. Recommended for desert.
E. ficifolia RED-FLOWERING GUM	25°–30°F.	Usually single-trunked, round-headed tree to 40 ft. Compact crown. Can be multistemmed big bush.	Leaves 3–7 in. long, shape and texture of rubber plant leaves. Bark red and stringy to gray and fibrous.	Spectacular 1-ft. clusters of flowers in cream, light pink, salmon, orange, or light red (most common); all year, peaking July–August. Seed capsules 1 in. wide, like miniature dice cups with swollen bottoms.	Aside from *E. calophylla*, not like other eucalypts. Prune off seed capsules from young trees so they won't pull branches down. Best on coast; seldom successful inland. Rarely good in lawns. Unpredictable flower color from seed.
E. formanii	15°F.	Bushy, billowy big shrub or small tree to 15–30 ft.	Silvery to tan, leaves, 2½ in. long, ⅛ in. wide.	Small white flowers are inconspicuous. Fruits small, rounded.	Slow-growing tree of unusual interest in desert.
E. forrestiana FUCHSIA EUCALYPTUS	23°–27°F.	Shrub or short-trunked tree to 12 ft. (needs staking, pruning as tree).	Narrow leaves, 1½–2½ in. long. Gray brown, smooth trunk, reddish branches.	Woody, pendant red flower bases resemble fuchsias, are decorative. Intermittent all year. Capsules 1 in. wide.	Fuchsialike flower bases last long when cut. Good performance coast or dry areas. Any soil. To strengthen, cut back when young.
E. globulus BLUE GUM	17°–22°F.	Tall, solemn trees of grandeur; reach 150–200 ft. Straight trunks. Heavy masses of foliage.	Sickle-shaped, dark green leaves, 6–10 in. long. Young leaves oval, silvery, soft. Bark sheds.	Flowers creamy white to yellow in winter and spring. Warty, ribbed, blue gray seed capsules, 1 in. wide. Fruit drop added to leaf and bark litter makes tree very messy.	Most common eucalypt in California. Very aromatic. Magnificent windbreak but too messy, greedy, and brittle for garden or city street. Needs deep soil and plenty of room. Best on coastal slopes. Poor in deserts.

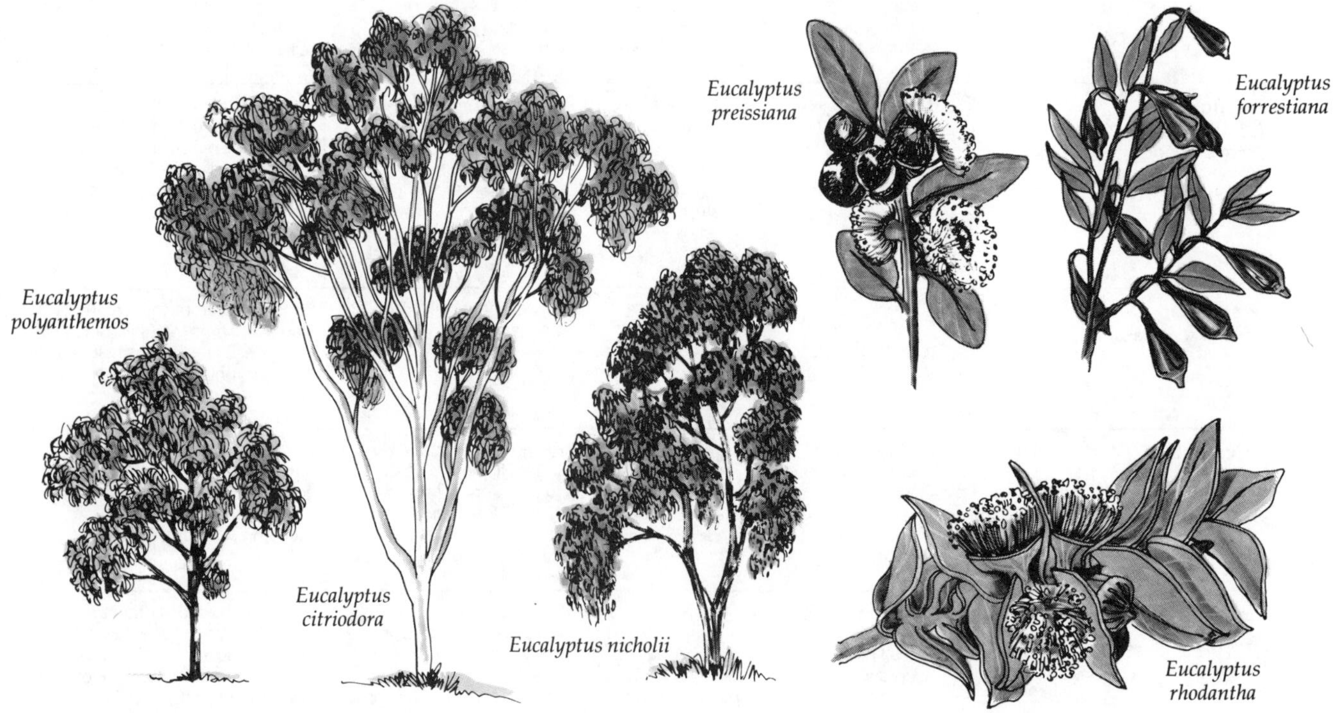

Three widely planted tree-type eucalypts show differences in form. Eucalyptus flower size and form vary. With **E. forrestiana**, *display comes from red, woody flower bases.*

E

NAME	HARD-INESS	FORM AND SIZE	LEAVES AND BARK	FLOWERS AND FRUIT	BEST FEATURES AND HOW TO ENCOURAGE THEM
E. g. 'Compacta' DWARF BLUE GUM	17°–22°F.	Multibranched, bushy, shrublike tree, as high as 60–70 ft.	Same as *E. globulus*. Foliage persists to ground for 10–15 years. Becomes treelike later.	Flowers and seed capsules same as on *E. globulus*.	Lacks noble silhouette of *E. globulus*, but is just as greedy, almost as messy. Good low windbreak in coastal areas—can be sheared as low as 10 ft.
E. grossa COARSE-FLOWERED MALLEE	22°–26°F.	Multitrunked, spreading shrub, 9–15 ft. tall. Sometimes dense.	Thick, glistening, deep green, 3-in., broad, oval leaves. Red and green stems.	Noticeable yellow flowers in clusters open from bullet-shaped buds in spring and summer. Cylindrical seed capsules, ⅜ in. wide.	Best feature is clean green foliage. Often erratic, can be made into dense hedge if pruned. Gets scraggly when old if watered heavily. Good desert choice.
E. gunnii CIDER GUM	5°–10°F.	Medium to large, dense, vertical tree, 40–75 ft.	Mature leaves lance shaped, 3–5 in. long. Smooth, green and tan bark.	Small creamy white flowers, April–June, from green, shiny, round buds. Seed capsules ¼ in. wide, bell shaped, in clusters.	Strong, vigorous, tall grower. Impressively healthy and vigorous looking. Good shade, windbreak, or privacy screening tree in cold areas (very hardy).
E. kruseana KRUSE'S MALLEE	25°–28°F.	Thin, open, angular shrub, almost ground cover; 5–8 ft. tall at most.	Silver blue, round, 1-in. leaves like tiny *E. pulverulenta*. Smooth bark.	Little (½-in.) yellow flowers along stems between round leaves. Flower bud caps cone shaped. Seed capsules size and shape of small (¼-in.) acorns.	Attractive foliage and flowers on slow-growing shrub, small and dainty enough for Japanese garden. Conversation plant. Cut back frequently. Useful in desert gardens.
E. lehmannii BUSHY YATE	25°–28°F.	Small tree, 20–30 ft. Dense, flat topped, wide spreading.	Light green, long-oval, 2-in. leaves; some turn red in fall. Old ones rough. Brown bark.	Apple green flowers in big (4-in.-wide), round clusters open from curved, horn-shaped buds in clusters. (Horns straight in variety 'Max Watson'.) Large fused seed capsules remain on branches.	Fast growing, densely leafed tree, very good for screening on coast; or street tree with lower branches pruned. Unpruned, branches persist to ground. Variety 'Max Watson' grows low and compact.
E. leucoxylon WHITE IRONBARK	14°–18°F.	Somewhat variable, usually slender, upright, open, with pendulous branches. Reaches 20–80 ft.	Gray green, sickle-shaped leaves, 3–6 in. long. Bark sheds, leaving white to mottled trunk.	White flowers intermittently, winter, spring. Goblet-shaped seed capsules, ⅜ in. wide. (*E. l.* 'Rosea' has pink flowers, larger seed capsules, may not come true from seed.)	Free-flowering, fast-growing, moderate-sized tree that tolerates many adverse conditions including heavy soil, light rocky soil, heat, wind.
E. l. macrocarpa 'Rosea' LARGE-FRUITED RED-FLOWERING GUM	14°–18°F.	Much-branched, shrublike tree. Variable 15–25 ft.	Gray green leaves. Gray to pinkish trunk.	Clear vivid crimson flowers borne profusely at early age. Goblet-shaped seed capsules, ¾ in. wide.	Very ornamental tree. Good in most soils, most sites, even near beach or in desert.
E. linearis		See *E. pulchella*.			
E. macrandra LONG-FLOWERED MARLOCK	8°–12°F.	Round-headed, open tree to 25–35 ft. Main branches often develop curves.	Light golden green, lance-shaped leaves, 2½–5 in. long. Slick bark peels in ribbons.	Cream to green flowers in clusters. Bud caps distinctive: light green fingers 1–1½ in. long, ⅛ in. wide. Seed capsules slightly elongated, too. Flowering is incidental.	Plant to hide utility pole or soften house corner. (Some nurseries mistakenly sell this as *E. angulosa*; real *E. angulosa* is a mallee with yellowish white flowers and prominently ribbed seed capsules.)
E. macrocarpa (*macrocarpa* means "big-fruited")	8°–12°F.	Erratic, sprawling shrub, 4–15 ft. Tries to be vine but stems are too stiff. Similar to *E. rhodantha*.	Light gray blue leaves, 2–5 in. long, round with definite point, set close to stem. Greenish white bark.	Golf ball–sized gray buds (point on top) open to show flat-topped, round, fluffy flowers 4–7 in. wide. Usually pink, also white, red, or yellowish white (seedlings vary). No stems on flowers; grow right on branch. Flat-topped, bowl-shaped seed capsules, 3 in. wide.	Sprawling plant good for seasonal display in dry, sunny place. Not for irrigated areas (overwatering causes blackening of leaves). New growth begins vertical, becomes horizontal when weighted down with buds and capsules. Stems tend to die back from pruning.
E. maculata (*maculata* means "spotted")	19°–23°F.	Erect single-trunked tree, branching to make wide head. Graceful, strong. To 50–75 ft.	Dark green leaves, 3–6 in. long. Pearl gray bark patched dark red to violet.	White flowers in branch-end clusters, 1–3 in. wide. Seed capsules urn shaped, ½ in. wide, rough on outside. Not grown for flowers; landscaping tree.	Good singly or in groves. Smooth, spotted trunks are usually quite handsome; they vary in degree of spottiness. Best in sandy, well-drained soil.

(Continued on next page)

E

NAME	HARD-INESS	FORM AND SIZE	LEAVES AND BARK	FLOWERS AND FRUIT	BEST FEATURES AND HOW TO ENCOURAGE THEM
E. mannifera maculosa RED-SPOTTED GUM	20°–25°F.	Tall, slender tree, 20–50 ft. tall. Gracefully pendant branches sway prettily in wind.	Leaves ½ in. wide, 4–6 in. long, light green with gray cast. Bark brown, gray, off white.	Unimportant light-colored flowers open from pointed oval buds in clusters of 3–7; leave ½-in., goblet-shaped seed capsules.	Landscaping tree to feature in place of honor. When mature, brownish and grayish bark flakes off in summer, leaving powdery white surface. Australian aborigines paint their faces with the white dust.
E. megacornuta (*megacornuta* means "big-horned")	20°–23°F.	Big shrub or small tree, 20–30 ft. Multistemmed or single trunked. Spindly.	Shiny, bronzy green leaves. Smooth, gray to tan bark.	Clusters of St. Patrick's green flowers, 1½ in. long, each shaped like a shaving brush, open from buds that look like warty fingers. Clawlike seed capsules.	Flower arrangers like 2-in.-long, bronzy green buds, flowers, and seed capsules. Sometimes the form makes it acceptable for landscaping purposes.
E. melliodora (*melliodora* means "honey-scented")	18°–20°F.	Upright, graceful tree, 30–100 ft., with slightly weeping branches. Top fills in well.	Boat-shaped to sickle-shaped leaves, 2–6 in. long, grayish green. Old bark scaly, flaky, tan.	Late winter, early spring flowers are off white, in clusters about 1½ in. wide; not showy but sweet smelling and attractive to bees. Seed capsules ¼ in. wide, in clusters.	Clean, well-mannered tree, very little litter. Good for shade tree, street tree, windbreak (takes wind very well). Form 'Rosea' has pink flowers.
E. microtheca (*microtheca* means "tiny capsules") COOLIBAH	5°–10°F.	Bushy, round-headed tree to 35–40 ft. May have one or many trunks.	Blue green, ribbonlike leaves, 8 in. long. Smooth bark.	Insignificant creamy white flowers. Seed capsules tiny (match head size) in clusters of 3–5. Seed capsules create no litter.	Strong-looking, strong-growing tree of character. Drought tolerant. No breakage from wind. One of Arizona's best eucalypts.
E. nicholii NICHOL'S WILLOW-LEAFED PEPPERMINT	12°–15°F.	Graceful, weeping tree to 40 ft. Upright main trunk. Spreading crown.	Light green, very narrow leaves, 3–5 in. long. Mature foliage coarser. Bark deeply furrowed, reddish brown.	Small, inconspicuous whitish flowers, mostly in summer. Very small, round seed capsules in roundish clusters.	Garden or street tree. Beauty is in fine-textured foliage and billowing, willowy form. Grows fast. Crushed leaves smell like peppermint. Excessive water can cause chlorosis.
E. niphophila SNOW GUM	0°–10°F.	Small, wide-spreading, open tree to 20 ft. Trunk usually crooked.	Silvery blue, lance-shaped, 1½–4-in. leaves. Smooth, white, peeling bark.	Creamy white flowers in tight clusters 1½ in. wide, summer. Seed capsules round, ⅜ in. wide, very gray, also in tight clusters, close to stem.	Acclaimed chiefly for hardiness and silvery look of leaves. Slow growing. Drought, wind tolerant. Good on slopes. Can be picturesque.
E. orbifolia ROUND-LEAFED MALLEE	23°–25°F.	Large mallee of irregular, clambering habit. Not a tree.	Leaves nearly round (slightly pointed), 2 in. long. Thin red bark.	Little (½-in.-wide) yellow flowers in late spring. Round flower bud cap has point like Kaiser Wilhelm helmet.	Use as ground cover in difficult sunny place; native to rocky desert. Can be espaliered to show off round leaves and flowers. Slender, vinelike stems.
E. papuana GHOST GUM	22°F.	Variable; can be short, crooked, 20-ft. tree with multiple trunks or 60-ft. tree.	Gray green leaves, tinted purplish by frosts. Smooth white bark.	Small white summer flowers. Fruit inconspicuous.	White bark is its most striking feature. Does well in desert soils.
E. pauciflora GHOST GUM	10°–15°F.	Tree. Branches spread to make crown as wide as tree is tall (40 by 40 ft.). Graceful, airy, open.	White trunk and branches and narrow, gray green 3–6-in. leaves give it the name "ghost gum."	Insignificant flowers and little or no seed setting. Among other good points, ghost gum doesn't litter ground beneath it.	White trunk and branches and open, see-through foliage make it valuable individual display tree. Takes almost every degree of soil moisture. Good in lawns. In youth, remove erratic branches.
E. perriniana ROUND-LEAFED SNOW GUM	10°–15°F.	Small, straggly tree, 15–30 ft. Best cut back as shrub.	Juvenile leaves silvery, form circle around stem, spin on stem when dry.	Many small white flowers in summer in clusters of 3. Seed capsules, also in clusters of 3, are cup shaped, ¼ in. wide.	Silvery foliage nice for arrangements. If you cut enough, silvery juvenile growth remains (mature leaves are long). Use as gray-leafed plant in border.
E. platypus ROUND-LEAFED MOORT	23°–26°F.	Large bush or small tree, 20–30 ft. Many stems; may ultimately form one trunk.	Dark, dull green leaves, round ended, 1–2 in. long, rough. Smooth tan bark.	Many flowers, red or green (2 forms), open at ends of flattened stems, make showy clusters 2 in. wide. Cluster of many ½-in., goblet-shaped seed capsules.	Dense, fast-growing, pyramidal form, good for solid screening (space 12 ft. apart). Plants give general effect of stiff birches. Hummingbirds enjoy flowers. Good desert selection.

NAME	HARD-INESS	FORM AND SIZE	LEAVES AND BARK	FLOWERS AND FRUIT	BEST FEATURES AND HOW TO ENCOURAGE THEM
E. polyanthemos SILVER DOLLAR GUM	14°–18°F.	Slender, erect tree, single or multistemmed, to 20–60 ft. Fairly fast growing.	Juvenile leaves gray green, oval or round, 2–3 in. Mature leaves lance shaped. Mottled bark.	Creamy white flowers in 1-in. clusters, spring and summer. Seed capsules are cylindrical cups, ½ in. wide, in clusters. Flowers incidental—grow tree for cut foliage or landscape.	Popular landscaping and street tree. Excellent cut foliage. Select young trees carefully; some have leaves less round and gray than others. Grows almost anywhere. Not good in wet places.
E. populnea (*populnea* means "poplarlike") BIMBLE BOX, POPLAR BOX	22°F.	Grows 35–70 ft. tall with short trunk and dense, roundish crown.	Leaves thickish, round, deep green.	Small white flowers.	Leaves shimmer in wind.
E. preissiana BELL-FRUITED MALLEE	24°–26°F.	Mallee—typically an open, many-stemmed shrub to 12 ft. Sometimes tree to 15 ft.	Oval leaves, 2–3 in. long, thick, dull bluish cast, red stems. Smooth gray bark.	Very showy. Circular, flat yellow flowers 2–3 in. wide open from brown, globelike buds, 1 in. wide. Seed capsules cup shaped, ¾ in. wide. Flower color contrasts nicely with leaf, stem, trunk.	First-rate flower producer that also can hold its own as garden shrub. Cut flowers keep well. Blooms most heavily January–March.
E. pulchella (*E. linearis*) WHITE PEPPERMINT	18°–22°F.	Graceful tree to 20–50 ft. with weeping branches. Can be either asymmetrical or round headed in form.	Long, very narrow, dark green, pendulous leaves. White to light tan bark peels in thin strips.	Clusters of tiny creamy white flowers open from pinhead-sized buds, June–October. Goblet-shaped seed capsules, 3⁄16 in. wide, in tight clusters.	Fine well-mannered landscaping and street tree. Beautiful willowy form. Dark, dense foliage masses contrast with light trunk. Good in light soils with little water.
E. pulverulenta (*pulverulenta* means "powdered as with dust") SILVER MOUNTAIN GUM	15°–21°F.	Irregular, sprawling small tree or large shrub, 15–30 ft. Poor form unless pruned.	Silver gray, shish kebab–style juvenile foliage (stems appear to go through leaves). Ribbony bark.	Creamy white, ½-in., fuzzy flowers in clusters of 3 sandwiched between round leaves along stems. Fall to spring. Flowers are simply an extra. They are followed by ½-in.-wide, cup-shaped seed capsules.	Use in garden as curiosity feature and source of branches for arrangements (use natural or gilded). Cut back often to get and encourage decorative juvenile leaf growth; mature leaves are usually long and pointed.
E. pyriformis (*pyriformis* means "pear shaped")	25°–28°F.	Shrub or treelike shrub (mallee), 10–20 ft. Long, weak, rangy stems.	Broad, oval, light green leaves 2–4 in. long. Light brown bark.	Showy, large (2–3-in.-wide) flowers in clusters, late winter to early summer. May be red, pink, orange, yellow, or cream. Pear-shaped, 1-in. seed capsules.	Collector's item. Sometimes an elegant, slender tree, sometimes weak, rangy shrub. Flowers are best feature. Good performance in dry or sandy soil.
E. rhodantha (*rhodantha* means "roselike")	8°–12°F.	Erratic, sprawling shrub, to 4–8 ft. Branches tend to grow horizontally.	Light gray blue leaves sometimes with greenish cast, 2–4 in. long, nearly round, close to stem. Greenish white bark.	Buds same as *E. macrocarpa* but with shorter point on lid. Flowers, on 1-2-in.-long stems, same shape as those of *E. macrocarpa* but 3–5 in. wide and almost always carmine red. Capsules like those of *E. macrocarpa*. The two are similar but differ in some ways; compare them.	Sprawling plant good for almost continual flower display. For dry, sunny place and little water, same as *E. macrocarpa*. Better for spilling down slope than *E. macrocarpa* (follows terrain better). Put supports under branches to keep mud off. Makes good espalier.
E. robusta SWAMP MAHOGANY	11°–15°F.	Tall, densely foliaged, ultimately round headed. To 80–90 ft.	Dark green, leathery, shiny leaves 4–7 in. long. Rough, dark red brown, stringy bark.	Attractive flowers for large tree: masses of pink-tinted, creamy white flowers any time, chiefly in winter. Cylindrical ⅜-in. seed capsules in clusters.	Big, strong tree performs well in moist or saline soil. Good for windy places at beach or inland. Windbreak. Attractive foliage. Darkest green eucalypt in deserts.
E. rudis FLOODED GUM	12°–18°F.	Upright, spreading, often weeping, 30–60 ft. high. Robust.	Mature leaves gray green to green, lance shaped, 4–6 in. long. Rough trunk.	White flowers in clusters, spring and summer (not showy but good for large tree). Seed capsules ¼ in. wide.	Good large shade tree or street tree. Tolerates valleys, beach, wind, much or little water, sandy soil (including saline soil). Not good in desert unless on deep, gravelly soils with excellent drainage.

(Continued on next page)

NAME	HARD-INESS	FORM AND SIZE	LEAVES AND BARK	FLOWERS AND FRUIT	BEST FEATURES AND HOW TO ENCOURAGE THEM
E. saligna SYDNEY BLUE GUM	18°–20°F.	Tall, slender, shaftlike tree, dense when young, thins out later. To 60–80 ft.	Mature leaves medium green, 4–8 in. long, lance shaped. Red to pinkish bark sheds.	Flowers pinkish to cream in spring and summer, not showy. Smooth seed capsules, ¼ in. wide, in tight clusters 1 in. wide.	Probably fastest growing eucalypt ("fastest gum in the West"); if gallon can plant not rootbound, can grow 10 ft. first year. Best near coast; not recommended inland. Can grow in lawns.
E. sargentii SALT RIVER MALLET	22°F.	Relatively short (25–30 ft.). Stout trunk or multiple trunks.	Narrow green leaves to 4 in. long, ¼ in. wide. Dark trunk.	Cream-colored flowers open from slender, long-horned buds in spring.	Exceptionally tough, exceptionally salt tolerant.
E. sideroxylon (often sold as *E. sideroxylon* 'Rosea') RED IRONBARK, PINK IRONBARK	10° (with risk)–15°F.	Varies: 20–80 ft. high, open or dense, slender or squat, weeping or upright.	Slim blue green leaves turn bronze in winter. Furrowed, nearly black trunk.	Fluffy flowers, light pink to pinkish crimson, in pendulous clusters, mostly from fall to late spring. Seed capsules goblet shaped, ⅜ in.	Use singly, as screen, or as street or highway tree. Wide variation in individuals—try to select according to characteristics you desire. Grows fast. Coast or inland. Gets chlorotic in wet adobe soils.
E. spathulata NARROW-LEAFED GIMLET, SWAMP MALLEE	15°–20°F.	Small, erect, multitrunked tree, 6–20 ft.	Ribbonlike leaves 2–3 in. long. Smooth red bark.	Cream and gold flowers open in summer from long, oval buds. Bell-shaped seed capsules.	Versatile. Tolerates poor soil drainage. Bushy wind screen. Branches move nicely in breezes. Good desert plant.
E. stellulata BLACK SALLY	12°–18°F.	Medium-sized (20–50-ft.), spreading tree with pendulous branches.	Broad elliptical leaves. Smooth gray bark changes to olive green.	White to cream flowers, October–April. Roundish seed capsules, size of small peas, in tight clusters along stem.	Unusual colored bark. Nice spreading form. Good screening tree or shade tree.
E. tetraptera SQUARE-FRUITED MALLEE	22°–26°F.	Shrub, 4–10 ft. (occasionally to 15 ft.). Straggly but interesting.	Thick, rubbery, dark leaves, 4–5 in. long. Green to gray bark.	Big (1½-in.) buds open to big, red flowers. Blooms almost continuously. Seed capsules, square with flanges, 1½ in. wide.	A novelty with striking flowers and fruit, unusual form. Not for basic landscaping. Grows in sand. Wind resistant, salt tolerant. Prune to make bushy.
E. torquata CORAL GUM	17°–22°F.	Slender, upright, narrow headed, to 15–20 ft. Branches often droop from weight of flowers, seed capsules.	Light green to golden green leaves, long and narrow or blunt and round. Rough, flaky bark.	Flower buds are like little (¾-in.) Japanese lanterns. From them open beautiful coral red and yellow flowers, on and off all year. Seed capsules ½ in. long, grooved.	Grown for bloom (good cut flowers) and small size. Good as free-standing tree in narrow area or as a grove. Stake and prune or head back to make it graceful and attractive. Select individuals by plant form. Good in desert.
E. viminalis (*viminalis* means "long, flexible shoot") MANNA GUM	12°–15°F.	Tall, spreading patriarch tree to 150 ft.; drooping willowlike branches.	Light green, narrow, 4–6-in.-long leaves. Trunk whitish; bark sheds.	Little white flowers in long, thin, open clusters all year—usually too high to be seen. Small, roundish seed capsules.	Can make significant silhouette. Grows best in good soil but can take poor soil. Needs room. For ranches, parks, highways, not small gardens. Creates debris.
E. woodwardii LEMON-FLOWERED GUM	17°–22°F.	To 40 ft., with irregular growth.	Gray leaves to 5 in. long, 2 in. wide.	Flowers are lemon yellow puffs, spectacular fall to summer.	Can grow on as little as 7 in. annual rainfall. Use lower plantings to mask bare base, awkward habit.

EUCOMIS. *Liliaceae.* PINEAPPLE FLOWER. Bulbs. Zones 4–24. Unusual looking: thick, 2–3-ft. spikes, closely set with ½-in.-long flowers, are topped with cluster of leaflike bracts like a pineapple top. Bloom period July–August, but persisting purplish seed capsules carry on the show even longer. Garden or container plant, good cut flower. Sun or light shade, rich soil with plenty of humus. Some water in summer. Divide when plants become crowded. Fairly easy to grow from spring-sown seed. Interesting potted plant.

Eucomis comosa

E. bicolor. To 2 ft.; flowers green, each petal edged with purple. Attractive leaves 1 ft. long, 3–4 in. wide, with wavy edges.

E. comosa *(E. punctata)*. Thick spikes 2–3 ft. tall are set with greenish white flowers tinged pink or purple. Stems are spotted purple at the base. Leaves grow to 2 ft. long and are less wavy than those of *E. bicolor.*

EUCRYPHIA. *Eucryphiaceae.* Evergreen or semievergreen small trees or large shrubs. Zones 5, 6, 15–17. Many attractive species and varieties, all quite rare. The most frequently sold kinds in West have shiny evergreen leaves and 2½-in.-wide, pure white flowers with big tufts of yellow stamens in center. Give them neutral or slightly acid soil, ample water, and shelter from strong winds. In Zones 5 and 6, protect young plants from temperatures below 15°F.

Eucryphia nymansensis

E. lucida. Slender evergreen tree to 30 ft. Smooth-edged, glossy leaves 1½–3 in. long. Fragrant white flowers in June, July. Native to Tasmania.

E. nymansensis. Group of hybrids between 2 species from Chile. 'Mt. Usher', best known, is small, columnar evergreen tree with toothed leaves, some simple, some divided into 3–5 leaflets 2–4 in. long. Flowers often double. 'Nymansay' is somewhat faster growing. Both bloom in August, September.

EUGENIA. *Myrtaceae.* Evergreen trees and shrubs, mostly tropical. Many have been reclassified.

E. myrtifolia. See *Syzygium paniculatum.*

E. paniculata. See *Syzygium paniculatum.*

E. smithii. See *Acmena smithii.*

E. uniflora. *Myrtaceae.* SURINAM CHERRY, PITANGA. Evergreen compact shrub or small tree. Zones 21–24. Very slow and open growth to 15–25 ft., usually to 6–8 ft., with equal spread. Leaves oval, to 2 in. long, glossy coppery green deepening to purplish or red in cold weather. White, fragrant flowers like little brushes, ½ in. across. Fruit, size of small tomatoes, changes color from green to yellow to orange to deep red, at which stage it is edible. Grow in well-drained soil; water freely. Best in moist atmosphere and sheltered spot in sun or partial shade. Can be sheared into hedge, but this will reduce flowering and fruiting. Prune to shape. Grafted varieties are sometimes available in southern California.

Eugenia uniflora

EULALIA GRASS. See *Miscanthus sinensis.*

EUONYMUS. *Celastraceae.* Evergreen or deciduous shrubs, evergreen vines. Evergreen kinds are highly valued for their foliage, texture, and form; they are almost always used as landscape structure plants, never for flower display. Some types display colorful fruit—pink, red, or yellow capsules which open to show orange red seeds in fall and attract birds. Most are best in full sun or a little shade. Need only moderate watering. Climate adaptation is quite significant because of varying degrees of hardiness and susceptibility to mildew.

Euonymus japonica

E. alata. WINGED EUONYMUS. Deciduous shrub. Zones 1–9, 14–16. Slow to medium growth to 7–10 ft. high, 10–15 ft. wide. Dense, twiggy, flat topped, with horizontal branching. Twigs have flat, corky wings which disappear on older growth. Dark green leaves turn rich rose red in fall. Inconspicuous flowers followed by sparse crop of bright orange red fruit. Background, screen, or isolated plant; best against dark evergreens.

Variety 'Compacta' grows 4–6 ft. tall and equally wide, has less prominent wings. Use as screen or unclipped hedge.

E. europaea. EUROPEAN SPINDLE TREE. Deciduous large shrub, small tree. Zones 1–17. To 25 ft., usually much less. Easily trained into single-trunked, broad-topped tree. Medium green, scallop-toothed, 3-in. leaves turn rose pink in fall. Flowers yellowish green, inconspicuous. Showy, pink to red fruit splits to show bright orange seeds. 'Aldenhamensis' has more profuse, longer-stalked, larger (over ¾ in.), bright pink and orange fruit.

E. fortunei (formerly *E. radicans acuta*). Evergreen vine or shrub. Zones 1–17. One of best broad-leafed evergreens where temperatures drop below 0°F. Trails or climbs by rootlets. If plant is used as shrub, its branches will trail and sometimes root; allowed to climb, it will be spreading mass to 20 ft. or more. Prostrate forms can be used to control erosion. In desert climates, takes full sun better than ivy (*Hedera*). Leaves dark rich green, 1–2½ in. long with scallop-toothed edges; flowers inconspicuous. Sun or full shade. Mature growth, like that of ivy, is shrubby and bears fruit; cuttings taken from this shrubby wood produce upright plants.

E. radicans (native to Korea, Japan), once thought to be the species, was later classed as variety of *E. fortunei.* Many nurserymen have not changed the names, and still sell many varieties as forms of *E. radicans;* translate *radicans* to *fortunei* wherever you see it, except in *E. fortunei radicans.* Varieties of *E. fortunei* listed below are better known than species itself.

'Canadale Gold'. Small, compact shrub with light green, yellow-edged leaves.

'Carrierei'. Shrubby, spreading form. Will not climb, so plant where it can lean or sprawl against wall or fence. Mature form bears handsome orange fruit.

'Colorata'. PURPLE-LEAF WINTER CREEPER. Same sprawling growth habit as *E. f. radicans.* Leaves turn dark purple in fall and winter. Provides more even ground cover than *E. f. radicans.*

'Emerald Gaiety'. Small, dense-growing, erect shrub with deep green leaves edged with white.

'Emerald 'n Gold'. Similar to above, but with gold-edged leaves.

'Golden Prince.' New growth tipped gold. Older leaves turn green. Extremely hardy; good hedge plant.

'Gracilis' (often sold as *E. radicans argentea variegata, E. fortunei variegata, E. f.* 'Silver Edge'). Trailing, less vigorous, more restrained than the species. Leaves variegated with white or cream; lighter portions turn pinkish in cold weather. Use in hanging baskets, as ground cover in small areas, to spill over wall.

'Greenlane'. Low, spreading shrub with erect branches, deep green foliage, orange fruit in fall.

'Ivory Jade'. Resembles 'Greenlane' but has creamy white leaf margins which show pink tints in cold weather.

'Kewensis' ('Minima'). Delightful trailing or climbing form with very small (¼-in.) leaves. Use it to create delicate traceries against stone or wood, or as dense, fine-textured ground cover.

E. f. radicans. COMMON WINTER CREEPER. Tough, hardy, trailing or vining shrub with dark green, thick-textured, 1-in.-long leaves. Given no support, it sprawls; given masonry wall to cover, it does the job completely.

'Sarcoxie'. As hardy as *E. fortunei,* but with upright habit of *E. japonica.* To 4 ft. high. Use for hedges, as sheared tubbed plant, or as espalier.

'Silver Queen'. Seems identical to 'Carrierei' except for having white leaf margins. (There is also an *E. japonica* 'Silver Queen'.)

'Sparkle 'n Gold'. Compact mound 1–1½ ft. tall. Deep green leaves edged with yellow.

'Vegeta'. BIG-LEAF WINTER CREEPER. Shrub woody enough to support itself in a mound; with support and training, grows as vine that will cover an area 15–20 ft. square. Irregular growth habit; sends out large branches, with side branches developing later. Attractive fruit—orange seeds in little "hatboxes"—in early fall. New spring growth an interesting chartreuse.

E. japonica. EVERGREEN EUONYMUS. Evergreen shrub. Zones 2–20. Upright, 8–10 ft. with 6-ft. spread, usually held lower by pruning or shearing. Flowers inconspicuous. Older shrubs attractive trained as trees with their curving trunks and umbrella-shaped tops. Can be grouped as hedge or screen. Leaves very glossy, leathery, deep green, 1–2½ in. long, oval to roundish.

This and its varieties are "cast-iron" shrubs where heat tolerance is important and soil conditions unfavorable. Notorious for mildew except in Zones 4–6, where plants grow well even in coastal wind and salt spray. To lessen risk of mildew farther south, locate plants in full sun, where air circulation is good. Since plants are also attacked by scale insects, thrips, and spider mites, it's a good idea to include them in your regular rose spray program for mildew and insects.

Variegated forms are most popular; they are among the few shrubs that maintain variegations in full sun in such hot-summer climates as Zones 8–14, 18–20. They are labeled in many ways; there may be some overlapping in names.

'Albomarginata'. Green leaves edged white.

'Aureo-marginata'. Dark green leaves have golden yellow edges.

'Aureo-variegata'. Leaves have brilliant yellow blotches, green edges.

'Gold Center'. Green leaves, yellow center.

'Golden'. Green leaves edged yellow.

'Gold Spot'. Green edges, yellow blotches. Probably same as 'Aureo-variegata'.

'Grandifolia'. Plants sold under this name have shiny dark green leaves larger than those of the species. Compact, well branched, good for shearing as pyramids, globes.

(Continued on next page)

'Microphylla' (*E. j. pulchella*). BOX-LEAF EUONYMUS. Compact, small leafed, 1–2 ft. tall and half as wide. Formal looking; usually trimmed as low hedge.

'Microphylla Variegata'. Like 'Microphylla', but with leaves splashed white.

'President Gauthier'. Deep green leaves with cream-colored margins.

'Silver King'. Green leaves with silvery white edges.

'Silver Queen'. Green leaves, creamy white edges.

E. kiautschovica *(E. patens).* Evergreen shrub. Zones 1–13. Spreading shrub to 9 ft. tall; lower branches sometimes root in moist soil. Leaves partially evergreen or completely evergreen, damaged near 0°F.; light green, thinner textured than other species of evergreen euonymus. Showy, pinkish fruit with red seeds. Takes desert conditions if watered.

'Du Pont'. Compact, dense, fast growing, with dark green leaves. Hedge, screen, sheared formal plant.

'Manhattan'. Upright growth, glossy dark green leaves. Hedge, sheared formal plant, espalier.

EUPHORBIA. *Euphorbiaceae.* SPURGE. Shrubs, subshrubs, perennials, biennials, annuals, succulents. Most have acrid, milky sap (poisonous in some species) which can irritate skin and cause pain in contact with eyes or open cuts. What is called "flower" is really group of colored bracts. True flowers, centered in bracts, are inconspicuous. Many euphorbias are succulents; these often mimic cacti in appearance and are as diverse in form and size. Full sun. Only a few are listed below, but specialists in cacti and succulents can supply scores of species and varieties.

Euphorbia characias wulfenii

E. biglandulosa. See *E. rigida*.

E. characias. Shrubby evergreen perennial. Zones 4–24. Upright stems make dome-shaped bush 4 ft. tall. Fairly drought resistant. Narrow, blue green leaves crowded all along stems. Clustered flowers make dense, round to cylindrical masses of chartreuse or lime green in late winter, early spring. Color holds with only slight fading until seeds ripen; then stalks yellow and should be cut out at base. New shoots have already made growth for next year's flowers. *E. c. wulfenii (E. veneta),* commonest form, has broader clusters of yellower flowers.

Euphorbia pulcherrima

E. cotinifolia. CARIBBEAN COPPER PLANT. Shrub or tree. Zones 21–24. Can become a small tree in frost-free, warm spots, but usually a multistemmed shrub. Long-stalked leaves to 4 in. long, 3 in. wide. *E. c.* 'Atropurpurea', the form commonly grown, has wine red leaves. Loose flower clusters have small white bracts. Likes heat, good drainage, average water; can't take frost.

For a similar plant sometimes sold under this name, see *Synadenium grantii.*

E. epithymoides *(E. polychroma).* Perennial. All Zones. Neatly rounded hemisphere of deep green leaves symmetrically arranged on closely set stems. Each stem ends in a branching, rounded cluster of tiny flowers surrounded by bright yellow bracts. Effect is of a 1–1½-ft. gold mound suffused with green. Spring bloom. Displays good fall color (yellow to orange or red) before going dormant. Use in rock gardens, perennial borders. Needs sun, good drainage, average soil and water.

E. griffithii. Perennial. Zones 4–9, 14–24. Erect stems to 3 ft., clad with narrow, medium-green leaves and topped by clusters of brick red bracts. 'Fireglow' is the variety commonly sold. Spreads by creeping roots, but is not aggressive.

E. heterophylla. MEXICAN FIRE PLANT. Summer annual. To 3 ft. tall. Bright green leaves of varying shapes, larger ones resembling those of poinsettia; flowers unimportant. In summer, upper leaves are blotched bright red and white, giving appearance of second-rate poinsettias. Useful in hot, dry borders in poor soil. Sow seed in place after frost danger is over.

E. lathyris. GOPHER PLANT, MOLE PLANT. Biennial. All Zones. Legend claims that it repels gophers and moles. Stems have poisonous, caustic milky juice; keep away from skin and especially eyes, since painful burns can result. Juice could conceivably bother a gopher or mole enough to make it beat a hasty retreat. Grows as tall single stem to 5 ft. by second summer, when it sets cluster of unspectacular yellow flowers at top of stem. Flowers soon become seeds and plant dies. Leaves long, narrow, pointed, at right angles to stem and to each other. Grow from seed.

E. marginata. SNOW-ON-THE-MOUNTAIN. Summer annual. To 2 ft. Leaves light green, oval; upper ones striped and margined white, uppermost sometimes all white. Flowers unimportant. Used for contrast with bright-colored bedding dahlias, scarlet sage or zinnias, or dark-colored plume celosia. Before using in arrangements, dip stems in boiling water or hold in flame for a few seconds. Sow seed in place in spring, in sun or part shade. Thin to only a few inches apart, as plants are somewhat rangy.

E. milii *(E. splendens).* CROWN OF THORNS. Woody perennial or subshrub. Zones 21–24 in gardens; elsewhere as greenhouse or house plant, or summer potted plant. Shrubby, climbing stems to 3–4 ft. armed with long, sharp thorns. Leaves roundish, thin, light green, 1½–2 in. long, usually found only near branch ends. Clustered pairs of bright red bracts borne nearly all year. Many varieties and hybrids vary in plant form, size, and color of bracts (yellow, orange, pink).

Train on small frame or trellis against sheltered wall or in container. Grow in porous soil, in full sun or light shade. Tolerates drought but does better with regular watering.

E. myrsinites. Perennial. All Zones. Stems flop outward from central crown, then rise toward tip to 8–12 in. Leaves stiff, roundish, blue gray, closely set around stems. Flattish clusters of chartreuse to yellow flowers top stem ends in late winter, early spring. Cut out old stems as they turn yellow. Withstands cold, heat, and drought, but is short lived in warm-winter areas. Use in rock gardens with succulents and gray-foliaged plants.

E. obesa. BASEBALL PLANT. Succulent. House plant or indoor/outdoor pot plant. Solid, fleshy, gray green sphere (or short cylinder) to 8 in., with brownish stripings and brown dots that resemble stitching on a baseball. Flowers unimportant. Good drainage, bright light, warmth, no sudden temperature change. Moderate water; keep dryish in winter.

E. pulcherrima. POINSETTIA. Evergreen or deciduous shrub. Outdoors in Zones 13, 16–24; greenhouse and house plant anywhere. Native to Mexico. Leggy, to 10 ft. tall or taller. Coarse evergreen leaves grow on stiffly upright canes. Showy part of plant consists of petal-like bracts; true flowers in center are yellowish, inconspicuous. Red single form most familiar; less well known are red doubles and forms with white, yellowish, pink, or marbled bracts. Bracts of these paler kinds often last until Easter. Poinsettia has typical milky euphorbia juice, but it is not poisonous; it is either completely harmless or at most mildly irritating to skin or stomach.

Useful garden plant in well-drained soil. Prune to prevent legginess. Grow as informal hedge in frostless areas; where frosty (not severely cold), plant against sunny walls, in sheltered corners, under south-facing eaves.

Where adapted outdoors, needs no special care. Give slightly acid soil. Thin branches in summer to produce larger bracts; prune back at 2-month intervals for bushy growth (but often smaller flowers). To improve red color, feed every 2 weeks with high-nitrogen fertilizer starting when color begins to show.

To care for Christmas gift plants, keep plants in sunny window. Avoid sudden temperature changes. Keep soil moist; don't let water stand in pot saucer. When leaves fall in late winter or early spring, cut stems back to 2 buds, reduce watering to minimum. Store in cool place until late spring. When frosts are past, set pots in sun outdoors. It's difficult to bring plants into bloom again indoors. They will probably grow too tall for indoor use next winter, but may survive winter if well sheltered. Plants bloom only when they experience long nights; don't keep them where artificial light will disturb their necessary 14-hour sleep. Starting in October, put plants in dark closet for the night. Start new plants by making late summer cuttings of stems with 4 or 5 eyes (joints).

E. rigida ***(E. biglandulosa).*** Evergreen perennial or subshrub. Zones 4–24. Stems angle outward, then rise up to 2 ft. Fleshy, gray green leaves to 1½ in. long are narrow and pointed, their bases tightly set against stems. Broad, domed flower clusters in late winter or early spring are chartreuse yellow fading to pinkish. After seeds ripen, stems die back and should be removed; new stems take their place. Showy display plant in garden or container. Drought tolerant.

E. tirucalli. MILKBUSH, PENCILBUSH, PENCIL TREE. Zones 13, 23, 24. House plant or indoor/outdoor plant anywhere. Tree or large shrub to possible 30 ft. tall in open ground, usually much smaller. Single or multiple trunks support tangle of light green, pencil-thick, succulent branches with no sign of a leaf. Flowers unimportant. Striking for pattern of silhouette or shadow. Thrives as house plant in driest atmosphere; needs all the light you can give it, routine soil, water, and feeding. Bleeds milky sap if cut.

E. veneta, E. wulfenii. See *E. characias.*

Euphorbiaceae. The euphorbia family contains annuals, perennials, shrubs, and an enormous number of succulents. Most have milky sap, and many have unshowy flowers made decorative by bracts or bractlike glands. Poinsettia (*Euphorbia pulcherrima*) is the best known example.

EURYA. *Theaceae.* Evergreen shrubs. Zones 4–6, 15–17, 21–24. Native to Japan. Grown for refined foliage. Yellowish green flowers are insignificant and ill-smelling, but are present only on old plants. Slow growing to 6–8 ft., but easily kept to 3–4 ft. by pruning to side buds or branches. Grow under same conditions as for azaleas.

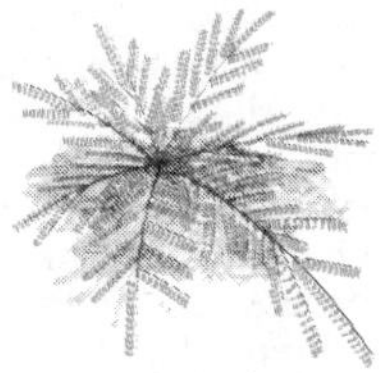

Eurya emarginata

E. emarginata. Branches rise at 45° angle from base of plant. Teardrop-shaped, dark green, leathery, ½-in.-long leaves are closely set on branches. *E. e. microphylla* has even tinier leaves—¼ in. long.

E. japonica. Leaves much larger (to 3 in. long) than those of *E. emarginata.* Cold weather gives them a purplish tint.

EURYOPS. *Compositae.* Shrubby evergreen perennials. Zones 14–17, 19–24. Native to South Africa. Leaves are finely divided; flower heads are daisylike. Long bloom season; cut back after flowering. Although plants need little water once established, they do require excellent drainage. Fast growing in full sun. They thrive in buffeting ocean winds but are damaged by sharp frosts. Keep old blooms picked off; prune in June.

Euryops pectinatus

E. acraeus. Mounded growth to 2 ft. Leaves silvery gray, ¾ in. long. Inch-wide, bright yellow daisies cover plant in May and June. Native to high South African mountains; hardier to frost than others. Has been used as a rock garden plant in western Washington and Oregon.

E. pectinatus. To 6 ft. One of California's most widely planted shrubby perennials. Easy maintenance and extremely long flowering season make it a good filler, background plant, or low screen. Leaves are gray green, deeply divided, 2 in. long. Bright yellow, 1½–2-in.-wide daisies on 6-in. stems bloom most of the year. Cut back to side branches to control size as needed. 'Viridis' is identical, but with deep green leaves.

EUSTOMA grandiflorum ***(Lisianthus russellianus).*** *Gentianaceae.* LISIANTHUS, TULIP GENTIAN, TEXAS BLUEBELL. Biennial or short-lived perennial. All Zones. Native to high plains of the West, but garden forms introduced from Japan. In summer, clumps of gray green foliage send up 1½-ft. stems topped by tulip-shaped, 2–3-in. flowers in purplish blue, pink, or white; plants bloom all summer if old blooms are cut off. Excellent cut flower. Buying started plants is easier, but eustoma can be grown with much care from dustlike seeds. Sprinkle seed on surface of potting soil; don't cover. Soak well, then cover pot with glass or plastic. At 4-leaf stage (about 2 months), transplant 3 or 4 plants into each 6-in. pot. Needs sun, good garden soil, drainage, average water and fertilizing. Use in pots, border, cutting garden. Yodel strain has rose and lilac as additional colors; Lion strain has double flowers.

Eustoma grandiflorum

EVENING PRIMROSE. See *Oenothera.*

EVERGREEN CANDYTUFT. See *Iberis sempervirens.*

EVERGREEN GRAPE. See *Rhoicissus capensis.*

EVERGREEN PEAR. See *Pyrus kawakamii.*

EVERGREEN WISTERIA. See *Millettia reticulata.*

EXACUM affine. *Gentianaceae.* GERMAN VIOLET, PERSIAN VIOLET. Summer annual grown as house or cool greenhouse plant. Small, rounded plant with egg-shaped, inch-long leaves and blue, sweet-scented, star-shaped flowers centered with tufts of bright yellow stamens. (A white variety is also available.) Plant seeds indoors in midwinter for summer bloom, in fall for spring bloom. Five plants in 5-in. pot make attractive showing. Needs rich soil, ample water.

Exacum affine

EXOCHORDA. *Rosaceae.* PEARL BUSH. Deciduous shrubs. Perform best in Zones 3–6, satisfactory in Zones 7–9, 14–18. Loose, spikelike clusters of white, 1½–2-in.-wide flowers open from profusion of pearl-like buds. Flowers bloom about same time as roundish, 1½–2-in.-long leaves expand. Give plants sunny spot, ordinary garden soil, average water. Prune after bloom to control size and form.

E. macrantha. Hybrid. The only variety available, 'The Bride', is a compact shrub to 4 ft. tall and as broad. Flowers in late April. Plant it beneath south- or west-facing windows.

Exochorda racemosa

E. racemosa ***(E. grandiflora).*** COMMON PEARL BUSH. Native to China. Loose, open, slender shrub to 10–15 ft. tall and wide. April bloom. In small gardens, trim it high to make upright, airy, multistemmed small tree. Resistant to oak root fungus.

Fagaceae. The beech family contains evergreen or deciduous trees characterized by fruit which is a nut enclosed in a cup, as in oak (*Quercus*) and tanbark oak (*Lithocarpus*), or burr, as in beech (*Fagus*) and chestnut (*Castanea*).

F

Fagus sylvatica

FAGUS. *Fagaceae.* BEECH. Deciduous trees. Zones 1–9, 14–24. Beeches can reach 90 ft., although they're usually much lower. Trees have a broad cone shape, with lower branches sweeping ground (unless pruned off). Smooth, gray bark contrasts well with dark, glossy foliage and looks handsome in winter. Leaves turn red brown in fall and hang on tree well into winter. Later, pointed winter buds and twig structure make lacy patterns; expanding new leaves have silky sheen. Little 3-sided nuts in spiny husks are edible but inconsequential; they often fail to fill out, especially on solitary trees.

Grow in any good garden soil. Best in full sun; moderate watering needed. Salts in soil or water stunt growth, turn leaves brown. Good lawn trees when young, but many feeder roots and heavy shade make lawn maintenance difficult under old or low-branched trees. Woolly beech aphids cause little trouble except dripping honeydew.

F. grandifolia. AMERICAN BEECH. Much less widely planted than the following plants. Leaves longer (to 5 in.), narrower, turning yellow before their long-lasting red brown phase.

F. sylvatica. EUROPEAN BEECH. Glossy green leaves to 4 in. long. Many garden varieties; here are some of the best:

'Asplenifolia'. Leaves narrow, deeply lobed or cut nearly to midrib. Delicate foliage on large, robust, spreading tree.

'Atropunicea'. COPPER BEECH, PURPLE BEECH. Leaves deep reddish or purple. Good in containers. Often sold as 'Riversii' or 'Purpurea'. Seedlings of copper beech are usually bronzy purple, turning bronzy green in summer.

'Fastigiata'. DAWYCK BEECH. Narrow, upright tree, like Lombardy poplar (*Populus nigra* 'Italica') in form; 8 ft. wide when 35 ft. tall. Broader in great age, but still narrower than species.

'Laciniata'. CUTLEAF BEECH. Narrow green leaves, deeply cut.

'Pendula'. WEEPING BEECH. Irregular, spreading form. Long, weeping branches reach to ground. Green leaves. Without staking to establish vertical trunk, it will grow wider than high.

'Purpurea Pendula'. WEEPING COPPER BEECH. Purple-leafed weeping form. Splendid container plant.

'Rohanii'. Purple leaves are oaklike, with rounded lobes.

'Spaethii' or 'Spaethiana'. Deepest black purple of the copper beech varieties; fades little or not at all in summer.

'Tricolor'. TRICOLOR BEECH. Green leaves marked white and edged pink. Slow to 24–40 ft., usually much less. Foliage burns in hot sun or dry winds. Choice container plant.

'Zlatia'. GOLDEN BEECH. Young leaves yellow, aging to yellow green. Subject to sunburn. Good container subject.

FAIRY DUSTER. See *Calliandra eriophylla.*

FAIRY LANTERN. See *Calochortus albus, C. amabilis.*

FAIRY LILY. See *Zephyranthes.*

FAIRY WAND. See *Dierama.*

Fallugia paradoxa

FALLUGIA paradoxa. *Rosaceae.* APACHE PLUME. Partially evergreen shrub. Zones 2–23. Native to mountains of east San Bernardino County, California; and to Nevada, southern Utah, Arizona, Colorado to western Texas, northern Mexico. Grows 3–8 ft. high, with straw-colored branches and flaky bark. Small, clustered, lobed leaves, deep green on top, rusty beneath. Flowers like single white roses (1½ in. wide) in April and May. Large clusters of feathery fruit follow; greenish at first, turning pink or reddish tinged later, they create a soft-colored, changing haze through which you can see rigid branch pattern. Plant in full sun; very tolerant of heat and drought. Important erosion control plant.

FALSE CYPRESS. See *Chamaecyparis.*

FALSE DRAGONHEAD. See *Physostegia virginiana.*

FALSE HEATHER. See *Cuphea hyssopifolia.*

FALSE INDIGO. See *Baptisia australis.*

FALSE LILY-OF-THE-VALLEY. See *Maianthemum dilatatum.*

FALSE MESQUITE. See *Calliandra eriophylla.*

FALSE SOLOMON'S SEAL. See *Smilacina racemosa.*

FALSE SPIRAEA. See *Astilbe, Sorbaria sorbifolia.*

FAN PALM. See *Washingtonia.*

FAREWELL-TO-SPRING. See *Clarkia amoena.*

FARFUGIUM. See *Ligularia tussilaginea.*

Fatshedera lizei

FATSHEDERA lizei. *Araliaceae.* Evergreen vine, shrub, ground cover. Zones 4–10, 12–24. Hybrid between *Fatsia japonica* and *Hedera helix,* it shows characteristics of both parents. Highly polished, 6–8-in.-wide leaves with 3–5 pointed lobes look like giant ivy leaves, and plant sends out long trailing or climbing stems like ivy; but in form, it is shrubby like fatsia. Variety 'Variegata' has white-bordered leaves.

Leaves are injured at 15°F., tender new growth at 20°–25°F.; seems to suffer more from late frosts than from winter cold. Will take full sun only in mild, cool-summer coastal gardens; inland, give it partial shade and protection from hot, drying winds. Will take heavy shade and can even thrive indoors. Give it plenty of water. Good near swimming pools.

Fatshedera tends to grow in a straight line, but it can be shaped if you work at it. Pinch tip growth to force branching. About 2 or 3 times a year, guide and tie stems before they become brittle. If plant gets away from you, cut it back to ground; it will regrow quickly. If you use it as ground cover, cut back vertical growth every 2–3 weeks during growing season. Grown as vine or espalier, plants are heavy, so give them strong supports. Even when well-grown, vine will be leafless at base. Protect leaves from pests.

Fatsia japonica

FATSIA japonica ***(Aralia sieboldii, A. japonica).*** *Araliaceae.* JAPANESE ARALIA. Evergreen shrub. Zones 4–9, 13–24. Tropical appearance with big, glossy, dark green, deeply lobed, fanlike leaves to 16 in. wide on long stalks. Moderate growth to 5–8 ft. (rarely more); sparsely branched. Many roundish clusters of small whitish flowers in fall and winter, followed by clusters of small, shiny black fruit.

Takes full shade. In cool-summer climates, tolerates all but hottest sun; foliage yellowish in full sun. Suffers in reflected heat from bright walls. Grows in nearly all soils except where too soggy. Adapted to containers. Responds quickly to ample feeding and watering. Where leaves are chronically yellow, add iron to soil. Foliage damaged in coldest Portland or Seattle winters. Wash occasionally with hose to clean leaves, lessen insect attack. Bait for snails, slugs. Established plants sucker freely; keep suckers or remove them with spade. Rejuvenate spindly plants by cutting back hard in early spring. Plants that set fruit often self-sow.

A natural landscaping choice where bold pattern is wanted. Most effective when thinned to show some branch structure. Year-round good looks for shaded entryway or patio. Useful near swimming pools. Good house plant in cool (not over 70°F.), bright room; north or east exposure good. Variety 'Moseri' grows compact and low. 'Variegata' has leaves edged golden yellow to creamy white.

FAVA BEAN. See Bean, Broad.

FAWN LILY. See *Erythronium californicum.*

FEATHER BUSH. See *Lysiloma thornberi.*

FEATHERED HYACINTH. See *Muscari comosum* 'Monstrosum'.

FEIJOA sellowiana. *Myrtaceae.* PINEAPPLE GUAVA. Evergreen shrub or small tree. Zones 7–9, 12–24. From South America. Hardiest of so-called subtropical fruits. Normally a large plant of many stems; reaches 18–25 ft. with equal spread if not trained or killed back by frosts. Can take any amount of pruning or training to almost any shape: espalier, screen, hedge, small tree with some features of olive. Prune in late spring. Oval leaves 2–3 in. long, glossy green above, silvery white beneath. Unusual inch-wide flowers have big tuft of red stamens and 4 fleshy white petals tinged purplish on inside. Petals edible; can be added to fruit salads. Blooms May or June. Attractive to bees and birds. Sun loving and drought tolerant but can take lawn watering.

Feijoa sellowiana

Fruit ripens 4–5½ months after flowering in southern California, 5–7 months in cooler areas; production is low in deserts. Fruit is 1–4 in. long, oval, grayish green, filled with soft, sweet-to-bland, somewhat pineapple-flavored pulp. Plants grow well in valley heat, but fruit seems to have better flavor in cooler coastal areas. Fruits sometimes seen in markets as "feijoas" or "guavas."

The improved varieties 'Beechwood', 'Coolidge', and 'Nazemetz' are self-fertile, although cross-pollination will give a better crop. Single plants of seedlings or other named varieties may need cross-pollination.

FELICIA. *Compositae.* South African shrubs or shrubby perennials. Daisy relatives with (generally) blue flowers.

F. amelloides ***(F. aethiopica, Agathaea coelestis).*** BLUE MARGUERITE. Shrubby perennial in Zones 8, 9, 13–24; grown and offered as summer annual in Zones 4–7. Called a marguerite, but not the true marguerite (*Chrysanthemum frutescens*). About 1½ ft. tall, spreading to 4–5 ft. unless pinched or pruned back, with roughish, rather aromatic green foliage. Leaves oval, an inch long. Produces 1¼-in.-wide, sky blue, yellow-centered daisies almost continuously if dead flowers are picked off. Blooms even in mild winters.

Felicia amelloides

Grow in pots or containers, let spill over wall or raised bed, or plant in any sunny spot in garden. Needs fair amount of water for good appearance. Vigorous and likely to overgrow and look ragged; trim severely for cut flowers and prune back hard in late summer to encourage new blooming wood. One of most satisfactory perennials for warm regions.

Improved varieties include 'George Lewis', 'Midnight', and 'Rhapsody in Blue', all with very dark blue flowers; 'San Luis', 'San Gabriel', and 'Santa Anita', with extra-large (to 2½–3-in.), medium blue flowers; 'Jolly', 1-ft.-tall dwarf with medium blue flowers; and 'Astrid Thomas', compact grower with medium blue flowers that stay open at night. There is also a white-flowered variety.

F. fruticosa ***(Aster fruticosus, Diplopappus fruticosus).*** SHRUB ASTER. Evergreen shrub. Zones 8, 9, 14–24. Bushy, densely branched, 2–4 ft. tall, 3 ft. wide. Leaves narrow, dark green, ½–¾ in. long. Flowers lavender, profuse, to 1 in. across. April–June bloom. Prune after flowering. Good in sunny, dry locations.

FELT PLANT. See *Kalanchoe beharensis.*

FENNEL. See *Foeniculum vulgare.*

FERN. Large group of perennial plants grown for their lovely and interesting foliage. They vary in height from a few inches to 50 ft. or more, and are found in all parts of the world; most are forest plants, but some grow in deserts, in open fields, or near the timberline in high mountains. Most have finely cut leaves (fronds). They do not flower, but reproduce by spores which form directly on the fronds—occasionally on fronds modified specifically for spore production.

Ferns are divided into several families, separated from each other by botanical differences of a largely technical nature. Such differences aside, these plants fall into several groups based on general appearance.

Most spectacular are tree ferns, which display their finely cut fronds atop a treelike stem. These need rich, well-drained soil, moisture, and shade (except in Zones 4–6, 17, 24, where they can stand sun). Most tree ferns are rather tender to frost, and all suffer in hot, drying winds and in extremely low humidity. Frequent watering of tops, trunks, and root area will help pull them through unusually hot or windy weather. For the various kinds of tree fern, see *Blechnum, Cibotium, Cyathea, Dicksonia.*

Native ferns do not grow as high as tree ferns, but their fronds are handsome and they can perform a number of landscape jobs. Naturalize them in woodland or wild gardens, or use them to fill shady beds, as ground cover, as interplantings between shrubs, or along a shady house wall. Many endure long, dry summers in California but look lusher if given ample summer water. Some ferns native to eastern U.S. grow well in Northwest and in northern California; these take extreme cold and are usually deciduous. For native ferns, see *Adiantum, Asplenium, Athyrium, Blechnum, Dryopteris, Onoclea, Osmunda, Pellaea, Phyllitis, Pityrogramma, Polypodium, Polystichum, Pteridium, Woodwardia.*

Many ferns from other parts of the world grow well in the West; although some are house, greenhouse, or (in mildest climates) lathhouse subjects, many are fairly hardy. Use them as you would native ferns, unless some peculiarity of habit makes it necessary to grow them in baskets or on slabs. Some exotic ferns will be found under *Adiantum, Asplenium, Ctenitis, Cyrtomium, Davallia, Humata, Lygodium, Microlepia, Nephrolepis, Pellaea, Pityrogramma, Platycerium, Polypodium, Polystichum, Pteris, Pyrrosia, Rumohra, Woodwardia.*

All ferns look best if groomed: cut off dead or injured fronds near ground or trunk—but don't cut back hardy outdoor ferns until new growth begins, since old fronds protect growing tips. Feed frequently during growing season, preferably with light applications of organic-base fertilizer such as blood meal or fish emulsion. Mulch with peat moss occasionally, especially if shallow fibrous roots are exposed by rain or irrigation.

FERNLEAF WANDERING JEW. See *Tripogandra multiflora.*

FERNLEAF YARROW. See *Achillea filipendulina.*

F

FERN-OF-THE-DESERT. See *Lysiloma thornberi*.

FERN PINE. See *Podocarpus gracilior*.

FEROCACTUS. *Cactaceae.* BARREL CACTUS. Zones 8–24. Medium to large cactus. Ribbed and spiny; globular when young, cylindrical with increasing age. Full sun; tolerates drought.

Ferocactus acanthodes

F. acanthodes. COMPASS BARREL CACTUS. Native to southern California, Nevada, Baja California. Grows slowly to 8–9 ft. Yellow to orange, bell-shaped flowers, 3 in. across, bloom May–July. Grows faster on shady side of plant than on sunny side, producing curve toward the south.

F. wislizenii. FISHHOOK BARREL CACTUS. Native to Arizona, Texas, Mexico. Similar to above, with yellow or yellow-edged red flowers July–September. Hardy to near 0°F.

FESTUCA. *Gramineae.* FESCUE. Grasses, several used for lawns, erosion control, or pasture; others have limited use as ornamental plants. All Zones. Lawn fescues are classified as fine or coarse.

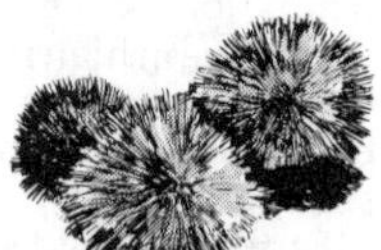

Festuca ovina glauca

F. elatior. TALL FESCUE. Coarse. Tall-growing (to 2½ ft.), clumping pasture grass also used for erosion control and rough, drought-resistant lawns. Tough blades, tolerance of compacted soils make it good play or sports lawn. Forms no runners, so plants must be close together to make dense turf; sow 8–10 pounds of seed per 1,000 sq. ft. in fall. After grass is 2–3 in. tall, soak deeply if rains fail; soak again to 1 ft. when blades begin to fold or curl. Feed lightly—monthly in summer, 3 times during fall, winter. Mow when 2 in. tall. Unmowed, makes excellent, deep-rooted erosion control on slopes, banks. 'Alta' is medium coarse and extremely tough against wear. 'Fawn' has narrowest leaf, finest texture. 'Goars' is fairly tolerant of saline and alkaline soils. 'Kentucky 31' is best adapted to hot-summer climates. Finer-textured new strains are being developed for use as lawn grasses, either alone or mixed with bluegrass. Such mixtures are available as sod in many parts of California. Among them are 'Houndog', 'Jaguar', and 'Olympic'.

F. ovina. SHEEP FESCUE. Fine. Low-growing (to 1 ft.), clumping grass with narrow, needle-fine, soft but tough leaves. *F. o. duriuscula*, HARD FESCUE, is sometimes used as lawn grass. *F. o. glauca*, BLUE FESCUE, forms blue gray tufts 4–10 in. tall. Useful ground cover for sunny or partially shaded areas, on slopes or level ground. Needs little water in Zones 1–9, 14–24; as much as lawn grass in Zones 10–13. No foot traffic. Clip back to near ground after flowering or any time plants look shabby. Does not make solid cover and needs frequent weeding. Dig overgrown clumps, pull apart, and replant as small divisions. Set 6–15 in. apart, depending on desired effect.

F. rubra. RED FESCUE. Fine blades. Principal use is as lawn grass in blends with bluegrass or other lawn grasses. Blades narrow, texture fine, color dark green. Not fussy about soil; takes some drought, some shade. Used alone, tends to grow clumpy. Mow to 1½–2 in. tall. Common red fescue is sometimes called creeping red fescue; it is one of most shade tolerant of good lawn grasses. Other creeping selections are sold as Creeping Red, 'Illahee', and 'Rainier'. *F. rubra commutata*, CHEWINGS FESCUE, tends toward clumpiness. Unmowed, red fescues make attractive meadow on slopes too steep to mow. They are also used to overseed Bermuda lawns in winter.

FEVERFEW. See *Chrysanthemum parthenium*.

FICUS. *Moraceae.* Ornamental figs. Evergreen or deciduous trees, vines, shrubs, house plants. The average gardener would never expect to find the commercial edible fig, small-leafed climbing fig, banyan tree, and potted rubber plant under one common heading—but they are classed together because they all bear small or large figs.

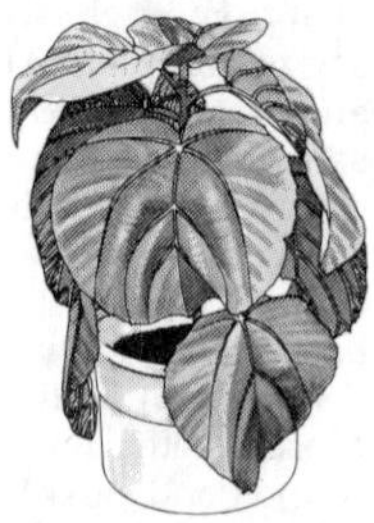

Ficus auriculata

F. auriculata *(F. roxburghii)*. Briefly deciduous. Zones 20–24. Native to India. Usually takes the form of large, spreading shrub or small tree to 25 ft. high and as wide. Full sun. Leaves are unusually large—broadly oval to round, about 15 in. across. New growth is interesting mahogany red, turning to rich green. Leaves have sandpapery texture. Large figs are borne in clusters on trunk and framework branches.

Can be shaped as small tree or espaliered. Beautiful in large container; good near swimming pools.

Grow in wind-protected locations. Water young plants until established.

Ficus benjamina

F. benjamina. WEEPING CHINESE BANYAN. Evergreen tree. Outdoors in Zones 13, 23, 24; indoor plant anywhere. Native to India. To 30 ft. high and broadly spreading. Leathery, poplarlike, 5-in.-long leaves densely clothe drooping branches in shining green. Red figs. In frost-free, wind-protected locations, grow it in sun or shade. Probably best fig for heat tolerance in Zone 13 (damaged there by any frost but recovers quickly as weather warms). Often used as small tree in entryway or patio. Good as espalier or screen. In mildest climates, can be used as clipped hedge.

Ficus deltoidea

Undoubtedly most popular indoor tree, and one of most popular house plants. Thrives on rich, steadily moist (not wet) soil, frequent light feeding, and abundant light. Dislikes overwatering, dark growing conditions, drafts, heat registers, and sudden changes in environment. If you get one growing happily, leave it where it is; moving it may cause it to drop leaves. (It will probably grow a new set.) Recently purchased plants often exhibit moving shock; don't rush to cure them with heavy watering and don't feed until plants recover. If green leaves drop, drought is the likely culprit; if leaves yellow and fall, light is probably inadequate.

New plants are easy to start from semihardwood cuttings taken between May and July.

Variety 'Exotica' has wavy-edged leaves with long, twisted tips; it is often sold simply as *F. benjamina*.

F. carica. EDIBLE FIG. See Fig, Edible.

F. deltoidea *(F. diversifolia)*. MISTLETOE FIG. Evergreen shrub. Outdoors in Zones 19–24; house plant anywhere. Native to Malaya. Grows very slowly to 8–10 ft. high. Interesting open, twisted branch pattern. Thick, dark green, roundish, 2-in. leaves are sparsely stippled with tan specks on upper surface and a few black dots below. Attractive, small, greenish to yellow fruit borne continuously. Most often grown in containers as patio and house plant. Grow in part shade or strong diffused light.

Ficus elastica

F. elastica. RUBBER PLANT. Evergreen shrub or tree. Outdoors in Zones 16, 17, 19–24; house plant anywhere. Native to India and Malaya. This is the familiar rubber plant found in almost every florist shop. One of most foolproof indoor pot subjects. Takes less light than most big indoor plants. Leaves are thick, glossy, leathery, dark green, 8–12 in. long by 4–6 in. wide. New leaves unfold from rosy pink sheaths which soon wither and drop. Let soil get fairly dry between waterings. Can become 40-ft.-high tree in Zones 23, 24. As small tree or shrub, useful in shaded "tunnel" garden entrances. Comes back in 3 months when cut to ground by frost.

If potted rubber plant becomes too tall and leggy, you can cut off top and select side branch to form new main shoot or get a new plant by air layering top section (see page 85). When roots form, cut branch section with attached roots and plant it in pot.

F. e. 'Decora' ***(F. e.*** **'Belgica').** Considered superior to the species because of its broader, glossier leaves, bronzy when young.

F. e. 'Rubra'. New leaves are reddish and retain red edge as rest of leaf turns green. Grown as shrub or small tree in Zones 22–24.

F. e. 'Variegata'. Leaves are long, narrow, variegated yellow and green. Variegation is interesting when viewed close up in container, but as outdoor tree, plant has an unhealthy look.

F. lyrata *(F. pandurata).* FIDDLELEAF FIG. Evergreen tree or large shrub. Outdoors in Zones 22–24. Native to tropical Africa. Dramatic structural form with huge, glossy-surfaced, dark green, fiddle-shaped leaves to 15 in. long and 10 in. wide, prominently veined. Highly effective as indoor pot plant. In protected outdoor position, can grow to 20 ft. with trunks 6 in. thick. Good near swimming pools.

Ficus lyrata

To increase branching, pinch back when young.

F. macrophylla. MORETON BAY FIG. Huge evergreen tree. Zones 17, 19–24. Native to north New South Wales and Queensland, Australia. Grows to enormous dimensions. A tree in Santa Barbara planted in 1877 has spread of 150 ft., with massive buttressed trunk and surface roots. Blunt, oval, leathery leaves, 10 in. long and 4 in. wide, glossy green above, brownish beneath. Rose-colored leaf sheaths appear like candles at ends of branches. Inch-long figs are purple spotted with white.

Although tender when young, acquires hardiness with size. Shows damage at 24°–26°F. Ample water. Plant only if you can give it plenty of room.

F. microcarpa *(F. retusa).* INDIAN LAUREL FIG. Evergreen tree. Zones 9, 15–24. Native to India, Malaya. Both this and its variety *nitida* are widely used along streets throughout southern California and in San Francisco Bay area. They differ markedly in growth habit and appearance. Both perform best with some summer water.

F. microcarpa grows at a moderate rate to 25–30 ft. It has beautiful weeping form, with long, drooping branches thickly clothed with blunt-tipped, 2–4-in.-long leaves. Light rose to chartreuse new leaves, produced almost continuously, give tree pleasing 2-tone effect. Slim, light gray trunk supporting massive crown may be concealed by lower trailing branches if these are not trimmed off.

F. m. nitida. Has dense foliage on upright-growing branches, and is admirably suited to formal shearing. Leaves are clear lustrous green, similar in size to those of *F. microcarpa* but more pointed at base and apex. *F. m. nitida* may be pruned at almost any time of year to size or shape desired.

Where this tree is pest free, it is difficult to find a more satisfactory tree or tub plant for warm climates. Unfortunately, a thrips which attacks both the species and its variety has become established in California. This insect is difficult to control because it quickly curls new leaves, stippling them and causing them to fall. Best control: systemic insecticides. The variety 'Green Gem' has thicker, darker green leaves and is apparently unaffected by thrips.

F. microphylla. Plants sold under this name in California are *F. rubiginosa*.

F. nekbudu *(F. utilis).* ZULU FIG. Evergreen tree. Zones 19–24. To 20 ft. tall (eventually much taller) and as wide. Leaves to 1 ft. long, 6 in. wide, thick, leathery, smooth. Foliage pattern is open, revealing branching structure and smooth, pale gray bark.

F. pumila *(F. repens).* CREEPING FIG. Evergreen vine. Zones 8–24. Native to China, Japan, Australia. A most unfiglike habit; it is one of few plants which attaches itself securely to wood, masonry, or even metal in barnacle fashion.

In young stages, gives very little indication of its potential vigor. Delicate tracery of tiny, heart-shaped leaves frequently seen patterned against a chimney or stucco wall is almost certain to be *F. pumila*, but in this growth phase gives no hint of its powerful character at maturity. There is almost no limit to size of vine and area it will cover. Neat little leaves of juvenile growth ultimately develop into large (2–4 in. long), leathery, oblong leaves borne on stubby branches which bear large oblong fruit. In time, stems will envelop a 3- or 4-story building so completely that it becomes necessary to keep them trimmed away from windows.

It is safe to use this fig on houses if it is cut to ground every few years; you may also control by removing fruiting stems from time to time as they form. Roots are invasive, probably more so than those of most other figs.

Because it is grown on walls, and thus protected, it is found in colder climates than any other evergreen fig. Will not climb on hot south or west wall—or, if it does grow there, will be unattractive yellow. Sometimes slow to begin climbing. Cut back to ground soon after planting to make new growth that will take off fast.

F. p. 'Minima'. Slender, small-leafed variety. Another tiny variety sold as *F. p.* 'Quercifolia' has lobed leaves something like tiny oak leaves. 'Variegata' has creamy white markings.

F. religiosa. PEEPUL, BO-TREE. Briefly deciduous tree. Zones 13, 19, 21, 23, 24. Native to India. Large, upright; less spread than *F. macrophylla*. Foliage is quite open and delicate, revealing structure of tree at all times. Bark is warm, rich brown. Roundish, pale green leaves are rather crisp and thin textured, 4–7 in. long with long tail-like point. They move easily even in slightest breeze, giving foliage a fluttering effect. Foliage drops completely in April or May—frightening experience for gardener who has bought an "evergreen" fig.

F. retusa. See *F. microcarpa*.

F. roxburghii. See *F. auriculata*.

F. rubiginosa. RUSTYLEAF FIG. Evergreen tree. Zones 18–24. Native to Australia. Grows to 20–50 ft., with broad crown and single or multiple trunks. Dense foliage of 5-in. oval leaves, deep green above and generally rust colored and woolly beneath.

Does well in sand on beach in Santa Monica and thrives in heat of interior valleys. A few trees in coastal gardens have developed hanging aerial roots that characterize many of the evergreen figs in tropical environments. Small-leafed form is widely sold as *F. microphylla*.

F. r. australis. Varies from the species (if it varies at all) in having slightly less rusty leaves. Varieties 'El Toro' and 'Irvine' have exceptionally dark green leaves; 'Florida', widely distributed, has lighter green leaves. 'Variegata', with leaves mottled green and cream, is sometimes sold as house plant.

FIG, EDIBLE. *Moraceae.* For ornamental relatives, see *Ficus*. Deciduous tree. Zones 4–9, 12–24. In Zones 1–3, 10, 11 as tubbed plant, protected in winter. Grows fairly fast to 15–30 ft., generally low branched and spreading; where hard freezes are common, fig wood freezes back severely and plant behaves as a big shrub. Can be held to 10 ft. in big container, or trained as espalier along fence or wall.

Edible Fig

Trunks heavy, smooth, gray barked, gnarled in really old trees, picturesque in silhouette. Leaves rough, bright green, 3–5 lobed, 4–9 in. long and nearly as wide. Winter framework, tropical-looking foliage, strong trunk and branch pattern make fig a top-notch ornamental tree, especially near patio where it can be illuminated from beneath. Fruit drop is problem immediately above deck or paving. Casts dense shade.

Not particular about soil. Needs sun, good drainage; drought resistant when established. In Zones 4–7, trees planted near south walls or trained against them benefit from reflected heat. Cut back tops hard at planting. As tree grows, prune lightly each winter, cutting out dead wood, crossing branches, low-hanging branches that interfere with traffic. Pinch back runaway shoots any season. Avoid deep cultivation (may damage surface roots) and high-nitrogen fertilizers (stimulate growth at expense of fruit). 'Kadota', 'Mission' are resistant to oak root fungus.

Home garden figs do not need pollinating, and most varieties bear 2 crops a year. The first comes in June (July in Northwest) on last year's wood; the second and more important comes in August–November from current summer's wood. Ripe figs will detach easily when lifted and bent back toward the branch. Keep fruit picked as it ripens; protect from birds if you can. In late fall, pick off any remaining ripe figs and clean up fallen fruit. California pocket gophers love fig roots; to foil their attacks, plant young figs in ample-sized wire baskets.

Varieties differ in climate adaptability; some thrive under cool coastal conditions, while others need prolonged high temperatures to bear good fruit. Familiar dried figs from the market are usually 'Calimyrna' or imported Smyrna figs. These require special pollinators (caprifigs) and special pollinating insect; not recommended for home gardens.

'Blue Celeste' ('Celeste', 'Celestial'). Hardy tree. Bronzy fruit tinged violet, pulp rosy amber; fruit resistant to spoilage, dries well on tree in California.

'Brown Turkey' ('San Piero'; sold in Northwest as 'Black Spanish'). Small tree; brownish purple fruit. Adaptable to most fig climates, Arizona to Northwest. Good garden tree. Cut back hard to scaffold limbs to lessen fruit formation and subsequent fruit-drop mess.

'Conadria'. Choice thin-skinned white fig blushed violet; white to red flesh, fine flavor. Best in hot areas.

'Desert King'. Green fig with red flesh. Good in Northwest. One late-summer crop.

'Genoa' ('White Genoa'). Greenish yellow skin, amber to yellow flesh. Good quality, good home garden variety in California coastal and coastal valley gardens.

'Italian Everbearing'. Resembles 'Brown Turkey', but fruit averages somewhat larger, with reddish brown skin.

'Kadota' ('White Kadota'). Tough-skinned fruit is greenish yellow in California's hot interior valleys (where tree bears best), green near coast. Commercial canning variety. Strong grower, needs little pruning. If given severe pruning, it will bear later, with fewer, larger fruits.

'Lattarula'. Also known as Italian honey fig. Green skin, amber flesh. Grown in Northwest, where it can ripen summer and fall crops in good seasons.

'Mission' ('Black Mission'). Purple black fig for desert and all California gardens. Large tree.

'Neveralla'. Purple skinned, with amber flesh. Can ripen summer and fall crops in Northwest.

'Osborn Prolific'. Purplish brown fruit; good bearer in California coastal areas.

'Peter's Honey' ('Rutara'). Greenish yellow skin, amber flesh. Needs hot exposure in Northwest and coastal areas.

'Texas Everbearing'. Medium to large, mahogany to purple fruit with strawberry-colored pulp. Bears young and gives good crop in short-season areas of Southwest.

FILBERT. *Betulaceae.* For ornamental relatives, see *Corylus*. Deciduous nut trees. Zones 2–7. More treelike in form (15–25 ft.) than ornamental forms of *Corylus* (this is *C. maxima*). Makes handsome, well-structured, small tree for garden or terrace. From spring to fall, roundish, ruffle-edged leaves cast pleasant spot of shade. Showy male catkins hang long and full on bare branches in winter. Crop of roundish to oblong nuts (ones sold in stores) comes as bonus in fall. A 10-year-old tree may yield up to 10 lbs. of nuts a year. Nuts form inside frilled husks.

Filbert

Set out plants in late winter or early spring, in well-drained, deep soil, full sun. Takes average water. Tree tends to sucker; clear these out 3 or 4 times a year if you wish to maintain clear trunk. For a boundary hedgerow, plant mixed varieties 4 ft. apart and permit suckers to grow. Spray for aphids, bud mites, and filbert blight. Since cross-pollination is necessary, plant at least 2 varieties.

'Barcelona'. Slow or moderate growth to 18 ft. with greater spread. Roundish, large nuts.

'Butler'. Good pollinator for 'Barcelona' or 'Ennis'. Oval nuts of good flavor.

'Du Chilly'. Slow to 15 ft. with equal spread. Shoots grow at right angles to limbs. Large, long nut of high quality, slow to drop; nuts adhere to husks.

'Ennis'. Slow growth. Very productive. Large, round nuts. Pollinates and is pollinated by 'Butler'.

'Purpurea'. Ornamental variety with dark purple leaves. Thrives in Zone 17, but does not bear nuts there.

'Royal'. Slow to 18 by 18 ft. Large nuts of excellent flavor.

'White Aveline' and 'Daviana'. Varieties used as pollinators. Light-crop varieties with medium-sized, high-quality nuts.

FILIPENDULA. *Rosaceae.* Perennials. Zones 1–9, 14–24. Like closely related *Astilbe*, characterized by plumed clusters of tiny flowers above coarsely divided leaves that look like fern fronds. Dormant in winter. Average soil, ample moisture, sun or light shade in cool-summer climates, light shade elsewhere. Use in borders or naturalistic plantings.

Filipendula rubra 'Venusta'

F. hexapetala. See *F. vulgaris.*

F. purpurea. Pink plumes 3–4 ft. tall rise above maplelike 5–7-in. leaves.

F. rubra. QUEEN OF THE PRAIRIE. When given ample water and rich soil, can reach 8 ft. Plumes are pink; purplish pink in the variety 'Venusta'.

F. vulgaris *(F. hexapetala).* White plumes on 3-ft. stems rise above 10-in., fernlike leaves with 1-in. leaflets. Double-flowered 'Flore Pleno' has heavier-looking plumes.

FINOCCHIO. See *Foeniculum vulgare azoricum.*

FIR. See *Abies.*

FIRECRACKER FLOWER. See *Dichelostemma ida-maia.*

FIRE FERN. See *Oxalis hedysaroides* 'Rubra'.

FIRETHORN. See *Pyracantha.*

FIREWHEEL TREE. See *Stenocarpus sinuatus.*

FIRMIANA simplex *(F. platanifolia).* *Sterculiaceae.* CHINESE PARASOL TREE. Deciduous tree. Zones 5, 6, 8, 9, 12–24. Native to China, Japan. Small (15–30 ft.), usually slow growing, with unique light gray green bark. Trunk often has no side branches to 4–5 ft., at which point it divides into 3 or more slender, upright, slightly spreading stems which carry lobed, tropical-looking, 1-ft. leaves. Each stem looks as if it could be cut off and carried away as a parasol. Large, loose, upright clusters of greenish white flowers at ends of branches in July. Interesting fruit looks like 2 opened green pea pods with seeds on margins. Goes leafless for long period in winter (unusual for tropical-looking tree).

Firmiana simplex

Has been grown in mild-climate areas in all types of soil, but does best in patios and courtyards or other full-sun or morning-sun locations protected from wind. Useful near swimming pools. Needs irrigation when young; drought resistant when established.

FISHTAIL PALM. See *Caryota.*

FITTONIA verschaffeltii. *Acanthaceae.* FITTONIA. Evergreen house plant or greenhouse plant. Native to South America. Low and creeping, with handsome foliage. Leaves dark green, oval, 4 in. long, conspicuously veined with red. Variety 'Argyroneura' has leaves veined with white.

Does best when grown in north light. High humidity, average watering, and warm, even temperatures are among its requirements. Grow from cuttings. Use in hanging pots or baskets, terrariums, or as ground cover with taller tropical plants in large indoor planting beds.

Fittonia verschaffeltii

FIVE-FINGER FERN. See *Adiantum pedatum.*

Flacourtiaceae. This family of evergreen trees and shrubs (most of them tropical or subtropical) includes *Azara, Idesia, Olmediella,* and *Xylosma.*

FLAG. See *Iris.*

FLAME PEA. See *Chorizema.*

FLAME TREE. See *Brachychiton acerifolius.*

FLAME VINE. See *Pyrostegia venusta.*

FLANNEL BUSH. See *Fremontodendron.*

FLAX. See *Linum.*

FLAX, NEW ZEALAND. See *Phormium.*

FLAXLEAF PAPERBARK. See *Melaleuca linariifolia.*

FLEABANE. See *Erigeron.*

FLOSS FLOWER. See *Ageratum houstonianum.*

FLOSS SILK TREE. See *Chorisia.*

FLOWERING ALMOND. See *Prunus triloba.*

FLOWERING CHERRY. See *Prunus.*

FLOWERING CRABAPPLE. See *Malus.*

FLOWERING MAPLE. See *Abutilon.*

FLOWERING NECTARINE, PEACH, PLUM. See *Prunus.*

FLOWERING QUINCE. See *Chaenomeles.*

FLOWERY SENNA. See *Cassia corymbosa.*

FOENICULUM vulgare. *Umbelliferae.* COMMON FENNEL. Perennial herb, usually grown as summer annual. To 3–5 ft. Similar to dill, but coarser. Yellow green, finely cut leaves; flat clusters of yellow flowers. Grow in light, well-drained soil, full sun. Very drought tolerant. Start from seed where plants are to be grown; thin seedlings to 1 ft. apart. Use seeds to season bread, pudding; use leaves as garnish for salads, fish. Young leaves and seeds have slight licorice taste. Plants often grow as roadside or garden weeds; they are attractive until tops turn brown, and even then seeds form favorite food for wild birds.

Foeniculum vulgare

F. v. azoricum. FINOCCHIO. Lower growing than the species, with larger, thicker leaf bases that are edible cooked or raw.

FORESTIERA neomexicana. *Oleaceae.* NEW MEXICAN PRIVET, DESERT OLIVE. All Zones (little used outside arid regions). Native to New Mexico, Colorado, Arizona west to California. Deciduous shrub. To 6–8 ft. tall, nearly as broad. Smooth, medium green leaves 1 to nearly 2 in. long. Flowers negligible. Egg-shaped, blue black fruit, ¼ in. long, not always produced (some plants do not have both male and female flowers). Fairly fast growth makes it a good screening plant in difficult climates. Full sun. Established plants withstand drought, but grow faster with some water.

Forestiera neomexicana

FORGET-ME-NOT. See *Myosotis.*

FORSYTHIA. *Oleaceae.* Deciduous shrubs. Zones 2–11, 14–16, 18, 19. Somewhat fountain-shaped shrubs; bare branches covered with yellow flowers February–April. During remainder of growing season, medium green foliage blends well with other shrubs in border background. Lush green, rounded leaves with pointed tips. Branches can be forced for indoor bloom in winter.

Use as screen, espalier, or bank cover. Or plant in shrub border. Tolerates most soils; likes sun, moderate water, and fertilizer. Prune established plants after bloom by cutting to ground ⅓ of branches that have bloomed. Remove oldest branches and weak or dead wood.

Forsythia intermedia

F. intermedia. Hybrids between *F. suspensa* and *F. viridissima.* Most grow 7–10 ft. tall and have arching branches. 'Arnold Dwarf', 20–36 in. tall and to 6 ft. wide, has few flowers which are not especially attractive, but it's a useful, fast-growing ground cover in hard climates. 'Beatrix Farrand', an upright grower to 10 ft. tall, 7 ft. broad, has branches thickly set with 2–2½-in.-wide, deep yellow flowers marked orange.

F. i. 'Karl Sax' resembles *F. i.* 'Beatrix Farrand' but is lower growing, neater, more graceful. *F. i.* 'Lynwood' ('Lynwood Gold') grows stiffly upright to 7 ft., with 4–6-ft. spread. Profuse tawny yellow blooms survive spring storms. *F. i.* 'Spectabilis' is dense, upright, vigorous shrub to 9 ft. with deep yellow flowers. *F. i.* 'Spring Glory' has heavy crop of pale yellow flowers.

F. suspensa. WEEPING FORSYTHIA. Dense, upright growth habit to 8–10 ft. with 6–8-ft. spread. Drooping, vinelike branches root where they touch damp soil. Golden yellow flowers. Useful large-scale bank cover. Can be trained as vine; if you support main branches, branchlets will cascade. *F. s.* 'Fortunei' is somewhat more upright, more available in nurseries.

F. viridissima. GREENSTEM FORSYTHIA. Stiff-looking shrub to 10 ft. with deep green foliage, olive green stems, greenish yellow flowers. 'Bronxensis' is slow-growing dwarf form to 16 in. tall, for smaller shrub borders or ground cover.

FORTNIGHT LILY. See *Dietes.*

FORTUNELLA margarita. See *Citrus,* Nagami Kumquat.

FOTHERGILLA. *Hamamelidaceae.* Deciduous shrubs. Zones 3–9, 14–17. Grown principally for fall color, but small white flowers in brushlike, 1–2-in. clusters are pretty. Plant in peaty soil, partial shade—especially where summers are long and hot. Average water.

Fothergilla monticola

F. major. Erect shrub to 9 ft. with roundish, 4-in.-long leaves turning orange to purplish red in autumn. Flowers appear with the leaves. Fall color early and good in San Francisco Bay area.

F. monticola. Spreading plant to 3–4 ft. tall. Broadly oval leaves; flower clusters somewhat larger than those of *F. major.* Fall color scarlet to crimson.

FOUNTAIN GRASS. See *Pennisetum setaceum.*

FOUQUIERIA splendens. *Fouquieriaceae.* OCOTILLO. Deciduous shrub with distinctive character. Zones 10–13, 18–20. Native to Mojave and Colorado deserts east to Texas, Mexico. Many stiff, whiplike gray stems 8–25 ft. high, heavily furrowed and covered with stout thorns. Fleshy, roundish, ½–1-in.-long leaves appear after rains, soon drop. Tubular, ¾–1-in.-long red flowers in very attractive foot-long clusters after rains in spring or summer. Can be used as screening, impenetrable hedge, or for silhouette against bare walls. Needs excellent drainage and full sun. Don't overwater. Cuttings stuck in ground will grow.

Fouquieria splendens

FOUR O'CLOCK. See *Mirabilis jalapa.*

FOXGLOVE. See *Digitalis.*

FRAGARIA chiloensis. *Rosaceae.* WILD STRAWBERRY, SAND STRAWBERRY. Evergreen ground cover. Grow in part shade in Zones 4–24; also in sun in Zones 4–6, 15–17, 20–24. Native of Pacific beaches and bluffs, North and South America. Forms low, compact, lush mats 6–12 in. high. Dark green, glossy leaves have 3-toothed leaflets. Leaves take on red tints in winter. Large (1-in.-wide) white flowers in spring; bright red, ¾-in., seedy fall fruit that attracts birds (fruit seldom sets in gardens). Plant rooted stolons in late spring or early summer. Flat-grown plants can be planted any time. Set plants 1–1½ ft. apart. Needs annual mowing or cutting back (early spring) to force new growth, prevent stem buildup. Feed annually in late spring. Needs regular watering in Zones 7–16, 18–21. In late summer, if leaves show yellowing, apply iron sulfate.

For fruiting or garden strawberry, see Strawberry.

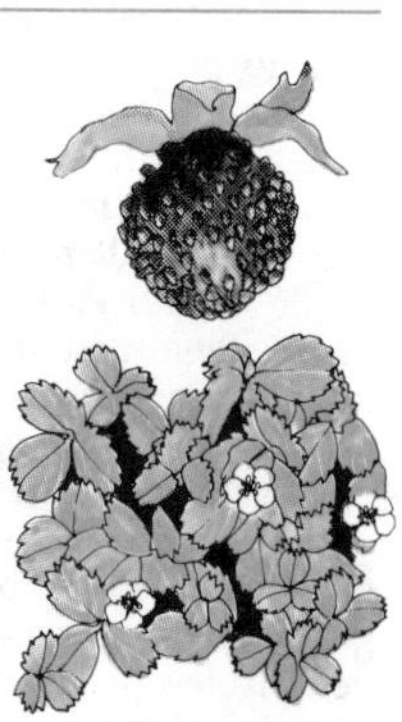

Fragaria chiloensis

FRANCESCHI PALM. See *Brahea elegans.*

FRANCOA ramosa. *Saxifragaceae.* MAIDEN'S WREATH. Perennial. Grown as evergreen in Zones 4, 5, 8, 9, 13–24. Native to Chile. Spreading plant with basal clumps (up to 1–2 ft. across) of large, wavy-margined leaves. In midsummer, graceful, almost leafless flowering stems stand 2–3 ft. high; upper portions carry spikes of many pure white (occasionally pinkish) tiny flowers. Ideal exposure is sun half the day or dappled sun all day. Needs only normal garden watering, very little fertilizer. Distribution seems mainly by neighborliness; more plants pass over back fences than through nursery channels. In just a few years, plants increase in size enough that you can divide and replant fresh new segments from outside edges of clumps.

Francoa ramosa

Good companion for foxgloves, primroses, azaleas, camellias. Good cut flowers.

FRANGIPANI. See *Plumeria rubra.*

FRANKLINIA alatamaha *(Gordonia alatamaha).* *Theaceae.* Deciduous tree. Zones 2–6, 14–17. Once native to Georgia, but apparently extinct in the wilds before 1800. Slender form, to 20–30 ft. high. Slow to moderate growth. Reddish brown bark with faint striping. Spoon-shaped leaves, 4–6 in. long, turn from bright green to scarlet in fall. White, 3-in.-wide flowers with center clusters of yellow stamens open from round white buds August–September, sometimes coinciding with fall foliage color. During wet autumns in Northwest, it blooms shyly. Give rhododendron conditions: well-drained, rich, light, acid soil, ample water, and partial shade in hot-summer areas. Easy to grow from seed, blooming in 6–7 years. Use for contrast in rhododendron-azalea plantings. Unusual lawn or patio tree with right soil and exposure.

Franklinia alatamaha

FRAXINELLA. See *Dictamnus albus.*

FRAXINUS. *Oleaceae.* ASH. Deciduous trees, one almost evergreen. Trees grow fairly fast, and most tolerate hot summers, cold winters, and many kinds of soil (including alkaline soil). Chiefly used as street trees, shade trees, lawn trees, patio shelter trees. Fairly pest free.

In most cases, leaves are divided into leaflets. Male and female flowers (generally inconspicuous, in clusters) grow on separate trees in some species, on same tree in others. In latter case, flowers are often followed by clusters of single-seeded, winged fruit, often in such abundance that they can be a litter problem. When flowers are on separate trees, you'll get fruit on female tree only if it grows near male tree.

Fraxinus velutina 'Modesto'

F. americana. WHITE ASH. Deciduous tree. Zones 1–11, 14–17. Native to eastern U.S. Grows to 80 ft. or more, with straight trunk and oval-shaped crown. Leaves 8–15 in. long with 5–9 dark green, oval leaflets, paler beneath; turn purplish in fall. Needs some watering. Edges show burning in hot, windy areas. Male and female flowers on separate trees, but plants sold are generally seedlings, so you don't know what you're getting. If you end up with both male and female trees, you will get heavy crop of seed; both litter and seedlings can be problem. Seedless selections include

'Autumn Applause' and 'Autumn Purple', both with exceptionally good, long-lasting purple fall color; 'Champaign County', a dense grower; 'Rosehill', with bronzy red fall color; and 'Skyline', an upright oval with brown and purple fall color.

F. dipetala. FOOTHILL ASH. Deciduous tree or large shrub. Zones 7–24. Native to foothills of California; also in Baja California. Treelike shrub to 6 ft. high or small tree to 18–20 ft. Drought tolerant. Leaves 2–5½ in. long; occasionally undivided, but usually with 3–9 leaflets about 1 in. long. White flowers in showy, branched clusters, March–June, followed by many 1-in.-long fruits.

F. excelsior. EUROPEAN ASH. Deciduous tree. All Zones. Native to Europe, Asia Minor. Round-headed tree 60–80 ft. high, or may grow to 140 ft. Dormant buds black. Leaves 10–12 in. long, divided into 7–11 oval, toothed leaflets, dark green above, paler beneath; do not change color but drop while green.

F. e. 'Kimberly'. All Zones, but especially valued as shade tree in Zones 1–3. A selected male variety that doesn't produce seed.

F. e. 'Pendula'. WEEPING EUROPEAN ASH. All Zones. Spreading, rather asymmetrical, umbrella-shaped tree with weeping branches that reach ground.

F. 'Fan West'. Seedless hybrid between green ash (*F. pennsylvanica*) and Modesto ash (*F. velutina* 'Modesto'). Light olive green leaves, good branch structure; tolerates cold, desert heat and wind.

F. holotricha. Deciduous tree. Zones 4–24. Native to eastern Balkan Peninsula. Upright, rather narrow tree to 40 ft. Leaves of 9–13 dull green, 2–3-in.-long leaflets with toothed edges. Casts light, filtered shade. Leaves turn yellow in fall, dry up, and sift down into lawn or ground cover, thus lessening litter problem.

F. h. 'Moraine'. Selected variety; more round headed than species, produces few seeds. Good lawn tree—neat, symmetrical, uniform bright yellow in fall.

F. latifolia *(F. oregona).* OREGON ASH. Deciduous tree. Zones 4–24. Native to Sierra Nevada and along coast from northern California to British Columbia. Grows to 40–80 ft. Leaves 6–12 in. long, divided into 5–7 oblong to oval, light green, hairy or smooth leaflets; end leaflet to 4 in. long, larger than side leaflets. Male and female flowers on separate trees. Will grow in standing water during winter months.

F. ornus. FLOWERING ASH. Deciduous tree. Zones 3–9, 14–17. Native to southern Europe and Asia Minor. Grows rapidly to 40–50 ft. with broad, rounded crown 20–30 ft. wide. Supplies luxuriant mass of foliage. Leaves 8–10 in. long, divided into 7–11 oval, medium green, 2-in.-long leaflets with toothed edges. Foliage turns to soft shades of lavender and yellow in fall. In May, displays quantities of fluffy, branched, 3–5-in.-long clusters of fragrant white to greenish white blossoms followed by unsightly seed clusters that hang on until late winter unless removed.

Fraxinus ornus

F. oxycarpa. Zones 3–9, 14–24. Compact, small-leafed, fine-textured ash with delicate, lacy look. The species is not known in the West: the following selection from Australia is choice.

F. o. 'Raywood'. RAYWOOD ASH, CLARET ASH. Compact, round-headed, fast-growing tree to 25–35 ft. Usually sold in California as container-grown rather than bare-root tree. Produces no seeds. Purple red fall color.

F. pennsylvanica *(F. lanceolata).* GREEN ASH, RED ASH. Deciduous tree. Zones 1–6. Native to eastern U.S. Moderate grower to 30–40 ft., forming compact oval crown. Gray brown bark; dense, twiggy structure. Leaves 10–12 in. long, divided into 5–9 bright green, rather narrow, 4–6-in.-long leaflets. Male and female flowers on separate trees. Takes wet soil and severe cold, but foliage burns in hot, dry winds.

Seedless varieties include: 'Marshall' and 'Summit' (below); 'Bergeson', fast growing, very cold tolerant; 'Emerald', yellow fall color; 'Patmore', tolerant of extreme cold; and 'Urbanite'.

F. p. 'Marshall'. MARSHALL SEEDLESS GREEN ASH. Selected male form with large, glossy, dark green leaflets. Fast grower with tapered crown.

F. p. 'Summit'. Fast growing to 50–60 ft. Uniform, erect growth.

F. quadrangulata. BLUE ASH. Deciduous tree. Zones 1–6. Native to central U.S. Grows rapidly to 60–80 ft. or more. Branches distinctly square, usually with flanges along edges. Oval, dark green leaflets (7–11 per leaf), 2–5 in. long, with toothed edges. Foliage turns purplish in fall. Fruit may become litter problem if you have both female and male trees.

F. uhdei. EVERGREEN ASH, SHAMEL ASH. Evergreen to semievergreen tree. Zones 9, 12–24. Native to Mexico. In mildest areas, leaves stay through winter; in colder sections, trees lose most or all foliage, but often only for a short time. Sharp frosts may kill back branch tips; serious damage at about 15°F. or lower. A top favorite in southern California and low-elevation deserts. 'Majestic Beauty' has exceptionally large leaves, is more reliably evergreen than the species.

Grows fast to 25–30 ft. in 10 years; 40 ft. in 20 years; eventually 70–80 ft. or more. Upright, narrow tree when young; eventually takes on a spreading form as it grows older. Leaves divided into 5–9 glossy dark green leaflets about 4 in. long, edged with small teeth. Foliage may burn if subjected to hot winds. Shallow rooted; encourage deeper rooting by watering deeply. Cut back any long branches to well-placed, strong side branches when tree is young. Eliminate deep crotches by pruning out weaker branches. Texas root rot sometimes causes dieback and will kill young trees, but established trees usually survive. Resistant to oak root fungus.

F. u. 'Sexton'. SEXTON ASH. Forms very compact, rounded crown. Leaflets larger and deeper green than those of *F. uhdei.*

F. u. 'Tomlinson'. TOMLINSON ASH. Grows more slowly than species (18 ft. in 10 years). More upright and dense when young. Leaflets deep green and more leathery, with wavy-toothed margins.

F. velutina. ARIZONA ASH. Deciduous tree. Zones 8, 9, 10–24. Native to Arizona. Tree withstands hot, dry conditions and cold to about −10°F. Pyramidal when young; spreading, more open when mature. Leaves divided into 3–5 narrow to oval, 3-in.-long leaflets. Male and female flowers on separate trees.

F. v. coriacea. MONTEBELLO ASH. Zones 8, 9, 13–24. Native mostly to southern California. Has broader, more leathery leaves than the species.

F. v. 'Modesto'. MODESTO ASH. Zones 3–24. Selection from tree in Westside Park, Modesto, Calif. Vigorous form of Arizona ash. Grows to about 50 ft. with 30-ft. spread. Medium green leaflets, glossier than those of the species, turn bright yellow in fall.

In many areas, Modesto ash leaves get scorched look following a wet spring. This is caused by fungus disease called anthracnose. Control by spraying with benomyl. Prune out and dispose of infected wood—it can reinfect. Verticillium wilt is prevalent in agricultural areas; there is no control once it's started in young trees, but established trees often survive. In desert, subject to ash decline syndrome, an ailment of unknown origin. Keep trees vigorous; if any are lost, replace with Raywood or Shamel ashes. Control aphids, psyllids, and spider mites with contact spray. Resistant to oak root fungus.

F. v. 'Rio Grande'. FAN-TEX ASH. Zones 8–24. Thrives in hot, dry climates and alkaline soils. Has very large, darker green, more succulent leaflets than Modesto ash; they unfold in early spring, turn golden yellow in late fall. Foliage resistant to wind burn.

FREESIA. *Iridaceae.* Corm. Outdoors in Zones 8, 9, 12–24; indoors in pots anywhere. Native to South Africa. Prized for rich fragrance of flowers. Slender, branched stems to 1–1½ ft., about same height as lowest leaves; stem leaves shorter. Flowers tubular, 2 in. long, in one-sided spikes. Older variety 'Alba' has fragrant white or creamy white blooms; newer, larger-flowered varieties with 1–1½-ft. stems are Tecolote and Dutch Hybrids with white, pink, red, lavender, purple, blue, yellow, and orange flowers, mixed or in single-color named varieties. Freesias will self-sow if faded flowers are not removed; volunteers tend to revert to cream marked with purple and yellow.

(Continued on next page)

In mild climates, plant 2 in. deep (pointed end up) in fall in sunny, well-drained soil. Plants dry up after bloom, start growing again in fall with rains or watering; increase rapidly. In cold climates, plant 2 in. deep, 2 in. apart in pots; grow indoors in sunny window. Keep room temperature as cool as possible at night. Easily grown from seed sown in July–August; often bloom following spring. Good in rock gardens or for cutting. Flowering potted freesias are available all year; they have been grown from chilled and stored corms.

Freesia hybrid

FREMONTODENDRON *(Fremontia).* *Bombacaceae.* FLANNEL BUSH. Evergreen shrubs or small trees. Zones 7–24. Fast growing to 6–20 ft. tall. Leathery leaves are dark green above, with feltlike coating beneath. Yellow, saucerlike flowers. Conical seed capsules, covered with bristly, rust-colored hairs, persist for a long time; some consider them unsightly. Plants need excellent drainage; hillside planting is best. Completely drought resistant. Give plants little summer water, especially in heavy soils. Roots shallow, so stake plants while young. Pinch and prune to shape. Usually short lived. Plant with other drought-tolerant shrubs—beautiful with ceanothus.

Fremontodendron 'California Glory'

F. 'California Glory'. Hybrid between *F. californicum* and *F. mexicanum.* To 20 ft. tall, possibly more. Flowers to 3 in. across, rich yellow inside, tinged red outside. Very prolific bloom over long period.

F. californicum. COMMON FLANNEL BUSH. Native to foothills of Sierra Nevada and Coast Ranges, and southern California mountains. Eye-catching show of lemon yellow, 1–1½-in.-wide flowers in May–June; flowers bloom all at once. Roundish unlobed or 3-lobed leaves, 1 in. long.

F. c. napense. Native to Napa, Lake, and Yolo counties in California. Somewhat shrubbier than species, with thinner leaves. Smaller yellow flowers, sometimes tinged with rose.

F. mexicanum. SOUTHERN FLANNEL BUSH. Native to San Diego County and Baja California. To 18 ft. Leaves have 3–5 distinct lobes, 1¼–3 in. long. Flowers are 1½–2½ in. wide, yellow often tinged orange. Blooms over longer period than *F. californicum,* but because flowers form among leaves, mass effect is not as showy.

F. 'Pacific Sunset'. Deep orange yellow flowers, 3½–4 in. wide. Peak bloom late April, May; sporadic bloom later.

F. 'San Gabriel'. Resembles *F.* 'California Glory', but leaves are more deeply cut (maplelike).

FRINGE BELLS. See *Shortia soldanelloides.*

FRINGECUPS. See *Tellima grandiflora.*

FRINGED WORMWOOD. See *Artemisia frigida.*

FRINGE HYACINTH. See *Muscari comosum.*

FRINGE TREE. See *Chionanthus.*

FRITILLARIA. *Liliaceae.* FRITILLARY. Bulbs. Zones 1–7, 15–17. Native to Europe, Asia, North America; American species most numerous in West. Give variable performance in gardens; some kinds short lived. Unbranched stems 6 in.–4 ft. high, topped by bell-like, nodding flowers, often unusually colored and mottled. Use in woodland, rock garden, or as border plants in filtered shade. In fall, plant bulbs in porous soil with ample humus. Set smaller bulbs 3–4 in. deep; set largest (crown imperial) 4–5 in. deep. Most kinds should gradually dry out as foliage yellows, remain dry until late fall. Bulbs sometimes rest a year after planting or after blooming; use enough for yearly display.

Fritillaria imperialis

F. assyriaca. Strong-growing plants 12–16 in. tall with blue green foliage, drooping maroon flowers lined with golden bronze. April–May bloom.

F. camschatcensis. Stems to 2 ft. carry 1–6 bell-shaped, nearly black flowers 1–1¼ in. long. Lance-shaped leaves to 4 in. long. Needs shade, leaf mold, cool soil. April–May bloom.

F. imperialis. CROWN IMPERIAL. Stout stalk 3½–4 ft. tall, clothed with broad, glossy leaves. At top of stalk are clusters of large, drooping, bell-shaped flowers in red, orange, or yellow; tuft of leaves above flowers. Use in borders, containers. Bulb and plant have somewhat unpleasant odor. Takes full sun near coast.

F. lanceolata. CHECKER LILY. Western native. Stems 2½ ft. high with several whorls of leaves. Flowers are bowl-shaped, brownish purple bells mottled with yellow, greenish yellow, or purple spots.

F. meleagris. CHECKERED LILY, SNAKESHEAD. Nodding 2-in. bells on 1–1½-ft. stems. Showy flowers, checkered and veined with reddish brown and purple, bloom in late spring. Lance-shaped leaves are 3–6 in. long. There is a white form. Native to damp meadows in Europe, Asia; tolerates occasional flooding. Long lived in colder regions.

F. persica 'Adiyaman'. Stems 2–3 ft. tall carry up to 30 drooping, deep plum purple, 1-in. flowers on upper half. Foliage is grayish. Plant is hardy and easy to grow, but emerging stems need protection from late frosts in colder regions.

F. pudica. YELLOW FRITILLARY. Western native. Stems 6–12 in. tall topped with 1–3 nodding bells, April–June; flowers yellow or orange at first, turning brick red with age. Alternate lance-shaped leaves to 8 in. long.

F. recurva. SCARLET FRITILLARY. Western native. Stems 2½ ft. high; flowers are scarlet bells marked yellow inside, tinged purple outside. Blooms March–July, depending on climate. Lance-shaped leaves in whorls, to 4 in. long.

F. verticillata thunbergii *(F. thunbergii).* To 2 ft. tall. Flowers white or cream, checkered with green or purplish markings. Early spring bloom.

FUCHSIA. *Onagraceae.* Evergreen in frost-free climates, deciduous elsewhere. Shrub. Popular, showy-flowered fuchsias that come in hundreds of named varieties are forms of *F. hybrida,* and are discussed under that heading. Other species are grown almost entirely by collectors, but some are good for basic landscaping purposes. Give plenty of water and partial shade.

Fuchsia hybrida

F. arborescens. Zones 16, 17, 22–24. Big shrub to 18 ft. tall, with 8-in. leaves and large clusters of small, erect, pinkish or purplish flowers like lilacs in summer.

F. hybrida. HYBRID FUCHSIA. Here belong nearly all garden fuchsias. Zones 4–6, 15–17, 22–24 constitute finest climate in North America for growing fuchsias and region in which most varieties were developed. The next strip—Zones 2, 3, 7–9, 14, 20, 21—finds fuchsias grown, but with more difficulty. Outside of those 2 strips, fuchsias are little known, grown as summer annuals in greenhouses, or as house plants.

Fuchsias bloom from early summer to first frost. At least 500 varieties in West, with wide variety of combinations within color range. Sepals (top parts that flare back) are always white, red, or pink. Corolla (inside part of flower) may be almost any color possible within range of white, blue violet, purple, pink, red, and shades approaching orange. Flowers have no fragrance, but hummingbirds visit them.

There are considerable differences in flower sizes and shapes. In size, fuchsias range from shelled-peanut size to giants as big as a child's fist. Within this range, some are single, meaning that there's just one layer of closely set petals in corolla; some are very double, with many sets of ruffled petals in corolla. Quite frequently, little-flowered types have small leaves, and big-flowered types have large leaves.

Plant forms vary widely—from erect-growing shrubs ranging from 3–12 ft. high to trailing types grown in hanging containers, with just about every possible intermediate form. Specifically, you can buy or train fuchsias in these forms: hanging basket, small shrub, medium shrub, large shrub, espalier, and standard (miniature tree shape).

Best environment. Fuchsias grow best in cool summer temperatures, modified sunlight, and with much moisture in atmosphere and soil. If you live where fog rolls in on summer afternoons, any place in your garden will supply these conditions. Where summers are warm, windy, dry, or sunny, seek or create favorable exposure protected from wind and in morning sun or all-day dappled shade—in short, a place where you yourself are comfortable on hot summer afternoons.

For containers or planting beds, soil mix should be porous (for aeration), water retentive, and rich in organic matter.

Watering. Water as often as you can. It's almost impossible to give thriving fuchsias in well-drained containers too much water. Hanging basket fuchsias need more watering than any other form. Fuchsias in ground can go longer between watering if drainage is good. In hot-summer climates, heavy mulching (1½–3 in. deep) helps maintain soil moisture. Frequent overhead sprinkling is beneficial in several ways: it keeps leaves clean, discourages pests, counteracts low humidity (especially important on windy days in inland climates). When foliage wilts in extreme heat regardless of watering, mist to cool it down.

Feeding. Apply complete fertilizer frequently. Light doses every 10 days–2 weeks, or label-recommended feedings every month, will keep plants growing and producing flowers. You can almost see fertilizer take effect. Liquid fertilizers work well.

Growing from cuttings. You can take cuttings of favorite variety and grow them into flowering plants in a few months, or—at longest—in a year. Just cut 2–3-in. stem pieces (tips preferred) and put lower halves in damp sand to root.

Summer pruning and pinching. If plant is growing leggier than you'd like, pinch out tips of branches whenever you can. Pinching forces growth into side branches, makes plant bushier. Pick off old flowers as they start to fade.

Spraying. Common pests in California are spider mites and whiteflies. If not controlled, they cause leaves to yellow and drop. Frequent overhead watering will discourage red spider mites; spray undersides of leaves with miticide to control them. Spray undersides of leaves with resmethrin or orthene at 5–7-day intervals to control whiteflies. In California, the fuchsia gall mite has recently become a serious pest, causing distortion of leaves and shoots. Cut off and destroy distorted tissue. Spray plants early in season with carbaryl (sevin) or thiodan; repeat in 2 weeks. In Northwest, aphids are worst pest. Spray to control, using any good general-purpose insecticide.

Winters in cold climates. Where frosts are light, fuchsias lose their leaves; sometimes tender growth is killed. Where freezes are hard, most plants die back to hard wood, sometimes to roots. A few varieties, including 'Royal Purple', 'Checkerboard', and 'Marinka', stand outdoor exposures in winter in Zones 4–7. In Northwest, best plan is usually to protect outdoor fuchsias by mounding 5–6 in. of sawdust over roots (tops will be killed), and to store potted plants in greenhouse or indoors (40°–50°F. is ideal) in damp sawdust. Keep soil moist (but not soggy) all winter.

Early spring pruning. Fuchsias everywhere need some pruning in early spring. In frost-free areas, cut out approximately the same volume of growth that formed the previous summer—leave about 2 healthy leaf buds on that growth. In mild-frost regions, cut out all frost-damaged wood and enough additional wood to remove most of the last summer's growth. In cold-winter regions, prune plants lightly (remove leaves and twiggy growth) before storing them. In spring, prune out all broken branches and cut back into live wood.

F. magellanica. Zones 2–9, 14–24. Many arching, 3-ft.-long stems loaded with drooping, 1½-in.-long, red and violet flowers, July to frost. Flowers frequented by hummingbirds. Leaves are oval, in groups of 2 or 3, ½–1 in. long. Where winters are mild, can reach 20 ft. trained against wall. Treat as perennial in cold-climate areas. Roots are hardy with mulching; tops will die back with the first hard frost.

F. procumbens. Zones 16, 17, 21–24. Prostrate, spreading fuchsia to 1 ft. high for containers, shady rock gardens. Leaves ½ in. long. Tiny flowers without petals in summer. Purple-tipped sepals pale orange marked green; anthers and pollen blue. Red berries, ¾ in. long, are showy.

F. triphylla. This West Indian species is seldom seen, but a hybrid descendant, 'Gartenmeister Bonstedt', is well known. It's a spreading, shrubby plant 2–3 ft. tall, with purplish leaf undersides and drooping clusters of intense orange red, long-tubed flowers. It is somewhat more tender than most fuchsia hybrids but is said to be more tolerant of heat. Blooms all year in mildest climates. Protect from frost.

Fuchsia flower types vary.

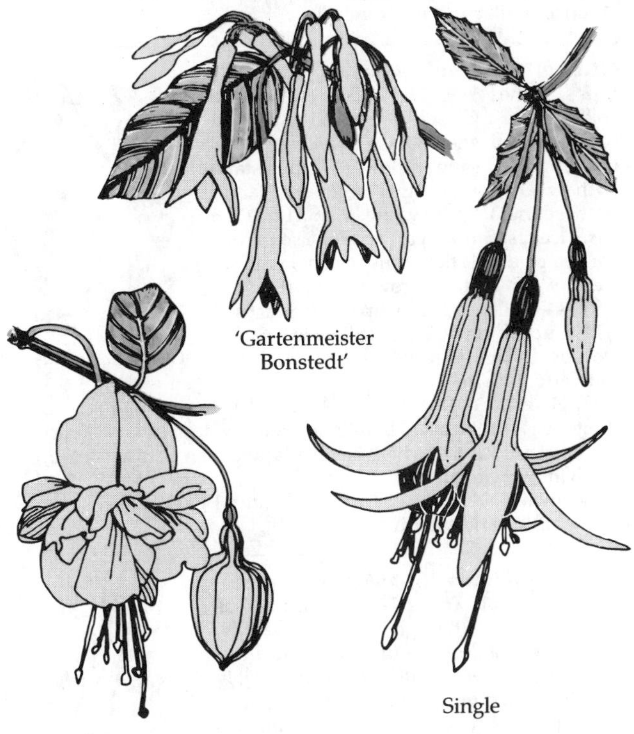

FUCHSIA EUCALYPTUS. See *Eucalyptus forrestiana.*

Fumariaceae. Closely related to the poppy family, this family consists of annuals and perennials, usually with irregularly-shaped flowers. *Corydalis* and *Dicentra* are examples.

FUNKIA. See *Hosta.*

G

GAILLARDIA. *Compositae.* Perennials and annuals. All Zones. Native to central and western U.S. Low-growing, sun-loving plants with daisylike flowers in warm colors—yellow, bronze, scarlet. They thrive in sun and heat, will take some drought, need good drainage. Easy to grow from seed and fine for cutting and borders. Often reseed.

Gaillardia grandiflora

G. grandiflora. BLANKET FLOWER. Perennial. To 2–4 ft. high. Developed from native species *G. aristata* and *G. pulchella.* Foliage roughish, gray green; flower heads 3–4 in. across, single or double. Much variation in flower color: warm shades of red and yellow with orange or maroon bands. Bloom June until frost.

Plants flower first year from seed. Many strains and varieties are obtainable, including dwarf kinds and types with extra-large flowers. 'Goblin' is an especially good compact variety (1 ft. tall) with large, deep red flowers bordered in bright yellow.

G. pulchella. Annual. Easy to grow. To 1½–2 ft. high. Flower heads 2 in. wide on long, whiplike stems in summer. Warm shades of red, yellow, gold. Leaves soft, hairy. Sow seeds in warm soil after frost danger is past.

G. p. 'Lorenziana'. Has no ray flowers (petals); instead, disk flowers are enlarged into little star-tipped bells, whole effect like balls of bright fluff. Double Gaiety strain (1½ ft.) has flowers that range from near-white to maroon, often with bicolors. Lollipop strain is similar, but 10–12 in. tall.

GALANTHUS. *Amaryllidaceae.* SNOWDROP. Bulbs. Zones 1–9, 14–17. Best adapted to cold climates. Closely related to and often confused with snowflake (*Leucojum*). White, nodding, bell-shaped flowers (1 per stalk) with green tips on inner segments; larger outer segments pure white. Plants have 2–3 basal leaves. Sun or part shade. Use in rock garden or under flowering shrubs, naturalize in woodland, or grow in pots. Plant in fall, 3–4 in. deep, 2–3 in. apart, in moist soil with ample humus. Do not allow to dry out. Do not divide often; when needed, divide right after bloom.

Galanthus nivalis

G. elwesii. GIANT SNOWDROP. Globular, 1½-in.-long bells on 1-ft. stems; 2 or 3 leaves, 8 in. long, ¾ in. wide. January–February bloom in mild areas (where better adapted than *G. nivalis*); March–April in cold climates.

G. nivalis. COMMON SNOWDROP. Dainty 1-in.-long bells on 6–9-in. stems in earliest spring.

GALAX urceolata ***(G. aphylla).*** *Diapensiaceae.* Perennial. Zones 1–6. Often used as ground cover, although it spreads slowly. Must have medium to full shade, acid soil with much organic material, and preferably mulch of leaf mold. Regular water essential. Space plants 1 ft. apart. Small white flowers on 2½-ft. stems in July. Leaves, in basal tufts, give plant its real distinction. They are shiny, heart shaped, 5 in. across; turn beautiful bronze color in fall. Leaves much used in indoor arrangements.

Galax urceolata

GALIUM odoratum ***(Asperula odorata).*** *Rubiaceae.* SWEET WOODRUFF. Perennial. Zones 1–6, 15–17. Attractive, low-spreading perennial that brings to mind deep-shaded woods. Slender, square stems 6–12 in. high, encircled every inch or so by whorls of 6–8 aromatic, bristle-tipped leaves. Clusters of tiny white flowers show above foliage in late spring and summer. Leaves and stems give off fragrant, haylike odor when dried; used to make May wine.

In the garden, sweet woodruff's best use is as ground cover or edging along path in shaded location. Will spread rapidly in rich soil with abundant moisture—can become a pest if allowed to grow entirely unchecked. Self-sows freely. Can be increased by division in fall or spring.

Galium odoratum

GALTONIA candicans. *Liliaceae.* SUMMER HYACINTH. Bulb. Zones 8–24. Native to South Africa. Straplike leaves, 2–3 ft. long; stout 2–4-ft. stems topped in summer with loose, spikelike clusters of fragrant white flowers—drooping, funnel-shaped, 1–1½ in. long, with 3 outer segments often tipped green. Best in moderate shade with some summer irrigation. Plant behind low, bushy plants. Plant bulbs 6 in. deep in rich soil in fall; they will grow well for many years without lifting, dividing. Where ground freezes, plant in spring; mulch deeply during winter or lift bulbs after foliage dies and store them at 55°–60°F. Bait for slugs and snails.

Galtonia candicans

GALVEZIA speciosa. *Scrophulariaceae.* ISLAND BUSH-SNAPDRAGON. Evergreen shrub. Zones 14–24. Native to Santa Catalina, San Clemente, Guadalupe islands. Usually 3–5 ft. across, slightly less in height, but can climb or lean on other shrubs and reach 8 ft. Leaves about 1 in. long, half as wide. Flowers scarlet, tubular, 1 in. long, clustering toward tips of branches. Bloom heaviest in midspring, but intermittent throughout year. Withstands drought once established, endures light or heavy soils if drainage is adequate. Sun near coast, light shade in interior. Once well rooted, plants need little summer water.

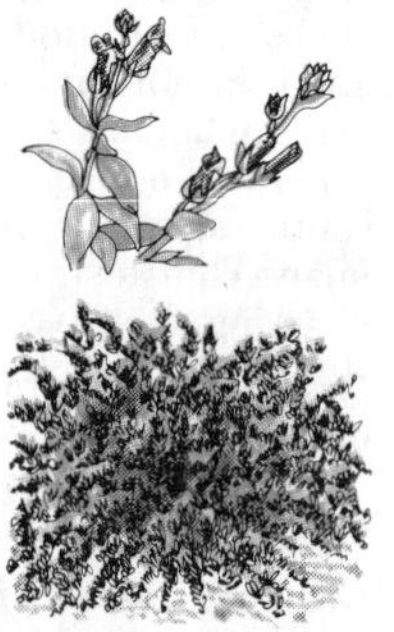

Galvezia speciosa

GARDENIA. *Rubiaceae.* Evergreen shrubs. White, intensely fragrant flowers.

G. jasminoides. Zones 7–9, 12–16, 18–23. Native to China. Glossy bright green leaves and double white, highly fragrant flowers. Vigorous when conditions are right: plants need ample warmth, ample water, and steady feeding. Though hardy to 20°F. or even lower, plants fail to grow and bloom well without summer heat. They are hard to grow in adobe soils. Take full sun in coastal valleys; best with filtered shade in hot inland valleys. Give north or east exposure in desert.

Soil should drain fast but retain water, too; use plenty of peat moss or ground bark in conditioning soil. Plant high (like azaleas and rhododendrons) and avoid crowding by other plants and competing roots. Mulch plants instead of cultivating. Syringe plants in early morning except when in bloom—unless water is high in salts (residue from this water may burn leaves). Keep soil moist; where water is poor, leach salts by monthly flooding. Feed every 3–4 weeks during growing season with acid plant food, fish emulsion, or blood meal. Treat chlorosis with iron sulfate or iron chelate. Prune to remove straggly branches, faded flowers. Use all-purpose spray or dust to control aphids, other sucking insects.

Gardenia jasminoides

All are useful in containers or raised beds, as hedges, espaliers, low screens, or as single plants. Here are named varieties:

'August Beauty'. Grows 4–6 ft. high and blooms heavily, May–October or November. Large double flowers.

'Golden Magic'. Plants reach 3 ft. tall, 2 ft. wide in 2–3 years; eventually larger. Extra-full flowers open white, gradually age to deep golden yellow. April–September bloom, peaking in May.

'Kimura Shikazaki' ('Four Seasons'). Compact plant 2–3 ft. tall. Flowers similar to those of 'Veitchii', but slightly less fragrant. Extremely long bloom season—spring to fall.

'Mystery'. Best-known variety; has 4–5-in. double white flowers, May–July. Tends to be rangy. Needs pruning to keep it neat. In warm southwestern gardens may bloom through November. Can reach 6–8 ft.

'Radicans'. Grows 6–12 in. high and spreads to 2–3 ft. Small dark green leaves often streaked with white. Summer flowers only 1 in. wide, but with gardenia form and fragrance. Good small-scale ground cover, container plant.

'Veitchii'. Compact 3–4½-ft. plant with many 1–1½-in. blooms May–November, sometimes even during warm winter. Prolific bloom, reliable grower.

'Veitchii Improved.' Taller (to 5 ft.) and produces larger number of slightly larger blooms.

G. thunbergia. Zones 16, 17, 21–24. Native to South Africa. Angular-branched shrub to 10 ft. tall, 20 ft. wide. Leaves to 6 in. long, very dark green (nearly black). Winter flowers long tubed, single, 3–4 in. across. Very fragrant. Seems somewhat more tolerant of cool conditions and less than perfect soil than common gardenia, but tender to frost. With age, becomes more vigorous, flowers more profusely.

GARLAND FLOWER. See *Hedychium coronarium.*

GARLIC. *Liliaceae.* For ornamental varieties, see *Allium.* Perennial. Seed stores and some mail-order seed houses sell mother bulbs ("sets") for planting. In mild-winter areas, plant October–December for early summer harvest. Where winters are cold, plant early in spring. Break bulbs up into cloves and plant base downward, 1–2 in. deep, 2–3 in. apart, in rows 1 ft. apart. Harvest when leafy tops fall over; air-dry bulbs, remove tops and roots, and store in cool place. GIANT or ELEPHANT GARLIC has unusually large (fist-sized) bulbs and mild garlic flavor. Same culture as regular garlic.

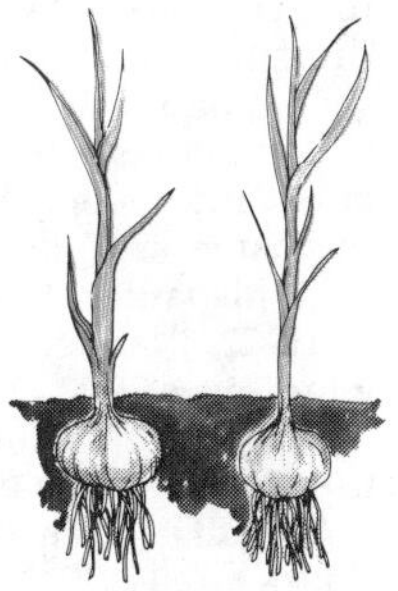

Garlic

GARLIC CHIVES. See *Allium tuberosum.*

GARRYA. *Garryaceae.* SILKTASSEL. Evergreen shrubs. Pendulous male and female catkins on separate shrubs; male catkins are long, slender, and decorative. Both plants must be present to produce grapelike clusters of purple fruit on female plant.

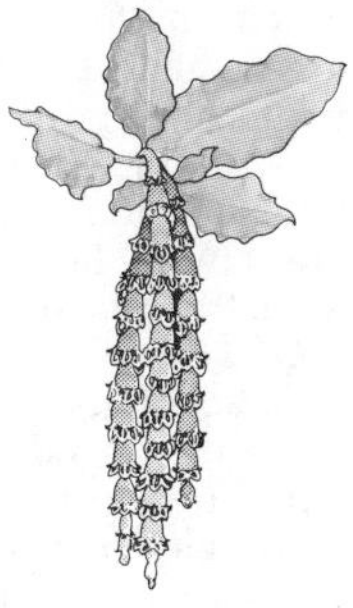

Garrya elliptica

G. elliptica. COAST SILKTASSEL. Zones 5–9, 14–21. Native to Coast Ranges from southern Oregon to San Luis Obispo County, California. Shrub to 4–8 ft. or small tree to 20–30 ft. Branches densely clothed with elliptical, wavy-edged leaves to 2½ in. long, dark green above, gray and woolly beneath. Clustered flower tassels December–February. Yellowish to greenish yellow male catkins are slender and graceful, 3–8 in. long; pale green, rather stubby female catkins are 2–3½ in. long. Female plants have clusters of purplish fruit which hang on June–September—even longer if not eaten by robins. Male variety 'James Roof' has unusually long catkins.

Excellent foliage plant for sun or part shade. Will take summer water and thrives near coast or inland as screen, informal hedge, or as display shrub.

G. fremontii. FREMONT SILKTASSEL. Zones 4–9, 14–17. Native to Cascade Mountains, Sierra Nevada, Coast Ranges. Differs from *G. elliptica* in its leaves—glossy, smooth edged, lively yellow green on both upper and lower surfaces. Catkins yellowish or purplish; fruit purple or black. Grows 4–8 ft. high. Does best in full sun. Tolerates drought, heat, cold better than *G. elliptica*. Gets rangy in dense shade.

GAS PLANT. See *Dictamnus albus.*

GAULTHERIA. *Ericaceae.* Evergreen shrubs or shrublets. Zones 4–7, 14–17 except as noted. All have urn-shaped flowers and berrylike fruit. They need woodland soil and partial shade (except for native *G. shallon*). Require routine watering through dry season; tolerate wet soil. Smaller kinds are favored for rock gardens, woodland plantings in Northwest. Larger kinds are good companions for other acid-soil shrubs such as rhododendrons and azaleas.

Gaultheria shallon

G. cuneata. Compact shrub, 1–1½ ft. tall. Glossy dark green leaves, ½–1 in. long and half as wide, on reddish brown branches. Short clusters of white flowers in summer. White fruit, ⅜ in. wide.

G. miqueliana. Native to Japan. Grows 1–1½ ft. tall, spreads to 3–4 ft. Oval, net-veined evergreen leaves turn bronzy in fall. Tiny white flowers are followed by ¼-in. white berries with wintergreen flavor.

G. ovatifolia. Native to mountains northern California to British Columbia, east to northern Idaho. Spreading, trailing, with upright branches to about 8 in. high. Oval, leathery dark green leaves, ¾–1½ in. long, nearly as wide. Tiny white to pinkish flowers in summer. Bright red berries ¼ in. wide in fall and winter are edible, wintergreen flavored. Small-scale ground cover in woodland.

G. procumbens. WINTERGREEN, CHECKERBERRY, TEABERRY. Zones 2–7, 14–17. Native to eastern U.S. Creeping stems, upright branches to 6 in. with 2-in., oval, glossy leaves clustered toward tips. Small white summer flowers followed by scarlet berries. Leaves and fruit have flavor of wintergreen (or teaberry). Use as ground cover; plant 1 ft. apart.

G. shallon. SALAL. Native Santa Barbara County, California, to British Columbia. In full sun and poor, dry soil, a tufted plant 1–2 ft. tall. In shade and good soil can reach 4–10 ft. Nearly round, glossy bright green leaves 1¾–4 in. long. White or pinkish, bell-like flowers on reddish stalks in loose, 6-in.-long clusters. Blooms March–June. Edible black fruits resemble large huckleberries but are bland in flavor. Birds like them.

In sun, good low bank cover. In shade and acid soil, good companion for rhododendrons, azaleas, ferns. Only neglected plantings need pruning; cut back in April, remove dead wood, and mulch with leaf mold or peat moss. Cut branches are sold by florists as "lemon leaves."

GAURA lindheimeri. *Onagraceae.* GAURA. Perennial. All Zones. Native to Southwest. Grows 2¼–4 ft. high. Stalkless leaves, 1½–3½ in. long, grow directly on stems. Branching flower spikes bear many 1-in.-long white blossoms that open from pink buds closely set on stems. Long blooming period, with only a few blossoms opening at a time. Blossoms drop off cleanly when spent, but seed-bearing spikes should be cut to improve appearance and prevent overly enthusiastic self-sowing. Plant in full sun. Can take neglect. Fairly drought tolerant. One of the few long-lived perennials in Southwest.

Gaura lindheimeri

G

GAYFEATHER. See *Liatris.*

GAZANIA. *Compositae.* Perennials in Zones 8–24. Summer annuals anywhere. Native to South Africa. Daisy flowers give dazzling color display during peak bloom in late spring, early summer. In mild areas, they continue to bloom intermittently throughout the year. Gazanias grow well in almost any soil. Once plants are established, water them about twice a month, more often in Zones 10–13. Feed once in spring with slow-acting fertilizer. Divide plants about every 3–4 years. In cold areas, carry gazanias through winter by taking cuttings in fall as you would for pelargoniums.

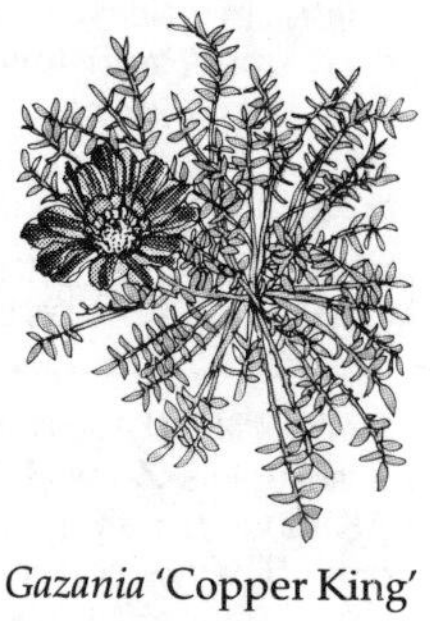

Gazania 'Copper King'

There are basically 2 types: clumping and trailing. The clumping kind (complex hybrids between a number of species) forms a mound of evergreen leaves—dark green above, gray and woolly beneath, often lobed. Flowers 3–4 in. wide, on 6–10-in.-long stems; they open on sunny days, close at night and in cloudy weather. You can buy clumping gazanias in single colors—yellow, orange, white, or rosy pink, with reddish purple petal undersides, often with dark blossom centers. Or you can get a mixture of hybrids (as plants or seeds) in different colors. Seed-grown kinds include Carnival (many colors, silver leaves); Chansonette (early blooming, compact; medium-sized round flowers); Harlequin (many colors, eyed and banded); Mini-Star (compact, floriferous plants; named selections include 'Mini-Star Yellow', 'Mini-Star Tangerine'); Sundance (5-in. flowers, striped or banded); and Sunshine (big, multicolored flowers, gray foliage).

Named hybrids of special merit are 'Aztec Queen' (multicolored), 'Burgundy', 'Copper King', and 'Fiesta Red'; these are best used in small-scale plantings, although the last is sturdy enough for large expanses. 'Moonglow' is double-flowered bright yellow of unusual vigor; its blossoms, unlike most, stay open even on dull days.

Clumping gazanias serve well as temporary fillers between young, growing shrubs and as a replaceable ground cover for relatively level areas that aren't subject to severe erosion. Try them in parking strips or as edgings along sunny paths. They also do well in rock gardens. They can be fire retardant if reasonably well-watered.

Trailing gazania (*G. rigens leucolaena*, formerly sold as *G. uniflora* or *G. leucolaena*) grows about as tall as clumping kinds, but spreads rapidly by long trailing stems. Foliage is clean silvery gray; flowers are yellow, white, orange, or bronze. New, larger-flowered hybrids are 'Sunburst' (orange, black eye) and 'Sunglow' (yellow). 'Sunrise Yellow' has large, black-eyed yellow flowers; leaves are green instead of gray. New hybrids are superior to older kinds in length of bloom, resistance to dieback. Trailing gazania is useful on banks, level ground. Or grow it at top of wall and allow it to trail over. Attractive in hanging baskets.

GEIJERA parviflora. *Rutaceae.* AUSTRALIAN WILLOW, WILGA. Evergreen tree. Zones 8, 9, 13–24. Graceful, fine textured, to 25–30 ft. high, 20 ft. wide. Main branches sweep up and out, little branches hang down. Distant citrus relative; called Australian willow because its 3–6-in.-long, narrow, medium green, drooping leaves give a kind of weeping willow effect. With age, produces loose clusters of unimportant small, creamy white flowers in early spring, early fall. Well-drained soil and full sun; plant tolerates light shade but tends to be thin in foliage. Established tree resists drought but responds to ample water with faster growth. Needs pruning only to correct form (much less pruning than willow). Quite pest free. Has much of the willow's grace and the eucalyptus's toughness. Moderate growth rate; deep, noninvasive roots. Casts light shade. Plant singly as patio or street tree, or in colonies for attractive grove effect.

Geijera parviflora

GELSEMIUM sempervirens. *Loganiaceae.* CAROLINA JESSAMINE. Evergreen vine. Zones 8–24. Shrubby and twining; moderate growth rate to about 20 ft. Clean pairs of shiny light green, 1–4-in.-long leaves on long, streamerlike branches make neat but not dense foliage pattern. Full sun. On trellis, vine will cascade and swing in wind; makes delicate green curtain of branches when trained on house. Vine can get top-heavy; if it does, cut it back severely. Fragrant, tubular yellow flowers, 1–1½ in. long, in late winter, early spring. 'Plena' is a double-flowered form. Can be used as ground cover; keep trimmed to 3 ft. high. Moderately drought tolerant but looks best if watered regularly. All parts of plant are poisonous.

Gelsemium sempervirens

GENISTA. *Leguminosae.* BROOM. Usually deciduous shrubs, but green branches give plants evergreen look. Leaves often small and short lived. Flowers yellow (rarely white or pink), sweet pea shaped. Less aggressive than other brooms (*Cytisus, Spartium*); will not run wild. Smaller kinds attractive in rock gardens, bank plantings. Need sun, good drainage; tolerate rocky or infertile soil, drought, conditions at seashore.

G. canariensis. See *Cytisus canariensis.*

G. fragrans. This white-flowered species is not in nursery trade. Plants sold under this name are *Cytisus spachianus.*

G. hispanica. SPANISH BROOM. Zones 2–9, 11–22. Mass of spiny stems, with ½-in.-long leaves, to 1–2 ft. high and spreading wide. Golden yellow flowers in clusters at tips of stems, May–June.

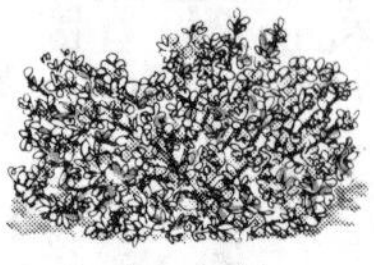

Genista lydia

G. lydia (often sold, erroneously, as *Cytisus lydia*). Shrublet. Zones 4–6, 14–17. Grows to 2 ft. high, with spreading habit. Makes a good ground cover. Bright yellow flowers are borne in profusion at ends of shoots in June. This plant sets little seed.

G. monosperma. BRIDAL VEIL BROOM. Zones 16, 17, 22–24. Upright growth to 20 ft. high, 10 ft. wide, with slender, graceful, gray green, almost leafless branches. Fragrant white flowers in late winter and spring.

G. pilosa. Zones 2–9, 11–22. Fairly fast-growing prostrate shrub, ultimately to 1–1½ ft. with 7-ft. spread. Intricately branched, gray green twigs. Roundish, ¼–½-in.-long leaves. Yellow flowers, May–June. 'Vancouver Gold' is best selection.

G. racemosa. See *Cytisus spachianus.*

G. sagittalis. Zones 2–9, 11–22. Plants spread along ground. Upright, winged, bright green branchlets appear jointed. Rather rapid grower to 1 ft. high with wide spread. Makes sheet of golden yellow bloom, late spring and early summer.

GENTIAN. See *Gentiana.*

GENTIANA. *Gentianaceae.* GENTIAN. Zones 1–6, 14–17. Perennials. Low, spreading, or upright plants, generally with very blue tubular flowers. Most are hard to grow, but prized by rock garden enthusiasts. Need full sun or light shade, perfect drainage, lime-free soil, ample moisture. If they thrive, they produce some of richest blues in garden.

G. acaulis. Leafy stems to 4 in. tall. Leaves 1 in. long. Rich blue flowers 2 in. long in summer. Grows well; often fails to bloom.

G. asclepiadea. Upright or arching stems to 1½ ft. Leaves willowlike, 3 in. long. Flowers blue, 1½ in. long, in late summer, fall. Fairly easy to grow in cool border or rock garden.

Gentiana acaulis

G. clusii *(G. acaulis clusii).* Similar to *G. acaulis.* Flowers generally somewhat larger.

G. septemfida. Arching or sprawling stems 9–18 in. long. Oval leaves to 1½ in. long. Clusters of blue 2-in. flowers in late summer. Fairly easy to grow.

G. sino-ornata. From 7-in. rosettes of bright green leaves come trailing stems which end in 2-in.-long flowers of brightest blue. Blooms in early fall. Fairly easy to grow in half shade.

Gentianaceae. The gentian family includes annuals and perennials from many parts of the world. Many have blue or purple flowers, including the gentians, Persian violet (*Exacum*), and *Eustoma.*

Geraniaceae. The cranesbill family of annuals and perennials (the latter sometimes shrubby) includes true geranium, *Erodium* (perennial, rarely annual), and *Pelargonium* (perennial or shrubby).

GERANIUM. *Geraniaceae.* CRANESBILL. Perennials. Here we consider true geraniums, hardy plants. Botanically, the more common indoor/outdoor plant most people know as geranium is *Pelargonium.* Several true geraniums have handsome, near-evergreen leaves and bloom over a long period in summer and fall. Flowers are attractive but not as showy as pelargonium "geranium." Borne singly or in clusters of 2 or 3, flowers have 5 overlapping petals, all alike in appearance. (Pelargonium flowers have 5 petals also, but 2 point in one direction, while other 3 point in opposite direction.) Colors include rose, blue, and purple; a few are pure pink or white. Leaves roundish or kidney shaped, lobed or deeply cut. Plants may be upright or trailing. Prefer full sun, but many tolerate light shade. Most need constant moisture for good performance. Good in rock gardens.

Geranium pratense

G. argenteum. Zones 1–6. To 3–5 in. high. Densely covered with silky, silvery hairs. Leaves basal, 5–7 lobed, 1 in. across. Flowers appear June–July: pink with darker veins, 1¼ in. across, with notched petals.

G. cinereum. All Zones. To 6 in. tall, much wider, with deeply cut dark green leaves and inch-wide pink flowers with darker veining. 'Ballerina' has lilac pink flowers with purple veining; blooms over a long summer season. Dormant in winter.

G. endressii. Zones 1–9, 14–24. Bushy, 1–1½ ft. high. Leaves 2–3 in. across, deeply cut in 5 lobes. Flowers rose pink, about 1 in. across; May–November.

G. himalayense *(G. grandiflorum).* All Zones. Wiry, branching stems 1–2 ft. high. Leaves roundish, 5 lobed, long stalked, 1¾ in. across. Flowers in clusters, lilac with purple veins and red purple eye, 1½–2 in. across. Blooms all summer.

G. incanum. Zones 14–24. South African trailing ground cover plant 6–10 in. high, spreading. Least hardy of true geraniums. Spreads fast to make wide cushions of finely cut leaves; 1-in.-wide flowers of magenta pink appear spring to fall. Affected by hard frost; evergreen where frosts are light. Cut back every 2–3 years to keep neat.

G. macrorrhizum. All Zones. Plants 8–10 in. tall, spreading by underground roots. Flowers are magenta red; 5–7-lobed leaves are fragrant and have attractive autumn tints. Good ground cover plant for small areas but can overwhelm delicate smaller plants. Pink- and white-flowered varieties exist.

G. pratense. All Zones. Common border perennial to 3 ft., branched above. Shiny green leaves, 3–6 in. across, cut in 7 deep lobes. Flowers about 1 in. wide, typically blue, red veined; often vary in color. Blooms June–August.

G. sanguineum. All Zones. Grows 1½ ft. high; trailing stems spread to 2 ft. Leaves roundish, 5–7 lobed, 1–2½ in. across; turn blood red in fall. Flowers deep purple to almost crimson, 1½ in. across. May–August bloom. Variety 'Prostratum' (*G. lancastriense*), neater, lower, more compact, has pure pink blooms.

G. wallichianum. Zones 1–9, 14–24. A foot tall and 3 ft. wide. Species has lilac flowers with a white eye; 'Buxton's Variety' has pure blue flowers. Blooms June to autumn.

GERBERA jamesonii. *Compositae.* TRANSVAAL DAISY. Perennial. Zones 8, 9, 12–24. Survives Zones 4–7 in cold frame with careful mulching, good drainage. House or greenhouse plant elsewhere. Native to South Africa. Most elegant and sophisticated of daisies. Lobed leaves to 10 in. long spring from root crowns which spread slowly to form big clumps. Slender-rayed, 4-in. daisies (one to a stem) rise directly from crowns on 1½-ft., erect or slightly curving stems. Colors range from cream through yellow to coral, orange, flame, and red. Flowers are first rate for arrangements; cut them as soon as fully open and slit an inch at bottom of stem before placing in water. Blooms any time of year with peaks in early summer, late fall.

Gerbera jamesonii

Best in full sun; partial shade in hottest areas. Needs good soil with excellent drainage. Where drainage is poor, grow in raised beds. Plant 2 ft. apart with crowns at least ¼ in. above surface. Protect against snails and slugs. Water deeply and prevent soil from washing over crowns, then allow soil to become nearly dry before watering again. Feed frequently. Keep old leaves picked off. Let plants remain until crowded; divide February–April, leaving 2 or 3 buds on each division. As house or greenhouse plant, grow in bright light with night temperature of 60°F.

Wild Transvaal daisy was orange red. Plants sold as hybrids are merely seedlings or divisions in mixed colors. Specialists have bred duplex and double strains. Duplex flowers have 2 rows of rays and are often larger (to 5–6 in. across) on taller (2–2½-ft.) stems. In doubles, all flowers are rays and flowers vary widely in form—some flat, some deep, some swirled, some bicolored. Happipot strain has 4-in. flowers on 6-in. stems. Double Parade strain has double flowers on 7–10-in. stems. Blackheart and Ebony Eyes strains have dark-centered flowers.

Plant as seedlings from flats, as divisions or clumps, or from cans. To grow your own from seed, sow thinly in sandy, peaty soil at 70°F. Water carefully; allow 4–6 weeks to sprout. Takes 6–18 months to flower. Seed must be fresh to germinate well; seed specialists can supply fresh seed of single, double, or duplex strains. Doubles come about 60 percent true from seed.

GERMANDER. See *Teucrium.*

GERMAN IVY. See *Senecio mikanioides.*

GERMAN VIOLET. See *Exacum affine.*

Gesneriaceae. The gesneriads are perennials, usually tropical or subtropical, grown for attractive flowers or foliage. Although a few are rock garden perennials, most are grown as house plants. African violet (*Saintpaulia*) and gloxinia (*Sinningia*) are examples.

GEUM. *Rosaceae.* Perennials. All Zones. Double, semidouble, or single flowers in bright orange, yellow, and red over long season (May to late summer) if dead blooms are removed. Foliage handsome; leaves divided into many leaflets. Plants evergreen except

G

in coldest winters. Borders, cut flowers.

Grow in sun (part shade where summers are hot). Ordinary garden soil and irrigation; need good drainage. Grow from seed sown in early spring, or divide plants in autumn or early spring.

Geum quellyon

G. 'Borisii'. Plants sold under this name make 6-in.-high mounds of foliage and have foot-high leafy stems with bright orange red flowers. Use in rock garden, front of border. True *G. borisii* has yellow flowers.

G. quellyon (often sold as *G. chiloense, G. coccineum*). Foliage mounds to 15 in. Leafy flowering stems to 2 ft.; flowers about 1½ in. wide. Varieties: 'Fire Opal', semidouble orange scarlet flowers; 'Lady Stratheden', double yellow; 'Mrs. Bradshaw', double scarlet; 'Princess Juliana', double copper.

GHOST GUM. See *Eucalyptus papuana, E. pauciflora*.

GIANT GARLIC. See Garlic.

GIANT REED. See *Arundo donax*.

GIANT SEQUOIA. See *Sequoiadendron giganteum*.

GILIA. *Polemoniaceae.* Summer annuals. Western natives related to phlox. Useful and colorful in wild garden or in borders. In early spring, sow seed in sunny spot, in open, well-drained soil. Thin plants to avoid crowding.

Gilia capitata

G. aggregata. See *Ipomopsis*.

G. capitata. BLUE THIMBLE FLOWER. Slender plants 8–30 in. tall. Finely cut leaves. Flowers pale blue to violet blue with blue pollen, in dense clusters like pincushions, ½–1½ in. across, June–October.

G. micrantha. See *Linanthus*.

G. rubra. See *Ipomopsis*.

G. tricolor. BIRD'S EYES. Branching plant ranging from 10–20 in. tall. Finely cut leaves. Flowers ½ in. wide or wider, carried single or in clusters of 2–5. Flower color varies from pale to deep violet in color, with yellow throat spotted purple; blue pollen. June–September.

GINGER. See *Zingiber officinale*.

GINGER LILY. See *Hedychium*.

GINKGO biloba. *Ginkgoaceae.* MAIDENHAIR TREE. Deciduous tree. Zones 1–9, 14–24. Graceful, hardy tree, attractive in any season, especially in fall when leathery, light green leaves of spring and summer suddenly turn gold. Fall leaves linger, then drop quickly and cleanly to make golden carpet where they fall. Related to conifers but differs in having broad (1–4-in.-wide), fan-shaped leaves rather than needlelike foliage. In shape and veining, leaves resemble leaflets of maidenhair fern, hence name. Can grow to 70–80 ft., but most mature trees are 35–50 ft. May be gawky in youth, but becomes well-proportioned with age—narrow to spreading or even umbrella shaped. Usually grows slowly, about 1 ft. a year, but under ideal conditions can grow up to 3 ft. a year.

Ginkgo biloba

Plant only male trees (grafted or grown from cuttings of male plants); female trees produce messy, fleshy, ill-smelling fruit in quantity. Named varieties listed below are reliably male. Use as street tree, lawn tree. Plant in deep, loose, well-drained soil. Be sure plant is not rootbound in can. Stake young trees to keep stem straight; young growth may be brittle, but wood becomes strong with age. Water through dry seasons until 10–20 ft. high, then let tree become self-sufficient. In general, ginkgos are not bothered by insects or diseases. They are resistant to oak root fungus.

G. b. 'Autumn Gold'. Upright, eventually rather broad.

G. b. 'Fairmount'. Fast-growing, pyramidal form. Straighter main stem than 'Autumn Gold', requires less staking and tying.

GLADIOLUS. *Iridaceae.* Corms. All Zones. All have sword-shaped leaves and tubular flowers, often flaring or ruffled, in simple or branching, usually one-sided spikes. Extremely wide color range. Bloom from spring to fall, depending on kind and on time of planting. Superb cut flowers. Good in borders or beds behind mounding plants that cover lower parts of stems, or in large containers with low annuals at base. Plant in sun in rich, sandy soil.

Gladiolus hybrid

G. callianthus *(Acidanthera bicolor)*. Grows 2–3 ft. tall, with 2–10 fragrant, creamy white flowers marked chocolate brown on lower segments. Flowers 2–3 in. wide, 4–5 in. long. Variety 'Murielae' is taller, with purple crimson blotches. Both are excellent cut flowers. Same culture as garden gladiolus.

Gladiolus callianthus

G. colvillei. BABY GLADIOLUS. Red and yellow hybrid, notable as ancestor of hybrid race called baby gladiolus. Latter have flaring, 2½–3¼-in. flowers in short, loose spikes on 1½-ft. stems. Flowers white, pink, red, or lilac, solid or blotched with contrasting color. May be left in ground from year to year and will form large clumps in border or among shrubs. Plant 4 in. deep, in October–November for May–June bloom in mild-winter areas (June–July in Northwest).

G. hortulanus. GARDEN GLADIOLUS. Commonly grown garden gladiolus are a complex group of hybrids derived by variation and hybridization from several species. These are the best-known gladiolus, with widest color range—white, cream, buff, yellow, orange, apricot, salmon, red shades, rose, lavender, purple, smoky shades, and, more recently, green shades. Individual blooms are occasionally as large as 8 in. across. Stems are 4–6 ft. tall.

Newer varieties of garden gladiolus, up to 5 ft. tall, have sturdier spikes bearing 12–14 open flowers at a time. They are better garden plants than older varieties and stand upright without staking. Another group, called miniature gladiolus, grows 3 ft. tall, with spikes of 15–20 flowers 2½–3 in. wide; useful in gardens and for cutting. All varieties of garden gladiolus combine nicely in borders with delphiniums, Shasta daisies, gypsophila, perennial phlox.

High-crowned corms, 1½–2 in. wide, are more productive than older, larger corms (over 2 in. wide). Plant as early as possible to avoid damage by thrips. In frostless areas along southern California coast, plant nearly all year. Along most of coast, growers plant every 15 days from January–March for succession of bloom. In Zones 12, 13, plant November–February to avoid heat during bloom. Plant April–June in Northwest, May–June where winters are severe. Corms bloom 65–100 days after planting.

If soil is poor, mix in complete fertilizer or superphosphate (4 lbs. per 100 sq. ft.) before planting; do not place fertilizer in direct contact with corms. Treat with bulb dust (insecticide-fungicide) before planting. Set corms about 4 times deeper than their height, somewhat less in heavy soils. Space big corms 6 in. apart, smaller ones 4 in. When plants have 5 leaves, apply complete fertilizer 6 in. from plants, water in thoroughly. Water regularly during growth. Control thrips and mites as necessary.

Cut flower spikes when lowest buds begin to open; keep at least 4 leaves on plants to build up corms. Dig corms when foliage starts to yellow; cut tops off just above corms. (In rainy areas, growers dig corms while leaves are still green to avoid botrytis infection.) Destroy tops; dry corms in shaded, ventilated area. In about 3 weeks, pull off old corms and roots, dust new corms with diazinon, and store at 40°–50°F. in single layers in flats or ventilated trays.

G. primulinus. This 3-ft.-tall African species with hooded, primrose yellow flowers is rarely grown, but the name has been applied to its hybrids with other tall and miniature gladiolus. Strain called Butterfly gladiolus also belongs here. Flowers medium sized, frilled, with satiny sheen, vivid markings in throat. Strong, wiry 2-ft. stems bear as many as 20 flowers; 6–8 open at a time. Colors include bright and pastel shades and pure white.

G. tristis. Dainty gladiolus with 2½–3-in. flowers on slender 1½-ft. stems. Blooms creamy to yellowish white, veined purple; fragrant at night. *G. t. concolor* has soft yellow to nearly white flowers. Blooms March and April; hardy except in severe winters. Plant corms October–November.

GLAUCIUM. *Papaveraceae.* HORNED POPPY, SEA POPPY. Annuals or perennials. Grow to about 2 ft. Gray green leaves, lobed or finely cut. Individual flowers 2 in. wide, cup shaped, 4 petaled; they are short lived, but bloom season continues June–August. Flowers followed by unusually long (to 1 ft.), slender seed capsules. Grow in full sun with other gray plants or with succulents. Fairly drought tolerant.

Glaucium flavum

G. corniculatum. Summer annual. Orange red flowers with dark spot at base.

G. flavum. YELLOW HORNED POPPY. Perennial or biennial, Zones 8–24; grows as annual elsewhere. Orange to brilliant yellow flowers look varnished. Cut back to new basal leaves once a year.

GLECHOMA hederacea *(Nepeta hederacea)*. *Labiatae.* GROUND IVY. Perennial. All Zones; evergreen where winters seldom dip below 20°F. Trailing plant with neat pairs of round, scalloped, bright green or white-edged leaves 1½ in. across, spaced along stems. Small, trumpet-shaped blue flowers in spring and summer not especially showy. Sometimes planted as small-scale ground cover or used to trail from hanging basket. To 3 in. tall with stems trailing to 1½ ft., rooting at joints. Can become pest in lawns.

Glechoma hederacea

GLEDITSIA triacanthos. *Leguminosae.* HONEY LOCUST. Deciduous tree. Zones 1–16, 18–20. Fast growing with upright trunk and spreading, arching branches. To 35–70 ft. Leaves divided into many oval, ¾–1½-in.-long leaflets. Late to leaf out; leaves turn yellow and drop early in fall. Inconspicuous flowers followed by broad, 1–1½-ft.-long pods filled with sweetish pulp and roundish, hard seeds.

Tolerant of acid or alkaline conditions; hardy to cold, heat, wind, some drought. Seems to do best in districts with sharply defined winters, hot summers. Good desert tree. A pod gall midge deforms leaves in some areas. No effective control.

Gleditsia triacanthos

Good lawn tree. Leafs out late and goes dormant early, giving grass added sunlight in spring and fall. Small leaflets dry up and filter into grass, decreasing raking chores. Stake until good basic branch pattern is established. Not good in narrow area between curb and sidewalk: roots on old plants will heave paving. Don't plant if you need dense shade over long season.

Trunks and branches of species are formidably thorny, and pods make a mess; several garden varieties of *G. t. inermis* are thornless, have few or no pods.

'Halka'. Fast growing, forms sturdy trunk early, has strong horizontal branching pattern.

'Imperial'. Tall, spreading, symmetrical tree to about 35 ft. More densely foliaged than other forms; gives heavier shade.

'Moraine'. MORAINE LOCUST. Best known. Fast-growing, spreading tree with branches angled upward, then outward. Subject to wind breakage.

'Rubylace'. Deep red new growth. Subject to wind breakage.

'Shademaster'. More upright and faster growing than 'Moraine'—to 24 ft. tall, 16 ft. wide in 6 years.

'Skyline'. Pyramidal and symmetrical.

'Sunburst'. Golden yellow new foliage. Looks unhealthy unless combined with dark green or bronzy foliage. Defoliates easily in response to temperature changes, drought. Wind breakage. Showy against background of deep green foliage.

'Trueshade'. Rounded head of light green foliage.

GLOBE AMARANTH. See *Gomphrena*.

GLOBEFLOWER. See *Trollius*.

GLOBE LILY, WHITE. See *Calochortus albus*.

GLOBE THISTLE. See *Echinops exaltatus*.

GLOBE TULIP, PURPLE. See *Calochortus amoenus*.

GLORIOSA DAISY. See *Rudbeckia hirta*.

GLORIOSA rothschildiana. *Liliaceae.* GLORY LILY, CLIMBING LILY. Outdoors in Zone 24; anywhere as greenhouse or summer container plant. Native to tropical Africa. Climbs to 6 ft. by tendrils on leaf tips. Lance-shaped leaves 5–7 in. long. Lilylike flowers 4 in. across with 6 wavy-edged, curved, brilliant red segments banded with yellow. Grow in light shade on terrace, patio; train on trellis or frame.

Gloriosa rothschildiana

Set tuberous root horizontally about 4 in. deep in light, spongy soil. Start indoors or in greenhouse in February; set out after frosts. Keep moist; feed with liquid fertilizer every 3 weeks. Dry off gradually in fall; store in pot, or lift tubers and store over winter. May survive outdoors in mild-winter areas, but likely to rot in cold, wet soil. All parts of the plant—especially the tubers—are poisonous.

GLORYBOWER. See *Clerodendrum*.

GLORY LILY. See *Gloriosa rothschildiana*.

GLORY-OF-THE-SNOW. See *Chionodoxa*.

GLORY OF THE SUN. See *Leucocoryne ixioides*.

GLOXINIA. See *Sinningia speciosa*.

GODETIA. See *Clarkia.*

GOLDBACK FERN. See *Pityrogramma.*

GOLDEN BRODIAEA. See *Triteleia ixioides.*

GOLDEN CANDLE. See *Pachystachys lutea.*

GOLDENCHAIN TREE. See *Laburnum.*

GOLDEN CUP. See *Hunnemannia fumariifolia.*

GOLDEN DEWDROP. See *Duranta repens.*

GOLDEN DROPS. See *Onosma tauricum.*

GOLDEN EARDROPS. See *Dicentra chrysantha.*

GOLDEN FAIRY LANTERN. See *Calochortus amabilis.*

GOLDEN FLEECE. See *Dyssodia tenuiloba.*

GOLDEN FRAGRANCE. See *Pittosporum napaulense.*

GOLDEN GARLIC. See *Allium moly.*

GOLDEN GLOW. See *Rudbeckia laciniata* 'Hortensia'.

GOLDEN LARCH. See *Pseudolarix kaempferi.*

GOLDEN MARGUERITE. See *Anthemis tinctoria.*

GOLDENRAIN TREE. See *Koelreuteria paniculata.*

GOLDENROD. See *Solidago.*

GOLDEN TRUMPET TREE. See *Tabebuia chrysotricha.*

GOLDEN WONDER SENNA. See *Cassia splendida.*

GOLDFISH PLANT. See *Alloplectus nummularia.*

GOLD MEDALLION TREE. See *Cassia leptophylla.*

GOMPHRENA. *Amaranthaceae.* GLOBE AMARANTH. Annuals. All Zones. Stiffly branching plants 9 in.–2 ft. tall, covered in summer and fall with rounded, papery, cloverlike heads ¾–1 in. wide. These may be dried quickly and easily, retaining color and shape for winter arrangements. Narrow oval leaves are 2–4 in. long.

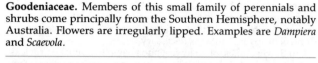

Gomphrena globosa

G. globosa. White, pink, lavender, or purple flower heads top 1-ft. stems. Dwarf varieties for use as edging or bedding plants are 9-in. 'Buddy' (purple) and 'Cissy' (white). 'Strawberry Fields' grows 2 ft. tall, has 1½-in. heads. Planted closely in large pots—6 to a shallow 10-in. pot—makes a long-lasting living bouquet.

G. haageana. To 2 ft. tall, with heads of tightly clustered, bright orange bracts that resemble inch-wide pine cones. Tiny yellow flowers peep from the bracts. Sold as 'Haageana Aurea' or simply 'Orange'.

Goodeniaceae. Members of this small family of perennials and shrubs come principally from the Southern Hemisphere, notably Australia. Flowers are irregularly lipped. Examples are *Dampiera* and *Scaevola.*

GOOSEBERRY. *Saxifragaceae.* For ornamental relatives, see *Ribes.* Deciduous shrub. Zones 1–6, 17. Same culture as currant. Grown for pies, canning. Lobed, somewhat maplelike leaves. Fruit often striped longitudinally, decorative. 'Oregon Champion', 3–5-ft. thorny bush, is the preferred variety; green fruit. 'Pixwell', extremely hardy and with few thorns, has pink fruit. 'Poorman', favorite in Zones 1–3, has red fruit sweet enough to eat off bush. 'Welcome', as hardy as 'Poorman', has medium large, dull red fruit with tart flavor; plants are productive, nearly spineless.

Gooseberry

GOOSE PLANT. See *Asclepias fruticosa.*

GOOSE PLUM. See *Prunus americana.*

GOPHER PLANT. See *Euphorbia lathyris.*

GORDONIA alatamaha. See *Franklinia alatamaha.*

GOURD. *Cucurbitaceae.* Summer annual vine. Many plants produce gourds; most commonly planted are the following: 1) *Cucurbita pepo ovifera,* YELLOW-FLOWERED GOURD. Produces great majority of small ornamental gourds in many shapes and sizes. These may be all one color or striped. 2) *Luffa aegyptiaca,* DISH CLOTH GOURD, VEGETABLE SPONGE GOURD. Also has yellow flowers. Bears cylindrical gourds 1–2 ft. long, fibrous interior of which may be used in place of sponge or cloth for scrubbing and bathing. 3) *Lagenaria siceraria (L. vulgaris),* WHITE-FLOWERED GOURD. Bears gourds 3 in.–3 ft. long. May be round, bottle shaped, dumbbell shaped, crooknecked, coiled, or spoon shaped.

Gourd

All grow fast and will reach 10–15 ft. Sow seeds in full sun, when ground is warm. Start indoors if growing season is short. Gourds need all the summer heat they can get to develop fruit by frost. If planting for ornamental gourd harvest, give vines wire or trellis support to hold ripening individual fruits off ground. Plant seedlings 2 ft. apart or thin seedlings to same spacing. Give deep regular watering. Harvest when vines are dry. Cut some stem with each gourd so you can hang it up to dry slowly in cool, airy spot. When thoroughly dry, preserve with coating of paste wax, lacquer, or shellac.

GOUTWEED. See *Aegopodium podagraria.*

GRAMA GRASS, BLUE. See *Bouteloua gracilis.*

Gramineae. The grass family is undoubtedly the most important plant family in terms of usefulness to man. All the important grains and pastures in the world are grasses; the bamboos (giant grasses) are useful in building and crafts. Many grasses are used as lawns or as ornamental annual or perennial plants. (Some botanists use *Poaceae* as the family name for grasses.)

GRANJENO. See *Celtis pallida.*

GRAPE. Deciduous vine. All Zones (but see limitations in chart). For fruit, wine, shade. Single grapevine can produce enough new growth every year to arch over a walk, roof an arbor, form leafy wall, or put umbrella of shade over deck or terrace. Grape is one of few ornamental vines with dominant trunk and branch pattern for winter interest, bold-textured foliage, and colorful, edible fruit.

Grape

To get quality fruit you must choose a variety that fits your climate, train it carefully, and prune it regularly.

Two basic classes are: European (*Vitis vinifera*)–tight skin, winelike flavor, generally high heat requirements, cold tolerance to about 5°F.; and American (*V. labrusca*)—slipskin, "foxy" Concord-type flavor, moderate summer heat requirements, cold tolerance well below 0°F. Hybrids between classes are available; most are reasonably hardy, fall between parents in flavor.

Choosing the right variety is important, since varieties differ widely in hardiness and in heat requirements. Northwest is primarily American grape country; long warm-season areas of California, Arizona favor European varieties. Short-season, high-elevation areas must choose from American grapes.

Ideal climate for most table grapes in California is that of California's Central Valley—a long season of high heat. Ideal climate in Northwest is in warmest parts of Columbia Basin. If your climate is cooler, or if growing season is shorter than ideal, look to *early-ripening* varieties.

Mildew is serious disease of European grapes (most American varieties are immune). To control, dust vines with sulfur when shoots are 6 in. long, again when they are 12–15 in., then every 2 weeks until harvest. Vines growing near lawns may need additional dustings.

To control grape leafhopper in California, add diazinon dust to sulfur at time of third sulfur dusting, just before blooming time. In Northwest, dust with diazinon in June and again in August. Grape mealybugs may infest vines in Northwest. Control with dormant oil spray in late winter and with malathion in June.

GRAPEFRUIT. See *Citrus*.

GRAPE HYACINTH. See *Muscari*.

GRAPE IVY. See *Cissus rhombifolia*.

Grape

VARIETY	ZONES	SEASON	PRUNING	REMARKS
AMERICAN & AMERICAN HYBRID VARIETIES				
'Agawam'	2, 3, 7	Midseason to late.	Cane.	Pinkish red, aromatic, slightly foxy. Keeps well after picking. Some winter injury in coldest areas.
'Black Spanish'	1–3, 10, 11	Early midseason.	Cane.	Heavy annual producer of small black berries for juice, jelly. Tough, disease resistant.
'Brilliant'	1–3, 10, 11	Very early.	Cane.	Light to dark red berries good for eating fresh. Very large leaves make it a good arbor vine.
'Caco'	1–3, 7	Midseason to late.	Cane.	Light red berries. Aromatic and vinous in flavor. Thick skinned. Good for arbors. Hardy, thrifty.
'California Concord' (See **'Pierce'**)				
'Campbell Early' ('Island Belle')	2–7, 17	Early.	Cane.	Dark purplish black with heavy bloom. High quality. Lacks foxy taste. Vine moderately vigorous. Excellent 'Concord' type where too cool for 'Concord'.
'Canadice'	1–17	Early.	Cane.	Hardy vine produces small, tight clusters of seedless red fruit with mild 'Concord' flavor.
'Champanel'	1–14	Early.	Cane.	Large blue black grape that holds well on vine. Takes heat, drought, alkaline soil.
'Concord'	1–3, 6–9, 14–16, 18–21	Midseason. Late in Northwest.	Cane.	Standard American slipskin. California's dry hot-summer areas are not to its liking. Fruit inferior to that grown in Northwest.
'Concord Seedless'	1–3, 6–9	Midseason to late.	Cane.	Smaller berries than 'Concord', not as vigorous a vine.
'Diamond' ('White Diamond')	3, 5–7, 17	Early midseason.	Cane.	Round, medium-sized, yellowish green berries of high quality. Slightly aromatic. Pleasantly tart. Vine fairly vigorous, very productive.
'Fredonia'	1–7, 17	Early.	Cane.	Large black berries with thick, tough skin. Similar to 'Concord' but larger. Vigorous vine, clean foliage. Excellent for arbors.
'George'	1–14	Early.	Cane.	Large blue black grape with pronounced 'Concord' flavor.
'Glenora'	1–7, 17	Early.	Cane.	Crisp, blue black, seedless berries in tight clusters.
'Golden Muscat' (American hybrid)	1–3, 6–9, 11–24	Early midseason.	Cane.	Golden green, with slipskin of American grapes but with Muscat flavor. Hybrid of 'Muscat' and green American grape, 'Diamond'. Vigorous.

(Continued on next page)

G

VARIETY	ZONES	SEASON	PRUNING	REMARKS
AMERICAN & AMERICAN HYBRID VARIETIES *(Continued from previous page)*				
'Himrod' ('Himrod Seedless') (American hybrid)	1–3, 5–7	Very early.	Cane.	Resembles 'Interlaken Seedless'.
'Interlaken Seedless' (American hybrid)	1–7	Very early.	Cane.	Small, sweet, crisp, firm, greenish white berries. Tight skinned. Excellent flavor. Vine moderately vigorous, productive.
'Lakemont'	1–3, 5–7	Early.	Cane.	Seedless white grape with large clusters of medium-sized berries.
'Moored'	1–7, 17	Early.	Cane.	Medium to large red grape with light gray bloom. Vigorous, productive, disease resistant.
'Moore Early'	1–3, 6, 7	Early.	Cane.	Medium clusters of large berries.
'Niabell'	7–9, 14–16, 18–22	Early.	Spur or cane.	Large black berries similar to 'Concord' at its best. Excellent arbor grape. Vigorous and productive in wide range of climates. Succeeds in hot interiors where 'Concord' fails.
'Niagara'	3, 6, 7	Midseason.	Cane.	Large, full clusters of medium to large green gold berries. Sweet and juicy with strong foxy flavor. Attractive, vigorous vine, excellent for arbors.
'Pierce'	7–9, 14–16, 18–21	Midseason.	Cane.	Called 'California Concord'. Berries larger, vine more vigorous than 'Concord'. Stands high heat better than 'Concord'.
'Romulus' (American hybrid)	3, 6, 7	Late midseason.	Cane.	Yellow seedless berries similar to 'Interlaken Seedless' but 2 weeks later. Moderate vigor but productive.
'Schuyler' (American hybrid)	3, 5–7	Early.	Spur or cane.	Medium-sized blue berries in large clusters. Very sweet and juicy. Vigorous and productive.
'Seneca'	1–7, 17	Very early.	Cane.	Sweet, aromatic, high-quality white berries. Skin thin and tender, adhering to pulp. Bunches sometimes loose; not heavy yielder.
'Suffolk Red'	1–7, 17	Early.	Cane.	Seedless red grape with fine flavor. Fruit holds well on vine. Slight susceptibility to mildew.
EUROPEAN VARIETIES				
'Black Monukka'	3, 7–9, 11–21	Early midseason.	Cane or spur.	Medium-sized reddish black seedless berries in large, loose clusters. Popular home variety. One of hardiest European grapes.
'Cardinal'	8, 9, 11–16, 18–21	Early.	Spur, short cane.	Large, deep red, firm, crisp. Slight 'Muscat' flavor when fully ripe. Heavy bearer. Thin some flower clusters off when shoots are 1–1½ ft. long.
'Csaba' ('Pearl of Csaba')	3, 6	Very early.	Spur.	Small to medium, yellowish white, moderately firm, some 'Muscat' flavor. One of hardiest European types. Grown in central Washington.
'Emperor'	8, 9, 18, 19	Late.	Cane or spur.	Large, reddish, very firm, crisp and crunchy. Neutral flavor.
'Flame' ('Flame Seedless')	6–9, 12–21	Early.	Cane.	Medium-sized, light to medium red seedless grapes. Crisp, productive.
'Italia' ('Italian Muscat')	8, 9, 11–14, 18–20	Midseason.	Spur.	Large amber yellow berries. Crisp, with sweet 'Muscat' flavor, tender skin.
'Lady Finger'	8, 9, 11–14, 18–20	Late midseason.	Cane.	Two varieties share this name: 'Olivette Blanche' and 'Rish Baba'. Grapes are greenish white, long, slender, with mild, sweet flavor.
'Muscat' ('Muscat of Alexandria')	8, 9, 11–14, 18–19	Late midseason.	Spur.	Large, green to amber, round berries in loose clusters. Strongly aromatic. Renowned for its sweet, musky, aged-in-the-vat flavor.
'Perlette'	3, 7–16, 18–21	Early.	Spur.	Earlier, larger, less sweet than 'Thompson Seedless'. Needs far less heat than most European varieties.
'Ruby Seedless' ('King's Ruby')	8, 9, 12–16, 18–20	Late midseason.	Spur or cane.	Large clusters of small to medium, red to reddish black seedless berries. Sweet as dessert fruit; make good raisins.
'Thompson Seedless'	8, 9, 11–14, 18, 19	Early to midseason.	Cane.	Small, sweet, mild flavored, greenish amber in big bunches. Widely planted but top quality in warm interior areas only.
'Tokay'	8, 9, 14–16, 18–20	Late midseason.	Spur.	Brilliant red to dark red. Crackling crisp with distinctive winy flavor. Reaches perfection where summer heat is high but not excessive—Zone 14.

Grape Pruning

1. ***December–March. Dig deep hole. Plant rooted cutting from nursery; leave only top bud exposed. Set stake for training. Mound soil over bud. Object is to secure deep rooting.***

2. ***First year: Let vine sprawl, develop as many leaves as possible to manufacture food for the developing roots. This growth made by November. Leaves have fallen.***

3. ***First winter: Prune vine to sturdiest cane; shorten it to 3 lowest buds. If cane is very vigorous, cut it at 2–3 ft., or at a good point for branching for arbor.***

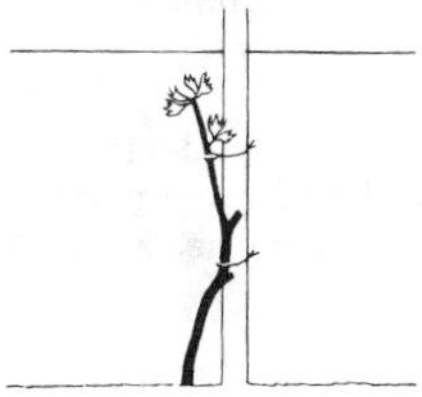

4. ***Second spring: When new shoots are 6–8 in. long, select 1 vigorous, upright shoot to form permanent trunk. Tie it loosely to the stake. Cut out all other shoots.***

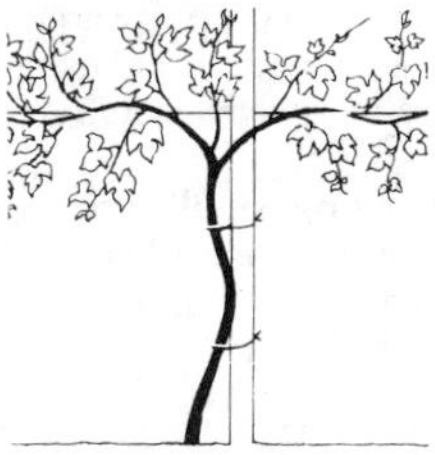

5. ***Second summer: When shoot reaches branching point, pinch out tip. Allow 2 strongest subsequent shoots to develop. Pinch out side shoots at 10 in.***

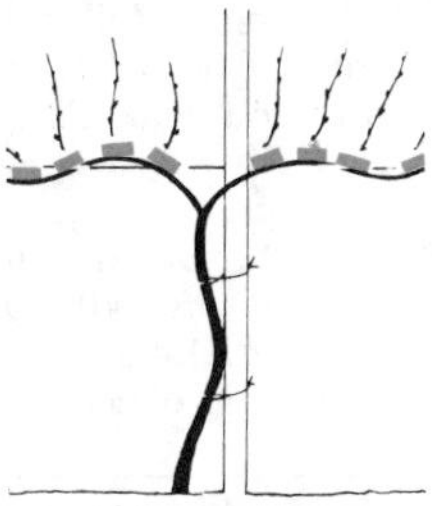

6. ***Third winter: Cut spindly canes on arms back to old wood. Don't prune yet for fruit production; vines are too immature. For fruit, leave 2 buds on each cane.***

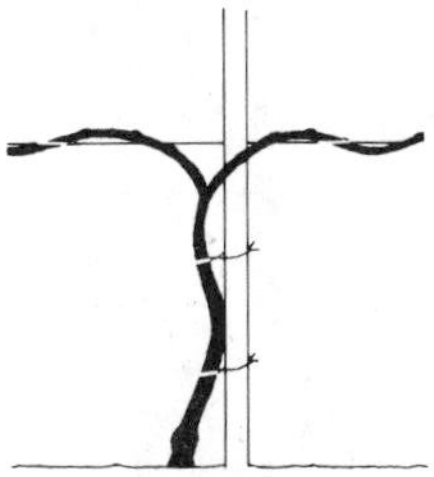

7. ***Third winter's finished product. On an arbor, arms would stretch out along roof level of structure. Length of arms determines size and permanent frame.***

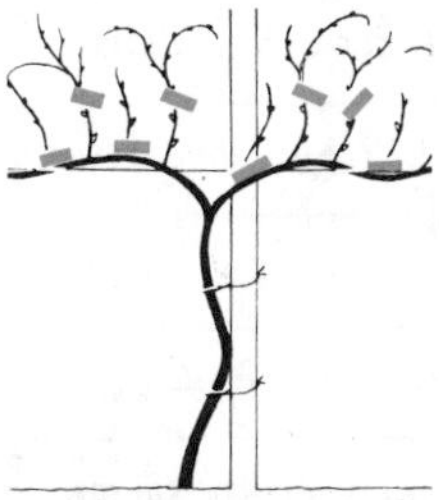

8. ***Fourth winter: These canes grew previous summer. To prune for fruit, cut out weak or crowding canes. Select sturdy canes 6–10 in. apart, cut each to 2 buds.***

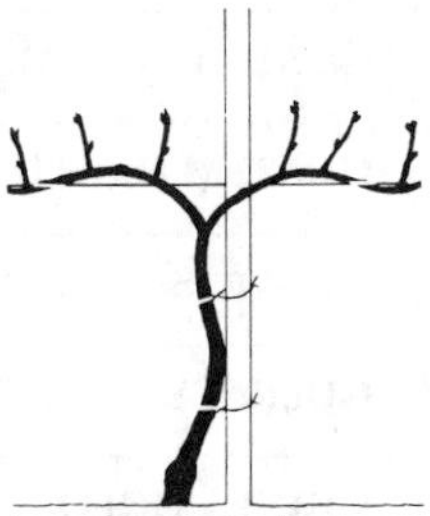

9. ***Fourth winter's finished product. Each bud will give 2 fruiting canes next summer. Following winter cut 1 out entirely, shorten the other to 2 buds. See Nos. 10, 11.***

10. ***Fifth winter: These canes bore fruit the previous autumn. Cut 1 off at base. Branch at left already pruned. These short, thick branches are called spurs.***

11. ***Fifth winter: Shorten remaining cane to 2 buds. These will give next year's fruiting canes. Pruning in subsequent years is the same.***

12. ***Well-pruned arm in its fifth year should look like this. Fruit spurs spaced approximately 6 in. apart, with 2 buds on each new cane at end of spurs.***

GRAPTOPETALUM. *Crassulaceae.* Succulents. Zones 8–24. Native to Mexico. Leaves very thick, in loosely packed, elongated rosettes. Full sun. Need little water. Good looking in pots or in rock gardens in mildest regions. Leaves have subtle, opalescent blending of colors. Detached leaves root easily.

Graptopetalum paraguayense

G. amethystinum. Stems to 4 in. tall, eventually leaning or sprawling. Leaves bluish gray with pinkish purple overcast.

G. paraguayense. Leaves whitish gray with pinkish overcast, thickly borne on stem to 7 in. tall.

GRASSES. *Gramineae.* The grasses in this book are either lawn or ornamental plants—except for corn, the only cereal commonly grown in home gardens. They are described under entries headed by their botanical names; to find these, check lists below. (Two lawns are not grasses: see *Dichondra* and *Phyla*. All bamboos, which are grasses, are charted under Bamboo.)

Lawn grasses are *Agropyron*, WHEAT GRASS; *Agrostis*, BENT GRASS, REDTOP; *Bouteloua*, BLUE GRAMA GRASS; *Buchloe*, BUFFALO GRASS; *Cynodon*, BERMUDA GRASS; *Festuca*, FESCUE; *Lolium*, RYEGRASS; *Poa*, BLUEGRASS; *Stenotaphrum*, ST. AUGUSTINE GRASS; *Zoysia*, ZOYSIA.

Ornamental grasses are: *Arundo*, GIANT REED; *Briza*, RATTLESNAKE GRASS; *Chasmanthium*, SEA OATS; *Coix*, JOB'S TEARS; *Cortaderia*, PAMPAS GRASS; *Festuca*, FESCUE; *Hakonechloa*, JAPANESE FOREST GRASS; *Helictotrichon*, BLUE OAT GRASS; *Imperata*, JAPANESE BLOOD GRASS; *Milium effusum* 'Aureum', BOWLES' GOLDEN GRASS; *Miscanthus*; *Pennisetum*, FOUNTAIN GRASS; *Phalaris*, RIBBON GRASS; and *Stipa*, GIANT FEATHER GRASS.

GRASS NUT. See *Triteleia laxa*.

GRASS TREE. See *Xanthorrhoea*.

GRECIAN LAUREL. See *Laurus nobilis*.

GREEN CARPET. See *Herniaria glabra*.

GREVILLEA. *Proteaceae.* Evergreen shrubs, trees. Native to Australia. New species and hybrids appear frequently. Plants vary in size and appearance, but generally have fine-textured foliage and long, slender, curved flowers, usually in dense clusters.

The grevilleas described below are all good garden plants; some of the newer arrivals may prove equally good, but many cannot tolerate salt-laden soils, poor water quality, and heavy summer irrigation. Still, most are attractive enough to warrant some risk-taking.

Grevillea robusta

The plants listed here all take full sun. Once established, they take poor, rocky, dry soil, but accept ordinary well-drained garden soil. Most are very drought tolerant. Rarely successful near lawns.

G. banksii (often sold as *G. banksii forsteri*). Shrub or small tree. Zones 20–24. To 15–20 ft. Leaves 4–10 in. long, deeply cut into narrow lobes. Erect, 3–6-in.-long clusters of dark red flowers bloom sporadically throughout the year, heaviest in late spring. Showy used singly against high wall, near entryway, or grouped with other big-scale shrubs. Freezes at 24°F.; takes wind, drought.

G. 'Canberra'. Shrub. Zones 8–9, 12–24. Open, graceful growth to 8 ft. tall, 12 ft. wide. Bright green, needlelike, 1-in. leaves. Clusters of red flowers in spring and intermittently at other times.

G. 'Constance'. Zones 8, 9, 12–24. Resembles 'Canberra' but broader in growth. Orange red flowers in large clusters.

(Continued on next page)

G

G. juniperina *(G. sulphurea).* Shrub. Zones 8, 9, 12–24. To 6 ft., with needlelike, bright green leaves, ½–1 in. long; clusters of pale yellow flowers in May and June.

G. lanigera. WOOLLY GREVILLEA. Shrub. Zones 15–24. Spreading, mounding plant 3–6 ft. tall, 6–10 ft. across. Closely set, narrow, ½-in.-long leaves; general foliage effect gray green. Clusters of narrow, curved, crimson and cream flowers profusely carried in summer; attractive to hummingbirds. Good bank cover in hot, sunny areas; good transition between garden and wild areas.

G. 'Noellii'. Shrub. Zones 8, 9, 12–24. Plant sold under this name reported to be a hybrid. To 4 ft. tall, 4–5 ft. wide. Densely foliaged; narrow, 1-in.-long, medium green glossy leaves. Clusters of pink and white flowers bloom for 6–8 weeks in early and mid-spring. Takes more water than *G. lanigera;* less drought resistant.

Grevillea 'Noellii'

G. robusta. SILK OAK. Tree. Zones 8, 9, 12–24. Fast growing to 50–60 (rarely 100) ft. Symmetrical, pyramidal when young. Old trees broad topped, picturesque against skyline, usually with a few heavy, horizontal limbs. Fernlike leaves are golden green to deep green above, silvery beneath. Heavy leaf fall in spring, sporadic leaf drop throughout year; frequent raking necessary. Large clusters of bright golden orange flowers in early spring; effective with jacaranda or with dark green background foliage.

Grows in poor, compact soils if not overwatered; takes fair amount of water in fast-draining soils. Brittle, easily damaged in high wind. Stake securely. To make sturdier branches and lessen wind damage, cut leading shoot back hard at planting time, shorten branches to well-balanced framework. Thrives in heat. Young trees damaged at 24°F.; older plants hardy to 16°F.

Use for quick, tall screening or clip as tall hedge. One of lushest greens for low desert. Fast shade producer, showy tree for unused space far from hose bibb. Good temporary tree while you wait for slower, tougher-wooded tree to grow up.

G. rosmarinifolia. ROSEMARY GREVILLEA. Compact shrub to 6 ft. tall, nearly as broad. Zones 8, 9, 12–24. Narrow, dark green, 1½-in.-long leaves (silvery beneath) somewhat like those of rosemary. Red and cream flower clusters (rarely pink or white) in fall and winter; scattered bloom in other seasons. Use as clipped or unclipped hedge in dryish places. Impervious to heat and drought.

G. sulphurea. See *G. juniperina.*

G. thelemanniana. HUMMINGBIRD BUSH, SPIDER-NET GREVILLEA. Shrub. Zones 9, 14–17, 19–24. Graceful, rounded, 5–8 ft. tall, equally wide. Dark green leaves 1–2 in. long, divided into very narrow segments. Bright red flower clusters tipped yellow. Can bloom at any season. Water plants until established, then taper off. Somewhat temperamental. Plants airier, more open, less adapted to hedge and screen use than *G. rosmarinifolia.*

G. tridentifera. Shrub. Zones 14–24. To 6 ft. tall and broader, with bright green, 3-pronged needlelike leaves; small, white, honey-scented flower clusters. Good bank cover.

GREWIA occidentalis (usually sold as *G. caffra*). *Tiliaceae.* LAVENDER STARFLOWER. Evergreen shrub. Zones 8, 9, 14–24. Native to South Africa. Fast-growing, sprawling habit. Tends to branch freely in flat pattern, making natural espalier if given some support. Becomes dense with pinching and pruning. Grows 6–10 ft. tall (sometimes higher), with equal spread if unstaked.

Deep green, oblong, finely toothed leaves 3 in. long. Flowers are 1 in. wide, starlike, lavender pink with yellow centers. Blooms late spring with scattered bloom into autumn, especially if pruned after first heavy bloom.

Plant against warm, sunny wall or fence. Can be planted 2 ft. apart and used as tall clipped hedge or screen. If upright growth is pruned out, can be used as bank cover. Can be trained and staked to make single-trunked tree or tied in place to cover arbor or trellis. Takes wind well. Needs water; needs iron if chlorotic. If plants become too large or woody for their situation, cut back hard, keeping 1 or 2 young basal branches to grow on for new framework.

Grewia occidentalis

GRISELINIA. *Cornaceae.* Evergreen shrubs. Zones 9, 15–17, 20–24. Native to New Zealand. Upright form and thick, leathery, lustrous leaves. Flowers and fruit are insignificant. Always look well groomed. Good near swimming pools.

G. littoralis. A 50-ft. tree in New Zealand, but usually seen in California as 10-ft.-high shrub of equal spread. Leaves roundish, 4 in. long. In full sun with ample water it can reach 8 ft. in 3 years. Dense, compact screen or windbreak. Fine beach plant. Good espalier. Variety 'Variegata' has leaves marked with cream.

Griselinia littoralis

G. lucida. Slower growing, smaller, more open and slender than *G. littoralis,* with larger, 7-in.-long leaves. Excellent foliage plant for partial shade. Thrives in container. Variety 'Variegata' has white markings on leaves.

GROUND CHERRY. See *Physalis pruinosa.*

GROUND IVY. See *Glechoma hederacea.*

GROUND MORNING GLORY. See *Convolvulus mauritanicus.*

GRU-GRU PALM. See *Acrocomia.*

GUADALUPE PALM. See *Brahea edulis.*

GUATEMALAN HOLLY. See *Olmediella betschlerana.*

GUAVA. See *Psidium.*

GUERNSEY LILY. See *Nerine sarniensis.*

GUINEA GOLD VINE. See *Hibbertia scandens.*

GUM. See *Eucalyptus.*

GUM MYRTLE. See *Angophora costata.*

GUNNERA. *Gunneraceae.* Perennials. Zones 4–6, 14–17, 20–24. Big, bold, awe-inspiring plants to 8 ft. high, with giant leaves (4–8 ft. across) on stiff-haired stalks 4–6 ft. long. Leaves are conspicuously veined, with lobed and cut edges. Given space (they need plenty) and necessary care, these plants can be the ultimate summertime conversation pieces. New sets of leaves grow each spring. In mild-winter areas, old leaves remain green for more than a year. Elsewhere, leaves die back completely in winter. Corncoblike 1½-ft. flower clusters form close to roots. Tiny fruits are red.

Gunnera tinctoria

Part shade. Soil must be rich in nutrients and organic material, continually moist (but never soggy around the root crown). Feed 3 times a year, beginning when new growth starts, to keep leaves maximum size. Give overhead sprinkling when humidity is low or drying winds occur. Use plants where they can be focal point in summer—beside a pool or dominating a bed of low, fine-textured ground cover. Makes confused scene when mixed with other plants with medium-sized to large leaves.

G. manicata. Leaves carried fairly horizontally. Spinelike hairs on leaf stalks and ribs are red. Leaf lobes are flatter, lack frills of *G. tinctoria*.

G. tinctoria *(G. chilensis).* Most common species. Lobed leaf margins are toothed and somewhat frilled. Leaves held in bowl-like way, half upright and flaring.

GUZMANIA. *Bromeliaceae.* Bromeliads grown as house plants or as indoor/outdoor plants in mildest coastal gardens. Most come from damp jungles. Pot in fast-draining organic mixes, give plenty of water and frequent light feeding, and keep out of direct, hot sunlight.

Guzmania monostachia

G. lingulata. Rosettes of glossy green leaves, 12–16 in. long, produce torchlike inflorescences of broad, brightly colored bracts and white flowers. Bracts vary from red (most common) to orange and yellow.

G. monostachia. Rosettes produce cylindrical spike tightly shingled with short bracts. Lower ones are white striped with dark brown parallel lines; upper are orange to red with white flowers peeping out. Leaves to 16 in. long.

G. sanguinea. Rosettes, 2 ft. wide or more, gradually turn from green to scarlet as plants reach blooming size. Flowers themselves are inconspicuous.

GYMNOCALYCIUM. *Cactaceae.* CHIN CACTUS. Small cacti usually grown as house plants. Plant bodies nearly globular, single or clustered, a few inches thick in most species. Long-tubed, showy flowers open from smooth buds and last several days; colors include white, shades of red, pink, and (rarely) yellow and chartreuse. Easy to grow in good potting soil with ample water in summer, coolness and dry soil in winter. Dislike scorching sun. Best known of many is *G. mihanovichii*, PLAID CACTUS, dark green plant with brown markings; these markings are even stronger in *G. m. friedrichii*. The latter also has forms with pure red or pure yellow bodies known by such names as 'Ruby Ball', 'Red Head', 'Blondie', or, lumped together, as MOON CACTUS. These are all grafted on green plants of the species.

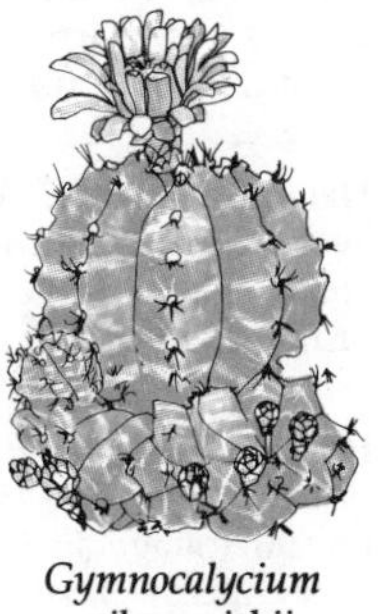

Gymnocalycium mihanovichii

GYMNOCLADUS dioica. *Leguminosae.* KENTUCKY COFFEE TREE. Deciduous tree. Zones 1–3, 7–10, 12–16, 18–21. Native to eastern U.S. Saplings grow very fast, but slow down at 8–10 ft. Trees ultimately reach 50 ft. Narrowish habit in youth. Older trees broader, with fairly few heavy, contorted branches. These, together with stout winter twigs, make bare tree picturesque. Leaves (1½–3 ft. long, divided into many leaflets 1–3 in. long) come out late in spring; they are pinkish when expanding, deep green in summer, yellow in autumn. Inconspicuous flowers are followed by 6–10-in.-long, flat, reddish brown pods containing hard black seeds. Average garden soil and routine watering. Established trees will take some drought, much heat and cold, poor soil. Effective for form in any cold-winter garden.

Gymnocladus dioica

GYNURA aurantiaca. *Compositae.* PURPLE VELVET PLANT. House plant from East Indies grown for its leaves and stems, which have plushlike covering of violet hairs. Leaves lance shaped, toothed, to 6 in. long, 2½ in. wide. Plant is somewhat shrubby, may reach 2–3 ft. Yellow to orange, ½-in. flowers have unpleasant odor; pinch out flower buds as they form. Needs strong indirect light for best color. Give plant warmth, average water, and rich, loose, well-drained soil. 'Purple Passion' ('Sarmentosa'), often sold as *G. sarmentosa*, has climbing or trailing habit.

Gynura aurantiaca 'Sarmentosa'

GYPSOPHILA. *Caryophyllaceae.* Annuals and perennials. All Zones in conditions noted below. Much-branched, upright or spreading, slender-stemmed plants 6 in.–4 ft. tall, profusely covered in summer with small, single or double, white, pink, or rose flowers in clusters. Leaves blue green; few when plant is in bloom. Use for airy grace in borders, bouquets; fine contrast with large-flowered, coarse-textured plants. Dwarf kinds ideal in rock gardens, trailing from wall pocket, or over top of dry rock walls.

Gypsophila repens

Full sun. Routine watering. Add lime to strongly acid soils. Thick, deep roots of some perennial kinds difficult to transplant; do not disturb often. Protect roots from gophers, tender top growth from snails and slugs. For repeat bloom on perennial kinds, cut back flowering stems before seed clusters form.

G. elegans. Annual. Upright, 1–1½ ft. Lance-shaped, rather fleshy leaves to 3 in. long. Profuse single white flowers ½ in. or more across. Pink and rose forms available. Plants live only 5–6 weeks; for continuous bloom, sow seed in open ground every 3–4 weeks from late spring into summer.

G. paniculata. BABY'S BREATH. Perennial. Zones 1–10, 14–16, 18–21. Much branched to 3 ft. or more. Leaves slender, sharp pointed, 2½–4 in. long. Single white flowers about 1/16 in. across, hundreds in a spray, July–October. Variety 'Bristol Fairy' is improved form, more billowy, to 4 ft. high, covered with double blossoms ¼ in. wide. Grow from root grafts or stem cuttings.

G. repens. Perennial. Zones 1–11, 14–16, 18–21. Alpine native 6–9 in. high, with trailing stems 1½ ft. long. Leaves narrow, less than 1 in. long. Clusters of small white or pink flowers in summer. Increase by cuttings in midsummer.

HABENARIA radiata. See *Pecteilis*.

HACKBERRY. See *Celtis*.

HAEMANTHUS katherinae *(Sciadoxus multiflorus katherinae).* *Amaryllidaceae.* BLOOD LILY. Bulb. Tender South African plant closely related to amaryllis. Grow in pots in greenhouse or as house plant; in mild climates, move to terrace or patio for bloom in late spring. Large (4-in.-diameter), white bulb stained red (hence common name). Leaves broad, wavy edged, bright green, 12–15 in. long. Sturdy succulent stem 2 ft. tall, topped by large, round clusters of salmon red flowers with protruding, showy red stamens.

Haemanthus katherinae

Put 1 bulb in 10-in. pot in rich potting mix in winter or early spring. Set bulb with tip at soil surface; water sparingly, keep at 70°F. When leaves appear (8–10 weeks), move outdoors (in frostless Zones) to sheltered, lightly shaded spot. Water thoroughly; feed monthly with complete fertilizer. Bait for snails. After bloom, gradually reduce watering; dry out plant in cool, protected place. Do not repot next season; add new mix on top or tip out root ball, scrape off some old soil, replace with fresh.

HAKEA. *Proteaceae.* Evergreen shrubs or trees. Zones 9, 12–17, 19–24. Native to Australia. Tough, drought tolerant, especially good for seacoast. Full sun. Take poor soil.

In addition to the 4 species described below, other hakeas are offered from time to time by experimentally-minded nurserymen. Remarkably diverse in foliage and flower, all are quality shrubs or small trees for difficult sites.

Hakea laurina

H. laurina. SEA URCHIN, PINCUSHION TREE. Small, dense, rounded tree or large shrub to 30 ft. Narrow, gray green, 6-in.-long leaves are often red margined. Showy flower clusters look like round crimson pincushions stuck with golden pins. Blooms in winter, sometimes in late fall. Stake young trees securely. Good small patio tree.

H. saligna. WILLOWLEAF HAKEA. Shrub to 8 ft.; rarely treelike to 20 ft. Narrow, gray green leaves up to 6 in. long. Many clusters of small white flowers.

H. suaveolens. SWEET HAKEA. Dense, broad, upright shrub to 10–20 ft. tall. Stiff, dark green, 4-in. leaves, branched into stiff, needlelike, stickery segments. Small, fragrant white flowers in dense, fluffy clusters, fall and winter. Useful, fast-growing barrier plant, background, or screen. Good with conifers. Can be pruned into tree form.

H. victoria. ROYAL HAKEA. Erect, narrow plant to 9 ft. tall, 5 ft. wide. Leaves broad, flat or slightly cupped, stemless, toothed, deep green beautifully netted with yellow and variegated with cream and orange. Flowers insignificant. Cut foliage dries well, lasts well in arrangements.

HAKONECHLOA macra 'Aureola'. *Gramineae.* JAPANESE FOREST GRASS. Perennial. All Zones. Graceful, slender, leaning or arching stems to 1½ ft. carry long, slender leaves with gold stripes. Effect is that of a tiny bamboo. Spreads very slowly by underground runners. Needs shade, good soil, average water. Choice plant for woodland garden or for close viewing in a container.

Hakonechloa macra 'Aureola'

HALESIA. *Styracaceae.* Deciduous trees. Zones 2–9, 14–24. Both kinds give best flower display in areas of winter cold and grow best in cool, deep, humus-rich soil with ample water.

Halesia carolina

H. carolina *(H. tetraptera).* SNOWDROP TREE, SILVER BELL. Moderate growth to 20–50 ft. with 15–30-ft. spread, depending on climate. Rates high as flowering tree in May, when clusters of snow white, ½-in., bell-shaped flowers hang from graceful branches just as leaves begin to appear. Oval, finely toothed, 4-in.-long leaves turn yellow in fall. Interesting brown fruit with 4 wings hangs on almost all winter. Prune plant to a single stem when young or it will grow as a large shrub. Flowers show off best when you can look up into tree. Attractive as overhead planting for azaleas, rhododendrons.

H. monticola. MOUNTAIN SILVER BELL. Larger tree, 40–60 ft., with larger (3–6-in.) leaves than *H. carolina.*

HALIMIOCISTUS sahucii. *Cistaceae.* Evergreen shrub. Zones 4–24. Hybrid between *Halimium umbellatum* and *Cistus salviifolius.* Combines best characteristics of both parents. Densely foliaged with 1-in., narrow, gray green leaves, it grows to 2 ft. high and spreads to 3 ft. or more. In summer, clusters of white, 1–2-in.-wide flowers with center tufts of yellow stamens almost hide foliage. Good in sunny rock garden, on dry bank, or cascading over concrete retaining wall. Or plant on sunny side of house under wide eaves where rains seldom reach. Will not live in wet soil, and can be watered with other plants only if drainage is excellent.

Halimiocistus sahucii

HALIMIUM. *Cistaceae.* Evergreen shrublets. Zones 7–9, 12–24. Closely related to sunrose (*Helianthemum*) and sometimes sold under that name; cultural requirements and uses are the same. Halimiums grow 2–3 ft. high, have gray green foliage, yellow flowers in loose clusters in spring.

Halimium lasianthum

H. lasianthum *(Helianthemum formosum).* Spreading plant with leaves ½–1½ in. long, ¼ in. wide. Flowers 1½ in. across, bright yellow with brownish purple blotch near base of petals.

H. ocymoides *(Helianthemum ocymoides).* Erect plant with leaves slightly narrower than those of above species. Flowers 1 in. wide, bright yellow, with black and purple blotch at base of petals.

H. umbellatum *(Helianthemum umbellatum).* Grows to 1½ ft. Leaves very narrow, resembling those of rosemary. Flowers ¾ in. across, white with yellow at petal bases, in 4–6-in.-long clusters.

Hamamelidaceae. The witch hazel family contains deciduous (rarely evergreen) trees and shrubs. Some have showy flowers (*Fothergilla, Hamamelis, Loropetalum*). Many of the deciduous kinds have brilliant fall color (*Liquidambar, Parrotia*).

HAMAMELIS. *Hamamelidaceae.* WITCH HAZEL. Deciduous trees or large shrubs. Yellow fall foliage. Fragrant yellow flowers with very narrow, crumpled-looking petals in nodding few-flowered clusters. Plants grow in sun or light shade and need moderate moisture and some peat moss, ground bark, or leaf mold in soil.

Hamamelis mollis

H. intermedia. Zones 4–7 15–17. Group of hybrids between *H. mollis* and a Japanese witch hazel. Big shrubs (to 15 ft. high) with spreading habit. The following varieties are widely grown in Zones 4–7: 'Diane', bright red flowers, fine fall color; 'Jelena' (also known as 'Copper Beauty' and 'Orange Beauty'), spreading plant with large leaves, large yellow flowers heavily suffused with red, and fall foliage color of orange, red, and scarlet; 'Magic Fire' ('Fire Charm', 'Feuerzauber'), upright plant with blossoms in coppery orange blended with red; and 'Ruby Glow', erect, with coppery red flowers and fine fall color. Bloom season for all these is December–March.

H. mollis. CHINESE WITCH HAZEL. Zones 4–7, 15–17. Moderately slow-growing shrub to 8–10 ft. or (eventually) small tree to 30 ft. Branches in loose zigzag pattern. Roundish leaves, 3½–6 in. long; dark green and rough above, gray and felted beneath, turning good clear yellow in fall. Fragrant, 1½-in.-wide, rich golden yellow flowers with red brown calyces bloom on bare stems, December–March. Effective against red brick or gray stone. Flowering branches excellent for flower arrangements.

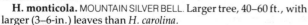

H. virginiana. COMMON WITCH HAZEL. Zones 1–9, 14–16, 18–21. Native to eastern U.S. Sometimes to 25 ft. tall but usually 10–15 ft. high; open, spreading, rather straggling habit. Moderately slow growing. Roundish leaves similar to those of *H. mollis* but not gray and felted beneath; turn yellow to orange in fall. Golden yellow, ¾-in.-wide blooms appear in October, November and tend to be lost in colored foliage.

HARDENBERGIA. *Leguminosae.* Evergreen shrubby vines. Native to Australia. Grow at moderate rate to 10 ft., climbing by twining stems. Flowers shaped like pea blossoms, several to many in clusters, late winter to early spring. Useful for light, delicate pattern on low walls, fences, screens, arches. Can be pegged down as a ground cover. Need light, well-drained soil in sun (partial shade in hot areas). Do not overwater. Provide support for climbing and cut back after bloom to prevent tangling. Subject to spider mites, nematodes; otherwise fairly free of pests and diseases.

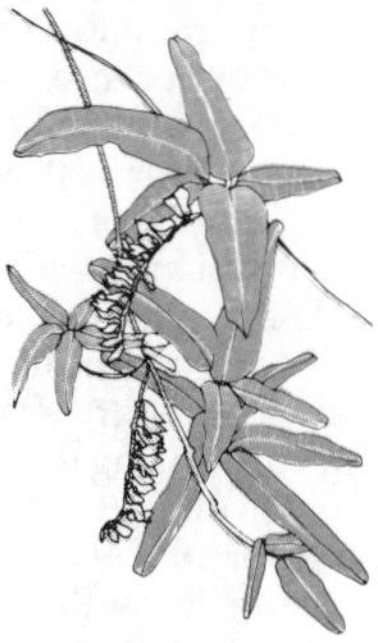

Hardenbergia comptoniana

H. comptoniana. LILAC VINE. Zones 15–24. Light, delicate foliage pattern; leaves divided into 3–5 dark green, narrow, 2–3-in.-long leaflets. Flowers violet blue, ½ in. long, in long, narrow clusters. Where temperatures drop below 24°F., shelter blossoms, buds, tender tops by planting under overhang.

H. violacea *(H. monophylla).* Zones 9–24. Coarser texture; leaves usually undivided, 2–4 in. long. Vining or shrubby. Flowers lilac or violet to rose or white. 'Happy Wanderer', pinkish purple, is a tough, hardy, vigorous selection that takes full sun, wind.

HAREBELL. See *Campanula rotundifolia.*

HARE'S FOOT FERN. See *Polypodium aureum.*

HARPEPHYLLUM caffrum. *Anacardiaceae.* KAFFIR PLUM. Evergreen tree. Zones 17, 19, 21–24. Fast growth to 30–35 ft. or higher, with 20–25-ft. spread. Freezes back in cold weather but makes quick recovery if temperature not below 25°F. (Usually has multiple trunks after such recovery.) Round headed, but easily trained to structurally interesting small tree. Leathery, glossy leaves, each with 13–15 narrow, 2½-in.-long leaflets, unfold rich red, then turn dark green. Clusters of very small white or greenish flowers are followed by tart but edible dark red fruit resembling large olives. Fruit drop is a problem near paving.

Harpephyllum caffrum

Tolerates considerable wind, heat; requires average water. Prune to shape and to remove frost-damaged wood. Well-groomed appearance and quick growth make it a good shade or decorative tree for the small garden. Striking silhouette against tall, light-colored wall.

HARRY LAUDER'S WALKING STICK. See *Corylus avellana* 'Contorta'.

HART'S TONGUE FERN. See *Phyllitis scolopendrium.*

HAWAIIAN TREE FERN. See *Cibotium glaucum.*

HAWORTHIA. *Liliaceae.* Succulents. Zones 8, 9, 12–24. Extremely variable in growth habit. Best-known ones resemble smaller aloes (to which the group is closely related); others make small towers of neatly stacked fleshy leaves; and there are other forms. Full sun; very drought tolerant. All make excellent pot plants, best in part shade. Here are 3 of dozens available from specialists.

Haworthia fasciata

H. attenuata. Dark green leaves heavily marked with raised white dots grow in stemless or short-stemmed rosettes to 6 in. wide. Spreads to make clumps. Dull pink flowers in 2-ft. clusters.

H. fasciata. Stemless rosettes with many narrow, 3-in.-long, dark green leaves, strongly marked with crosswise bands of raised white dots. Flowers greenish white, in 6-in. clusters. Spreads freely by offsets.

H. setata. LACE HAWORTHIA. Small, stemless rosettes of many leaves to 1¼ in. long, half as wide. Leaves dark green marked with whitish translucent areas and edged with long, bristly, white teeth that give lacy look.

HAWTHORN. See *Crataegus.*

HAZELNUT. See *Corylus.*

HEART OF FLAME. See *Bromelia balansae.*

HEATH. See *Erica, Daboecia.*

HEATHER. See *Calluna.*

HEAVENLY BAMBOO. See *Nandina domestica.*

HEBE. *Scrophulariaceae.* Evergreen shrubs. Zones 14–24 except as noted. Closely related to *Veronica* and often still sold under that name. Native to New Zealand. Most are fast growers. Landscaping plants grown principally for form and foliage; some give good flower display. All do better in cool coastal gardens than in interior, where dry summer heat and winter frosts shorten their lives. Lower kinds are useful for edgings or ground cover; taller ones are good shrubs where sea winds and salt air are problems.

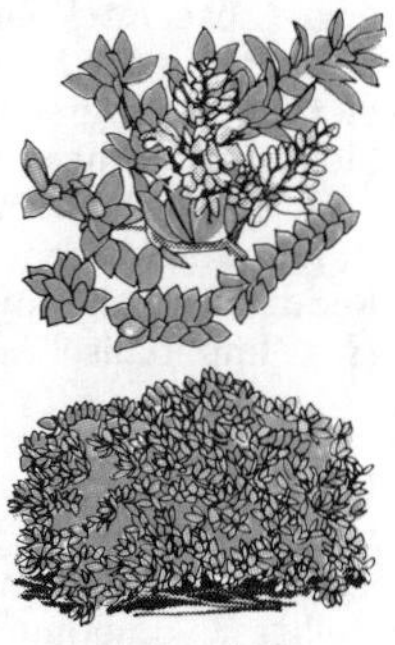

Hebe buxifolia

Will take full sun on coast; give partial shade in warm valleys. Good drainage is essential, with plenty of moisture. Prune after bloom, shortening flowering branches considerably to keep plants compact. In southern California, fusarium wilt may cause wilting leaves or death of branches or whole plant. Shop carefully, rejecting plants that look unhealthy; signs of fusarium wilt include dying leaves and brown discoloration inside stems. Don't replant hebes where one has died.

H. andersonii. Hybrid between *H. speciosa* and *H. salicifolia.* Compact, to 5–6 ft. Leaves fleshy, deep green. Summer flowers in 2–4-in. spikes; white at base, violet at tip.

H. 'Autumn Glory'. Zones 5, 6, 14–24. Mounding, compact, 2 ft. high, 2 ft. wide. Oval leaves 1½ in. long. Many 2-in.-long, dark lavender blue flower spikes in late summer, fall.

H. buxifolia. BOXLEAF HEBE. Rounded, symmetrical habit. Eventually reaches 5 ft. tall; easily shaped into 3-ft. hedge. Deep green, ⅓-in.-long leaves densely cover branches. Small white flowers in headlike clusters in summer. One of the hebes most resistant to heat, drought, cold.

H. 'Carnea'. Grows 3–5 ft. tall. Deep green, willowlike leaves 2½ in. long. Rosy crimson flowers in 2½-in.-long spikes, August–September.

H. chathamica. Ground cover shrub to 1½ ft. tall, stems trailing to 3 ft. Leaves ½ in. long, deep green. Lavender flowers in summer.

(Continued on next page)

H. 'Coed'. Compact plant to 3 ft. tall and as broad. Reddish stems densely clothed with 1½-in.-long, dark green leaves. Blooms profusely May–August, bearing spikelike clusters of small, pinkish purple flowers.

H. cupressoides. Slow grower to 4–5 ft. Slender branches clothed in bright green, scalelike leaves that look like those of cypress; small bluish flowers seldom produced. More widely sold is variety 'Nana', a compact, rounded, slow-growing plant to 2 ft. high. Often used in containers and rock gardens, and as bonsai.

H. 'Desilor'. Dense, rounded shrub to 3 ft. tall and as broad. Leaves somewhat smaller than those of *H. elliptica*. Flowers deep purple blue in 1½-in.-long clusters, May–October.

H. elliptica *(H. decussata)*. Much-branched shrub 5–6 ft. high. Medium green leaves 1¼ in. long. Fragrant bluish flowers in 1½-in.-long clusters bloom in summer.

H. glaucophylla. Broad, compact, rounded shrub about 2 ft. wide. Roundish, blue green, ½-in.-long leaves. White summer flowers in short, dense clusters. Use as low foundation plant or divider between walk and lawn.

H. imperialis. See *H. speciosa* 'Imperialis'.

H. 'Lake' ('Veronica Lake'). Dense shrub 3 ft. tall, with 1½-in., dark green leaves and abundant short spikes of lilac flowers in summer.

H. menziesii. Can reach 5 ft.; usually much lower. Narrow, closely spaced ¾-in.-long leaves are shiny bright green and slightly toothed. White flowers tinged lilac in short clusters; summer bloom. Spreading habit; good ground cover.

H. 'Patty's Purple'. To 3 ft. high. Stems wine red; leaves ½ in. long, dark green. Purple flowers on slender spikes in summer. Mass in groups or use to back flower border.

H. pinguifolia. Zones 5, 6, 14–24. Erect or creeping shrub 1–3 ft. tall with roundish, ¾-in.-long, blue green leaves, often red edged. Fat, 1-in.-long, white flower spikes in summer. *H. p.* 'Pagei' grows 9 in. high, 5 ft. across, has ½-in.-wide leaves of blue gray edged rose. Rock garden plant.

H. 'Reevesii' *(H. 'Evansii')*. To 3 ft. high. Two-in.-long leaves are blend of dark green and reddish purple; reddish purple flowers bloom in summer.

H. speciosa. SHOWY HEBE. Dense, broad, spreading shrub 2–5 ft. high. Stout stems bear dark green, glossy leaves, 2–4 in. long. Reddish purple flowers in 3–4-in.-long spikes, July–September. *H. s.* 'Imperialis' has reddish foliage, magenta flowers in summer.

HEDERA. *Araliaceae.* IVY. Evergreen woody vines. Most widely planted ground cover in California; also often climbs on walls, fences, trellises. Sometimes planting does both—wall ivy spreads to become surrounding ground cover or vice versa. Ivy is dependable, uniform, neat. It is good for holding soil—discouraging soil erosion and slippage on slopes. Roots grow deep and fill soil densely. Branches root as they grow, further knitting soil.

Hedera helix

Ivy climbs almost any vertical surface by aerial rootlets—a factor to consider in planting against walls that need painting. Chain link fence planted with ivy soon becomes wall of foliage.

Ivy grows in sun or shade in most climates; must have shade in Zones 12, 13. Its only real shortcoming is monotony. All year long you get nothing from it but green or green and white (except in the case of *H. helix* 'Baltica').

Thick, leathery leaves are usually lobed. Mature plants will eventually develop stiff branches toward top of vine which bear round clusters of small greenish flowers followed by black berries. These branches have unlobed leaves; cuttings from such branches will have same kind of leaves and will be shrubby, not vining. Such shrubs taken from variegated Algerian ivy are called "ghost ivy." *H. helix* 'Arborescens' is another variety of that type.

You can grow regular ivy from cuttings, but many will die and growth will be very slow. Plants from flats grow much faster. Standard spacing: 1–1½ ft. Best planting time is early spring (March in California and Arizona, May in Colorado), but fall plantings, where winters are not excessively cold, require less water to get started.

When you plant, it is critical that soil be thoroughly premoistened; in addition, the ivy's roots must be moist and its tissues full of moisture (not wilted). Mix peat moss or ground bark into planting soil to a depth of 9–12 in., if possible. On steep slope, dig conditioner into each planting hole (6 in. deep, 6 in. wide). After spring planting, feed with high-nitrogen fertilizer. Feed again in August. For best possible growth, continue to feed in early spring and August of every year. In hot climates, the more water you give an ivy planting, the better it will hold up through summer. Nevertheless, established English ivy is fairly drought tolerant.

Most ivy ground covers need trimming around edges (use hedge shears or sharp spade) 2 or 3 times a year. Fence and wall plantings need shearing or trimming 2 or 3 times a year. When ground cover builds up higher than you want, mow it with rugged power rotary mower or cut it back with hedge shears. Do this in spring so ensuing growth will quickly cover bald look.

Many trees and shrubs grow quite compatibly in ivy. But small, soft, or fragile plants will never exist for long with healthy ivy—it simply smothers them.

To kill Bermuda grass in ivy, spray with dalapon 2 or 3 times during Bermuda's active growing season. Chemical doesn't hurt ivy when used as directed for Bermuda. Add wetting agent to make dalapon more effective.

A bacterial leaf spot causes light green, water-soaked spots on leaves. Spots turn brown or black, edged with red or brown; ultimately stems shrivel and blacken. Physiological trouble called edema brings on same symptoms. Prevent either malady by watering early in day so foliage is dry by night. There is no chemical control for edema. To control the bacterial disease, spray infected beds with copper-bearing compounds or other locally recommended products.

If dodder, a yellow, threadlike parasite, grows among ivy plants, use ammonium sulfate at 1 lb. per gal. of water. Treatment will kill ivy leaves, but new leaves will replace them.

Ivy can be a haven for slugs and snails. If your garden has these pests, put slug-snail poison in ivy often. Ivy also harbors rodents.

H. canariensis. ALGERIAN IVY. Zones 8, 9, 12–24. Shiny, rich green leaves 5–8 in. wide with 3–5 shallow lobes, more widely spaced along stems than on English ivy. Requires more moisture than English ivy.

H. c. 'Variegata'. VARIEGATED ALGERIAN IVY. Leaves edged with yellowish white; white edges are sometimes suffused with reddish purple in cold weather. Avoid extreme heat or desert sun.

H. colchica. PERSIAN IVY. Zones 7–9, 12–24. Evergreen, egg-shaped to heart-shaped leaves, 3–7 in. across, up to 10 in. long (largest leaves of all ivies). Best known for its variety 'Dentata', with faintly toothed leaves. 'Dentata Variegata' is marbled with deep green, gray green, and creamy white.

H. helix. ENGLISH IVY. All Zones. Dull dark green leaves with paler veins are 3–5 lobed, 2–4 in. wide at base and as long. Not as vigorous as Algerian ivy, better for small spaces.

H. h. 'Baltica'. Hardiest; has whitish-veined leaves half size of English ivy leaves. Turns purplish in winter. 'Bulgarica', also hardy, has larger leaves.

Many small- and miniature-leafed forms are useful for small-area ground covers, hanging baskets, and training to intricate patterns on walls and in pots. These varieties are also used to create topiary shapes—globes, baskets, animals—on wire frames. Some of small-leafed forms are: 'Hahn's Self Branching,' light green leaves, dense branching, part shade best; 'Conglomerata', slow-growing dwarf; 'Minima', leaves ½–1 in. across with 3–5 angular lobes. Other varieties to be had: 'California', 'Fluffy Ruffles', 'Gold Dust', 'Gold Heart', 'Heart', 'Needlepoint', 'Ripple', 'Shamrock', and 'Star'.

HEDYCHIUM. *Zingiberaceae.* GINGER LILY. Perennials. Outdoors in Zones 17, 22–24; greenhouse plants anywhere. Foliage handsome under ideal conditions. Leaves on 2 sides of stems but in a single plane. In late summer or early fall, richly fragrant flowers in dense spikes open from cone of overlapping green bracts at ends of stalks. Remove old stems after flowers fade to encourage fresh new growth. Very useful in large containers but will not grow as tall as in open ground. Container plants can be moved out of sight when unattractive. Grow in light shade in soil high in organic matter. Keep moist at all times. Frosts in mild areas can kill plants to ground, but new stalks appear in early spring. Useful next to swimming pools. Attractive with palms, ferns, other tropical-looking plants.

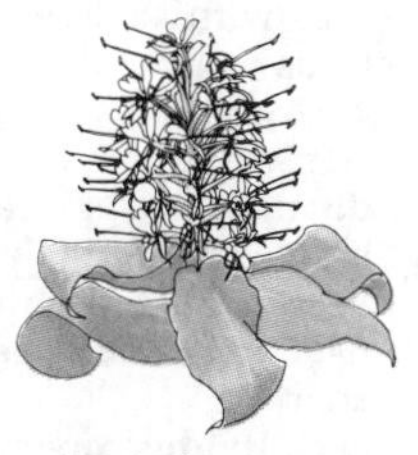
Hedychium gardneranum

H. coronarium. WHITE GINGER LILY, GARLAND FLOWER. Native to India, Indonesia. Grows 3–6 ft. high. Leaves 8–24 in. long, 2–5 in. broad. Foliage usually unattractive in California because leaves will burn if plant is given enough heat to bloom well. White, wonderfully fragrant flowers in 6–12-in.-long clusters; good cut flowers.

H. gardneranum. KAHILI GINGER. Native to India. Grows to 8 ft. high; 8–18-in.-long leaves 4–6 in. wide. Clear yellow flowers with red stamens, in 1½-ft.-long spikes, tip branches from July to onset of cool weather.

HEDYSCEPE canterburyana. *Palmae.* Palm. Outdoors in Zones 17, 23, 24; anywhere as house or greenhouse plant. Comes from Lord Howe Island in the South Pacific. Related to better-known Kentia palms (see *Howea*) but smaller, broader, and lower growing, with broader leaf segments and more arching, lighter green feather-type leaves. To 30 ft. Needs ample water.

Hedyscepe canterburyana

HEIMERLIODENDRON brunonianum. See *Pisonia umbellifera.*

HELENIUM autumnale. *Compositae.* COMMON SNEEZEWEED. Perennial. All Zones. Many branching, leafy stems to 1–6 ft., depending on variety. Daisylike flowers summer to early fall—rays in shades of yellow, orange, red, and copper, surrounding brown, pomponlike center. Leaves 2–4 in. long, toothed. Needs full sun. Fairly drought resistant. Flowers best where summers are hot. Trim off faded blossoms to encourage more blooms. Plants can take some neglect.

Helenium autumnale

HELIANTHEMUM nummularium. *Cistaceae.* SUNROSE. Evergreen shrublet. All Zones. Commonly sold under this name are a number of forms as well as hybrids between this species and others. They grow about 6–8 in. high and spread to 3 ft. Depending on the kind, the ½–1-in.-long leaves may be glossy green above and fuzzy gray beneath, or gray on both sides. Sunroses put on a delightful display of 1-in.-wide, clustered single or double flowers in lovely, sunny colors—flame red, apricot, orange, yellow, pink, rose, peach, salmon, and white. Plants bloom April–June in California and Arizona, May–July in Northwest. Each blossom lasts only a day, but new buds continue to open. Shear plants back after flowering to encourage fall bloom.

Helianthemum nummularium

Plant sunroses in full sun. Let them tumble over rocks, give them niche in dry rock wall, or set them in planter inset in sunny patio. Use them at the seashore or in rock gardens. Allow them to ramble over gentle slope. If used as ground cover, plant 2–3 ft. apart. Plant in fall or early spring—from flats, if possible. Soil drainage must be good. Do not overwater. In cold-winter areas, lightly cover plants with branches from evergreens in winter to keep foliage from dehydrating.

HELIANTHUS. *Compositae.* SUNFLOWER. Annuals and perennials. All Zones. Coarse, sturdy plants with bold flowers. All are tough, tolerant plants for full sun, any garden soil. Perennial kinds spread rapidly, may become invasive. Not for tidy gardens. All bloom in late summer, fall.

Helianthus annuus

H. annuus. COMMON SUNFLOWER. Annual. From this rough, hairy plant with 2–3-in.-wide flower heads have come many ornamental and useful garden varieties. Some ornamental varieties have double yellow flower heads 5–7 in. across ('Teddy Bear', 'Sungold', 'Chrysanthemum-Flowered'); others have large orange, red brown, or mahogany heads. Best-known form is coarse, towering (to 10-ft.) plant with small rays outside and cushiony center of disk flowers, 8–10 in. across. Usually sold as 'Mammoth Russian'. People eat the roasted seeds; birds like them raw, and visit flower heads in fall and winter. For children, annual sunflowers are big, easy to grow, and bring sense of great accomplishment. Sow seeds in spring where plants are to grow. Large-flowered kinds need rich soil, lots of water.

H. multiflorus. Perennial. To 5 ft. with thin, toothed, 3–8-in.-long leaves and numerous 3-in.-wide flower heads with yellow centers. 'Loddon Gold' is double-flowered variety. Excellent for cutting.

Helianthus tuberosus

H. salicifolius ***(H. orgyalis).*** Perennial. Clumps of tall (3–6-ft.) stems clothed with long, narrow, drooping leaves carry sheaves of long-stemmed yellow, 2-in. flower heads with brown centers. Endures heat and some drought when established.

H. tuberosus. JERUSALEM ARTICHOKE. Perennial. Also grown as a commercial crop; tubers are edible and sold in markets as "sunchokes." Plants 6–7 ft. tall, with bright yellow flower heads. Oval leaves 8 in. long. Spreads readily and can become pest. Best to harvest tubers every year and save out 2 or 3 for replanting. If controlled, makes a good, quick temporary screen or hedge.

HELICHRYSUM. *Compositae.* Annuals, perennials. Best known is the annual strawflower. Others are little-known but choice perennials or subshrubs for landscape use.

H. bracteatum. STRAWFLOWER. Summer annual. Grows 2–3 ft. high with many flower heads. (Dwarf forms also available.) Known as "everlasting" because 2½-in. pomponlike flowers are papery and last indefinitely when dried. Also good in fresh arrangements. Flowers may be yellow, orange, red, pink, or white (seeds come in mixed colors). Alternate leaves 2–5 in. long. Plant seed in place in late spring or early summer (same time as zinnias). Full sun. Once plants are well started, keep on dry side. Inclined to have dry leaves at base. Best for hillside or dry areas. Two named varieties are perennial in mild-winter climates: 'Dargan Hill Monarch' and 'Diamond Head'. The former is 1½–2 ft. tall, with gray green leaves and 3-in., golden yellow flowers. 'Diamond Head' is somewhat lower and more compact, with deeper yellow flowers.

Helichrysum bracteatum

(Continued on next page)

H. petiolatum ***(Gnaphalium lanatum).*** Shrubby perennial. Zones 16, 17, 22–24. Woody-based plants to 2 ft. with trailing stems that spread 4 ft. or more. Grown for 1-in.-long, oval, white-woolly leaves. If flower heads form, they are ⅛ in. wide in clusters 1–2 in. wide. Full sun. Drought tolerant. Needs room; trim to keep tidy. Good in sandy soils. There are dwarf (less than half-sized) and variegated forms.

HELICTOTRICHON sempervirens ***(Avena sempervirens).*** *Gramineae.* BLUE OAT GRASS. Perennial. All Zones. Evergreen, 2–3-ft. fountains of bright blue gray, narrow leaves resemble giant clumps of blue fescue (*Festuca ovina glauca*), but are more graceful. Plants need full sun, good drainage. They combine well with other grasses and broadleafed plants, and with boulders in rock gardens. Groom by pulling out occasional withered leaves.

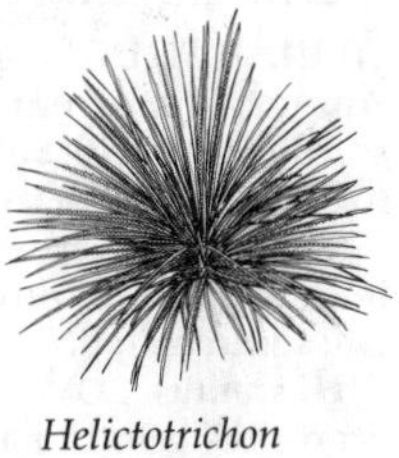
Helictotrichon sempervirens

HELIOTROPE, GARDEN. See *Valeriana officinalis*.

HELIOTROPIUM arborescens ***(H. peruvianum).*** *Boraginaceae.* COMMON HELIOTROPE. Perennial. House or summer annual everywhere; outdoor plant Zones 8–24. Rather tender old-fashioned plant grown for delicate, sweet fragrance of its flowers. In mild climates, it's a shrubby plant up to 4 ft. high. Flowers dark violet to white, arranged in tightly grouped, curved, one-sided spikes which form rounded, massive clusters. Veined leaves have darkish purple cast. If in pots, can be protected in winter and moved into patio or garden for spring and summer enjoyment. It takes sun or partial shade (latter best in hot-summer climates). Avoid overwatering. 'Black Beauty' and 'Iowa' are forms with deep purple flowers.

Heliotropium arborescens

HELIPTERUM roseum ***(Acroclinium roseum).*** *Compositae.* Annual. Although grown for summer color in garden, valued mostly for dried cut flowers. Grows to 2 ft. tall. Daisy flower heads 1–2 in. across, carried singly; pink or white rays are thicker, brownish or greenish near base. Leaves narrow, numerous near top of stems. Easily grown in full sun in warm, dry soil. Sow seeds after frost where plants are to grow. Thin to 6–12 in. apart. To dry flowers, cut when fully open, after dew has dried from flowers. Tie in small bunches; hang upside down by stems in dry, cool, airy place until stems harden and leaves become brittle.

Helipterum roseum

HELLEBORUS. *Ranunculaceae.* HELLEBORE. Perennials. Distinctive, long-lived evergreen plants for shade or half shade, blooming for several months in winter and spring. Basal clumps of substantial, long-stalked leaves, usually divided fanwise into leaflets. Flowers large, borne singly or in clusters, centered with many stamens. Good cut flowers; sear ends of stems or dip in boiling water, then place in deep, cold water.

Helleborus lividus corsicus

Plant in good soil with lots of organic material added. Ample water. Feed once or twice a year. Do not move often; plants reestablish slowly. Mass under high-branching trees on north or east side of walls, in beds bordered with ajuga, wild ginger, primroses, violets. Use in plantings with azaleas, fatsia, pieris, rhododendrons, skimmia, and ferns.

H. foetidus. All Zones. Grows to 1½ ft. Attractive leaves—leathery, dark green, divided into 7–11 leaflets. Flowers 1 in. wide, light green with purplish margin; bloom February–April. Drought tolerant. Good with naturalized daffodils. Self-sows freely where adapted.

Helleborus lividus corsicus

H. lividus corsicus (sometimes sold as *H. corsicus* or *H. lividus*). CORSICAN HELLEBORE. Zones 4–24. Leafy stems to 3 ft. Leaves divided into 3 pale blue green leaflets with sharply toothed edges. (Species *H. lividus* has leaflets with smooth edges or only a few fine teeth.) Clusters of large, firm-textured light chartreuse flowers among upper leaves. In mild-winter climates, blooms late fall to late spring; in Northwest, blooms March–April. After shedding stamens, flowers stay attractive until summer. Best hellebore for southern California. Neutral soil. Established plants take more sun than other hellebores. Drought tolerant when established.

H. niger. CHRISTMAS ROSE. Zones 1, 7, 14–17. Elegant plant to 1½ ft. tall, blooming December–April. Often planted in mild-winter climates but seldom thrives there. Lustrous dark green leaves divided into 7–9 leaflets with few large teeth. Flowers about 2 in. wide, white or greenish white turning purplish with age.

H. orientalis. LENTEN ROSE. All Zones. Much like *H. niger* in growth habit, but easier to transplant. Basal leaves with 5–11 sharply toothed leaflets. Blooms March–May. Flowering stems branched, with leaflike bracts at branching points and beneath flowers. Flowers greenish, purplish, or rose, often spotted or splashed with deep purple. Lenten rose often sold as Christmas rose, but Lenten rose has different flower color and many small teeth on leaflets (few large teeth on those of Christmas rose). Lenten rose does better in southern California than Christmas rose.

HELXINE. See *Soleirolia*.

HEMEROCALLIS. *Liliaceae.* DAYLILY. Perennials with tuberous, somewhat fleshy roots; deciduous and evergreen. All Zones. Large clumps of arching, sword-shaped leaves. Lilylike flowers in open or branched clusters at ends of generally leafless stems that stand well above foliage. Older yellow, orange, and rust red daylilies have mostly been replaced by newer kinds (see below); both tall and dwarf varieties are available.

Use in borders with bearded iris, Michaelmas and Shasta daisies, poker plant (*Kniphofia*), dusty miller, agapanthus. Mass on banks under high-branching, deciduous trees, along driveways and roadsides in country gardens. Group among evergreen shrubs, near pools, along streams. Plant dwarf daylilies in rock gardens, as edgings, as low ground covers. Good cut flowers. Cut stems with well-developed buds; buds open on successive days, though each flower is slightly smaller than preceding one. Arrange individual blooms in low bowls. Snap off faded flowers daily.

Hemerocallis hybrid

Few plants are tougher, more persistent, or more pest free. Adapt to almost any kind of soil. Sun or part shade (in hottest areas, flowers fade in full sun all day, so give some afternoon shade). Red-flowered daylilies need warmth to develop best color. Water thoroughly while blooming; feed with complete fertilizer in spring and midsummer. Divide crowded plants in early spring or late fall.

H. fulva. TAWNY DAYLILY, COMMON ORANGE DAYLILY. Deciduous. To 6 ft. Leaves 2 ft. long or longer, 1 in. wide; tawny orange red, 3–5-in.-long flowers bloom in summer. Old double-flowered variety 'Kwanso' superseded by newer, more handsome hybrids.

H. hybrids. Deciduous or evergreen. Modern hybrids grow 1–6 ft. tall, with flowers 3–8 in. across. Color range extends far beyond basic yellow, orange, rust red; includes shell pink, vermilion, buff, apricot, creamy white, many bicolors. Early, midseason, late varieties insure bloom from May to September or October (in mild climates). Some varieties bloom twice a year (or even more often); some bloom in evening. 'Stella d'Oro', 2 ft. tall, produces bright yellow flowers throughout warm weather. Flowers single, semidouble, double; vary in shape from broad-petaled to narrow and twisted. Especially noteworthy are tetraploids ("tetras"), which have unusually heavy-textured flowers.

H. lilioasphodelus *(H. flava).* LEMON DAYLILY. Deciduous. To 3 ft. Leaves 2 ft. long. Fragrant, clear yellow, 4-in. flowers in June. Old-timer, worthwhile for fragrance and moderate size.

HEMLOCK. See *Tsuga.*

HEN AND CHICKENS. See *Sempervivum tectorum.*

HEN AND CHICKS. See *Echeveria.*

HERALD'S TRUMPET. See *Beaumontia grandiflora.*

HERB-OF-GRACE. See *Ruta graveolens.*

HERBS. This category includes all plants that at some time in history have been considered valuable for seasoning, medicine, fragrance, or general household use. As you look through lists of plants, you can recognize certain herbs because they bear the species name *officinalis*—meaning sold in shops, edible, medicinal, recognized in the pharmacopoeia. Today's herb harvest is used almost entirely for seasoning foods.

Herbs are versatile as garden plants. Some creep along the ground, making fragrant carpets. Others are shrublike and can be clipped to make formal hedges or grown informally in shrub or perennial borders. Many make attractive container plants. Those with gray foliage offer striking contrast to green-leafed plants. However, many herbs do have a distinctly weedy look, especially when planted beside regular ornamental plants.

Many herbs are hardy and adaptable. Although hot, dry, sunny conditions with poor but well-drained soil are usually considered best for most herbs, some thrive in shady, moist locations with light soil rich in humus.

Following are lists of herbs for specific landscape situations.

Kitchen garden. This can be a sunny raised bed near the kitchen door, planter box near the barbecue, or part of vegetable garden. Plant basic cooking herbs: basil (*Ocimum*), chives, dill (*Anethum graveolens*), sweet marjoram (*Origanum majorana*), mint (*Mentha*), oregano (*Origanum vulgare*), parsley, rosemary (*Rosmarinus*), sage (*Salvia officinalis*), savory (*Satureja*), tarragon (*Artemisia dracunculus*), thyme (*Thymus*). The connoisseur may wish to plant angelica, anise (*Pimpinella anisum*), caraway (*Carum carvi*), chervil (*Anthriscus cerefolium*), coriander (*Coriandrum sativum*), common fennel (*Foeniculum vulgare*).

Ground cover for sun. Prostrate rosemary, mother-of-thyme (*Thymus praecox arcticus, T. serpyllum*), lemon thyme (*T. citriodorus*), woolly thyme (*T. pseudolanuginosus*), caraway-scented thyme (*T. herba-barona*).

Ground cover for shade or part shade. Chamomile (*Chamaemelum nobile*).

Ground cover for shade. Sweet woodruff (*Galium odoratum*).

Perennial or shrub border. Common wormwood (*Artemisia absinthium*), Roman wormwood (*A. pontica*), small burnet (*Poterium sanguisorba*), lavenders (*Lavandula*), monarda, rosemary, rue (*Ruta graveolens*), scented geraniums (*Pelargonium*), tansy (*Tanacetum vulgare*).

Hedges. Formal clipped hedge—hyssop (*Hyssopus officinalis*), santolina, germander (*Teucrium*). Informal hedge—lavenders, winter savory (*Satureja montana*).

Gray garden. Common wormwood, Roman wormwood, English lavender (*Lavandula angustifolia*), germander, horehound (*Marrubium vulgare*), sage, woolly thyme.

Rock garden. French lavender (*Lavandula dentata*), sage, woolly thyme, mother-of-thyme, winter savory.

Herbs for moist areas. Angelica, mints, parsley, sweet woodruff.

Herbs for part shade. Chervil, costmary (*Chrysanthemum balsamita*), lemon balm (*Melissa officinalis*), parsley, sweet woodruff.

Herbs for containers. Crete dittany (*Origanum dictamnus*), chives, costmary, lemon verbena (*Aloysia triphylla*), sage, pineapple sage (*Salvia elegans*), summer savory (*Satureja hortensis*), sweet marjoram, mints, small burnet.

Potpourris and sachets. Costmary, English lavender, lemon balm, sweet woodruff, lemon verbena, lemon-scented geranium (*Pelargonium crispum*), rose geranium (*P. graveolens*), monarda.

To dry leafy herbs for cooking, cut them early in day before sun gets too hot, but after dew has dried on foliage. (Oil content is highest then.) Leafy herbs are ready to cut from time flower buds begin to form until flowers are half open. (Exceptions: parsley can be cut any time; sage and tarragon may take on strong taste unless cut early in summer.) Don't cut perennial herbs back more than ⅓; annual herbs may be sheared back to about 4 in. from ground. Generally you can cut 2 or 3 crops for drying during summer. Don't cut perennial herbs after September or new growth won't have chance to mature before cold weather.

Before drying, sort weeds and grass from herbs; remove dead or insect-damaged leaves. Wash off loose dirt in cool water; shake or blot off excess moisture. Tie woody-stemmed herbs such as sweet marjoram or thyme in small bundles and hang upside down from line hung across room. Room for drying herbs should be dark to preserve color, have good air circulation and warm temperature (about 70°F.) for rapid drying to retain aromatic oils. If drying area is fairly bright, surround herb bundles with loose cylinders of paper.

For large-leafed herbs such as basil, or short tips that don't bundle easily, dry in tray made by knocking bottom from nursery flat and replacing it with screen. On top of screen place double thickness of cheesecloth. Spread leaves out over surface. Stir leaves daily.

With good air circulation and low humidity, leafy herbs should be crumbly dry in a few days to a week. Strip leaves from stems and store whole in airtight containers—glass is best—until ready to use. Label each container with name of herb and date dried. Check jars first few days after filling to make sure moisture has not formed inside. If it has, pour out contents and dry for a few more days.

To gather seeds, collect seed clusters such as dill, anise, fennel, caraway when they turn brown. Seeds should begin to fall out when clusters are gently tapped. Leave a little of stem attached when you cut each cluster. Collect in box. Flail seeds from clusters and spread them out in sun to dry for several days. Then separate chaff from seed and continue to dry in sun for another 1½–2 weeks. Store seed herbs same way as leafy ones.

HERNIARIA glabra. *Caryophyllaceae.* GREEN CARPET, RUPTURE WORT. Evergreen perennial. All Zones. Trailing plant under 2–3 in. tall with crowded, tiny, bright green leaves less than ¼ in. long. Bloom negligible.

Grows vigorously in full sun in hottest places, but does well in moist shade too. Foliage turns bronzy red in cold winters.

Spreads well, but won't grow out of control; use it between stepping stones, on mounds, with rocks, or in parking strips.

Herniaria glabra

(Continued on next page)

Endures occasional footsteps, but not constant traffic.

Hesperaloe parviflora

HESPERALOE parviflora. *Agavaceae.* Evergreen perennial. Zones 10–16, 18–21. Native to Texas, northern Mexico. Makes dense, yuccalike clump of very narrow, swordlike leaves 4 ft. long, about 1 in. wide. Pink to rose red, 1¼-in.-long, nodding flowers in slim, 3–4-ft.-high clusters in early summer, with repeat bloom frequent in milder climates. On older plants, spikes can reach 8–9 ft. Effective combined with other desert plants. Good large container plant with loose, relaxed look. Full sun; drought tolerant.

H. p. engelmannii is similar to species, but its 1-in.-long flowers are more bell shaped.

Heterocentron elegans

HETEROCENTRON elegans *(Schizocentron elegans).* *Melastomataceae.* SPANISH SHAWL. Perennial in Zones 17, 21–24; with protection from frost, lives over in Zones 15, 16, 18–20. Creeping, vinelike habit. Oval leaves up to ½ in. wide with 3 well-marked veins. Leaves and stems often acquire a red color as the season advances. In summer, 1-in.-wide magenta flowers appear among the leaves; calyces remain after blossoms have withered. Grow in shade. When used as ground cover, plants in bloom give appearance of a carpet covered with bougainvillealike blossoms. Good subject for hanging baskets.

Heteromeles arbutifolia

HETEROMELES arbutifolia *(Photinia arbutifolia).* *Rosaceae.* TOYON, CHRISTMAS BERRY, CALIFORNIA HOLLY. Evergreen shrub or small tree. Zones 5–24. Native to Sierra Nevada foothills, southern California to Baja California, Coast Ranges. Dense shrub 6–10 ft. tall or multitrunked small tree 15–25 ft. tall; can be pruned to form small single-trunked tree. Thick, leathery, glossy dark green leaves 2–4 in. long with bristly, pointed teeth. Small white flowers in flattish clusters, June–July. Bright red (rarely yellow) berries in clusters, November–January; birds relish them. Bees also attracted to plant. *H. a. macrocarpa,* from Channel Islands, has larger berries.

Improves under cultivation. Drought tolerant, but thrives with summer water in well-drained soil. Needs some summer water in desert. Full sun or part shade. If trimmed to give abundance of year-old wood, it produces even more berries than in the wilds. Valuable as screen or bank planting or for erosion control. Fire retardant if kept moist.

Heuchera sanguinea

HEUCHERA. *Saxifragaceae.* ALUM ROOT, CORAL BELLS. Perennials. Compact, evergreen clumps of roundish leaves with scalloped edges. From April–August, slender, wiry stems 15–30 in. high bear open clusters of nodding, bell-shaped flowers ¼ in. or more across, in carmine, reddish pink, coral, crimson, red, rose, greenish, and white. Use as edging in rock gardens, as ground cover; mass in borders, in front of shrubs. Flowers dainty, long lasting in cut arrangements, attractive to hummingbirds.

Sun, light shade in hot inland areas. Best with plenty of water. Divide clumps every 3 or 4 years in fall (in spring in colder areas). Use young, vigorous, rooted divisions; discard older, woody rootstocks. Sow seed in spring.

H. maxima. ISLAND ALUM ROOT. Zones 15–24. Native to Channel Islands, southern California. Foliage clumps 1–2 ft. across. Leaves roundish, heart shaped, lobed, shining dark green. Flowers whitish or pinkish; hundreds in each narrow, 1½–2½-ft.-long cluster. Blooms February–April. Partial shade. Needs moisture except near coast, where established plants need very little water. Good ground cover in untamed parts of garden.

H. micrantha. All Zones. Native to California, Washington, Oregon, Idaho. Adapts easily to garden conditions. Plant in protected spots in cold areas. Long-stalked, roundish leaves 1–3 in. long, hairy on both sides, toothed and lobed. Flowers whitish or greenish, about ⅛ in. long, in loose clusters on leafy, 2–3-ft. stems.

H. 'Palace Purple'. All Zones. Described variously as a form of *H. micrantha* or the very similar species *H. americana.* Maplelike leaves are rich brownish or purplish red. Plant grows 1½ ft. tall, keeps its color year round. Tiny flowers are pinkish.

H. sanguinea. CORAL BELLS. All Zones. Native to Mexico and Arizona. Universal favorite. Makes neat foliage tufts of round, 1–2-in.-long leaves with scalloped edges. Slender, wiry stems 14–24 in. tall bear open clusters of nodding, bell-shaped, bright red or coral pink flowers. White, pink, crimson varieties available. Good edging for beds of delphinium, iris, lilies, peonies, roses.

H. 'Santa Ana Cardinal'. Zones 14–24. Outstanding hybrid between garden forms of *H. sanguinea* and *H. maxima.* Unusually vigorous, free flowering. Clumps 3–4 ft. wide. Vibrant rose red flowers, 50–100 on a spike, on 2-ft. stems. Bloom season covers 3–5 months, lasts almost all year in mild areas.

Hibbertia cuneiformis

HIBBERTIA. *Dilleniaceae.* Evergreen shrubs and vines with yellow flowers. Most are native to Australia. Prostrate species with tiny leaves and nickel-sized gold flowers are occasionally offered at botanic garden plant sales.

H. cuneiformis *(Candollea cuneiformis).* Evergreen shrub. Zones 13, 15–24. Native to Australia. Pleasing appearance and substance, to 4 ft. and somewhat broader. Small, 1-in.-long, polished green leaves are tapered at base and toothed at tip. Flowers resembling clear yellow wild roses are carried all along new growth, March–June. Prune after flowering to control outline. Needs food and water in average amounts; requires exceptionally fast drainage. Takes sun or light shade. Resists wind well. Group with rockroses (*Cistus*), sunroses (*Helianthemum*), and *Aster frikartii.*

Hibbertia scandens

H. scandens *(H. volubilis).* GUINEA GOLD VINE. Evergreen vine. Zones 16, 17, 21–24. Native to Australia. Fast growing, shrubby, climbing by twining stems to 8–10 ft. In ideal climate, luxuriant foliage is handsome all year: waxy dark green leaves, 3 in. long by 1 in. wide. Clear bright yellow flowers, like single roses, first appear in May and continue to bloom into October. Thrives in part shade, but will also grow in hot sun. Requires ample water. Recovers quickly from burning by light frosts. Use it as ground cover or to cover stone or tile walls. Good for small garden areas if trained on trellis or against low fence. Can also be grown in containers.

HIBISCUS. *Malvaceae.* Five species are grown in the West—an annual, a perennial, 2 deciduous shrubs, and an evergreen shrub. In Hawaii and warmest areas of coastal southern California, several more species are grown.

H. huegelii. See *Alyogyne.*

Hibiscus rosa-sinensis

H. moscheutos. PERENNIAL HIBISCUS, ROSE-MALLOW. Perennial. Zones 1–21. Hardy. To 6–8 ft. high. Stems rise each year; bloom starts in late June and continues until frost. Plants die down in winter. Oval, toothed leaves deep green above, whitish beneath. Flowers largest of all hibiscus; some reach 1 ft. across. Plants need regular deep watering and protection from winds that may burn flowers. A 2-in.-deep mulch will help conserve moisture. Feed at 6–8-week intervals during growing season. Sun.

Named varieties grown from cuttings are sometimes available. Most are grown from seed, often flowering the first year if sown indoors and planted out early. Southern Belle is tall (4-ft.) strain; 2–2½-ft.-tall strains are Disco Belle, Frisbee, and Rio Carnival. Flowers are 8–10 in. wide, in red, pink, rose, or white, often with red eye.

H. mutabilis. CONFEDERATE ROSE. Deciduous shrub. Zones 4–24. Shrubby or treelike in warmest climates, it behaves more like perennial in colder areas, growing flowering branches from woody base or short trunk. Broad, oval, 3–5-lobed leaves. Summer flowers 4–6 in. wide, opening white or pink and changing to deep red by evening. Variety 'Rubra' has red flowers. Requires sun, average water.

H. rosa-sinensis. CHINESE HIBISCUS, TROPICAL HIBISCUS. Evergreen shrub. Zones 9, 12, 13, 15, 16, 19–24. House plant or indoor/outdoor plant in cold-winter areas. One of showiest flowering shrubs. Reaches 30 ft. in tropics, but seldom over 15 ft. tall in U.S., even in mildest parts of California. Glossy foliage varies somewhat in size and texture depending on variety. Growth habit may be dense and dwarfish or loose and open. Summer flowers single or double, 4–8 in. wide. Colors range from white through pink to red, from yellow and apricot to orange.

Plants require good drainage; to check, dig hole 1½ ft. wide and deep. Fill with water; if water hasn't drained in an hour or so, find another planting area, improve drainage, or plant in raised bed or container. Plants also need sun, heat, and protection from frost and wind (especially ocean wind). In warm inland areas, they generally grow best if partially shaded from very hot afternoon sun. In cool coastal climates such as San Francisco's, they never get enough heat to thrive or bloom. Where winter temperatures frequently drop below 30°F., even the hardier varieties will need overhead protection of roof overhang or evergreen tree. Where temperatures drop much lower, grow plants in containers and shelter them indoors over winter. Or grow them as annuals, setting out fresh plants each spring.

Feed plants monthly (container plants twice monthly) from April to early September. Let growth harden after that. Water deeply and frequently. All varieties are quite susceptible to aphids.

Can be used as screen planting, in containers, as espaliers, or as free-standing shrubs or small trees. To keep mature plants growing vigorously, prune out about ⅓ of old wood in early spring. Pinching out tips of stems in spring and summer increases flower production. To develop good branch structure, prune poorly shaped young plants when set out in spring. Here are a few of the many varieties sold in the West:

'Accra'. Full-foliaged plant 6–7 ft. tall carries 4-in., single golden yellow flowers with orange centers.

'Agnes Galt'. Big single pink flowers. Vigorous, hardy plant to 15 ft. Prune to prevent legginess.

'All Aglow'. Tall (10–15-ft.) plant has large single flowers with broad, gold-blotched orange petals, pink halo around a white throat.

'American Beauty'. Broad, deep rose flowers. Slow growth to 8 ft. tall. Irregular form.

'Amour'. Large single soft pink flowers on sturdy 10-ft. plant.

'Bridal Veil'. Large pure white single flowers last 3–4 days. Plant 10–15 ft. tall.

'Bride'. Very large, palest blush to white flowers. Slow or moderate growth to open-branched 4 ft.

'Brilliant' ('San Diego Red'). Bright red single flowers in profusion. Tall, vigorous, compact, to 15 ft. Hardy.

'Butterball'. Fully double pure yellow flowers on compact bush, 4–6 ft. tall.

'Butterfly'. Small, single bright yellow flowers. Slow, upright growth to 7 ft.

'California Gold'. Heavy yield of yellow, red-centered, single flowers. Slow or moderate growth to a compact 7 ft.

'Cherie'. Single bright yellow flowers with deep maroon throat. Grows to 10–15 ft. tall.

'Crown of Bohemia'. Double gold flowers; petals shade to carmine orange toward base. Moderate or fast growth to 5 ft. Bushy, upright. Hardy.

'Diamond Head'. Large double flowers in deepest red (nearly black red). Compact growth to 5 ft.

'Ecstasy'. Large (5–6-in.) single bright red flowers with striking white variegation. Upright growth to 4 ft.

'Empire'. Profusion of single orange red flowers on 10–15-ft. plant.

'Fiesta'. Single bright orange flowers 6–7 in. wide; white eye zone at flower center edged red. Petal edges ruffled. Strong, erect growth to 6–7 ft.

'Fullmoon'. Double pure yellow flowers. Moderately vigorous growth to a compact 6 ft.

'Golden Dust'. Bright orange single flowers with yellow orange centers. Compact, thick-foliaged plant 4 ft. tall.

'Hula Girl'. Large single canary yellow flowers have deep red eye. Compact growth to 6 ft. Flowers stay open several days.

'Itsy Bitsy Peach', 'Itsy Bitsy Pink', and 'Itsy Bitsy Red' are all tall (10–15-ft.) plants with small leaves and small (2–3-in.) single flowers.

'Izumi'. Long-lasting double orange flowers with red petal bases. Grows 6 ft. tall.

'Jason Okumoto'. Semidouble scarlet-throated orange flowers surrounded by collar of large pink petals (blooms have a cup-and-saucer look). Grows 10–15 ft. tall.

'Kate Sessions'. Flowers large, single, broad petaled, red tinged gold beneath. Moderate growth to 10 ft. Upright, open habit.

'Kona'. Ruffled double pink flowers. Vigorous, upright, bushy, to 15–20 ft. Prune regularly. 'Kona Improved' has fuller flowers of richer pink color.

'Morning Glory'. Single blush pink flowers changing to warmer pink with white petal tips. Grows 8–10 ft. tall.

'Powder Puff'. Creamy double flowers develop pink blush in cool weather. To 8 ft. tall.

'President'. Flowers single, 6–7 in. wide, intense red shading to deep pink in throat. Upright, compact, 6–7 ft. tall.

'Red Dragon' ('Celia'). Flowers small to medium, double, dark red. Upright, compact, 6–8 ft. tall.

'Rosea'. Heavy producer of double rose red flowers.

'Ross Estey'. Flowers very large, single, with broad, overlapping petals of pink shading coral orange toward tips. Heavy-textured flowers last 2–3 days on bush. Vigorous grower to 8 ft. Leaves unusually large, ruffled, polished dark green.

'Sundown' ('Jigora'). Double salmon orange flowers. Plant bushy, to 7 ft.

'Vulcan'. Large single red flowers with yellow on back of petals open from yellow buds. Flowers often last more than a day. Compact grower, 4–6 ft. tall.

'White Wings'. Single white, narrow-petaled flowers with small red eye. Profuse. Vigorous, open, upright growth to 20 ft.; prune to control legginess. Compact form with somewhat smaller flowers is available; it is generally sold under the name 'White Wings Compacta'.

H. sabdariffa. ROSELLE, JAMAICA SORREL, JAMAICA FLOWER. Annual. Tall (4–5-ft.), narrowish plant with oval, 3–5-lobed leaves, grown for fleshy red calyces which surround bases of yellow flowers. These calyces are used for making sauce, jelly, cool drinks, or teas; dried, they are known as Jamaica flowers. Their flavor is reminiscent of cranberry or currant. Plants need long, hot summer to ripen flowers; they do well in all interior valleys where frosts come late. Bloom begins as days shorten; early frosts prevent

H

harvest. Give tomato culture; space plants 1½–2 ft. apart in rows. Can be used as narrow temporary hedge.

H. syriacus. ROSE OF SHARON, SHRUB ALTHAEA. Deciduous shrub. Zones 1–21. To 10–12 ft. tall, upright and compact when young, spreading and open with age. Easily trained to single trunk with treelike top. Leaves medium sized, often 3 lobed, coarsely toothed. Summer flowers single or double, 2½–3 in. across. Single flowers are slightly more effective, opening somewhat wider, but they produce many unattractive capsule-type fruits.

Grows easily in sun or part shade. Water requirements moderate; established plants take some drought. Prune to shape; for bigger flowers, cut back (in winter) previous season's growth to 2 buds. Resistant to oak root fungus.

Best varieties, some hard to find, are these: 'Albus', single pure white, 4-in. flowers; 'Anemoniflora' ('Paeoniflora'), semidouble red with deeper crimson eye; 'Ardens', double purple; 'Boule de Feu', double deep violet pink; 'Coelestis', single violet blue with reddish purple throat; 'Collie Mullens', double magenta rose with crimson eye; 'Diana', large single pure white that drops clean and forms few seed pods; 'Lucy', double magenta rose with red eye; 'Purpurea', semidouble purple, red at base of petals; 'Red Heart', single pure white with deep red center; 'Woodbridge', single magenta rose with red eye.

HIMALAYAN POPPY. See *Meconopsis betonicifolia*.

HINDU-ROPE PLANT. See *Hoya carnosa* 'Compacta'.

HIPPEASTRUM. *Amaryllidaceae*. AMARYLLIS. Bulbs. Zones 12, 13, 19, 21–24; elsewhere as pot plant indoors or in greenhouse or frostproof outdoor area. Native to tropics and subtropics. Many species are useful in hybridizing, but only hybrids are generally available; these are usually sold as giant amaryllis or Royal Dutch amaryllis (though many are grown in South Africa or elsewhere). Named varieties or color selections in reds, pinks, white, salmon, near-orange, some variously marked and striped. Two to several flowers, often 8–9 in. across, form on stout, 2-ft. stems. Where plants are grown outdoors, flowers bloom in spring; indoors, they bloom just a few weeks after planting. Broad, strap-shaped leaves usually appear after bloom, grow through summer, disappear in fall.

Hippeastrum hybrid

Usually grown in pots. Plant November–February, in rich, sandy mix with added bonemeal or superphosphate. Allow 2-in. space between bulb and edge of pot. Set upper half of bulb above soil surface. Firm soil, water well, then keep barely moist until growth begins. Wet, airless soil causes root rot.

To force early bloom indoors, keep in warm, dark place until rooted. Growers maintain bottom heat and air temperatures of 70°–85°F. until flower stalk is 6 in. tall, then put in a warm place in light shade. In homes, keep in warm room where air is not too dry; can grow in sunny indoor window boxes. Increase watering as leaves form. Feed lightly every 2 weeks through flowering period.

When flowers fade, cut off stem, keep up watering; feed to encourage leaf growth. When leaves yellow, withhold water, let plants dry out. Repot in late fall or early winter.

HIPPOCREPIS comosa. *Leguminosae*. Perennial ground cover. Zones 8–24. Forms mat 3 in. high; spreads to 3 ft. Leaves divided into 7–15 medium green, oval, ¼–½-in.-long leaflets. Flowers golden yellow, sweet pea shaped, ½ in. long, in loose clusters of 5–12. Blooms in spring; some repeat bloom in summer. Drought resistant and takes poor soils, but lusher looking with good soil, adequate water. Sun. Roots bind soil on steep banks. Bank cover, rock garden, small-scale lawn substitute (mow once just after flowers fade). Set 1 ft. apart. Takes light foot traffic.

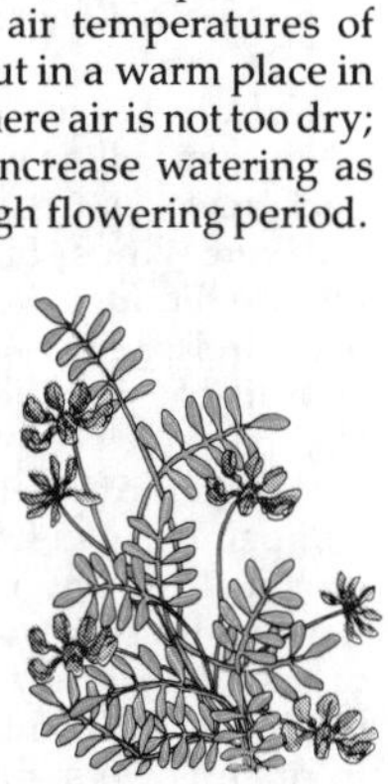

Hippocrepis comosa

HOGAN CEDAR. See *Thuja plicata* 'Fastigiata'.

HOHERIA. *Malvaceae*. Evergreen trees and deciduous trees or shrubs. Native to New Zealand. Leaves are bright green, leathery, toothed, 3–5 in. long, 1½–2 in. wide. Pure white flowers about 1 in. wide form in clusters among leaves. Keep moist.

H. glabrata. MOUNTAIN RIBBONWOOD. Deciduous tree or large shrub. Zones 5, 6. To 40 ft. high, usually much less. Attractive with azaleas or rhododendrons. Summer bloom.

H. populnea. NEW ZEALAND LACEBARK. Evergreen tree. Zones 4–6, 15–17, 21–24. In growth habit, as graceful as birch; in addition, it puts on good show of flowers from late summer into fall. Grows fast to eventual 50–60 ft., but enjoyable for many years as 20–30-ft., slender tree. Like birch, it's ideal for multiple planting and groves. Has deep, well-behaved root system. Inner bark is interestingly perforated; in New Zealand, it is used for ornamental purposes. Rarely seen but worth seeking out for coastal gardens. Needs humid air to thrive, but dislikes cold ocean winds. Self-sows where adapted, and seedling volunteers could be a problem where tree is growing in ground cover.

Hoheria glabrata

HOLLY. See *Ilex*.

HOLLYFERN. See *Cyrtomium falcatum*.

HOLLYHOCK. See *Alcea rosea*.

HOLLYLEAF CHERRY. See *Prunus ilicifolia*.

HOLLYLEAF REDBERRY. See *Rhamnus crocea ilicifolia*.

HOLLYLEAF SWEETSPIRE. See *Itea ilicifolia*.

HOLODISCUS. *Rosaceae*. Deciduous shrubs related to *Spiraea* and similar in appearance. All are western natives.

H. discolor. CREAM BUSH, OCEAN SPRAY. Zones 1–7, 14–17. Native to Coast Ranges, Sierra Nevada; north to British Columbia, east to Rocky Mountains. May grow to 20 ft. in moist, rich soil and partial shade. Fairly drought tolerant. In dry, sunny situations, such as east of Cascades in Oregon and Washington, may grow only 3 ft. tall. Triangular leaves to 3 in. long are deep green above, white and hairy beneath; edges are coarsely toothed. Nodding, branched clusters (sometimes to 1 ft. long) of small, creamy white flowers tip branches May–July, make quite a show, attract birds. Flowers fade to tannish gold, remain attractive for a long time. Prune back after flowers turn brown and clusters wither.

Holodiscus discolor

H. dumosus. MOUNTAIN SPRAY, ROCK SPIRAEA. Zones 1–3, 10. Native to shady canyons in Rockies from Wyoming south. Generally smaller than *H. discolor* and with narrower flower clusters, but may reach 15 ft. Coarsely toothed leaves less than 1 in. long.

H

HOMALOCLADIUM platycladum. *Polygonaceae.* RIBBON BUSH, CENTIPEDE PLANT. Strange shrubby plant. Zones 8, 9, 12–24. Novelty or collector's plant, sometimes grown in raised beds or containers. Grows in sun or shade. Usually leafless, with long, narrow, flat, bright green, jointed stems reaching 2–4 ft. tall, usually less in pots. Small, narrow leaves sometimes show on stem edges. Flowers inconspicuous. Berrylike red fruit.

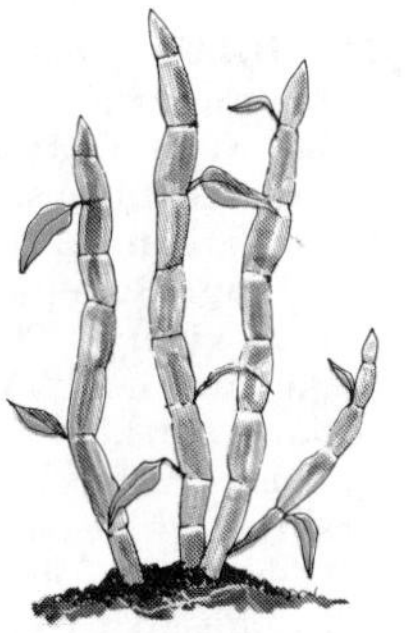

Homalocladium platycladum

HOMERIA collina. *Iridaceae.* Corm. Zones 4–24. Branching or unbranched 1½-ft. stems bear 2½–3-in.-wide flowers in California poppy colors—golden yellow or muted orange. Corms planted in September or October send up a single floppy, grasslike leaf; flowers follow in March or April. Give sun (part shade in hottest areas), good drainage; water only if winter rains are insufficient. Plants are dormant in summer. They multiply freely.

Homeria collina

HONEY BUSH. See *Melianthus major.*

HONEY LOCUST. See *Gleditsia triacanthos.*

HONEYSUCKLE. See *Lonicera.*

HONG KONG ORCHID TREE. See *Bauhinia blakeana.*

HOOP PINE. See *Araucaria cunninghamii.*

HOP. See *Humulus.*

HOP BUSH, HOPSEED BUSH. See *Dodonaea viscosa.*

HOP TREE. See *Ptelea trifoliata.*

HOREHOUND. See *Marrubium vulgare.*

HORNBEAM. See *Carpinus.*

HORNED POPPY. See *Glaucium.*

HORSE BEAN. See Bean, Broad.

HORSECHESTNUT. See *Aesculus.*

HORSERADISH. *Cruciferae.* All Zones. A large, coarse, weedy-looking perennial plant grown for its large, coarse, white roots, which are peeled, grated, and mixed with vinegar or cream to make a condiment. Does best in rich, moist soils in cool regions. Grow it in some sunny out-of-the-way corner. Start with roots planted 1 ft. apart in late winter or early spring. Dig full-grown roots in fall, winter, or spring. It's best to dig just a few outside roots at a time; then you'll have your horseradish fresh and hot.

Horseradish

HORSETAIL. See *Equisetum hyemale.*

HORSETAIL TREE. See *Casuarina equisetifolia.*

HOSTA *(Funkia).* *Liliaceae.* PLANTAIN LILY. Perennials. Zones 1–10, 12–21. Their real glory is in their leaves—typically heart shaped, shiny, distinctly veined. Flowers come as a dividend: thin spikes topped by several trumpet-shaped flowers grow up from foliage mounds in summer, last for several weeks. Give sun, light shade, or heavy shade (north side of house); water regularly in summer. Feeding once a year will bring on extra leafy splendor. Blanket of peat moss around plants will prevent mud from splattering leaves. Slugs and snails love hostas; bait 3–4 times a year. All forms go dormant (collapse almost to nothing) in winter; fresh new leaves grow from roots in early spring. Good in containers. In ground, plants last for years; clumps expand in size and shade out weed growth. Few plants have undergone so many name changes; to be quite sure you are getting the one you want, buy it in full leaf.

Hosta decorata

New garden varieties are entering the scene in ever-increasing numbers; you'll find dwarf (6-in.) and giant (5-ft.) varieties, blue-leafed and gold-leafed types, and every gradation between. Many are available only from mail-order specialists. All are splendid companies for ferns and fernlike foliage plants such as *Dicentra.*

H. decorata (*H.* 'Thomas Hogg'). Plants to 2 ft. high. Oval leaves, 6 in. long, bluntly pointed at tips, green with silvery white margins. Lavender, 2-in.-long flowers.

H. 'Honeybells'. Large grass green leaves. Fragrant lavender flowers on 3-ft. stems.

H. 'Krossa Regal'. Big bluish green leaves arch upward and outward to make a 3-ft. vase-shaped plant. Lavender flower spikes can reach 5–6 ft. in late summer.

H. lancifolia *(H. japonica).* NARROW LEAFED PLANTAIN LILY. Leaves dark green, 6 in. long; not heart shaped, but tapering into the long stalk. Pale lavender, 2-in.-long flowers on 2-ft. stems.

H. plantaginea *(H. grandiflora, H. subcordata).* FRAGRANT PLANTAIN LILY. Scented white flowers, 4–5 in. long, on 2-ft. stems. Leaves bright green, to 10 in. long.

H. sieboldiana *(H. glauca).* Blue green leaves, 10–15 in. long, heavily veined. Many slender, pale lilac flowers nestle close to leaves. A showpiece plant near shaded pool or woodland path. The variety 'Frances Williams', sometimes called 'Gold Edge' or 'Gold Circle', makes clumps 4 ft. tall and as wide, with the typical blue green leaves of the species boldly edged in yellow.

H. undulata *(H. media picta, H. variegata).* WAVY-LEAFED PLANTAIN LILY. Wavy-margined, 6–8-in.-long leaves are variegated white on green. Foliage used in arrangements. Pale lavender flowers on 3-ft. stalks.

H. ventricosa *(H. caerulea).* BLUE PLANTAIN LILY. Deep green, broad, prominently ribbed leaves. Blue flowers on 3-ft. stems.

HOUSELEEK. See *Sempervivum.*

HOUTTUYNIA cordata. *Saururaceae.* Perennial. Zones 4–9, 14–24. Underground rhizomes send up 2–3-in. leaves that look much like those of English ivy, have odd scent of orange peel when crushed. Inconspicuous clusters of white-bracted flowers like tiny dogwood blossoms. Disappears completely in winter. Unusual ground cover in light or deep shade inland, sun near coast. Can spread aggressively in wet ground. 'Variegata' ('Chameleon') has showy splashes of cream, pink, yellow, and red on foliage, is attractive in container or (curbed) in shady garden.

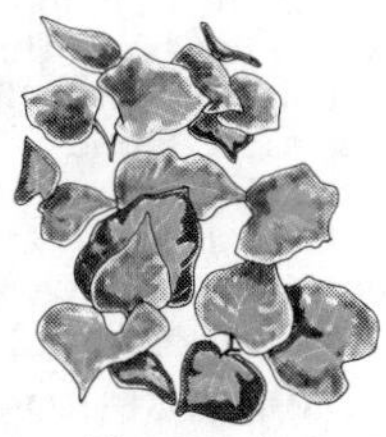

Houttuynia cordata

HOWEA. *Palmae*. Palms. Outdoors in Zones 17, 21–24; anywhere as house or greenhouse plant. Native to Lord Howe Island. These feather palms are the kentia palms of florists, and are usually sold under the name "kentia." Slow growing; with age, leaves drop to show clean, green trunk ringed with leaf scars.

Howea forsterana

Howeas are ideal pot plants—the classic parlor palms. Keep fronds clean and dust free to minimize spider mite problem.

H. belmoreana. SENTRY PALM. Less common than *H. forsterana*, smaller and more compact, with overarching leaves 6–7 ft. long. Stands some watering neglect, drafts, dust.

H. forsterana. PARADISE PALM. Larger than *H. belmoreana*, with leaves to 9 ft. long and long, drooping leaflets. Average water.

HOYA. *Asclepiadaceae*. WAX FLOWER, WAX PLANT. Shrubby or climbing house plants; *H. carnosa* used outdoors in mild climates. Thick, waxy, evergreen leaves and tight clusters of small waxy flowers. Commonly grown in sunny windows. Do best in rich, loose, well-drained soil. Bloom best when potbound; usually grown in containers even outdoors. Do not prune out flowering wood; new blossom clusters appear from stumps of old ones.

Hoya carnosa

H. bella. House or greenhouse plant. Shrubby, small leafed, to 3 ft., with slender, upright branches which droop as they grow older. Tight clusters of purple-centered white, ½-in. flowers in summer. Best in hanging basket. Average water.

H. carnosa. WAX FLOWER, WAX PLANT. Indoor plant or outdoors in Zones 15–24 with overhead protection—but even there it is quickly damaged by temperatures much below freezing. Vining to 10 ft. Leaves are oval, 2–4 in. long. Fragrant summer flowers are borne in big, round, tight clusters; each ½-in.-wide blossom is creamy white, centered with a perfect 5-pointed pink star. Red young leaves give additional touch of color. Water deeply in summer, then allow soil to go partially dry before watering again. In cool climates, let plant go dormant in winter, giving only enough water to keep it from shriveling. Outdoors, train on pillar or trellis in shade; indoors, train on wire in sunny window.

'Variegata' has leaves edged with white suffused with pink; it is not as vigorous or hardy as the green form. 'Exotica' shows yellow and pink variegation. 'Krinkle Kurl' has crinkly leaves very closely spaced on short stems; it is often sold as *H. c.* 'Compacta' or as HINDU-ROPE PLANT.

HUCKLEBERRY. See *Vaccinium ovatum, V. parvifolium.*

HUMATA tyermannii. *Polypodiaceae*. BEAR'S FOOT FERN. Outdoors in Zones 17, 23, 24; elsewhere an indoor or greenhouse plant. Native to China. This small fern has furry, creeping rhizomes that look something like bear's feet. Fronds 8–10 in. long, very finely cut, rising at intervals from the rhizome. Like *Davallia* in appearance and uses, but slower growing. Average water, partial shade.

Humata tyermannii

HUMMINGBIRD BUSH. See *Grevillea thelemanniana.*

HUMMINGBIRD FLOWER. See *Zauschneria.*

HUMULUS. *Cannabaceae*. HOP. Annual and perennial vines. Extremely fast growth. Need much water. Full sun. Large, deeply lobed leaves. Useful for summer screening on trellises or arbors.

Humulus lupulus

H. japonicus. JAPANESE HOP. Summer annual vine. To 20–30 ft. Flowers do not make true hops. Variety 'Variegatus' has foliage marked with white. Flowers in greenish clusters like pine cones. Sow seeds in spring where plants are to grow.

H. lupulus. COMMON HOP. Perennial vine. All Zones. This plant produces the hops used to flavor beer. Grow from roots (not easy to find in nurseries) planted in rich soil in early spring. Place thick end up, just below soil surface. Furnish supports for vertical climbing. Shoots appear in May and grow quickly to 15–25 ft. by midsummer. Give roots copious water once rapid growth starts. Leaves 3–5 lobed, toothed. Squarish, hairy stems twine vertically; to get horizontal growth, twine stem tips by hand. Light green hops (soft, flaky, 1–2-in. cones of bracts and flowers) form in August–September. They're attractive and have fresh, piny fragrance. Cut back stems to ground after frost turns them brown. Regrowth comes the following spring. Tender hop shoots can be cooked as a vegetable.

H. l. neomexicanus *(H. americanus).* Native to central and southern Rockies; scarcely differs from the cultivated hop noted above.

HUNNEMANNIA fumariifolia. *Papaveraceae*. MEXICAN TULIP POPPY, GOLDEN CUP. Perennial, usually treated as annual. Related to California poppy (*Eschscholzia californica*). Bushy, open, 2–3 ft. high, with very finely divided blue green leaves. Clear soft yellow, cup-shaped flowers with crinkled petals are about 3 in. across, bloom July–October. Showy plant in masses; striking with scarlet *Zauschneria californica* or with blues of ceratostigma, echium, or penstemon. Blooms last for a week in water if cut in bud. Plant from nursery flats or sow seed in place in warm, dry, sunny position; thin seedlings to 1 ft. apart. Reseeds. Plants need excellent drainage, will die out if overwatered.

Hunnemannia fumariifolia

HYACINTH BEAN. See *Dolichos lablab.*

HYACINTHUS. *Liliaceae*. HYACINTH. Bulbs. All Zones. As garden plants, best adapted in cold-winter climates. Bell-shaped, fragrant flowers in loose or tight spikes rise from basal bundle of narrow bright green leaves. All are spring blooming. Plant in fall. Where winters are cold, plant September–October. In mild areas, plant October–December.

Hyacinthus orientalis

H. amethystinus. See *Brimeura.*

H. azureus. See *Muscari azureum.*

H. orientalis. COMMON HYACINTH. Grows to 1 ft., with fragrant, bell-shaped flowers in white, pale blue, or purple blue. Two basic forms are the Dutch and the Roman or French Roman.

DUTCH HYACINTH, derived from *H. orientalis* by breeding and selection, has large, dense spikes of waxy, bell-like, fragrant flowers in white, shades of blue, purple, pink, red, cream, buff, and salmon. The size of the flower spike is directly related to the size of the bulb.

Biggest bulbs are desirable for exhibition plants or for potting; next largest size is most satisfactory for bedding outside. Small bulbs give smaller, looser clusters with more widely spaced flowers. These are sometimes called miniature hyacinths. Set the larger bulbs 6 in. deep, smaller bulbs 4 in. Hyacinth bulbs have invisible barbs on their surfaces that can cause some people's skin to itch; after handling, wash hands before touching face or eyes.

Hyacinths look best when massed or grouped; rows look stiff, formal. Mass bulbs of a single color beneath flowering tree or in border. Leave bulbs in ground after bloom, continue to feed and water until foliage yellows. Flowers tend to be smaller in succeeding years, but maintain same color and fragrance.

Choice container plants. Pot in porous mix with tip of bulb near surface. After potting, cover containers with thick mulch of sawdust, wood shavings, or peat moss to keep bulbs cool, moist, shaded until roots well formed; remove mulch, place in full light when tops show. Also grow hyacinths in water in special hyacinth glass, the bottom filled with pebbles and water. Keep in dark, cool place until rooted, give light when top growth appears; place in sunny window when leaves have turned uniformly green.

ROMAN or FRENCH ROMAN HYACINTH *(H. o. albulus)* has white, pink, or light blue flowers loosely carried on slender stems; usually several stems to a bulb. Earlier bloom than Dutch hyacinths. These are well adapted to mild-winter areas, where they naturalize under favorable conditions. Where winters are cold, grow in pots for winter bloom.

HYDRANGEA. *Saxifragaceae.* Deciduous shrubs or vine. Big, bold leaves and large clusters of long-lasting flowers in white, pink, red, or (under some conditions) blue. Summer, fall bloom. Flower clusters may contain sterile flowers (conspicuous, with large, petal-like sepals) or fertile flowers (small, starry petaled); or they may feature a cluster of small fertile flowers surrounded by ring of big sterile ones (these are called the lace cap hydrangeas). Sterile flowers last long, often holding up for months, gradually fading in color. Effective when massed in partial shade or planted in tubs on paved terrace.

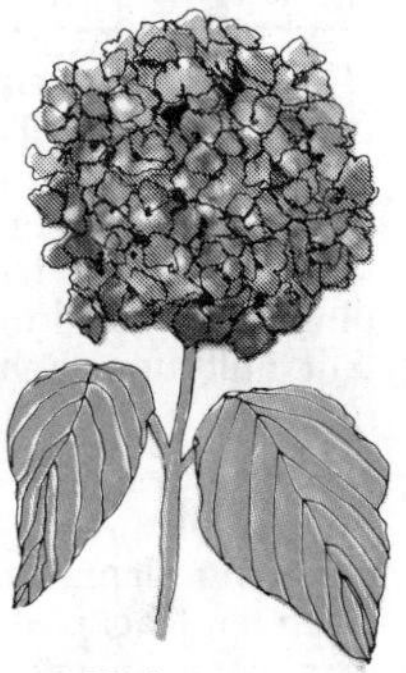

Hydrangea macrophylla

Easy to grow in rich, porous soil; dependent on heavy watering. Protect against overhead sun inland; in cool coastal gardens, plants can take full sun. Fast growing—prune to control size and form; cut out stems that have flowered, leaving those which have not. To get biggest flower clusters, reduce number of stems; for numerous middle-sized clusters, nicely spaced, keep more stems.

H. anomala. CLIMBING HYDRANGEA. Deciduous vine. Zones 1–21. Climbs high by clinging aerial rootlets. Shrubby and sprawling without support. Roundish, 2–4-in.-long, green, heart-shaped leaves. Mature plants develop short, stiff, flowering branches with flat white flower clusters, 6–10 in. wide, in lace cap effect. *H. a. petiolaris (H. petiolaris),* more common form in cultivation, differs hardly at all.

H. arborescens. SMOOTH HYDRANGEA. Deciduous shrub. Zones 1–21. Upright, dense to 10 ft. Oval, grayish green, 4–8-in. leaves. White flowers in 6-in. roundish clusters, June to frost; a few large sterile flowers. Much better is variety 'Grandiflora', with very large clusters made up of large sterile flowers. The variety 'Annabelle' is lower growing (to 4 ft.), yet produces enormous (to 12 in.) globular clusters of sterile white flowers throughout the summer.

H. macrophylla *(H. hortensia, H. opuloides, H. otaksa).* BIGLEAF HYDRANGEA, GARDEN HYDRANGEA. Deciduous shrub. Zones 2–24. Symmetrical, rounded habit; grows to 4–8 or even 12 ft. Thick, shining, coarsely toothed leaves to 8 in. long; white, pink, red, or blue flowers in big clusters.

Great performer in areas where winters are fairly mild, but disappointing where plants freeze to ground every year (may never bloom under these conditions). Protect in Zones 2 and 3 by mounding soil or leaves over bases of plants.

There are hundreds of named varieties, and plants may be sold under many names. Florists' plants are usually French hybrids, dwarfer (1–3 ft. tall) and larger flowered than old garden varieties. Two varieties are unmistakable: 'Domotoi' has clusters of pink or blue double sterile flowers; 'Tricolor' (usually sold as 'Variegata'), a lace cap, has dark green leaves strongly marked with cream and light green.

Pink and red garden hydrangeas often turn blue or purple in acid soils. Florists grow French hybrids as pot plants, controlling flower color by controlling soil mix; blue-flowering plants from the florist may show pink flowers when planted out in neutral or alkaline soil. Plants can be made (or kept) blue by applying aluminum sulfate to soil; plants can be kept red or made redder by liming or applying superphosphate in quantity. Treatment is not effective unless started well ahead of bloom.

H. paniculata 'Grandiflora'. PEEGEE HYDRANGEA. Deciduous shrub. Zones 1–21. Upright, of coarse texture. Can be trained as a 25-ft. tree, but best as a 10–15-ft. shrub. Leaves 5 in. long, turn bronzy in fall. Flowers in upright 10–15-in.-long clusters are white, slowly fading to pinky bronze.

H. quercifolia. OAKLEAF HYDRANGEA. Deciduous shrub. Zones 1–22. Broad, rounded shrub to 6 ft. with very handsome, deeply lobed, oaklike, 8-in.-long leaves that turn bronze or crimson in fall. Creamy white flowers in open clusters, June. Pruned to ground each spring, it makes compact, 3-ft. shrub. Thinned out to well-spaced branches, it makes a distinguished container plant.

Hydrangea quercifolia

Hydrophyllaceae. The waterleaf family, largely but not entirely native to North America, includes annuals, perennials, and a few shrubs. Many have flowers in crosier-shaped clusters. *Nemophila,* and *Phacelia* are sometimes grown in gardens.

HYMENOCALLIS. *Amaryllidaceae.* Bulbs. Zones 5, 6, 8, 9, 14–24. Clumps of strap-shaped leaves like those of amaryllis. In June and July, 2-ft. stems bear several very fragrant flowers; blooms resemble daffodils, but the center cup has 6 slender, spidery free segments. Unusual summer-blooming plant for borders or containers. Plant in rich, well-drained soil—in late fall or early winter in frostless areas, after frosts in colder climates. Likes sun or light shade. Set bulbs with tips 1 in. below surface. Water well during growth and bloom; dry off when foliage begins to yellow. Dig and wash bulbs, dry in inverted position; do not cut off fleshy roots. Store in open trays at 60°–75°F.

Hymenocallis narcissiflora

H. festalis. Free flowering, with 4 or more pure white flowers, the cup with very narrow curved segments. Leaves resemble those of *H. narcissiflora.*

H. narcissiflora *(Ismene calathina).* BASKET FLOWER, PERUVIAN DAFFODIL. Leaves 1½–2 ft. long, 1–2 in. wide. White, green-striped flowers in clusters of 2–5. Variety 'Advance' has pure white flowers, faintly lined with green in throat.

H. 'Sulfur Queen'. Primrose yellow flowers with light yellow, green-striped throat. Leaves like those of *H. narcissiflora.*

HYMENOCYCLUS. See *Malephora.*

HYMENOSPORUM flavum. *Pittosporaceae.* SWEETSHADE. Evergreen small tree or large shrub. Zones 8, 9, 14–23. Native to Australia. Slow to moderate growth to 20–40 ft. with 15–20-ft. spread. Graceful, upright,

Hymenosporum flavum

slender, open habit in first 10 years. Leaves shiny dark green, 2–6 in. long, 1–2 in. wide, with tendency to cluster near ends of twigs and branches. In early summer, bears clusters of yellow flowers with pronounced fragrance of orange blossom honey.

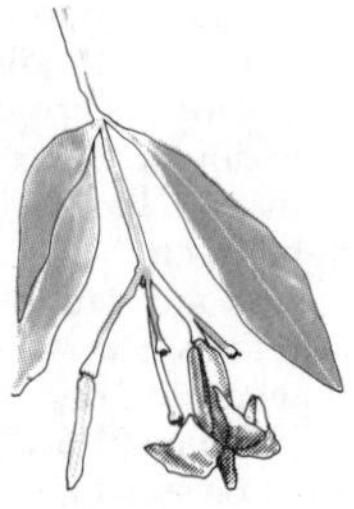

Hymenosporum flavum

Best away from coastal winds. Should have fast soil drainage, routine feeding, and well-spaced deep watering rather than lawn watering. Full sun or light shade. Early training is necessary, since branches spread out in almost equal threes, creating weak crotches that are likely to split. Strengthen branches by frequent pinching and shortening. As single tree, needs staking for several years. Attractive planted in small groves, in which case trees need no staking or training.

HYPERICUM. *Hypericaceae.* ST. JOHNSWORT. Shrubs and perennials, evergreen or semi-evergreen. Zones 4–24, except as noted below. Best in mild, moist coastal areas. Open, cup-shaped, 5-petaled flowers range in color from creamy yellow to gold, and have prominent sunburst of stamens in center. Neat leaves vary in form and color. Plants useful for summer flower color and fresh green foliage. Mass planting, ground cover, informal hedges, borders. Sun near coast, part shade in hot-summer areas. Any soil. Most kinds stand some drought, but perform better with water.

Hypericum calycinum

H. androsaemum. Shrub to 3 ft. tall, with stems arching toward the top. Leaves to 4 in. long, 2 in. wide. Clusters of ¾-in., golden yellow flowers at tops of stems and at ends of side branches. Blossoms followed by berrylike fruits—first red, then purple, then black. Useful as tall ground cover at edge of woods, shaded slopes, wild garden.

H. beanii *(H. patulum henryi).* To 4 ft., with light green, oblong leaves on graceful, willowy branches. Evergreen. Flowers brilliant golden yellow, 2 in. across, July–October. Shabby winter appearance in cold-winter areas. Good for low, untrimmed hedge, mass planting.

H. calycinum. AARON'S BEARD, CREEPING ST. JOHNSWORT. Evergreen shrub; semideciduous where winters are cold. Zones 2–24. Grows to 1 ft. tall; spreads by vigorous underground stems. Short-stalked leaves to 4 in. long; medium green in sun, yellow green in shade. Flowers bright yellow, 3 in. across. Tough, dense ground cover for sun or shade; competes successfully with tree roots, takes poor soil, some drought. Fast growing, will control erosion on hillsides. Can invade other plantings unless confined. Plant from flats or as rooted stems; set 1½ ft. apart. Clip or mow off tops every 2–3 years during dormant season.

H. coris. Evergreen subshrub. To 6–12 in. tall or taller. Leaves narrow, ½–1 in. long, in whorls of 4–6. Flowers yellow, ¾ in. across, in loose clusters. Blooms April–June. Good ground cover or rock garden plant.

H. frondosum. Zones 2–24. Native to Georgia. Evergreen or semievergreen in mild climates. Grows 1 ft. tall, twice as wide. Clusters of 1½-in., bright yellow flowers form at branch tips throughout summer. Grows in sun or shade; tolerates drought.

H. 'Hidcote' *(H. patulum* 'Hidcote'). Rounded shrub to 4 ft.; semievergreen in colder climates, where freezing keeps height closer to 2 ft. Leaves 2–3 in. long. Flowers yellow, 3 in. wide; blooms all summer.

H. kouytchense. Semievergreen. Twiggy, rounded shrub 1½–2 ft. tall, 2–3 ft. wide, with pointed oval, 2-in. leaves. Flowers golden yellow, 2–3 in. across, heavily produced July–August.

H. moseranum. GOLD FLOWER. Evergreen shrub or perennial. To 3 ft. tall where winters are mild; grows as hardy perennial in cold-winter areas. Moundlike habit with arching, reddish stems. Leaves 2 in. long, blue green beneath. Flowers golden yellow, 2½ in. across; borne singly or in clusters of up to 5 blossoms. Blooms June–August. Cut back in early spring.

H. patulum henryi. See *H. beanii.*

H. patulum 'Hidcote'. See *H.* 'Hidcote'.

H. reptans. Flat-growing shrublet that roots along ground. Leaves ¼–½ in. long, crowded along stems; flowers to 1¾ in. wide. Rock garden plant. Give protection from frosts in colder regions.

H. 'Rowallane'. Evergreen shrub. Upright to 3–6 ft., rather straggly growth. Flowers bright yellow, 2½–3 in. across, profuse in late summer and fall. Leaves 2½–3½ in. long. Remove older branches annually.

H. 'Sungold'. See *H. kouytchense.*

HYPOCYRTA nummularia. See *Alloplectus nummularia.*

HYPOESTES phyllostachya *(H. sanguinolenta).* *Acanthaceae.* FRECKLE FACE, PINK POLKA-DOT PLANT. Indoor foliage plant. Can reach 1–2 ft. tall. Slender stems bear oval, 2–3-in.-long leaves spotted irregularly with pink. A selected form known as 'Splash' has larger spots. Blooms very rarely. Plant in loose, peaty mixture in pots or planters. Feed with liquid fertilizer. Pinch tips to make bushy.

Hypoestes phyllostachya

HYSSOPUS officinalis. *Labiatae.* HYSSOP. Perennial herb. All Zones. Compact growth to 1½–2 ft. Narrow, dark green, pungent leaves; profusion of dark blue flower spikes, July–November. There are also white- and pink-flowered forms. Fairly drought resistant. Full sun or light shade.

Hyssopus officinalis

IBERIS. *Cruciferae.* CANDYTUFT. Annuals, perennials. All Zones. These are free-blooming plants bearing clusters of white, lavender, lilac, pink, rose, purple, carmine, or crimson flowers from early spring to summer. Use annuals for borders, cutting; perennials for edging, rock gardens, small-scale ground covers, containers.

In fall (in mild areas) or early spring, sow seed of annual kinds in place or in flats. Set transplants 6–9 in. apart. Plant perennials in sun or partial shade in fall or spring; water deeply and infrequently. Shear lightly after bloom to stimulate new growth.

I. amara. HYACINTH-FLOWERED CANDYTUFT, ROCKET CANDYTUFT. Annual. Fragrant white flowers in tight, round clusters that elongate into hyacinthlike spikes on 15-in. stems. Narrow, slightly fuzzy leaves.

Iberis sempervirens

I. sempervirens. EVERGREEN CANDYTUFT. Perennial. Grows 8 in. to 1 ft. or even 1½ ft. high, spreading about as wide. Leaves narrow, shiny dark green, good looking all year. Flower clusters pure white, on stems long enough to cut for bouquets. Plants bloom early spring to June, but first flowers may appear as early as November in mild areas. Lower, more compact varieties are 'Little Gem', 4–6 in. tall; 'Purity', 6–12 in. tall, wide spreading; 'Snowflake', 4–12 in. tall, 1½–3 ft. wide. 'Snowflake' differs from species in its broader, more leathery leaves, larger flowers in larger clusters on shorter stems; it is extremely showy in spring and blooms sporadically all year in milder areas.

I. umbellata. GLOBE CANDYTUFT. Annual. Bushy plants 12–15 in. high. Lance-shaped leaves to 3½ in. long. Flowers in pink, rose, carmine, crimson, salmon, lilac, and white. Dwarf strains 'Dwarf Fairy' and 'Magic Carpet' grow to 6 in. tall, in the same colors.

ICE PLANT. *Aizoaceae.* Succulent perennials, subshrubs, or annuals. Once conveniently lumped together as *Mesembryanthemum,* but now classified under several different names. A brief summary of plants under new names:

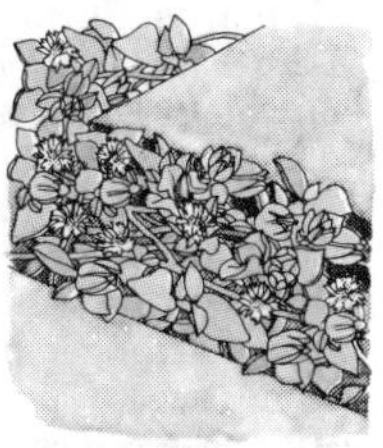

Delosperma 'Alba'

Aptenia. Ground cover with small red flowers. Brightest green foliage in class.

Carpobrotus. Coarse, sturdy ice plants of beach and highway plantings.

Cephalophyllum. Slow spreading, hardy, showy flowers.

Delosperma. Good ground cover and bank cover.

Dorotheanthus. Annuals for summer bloom.

Drosanthemum. Profuse pink or purple flowers, useful on steep banks.

Lampranthus. Large flowering, brilliantly colorful as ground cover, in rock gardens.

Malephora. Ground covers with good-looking foliage, long bloom season.

Mesembryanthemum. Annuals of little ornamental value are the only plants left here. One is sometimes seen as naturalized roadside planting in California.

Oscularia. Dainty form, fragrance.

Descriptions of each of above are given under the listed names. All tolerate drought when established, but look best with some summer water; amount depends on heat, humidity. Plants require little summer water in coastal areas, more inland. Too much water can lead to dieback. Give just enough to keep plants looking lively. Feed lightly when fall rains begin, again after bloom. All need full sun, take most soils; won't take foot traffic.

IDESIA polycarpa. *Flacourtiaceae.* Deciduous tree. Zones 4–9, 14–17, 19–24. Native to Japan, China. To 50 ft. tall, usually much less, with strongly horizontal branch structure and broad crown. Thick, heart-shaped leaves, 6–10 in. long and nearly as wide, on 5–7-in. stalks. Yellow green flowers (June and July) in 10-in.-long, drooping clusters, fragrant but not showy; male and female flowers usually on separate trees. Female trees bear ornamental clusters of pea-sized fruit that turns from green to brown to red. Needs some summer water. Unusual lawn or shade tree. Large leaves and broad crown give idesia an exotic look; berries are handsome in fall and early winter, but you must have both male and female plants for fruiting.

Idesia polycarpa

ILEX. *Aquifoliaceae.* HOLLY. Evergreen shrubs or trees (deciduous types rarely grown in the West). English holly is most familiar, but other species are becoming popular, especially in warmer, drier parts of the West. Hollies range from foot-high dwarfs to 50-ft. trees. Leaves may be tiny or large, toothed or smooth, green or variegated. Plants sold as Dutch holly are simply hollies without marginal spines. Berries may be red, orange, yellow, or black.

Ilex aquifolium

Most holly plants are either male or female, and in general, both plants must be present for female to bear fruit. There are exceptions: some female holly plants will set fruit without pollination, and hormone sprays may induce berry set on female flowers. Safest way to get berries is to have plants of both sexes, or to graft male branch onto female plant. Male plants will have no berries.

Holly prefers rich, slightly acid, good garden soil with good drainage; it tolerates sun or shade, is most compact and fruitful in sun. (See descriptions for exceptions.) It needs ample water. Add thick mulch rather than cultivating around plant. Attractive background plant, useful as barrier.

Scale and mealybugs can attack in all holly-growing areas. Holly bud moth and leaf miner need attention on English holly in Northwest. Two sprays a year generally give good control. Use an oil in late March for scale and bud moth; spray with systemics or malathion during May for leaf miner. Birds will eat fruit. Diseases rarely a problem to the home gardener.

I. altaclarensis 'Wilsonii' ***(I. wilsonii).*** WILSON HOLLY. Shrub or tree. Zones 3–24. Hybrid between English holly and a Canary Island species. One of best hollies, especially in warmer regions. Takes sun, shade, wind, almost any soil. Moderately drought tolerant. Usually a 6–8-ft. shrub, but easily grown as 15–20-ft. single-stemmed tree. Evenly spine-toothed leaves to 5 in. long, 3 in. wide; thick, leathery, rich green. Heavy producer of bright red berries. Use as standard tree, espalier, shrub, screen, clipped hedge.

I. aquifolium. ENGLISH HOLLY, CHRISTMAS HOLLY. Shrub or tree. Zones 4–9, 14–24; at its best in Zones 4–6, 15–17. Occasionally seen in sheltered locations in colder climates. Native to southern and central Europe, British Isles. Slow growth to 40 ft., usually much less. Highly variable in leaf shape, color, and degree of spininess. Note that male plants will not have berries; females may or may not. Some varieties produce infertile berries without a pollinator but these berries are usually small, slow to develop, and quick to drop. English holly needs protection from sun in hot, dry areas and requires soil conditioning where soils are alkaline. Resistant to oak root fungus. Best-known varieties include:

'Angustifolia'. Grows as compact, narrow pyramid. Spiny leaves are ½ in. wide, 1½ in. long. Small, brilliant red berries.

'Balkans'. Hardiest of English hollies, this is grown from seed collected in the Balkan mountains. Upright plants with smooth, dark green leaves. Male and female (fruiting) forms are available.

'Big Bull'. Very ornamental male with large, nearly smooth-edged leaves.

'Boulder Creek'. Typical English holly with large leaves. Brilliant red berries.

'Ciliata Major'. Vigorous, erect holly with purple bark on young shoots. Large, olive-tinged dark green leaves are flat, long spined, with high gloss. Good berry producer.

'Ferox'. HEDGEHOG, PORCUPINE HOLLY. Male with sterile pollen. Twisted, fiercely spined leaves give it its common names.

'Fertilis'. Sets light crop of seedless berries without pollination.

'Gold Coast'. Male selection grown for bright yellow edging on its leaves. Dense growth to 6–8 ft.

'Little Bull'. Very ornamental compact male with small leaves.

'San Gabriel'. Bears seedless berries without pollination.

'Sparkler'. Strong, upright grower. Heavy crop of glistening red berries at an early age.

'Teufel's Deluxe'. Exceptionally dark green leaves. Large, early-ripening red berries.

'Teufel's Zero'. Upright with long slender branches, weeping. Dark red berries ripen early. Unusually hardy.

'Van Tol'. Smooth, glossy green leaves. Early to mature. Large dark red berries.

Varieties with variegated leaves are also sold. Types with silver-edged leaves: 'Argenteo-marginata', 'Silvery', 'Silver Queen' (male), 'Silver King'. Silver-centered leaves: 'Argentea-mediopicta', 'Silver Star', 'Silver Milkmaid'. Gold-edged leaves: 'Aureo-marginata', 'Golden Queen' (male), 'Lily Gold'. Gold-centered leaves: 'Golden Milkmaid', 'Pinto'.

I. aquipernyi. Shrub. Zones 4–9, 14–24. Hybrid between *I. aquifolium* and *I. pernyi.* Varieties 'Brilliant' and 'San Jose' grow 8–10 ft. (possibly to 20 ft.), with cone-shaped habit and dense foliage. Leaves short stalked, densely set on branches, twice as large as those of *I. pernyi,* with few but very pronounced teeth. Heavy crop of red berries without pollination. Resistant to oak root fungus.

(Continued on next page)

I

I. cornuta. CHINESE HOLLY. Shrub or small tree. Zones 4–24; best in Zones 8, 9, 14–16, 18–21. Needs long warm season to set fruit. Give it east or north exposure in desert climates. Dense or open growth to 10 ft. Typical leaves glossy, leathery, nearly rectangular, with spines at the 4 corners and at tip. Berries exceptionally large, bright red, long lasting. Great variation among varieties in fruit set, leaf form, spininess. In following list, all bear fruit without pollinator except those noted:

'Berries Jubilee'. Dwarf, dome-shaped plant with large leaves and very heavy crop of large, bright red berries. Leaves larger, spinier than those of 'Burfordii', on much smaller plant.

'Burfordii'. BURFORD HOLLY. Widely planted in low-elevation California. Leaves nearly spineless, cupped downward. Useful as espalier.

'Carissa'. Extremely dwarf, dense grower with small leaves; smaller than 'Rotunda'. Use for small containers, low hedge. No berries.

'Dazzler'. Compact, upright growth. Glossy leaves have a few stout spines along wavy margins. Loaded with berries.

'Dwarf Burford' ('Burfordii Nana'). Resembles 'Burfordii' but is much smaller; 5-year-old plants not likely to exceed 1½ ft. in height, spread. Small (1½-in.), light green, spineless leaves, densely set.

'Femina'. Very spiny leaves. Good berry producer.

'Rotunda'. DWARF CHINESE HOLLY. Compact low grower. A 6-year-old may be 1½ ft. high and as wide. Does not produce berries. A few stout spines and rolled leaf margins between spines make medium light green leaves nearly rectangular.

'Willowleaf'. Large shrub or small tree with dense, spreading growth pattern. Long, narrow, dark green leaves. Good crop of dark red berries.

I. crenata. JAPANESE HOLLY. Shrub. Zones 2–9, 14–24. Looks more like a boxwood than a holly. Dense, erect, usually to 3–4 ft., sometimes to 20 ft. Narrow, fine-toothed leaves, ½–¾ in. long. Berries are black. Extremely hardy and useful where winter cold limits choice of polished evergreens for hedges, edgings. All grow best in slightly acid soil. Sun or shade. Varieties sold:

'Compacta'. Dense, compact form useful for untrimmed hedge.

'Convexa' (often sold as *I. c. bullata*). Compact, rounded shrub to 4–6 ft.; broader than tall. Leaves are ½ in. long, roundish with edges cupped downward. Handsome clipped or unclipped.

'Glory'. Small, dense grower; round bush with tiny leaves. Male plant (no fruit).

'Green Island'. Low and spreading, to 2 ft. high.

'Green Thumb'. Compact, upright to 20 in. Deep green leaves.

'Helleri'. Dwarf to 1 ft. high, 2 ft. wide.

'Hetzii'. Similar to 'Convexa' but with larger leaves, more vigorous growth.

'Mariesii'. Smallest and slowest growing of Japanese hollies. Only 8 in. high in 10 years.

'Northern Beauty'. Resembles 'Hetzii' but is more compact.

I. dimorphophylla. OKINAWAN HOLLY. Shrub. Zones 16, 17, 19–24. Dwarf tropical evergreen holly with leaves less than 1 in. long, closely set with short spines. Red berries. Tender to frost.

I. latifolia. Tree. Zones 4–7, 15–17, 20–24. Native to China and Japan. Slow-growing, stout-branched tree to 50–60 ft. Largest leaves of all hollies: 6–8 in. long, dull dark green, thick and leathery, fine toothed. Large, dull red berries in large clusters.

I. meserveae. Zones 3–24. Hybrids between *I. aquifolium* and species from far northern Japan. Apparently the hardiest of hollies that have true holly look. Dense, bushy plants 6–7 ft. tall with purple stems and spiny, blue green, glossy leaves. Female forms include 'Blue Angel', 'Blue Girl', and 'Blue Princess'; male pollinators are 'Blue Boy' and 'Blue Prince'.

I. 'Nellie Stevens'. Shrub. Zones 4–9, 14–24. Hybrid between *I. cornuta* and *I. aquifolium.* Leaves suggest both parents. Showy berries. Large, fast growing; can be trained as tree.

I. opaca. AMERICAN HOLLY. Tree. Zones 2–9, 15, 16, 19–23. Native to eastern U.S. Slow-growing, pyramidal or round-headed tree to 50 ft. Leaves 2–4 in. long, dull or glossy green with spiny margins. Berries red, not as numerous as on *I. aquifolium.* Resistant to oak root fungus. Some of the many varieties are occasionally available in the West. They include: 'Brilliantissima', 'East Palatka', 'Howard', 'Manig', 'Mrs. Sarver', 'Old Heavy Berry', 'Rosalind Sarver'.

I. pernyi. Shrub or small tree. Zones 4–9, 14–24. Slow growth to 20–30 ft. Glossy, square-based leaves closely packed against branchlets; leaves are 1–2 in. long, with 1–3 spines on each side. Red berries are set tightly against stem.

I. 'San Jose Hybrid'. Shrub or small tree. Zones 4–9, 14–24. Probably a variety of *I. koehneana* (hybrid between *I. aquifolium* and *I. latifolia*). To 15–20 ft. Resembles *I. altaclarensis* 'Wilsonii', but has somewhat longer, narrower leaves. Growth upright, berry production heavy.

I. vomitoria. YAUPON. Shrub or small tree. Zones 3–9, 11–24. Native to southeastern U.S. Stands extremely alkaline soils better than other hollies. Large shrub or small tree to 15–20 ft. Often sheared into columnar form or grown as standard. Narrow, inch-long, dark green leaves. Tiny scarlet berries borne in profusion without pollinator. The following varieties are available:

'Nana'. DWARF YAUPON. Low shrub. Compact to 1½ ft. high and twice as wide. Refined, attractive. Formal when sheared.

'Pendula'. Weeping branches show to best effect when plant is trained as standard.

'Pride of Houston'. Large shrub or small tree, upright, freely branching. Use as screen or hedge.

'Stokes'. Dark green leaves, close set, compact. Smaller growing than 'Nana'.

IMMORTELLE. See *Xeranthemum annuum.*

IMPATIENS. *Balsaminaceae.* BALSAM, TOUCH-ME-NOT, SNAPWEED. Summer annuals, perennials. Annual kinds grow best in sun, perennials in partial shade in all but coastal areas. Ripe seed capsules burst open when touched lightly and scatter seeds explosively.

Impatiens wallerana

I. balsamina. BALSAM. Summer annual. Erect, branching, 8–30 in. tall. Leaves 1½–6 in. long, sharply pointed, deeply toothed. Flowers large, spurred, borne among leaves along main stem and branches. Colors plain or variegated, in white, pink, rose, lilac, red. Compact, bushy, double camellia-flowered forms are most frequently used. Sow seeds in early spring; set out plants after frost in full sun (light shade in hot areas). Needs lots of water.

I. glandulifera ***(I. roylei).*** Summer annual. Coarse, much branched, to 3–4 ft. Sharp-toothed leaves 2–6 in. long; large, pale lavender to purple flowers in clusters of 3 or more on long stalks.

I. holstii. See *I. wallerana.*

I. New Guinea Hybrids. Perennials grown as summer annuals. A varied group of striking plants developed from number of species native to New Guinea. Plants can be upright or spreading; they usually have very large leaves, often variegated with cream or red. Flowers are usually large (though not profuse); colors include lavender, purple, pink, red, orange. Best used as pot plants. Give ample water and fertilizer; need somewhat more light than conventional bedding impatiens. Many named kinds, ranging from spreading 8 in. to erect 2 ft. 'Sweet Sue', with bronzed foliage and bright orange, 2–3-in. flowers, can be grown from seed.

I. oliveri. POOR MAN'S RHODODENDRON. Perennial. Zones 15–17, 21–24; elsewhere as greenhouse or indoor/outdoor container plant. Shrubby to 4–8 ft. tall, up to 10 ft. wide. Bears many slender-spurred lilac, pale lavender, or pinkish flowers 2¼ in. across. Glossy dark green leaves to 8 in. long in whorls along stems. Blooms in partial or deep shade. Along coast grows in full sun, takes sea breezes, salt spray. Needs some summer water. Inland, frosts kill it to ground; regrows in spring.

I. repens. House plant. Trailer, with juicy red stems, tiny (fingernail-sized) bright green leaves. Bright yellow, 1½-in. flowers appear from time to time, with heaviest bloom in summer, early fall. Best in hanging pot with rich soil, summer feeding, regular watering, strong indirect light.

I. sultanii. See *I. wallerana.*

I. wallerana. BUSY LIZZIE. Perennial, usually grown as summer annual. Includes plants formerly known as *I. holstii* and *I. sultanii.* Rapid, vigorous growth: tall varieties (usually called *I. holstii*) to 2 ft.; dwarf, 4–12 in. Dark green, glossy, narrow, 1–3-in.-long leaves on pale green, juicy stems. Flowers 1–2 in. wide, in scarlet, pink, rose, violet, orange, or white.

Useful for bright flowers for many months in partial shade with begonias, fatsia, ferns, fuchsias, hydrangeas. Grow from seed, cuttings, or buy plants from flats. Rich, moist soil. Perhaps *the* most useful summer annual for shady gardens—especially in warm-summer climates.

Strains exist in bewildering variety. Single-flowered kinds are best for massing or bedding; they nearly cover themselves with flowers. Doubles have attractive flowers like little rosebuds, but don't match singles for mass show; use them in pots.

Dwarf strains and tall strains will all grow considerably taller if planted close together, but will still produce sheets of flowers throughout warm weather. All are available in single colors or as mixes. Some strains (Cinderella and ZigZag, for instance) have flowers striped or splashed with white. Improved strains of dwarf 6–12-in. plants are Cinderella, Elfin, and Minette.

IMPERATA cylindrica 'Rubra' ('Red Baron'). *Gramineae.* JAPANESE BLOOD GRASS. Perennial. Zones 4–24. Clumping grass with erect stems 1–2 ft. tall, the top half rich blood red. Striking in borders, especially where sun can shine through blades. Completely dormant in winter. Sun or part shade, average soil and water.

Imperata cylindrica 'Rubra'

INCARVILLEA delavayi. *Bignoniaceae.* Perennial. All Zones. Fleshy roots. Basal leaves 1 ft. long, divided into toothed leaflets. Stems to 3 ft., topped with clusters of 2–12 trumpet-shaped flowers 3 in. long and wide; rosy purple outside, yellow and purple inside. Blooms May–July. Sun or light shade. Needs deep, porous soil; roots rot in winter in waterlogged soils. In extremely cold climates, lift and store roots as you would dahlias. Cover roots with soil; do not let them dry out.

Incarvillea delavayi

INCENSE CEDAR. See *Calocedrus decurrens.*

INDIA HAWTHORN. See *Rhapiolepis indica.*

INDIAN MOCK STRAWBERRY. See *Duchesnea indica.*

INSIDE-OUT FLOWER. See *Vancouveria planipetala.*

IOCHROMA cyaneum ***(I. lanceolatum, I. purpureum, I. tubulosum).*** *Solanaceae.* Evergreen shrub. Zones 16, 17, 19–24. To 8 ft. or more. Dull dark green, oval to lance-shaped leaves, 5–6 in. long. Clusters of purplish blue, tubular, drooping, 2-in.-long flowers in summer; flower color of seedlings may vary to purplish rose or pink. Buy plants in bloom to get color you want. Fast-growing, soft-wooded shrub that looks best espaliered or tied up against wall. Best in full sun. Prune it hard after bloom; give plenty of water and protect from hard frosts. Control measuring worms with insecticide.

Iochroma cyaneum

IPHEION uniflorum ***(Brodiaea uniflora, Triteleia uniflora).*** *Amaryllidaceae.* SPRING STAR FLOWER. Bulb. Zones 4–24. Native to Argentina. Flattish, bluish green leaves which smell like onions when bruised. Spring flowers 1½ in. across, broadly star shaped, pale to deep blue, on 6–8-in. stems. Edging, ground cover in semiwild areas, under trees, large shrubs. Plant in fall in any soil; sun or part shade. Not fussy about water. Easy to grow; will persist and multiply for years.

Ipheion uniflorum

IPOMOEA. *Convolvulaceae.* MORNING GLORY. Perennial or annual vines. Includes many ornamental vines and the sweet potato; does not include wild morning glory or bindweed (*Convolvulus arvensis*). Ipomoeas may self-sow, but they don't spread by underground runners. Full sun. Don't need much water once established.

I. acuminata ***(I. leari).*** BLUE DAWN FLOWER. Perennial. Zones 8, 9, 12–24. Vigorous, rapid growth to 15–30 ft. Leaves dark green; flowers bright blue, fading pink, 3–5 in. across, clustered. Use to cover large banks, walls. Blooms in 1 year from seed; grows from cuttings, divisions, and layering of established plants.

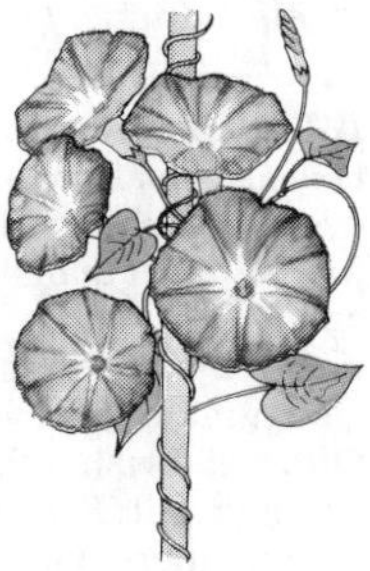

Ipomoea tricolor

I. alba ***(Calonyction aculeatum).*** MOONFLOWER. Perennial vine grown as summer annual, as greenhouse plant in coldest climates. Fast-growing (20–30 ft. in a season); provides quick summer shade for arbor, trellis, or fence. Effective combined with annual morning glory 'Heavenly Blue'. Luxuriant leaves 3–8 in. long, heart shaped, closely spaced on stems. Flowers fragrant, white (rarely lavender pink), often banded green, 6 in. long and wide. Theoretically flowers open only after sundown, but will stay open on dark, dull days. Seeds are hard; abrade or soak 1–2 days for faster sprouting.

I. batatas. See Sweet Potato.

I. nil. MORNING GLORY. Summer annual. Includes rare large-flowered Imperial Japanese morning glories and a few varieties of common morning glory, including rosy red 'Scarlett O'Hara'. For culture, see *I. tricolor.*

I. quamoclit ***(Quamoclit pennata).*** CYPRESS VINE, CARDINAL CLIMBER. Summer annual, twining to 20 ft. Leaves 2½–4 in. long, finely divided into slender threads. Flowers are tubes 1½ in. long, flaring at mouth into 5-pointed star; they are usually scarlet, rarely white.

I. tricolor. MORNING GLORY. Summer annual. Flowers showy, funnel shaped to bell-like, single or double, in solid colors of blue, lavender, pink, red, white, usually with throats in contrasting colors; some bicolored, striped. Most morning glories open only in morning, fade in afternoon. Bloom lasts until frost. Large, heart-shaped leaves.

Use on fence, trellis, as ground cover. Or grow in containers—train vine on stakes or wire cylinder or allow it to cascade. For cut flowers, pick stems with buds in various stages of development, place in deep vase. Buds open on consecutive days.

Sow seed in place in full sun after frost. To speed sprouting, notch seed coat with knife or file, or soak in warm water for 2 hours. Some growers sell scarified seed. For earlier start, sow seeds indoors in small pots or plant bands. Set out plants 6–8 in. apart. Ordinary soil, moderate water; no fertilizer.

'Heavenly Blue' morning glory twines to 15 ft. Flowers 4–5 in. across, pure sky blue, yellow throat. Early Call strain blooms early, is useful where summers are short. A dwarf strain with white markings on the leaves is known as Spice Islands or simply as Variegated. Plants grow 9 in. tall and spill to 1 ft. in width. Colors include red, pink, blue, and bicolors.

I

IPOMOPSIS. *Polemoniaceae.* Biennials or short-lived perennials. Erect single stems, finely divided leaves, and tubular red (or yellow and red) flowers. Startling in appearance, best massed; individual plants are very narrow. Sow seed in spring or early summer for bloom the following year. Sun, good drainage; quite drought tolerant.

I. aggregata *(Gilia aggregata).* Biennial. Native California to British Columbia, east to Rocky Mountains. To 2½ ft. tall. Flowers are red marked yellow (sometimes pure yellow), an inch or so long; borne in long, narrow clusters. June–September bloom.

I. rubra *(Gilia rubra).* Biennial or perennial. Native to southern U.S. To 6 ft. tall. Flowers red outside, yellow marked red inside. Summer bloom.

Ipomopsis aggregata

IRESINE herbstii. *Amaranthaceae.* BLOODLEAF. Annual or indoor plant in all Zones, evergreen shrub in Zones 22–24. Desirable for leaf rather than flower color. Stalked leaves are 1–2 in. long, oval to round, usually notched at tip; may be purplish red with lighter midrib and veins, or green or bronzed with yellowish veins. Leaf display best in summer, fall. Flowers inconspicuous. Good in containers. Give plants as much sun as possible. Except in mildest coastal climates, plants must be wintered indoors or treated as annuals. Easy to propagate from cuttings taken in fall and grown for spring and summer display. Similar is *I. lindenii,* with red leaves pointed instead of notched at the ends.

Iresine herbstii

Iridaceae. The large iris family includes many familiar (and unfamiliar) garden bulbs, corms, and fibrous-rooted perennials. Leaves are swordlike or grasslike, often in 2 opposing rows. Flowers may be simply arranged with 6 equal segments (crocus, for example) or highly irregular in appearance (as in iris).

IRIS. *Iridaceae.* Bulbs, rhizomes. All Zones, exceptions noted below. Large and remarkably diverse group of about 200 species, varying in flower color and form, cultural needs, and blooming season, although majority flower in spring or early summer. Leaves swordlike or grasslike; flowers showy, complex in structure. The 3 inner segments (petals or standards) are usually erect, arching or flaring; 3 outer ones (sepals or falls) hang or curve back. The following best-known and most widely adapted species and varieties are listed in 4 main groups: bulbous, crested, beardless, and bearded. The last 3 have rhizomes. The "beard" is a tuft of hair on falls.

Tall Bearded Iris

Listings below are necessarily incomplete. Iris specialists devote whole catalogues to varieties of irises (the most widely grown of which are tall bearded); many new varieties appear every year. Other specialists can furnish lesser-known species. Few irises (except bulbous) appear in retail nurseries.

Bulbous Irises

All have bulbs that become dormant in summer, can be lifted, stored until time to plant in fall. Flowers dainty, sometimes orchidlike.

I. reticulata. VIOLET-SCENTED IRIS. Bulb has netted outer covering. Long-tubed, 2–3-in., delicately fragrant, violet purple flowers edged gold. Stems 6–8 in. tall. Blooms March–April (late January–early February in mild areas). Thin, 4-sided, blue green leaves appear after bloom. Well adapted to pot culture. Named varieties are sometimes obtainable: 'Cantab' has pale blue flowers with orange markings, 'Harmony' is sky blue marked yellow, and 'J. S. Dijt' is reddish purple. These are sometimes sold in mixture. Similar in appearance but bright yellow in color is *I. danfordiae.* Plant bulbs 3–4 in. deep, 3 in. apart in well-drained soil, full sun. Good in rock gardens.

I. xiphioides. ENGLISH IRIS. Zones 1–6, 15–17, 21–24. Plant to 1½ ft.; flowers larger than Dutch irises, with velvety texture of Japanese irises. Early summer blooms (after Dutch iris) are bluish purple, wine red, maroon, blue, mauve, white; no yellows. Needs partial shade in warm-summer areas, full sun where cool. Give moist, cool, acid soil. In Zones 1–3, some gardeners find it hardier than Dutch irises; it has no top growth in autumn that is liable to freeze. Set bulbs 3–4 in. deep, 4 in. apart in fall.

Spanish irises. Derived from species native to Spain, its surrounding areas, and north Africa. The species are not grown commercially, but many varieties and color strains have been developed from them. Related to the 2 following kinds, Spanish irises have smaller flowers and bloom about 2 weeks later than Dutch irises. Culture is the same as for Dutch irises.

Dutch irises. Some growers lump Spanish and Dutch irises together; others consider them separate. Dutch irises acquired their name because the process of selecting and hybridizing them was first carried out by Dutch growers. The result was a group of lovely irises with long, straight stems and flowers in many clear colors—white, blue, orange, purple, mauve, yellow brown, and bicolors. They flower in March–April in warm climates, May–June in colder areas. Flowers are 3–4 in. across on stems 1½–2 ft. tall. They make excellent cut flowers.

Dutch Iris

Plant 4 in. deep, 3–4 in. apart, in October–November, in full sun. Bulbs are hardy, but in coldest climates, mulch in winter. Give ample water during growth. After bloom, let foliage ripen before digging; store bulbs in cool, dry place for no more than 2 months before replanting. Dutch irises are good in containers; plant 5 bulbs in 5–6-in. pot.

Wedgwood irises. Zones 4–24. These are often sold as Dutch irises, but actually they are the result of a series of crosses between Dutch iris antecedents and Moroccan native *I. tingitana.* Flowers are large, in shades of lavender blue with yellow markings. Bulbs are larger than those of Dutch irises. They are also more tender; plants bloom several weeks earlier. Outstanding for cutting, containers, early color in borders (plant behind bushy annuals or perennials to hide floppy leaves). The light blue 'Wedgwood' is best known; it blooms at same time as 'King Alfred' daffodils.

Crested Irises

Dainty, closely related to bearded irises, generally shade tolerant. Flowers distinguished by small, narrow crest at base of falls (outer petals). All are subject to slug, snail damage.

I. cristata. Leaves 4–6 in. long, ½ in. wide, from slender, greenish, free-running rhizomes. Lavender, light blue, or white flowers with golden crests, April–May. Hardy to −10°F. Cool, damp soil, light shade, summer water. Divide crowded plantings right after bloom or in fall after leaves die down. Good in rock gardens.

I. japonica. Sometimes called orchid iris; considered most beautiful of crested irises. Widely branched, 2-ft. stems bear pale lavender, fringed flowers with orange crests, late spring. Outside only in milder climates; grow in containers in coldest areas.

I. tectorum. ROOF IRIS. Broad, ribbed leaves 1 ft. tall. Late spring flowers purple blue with white crests, or pure white. Rich, somewhat acid soil, half shade, ample water. Best in mild, moist areas; short lived in very cold or dry climates. Planted on thatched roofs in Japan; good in rock gardens.

Beardless Irises

This group varies in size, appearance, and garden use. Distinguished by lack of beard (tufts of hairs on falls), rhizomes with many fibrous roots, need for moisture (some need much more than others).

I. ensata (formerly *Iris kaempferi*). JAPANESE IRIS. Graceful, upright, sword-shaped leaves with distinct raised midrib. Stems to 4 ft. bear 1, 2, or more large (4–12-in.), flat, velvety, single or double flowers in late June–July. Colors are purple, violet, pink, rose, red, or white, often edged in contrasting shade.

Iris ensata

Use in moist borders, at edge of pools or streams, or in boxes or pots plunged halfway to rim in pond or pool during growing season. Plant in fall or spring. Set rhizomes 2 in. deep, 1½ ft. apart, in rich, moist, acid soil. Sun in cool-summer areas, light shade in warm sections; shelter from wind. Give lots of water during growth, bloom. Not adapted to hot, dry climates. If soil or water is alkaline, apply aluminum sulfate or iron sulfate (1 oz. to 2 gal. water) several times during growing season. Divide crowded clumps in late summer or fall. Use rhizomes from clump edges, cut back foliage halfway, replant quickly.

I. foetidissima. GLADWIN IRIS. Hardy iris with evergreen leaves to 2 ft., ill smelling if bruised. Stems 1–1½ ft. tall; spring flowers unshowy, subtly attractive in shades of blue gray and chartreuse (a rare form is pale yellow). Real attraction is large seed capsules which open in fall to show numerous round, scarlet seeds, admired by flower arrangers. Plant will grow in sun or quite deep shade. Needs little care; extremely drought resistant.

I. missouriensis. WESTERN BLUE FLAG. Native to meadows and streambeds throughout the West, including Rocky Mountains. Grows 1–2 ft. tall. Spring flowers nearly 3 in. wide, pale lavender blue or white, veined bluish purple. Full sun to light shade. Established clumps tolerate drought after blooming season.

I. pseudacorus. YELLOW FLAG, YELLOW WATER IRIS. Tall iris (leaves to 5 ft., flower stems to 6–7 ft.) with 2–3-in., bright yellow flowers (there are forms with ivory-colored flowers). Needs acid, damp to wet soil. Thrives in shallow water. Decorative in pools or at edges of ponds. Full to light shade. Can seed itself prolifically; may become a pest in favored locations unless seed capsules are removed.

Siberian iris. Name given to group of hybrids based on *Iris sibirica* and *I. sanguinea* (*I. orientalis*). Graceful iris for perennial borders, cut flowers. Leaves somewhat grassy, narrow, erect, 1–2½ ft. high. Flowers shaped like Dutch irises appear on 2–3½-ft. stems as midseason bearded irises fade; colors include pale to deep blue, purple, purple red, and white. Excellent named varieties. Full sun. Acid to neutral soil; plenty of water during growing season. Well-established clumps perform best; divide (in September–October) only when old clumps begin to get hollow in center.

I. unguicularis (*I. stylosa*). WINTER IRIS. Zones 5–24. Dense clumps of narrow, dark green, 1–2-ft. leaves. Lavender blue flowers, with 6–9-in. tubes that look like stems, appear in November (where winters are mildest) to January–March. Use along paths, in borders. In Zones 5–7, grow next to sunny wall or house foundation. Slugs attracted to flowers. Sun or shade, any soil, much or little water. To reveal flowers partly concealed by foliage, cut back tallest leaves in September; also divide overgrown clumps at this time, or in March–April after flowering.

Louisiana irises. A group consisting of 3 or more species, mostly native to Mississippi delta, has given rise to hybrids of great beauty and grace. Among the species are: *I. fulva*, with unusual coppery red color; *I. giganticaerulea*, great size, height, good blue color; *I. brevicaulis*, hardy plant with long-lasting blue blooms. Hybrids somewhat like Japanese irises, but more graceful in form, with colors including red, white, yellow, pink, purple, blue. Height ranges from 2–5 ft. Mulch where ground freezes. Need rich, neutral or acid soil, ample water during growing season, partial shade in hot regions.

Pacific Coast irises. Following 3 species native to Pacific Coast are used in western gardens. Selections and hybrids of these irises also available from specialists. Where summer temperatures are high and soils are heavy, these irises are difficult to grow; give them light shade and lighten soil with organic material. Under these conditions, selections and hybrids of *I. douglasiana* are tougher than the others. Good in rock gardens.

I. douglasiana. Zones 4–24. Native to California coast from Santa Barbara north to Oregon. Large clump of evergreen 1–1½-ft. leaves. Stems 1–2 ft., often branched, with 2 to 3 or more flowers in white, cream, yellow, or lavender blue to deep reddish purple. Naturalize on banks, in fringe areas of garden. Full sun or light shade; tolerates many soils. Once established, withstands summer drought, but will also accept some summer water.

I. innominata. Zones 4–24. From mountains of northern California, southwestern Oregon. Clumps of evergreen, 15-in. leaves. Flowers on 6–10-in. stems; colors include clear yellow to orange, lavender, purple, brick red. Best forms are golden yellow with brown stripes. Woodland or rock garden plant.

I. tenax. Zones 4–17. From Washington and Oregon. Dense clumps of 6–12-in. deciduous leaves. Dainty flowers in white, dark purple blotched white, blue, lavender, pink, apricot, and cream on 6–12-in. stems. Rock garden. Porous soil, sun or light shade.

Spuria irises. This name was originally given to a group of species with similar habits, flower form, and culture. Of these, only an iris usually sold as *I. ochroleuca* is much grown today. It grows 3–5 ft. tall, and its white flowers have deep yellow blotches on the falls. Improved hybrids are replacing the species. They vary in height from 2–6 ft. They have somewhat larger flowers than the species and come in many shades—yellow, buff, bronze, lavender, blue, chartreuse, white.

All form clumps of stiff, erect, narrow, deep green leaves. Flowers similar to Dutch irises form on one side of tall, rigid stems, bloom in spring, early summer. Stately plants in borders, for cutting. Full sun or light shade, rich soil, ample moisture while growing, little or no summer water needed. Best dividing time is early fall. Difficult to dig after firmly established. Best performance when established. Plants often fail to bloom first year after dividing.

Bearded Irises

Probably most irises grown fall into this group. Many species, varieties, and many years of hybridizing by growers and iris fanciers have contributed to this great array of beautiful irises. All are characterized by having a beard (tuft of hairs) on the falls. Bearded irises can be separated into dwarf and median irises, tall bearded irises, and aril irises; the dwarf and median group can be further divided into 5 classes. (Note that the aril group has slightly different cultural requirements.)

Bearded irises need good drainage, full sun in cool climates, light shade in hottest areas. Adapt to most soils; feeding in early spring and after bloom will suffice.

Plant between July 1 and October 31; in cold-winter climates, the earlier part of this season is safer. Near coast, plant any time during this period. Set rhizomes 1–2 ft. apart, with top just below surface; spread roots well. Rhizomes grow from end with leaves; point that end in direction you want growth to take. For quick show, plant 3 rhizomes 1 ft. apart, 2 with growing ends pointed outward, the third aimed to grow into the space between them. On slopes, set rhizomes with growing end facing upward. Water to settle soil, start growth. Take care not to overwater later—once in 2 weeks sufficient in most sections; established clumps need only occasional watering in cool areas. In warm climates, soak deeply 2 or 3 times during hot season. After 3 or 4 years clumps are likely to be overcrowded. Lift and divide at best season for planting in your growing area. Divide rhizomes with sharp knife; discard older woody center; plant healthy sections with good fan of leaves. Trim leaves, roots to 6 in. for convenient handling. Let cut ends heal for several hours to a day before planting.

In late autumn, remove old or dry leaves. Where winters are severe, mulch plantings to prevent alternate freezing, thawing.

(Continued on next page)

I

Dwarf and Median Irises

These are smaller in plant size, stature, and flower size than taller beardeds but generally have flowers of tall bearded iris form. Median iris is a collective term for Standard Dwarfs, Intermediates, Border Beardeds, and Miniature Tall Beardeds.

Miniature Dwarf Bearded Irises. To 10 in. tall; flowers large for size of plant. Earliest to bloom of bearded irises (about 6 weeks before main show of tall beardeds). Hardy; multiplies quickly. Fine in rock gardens, front of borders. Wide range of colors.

Standard Dwarf Bearded Irises. Larger than miniature dwarfs, these range from 10–15 in. tall; flowers are larger (2–3 in. across) and bloom is very profuse.

Intermediate Bearded Irises. These bloom later than dwarfs but 1–3 weeks before tall bearded irises. Height is 15–28 in.; flowers are 3–5 in. across. Most are hybrids between standard dwarfs and tall bearded varieties, resemble larger standard dwarfs (as compared to border bearded irises in same height range, which are slightly smaller replicas of tall beardeds). Some give second bloom in fall.

Border Bearded Irises. Blooming at the same time as tall bearded irises, these are useful in smaller gardens. They grow 15–28 in. tall—proportionately smaller versions of tall beardeds in the same range of colors.

Miniature Tall Bearded Irises. Ranging from 15–28 in. high, these resemble tall bearded irises reduced in every proportion—slim stems, small flowers (2–3 in. wide), narrower, finer foliage. Blooming same time as tall beardeds, they are especially favored for cutting and arrangements—hence their original name, Table Irises.

Tall Bearded Irises

Among very choicest perennials for borders, massing, cutting. Adapted in all climates, easy to grow. From 2½–4 ft. high. All colors but pure red and green; patterns of 2 or more colors, blendings of colors produce infinite variety. Many named selections available. Modern hybrids free-branching, some with flowers ruffled, fringed. Some rebloom in late summer, fall, or winter. Climate, growing conditions, and varieties must be right; consult specialists' catalogues for most suitable reblooming varieties.

Aril Irises

Little-grown group with strange and often remarkably beautiful flowers. Mostly from semidesert areas of the Near East and central Asia, they need perfect drainage, limy soil, and no summer water. Two main groups are Oncocyclus, in which a number of species have huge, domed flowers in lavender, gray, silver, maroon, and gold, often subtly veined and stippled with deeper hues; and Regelias, with smaller, narrower blooms. Oncocyclus are difficult; Regelias and Oncogelias (hybrids between the 2) are only relatively easy to grow. For the average gardener, arilbred (or Oncobred) irises—crosses between arils and bearded irises—are more satisfactory, being nearly as easy to grow as the latter and having some of the exotic beauty of the former.

IRISH MOSS. See *Sagina subulata.*

IRONBARK. See *Eucalyptus.*

ISLAND BUSH SNAPDRAGON. See *Galvezia.*

ISMENE calathina. See *Hymenocallis narcissiflora.*

ISOTOMA fluviatilis. See *Laurentia.*

ITEA ilicifolia. *Saxifragaceae.* HOLLYLEAF SWEETSPIRE. Evergreen shrub or small tree. Zones 4–24. Usually graceful, open, arching shrub, 6–10 ft. tall, rarely to 18 ft. Leaves glossy, dark green, oval, 4 in. long, spiny toothed. Small, greenish white, lightly fragrant flowers in nodding or drooping narrow clusters to 1 ft. long. Fall bloom. Blooms sparsely where winters are very mild. Not a striking plant, but extremely graceful. Needs ample moisture and good soil; stands sun or partial shade near coast, should have part shade inland. Good near pools or waterfalls, as espalier against dark wood or stone backgrounds. Good informal screen.

Itea ilicifolia

ITHURIEL'S SPEAR. See *Triteleia laxa.*

IVY. See *Hedera.*

IXIA. *Iridaceae.* AFRICAN CORN LILY. Corm. Zones 5–24. Garden kinds are hybrids of several South African species particularly *I. maculata.* Swordlike leaves, wiry stems 18–20 in. long, topped in May–June with spikelike clusters of 1–2-in., cup-shaped flowers in cream, yellow, red, orange, pink, all with dark centers. Long-lasting when cut. In mild areas, plant corms 3 in. deep in early fall; in Zones 5, 6, delay planting until after November 1. Set corms 4 in. deep in sheltered spot, full sun. Apply protective mulch. Can be left in ground several seasons; when crowded, lift in summer, replant in fall. In mild climates, plants reseed freely and are quite drought tolerant. In coldest areas, grow in pots like freesias; plant 6–8 corms 1 in. deep in 5-in. pot. Keep cool after bringing indoors—not over 55°F. night temperature.

Ixia maculata

IXIOLIRION tataricum *(I. montanum).* *Amaryllidaceae.* Bulb. Zones 5–24. Native to central Asia. Narrow, greenish gray leaves. Wiry, 12–16-in.-high stems bear loose clusters of violet blue, trumpet-shaped, 1½-in. flowers in late May–June. Plant in sun in fall; set bulbs 3 in. deep, 6 in. apart. In cold areas, plant in warm, sheltered location and mulch to protect leaves from severe frost in spring.

Ixiolirion tataricum

JACARANDA mimosifolia (often sold as *J. acutifolia*). *Bignoniaceae.* JACARANDA. Deciduous to semievergreen tree. Zones 12, 13, 15–24. Native to Brazil. Grows 25–40 ft. high, 15–30 ft. wide. Open, irregular, oval headed; sometimes multitrunked or even shrubby. Finely cut, fernlike leaves, usually dropping in February–March. New leaves may grow quickly or branches may remain bare until tree flowers—usually in June, but bloom is possible any time from April–September. Blossoms lavender blue, tubular, 2 in. long, in many 8-in.-long clusters. White-flowered 'Alba' is sometimes seen; it has lusher foliage, longer blooming period, and sparser flowers. All forms have roundish, flat seed capsules, quite decorative in arrangements.

Jacaranda mimosifolia

Plant is fairly hardy after it attains some mature, hard wood; young plants are tender below 25°F. but often come back from freeze to make multistemmed, shrubby plants. Takes wide variety of soils but does best in sandy soil. Needs regular but not frequent irrigation. Too little water stunts it; too much encourages lush, loose, tender growth. Often fails to flower in path of ocean winds or where heat is inadequate. Resistant to oak root fungus.

Stake to produce single, sturdy trunk. Prune to shape. Usually branches profusely at 6–10 ft. In hillside gardens, a nice tree to look down on from above (downslope from deck or terrace) or to view against sky (planted on top of knoll). But it's also widely used in flat valley floor gardens.

JACOBEAN LILY. See *Sprekelia formosissima.*

JACOBINIA carnea. See *Justicia carnea.*

JACOB'S LADDER. See *Polemonium caeruleum.*

JADE PLANT. See *Crassula argentea.*

JAMAICA FLOWER, JAMAICA SORREL. See *Hibiscus sabdariffa.*

JAPANESE ANGELICA TREE. See *Aralia elata.*

JAPANESE ARALIA. See *Fatsia.*

JAPANESE BLOOD GRASS. See *Imperata cylindrica.*

JAPANESE FELT FERN. See *Pyrrosia lingua.*

JAPANESE FLOWERING APRICOT, JAPANESE FLOWERING PLUM. See *Prunus mume.*

JAPANESE LACE FERN. See *Polystichum polyblepharum.*

JAPANESE PAGODA TREE. See *Sophora japonica.*

JAPANESE SNOWBALL. See *Viburnum plicatum.*

JAPANESE SNOWBELL, JAPANESE SNOWDROP TREE. See *Styrax japonicus.*

JAPANESE SPURGE. See *Pachysandra terminalis.*

JAPAN PEPPER. See *Zanthoxylum piperitum.*

JASMINUM. *Oleaceae.* JASMINE. Evergreen or deciduous shrubs or vines. This is one of the first plants that comes to mind when one thinks of fragrance. Yet not all jasmines are fragrant—and the well-known star jasmine, one of the most fragrant plants commonly called jasmine, is not a true jasmine at all (it belongs to the genus *Trachelospermum*). All jasmines thrive in regular garden soil, sun or partial shade, and need frequent pinching and shaping to control growth. All need some watering; the larger-leafed kinds suffer from drought the most. Low-growing, shrubby kinds make good hedges.

Jasminum mesnyi

J. floridum. Evergreen or partially evergreen, shrubby, sprawling, or half-climbing shrub. Zones 4–9, 12–24. To 3–4 ft. Leaves divided into 3 (rarely 5) small leaflets, each ½–1½ in. long. Clusters of golden yellow, scentless, ½–¾-in. flowers over a long season in spring, summer, fall.

J. grandiflorum *(J. officinale grandiflorum).* SPANISH JASMINE. Semievergreen to deciduous vine. Zones 5–9, 12–24. Rapid growth to 10–15 ft. Glossy green leaves with 5–7 leaflets, each 2 in. long. Fragrant white flowers, 1½ in. across, in loose clusters. Blooms all summer. Dry flowers stay on plant. Gives open, airy effect along fence tops or rails.

J. humile. ITALIAN JASMINE. Evergreen shrub or vine. Zones 5–9, 12–24. Erect, willowy shoots reach to 20 ft. and arch to make 10-ft. mound. Can be trained as shrub or, planted in a row, clipped as hedge. Light green leaves with 3–7 leaflets, each 2 in. long. Clusters of fragrant, bright yellow, ½-in. flowers July–September. *J.h.* 'Revolutum' has larger, dull dark green leaves; flowers 1 in. across, up to 12 per cluster. Side clusters make even larger show.

J. magnificum. See *J. nitidum.*

J. mesnyi *(J. primulinum).* PRIMROSE JASMINE. Evergreen shrub. Zones 4–24; protected spots in Zone 3. Long, arching branches 6–10 ft. long. Leaves dark green with 3 lance-shaped, 2–3-in. leaflets; square stems. Flowers bright lemon yellow, to 2 in. across, semidouble or double, unscented. They are scattered singly through plant, November–April in mild-winter areas, February–April in colder climates. Needs space. Best tied up at desired height and permitted to spill down in waterfall fashion. Use to cover pergola, banks, large walls. Will control erosion. Can be clipped as 3-ft.-high hedge. In whatever form, plants may need occasional severe pruning to avoid brushpile look. Sun or part shade.

J. nitidum (often sold as *J. magnificum*). ANGELWING JASMINE. Evergreen vine. Zone 13; semideciduous Zones 12, 16, 19–21. Needs long, warm growing season to bloom satisfactorily. Not reliably hardy below 25°F. Moderate growth to 10–20 ft. Leathery, uncut, glossy medium green leaves to 2 in. long. Very fragrant flowers shaped like 1-in.-wide pinwheels are borne in clusters of 3 in late spring and summer; flowers are white above, purplish beneath, purplish in bud. Responds well to drastic pruning. Shrubby ground cover. Good container plant.

Jasminum nitidum

J. nudiflorum. WINTER JASMINE. Deciduous viny shrub. Zones 3–21; best adapted in cooler climates. To 10–15 ft. with slender, willowy branches. Glossy green leaves with 3 leaflets. Yellow, 1-in. flowers January–March, before leaves unfold. Not fragrant. Train like *J. mesnyi.* Will control erosion.

J. officinale. COMMON WHITE JASMINE, POET'S JASMINE. Semievergreen to deciduous twining vine. Zones 5–9, 12–24. Resembles *J. grandiflorum* but is taller (to 30 ft.), with smaller flowers (to 1 in. across). Somewhat more tender than *J. grandiflorum.*

J. parkeri. DWARF JASMINE. Evergreen shrub. Zones 5–9, 12–24. Dwarf, twiggy, tufted habit. To 1 ft. tall, 1½–2 ft. across. Leaves bright green, ½–1 in. long, made up of 3–5 tiny leaflets. Small, yellow, scentless flowers profusely borne in May, June. Good shrub for rock garden or containers. Drought tolerant.

J. polyanthum. Evergreen vine. Zones 5–9, 12–24. Fast climbing, strong growing to 20 ft. Finely divided leaflets. Dense clusters of fragrant flowers, white inside, rose colored outside; February–July in Zones 22–24, April–July in colder areas. Needs sun to bloom well. Give regular summer watering; prune annually to prevent tangling. Use as climber, ground cover, in containers.

J. sambac. ARABIAN JASMINE. Evergreen shrub. Zones 13, 21, 23. In Hawaii also called pikake; favorite flower for leis and used in making perfume. In Orient, added to tea to make jasmine tea. Tender. To 5 ft. tall. Leaves undivided, glossy green, to 3 in. long. Flowers white, ¾–1 in. across, powerfully fragrant, in clusters. Grow as small, compact shrub on trellis or in container.

J. stephanense. Evergreen vine. Zones 5–9, 12–24. Hybrid between *J. officinale* and a red-flowered Chinese species. Vine of moderate size; leaves may be solitary or divided into 5 leaflets. Clusters of fragrant, soft pink flowers in summer.

JERUSALEM ARTICHOKE. See *Helianthus tuberosus.*

JERUSALEM CHERRY. See *Solanum pseudocapsicum.*

JERUSALEM SAGE. See *Phlomis fruticosa.*

J

JERUSALEM THORN. See *Parkinsonia aculeata.*

JEWEL MINT OF CORSICA. See *Mentha requienii.*

JICAMA. See *Pachyrhizus erosus.*

JOB'S TEARS. See *Coix lacryma-jobi.*

JOHNNY-JUMP-UP. See *Viola tricolor.*

JOJOBA. See *Simmondsia chinensis.*

JONQUIL. See *Narcissus jonquilla.*

JOSEPH'S COAT. See *Amaranthus tricolor.*

JOSHUA TREE. See *Yucca brevifolia.*

Jubaea chilensis

JUBAEA chilensis *(J. spectabilis).* *Palmae.* CHILEAN WINE PALM. Palm with fat trunk patterned with scars of leaf bases. Zones 15–24. Slow grower to 50–60 ft. Feather-type leaves 6–12 ft. long; flowers insignificant. Needs regular watering during dry seasons until well established. Very hardy for a palm (20°F).

JUDAS TREE. See *Cercis siliquastrum.*

Juglandaceae. The walnut family consists of nut-bearing trees with leaves divided into many paired leaflets. Pecans and hickories (*Carya*), walnuts (*Juglans*), and wingnuts (*Pterocarya*) are examples.

JUGLANS. See Walnut.

JUJUBE. See *Ziziphus.*

JUNIPER MYRTLE. See *Agonis juniperina.*

JUNIPERUS. *Cupressaceae.* JUNIPER. Evergreen shrubs and trees. All Zones; those that do not tolerate extreme desert heat or mountain cold are not sold in these critical areas. Coniferous plants with fleshy, berrylike cones. Foliage is needlelike, scalelike, or both. Junipers are the most widely used woody plants in West; there's a form for almost every landscape use. Western nurserymen offer more than a hundred junipers under well over a hundred names. In the chart, these offerings are grouped by common use and listed by botanical names with accompanying synonyms, nurserymen's names, and common names. If you can't locate a juniper in the first column, look for one of its alternate names in next column to the right.

Juniperus chinensis 'Torulosa'

The ground cover group includes types ranging from a few inches to 2–3 ft. If you are planning large-scale plantings, some of the taller junipers (such as the Pfitzer) could be included in this group. Prostrate and creeping junipers are almost indispensable to rock gardens. As ground cover, space plants 5–6 ft. apart; for faster coverage, space plants 3–4 ft. apart and remove every other one when plants begin to crowd. In early years, mulch will help keep soil cool and weeds down. Or interplant with annuals until junipers cover.

Juniperus conferta

Juniperus horizontalis

Shrub types range from low to quite tall, from spreading to stiffly upright and columnar. You can find a juniper in almost any height, width, shape, or foliage color. Use columnar forms with care; they become quite large with age. Many serve well as screens or windbreaks in cold areas.

Tree types are not widely used. They are tough and drought resistant, interesting for picturesque habit of trunk and branch.

Junipers succeed in every soil type the West offers—acid or alkaline, heavy or light. However, you can expect root rot (yellowing and collapse) if soil is waterlogged. Avoid planting junipers so close to lawn sprinkling systems that their roots stay wet. Well-established junipers in reasonably retentive soil can thrive on little or no summer water—except in hottest interior or desert areas. In cool-summer climates, they are best grown in full sun but will accept light shade. In hot areas, they do well with partial shade.

Pests to watch for: spider mites (gray or yellow, dry-looking plants, fine webbing on twigs); aphids (sticky deposits, falling needles, sooty mildew); twig borers (browning and dying branch tips). Control mites and aphids with malathion or other contact spray. Sevin or diazinon sprays in mid-June and early July (1 month earlier in southern California) will control borers. One important disease is juniper blight; twigs and branches die back. Control with copper sprays in July and August.

JUPITER'S BEARD. See *Centranthus ruber.*

JUSTICIA. *Acanthaceae.* Subtropical shrubs, a few growing in deserts of California and Arizona. Includes plants formerly known as *Beloperone* and *Jacobinia.*

Justicia brandegeana

J. brandegeana *(Beloperone guttata).* SHRIMP PLANT. Evergreen. Zones 12, 13, 15–17, 21–24; anywhere as indoor/outdoor plant or annual. Native to Mexico. Will grow to 3- by 4-ft. mound but can be kept much lower. Egg-shaped, apple green leaves to 2½ in. long often drop in cold weather or if soil is too wet or too dry. Tubular white flowers spotted with purple are enclosed in coppery bronze, overlapping bracts to form compact, drooping spikes 3 in. long (lengthening to 6–7 in. if allowed to remain on plant). In total, spike formation somewhat resembles large shrimp. Flowers attract birds.

Justicia carnea

Plants will take sun, but bracts and foliage fade unless grown in partial shade. Variety 'Chartreuse' has chartreuse yellow spikes which sunburn more easily than those with coppery bracts. To shape plant, pinch continuously in early growth until compact mound of foliage is obtained, then let bloom. To encourage continued bushiness, cut back stems when flower bracts turn black. Good for pot or tub, for close-up planting near terraces, patios, entryways.

J. californica. CHUPAROSA, CALIFORNIA BELOPERONE. Deciduous. Zones 10–13. Native to edges of Colorado Desert to Arizona and northern Mexico. A low, gray green shrub 2–5 ft. high, spreading to 4 ft. Arching branches appear almost leafless. Small, roundish, ¼-in. leaves. Bright red, tubular flowers, 1½ in. long in clusters, give good show of color in April–May. Full sun. Often freezes to ground in winter but comes back quickly in spring. Very drought tolerant.

J. carnea *(Jacobinia carnea).* BRAZILIAN PLUME FLOWER. Evergreen shrub. Zones 8, 9, 13–24; house or greenhouse plant any-

(Continued on page 392)

Junipers

NAME	SYNONYMS OR NURSERYMEN'S NAMES	SIZE, HABIT	CHARACTERISTICS
GROUND COVERS			
Juniperus chinensis 'Alba' VARIEGATED PROSTRATA JUNIPER	*J. prostrata variegata. J. squamata variegata. J. davurica variegata.*	To 1½ ft. by 4–5 ft.	See *J. c.* 'Parsonii'. Patches of creamy yellow variegation. Not as rugged a grower as green forms. Variegations burn in hot sun.
J. c. 'Parsonii' PROSTRATA JUNIPER	*J. squamata* 'Parsonii'. *J. davurica* 'Parsonii'. *J. prostrata.*	To 1½ ft. by 8 ft. or more.	Selected form. Slow growing. Dense short twigs on flat, rather heavy branches.
J. c. procumbens JAPANESE GARDEN JUNIPER	*J. procumbens.*	To 3 ft. by 12–20 ft.	Feathery yet substantial blue green foliage on strong, spreading branches.
J. c. procumbens 'Nana'	*J. procumbens* 'Nana'. *J. procumbens* 'Compacta Nana'. *J. compacta* 'Nana'.	To 1 ft. by 4–5 ft. Curved branches radiating in all directions.	Shorter needles and slower growth than *J. procumbens*. Blue green foliage spreads rapidly. Give it some protection in hot climates.
J. c. 'San Jose'	*J. procumbens* 'San Jose'. *J. japonica* 'San Jose'. *J. chinensis procumbens* 'San Jose'.	To 2 ft. by 6 ft. or more. Prostrate, dense.	Dark sage green with both needle and scale foliage. Heavy trunked, slow growing. One of the best.
J. c. sargentii SARGENT JUNIPER, SHIMPAKU	*J. sargentii. J. sargentii viridis.*	To 1 ft. by 10 ft. Ground hugging.	Gray green or green. Feathery. Classic bonsai plant. *J. c. sargentii* 'Glauca' has blue green foliage; *J. c. sargentii* 'Viridis' has bright green foliage.
J. communis 'Hornibrookii'		To 1 ft. by 4 ft.	Attractive, rugged branching pattern.
J. c. saxatilis	*J. c. montana. J. c. sibirica.*	To 1 ft. by 6–8 ft. Prostrate, trailing.	Variable gray, gray green. Upturned branchlets like tiny candles. Native alpine.
J. conferta SHORE JUNIPER	*J. conferta littoralis.* Plants so named may be a grower's selected form.	To 1 ft. by 6–8 ft. Prostrate, trailing.	Bright green, soft needled. Excellent for seashore and will stand valley heat if given moist, well-drained soil. 'Blue Pacific' is denser, bluer, more heat-tolerant form. 'Emerald Sea' is bright green.
J. horizontalis 'Bar Harbor' BAR HARBOR JUNIPER		To 1 ft. by 10 ft. Hugs ground.	Fast growing. Feathery, blue gray foliage turns plum color in winter. Foliage dies back in center to expose limbs as plant ages, especially in hot climates.
J. h. 'Blue Chip'		To 1 ft. tall.	Silvery blue foliage.
J. h. 'Blue Mat'		9–12 in. by 6–7 ft.	Dense mat of gray green foliage.
J. h. 'Douglasii' WAUKEGAN JUNIPER		To 1 ft. by 10 ft. Trailing.	Steel blue foliage turns purplish in fall. New growth rich green.
J. h. 'Emerald Spreader'		To 6 in. tall.	Dense, feathery, bright green foliage.
J. h. 'Hughes'		To 6 in. tall.	Showy silvery blue.
J. h. 'Huntington Blue'		9–12 in. by 6–7 ft.	Dense, bright blue gray foliage.
J. h. 'Plumosa' ANDORRA JUNIPER	*J. depressa plumosa.*	To 1½ ft. by 10 ft. Wide spreading.	Gray green in summer, plum color in winter. Flat branches, upright branchlets. Plumy.
J. h. 'Prince of Wales'		To 8 in. tall.	Medium green foliage turns purplish in fall.
J. h. 'Turquoise Spreader'		To 6 in. tall.	Dense turquoise green foliage.
J. h. 'Wiltonii' BLUE CARPET JUNIPER	*J. h.* 'Blue Rug'.	To 4 in. by 8–10 ft. Flattest juniper.	Intense silver blue. Dense, short branchlets on long, trailing branches. Similar to 'Bar Harbor' but tighter; it rarely exposes limbs.
J. h. 'Youngstown'		To 1 ft. by 6 ft.	Resembles *J. h. 'Plumosa'* but is flatter, more compact.
J. h. 'Yukon Belle'		To 6 in. tall.	Silvery blue foliage. Hardy in coldest climates.
J. sabina 'Arcadia'		To 1 ft. by 10 ft.	Bright green, lacy foliage.
J. s. 'Blue Danube'		To 1½ ft. by 5 ft.	Blue green foliage.
J. s. 'Broadmoor'		To 14 in. by 10 ft. Dense, mounding.	Soft, bright green foliage.
J. s. 'Buffalo'		8–12 in. by 8 ft. Lower than tamarix juniper.	Soft, feathery, bright green foliage. Very wide spreading.

(Continued on next page)

J

NAME	SYNONYMS OR NURSERYMEN'S NAMES	SIZE, HABIT	CHARACTERISTICS
GROUND COVERS			
J. s. 'Calgary Carpet'		6–9 in. by 10 ft.	Soft green foliage. Extremely cold hardy.
J. s. 'Scandia'		To 1 ft. by 8 ft.	Low, dense, bright green.
J. s. 'Tamariscifolia' TAMARIX JUNIPER, TAM	*J. tamariscifolia.*	To 1½ ft. by 10–20 ft. Symmetrically spreading.	Dense, blue green. Widely used. Recently introduced is 'New Blue'.
J. scopulorum 'Blue Creeper'		To 2 ft. tall, 6–8 ft. wide.	Spreading, mounding habit, bright blue green color.
J. scopulorum 'White's Silver King'		To 10 in. by 6–8 ft. Dense, spreading.	Pale silver blue foliage. *J. s.* 'Blue Creeper' is similar.
J. squamata 'Blue Carpet'		To 1 ft. tall, 5 ft. wide	Bright blue gray foliage, slow growth.
J. virginiana 'Silver Spreader'	*J. v. prostrata.*	To 1½ ft. by 6–8 ft.	Silvery green, feathery, fine textured. Older branches become dark green.
SHRUBS			
J. chinensis 'Ames'		To 6 ft. Broad-based pyramid.	Blue green foliage. Slow growing. Massive.
J. c. 'Armstrongii' ARMSTRONG JUNIPER		To 4 ft. by 4 ft. Upright.	Medium green. More compact than Pfitzer juniper.
J. c. 'Blaauw' BLAAUW'S JUNIPER, BLUE SHIMPAKU		To 4 ft. by 3 ft. Vase shaped.	Blue foliage. Dense. Compact.
J. c. 'Corymbosa Variegata' VARIEGATED HOLLYWOOD JUNIPER	*J. c.* 'Torulosa Variegata'.	To 8–10 ft. Irregular cone.	Variegation of creamy yellow. Growth more regular than Hollywood juniper.
J. c. 'Fruitland'		To 3 ft. by 6 ft. Compact, dense.	Like a Pfitzer juniper but more compact.
J. c. 'Gold Coast'	*J.* 'Coasti Aurea'.		Similar or identical to *J. c.* 'Golden Armstrong'.
J. c. 'Golden Armstrong'		To 4 ft. by 4 ft. Full, blocky.	Between golden Pfitzer and Armstrong juniper in appearance.
J. c. 'Hetzii' HETZ BLUE JUNIPER	*J. c. hetzi glauca. J. glauca hetzi.*	To 15 ft. Fountainlike.	Blue gray. Branches spread outward and upward at 45° angle.
J. c. 'Maneyi'		To 15 ft. Semierect, massive.	Blue gray. Steeply inclined, spreading branches.
J. c. 'Mint Julep'		4–6 ft. by 6 ft. Vase shaped.	Mint green foliage, arching branches.
J. c. 'Pfitzerana' PFITZER JUNIPER		5–6 ft. by 15–20 ft. Arching.	Feathery, gray green. Sharp-needled foliage. 'Pfitzerana Aurea' is golden form.
J. c. 'Pfitzerana Aurea' GOLDEN PFITZER JUNIPER		3–4 ft. by 8–10 ft.	Blue gray foliage with current season's growth golden yellow.
J. c. 'Pfitzerana Compacta' NICK'S COMPACT PFITZER JUNIPER	*J. pfitzeriana nicksi, J. nicksi compacta.*	To 2 ft. by 4–6 ft. Densely branched.	Compact. Gray green foliage.
J. c. 'Pfitzerana Glauca'		5–6 ft. by 10–15 ft. Arching branches.	Silvery blue foliage.
J. c. 'Pfitzerana Mordigan Aurea'		To 3 ft. by 5 ft.	A denser, smaller golden Pfitzer.
J. c. 'Pfitzerana Nana'		To 4 ft. by 2 ft.	Dense, nearly globular green juniper.
J. c. 'Pfitzerana Old Gold'	May be same as *J. c.* 'Golden Armstrong'.		See *J. c.* 'Golden Armstrong'.
J. c. 'Plumosa Aurea'	*J. japonica aurea. J. bandai-sugi aurea. J. procumbens aurea.*	To 3 ft. by 3 ft. Vase shaped.	Semiupright, spreading, with bright gold new growth.
J. c. 'Sea Green'		To 4–5 ft. by 4–5 ft.	Compact, dark green, with arching, fountainlike habit.
J. c. 'Torulosa' HOLLYWOOD JUNIPER	*J. c.* 'Kaizuka'.	To 15 ft. Irregular, upright.	Rich green. Branches with irregular, twisted appearance. Give it enough room.

NAME	SYNONYMS OR NURSERYMEN'S NAMES	SIZE, HABIT	CHARACTERISTICS
SHRUBS			
J. sabina 'Moor-Dense'		To 1½ ft. by 8 ft.	Resembles *J. sabina* 'Broadmoor' but more dense. Has layered look.
J. s. 'Variegata' HOARFROST JUNIPER		3–4 ft. by 6 ft.	Upright, spreading; lacy branch pattern. Every twig bears small white tip.
J. scopulorum 'Table Top Blue'		To 6 by 8 ft.	Gray. Massive. Flat topped.
J. squamata 'Blue Star'		To 2 ft. by 5 ft.	Regular branching. Silver blue.
J. s. 'Meyeri' MEYER or FISHBACK JUNIPER		6–8 ft. by 2–3 ft. Upright.	Oddly angled stiff branches. Broad needled. Blend of green, gray, and reddish foliage.
COLUMNAR TYPES			
J. chinensis 'Columnaris' CHINESE BLUE COLUMN JUNIPER	*J. c.* 'Columnaris Glauca'.	12–15 ft.	Blue green, narrow pyramid.
J. c. 'Hetz's Columnaris'		12–15 ft.	Rich green. Dense column. Scale foliage predominant, branchlets threadlike.
J. c. 'Keteleeri' KETELEER JUNIPER		To 20 ft.	Bright green, broad pyramid with loose, ascending branches.
J. c. 'Pyramidalis'	*J. excelsa* 'Stricta'.	15–30 ft.	Blue gray needlelike foliage. Narrow pyramid broadening with age.
J. c. 'Robusta Green'		To 20 ft.	Brilliant green, dense-tufted column.
J. c. 'Spartan'	*J. c. densaerecta* 'Spartan'.	To 20 ft.	Rich green, dense column.
J. c. 'Wintergreen'		To 20 ft.	Deep green, dense-branching pyramid.
J. communis 'Compressa'		To 2 ft.	Dwarf, for rock gardens.
J. c. 'Stricta' IRISH JUNIPER	*J. c. hibernica*, *J. c. fastigiata*.	12–20 ft.	Dark green. Very narrow column with closely compact branch tips.
J. scopulorum 'Cologreen'			Narrow, bright green column.
J. s. 'Gray Gleam'			Gray blue, symmetrical column. Slow grower.
J. s. 'Moffetii'			Silvery green column.
J. s. 'Pathfinder'		To 25 ft.	Gray blue, upright pyramid.
J. s. 'Welchii'			Silvery green. Very narrow spire.
J. s. 'Wichita Blue'			Broad, silver blue pyramid.
J. virginiana 'Cupressifolia' HILLSPIRE JUNIPER		15–20 ft.	Dark green, compact pyramid.
J. v. 'Manhattan Blue'	*J. scopulorum* 'Manhattan Blue'.	10–15 ft.	Blue green, compact pyramid.
J. v. 'Skyrocket'		10–15 ft.	Narrowest blue gray spire.
TREES			
J. californica CALIFORNIA JUNIPER		Shrubby or to 40 ft.	Yellowish to rich green. Useful in desert areas.
J. deppeana pachyphlaea ALLIGATOR JUNIPER	*J. pachyphlaea*.	Shrubby or to 60 ft.	Blue gray foliage, strikingly checked bark like alligator hide.
J. monosperma		To 40 ft.	Similar to *J. osteosperma;* bluish green.
J. occidentalis WESTERN JUNIPER		50–60 ft.	Massive, long-lived mountain native.
J. osteosperma UTAH JUNIPER	*J. utahensis*.	Shrubby or to 20–30 ft.	Yellowish green foliage. Adapted to high desert.
J. scopulorum			Seldom grown; see varieties above.
J. virginiana EASTERN RED CEDAR		40–50 ft. or more.	Conical dark green tree that turns reddish in cold weather.

J

where. Erect, soft-wooded plant with heavily veined leaves to 10 in. Dense clusters of pink to crimson, tubular flowers bloom on 4–5-ft. stems, midsummer to fall. Shade, rich soil, ample water. Cut back in early spring to encourage strong new growth. Tops freeze back at 29°F. in any case.

J. ghiesbreghtiana. See *J. spicigera.*

J. leonardii. Zones 12–24. Shrub to 3 ft. with velvety leaves to 6 in. long. Small clusters of 1½-in., scarlet flowers appear off and on through warmer weather. Often sold in California as *Anisacanthus thurberi,* a related plant. Full sun. Drought tolerant.

J. spicigera (often sold as *J. ghiesbreghtiana* or, in Arizona, as *Anisacanthus thurberi*). To 6 ft., with smooth or velvety leaves and few-flowered clusters of 1½-in., orange or orange red flowers. Full sun. Drought tolerant.

KAFFIR LILY. See *Clivia miniata, Schizostylis coccinea.*

KAFFIR PLUM. See *Harpephyllum caffrum.*

KAHILI GINGER. See *Hedychium gardneranum.*

KALANCHOE. *Crassulaceae.* Succulents grown principally as house plants. Some hardy outdoors in mildest coastal regions, but safest even there with protection of lath, eaves, or other overhead structure. Shapes and sizes vary. Flowers fairly large, bell shaped, erect or drooping. Sun or light shade. Need very little water.

Kalanchoe blossfeldiana

K. beharensis (often sold as *Kitchingia mandrakensis*). FELT PLANT. Outdoors Zones 21–24, house plant anywhere. Stems usually unbranched, to 4–5 ft., possibly 10 ft. Thick, triangular to lance-shaped leaves—usually 6–8 pairs of them—at stem tips. Each leaf 4–8 or more in. long and half as wide, covered with a dense, feltlike coating of white to brown hairs. Flowers not showy; foliage strikingly waved and crimped at edges. Hybrids between this and other species differ in leaf size, color, and degree of felting and scalloping. Striking in big rock garden, raised bed, in sun or considerable shade.

K. blossfeldiana. House plant; some hybrids hardy Zones 17, 21–24. Fleshy, shiny dark green leaves edged red; smooth edged or slightly lobed, 2½ in. long, 1–1½ in. wide. Small bright red flowers in big clusters held above leaves. Hybrids and named varieties come in dwarf (6-in.) and extra-sturdy (1½-ft.) sizes and in different colors, including yellow, orange, salmon. 'Pumila' and 'Tetra Vulcan' are choice dwarf seed-grown selections. Blooms winter, early spring. Popular house plant at Christmas time.

K. daigremontiana. MATERNITY PLANT. House plant. Upright, single-stemmed plant 1½–3 ft. tall. Leaves fleshy, 6–8 in. long, 1¼ in. wide or wider, gray green spotted red. Leaf edges are notched; young plants sprout in notches and may root even on the plant. Clusters of small, grayish purple flowers.

K. fedtschenkoi. Zones 17, 21–24. Flowering stems upright, to 2 ft. Sterile stems spreading, rooting. Grown chiefly for leaves—fleshy, scallop toothed, lavender gray in color, ½–2 in. long. Brownish pink flowers attractive, not showy. Used as pot plant or for foliage color in mixed plantings of succulents.

K. flammea. House plant; some hybrids hardy Zones 17, 21–24. Lightly branched, 12–16 in. tall, with fleshy, gray green, 2½-in. leaves and many-flowered clusters of orange red or yellow flowers in winter and spring.

K. laciniata *(K. coccinea).* Zones 17, 21–24. To 4 ft. Fleshy leaves greenish bronze to red, to 5 in. long; may be smooth edged, scalloped, or cut. Clusters of ¼-in. yellow, orange, or red flowers in late winter and spring.

K. manginii. Zones 17, 21–24. Stems spreading or trailing, to 1 ft. long. Inch-long green leaves thick and fleshy. Drooping, bell-shaped, inch-long flowers are bright red. Hanging basket plant.

K. pinnata *(Bryophyllum pinnatum).* AIR PLANT. Zones 17, 21–24. Fleshy stems eventually 2–3 ft. tall. Leaves also fleshy. First leaves to form are undivided and scallop edged; later ones divided into 3–5 leaflets, these also scalloped. Produces many plantlets in notches of scallops. Leaves can be removed and pinned to curtain, where they will produce plantlets until they dry up. Flower color ranges from greenish white to reddish. Takes sun or considerable shade. Likes moisture.

K. tomentosa. PANDA PLANT. House plant. Eventually 1½ ft. tall, branched. Leaves very fleshy, 2 in. long, densely coated with white, felty hairs. Leaf tips and shallow notches in leaves strongly marked dark brown.

K. uniflora. Zones 17, 21–24. Trailing plant; inch-long, thick, fleshy leaves have a few scallops near rounded tips. Inch-long flowers are pinkish or purplish red. Hanging basket plant.

KALE and COLLARDS. *Cruciferae.* Vegetable crops that live 1–2 years. The type of kale known as collards is a large, smooth-leafed plant like a cabbage that does not form a head. Planted in early spring or late summer, collards will yield edible leaves in fall, winter, and spring. 'Georgia' and 'Vates' are typical varieties. Collards are not widely grown in the West.

Kale

Slightly more popular are curly kales like 'Dwarf Blue Curled' and 'Dwarf Siberian'; these are compact clusters of tightly curled leaves. They make decorative garden or container plants as well as supplying edible leaves. One kind, called flowering kale (see Cabbage, flowering), has brightly colored foliage, especially toward centers of rosettes. Grow just like late cabbage. Harvest leaves for cooking by removing them from outside of cluster; or harvest entire plant.

KALMIA. *Ericaceae.* Evergreen shrubs. Zones 1–7, 16, 17. Related to rhododendron. All have clusters of showy flowers and grow in part shade. All need regular watering.

Kalmia latifolia

K. latifolia. MOUNTAIN LAUREL, CALICO BUSH. Native to eastern U.S. Slow growing to 6–8 ft. or more, with equal spread. Glossy, leathery, oval leaves, 3–5 in. long, dark green on top, yellowish green beneath. Clusters of pink buds open to pale pink flowers in apple blossom effect, May–June. Varieties range from white to near red. Named varieties come in red, white, and many shades of pink. Some show spots or bands of contrasting colors. 'Elf' is a dwarf variety. Flowers 1 in. across, in clusters to 5 in. across. Hardy well below 0°F. Shares rhododendron's cultural needs—moist atmosphere, partial shade, acid soil rich in humus. Has proved difficult to grow in Zones 16, 17 even under these conditions; seems to do better in containers there.

K. microphylla *(K. polifolia microphylla).* WESTERN LAUREL, ALPINE LAUREL. Low plant has spreading branches with erect branchlets, small leaves (dark green above, whitish beneath), and rounded clusters of extremely showy, ½-in., rose to purple flowers in summer. Full sun. Will grow in very moist, acid soils.

Typical high mountain form is 8–11 in. tall with leaves up to ¾ in. long. A taller variety, *K. m. occidentalis,* to 2 ft. tall and with slightly larger leaves, grows in coastal lowlands north to Alaska.

Kalmiopsis leachiana

KALMIOPSIS leachiana. *Ericaceae.* Evergreen shrub. Zones 4–6, 14–17. Rhododendron relative native to mountains of southwest Oregon. Slow growing to 1 ft. tall, with 2-ft. spread. Many branches densely clothed with thick, dark green leaves. Blooms abundantly in early spring, with leafy clusters of ½-in., rose pink flowers. Does best in light shade. Takes same culture as rhododendron or azalea. Sometimes reblooms.

KANGAROO PAW. See *Anigozanthos*.

KANGAROO THORN. See *Acacia armata*.

KANGAROO TREEBINE. See *Cissus antarctica*.

KATSURA TREE. See *Cercidiphyllum japonicum*.

KENILWORTH IVY. See *Cymbalaria muralis*.

KENTIA PALM. See *Howea*.

KENTUCKY COFFEE TREE. See *Gymnocladus dioica*.

KENYA IVY. See *Senecio macroglossus*.

KERRIA japonica. *Rosaceae.* Deciduous shrub. Zones 1–21. Green branches give welcome winter color in cold areas. Open, graceful, rounded shrub to 8 ft., with 5–6-ft. spread. Leaves tooth edged, heavily veined, somewhat triangular, 2–4 in. long, bright green turning to yellow in fall. Flowers (March–May) like small, single yellow roses. Variety 'Pleniflora' has double yellow, inch-wide flowers and is the more commonly planted form.

Give kerria part shade (will take sun in cooler areas) and room to arch and display its form. Needs water until established and growing; drought tolerant thereafter. Remove suckers and prune heavily after bloom, cutting out branches that have flowered and all dead or weak wood. Cut green branches are a favorite subject in Japanese arrangements.

Kerria japonica 'Pleniflora'

KHAT. See *Catha edulis*.

KING PALM. See *Archontophoenix cunninghamiana*.

KINNIKINNICK. See *Arctostaphylos uva-ursi*.

KIWI, HARDY KIWI. See *Actinidia*.

KLEINIA. See *Senecio*.

KNIPHOFIA uvaria ***(Tritoma uvaria).*** *Liliaceae.* RED-HOT POKER, TORCH-LILY, POKER PLANT. Perennial. Zones 1–9, 14–24. Native to South Africa. Likes full sun or a little shade. Quite heat and drought tolerant. Has been in cultivation long enough to give rise to garden varieties with some range in size, color. Typical plant is coarse with large, rather dense clumps of long, grasslike leaves. Flower stalks (always taller than leaves) are about 2 ft. high in dwarf kinds, 3–6 ft. in larger kinds. The many drooping, orange red or yellow, tubular flowers of the typical plant overlap, forming pokerlike clusters 1 ft. long. Named varieties, in both dwarf and taller forms, come in soft or saffron yellow, creamy white, or coral. Flowers attract hummingbirds, are good in flower arrangements.

Kniphofia uvaria

Blooms from spring through summer (exact flowering time varies). Cut out flower spikes after bloom. Cut old leaves at base in fall; new leaves will replace them by spring. Increase by root divisions. Poker plant is useful in large borders with other robust perennials such as daylilies (*Hemerocallis*), *Echinops exaltatus*.

KNOTWEED. See *Polygonum*.

KOCHIA scoparia. *Chenopodiaceae.* SUMMER CYPRESS. Summer annual. Grow these foliage plants close together as low, temporary hedge, or individually for their gently rounded form—like fine-textured coniferous shrubs. To 3 ft. Branches densely clothed with very narrow, soft, light green leaves, making plants too dense to see through. Insignificant flowers. Sow in full sun. Tolerates high heat and will perform well in short-summer areas. Shear to shape if necessary.

K. s. trichophylla. MEXICAN FIRE BUSH, BURNING BUSH. Same as above, but foliage turns red at first frost. Can reseed profusely enough to become pest; hoe out unwanted seedlings when small.

Kochia scoparia

KOELREUTERIA. *Sapindaceae.* Deciduous trees. Small yellow flowers in large, loose clusters in summer. Colorful fruits are fat, papery capsules which seem to resemble clusters of little Japanese lanterns; used in arrangements.

K. bipinnata ***(K. integrifoliola).*** CHINESE FLAME TREE. Zones 8–24. Slow to moderate growth to 20–40 ft. or taller, spreading, eventually flat topped. One- to 2-ft.-long leaves, divided into many oval leaflets, hold onto tree until December, then turn yellow for a short time before dropping. Capsules 2 in. long, orange, red, or salmon-colored, showy in late summer and fall, in large clusters. Fruit formation not always dependable. Takes to most well-drained soils and moderate watering. Stake and prune to develop high branching. Good patio shade tree, lawn tree, or street tree. Roots deep, not invasive. Good tree to plant under. A similar species, *K. elegans (K. formosana, K. henryi)*, is occasionally seen. It is less hardy and less widely sold.

Koelreuteria paniculata

K. paniculata. GOLDENRAIN TREE. Zones 2–21. Slow to moderate growth to 20–35 ft. with 10–40-ft. spread. Open branching, giving slight shade. Leaves to 15 in. long, with 7–15 toothed or lobed leaflets, each 1–3 in. long. Flower clusters in summer, 8–14 in. long. Fruit buff to brown in fall, hanging late. Takes cold, heat, drought, wind, alkaline soil; needs regular watering when young. Prune to shape; can be gawky without pruning. Valuable as street, lawn, or terrace tree in difficult soils and climates. The variety 'Kew' or 'Fastigiata' is erect and narrow—3 ft. wide by 25 ft. tall.

KOHLRABI. *Cruciferae.* All Zones in conditions noted below. Cool-season, annual vegetable related to cabbage. The edible portion is an enlarged, bulblike portion of the stem, formed just above soil surface. Ordinary leaves grow above. Varieties are 'Early White Vienna' and 'Early Purple Vienna'—similar in size and flavor, differing only in skin color. Sow seed ½ in. deep in full sun and rich soil, about 2 weeks after average date of last frost. Follow first planting with successive plantings 2 weeks apart. In warm-winter areas,

Kohlrabi

K

plant again in late fall and early winter. Space rows 1½ ft. apart; thin seedlings to 4 in. apart. To control aphids, dust or spray with rotenone. Harvest when round portions are 2–3 in. wide; slice and eat raw like cucumbers or cook like turnips.

KOLKWITZIA amabilis. *Caprifoliaceae.* BEAUTY BUSH. Deciduous shrub. Zones 1–11, 14–20. Growth upright, graceful to 10–12 ft., arching in part shade, denser and lower in full sun. Leaves gray green. Clusters of small, pink, yellow-throated flowers bloom heavily in May in California, June in Northwest and mountain states. Flowers followed by conspicuous pinkish brown, bristly fruit that prolongs color. Thin out after bloom; to enjoy the fruit, prune lightly in early spring, removing wood which has bloomed year before. Brown, flaky bark gradually peels from stems during winter. Sun. Average water needs.

Kolkwitzia amabilis

KOREAN GRASS. See *Zoysia tenuifolia*.

KOWHAI. See *Sophora tetraptera*.

KUMQUAT. See *Citrus*.

Labiatae. Members of the mint family of herbaceous plants and shrubs are easily recognized by their square stems, leaves in opposite pairs, and whorled flowers in spikelike clusters (sometimes branched). Many of the group are aromatic; the family contains most of the familiar kitchen herbs, including basil (*Ocimum*), mint (*Mentha*), oregano (*Origanum*), and sage (*Salvia*). Many have attractive foliage or flowers (coleus, salvia).

LABURNUM. *Leguminosae.* GOLDENCHAIN TREE. Deciduous trees or large shrubs. Zones 1–10, 14–17. Upright growth; usually pruned into single-stemmed tree, but can be shrubby if permitted to keep basal suckers and low branches. Green bark, bright green leaves divided into 3 leaflets (like clover). Handsome in bloom: yellow, sweet pea–shaped flowers in hanging clusters like wisteria.

Laburnum watereri

Protect from afternoon sun in hot regions. Well-drained soil, adequate water. Subject to chlorosis in alkaline soils; use iron. Prune and trim regularly to keep plants tidy. Remove seed pods if possible; not only are they poisonous, but too heavy a crop is a drain on plant's strength. Use as a single tree in lawn or border, group in front of neutral background, or space regularly in long borders of perennials, rhododendrons, or lilacs. In Wales, a tunnel of laburnums (plants are trained over a series of arches) is one of the world's most startling horticultural sights when plants are in bloom. Pests are seldom a problem, but beware of mites.

L. alpinum. SCOTCH LABURNUM. To 30–35 ft. Flower clusters 10–15 in. long. Blooms in late spring. The variety 'Pendulum' has weeping branches.

L. anagyroides. COMMON GOLDENCHAIN. To 20–30 ft. high; often bushy and wide spreading. Flower clusters are 6–10 in. long in late spring. Like Scotch laburnum, common goldenchain has a weeping variety, 'Pendulum'.

L. watereri. Hybrid between the 2 preceding species; has flower clusters 10–20 in. long. Most widely grown variety is 'Vossii', most graceful of the lot. Can be espaliered.

LACEBARK. See *Hoheria*.

LACE FERN. See *Microlepia strigosa*.

LACHENALIA. *Liliaceae.* CAPE COWSLIP. Bulbs. Hardy outdoors only in Zones 16, 17, 24; usually grown in pots indoors or in greenhouses. Native to South Africa. Strap-shaped, succulent leaves, often brown spotted. Tubular, pendulous flowers in spikes on thick, fleshy stems; bloom in winter, early spring. Plant in August–September; put 6 bulbs in 5–6-in. pot, setting 1–1½ in. deep to prevent flowering stems from falling over. Water and keep cool and dark until roots form and leaves appear. When growth becomes active, water thoroughly and bring plants into light. Keep cool (50°F. night temperature). Feed when flower spikes show. When leaves start to yellow, gradually let plants dry out. Keep dry during summer.

Lachenalia bulbiferum

L. aloides *(L. tricolor)*. Flowers yellow, inner segments tipped red, outer tipped green, on stems 1 ft. tall or less. Leaves usually 2 to a plant, 1 in. wide, about as tall as or taller than flower stems. Variety 'Aurea' is bright orange yellow; 'Nelsonii', bright yellow tinged green; 'Pearsonii' slightly taller, yellow orange with reddish orange buds and flower bases.

L. bulbiferum *(L. pendula)*. Basal leaves to 2 in. wide. Flowers 1½ in. long, coral red and yellow, purple tipped, in spikes 12–15 in. tall. 'Superba', improved form, has orange red flowers.

L. contaminata. Leaves bright green, to 9 in. long, nearly erect. Flower spikes to 8 in. long, narrow, packed with roundish, ½-in. flowers in white tinged red or brown.

LADY FERN. See *Athyrium filix-femina*.

LADY-OF-THE-NIGHT. See *Brassavola nodosa*.

LADY PALM. See *Rhapis*.

LADY'S SLIPPER. See *Paphiopedilum*.

LAELIA. *Orchidaceae.* EPIPHYTIC ORCHIDS. Greenhouse or house plants; the 3 listed below are also hardy in sheltered locations outdoors in Zones 16, 17, 21–24. Resemble cattleyas in foliage and flowers. Color range includes red, orange, and yellow, but most are in the white-pink-lavender-purple range. Plants perform best in filtered shade. Grow on slab of tree bark or tree fern (hapuu) or in media used for cattleyas. Tack slabs on wall in patio, hang from tree trunk, or grow in pots on patio. During summer, feed several times with fish emulsion or fertilizer packaged especially for orchids. Let potting medium dry out between waterings.

Laelia anceps

L. albida. Transparent white, 2-in. flowers with yellow rib in throat, lavender flush in lip, 2–8 per stem. Bloom in winter and early spring. Fragrant. Oval, 1–2-in.-high pseudobulbs topped by pair of narrow leaves.

L. anceps. Rose violet flowers with yellow throat lined purple. Up to 4 in. across, carried 2–6 per stem. Blooms in autumn and winter. Four-sided pseudobulb, 3–5 in. high, bears 1 or 2 leaves, each 5–9 in. long. Repot these plants as infrequently as possible.

L. autumnalis. Rose purple, 4-in. flowers with white at base of lip. Fragrant blooms, 3–9 on erect stem, in fall and winter. Pseudobulbs 2–4 in. high bear 2 or 3 leathery, 4–8-in.-long leaves.

LAGENARIA. See Gourd.

LAGERSTROEMIA indica. *Lythraceae.* CRAPE MYRTLE. Deciduous shrub or tree. Root hardy and sometimes treated as perennial in Zones 1–3. Hardy in Zones 4–6 but doesn't flower freely except in hottest summers; excellent in Zones 7–9, 12–14, 18–21. Generally a shrub in Zones 10, 11. Mildew is serious problem in Zones 15–17, 22–24. Native to China. Dwarf shrubby forms and shrub-tree forms, 6–30 ft. tall, are available. Slow growing as shrub, spreads as wide as high; trained as tree, becomes vase shaped with very attractive trunk and branch pattern. Smooth gray or light brown bark flakes off to reveal smooth pinkish inner bark.

Lagerstroemia indica

Spring foliage is light green tinged bronze red; mature leaves 1–2 in. long, oval, deep glossy green. Fall foliage is yellow, more rarely orange to red. Crinkled, crepelike, 1½-in. flowers in rounded, slightly conical clusters, 6–12 in. long, at ends of branches; smaller clusters form lower down on branches. Colors in shades of red, rose, deep or soft pink, rosy orchid, purple, white. Long flowering period, July–September.

Plant in full sun. Feed moderately; water infrequently but deeply (plants are drought resistant). Where soil is alkaline or water high in salts, treat chlorosis or marginal leaf burn by occasional leaching and applications of iron. Check mildew with sprays just before plants bloom. Prune in dormant season to increase flowering wood the next summer. Remove spent flower clusters and prune out small twiggy growth from dwarf shrub forms. On large shrubs and trees, cut back branches 1–1½ ft.

Many color selections are available in bush form and trained as trees. In whites: 'White', 'Glendora White'. Pinks: 'Shell Pink' ('Near East'), 'Pink'. Reds: 'Durant Red', 'Gray's Red', 'Rubra', 'Watermelon Red', 'Watermelon Red Improved'. Other colors: 'Lavender', 'Purple', 'Select Purple', 'Majestic Orchid'. 'Peppermint Lace' has rose pink flowers edged with white.

These are the dwarfer, shrubby forms (to 5–7 ft.): 'Petite Embers' (rose red), 'Petite Orchid', 'Petite Pinkie', 'Petite Red Imp' (dark red), 'Petite Snow', 'Snow White'.

Selections called Indian Tribes have heavy foliage with considerable resistance to mildew. 'Catawba' has dark purple flowers, 'Cherokee' bright red blooms. 'Potomac' and 'Seminole' have pink blooms. 'Powhatan' is a dense, globular shrub with light lavender flowers.

Hybrids between *L. indica* and the species *L. fauriei* have even greater resistance to mildew than the Indian Tribes. 'Muskogee' is light lavender, 'Natchez' pure white, and 'Tuscarora' coral pink.

The strain called Crape Myrtlettes grows from seed, flowering in late summer from March sowing. Plants in this group have the full range of crape myrtle colors; they grow to 12–14 in. during first year, eventually to 3–4 ft. They can be grown in pots or hanging baskets, or espaliered.

LAGUNARIA patersonii. *Malvaceae.* PRIMROSE TREE, COW ITCH TREE. Evergreen tree. Zones 13, 15–24. Native to South Pacific and Australia. Rather fast growth to 20–40 ft. Young trees narrow and erect; old trees sometimes spreading, flat topped. Densely foliaged. Thick, oval, 2–4-in.-long leaves are olive green above, gray beneath. Flowers hibiscuslike, 2 in. wide, pink to rose, fading nearly white in summer. Brown seed capsules hang on for a long time; flower arrangers like them because they split into 5 sections, revealing bright brown seeds. Handle carefully; pods also contain short, stiff fibers which can cause skin irritation.

Lagunaria patersonii

Tolerates wide variety of soils and growing conditions. Resists ocean wind, salt spray; tolerates soils and heat of low deserts. Foliage burns at 25°F. but recovers quickly. Best flowering under coastal conditions. Plant individually as garden tree or in groups as showy windbreak or screen. Needs little water once established.

LAMB'S EARS. See *Stachys byzantina.*

LAMB'S QUARTERS. See *Chenopodium album.*

LAMIUM maculatum. *Labiatae.* DEAD NETTLE. Perennial. All Zones. Trailing stems sprawl along ground or hang from wall or container. Heart-shaped, 1½–2-in. leaves in neat pairs are bluntly toothed at edges; hooded flowers are carried in short spikes. 'Variegatum' has silvery markings along leaf midrib, pink flowers; 'Beacon Silver' has silvery gray leaves with narrow green edge, pink flowers; 'White Nancy' is a 'Beacon Silver' with white flowers. Usually seen as hanging basket plant; can be used as ground cover in shade. Needs rich soil, plenty of water. Deciduous in cold winters. Partially evergreen where winters are mild, but old, shabby stems should be cut off to make room for fresh new growth.

Lamium maculatum

LAMPRANTHUS. *Aizoaceae.* ICE PLANT. Succulent subshrub. Zones 14–24. Most of the blindingly brilliant ice plants with large flowers belong here. Plants erect or trailing, woody at base; leaves fleshy, cylindrical or 3-sided. Select in bloom for the color you want. Plant in full sun. Need little or no summer water. Cut back lightly after bloom to eliminate fruit capsules, encourage new leafy growth. Good at seashore. Attract bees.

L. aurantiacus. To 10–15 in. tall. Gray green, inch-long, 3-sided leaves. Flowers (February–May) 1½–2 in. across, bright orange. Variety 'Glaucus' has bright yellow flowers; 'Sunman' has golden yellow flowers. Plant 15–18 in. apart for bedding, borders, low bank cover.

Lampranthus spectabilis

L. filicaulis. REDONDO CREEPER. Thin, creeping stems, fine-textured foliage. Spreads slowly to form mats 3 in. deep. Small pink flowers in early spring. Use for small-scale ground cover, mound or low bank cover.

L. productus. To 15 in. tall, spreading to 1½–2 ft. Gray green, fleshy leaves tipped bronze. Purple flowers an inch wide. Blooms heavily January–April; scattered bloom at other times. Plant 1–1½ ft. apart.

L. spectabilis. TRAILING ICE PLANT. Sprawling or trailing, to 1 ft. tall, 1½–2 ft. wide. Gray green foliage. Makes carpets of gleaming color, March–May. Flowers 2–2½ in. across, very heavily borne. Available in pink, rose pink, red, purple. Set plants 1–1½ ft. apart.

LANTANA. *Verbenaceae.* Evergreen and deciduous vining shrubs—deciduous only in very cold winters. Seldom freeze in Zones 17, 23, 24. May freeze but recover quickly in Zones 12, 13, 15, 16, 18–22. In Zones 8–10 and 14, they often persist, but may need replacement after hard winter. Elsewhere, an annual. Fast growing, valued for profuse show of color over long season—every month of the year in frost-free areas.

Not particular as to soil. Plant in full sun. Subject to mildew in shade or continued

Lantana montevidensis

L overcast. Prune hard in spring to remove dead wood and prevent woodiness. Water deeply but infrequently; feed lightly. Too much water and fertilizer cuts down on bloom. Shrubby kinds used as substitutes for annuals in planting beds or containers, as low hedges, foundation shrubs. Spreading kinds excellent bank covers, will control erosion. Effective spilling from raised beds, planter boxes, or hanging baskets. Crushed foliage has a strong, pungent odor that is objectionable to some people. Birds are attracted to the plants.

L. camara. One species used in development of kinds sold at nurseries. Coarse, upright to 6 ft. Rough dark green leaves. Flowers in 1–2-in. clusters, yellow, orange, or red.

L. montevidensis *(L. sellowiana).* The other species used in cross breeding. This one is sold at nurseries. A little hardier than *L. camara,* it's a well-known ground cover with branches trailing to as much as 3 or even 6 ft. Dark green leaves, 1 in. long, with coarsely toothed edges; sometimes tinged red or purplish, especially in cold weather. Rosy lilac flowers in 1–1½-in.-wide clusters.

The following list gives some of the named kinds of lantana that are available. Some are merely forms of *L. camara,* or hybrids between the forms. Others are hybrids between *L. camara* and *L. montevidensis.*

'Carnival' ('Dwarf Carnival'). 1½–2 ft. by 4 ft. Pink, yellow, crimson, lavender.

'Christine'. To 6 ft. tall, 5 ft. wide. Cerise pink. Can be trained into small patio tree.

'Confetti'. To 2–3 ft. by 6–8 ft. Yellow, pink, purple.

'Cream Carpet'. To 2–3 ft. by 6–8 ft. Cream with bright yellow throat.

'Dwarf Pink'. To 2–4 ft. by 3–4 ft. Light pink. Rather tender.

'Dwarf White'. To 2–4 ft. by 3–4 ft.

'Dwarf Yellow'. To 2–4 ft. and as wide as high.

'Gold Mound'. To 1½–2 ft. by 6 ft. Yellowish orange.

'Irene'. To 3 ft. by 4 ft. Compact. Magenta with lemon yellow.

'Kathleen'. To 2 ft. by 5–6 ft. Blend of soft rose and gold.

'Lemon Swirl'. Slow growing to 2 ft. tall, 3 ft. wide. Yellow flowers, bright yellow band around each leaf.

'Orange'. To 4 ft. by 3 ft.

'Pink Frolic'. To 2–3 ft. by 6–8 ft. Pink and yellow.

'Radiation'. To 3–5 ft. and as wide as high. Rich orange red. Try it as staked small patio tree.

'Spreading Sunset'. To 2–3 ft. by 6–8 ft. Vivid orange red.

'Spreading Sunshine'. To 2–3 ft. by 6–8 ft. Bright yellow.

'Sunburst'. To 2–3 ft. by 6–8 ft. Bright golden yellow.

'Tangerine'. To 2–3 ft. by 6–8 ft. Burnt orange.

LAPAGERIA rosea. *Liliaceae.* CHILEAN BELLFLOWER. Evergreen vine. Zones 5, 6, 15–17, 23, 24. The national flower of Chile. Likes high humidity, moderate summer temperatures. Slender stems twine to 10–20 ft. Leaves glossy, leathery, oval, to 4 in. long. Blooms scattered through late spring, summer, and fall. Beautiful, 3-in.-long, rosy red, pendant, bell-shaped flowers (frequently spotted with white) have unusually heavy, waxy substance; hold up as long as 2 weeks after cutting. Give it partial shade, wind protection, ample water, and loose soil with plenty of peat moss, ground bark, or sawdust. Protect from snails and slugs.

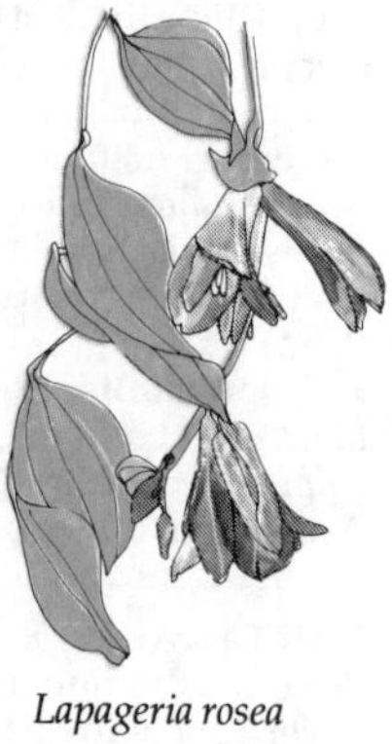

Lapageria rosea

LARCH. See *Larix.*

LARIX. *Pinaceae.* LARCH. Deciduous conifers. Slender pyramids with horizontal branches and drooping branchlets. Needles (½–1½ in. long) soft to touch, in fluffy tufts. Woody, roundish cones, ½–1½ in. long, are scattered all along branchlets. Notable for color in spring and fall and pattern in winter. In spring, new needle tufts are pale green and new cones bright purple red. In fall, needles turn brilliant yellow and orange before dropping. Winter interest is enhanced by many cones which create a delightful polka dot pattern against sky. Not particular about soils; accept lawn watering. Not for warm winter climates or dry soils. Plant with dark evergreen conifers as background or near water for reflection. Larches attract birds.

Larix decidua

L. decidua *(L. europaea).* EUROPEAN LARCH. Zones 1–9, 14–17. Moderate to fast growth to 30–60 ft. Summer color is grass green, lighter than the other species. In variety 'Pendula', branches arch out and down; branchlets hang nearly straight down.

L. kaempferi. JAPANESE LARCH. Zones 1–9, 14–19. Most frequently planted larch in West. Fast growing to 60 ft. or more, but can be dwarfed in containers. Summer foliage is a soft bluish green.

L. occidentalis. WESTERN LARCH, TAMARACK. Zones 1–7. Native to Cascades of Washington and Oregon, eastern Oregon, northern Rocky Mountains. Needles sharp and stiff. Grows to 150–200 ft. as timber tree, 30–50 ft. in gardens.

LARKSPUR. See *Consolida ambigua.*

LARREA tridentata (sometimes sold as *L. divaricata*). *Zygophyllaceae.* CREOSOTE BUSH. Evergreen shrub. Zones 10–13, 19. One of most common native shrubs in deserts of southeastern California, Arizona, southern Utah, Texas, northern Mexico. Grows 4–8 ft. tall with many upright branches. Straggly and open in shallow, dry soil; attractive, dense, rounded but spreading where water accumulates. Leathery, yellow green to dark green leaves divided into 2 tiny, ⅜-in.-long crescents. Gummy secretion makes leaves look varnished and yields distinctive creosote odor, especially after rain. Small yellow flowers off and on all year, followed by small roundish fruit covered with shiny white or rusty hairs. Full sun. With water and fertilizer, grows taller, denser, with larger shiny dark green leaves. Use as wind or privacy screen, or trim into more formal hedge.

Larrea tridentata

LATHYRUS. *Leguminosae.* Annual vines or bushlike perennial vine. In this group is one of the best-known garden flowers—the delightfully fragrant and colorful sweet pea.

Throughout this book, you will find flowers described as "sweet pea shaped." The flower of the sweet pea is typical of the many members of the pea family (*Leguminosae*). Each flower has 1 large, upright, roundish petal (banner or standard), 2 narrow side petals (wings), and 2 lower petals that are somewhat united, forming a boat-shaped structure (keel). Leaves are alternate.

Lathyrus odoratus

L. latifolius. PERENNIAL SWEET PEA. All Zones. Strong-growing vine up to 9 ft., with blue green foliage. Flowers usually reddish purple, often white or rose. Single colors—white and rose—sometimes sold. Long bloom season (June–September) if not allowed to go to seed. Plants grow with little care. May escape and become naturalized. Use as bank cover, trailing over rocks, on trellis or fence. Sun.

L. odoratus. SWEET PEA. Spring or summer annual. Bears many spikelike clusters of crisp-looking flowers with a clean, sweet fragrance, in single colors and mixtures. Color mixtures include deep rose, blue, purple, scarlet, white, cream, amethyst on white ground, salmon, salmon pink on cream. Sweet peas make magnificent cut flowers in quantity. Bush types offer cut flowers the same as vine types, and require no training; both need sun.

To hasten germination, soak seeds for a few hours before planting. Treat seeds with fungicide. Sow seeds 1 in. deep and 1–2 in. apart. When seedlings are 4–5 in. high, thin to not less than 6 in. apart. Pinch out tops to encourage strong side branches. Where climate prevents early planting or soil is too wet to work, start 3 or 4 seeds in each 2¼–3-in. peat pot, indoors or in protected place, and set out when weather has settled. Plant 1 ft. apart, thinning to 1 strong plant. This method is ideal for bush types. Protect young seedlings from birds with wire screen. Set out bait for slugs and snails. Never let vines lack for water. Soak heavily when you water. Cut flowers at least every other day and remove all seed pods.

For vining sweet peas, provide trellis, strings, or wire before planting. Seedlings need support as soon as tendrils form. Freestanding trellis running north and south is best. When planting against fence or wall keep supports away from wall to give air circulation.

Here is a special method of soil preparation—not essential, but producing most perfect flowers on extra-long stems. Dig trench 1–1½ ft. deep. Mix 1 part peat moss, ground bark, or sawdust to 2 parts soil. Add complete commercial fertilizer according to label directions as you mix. Backfill trench with mix. (This extra-deep digging is not necessary in good garden soils.) Regular monthly feeding with commercial fertilizer will keep vines vigorous and productive.

The many varieties of vine-type sweet peas are best understood if grouped by time of bloom.

Early flowering. (Early Flowering Multiflora, Early Multiflora, formerly Early Spencers.) The name "Spencer" once described a type of frilled flower (with wavy petals) that is now characteristic of almost all varieties. The "Multiflora" indicates that the plants carry more flowers per stem than the old "Spencers." The value of early-flowering varieties is that they will bloom in midwinter when days are short. (Spring- and summer-flowering types will not bloom until days have lengthened to 15 hours or more.) Where winter temperatures are mild (Zones 12, 13, 17, 21–24), sow seeds in August or early September for late December or January bloom. Use these varieties for forcing in greenhouse. They are not heat resistant. Generally sold in mixed colors.

Spring flowering. (Spring-Flowering Heat-Resistant Cuthbertson Type, Cuthbertson's Floribunda, Floribunda—Zvolanek strain.) Seeds are packed in both mixtures and single-color named varieties. Wide color range: pink, lavender, purple, white, cream, rose, salmon, cerise, carmine, red, blue. Royal or Royal Family are somewhat larger flowered, more heat resistant.

In Zones 7–9, 12–24, plant between October and early January. Elsewhere, plant February to April (just as soon as soil can be worked).

Summer flowering. (Galaxy, Plenti-flora.) Available in named varieties and mixtures in wide color range. Heat resistant; bloom from early summer on. Large flowers, 5–7 on long stems. Heat resistance is relative; not enough for Zones 7–15, 18–21.

Bush type. The so-called bush type sweet peas are strong vines with predetermined growth, heights. Unlike vining types that reach 5 ft. and more, these stop their upward growth at 1–2½ ft.

Bijou. To 1 ft. Full color range in mixtures and single varieties. Flowers 4 or 5 on 5–7-in. stems. Useful and spectacular in borders, beds, window boxes, containers. Not as heat resistant or as long stemmed as Knee-Hi; performs better in containers.

Cupid. Grows 4–6 in. tall, 1½ ft. wide. Trails on ground or hangs from container.

Jet Set. Bushy, self-supporting plants 2–3 ft. tall. All colors.

Knee-Hi. To 2½ ft. Large, long-stemmed flowers, 5 or 6 to the stem. Has all the virtues and color range of Cuthbertson's Floribundas in self-supporting, bush-type vines. Provides cutting-type flowers in mass display in beds and borders. Growth will exceed 2½ ft. where planting bed joins fence or wall. Keep in open area for uniform height. Follow same planting dates as for spring-flowering sweet peas.

Little Sweethearts. Rounded bushes, 8 in. tall, bloom over a long season. Full range of colors. Patio strain grows 9 in. tall. Snoopea (12–15 in.) and Supersnoop (2 ft.) need no support, come in full range of sweet pea colors.

L. splendens. PRIDE OF CALIFORNIA. Perennial vine to 8–10 ft. Zones 14–24. Clusters of 3–10 deep red sweet peas per stem, March–April. Native to chaparral in San Diego County and adjacent Baja California. Start from seed in pots in fall or spring, plant out in fall or winter. Needs little water first year or so, none once established. Long lived in dry, well-drained soil.

Lauraceae. The laurel family contains evergreen or deciduous trees and shrubs with inconspicuous flowers and (usually) aromatic foliage. Fruits are fleshy and single seeded. Examples are avocado, camphor (*Cinnamomum*), sweet bay (*Laurus nobilis*), and California laurel (*Umbellularia californica*).

LAUREL. See *Laurus, Prunus, Umbellularia californica*.

LAURENTIA fluviatilis *(Isotoma fluviatilis)*. *Lobeliaceae.* BLUE STAR CREEPER. Perennial ground cover plant. Zones 4, 5, 8, 9, 14–24. Creeping, spreading plant that grows only 2–3 in. tall. Pointed, oval leaves ¼ in. long give plant look of baby's tears (*Soleirolia*). Pale blue, starlike flowers, slightly broader than the leaves, spangle plantings in late spring, summer, with a scattering at other times. Will grow in part shade or full sun and can take foot traffic. Plant pieces 6–12 in. apart for cover within a year. Feed lightly once a month, spring to fall. Looks good around stepping stones.

Laurentia fluviatilis

LAURUS nobilis. *Lauraceae.* SWEET BAY, GRECIAN LAUREL. Evergreen tree or shrub. Zones 5–9, 12–24. Slow growth to 12–40 ft. Natural habit is compact, broad-based, often multistemmed, gradually tapering cone. Leaves leathery, aromatic, oval, 2–4 in. long, dark green; traditional bay leaf of cookery. Clusters of small yellow flowers are followed by ½–1-in.-long, black or dark purple berries.

Not fussy about soil, but needs good drainage; requires little water when established. In hot-summer climates, best in filtered shade or afternoon shade. Spray for black scale and laurel psyllid. Tends to sucker heavily. Dense habit makes it a good large background shrub, screen, or small tree. Takes well to clipping into formal shapes—globes, cones, topiary shapes, standards, or hedges. A classic formal container plant. 'Saratoga' has broader leaves and a more treelike habit, and is resistant to psyllid.

Laurus nobilis

LAURUSTINUS. See *Viburnum tinus*.

LAVANDULA. *Labiatae.* LAVENDER. Evergreen shrubs or subshrubs. Native to Mediterranean region. Prized for fragrant lavender or purple flowers used for perfume, sachets. Grayish or gray green aromatic foliage. Plant as hedge or edging, in herb gardens, or in borders with plants needing similar conditions—cistus, helianthemum, nepeta, rosemary, santolina, verbena.

All need full sun and loose, fast-draining soil. Little water or fertilizer. Prune immediately after bloom to keep plants compact and neat. For sachets, cut flower clusters or strip flowers from stems just as color shows; dry in cool, shady place.

(Continued on next page)

L

L. angustifolia ***(L. officinalis, L. spica, L. vera).*** ENGLISH LAVENDER. Zones 4–24. Most widely planted. Classic lavender used for perfume and sachets. To 3–4 ft. high and wide. Leaves gray, smooth on margins, narrow, to 2 in. long. Flowers lavender, ½ in. long, on 1½–2-ft.-long spikes in July–August. Dwarf varieties: 'Compacta' ('Compacta Nana'), to 8 in. tall, 12–15 in. wide; 'Hidcote', slow growing to 1 ft. tall, with very gray foliage and deep purple flowers; 'Munstead', most popular dwarf, 1½ ft. tall, with deep lavender blue flowers a month earlier than the species; 'Twickel Purple', 2–3 ft. high, with purple flowers in fanlike clusters on extra-long spikes. Attractive to bees.

Lavandula angustifolia

L. dentata. FRENCH LAVENDER. Zones 8, 9, 12–24. To 3 ft. tall. Gray green, narrow leaves, 1–1½ in. long, with square-toothed edges. Lavender purple flowers in short spikelike clusters topped with tuft of petal-like bracts. In mild-winter areas, blooms almost continually.

L. d. candicans. Has somewhat larger leaves than French lavender and dense, grayish white down on young foliage.

L. latifolia. SPIKE LAVENDER. Zones 4–24. Much like English lavender in appearance, but with broader leaves and flower stalks frequently branched.

L. stoechas. SPANISH LAVENDER. Zones 4–24. Stocky plant 1½–3 ft. tall, with narrow gray leaves ½–1 in. long. Flowers dark purple, about ⅛ in. long, in dense, short spikes topped with tuft of large, purple, petal-like bracts. Blooms in early summer.

LAVATERA. *Malvaceae.* TREE MALLOW. Annuals, shrubs. Flowers resemble single hollyhocks. Needs sun; accepts routine watering or drought, good or poor soil.

L. assurgentiflora. Zones 14–24. Native to Channel Islands, but naturalized on California coastal mainland. Erect shrub to 12 ft., or treelike. Maplelike leaves 3–5 in. long, lobed and toothed. Rosy lavender, white-striped, 2–3-in.-wide flowers bloom almost throughout the year, heaviest April–August. Resists drought, wind, salt spray. Use as fast-growing windbreak hedge. Will reach 5–10 ft. and bloom first year from seed. Shear to keep dense.

Lavatera assurgentiflora

L. trimestris. ANNUAL MALLOW. Annual. To height of 3–6 ft. from spring-sown seed. Leaves roundish, angled on upper part of plant, toothed. Flowers satiny, to 4 in. across; named varieties in white, pink, rosy carmine. July–September bloom if spent flowers are removed to halt seed production. Thin seedlings to allow ample room to spread. Colorful, fast-growing summer hedge or background planting. Compact (2–3-ft.) varieties include 'Mont Rose' (rose pink), 'Mont Blanc' (white), and 'Silver Cup' (bright pink).

LAVENDER. See *Lavandula.*

LAVENDER COTTON. See *Santolina chamaecyparissus.*

LAVENDER MIST. See *Thalictrum rochebrunianum.*

LAVENDER STARFLOWER. See *Grewia occidentalis.*

LAYIA platyglossa. *Compositae.* TIDYTIPS. Spring and summer annual. California native. Member of sunflower family. Often obtained in mixed wildflower packets, or from dealers in seeds of native plants. Rapid growth to 5–16 in. high. Flower heads about 2 in. across; the rays are light yellow with neatly marked white tips. Can grow in rather heavy soil but won't take standing water. Will naturalize on banks or other well-drained sites with poor soil and little competition from grasses. Give seedlings a good start by preparing soil as for any garden bed. Sow seeds in sunny place in autumn; water occasionally if winter rains fail to materialize.

Layia platyglossa

LEATHERLEAF FERN. See *Rumohra adiantiformis.*

LEEA coccinea. *Leeaceae.* Large house plant; outdoors in sheltered gardens Zones 23, 24. Vigorous, upright grower to 6 ft. or more. Large leaves divided and subdivided into 4–6-in.-long leaflets. General effect is fernlike and lacy. Grows well in bright light (not hot sunlight); survives fairly heavy shade, but grows very little. Feed regularly; let soil surface dry between waterings. Best with room to spread up and out. Flowers red, not especially showy.

Leea coccinea

LEEK. *Liliaceae.* For ornamental relatives, see *Allium.* An annual vegetable—an onion relative that doesn't form distinct bulb. Edible (mild-flavored) bottoms resemble long, fat green onions. Leeks need very rich soil that should never completely dry out. Best in cool weather. Sow in early spring in sunny spot. (In cold-winter areas, sow indoors and set out plants in June or July.) When plants have made considerable top growth, draw soil up around fat, round stems to make bottoms white and mild. Plants grow 2–3 ft. high. Do not let soil into bases of leaves. Begin to harvest in late autumn. Where winters are cold, dig plants with roots and plant them closely in boxes of soil in cool but frost-free location. Where winters are mild, dig as needed from late fall until spring. Any offsets may be detached and replanted. If leeks bloom, small bulbils may appear in the flower clusters. These may be planted for later harvest.

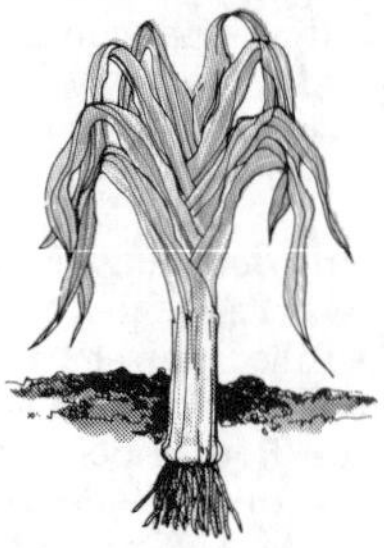

Leek

Leguminosae. The pea family is an enormous group containing annuals, perennials, shrubs, trees, and vines. Many are useful as food (beans, peas), while others furnish timber, medicines, pesticides, and a host of other products. Many are ornamental.

The best-known kinds—sweet peas (*Lathyrus*), for example—have flowers shaped like butterflies, with 2 winglike side petals, 2 partially united lower petals (called the keel), and 1 erect upper petal (the banner or standard). Others have a more regular flower shape (bauhinias, cassias); still others have tightly clustered flowers that appear to be puffs of stamens, as in acacia and silk tree (*Albizia*). All bear seeds in pods (legumes). Many have on their roots colonies of bacteria which can extract nitrogen from the air and convert it into compounds useful as plant food; clovers are a familiar example.

LEMAIREOCEREUS thurberi. *Cactaceae.* ORGANPIPE CACTUS. Zones 12–24. Native to Arizona, Mexico. Columnar, treelike cactus branching from base (also from top, if injured). Dark green or gray green stems, with 12–17 ribs, grow slowly to 15 ft. Spines black, ½–1 in. long. Purplish, white-edged, 3-in. flowers May–June. Full sun. Needs

Lemaireocereus thurberi

deep rose, blue, purple, scarlet, white, cream, amethyst on white ground, salmon, salmon pink on cream. Sweet peas make magnificent cut flowers in quantity. Bush types offer cut flowers the same as vine types, and require no training; both need sun.

To hasten germination, soak seeds for a few hours before planting. Treat seeds with fungicide. Sow seeds 1 in. deep and 1–2 in. apart. When seedlings are 4–5 in. high, thin to not less than 6 in. apart. Pinch out tops to encourage strong side branches. Where climate prevents early planting or soil is too wet to work, start 3 or 4 seeds in each 2¼–3-in. peat pot, indoors or in protected place, and set out when weather has settled. Plant 1 ft. apart, thinning to 1 strong plant. This method is ideal for bush types. Protect young seedlings from birds with wire screen. Set out bait for slugs and snails. Never let vines lack for water. Soak heavily when you water. Cut flowers at least every other day and remove all seed pods.

For vining sweet peas, provide trellis, strings, or wire before planting. Seedlings need support as soon as tendrils form. Freestanding trellis running north and south is best. When planting against fence or wall keep supports away from wall to give air circulation.

Here is a special method of soil preparation—not essential, but producing most perfect flowers on extra-long stems. Dig trench 1–1½ ft. deep. Mix 1 part peat moss, ground bark, or sawdust to 2 parts soil. Add complete commercial fertilizer according to label directions as you mix. Backfill trench with mix. (This extra-deep digging is not necessary in good garden soils.) Regular monthly feeding with commercial fertilizer will keep vines vigorous and productive.

The many varieties of vine-type sweet peas are best understood if grouped by time of bloom.

Early flowering. (Early Flowering Multiflora, Early Multiflora, formerly Early Spencers.) The name "Spencer" once described a type of frilled flower (with wavy petals) that is now characteristic of almost all varieties. The "Multiflora" indicates that the plants carry more flowers per stem than the old "Spencers." The value of early-flowering varieties is that they will bloom in midwinter when days are short. (Spring- and summer-flowering types will not bloom until days have lengthened to 15 hours or more.) Where winter temperatures are mild (Zones 12, 13, 17, 21–24), sow seeds in August or early September for late December or January bloom. Use these varieties for forcing in greenhouse. They are not heat resistant. Generally sold in mixed colors.

Spring flowering. (Spring-Flowering Heat-Resistant Cuthbertson Type, Cuthbertson's Floribunda, Floribunda—Zvolanek strain.) Seeds are packed in both mixtures and single-color named varieties. Wide color range: pink, lavender, purple, white, cream, rose, salmon, cerise, carmine, red, blue. Royal or Royal Family are somewhat larger flowered, more heat resistant.

In Zones 7–9, 12–24, plant between October and early January. Elsewhere, plant February to April (just as soon as soil can be worked).

Summer flowering. (Galaxy, Plenti-flora.) Available in named varieties and mixtures in wide color range. Heat resistant; bloom from early summer on. Large flowers, 5–7 on long stems. Heat resistance is relative; not enough for Zones 7–15, 18–21.

Bush type. The so-called bush type sweet peas are strong vines with predetermined growth, heights. Unlike vining types that reach 5 ft. and more, these stop their upward growth at 1–2½ ft.

Bijou. To 1 ft. Full color range in mixtures and single varieties. Flowers 4 or 5 on 5–7-in. stems. Useful and spectacular in borders, beds, window boxes, containers. Not as heat resistant or as long stemmed as Knee-Hi; performs better in containers.

Cupid. Grows 4–6 in. tall, 1½ ft. wide. Trails on ground or hangs from container.

Jet Set. Bushy, self-supporting plants 2–3 ft. tall. All colors.

Knee-Hi. To 2½ ft. Large, long-stemmed flowers, 5 or 6 to the stem. Has all the virtues and color range of Cuthbertson's Floribundas in self-supporting, bush-type vines. Provides cutting-type flowers in mass display in beds and borders. Growth will exceed 2½ ft. where planting bed joins fence or wall. Keep in open area for uniform height. Follow same planting dates as for spring-flowering sweet peas.

Little Sweethearts. Rounded bushes, 8 in. tall, bloom over a long season. Full range of colors. Patio strain grows 9 in. tall. Snoopea (12–15 in.) and Supersnoop (2 ft.) need no support, come in full range of sweet pea colors.

L. splendens. PRIDE OF CALIFORNIA. Perennial vine to 8–10 ft. Zones 14–24. Clusters of 3–10 deep red sweet peas per stem, March–April. Native to chaparral in San Diego County and adjacent Baja California. Start from seed in pots in fall or spring, plant out in fall or winter. Needs little water first year or so, none once established. Long lived in dry, well-drained soil.

Lauraceae. The laurel family contains evergreen or deciduous trees and shrubs with inconspicuous flowers and (usually) aromatic foliage. Fruits are fleshy and single seeded. Examples are avocado, camphor (*Cinnamomum*), sweet bay (*Laurus nobilis*), and California laurel (*Umbellularia californica*).

LAUREL. See *Laurus, Prunus, Umbellularia californica.*

LAURENTIA fluviatilis *(Isotoma fluviatilis)*. *Lobeliaceae.* BLUE STAR CREEPER. Perennial ground cover plant. Zones 4, 5, 8, 9, 14–24. Creeping, spreading plant that grows only 2–3 in. tall. Pointed, oval leaves ¼ in. long give plant look of baby's tears (*Soleirolia*). Pale blue, starlike flowers, slightly broader than the leaves, spangle plantings in late spring, summer, with a scattering at other times. Will grow in part shade or full sun and can take foot traffic. Plant pieces 6–12 in. apart for cover within a year. Feed lightly once a month, spring to fall. Looks good around stepping stones.

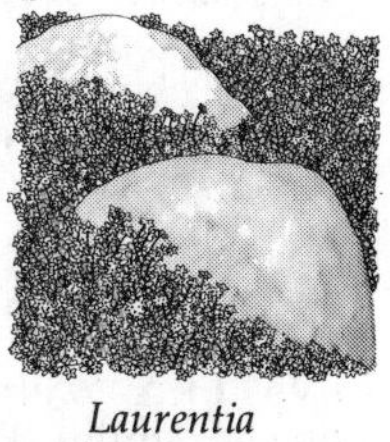

Laurentia fluviatilis

LAURUS nobilis. *Lauraceae.* SWEET BAY, GRECIAN LAUREL. Evergreen tree or shrub. Zones 5–9, 12–24. Slow growth to 12–40 ft. Natural habit is compact, broad-based, often multistemmed, gradually tapering cone. Leaves leathery, aromatic, oval, 2–4 in. long, dark green; traditional bay leaf of cookery. Clusters of small yellow flowers are followed by ½–1-in.-long, black or dark purple berries.

Not fussy about soil, but needs good drainage; requires little water when established. In hot-summer climates, best in filtered shade or afternoon shade. Spray for black scale and laurel psyllid. Tends to sucker heavily. Dense habit makes it a good large background shrub, screen, or small tree. Takes well to clipping into formal shapes—globes, cones, topiary shapes, standards, or hedges. A classic formal container plant. 'Saratoga' has broader leaves and a more treelike habit, and is resistant to psyllid.

Laurus nobilis

LAURUSTINUS. See *Viburnum tinus.*

LAVANDULA. *Labiatae.* LAVENDER. Evergreen shrubs or subshrubs. Native to Mediterranean region. Prized for fragrant lavender or purple flowers used for perfume, sachets. Grayish or gray green aromatic foliage. Plant as hedge or edging, in herb gardens, or in borders with plants needing similar conditions—cistus, helianthemum, nepeta, rosemary, santolina, verbena.

All need full sun and loose, fast-draining soil. Little water or fertilizer. Prune immediately after bloom to keep plants compact and neat. For sachets, cut flower clusters or strip flowers from stems just as color shows; dry in cool, shady place.

(Continued on next page)

Lavandula angustifolia

L. angustifolia ***(L. officinalis, L. spica, L. vera).*** ENGLISH LAVENDER. Zones 4–24. Most widely planted. Classic lavender used for perfume and sachets. To 3–4 ft. high and wide. Leaves gray, smooth on margins, narrow, to 2 in. long. Flowers lavender, ½ in. long, on 1½–2-ft.-long spikes in July–August. Dwarf varieties: 'Compacta' ('Compacta Nana'), to 8 in. tall, 12–15 in. wide; 'Hidcote', slow growing to 1 ft. tall, with very gray foliage and deep purple flowers; 'Munstead', most popular dwarf, 1½ ft. tall, with deep lavender blue flowers a month earlier than the species; 'Twickel Purple', 2–3 ft. high, with purple flowers in fanlike clusters on extra-long spikes. Attractive to bees.

L. dentata. FRENCH LAVENDER. Zones 8, 9, 12–24. To 3 ft. tall. Gray green, narrow leaves, 1–1½ in. long, with square-toothed edges. Lavender purple flowers in short spikelike clusters topped with tuft of petal-like bracts. In mild-winter areas, blooms almost continually.

L. d. candicans. Has somewhat larger leaves than French lavender and dense, grayish white down on young foliage.

L. latifolia. SPIKE LAVENDER. Zones 4–24. Much like English lavender in appearance, but with broader leaves and flower stalks frequently branched.

L. stoechas. SPANISH LAVENDER. Zones 4–24. Stocky plant 1½–3 ft. tall, with narrow gray leaves ½–1 in. long. Flowers dark purple, about ⅛ in. long, in dense, short spikes topped with tuft of large, purple, petal-like bracts. Blooms in early summer.

LAVATERA. *Malvaceae.* TREE MALLOW. Annuals, shrubs. Flowers resemble single hollyhocks. Needs sun; accepts routine watering or drought, good or poor soil.

Lavatera assurgentiflora

L. assurgentiflora. Zones 14–24. Native to Channel Islands, but naturalized on California coastal mainland. Erect shrub to 12 ft., or treelike. Maplelike leaves 3–5 in. long, lobed and toothed. Rosy lavender, white-striped, 2–3-in.-wide flowers bloom almost throughout the year, heaviest April–August. Resists drought, wind, salt spray. Use as fast-growing windbreak hedge. Will reach 5–10 ft. and bloom first year from seed. Shear to keep dense.

L. trimestris. ANNUAL MALLOW. Annual. To height of 3–6 ft. from spring-sown seed. Leaves roundish, angled on upper part of plant, toothed. Flowers satiny, to 4 in. across; named varieties in white, pink, rosy carmine. July–September bloom if spent flowers are removed to halt seed production. Thin seedlings to allow ample room to spread. Colorful, fast-growing summer hedge or background planting. Compact (2–3-ft.) varieties include 'Mont Rose' (rose pink), 'Mont Blanc' (white), and 'Silver Cup' (bright pink).

LAVENDER. See *Lavandula.*

LAVENDER COTTON. See *Santolina chamaecyparissus.*

LAVENDER MIST. See *Thalictrum rochebrunianum.*

LAVENDER STARFLOWER. See *Grewia occidentalis.*

LAYIA platyglossa. *Compositae.* TIDYTIPS. Spring and summer annual. California native. Member of sunflower family. Often obtained in mixed wildflower packets, or from dealers in seeds of native plants. Rapid growth to 5–16 in. high. Flower heads about 2 in. across; the rays are light yellow with neatly marked white tips. Can grow in rather heavy soil but won't take standing water. Will naturalize on banks or other well-drained sites with poor soil and little competition from grasses. Give seedlings a good start by preparing soil as for any garden bed. Sow seeds in sunny place in autumn; water occasionally if winter rains fail to materialize.

Layia platyglossa

LEATHERLEAF FERN. See *Rumohra adiantiformis.*

LEEA coccinea. *Leeaceae.* Large house plant; outdoors in sheltered gardens Zones 23, 24. Vigorous, upright grower to 6 ft. or more. Large leaves divided and subdivided into 4–6-in.-long leaflets. General effect is fernlike and lacy. Grows well in bright light (not hot sunlight); survives fairly heavy shade, but grows very little. Feed regularly; let soil surface dry between waterings. Best with room to spread up and out. Flowers red, not especially showy.

Leea coccinea

LEEK. *Liliaceae.* For ornamental relatives, see *Allium.* An annual vegetable—an onion relative that doesn't form distinct bulb. Edible (mild-flavored) bottoms resemble long, fat green onions. Leeks need very rich soil that should never completely dry out. Best in cool weather. Sow in early spring in sunny spot. (In cold-winter areas, sow indoors and set out plants in June or July.) When plants have made considerable top growth, draw soil up around fat, round stems to make bottoms white and mild. Plants grow 2–3 ft. high. Do not let soil into bases of leaves. Begin to harvest in late autumn. Where winters are cold, dig plants with roots and plant them closely in boxes of soil in cool but frost-free location. Where winters are mild, dig as needed from late fall until spring. Any offsets may be detached and replanted. If leeks bloom, small bulbils may appear in the flower clusters. These may be planted for later harvest.

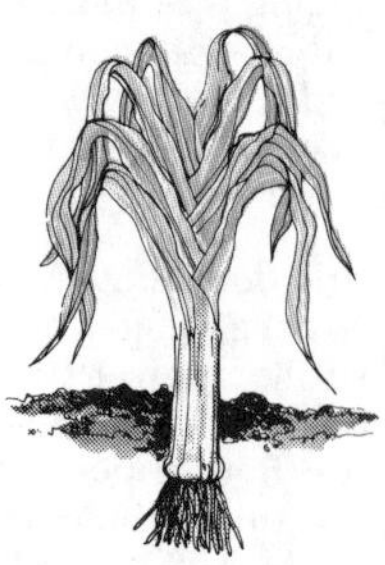
Leek

Leguminosae. The pea family is an enormous group containing annuals, perennials, shrubs, trees, and vines. Many are useful as food (beans, peas), while others furnish timber, medicines, pesticides, and a host of other products. Many are ornamental.

The best-known kinds—sweet peas (*Lathyrus*), for example—have flowers shaped like butterflies, with 2 winglike side petals, 2 partially united lower petals (called the keel), and 1 erect upper petal (the banner or standard). Others have a more regular flower shape (bauhinias, cassias); still others have tightly clustered flowers that appear to be puffs of stamens, as in acacia and silk tree (*Albizia*). All bear seeds in pods (legumes). Many have on their roots colonies of bacteria which can extract nitrogen from the air and convert it into compounds useful as plant food; clovers are a familiar example.

LEMAIREOCEREUS thurberi. *Cactaceae.* ORGANPIPE CACTUS. Zones 12–24. Native to Arizona, Mexico. Columnar, treelike cactus branching from base (also from top, if injured). Dark green or gray green stems, with 12–17 ribs, grow slowly to 15 ft. Spines black, ½–1 in. long. Purplish, white-edged, 3-in. flowers May–June. Full sun. Needs

Lemaireocereus thurberi

excellent drainage and very little watering. Night blooming. Fruit 1½ in. long, red tinged olive green, filled with edible sweet red pulp.

LEMON. See *Citrus.*

LEMONADE BERRY. See *Rhus integrifolia.*

LEMON BALM. See *Melissa.*

LEMON-SCENTED GUM. See *Eucalyptus citriodora.*

LEMON VERBENA. See *Aloysia triphylla.*

LENTEN ROSE. See *Helleborus orientalis.*

LEONOTIS leonurus. *Labiatae.* LION'S TAIL. Perennial. Zones 8–24. Shrubby, branching, to 3–6 ft. Hairy stems; 2–5-in.-long leaves with coarsely toothed edges. Dense whorls of tubular, deep orange, 2-in.-long flowers covered with furlike coat of fine hairs. Blooms summer into fall. Plant in full sun. Drought resistant. Striking if kept well-groomed.

Leonotis leonurus

LEONTOPODIUM alpinum. *Compositae.* EDELWEISS. Perennial. Zones 1–9, 14–24. Short-lived, white, woolly plants 4–12 in. high, with small flower heads closely crowded on tips of stems and surrounded by collar of slender white, woolly leaves radiating out from below flower heads like arms of starfish. The tiny bracts of flower heads, also white and woolly, are tipped with black. Blooms June–July. Needs sun, plenty of water, and excellent drainage. Seeds germinate easily. Good in rock gardens.

Leontopodium alpinum

LEOPARD PLANT. See *Ligularia tussilaginea* 'Aureo-maculata'.

LEOPARD'S BANE. See *Doronicum.*

LEPTOSPERMUM. *Myrtaceae.* TEA TREE. Evergreen shrubs or small trees. Zones 14–24. Native to Australia, New Zealand. Soft and casual looking (never rigid or formal), partly because of branching habit. Substantial, useful landscape structure plants the year around. All make springtime display of flowers along stem among small leaves. The flowers (white, pink, or red) are basically alike; about ½ in. wide with petals arranged around hard central cone or cup. Single flowers look like tiny single roses. Petals fall to leave woody, long-lasting seed capsules about ¼ in. wide.

Leptospermum laevigatum

Need good soil drainage and full sun. Need moisture when first planted; established plants are drought tolerant. Subject to chlorosis in alkaline soils. Apparently pest free above ground; sometimes succumb quickly to root troubles where drainage is poor. All take some surface shearing; in real pruning, cut back only to side branches, never into bare wood. Called "tea tree" because Captain Cook brewed leaves of *L. scoparium* into tea to prevent scurvy among his crew. Good near ocean.

L. citratum. See *L. petersonii.*

L. laevigatum. AUSTRALIAN TEA TREE. Large shrub or small tree. To 30 ft. high, often as wide. With the right soil—well drained, slightly acid—lives long and well with little care. Oval or teardrop-shaped, dull green to gray green leaves to ⅜ in. wide, 1 in. long. The plant has 2 basic uses; the use determines appearance.

(1) Solitary plants allowed to grow to full size develop picturesque character with muscular-looking, twisted and gracefully curved, shaggy, gray brown trunks up to 2 ft. across at the base. Equally handsome branches range out from trunk and carry canopies of fine-textured foliage. Some pendulous branches weep down from foliage canopies. Single white flowers appear in great numbers along branches in spring.

(2) Planted close together (1½–6 ft.) to make windbreak, thick natural screen, or clipped hedge, plants do not develop any visible branching character but do make solid bank of fine-textured green foliage, highlighted in spring by white flowers.

L. l. 'Compactum'. Similar to species but smaller—to 8 ft. high, 6 ft. wide—and slightly more open and loose. Does not flower as heavily as *L. laevigatum.*

L. l. 'Reevesii'. Leaves are rounder, slightly bigger and more densely set than those of *L. laevigatum,* and plant grows only 4–5 ft. high and wide. Heavier looking than either of the preceding 2 kinds.

L. nitidum 'Macrocarpum' (*L. lanigerum* 'Macrocarpum'). Shrub 6 ft. tall with reddish new growth, purplish bronze older foliage. Leaves are tiny and narrow—½ in. long, ⅛ in. wide. Spring flowers nearly 1 in. wide, chartreuse yellow with dark green disk.

L. petersonii *(L. citratum).* Big shrub or small tree 15–20 ft. tall with open-branching, see-through quality and graceful weeping branches. Pale green leaves, 1–2 in. long, less than ¼ in. wide, have strong, pleasant lemon scent when crushed. White flowers with green centers in summer. Attractive multistemmed small tree.

L. rotundifolium *(L. scoparium rotundifolium).* Shrub to 6 ft. tall, 9 ft. wide. Variable size and habit, but usually with spreading, arching branches. Tiny leaves are roundish rather than needlelike. Spring flowers are large (1 in. wide) and vary from white to deep purplish pink. Extremely showy in bloom, but has shorter bloom period than *L. scoparium.* Scarce, hard to propagate.

L. scoparium. NEW ZEALAND TEA TREE, MANUKA. Ground cover to large shrub. True species *L. scoparium* is of no interest in western U.S., but its many varieties are valuable. These are not as bold of form or quite as serviceable in hedges and screens as the kinds listed above, but they have showier flowers. Hardier than other species. Leaves are tiny (from almost needlelike and ¼ in. long to ⅛ in. wide and ½ in. long), pointed, densely set. Many white to pink flowers to ½ in. across in spring or summer.

L. s. 'Gaiety Girl'. Slow growing to 5 ft. Midspring flowers double, pink with lilac tint. Foliage reddish.

L. s. 'Helene Strybing'. Seedling of *L. s.* 'Keatleyi'; resembles parent except that flowers are somewhat smaller, much deeper pink.

L. s. 'Keatleyi'. Tallest (6–10 ft.), most open and rangy of *L. scoparium* varieties—and most inclined to develop picturesque habit. Single pink flowers, paler at edges, are extra large, sometimes as big as a quarter. Spring bloom, may repeat in summer.

L. s. 'Nanum Tui'. Low, rounded shrub to 2 ft. high. Single flowers light pink, darker at center.

L. s. 'Pink Cascade'. To 1 ft. tall by 3–4 ft. wide. Single pink flowers on sprawling, weeping branches. Attractive trailing over walls, among rocks.

L. s. 'Pink Pearl'. To 6–10 ft. Pale pink buds open to double blush pink to white flowers.

L. s. 'Red Damask'. To 6–8 ft. Dense in habit. Double ruby red flowers, red-tinged leaves. Heavy bloom midwinter to spring.

L. s. 'Ruby Glow'. Compact, upright 6–8-ft. shrub with dark foliage. Double oxblood red flowers (¾ in. wide) in winter and spring, borne in great profusion—entire shrub looks red.

L. s. 'Snow White'. Spreading, compact plant 2–4 ft. high. Medium-sized double white flowers with green centers, December to spring.

L

LETTUCE. *Compositae.* Summer annual in Zones 1–7, 10, 11. Cool-season annual in Zones 8, 9, 12–24. Indispensable salad plant and easy to grow. There are 4 principal types.

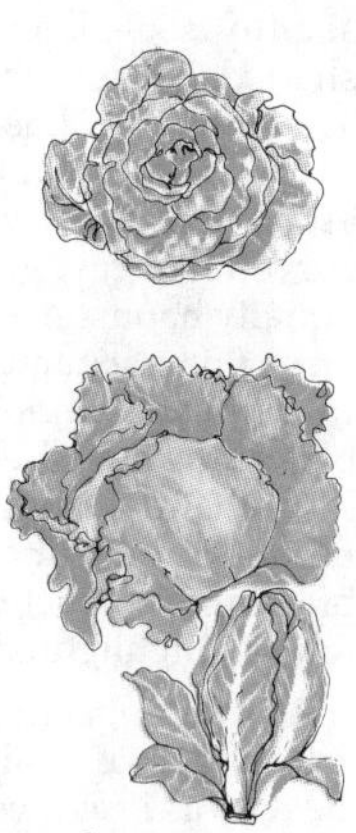

Lettuce

Crisphead lettuce is most familiar kind in markets, most exasperating for home gardener to produce. Heads best when monthly average temperatures are around 55°–60°F. In cool coastal areas it does well over long season; inland, timing becomes critical. Best varieties: various strains of 'Great Lakes', 'Imperial', and 'Iceberg'.

Butterhead or Boston types have loose heads with green, smooth outer leaves and yellow inner leaves. Good varieties: 'Bibb' ('Limestone') and 'Buttercrunch'. 'Mignonette' ('Manoa') stands heat without bolting (going to seed) quickly.

Loose-leaf lettuce makes rosettes rather than heads, stands heat better than the others, is summer mainstay in warm climates. Choice selections: 'Black-seeded Simpson', 'Oak Leaf', 'Slobolt', 'Prizehead' or 'Ruby' (red-tinged varieties), and 'Salad Bowl', with deeply cut leaves.

Romaine lettuce has erect, cylindrical heads of smooth leaves, the outer green, the inner whitish. Stands heat moderately well. Try 'White Paris', 'Parris Island', 'Dark Green Cos', or 'Valmaine'.

Lettuces with bronzy to pinkish red leaves add a colorful touch to a salad. 'Lollo Rosso', 'Red Sails', 'Red Oak Leaf', and 'Ruby' are loose-leaf varieties; 'Merveille des Quatre Saisons' and 'Perella Red' are butterheads; 'Rouge d'Hiver' is a romaine.

Lettuce needs loose, well-drained soil; in hot-summer areas, light shading at midday helps. Water regularly; feed lightly and frequently. Sow in open ground at 10-day intervals, starting after frost as soon as soil is workable. Barely cover seeds; space rows 8–12 in. apart. Thin head lettuce or romaine to 1 ft. apart, moving seedlings with care to extend the plantings. Leaf lettuce can be grown 4 in. apart; harvest some whole plants as they begin to crowd.

In milder climates, make later sowings in late summer, fall. Where summers are very short, sow indoors, then move seedlings outdoors after last frost. Control snails, slugs, and earwigs with bait *on the ground*—not on the plants. Harvest when heads or leaves are of good size; lettuce doesn't stand long before going to seed, becoming quite bitter in the process. Loose-leaf lettuce can be harvested over a long period; remove a few leaves from each plant in the row until bloom stalks start to grow.

LEUCOCORYNE ixioides *(L. odorata).* *Amaryllidaceae.* GLORY OF THE SUN. Bulb. Zones 13, 16, 19, 21–24. Native to Chile. Closely related to *Brodiaea.* Narrow, grass-like leaves to 1 ft. Blooms March–April: slender, wiry stems, 1–1½ ft. high, bear 4–6 lavender blue, white-centered, beautifully scented flowers, 2 in. across. Excellent, long-lasting cut flowers. In mild-winter climates, use in rock gardens or naturalize in sections that get little summer watering. Use with ixia, sparaxis, freesia, tritonia; or grow in pots like freesias.

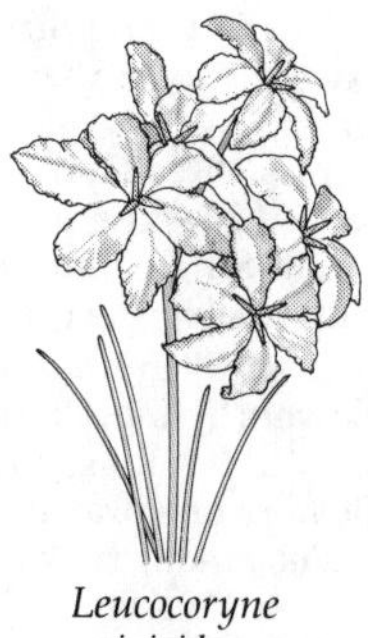

Leucocoryne ixioides

Outdoors, plant bulbs in fall, 6 in. deep, 3–4 in. apart, in sunny spot with light, perfectly drained soil. Give ample water until after bloom, then let bulbs dry out. Bulbs tend to move downward in soil; confine them by planting in containers or laying wire screen across bottom of planting area.

LEUCODENDRON. *Proteaceae.* Evergreen shrubs, trees. Zones 16, 17, 20–24. Native to South Africa. Related to proteas. Male and female flowers are borne on separate plants. Some shrubby species have showy colored bracts beneath the conelike male flower clusters, giving clusters the look of giant daisies. Female flower clusters are less showy and develop into conelike seed clusters. All leucodendrons need good drainage; most prefer acid soil. The following tolerate neutral or mildly alkaline conditions.

Leucodendron argenteum

L. argenteum. SILVER TREE. Young trees (the most spectacular in effect) narrow and stiffly upright; mature trees spreading, with tortuous, gray-barked trunk, irregular silhouette. Can reach 40 ft. Silky, silvery white, 3–6-in.-long leaves densely cover the branches. This is a foliage plant; flowers and fruit are inconsequential. Foliage good for arrangements.

Needs fast-draining soil, some water during summer. Will not thrive in clay, alkaline soil, or soil with animal manure. Needs sunlight and humid air; takes ocean winds but not dry winds. Striking appearance and cultural problems make it hard to use. Small plants are picturesque container subjects for 3–4 years. Larger plants are effective on slopes when combined with boulders, succulents, and pines in sheltered seaside gardens. Use singly or in groups.

L. discolor. Upright, slightly spreading shrub 4–8 ft. tall and as wide (smaller in container), its stems densely set with gray green leaves. Red-centered gold inflorescences at stem tips in early fall or winter; these make striking cut flowers which dry well.

L. tinctum. Upright, slender shrub to 8 ft. tall, 3–4 ft. wide. March inflorescences rose to red, sometimes yellow.

LEUCOJUM. *Amaryllidaceae.* SNOWFLAKE. Bulbs. Strap-shaped leaves and nodding, bell-shaped white flowers with segments tipped green. Easy to grow and permanent. Naturalize under deciduous trees, in shrub borders, orchards, or cool slopes. Plant 4 in. deep in fall. Do not disturb until really crowded; then dig, divide, and replant after foliage dies down.

Leucojum aestivum

L. aestivum. SUMMER SNOWFLAKE. All Zones. Most commonly grown. Leaves 1–1½ ft. long. Stems 1½ ft. tall carry 3–5 flowers; variety 'Gravetye Giant' has as many as 9 flowers to a stem. In mild-winter areas, blooms November through winter; blooms with narcissus in colder areas.

L. vernum. SPRING SNOWFLAKE. Zones 1–6; not successful in hot, dry climates. Leaves 9 in. long. Stems 1 ft. tall bear single large, nodding, white flowers in very early spring (late winter in warmer areas). Needs rich, moist soil.

LEUCOPHYLLUM frutescens *(L. texanum).* *Scrophulariaceae.* TEXAS RANGER. Evergreen shrub. Zones 7–24. Native to Texas, Mexico. Compact, slow-growing, silvery-foliaged shrub to 5–12 ft. tall, 4–6 ft. wide. Does well in desert areas, taking any degree of heat and wind. Tolerates some alkali if drainage is good. Thrives with little water near sea, but needs heat to produce its rose purple, 1-in.-long, bell-shaped summer flowers. Leaves small, silvery white beneath. Useful either as round-headed gray mass, as clipped hedge, or in mixed dry plantings. *L. f. alba* has white flowers; purple-flowered variety 'Compactum' is smaller and denser than the species. 'Green Cloud' and 'Silver Cloud' are selections, the former with deep green foliage, the latter especially silvery.

Leucophyllum frutescens

L

LEUCOSPERMUM. *Proteaceae.* PINCUSHION. Evergreen shrubs. Zones 15–17, 21–24. South African shrubs related to *Protea;* see that entry for culture. Like proteas, these shrubs are difficult to grow, but extra effort is rewarded with spectacular flower clusters: many long, slender tubular flowers in a large thistlelike head. These make stunning cut flowers, lasting a month in water. Leaves are narrow ovals, stalkless and crowded along stems. Bloom peaks in late winter, early spring, but can start earlier, last up to 6 months in mild winters. Well-established plants can take several degrees of frost, and side buds will produce flowers even if main flower buds freeze.

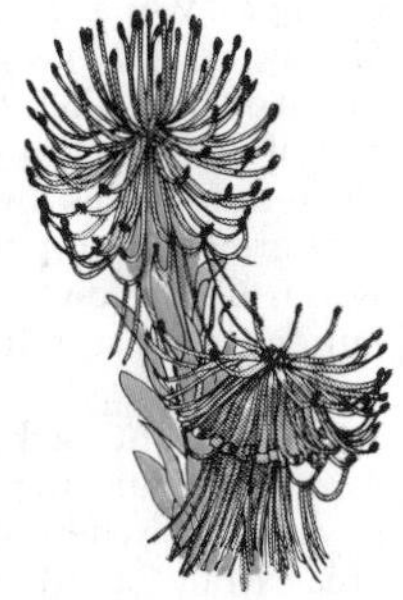

Leucospermum reflexum

L. nutans. NODDING PINCUSHION. Compact plants 4 ft. tall and as wide. Flower clusters 4 in. across, individual tube flowers curving gracefully outward, then inward again, coral with yellow tips. Best kind for cut flowers.

L. reflexum. ROCKET PINCUSHION. Sprawling plant to 12 ft. tall with attractive gray foliage. Orange rose, 4-in. heads; as flowers age, "pins" curl downward, giving shaggy look.

LEUCOTHOE. *Ericaceae.* Evergreen shrubs. Related to *Pieris.* All have leathery leaves and clusters of urn-shaped white flowers. Need acid, woodsy, deep soil and some shade; do best in woodland gardens or as facing for taller broad-leafed evergreens. Best used in masses; not especially attractive individually. Bronze-tinted winter foliage is a bonus.

Leucothoe fontanesiana

L. davisiae. SIERRA LAUREL. Zones 1–7, 15–17. Grows in bogs and wet places in Sierra Nevada, Trinity, and Siskiyou mountains. Upright shrub to 3½ ft. Oblong or egg-shaped leaves to 3 in. long, glossy rich green. White flowers in erect, 2–4-in.-long clusters. Blooms in summer.

L. fontanesiana *(L. catesbaei).* DROOPING LEUCOTHOE. Zones 4–7, 15–17. Borderline hardiness in Zones 1–3. Native to eastern U.S. Slow grower to 2–6 ft.; branches arch gracefully. Leathery, 3–6-in.-long leaves turn bronzy purple in fall (bronzy green in deep shade). Spreads from underground stems. Drooping clusters of creamy white flowers resembling lily-of-the-valley in spring. Variety 'Rainbow', with leaves marked yellow, green, and pink, grows 3–4 ft. tall.

Requires summer water in first 2 or 3 summers, but later can take fair amount of drought. Can be controlled in height to make 1½-ft. ground cover in shade; just cut older, taller stems to ground. Blooming branches are decorative cut flowers.

L. populifolia. Zones 7–9, 14–24. Native to swamps, South Carolina to Florida; needs ample water. To 10 ft. tall, with pointed oval leaves to 4 in. long and white flowers in short clusters.

LEVISTICUM officinale. *Umbelliferae.* LOVAGE. Perennial. All Zones. This herb is sometimes grown for its celery-flavored seeds, leaves, and stems. Reaches 2–3 ft. tall, sometimes even 6 ft. Cut and divided, glossy deep green leaves; flattish clusters of small greenish yellow flowers. Full sun. Ordinary garden care suits it. Grow from seeds or divisions.

Levisticum officinale

LEWISIA. *Portulacaceae.* Perennials. Zones 1–7. Beautiful, often difficult plants for rock gardens, collections of alpine plants. All need excellent drainage; plant with fine gravel around crowns. Of many offered by specialists, these are outstanding:

Lewisia tweedyi

L. cotyledon. Native to northern California and southern Oregon. Rosettes of narrow, fleshy, evergreen leaves bear 10-in. stems topped by large clusters of 1-in., white or pink flowers striped with rose or red. Spring to early summer bloom is extremely showy. *L. c. howellii* is similar, but leaves are wavy edged and flowers somewhat larger. Same culture as *L. tweedyi.* Can be grown in pots in fast-draining sterilized soil or growing mixes.

L. rediviva. BITTERROOT. Native to mountains of the West. State flower of Montana. Fleshy roots; short stems with short, succulent, strap-shaped leaves to 2 in. long that usually die back before flowers appear (seemingly from bare earth) in spring. Flowers, borne singly on short stems, look like 2-in.-wide, rose or white waterlilies. Full sun. Water sparingly. Not difficult if drainage is excellent.

L. tweedyi. Native to mountains, south central Washington. Stunning big, satiny, salmon pink flowers, 1–3 to a stem, bloom above fleshy, evergreen, 4-in. leaves. Grow in full sun or light shade. Water sparingly. Needs perfect drainage around root crown to prevent rot. Prune out side growths.

LIATRIS. *Compositae.* GAYFEATHER. Perennials. Zones 1–3, 7–10, 14–24. Native to eastern and central United States. Showy plants. Basal tufts of narrow, grassy leaves grow from thick, often tuberous rootstocks. Tufts lengthen in summer to tall, narrow stems densely set with narrow leaves and topped by narrow plume of small, fluffy, rose purple (sometimes white) flower heads. Choice cut flowers.

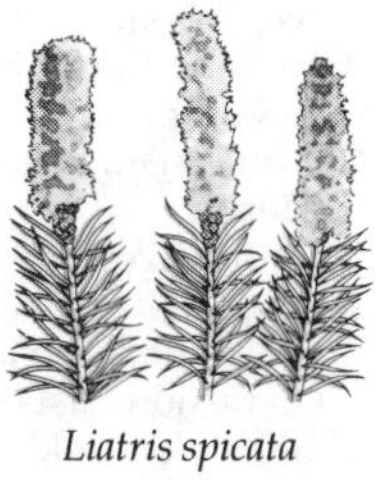

Liatris spicata

These plants need full sun and endure heat, cold, drought, and poor soil. They are best used in mixed perennial borders, although the rosy purple color calls for careful placing to avoid color clashes.

L. callilepis. Plants grown and sold under this name by Dutch bulb growers are *L. spicata.*

L. spicata. To 6 ft., usually only 2–3 ft., with 15-in.-long flower plumes; each individual flower head to ⅓ in. wide. 'Kobold', a 2-ft. dwarf variety, is widely sold.

LIBOCEDRUS. See *Calocedrus.*

LICORICE FERN. See *Polypodium glycyrrhiza.*

LIGULARIA. *Compositae.* Stately perennials with big leaves and yellow to orange daisy flowers. Some are hardy and winter dormant; one is less hardy and evergreen. All need rich soil and ample water. Winter-dormant kinds grow in full sun near the coast but need shade inland. Hardy anywhere (mulch in coldest winter climates), they perform poorly in poor soils and low humidity.

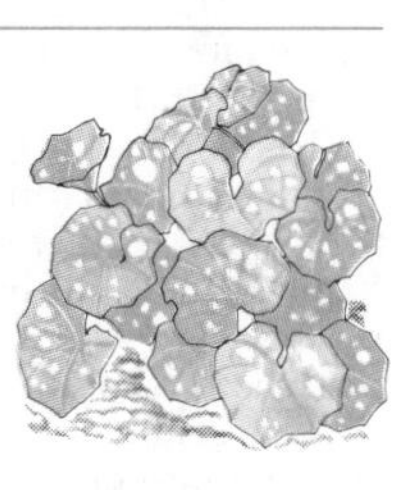

Ligularia tussilaginea 'Aureo-maculata'

L. dentata. Zones 3–9, 15–17. Roundish leaves, heart shaped at the base, are more than 1 ft. wide. Orange yellow daisies to 4 in. wide appear in midsummer to early fall on 3–5-ft. stalks. 'Desdemona' has deep purple leaf stalks, veins, and leaf undersurfaces; upper surfaces are green. 'Othello', somewhat larger, has purple leaf undersurfaces.

L. stenocephala. Zones 3–9, 15–17. Usually represented by variety 'The Rocket'. Foot-wide leaves are deeply cut; yellow daisies form along tall, narrow spires to 5 ft.

(Continued on next page)

L

L. tussilaginea ***(L. kaempferi, Farfugium japonicum).*** Zones 4–10, 14–24; house plant or indoor/outdoor plant anywhere. Speckled variety 'Aureo-maculata', LEOPARD PLANT, has evergreen leaves 6–10 in. wide, thick and rather leathery, speckled and blotched with cream or yellow, nearly kidney shaped but shallowly angled and toothed. All leaves rise directly from rootstock on 1–2-ft. stems. Flower stalks 1–2 ft. tall bear a few yellow-rayed, 1½–2-in.-wide flower heads.

Choice foliage plant for shady beds or entryways. Good container plant. Tops hardy to 20°F.; plants die back to roots at 0°F., put on new growth again in spring. Needs routine summer watering. Bait for snails and slugs. *L. t.* 'Argentea' has deep green leaves irregularly mottled, particularly on edges, with gray green and ivory white. 'Crispata' has curled and crested leaf edges.

LIGUSTRUM. *Oleaceae.* PRIVET. Deciduous or evergreen shrubs or small trees. Most widely used in hedges. Can also be clipped into formal shapes and featured in tubs or large pots. One type is a common street tree. All have abundant, showy clusters of white to creamy white flowers in late spring or early summer. (Clipped hedges bear fewer flowers because most of the flower-bearing branches get trimmed off.) Fragrance is described as "pleasant" to "unpleasant" (never "wonderful" or "terrible"). Flowers draw bees. Small, blue black, berrylike fruit follows blossoms. Birds eat fruit, thus distributing seeds—resulting in multitudes of seedlings.

Ligustrum lucidum

Most privets are easily grown in sun or some shade, and in any soil. Give them lots of water. In some areas they are subject to lilac leaf miner, which disfigures leaves.

Confusion exists concerning identity of certain privets in nurseries. The plant sold as *L. japonicum* usually turns out to be the small tree *L. lucidum.* The true *L. japonicum* is available in 2 (or more) forms. The tall, shrubby kind is the true species; the lower-growing, more densely foliaged form is typically sold as *L. texanum,* and probably should be called *L. japonicum* 'Texanum'. In a similar fashion, the smaller-leafed hardy privets used for hedging are often confused: *L. amurense, L. ovalifolium,* and *L. vulgare* look much alike, and any is likely to be sold as common privet—a name that belongs to *L. vulgare.*

L. amurense. AMUR PRIVET, AMUR RIVER NORTH PRIVET. Shrub. All Zones. Deciduous in coldest areas, where it is much used for hedge and screen planting. Partially evergreen in milder climates, but seldom planted there. Much like *L. ovalifolium* in appearance, but foliage is less glossy.

L. ibolium 'Variegata'. Zones 3–24. Semideciduous shrub. Variegated form of a hybrid between *L. ovalifolium* and another Japanese privet. Resembles *L. ovalifolium,* but has bright green leaves with creamy yellow edges.

L. japonicum (often sold as *L. texanum*). JAPANESE PRIVET, WAXLEAF PRIVET. Evergreen shrub. Zones 4–24. Dense, compact growth habit to 10–12 ft., but can be kept lower by trimming. Roundish oval leaves 2–4 in. long, dark to medium green and glossy above, distinctly paler to almost whitish beneath; have thick, slightly spongy feeling. Excellent plants for hedges or screens, or for shaping into globes, pyramids, other shapes, or small standard trees. Sunburns in hot spells. In areas of caliche soil, or where Texas root rot prevails, grow it in containers.

L. j. 'Rotundifolium' (*L. j.* 'Coriaceum'). Grows to 4–5 ft. and has nearly round leaves to 2½ in. long. Part shade in inland valleys.

L. j. 'Silver Star'. Leaves are deep green, with gray green mottling and startling creamy white edges. Provides a good contrast to deep green foliage.

L. j. 'Texanum'. Very similar to species but lower growing (to 6–9 ft.) with somewhat denser, lusher foliage. Useful as windbreak.

L. lucidum. GLOSSY PRIVET. Evergreen tree. Zones 5, 6, 8–24. Makes a round-headed tree that eventually reaches 35–40 ft. Can be kept lower as a big shrub, or may form multiple-trunked tree. Glossy, 4–6-in.-long leaves are tapered and pointed, dark to medium green on both sides. They feel leathery but lack the slightly spongy feel of *L. japonicum's* leaves. Flowers in especially large, feathery clusters followed by profusion of fruit. Fine street or lawn tree. Fast growing; somewhat drought resistant but looks better with water. Can grow in narrow areas. Performs well in large containers. Or plant 10 ft. apart for tall privacy screen. Useful as windbreak.

Before planting this tree, weigh the advantages listed above very carefully against the disadvantages. Eventual fruit crop is immense; never plant where fruits will fall on cars, walks, or other paved areas (they stain). Fallen seeds (and those dropped by birds) sprout profusely in ground cover and will need pulling. Many people dislike the flower odor, and fruiting clusters are bare and unattractive after fruit drops.

L. ovalifolium. CALIFORNIA PRIVET. Semideciduous shrub; evergreen only in mildest areas. Zones 4–24. Inexpensive hedge plant, once more widely used in California. Grows rapidly to 15 ft., but can be kept sheared to any height. Dark green, oval, 2½-in.-long leaves. Set plants 9–12 in. apart for hedges. Clip early and frequently to encourage low, dense branching. Greedy roots. Well-fed, well-watered plants hold leaves longest. Tolerates heat.

L. o. 'Aureum' (sold as *L. o.* 'Variegatum'). GOLDEN PRIVET. Leaves have broad yellow edge.

L. 'Suwannee River'. Evergreen shrub. All Zones. Reported to be hybrid between *L. japonicum* 'Rotundifolium' and *L. lucidum.* Slow growing to 1½ ft. tall in 3 years, eventually 3–4 ft.; compact habit. Leathery, dark green, somewhat twisted leaves; no fruit. Low hedge, foundation planting, containers.

L. 'Vicaryi'. VICARY GOLDEN PRIVET. Deciduous shrub. All Zones. This one has yellow leaves—color strongest on plants in full sun. To 3–4 ft. high. Best planted alone; color does not develop well under hedge shearing.

L. vulgare. COMMON PRIVET. Deciduous shrub. All Zones. To 15 ft., unsheared. Light green leaves less glossy than those of *L. ovalifolium.* Clusters of black fruit conspicuous on unpruned or lightly pruned plants. Root system less greedy than that of California privet. Variety 'Lodense' ('Nanum') is dense, dwarf form which reaches only 4 ft. with equal spread.

LILAC. See *Syringa.*

LILAC VINE. See *Hardenbergia comptoniana.*

Liliaceae. The lily family contains hundreds of species of ornamental plants, as well as such vegetables as asparagus and the whole onion tribe. Most have bulbous, cormous, or rhizomatous rootstocks. Flowers are often showy, usually with 6 equal-size segments.

LILIUM. *Liliaceae.* LILY. Bulbs. All Zones. Most stately and varied of bulbous plants. For many years, only species—same as plants growing wild in parts of Asia, Europe, and North America—were available, and many of these were difficult and unpredictable.

Around 1925, lily growers began a significant breeding program. They bred new hybrids from species with desirable qualities and also developed strains and varieties that were healthier, hardier, and easier to grow than the original species. They were able to produce new forms and new colors; what is more important, they evolved the methods for growing healthy lilies in large quantities. Today, the new forms and new colors are the best garden lilies, but it is still possible to get some desirable species lilies.

Lilium auratum

Lilies have 3 basic cultural requirements: (1) deep, loose, well-drained soil; (2) ample moisture year round (plants never completely stop growing); (3) coolness and shade at roots, and sun or filtered shade at tops where flowers form.

Plant bulbs as soon as possible after you get them. If you must wait, keep them in a cool place until you plant. If bulbs are dry, place them in moist sand or peat moss until scales get plump and new roots begin to sprout.

In coastal fog belts, plant lilies in an open, sunny position, but protect them from strong winds. In warmer, drier climates, light or filtered shade is desirable.

Deep, well-drained soil that contains ample organic materials will grow good lilies. If you want to plant lilies in heavy clay or soil that is very sandy and deficient in organic matter, you will need to add peat moss, ground bark, or sawdust. Spread a 3–4-in. layer of such material over surface; broadcast complete fertilizer (follow label directions for preplanting application) on top of it, then thoroughly blend both into soil as you dig to a depth of at least 1 ft.

Before planting bulbs, remove any injured portions and dust cuts with sulfur or a special antifungus seed and bulb disinfectant.

For each bulb, dig a generous planting hole (6–12 in. deeper than depth of bulb). Place enough soil at bottom of hole to bring it up to proper level for bulb (see below). Set bulb with its roots spread; fill in hole with soil, firming it in around bulb to eliminate air pockets. If your area is infested with gophers, you may have to plant each bulb in a 6-in.-square wire basket made of ½-in. hardware cloth. The depth of the basket will depend on the planting depth—see next paragraph.

Planting depths vary according to size and rooting habit of bulb. General rule is to cover smaller bulbs with 2–3 in. of soil, medium-sized bulbs with 3–4 in., and larger bulbs with 4–6 in. (but never cover Madonna lilies with more than 1 in. of soil). Planting depth can be quite flexible. It's better to err by planting shallowly than too deeply; lily bulbs have contractile roots that draw them down to proper depth. Ideal spacing for lily bulbs is 1 ft. apart, but you can plant as close as 6 in. for densely massed effect.

After planting, water well and mulch area with 2–3 in. of organic material to conserve moisture, keep soil cool, and reduce weed growth.

Lilies need constant moisture to about 6 in. deep. You can reduce watering somewhat after tops turn yellow in fall, but never allow roots to dry out completely. Flooding is preferable to overhead watering, which may help to spread disease spores. Pull weeds by hand if possible; hoeing may injure roots.

Virus or mosaic infection is a problem. No cure exists. To avoid it, buy healthy bulbs from reliable sources. Dig and destroy any lilies that show mottling in leaves or seriously stunted growth. Control aphids, which spread the infection. Control botrytis blight, a fungus disease, with appropriate fungicide. Control gophers; they relish lily bulbs.

Remove faded flowers. Wait until stems and leaves turn yellow before you cut plants back.

If clumps become too large and crowded, dig, divide, and transplant them in spring or fall. If you're careful, you can lift lily clumps at any time, even in bloom.

Lilies are fine container plants. Place 1 bulb in a deep 5–7-in. pot or 5 in a 14–16-in. pot. First, fill pot ⅓ full of potting mix. Then place bulb with roots spread and pointing downward; cover with about an inch of soil. Water thoroughly and place in deep cold-frame or greenhouse that is heated (in colder climates) just enough to keep out frost. During root-forming period, keep soil moderately moist. When top growth appears, add more soil mixture and gradually fill pot as stems elongate. Leave 1 in. space between surface of soil and rim of pot for watering. Move pots onto partially shaded terrace or patio during blooming period.

When foliage turns yellow, withhold water somewhat but do not let soil become bone dry, since lilies never go completely dormant. You can repot bulbs in late fall or early spring.

The official classification of lilies lists 8 divisions of hybrids (not all of them available in nurseries) and a ninth division of species. Following are the lilies ordinarily available to western gardeners (members of Divisions 1–4, 6, 7, and 9).

Division 1. Asiatic Hybrids

Subdivision a. Upright flowering. Compact growth.

Golden Chalice Hybrids. Stems 1½–3 ft. tall. Colors range from lemon yellow to apricot orange. 'Golden Wonder', 2½–4½ ft. tall, is soft golden yellow variety. Blooms in May.

Mid-Century Hybrids. Strong growing, hardy, tolerant of most soils. Plants are 2–4 ft. tall. July bloom in most climates, June in Zones 18–24. Colors range from yellow through orange to red; most dotted with black. Upward-facing, wide open flowers spread like branches of candelabra. Many excellent named varieties; notable ones are: 'Enchantment' (nasturtium red), especially adapted to warm climates and pot culture, 'Chinook' (salmon), 'Cinnabar' (orange red), 'Connecticut King' (yellow), and 'Sterling Star' (white to cream).

Rainbow Hybrids. Tulip-shaped flowers in golden yellow through orange to dark red, usually with dark spots, in upward-facing clusters; bloom in June. Stems 3–4 ft. tall.

Subdivision b. Outward-facing flowers, but otherwise similar to group 1a. Varieties include 'Connecticut Lemonglow', 'Corsage', 'Paprika', 'Prosperity', and 'Sunrise'.

Subdivision c. Drooping flowers on long stalks, but otherwise similar to groups 1a and 1b.

Fiesta Hybrids. Hardy, vigorous, sun loving. Bloom in July. Nodding flowers with strongly recurved segments in pale yellow through gold to deep maroon. Selections from Fiesta Hybrids are: Bronzino strain (sand, mahogany, and amber); Burgundy strain (cherry red, claret, and burgundy); Citronella strain (golden and lemon yellow flowers with small black dots); Golden Wedding strain (large golden yellow flowers).

Harlequin Hybrids. Largely derived from *L. cernuum.* June–July bloom. To 5 ft. tall. Open flowers with segments recurved (curved sharply backward); ivory white through pale lilac and old rose to violet and purple, with intermediate shades of salmon, terra cotta, and amber pink. Most are pink and tangerine. Selected varieties are 'Bittersweet', 'Connecticut Yankee', 'Discovery', Hallmark strain, 'Hornback's Gold', and 'Sonata'.

Division 2

Mostly hybrids between *L. martagon* and *L. hansonii.* All bloom in June. Paisley strain, 3½–5 ft. tall, has many flowers to a stem. Segments recurved; colors range through yellow, orange, tangerine, lilac, purple, and mahogany.

Division 3. Candidum Hybrids

As with *L. candidum* (see Division 9), plant bulbs in fall, only 1–2 in. deep. Lime loving; profits by addition of lime when growing in strongly acid soils.

L. testaceum. Handsome apricot yellow flowers, 6–12 on a stem. Same waxlike appearance and perfume as *L. candidum,* a parent. (*L. chalcedonicum* is other parent.) 'Uprising' (pale yellow to white erect flowers with dark speckles) and 'Limerick' (soft green to chartreuse, fragrant) are recent additions to this small class.

Division 4. American Hybrids

Derived from *L. parryi, L. pardalinum,* and other North American species. Tall growers. Plant 4 in. deep in well-drained, enriched soil. Bellingham and San Juan strains are the result of crosses of West Coast native lilies. Colors range from yellow through orange to red and pink, spotted brown or reddish brown.

Division 6. Aurelian Hybrids

Derived from Asiatic species, excluding *L. auratum* and *L. speciosum.* All grow 3–6 ft. high, bloom July–August.

Subdivision a. Trumpet-type flowers in clusters of 12–20, topping 5–6-ft. stems. Includes golden and lemon yellow strains such as Golden Clarion, Golden Splendor, and Royal Gold; other strains, such as Copper King, Moonlight, and Regale; and the Olympic Hybrids.

Olympic Hybrids. Trumpet-shaped lilies bloom July–August

L on plants to 6 ft. high. Flowers range from pure white through cream, yellow, soft pink, and icy green, shaded on outside with greenish brown or wine. Many choice named varieties are available, such as 'Green Dragon', 'Quicksilver', 'Carrara'. Also available in strains such as Black Dragon, Green Magic, and pure white Sentinel.

Subdivision b. Shallow, bowl-shaped, outward-facing flowers. Colors include white, yellow, and cream, often with orange throats shading into cream at segment tips. Includes Heart's Desire strain and 'Thunderbolt'.

Subdivision c. Pendant flower type. Includes 'Pendant'.

Subdivision d. Sunburst type with flared flowers that open flat and have narrow segments. Includes Golden Sunburst and Sunburst Hybrids.

Division 7. Oriental Hybrids

Lilies derived from Far Eastern species *L. japonicum, L. rubellum, L. speciosum,* and *L. auratum* (the latter 2 being the most important Japanese species) and any crosses of these with *L. henryi.*

Subdivision b. Hybrids bearing bowl-shaped flowers. Derived from *L. auratum* and *L. speciosum.* Exquisitely beautiful flowers in August—"queens" of all lilies. Includes *L. auratum* Melridge strain, 'Cover Girl', 'Empress of India', Little Rascal, Magic Pink, Red Band Hybrids, and 'Red Baron'.

Subdivision c. Flat-faced flowers with recurving blooms. Includes Imperial Crimson, Imperial Gold, Imperial Pink, Imperial Silver, and Oriental Hybrids.

Subdivision d. Hybrids with flat flowers. Includes 'Black Beauty', Celebrity, Jamboree, and 'Journey's End'.

Division 9. Species and Variants

L. auratum. GOLD-BAND LILY. August or early September bloom on 4–6-ft. plants. Flowers fragrant, waxy white spotted crimson, with golden band on each segment. 'Platyphyllum' is most robust selection, with flowers nearly a foot wide.

L. candidum. MADONNA LILY. Pure white, fragrant blooms on 3–4-ft. stems in June. Unlike most lilies, dies down soon after bloom, makes new growth in fall. Plant while dormant in August. Does not have stem roots; set top of bulb only 1–2 in. deep in sunny location. Bulb quickly makes foliage rosette which lives over winter, lengthens to blooming stem in spring. Subject to diseases that shorten its life. Cascade strain, grown from seed, is healthier than imported bulbs. The lily of medieval romance, a sentimental choice for many gardeners.

Lilium candidum

L. cernuum. Only 12–20 in. tall, with lilac flowers often dotted dark purple. Summer blooming; perfectly hardy. Sun.

L. chalcedonicum. The famous scarlet Turk's cap lily from the Near East. Now rare. Sweet-scented blooms, 6–10 per stem (each stem to 4½ ft. high), in July.

L. columbianum. COLUMBIA LILY. Dainty species bearing about 20–30 golden orange lilies on 2-ft. stems in July and August. Native from British Columbia to northern California.

L. concolor. To 2 ft., with 5–7 scarlet, unspotted, star-shaped flowers on wiry stems in early summer. Needs full sun and perfect drainage. 'Coridion' is a citron yellow variety.

L. formosanum. Long white Easter lily flowers appear very late. Plant bulbs 5–6 in. deep to allow for heavy stem roots. Easy and fast to grow from seed, but tender and virus prone. Stems to 5 ft. tall.

L. hansonii. Sturdy lily to 4 ft. or more, with many thick-textured orange flowers spotted brown. June–July. Needs light shade. Highly resistant or immune to virus.

L. henryi. Slender stems to 8–9 ft. topped by 10–20 bright orange flowers with sharply recurved segments. Summer bloom. Best in light shade.

L. humboldtii. HUMBOLDT LILY. Native of open woodlands in Sierra Nevada. Grows 3–6 ft. tall. Nodding, recurved, bright orange flowers with large maroon dots. Early summer bloom. *L. h. ocellatum* (*L. h. magnificum*) is larger, finer, easier to grow.

L. lancifolium *(L. tigrinum).* TIGER LILY. To 4 ft. or taller with pendulous orange flowers spotted black. Summer bloom. An old favorite. Newer tiger lilies are available in white, cream, yellow, pink, and red, all with black spots.

L. lankongense. Long-lived lily in garden. Heavily scented, crimson-spotted, rosy mauve Turk's cap blooms, 20–30 on a stem. Grows to 3 ft. tall; blooms in August.

L. longiflorum. EASTER LILY. Very fragrant, long white trumpet-shaped flowers on short stems. Usually purchased in bloom at Easter as forced plant. Set out in garden after flowers fade. Sun or part shade, good drainage. Stem will ripen and die down. Plant may rebloom in fall; in 1–2 years may flower in midsummer, its normal bloom season. Varieties include 'Ace', 1½ ft. tall; 'Tetraploid', 1–1½ ft. tall; 'Croft', 1 ft. tall; 'Estate', to 3 ft. Not for severe winter climates. Don't plant forced Easter lilies near other lilies; they may transmit a virus.

L. martagon. TURK'S CAP LILY. Purplish pink, recurved, pendant flowers in June–July on 3–5-ft. stems. This lily is slow to establish, but it is long lived and eventually forms big clumps. *L. m. album,* pure white, is one of the most appealing lilies. There is also a deep wine purple variety that blooms July–August and may be sold as *L. m. dalmaticum* (it is properly *L. m. cattaniae*).

L. pardalinum. LEOPARD LILY. California native. Recurved flowers orange or red orange shading to yellow, with brown spotting in center. Spring–summer bloom on stems 4–8 ft. high.

L. pumilum. A coral red lily that loves sun, but needs shade for its roots. Each wiry, 1–1½-ft. stem carries 1–20 scented flowers. Blooms May–June.

L. regale. REGAL LILY. Superseded in quality by modern hybrid trumpet lilies, but still popular and easy to grow. To 6 ft., with white, fragrant flowers in July.

L. speciosum. Grows 2½–5 ft. tall. Large, wide, fragrant flowers with broad, deeply recurved segments, August–September; white, heavily suffused rose pink, sprinkled with raised crimson dots. 'Rubrum', red; 'Album', pure white; also other named forms. Best in light and afternoon shade; needs rich soil with plenty of leaf mold. Newer varieties are 'Crimson Glory', 'Grand Commander', and 'White Glory'.

L. superbum. TURK'S CAP LILY. Eastern North American native. Grows to 6 ft. and more. Blooms July–August. Brilliant orange flowers like those of *L. pardalinum,* but larger; flowers are flushed with yellow at center and spotted with brown. Effective red anthers. Likes wet conditions while growing.

L. tigrinum. See *L. lancifolium.*

L. washingtonianum. West Coast native. Waxy-textured, translucent lilies in large, open clusters change from white to deep rose. Carnation scented. Grows to 4–6 ft. Plant bulbs 10 in. deep in partial shade. Blooms June–July. Keep on dry side after bloom. Difficult; needs acid soil, fast drainage.

LILLY-PILLY TREE. See *Acmena smithii.*

LILY. See *Lilium.*

LILY-OF-THE-NILE. See *Agapanthus.*

LILY-OF-THE-VALLEY. See *Convallaria majalis.*

LILY-OF-THE-VALLEY SHRUB. See *Pieris japonica.*

LILY-OF-THE-VALLEY TREE. See *Clethra arborea, Crinodendron patagua.*

LILY TURF. See *Liriope and Ophiopogon.*

LIME. See *Citrus.*

LIMEQUAT. See *Citrus.*

LIMONIUM ***(Statice).*** *Plumbaginaceae.* SEA LAVENDER. Annuals, perennials. Large, leathery basal leaves contrast with airy clusters of small, delicate flowers on nearly leafless, many-branched stems. Tiny flowers consist of 2 parts: an outer, papery envelope (the calyx) and an inner part, the corolla, which often has a different color. Flowers are good for cutting, keeping their color even when dried.

Limonium perezii

Tolerate heat, strong sun, some drought when established. Need good drainage; otherwise tolerant of many soils. Often self-sow.

For spring–summer bloom, sow annual kinds indoors and move to garden when weather warms up. Or sow outdoors in early spring for later bloom.

L. bonduellii. Summer annual or biennial. All Zones. Grows 2 ft. tall, with 6-in. basal leaves lobed nearly to midrib. Flower stems are distinctly winged; calyx is yellow, tiny corolla deeper yellow.

L. latifolium. Perennial. Zones 1–10, 14–24. To 2½ ft. tall. Smooth-edged leaves to 10 in. long. Calyx is white and corolla bluish; white and pink kinds exist. Summer bloom. Vigorous plants may show a 3-ft.-wide haze of flowers.

L. perezii. Perennial. Zones 13, 15–17, 20–24. Often freezes in Zones 14, 18, 19. Rich green leaves up to 1 ft. long, including stalks. Summer bloom over long season. In the flowers, calyx is rich purple and the tiny corolla white. Flower clusters may be 3 ft. tall, nearly as wide. First-rate beach plant; can be fire retardant. Often naturalizes along southern California coast. Damaged by 25°F. temperatures, but useful even where it freezes out occasionally; nursery-grown seedlings develop fast.

L. sinuatum. Summer annual. Growth habit like *L. bonduellii,* with lobed leaves and winged stems, but calyx blue, lavender, or rose, corolla white. Widely grown as a fresh or dried cut flower.

L. suworowii. See *Psylliostachys.*

Linaceae. The flax family of annuals, perennials, and shrubs displays cup- or disk-shaped flowers with 4 or 5 petals. Flowers are often showy. Individually short lived, they appear over a long season. Examples are flax (*Linum*) and yellow flax (*Reinwardtia*).

LINARIA. *Scrophulariaceae.* TOADFLAX. Annuals or perennials with brightly colored flowers that resemble small, spurred snapdragons. Very narrow, medium green leaves. Easy to grow. Full sun or light shade. Best in masses; individual plants are rather wispy.

L. cymbalaria. See *Cymbalaria muralis.*

L. maroccana. BABY SNAPDRAGON, TOADFLAX. Summer annual; winter annual Zones 10–13. To 1½ ft. Flowers in red and gold, rose, pink, mauve, chamois, blue, violet, and purple, blotched with different shade on the lip. Spur is longer than flower. Fairy Bouquet strain is only 9 in. tall and has larger flowers in pastel shades. Northern Lights strain has reds, oranges, and yellows as well as bicolors. Blooms June–September. Sow in quantity for a show.

Linaria maroccana

L. purpurea. Perennial. All Zones. Narrow, bushy, erect growth to 2½–3 ft. Blue green foliage and violet blue flowers. 'Canon Went' is a pink form. Summer blooming. Fairly drought tolerant.

LINDEN. See *Tilia.*

LINGONBERRY. See *Vaccinium vitis-idaea minus.*

LINNAEA borealis. *Caprifoliaceae.* TWINFLOWER. Low, delicate perennial. Zones 1–7, 14–17. Native northern California to Alaska, Idaho, and much of northern hemisphere. Dainty, flat, evergreen mats with 1-in.-long, glossy leaves. Spreads by runners. Pale pink, paired, fragrant, trumpet-shaped flowers, ⅓ in. long on 3–4-in. stems. Collector's item or small-scale ground cover for woodland garden. Keep area around plants mulched with leaf mold to induce spreading. In Zones 4–6 will grow in full sun if well watered. Must have shade in Zones 14–16.

Linnaea borealis

LINUM. *Linaceae.* FLAX. Annuals, perennials. All Zones. Flaxes are drought-resistant, sun-loving plants with erect, branching stems, narrow leaves, and abundant, shallow-cupped, 5-petaled flowers blooming from late spring into summer or fall. Each bloom lasts but a day, but others keep coming on. (The flax of commerce—*L. usitatissimum*—is grown for its fiber and seeds, which yield linseed oil.)

Linum perenne

Use in borders; some naturalize freely in waste places. Full sun. Light, well-drained soil. Most perennial kinds live only 3–4 years. Easy from seed; perennials also can be grown from cuttings. Difficult to divide.

L. flavum. GOLDEN FLAX. Perennial. (Often called yellow flax, a name correctly applied to closely related *Reinwardtia indica.*) Erect, compact, 12–15 in. tall, somewhat woody at base; grooved branches, green leaves. Flowers golden yellow, about 1 in. wide, in branched clusters, April–June.

L. grandiflorum 'Rubrum'. SCARLET FLAX. Annual. Bright scarlet flowers, 1–1½ in. wide, on slender, leafy stems 1–1½ ft. tall. Narrow, grayish green leaves. Also comes in a rose-colored form. Sow seed thickly in place in fall (in mild areas) or early spring. Quick, easy color in borders, over bulbs left in ground. Good with gray foliage or white-flowered plants. Reseeds, but doesn't become a nuisance. Seed often incorporated into wild flower seed mixtures.

L. narbonense. Perennial. Wiry stems to 2 ft. high. Leaves blue green, narrow. Flowers large (1¾ in. across), azure blue with white eye, in open clusters. Best variety, 'Six Hills', has rich sky blue flowers.

L. perenne. PERENNIAL BLUE FLAX. Most vigorous blue-flowered flax with stems to 2 ft., usually leafless below. Branching clusters of light blue flowers, profuse from May–September. Flowers close in shade or late in the day. Self-sows freely.

LION'S TAIL. See *Leonotis leonurus.*

LIPPIA citriodora. See *Aloysia triphylla.*

LIPPIA repens. See *Phyla nodiflora.*

LIPSTICK PLANT. See *Aeschynanthus radicans.*

LIQUIDAMBAR. *Hamamelidaceae.* SWEET GUM. Deciduous trees. Valuable for form, foliage, and fall color, easy culture. Moderate growth rate; young and middle-aged trees generally upright, somewhat cone shaped, spreading in age. Lobed, maplelike leaves. Flowers inconspicuous; fruits are spiny balls which ornament trees in winter, need raking in spring.

(Continued on next page)

L

Give neutral or slightly acid good garden soil; chlorosis in strongly alkaline soils is hard to correct. Plant from containers or from ball and burlap; be sure roots are not can-bound. Stake well. Prune only to shape. Trees branch from ground up and look most natural that way, but can be pruned high for easier foot traffic.

Good street trees. Form surface roots which can be nuisance in lawns or parking strips. Effective in tall screens or groves, planted 6–10 ft. apart. Brilliant fall foliage. Leaves color best when trees are in full sun and well-drained soil; fall color less effective in mildest climates or in mild, late autumns.

Liquidambar styraciflua

For best appearance, should be watered deeply once a month in heavy soils, twice a month in sandy soils through dry season.

L. formosana. CHINESE SWEET GUM. Zones 4–9, 14–24. To 40–60 ft. tall, 25 ft. wide. Free-form outline; sometimes pyramidal, especially when young. Leaves 3–5 lobed, 3–4½ in. across, violet red when expanding, then deep green. In southern California, leaves turn yellow beige in late December–January before falling. Farther north, leaves turn red. Variety 'Afterglow' has lavender purple new growth, rose red fall color.

L. orientalis. ORIENTAL SWEET GUM. Zones 5–9, 14–24. Native to Turkey. To 20–30 ft., spreading or round headed. Leaves 2–3 in. wide, deeply 5 lobed, each lobe again lobed in lacy effect. Leafs out early after short dormant period. Fall color varies from deep gold and bright red in cooler areas to dull brown purple in coastal southern California. Resistant to oak root fungus.

L. styraciflua. AMERICAN SWEET GUM. Zones 1–11, 14–24. Grows to 60 ft. (much taller in its native eastern U.S.). Narrow and erect in youth, with lower limbs eventually spreading to 20–25 ft. Tolerates damp soil; resistant to oak root fungus. Good all-year tree. In winter, branching pattern, furrowed bark, corky wings on twigs, and hanging fruit give interest; in spring and summer, leaves (5–7 lobed, 3–7 in. wide) are deep green; in fall, leaves turn purple, yellow, or red. Even seedling trees give good color (which may vary somewhat from year to year), but for uniformity, match trees while they are in fall color or buy budded trees of a named variety, such as the following:

'Burgundy'. Leaves turn deep purple red, hang late into winter or even early spring if storms are not heavy.

'Festival'. Narrow, columnar. Light green foliage turns to yellow, peach, pink, orange, and red.

'Palo Alto'. Turns orange red to bright red in fall.

LIRIODENDRON tulipifera. *Magnoliaceae.* TULIP TREE. Deciduous tree. Zones 1–12, 14–23. Native to eastern U.S. Fast growth to 60–80 ft., with eventual spread to 40 ft. Straight columnar trunk, with spreading, rising branches that form tall pyramidal crown. Lyre-shaped leaves, 5–6 in. long and wide, turn from bright yellow green to bright yellow (or yellow and brown) in fall. Tulip-shaped flowers in late spring are 2 in. wide, greenish yellow, orange at base. Handsome at close range, they are not showy on the tree, being high up and well-concealed by leaves. They are not usually produced until tree is 10–12 years old.

Liriodendron tulipifera

Give this tree room; deep, rich, well-drained neutral or slightly acid soil; and plenty of summer water. Best where constant wind from one direction won't strike it. Control scale insects and aphids as necessary. Not bothered by oak root fungus.

Good large shade, lawn, or roadside tree. One of the best deciduous trees for southern California; it turns yellow there most autumns. Spreading root system makes it hard to garden under. Columnar variety 'Arnold' is useful in narrow planting areas; it will bloom 2–3 years after planting. 'Majestic Beauty' (*L. t.* 'Aureo-marginatum') has leaves edged with yellow. Moderate growth rate, size.

LIRIOPE and OPHIOPOGON. *Liliaceae.* LILY TURF. Evergreen grasslike perennials. Zones 5–10, 12–24 (*L. spicata* in all Zones). These 2 plants are similar in appearance: both form clumps or tufts of grasslike leaves and bear white or lavender flowers in spikelike or branched clusters (quite showy in some kinds). Last well in flower arrangements.

Liriope muscari

Use as casual ground cover in small areas. Also attractive as borders along paths, or between flower bed and lawn, among rock groupings, or in rock gardens. Grow well along streams and around garden pools. Try under bamboo or to cover bare soil at base of trees or shrubs in large containers. None satisfactory as mowed lawn. Tolerate indoor conditions in pots or planter beds.

Plant in well-drained soil. Give shade in inland areas or foliage may turn yellow; along coast, plant in sunny location. Ample moisture is needed, but fleshy roots enable plants to withstand brief lapses in watering. Become ragged and brown with neglect. Cut back shaggy old foliage after new leaves appear. Plants don't need heavy feeding. Bait or spray for snails and slugs. Increase plants by dividing in early spring before new growth starts.

Plants look best from spring until cold weather of winter. Extended frosts may cause plants to turn yellow; it takes quite a while for them to recover. Can show tip burn on leaves if there are excess salts in soil or if plants are kept too wet where drainage is poor.

The chart at right compares the kinds you can buy, describes leaves and flowers, and mentions uses and cultural needs.

LISIANTHUS. See *Eustoma.*

LITCHI chinensis. *Sapindaceae.* LITCHI, LITCHI NUT. Evergreen tree. Zones 21–24. Slow-growing, round-topped, spreading, 20–40-ft.-tall tree. Leaves have 3–9 leathery, 3–6-in.-long leaflets that are coppery red when young, dark green later. Inconspicuous flowers. When fruit is ripe, the brittle, warty rind surrounding it turns red. Fruit is sweet in flavor; juicy when fresh, raisinlike when dried.

Litchi chinensis

Needs frost-free site, acid soil, ample water, moist air, feeding with nitrogen. Has fruited in a few warm areas near San Diego. Look for named varieties if you're interested in fruit production. 'Brewster', 'Kate Sessions', 'Kwai Mi', 'Mauritius', and 'Sweet Cliff' are grown.

LITHOCARPUS densiflorus. *Fagaceae.* TANBARK OAK. Evergreen tree. Zones 4–7, 14–24. Native to Coast Ranges from southern Oregon to Santa Barbara County, California. Reaches 60–90 ft. under forest conditions; in the open, tree is lower, broader, its lower branches sometimes touching the ground. Leathery, 1½–4-in., sharply toothed leaves are covered with whitish or yellowish wool upon expanding; later, they are smooth green above, gray green beneath. Tiny, whitish male flowers in large branched clusters have odd odor which some people find offensive. Acorns in burrlike cups.

Lithocarpus densiflorus

Tanbark oak will withstand some drought

L

Liriope and Ophiopogon

NAME	GROWTH FORM	LEAVES	FLOWERS	COMMENTS
LIRIOPE muscari BIG BLUE LILY TURF	Forms large clumps but does not spread by underground stems. Rather loose growth habit 1–1½ ft. high.	Dark green. To 2 ft. long, ½ in. wide.	Dark violet buds and flowers in rather dense, 6–8-in.-long spikelike clusters on 5–12-in.-long stems (resemble grape hyacinths), followed by a few round, shiny black fruits.	Profuse flowers July–August. Flowers held above leaves in young plants, partly hidden in older plants. Many garden varieties. 'Lilac Beauty' has paler violet flowers.
L. m. 'Majestic'	Resembles *L. muscari* but forms more open clumps and is somewhat taller growing.	Similar to above.	Dark violet flowers and buds in clusters that look somewhat like cockscombs on 8–10-in.-long stems.	Heavy flowering. Clusters show up well above leaves on young plants.
L. m. 'Silvery Sunproof'	Open growth, strongly vertical, partly arching, 15–18 in. high.	Leaves with gold stripes that turn white as they mature.	Lilac flowers in spikelike clusters rise well above foliage in early summer.	One of the best for open areas and flowers. Best in full sun along coast; inland partial or full shade.
L. m. 'Variegata' (May be sold as *Ophiopogon jaburan* 'Variegata')	Resembles *L. muscari*, but somewhat looser, softer.	New leaves green, 1–1½ ft. long, edged with yellow, becoming dark green second season.	Violet buds and flowers in spikelike clusters well above foliage. Flower stalk 1 ft. high.	Does best in part shade.
L. spicata CREEPING LILY TURF	Dense ground cover that spreads widely by underground stems. Grows 8–9 in. high.	Narrow (¼ in. wide), deep green, grasslike leaves, soft and not as upright as those of *L. muscari*. 'Silver Dragon' has white-striped leaves.	Pale lilac to white flowers in spikelike clusters barely taller than leaves.	Hardy in all Zones. Inland, it looks rather shabby in winter. Should be mowed every year in spring prior to new growth development to get best effect. Good ground cover for cold areas where *Ophiopogon japonicus* won't grow.
OPHIOPOGON jaburan (Often sold as *Liriope gigantea*)	Eventually forms large clump growing from fibrous roots.	Dark green, somewhat curved, firm leaves 1½–3 ft. long, about ½ in. wide.	Small, chalk white flowers in nodding clusters, somewhat hidden by leaves in summer. Metallic violet blue fruit.	Does best in shade. Fruit is very attractive feature; good for cutting. *O. j.* 'Vittatus' has leaves striped lengthwise with white, aging to plain green. Similar, perhaps identical, is *Liriope muscari* 'Variegata', sometimes sold as *L. exiliflora* 'Vittata'.
O. japonicus MONDO GRASS	Forms dense clumps that spread by underground stems, many of which are tuberlike. Slow to establish as ground cover.	Dark green leaves ⅛ in. wide, 8–12 in. long. 'Nana' or 'Kyoto Dwarf' has half-sized leaves in tight clumps. Slow, sure spreader.	Flowers light lilac in short spikes usually hidden by the leaves. Summer blooming. Fruit blue.	In hot, dry areas, grow in some shade. Can be cut back. Easy to divide. Set divisions 6–8 in. apart. Roots will be killed at 10°F. Looks best in partial shade but will take full sun along coast.
O. planiscapus 'Nigrescens' (*O. p.* 'Nigricans', *O. p.* 'Arabicus')	Makes tuft 8 in. high and about 1 ft. wide.	Leaves to 10 in. long. New leaves green but soon turn black.	White (sometimes flushed pink) in loose spikelike clusters in summer.	Probably best grown in container; valuable as a novelty, as black-leafed plants are rather rare.

when it is established. As street or lawn tree, it resembles holly oak (*Quercus ilex*), but has lusher foliage.

LITHODORA diffusa *(Lithospermum diffusum, L. prostratum).* *Boraginaceae.* Perennial. Zones 5–7, 14–17. Prostrate, somewhat shrubby, slightly mounded, broad mass 6–12 in. tall. Narrow evergreen leaves, ¾–1 in. long; both foliage and stems are hairy. In May–June (and often later), plants are sprinkled with brilliant blue, tubular flowers ½ in. long. Full sun or light shade in hot exposures. Loose, well-drained, lime-free soil. Needs some summer watering. Rock gardens, walls.

Lithodora diffusa

'Heavenly Blue' and 'Grace Ward' are selected varieties.

LITHOPS. *Aizoaceae.* STONEFACE. Succulents. Best grown indoors. Among the best-known "living rocks" or "pebble plants" of South Africa. Shaped like inverted cones 2–4 in. high; tops are shaped like stones with a fissure across the middle. From this fissure emerges the large flower (it looks like an ice plant flower) and new leaves. Many species, all interesting. Grow in pots of fast-draining soil. Water sparingly in summer; must be kept dry during cool winter weather. Fairly hardy in mild winters but subject to rot outdoors in damp winter air and cold, wet soil.

Lithops

L

LITHOSPERMUM. See *Lithodora.*

LIVINGSTONE DAISY. See *Dorotheanthus bellidiformis.*

LIVISTONA. *Palmae.* Palms. Zones 13–17, 19–24. Native from China to Australia. These fan palms somewhat resemble *Washingtonia,* but generally have shorter, darker, shinier leaves. All are hardy to about 22°F. Irrigate regularly for luxuriant appearance.

Livistona australis

L. australis. In ground, grows slowly to 40–50 ft. Has clean, slender trunk with interesting-looking leaf scars. Dark green leaves 3–5 ft. wide. Good potted plant when young.

L. chinensis. CHINESE FOUNTAIN PALM. Slow growing; 40-year-old plants are only 15 ft. tall. Self-cleaning (no pruning of old leaves needed) with leaf-scarred trunk. Roundish, bright green, 3–6-ft. leaves droop strongly at outer edges.

L. decipiens. To 30–40 ft. in 20 years. Stiff, open head of leaves 2–5 ft. across, green on top, bluish beneath, on long, spiny stems. Good in pots, gardens.

L. mariae. From hot, dry interior Australia. Grows slowly to 10–15 ft. Young or potted plants have attractive reddish leaves and leaf stems. Leaves 3–4 ft. wide.

LOBELIA. *Lobeliaceae.* Perennials or annuals. Tubular, lipped flowers look like those of honeysuckle or salvia.

Lobelia erinus

L. cardinalis. CARDINAL FLOWER. Perennial. Zones 1–7, 13–17. Native to eastern U.S. and to a few sites in mountains of the Southwest. Erect, single-stemmed, 2–4-ft.-high plant with saw-edged leaves set directly on the stems. Spikes of flame red, inch-long flowers. Summer bloom. A bog plant in nature, it needs rich soil and constant moisture through growing season. Sun or part shade.

Hybrids of this and other species are sometimes seen; some have deep beet red foliage in addition to scarlet flowers.

L. erinus. Summer annual. All Zones. Popular and dependable edging plant. Compact or trailing growth habit with leafy, branching stems. Flowers are ¾ in. across and are light blue to violet (sometimes pink, reddish purple, or white) with white or yellowish throat. Blooms from early summer to frost; lives over winter in mild areas.

Takes about 2 months for the seed in flats to grow to planting-out size. Moist, rich soil. Part shade in hot areas, full sun where summers are cool or foggy. Self-sows where adapted.

Trailing kinds are graceful as ground cover in large planters or in smaller pots, where stems, loaded with flowers, spill over the edges. Compact varieties make good edging, masses.

'Cambridge Blue' has clear, soft blue flowers, light green leaves on compact 4–6-in. plant. 'Crystal Palace' has rich, dark blue flowers on a compact plant with bronze green leaves. Takes morning or late afternoon sun inland. 'Rosamond' has carmine red flowers with a white eye. 'White Lady' is pure white. Three trailing varieties for hanging baskets or wall plantings are 'Hamburgia', 'Blue Cascade', and 'Sapphire'.

L. laxiflora. Perennial. Zones 7–9, 12–24. Mexican native. Narrow, erect, 2-ft. stems from creeping underground rootstocks bear narrow leaves and open clusters of tubular, orange red flowers over a long summer season. Once established, withstands considerable drought and neglect; often persists in abandoned gardens.

L. syphilitica. Perennial. Zones 2–9, 14–17. Native to eastern U.S. Leafy plants send up 3-ft. stalks set with blue flowers. Needs ample moisture, part shade.

Lobeliaceae. The lobelia family contains plants with irregular, 2-lipped flowers, usually in shades of red or blue. Garden kinds are annual or perennial herbaceous plants, including *Laurentia, Lobelia,* and *Pratia.*

LOBIVIA. *Cactaceae.* Cactus. Outdoors in part shade in Zones 16, 17, 21–24; as house plant or indoor/outdoor plant anywhere. Small globular or cylindrical shapes with big, showy flowers in shades of red, yellow, pink, orange, purplish, lilac. Flowers sometimes nearly as big as plants, like flowers of *Echinopsis* but shorter, broader. Many species offered. Usually grown in pots by collectors. Give full sun or light shade (part shade for outdoor plants in Zones noted above), porous soil, ample water during summer bloom and growth, occasional feeding.

Lobivia hybrid

LOBIVOPSIS. *Cactaceae.* Cactus. Hybrids between *Lobivia* and *Echinopsis.* Extremely free flowering with big, long-tubed flowers on small plants. Culture, hardiness same as for *Echinopsis;* grow in fairly good-sized pots (5-in. pot for a 3-in. plant), feed monthly in summer, and water freely during bloom season. Paramount Hybrids come in red, pink, orange, rose, and white. Some may show a dozen or more 6-in.-long flowers on a 3–4-in. plant. Will take part shade, but bloom most heavily in full sun. Keep cool and dry in winter.

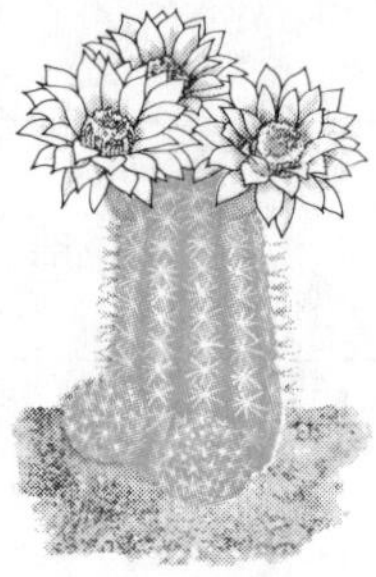

Lobivopsis hybrid

LOBULARIA maritima. *Cruciferae.* SWEET ALYSSUM. Summer or winter annual in Zones 10–24; summer annual anywhere. Low, branching, trailing plant to 1 ft. tall. Leaves narrow or lance shaped, ½–2 in. long. Tiny, white, 4-petaled flowers crowded in clusters; honeylike fragrance. Spring and summer bloom in cold regions; where winters are mild, blooms all year from self-sown seedlings. Has run wild in parts of the West. Sometimes included in wildflower mixes or erosion control mixes for bare or disturbed earth.

Lobularia maritima

Easy, quick, dependable. Blooms from seed in 6 weeks, grows in almost any soil. Best in sun, but takes light shade. Useful for carpeting, edging, bulb cover, temporary filler in rock garden or perennial border, between flagstones, in window boxes or containers. Attracts bees. If you shear plants halfway back 4 weeks after they come into bloom, new growth will make another crop of flowers, and plants won't become rangy.

Garden varieties better known than the species; these varieties self-sow too, but seedlings tend to revert to taller, looser growth, less intense color, smaller flowers.

'Carpet of Snow' (2–4 in. tall), 'Little Gem' (4–6 in.), and 'Tiny Tim' (3 in.) are good compact whites. 'Tetra Snowdrift' (1 ft.) has long stems, large white flowers. 'Rosie O'Day' (2–4 in.) and 'Pink Heather' (6 in.) are lavender pinks. 'Oriental Night' (4 in.) and 'Violet Queen' (5 in.) are rich violet purples.

LOCUST. See *Robinia.*

LOGANBERRY. See Blackberry.

LOLIUM. *Gramineae.* RYEGRASS. Annual or perennial lawn grasses used for lawns, pasture, and soil reclamation. Not considered choicest lawn grass, but useful in special conditions and for special uses. Plants clump instead of running, and do not make tight turf;

heavy sowing helps overcome this. Often mixed with other lawn grass species for low-cost, large-area coverage in cool-summer climates. In Bermuda grass country, often sown in fall on reconditioned Bermuda lawns to give winter green.

L. multiflorum. ITALIAN RYEGRASS. Larger, coarser than perennial ryegrass. Basically an annual; some plants live for several seasons in mild climates. Fast growing, deep rooted. Hybrid between *L. multiflorum* and *L. perenne* is COMMON or DOMESTIC RYEGRASS, often used as winter cover on soil or winter-dormant lawns.

Lolium perenne

L. perenne. PERENNIAL RYEGRASS. Finer in texture than above, deep green with high gloss. Disadvantages are clumping tendency and tough flower and seed stems that lie down under mower blades. Advantages are fast sprouting and growth. Best in cool-summer climates. 'Manhattan' is finer, more uniform. Other varieties are 'Pennfine', 'Derby', 'Yorktown', 'Loretta'. Mow at 1½–2 in., higher in the summer.

LOMARIA. See *Blechnum*.

LONAS annua *(L. inodora)*. *Compositae.* Annual. All Zones. Stems to 1 ft. tall. Finely divided leaves; 2-in.-wide, flat-topped clusters of yellow flower heads that suggest yarrow. Takes coastal fog and wind. Sow where plants will bloom, or grow in flats, then transplant. Summer bloom in most areas, year-round bloom in Zone 17.

Lonas annua

LONDON PRIDE. See *Saxifraga umbrosa*.

LONICERA. *Caprifoliaceae.* HONEYSUCKLE. Evergreen or deciduous shrubs or vines. Most kinds valued for tubular, often fragrant flowers. Easily grown in sun (light shade inland). Vining kinds need support when starting out. Flowers of most kinds yield abundant nectar for hummingbirds; fruit of shrubby kinds attracts many seed- and fruit-eating birds. Most need average summer water once established.

Lonicera hildebrandiana

L. 'Clavey's Dwarf'. Deciduous shrub. Zones 1–9, 14–24. Dense growing. To 3 ft. (rarely to 6 ft.) tall, with equal spread. Flowers white, small, not showy. Blue green leaves. Useful foundation plant or low unclipped hedge in colder regions.

L. fragrantissima. WINTER HONEYSUCKLE. Deciduous shrub, partially evergreen in mild-winter areas. Zones 1–9, 14–24. Arching, rather stiff growth to 8 ft. Leaves oval, dull dark green above, blue green beneath, 1–3 in. long. Creamy white flowers ⅝ in. long on previous year's wood, in early spring to fall depending on climate. Flowers richly fragrant (like *Daphne odora*) but not showy. Berrylike red fruit. Can be used as clipped hedge or background.

L. heckrottii. GOLD FLAME HONEYSUCKLE, CORAL HONEYSUCKLE. Deciduous or semideciduous vine, or small shrub. Zones 2–24. Vigorous to 12–15 ft., with oval, 2-in., blue green leaves. Free blooming from spring to frost. Clustered 1½-in.-long flowers, bright coral pink outside and rich yellow within, open from coral pink buds. Train as espalier, or on wire along eaves. Susceptible to aphids. Varieties sold as 'Gold Flame' and 'Pink Gold Flame' are similar, if not identical to the species.

L. hildebrandiana. GIANT BURMESE HONEYSUCKLE. Fast-growing evergreen vine. Zones 9, 14–17, 19–24. Big plant with 4–6-in., oval, glossy dark green leaves on supple, ropelike stems. Blooms in summer: tubular, fragrant flowers up to 6–7 in. long that open white, then turn yellow to dull orange. Blossoms are slow to drop. Plants occasionally have dark green, inch-wide, berrylike fruit. Most widely planted honeysuckle in southern California. Any good soil, occasional feeding, plenty of water. Thin out older stems occasionally and remove some growth that has bloomed. Striking along eaves, on arbor or wall.

L. japonica. JAPANESE HONEYSUCKLE. Evergreen vine, partly or wholly deciduous in coldest regions. Zones 2–24. Rampant. Deep green, oval leaves; purple-tinged white flowers with sweet fragrance. Late spring, summer bloom. Several varieties are grown, all better known than the species itself. *L. j.* 'Aureoreticulata', GOLDNET HONEYSUCKLE, has leaves veined yellow, especially in full sun. *L. j.* 'Halliana', HALL'S HONEYSUCKLE, most vigorous and most widely grown, climbs to 15 ft., covers 150 sq. ft.; flowers pure white changing to yellow, attractive to bees. *L. j.* 'Purpurea', probably same as *L. j. chinensis*, has leaves tinged purple underneath, purplish red flowers that are white inside.

Of the above, Hall's honeysuckle most commonly used as bank and ground cover, for erosion control in large areas; unless curbed, it can become a weed, smothering less vigorous plants. Needs severe pruning once a year to prevent undergrowth from building up and becoming fire hazard. Cut back almost to framework with shears. Train as privacy or wind screen on chain link or wire fence. Fairly drought resistant when established; tolerates poor drainage. As ground cover, set 2–3 ft. apart.

L. korolkowii. Deciduous shrub. Zones 1–9, 14–24. Arching form to 12 ft. Leaves oval, 2 in. long, bluish green. Profuse small rose-colored flowers in May–June are followed by bright red fruit in early fall. Use in cold areas as big background shrub. Takes desert heat. *L. k.* 'Zabelii' has broader leaves, deeper rose flowers.

L. nitida. BOX HONEYSUCKLE. Evergreen shrub. Zones 4–9, 14–24. To 6 ft. with erect, densely leafy branches. Tiny (½-in.), oval, dark green, shiny leaves. Attractive bronze to plum-colored winter foliage. Flowers (in June) fragrant, creamy white, ½ in. long. Berries translucent, blue purple. Rapid growth, tending toward untidiness, but easily pruned as hedge or single plant. Takes salt spray; resistant to oak root fungus.

L. periclymenum. WOODBINE. Zones 2–24. Evergreen vine in mild-winter areas, deciduous elsewhere. Resembles Japanese honeysuckle but is less rampant. Whorls of 2-in.-long, fragrant flowers in summer, fall. Blooms of 'Serotina' are purple outside, yellow inside; 'Berries Jubilee' has yellow flowers followed by profusion of red berries.

L. pileata. PRIVET HONEYSUCKLE. Semievergreen shrub. Zones 2–9, 14–24. Low, spreading, with stiff horizontal branches, to 3 ft. Dark green, 1½-in., privetlike leaves; small, fragrant white flowers in May; translucent violet purple berries. Sun (light shade inland). Good bank cover with low-growing euonymus or barberries. Does well at seashore.

L. sempervirens. TRUMPET HONEYSUCKLE. Evergreen or semi-evergreen twining vine, shrubby if not given support. Zones 3–24. Showy, unscented, orange yellow to scarlet, trumpet-shaped flowers 1½–2 in. long, in whorls at ends of branches in summer. Scarlet fruit. Oval leaves, 1½–3 in. long, bluish green beneath.

L. tatarica. TATARIAN HONEYSUCKLE. Deciduous shrub. Zones 1–9, 14–21. Forms big, upright, dense mass of twiggy branches; looser and more attractive in partial shade. Oval, 2-in.-long, dark green or bluish green leaves. Small pink or rose flowers in late spring, early summer. Bright red fruit. Tidy-looking plants for backgrounds, screens, windbreaks. 'Arnold Red' is smaller, compact.

LOOSESTRIFE. See *Lysimachia, Lythrum*.

LOQUAT. See *Eriobotrya japonica*.

Loropetalum chinense

LOROPETALUM chinense. *Hamamelidaceae.* Evergreen shrub. Zones 6–9, 14–24. Borderline Zones 4, 5. Generally 3–5 ft. tall, possibly up to 12 ft. in great age. Neat, compact habit, with tiered, arching or drooping branches. Leaves roundish, light green, soft,

L

1–2 in. long. Occasional leaf turns yellow or red throughout the year for nice touch of color. Flowers white to greenish white, in clusters of 4–8 at ends of branches. Each flower has 4 narrow, inch-long, twisted petals. Blooms most heavily March–April, but some bloom is likely to appear any time.

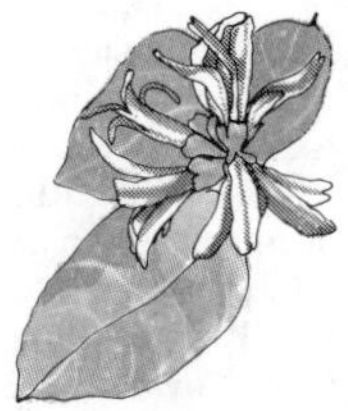

Loropetalum chinense

Full sun in fog belt; sun or partial shade inland. Needs rich, well-drained soil and lots of water. Subtly beautiful plant, good in foregrounds, raised beds, hanging baskets, woodland gardens, as ground cover. In Northwest, needs protection against hard freezes.

LOTUS. *Leguminosae.* Subshrubs or perennials, often with completely prostrate trailing stems. (For plants with common name LOTUS, see *Nelumbo*.) Leaves divided into leaflets. Flowers sweet pea shaped, pink through shades of red to yellow. Full sun to part shade. Need some summer water.

Lotus berthelotii

L. berthelotii. PARROT'S BEAK. Zones 9, 15–24. Trailing perennial with stems 2–3 ft. long, thickly covered with silvery gray foliage and very narrow, 1-in.-long, scarlet blossoms. Blooms June–July. Dies back in cold weather, suffers root rot in poor drainage. Space 2 ft. apart as ground cover; cut back occasionally to induce bushiness. Also very effective in hanging baskets, as cascade over wall or rocks.

L. corniculatus. BIRDSFOOT TREFOIL. All Zones. Goes dormant where winters are cold. Use as ground cover or coarse lawn substitute. Makes mat of dark green, cloverlike leaves. Forms clusters of small yellow flowers in summer and fall. Seed pods at top of flower stems spread like bird's foot, hence common name. Sow seeds or set out plants. Takes much water in hot, dry months. Should be mowed occasionally.

LOVAGE. See *Levisticum officinale*.

LOVE-IN-A-MIST. See *Nigella damascena*.

LOVE-LIES-BLEEDING. See *Amaranthus caudatus*.

LUFFA. See Gourd.

LUMA apiculata *(Myrceugenella apiculata, Myrtus luma).* *Myrtaceae.* Evergreen shrub or small tree. Zones 14–24. Slow growth to 6–8 (possibly 20) ft. tall, equally wide. Old plants develop beautiful, smooth, cinnamon-colored bark. Dense foliage; dark green, oval to roundish, ½–1-in.-long leaves close together. Flowers white to pinkish, a little more than ½ in. across, with 4 petals and a large brush of stamens in the center. Blue black fruit less than ½ in. wide; it is edible but not especially tasty. Resembles common myrtle (*Myrtus*) but is denser and darker green. Fairly drought tolerant.

Luma apiculata

LUNARIA annua *(L. biennis).* *Cruciferae.* MONEY PLANT. Biennial. Zones 1–10, 14–24. Old-fashioned garden plant, grown for the translucent silvery circles (about 1¼ in. across) that stay on flower stalks and are all that remain of ripened seed pods after outer coverings drop with seeds. Plants 1½–3 ft. high, with coarse, heart-shaped, toothed leaves. Flowers resemble wild mustard blooms, but are purple or white, not yellow. Plant in an out-of-the-way spot in poor soil, or in a mixed flower bed where shining pods can be admired before they are picked for dry bouquets. Tough, persistent; can reseed and become weedy.

Lunaria annua

LUNGWORT. See *Pulmonaria*.

LUPINUS. *Leguminosae.* LUPINE. Annuals, perennials, shrubs. Leaves are divided into many leaflets (like fingers of a hand). Flowers sweet pea shaped, in dense spikes at ends of stems. Many species native to western U.S., ranging from beach sand to alpine rocks. Only best, easiest-to-grow kinds covered here; native plant seed specialists can supply many others.

Lupinus Russell Hybrids

All need good drainage, but otherwise are not fussy about soil. Start from seed sown in winter or early spring. Hard-coated seeds are often slow to sprout; they germinate faster if you soak them in hot water or scratch or cut seed coats.

L. arboreus. Shrub. Zones 14–17, 22–24. Native to California coastal areas. Grows 5–8 ft. tall. Flower clusters March–June, 4–16 in. long; usually yellow, but sometimes lilac, bluish, white, or some mixture of those colors. Drought resistant. Striking beach plant.

L. hartwegii. Summer annual. Native to Mexico. Grows 1½–3 ft. tall and comes in shades of blue, white, and pink. Easy to grow from seed sown in place in April or May. Flowers July–September.

L. nanus. SKY LUPINE. Spring annual; Zones 8, 9, 14–24. California native, 8–24 in. high; flowers rich blue marked white. Sow seeds in fall or winter for spring bloom. Sow California poppies with it for contrast. April–May flowers. Self-sows readily where it gets little competition. Excellent for barren banks.

L. polyphyllus. Perennial. All Zones. Native to moist places, northern California to British Columbia. Grows 1½–4 ft. tall, with dense flower clusters, 6–24 in. long, in summer. Flowers blue, purple, or reddish. One important ancestor of the Russell Hybrids. Needs fair amount of water. Control aphids.

L. Russell Hybrids. RUSSELL LUPINES. Perennials. Zones 1–7, 14–17. Large, spreading plants to 4–5 ft., with long, dense spikes of flowers in May–June. Little Lulu and Minarette strains are smaller growing (to 1½ ft.). Colors white, cream, yellow, pink, blue, red, orange, purple. Many bicolors. Grow from seed or buy started plants from flats, pots. Striking border plant where summers aren't too hot and dry. Keep soil moist, give plants good air circulation to help avoid mildew. Often short lived.

LYCHNIS. *Caryophyllaceae.* Annuals, perennials. Hardy, old-fashioned garden flowers, all very tolerant of adverse soils.

Lychnis coronaria

L. chalcedonica. MALTESE CROSS. Perennial. Zones 1–9, 11–24. Loose, open, growing 2–3 ft. high, with hairy leaves and stems. Grow in full sun to light shade; keep moist. Scarlet flowers in dense terminal clusters, the petals deeply cut. June–July bloom. Plants effective in large borders with white flowers, gray foliage. There is a white variety, 'Alba'.

L. coeli-rosa *(Silene coeli-rosa, Agrostemma coeli-rosa, Viscaria coeli-rosa).* Summer annual. Single, saucer-shaped, 1-in. flowers cover foot-tall plants in summer. Blue and lavender are favorite colors; white and pink are also available, most with contrasting lighter or darker eye spot. Leaves long, narrow, and pointed. Good cut flowers with long bloom season. Sow seed March–April in moist, rich soil. In Zones 8, 9, 12–24, sow in fall for winter, spring bloom.

L. coronaria. CROWN-PINK, DUSTY MILLER, MULLEIN-PINK. Annual or perennial. All Zones. Plants 1½–2½ ft. tall, with attractive, silky, white foliage and, in spring and early summer, magenta to crimson flowers a little less than an inch across. Effective massed. Reseeds copiously, but surplus plants are easily weeded out.

L. viscaria 'Splendens'. Perennial. Zones 1–9, 11–24. Compact, low, evergreen clumps of grasslike leaves to 5 in. long. Flower stalks to 1 ft. with clusters of pink to rose, ½-in. flowers in summer. A double-flowered variety, 'Splendens Flore Pleno', is a good rock garden plant that lasts well when cut.

LYCIANTHUS rantonnei (often sold as *Solanum rantonnetii*). *Solanaceae*. Evergreen or deciduous shrub or vine. Zones 12, 13 (in protected patios), 15–24. As free-standing plant makes 6–8-ft. shrub, but can be staked into tree form or, with support, grown as a vine to 12–15 ft. or more. Can also be allowed to sprawl as a ground cover. Informal, fast growing, not easy to use in tailored landscape. Evergreen in mild winters; in severe cold, leaves drop and branch tips may die back. Bright green, oval leaves to 4 in. long; violet blue, yellow-centered, 1-in.-wide flowers throughout warm weather, often nearly throughout year. Apparently all plants in cultivation are variety 'Grandiflorum'. Wild species has flowers only half as large.

Lycianthus rantonnei

If you use this plant as a shrub, prune it severely to keep neat.

LYCORIS. *Amaryllidaceae*. SPIDER LILY. Bulbs. Narrow, strap-shaped leaves appear in spring, ripen, and die down before bloom starts. Clusters of red, pink, or yellow flowers on bare stems up to 2 ft. tall in late summer, fall. Flowers are spidery looking, with long stamens and narrow, wavy-edged segments curved backward. Grow in garden beds, depending on hardiness, or as pot plants. Some kinds are tender, some half hardy. Bulbs available July–August. Set 3–4 in. deep (note exception for *L. squamigera* below) in good soil, in full sun to light shade; give ample water during growth, but let plants dry out during dormant period in late summer. Don't disturb plantings for several years. When potting, set with tops exposed. Don't use pots that are too large, since plants with crowded roots grow best.

Lycoris radiata

L. africana ***(L. aurea)***. GOLDEN SPIDER LILY. Outdoors in Zones 16, 17, 19–24; indoor/outdoor container plants elsewhere. Bright yellow, 3-in. flowers in September–October.

L. radiata. Zones 4–9, 12–24. Best known and easiest to grow. Coral red flowers with gold sheen; 1½-ft. stems. 'Alba' has white flowers. Will take light shade. Give protection in cold-winter climates. August–September bloom.

L. sanguinea. Zones 4–9, 12–24. To 2 ft. tall, with bright red to orange red, 2–2½-in. flowers in fall.

L. sprengeri. Zones 4–9, 12–24. Similar to *L. squamigera*, but with slightly smaller purplish pink flowers.

L. squamigera ***(Amaryllis hallii)***. All Zones. Funnel-shaped, fragrant, pink or rosy lilac, 3-in. flowers in clusters on 2-ft. stems. August bloom. Hardiest lycoris; overwinters in colder regions if bulbs are planted 6 in. deep in protected location, as against a south wall.

LYGODIUM japonicum. *Schizaeaceae*. CLIMBING FERN. Perennial. Zones 8, 9, 14–24. Native to Southeast Asia. Delicate, lacy-textured, tightly twining climber to 8 ft., with light green leaflets. Fertile (spore-bearing) leaflets much narrower than sterile ones. Grow on post or trellis, or in hanging basket. Give light to heavy shade and keep roots moist. Hardy to 30°F.

Lygodium japonicum

LYONOTHAMNUS floribundus. *Rosaceae*. CATALINA IRONWOOD. Evergreen tree. Zones 15–17, 19–24. Native to Channel Islands off coast of southern California. The species, with lobed or scallop-toothed leaves (not divided into leaflets), is seldom seen in cultivation; *L. f. asplenifolius*, FERNLEAF CATALINA IRONWOOD, is well known. Moderate growth to 30–60 ft. with 20–40-ft. spread. Redwood-colored bark peels off in long, thin strips. Young twigs often reddish. The 4–6-in. leaves are divided into 3–7 deeply notched or lobed leaflets, deep glossy green above, gray and hairy beneath. Small white blossoms in large, flat, 8–18-in. clusters stand out well from foliage, but should be cut off when they fade; old clusters turn brown and look unattractive.

Lyonothamnus floribundus

Needs excellent drainage and should be pruned in winter to shape and control growth. Sometimes shows chlorosis in heavy soils. Easiest to grow near coast, where it tolerates much drought. Handsome in groves (like redwood); effective with redwood, Torrey pines.

LYSILOMA thornberi. *Leguminosae*. FEATHER BUSH, FERN-OF-THE-DESERT. Shrub or small tree, evergreen in frostless areas, deciduous elsewhere. Zones 10, 12–24. Native to foothills of Rincon Mountains of Arizona. To 12 ft. Makes broad canopy of finely cut bright green leaves somewhat like acacia. Sometimes killed by heavy frosts, but usually comes back. Flowers tiny, white, in ½-in. heads, May–June. Seed pods flat, ridged, 4–8 in. long, 1 in. wide. Takes desert heat and drought when established. Good informal background shrub, patio tree, transitional planting between garden and desert.

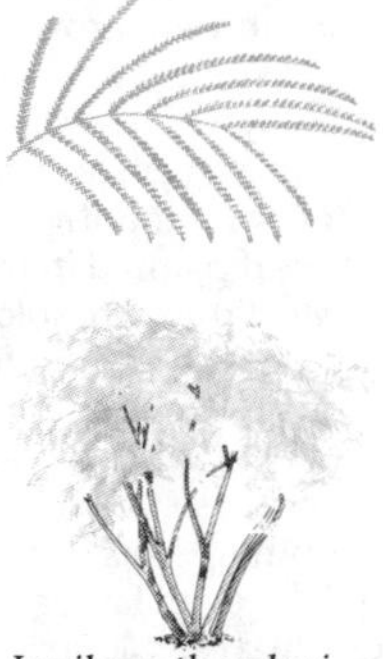

Lysiloma thornberi

LYSIMACHIA. *Primulaceae*. Vigorous perennials—one a widely grown ground cover, another a free-growing perennial for casual gardens.

L. ephemerum. Zones 3–10, 14–24. Grows to 3 ft., with a neat clump of leathery, gray green foliage topped by long, slender clusters of long-lasting white flowers.

L. nummularia. MONEYWORT, CREEPING JENNY. Zones 1–9, 14–24. Evergreen creeping plant with long runners (to 2 ft.) that root at joints. Forms pretty light green mat of roundish leaves. Flowers about 1 in. across, yellow, form singly in leaf joints. Summer blooming. Requires moisture and shade (full sun near coast). Best use is in corners where it need not be restrained. Will spill from wall, hanging basket. Good ground cover (plant 1–1½ ft. apart) near streams. 'Aurea' has yellow leaves, needs shade.

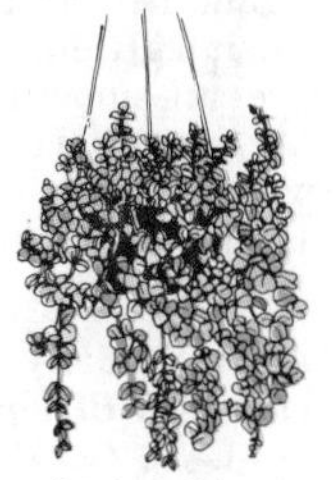

Lysimachia nummularia

L. punctata. Zones 1–9, 14–24. LOOSESTRIFE. To 4 ft. tall, 2 ft. wide, spreading freely by underground roots. Erect stems have narrow leaves in whorls, whorled yellow flowers on the upper third. Useful at edge of wood or in outer garden borders. Can be invasive.

Lythraceae. The loosestrife family is represented here by *Cuphea*, *Lagerstroemia*, and *Lythrum*.

LYTHRUM virgatum. *Lythraceae.* PURPLE LOOSESTRIFE. Perennial. All Zones. Showy magenta-flowered plants for pond margins or moist sunny areas. Grows in 2-ft.-wide clumps. Stems are 2½–5 ft. tall, the upper 8–18 in. densely set with ¾-in. flowers in late summer, fall. Narrow leaves clothe lower stem. Hybrids known as 'Roseum Superbum', 'Morden's Pink', or 'Morden's Gleam' are grown in the West. Valued for cut flowers. In borders, tone down magenta by planting with white flowers. Garden varieties are often offered as varieties of *L. salicaria*, a similar plant.

Lythrum virgatum

MACADAMIA. *Proteaceae.* MACADAMIA NUT, QUEENSLAND NUT. Evergreen trees. Zones 9, 16, 17, 19–24. Clean, handsome ornamental tree where frosts are light. Where best adapted (Zones 23, 24), produces clusters of hard-shelled, delicious nuts; pick them up as they fall from trees.

Best in deep, rich soil. Takes some drought when established but grows slowly if kept dry. Stake young trees. Prune to shape. Young plants tend to develop multiple trunks; eliminate the weaker ones and train the best to branch at 5 ft. above the ground. Yellow color in new growth flushes during winter is caused by cold and is not serious. Later growth will be green.

Macadamia tetraphylla

You can plant a macadamia from a container any month of the year, but trees suffer less heat and water stress if planted in the fall. Expect nuts in 3–5 years.

Most trees are sold under the name *M. ternifolia.* They are nearly always one of the species described below. 'Beaumont' ('Dr. Beaumont'), 'Cooper', and 'Vista' are hybrids between the 2 species. Look for grafted, named varieties of proven nut-bearing ability. All are resistant to oak root fungus.

Both species reach 25–30 ft. tall or taller, 15–20 ft. wide (trees will be even larger when very old). Long (5–12-in.), glossy, leathery leaves. Mature foliage is durable and attractive for cutting. Small flowers in winter and spring are white to pink in dense, hanging, 1-ft. clusters.

M. integrifolia. SMOOTH-SHELL MACADAMIA. Best near coast. Leaves are smooth edged. Nuts ripen in late fall to May.

M. tetraphylla. ROUGH-SHELL MACADAMIA. Best inland. Spiny leaves. Thinner-shelled nuts on more open tree than *M. integrifolia.* Nuts appear fall through February.

MACFADYENA unguis-cati *(Doxantha unguis-cati, Bignonia tweediana).* *Bignoniaceae.* CAT'S CLAW, YELLOW TRUMPET VINE. Partly deciduous vine that loses all its leaves when winters are cold. Zones 8–24. Climbs high and fast by hooked, clawlike, forked tendrils. To 25–40 ft. Leaves divided into 2 oval, glossy green, 2-in. leaflets. Blooms in early spring, bearing yellow trumpets to 2 in. long, 1¼ in. across.

Macfadyena unguis-cati

Grows near coast, but faster growing and stronger where summers are hot—even on south walls in Zones 12, 13. Clings to any support—stone, wood, fence, tree trunk. Some are even seen clinging to undersides of freeway overpasses. Tends to produce leaves and flowers at ends of stems. Cut back some stems nearly to ground to stimulate new growth lower down; prune whole plant hard after bloom. Needs little dry-season water once established.

MACKAYA bella. *Acanthaceae.* Evergreen shrub. Zones 15–24. South African native; 4–5 ft. tall, sometimes much taller, with glossy, dark green leaves 4–5 in. long. In spring, produces loose, 9–10-in.-long clusters of pale lavender, 2-in. flowers with deep purple lines in the throat. Likes average soil, ample water, and part shade, but survives and looks good in dense shade with little water.

Mackaya bella

MACLEAYA cordata *(Bocconia cordata).* *Papaveraceae.* PLUME POPPY. Perennial. All Zones. Stately plant with 3-ft.-wide clumps of grayish green, deeply lobed leaves up to 10 in. wide. Branched flower stems to 7–8 ft. carry clouds of tiny, pinkish tan flowers. Plants thrive in average good garden soil, with ample water and sun for at least half the day. They can crowd out smaller plants, so group them with sturdy shrubs or plant them alone.

Macleaya cordata

MACLURA pomifera. *Moraceae.* OSAGE ORANGE. Deciduous tree. All Zones; little planted outside Zones 1, 3, 10–13. Fast growth to 60 ft. with spreading, open habit. Thorny branches. Leaves to 5 in. long, medium green. If there's a male plant present, female plants may bear inedible, 4-in. fruits (hedge-apples) which somewhat resemble bumpy, yellow green oranges. Can stand heat, cold, wind, drought, poor soil, moderate alkalinity. Easily propagated by seed, cuttings, root cuttings; easily transplanted. Useful as big, tough, rough-looking hedge or background. Prune to any size from 6 ft. up. Pruned high, becomes desert shade tree, but needs some water until established. Not bothered by oak root fungus.

Maclura pomifera

MADAGASCAR JASMINE. See *Stephanotis floribunda.*

MADAGASCAR PALM. See *Pachypodium lamieri.*

MADAGASCAR PERIWINKLE. See *Catharanthus roseus.*

MADEIRA VINE. See *Anredera cordifolia.*

MADRONE, MADROÑO. See *Arbutus menziesii.*

MAGNOLIA. *Magnoliaceae.* Deciduous or evergreen trees and shrubs. A great number of magnificent flowering plants with a remarkable variety of colors, leaf shapes, and plant forms. The following classification by general appearance may help you find the magnolias that interest you (the chart lists all the kinds alphabetically).

Evergreen Magnolias

To gardeners in California and Arizona, magnolia usually means *M. grandiflora,* the big evergreen with glossy leaves and big, white, fragrant flowers. This one stands pretty much by itself. Generally considered a street or lawn tree, it can also be used as an espalier or grown in a large container for a

Magnolia grandiflora

(Continued on page 418)

Magnolia

NAME	ZONES	DEC. or EV.	HEIGHT	SPREAD	BLOOMS AT AGE:	FLOWERS	USES	REMARKS
Magnolia acuminata CUCUMBER TREE	1–9, 14–21	Decid-uous.	60–80 ft.	25 ft.	12 yrs.	Small, greenish yellow, appear after leaves. Late spring, summer. Handsome reddish seed capsules, red seeds.	Shade or lawn tree.	Dense shade from glossy 5–9-in. leaves. Hardy to cold; dislikes hot, dry winds.
M. a. cordata (*M. cordata*) YELLOW CUCUMBER TREE, YELLOW MAGNOLIA	4–9, 14–21	Decid-uous.	To 35 ft.	To 35 ft.	12 yrs.	Larger (to 4 in.), chartreuse yellow outside, pure yellow within; appear as leaves start to expand. Mild lemon scent.	Lawn or border tree for large properties. Slow growing.	Lower, shrubbier than *M. acuminata*. Showier, but not ordinarily a tree you can walk or sit under. 'Elizabeth', a cross with *M. denudata*, is a shrubby tree with fragrant, light yellow blooms. 'Miss Honeybee' is good selection with pale yellow flowers.
M. campbellii	6–9, 14–21	Decid-uous.	60–80 ft.	To 40 ft.	20 yrs. Grafts bloom younger.	Magnificent 6–10-in. bowls, deep rose outside, paler within. Central petals cupped over rose stamens. Very early flowering.	Plant in lee of evergreens to protect flowers from storm winds. Make it focus of garden and give it room.	Best in Zones 15–17. 'Alba', 'Strybing White' are white forms; 'Hendricks Park', 'Late Pink' are good pinks.
M. dawsoniana DAWSON MAGNOLIA	4–9, 14–21	Decid-uous.	40–50 ft.	25–30 ft.	10 yrs. from grafts.	Large (8–10 in.), white with rose shading. Narrow petals, slightly pendulous. Profuse bloom. Early flowering. Slight perfume.	Big plant for big garden. Makes magnificent show—a little untidy close up.	Very dark green leaves. Quite cold hardy when established, needs hardening off in fall. 'Chyverton' is selected salmon, fading pink.
M. delavayi	7–9, 14–21	Evergreen.	20–30 ft.	To 20 ft.	4–5 yrs.	Dull creamy white, 6–8 in. wide. Fragrant, short-lived; flowers shatter day they open. Long summer bloom.	Use as single tree or giant shrub in lawn or large corner. Hard to train as single-stemmed tree.	Foliage is the feature; leaves 8–14 in. long, 5–8 in. wide, stiff, leathery, gray green, tropical looking.
M. denudata (*M. conspicua, M. heptapeta*) YULAN MAGNOLIA	2–9, 14–24	Decid-uous.	To 35 ft.	To 30 ft.	6–7 yrs.	White, fragrant, sometimes tinged purple at base. Held erect, somewhat tulip shaped, 3–4 in. long spreading to 6–7 in. Early; often a few in summer.	Place it where it can be shown off against dark background or sky. Cut flowers striking in Oriental arrangements.	Tends toward irregular form—no handicap in informal garden or at woodland edge. Leaves 4–7 in. long.
M. fraseri (*M. auriculata*)	2–9, 14–21	Decid-uous.	To 50 ft.	20–30 ft.	10–12 yrs.	Creamy to yellowish white, 8–10 in. wide. Blooms May–June when leaves are full grown.	Single lawn tree or woodland tree. Rose red, 5-in. seed capsules showy in summer.	Leaves 16–18 in. long, parchmentlike, in whorls at ends of branches. Effect is that of parasols. Handsome dark brown fall color.
M. 'Freeman'	4–12, 14–24	Evergreen.	10–15 ft.	To 5 ft.	8 yrs. from seed.	White, 5 in. across, very fragrant. Summer bloom.	Narrow, dense, columnar evergreen tree for small gardens. Leaves like those of *M. grandiflora* but smaller.	Hybrid between *M. virginiana* and *M. grandiflora*. A very old tree has been known to reach 50 ft.

(Continued on next page)

M

NAME	ZONES	DEC. or EV.	HEIGHT	SPREAD	BLOOMS AT AGE:	FLOWERS	USES	REMARKS
M. globosa	5–9, 14–21	Deciduous.	To 20 ft.	To 20 ft.	10 yrs.	White, fragrant, cupped or globe shaped, nodding or drooping. June.	Use as big shrub in lawn, woodland edge, above a wall (to look up into flowers).	Leaves 5–8 in. long, half as wide, rusty and furry beneath. Tree tender when young.

The southern magnolia in all its forms is something of a "sacred cow" in western gardens: on the one hand it is loved for its pretty foliage (while it's on the tree) and its glorious flower display; on the other hand, it is cursed or tolerated for the big, hard (almost like plastic) fallen leaves, fallen flower parts, and fallen seedheads that need to be picked or raked up daily or weekly from May through September. Trees seldom thrive for long in narrow parking strips, and they have a tendency to lift sidewalks if planted there. Surface rooting and dense year-round shade prevent healthy lawn growth. Although established trees can take some drought, they look their best only when amply supplied with water.

NAME	ZONES	DEC. or EV.	HEIGHT	SPREAD	BLOOMS AT AGE:	FLOWERS	USES	REMARKS
M. grandiflora SOUTHERN MAGNOLIA, BULL BAY	4–12, 14–24	Evergreen.	To 80 ft.	To 40 ft.	15 yrs., sometimes much less. From grafts or cuttings, 2–3 yrs.	Pure white, aging buff; large (8–10 in. across), powerfully fragrant. Carried throughout summer and fall.	Street or lawn tree, big containers, wall or espalier plant. In cool-summer areas, it appreciates warm wall or pocket. Glossy, leathery leaves, 4–8 in. long.	Unpredictable in form and age of bloom. Grafted plants more predictable. Does well in desert heat if out of wind. Needs warm wall in Zones 4, 5. Expect breakage, yearly pruning in Zones 6, 7.
M. g. 'Edith Bogue'	Same.	Same.	To 35 ft.	To 20 ft.	2–3 yrs. from grafts.	As in *M. grandiflora*. Young plants slower to come into heavy bloom than some other varieties.	One of hardiest selections of *M. grandiflora*. Original tree was from New Jersey. Shapely, vigorous tree.	Has withstood −24°F. The one to try in coldest regions. Keep it out of strong winds.
M. g. 'Little Gem'	Same.	Same.	Slow to 15–20 ft.	To 10 ft.	2 yrs. from grafts.	Small (5–6 in. wide).	Good in containers, as espalier, confined area.	Blooms young. Half-size foliage, rusty beneath. Branches to ground unless trimmed.
M. g. 'Majestic Beauty'	Same.	Same.	35–50 ft.	To 20 ft.	2 yrs. from grafts.	Very large, to 1 ft. across, with 9 petals.	Vigorous, dense-branching street or shade tree of broadly pyramidal form.	Leaves exceptionally long, broad, and heavy. Most luxuriant of southern magnolias; however, not the densest or most symmetrical. 'Timeless Beauty' is more erect, denser, has slightly smaller (10-in.) flowers.
M. g. 'Samuel Sommer'	Same.	Same.	30–40 ft.	To 30 ft.	Same.	Very large and full; to 10–14 in. across, with 12 petals.	Like the other grafted magnolias that bloom young, this will need pruning to become single-trunked tree. Can grow as multitrunked tree.	Leaves large, leathery, glossy, with heavy, rusty red felting on underside; very dark green above. Fairly fast growing.
M. g. 'St. Mary'	Same.	Same.	Usually 20 ft. Much larger in old age.	To 20 ft.	Same.	Heavy production of full-sized flowers on small tree.	Fine where standard-sized magnolia would grow too large too fast. Good espalier and pot subject.	Left alone, it will form a big, dense bush. Pruned and staked, it makes a small tree.
M. g. 'Victoria'	Same.	Same.	To 20 ft.	To 15 ft.	2–3 yrs. from grafts.	Same as *M. grandiflora*.	Withstands −10°F. with little damage, but plant out of wind.	Parent plant grew in Victoria, B.C. Foliage exceptionally broad, heavy, dark green. 'Pioneer' is as hardy but leaves are not as dark green.
M. heptapeta See *M. denudata*								

NAME	ZONES	DEC. or EV.	HEIGHT	SPREAD	BLOOMS AT AGE:	FLOWERS	USES	REMARKS
M. hypoleuca (*M. obovata*)	4–9, 14–21	Decid-uous.	To 50 ft.	To 25 ft.	15 yrs.	To 8 in. across, creamy, fragrant. Appear in summer after leaves expand.	Only for big lawn or garden. Flowers are high up in tree.	Leaves impressive—up to 1½ ft. long. They tend to obscure flowers.
M. kobus KOBUS MAGNOLIA	2–9, 14–24	Decid-uous.	To 30 ft.	To 20 ft.	15 yrs.	White, to 4 in. across; early.	Hardy, sturdy tree for planting singly on lawn or in informal shrub and tree groupings.	Variety 'Wada's Memory' (*M. kewensis* 'Wada's Memory') is a better garden plant; blooms young, grows faster, has bigger flowers, copper red new growth. *M. k. borealis* is much larger (to 75 ft.) tree with larger (6 in.) leaves.
M. k. stellata See *M. stellata*.								
M. liliiflora (*M. quinquepeta*) LILY MAGNOLIA	2–9, 14–24	Decid-uous	To 12 ft.	To 15 ft.	4–5 yrs.	White inside, purplish outside. Selections sold as 'Gracilis', 'Nigra' and 'O'Neill' darker purple red outside, pink inside.	Shrub border; strong vertical effect in big flower border. Blooms over long spring, summer season.	Good cut flower if buds taken before fully open. Spreads slowly by suckering. Leaves 4–6 in. long. 'Royal Crown', hybrid with *M. veitchii*, has pink, candle-shaped buds which open to 10-in. flowers.
M. loebneri	2–9, 14–24	Decid-uous.	Slow to 12–15 ft.	12–15 ft.	3 yrs.	Narrow, strap-shaped petals like star magnolia, but fewer, larger. Plants bloom early and young.	Use in lawn, shrub border or woodland edge.	Group of hybrids between *M. kobus* and *M. stellata*. 'Ballerina' is white with faint pink blush on opening; 'Leonard Messel' has pink flowers, deeper in bud; 'Merrill' ('Dr. Merrill') is a very hardy, free-flowering white. 'Spring Snow' can reach 30 ft., with pure white flowers.
M. macrophylla BIGLEAF MAGNOLIA	2–9, 14–21	Decid-uous.	Slow to 50 ft.	To 30 ft.	12–15 yrs.	White, fragrant, to 1 ft. across, appearing May–July, after leaves are out.	Show-off tree with leaves 1–2½ ft. long, 9–12 in. wide. Needs to stand alone. Striking foliage but hard to blend with other textures.	Plant where it is out of the wind; huge leaves are easily tattered and branches are brittle. *M. m. ashei* is smaller grower (to 25 ft.) with 8–12-in. flowers. Blooms very young.
M. officinalis	4–9, 14–21	Decid-uous.	To 50 ft.	To 25 ft.	15 yrs.	To 8 in. wide, fragrant, creamy white. Appear after leaves in May.	Much like *M. hypoleuca*. Use for big, exotic-looking tree.	*M. o. biloba* has 1½-ft.-long leaves notched at tips.
M. quinquepeta See *M. liliiflora*								
M. salicifolia ANISE MAGNOLIA	2–9, 14–21	Decid-uous.	Slow to 18–30 ft.	To 12 ft.	2–10 yrs.	White, narrow petaled, to 4 in. across. Early.	Usually upright with slender branches, graceful appearance. In front of trees, use as shrub border. Leaves (3–6 in. long) bronze red in fall.	'Kochanakee' and 'W. B. Clarke' are large flowered, bloom young and heavily. 'Miss Jack' has narrow, anise-scented leaves, blooms heavily.

(Continued on next page)

M

NAME	ZONES	DEC. or EV.	HEIGHT	SPREAD	BLOOMS AT AGE:	FLOWERS	USES	REMARKS
M. sargentiana robusta	5–9, 14–24	Deciduous.	To 35 ft.	To 35 ft.	10–12 yrs.; 8–10 yrs. from grafts.	Huge (8–12-in.), mauve pink bowls which open erect, then nod to horizontal. Early to midseason.	Must have ample room and protection from stormy winds which would tear early blooms.	One of most spectacular of flowering plants. Leaves 6–8 in. long. Not for hot, dry areas. 'Caerhays Belle' and 'Marjory Gossler', hybrids of this and other large-flowered species, are vigorous trees that have dinner plate–sized pink flowers. Both are rare, choice.
M. sieboldii (Sometimes sold as *M. parviflora*) OYAMA MAGNOLIA	4–9, 14–24	Deciduous.	6–15 ft.	6–15 ft.	5 yrs.	White, cup shaped, centered with crimson stamens; fragrant. Begins blooming in May; flowers over long period.	Nice planted upslope or at the top of wall so people can look into flowers. Good for small gardens.	Popular in Zones 4–6 for fragrance, long bloom, restrained growth. Buds like white Japanese lanterns. Leaves 3–6 in. long.
M. soulangiana SAUCER MAGNOLIA (Often erroneously called TULIP TREE)	1–10, 12–24	Deciduous.	To 25 ft.	To 25 ft. or more.	3–5 yrs.	White to pink or purplish red, variable in size and form, blooming before leaves expand. Generally about 6 in. across.	Lawn ornament, anchor plant in big corner plantings. Foliage good green, rather coarse; leaves 4–6 in. (or more) long.	Seedlings highly variable; shop for named varieties. Hybrid of *M. denudata* and *M. liliiflora*.
M. s. 'Alba' (*M. s.* 'Amabilis', *M. s.* 'Alba Superba')	Same.	Same.	To 30 ft.	Same.	Same.	Flowers suffused purple, opening nearly pure white.	As above. Rather more upright in growth than most.	Large flowers bloom early.
M. s. 'Alexandrina'	Same.	Same.	To 25 ft.	Same.	Same.	Deep purplish pink, white inside, large. Midseason.	As above. Large, rather heavy foliage.	Late bloom helps it escape frosts in colder sections.
M. s. 'Brozzonii'	Same.	Same.	Same.	Same.	Same.	Huge, to 8 in. across. White, very slightly flushed at base. Early.	Large, vigorous plant.	One of handsomest whites.
M. s. 'Burgundy'	Same.	Same.	Same.	Same.	Same.	Large, well-rounded, deep purple halfway up to petal tips, then lightening to pink. Early.	San Francisco's Japanese Tea Garden has many of these, pruned to picturesque shapes.	
M. s. 'Coates'	Same.	Same.	Same.	Same.	Same.	Large, attractive flowers resemble those of *M. quinquepeta* 'Royal Crown'.	Large, shrubby.	Quick grower.
M. s. 'Lennei' (*M. lennei*)	Same.	Same.	Same.	Same.	Same.	Very large, globe shaped, deep purple on outside, white on inside.	Spreading, vigorous plant.	Very late bloom helps it escape frosts in cold areas.
M. s. 'Lennei Alba' (*M. lennei* 'Alba')	1–10, 12–24	Deciduous.	To 25 ft.	To 25 ft. or more.	3–5 yrs.	Same as *M. s.* 'Lennei', but white in color, slightly smaller, earlier (midseason).	Plant spreading, vigorous.	Two plants sold under this name. One form common in California is smaller in flower, creamy white, and earlier.
M. s. 'Lilliputian'	Same.	Same.	Smaller grower than others.	Same.	Same.	Pink and white, somewhat smaller than other *M. soulangiana* varieties. Late flowering.	Good where a smaller magnolia is called for.	Late blooming.

NAME	ZONES	DEC. or EV.	HEIGHT	SPREAD	BLOOMS AT AGE:	FLOWERS	USES	REMARKS
M. s. 'Norbertii'	1–10, 12–24	Deciduous.	To 25 ft.	To 25 ft. or more.	3–5 yrs.	White, stained purple on outside. Late.	Upright dense habit.	
M. s. 'Pink Superba'	Same.	Same.	Same.	Same.	Same.	Large, deep pink, white inside. Early.	Best where late frosts are not a problem.	Identical to *M. s.* 'Alba' except for flower color.
M. s. 'Rustica Rubra'	Same.	Same.	Same.	Same.	Same.	Large, cup shaped, deep reddish purple. Midseason.	Tall, vigorous grower for large areas. More treelike than many varieties.	Blooms somewhat past midseason. Big (6-in.) seed pods of dark rose.
M. s. 'San Jose'	Same.	Same.	Same.	Same.	Same.	Large, white flushed pink.	Earliest *M. soulangiana.*	Blooms January–February.
M. sprengeri 'Diva'	5–9, 14–24	Deciduous.	To 40 ft.	To 30 ft.	7 yrs. from grafts.	To 8 in. wide, rose pink outside, white suffused pink with deeper lines inside. Scented. Early to midseason.	One of the brightest in color; young plants broad, twiggy.	Highly colored, erect, spectacular flowers. Buds seem more frost resistant than those of *M. sargentiana robusta.* Hybrids between this and *M. liliiflora* are 'Nigra' and 'Galaxy', with large purple flowers that open late in the spring to avoid frost; and 'Spectrum', with larger but fewer flowers. All are big shrubs that can be trained as small trees.
M. stellata STAR MAGNOLIA	1–9, 14–24	Deciduous.	To 10 ft.	To 20 ft.	3 yrs.	Very early white flowers with 19–21 narrow, strap-shaped petals. Profuse bloom in late winter, early spring.	Slow growing, shrubby, fine for borders, entryway gardens, edge of woods.	Quite hardy, but flowers often nipped by frost in Zones 1–7. Fine texture in twig and leaf. Fair yellow and brown fall color.
M. s. 'Centennial'	Same.	Same.	Same.	Same.	Same.	Large (5 in.), white, faintly marked pink.	Same.	Like an improved *M. s.* 'Waterlily'.
M. s. 'Dawn'	Same.	Same.	Same.	Same.	Same.	To 40–50 pink petals.	Same.	
M. s. 'Rosea' PINK STAR MAGNOLIA	Same.	Same.	Same.	Same.	Same.	Pink buds, flowers flushed pink, fading white.	As for species. Place where you can see flowers from living or family room; they often bloom so early that you won't want to walk out to see them.	In cold regions, plant these early-flowering sorts in a north exposure to delay bloom as long as possible, lessen frost damage.
M. s. 'Royal Star'	Same.	Same.	Same.	Same.	Same.	White, 25–30 petals, blooms 2 weeks later than *M. stellata.*	Same uses as above. Faster growing.	
M. s. 'Rubra'	Same.	Same.	Same.	Same.	Same.	Rosy pink flowers.	More treelike in form than other *M. stellata* varieties.	
M. s. 'Waterlily'	1–9, 14–24	Deciduous.	To 10 ft.	To 20 ft.	3 yrs.	White. Larger flowers than *M. stellata;* broader, more numerous petals.	Leaves, like those of all star magnolias, are modest in size (2–4 in. long); give finer foliage texture than other magnolias.	Faster growing than most star magnolias.

(Continued on next page)

M

NAME	ZONES	DEC. or EV.	HEIGHT	SPREAD	BLOOMS AT AGE:	FLOWERS	USES	REMARKS
M. veitchii VEITCH MAGNOLIA	4–9, 14–24	Deciduous.	30–40 ft.	To 30 ft.	4–5 yrs.	Blooms early, before leaves. Rose red at base, shading to white at tips, to 10 in. across.	Needs plenty of room and protection from wind. Fast-growing branches are brittle. Spectacular tree.	This hybrid between *M. campbellii* and *M. denudata* is exceptionally fast growing and vigorous. 'Rubra' has smaller purple red flowers.
M. virginiana (*M. glauca*) SWEET BAY	4–9, 14–24	Deciduous or semi-evergreen.	To 50 ft. Usually less.	To 20 ft.	8–10 yrs.	Nearly globular, 2–3 in. wide, creamy white, fragrant, June–September.	Prefers moist, acid soil. Grows in swamps in eastern U.S. Usually a massive, semievergreen shrub.	Variable in leaf drop. Some plants quite evergreen. Leaves grayish green, nearly white beneath, 2–5 in. long.
M. wilsonii WILSON MAGNOLIA	4–9, 14–24	Deciduous.	To 25 ft.	To 25 ft.	10 yrs.	White, with red stamens, pendulous, 3–4 in. across, fragrant. May and June.	Blooms at 4 ft. and tends to remain shrubby. Plant high on bank where flowers can be looked up at. Better in light shade.	Rich purple brown twigs and narrow, tapered leaves, 3–6 in. long with silvery undersides.

few years. Foliage is good in arrangements. Known for heat resistance and tolerance of damp soil, it has many named forms for different uses.

Other evergreen magnolias are *M. delavayi, M. virginiana*, and *M.* 'Freeman'.

Magnolia soulangiana

Deciduous Magnolias with Saucer Flowers

This group includes the saucer magnolia (*M. soulangiana*) and its many varieties, often erroneously called "tulip trees" because of the shape and bright colors of their flowers. Included here are the yulan magnolia (*M. denudata*) and lily magnolia (*M. liliiflora*). All are hardy to cold, thriving in various climates throughout the West—but early flowers of all forms are subject to frost damage, and all do poorly in hot, dry, windy areas. Related to these, but more tender to cold (and heat), are the big, spectacular Oriental magnolias from western China and the Himalayas—*M. campbellii, M. dawsoniana, M. sargentiana robusta, M. sprengeri* 'Diva'. These are barely hardy in Zones 4 and 5, subject to frost and storm damage to early flowers.

Deciduous Magnolias with Star Flowers

This garden group includes *M. kobus, M. stellata* and its varieties (the star magnolias), and *M. salicifolia*. All are hardy, slow-growing, early-blooming plants with wide climatic adaptability.

Other Magnolias

Less widely planted is a group of magnolias which bloom with or after the appearance of the leaves but are generally considered foliage plants or shade trees. Among them are: *M. acuminata*, a big shade tree with inconspicuous flowers; *M. hypoleuca* and *M. officinalis*, big trees with big leaves and large but not noticeable flowers; and the eastern American *M. fraseri* and *M. macrophylla*, middle-sized trees with huge leaves and flowers.

Magnolia Culture

For any magnolia, pick planting site carefully. Except for *M. grandiflora*, magnolias are hard to move once established, and many grow quite large. They never look their best when crowded, and may be severely damaged by digging around their roots. They need moist, well-drained, rich, neutral or slightly acid soil. Add plenty of organic matter at planting time—leaf mold, peat moss, or ground bark. Full sun (light shade in desert regions).

Balled and burlapped plants are available in late winter and early spring; container plants are sold any time. Do not set plants lower than their original soil level. Stake single-trunked or very heavy plants against rocking by wind, which will tear the thick, fleshy, sensitive roots. Set stakes in planting hole before placing tree (to avoid damaging roots). If you plant your magnolia in a lawn, try to provide a good-sized area free of grass for a watering basin. Water deeply and thoroughly, but do not drown the plants. Thick mulch will help hold moisture and reduce soil temperature. Surrounding grass will decrease reflected heat, but do not let grass invade watering basin. Keep root crown shaded and damp.

Prevent soil compaction around root zone; this means reducing foot traffic to a minimum. Prune only when absolutely necessary. Best time is right after flowering, and best way is to remove the entire twig or limb right to the base.

Damaging creatures and diseases are few. Watch for scale and aphids at any time and for spider mites in hot weather. Snails and slugs eat lower leaves of shrubby magnolias. Bait or spray will control them. Magnolias are not immune to oak root fungus, but they seem somewhat resistant.

More bothersome are deficiency problems: chlorosis from lack of iron in alkaline soils, and nitrogen starvation. Iron chelates will remedy the first condition; fertilizer will fix the second. Burned leaf edges usually mean salt damage from overfertilizing, mineral salts in the soil, or salts in the irrigation water. This last, a problem in southern California, is usually the factor limiting success of magnolias in deserts. Regular, frequent, deep, heavy waterings help leach out salts and carry them to lower soil levels—*if* drainage is good. In the Northwest, late frosts may burn leaf edges.

Uses are discussed in more detail in the chart. Generally speaking, larger deciduous magnolias are at their best standing alone against some background that will display their flowers and, in winter, their strongly patterned, usually gray limbs and big, fuzzy flower buds. Smaller deciduous magnolias show up well in large flower or shrub borders, and make choice ornaments in the Oriental garden. And all magnolias are excellent lawn trees. Be aware of a magnolia's eventual size before planting it near house or drive.

Magnoliaceae. The magnolia family contains evergreen and deciduous trees and shrubs with large, showy flowers, usually with a large number of petals, sepals, and stamens. Tulip tree (*Liriodendron*) Michelia, and magnolia are examples.

MAHONIA. *Berberidaceae.* Evergreen shrubs. Related to *Berberis* (barberry) and described under that name by some botanists. Easily grown; good looking all year. Leaves divided into leaflets that usually have spiny teeth on edges. Yellow flowers in dense, rounded to spikelike clusters, followed by blue black (sometimes red), berrylike fruit. Generally disease resistant, though foliage is sometimes disfigured by small looper caterpillar. All are drought tolerant, attract birds.

Mahonia aquifolium

M. aquifolium. OREGON GRAPE. Zones 1–21. Native British Columbia to northern California. State flower of Oregon. To 6 ft. or more with tall, erect habit; spreads by underground stems. Leaves 4–10 in. long, with 5–9, very spiny-toothed, oval, 1–2½-in.-long leaflets that are glossy green in some forms, dull green in others. Young growth ruddy or bronzy; scattered mature red leaves through year (more pronounced in fall). Purplish or bronzy leaves in winter, especially in cold-winter areas or where plants are grown in full sun. Flowers in 2–3-in.-long clusters, March–May; edible blue black fruit with gray bloom (makes good jelly).

Takes any exposure in most areas. North exposure best in Zones 12, 13 (where chlorosis is also a problem); in Zones 9–14, 18–21, it looks best if grown in shade. Control height and form by pruning; cut to ground any woody stems that extend too far above mass (new growth fills in quickly). At first sign of caterpillar damage (lacelike perforations on leaves), spray with BTU (*Bacillus thuringiensis*).

For uniformity, plant one of the varieties grown from cuttings or divisions. 'Compacta' averages about 2 ft. tall and spreads freely to make broad colonies. New foliage is glossy, light to coppery green; mature foliage is matte medium green. 'Orange Flame', 5 ft. tall, has bronzy orange new growth, glossy green mature leaves that turn wine red in winter.

Plant in masses as foundation planting, in woodland, in tubs, as low screen or garden barrier. Resistant to oak root fungus and especially valuable where gardens are heavily infested by it.

M. bealei. LEATHERLEAF MAHONIA. All Zones. To 10–12 ft., with strong pattern of vertical stems, horizontal leaves. Leaves are over a foot long, divided into 7–15 thick, leathery, broad leaflets as much as 5 in. long, yellowish green above, gray green below, edges spiny toothed. Flowers in erect, 3–6-in.-long, spikelike clusters at ends of branches in earliest spring. Powdery blue berries. Takes sun in fog belt; best in partial shade elsewhere. Plant in rich soil with ample organic material incorporated. Water generously. Truly distinguished plant against stone, brick, wood, glass.

M. fremontii. DESERT MAHONIA. Zones 8–24. Native to deserts of Southwest. Erect habit, many stems, 3–12 ft. tall. Gray green to yellowish green leaves with 3–5 thick, 1-in.-long leaflets; edges have very sharp, tough spines. Flowers in 1–1½-in.-long clusters, May–June; dark blue to brown fruit. Grow in full sun or light shade.

M. 'Golden Abundance'. Zones 1–21. Dense, heavily foliaged shrub, 5–6 ft. tall. Glossy green leaves with red midribs; heavy bloom and fruit set.

M. lomariifolia. Zones 6–9, 14–24. Showy plant with erect, little-branched stems to 6–10 ft. Young plants often have single, vertical unbranched stem; with age, plants produce more almost vertical branches from near base. Clustered near ends of these branches are horizontally-held leaves to 2 ft. long. In outline, leaves look like stiff, crinkly, barbed ferns; each has as many as 47 thick, spiny, glossy green leaflets arranged symmetrically along both sides of central stem. Yellow flowers in winter or earliest spring grow in long, erect clusters at branch tips, just above topmost cluster of leaves. Powdery blue berries, appealing to birds, follow the flowers.

Mahonia lomariifolia

Needs shade at least in afternoon to keep its deep green color. Prune stems at varying heights to induce branching. Dramatic in entryways, on shaded patios, against shaded wall, in containers. Vertical habit, high leaf masses make it a dramatic plant for silhouette lighting effect. Good choice for narrow areas. Just don't place it so close to walk that sharp needles on its leaflets scratch passers-by.

M. nervosa. LONGLEAF MAHONIA. Zones 2–9, 14–17. Native British Columbia to northern California. Low shrub, 2 ft. (rarely 6 ft.) tall. Spreads by underground stems to make good cover. Leaves clustered at stem tips; 10–18 in. long, with 7–21 glossy, bristle-toothed, green, 1–3¾-in.-long leaflets. Creates the impression of a stiff, leathery fern. Yellow flowers in upright clusters 3–6 in. long, April–June. Blue berries. Best in shade; will take sun in cooler areas, becoming very compact. Woodland ground cover, facing for taller mahonias, low barrier planting.

M. nevinii. NEVIN MAHONIA. Zones 8–24. Native to scattered localities, southern California. Many-branched shrub, 3–10 ft. tall, with gray foliage. Leaves with 3–5 leaflets, about 1 in. long, bristly or spiny. Flowers in loose, 1–2-in.-long clusters, March–May, followed by red berries. Sun or light shade, any soil, much or little water. Resistant to oak root fungus. Use individually or as screen, hedge, barrier. Extremely rare in nature; population was once reduced to 100 plants or so. It may now be extinct in the wild.

M. pinnata. CALIFORNIA HOLLY GRAPE. Zones 7–9, 14–24. Native southern Oregon to southern California. Similar to Oregon grape—but leaves are more crinkly and spiny, new growth often shows lots of red and orange, and plants may grow taller than Oregon grape in ideal coastal conditions. Takes drought better than Oregon grape. In Zones 8, 9, 14, 18–21, it's best in light shade. For uniformity, plant selection 'Ken Hartman'.

M. repens. CREEPING MAHONIA. Zones 1–21. Native northern California, eastward to Rocky Mountains. Creeps by underground stems. To 3 ft. tall, spreading habit. Dull bluish green leaves have 3–7 spine-toothed leaflets, turn bronzy in winter. Yellow flowers, April–June, followed by blue berries in short clusters. Good ground cover in sun, partial shade. Will control erosion.

MAIANTHEMUM dilatatum ***(M. bifolium, M. d. camtschaticum).*** *Liliaceae.* FALSE LILY-OF-THE-VALLEY. Perennial. Zones 1–9, 14–17. Native to northern California, the Northwest. Creeping rootstocks send up neat, roundish, heavily veined leaves to 8 in. long, half as wide, on 2–6-in. stems. Foamy clusters of white flowers in spring are followed by red berries in summer. Attractive woodland ground cover, but capable of overwhelming delicate plant neighbors. Disappears in winter.

Maianthemum dilatatum

MAIDEN GRASS. See *Miscanthus sinensis* 'Gracillimus'.

MAIDENHAIR FERN. See *Adiantum*.

MAIDENHAIR TREE. See *Ginkgo biloba*.

MAIDEN'S WREATH. See *Francoa ramosa*.

MAJORANA hortensis. See *Origanum majorana*.

M

MALCOLMIA maritima. *Cruciferae.* VIRGINIAN STOCK. Summer annual. To 8–15 in., single stemmed or branching from base, covered with nearly scentless, 4-petaled flowers. Colors include white, yellow, pinks, and lilacs to magenta. Leaves are oblong. Sow in place any time except in hot or very cold weather. As with sweet alyssum (*Lobularia maritima*), plants bloom only 6 weeks after seeds are sown. Does not readily reseed. Demands moderately rich soil and full sun for best performance. Good bulb cover.

Malcolmia maritima

MALEPHORA (*Hymenocyclus*). *Aizoaceae.* ICE PLANT. For comparison with other ice plants, see Ice Plant. Dense, smooth, gray green to blue green foliage highly resistant to heat, wind, exhaust fumes, fire. Widely used in streetside and freeway plantings. Drought tolerant. Full sun. Flowers over long season, but blooms are scattered rather than in sheets. Attractive to bees.

Malephora luteola

M. crocea. Zones 11–24. Trailing plant to 6 in. high with smooth, gray green foliage, sparse production of reddish yellow flowers nearly throughout year, heaviest in spring. *M. c. purpureo-crocea* has salmon flowers, bluish green foliage.

Good for erosion control on moderately steep slopes. Hardiest of trailing ice plants. Plant 1–1½ ft. apart.

M. luteola. Zones 15–24. To 1 ft. Light gray green foliage. Yellow flowers, May–June and throughout year. Bloom sparse. Not for erosion control.

MALLEE. See *Eucalyptus.*

MALLOW. See *Malva.*

MALTESE CROSS. See *Lychnis chalcedonica.*

MALUS. *Rosaceae.* CRABAPPLE. Deciduous trees, rarely shrubs. Zones 1–11, 14–21. Handsome pink, white, or red flowers and fruit which is edible, showy, or sometimes both. For crabapples used in jellies, see Crabapple. Ornamental crabapples include at least 200 named kinds, and new ones appear with each year's new catalogues. Chart describes most frequently used kinds.

Most types grow 6–30 ft. high. Leaves are pointed ovals, often fuzzy, from deep green to nearly purple. Longer lived than flowering peaches, hardier and more tolerant of wet soil than flowering cherries or other flowering stone fruits, flowering crabapples are among the most useful and least troublesome of flowering trees—even if spring color is less striking than that of flowering peach or cherry. Plant bare-root trees in winter or early spring; set out container plants any time. Good, well-drained garden soil is best, but crabapples will take rocky or mildly acid or alkaline soil. They take heat. Prune only to build good framework or to correct shape; annual pruning is not necessary.

Malus floribunda

Malus sargentii

(*Continued on page 422*)

Malus-Crabapple

NAME	GROWTH RATE, HEIGHT & SPREAD	STRUCTURE	FOLIAGE	FLOWERS	FRUIT
Malus 'Almey'	Moderate to 15 by 15 ft.	Upright growth.	Purplish to bronzy green. Susceptible to disease.	Single; scarlet, white at base. April bloom.	Scarlet, hangs on well.
M. arnoldiana ARNOLD CRABAPPLE	Fairly rapid, 20 by 30 ft.	Broad, spreading, with long, arching branches.	Medium texture, fairly large leaf.	Buds red. Flowers pink, fading white, fragrant, to 2 in.	Yellow and red. Sept.–Nov.
M. atrosanguinea CARMINE CRABAPPLE	Moderate to 18 by 18 ft.	Upright branches, drooping tips. Open, irregular.	Purplish green, with more sheen than average crabapple.	Fragrant, crimson to rose pink. Profuse. Late April–May.	Yellow aging to brown. Hangs on through winter in withered state.
M. coronaria 'Charlotte'	Moderate to 30 by 30 ft.	Rounded, broad at base of crown.	Dense.	Pink, double, 2 in. May; fragrant.	Large, green, sparsely produced.
M. 'Dolgo'	Moderate to 40 by 40 ft.	Willowy, spreading; prune for good framework.	Reddish green, dense. Good disease resistance.	Profuse, white, single. Early spring bloom.	Cherrylike clusters of red, 1¼-in. fruit with good flavor, August–October.
M. 'Dorothea'	Moderate to 25 by 25 ft.	Dense, rounded.	Dense, fine textured.	May blooming; double, 2-in. pink flowers.	Marble sized, bright yellow; effective.
M. floribunda JAPANESE FLOWERING CRABAPPLE	Moderate to 20 by 30 ft.	One form is rounded, dense. The other is more upright.	Dense, fine textured. Good disease resistance.	Red to pink in bud, opening white. Extremely profuse.	Small, yellow and red, August–October.
M. 'Hopa'	Fast to 25 by 20 ft.	Upright branches spreading with weight of fruit.	Dense, dark green with brownish cast. Subject to rust, scab, and fireblight.	Fragrant, rose red, 1½-in. single flowers in April. One of best in southern California.	Orange red, coloring early. Profuse. Good for jelly.
M. hupehensis (*M. theifera*) *TEA CRABAPPLE*	Moderate to 15 by 20 ft.	Rigid branches grow at 45° angles from short trunk.	Dense on side branches, but these are spaced well apart.	Deep pink buds, pink flowers fading white, fragrant. Early May.	Not ornamental.

NAME	GROWTH RATE, HEIGHT & SPREAD	STRUCTURE	FOLIAGE	FLOWERS	FRUIT
M. ioensis 'Plena' BECHTEL CRABAPPLE	Moderate to 25 by 20 ft. 'Klehm's Improved Bechtel' is a better grower.	Coarse branches, rather angular, eventually vase shaped.	Sparse, coarse, soft green.	Large, very double, pink, fragrant. Resemble rambler rose flowers.	Rarely borne, green, not ornamental.
M. 'Katherine'	Slow to 20 by 20 ft.	Loose and open.	Dark green, not dense.	Double, light pink fading white, very large—to 2¼ in. Alternate bloom; heavy one year, light the next.	Dull red, not especially showy.
M. micromalus (*M. kaido*) MIDGET CRABAPPLE (*kaido* is Japanese for "crabapple")	Slow to 20 by 15 ft.	One strain is upright and dense. The other is smaller with irregular branches.	Dark green.	Single, unfading pink, fragrant. Very profuse in April.	Red or greenish red, not showy.
M. 'Oekonomierat Echtermeyer' ('Pink Weeper') WEEPING CRABAPPLE	Moderate to 15 ft. Spread depends on pruning.	Weeping branches. Usually grafted high on a standard crabapple. Cut out branches that grow stiffly upright.	Opening purplish, later bronzy green.	Purplish red, 1½ in. wide, all along drooping branchlets.	Purple red, 1 in., effective in fall.
M. 'Pink Perfection'	Moderate to 20 by 20 ft.	Full, rounded crown.	Thick, heavy, green; holds color to fall. Resists rust, mildew.	Red buds open to large, double pink flowers.	Yellow and insignificant.
M. 'Pink Spires'	Moderate to 15 by 10 ft.	Narrow, upright grower.	Red purple in spring, turning bronzy green. Good disease resistance.	Rose pink.	Small, purplish red.
M. 'Purple Wave'	Moderate to 10–15 by 10 ft.	Spreading, broad headed.	Dark purplish green.	Large, single to semidouble; rose red fading to purplish pink.	Dark purple red, 1 in.
M. purpurea 'Aldenhamensis' ALDENHAM CRABAPPLE	Fast to 20 by 20 ft.	Somewhat irregular round head, dense.	Purplish leaves and purplish bark on twigs.	Semidouble, purplish red, large. May, sometimes reblooming in fall.	Purplish red, 1 in.
M. p. 'Eleyi' ELEY CRABAPPLE	Fast to 20 by 20 ft.	Irregular, open, graceful.	Dark green, with reddish veins and stalks. Subject to apple scab.	Wine red, 1¼ in., April.	Heavy bearer of ¾-in. purple red fruit.
M. 'Radiant'	Fast to 20 by 20 ft.	Broad, rounded crown.	New foliage purple red, aging green.	Deep red buds open to deep pink blooms.	Bright red, ½ in. wide. Color in midsummer.
M. 'Red Jade'	Moderate to 15 by 15 ft.	Long, slender, weeping branches. Charming, irregular habit.	Dark green.	Small, white, profuse in April–May.	Heavy crop of bright red fruit holds late into fall, is showy on weeping branches.
M. 'Red Silver'	Fast to 15 by 15 ft.	Irregular, branches angular with tips drooping slightly.	Reddish or purplish bronze silvered with silky hairs.	Deep wine red, April.	Dark purplish red, ¾ in., good for jelly.
M. 'Royalty'	Moderate to 15 by 15 ft.	Dense, moundlike crown. Extremely cold hardy.	Same dark purple as purple-leaf plum. Resists scab.	Single, purplish crimson.	Dark red, nearly ¾ in. across.
M. sargentii SARGENT CRABAPPLE	Slow to 10 by 20 ft.	Dense, broad shrub with zigzag branching.	Dark green, often lobed at base. Good disease resistance.	White, small, profuse, fragrant. Pink in *M. s.* 'Rosea'. Mid-May.	Red, tiny, profuse, lasting late.
M. 'Snowdrift'	Moderate to 20–25 by 20 ft.	Rounded, dense crown.	Good green; scab resistant.	Red buds open to single white flowers. Long bloom period.	Orange red, under ½ in. wide; hangs on for a long time.
M. 'Strathmore'	Moderate to fast to 20 by 10 ft.	Narrow, upright, pyramidal.	Reddish purple leaves in summer; deepen to scarlet in fall. Subject to apple scab.	Deep pink to reddish pink.	Small red fruit.
M. zumi calocarpa	Moderate to 25 by 15 ft.	Pyramidal, dense, branching, branchlets weeping.	Densely foliaged; larger leaves lobed. Good disease resistance.	Opening soft pink, fading white; fragrant. Late April–early May.	Small, ½ in., glossy, bright red. Holds on well into winter.

M

Diseases and pests are few; fireblight can be a problem, but usually is not. The same pests that affect apple also prey on crabapple; controls are simple. If you or your neighbors grow apples, or if you wish to use crabapples from your tree, spray to control codling moths. Scale, aphids, spider mites, and tent caterpillars may require spraying. Scab, powdery mildew, and crabapple rust are serious problems in the Northwest.

Northwestern varieties especially selected for disease resistance (particularly to scab) are: 'Adams' (rounded tree to 20 ft., pink flowers, red fruit); 'Beverly' (spreading habit to 20 ft., pink flowers, red fruit); 'Liset' (spreading tree to 15 ft., rose flowers, purple leaves, maroon fruit); 'Robinson' (to 25 ft., deep pink flowers, purple leaves, red fruit); Sargent crab (see chart, page 421); 'Snowdrift' (see chart, page 421); and *M. yunnanensis* 'Veitchii' (upright, narrow to 20 ft., small white flowers, purple brown fruit, orange and red fall color).

Crabapples are fine lawn trees and may be used in rows along driveways or walks. Planted near fences, they will heighten screening effect, provide blossoms and fruit, and still give planting room for primroses, spring bulbs, or shade-loving summer bedding plants. Good espaliers.

MALVA. *Malvaceae.* MALLOW. All Zones. Herbaceous plants related to and somewhat resembling hollyhock (*Alcea*), but bushier, with smaller, roundish leaves. Easy to grow; need sunshine, good drainage, average soil. Grow from seed; usually bloom first year. Use in perennial borders or for a quick tall edging. Plants not long lived.

Malva alcea

M. alcea. Perennial. Grows to 4 ft. tall, 2 ft. wide. Saucer-shaped, 2-in.-wide, pink flowers appear from late spring to fall. Common kind is the variety 'Fastigiata', which is a narrow grower and looks much like a hollyhock.

M. sylvestris. Perennial or biennial. Erect, bushy growth to 2–4 ft. Flowers 2 in. wide appear all summer. Common variety (often sold as *M. zebrina*) has pale lavender pink flowers with pronounced deep purple veining. The variety 'Mauritiana' has deeper-colored flowers, often semidouble.

MAMMILLARIA. *Cactaceae.* Cactus. Zones 8–24. Small, cylindrical or globe shaped, either single stemmed or clustered. Plants mostly grow 2–6 in. high. Flowers generally small, arranged in circle near top of plant; red, pink, yellow, or white. Easy to grow in sun; give ample water during summer. These cacti are chiefly grown in pots by collectors. Specialists offer as many as a hundred species.

For the plant sold as *M. vivipara,* see *Coryphantha.*

Mammillaria candida

MANDARIN ORANGE. See *Citrus.*

MANDEVILLA. *Apocynaceae.* Evergreen or deciduous vines. Known for showy flowers. Includes plants formerly known as *Dipladenia.*

M. 'Alice du Pont' ***(Mandevilla splendens, M. amabilis, Dipladenia splendens, D. amoena).*** House or greenhouse plant; outdoors Zones 21–24. Evergreen vine to 20–30 ft., much less in pots or tubs (where it is usually grown). Twining stems produce dark green, glossy, oval leaves 3–8 in. long. Clusters of 2–4-in.-wide, pure pink flowers appear among leaves from April–November. Even very small plant in 4-in. pot will bloom. Plant in rich soil and provide frame, trellis, or stake for support. Pinch young plant to induce bushiness. Ample water during growth period; full sun coastal areas, part shade inland. Spray for spider mites.

Mandevilla 'Alice du Pont'

M. laxa ***(M. suaveolens).*** CHILEAN JASMINE. Deciduous vine. Zones 4–9, 14–21. Twines to 15 ft. or more. Leaves are long ovals, heart shaped at base, 2–6 in. long. Clustered summer flowers are white, 2 in. across, trumpet shaped, powerfully fragrant (like gardenia). Sun, rich soil, ample water. If plant becomes badly tangled, cut it to ground in winter; it will bloom on new growth. Root hardy to about 5°F.

M. splendens ***(M. amabilis, M.*** **'Profusa',** ***M.*** **'Red Riding Hood',** ***M. sanderi).*** Same Zones as 'Alice du Pont'. Lower growing, shrubbier than 'Alice du Pont', with deeper pink blooms. Superb hanging basket plant.

MANGIFERA indica. *Anacardiaceae.* MANGO. Evergreen tree. Zones 23, 24. Grows to large size in tropics. In mildest parts of southern California often survives for years, but may remain shrubby and is likely to fruit only in most favored, frost-free locations. Yellow to reddish flowers in long clusters at branch ends. Fruits that follow are oval, to 6 in. long, green to reddish or yellowish, with large seeds and peach-flavored flesh with varnish or turpentine overtones. Leaves are large and handsome, often coppery red or purple at time of expanding, later dark green and 8–16 in. long. Needs steady moisture, but tolerates fairly poor, shallow soils. Fruiting varieties include 'Alolia', 'Edgehill', 'Haden', and 'Manila'.

Mangifera indica

MANZANITA. See *Arctostaphylos.*

MAPLE. See *Acer.*

Marantaceae. The arrowroot family consists of tropical or subtropical herbaceous plants with fleshy rhizomes or tubers and highly irregular flowers. Most are grown for handsome foliage, a few for flowers. Examples are *Calathea* and *Maranta.*

MARANTA leuconeura. *Marantaceae.* PRAYER PLANT, RABBIT TRACKS. House or greenhouse plant with leafy stems, usually less than 1 ft. high. Leaves 7–8 in. long and half as wide, short stalked, becoming whitish along midrib and veins; brown spots toward margin account for name "rabbit tracks." Leaves fold upward at night; hence other common name, "prayer plant." In variety *kerchoviana,* undersurface of leaves is grayish and spotted with red. Small flowers are white with purple spots.

Maranta leuconeura

Grow out of direct sunlight. Must have warmth, occasional trimming, lots of water, and regular feeding (fish emulsion is good) to be at its best. Excellent in dish gardens, terrariums, or shallow pots.

MARGUERITE. See *Chrysanthemum frutescens.*

MARIGOLD. See *Tagetes.*

MARIGOLD, DESERT. See *Baileya multiradiata.*

MARIPOSA LILY. See *Calochortus venustus.*

MARJORAM. See *Origanum majorana.*

MARMALADE BUSH. See *Streptosolen jamesonii.*

MARRUBIUM vulgare. *Labiatae.* HOREHOUND. Perennial herb. All Zones. To 1–3 ft. Wrinkled, woolly, aromatic, gray green leaves; whorls of white mintlike flowers on footlong, branching stems. Grows in poor, sandy, dry soil, full sun. Sow seeds in spring in flats; later transplant to 1 ft. apart. As garden plant, it's rather weedy looking but can serve as edging in gray garden. Used for medicinal purposes and in candy. Foliage lasts well in bouquets.

Marrubium vulgare

MARSH MARIGOLD. See *Caltha palustris.*

MATILIJA POPPY. See *Romneya coulteri.*

MATRICARIA recutita *(M. chamomilla).* *Compositae.* CHAMOMILE. Summer annual. This is the chamomile which yields a fragrant tea with overtones of pineapple. Plants grow 2–2½ ft. tall, with finely cut, almost fernlike foliage and daisylike white and yellow flower heads an inch (or less) wide. Grows easily in full sun, ordinary soil from seed sown in late winter or spring. Needs little or no irrigation once started. Has become naturalized in some areas. Dried flowers are the parts used in making tea.

Matricaria recutita

Plants or seeds sold as *Matricaria* 'White Stars', 'Golden Ball', and 'Snowball' are varieties of *Chrysanthemum parthenium.* Chamomile sold as walk-on ground cover is *Chamaemelum nobile* (*Anthemis nobilis*). Its flowers yield medicinal-tasting, rather bitter tea.

MATTEUCCIA struthiopteris. *Polypodiaceae.* OSTRICH FERN. Zones 1–10, 14–24. Native to northern Europe and Asia. Hardy to extreme cold, but indifferent grower in mild-winter areas. Clumps narrow at base, spreading at top in shuttlecock effect. Can grow to 6 ft. in moist, moderate climates, but reaches only 1½–2 ft. in mountains where season is short, humidity low. Spreads slowly by underground rhizomes. Dormant in winter. *M. pensylvanica* (from eastern North America) is similar. Both are attractive woodland or waterside plants, needing rich soil, ample water, shade except near coast.

Matteuccia struthiopteris

MATTHIOLA. *Cruciferae.* STOCK. Annuals (technically, biennials or perennials grown as annuals). All have long, narrow, gray green leaves and flowers in erect clusters.

M. incana. STOCK. Valued for fragrance, cut flowers, garden decoration. Leaves oblong to 4 in. long. Flowers single or double, 1 in. wide, in spikes. Colors include white, pink, red, purple, lavender, cream. Blues and reds are purple toned, yellows tend toward cream. Spicy-sweet fragrance.

Stock needs light, fertile soil, good drainage, cool weather. Valuable winter flowers in Zones 8, 9, 12–24—there, set out plants in early fall for winter or early spring bloom. Plants take moderate frost, but will not set flower buds if nights are too chilly; late planting will mean late flowers. Where rainfall is heavy, plant in raised beds to ensure good drainage, prevent root rot. In Zones 1–7, 10, 11, plant in earliest spring to get bloom before hot weather.

Matthiola incana

Many strains available. Column stock and Double Giant Flowering are unbranched, 2–3 ft. tall, and can be planted 6–8 in. apart in rows; ideal for cutting. Giant Imperial strain is branched, 2–2½ ft. tall, comes in straight colors or mixed. Trysomic or Ten Weeks stock is branched, 15–18 in. tall. Trysomic Seven Weeks strain is 12–15 in. tall.

M. longipetala bicornis. EVENING SCENTED STOCK. Summer annual. Foot-tall plant with lance-shaped leaves to 3½ in. long. Small purplish flowers are closed and inconspicuous by day, wonderfully fragrant at night. Full sun. Routine watering.

MATTRESS VINE. See *Muehlenbeckia complexa.*

MAYBUSH, MAYDAY TREE. See *Prunus padus.*

MAYTENUS boaria. *Celastraceae.* MAYTEN TREE. Evergreen tree. Zones 8, 9, 14–21. Slow to moderate growth to an eventual 30–50 ft.; 20 ft. tall by 15 ft. wide at 12 years is typical. Long, pendulous branchlets hang down from branches, giving tree daintiness and grace. Habit and leaves (1–2 in. long) give tree the look of a small-scale weeping willow. Better tree for patio than weeping willow—neater and with less invasive roots. Without deep watering, it will root voraciously near surface of soil and invade planting beds. Flowers and fruit inconspicuous.

Maytenus boaria

Good drainage is crucial. Stake securely when planting. There will be much side growth; remove unwanted growth along trunk, or, if you wish, preserve some side branches for multiple trunk effect. Will take some drought when established, but is lusher and greener with adequate water. Sometimes may show partial defoliation after cold snaps or at blooming time; recovery is rapid. Resistant to oak root fungus. For uniformity, plant cutting-grown variety 'Green Showers'; its weeping branchlets are densely clad with deep green leaves that are a little broader than those of most seedling trees.

Will thrive in a lawn, but can send up suckers, especially if roots are disturbed. Locate to display its pattern effectively—against walls in entryway or patio, in featured raised planting beds, near outdoor living areas.

MAZUS reptans. *Scrophulariaceae.* Perennial. Zones 1–7 (freezes to ground in winter), 14–24 (evergreen). Slender stems creep and root along ground, send up leafy branches 1–2 in. tall. Leaves an inch long, narrowish, bright green, with a few teeth on edges. Flowers (spring, early summer) in clusters of 2–5, purplish blue with white and yellow markings, about ¾ in. across. In shape, flowers resemble those of mimulus. Sun or very light shade; rich, moist soil. Rock gardens or small-scale ground cover. Takes very light foot traffic.

Mazus reptans

MEADOW RUE. See *Thalictrum.*

MEADOW SAFFRON. See *Colchicum autumnale.*

MECONOPSIS. *Papaveraceae.* Perennials. Ardent collectors and shade garden enthusiasts sometimes attempt the many species offered by specialist seed firms. Most are difficult, but the 2 listed here are not too hard to grow in right climate.

M. betonicifolia *(M. baileyi).* HIMALAYAN POPPY. Zones 1–7, 17.

(Continued on next page)

M

Tall, leafy, short-lived perennial 2–4 ft. tall with hairy leaves and silky, 3–4-in.-wide poppies of sky blue or rosy lavender, centered with yellow stamens. Needs shade, humid air, coolness, loose, acid soil, summer watering. Try it with rhododendrons.

Meconopsis betonicifolia

M. cambrica. WELSH POPPY. Zones 1–9, 14–17. Short-lived perennial with 3-in., yellow or orange flowers on 1-ft. stems. Gray green divided leaves. Full sun or light shade near coast, part shade inland. Can take a little or a lot of summer water. Self-sows.

MEDITERRANEAN FAN PALM. See *Chamaerops humilis.*

MELALEUCA. *Myrtaceae.* Evergreen trees and shrubs. Narrow, sometimes needlelike leaves; clustered flowers with prominent stamens. Each cluster resembles a bottlebrush, and some melaleucas are called bottlebrushes, although that name is more generally applied to *Callistemon.* Clusters of woody seed capsules hang on for several years, forming odd, decorative cylinders around twigs and branches. Flowers attract birds.

Melaleuca linariifolia

Most melaleucas stand heat, wind, poor soil, drought, and salt air; exceptions, noted below, are important. Most are vigorous and fast growing; control by cutting back selected branches to a well-placed side branch. Shearing makes plants dense and lumpish. Smaller melaleucas are good screening materials; some of the larger ones are useful as flowering or shade trees. Many have interestingly contorted branches and bark that peels in thick, papery layers.

Australia is home to 140 or more species, and it is likely that many of these will show up in Western gardens. All are easy to grow.

M. armillaris. DROOPING MELALEUCA. Shrub or small tree. Zones 9, 12–24. To 15–30 ft. Furrowed gray bark peels off in strips near base of trunk. Drooping branches. Light green, needlelike leaves to 1 in. long. Fluffy white flowers in 1–3½-in.-long spikes, spring to fall. Tough and adaptable, especially useful in sea winds. Clipped hedge or unclipped informal screen (prickly leaves a real deterrent), or, with training, a sprawling shrub or small tree.

M. decussata. LILAC MELALEUCA. Large shrub or small tree. Zones 9, 12–24. Grows 8–20 ft. tall with equal spread. Brown, shredding bark. Tiny (½-in.-long) leaves close-set on arching, pendulous branches. Lilac to purple flowers in 1-in. spikes, late spring to summer. Will stand some neglect. Use it to supply big masses of fine-textured, bluish foliage. Thinning will improve its appearance by showing off trunk, branch character.

M. elliptica. Shrub or small tree. Zones 9, 12–24. To 8–15 ft. high. Brown, shredding bark. Roundish, ½-in.-long leaves mostly at ends of fanlike branches. Large, showy, red to crimson bottlebrushes to 3½ in. long, on side branches, early spring to fall.

M. ericifolia. HEATH MELALEUCA. Shrub or small tree. Zones 9, 12–24. To 10–25 ft. Bark tan or gray, soft, fibrous. Dark green, needlelike, 1-in. leaves like those of heather. Yellowish white flowers in 1-in. spikes, in early spring. Fast growing and tolerant of alkaline soil and poor drainage; good near beach. Attractive multitrunked tree.

M. hypericifolia. DOTTED MELALEUCA. Shrub. Zones 9, 12–24. Grows 6–10 ft. tall, with thin, peeling bark, drooping branches. Coppery green to dull green, 1¼-in. leaves, bright orange red flowers in dense 2-in. clusters, late spring through winter (often hidden by foliage). Can be clipped into hedge, but will bloom more profusely as informal, unclipped screen. Not suitable for planting right at beach, but takes ocean wind, drought.

M. linariifolia. FLAXLEAF PAPERBARK. Tree. Zones 9, 13–23. To 30 ft., with umbrellalike crown. White bark sheds in papery flakes. Slender branchlets. Bright green or bluish green, 1¼-in.-long leaves are stiff, needlelike. Numerous fluffy spikes of small white flowers in summer give effect of snow on branches. Young plants willowy, need staking until trunk firms up; prune out lower branches to shape.

M. nesophila. PINK MELALEUCA. Tree or large shrub. Zones 13, 16–24. Fast growth to 15–20 or possibly 30 ft. Grows naturally as small tree; unpruned, produces gnarled, heavy branches that sprawl or ascend in picturesque patterns. Thick, spongy bark. Gray green, thick, roundish, 1-in. leaves. Roundish (to inch-wide) mauve flower brushes at branch ends, produced most of year, fade to white with yellow tips. Takes beach winds and spray; poor, rocky soil; desert heat; much or practically no water. Use as tree or big informal screen, or shear as hedge.

M. quinquenervia (usually sold as *M. leucadendra*). CAJEPUT TREE. Tree. Zones 9, 13–17, 20–24. Upright, open growth to 20–40 ft. Young branches pendulous. Trunk has thick, spongy, light brown to whitish bark that peels off in sheets. (You can use these sheets to line wire hanging baskets.) Leaves stiff, narrowly oval, pale green, shiny, 2–4 in. long. Young leaves have silky hairs. Foliage turns purple with light frost. Flowers yellowish white (sometimes pink or purple), in 2–3-in. spikes, summer and fall. Can take much or little water. Good street tree. Planted 8–10 ft. apart and thinned occasionally, trees make pleasant groves.

M. styphelioides. Tree. Zones 9, 13–24. To 20–40 ft. Pendulous branchlets; lacy, open growth habit. Thick, pale, spongy, light tan bark becomes charcoal with age, peels off in papery layers. Light green leaves to ¾ in. long, ¼ in. wide, sometimes twisted, prickly to touch. Creamy white flowers in 1–2-in. brushes, summer through fall. Thrives in any soil; resistant to oak root fungus. Good lawn tree. Best trained with multiple trunks.

MELAMPODIUM leucanthum. *Compositae.* BLACKFOOT DAISY. Short-lived perennial. Zones 1–3, 10–13. Native to Arizona, New Mexico, Mexico, Texas. Foot-tall, foot-wide clumps of narrow gray leaves are topped by clouds of inch-wide daisies, white with yellow centers. Rays are broad and full; plant is showy when in bloom. In mild-winter climates, it blooms off and on during winter months and more heavily April–October—if given water. Where freezing temperatures are routine, expect spring and summer bloom only. Plants need full sun and fast-draining soil; in nature, they grow principally in decomposed granite. If plants become too straggly for good looks, cut them back in autumn.

Melampodium leucanthum

Melastomataceae. The melastoma family consists almost entirely of tropical shrubs and trees with strongly veined leaves and regular (symmetrical) flowers. Examples are Spanish shawl (*Heterocentron*) and princess flower (*Tibouchina*).

MELIA azedarach. *Meliaceae.* CHINABERRY. Deciduous tree. Zones 6, 8–24. Spreading tree to 30–50 ft. high. Leaves 1–3 ft. long, cut into many 1–2-in.-long, narrow or oval, toothed leaflets. Loose clusters of lilac flowers in spring or early summer, fragrant in evening, followed by yellow, hard, berrylike fruit ½ in. across. Fruit poisonous if eaten in quantity, but birds enjoy it.

M. a. 'Umbraculiformis'. TEXAS UMBRELLA TREE. Less picturesque but far more common, with a dense, spreading, dome-shaped crown and drooping leaves. Grows to 30 ft.

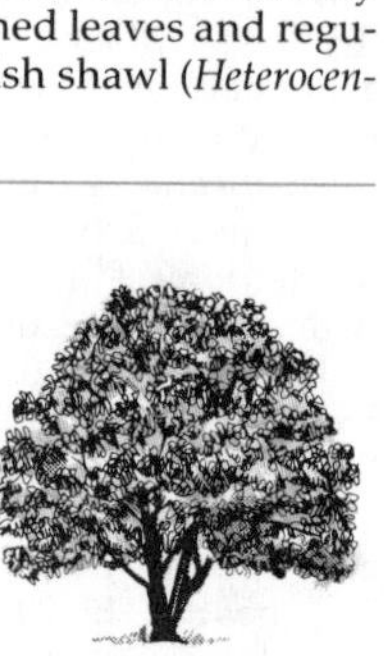

Melia azedarach 'Umbraculiformis'

Gives rich green color, dense shade in hottest, driest climates; grows even in poor alkaline soil. Leaves turn gold in autumn. Stands all but strongest ocean winds. Has brittle wood and sometimes suckers, but is valuable where trees are hard to grow.

Melia azedarach 'Umbraculiformis'

Meliaceae. The mahogany family, consisting largely of tropical trees or shrubs, contains 2 plants grown in the West: *Cedrela* and *Melia*. Both have finely divided leaves and clustered flowers.

MELIANTHUS major. *Melianthaceae.* HONEY BUSH. Evergreen shrub. Zones 8, 9, 12–24. Soft-wooded plant of very fast growth to 12–14 ft., but easily kept much lower. Stems slightly branched, upright or sprawling and spreading. Striking foliage: 1-ft.-long, grayish green leaves divided into 9–11 strongly toothed leaflets (leaves smell disagreeable when brushed or bruised). Foot-long spikes of reddish brown, 1-in.-long flowers in late winter, early spring.

Melianthus major

Adapts to most soils and most locations, but best in some shade in desert and other hot gardens. To get tall plants, stake a few stems; for sprawling, bulky effect, shorten some stems in early spring before new growth begins. Needs grooming. Spray to control whitefly. Excellent when used as silhouette in raised beds, sprawling over wall, in containers, with succulents or foliage plants.

M. minor. Rare plant occasionally seen at plant sales or in collectors' gardens. Leaves are much smaller (6–7 in.), on shorter (3-ft.) plants.

MELISSA officinalis. *Labiatae.* LEMON BALM, SWEET BALM. Perennial herb. All Zones. To 2 ft. Light green, heavily veined leaves with lemon scent. White flowers unimportant. Shear occasionally to keep compact. Spreads rapidly. Grow in rich, moist soil, in sun or part shade. Very hardy. Propagate from seed or root divisions. Self-sows. Leaves used in drinks, fruit cups, salads, fish dishes. Dried leaves help give lemon tang to sachets, potpourris.

Melissa officinalis

MELON, MUSKMELON, CANTALOUPE. *Cucurbitaceae.* Annual. (The true cantaloupe, a hard-shelled melon, is rarely grown in this country.) To ripen to full sweetness, a melon needs 2½–4 months of heat. Foggy or cool summer days don't help. Gardeners in cool-summer climates should plant melons in warmest southern exposures. In both cool-summer climates and interior short-summer climates, start plants indoors in peat pots a few weeks before last frost date; truly tropical plants, melons perish in even light frost. Black plastic mulch under melons warms soil, speeds harvest, helps keep melons from rotting. Plastic row covers permit earlier planting out of doors.

Melon

Melons need considerable space (dimensions described below) in full sun. You can grow melons on sun-bathed trellises, but heavy fruit must be supported in individual cloth slings.

Principal types are muskmelons ("cantaloupes") and late melons. The former are ribbed, with netted skin and (usually) salmon-colored flesh; these are most widely adapted to various western climates. Good ones (best types for cooler climates) are 'Hale's Best', 'Honey Rock', and the hybrids 'Ambrosia', 'Mainerock' (early), 'Samson', and 'Saticoy'. Hybrids are superior to others in disease resistance and uniformity of size and quality. Small, tasty, highly perfumed melons from Mediterranean (and hybrids of these) are white-fleshed 'Ha-Ogen' and orange-fleshed 'Chaca' and 'Charentais'. Late melons ripen only where there is a long, hot, rather dry summer (Zones 8, 9, 12–14, 18, 19); members of this group are 'Persian', 'Honey Dew', 'Honey Ball', 'Golden Beauty Casaba', and 'Crenshaw'.

Except as noted above, sow seeds 2 weeks after average date of last frost. Soil should be light and well drained. Best planted on gently rounded mounds 6 ft. wide, a few inches high at center, and as long as your garden will permit. On south side of mounds make furrows 10 in. wide and 6 in. deep for irrigation. Water well until furrows are filled. Plant 6 or 7 seeds about 1 in. deep, spaced within an 8–10-in. circle, 6 in. or so away from furrow. Space these circles (hills) 3 ft. apart. This system permits watering plants from below without wetting foliage.

When plants are well established, thin each hill to the best 2, and begin to train them away from furrow. Fill furrow with water from time to time, but do not keep soil soaked. Feed (again in furrow) every 6 weeks. Harvest muskmelon and 'Persian' melon when stems begin to crack away from melon end. 'Honey Dew' and 'Casaba' are ready when rinds turn yellow; 'Crenshaw' melons turn mostly yellow, but show some green even when ripe. Most reliable way to determine degree of ripeness of these melons is to smell blossom end. Ripe ones have pleasant, fruity perfume.

MENTHA. *Labiatae.* MINT. Perennial herbs and ground cover. Spread rapidly by underground stems. Once established, surprisingly drought tolerant. Can be quite invasive. Grow almost anywhere but perform best in light, medium-rich, moist soil, partial shade. Contain in pot or box to keep in bounds. Propagate from runners. Keep flowers cut off. Replant every 3 years.

Mentha spicata

M. gentilis. GOLDEN APPLE MINT. All Zones. To 2 ft. Smooth, deep green leaves, variegated yellow. Flowers inconspicuous. Use in flavoring foods. Foliage excellent in mixed bouquets.

M. piperita. PEPPERMINT. All Zones. To 3 ft. Strong-scented, toothed, 3-in.-long leaves. Small purple flowers in 1–3-in. spikes. Leaves good for flavoring tea. *M. p. citrata*, ORANGE MINT, BERGAMOT MINT, grows to 2 ft. and has broad, 2-in.-long leaves, small lavender flowers. It is used in potpourris or like other mints in flavoring foods. Crushed leaves have slight orange flavor.

M. pulegium. PENNYROYAL. Zones 4–24. Creeping plant grows a few inches tall with nearly round 1-in. leaves. Small lavender flowers in tight, short whorls. Strong mint fragrance and flavor. Poisonous in large quantities, but safe as a flavoring. Needs cool, moist site, with shade in hottest areas.

M. requienii. JEWEL MINT OF CORSICA. Creeping, mat-forming perennial. Zones 5–9, 12–24. Spreads at moderate to rapid rate, grows only ½ in. high. Tiny, round, bright green leaves give mossy effect. Tiny light purple flowers in summer. Set divisions 6 in. apart for ground cover in sun or part shade. Needs moisture; disappears during winter in colder areas. Delightful minty or sagelike fragrance when leaves are bruised or crushed underfoot.

M. spicata. SPEARMINT. All Zones. To 1½–2 ft. Dark green leaves, slightly smaller than those of peppermint; leafy spikes of purplish flowers. Use leaves fresh from garden or dried, for lamb, in cold drinks, as garnish, in apple jelly.

M. suaveolens (usually sold as *M. rotundifolia*). APPLE MINT. All Zones. Stiff stems grow 20–30 in. tall. Rounded leaves are slightly hairy, gray green, 1–4 in. long. Purplish white flowers in 2–3-in. spikes. Leaves have apple-mint fragrance. *M. s.* 'Variegata', PINEAPPLE MINT, has leaves with white markings, faint fragrance of pineapple.

M

MENTZELIA. *Loasaceae.* BLAZING STAR. Annuals, biennials, or perennials. All Zones. Native to desert or semidesert areas of western U.S. They tolerate heat, wind, and poor soil but require good drainage and full sun. Star-shaped yellow blossoms are large and showy.

Mentzelia lindleyi

M. laevicaulis. Biennial or short-lived perennial grows to 3–3½ ft. tall, rough and ungainly. Narrow, 3–7-in.-long leaves. Spectacular pale yellow, 4-in.-wide stars open in the evening; plant is often called evening star. It requires summer drought and excellent drainage. Best use is on bare banks, where it's perfectly at home.

M. lindleyi. Summer annual 1–4 ft. tall, usually narrow, sometimes spreading to 1½ ft. Light green, rough-textured leaves with short hairs. Flowers bright yellow with orange or reddish center ring and big brush of yellow stamens. Blooms April–June. Sow seed in fall, winter, or earliest spring where plants are to bloom; give ample water until plants come into bloom, then reduce or stop watering. Use alone or in wildflower mixtures.

MERTENSIA. *Boraginaceae.* Perennials. Zones 1–21. Resemble giant-size forget-me-nots (*Myosotis*) and are related to them. Plants appear and flower early, go dormant soon after seeding, usually before midsummer. Foliage usually smooth gray green or blue green. Flowers nodding, in loose, gradually uncoiling clusters, pink or lavender in bud opening to blue bells, sometimes with pinkish cast. Hardy and attractive in shade with ample moisture during growth and bloom. Good with naturalized daffodils or with ferns, trilliums in woodland gardens.

Mertensia virginica

M. ciliata. CHIMING BELLS, MOUNTAIN BLUEBELL. Native to damp places in Rocky Mountains. Grows 1–3 ft. tall, with ½–¾-in. flowers. Several other species grow in mountainous areas of West; most are lower growing.

M. virginica. VIRGINIA BLUEBELLS. From eastern U.S. Most widely planted species. Grows 1–2 ft. tall; flowers are 1 in. long. Widely available from mail-order bulb or plant catalogues.

MERYTA sinclairi. *Araliaceae.* PUKA. Shrub or small tree. Zones 17, 23, 24; house plant anywhere. Not often seen outside its native New Zealand. Young plants have single, upright stems several feet tall with huge (8–20-in.), leathery, oval, dark green leaves. Older plants eventually branch and become broad, rounded trees 15–18 ft. tall. Flowers, fruit inconspicuous. Rich soil, ample water and feeding, light shade.

Meryta sinclairi

MESCAL BEAN. See *Sophora secundiflora.*

MESEMBRYANTHEMUM crystallinum. *Aizoaceae.* ICE PLANT. Summer annual. Least ornamental of many plants commonly called *Mesembryanthemum* or ice plant, but now considered the only true *Mesembryanthemum.* Grow in full sun. Needs little or no water once established. For other, showier kinds used as ground covers or ornamentals, see entry under Ice Plant.

Mesembryanthemum crystallinum

M. crystallinum is a sprawling plant a few inches tall and several feet wide. Oval, flat, stalked, fleshy leaves grow up to 4 in. long, turn red in dry season. Leaves covered with tiny transparent blisters that glisten like flecks of ice. Foliage is edible and resembles New Zealand spinach. Inch-wide flowers white to pinkish. Easy to grow from seed. Plant has become wild in parts of California.

MESQUITE. See *Prosopis.*

METASEQUOIA glyptostroboides. *Taxodiaceae.* DAWN REDWOOD. Deciduous conifer. Zones 3–9, 14–24. To 80–90 ft. high. Looks somewhat like coast redwood (*Sequoia sempervirens*) but differs in several ways. Cones are much smaller; leaves are soft to the touch and light, bright green, while those of coast redwood are dark green and somewhat stiff. Dawn redwood's light brown branchlets turn upward; those of coast redwood usually stand out horizontally. Most important, foliage of dawn redwood turns light bronze in autumn, then falls; coast redwood is evergreen.

Metasequoia glyptostroboides

Stands temperatures from −15° to 105°F., but suffers winter wind damage in cold, dry areas. Salt winds cause foliage burn, as does hot sunlight in enclosed areas. Grows best in moist, well-drained soil containing peat moss or leaf mold; takes lawn watering well. Resistant to oak root fungus.

Best use is in groves, where it brings something of the beauty of a redwood grove to cold-winter areas. However, also good for single planting—swelling buds and bright, silky new needles are a real treat in spring. Structurally interesting even when bare. Trunks of older trees show rugged, fluted bases. Grows very fast when young, sometimes 4–6 ft. a year in California, less in colder areas. Young tree grows satisfactorily in large tub or box.

METROSIDEROS. *Myrtaceae.* Evergreen trees or large shrubs. Native to New Zealand. Plants generally branch heavily from ground up, require careful staking and pruning to bring into tree form. Leaves firm, leathery, densely spaced on branches. Flowers, clustered at ends of branches, are red (rarely yellow or white). Dense, clustered stamens make the show; along coast, trees rival *Eucalyptus ficifolia* in flower color.

Metrosideros excelsus

Best near coast; frost, dry air limit success inland. Most dependable first-line trees near beach, since they tolerate wind and salt spray. Water through the first 2 dry seasons; thereafter, they should be drought resistant. Useful lawn trees; good street trees, but if growing in narrow parking strip, can break sidewalk.

M. excelsus *(M. tomentosus).* NEW ZEALAND CHRISTMAS TREE, POHUTUKAWA. Zones 17, 23, 24. Grows to 30 ft. or more. Foliage on young plants smooth, glossy green; older plants develop leaves which are dark green above, white and woolly underneath. Dark scarlet flowers in big clusters cover ends of branches May–July (in December in New Zealand, hence common name "Christmas tree"). *Pohutukawa* means "drenched with spray," and describes very well seashore conditions where wild plants grow. There is a yellow-flowered variety, 'Aurea'. In humid coastside gardens old plants sometimes grow aerial roots which reach the ground.

M. kermadecensis *(M. villosus).* Zones 17, 20–24. Shrubby, fairly upright plant. Smaller than *M. excelsus,* with smaller grayish leaves, red flowers produced sporadically through year. Showier than *M. excelsus* when in bloom. Has withstood 22°F. *M. k.* 'Variegata' has leaves with creamy markings.

M. robustus. NORTH ISLAND RATA. Zones 17, 23, 24. To 45 ft. or more. Leaves 1–1½ in. long, dark green, roundish. New shoots and foliage coppery red. Flowers (in midsummer) scarlet. Blooms young.

M. umbellatus *(M. lucidus).* SOUTHERN RATA. Zones 16, 17, 20–24. Slow growth to large bush; eventually may become tree 45–60 ft. tall. New leaves flushed red; mature leaves 1–3½ in. long, silky when young, later glossy. Midsummer flowers are scarlet. This bush is slow-growing, as well as very slow to come into bloom (15–20 years). Tolerant of frosts and constant wind. Needs plenty of water.

MEXICAN BLUE PALM. See *Brahea armata*.

MEXICAN DAISY. See *Erigeron karvinskianus*.

MEXICAN FAN PALM. See *Washingtonia robusta*.

MEXICAN FIRE BUSH. See *Kochia scoparia trichophylla*.

MEXICAN FIRE PLANT. See *Euphorbia heterophylla*.

MEXICAN FLAME VINE. See *Senecio confusus*.

MEXICAN ORANGE. See *Choisya ternata*.

MEXICAN PALO VERDE. See *Parkinsonia aculeata*.

MEXICAN SHELL FLOWER. See *Tigridia pavonia*.

MEXICAN SUNFLOWER. See *Tithonia rotundifolia*.

MEXICAN TREE FERN. See *Cibotium schiedei*.

MEXICAN TULIP POPPY. See *Hunnemannia fumariifolia*.

MICHAELMAS DAISY. See *Aster*.

MICHELIA. *Magnoliaceae*. Evergreen trees or shrubs. Related to magnolias, but with numerous flowers borne among leaves rather than singly at ends of branches.

Michelia doltsopa

M. doltsopa. Big evergreen shrub or tree. Zones 14–24. Ultimate size in this country not known, but tall tree in its native Himalayas. Has grown to 25 ft. in as many years in San Francisco. Varies from bushy to narrow and upright; choose plants for desired form and prune to shape. Leaves thin, leathery, dark green, 3–8 in. long, 1–3 in. wide. Flowers open January–March from brown, furry buds that form in profusion among leaves near branch ends. Flowers creamy or white, slightly tinged green at base of petals, 5–7 in. wide, fragrant, with 12–16 about 1-in.-wide petals. They somewhat resemble flowers of saucer magnolia (*M. soulangiana*). Needs rich soil, ample water.

Because of propagation difficulties, plant availability is unpredictable. Seedlings are somewhat variable in form and grafting is not always successful.

M. figo *(M. fuscata).* BANANA SHRUB. Evergreen shrub. Zones 9, 14–24. Slow growth to 6–8 ft., possibly to 15 ft. Dense habit, with glossy, 3-in.-long, medium green leaves. Heavy bloom season March–May, but plants often show scattered bloom throughout the summer. Flowers 1–1½ in. wide, creamy yellow shaded brownish purple, resembling small magnolias. Notable feature is powerful, fruity fragrance; most people think it resembles smell of ripe bananas. Rich, well-drained soil in sun; partial shade best in hottest climates. Ample water. Fragrance best in warm, wind-free spot. Choice plant for entryway or patio.

MICKEY MOUSE PLANT. See *Ochna serrulata*.

MICROBIOTA decussata. *Cupressaceae*. All Zones. Native to Siberian mountains and hardy to any amount of cold. Neat, sprawling shrub that resembles a trailing arborvitae. Grows to 1½ ft. tall, 7–8 ft. wide, with many horizontal or trailing plumelike branches closely set with scalelike leaves. Foliage green in summer, reddish brown in winter. Average soil and water; sun (light shade in hottest climates). Bank cover.

Microbiota decussata

MICROLEPIA. *Polypodiaceae*. Ferns. Zones 17, 23, 24. Sturdy plants, useful for landscaping shaded areas in mild climates. Both species below can take fairly dry soil.

M. firma. Native to India. Fronds dull green, delicately cut, triangular, to 3 ft. long. Surfaces densely hairy. Hardy to 28°F.

M. strigosa (sometimes sold as *M. speluncae*). LACE FERN. Native to tropical Asia. Robust fern with delicate fronds. Grows 2–3 ft. tall. Hardy to 28°F.

Microlepia strigosa

MICROMERIA chamissonis. See *Satureja douglasii*.

MIGNONETTE. See *Reseda odorata*.

MILFOIL. See *Achillea millefolium*.

MILIUM effusum 'Aureum'. *Gramineae*. BOWLES' GOLDEN GRASS. Perennial. All Zones. Attractive clumping grass to 2 ft. tall, usually less. Leaves erect, then arching and weeping, bright greenish gold in color. Effective for spot of color in woodland garden, shaded rock garden.

Milium effusum

MILKBUSH. See *Euphorbia tirucalli*.

MILLA biflora. *Amaryllidaceae*. Bulb. Zones 13, 16–24. Native to Arizona, New Mexico, northern Mexico. Grasslike basal leaves. Clusters of white, green-striped buds open to flat, starlike, fragrant flowers that are white inside, green outside. Spring bloom. Stems to 1½ ft. high. Hardy (with mulch) in fairly cold winters. Average water. Plant in October in sunny border, rock garden, or as edging. Or plant in pots for late winter, early spring bloom indoors. Plants sold under this name are often *Zephyranthes candida*, a plant with rushlike leaves and white, long-tubed flowers in late summer, fall.

Milla biflora

MILLETTIA reticulata. *Leguminosae*. EVERGREEN WISTERIA. Zones 20–24. Vigorous, twining vine that can reach great size. Shiny, leathery leaves divided into leaflets like those of wisteria; evergreen only in frost-free areas. Tight clusters of dark purple red flowers in fall have odor of cedar and camphor. An extremely fast grower when established; if permitted to climb into trees, it can overwhelm them. Best use is as cover for large arbor or pergola, or as chain-link fence cover.

Millettia reticulata

M

MILTONIA. *Orchidaceae.* PANSY ORCHID. Epiphytic orchids. Greenhouse or indoors. Native to tropical or subtropical Americas. Many lovely large-flowered hybrids listed in catalogues. Flower colors include yellow, white, red, and blends of these colors. Flat, pansylike blooms, borne singly or in clusters on arching stems, last a month or more on plant (not good cut flowers). Plants have short pseudobulbs and long, graceful, light green leaves that produce clump of foliage a foot or more in diameter. Thrive in shade in cool night temperatures (50°–60°F. is ideal). Keep moist and medium warm when flower spikes are forming; water less frequently in winter. Grow in finely cut but firmly packed osmunda fiber or in fine-sized ground bark or prepared, bark-based mix.

Miltonia hybrid

MIMOSA. Gardeners from East and South often use this name for silk tree (*Albizia julibrissin*). *Acacia baileyana* and other fine-leafed acacias are also sometimes called "mimosa."

MIMOSA pudica. *Leguminosae.* SENSITIVE PLANT. Tender perennial usually grown as house plant curiosity. To 1½ ft. or less. Leaves finely cut into tiny leaflets. When touched or otherwise disturbed, leaves and branchlets droop and fold up with astonishing speed. (They quickly expand again.) Small pink "silk tree" blossoms. Grow from seed indoors or in bright light in a warm greenhouse. They will grow outdoors, but are not sufficiently attractive for garden. Transplant carefully to 4-in. pots. Avoid overwatering. Their only use is to demonstrate movement in plants; children find them fascinating. Plant is a weed in Hawaii.

Mimosa pudica

MIMULUS. *Scrophulariaceae.* MONKEY FLOWER. Perennials, some grown as annuals, or shrubby evergreen perennials. The latter, often known as *Diplacus*, are showy, drought-tolerant plants for Zones 7–9, 14–24. They grow 1–4 ft. tall and branch from base. Narrow, glossy dark green leaves are often sticky. Tubular, lipped flowers, 1–3 in. long, bloom over a long period in late spring, summer. Pruned after first flowering, they often bloom again in fall or, with some water, flower repeatedly throughout most of the year. Prune in spring before growth starts. Sow seed or set out plants in fall for bloom next summer. Make cuttings of most desirable plants to preserve best colors (easy to root in moist sand). Need sun, well-drained soil. Monkey flower plants are among the most colorful of native Western plants.

Mimulus hybridus

Of the species described below, *M. cardinalis*, *M. hybridus*, and *M. lewisii* need partial shade except in fog belt, damp soil. Good in pots.

M. aurantiacus *(Diplacus aurantiacus).* STICKY MONKEY FLOWER. California native to 4 ft. tall, with sticky foliage and 1½-in., buff orange, funnel-shaped flowers. Drought tolerant.

M. bifidus *(Diplacus grandiflorus).* PLUMAS MONKEY FLOWER. Large, pale yellow to peach pink flowers resemble those of deciduous azaleas.

M. cardinalis. Perennial. Zones 4–24. Native to Oregon, California, Nevada, and Arizona. To 1–2 ft. with rather floppy stems. Leaves light green, 1–4½ in. long, sharply toothed, sticky. Flowers 1½–2 in. long, scarlet, 2 lipped, bloom July–October. Takes lots of heat if given partial shade and plenty of water.

M. hybridus. Short-lived perennial, usually grown as annual. All Zones. Smooth, succulent leaves and stems; leaves veined, toothed. Flowers 2–2½ in. wide, ivory to yellow, orange, rose, scarlet, and brown, usually with heavy brownish maroon spotting or mottling. Need shade, moisture, soil with high organic content. Can take sun in Zones 17, 24. Use in pots, hanging baskets, with ferns, primroses. Sow in spring for summer bloom, or set out nursery plants. Choice strains are Calypso, Malibu, and Queen's Prize.

M. lewisii. Perennial, often grown as annual. All Zones. Native to streams and wet places in western mountains. Plants erect to 2½ ft. high, slightly sticky. Leaves 1–3 in. long, irregularly toothed. Flowers rose red or pink, about 2 in. long, sometimes blotched or streaked maroon, with yellow lines in throat. Adapted to wet but well-drained places in rock gardens.

M. longiflorus *(Diplacus longiflorus).* Much-branched, 3-ft. shrub. Zones 16, 17, 20–24. Native to coastal southern California. Flowers vary from cream to orange yellow; *M. l. rutilus* has velvety red flowers. Many hybrids have been raised in shades of cream, yellow, orange, copper, rose, salmon, red, and mahogany. These are not quite as tough as wild species; they appreciate water every 1–2 weeks in summer.

Mimulus longiflorus

MING ARALIA. See *Polyscias fruticosa*.

MINT. See *Mentha*.

MIRABILIS jalapa. *Nyctaginaceae.* FOUR O'CLOCK. Perennial in Zones 4–24; summer annual in Zones 1–3. Tuberous roots can be dug and stored like dahlia roots. Erect, many-branched stems grow quickly to form mounded clumps, 3–4 ft. high and wide. Trumpet-shaped flowers, in red, yellow, or white with variations of shades between, open in midafternoon. Deep green, oval, 2–6-in.-long leaves and strong, bushy habit give plants the substance and character of shrubs (even though only temporary or seasonal). Jingles strain is lower growing than old-fashioned kinds, has elaborately splashed and stained flowers in 2 or 3 colors all at once. Sow seed in sunny, open location in early spring for blooms from midsummer through fall. Reseeds readily. Drought tolerant.

Mirabilis jalapa

MIRROR PLANT. See *Coprosma repens*.

MISCANTHUS sinensis. *Gramineae.* EULALIA GRASS. Perennial. All Zones. Tall (5–6-ft.), graceful, clumping grasses to stand out in border or at focal points in garden. Grow in sun or shade, any soil; turn tan or brown in winter and should be cut back before new growth starts in spring. Garden varieties are:

'Gracillimus'. MAIDEN GRASS. Slender, weeping leaves topped by loose, lacy, drooping, feathery beige flower clusters that can be cut for fresh or dry arrangements.

'Variegatus'. Leaves striped lengthwise with white.

'Zebrinus'. Bands of yellow running across leaves.

Miscanthus sinensis

MOCK ORANGE. See *Philadelphus*. Some people call Mexican orange (*Choisya*) mock orange.

MOLE PLANT. See *Euphorbia lathyris*.

MOLUCCELLA laevis. *Labiatae.* BELLS-OF-IRELAND, SHELL FLOWER. Summer annual. Single stemmed or branched, about 2 ft. high.

M

Flowers are carried almost from base in whorls of 6. Showy part of flower is large shell-like or bell-like, apple green calyx, very veiny and crisp textured; small white tube of united petals in center is inconspicuous. As cut flowers, spikes of little bells are attractive fresh (long lasting) or dried (be sure to remove unattractive leaves).

Needs sunny location and loose, well-drained soil. Sow seeds in early spring or late fall; if weather is warm, refrigerate seeds for a week before planting. For long spikes, water and fertilize regularly.

Moluccella laevis

MOMORDICA charantia. *Cucurbitaceae.* BALSAM PEAR, BITTER MELON. Annual vine that sprawls or climbs by tendrils. All Zones. Deeply lobed leaves; white, fringed flowers 1 in. across. Fruit to 8 in. long, cylindrical with tapered ends, ridged and warty, bright yellow when ripe, splitting to show scarlet seeds. Immature fruits cherished in Oriental cooking despite bitter flavor. Ripe fruits showy, sometimes used in arrangements. Sow seed when soil warms, water and feed generously, and provide a trellis or other support.

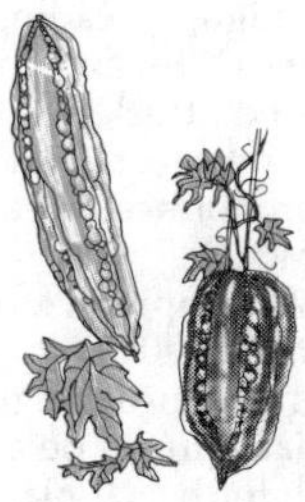
Momordica charantia

MONARDA. *Labiatae.* BEE BALM, OSWEGO TEA, HORSEMINT. Perennials. All Zones, but not long lived where winters are warm, summers long and hot. Bushy, leafy clumps, 2–4 ft. tall, spread rapidly at edges but are not really invasive. Oval, 6-in.-long, dark green leaves have strong, pleasant odor like blend of mint and basil. In summer, stems are topped by tight clusters of long-tubed flowers much visited by hummingbirds. Sun (light afternoon shade in hottest summer climates). Need lots of water. Plant 10 in. apart. Divide every 3–4 years.

Monarda didyma

M. didyma. Scarlet flowers. Heavily aromatic leaves to 4 in. long. Native to eastern U.S.

Garden selections and hybrids include scarlet 'Adam', pink 'Croftway Pink' and 'Granite Pink', lavender 'Violet Queen', and 'Snow White'. A very old variety, 'Cambridge Scarlet', is still widely grown. Pale colors may be best in some color schemes, but scarlets are showiest and most typical.

M. fistulosa. Rosy lavender flowers. Takes moist or average soils. Native from eastern U.S. to Rocky Mountains.

MONDO GRASS. See *Ophiopogon japonicus* under *Liriope and Ophiopogon.*

MONEY PLANT. See *Lunaria annua.*

MONEYWORT. See *Lysimachia nummularia.*

MONKEY FLOWER. See *Mimulus.*

MONKEY HAND TREE. See *Chiranthodendron pentadactylon.*

MONKEY PUZZLE TREE. See *Araucaria araucana.*

MONKSHOOD. See *Aconitum.*

MONSTERA. *Araceae.* Evergreen vines. Related to philodendrons and resembling them in leaf gloss and texture. Most have cut and perforated foliage.

M. deliciosa (often sold as *Philodendron pertusum).* SPLIT-LEAF PHILODENDRON. Zones 21–24; house plant anywhere. Eventually of great size if planted in open ground bed in greenhouse or (in mildest areas) outdoors. Long, cordlike roots hanging from stems root into soil, help support plant on trees or on moss "totem poles." Leaves on youngest plants uncut; mature leaves heavy, leathery, dark green, deeply cut and perforated. Big plants may bear flowers something like callas, with a thick, 10-in. spike surrounded by a white, boatlike bract. If heat, light, and humidity are high, spike may ripen into edible fruit—delicious only when fully ripe (intensely irritating when immature).

Monstera deliciosa

Best in filtered shade with rich soil, ample water, stout support. For best results indoors, grow in container with good drainage, feed occasionally, and keep leaves clean. In poor light or low humidity, new leaves will be smaller. If tall plants get bare at base, replant in larger container and add younger, lower plant to fill in; or cut plant back and let new shoots start.

M. friedrichsthalii. SWISS CHEESE PLANT. House or greenhouse plant. Leaves smaller, thinner in texture than those of *M. deliciosa;* edges are wavy, not deeply cut. Leaves are perforated by series of oval holes on either side of midrib.

MONTANOA. *Compositae.* DAISY TREE. Evergreen shrubs or small trees. Zones 16, 17, 20–24. Give them good soil, ample water, and full sun; groom by cutting off dead flower heads. Useful for winter flowers, tropical effects, background.

M. arborescens. To 12 ft. or more. Usually seen as multitrunked tree branching from base. Oval, 6-in. leaves are medium green, slightly toothed and rough textured. Covered with small, white, daisylike flower heads in winter. Needs little pruning.

M. bipinnatifida. To 7–8 ft. Bold-textured shrub with large, deeply lobed leaves. Flower heads to 3 in. across, mostly composed of white ray flowers to give double effect; some yellow in center of heads. Blooms all autumn, into early winter. Prune hard after bloom; new stems grow quickly.

Montanoa bipinnatifida

M. grandiflora. To 12 ft., with large, deeply cut leaves; 3-in. daisies in fall, winter. Flowers smell like freshly baked cookies.

MONTBRETIA. See *Crocosmia crocosmiiflora, Tritonia.*

MOON CACTUS. See *Gymnocalycium mihanovichii friedrichii.*

MOONFLOWER. See *Ipomoea alba.*

Moraceae. The mulberry family includes deciduous or evergreen trees, shrubs, and vines. Individual fruits are tiny and single-seeded, but often aggregated into clusters. Fig (*Ficus*) and mulberry (*Morus*) are examples.

MORAEA IRIDIOIDES. See *Dietes.*

MORAINE ASH. See *Fraxinus holotricha* 'Moraine'.

MORAINE LOCUST. See *Gleditsia triacanthos* 'Moraine'.

M

MORETON BAY CHESTNUT. See *Castanospermum australe.*

MORNING GLORY. See *Convolvulus, Ipomoea.*

MORUS. *Moraceae.* MULBERRY. Deciduous trees. Leaves of variable form, size, and shape—often on same tree. Fruits look like miniature blackberries and are favored by birds. For home gardeners, however, the most important kinds are fruitless forms of *M. alba.*

M. alba. WHITE MULBERRY, SILKWORM MULBERRY. All Zones. Fruit-bearing form grows to 20–60 ft., has inconspicuous flowers followed by sweet but rather insipid fruit which stains patios, clothing. 'Pendula' or 'Teas' Weeping' is a low-growing, strongly weeping variety; 'Chaparral' is another weeping mulberry (nonfruiting) with deeply cut, dark green leaves.

Morus alba

Fruitless forms are better for home gardens. They grow well in the desert and provide quick shade; they tolerate heat and alkaline soil and are resistant to Texas root rot. On the other hand, they produce pollen in prodigious amounts and, like fruiting forms, are subject to sooty canker disease. Take some drought once established, but grow faster with water and feeding. Beach plantings in southern California very successful. Difficult to garden under because of heavy surface roots. To 35 ft. tall with somewhat wider spread; often 20 ft. by 20 ft. in 3 years (slower in cool climates). 'Fan-San', 'Fruitless', 'Kingan', and 'Stribling' ('Mapleleaf') are good varieties.

Stake new plants carefully; they develop large crowns rather quickly, and these may snap from slender young trunks in high winds. For first few years, branches may grow so long that they droop from their own weight; shorten such branches to a well-placed, upward-growing bud. Do not prune heavy branches to stubs; these are likely either to rot or to furnish entry for sooty canker fungus.

M. nigra. BLACK or PERSIAN MULBERRY. Zones 4–24. To 30 ft. with short trunk and dense, spreading head. Takes some drought once established. Heart-shaped leaves to 8 in. long. Fruit large, juicy, dark red to black. 'Black Beauty' is semidwarf (15 ft.).

M. papyrifera. See *Broussonetia.*

MOSES-IN-THE-BOAT, MOSES-IN-THE-CRADLE. See *Rhoeo spathacea.*

MOSS CAMPION. See *Silene acaulis, S. schafta.*

MOSS, IRISH and SCOTCH. See *Sagina.*

MOSS PINK. See *Phlox subulata.*

MOTHER FERN. See *Asplenium bulbiferum.*

MOTH ORCHID. See *Phalaenopsis.*

MOUNTAIN ASH. See *Sorbus.*

MOUNTAIN GARLAND. See *Clarkia unguiculata.*

MOUNTAIN IRONWOOD. See *Cercocarpus betuloides.*

MOUNTAIN LAUREL. See *Kalmia latifolia.*

MOUNTAIN MAHOGANY. See *Cercocarpus.*

MOUNTAIN PRIDE. See *Penstemon newberryi.*

MOUNTAIN SPRAY. See *Holodiscus dumosus.*

MOURNING BRIDE. See *Scabiosa atropurpurea.*

MUEHLENBECKIA. *Polygonaceae.* WIRE VINE. Evergreen vines. Unusual plants with thin, wiry stems, tiny leaves, insignificant flowers. Routine summer watering. Sun to medium shade.

M. axillaris *(M. nana).* CREEPING WIRE VINE. Zones 3–9, 14–24. Small, dense, creeping plant to a few inches tall or mounding up to 1 ft. high, spreading by underground stems. Leaves ⅛ in. long, dark glossy green, closely spaced. Rock garden plant or small-scale ground cover. Deciduous where winter chill is pronounced. Translucent white fruits with black seeds can be attractive.

Muehlenbeckia axillaris

M. complexa. MATTRESS VINE, WIRE VINE. Zones 8, 9, 14–24. Vine climbs to 20–30 ft. or more, or sprawls when there is no support. Has a dense tangle of thin black or brown stems. Leaves are variable in shape and are ⅛–¾ in. long. Mattress vine is a tough vine for beach planting. It is also a good screen for old stump or rock pile.

MULBERRY. See *Morus.*

MULLEIN. See *Verbascum.*

MULLEIN PINK. See *Lychnis coronaria.*

MURRAYA paniculata *(M. exotica).* *Rutaceae.* ORANGE JESSAMINE. Evergreen shrub. Zones 21–24. To 6–15 ft. tall and wide, sometimes grown as small single or multitrunked tree. Open habit; graceful, pendulous branches with dark green, glossy leaves divided into 3–9 oval, 1–2-in. leaflets. White, ¾-in., bell-shaped flowers have jasmine fragrance. Blooms late summer and fall, sometimes spring as well. Mature plants have small red fruit.

Best in high shade or half-day sun without reflected heat. Needs rich soil, ample water, frequent feeding. Recovers beauty slowly after cold, wet winters. Good as hedge or filler; also for shaping. Fast growing; attracts bees.

Murraya paniculata

A dwarf variety of orange jessamine is usually sold as *M. exotica.* It is slower growing, more upright and compact, to 6 ft. tall, 4 ft. wide. Leaves are lighter green; leaflets smaller, stiffer. Bloom is usually less profuse.

MUSA. *Musaceae.* BANANA. Perennials, some treelike in size. For most common bananas, see *Ensete.* Kinds described here include tall, medium, and dwarf (2–5-ft.) plants. All have soft, thickish stems and spread by suckers or underground roots to form clumps. Spectacular long, broad leaves are easily tattered by strong winds (a banana plant outdoors should be in wind-sheltered spot). Most kinds are tender and should be grown in tubs, either beside a sunny window or in a greenhouse (or in such a location in winter and outdoors in warm season). Attractive near

Musa paradisiaca seminifera

swimming pools. Give all types rich soil, plenty of water, heavy feeding. Fast growing.

M. acuminata 'Dwarf Cavendish' ***(M. cavendishii, M. nana).*** Zones 21–24. Plants 6–8 ft. tall have leaves 5 ft. long, 2 ft. wide. Large, heavy flower clusters with reddish to dark purple bracts, yellow flowers. In warmest southern California coastal gardens, can bear sweet, edible 6-in. bananas. Plant out of wind near south wall.

M. coccinea. Zones 21 (warmest parts), 23, 24. Grows 6–8 ft. tall; leaves 2–3 ft. long. Flower bracts are fiery red tipped yellow. Striking cut flower.

M. ensete. See *Ensete ventricosum.*

M. mannii. Zones 23, 24. To 6–8 ft., with 4-ft. leaves; stems and midribs black. Rose-colored bracts, seedy 3-in. bananas.

M. maurelii. See *Ensete ventricosum* 'Maurelii'.

M. ornata *(M. rosacea, M. rosea).* Zones 23, 24. Grows 8–12 ft. tall, with 5-ft. leaves. Short, erect flower stalk has pinkish bracts, yellow orange flowers.

M. paradisiaca *(M. sapientum).* Zones 16, 19–24; root hardy but damaged by frost in Zones 9, 14, 15. Many ornamental and edible forms. Most common type is often called *M. p. seminifera.* Grows to 20 ft., with leaves to 9 ft. Makes large clumps. Drooping flower stalk with powdery purple bracts; fruit (usually seedy and inedible) sometimes follows.

M. velutina. Zones 23, 24. Grows to 3–4 ft., with 3-ft. leaves that are green above, bronzy beneath. Upright pink bracts, orange flowers, velvety pink fruit.

Musaceae. The banana family consists of giant herbaceous plants that resemble palm trees; the bases of the enormous leaves form a false trunk. *Ensete* and *Musa* are grown in the West.

MUSCARI. *Liliaceae.* GRAPE HYACINTH. Bulbs. All Zones. Clumps of narrow, grassy, fleshy leaves appear in autumn and live through cold and snow. Small, urn-shaped, blue or white flowers in tight spikes appear in early spring. Plant 2 in. deep in fall, setting bulbs in masses or drifts under flowering fruit trees or shrubs, in edgings and rock gardens, or in containers. Grow in sun or light shade. Need little or no water in summer. Very long lived. Lift and divide when bulbs become crowded.

Muscari armeniacum

M. armeniacum. Bright blue flowers on 4–8-in. stems above heavy cluster of floppy foliage. 'Cantab' has clear light blue flowers, blooms later, is lower growing, has neater foliage. 'Blue Spike' has double blue flowers in a tight cluster at the top of the spike.

M. azureum *(Hyacinthella azurea, Hyacinthus azureus).* Something between hyacinth and grape hyacinth in appearance. The 4–8-in. stalks have tight clusters of bell-shaped (not urn-shaped), fragrant sky blue flowers.

M. botryoides. Medium blue flowers on 6–12-in. stems. 'Album' is white variety.

M. comosum. FRINGE or TASSEL HYACINTH. Unusual, rather loose cluster of shredded-looking flowers—greenish brown fertile ones, bluish purple sterile ones. Stems 1–1½ ft. high. Leaves about same length as stems, ⅜–1 in. wide.

M. c. 'Monstrosum' (*M. c.* 'Plumosum'). FEATHERED or PLUME HYACINTH. Sterile violet blue to reddish purple flowers with finely divided and twisted segments. Stems 1–1½ ft. high.

M. tubergenianum. Stems to 8 in. tall. Flowers at top of spike dark blue; lower flowers light blue.

MUSTARD. *Cruciferae.* Summer annual. All Zones in conditions noted below. Curly-leaf mustards somewhat resemble curly-leaf kales in appearance. They are cooked like spinach or cabbage; young leaves are sometimes eaten raw in salads or used as garnishes. Fast and easy to grow; ready for the table in 35–60 days. Sow in early spring and make successive sowings when young plants are established. Plants thrive in cool weather but quickly go to seed in heat of summer. Sow in late summer for fall use. In mild-winter areas, plant again in fall and winter. Thin seedlings to stand 6 in. apart in rows. Water well. Harvest leaves from outside as needed. Mustard spinach or tendergreen mustard has smooth, dark green leaves. It ripens earlier than curly mustard and is more tolerant of hot, dry weather.

Mustard

MYOPORUM. *Myoporaceae.* Evergreen shrubs or small trees. Bell-shaped flowers attractive at close range but not showy; fruit small but colorful. Shiny dark green leaves with translucent dots. Tough and fast growing; all take full sun, are fire retardant.

Myoporum laetum

M. debile. Shrub. Zones 15–17, 19–24. Low growing (to 1 ft. tall, 2–4 ft. wide) with trailing branches. Narrow, dark green leaves. Pink, ½-in.-wide flowers in spring; rose colored, ½-in. fruit. Drought resistant. Rock garden, banks.

M. insulare. Shrub or tree. Zones 8, 9, 15–17, 19–24. Generally shrubby near coast, taller and more treelike inland. Grows to 20–30 ft. Leaves and flowers much like those of *M. laetum* but somewhat smaller. Fruit is bluish purple. Culture and uses same as for *M. laetum;* plants more drought resistant.

M. laetum. Shrub or tree. Zones 8, 9, 14–17, 19–24. Temperatures in low 20s can inflict severe damage. Exceptionally fast growth to 30 ft. tall, 20 ft. wide. Dense foliage of rather narrow, 3–4-in.-long leaves. If allowed to assume natural habit, it's a broad-based, billowing mass of dark green. Attractive multitrunked tree if staked and pruned; thin to prevent topheaviness and wind damage. Summer flowers about ½ in. wide, white with purple markings, borne in clusters of 2–6. Small reddish purple fruit is poisonous.

Superb for seaside use—effectively blocks sound, wind, sun, blown sand (won't take drought, however). Can also make good ground cover; keep branches pegged down so they'll root and spread. Not good for tailored garden areas or near pools; some leaf drop at all times, invasive roots.

M. l. 'Carsonii'. Cutting-grown selection. Has darker, larger, broader leaves with fewer translucent dots; keeps its foliage right down to base of plant. Grows even faster than species.

M. 'Pacificum'. Shrub. Zones 16–24. Hybrid selection of extremely fast growth to 2 ft. tall, up to 30 ft. wide; as ground cover, can cover 100 square feet a year. Elongated oval, medium green leaves; small white flowers in summer. Best near coast; full sun everywhere, little water (once established) except in hot interior. Trim as needed; regrowth is rapid.

M. parvifolium (*M. p.* 'Prostratum'). Ground cover. Zones 8, 9, 14–16, 18–24. Bright green, ½–1-in. leaves densely cover plant. White summer flowers, ½ in. wide, are followed by purple berries. Grows to 3 in. high, 9 ft. wide. Plant 5 ft. apart. Plants will fill in within 6 months, branches rooting where stems touch moist ground. No traffic. Moderately drought resistant but better with some summer water. 'Putah Creek' is a vigorous selection to 1 ft. tall, 8 ft. across. Thrives in interior valley heat. Needs good drainage.

MYOSOTIS. *Boraginaceae.* FORGET-ME-NOT. Annual or biennial, perennial. Exquisite blue flowers, tiny but profuse. Best in partial shade; grows easily and thickly as ground cover. Give ample water.

M. scorpioides. Perennial. All Zones. Similar in most respects to *M. sylvatica,* but grows lower and blooms even longer, and

Myosotis sylvatica

M

roots live over from year to year. Flowers, ¼ in. wide, are blue with yellow centers, pink, or white. Bright green, shiny, oblong leaves. Spreads by creeping roots.

M. sylvatica (often sold as *M. alpestris*). Annual or biennial. All Zones. To 6–12 in. Soft, hairy leaves, ½–2 in. long, set closely along stem. Tiny, clear blue, white-eyed flowers to ⅓ in. wide loosely cover upper stems. Flowers and seeds profusely for a long season; beginning in late winter or early spring. With habit of reseeding, will persist in garden for years unless weeded out. Improved strains are available, best of which are 'Blue Ball', 'Blue Bird', and 'Ultramarine'.

MYRICA. *Myricaceae.* Evergreen and deciduous shrubs. *M. californica* is from the Pacific Coast, *M. pensylvanica* from the Atlantic.

M. californica. PACIFIC WAX MYRTLE. Evergreen shrub or tree. Zones 4–6, 14–17, 20–24. Native to coast and coastal valleys, southern California to Washington. At the beach, it's a low, flattened mass; out of wind, it's a big shrub or tree to 30 ft., usually with many upright trunks. In garden, one of best-looking native plants; its great virtue is clean-looking foliage throughout the year. Branches are densely clad with tooth-edged, glossy, dark green leaves, paler beneath, 2–4½ in. long, about ½ in. wide. Spring flowers inconspicuous; fall fruits are purplish nutlets coated with wax, attractive to birds. Useful screen or informal hedge, 6–25 ft. tall. Can be used as clipped hedge. Drought tolerant.

Myrica californica

M. pensylvanica *(M. caroliniensis).* BAYBERRY. Deciduous or partly evergreen shrub. Zones 4–7. Native to eastern U.S. Dense, compact growth to 9 ft. Leaves to 4 in. long, narrowish, glossy green, dotted with resin glands, fragrant. Flowers inconspicuous. Fruit tiny, roundish, covered with white wax—the bayberry wax used for candles. Tolerates poor, sandy soil; takes sun. Resistant to oak root fungus. Usually needs some summer water.

MYROBALAN. See *Prunus cerasifera.*

Myrsinaceae. This plant family consists of evergreen shrubs and trees with (usually) inconspicuous flowers, attractive foliage and habit, and sometimes showy fruits. Representatives are *Myrsine* and *Ardisia.*

MYRSINE africana. *Myrsinaceae.* AFRICAN BOXWOOD. Evergreen shrub. Zones 8, 9, 14–24. To 3–8 ft.; slightly floppy when young, but stiffens up into dense, rounded bush easily kept at 3–4 ft. with moderate pinching, clipping. Stems vertical, dark red, closely set with very dark green, glossy, roundish, ½-in. leaves (excellent cut foliage). Insignificant flowers.

Grows well in full sun or part shade with reasonable drainage. Smog resistant; relatively pest free, although susceptible to red spider mites and, occasionally, brown scale. Drought tolerant. Good for low hedges, clipping into formal shapes, low backgrounds, foundations, narrow beds, containers.

Myrsine africana

Myrtaceae. The immense myrtle family of trees and shrubs is largely tropical and subtropical. Leaves are evergreen and often aromatic. Flowers are conspicuous thanks to large tufts of stamens, often showy. Fruits may be fleshy (*Feijoa*) or dry and capsular (*Eucalyptus*). Bottlebrush (*Callistemon*) and guava (*Psidium*) are two other familiar examples.

MYRTLE. See *Myrtus, Vinca.*

MYRTUS. *Myrtaceae.* MYRTLE. Evergreen shrubs. Included here are several of the most useful, basic evergreen shrubs for California and Arizona gardens. Drought tolerant.

M. communis. TRUE MYRTLE. Zones 8–24. Rounded form to 5–6 ft. high and 4–5 ft. wide; old plants can reach treelike proportions—15 ft. tall, 20 ft. across. Glossy bright green, pointed, 2-in. leaves, pleasantly aromatic when brushed or bruised. White, sweet-scented, ¾-in.-wide flowers with many stamens in summer, followed by bluish black, ½-in. berries. Grows well in part shade but also will take hot bright sun. Any soil, but good drainage is essential—tip chlorosis occurs if drainage is poor. Good formal or informal hedge or screen. Can also be trained to reveal attractive branches.

Myrtus communis

M. c. 'Boetica'. Heavy, stiff, gnarled branches rise 4–6 ft. from base. Leaves large, leathery, very dark green, upward pointing, very fragrant. Popular in desert.

M. c. 'Buxifolia'. BOXLEAF MYRTLE. Small elliptical leaves.

M. c. 'Compacta'. DWARF MYRTLE. Slow growing, small, compact plant densely set with small leaves. Very popular for low edgings and foundation plantings. Excellent for use as a low, compact, formal hedge.

M. c. 'Compacta Variegata'. VARIEGATED DWARF MYRTLE. Similar to 'Compacta', but leaves are edged in white.

M. c. 'Microphylla'. Dwarf myrtle with tiny, close-set leaves.

M. c. 'Variegata'. VARIEGATED MYRTLE. White-edged leaves.

M. luma. See *Luma apiculata.*

M. ugni. See *Ugni molinae.*

NAKED LADY. See *Amaryllis belladonna.*

NANDINA domestica. *Berberidaceae.* HEAVENLY BAMBOO, SACRED BAMBOO. Evergreen or semideciduous shrub. Zones 5–24. Loses leaves at 10°F.; killed to ground at 5°F., but usually recovers fast. Nandina belongs to the barberry family, but is reminiscent of bamboo in its lightly branched, canelike stems and delicate, fine-textured foliage.

Slow to moderate growth to 6–8 ft. (can be held to 3 ft. indefinitely by pruning oldest canes to ground). Leaves intricately divided into many 1–2-in., pointed, oval leaflets, creating lacy pattern. New foliage pinkish and bronzy red when it expands, later soft, light green. Picks up purple and bronze tints in fall; often turns fiery crimson in winter, especially in some sun and with some frost. Flowers pinkish white or creamy white in loose, erect, 6–12-in. clusters at branch ends, late spring or summer. Shiny red berries follow if plants are grouped; single plants seldom fruit heavily.

Nandina domestica

Sun or shade; colors better in sun, but needs some shade in low desert and hot valley regions. Best in rich soil with ample water, but plants tolerate drought when established, even competing with tree roots in dry shade. Apply iron sulfate or chelates to correct chlorosis in alkaline soils. Resistant to oak root fungus. Most useful for light, airy vertical effects; narrow, restricted areas. Good for hedge or screen, as tub plant, for bonsai. Dramatic with night lighting. Highly satisfactory indoor plant if given plenty of light and placed away from warm, dry air currents.

Varieties include:

'Alba' (*'Aurea'*). White berries; light yellow foliage turns golden in fall.

'Compacta'. Lower growing than species (4–5 ft.), with narrower, more numerous leaflets; has very lacy look.

N

'Filamentosa' ('Filamentosa San Gabriel'). Grows slowly to 4 ft. by 4 ft. Soft green foliage turns apricot in fall; leaflets are reduced to mere threads, giving plant a filmy appearance.

'Harbour Dwarf'. Lower growing (1½–2 ft.) than 'Compacta', much more freely spreading. Underground rhizomes send up stems several inches from parent plants. Orange red to bronzy red winter color. Good ground cover.

'Moyers Red'. Standard-sized plant with broad leaflets. Brilliant red winter color in Zones 5–7.

'Nana' ('Nana Compacta', 'Nana Purpurea'). At least 2 plants are grown under these names; they are often mixed in nurseries, so select plants carefully to get the kind you want. Both grow about 1 ft. tall. One has coarse foliage (purplish green in summer, reddish purple in winter) with broad, somewhat cupped leaflets. Very slow to spread, it is best as container plant or as single plant among rocks or in prominent corner where its domelike growth is emphasized. The other has finely cut leaves with narrow leaflets; it is green in summer, bright red in winter. It spreads fairly fast, making good small-scale ground cover.

'Pygmaea'. Dwarf nandina with extremely dense clumping habit. Stems mostly 8–10 in. tall, with occasional stems to 3 ft. Turns bright red in fall, winter. (Other varieties may be sold under this name.)

'Royal Princess' ('Chinensis', 'Chinese Princess'). Clumps are open rather than tight, making for broad shrubs with see-through quality. Fine-textured foliage colors well in winter.

'Umpqua Chief'. Shorter than species (5–6 ft.), fast growing, vigorous. Red spots appear on foliage early in fall, deepening and blending to overall bright red in winter.

'Umpqua Princess'. Clumps grow 3–4 ft. tall. Leaves narrow, giving fine texture, see-through look. Winter color not especially bright.

'Umpqua Warrior'. Tallest and fastest growing of named forms, inclined to floppiness in its tallest stems. Large leaflets, good winter color.

NANKING CHERRY. See *Prunus tomentosa*.

NARCISSUS. *Amaryllidaceae.* DAFFODIL. Bulbs. All Zones. Most valuable spring-flowering bulbous plants for most regions of West. They are permanent, increasing from year to year; they are hardy in cold and heat; they are useful in many garden situations; they provide fascinating variety in flower form and color; and gophers won't eat them.

Narcissus—daffodil

Leaves are straight and flat (strap shaped) or narrow and rushlike. Flowers are composed of ring of segments ("petals") which are at right angles to the trumpet or crown (also called cup) in center. Flowers may be single or clustered. Colors are basically yellow and white, but there are also many variations—orange, red, apricot, pink, cream.

Use under trees and flowering shrubs, among ground cover plantings, near water, in rock gardens and patios, or in borders. Naturalize in sweeping drifts where space is available. Good in containers, fine cut flowers.

Flowers usually face sun; keep that in mind when selecting planting place.

Plant bulbs as early in fall as obtainable. In southern California and the deserts of Arizona, wait until November so soil can cool. Look for solid, heavy bulbs. Number One double-nose bulbs are best; Number One round, single-nose bulbs are second choice. Plant with 5–6 in. of soil over top of bulbs (4–5 in. for smaller bulbs). Set bulbs 8 in. apart and you won't have to divide for at least 2–3 years. Full sun is best, but flowers of late-blooming kinds last better in light shade.

Water well after planting; if fall rains are on schedule, further watering is usually unnecessary. Continued watering may be necessary where winters are dry. Water while growing and blooming. Control snails and slugs; they relish leaves and flowers of all kinds of narcissus and are particularly abundant during the flowering season.

Let foliage ripen naturally after bloom. Lift and divide clumps of daffodils when flowers get smaller and fewer in number; wait until foliage has died down. Don't break away forcibly any bulbs that are tightly joined to mother bulb; remove only those that come away easily. Replant at once, or store for only a short time—preferably not over 3 weeks.

To grow in containers, set bulbs close together, with tips level with soil surface. Place pots in well-drained trench or cold frame and cover with 6–8 in. of moist peat moss, wood shavings, sawdust, or sand. Look for roots in 8–10 weeks (tip soil mass from pot carefully). Remove pots with well-started bulbs to greenhouse, cool room, or sheltered garden spot to bloom. Keep well watered until foliage yellows; then plant in garden. You can sink pots or cans of bulbs in borders when flowers are almost ready to bloom, then lift containers when flowers fade.

Following are the 11 generally recognized divisions of daffodils, and representative varieties in each division.

Trumpet daffodils. Trumpet is as long as or longer than surrounding flower segments. Yellows are most popular; old variety 'King Alfred' best known, top seller, although newer 'Unsurpassable' and 'William the Silent' are superior. White varieties include 'Mount Hood', 'Cantatrice', 'Empress of Ireland'. Bicolors with white segments, yellow cup are 'Spring Glory', 'Trousseau'. Reverse bicolors like 'Spellbinder' have white cup and yellow segments.

Large-cupped daffodils. Cups are more than ⅓ the length of flower segments, but not as long as segments. Yellow: 'Carlton' and 'Carbineer'. White: 'Ice Follies'. Bicolors: 'Binkie', 'Mrs. R. O. Backhouse'.

Small-cupped daffodils. Cups less than ⅓ the length of segments. Less widely available, for specialists.

Double daffodils. 'Golden Ducat'; 'Mary Copeland', white and bright red; 'White Lion', creamy white and yellow; 'Texas', yellow and orange scarlet; 'Windblown', white and pale lemon.

Narcissus—double

Triandrus Hybrids. Cups at least ⅔ the length of flower segments. Clusters of medium-sized, slender-cupped flowers. 'Thalia' is a favorite white with 2 or 3 beautifully proportioned flowers per stem. 'Silver Chimes' has 6 or more yellow-cupped white flowers per stem.

Cyclamineus Hybrids. Early medium-sized flowers with recurved segments. Gold, yellow, primrose, and white with yellow cup. Examples are 'February Gold', 'February Silver', 'Peeping Tom'.

Jonquilla Hybrids. Clusters of 2–4 rather small, very fragrant flowers. Yellow (like 'Trevithian' and 'Suzy'), orange, ivory.

Tazetta and Tazetta Hybrids. These are Polyanthus or bunch-flowered daffodils with small-cupped white and yellow flowers in clusters. Good double varieties are 'Cheerfulness' (white) and 'Golden Cheerfulness'. Also includes Poetaz narcissus, such as 'Geranium', paper white narcissus, and *N. tazetta* 'Orientalis' (Chinese sacred lilies). These last 3, along with 'Cragford' (white, scarlet cup) and 'Grand Soleil d'Or' (golden yellow), can be grown indoors in bowls of pebbles and water. Keep dark and cool until growth is well along, then bring slowly into light.

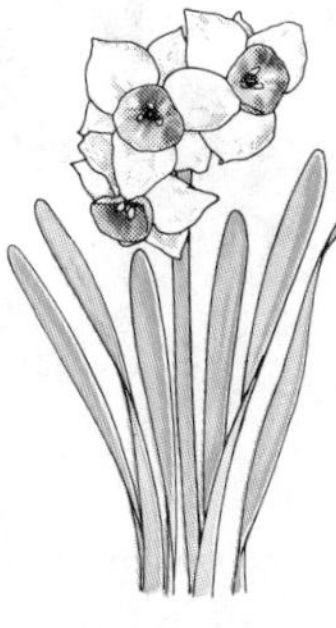

Narcissus tazetta 'Orientalis'

Poeticus narcissus. POET'S NARCISSUS. White flowers with shallow, broad yellow cups edged red. 'Actaea' is largest.

(Continued on next page)

N

Narcissus bulbocodium

Species, varieties, and hybrids. Many species and their varieties and hybrids delight the collector. Most are small; some are true miniatures for rock gardens or very small containers. *N. bulbocodium*, HOOP PETTICOAT DAFFODIL. To 6 in. tall, with little, upward-facing flowers that are mostly trumpet, with very narrow pointed segments. Deep and pale yellow varieties. *N. cyclamineus*, 6 in. high, backward-curved lemon yellow segments and narrow, tubular golden cup. *N. jonquilla*, JONQUIL. Cylindrical, rushlike leaves. Clusters of early, very fragrant, golden yellow flowers with short cups. *N. asturiensis* (usually sold as *N.* 'Minimus'), very early miniature trumpet flowers on 3-in. stems. *N. triandrus*, ANGEL'S TEARS. Clusters of small white flowers.

Miscellaneous. This group serves as a catch-all for a variety of new flower forms. Typical are 'Baccarat', light yellow with deeper yellow trumpet cut into 6 equal lobes; and 'Cassata', white with ivory split trumpet; segments of trumpet lie flat along petals.

NASTURTIUM. See *Tropaeolum*.

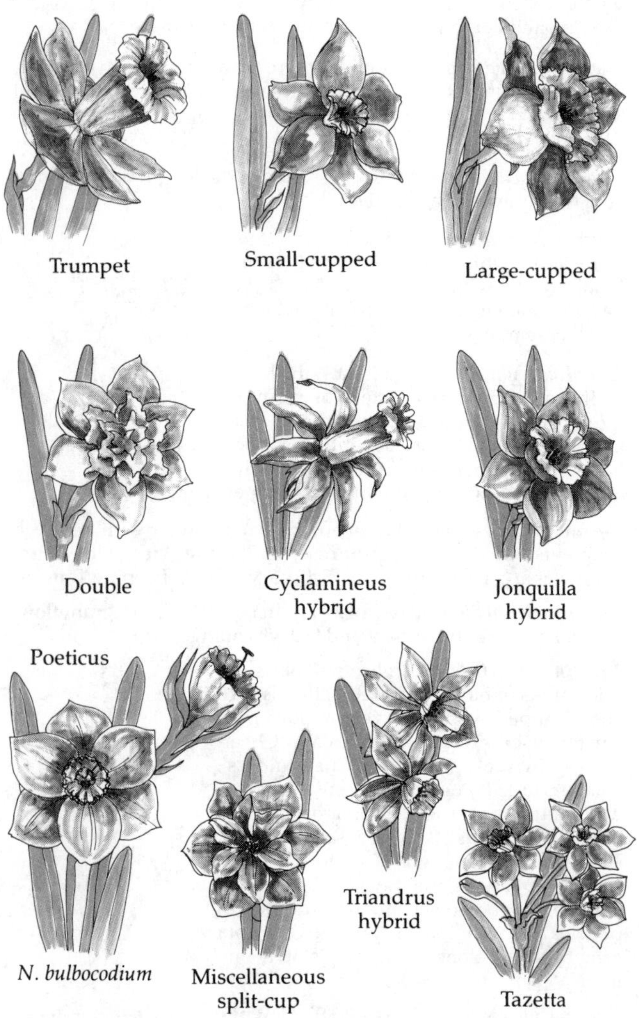

Narcissus come in groups called "divisions." Flowers (except doubles) have 6 segments (perianth) and a cup.

NATAL IVY. See *Senecio macroglossus*.

NATAL PLUM. See *Carissa macrocarpa*.

NEANTHE bella. See *Chamaedorea elegans*.

NECTARINE. See Peach and Nectarine.

NEEDLE PALM. See *Rhapidophyllum hystrix*.

NELUMBO *(Nelumbium).* *Nymphaeaceae.* LOTUS. Perennials. All Zones. These are water plants. If you acquire started plants in containers, put them in pond with 8–12 in. of water over soil surface. If you get roots, plant in spring, horizontally, 4 in. deep, in 1–1½-ft.-deep container of fairly rich soil. Place soil surface 8–12 in. under water. Huge round leaves attached at center to leaf stalks grow above water level. Large fragrant flowers, growing above or lower than leaves, form in summer. Ornamental woody fruit perforated with holes in salt shaker effect. Good for dried arrangements. Roots should not freeze; where freezing is possible, cover pond or fill it deeper with water.

Nelumbo nucifera

N. lutea *(Nelumbium luteum).* AMERICAN LOTUS. Similar to following but somewhat smaller in leaf and flower. Flowers are pale yellow.

N. nucifera *(Nelumbium nelumbo).* INDIAN or CHINESE LOTUS. Round leaves, 2 ft. or wider, carried 3–6 ft. above water surface. Pink, 4–10-in.-wide flowers carried singly on stems. Both tubers and seeds are esteemed in Chinese cookery, and the entire plant holds great religious significance for Buddhists. White, rose, and double varieties exist; dwarf forms suitable for pot culture are becoming available.

NEMESIA strumosa. *Scrophulariaceae.* Winter/spring annual in Zones 15–17, 21–24; summer annual elsewhere. To 10–18 in. Full sun. Lance-shaped, toothed leaves. Flowers ¾ in. wide, of irregular shape, in 3–4-in.-long spikes; every color of spectrum (except green), including some bicolors. Sutton's strain is larger flowered. There is also dwarf form, 'Nana Compacta'.

Nemesia strumosa

Sow outdoors in spring in cold climates, spring or fall where winters are mild; or buy in flats. Time plantings of this rapid grower to avoid frost but to bloom during cool weather. Does best in rich soil, moist but not wet. Pinch back to induce bushiness. Excellent bulb cover and container subject (handsome hanging basket plant). Small bed of nemesia edged with blue lobelias or violas makes dazzling patio planting.

NEMOPHILA. *Hydrophyllaceae.* Annuals. Often used as low cover for bulb beds. Broadcast seed in fall (mild winter regions) or early spring, in sun or part shade. Will reseed if growth conditions are ideal. Need constant moisture. Both listed here are native to western U.S.

Nemophila menziesii

N. maculata. FIVE-SPOT NEMOPHILA. To 6 in. tall; growth habit, foliage, flower size same as *N. menziesii*. Flowers white, with fine purple lines; small dots and 1 large dot on each of the 5 lobes.

N. menziesii *(N. insignis).* BABY BLUE EYES. To 6–10 in. tall, branching from base. Blooms as freely in gardens as it does in the wilds. Cup-shaped spring flowers about 1 in. across are sky blue with whitish center. Leaves have rounded lobes. Short blooming period. Nice bulb cover.

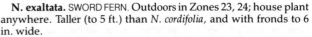

Neodypsis decaryi

NEODYPSIS decaryi. *Palmae.* TRIANGLE PALM. Palm. Zones 20–24. Slow grower to 18–20 ft. Native to arid parts of Madagascar, it needs little water once established. Trunk is triangular in cross-section because heavily keeled leaf bases grow in 3 ranks about the stem. Gray green, featherlike fronds to 15 ft., strongly upright but arching at tips.

Neoregelia carolinae

NEOREGELIA. *Bromeliaceae.* House plants. Sometimes grown in sheltered gardens in Zones 21–24. Bromeliads with rosettes of leathery leaves, often strikingly colored or marked; short spikes of usually inconspicuous flowers are buried in hearts of rosettes. Need light, open, fast-draining planting mix that holds moisture but does not exclude air. Feed lightly. Keep water in cup at the base of rosette. Can also be grown on tree branch with sphagnum moss around roots. Filtered shade or strong indirect light.

N. carolinae. Many narrow, shiny leaves 1 ft. long, 1½ in. wide. Medium green leaves turn rich red at base as plant approaches bloom. *N. c.* 'Tricolor' has leaves striped lengthwise with white. Center turns bright red.

N. spectabilis. PAINTED FINGERNAIL PLANT. Leaves 1 ft. long, 2 in. wide are olive green with bright red tips. In strong light, plant takes on bronzy color.

Nepeta cataria

NEPETA. *Labiatae.* Perennials, ground covers. All Zones. Vigorous, spreading plants of mint family. Plant in full sun. Normal watering.

N. cataria. CATNIP. Perennial plant 2–3 ft. high with downy, gray green leaves and clustered lavender or white flowers at branch tips in June. Easy grower in light soil; reseeds readily. Attractive to cats. Sprinkle its dried leaves over their food, or sew some into toy cloth mouse. Some people use it to flavor tea.

N. faassenii (usually sold as *N. mussinii*). CATMINT. Makes soft, gray green, undulating mounds to 2 ft. high. Leaves aromatic and (like catnip) attractive to cats, who enjoy rolling in plantings. Lavender blue, ½-in. flowers in loose spikes make display in early summer. If dead spikes prove unsightly, shear them back; this may bring on another bloom cycle. Set 1–1½ ft. apart for ground cover.

N. hederacea. See *Glechoma*.

Nephrolepis exaltata 'Bostoniensis'

NEPHROLEPIS. *Polypodiaceae.* SWORD FERN. (For native western sword fern, see *Polystichum munitum.*) Tough, easy-to-grow ferns for garden or house.

N. cordifolia (often sold as *N. exaltata*). SOUTHERN SWORD FERN. Zones 8, 9, 14–24. Bright green, narrow, upright fronds in tufts to 2–3 ft. tall. Fronds have closely spaced, finely toothed leaflets. Roots often have small roundish tubers. Plant spreads by thin, fuzzy runners and can be invasive if not watched. Will not take hard frosts but otherwise adaptable—easily moved, tolerant of poor soil, light or heavy shade, erratic watering. Can be used in narrow, shaded beds. Effective ground cover in sunny or shady tropical landscapes if adequately watered.

N. exaltata. SWORD FERN. Outdoors in Zones 23, 24; house plant anywhere. Taller (to 5 ft.) than *N. cordifolia,* and with fronds to 6 in. wide.

N. e. 'Bostoniensis'. BOSTON FERN. House plant. Spreading and arching in habit, with graceful, eventually drooping fronds. Classic parlor fern of grandmother's day. Many more finely cut and feathery forms exist; 'Fluffy Ruffles', 'Rooseveltii', and 'Whitmanii' are among best known. North light in cool room suits it. Plant in well-drained fibrous soil. Feed every month with dilute liquid fertilizer; water whenever soil surface dries out.

N. obliterata. House plant. From northwestern Australia. A selection called 'Kimberley Queen' has fronds to 3 ft. in length. Habit is stiffer, more erect than that of Boston fern, and plant is more tolerant of low humidity and both low and high light conditions.

NEPHTHYTIS. See *Syngonium*.

Nerine curvifolia 'Fothergillii Major'

NERINE. *Amaryllidaceae.* Bulbs. Zones 5, 8, 9, 13–24. Native to South Africa. Usually grown in pots, but can grow outdoors year around in mildest regions. Wide-leafed kinds need shade in warmer climates. Funnel-shaped flowers with 6 spreading segments bent back at tips, carried in rounded clusters on 1–2-ft. stems. Bloom August–January, depending on kind. Strap-shaped basal leaves appear during or after bloom.

Plant August–December. Put 1 bulb in 4-in. pot, 3 in 5–6-in. pot. Cover only lower half of bulb. Wait for signs of flower stalk before watering. Water through winter and spring. In May, move pots outdoors to lightly shaded spot. Gradually dry off. Withhold water from July until growth resumes. Do not repot until quite crowded. To grow outdoors, plant in sun in perfectly drained soil; set bulb 3 in. deep. Do not disturb or divide for several years.

N. bowdenii. The hardiest; grows outdoors in milder parts of Northwest. Glossy green leaves 1 in. wide, 6–12 in. long. Flowers to 3 in. long, soft pink, marked deeper pink, in clusters of 8–12 on 2-ft. stems. Forms with taller stems, larger flower clusters come in deeper pink, crimson, and red. 'Crispa' is 1 ft. tall, has pale pink, wavy-edged segments; 'Pink Triumph' blooms latest, is larger. Blooms in fall; as late as December in southern California.

N. curvifolia. Best known is variety 'Fothergillii Major', with clusters of 2-in.-wide, scarlet flowers overlaid with shimmering gold. Long stamens topped by greenish yellow anthers. Bloom stalks to 1½ ft.; leaves 1 ft. long.

N. filifolia. Leaves narrow, grassy, evergreen, 6–8 in. long. Flowers 1 in. wide, rose red with narrow, crinkled petals, in clusters of 8–12 on stems 1 ft. tall. Fast multiplier.

N. masonorum. Like *N. filifolia* but smaller, with 1-in.-wide flowers in clusters of 4–12 on 9-in. stems.

N. sarniensis. GUERNSEY LILY. Large clusters of iridescent crimson, 1½-in.-long flowers on 2-ft. stalks. Pink, orange scarlet, and pure white varieties. Green leaves, 1 ft. long, ¾ in. wide.

Nerium oleander

NERIUM oleander. *Apocynaceae.* OLEANDER. Evergreen shrub. Zones 8–16, 18–23. One of the basic shrubs for desert and hot interior valleys. Moderate to fast growth; most varieties reach maximum height of 8–12 ft. and as wide. Ordinarily broad and bulky, but easily trained into handsome single or many-trunked tree resembling (when out of bloom) an olive tree. Narrow, 4–12-in.-long leaves are dark green, leathery, and glossy, attractive all seasons; form with golden variegations in leaves is sometimes available. Flowers 2–3 in. across, clustered at twig or branch ends, May or June to October. Many

N

varieties have fragrant flowers. Forms with double and single flowers are sold, with color range from white to shades of yellow, pink, salmon, and red. 'Sister Agnes', single white, is most vigorous grower, often reaching 20 ft. tall; 'Mrs. Roeding', double salmon pink, grows only 6 ft. tall and has proportionally smaller leaves, finer foliage texture than big oleanders. Double varieties exist in other colors, but all share a drawback: double flowers hang on after bloom, turn brown. 'Hawaii' is a single-flowered oleander with the same luscious color as 'Mrs. Roeding'; its flowers drop clean. It is, however, tender in cold-winter areas.

'Petite Pink' and 'Petite Salmon' can easily be kept to 3–4 ft. with moderate pruning and make excellent informal flowering hedges, though they are not as cold hardy as regular oleanders. 'Little Red', bright red, is completely hardy—as are the following, intermediate in size between dwarfs and full-sized plants: 'Algiers' (deep red), 'Casablanca' (white), 'Ruby Lace' (bright red with 3-inch, wavy-edged individual flowers), and 'Tangier' (soft pink).

Oleanders are not at all particular about soil and withstand considerable drought, poor drainage, soil with relatively high salt content. They thrive in heat and strong light, even reflected light from paving. Weak or leggy growth and few flowers in shade or ocean fog.

Prune in early spring to control size and form. Cut out old wood that has flowered. Cut some branches nearly to ground. To restrict height, pinch remaining tips or prune them back lightly. To prevent bushiness at base, pull (don't cut) unwanted suckers.

Chief insect pests are yellow oleander aphid (one spring spraying usually controls) and scale insects (spray in midsummer crawler stage—see page 100 for choices in controls). One disease is bacterial gall, which causes blackened, deformed flowers, and warty growth and splitting on branches. Control by pruning out infected parts, making cuts well below visible damage—or completely remove infected plants.

All parts of plant are poisonous if eaten. Caution children against eating leaves or flowers; keep prunings, dead leaves away from hay or other animal feed; don't use wood for barbecue fires or skewers. Smoke can cause severe irritation. However, dwarf kinds are fire retardant.

Use as screens, windbreaks, borders for road or driveway, tubs, background plantings, small single or multitrunked trees. Use freely where deer are a problem—they don't touch it. Single white oleanders give cool look to hot-climate garden.

For a plant called YELLOW OLEANDER, see *Thevetia*.

NERTERA granadensis *(N. depressa)*. *Rubiaceae*. BEAD PLANT. Perennial. Extremely tender, generally grown as house plant. Sometimes used as rock garden subject or small-scale ground cover in Zones 17, 22–24. Prostrate habit. Tiny, smooth, rounded leaves make dense green mat an inch or so high; berrylike, ¼-in., bright orange fruit may last from midsummer into winter. Small green flowers are a lesser attraction. Plant in sandy loam with some leaf mold. Must have shade, constant moisture. Fine terrarium or dish-garden plant.

Nertera granadensis

NET BUSH. See *Calothamnus*.

NEW MEXICAN PRIVET. See *Forestiera neomexicana*.

NEW ZEALAND BRASS BUTTONS. See *Cotula squalida*.

NEW ZEALAND BUR. See *Acaena microphylla*.

NEW ZEALAND CHRISTMAS TREE. See *Metrosideros excelsus*.

NEW ZEALAND FLAX. See *Phormium*.

NEW ZEALAND LAUREL. See *Corynocarpus laevigata*.

NEW ZEALAND SPINACH. *Tetragoniaceae*. Perennial vegetable in Zones 15–17, 21–24; summer annual elsewhere. Cook and serve it like spinach. Differs chiefly in that it can be harvested through warm season; real spinach comes in cool season. You harvest greens from plants by plucking off top 3 in. of tender stems and attached leaves. A month later new shoots grow up for another harvest. Plants are spreading, 6–8 in. high, evergreen in mild-winter areas but going dormant in heavy frosts. Sow seed in full sun in early spring after frosts. Water deeply and often. Feed 1 or 2 times a year with complete fertilizer. Though heat tolerant, also thrives in cool, damp conditions at shore and is often seen growing wild.

New Zealand Spinach

NEW ZEALAND TEA TREE. See *Leptospermum scoparium*.

NICOTIANA. *Solanaceae*. Tender perennials grown as summer annuals; shrub. May live over in mild-winter areas. Upright-growing plants with slightly sticky leaves and stems. Usually grown for their fragrant flowers, which often open at night or on cloudy days; some kinds open during day time. Flowers tubular, usually broadly flaring at ends into 5 pointed lobes; grow near top of branched stems in summer. Large, soft, oval leaves. Plant in full sun or part shade. Require normal summer watering. Some kinds reseed readily.

N. alata *(N. affinis)*. Wild species is a 2–3-ft. plant with large, very fragrant white flowers that open toward evening. Seed is available. Selection and hybridization with other species have produced many garden strains that stay open day and night and come in colors ranging from white through pink to red (including lime green), but scent is not as strong as in the "unimproved" species.

Nicotiana alata

Domino strain grows to 12–15 in. and has upward-facing flowers that can take heat and sun better than taller kinds. Nicki strain is taller (to 15–18 in.). The older Sensation strain is taller still—up to 4 ft.—and looks more at home in informal mixed borders than as a bedding plant. Fragrance is erratic. If you particularly want fragrance—especially evening fragrance—plant *N. alata* 'Grandiflora'.

N. glauca. TREE TOBACCO. Zones 7–24. Naturalized South American species. Shrubby or treelike to 20 ft.; bluish green leaves to 6 in. long and small yellow green flowers. All the tobaccos are poisonous if eaten, but only this species has been implicated in deaths.

N. sylvestris. To 5 ft. Intensely fragrant, long, tubular white flowers grow in tiers atop a statuesque, coarse-foliaged plant. Plant is striking in a night garden.

NIDULARIUM innocentii. *Bromeliaceae*. Perennial. Outdoors in Zones 23, 24; greenhouse plant anywhere. Stemless bromeliad, best adapted to pot culture and shady, moist, warm atmosphere. Leaves straplike, 8 in. long or more, spiny toothed along margin to pointed tip, reddish purple on underside. Smaller, bractlike, brilliant red leaves make flattened, nestlike rosette at center of leaves, from which rises dense bunch of white flowers with erect petals. Appropriately named—*nidularium* means "bird's nest."

Nidularium innocentii

NIEREMBERGIA. *Solanaceae.* CUP FLOWER. Perennials. Flowers tubular but flaring into saucerlike or bell-like cup. Need sun, good soil, average water.

Nierembergia repens

N. hippomanica violacea *(N. h. caerulea).* DWARF CUP FLOWER. Zones 8–24. Grows to 6–12 in. high. Much-branched mounded plant. Stiff, very narrow, ½–⅔-in.-long leaves. Throughout the summer months, the plants are covered with blue to violet, widely spreading, bell-like flowers almost an inch across. Trimming plant back after flowering to induce new growth seems to lengthen life. Dwarf cup flower is a good edging plant for semishade beds in desert regions. 'Purple Robe' is a readily available variety.

N. repens *(N. rivularis).* WHITE CUP. Zones 5–9, 14–24. Prostrate 4–6-in. mat of bright green leaves covered in summer with white flowers of the same shape and size as (sometimes larger than) those of dwarf cup flower. For best performance, don't crowd it with more aggressive plants and water it occasionally during the dry season.

NIGELLA damascena. *Ranunculaceae.* LOVE-IN-A-MIST. Spring annual. Branching, to 1–2½ ft. high. All leaves, even those that form collar under each flower, are finely cut into threadlike divisions. Blue, white, or rose flowers, 1–1½ in. across, are solitary on ends of branches. Curious papery-textured, horned seed capsules very decorative in dried bouquets; fresh material gives airiness in bouquet or in mixed border. Sow seed on open ground in full sun or part shade. Plants come quickly into bloom in spring and dry up in summer. Will reseed. 'Miss Jekyll', with semidouble cornflower blue blossoms, is superior variety; 'Persian Jewels' is superior mixed strain.

Nigella damascena

N. hispanica. Grows to 2 ft., with slightly larger flowers than the *N. damascena;* blooms have prominent orange anthers. Seeds of both species have been used as a spice under the name of black cumin.

NIGHT JESSAMINE. See *Cestrum nocturnum.*

NIKAU PALM. See *Rhopalostylis sapida.*

NINEBARK. See *Physocarpus.*

NOLANA paradoxa. *Nolanaceae.* Annual. All Zones. Unusual plant from Chile. Plant looks like a trailing sky blue petunia: trailing stems bear 2-in.-long, ¾-in.-wide leaves and bright blue, 2-in. flowers with white throats. A variety is sold as 'Blue Bird' or *N. napiformis* 'Blue Bird'. Use as edging or in hanging basket. Withstands wide range of temperatures, sun or light shade, but best in sunny, relatively dry, well-drained soil.

Nolana paradoxa

NOLINA. *Agavaceae.* Evergreen shrubs. Yucca and century plant relatives with narrow, tough, grassy leaves on thick trunk. Desert or dry landscape plants. Sun, any soil, good drainage. Take much drought when established. Flowers not important.

Nolina longifolia

N. longifolia. MEXICAN GRASSTREE. Zones 12–24. Native to central Mexico. In youth forms fountain of 3-ft.-long, 1-in.-wide grasslike leaves. In time, fountains top thick trunks (6–10 ft. tall, sometimes with a few branches). Grows fast with plenty of water and feeding, but needs neither when established.

N. parryi. Zones 11–24. Native to southern California deserts. Smaller than above: 3-ft. trunk, leaves to 3 ft. long, ¾ in. wide.

NORFOLK ISLAND PINE. See *Araucaria heterophylla.*

NOTHOFAGUS. *Fagaceae.* SOUTHERN BEECH, FALSE BEECH. Trees. Zones 5, 6, 14–17. Southern hemisphere representatives of beech; many species grow in Chile, New Zealand, Australia. Small leaf size and open branch structure give all a graceful look. They require high humidity, neutral to acid soil, ample water, and good drainage. The nuts are so tiny as to be unnoticeable. Two Chilean species are available but scarce; evergreen species from Australia and New Zealand are rarely available.

Nothofagus antarctica

N. antarctica. Deciduous tree to 50 ft. Closely set, oval, ½–1½-in. leaves line long, graceful shoots of young trees; open growth makes for handsome silhouette against a wall or the sky. Fairly fast growth as a young tree; fills out with maturity, but maintains graceful, frondlike branch structure.

N. dombeyi. Evergreen tree to 50–70 ft. Leaves to 1½ in. long, ½ in. wide, shiny dark green. Good tree for shading rhododendrons, azaleas; open branch structure admits filtered light.

N. obliqua. Deciduous tree to 100 ft.; leaves to 3 in. long, half as wide. Fast growing. Called *roble* (oak) in Chile.

Nyctaginaceae. The four-o'clock family contains annuals, perennials, shrubs, and vines in which the conspicuous elements of the flowers consist either of a showy calyx (rather than petals) or bracts. Examples are bougainvillea and four-o'clock (*Mirabilis*).

NYMPHAEA. *Nymphaeaceae.* WATER LILY. Water plants. All Zones. Leaves float and are rounded, with deep notch at one side where leaf stalk is attached. Showy flowers either float on surface or stand above it on stiff stalks. Cultivated water lilies are largely hybrids that cannot be traced back to exact parentage. There are hardy and tropical types. Both kinds need full sun in order to bloom. Hardy kinds come in white, yellow, copper, pink, and red. Tropical types add blue and purple; recent introductions in tropicals include yellows and an unusual greenish blue. Some tropicals in the white-pink-red color range are night bloomers; all others close at night.

Nymphaea

Hardy kinds are easiest for beginners. Plant them from February–October in mild-winter areas, April–July where freezes prevail. Set 6-in.-long pieces of rhizome in nearly horizontal position with bud end up, on soil at pool bottom or in boxes at least 8 in. deep. Top of soil should be 8–12 in. below water surface. Do not use redwood containers; they can discolor water. Enrich soil with 1 lb. of complete fertilizer (3–5 percent nitrogen) for each lily you plant.

Groom plants by removing spent leaves and blooms. They usually bloom throughout warm weather and go dormant in fall, reappearing in spring. If you live in very cold area, protect as you would *Nelumbo.* Tropical kinds begin to grow and bloom later in summer, but they last longer in fall, too, often up to first frost. Buy started tropical plants and set at same depth as hardy rhizomes. Tropical types go dormant but do not survive really low winter temperatures. They usually live longer where orange trees grow. Where winters are colder, store dormant tubers in damp sand over winter or buy new plants each year.

N

Nymphaeaceae. The waterlily family consists of aquatic plants with (usually) floating leaves and flowers. Lotus (*Nelumbo*) and waterlily (*Nymphaea*) are examples.

Nyssaceae. Deciduous trees from Asia and North America. Two grown in the West are dove tree (*Davidia*) and *Nyssa*.

NYSSA sylvatica. *Nyssaceae.* SOUR GUM, TUPELO, PEPPERIDGE. Deciduous tree. Zones 3–10, 14–21. One of best lawn trees for fall color; dependable color even in mild-winter areas. Slow to moderate growth to 30–50 ft., spreading to 15–25 ft. Pyramidal when young; spreading, irregular, and rugged in age. Crooked branches, twigs, and dark, red-tinged bark make dramatic picture against winter sky. Leaves dark green, glossy, 2–5 in. long, turning hot, coppery red in fall before dropping; come out rather late in spring. Flowers are inconspicuous. Bluish black fruit shaped like small olives is attractive to birds. Grows well in any soil, takes much or little water, withstands occasional drought, tolerates poor drainage.

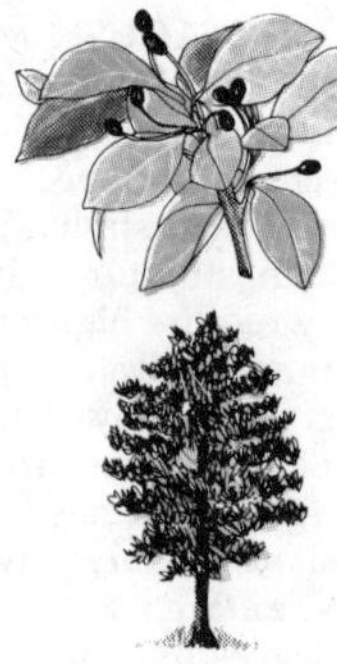
Nyssa sylvatica

OAK. See *Quercus*.

OAT GRASS, BLUE. See *Helictotrichon*.

OCEAN SPRAY. See *Holodiscus discolor*.

OCHNA serrulata *(O. multiflora)*. *Ochnaceae.* BIRD'S-EYE BUSH, MICKEY MOUSE PLANT. Evergreen shrub. Zones 14–24. Slow, spreading growth to 4–8 ft. high and as wide. Oblong leaves, 2–5 in. long, are leathery, fine toothed, bronzy in spring, deep green later. Early summer flowers are size of buttercups; when yellow petals fall, sepals turn vivid red. Next, 5 or more green, seedlike fruits protrude from red center. They later turn glossy jet black, in strong contrast with red sepals; at this stage children see the configuration as bright eyes and big ears of a mouse.

Ochna serrulata

Partial shade, slightly acid soil; fairly drought tolerant once established. Good tub or box subject; makes good small espalier. Sometimes grown indoors.

OCIMUM. *Labiatae.* BASIL. Summer annual herbs. One of the basic cooking herbs. Leaves in varying shades of green and purple. One type—'Dark Opal'—is attractive enough to be sold for borders and mass plantings. Sow seed of any basil in early spring; make successive sowings 2 weeks apart to have replacements for the short–lived older plants. Or set out plants outdoors after frost. Requires warm soil, full sun. Space plants 10–12 in. apart. Fertilize once during growing season with complete fertilizer. Water regularly to keep growth succulent. Occasional overhead watering keeps foliage clean and bright. Keep flower spikes pinched out to prevent seeding, subsequent death of plant.

Ocimum basilicum

O. basilicum. SWEET BASIL. To 2 ft. Green, shiny, 1–2-in.-long leaves; spikes of white flowers. Forms with purple or variegated leaves have purple flowers. Most popular basil for cooking. Used fresh or dry, it gives a pleasant, sweet, mild flavor to tomatoes, cheese, eggs, fish, shellfish, poultry stuffing, salads. There is a dwarf, small-leafed kind that thrives in pots.

O. 'Dark Opal'. Large-leafed basil, known for its ornamental qualities. Dark purple bronze foliage; spikes of small lavender pink flowers. Grows 1–1½ ft. tall with spread of about 1 ft. Attractive in mass planting with dusty miller or 'Carpet of Snow' sweet alyssum.

OCONEE BELLS. See *Shortia galacifolia*.

O'CONNOR'S LEGUME. See *Trifolium fragiferum*.

OCOTILLO. See *Fouquieria splendens*.

OCTOPUS TREE. See *Schefflera actinophylla*.

ODONTOGLOSSUM. *Orchidaceae.* Epiphytic orchids. Outdoors in Zones 23, 24; greenhouse or indoors in winter everywhere. Few other orchids have as many natural crosses or as much variation between species. In general, pseudobulbs are flat and oval in shape, with small leaves sheathing base and 1 or 2 larger leaves at top. Flower stalks usually reach well above foliage.

Odontoglossum crispum

Plant in medium or fine ground bark. Transplant after flowering in fall or in early spring, never in hot summer weather. Don't plant in oversize pot; plants thrive when crowded. Give abundant moisture all year, good ventilation but no drying winds; 45°–55°F. temperature preferable (not above 65°F. in winter and as low as possible in summer). Thrive in well-lighted location, but burn in hot summer sun. Species listed here can be grown in garden beds in Zones 23, 24. Elsewhere, grow in pots or on slabs; suspend from trees or place in protected patio or lathhouse in summer, then bring indoors or into cool greenhouse in winter.

O. crispum. Large (2–3-in.) white flowers, often tinged rose, blotched with red, crowded on 15–30-in.-long stem. Usually blooms late spring, early summer, but may bloom any time. Oval, 2–4-in.-high pseudobulbs; narrow, 9–15-in.-long leaves.

O. grande. TIGER ORCHID. Bright yellow flowers with mahogany brown stripes, 5–7 in. across, arranged 3–7 per stalk; stalks to 1 ft. long. Blooms in fall, lasting 3–4 weeks. Pseudobulbs 2–4 in. high with 2 dull green, broad, lance-shaped leaves 8–10 in. long. After bulbs mature, keep plant on dry side until growth shows again. Good cut flower.

OENOTHERA. *Onagraceae.* EVENING PRIMROSE. Biennials, perennials. All Zones. Valued for showy early summer flowers in tough, rough places.

O. berlandieri *(O. speciosa childsii)*. MEXICAN EVENING PRIMROSE. Perennial. During summer bloom period, profuse rose pink, 1½-in. flowers are carried on stems 10–12 in. high; stems die back after bloom. Blooms in daytime. Once established, thrives with little or no care. Invasive if not controlled. Good ground cover for dry slopes, parking strips.

Oenothera berlandieri

O. hookeri. Biennial. Western native. To 2–6 ft. high. Bright yellow, 3½-in. flowers open late afternoon to sunrise. Hairy, elliptical leaves.

O. missourensis. Perennial. Prostrate, sprawling stems to 10 in. long. Soft, velvety, 5-in. leaves. In late spring or summer, clear yellow flowers 3–5 in. across. One of most beautiful of evening primroses. Good rock garden subject.

O. stubbei (often sold as *O. drummondii*). BAJA EVENING PRIMROSE. Perennial. Desert native that makes a 5-in.-deep mat of dark green foliage. Blooms in spring and sporadically throughout the year; yellow, 2½-in. flowers rise on individual stems 6–8 in. above foliage. Endures heat and drought, but does better with occasional water.

O. tetragona. SUNDROPS. Perennial. Grows to 2 ft. with reddish stems and good green foliage. Daytime display of 1½-in.-wide, yellow blossoms throughout summer. Needs very little attention. Several varieties.

OKRA. *Malvaceae.* Warm-season annual vegetable crop that grows well under same conditions as sweet corn. Plant when ground begins to warm up. Soak seed 24 hours before planting to speed germination. Water regularly and fertilize at least once. Pods grow on large, erect, bushy plants with tropical-looking leaves. Harvest pods every 2 or 3 days. Best size is 1–3 in. long; overripe pods are tough, and they shorten plant's bearing life. In containers, variety 'Red River' has tropical look. In large tub in warm spot, a single plant can yield enough to make it worth growing.

Okra

OLD MAN CACTUS. See *Cephalocereus senilis.*

Oleaceae. The olive family contains trees and shrubs with leaves in opposite pairs and flowers with a 4-lobed calyx and 4-lobed corolla. (They appear to have 4 petals.) *Ligustrum* (privet), olive (*Olea*), and lilac (*Syringa*) are typical.

OLEA europaea. *Oleaceae.* OLIVE. Evergreen tree. Zones 8, 9, 11–24. Along with palms, citrus, and eucalyptus, olives stand out like regional trademarks along avenues and in gardens of California and southern Arizona. The trees' beauty has been appreciated in those areas since they were introduced to mission gardens for their oil.

Olea europaea

Willowlike foliage is a soft gray green that combines well with most colors. Smooth gray trunks and branches become gnarled and picturesque in maturity. Trees grow slowly, eventually reaching 25–30 ft. high and as wide; however, young trees put on height (if not substance) fairly fast. Begin training early. For single trunk, prune out or shorten side branches below point where you want branching to begin, stake tree firmly, and cut off basal suckers. For several trunks, stake lower branches or basal suckers to continue growth at desired angles.

Large old olive trees can (with reasonable care) be boxed and transplanted with near certainty of survival.

Olive trees need full sun. They're most lush when growing in deep, rich soil, but will also grow in shallow, alkaline, or stony soil and with little fertilizer. They thrive in areas with hot, dry summers, but also perform adequately in coastal areas. Take temperatures down to 15°F. Withstand heavy pruning—thinning each year shows off branch pattern to best advantage, and removing flowering-fruiting branches reduces or eliminates fruit crop, which is usually a nuisance.

Olives blacken and drop from tree late in the year. Without leaching and processing, they are inedible, and they can stain paving and harm a lawn if not removed. In addition to pruning, reduce crop by spraying with fruit-control hormones when tiny white flowers appear. Or spread tarpaulin at dropping time, knock off all fruit, and dispose of it. So-called fruitless varieties are not always reliably barren; see list.

Watch for scale insects; spray as needed. Olive knot occasionally forms galls on twigs and branches, eventually killing them; prune out infected wood, sterilizing instruments after making each cut. Verticillium wilt is a serious problem in some areas; you may be able to get olives grown on resistant understocks. The variety 'Swan Hill' has some tolerance; 'Oblonga' (purely an understock) has high resistance.

These varieties are sold:

'Fruitless'. Landscaping variety. Advertised as nonfruiting, but some have borne fruit.

'Little Ollie'. Dwarf, dense-growing fruitless olive suitable for hedge or low screen.

'Majestic Beauty'. Smaller than standard olive, more open in growth, with lighter green, longer, narrow leaves, no mature fruit.

'Manzanillo'. Landscaping and commercial variety with lower, more spreading growth habit than most. Large fruit.

'Mission'. Landscaping and commercial variety. Taller, more compact, and hardier than 'Manzanillo'. Smaller fruit than most, but has fine flavor and high oil content.

'Sevillano'. Commercial variety. Very large fruit, low oil content.

'Skylark Dwarf'. Neat, compact, large, dense shrub. Sets fruit very lightly. Leaves smallish (1–1½ in. long), deep blue green above, gray beneath.

'Swan Hill'. Landscaping variety. Fruitless because of flower deformity, which also results in little or no pollen to blow about—a boon to allergy sufferers.

OLEANDER. See *Nerium oleander.*

OLIVE. See *Olea europaea.*

OLMEDIELLA betschlerana. *Flacourtiaceae.* GUATEMALAN HOLLY, COSTA RICAN HOLLY, MANZANOTE. Evergreen shrub or small tree. Zones 9, 14–24. Fairly fast to 20–25 ft., 10–15-ft. spread. Dense foliage is bronzy when new, later turning dark green. Leaves resemble those of English holly, but have less prominent spines. Inconspicuous flowers. Female trees are capable of producing a few inedible fruits the size of a small orange. Young plants tender (plant after spring frosts); established plants hardy to 19°F. Sun or shade on coast; partial shade and ample water in inland valleys. Train as single or multi-trunked tree, or as big bush densely foliaged to base. Use as background plant, street or lawn tree, tall screen, barrier, trimmed hedge, or container plant. Do not use near swimming pools, though, since dry leaves are very stickery.

Olmediella betschlerana

OLNEYA tesota. *Leguminosae.* DESERT IRONWOOD. Evergreen tree. Zones 12, 13. Grows slowly to 25–30 ft. with equal spread. Branches erect in youth, later spreading. Gray green leaves, each with 2 spines at base, divided into many ¾-in. leaflets. In early summer, clusters of pinkish lavender, ½-in.-long, sweet pea–shaped flowers put on good show; 2-in.-long pods follow. Old leaves fall after bloom, with new ones replacing them quickly.

Name comes from extremely hard, heavy heartwood. Plant grows near washes where some deep water is usually available. Tree is deciduous in hard frosts and cannot endure prolonged freezes, but tolerates any amount of summer heat.

Olneya tesota

Onagraceae. Most members of the evening primrose family have flower parts in fours; otherwise, they are diverse in appearance and structure. Those that grow in Western gardens are all annuals

O

or perennials except for fuchsias. Many are Western natives (*Clarkia, Gaura, Zauschneria*).

ONCIDIUM. *Orchidaceae.* Epiphytic orchids. Greenhouse or indoors. Native from Florida to Brazil, and from sea level to high, cool mountains. In general, growth habit similar to odontoglossums. Hundreds of species and hybrids available. Most species have yellow flowers spotted or striped with brown; a few have white or rose-colored blooms.

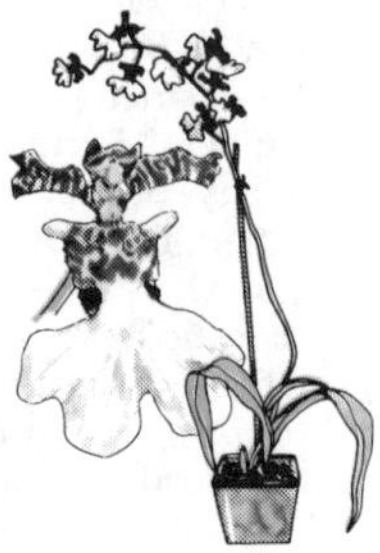

Oncidium splendidum

Water generously during growing season, sparingly during dormant period—just enough to keep pseudobulbs from shriveling. Give more light than odontoglossums. Give definite rest period to Mexican and Central American species. Potting medium same as for odontoglossums. Most species grow well under conditions recommended for cattleyas. Excellent cut flower.

O. cheirophorum. Colombia. Miniature species with fragrant, bright yellow, ½-in. flowers with green sepals. Dense, branched clusters in fall. Plant is seldom over 6 in. high, with bright green, grasslike leaves.

O. crispum. Brazil. Shiny brown, 1½–3-in. flowers with yellow and red at base of segments. Borne in profusion on 1–1½-ft., arching stems any time throughout year. Rough, flat, usually dark brown pseudobulbs 3–4 in. high; leathery, 6–9-in., lance-shaped leaves. Never let plants dry out completely.

O. flexuosum. Brazil. Many 1-in. flowers on branched stems 2–3 ft. long. Sepals and petals very small, barred green and brown, lip quite large and bright yellow. Flattened, egg-shaped pseudobulbs to 2 in., with 2 strap-shaped, thin leaves below and 2 above. Blooms well in great range of temperatures and light conditions. Excellent orchid for beginners.

O. papilio. BUTTERFLY ORCHID. West Indies. Flowers 4–5 in. long, 2½ in. across. Top sepals and petals stand erect, are brown with bands of yellow; lower sepals and petals curve downward and are yellow with bands of brown. Lip yellow, edged brown. Flowers open 1 at a time on 2–3-ft.-long stalk which continues to produce buds on old flower stems for several years. Blooms any time of year. Rounded, dark purple pseudobulbs. Olive green leaves, mottled with brownish purple.

O. splendidum. Guatemala and Mexico. Branched, 2–3-ft., erect flower stems produce profusion of 3-in. flowers in winter. Sepals and petals yellow green, barred and blotched with reddish brown, recurved at tips; large, flat, clear yellow lip. Two-inch pseudobulbs bear a single stiff, leathery leaf 9–15 in. high.

O. varicosum. DANCING LADY. Brazil. Golden yellow, 2-in. flowers barred with reddish brown appear in great profusion in 3-ft.-long, branched, arching sprays in fall and winter. Oblong, 3–4-in.-high pseudobulbs bear pair of 6–9-in.-long leaves.

ONION. *Amaryllidaceae.* For ornamental relatives, see *Allium*. Onions are biennials grown as annuals. Grow them from seed or sets (small bulbs). Sets are easiest for beginners, but seed gives larger crop for smaller investment. In mild climates, sets can go in 1–1½ in. deep and 1–2 in. apart all winter long and through April. Where winters are cold, plant sets in earliest spring. Start pulling green onions in 3 weeks or so; any not needed as green onions can grow on for later harvest as dry onions when tops wither. Plant seed in early spring in rows 15–18 in. apart. Soil should be loose, rich, and well drained. When seedlings are pencil sized, thin to 3–4 in. apart, transplanting thinnings to extend plantings. Trim back tops of transplants about halfway. In some areas, onion plants (field-grown, near pencil-sized transplants or seedlings growing in pots) are available.

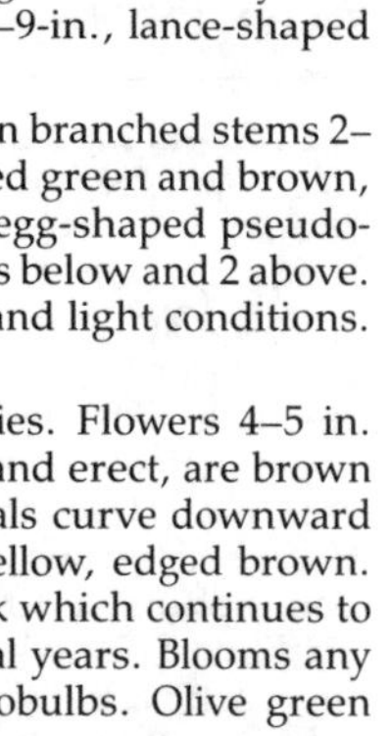

Onion

Do not let onions go dry; they are shallow rooted and need moisture fairly near the surface. Also feed plants, especially early in season: the larger and stronger the plants grow, the larger bulbs they form. For same reason, carefully eliminate weeds that compete for light, food, and water. When most of the tops have begun to yellow and fall over, dig bulbs and let them cure and dry on top of ground for several days. Then pull off tops, clean, and store in dark, cool, airy place.

Of the more familiar varieties, look for 'Crystal Wax Bermuda', 'Southport White Globe', and 'White Sweet Spanish' if you like white onions. Good yellow varieties are 'Early Yellow Globe', 'Yellow Globe Danvers', and 'Utah Sweet Spanish'. Fine red variety is 'Southport Red Globe'. An unusual onion is the long, red, very mild 'Italian Red' or 'Red Torpedo'.

ONOCLEA sensibilis. *Polypodiaceae.* SENSITIVE FERN. Zones 1–9, 14–24. Native to eastern U.S. Coarse-textured fern with 2–4-ft. sterile fronds divided nearly to midrib; fertile fronds smaller, with clusters of almost beadlike leaflets. Fronds come from underground creeping rhizome which can be invasive in wet, rich soil. Dies down in winter. Takes sun if moisture is adequate. Fronds seem coarse to many gardeners.

Onoclea sensibilis

ONOSMA tauricum. *Boraginaceae.* GOLDEN DROPS. Perennial. Zones 1–9, 14–17. Low-growing, irregular clumps to 8 in. high, spreading to 1½ ft. wide, with rough, dull green, narrow, 1–2-in.-long leaves. One main vertical stem with smaller, drooping side branches. Fragrant, long, tubular, yellow, 1½-in.-long flowers in fiddleneck clusters at tips of main stalk and side branches. Sun or part shade. Plant in well-drained soil and avoid overwatering. Use in rock gardens or include in low planting scheme of grays and yellows.

Onosma tauricum

OPHIOPOGON. See *Liriope and Ophiopogon*.

OPUNTIA. *Cactaceae.* Cactus. Many kinds, with varied appearance. Most species fall into 1 of 2 sorts: those having flat, broad joints or those having cylindrical joints. Members of the first group are often called PRICKLY PEAR, the second CHOLLA, but terms are rather loose. Hardiness is variable. Flowers are generally large and showy. The fruit is a berry, often edible. Need little or no water once established.

Opuntia microdasys

O. bigelovii. TEDDYBEAR CACTUS. Zones 11–24. Native to Arizona, Nevada, California, northern Mexico. Treelike plant of slow growth to 2–8 ft. Woody trunk covered with black spines. Branches cylindrical, easily detached, covered with vicious, silvery yellow spines. Flowers pale green, yellow, or white marked with lavender, 1–1½ in. wide. April bloom. Grows freely in hottest, driest deserts.

O. ficus-indica. Zones 8, 9, 12–24. Big shrubby or treelike cactus to 15 ft., with woody trunks and smooth, flat, green joints 15–20 in. long. Few or no spines, but has clusters of bristles. Yellow flowers 4 in. across, spring or early summer. Large, edible, red or yellow fruit, often sold in markets. Handle it carefully—bristles break off easily and are irritating. Use rubber gloves when peeling fruit, or impale fruit on a fork and strip skin carefully, avoiding bristly areas.

O. microdasys. BUNNY EARS. Zones 13–24. Mexico. Fast growth to 2 ft. high, 4–5 ft. wide (much smaller in pots). Pads flat, thin, nearly round, to 6 in. across, velvety soft green with neatly spaced tufts of short golden bristles in polka dot effect. *O. m.* 'Albispina' has white bristles. Small round new pads atop larger old ones give plant silhouette of animal's head. Favorite with children.

ORANGE. See *Citrus.*

ORANGE CLOCK VINE. See *Thunbergia gregorii.*

ORANGE JESSAMINE. See *Murraya paniculata.*

ORANGEQUAT. See *Citrus.*

Orchidaceae. Each of the kinds of orchids available to westerners is described fully in this book under its name (e.g., *Cattleya, Cymbidium, Laelia,* etc.). Here we explain the terms used in those descriptions and provide some information on basic culture.

Orchid growers' terms. Here are the orchid growers' terms you'll encounter in this book.

Epiphytic. Some orchids are epiphytic, growing high in branches of trees in tropical or subtropical jungles, clinging to bark, but obtaining their nourishment from air, rain, and whatever decaying vegetable matter they can trap in their root systems.

Pseudobulb. Epiphytic orchids have thickened stems called pseudobulbs which store food and water, making it possible for the plants to survive drought. These may be short and fat like bulbs, or erect and slender. They vary from green to brown in color. Leaves may grow along pseudobulbs or from their tips.

Terrestrial. Some orchids (including most native orchids) are terrestrial, with their roots growing in loose, moist soil rich in humus—often in wooded areas, but sometimes in open meadows as well. These orchids require constant moisture and food.

Sepals, petals, lip, and pouch. Segments of an orchid flower include 3 sepals and 3 petals; one of the petals, usually the lowest one, is referred to in descriptions as a lip. This lip is usually larger and more brightly colored than other segments. Sometimes it is fantastically shaped, with various appendages and markings. It may be folded into a slipperlike "pouch."

Rafts, bark. Nearly all orchids, terrestrial or epiphytic, are grown in pots. A few are grown on "rafts" or slabs of bark or wood, or in baskets of wood slats; a few natives are grown in open ground.

Basic orchid culture. For more information, refer to the *Sunset* book *How to Grow Orchids.*

Potting and growing. Potting materials for cattleyas (most commonly grown orchids) will work for most epiphytic orchids: osmunda fiber, hapuu (tree fern stem), or ground bark. Most popular now is bark, which is readily available, easy to handle, and fairly inexpensive. Use fine grade for 3-in. or smaller pots, medium grade for 4-in. or larger pots. It's sensible to use ready-made mixes sold by orchid growers; these are blended for proper texture and acidity.

Water plants about once a week—when mix dries out and becomes lightweight. Feed with a commercial water-soluble orchid fertilizer once every 2 weeks during growing season. To provide humidity for plants in house, fill a metal or plastic tray with gravel and add just enough water to reach almost to top of gravel. Stretch hardware cloth over pan, leaving an inch between gravel and wire for air circulation. Set pots on top. Maintain water level.

Temperature requirements. Below, we list orchids according to their temperature requirements. Many of the cool-growing orchids are hardy enough to grow outdoors in mild-winter areas; some are native to our western states.

Temperate-climate orchids can be grown in pots on a window sill with other house plants, but will perform best if given additional humidity. An excellent method of supplying humidity is described in "Potting and growing," above. Most temperate-climate orchids can be moved outdoors in summer; place them in the shade of high-branching trees, on the patio, or in a lathhouse.

Warm-climate orchids need greenhouse conditions to provide uniform warmer temperatures and high humidity they require.

Cool-climate orchids: *Bletilla, Calypso, Cymbidium, Epidendrum, Epipactis, Laelia, Odontoglossum, Paphiopedilum* (green-leafed forms), *Pleione.* Some of these are hardy out of doors in mildest parts of California. Some are thoroughly hardy.

Temperate-climate orchids: *Brassavola, Cattleya, Coelogyne, Dendrobium, Epidendrum, Laelia, Lycaste, Oncidium, Paphiopedilum* (mottled-leafed forms).

Warm-climate orchids: *Phalaenopsis, Vanda.*

ORCHID CACTUS. See *Epiphyllum.*

ORCHID TREE. See *Bauhinia.*

ORCHID VINE. See *Stigmaphyllon ciliatum.*

OREGANO. See *Origanum vulgare.*

OREGON BOXWOOD. See *Paxistima myrsinites.*

OREGON GRAPE. See *Mahonia aquifolium.*

OREGON MYRTLE. See *Umbellularia californica.*

ORGANPIPE CACTUS. See *Lemaireocereus thurberi.*

ORIENTAL ARBORVITAE. See *Platycladus orientalis.*

ORIENTAL GARLIC. See *Allium tuberosum.*

ORIENTAL POPPY. See *Papaver orientale.*

ORIGANUM. *Labiatae.* Subshrubs or perennials, some short-lived. Mint relatives with tight clusters of small flowers and foliage with a strong, pleasant scent. Bracts in flower clusters overlap, giving effect of small pine cones. Sun; little water; good drainage. Not fussy about soil type.

Origanum majorana

O. dictamnus *(Amaracus dictamnus).* CRETE DITTANY. Perennial. Zones 8–24. Native to Mediterranean area. Aromatic herb with slender, arching stems to 1 ft. long. Thick, roundish, woolly white leaves to ¾ in. long; somewhat mottled. Flowers pink to purplish, ½ in. long; rose purple fruit in conelike heads. Blooms summer to fall. Shows up best when planted individually in rock garden, container, or hanging basket.

O. majorana *(Majorana hortensis).* SWEET MARJORAM. Perennial herb in Zones 4–24; summer annual elsewhere. To 1–2 ft. Tiny, oval, gray green leaves; spikes of white flowers in loose clusters at top of plant. Grow in fairly moist soil, full sun. Keep blossoms cut off and plant trimmed to prevent woody growth. Propagate from seeds, cuttings, or root divisions. It's a favorite herb for seasoning meats, salads, vinegars, casserole dishes. Use leaves fresh or dried. Often grown in container indoors on window sill in cold-winter areas.

O. vulgare. OREGANO, WILD MARJORAM. Perennial herb. All Zones. Upright growth to 2½ ft. Spreads by underground stems. Medium-sized oval leaves; purplish pink blooms. Grow in sun, medium-rich soil; needs good drainage, average watering. Keep trimmed to prevent flowering. Replant every 3 years. Fresh or dried leaves are used in many dishes, especially Italian and Spanish ones.

O

ORNAMENTAL PEAR. See *Pyrus.*

ORNITHOGALUM. *Liliaceae.* Bulbs. Zones 5–24. Leaves vary from narrow to broad and tend to be floppy. Flowers mostly star shaped, in tall or rounded clusters. Most bloom in April–May. Grow in sun. Use in borders or grow in pots.

Ornithogalum caudatum

O. arabicum. STAR OF BETHLEHEM. Handsome clusters of 2-in., white, waxy flowers with beady black pistils in centers. Stems 2 ft. tall. Floppy leaves to 2 ft. long, 1 in. wide, bluish green. Bulbs hardy except in coldest winters; in cool-summer climates, bulbs may not bloom second year after planting because of lack of sufficient heat. Wet-winter, dry-summer plant. Can be grown in pots. Excellent cut flower.

O. caudatum. PREGNANT ONION, FALSE SEA ONION. House plant. Grown for bulb and foliage rather than for tall wands of small green and white flowers. Strap-shaped leaves hang downward and grow to 5 ft. long. Big, gray green, smooth-skinned bulb (3–4 in. thick) grows on, not in, the ground. Bulblets form under skin and grow quite large before they drop out and root. Hardy to 25°F.; will lose leaves in extended drought. Does best with 4 hours of sun daily.

O. thyrsoides. CHINCHERINCHEE. Tapering, compact clusters of white, 2-in. flowers with brownish green centers. Leaves bright green, upright, 2 in. wide, 10–12 in. long. Flower stems 2 ft. high. Usually considered tender, but has survived cold winters in sheltered south or southwest location when well mulched. Average water. Long-lasting cut flower.

O. umbellatum. STAR OF BETHLEHEM. Probably hardiest of group. May naturalize widely once it's established—can become pest. Clusters of 1-in.-wide flowers, striped green on outside, top 1-ft. stems. Grasslike leaves about as long as flower stems. Cut flowers last well but close at night. Give adequate water for good performance.

OSAGE ORANGE. See *Maclura pomifera.*

OSCULARIA. *Aizoaceae.* Subshrubs. Zones 15–24. Low plants with erect or trailing branches. To 1 ft. tall. Leaves very thick and fleshy, triangular, blue green with pink flush. Fragrant flowers to ½ in. across in late spring, early summer. Full sun. Need little water. Best in pots, hanging baskets, rock gardens, borders. Can be used for small-scale ground cover.

Oscularia deltoides

O. deltoides. Has purplish rose flowers.

O. pedunculata. Has paler, mauve pink flowers.

OSMANTHUS. *Oleaceae.* Evergreen shrubs or trees. All have clean, leathery, attractive foliage and inconspicuous but fragrant flowers. Take considerable drought once established. Good in full sun but perform well in light to medium shade. Tolerate broad range of soils, including heavy clays.

Osmanthus fragrans

O. decorus. See *Phillyrea decora.*

O. delavayi *(Siphonosmanthus delavayi).* DELAVAY OSMANTHUS. Shrub. Zones 4–9, 14–21. Slow growing, graceful, to 4–6 ft., with arching branches spreading wider. Leaves dark green, oval, to 1 in. long, with toothed edges. White, fragrant flowers (largest of any osmanthus) in profusion in clusters of 4–8, March–May. Attractive all year. Easily controlled by pruning. Good choice for foundations, massing. Handsome on retaining wall where branches hang down. In hot-summer areas, give partial shade.

O. fortunei. Shrub. Zones 5–10, 14–24. Hybrid between *O. heterophyllus* and *O. fragrans.* Slow, dense growth to eventual 20 ft. tall; usually seen at height of about 6 ft. Leaves are oval, hollylike, up to 4 in. long. Small, fragrant white flowers bloom during spring, summer.

O. f. 'San Jose'. Similar in appearance to species but has cream to orange flowers in October.

O. fragrans. SWEET OLIVE. Shrub. Zones 8, 9, 12–24. Moderate growth to 10 ft. and more with age. Broad, dense, compact. Can be pruned to upright growth where space is limited. Can be trained as small tree, hedge, screen, background, espalier, container plant. Pinch out growing tips of young plants to induce bushiness.

Leaves glossy, medium green, oval, to 4 in. long, toothed or smooth edged. Flowers tiny, white, inconspicuous except in their powerful, sweet, apricotlike fragrance. Bloom heaviest in spring and early summer, but plants flower sporadically throughout year in mild-winter areas. Young plants grow best in some shade, but tolerate sun as they mature. In Zones 12, 13, grow in east or north exposure.

O. f. aurantiacus. Leaves narrower and less glossy than those of *O. fragrans.* Concentrates its crop of wonderfully fragrant orange flowers in October.

O. heterophyllus *(O. aquifolium, O. ilicifolius).* HOLLY-LEAF OSMANTHUS. Shrub. Zones 3–10, 14–24. Useful as hedge. A number of varieties are available:

'Gulftide'. Similar to 'Ilicifolius' but more compact.

'Ilicifolius'. Dense, symmetrical upright growth to 6–8 ft., eventually to 20 ft. Leaves dark green, strongly toothed, hollylike, to 2½ in. long. Fragrant white flowers in fall, winter, early spring. Excellent for screening, background.

'Purpureus' ('Purpurascens'). Dark purple new growth, with purple tints through summer.

'Rotundifolius'. Slow growing to 5 ft. Roundish small leaves are lightly spined along edges.

'Variegatus'. Slow growing to 4–5 ft., with densely set leaves edged creamy white. Useful to light up shady areas.

OSMAREA burkwoodii. *Oleaceae.* Evergreen shrub. Zones 4–9, 14–17. Hybrid between *Osmanthus delavayi* and *Phillyrea decora.* Similar to *Osmanthus delavayi* but does not flower as freely. Slow growing to 6 ft. and as wide. Bushy, compact, and well foliaged, with dark green, glossy, toothed leaves 1–2 in. long. Small, fragrant white flowers in clusters, April–May. Sun or part shade. Drought tolerant. Good hedge.

Osmarea burkwoodii

OSMUNDA regalis. *Osmundaceae.* ROYAL FERN. All Zones; best in Zones 4–6. Big, extremely handsome fern with twice-cut fronds and large leaflets; texture coarser than that of most ferns. Fertile leaflets small, clustered at tips of fronds. Can reach 6 ft. in moist, shady places. Leaves die back in winter.

Osmunda regalis

OSTEOSPERMUM. *Compositae.* AFRICAN DAISY. (For other African daisies, see *Arctotis, Dimorphotheca.*) Evergreen subshrubs or perennials. Zones 8, 9, 14–24. South African plants closely related to *Dimorphotheca* (Cape marigold) and often sold as such. Except for trailing perennial *O. fruticosum,* all are spreading, mounded shrubby plants with medium-green foliage and profusion of daisylike flowers over long season (best spring, summer). Leaves variable in size and shape, larger on young plants and vigorous young shoots, 2–4 in. long, narrowish oval, smooth edged or with a few large teeth. Flowers, on long stems, open only in sunlight.

Osteospermum fruticosum

Grow in full sun. Plants look best with moderate watering and good garden soil, but will stand drought and neglect when established. Tip-pinching young plants will induce bushiness; cutting back old, sprawling branches to young side branches will keep plants neat, often induce repeat bloom. Use in borders or mass plantings along driveways or paths, on slopes, in front of screening shrubs. Grow from seeds or cuttings (named varieties from cuttings only).

O. barberae *(Dimorphotheca barberae)*. To 2–3 ft. tall, a little wider. Flower heads 2–3 in. across. Rays pinkish lilac inside, with deep purplish blue stripes on reverse; dark purple blue centers. Blooms from fall through spring, frequently through summer. This and other related daisies hybridize freely, and seedlings vary in height and color. Most will be lavender pink.

O. 'Buttersweet'. Plant form resembles that of *O. barberae.* Flower heads have primrose yellow rays fading to cream near center, lavender to brownish zone at base, lavender blue to brownish center. Backs of rays yellow with pronounced brown stripe. Spring to frost.

O. ecklonis *(Dimorphotheca ecklonis)*. Grows 2–4 ft. tall, equally broad. Long stems bear 3-in. flower heads with white rays (tinged lavender blue on backs), dark blue center. Blooms early summer to frost.

O. fruticosum *(Dimorphotheca fruticosa)*. TRAILING AFRICAN DAISY, FREEWAY DAISY. Spreads rapidly by trailing, rooting branches. Rooted cuttings will cover circle 2–4 ft. across in year; plants grow to 6–12 in. tall. Leaves shorter, thicker than those of other species. Blooms intermittently during year, most heavily November–March. Heads to 2 in. across; rays lilac above, fading nearly white by second day, deeper lilac beneath and in bud; dark purple center. Excellent ground cover for sunny areas; good bank cover. Needs well-drained soil. Does well at seashore. Fire retardant when well watered. Will spill over wall or grow in hanging basket (tip-pinch to induce bushiness). Used as annual (fall planting) in Zones 12, 13. White form (sold as 'Hybrid White', 'White Cloud', 'Snow White') grows more upright, blooms in sheets in late winter and early spring. Deep purple varieties are 'African Queen' and 'Burgundy Mound'.

O. 'Golden Charm'. Resembles *O.* 'Buttersweet', but rays and centers are bright yellow.

OSTRICH FERN. See *Matteuccia struthiopteris.*

OSWEGO TEA. See *Monarda.*

OTACANTHUS coeruleus. *Scrophulariaceae.* Perennial grown as an annual, or a house plant. All Zones. Shrubby-based plant to 2–2½ ft. tall and as wide. Paired oval leaves are 3 in. long, less than 1 in. wide. Stalks are topped by clusters of bright blue, 1½-in., 2-lipped flowers with white spot in throat. Attractive pot plant; can be used outdoors as a summer bedding plant. Full sun or part shade near coast, afternoon shade in interior. Rich soil, ample water and feeding. Tender to frost.

Otacanthus coeruleus

OTATEA. See Bamboo.

OUR LORD'S CANDLE. See *Yucca whipplei.*

OXALIS. *Oxalidaceae.* Perennials; some grow from bulbs or rhizomes. Leaves divided into leaflets; usually have 3 leaflets, like clover leaves. Flowers pink, white, rose, or yellow. Most can go completely dry in summer. Two species can be aggressive weeds: *O. corniculata* and its red-leafed form, with small yellow flowers and creeping, rooting stems; and the Bermuda buttercup (*O. pes-caprae*), an attractive plant with large yellow flowers on long (to 1-ft.) stalks. All species except *O. oregana* can be grown as house plants anywhere—keep them in a sunny window.

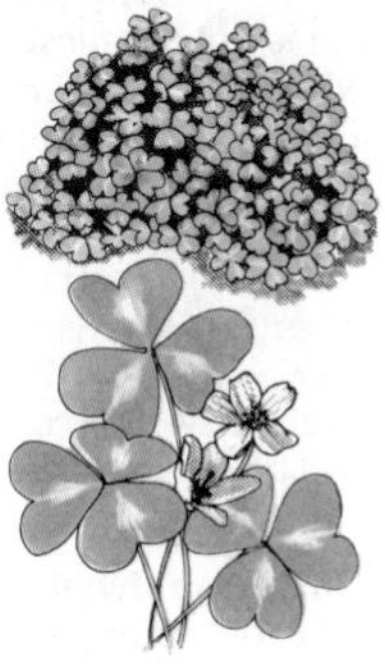

Oxalis oregana

O. acetosella. WOOD SORREL, SHAMROCK. One of several plants known as shamrock. See Shamrock.

O. adenophylla. Zones 4–9, 12–24. Low (4-in.-high), dense, compact tuft of leaves, each leaf with 12–22 crinkly, gray green leaflets. Flowers are 1 in. wide, on 4–6-in. stalks, bell shaped, lilac pink with deeper veins, in late spring. Plant roots in fall. Needs good drainage, full sun. Good rock garden plant or companion to bulbs such as species tulips or the smaller kinds of narcissus, in pots or in the ground.

O. bowiei. Zones 4–9, 12–24. Has survived 0°F. with only light mulching, but better known as house plant. Cloverlike leaves of 3 leaflets topped by 1-ft.-high stems with pink or rose purple summer flowers 1½–2 in. across.

O. corymbosa *(O. martiana)*. Zones 8, 9, 12–24. House plant everywhere. Plant 8–12 in. tall, with 3 heart-shaped leaflets to each leaf and a cluster of many reddish purple flowers on each bloom stalk.

O. crassipes. Zones 8, 9, 12–24. Compact evergreen plant seems to bloom at all seasons. At top of 6–18-in.-high stalks are small pink flowers. Enough open at one time to be effective. There is a white-flowered form, *O. c.* 'Alba', and a blush pink one, *O. c.* 'Pinkie'.

O. hedysaroides 'Rubra'. FIRE FERN. House plant. Shrubby, with erect stems to 3 ft. Flowers yellow, not especially showy. Maroon red leaves of 3-in. leaflets. Bright light. Let soil dry out between waterings.

O. hirta. Zones 8, 9, 14–24. Many upright, branching stems to 1 ft. high that gradually fall over with weight of leaves and flowers. Leaves cloverlike, small, set directly against stems or on very short stalks. General effect is feathery. Flowers (late fall or winter) bright rose pink, 1 in. wide. Plant bulbs in fall. Quite drought tolerant. Good in rock gardens, hanging baskets.

O. lasiandra. Zones 8, 9, 12–24. Leaves wheel shaped, with as many as 10 narrow leaflets. Foot-tall stems carry many dark red flowers slightly under 1 in. long.

O. latifolia. Zones 8, 9, 12–24. Clumps of 6-in. leaf stalks topped by leaves that resemble those of *O. regnellii* (see below). Small pink to purple flowers. The common garden kind has dark red leaves.

O. martiana. See *O. corymbosa.*

O. oregana. REDWOOD SORREL, OREGON OXALIS. Zones 4–9, 14–24. Native to coastal forests from Washington to California. Creeping white roots send up velvety, medium green, cloverlike leaves 1½–4 in. wide on stems 2–10 in. high. Flowers to 1 in. across, pink or white veined with lavender, borne in spring, sometimes again in fall. Interesting ground cover for part shade to deep shade in mild-winter, cool-summer areas. Good with ferns. Looks most lush when watered frequently.

O. pes-caprae *(O. cernua)*. BERMUDA BUTTERCUP. Zones 8, 9, 12–24. Clusters of bright green cloverlike leaves (often spotted with dark brown) spring directly from soil in fall. Above them in winter and spring rise stems up to 1 ft. long topped with clusters of inch-wide, bright yellow flowers. This handsome plant is best grown in pots or baskets; it spreads rapidly by rhizomes and bulbs, and it can become a troublesome pest in an open garden.

(Continued on next page)

O. purpurea *(O. variabilis)*. Zones 8, 9, 12–24. Low growing (4–5 in. tall), with large cloverlike leaves and rose red flowers an inch across, November–March. Spreads by bulbs and rhizomelike roots, but is not aggressive or weedy. Plant bulbs in fall. Improved kinds with larger flowers sold under the name Grand Duchess; flowers are rose pink, white, or lavender.

O. regnellii. House plant. Erect stem to nearly 1 ft. tall has many long-stemmed, drooping leaves, each with 3-in.-long leaflets shaped like triangles attached by their points—three-quarters of an iron cross. Flowers white, dainty. Same culture as *O. hedysaroides* 'Rubra'.

O. versicolor. Zones 8, 9, 12–24. To 8 in. tall, with ½-in. leaflets and inch-long, candy-striped flowers of creamy white to yellow and purplish violet.

OXERA pulchella. *Verbenaceae.* Evergreen vine or vining shrub. Zones 22–24. As a shrub, mounding to 6 ft. tall; with support, can be trained to 10 ft. Leaves leathery, glossy, very dark green, oblong, to 5 in. long. Clusters of white, waxy, 2-in. trumpets give winter or spring display of unusual quality at varying times of year. Refined appearance. Best in high shade or cool, sunny spot. Average water.

Oxera pulchella

OXYDENDRUM arboreum. *Ericaceae.* SOURWOOD, SORREL TREE. Deciduous tree. Zones 3–9, 14–17. Native to eastern U.S. Slow growth to 15–25 ft., eventually to 50 ft. Slender trunk, slightly spreading head. Leaves 5–8 in. long, narrow, somewhat resemble peach leaves; bronze tinted in early spring, rich green in summer, orange and scarlet in autumn. Creamy white, bell-shaped flowers in 10-in.-long, drooping clusters at branch tips, late July–August. In autumn, when foliage is brilliant scarlet, branching clusters of greenish seed capsules extend outward and downward like fingers; capsules turn light silver gray and hang on late into winter.

Oxydendrum arboreum

Best known in areas with cool summers, well-defined winters. Requires acid soil, ample water. Not competitive—doesn't do well in lawns or under larger trees. Avoid underplanting with anything needing cultivation. Good shade tree for patio or terrace. Distinguished branch and leaf pattern, spring leaf color, summer flowers, fall color. Young plants are good container subjects.

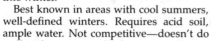

PACHISTIMA. See *Paxistima*.

PACHYPODIUM lamieri. *Apocynaceae.* MADAGASCAR PALM. House or indoor/outdoor plant. Not a palm, though somewhat palmlike. Easy-to-grow succulent with impressive silhouette: succulent trunk 2–4 ft. tall (or more, with age) is unbranched, spiny, topped with a circle of strap-shaped leaves to 10 in. long, 1 in. wide. White flowers seldom seen. Needs excellent drainage, bright light. Water only when soil becomes dry.

Pachypodium lamieri

PACHYRHIZUS erosus. *Leguminosae.* JICAMA. Annual vine. Zones 7–16, 18–24. Grown for its edible root, which looks like a large brown turnip and tastes something like a water chestnut. Twining or scrambling vines are attractive, with luxuriant deep green foliage and pretty purple or violet flower clusters. Leaves have 3 leaflets, each the size of a hand; upright spikes of sweet pea-shaped flowers appear in late summer. They should be pinched out for maximum root production, but you can allow seed for next year's crop to form on 1 or 2 plants. Needs long, warm growing season and good garden soil. Sow seeds in full sun after danger of frost is past, 1–1½ in. deep, 6–12 in. apart in rows. Do not let plants go dry, and feed once or twice in early or midsummer. Tubers form as days begin to grow shorter and should be harvested before first frost.

Although roots are delicious, seeds are poisonous and should not be eaten.

Pachyrhizus erosus

PACHYSANDRA terminalis. *Buxaceae.* JAPANESE SPURGE. Evergreen subshrub. Zones 1–10, 14–21. Use it as ground cover in shade. Spreads by underground runners. In deep shade, stems reach 10 in.; in dappled shade, 6 in. Leaves are rich dark green (yellowish in full sun), 2–4 in. long, in clusters atop stems. 'Variegata' has leaves edged with white. Small, fluffy spikes of fragrant white flowers in summer; white fruit follows.

Pachysandra terminalis

Set 6–12 in. apart in rich, preferably acid soil. Give plenty of water, especially while plants are getting established. Feed during growing season for best color. May spread moderately, but is not aggressive or weedy. Good transition between walks or lawns and shade-loving shrubs.

PACHYSTACHYS lutea. *Acanthaceae.* GOLDEN CANDLE. Evergreen shrub. Zones 21–24. House plant anywhere. Soft-wooded shrub related to and resembling shrimp plant (*Justicia brandegeana*), but broader, more erect and open, with brighter green foliage. Leaves to 6 in. long, 2 in. wide. Branches tipped with 3–6-in. spikes of neatly overlapping golden yellow bracts. True flowers are slender white tubes that appear from between bracts. Flowers last only a few days, but spike is attractive for many weeks. Blooms throughout warm weather—nearly all year in greenhouse, with peak production in summer. Needs rich soil, partial shade, ample water. Occasional thorough leaching will prevent salt burn in areas where water is salt laden. Pinch tips to encourage bushy growth; plant can grow to 5–6 ft. high and as wide under the most favorable conditions, but usually tops out at 3 ft. Where grown outdoors, may need protection from frost.

Pachystachys lutea

PAEONIA. *Paeoniaceae.* PEONY. Practically all garden peonies are hybrids. These fall into 2 principal classes, herbaceous and tree peonies.

Herbaceous peonies. Perennials growing from thickened, tuberous roots. Zones 1–11, 14–16. Well-grown clumps reach 2–4 ft. tall and spread wider. Large, deep green, attractively divided leaves make effective background for spectacular mid to late spring flowers. These may be: single (uncommon but very effective); single filled with mass of narrow, yellow, petal-like structures (Japanese type); semidouble; or fully double. Colors range from pure white through pale creams and pinks to red. Flowers may reach 10 in. across. Newer kinds have deeper reds and chocolate tones; there is even a pure yellow. Many have fragrance of old-fashioned roses.

Paeonia

Paeonia

Herbaceous peonies bloom really well only when they experience a period of pronounced winter chill. Winter cold and summer heat are not problems, but flowers do not last well where spring days are hot and dry; in such areas, choose early-blooming varieties and give plants some afternoon shade and ample water. Where they grow best—in Zones 1–7—they thrive in full sun.

Herbaceous peonies can grow in most soils, but because they are long lived, prepare soil well to at least 1½ ft. deep. Keep manure from direct contact with roots. Plant in early fall, being careful that eyes on tubers are no deeper than 2 in.; deeper planting may prevent blooming. Feed established clumps like other plants. Provide support for heavy flowers. Cut off stems carefully just below soil surface in fall after leaves turn brown. Fairly pest free. To control botrytis, which browns buds and spots leaves, spray with copper fungicide or benomyl before buds open; cut out and destroy all withered buds, stems, and brown-spotted leaves.

Divide clumps only when absolutely necessary, in early fall. To divide, dig plants, cut off foliage, hose dirt from root cluster, and divide carefully into sections with at least 3 eyes (pink growth buds).

These peonies are choice cut flowers and a mainstay of big perennial borders. Can be planted in bays of big shrub borders.

Tree peonies. Deciduous shrubs. Zones 2–12, 14–21. Descendants of *P. suffruticosa,* Chinese shrub to 6 ft. tall; yellow and salmon varieties are hybrids of this and *P. lutea,* Tibetan plant with yellow flowers. Irregular, picturesque branching habit; plants grow 3–6 ft. tall, eventually as wide. Leaves large, divided, blue green to bronzy green.

Flowers very large, up to 1 ft. across, single to fully double. Japanese types have single to double flowers held erect above foliage; silky petals range from white through pink and red to lavender and purple. European types have very heavy double flowers that tend to droop and hide their heads; colors range chiefly through pinks and rosy shades. Hybrids with *P. lutea* have single to fully double flowers in yellow, salmon, or sunset shades; singles and semidoubles hold up their flowers best.

Very hardy to cold and less dependent on winter chill than herbaceous peonies; can get botrytis in humid climates. Fragile blooms come in early to midspring and should be sheltered from strong winds. Give plants afternoon shade in hot-summer climates. Plant in fall or earliest spring (from containers any time) in rich, deep, well-prepared soil away from competing tree roots. Plants are long-lived, so take special pains to improve soil with peat moss or ground bark. Plant deep, setting plant several inches deeper than it grew in nursery can or growing field. Water regularly in summer. To prune, remove spent flowers and cut back to live wood in spring when buds begin to swell.

Many varieties are available, and some nurseries sell unnamed seedlings; select the latter in bloom to get desired form and color. Bare-root grafted plants are offered in winter, earliest spring.

PAINTED DAISY. See *Chrysanthemum coccineum.*

PAINTED FINGERNAIL PLANT. See *Neoregelia spectabilis.*

PAINTED-TONGUE. See *Salpiglossis sinuata.*

Palmae. It's difficult to generalize about any plant family as large and widespread as palms. Generally speaking, they have single, unbranched trunks of considerable height; some grow in clusters, though, and some are dwarf or stemless. The leaves are usually divided into many leaflets, either like ribs of a fan (fan palms) or like a feather, with many parallel leaflets growing outward from a long central stem (feather palms). But some palms have undivided leaves.

Most palms are tropical or subtropical; a few are surprisingly hardy (seen in Edinburgh, London, and southern Russia, as well as Portland and Seattle).

Palms offer great opportunity for imaginative planting. In nature they grow not only in solid stands but also in company with other plants, notably broad-leafed evergreen trees and shrubs. They are effective near swimming pools.

Most young palms prefer shade and all tolerate it; this fact makes them good house or patio plants when they are small. As they grow, they can be moved into sun or part shade, depending on species.

Growth rates vary, but keeping plants in pots usually slows growth of faster-growing kinds. If temperatures are in the 60s or higher, fertilize potted palms often; also wash them off frequently to provide some humidity and clean the foliage. Washing also dislodges insects, which (indoors, at any rate) are protected from their natural enemies and can increase at an unnatural rate.

To pot a palm, supply good potting soil, adequate drainage, and not too big a container. As with all potted plants, pot or repot a palm in a container just slightly larger than the one it's in.

Some shade-tolerant palms such as *Rhapis, Chamaedorea,* and *Howea* may spend decades in pots indoors. Others that later may reach great size—*Phoenix, Washingtonia, Chamaerops*—make charming temporary indoor plants but must eventually be moved.

To plant a palm of 5-gallon size in the ground, dig a hole 3 ft. wide and 8 in. deeper than root ball. At bottom, place 1–2 cubic ft. of manure, fortified sawdust, or other organic amendment, with a handful or two of blood meal added. Put 6-in. layer of soil over this, set palm, and fill around it with mixture of half native soil and half fortified sawdust, ground bark, or peat moss. Water well; continue watering throughout summer and fall. Give gallon-sized palms the same treatment (scaled down).

Palms, even big ones, transplant easily in late spring or early summer. Since new roots form from base of trunk, root ball need not be large. New root system will form and produce lush new growth. During transplant of large palms, tie leaves together over center "bud" or heart, and stiffen or secure the latter by tying leaf mass to a length of 2-by-4 tied to trunk.

Palms need little maintenance; plants thrive with reasonably fertile soil and adequate water. All palms with a tropical background do their growing during warm times of year. Winter rains wash them down and leach accumulated salts from soil. Washing with a hose is beneficial, especially for palms exposed to dust and beyond reach of rain or dew; it helps keep down spider mites and sucking insects which find refuge in long leaf stems.

Feather palms and many fan palms look neater when old leaves are removed after they have turned brown. Make neat cuts close to trunk, leaving leaf bases. Some palms shed old leaf bases on their own. Others, including arecastrums and chamaedoreas, may hold old bases. You can remove them by slicing them off at the very bottom of base (be careful not to cut into trunk).

Many palm admirers say that dead leaves of *Washingtonia* should remain on the tree, the thatch being part of the palm's character. If you also feel this way, you can cut lower fronds in a uniform way close to trunk, but leave leaf bases, which present a rather pleasant lattice surface.

Here are 10 roles that the right kinds of palms can fill (palms named in each listing are described under their own names elsewhere in this book):

Sturdy palms for park and avenue plantings, and for vertical effects in large gardens: *Archontophoenix, Arecastrum, Brahea, Jubaea, Livistona, Phoenix canariensis, P. dactylifera, P. loureiri, P. rupicola, Rhopalostylis, Sabal, Washingtonia.*

Small to medium-sized palms for sheltered areas in frost-free gardens: *Archontophoenix, Caryota, Chamaedorea, Chamaerops, Chrysalidocarpus, Hedyscepe, Howea.*

Small to medium-sized palms for gardens in areas of occasional frosts: *Acoelorrhaphe, Acrocomia totai, Brahea, Butia, Chamaedorea cataractarum, C. elegans, C. klotzschiana, C. seifrizii, Chamaerops, Livistona, Neodypsis, Phoenix roebelenii, Rhapidophyllum, Trachycarpus.*

(Continued on next page)

P

Hardy palms for cold areas (those marked with asterisk have withstood very cold winters in various parts of the world): *Brahea armata, B. edulis,* **Chamaerops,* **Jubaea, Livistona,* **Phoenix canariensis, P. dactylifera, P. loureiri,* **Rhapidophyllum, Rhapis, Sabal mexicana, S. minor, S. palmetto,* **Trachycarpus, Washingtonia filifera.*

Frost becomes more damaging to palms as it extends its stay and is repeated. Light frosts for half an hour may leave no damage, but the same degree during a period of 4 hours may damage some palms, kill others. Simplest damage is burned leaf edges, but frost may affect whole leaves, parts of trunks, or crown. Damage in crown is usually fatal (some have recovered). Hardiness is also a matter of size; larger plants may pass through severe frosts unharmed while smaller ones perish.

Garden palms for seaside planting: Palms in southern California beach plantings should be washed off occasionally to keep them free from salt accumulations. The following palms are listed in order of their salt tolerance, most tolerant first: *Washingtonia robusta, Phoenix dactylifera, P. canariensis, P. reclinata, Chamaerops, Brahea edulis, Butia, Sabal domingensis, S. palmetto.*

Palms for inland and desert: *Brahea armata, Butia, Chamaerops, Livistona chinensis, L. mariae, Phoenix canariensis, P. dactylifera, P. loureiri, P. sylvestris, Sabal mexicana, S. minor, Washingtonia.*

Palms to grow under trees, lath, overhangs, or indoors (indoor palms should occasionally be brought outdoors into mild light): *Acoelorrhaphe, Archontophoenix, Caryota mitis, C. ochlandra, C. urens, Chamaedorea, Hedyscepe, Howea,* young *Livistona, Phoenix reclinata* (when young), *P. roebelenii, Rhapis, Rhopalostylis, Trachycarpus* (when young).

Palms near swimming pools: Palms have great value near swimming pools because they do not drop leaves. Mature plants of *Phoenix reclinata* or *Chamaerops humilis,* with their curved trunks arching near the pool, create a tropical island effect. But whether palm trunks are curved or upright, or topped with fan or feather leaves, they can create beautiful mirror effects in the water.

Palms as ground covers: Young palms, especially slow growers such as *Livistona chinensis* or *Chamaerops humilis,* can be used effectively as ground covers. They'll stay low from 5–10 years, especially if they're in gardens that need little care. When they get too tall, move them to another location in garden where you need height.

Palms to light at night: Because of their stateliness and their spectacular leaves, all palms are good subjects for night lighting. You can backlight them, light them from below, or direct lights to silhouette them against light-colored building wall.

PALMETTO. See *Sabal.*

PALO VERDE. See *Cercidium.*

PAMPAS GRASS. See *Cortaderia selloana.*

PANAMIGA, PANAMIGO. See *Pilea involucrata.*

PANDA PLANT. See *Kalanchoe tomentosa.*

PANDOREA. *Bignoniaceae.* Evergreen vines. Zones 16–24. Leaves divided into glossy oval leaflets; clusters of trumpet-shaped flowers. Climb by twining.

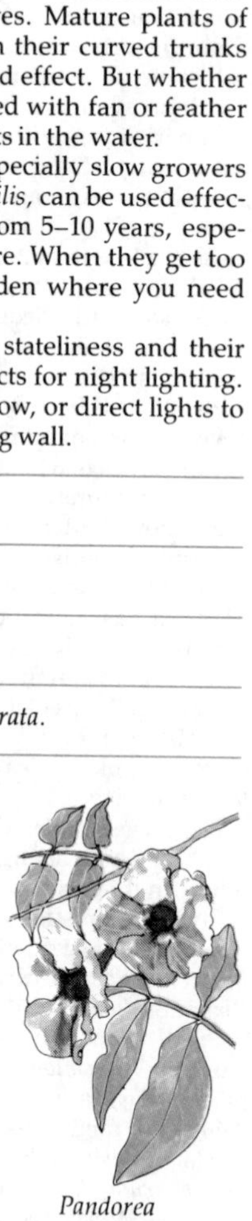

Pandorea jasminoides

P. jasminoides *(Bignonia jasminoides, Tecoma jasminoides).* BOWER VINE. Fast to 20–30 ft. Slender stems, distinguished glossy medium to dark green foliage. Leaves have 5–9 egg-shaped leaflets 1–2 in. long. Flowers (June–October) are 1½–2 in. long, white with pink throats, dropping cleanly after bloom. 'Alba' has pure white flowers; 'Rosea' has pink flowers with rose pink throats. Plant in lee of prevailing wind. Ample moisture, sun near coast, part shade inland. Prolonged freezes will kill it.

P. pandorana *(Bignonia australis, Tecoma australis).* WONGA-WONGA VINE. Glossy foliage handsome in all seasons. Flowers smaller (to ¾ in. long), yellow or pinkish white, usually spotted brown purple in throat. Grows in sun or shade. Needs room to grow. Requires little water once established. Prune ends of branches heavily after spring bloom.

PANSY. See *Viola.*

PANSY ORCHID. See *Miltonia.*

PAPAVER. *Papaveraceae.* POPPY. Annuals, perennials. Poppies provide gay color in spring and summer for borders and cutting. All kinds need full sun, ordinary soil, good drainage, not too much water, light feeding until established.

Papaver orientale

P. burseri *(P. alpinum).* ALPINE POPPY. Perennial. All Zones; best adapted in colder climates. Will bloom first spring from fall or early spring sowing. Short-lived rock garden poppy with leaves in a basal rosette and flower stalk 5–8 in. high. Blue green, nearly hairless, divided leaves. Spring flowers 1–1½ in. across, white, orange, yellow, salmon.

P. nudicaule. ICELAND POPPY. Perennial, grown as annual in warm-winter areas. All Zones. Divided leaves with coarse hairs. Slender, hairy stems 1–2 ft. high. Cup-shaped, slightly fragrant flowers to 3 in. across, in yellow, orange, salmon, rose, pink, cream, or white. In mild climates, blooms winter and early spring from plants set out in fall. Where winters are cold, sow seed in earliest spring for summer bloom. To prolong bloom, pick flowers frequently. Several good strains available; Champagne Bubbles is most widely grown. Wonderland strain is lower growing (10 in.), sold in mixed or single colors—white to cream, pink, yellow, or orange. Oregon Rainbows has larger flowers in a wider color range, including bicolors and picotees. Excellent in the Northwest, it is less successful in warmer climates, producing a number of blind buds (buds that fail to open). Misato Carnival strain has 6-in. flowers on 2–3-ft. stems. Cover young plants with screen to protect them from birds. Both Iceland poppy and Alpine poppy make excellent cut flowers; sear cut stem ends in flame before placing flowers in water.

P. orientale. ORIENTAL POPPY. Perennial. Zones 1–17. Short-lived in warm-winter climates. Strong, bold plants to 4 ft. Coarse, hairy, divided leaves. Flowers single or double, 3–6 in. across, in brilliant and pastel shades. Many named varieties. Plants die back in midsummer; new leafy growth appears in early fall, lasts over winter, develops rapidly in warm weather. Baby's breath (*Gypsophila*) makes good summer filler when poppies go dormant.

Minicaps, a series of hybrids involving Oriental poppy, set no seed and have extended blooming seasons; they come in dwarf (1–2-ft.), medium (2–4-ft.), and tall (4–6-ft.) forms. Colors are pink to red.

P. rhoeas. FLANDERS FIELD POPPY, SHIRLEY POPPY. Summer annual. Slender, branching, hairy, 2–5 ft. high. Leaves short, irregularly divided. Flowers 2 in. or more across, single or double, in red, pink, white, orange, scarlet, salmon, bicolors. Selections with single scarlet flowers, black bases sold as 'American Legion' or 'Flanders Field'. Broadcast seed mixed with fine sand. Sow successively for bloom from spring through summer. Take cut flowers when buds first show color. Remove seed capsules (old flower bases) weekly to prolong the bloom season.

PAPAYA. See *Carica papaya.*

PAPER MULBERRY. See *Broussonetia papyrifera.*

P

PAPHIOPEDILUM. *Orchidaceae.* LADY'S SLIPPER. Terrestrial orchids. Cool greenhouse or indoor plants. This name applies to lady's slipper orchids (sometimes sold as *Cypripedium*) native to tropical regions of Asia. The group includes large-flowered hybrids grown commercially for cut flowers. Blooms are perky, usually one to a stem, occasionally 2 or more. Many of them shine as if lacquered. Flowers may be white, yellow, green with white stripes, pure green, or combination of background colors and markings in tan, mahogany brown, maroon, green, and white.

Paphiopedilum insigne

Graceful, arching foliage (no pseudobulbs) is either plain green or mottled. Plain-leafed forms usually flower in winter, mottled-leafed forms in summer. Most plants at orchid dealers' establishments are hybrids.

In general, mottled-leafed forms do best with temperatures at about 60°–65°F. at night, 70°–85°F. in the day. Plain-leafed forms require 55°–65°F. at night, 65°–75°F. during the day. They have no rest period, so should be kept moist at all times. Combine equal parts ground bark and sandy loam for a good potting medium. Don't plant in oversize pot; plants thrive when crowded. Hardiest kinds can be grown in pots indoors, treated as house plants. They thrive in less light than most orchids require.

P. insigne. Polished lady's slipper–type flowers on stiff, brown, hairy stems any time October–March. Sepals and petals green and white, with brown spots and stripes; pouch reddish brown. Hardy to brief exposures of 28°F.

PAPYRUS. See *Cyperus papyrus.*

PARADISE PALM. See *Howea forsterana.*

PARKINSONIA aculeata. *Leguminosae.* JERUSALEM THORN, MEXICAN PALO VERDE. Deciduous tree. Zones 11–24; especially valuable in Zones 12, 13. Rapid growth at first, then slowing; eventually reaches 15–30 ft. high and wide. Yellow green bark, spiny twigs, picturesque form. Sparse foliage; leaves 6–9 in. long, with many tiny leaflets which quickly fall in drought or cold. Numerous yellow flowers in loose, 3–7-in.-long clusters. Long bloom season in spring, intermittent bloom throughout year.

Parkinsonia aculeata

Tolerates alkaline soil. Very drought tolerant. Stake young trees, train for high or low branching. Requires minimum attention once established. Does not do well with lawn watering. As shade tree, it filters sun rather than blocking it. Thorns, sparse foliage rule it out of tailored gardens. Flowering branches attractive in arrangements. Litter drop a problem on hard surfaces.

PARROT BEAK. See *Clianthus puniceus.*

PARROTIA persica. *Hamamelidaceae.* PERSIAN PARROTIA. Deciduous tree or large shrub. Zones 4–6, 15–17. Native to Persia. Drought tolerant once established. Choice and colorful; attractive all seasons of year. Most dramatic display comes in fall: leaves usually turn from golden yellow to orange to rosy pink and finally scarlet. Slow growing to 30 ft. or more, but tends to be shrub or multitrunked tree to 15 ft. Bark attractive in winter: smooth, gray, flaking off to leave white patches. Thick foliage is made up of lustrous, dark green, oval, 3–4-in.-long leaves. Flowers with red stamens are in dense heads surrounded by woolly brown bracts; they appear in spring before leaves open, giving a hazy red effect.

Parrotia persica

Parrotia persica

To train as tree, stake and shorten lower side branches. Allow upper branches to take their wide-spreading habit. When tree reaches desired height, remove lower shortened side branches cleanly.

PARROT'S BEAK. See *Lotus berthelotii.*

PARSLEY. *Umbelliferae.* Biennial herb treated as annual. All Zones. Attractive edging for herb, vegetable, or flower garden: plants are 6–12 in. high, with tufted, finely cut, dark green leaves. Attractive in boxes and pots. You can use the leaves fresh or dried as seasoning, fresh as garnishes. Parsley is most satisfactorily grown anew every year. Grow in partial shade if possible, or in sun. Buy plants at nursery or sow seed in place (April in Zones 1–7; December–May in Zones 8–11, 14–24; September–October in Zones 12, 13). Soak seed in warm water 24 hours before planting. Even then, it may not sprout for several weeks—an old story says that parsley seeds must go to the devil and come back before sprouting. Thin seedlings to 6–8 in. apart. Water regularly.

Parsley

Most attractive and most widely used are curled leaf kinds. For quantity production, ease of culture (and possibly superior flavor), try Italian or flat-leafed parsley (grows 2–3 ft. tall). Turnip-rooted or Hamburg parsley is grown for its fleshy, turnip-shaped root, which is used as a cooked vegetable; leaves also make acceptable garnish.

PARSNIP. *Umbelliferae.* Biennial vegetable. All Zones. Needs deep, well-prepared, loose soil for long roots; some varieties are 15 in. long. Grow in full sun. In cold-winter areas, plant seeds in late spring and harvest in fall; leave surplus in ground to be dug as needed in winter. In mild-climate areas, sow in fall and harvest in spring; in such areas, mature roots will continue to grow if they are left in ground, becoming tough and woody. Soak seeds in water 24 hours before planting to improve germination. Sow seeds ½ in. deep in rows spaced 2 ft. apart; thin seedlings to 3 in. apart.

Parsnip

PARTHENOCISSUS *(Ampelopsis).* *Vitaceae.* Deciduous vines. Cling to walls by sucker discs at ends of tendrils. Superb and dependable fall leaf color, orange to scarlet. Flowers are insignificant. Ample water, moderate feeding. Grow in most exposures, sun or quite a bit of shade. Attractive to birds. Think twice before planting them against wood or shingle siding; they can creep under, and their clinging tendrils are hard to remove at repainting time.

Parthenocissus quinquefolia

P. henryana. SILVERVEIN CREEPER. Zones 4–9, 14–17. Resembles smaller (to 20 ft.), less aggressive Virginia creeper. Leaves formed by 5 leaflets, each 1–2½ in. long, which open purplish, turn dark bronzy green with pronounced silver veining and purple undersides. Color is best in shade, fades to plain green in strong light. Rich red autumn foliage.

(Continued on next page)

Clings to walls, but needs some support to get started. Also good wall spiller, small-scale ground cover. Rare.

P. inserta. VIRGINIA CREEPER, WOODBINE. All Zones. Western form of *P. quinquefolia.* Native to Rocky Mountains and eastward. Scrambles rather than clings: tendrils have few or no sucker discs.

P. quinquefolia. VIRGINIA CREEPER. All Zones. Big, vigorous vine that clings or runs over ground, fence, trellis. Looser growth than Boston ivy; will drape its trailing branches over trellis. Leaves divided into 5 separate 6-in. leaflets with saw-toothed edges. Good ground cover on slopes; can control erosion. Sun or shade. *P. q.* 'Engelmannii' has smaller leaves, denser growth.

P. tricuspidata. BOSTON IVY. All Zones. Semievergreen in mild-winter areas. Glossy leaves variable in shape, usually 3 lobed or divided into 3 leaflets, up to 8 in. wide. Clings tightly, grows fast to make dense, even wall cover. This is ivy of the "Ivy League"; covers brick or stone in areas where English ivy freezes. North or east walls only in Zones 12, 13. Variety 'Beverly Brooks' has large leaves and good fall color, grows fast. Most leaves are divided into 3 leaflets. 'Green Showers' has large leaves, burgundy fall color. 'Lowii' has smaller (1½-in.), deeply lobed leaves. 'Veitchii' has small leaves, the younger ones purplish. Vine with leaves strongly resembling those of *P. tricuspidata* is *Ampelopsis brevipedunculata*.

Parthenocissus tricuspidata

PASPALUM vaginatum. *Gramineae.* SEASHORE PASPALUM. Zones 17, 24. Lawn grass native to southeastern U.S. Makes an attractive lawn near coast; tolerates salty soil, heat, drought, wear. Color is close to that of bluegrass, and lawns are pest free. In interior climates, it develops tough stems that turn brown after cutting. Mow to ¾ in. with a front-throw mower and feed only between late October and early May. Usually sold as sod, under names like Adalayd and Excalibre.

Paspalum vaginatum

PASQUE FLOWER. See *Anemone pulsatilla.*

PASSIFLORA. *Passifloraceae.* PASSION VINE. Evergreen, semievergreen, or deciduous vines. Climb by tendrils to 20–30 ft. Name comes from manner in which flower parts symbolize elements of passion of the Lord: the lacy crown could be a halo or crown of thorns; the 5 stamens the 5 wounds; the 10 petal-like parts the 10 faithful apostles.

Vigorous, likely to overgrow and tangle; to keep plant open and prevent buildup of dead inner tangle, prune annually after second year, cutting excess branches back to base or juncture with another branch. Tolerant of many soils. Average water and feeding. Favorite food of caterpillars of gulf fritillary butterfly.

Passiflora alatocaerulea

Use vines on trellises or walls for their vigor and bright, showy flowers; or use as soil-holding bank cover. Full sun. In cold-winter climates, use as greenhouse or house plants, training plants on a trellis or winding them on hoops of wire for wreath effect.

P. alatocaerulea *(P. pfordtii).* Evergreen or semievergreen vine. Zones 12–24; root-hardy perennial in Zones 5–9. Hybrid between *P. alata, P. caerulea.* Best known, most widely planted, probably least subject to caterpillars. Leaves 3 in. long, 3 lobed. Fragrant 3½–4-in. flowers, white shaded pink and lavender. Crown deep blue or purple. Blooms all summer. In colder areas, give it a warm place out of wind, against wall or under overhang. Mulch roots in winter. Forms no fruit.

P. caerulea. BLUE CROWN PASSION FLOWER. Evergreen or semievergreen vine. Zones 12–24; root-hardy perennial in Zones 5–9. Leaves smaller than those of *P. alatocaerulea,* 5 lobed. Flowers smaller, greenish white, crown white and purple. Edible small, oval fruit with orange rind and red seeds.

P. edulis. PASSION FRUIT. Semievergreen vine. Zones 15–17, 21–24. Leaves 3 lobed, deeply toothed, light yellow green. Flowers white with white and purple crown, 2 in. across. Fruit produced in spring and fall: deep purple, fragrant, 3 in. long, delicious in beverages, fruit salads, sherbets. There is a yellow-fruited variety.

P. incarnata. MAYPOP. Perennial vine. All Zones. Native to eastern U.S. A very hardy passion flower for really cold areas. Spreads prodigiously by root runners, dies back at first frost. Flowers 2 in. across, white with purple and white crown. Fruit 2 in. long, yellowish green, edible. Grow from seed.

P. 'Incense'. Zones 5–24. Hybrid between the preceding and an Argentinian species. Hardy to 0°F., even holding its foliage through short cold spells—deciduous otherwise. Flowers are 5 in. wide, violet with lighter crown, scented like sweet peas. Egg-shaped, 2-in. fruit; when ripe, it turns from olive to yellow green and then drops. Fragrant, tasty pulp.

P. jamesonii. Evergreen vine. Zones 14–24. Especially good in Zones 17, 24. Glossy, 3-lobed leaves. Long-tubed (to 4-in.) flowers are salmon to coral, profuse all summer. Fast bank, fence cover.

P. manicata. Evergreen vine. Zones 17, 23, 24. Leaves 3 lobed. Flowers to 4 in. across, scarlet with narrow blue crown.

P. mollissima. Evergreen vine. Zones 12–24. Soft green foliage; leaves 3 lobed, deeply toothed. Long-tubed pink to rose flowers 3 in. across. Yellow, 4–6-in.-long fruit. Rampant growth makes it a good bank cover, but a problem if planted with trees, shrubs.

P. racemosa *(P. princeps).* Evergreen vine. Zones 23, 24. Tall, slender. Leathery leaves. Showy flowers, deep rose maroon to coral with purple and white crowns, hang from main stems in long, wiry clusters. Fairly pest free.

PASSION FRUIT. See *Passiflora edulis.*

PASSION VINE. See *Passiflora.*

PAULOWNIA tomentosa *(P. imperialis).* *Bignoniaceae.* EMPRESS TREE. Deciduous tree. All Zones. Young trees may need protection in Zones 1–3; flowers to be expected only in Zones 4–9, 11–24. Somewhat similar to catalpa in growth habit, leaves. Fast to 40–50 ft. with nearly equal spread. Heavy trunk and heavy, nearly horizontal branches. Foliage gives tropical effect; leaves are light green, heart shaped, 5–12 in. long, 4–7 in. wide. Best with some summer irrigation. If tree is cut back annually or every other year, it will grow as billowy foliage mass with giant-sized leaves up to 2 ft. However, such pruning will reduce flower production.

Paulownia tomentosa

Brown flower buds about the size of small olives form in autumn and persist over winter; they open before leaves in early spring to form upright clusters (6–12 in. long) of trumpet-shaped, 2-in.-long, fragrant flowers of lilac blue with darker spotting and yellow stripes inside. Flowers are followed by top-shaped, 1½–2-in.-long seed capsules; these hang on tree, so that both seed capsules and flower buds are present at same time. Does not flower well where winters are very cold (buds freeze) or very mild (buds may drop off). In areas of strong winds, leaves will be damaged. Bark tends to sunburn in Zones 7–14, 18–21. Plant where falling flowers and leaves are not objectionable. Not tree to garden under because of dense shade, surface roots.

PAUROTIS wrightii. See *Acoelorrhaphe wrightii.*

PAXISTIMA ***(Pachystima, Pachistima).*** *Celastraceae.* Evergreen shrubs. Zones 1–10, 14–21. Low growing with small, shiny, leathery leaves, insignificant flowers. Hardiness and compact habit make them useful as low hedges, edgings, ground cover. Full sun near coast; partial shade, ample water in hot interiors. Best in well-drained soil.

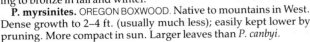

Paxistima canbyi

P. canbyi. Native to mountains of eastern U.S. Makes mat 9–12 in. tall. Narrow (¼-in.-wide), ¼–1-in.-long leaves, dark green turning to bronze in fall and winter.

P. myrsinites. OREGON BOXWOOD. Native to mountains in West. Dense growth to 2–4 ft. (usually much less); easily kept lower by pruning. More compact in sun. Larger leaves than *P. canbyi.*

PEA. *Leguminosae.* Cool-season vegetable. Easy crop to grow when conditions are right, and delicious when freshly picked. They need coolness and humidity and must be planted at just the right time. If you have space and don't mind the bother, grow tall (vining) peas on trellises, strings, or screen; tall peas reach 6 ft. or more and bear heavily. Bush types are more commonly grown in home gardens; they require no support. Grow either type in full sun. A good tall variety is 'Alderman'. Fine bush varieties are 'Green Arrow', 'Little Marvel', 'Morse's Progress No. 9', 'Freezonian', and 'Blue Bantam'. An unusually good vegetable (and one indispensable to Oriental cooking) is edible-pod snow or sugar pea; 'Mammoth Melting Sugar' is a tall-vining variety, 'Dwarf Gray Sugar' a bushy one. 'Sugar Snap' is an edible-pod pea with full complement of full-sized peas inside; instead of shelling, you merely string and snap, just like green beans.

Pea

Peas need nonacid soil that is water retentive but fast draining. They are hardy and should be planted just as early in spring as ground can be worked. Where winters are mild and spring days quickly become too warm for peas, plant October–February, later dates applying where winters are coldest. Sow 2 in. deep in light soil, shallower (½–1 in.) in heavy soil or in winter. Moisten ground thoroughly before planting; do not water again until seedlings have broken through surface. Leave 2 ft. between rows and thin seedlings to stand 2 in. apart. Successive plantings several days apart will lengthen bearing season, but don't plant so late that summer heat will overtake ripening peas; most are ready to bear in 60–70 days.

Plants need little fertilizer, but if soil is very light give them 1 application of complete fertilizer. If weather turns warm and dry, supply water in furrows; overhead water encourages mildew. Provide support for climbing peas as soon as tendrils form. When peas begin to mature, pick *all* pods that are ready; if seeds ripen, plant will stop producing. Vines are brittle; steady them with one hand while picking with the other. Above all—shell and cook (or freeze) peas right after picking.

PEACH and NECTARINE. *Rosaceae.* Peach ***(Prunus persica)*** and nectarine ***(Prunus persica nucipersica)*** trees look alike and have the same general cultural needs. In terms of fruit, nectarines differ from peaches only in having smooth skins and (in some varieties) a slightly different flavor. Climate adaptation of nectarine is more limited.

In terms of landscaping and fruit growing, there are 4 kinds of peaches: flowering peaches, fruiting peaches, flowering-fruiting (dual-purpose) peaches, and genetic dwarf fruiting peaches that form large bushes. Here we consider the 3 groups of fruiting peaches. For strictly flowering peaches, see *Prunus.*

A regular fruiting peach tree grows fast to 25 ft. high and as wide; well-pruned trees are usually less than 15 ft. tall and 15–18 ft. wide. The peach starts bearing large crops when 3–4 years old and reaches peak productivity at 8–12 years.

Peach

Peaches do best if they get some chilling in winter (chilling requirement is usually given as the number of hours below 45°F. a tree must experience during its dormant season to grow and bear satisfactorily). Only specially selected varieties do well in extremely mild-winter areas. Lack of winter chilling results in delayed foliation, few fruits, and eventual death of tree. The high desert satisfies chilling requirements, but late frosts make early-blooming varieties risky. Few are satisfactory in mild-winter areas of low desert.

Peach trees also need clear, hot weather during the growing season; where spring is cool and rainy, they generally set few flowers and pollinate poorly.

To save space, you can graft different varieties on one tree or plant 3 or 4 varieties in a single hole.

Peaches require well-drained soil, a regular fertilizing program, and heavier pruning than any other fruit trees. When planting a bare-root tree, cut back to 2 ft. above ground. New branches will form below cut. After first year's growth, select 3 well-placed branches for scaffold limbs. Remove all other branches. On mature trees, in each dormant season, cut off ⅔ of previous year's growth by removing 2 of every 3 branches formed last year; or head back each branch to ⅓ its length. Or head back some branches and cut out others. Peach trees can be trained as espaliers.

Peaches and nectarines tend to form too much fruit even with good pruning. When fruits are about 1 in. wide, remove (thin) some of the excess. If growth becomes weak and leaves yellowish, feed with nitrogen fertilizer. In hot, dry summers, irrigate several times while fruit is on tree.

Protect all kinds of peaches and nectarines from peach leaf curl and peach tree borer. Two dormant sprayings, the first in November and the second in January before buds swell, will control leaf curl. Use fixed copper, Bordeaux mixture, or lime sulfur. Sprays combining oil and lime sulfur or fixed copper will control both scale insects and peach leaf curl. Borers attack at or just below ground level. Pull away soil to expose 2–3 in. of roots. Spray with dursban every 3 weeks from early June to mid-August.

Flowering-Fruiting Peaches

These dual-purpose peaches were developed in southern California for southern California conditions, but are widely adapted and will grow in Zones 7–9, 12–22. Most likely to succeed in Zone 13 is 'Daily News Four Star'.

'Daily News Four Star'. Salmon pink double flowers. Highly colored red freestone with white flesh. Midseason.

'Daily News Three Star'. Deep pink double flowers. Highly colored red freestone with white flesh. Midseason.

'Saturn'. Large, deep pink double flowers. High-quality yellow-fleshed freestone. Midseason.

Natural Dwarf Peaches and Nectarines

Most fruit trees are dwarfed by grafting standard varieties on dwarfing rootstocks. In case of peaches and nectarines, best dwarfs are genetic (natural) dwarf varieties. Look for these varieties, all with medium-sized fruit unless otherwise noted:

'Bonanza'. Peach. Blooms and bears fruit at 2 ft. high, 2 years old. Will eventually reach 6 ft. Semidouble rose pink flowers. Early red-blushed, yellow-fleshed freestone of bland flavor. Very low chilling requirement.

'Empress'. Peach. Semidwarf, reaching 4–5 ft. Pink to red skin. Yellow-fleshed clingstone of fine flavor. Early August.

'Garden Delight'. Nectarine. Slow to 5–6 ft. Large, yellow-fleshed freestone. Midseason.

'Garden Gold'. Peach. To 5–6 ft. Large, yellow-fleshed freestone. Late midseason.

(Continued on next page)

P

'Garden Sun'. Peach. To 5–6 ft. Yellow-fleshed freestone. Midseason.

'Golden Gem'. Peach. To 5–6 ft. Double pink blooms. Yellow-fleshed freestone with yellow skin blushed red. Midseason.

'Golden Glory'. Peach. To 5 ft. Yellow-fleshed freestone. Golden skin with red blush. Heavy bearer. Mid to late August.

'Golden Prolific'. Nectarine. Slow growing to 5 ft. Yellow-fleshed freestone. Yellow skin mottled with orange red. Midseason.

'Golden Treasure'. Peach. To 5–6 ft. Large, golden, red-blushed, yellow-fleshed freestone. Early August.

'Honey Babe'. Peach. To 5–6 ft. Sweet, flavorful yellow-fleshed freestone. Red-blushed skin. Midseason.

'Nectar Babe'. Nectarine. High-quality yellow-fleshed freestone with dark red skin. Needs pollinator (any other dwarf peach or nectarine). Midseason.

'Nectarina'. Nectarine. To 5–6 ft. Skin deep red and yellow. Orange-fleshed freestone ripening in late July.

'Necta Zee'. Nectarine. High-quality yellow-fleshed semifreestone. Ripens in June.

'Pix Zee'. Peach. High-quality yellow-fleshed semifreestone. Ripens in June.

'Sensation'. Peach. Medium yellow-fleshed freestone. To 6–8 ft. Early.

'Silver Prolific'. Nectarine. Slow growing to 5–7 ft. Yellow-fleshed freestone. Light yellow skin blushed red. Rich flavor. Midseason.

'Southern Belle'. Nectarine. To 5 ft. Yellow-fleshed freestone. Midseason. Low chilling requirement.

'Southern Flame'. Peach. To 5 ft. Yellow with red blush, yellow flesh. Freestone. Moderately low chilling requirement. Early midseason.

'Southern Rose'. Peach. To 5 ft. Yellow blushed red. Freestone. Needs little chilling. Midseason.

'Southern Sweet'. Peach. To 5 ft. Medium-sized yellow fruit of good flavor. Freestone. Heavy bearer. Fairly low chilling requirement. Early ripening.

'Sunbonnet'. Nectarine. To 5 ft. Red skin, yellow flesh. Clingstone. Fairly low chilling requirement. Early midseason.

Peach and Nectarine

NAME	ZONES	FRUIT	COMMENTS
PEACHES			
'August Pride'	8, 9, 14–16, 18–23	Large yellow-fleshed freestone of high quality. Late July, early August.	One of best peaches with low chilling requirement.
'Autumn Gold'	3, 6–9, 14–16	Medium to large yellow freestone. Yellow skin striped red. Good quality. Ripens late September.	Keeps well if picked when firm-ripe.
'Babcock'	15–16, 19–24	White freestone, small to medium, sweet flavor with some tang. Early.	Needs little winter chilling. Old-timer.
'Belle of Georgia'	10–12, 18–19	Large white freestone of fine flavor, attractive appearance. Early midseason.	Old favorite for table use.
'Blazing Gold'	3, 6, 8, 9, 14–16	Yellow freestone, small to medium, firm fleshed, good flavor. Early.	Not as high quality in Zones 3, 6 as in 8, 9, 14–16.
'Bonita'	15–24	Large yellow freestone with medium blush, firm flesh, fine flavor. Ripens in midseason.	Bred for mild-winter areas.
'Desertgold'	8, 9, 12, 13, 23	Medium-sized yellow semiclingstone of good quality. Late April or early May in low desert; early June in San Joaquin Valley.	Very early bloom rules it out wherever spring frosts are likely.
'Earligrande'	18–23	Medium to large yellow-fleshed semifreestone. Yellow skin with red blush.	Very early peach for mild-winter areas.
'Early Elberta' ('Improved Elberta', 'Gleason Elberta', 'Lemon Elberta')	2–11, 14, 15	Superior in color and flavor to 'Elberta'. Freestone. Ripens 1 week earlier than 'Elberta'.	Needs somewhat less heat and less winter chill than 'Elberta'; less subject to fruit drop. Thin well for good-sized fruit.
'Elberta'	1–3, 6–11, 14	Medium to large yellow freestone, skin blushed red, high quality. Midseason (later in Zone 6).	Needs good amount of winter chilling, high summer heat to ripen to full flavor.
'Fay Elberta' ('Gold Medal' in Northwest)	2, 3, 6–11, 14, 15, 18, 19	More colorful than 'Elberta', keeps a little better. Yellow-fleshed freestone. Ripens with 'Elberta'.	Has large, handsome single flowers. Thin it well.
'Flordaking'	8, 9, 13–16, 18–23	Early yellow semifreestone. Good quality.	Needs 300–400 hours of chilling.
'Flordaprince'	13, 18–24	Very early yellow peach; ripens late April, early May. Freestone when fully ripe.	Needs only 150 hours of chilling.
'Flordasun'	18–23	Small yellow semiclingstone. Faint blush over yellow skin. Fair to good flavor. Mid to late April.	Fruit becomes freestone when fully ripe.
'Fortyniner'	5–9, 14–16, 18	Large yellow freestone. Bright red blush over yellow. Good to excellent flavor. Early midseason.	Resembles 'J. H. Hale', the parent; about 1 week earlier.

NAME	ZONES	FRUIT	COMMENTS
'Frost'	4–6	Medium-sized fruit with red-blushed skin, yellow flesh. Freestone.	Resistant to peach leaf curl.
'Gold Dust'	6–9, 11, 14–16	Small to medium yellow freestone, high blush, good quality. Early.	Like 'Blazing Gold', but ripens 1 week later.
'Golden Jubilee'	2, 3, 5, 6	Medium yellow freestone of fair flavor. Tender. Ripens 3 weeks before 'Elberta'.	Good early peach in Zones 2, 3.
'Halberta' ('Hal-Berta Giant')	1–3, 6–11, 14, 18	Very large yellow freestone, very smooth skinned. Ripens with 'Elberta'.	Needs pollinating; any other peach except 'J. H. Hale' or 'Indian Free' will do.
'Halehaven'	1–3, 6–11, 14–16	Medium to large, highly colored yellow freestone. Ripens 2 weeks before 'Elberta'.	Fine large yellow freestone to use fresh or canned. Flower and leaf buds are very winter hardy.
'Halford'	1–3, 7–12, 14–16, 18	Large yellow clingstone. Heavy bearer. Mid to late August.	Basically a commercial canning peach.
'Halloween'	3, 7–9, 14, 15	Large yellow freestone. Yellow skin, red blush. Early October.	Productive tree. Fruits very late.
'Indian Blood Cling' ('Indian Cling')	1–3, 6–11, 14–16	Medium-sized, red-skinned clingstone. Flesh firm, yellow streaked red. Late.	Old variety with small but devoted band of enthusiasts. Good for preserves.
'Indian Free'	7–11, 14–16	Large, round, yellow freestone, deep red at pit. Tart until fully ripe. Late midseason.	Needs pollinating by any other peach.
'J. H. Hale'	1–3, 7–11, 14–16	Very large, highly colored yellow freestone of high quality. Fine keeper. Ripens with 'Elberta'.	Needs pollinating by any other peach except 'Halberta', 'Indian Blood Cling'.
'July Elberta' ('Kim Elberta')	2, 3, 6–12, 14–16, 18, 19	Medium-large, yellow-fleshed freestone of high quality. Ripens a month before 'Elberta'.	Prolific bearer. May need extra thinning to get size.
'Loring'	2, 3, 6–9, 14, 15	Large, attractive yellow freestone. Skin with red blush, little fuzz. Very good quality. Midseason.	Bears well where spring brings unpredictable weather.
'Madison'	4–6	Large. Red blush over yellow skin; orange flesh of good flavor. Freestone when ripe. Late midseason.	Tolerates frost in blossom season. Needs thinning.
'Melba'	2, 3, 10, 11	Large white freestone. Pale yellow skin. Sweet, juicy. Long ripening season.	Sets fruit well in cold, unsettled spring weather.
'Midpride'	8, 9, 13, 23	High-quality yellow freestone for mild-winter climates. Early to mid-July.	Needs only 250 hours of chilling.
'Miller's Late'	7–11, 14, 18	Medium-sized yellow freestone peach of fair flavor. Very late.	If you must have peaches in mid-October, this is the tree to plant. In cool-autumn areas, ripen off tree.
'Nectar'	7–11, 14–16	Medium to large white freestone of excellent flavor. Early midseason.	Those who fancy white peaches consider it the best.
'O'Henry'	7–10, 14–16, 18	Large yellow freestone of fine flavor. Skin blushed red, flesh streaked red. Ripens early August.	Good commercial and home garden tree.
'Orange Cling' ('Miller Cling')	1–3, 7–12, 14–16, 18	Large, late clingstone peach with firm, deep yellow flesh.	A favorite for home canning.
'Polly'	1–3, 10	Medium-sized white freestone. White skin blushed red. Juicy, excellent flavor. Late midseason.	Tree and buds very hardy to cold.
'Ranger'	3, 5–9, 14–16, 18	Medium-large, highly colored freestone, yellow fleshed, good flavor. Early midseason, a month before 'Elberta'.	Heavy fruit bud set. High yielder. Excellent early canner.
'Redglobe'	3, 6–11, 14–16	Highly colored, firm-fleshed yellow freestone of good flavor. Three weeks before 'Elberta'.	Good for canning or freezing. Sometimes sets light crop in Zone 6.
'Redhaven'	3, 5, 12, 14–16	Brightly blushed yellow freestone. Long ripening season permits numerous pickings. Ripens 3–4 weeks ahead of 'Elberta'.	Colors up early, so taste-test for ripeness. Thin early and well. One of best for planting. 'Early Redhaven' ripens 2 weeks earlier.
'Redskin'	1–3, 6–12, 14–16	Medium to large yellow freestone. Heavy red blush. Excellent quality fresh, canned, or frozen. Midseason.	Productive tree. Needs only a little less winter chilling than 'Elberta'.
'Redtop'	4–6	Red-on-yellow freestone. Ripens just after 'Redhaven'.	Fruit hangs well on tree.

(Continued on next page)

P

NAME	ZONES	FRUIT	COMMENTS
'Redwing'	18–24	Small, highly colored white freestone. Soft fleshed. Early.	Low winter chilling requirement.
'Reliance'	4–9	Yellow skin blushed dull-medium red; soft yellow flesh of good flavor. Freestone. Ripens with 'Redhaven'.	Has outstanding cold hardiness.
'Rio Grande'	8–10, 15, 18–20	Medium to large yellow freestone. Red blush. Good quality. Early June.	Medium-sized productive tree with showy flowers.
'Rio Oso Gem'	3, 7–9, 14, 15	Medium-large, yellow-fleshed freestone of excellent flavor. A week later than 'Elberta'.	Small tree. Not vigorous. One of best.
'Rubidoux'	18, 20	Medium-large yellow freestone with firm flesh. Good keeper. Late midseason.	Developed specifically for Zones 18 and 20.
'Sam Houston'	2, 3, 6–11, 14–16, 18–20	Medium to large yellow freestone of 'Elberta' type. Ripens late June.	Needs less winter chilling than 'Elberta'. Sets heavy crop, needs thinning.
'Shanghai'	14–16, 18–24	Medium-sized white freestone. Red blush. Soft, juicy, very sweet flesh. Late midseason.	Vigorous tree. Fruit too soft for canning, freezing. Very fine flavor.
'Springcrest'	4–9	Small to medium fruit, bright red over yellow. Semifreestone when fully ripe. Good flavor.	Good early-ripening variety.
'Springtime'	18–23	White semiclingstone of high color, mild flavor. Ripens late May, early June.	One of earliest; sweet and juicy.
'Strawberry Cling'	7–9, 14–16, 18–20	Large, creamy white marbled red. Clingstone. Flesh white, juicy, richly flavored. Early midseason.	Favorite with home canners.
'Strawberry Free'	7–9, 14–16, 18–20	Medium-sized white freestone. Medium blush, firm flesh, excellent flavor. Early midseason.	Old favorite of those who like white peaches.
'Summerset'	7–9, 14–16, 18, 19	Large yellow freestone with attractive red blush. Firm flesh makes it good for canning, freezing. Late.	Vigorous, productive tree.
'Tejon'	18–22	Small to medium semifreestone, very juicy, yellow flesh. Very early.	Very low chilling requirement.
'Tropi-berta'	8, 9, 14–16, 18–24	Large yellow freestone with red blush. Juicy; good flavor. Late midseason.	Needs somewhat less chilling than 'Elberta'.
'Ventura'	18–24	Medium-sized, attractive yellow freestone. Very smooth skin. Midseason.	Developed especially for Zones 18–24.
'Veteran'	4–6	Medium-sized yellow freestone of good flavor. Ripens 10 days earlier than 'Elberta'.	Resembles 'Elberta' but rounder, less fuzzy. Sets fruit under adverse conditions.
'White Heath Cling' ('Heath')	7–11, 14–16	Medium to large, firm-fleshed white clingstone of excellent flavor. Late.	Distinctive flavor; a favorite for home canning.
NECTARINES			
'Desert Dawn'	8, 9, 13–24	High-quality red-skinned, yellow-fleshed semifreestone. Very early (May).	Very low chilling requirement.
'Double Delight'	7–9, 14–16, 18, 19	High-quality red-skinned, yellow-fleshed freestone. Midseason.	Double pink flowers in spring a showy bonus.
'Fantasia'	3, 7–9, 14–16, 18–22	Large, bright yellow and red, freestone. Firm flesh. Ripens mid-July.	Relatively low chilling requirement.
'Flame Kist'	7–9, 14–16, 18–22	Large, yellow blushed red, clingstone. Late.	Resistant to cracking; thin out tree to bring sunshine in on fruit and improve color.
'Flavortop'	3, 7–9, 14–16, 18, 19	Large, red with yellow undertone, freestone. Good quality.	Vigorous, productive tree.
'Freedom'	7–9, 11	Large, highly colored, yellow-fleshed freestone of high quality. Early midseason.	Beautiful fruit.
'Gold Mine'	7–9, 14–16, 18–24	Red-blushed, white-fleshed freestone. Late midseason. Tough skin, firm flesh; excellent for frozen halves.	Low winter chilling requirement. Excellent, distinctive flavor.
'Heavenly White'	7–9, 14–16, 18	Very large white-fleshed freestone of especially fine flavor. Midseason.	Has been called a connoisseur's delight.

NAME	ZONES	FRUIT	COMMENTS
'Independence'	7–9, 14–16, 18, 19	Large red freestone with yellow flesh of good flavor. Early.	Moderately vigorous, productive tree.
'John Rivers'	7–9, 14, 15	White freestone or semifreestone. Early.	Earliest good variety.
'Mericrest'	2, 3, 6–10, 14–16	High-quality freestone with dark red skin, yellow flesh. Midseason.	Blooms late; recommend where spring frosts are a problem.
'Panamint'	7–9, 14–16, 18–24	Freestone with bright red skin, yellow flesh, very good flavor. Midseason.	Very low chilling requirement.
'Pioneer'	7–9, 14–16, 18–23	Yellow overlaid with red. Flesh yellow touched with red. Freestone. Rich, distinctive flavor. Midseason.	Large pink flowers.
'Silver Lode'	7–9, 14–16, 18–20	White-fleshed freestone with scarlet and white skin. Early.	Low chilling requirement.
'Stanwick'	7–9, 14, 15	Greenish white shaded purple red. White-fleshed freestone. Late.	Excellent flavor. Good for freezing.
'Stribling Giant Free'	7–9, 11	Resembles 'Freedom'.	More uniform production than 'Freedom'.
'Stribling White Free'	7–9, 11, 14–16	Large white nectarine blushed red. Sweet white flesh. Early.	Good home orchard tree.
'Sunred'	18–23	Medium, bright red. Semifreestone. Yellow flesh, good flavor. Very early.	Best in warm-winter areas.

PEANUT. *Leguminosae.* Summer annual. Best production where summers are long and warm and soil is not acid. Tender to frost but worth growing as novelty even in cool regions. Plants resemble small sweet pea bushes 10–20 in. high. After bright yellow flowers fade, a "peg" (shootlike structure) develops at each flower's base, grows down into soil and develops peanuts underground. Soil must be light-textured to admit penetration by pegs. Sandy soil in full sun is ideal.

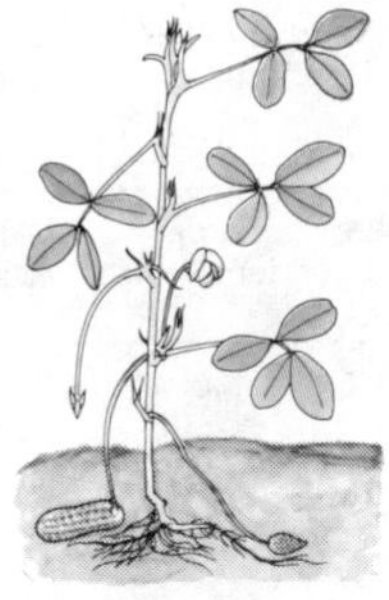
Peanut

Buy seeds (unroasted peanuts) from mail-order seed firms. Plant when soil warms up, setting nuts 2 in. deep in rows 3 ft. apart. Space shelled 'Jumbo Virginia' seeds 10 in. apart, 'Spanish' 4 in. apart (unshelled seeds of either variety 20 in. apart). Fertilize at planting time. Water regularly, especially at blossom time, up to 2 weeks before harvest. In 110–120 days after planting, foliage yellows and plants are ready to dig; loosen soil, then pull plants up. Cure peanuts on vines in warm, airy place out of sunlight for 2–3 weeks, then strip from plants.

PEANUT CACTUS. See *Chamaecereus sylvestri.*

PEAR *(Pyrus communis).* *Rosaceae.* Deciduous fruit tree. Zones 1–11, 14–18. (For ornamental relatives, see *Pyrus.*) Pyramidal tree with strongly vertical branching; grows 30–40 ft. tall, sometimes more. Long lived. Leaves are leathery, glossy, bright green. Clustered white flowers are handsome in early spring.

Pear

Takes damp, heavy soil better than most fruit trees; resistant to oak root fungus. Good looking enough for garden use and needs little pruning when mature, but requires spraying for codling moth, aphids, and other pests. Fireblight can be a serious problem; it makes entire branches die back quickly. Cut out blighted branches well below dead part; wash pruning tools with disinfectant between each cut.

Train trees early to good framework of main branches, then prune lightly to keep good form, eliminate crowding branches. Pears on dwarfing understock are good small garden trees, excellent espaliers.

See chart on pages 454–455 for description of pear varieties.

PEAR, ORIENTAL or ASIAN. *Rosaceae.* Deciduous trees. All Zones. Descendants of 2 Asiatic species: *Pyrus pyrifolia (P. serotina)* and *P. ussuriensis.* Fruit differs from European pears in being generally round, crisp and firm to hard in texture, and usually gritty to the bite. Asian pears are often called apple pears because of roundness and crispness, but they are not hybrids of these 2 fruits. Disease and pest problems are the same as those afflicting European pear. All need pollination by a second variety or by 'Bartlett' European pear.

Because of their unpearlike texture and taste, Asian pears should not be compared to European varieties for eating fresh. They're especially valuable for cooking and mixing with other fruits and vegetables in salads. Culture is same as for other pears. Varieties available include: 'Chojuro', 'Hosui', 'Ishiiwase', 'Kikusui', 'Niitaka', 'Nijisseiki' ('Twentieth Century'), 'Okusankichi' ('Late Korean'), 'Shinko', 'Shinseiki', 'Tsu Li', 'Ya Li', and 'Yakumo'.

PEARL BUSH. See *Exochorda.*

PEASHRUB. See *Caragana.*

PECAN. See *Carya illinoensis.*

PECTEILIS radiata *(Habenaria radiata).* *Orchidaceae.* EGRET FLOWER. House plant. Plants 8–16 in. tall, with a few narrow, 2–4-in. leaves and 1–3 white, 1½-in. flowers of complex form. Flower lip has 2 outspread, deeply fringed wings.

Plant 3 of the tiny bulbs in a 5-in. pot, just beneath surface of a rich potting mix. Set in a sunny window; keep moist until flowering is finished, then allow plants to go dormant. Keep dry 3–4 months, then replant.

Pecteilis radiata

P

Pear

NAME	CLIMATE ADAPTABILITY	FRUIT CHARACTERISTICS	COMMENTS
'Anjou', 'd'Anjou' ('Beurre d'Anjou')	A favorite late variety in Northwest, northern California mountains.	Medium to large, round or short necked, yellow to russeted yellow. Fine flavor, late ripening. Ripens after cold storage.	Tree upright and vigorous. Tie down limbs for more consistent bearing. Moderately susceptible to fireblight. There is a red-skinned selection, 'Red d'Anjou'.
'Bartlett'	Widely adaptable, but not at its best in mild winters. In southern California will succeed at high elevations or in cold canyon or valley floors.	Medium to large, with short but definite neck. Thin skinned, yellow or slightly blushed, very sweet and tender. Standard summer pear of fruit markets.	Generally sets fruit without pollination, but may require pollinator in cool California coastal areas and Northwest. Any variety except 'Seckel' will do. Tree form not the best, and somewhat subject to fireblight. Nevertheless a good home variety.
'Bosc' ('Beurre Bosc', 'Golden Russet')	Best in Northwest or at high altitudes farther south.	Medium to large, quite long necked, interesting and attractive in form. Heavy russeting on green or yellow ground color. Fine flavor. Midseason. Firm-fleshed, holds shape when cooked.	Large, upright, vigorous tree. Needs attention to pruning in youth. Highly susceptible to fireblight. Ripen it at room temperature after cold storage.
'Cascade'	Pacific Northwest.	Large, roundish fruit; outstanding flavor. Late.	Does not need cold storage to ripen.
'Clapp Favorite'	Very hardy to cold; good garden tree in Northwest, intermountain areas.	Resembles 'Bartlett'. Early, soft, and sweet.	Tree productive and shapely. Good foliage; highly susceptible to fireblight. 'Starkcrimson' and 'Super Red Clapp' are red-skinned strains.
'Comice' ('Doyenne du Comice', 'Royal Riviera')	At its best in Hood River and Medford regions of Oregon, Santa Clara County in California.	Large to very large, roundish to pear shaped, thick skinned, russeted greenish yellow, sometimes blushed. Superb flavor and texture. Late.	Big, vigorous tree but slow to reach bearing age. Moderately susceptible to fireblight. Bears well only when soil, climate, and exposure are right. Bears better in Northwest with pollinator. Ripens best after cold storage.
'Douglas'	Has low chilling requirement, but is also quite hardy.	Small to medium, oval in shape, greenish yellow. Flavor sweet to acid. Tender texture; some grittiness. Mid-August.	Like other hybrids with Asian pear, this one is highly resistant to fireblight.
'Fan Stil'	Low winter chilling requirements, high tolerance to heat and cold. Grown in high desert.	Medium sized, yellow with slight red blush. Crisp, juicy. August.	Vigorous, upright growth. Highly resistant to fireblight. Consistent bearer.
'Flemish Beauty'	Grown in Northwest.	Medium to large roundish pear, yellow, with pronounced red blush. Fine flavor. Early midseason.	Large, productive, very hardy tree. Fruit best ripened off tree.
'Flordahome'	Same as 'Fan Stil'.	Small to medium light green fruit. Juicy, not too gritty. Early.	Resistant to fireblight. With 'Hood', has lowest chilling requirement. Pollinate with 'Hood'.
'Garber'	Same as 'Fan Stil'.	Resembles 'Kieffer' but more rounded in form, lighter in color. Quality similar.	Tree moderately vigorous, somewhat resistant to fireblight.
'Hood'	Same as 'Fan Stil'.	Large yellow green fruit. Ripens a little later than 'Flordahome'.	Vigorous tree resistant to fireblight. Pollinate with 'Flordahome'.
'Kieffer'	Same as 'Fan Stil'.	Medium to large, oval, greenish yellow blushed dark red. Gritty in texture, fair in flavor. Best picked from tree and ripened at 65°F. Late.	Asian pear hybrid; quite resistant to fireblight. Good pear for extreme climates.
'Le Conte'	Same as 'Fan Stil'.	Resembles 'Kieffer'. Roundish, gritty, late.	Most tolerant to summer heat; somewhat resistant to fireblight.
'Max-Red Bartlett'	Same as 'Bartlett'.	Like 'Bartlett' except bright red in skin color and somewhat sweeter.	Red color extends to twigs and tints leaves. Needs pollinator in Northwest.
'Monterrey'	Same as 'Fan Stil'. Originated in Monterrey, Mexico.	Large, apple-shaped fruit with yellow skin. Flavor good; texture not too gritty. August–September.	Probably cross between an Asian and a European pear.
'Moonglow'	Wide climate tolerance.	Somewhat like 'Bartlett' in looks. Flesh juicy, soft. Flavor good. Ripens 2 weeks before 'Bartlett'.	Tree upright, vigorous, very heavy bearer. Very resistant to fireblight.
'Seckel' ('Sugar')	Widely adaptable.	Very small, very sweet and aromatic. Roundish to pear shaped, yellow brown. Flesh granular. Early midseason. A favorite for home gardens, preserving.	Tree fairly resistant to fireblight, highly productive.

NAME	CLIMATE ADAPTABILITY	FRUIT CHARACTERISTICS	COMMENTS
'Sure Crop'	Prolonged bloom period makes it safe bearer where spring frosts come late.	Resembles 'Bartlett' in looks and flavor. Bears August–September.	Consistent annual bearer. Fairly resistant to fireblight.
'Winter Bartlett'	Same as 'Bartlett'.	Smaller than 'Bartlett', firmer, later in ripening.	Tree spreading, loose, somewhat susceptible to fireblight.
'Winter Nelis'	Northwest. Mountains, cold valley floors in Southern California.	Small to medium, roundish, dull green or yellowish, rough. Very fine flavor. Late.	Very fine keeper, fine for baking but not attractive pear. Tree moderately susceptible to fireblight. Needs pollinator.

PEDILANTHUS tithymaloides. *Euphorbiaceae.* DEVIL'S BACKBONE. House plant. Cultivated varieties seldom exceed 1½ ft., are usually much shorter. Erect, fleshy, cylindrical stems have milky juice. Leaves in 2 rows, like ribs attached to backbone. Flowers small, in dense clusters atop stems; red bracts are showy parts. Commonest is 'Variegatus', with 4-in.-long, oval, light green leaves variegated with white and pink. 'Nana Compacta' has dark green leaves crowded together on erect 6–10-in. stems. Plants need warmth, good light, house plant soil, regular water.

Pedilanthus tithymaloides 'Variegatus'

PELARGONIUM. *Geraniaceae.* GERANIUM. Shrubby perennials. Zones 17, 24 are ideal climates; next best are Zones 15, 16, 22, 23; possible but not as easy are Zones 8, 9, 12–14, 18–21. Elsewhere, a pelargonium or geranium is house plant or summer bedding plant.

"Geranium" here is used as a common name; it's hard to be both botanically correct and conversationally clear. To the botanist, pelargoniums are all evergreen perennials or shrubby perennials that endure light frosts but not hard freezes and have slightly asymmetrical flowers in clusters. Most come from South Africa. A geranium, on the other hand, is one of many annual or perennial plants, most from the northern hemisphere, having symmetrical flowers borne singly or in clusters; some are weeds, some valued perennial border or rock garden plants.

Pelargonium crispum

In gardeners' conversation, a pelargonium is a Martha Washington (Lady Washington) geranium (or pelargonium). A geranium is an ivy geranium, a fancy-leafed geranium, a common geranium, or a scented geranium; all are species or varieties of *Pelargonium.* Gardeners also use the word to speak of the whole works—all true geraniums and all true pelargoniums.

Pelargonium domesticum

Most garden geraniums can be divided among 3 species of *Pelargonium: P. domesticum,* Martha Washington geranium; *P. hortorum,* common geranium (this group also includes variegated forms usually referred to as fancy-leafed or colored-leafed geraniums); and *P. peltatum,* ivy geranium. In addition, many other species have scented leaves.

Pelargonium graveolens

All geraniums do well in pots. Common geraniums grow well in garden beds; Martha Washington geraniums are also planted in beds, but tend to get rangy. Some varieties of Martha Washington are used in hanging baskets. Ivy geraniums are good in hanging containers, raised beds, and as a bank or ground cover. Use scented geraniums in close-up situations—in pots or in ground (in mild areas). For good bloom on potted geranium indoors, place it in a sunny window or in the brightest light possible.

Pelargonium hortorum

In the garden, plant geraniums in full sun in coastal areas, light shade in hot-summer climates; never plant in dense shade. Plant in any good, fast-draining soil. If soil is alkaline, add peat moss or nitrogen-fortified ground bark or sawdust to planting bed. Water common geraniums growing in ground when soil dries to about 1 in. below surface—best slightly on dry side. In warm weather, water Martha Washington geraniums deeply once a week. Water ivy geraniums every 10 days–2 weeks. Geraniums of any kind in good garden soil need little feeding; if in light sandy soil, feed 2 or 3 times during active growing season.

Pelargonium peltatum

Remove faded geranium flowers regularly to encourage new bloom. Pinch growing tips in early growth stages to force side branches. Prune after last frost, using tip cuttings to start new plants. With proper pinching and support, it is possible to raise standard ("tree") or espalier geraniums.

Geraniums in pots bloom best when somewhat potbound. When needed, repot only in next larger pot. In warm weather, water common geraniums in pots every other day; Martha Washington geraniums may need daily watering.

Pelargonium tomentosum

Tobacco budworm may be a problem in some areas. See "Geranium (tobacco) budworms," page 98, for control. Control aphids and whiteflies on Martha Washington geraniums with all-purpose spray. Use a miticide to control red spider mites on ivy geraniums.

P. domesticum. LADY WASHINGTON PELARGONIUM, MARTHA WASHINGTON GERANIUM, REGAL GERANIUM. Erect or somewhat spreading, to 3 ft. More rangy than common geranium. Leaves heart shaped to kidney shaped, dark green, 2–4 in. wide, with crinkled margins, unequal sharp teeth. Large, showy flowers 2 in. or more across in loose, rounded clusters, in white and many shades of pink, red, lavender, purple, with brilliant blotches and markings of darker colors. Blooms in spring and summer.

P. hortorum. COMMON GERANIUM, GARDEN GERANIUM. Most popular, widely grown. Shrubby, succulent stemmed, to 3 ft. or more; older plants grown in the open (in mild areas) become woody. Round or kidney-shaped leaves are velvety and hairy, soft to the touch, with edges indistinctly lobed and scallop toothed; most varieties show zone of deeper color just inside leaf margin. Some are plain green; others (color-leafed or fancy-leafed varieties) have zones, borders, or splashes of brown, gold, red, white, or green in various combinations. Some also have highly attractive flowers. Single or double flowers are flatter and smaller than those of Lady Washington, but plants bear many more blossoms to a cluster. Flowers are usually in solid colors. Many varieties in white and shades of pink, rose, red, orange, and violet. Blooms spring through fall.

There are also dwarf-growing, cactus-flowered, and other novelty kinds. Tough, attractive geraniums for outdoor bedding can be grown from seed, flowering the first summer. Widely available strains are Diamond and Elite (quick to reach bloom stage, compact, need no pinching), Orbit (distinct leaf zoning, broad, rounded flower clusters), and Sprinter.

P. peltatum. IVY GERANIUM. Trailing plants to 2–3 ft. or longer. Leaves rather succulent, glossy bright green, 2–3 in. across, ivy-like, with pointed lobes. Single or double, 1-in. flowers in rounded clusters are white, pink, rose, red, and lavender, 2 upper petals blotched or striped; 5–10 blooms per cluster. Many named varieties. Flat-grown plants for ground cover usually labeled only by color. 'L'Elegante' has foliage strongly edged with white; other varieties have white or yellow veins in leaves. Summer Showers strain may be grown from seed; it comes as a mixture of white, pink, red, lavender, and magenta.

Scented geraniums. Many species and varieties are grown for fragrance of their leaves, which may have the scent of various fruits, flowers, herbs, or spices. They are fun to collect and have a few uses—in sachets, for flavoring sauces or jellies, for scenting fingerbowls. Mostly, people just like to brush the foliage and enjoy the perfume. Common names describe fragrances. Fairly common are lemon-scented geranium, *P. crispum;* rose geranium, *P. graveolens* (there are other rose geraniums); lime-scented geranium, *P. nervosum;* and apple-scented geranium, *P. odoratissimum.*

P. tomentosum. PEPPERMINT-SCENTED GERANIUM. Large, 3–5-in.-wide, lobed leaves, velvety to the touch. Spreads to about 2–4 ft. Small white flowers in fluffy clusters. Use as ground cover in partial shade in frost-free gardens. Leafy branches are striking draped over wall or hanging from basket.

PELLAEA. *Polypodiaceae.* CLIFF-BRAKE. Ferns. Small plants, not striking in appearance, but with charmingly detailed foliage. The first 2 tolerate summer drought, but look dry. Second 2 are good house plants.

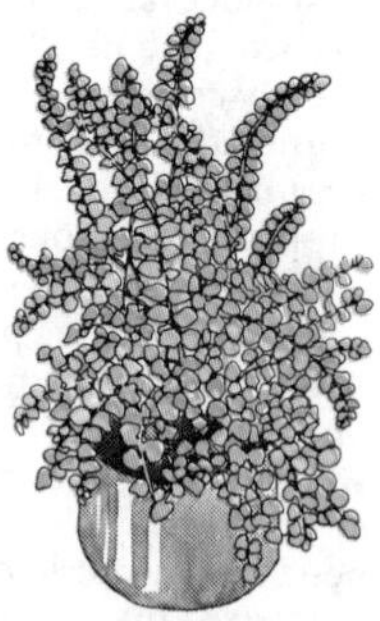
Pellaea rotundifolia

P. andromedifolia. COFFEE FERN. Zones 6–9, 14–24. Native to California, southern Oregon. Finely cut, gray green to bluish green fronds on thin, wiry stalks. To 1½ ft. high. With shade and ample water, will remain green.

P. mucronata. BIRD'S-FOOT FERN. Zones 2–11, 14–24. Larger than coffee fern, with gray green, airy fronds and narrow leaflets arranged in groups of 3.

P. rotundifolia. ROUNDLEAF FERN. Zones 14–17, 19–24. Small fern with spreading fronds to 1 ft. long. Nearly round leaflets, about ¾ in. across, are evenly spaced. Pretty fern to contrast with finer-textured ferns or to show off in pots, baskets, or raised beds. Filtered shade. Hardy to 24°F.

P. viridis *(P. adiantoides).* Zones 14–17, 19–24. Fronds to 2 ft. long, fresh green leaflets oval to lance shaped. Ground cover, rock garden, containers. Filtered shade. Hardy to 24°F.

PENCILBUSH, PENCIL TREE. See *Euphorbia tirucalli.*

PENNISETUM setaceum *(P. ruppelii).* *Gramineae.* FOUNTAIN GRASS. Perennial grass. All Zones. Dense, rounded clump to 4 ft. Narrow, arching leaves 2 ft. long. In summer, hollow 3–4-ft. stems are tipped with fuzzy, showy, coppery pink or purplish flower spikes. Use in dry locations, as in gravel beds, or as focal point in low ground covers. Any soil; full sun. Drought resistant. Goes dormant in winter. Cut stems for arrangements *before* flowers go to seed, since plant is a pest if not controlled. Variety 'Cupreum', with reddish brown leaves and dark plumes, does not set seed; grow it from divisions or cuttings.

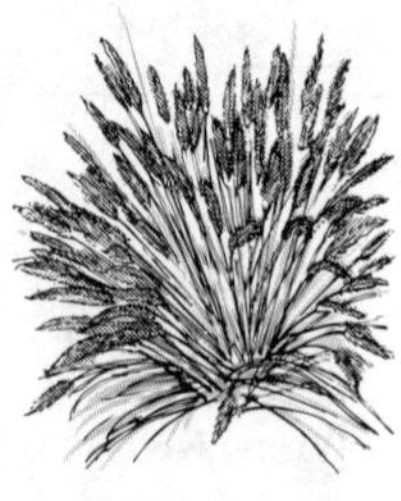
Pennisetum setaceum

PENNYROYAL. See *Mentha pulegium.*

PENSTEMON. *Scrophulariaceae.* BEARD TONGUE. Perennials, evergreen shrubs and shrublets. A few are widely grown; most others are sold only by specialists. All have tubular flowers. Bright reds and blues are the most common colors, but there are penstemons with blooms in soft pinks through salmon and peach to deep rose, lilac, deep purple, white, and rarely yellow. Hummingbirds are attracted to flowers. Of some 250 species, most are native to western U.S.—some on highest mountains, some in the desert, others in forest glades, foothills, or plains, from Canada into Mexico. Many are showy in bloom, and possibilities for hybridization are rich.

Penstemon heterophyllus purdyi

All penstemons do best in full sun (light shade in hot-summer climates). Need fast drainage; many kinds best in loose, gravelly soil, with infrequent watering. Usually short lived (3–4 years). In dry years or with little water, plants of wild species may thrive; if given too-rich soil and too much water, they may die quickly. Hybrids and selections tend to be easier to grow alongside regular garden plants.

P. antirrhinoides. Evergreen shrub. Zones 8–24. Native to southern California and northern Baja California. Stiffly spreading, much branched, 3–6 ft. tall. Leaves are narrow, to ½ in. long. Flowers bright yellow, ½–¾ in. long, very broad, in leafy clusters; buds brownish red. Blooms April–June. Use in fringe areas of garden, since it goes dormant in summer and loses lower leaves. Water sparingly in summer.

P. barbatus. Perennial. All Zones. Native to mountains from Colorado and Utah to Mexico. Open, somewhat sprawling habit, to 3 ft. Bright green leaves, 2–6 in. long. Long, loose spikes of red flowers about 1 in. long; early summer bloom. Selections include 'Prairie Dusk', deep purple flowers on 2-ft. spikes; 'Prairie Fire', scarlet on 2½-ft. spikes; and 'Rose Elf', deep rose on 2½-ft. spikes. All are short lived in warm-winter areas, tolerate extreme cold.

P. barrettiae. Perennial. Zones 1–7. Native to Columbia River gorge in Oregon and Washington. Shrubby, branching, to 1 ft. high. Leaves leathery, blue green, to 3 in. long, toothed. Abundant rose purple, 1–1½-in.-long flowers in short spikes, April–June.

P. cordifolius. Evergreen shrub. Zones 8, 9, 14–24. Native to coast of southern California. Loose branching, half climbing, with flexible, arching branches to 10 ft.; fuchsialike leaves ½–1½ in. long. Red, tubular flowers 1–1½ in. long, in dense clusters at tips of stems, April–June. Yellow-flowered forms exist. Give little summer water if soil is heavy.

P. davidsonii *(P. menziesii davidsonii).* Perennial. Zones 1–7. Native to high mountains of Sierra Nevada and western Nevada north to Washington. Mat-forming alpine to 3 in. high. Leaves oval, to ½–¾ in. long. Flowers violet blue, 1–1½ in. long, July–August. Ideal for gravelly slope in rock garden.

P. gloxinioides. BORDER PENSTEMON, GARDEN PENSTEMON. Perennial treated as annual in cold-winter climates. All Zones. Plants with this name are selections of *P. hartwegii* or hybrids between it and *P. cobaea*. Compact, bushy, upright stems to 2–4 ft. tall. Tubular flowers in loose spikes at ends of stems, in almost all colors but blue and yellow. Mass in borders or group with other summer-flowering plants.

Penstemon gloxinioides

Plant in full sun; partial shade in hot-summer areas. Subject to root rot in heavy, wet soil. In mild climates, set out flat-grown plants in fall for bloom in April. Older plants, if cut back after main bloom, flower again later in summer on side branches. Easy to grow from seed; several good mixed-color strains available. For plants in separate colors, make softwood cuttings from desirable plants. Some nurseries sell cutting-grown plants in separate colors.

P. heterophyllus purdyi. Perennial. Zones 6–24. Native to Sierra Nevada foothills and Coast Ranges of California. Stems upright or spreading, 1–2 ft. high. Narrow, pointed leaves 1–3 in. long. Blooms April–July, bearing spikelike clusters of flowers varying from rosy lavender to intense gentian blue. Most nurseries stocking this plant sell it as 'Blue Bedder' penstemon.

P. newberryi. MOUNTAIN PRIDE. Perennial. Zones 1–9. Native to higher elevations of Sierra Nevada. Matted plant to 20 in. high, woody at base. Leaves thick, roundish, toothed, ½–1½ in. long. Flowers rose red, about 1 in. long, June–August.

P. pinifolius. Small shrublet. All Zones. Spreading, 4–6 in. tall (rarely to 2 ft.), with crowded needlelike leaves ¾ in. long. Coral to scarlet flowers 1½ in. long. Rock garden or low border plant.

P. rupicola. Evergreen subshrub. Zones 1–7. Native to Cascade and Siskiyou mountains. Trailing, much branched, to 4 in. high. Leaves roundish, blue green, fine toothed, ⅓–¾ in. long. Flowers bright rose crimson, ½–1½ in. long, June–August. Gravel or perfectly drained soil is a must. Beautiful in rock gardens, in dry wall near miniature campanulas. Lesser-known, white-flowered form is available; it needs half shade, is somewhat harder to grow than species.

PENTAS lanceolata. *Rubiaceae.* STAR CLUSTERS. Perennial usually grown as an annual. All Zones. Can also be grown as a house plant. Spreading, multistemmed plant to 2–3 ft. tall. Leaves are long, somewhat hairy ovals; stems are topped by tight 4-in.-wide clusters of small, star-shaped flowers in white, pink, lilac, or red. Grow in full sun; give ample water and feeding. Remove dead flowers for a long bloom season. If growing as a house plant, give it as much sunlight as possible: set in a bright west or south window.

Pentas lanceolata

PEONY. See *Paeonia.*

PEPEROMIA. *Piperaceae.* Perennials. House or greenhouse plants grown for foliage. Evergreen, often succulent; usually prostrate or trailing. Tiny flowers in small, dense, slender spikes. Use in planters, dish gardens, other containers. Can be used as ground cover in large indoor plantings. Grow in north light, or in diffused light protected from direct sun (as by wide overhang). Cool or warm temperatures. Light, well-drained soil; not too much water. Propagate by stem, crown, or leaf cuttings (insert lower ½ of leaf in 2-in. pot of ½ sand, ½ leaf mold).

Peperomia caperata

Following are a few of many sold by house plant specialists.

P. argyreia *(P. sandersii).* WATERMELON PEPEROMIA. Compact, nearly stemless, with rosette of round, 3-5-in.-long, gray-striped leaves on long red stems.

P. caperata. EMERALD RIPPLE. Plants 3–4 in. tall. Leaves rich green, heart shaped, deeply veined, borne densely on very short, reddish stalks. Tiny greenish white flowers in spikes. 'Little Fantasy' is miniature variety.

P. metallica. Erect, dark red stems. Narrow, waxy, copper-colored leaves with a metallic luster and silver green band down leaf center.

P. obtusifolia. Old favorite with thick, upright or trailing stems to 6 in.; dark green, round, fleshy, 4-in. leaves. 'Minima', miniature form, has dense stems and oval, stalked leaves 1½–2 in. long, dark green above, paler beneath. Several variegated forms are available.

P. rotundifolia *(P. nummulariifolia, P. prostrata).* Tiny, dark green, round, ¼-in. leaves, often reddish underneath, borne along slender, trailing stems.

PEPINO. See *Solanum muricatum.*

PEPPER. *Solanaceae.* The 2 basic kinds of peppers are sweet and hot.

Pepper (Bell)

Sweet peppers always remain mild, even when flesh ripens to red. This group includes big stuffing and salad peppers commonly known as bell peppers; best known of these are 'California Wonder' and 'Yolo Wonder'. Hybrid varieties have been bred for early bearing, high yield, or disease resistance. Big peppers are also available in bright yellow and purple (purple types turn green when cooked). Other sweet types are thick-walled, very sweet pimientos used in salads or for cooking or canning; sweet cherry peppers for pickling; and long, slender Italian frying peppers and Hungarian sweet yellow peppers, both used for cooking.

Hot peppers range from tiny (pea-sized) types to narrow 6–7-in.-long forms, but all are pungent, their flavor varying from the mild heat of Italian peperoncini to the near-incandescence of the chilipiquin. 'Anaheim' is mild but spicy pepper used for making canned green chiles. 'Long Red Cayenne' is used for drying; 'Hungarian Yellow Wax (Hot)', 'Jalapeno', and 'Fresno Chile Grande' are used for pickling. Mexican cooking utilizes an entire palette of peppers, among them 'Ancho', 'Mulato', and 'Pasilla'.

All peppers grow on handsome, bushy plants, 1½–2 ft. tall. Use plants as temporary low informal hedge, or grow and display them in containers. Certain kinds have been bred for house plant use: 'Holiday Flame', 'Midnight Special' (black leaves), and 'Red Missile' are typical ornamental forms with small erect fruit that changes from green through whitish and purple to bright red.

Buy started plants at nursery, or sow seed indoors 8–10 weeks before average date of last frost. Set out when weather becomes warm, spacing plants 1½–2 ft. apart. Grow in full sun. Water thoroughly but not frequently as plants grow, and feed once or twice with commercial fertilizer after plants become established, before blossoms set. Sweet peppers are ready to pick when they have reached good size, but keep their flavor until red-ripe. Pimientos should only be picked when red-ripe. Pick hot peppers when they are fully ripe. Control cutworms with baits. Control aphids, whiteflies with all-purpose vegetable garden dust or spray.

PEPPERMINT. See *Eucalyptus, Mentha piperita.*

PEPPERMINT TREE. See *Agonis flexuosa.*

PEPPER TREE. See *Schinus.*

PEPPERWOOD. See *Umbellularia californica.*

P

PERILLA frutescens. *Labiatae.* SHISO. Summer annual. Sturdy, leafy plant to 2–3 ft. tall. Deeply toothed egg-shaped leaves to 5 in. long. Kind most commonly seen has bronzy or purple leaves that look much like those of coleus. Fancy Fringe strain has leaves deeply cut and fringed, deep bronzy purple in color. Use leaves as vegetable or flavoring (they taste something like mint, something like cinnamon); use long, thin clusters of flower buds as a vegetable to fry in tempura batter. Extremely fast and easy to grow in sun or light shade with average water. In the Orient, seeds are pressed for edible oil.

Perilla frutescens

PERIWINKLE. See *Catharanthus, Vinca.*

PERNETTYA mucronata. *Ericaceae.* Evergreen shrub. Zones 4–7, 15–17. Compact growth to 2–3 ft. tall, spreading by underground runners to make clumps. Glossy, dark green, oval or narrow, ⅓–¾-in.-long leaves give fine-textured look. Some leaves turn red or bronzy in winter. Tiny white to pink, bell-shaped flowers in late spring, followed by very colorful berries: purple, white, red, rose, pink, or near black, all with metallic sheen. Berries are fleshy, ½ in. across; they hold until knocked off by hard rain or frost, possibly until early spring. Plants set more fruit if you grow several for cross-pollination.

Pernettya mucronata

Acid, peaty soil; ample water. Full sun in cold-winter regions, partial shade where summers are long and hot. Can be invasive; control by root-pruning with spade. Tops often need regular pruning to stay attractive. Use as informal low hedge or border, in tubs or window boxes.

PEROVSKIA atriplicifolia. *Labiatae.* RUSSIAN SAGE. Perennial. All Zones (best with pronounced winter chill). Woody-based, multistemmed plant to 3 ft. tall. Leaves gray green, lower ones finely cut, upper merely toothed, small. Lavender blue flowers in many-branched, slender, spikelike clusters that form a haze above the foliage. Long summer bloom if old flowers are trimmed off. Tolerates some drought when established. Likes heat, full sun, winter chill. Dormant in winter. Effective with lavender and other gray-foliaged plants.

Perovskia atriplicifolia

PERSIAN VIOLET. See *Exacum affine.*

PERSIMMON ***(Diospyros).*** *Ebenaceae.* Deciduous trees. Two species are grown in the West, one a well-known fruit tree with outstanding ornamental qualities. Both are resistant to oak root fungus.

Oriental or Japanese persimmon ***(Diospyros kaki).*** Zones 7–9, 14–16, 18–23; borderline in Zones 4–6; grows in Zones 10–13, but rarely fruits. To 30 ft. or more with wide-spreading branches. New leaves soft, light green in spring, becoming dark green, leathery, broad ovals to 6–7 in. long, 2–3½ in. wide. In late autumn, leaves turn yellow, orange, or scarlet even in warm-winter climates. After leaves drop, orange scarlet fruit lights tree for weeks; after fruit drops, handsome branch structure justifies featured spot in garden.

Persimmon

Easy to grow. Prune only to remove dead wood, shape tree, or open up too-dense interior. Only problem is fruit drop, common in young trees. To avoid it, be consistent in feeding and watering. Space deep irrigations so that root zone is neither too wet nor too dry. Feed plants in late winter or early spring; overfeeding with nitrogen causes excessive growth, excessive fruit drop. Mature plants usually bear consistently.

Persimmon fruit can be dried; pick when hard-ripe with some stem remaining. Peel and hang up by string in sun. Dried fruit has flavor something like litchi or very high-quality prune.

One of best fruit trees for ornamental use; good garden or small shade tree. Can be espaliered. Available varieties:

'Chocolate'. Brown-flecked, very sweet flesh.

'Fuyu'. Nonastringent even when underripe; firm fleshed (like an apple), reddish yellow, about size of baseball but flattened like tomato. Similar but larger is 'Gosho', widely sold as 'Giant Fuyu'.

'Hachiya'. Shapeliest tree for ornamental use. This variety yields big (4-in.-long, 2½–3-in.-broad), slightly pointed persimmons usually found in produce stores. Pick before fully ripe to save crop from birds, but allow to become soft-ripe before eating; astringent unless mushy.

'Tamopan'. Very large, turban-shaped, astringent until fully ripe.

American persimmon ***(Diospyros virginiana).*** Zones 3–9, 14–16, 18–23. Moderate-growing small tree to 20–30 ft. with broad, oval crown, attractive gray brown bark fissured into deep checkered pattern. Glossy, broad, oval leaves to 6 in. long. New foliage bronzy or reddish; leaves turn yellow, pink, and red in fall. Fruit round, yellow to orange (often blushed red), 1½–2 in. wide, very astringent until soft-ripe, then very sweet.

PERUVIAN DAFFODIL. See *Hymenocallis narcissiflora.*

PERUVIAN LILY. See *Alstroemeria.*

PETREA volubilis. *Verbenaceae.* QUEEN'S WREATH. Evergreen vine. Zones 23, 24; possibly in sheltered, frost-free site Zones 19–22.

Elsewhere, house or greenhouse plant (can be grown in large container). To 40 ft., but can be kept much smaller. Deep green, rough-surfaced leaves. Stunning displays of purplish blue, star-shaped flowers in long, slender clusters, several times a year during warm weather. Flowers are individually small but borne in profusion. Likes heat, sun, ample water, average soil.

Petrea volubilis

PETUNIA hybrida. *Solanaceae.* COMMON GARDEN PETUNIA. Tender perennial grown as summer annual. In mild-winter desert areas, planted in fall for color from spring to early summer. Fragrant flowers are single and funnel shaped to very double, in many colors from soft pink to deepest red, light blue to deepest purple, cream, yellow, and pure white. Leaves thick, broad, and slightly sticky to touch.

Petunia hybrida

Plant in full sun in good garden soil; water regularly. Single-flowered kinds tolerate alkalinity, will grow in poor soil if it's well drained. Plant 8–18 in. apart depending on size of variety. After plants are established, pinch back halfway for compact growth. Feed monthly with complete fertilizer. Near end of summer, cut back rangy plants about half to force new growth. In some areas, smog causes spots on leaves of seedlings—plants outgrow damage in clear periods. White-flowered kinds are most susceptible. Tobacco budworm may be a problem in some areas. See "Geranium (tobacco) budworms," page 98, for control.

To most gardeners, petunias are of 2 main types: doubles or singles. Doubles are heavily ruffled, many-petaled flowers resembling carnations; singles are funnel shaped (either ruffled or smooth edged) with open throats. Both doubles and singles come as Grandifloras (very large flowers) or Multifloras (smaller but more numerous flowers).

Most newer varieties of petunias (F_1 hybrids, produced by crossing 2 different varieties) are more vigorous and more uniform in color, height, and growth habit than ordinary petunias. Most are hand-pollinated to produce seed and are thus somewhat more expensive than petunias grown from open-pollinated seed.

F_1 Hybrid Grandiflora. Sturdy plants, 15–27 in. high, 2–3 ft. across. Flowers usually single, ruffled or fringed, to 4½ in. across, in pink, rose, salmon, red, scarlet, blue, white, pale yellow, or striped combinations. Cascade, Countdown, and Supercascade series of petunias belong here; cascading growth habit makes them good for hanging baskets. Magic and Supermagic strains give heavy bloom on compact plants; large, single flowers are 4–5 in. across, in white, pink, red, blue. Double Hybrid Grandifloras with heavily ruffled flowers come in all petunia colors except yellow.

F_1 Hybrid Multiflora. Plants about same size as F_1 Hybrid Grandiflora, but flowers generally smooth edged and smaller (to 2 in. across), single or double. Neat, compact growth, ideal for bedding, massed planting. Many named varieties in pink, rose, salmon, yellow, white, blue. Multifloras are resistant to botrytis disease, which disfigures blossoms and later foliage of other kinds in humid weather. Joy and Plum series of petunias belong in F_1 Hybrid Multiflora strain. Flowers single, satiny textured, to 2½ in. wide, in white, cream, pink, coral, red, and blue. 'Summer Sun' is genuinely bright yellow petunia.

F_2 Hybrid Grandiflora and Multiflora. These petunias look like their F_1 seed parents, but are variable in color and somewhat so in growth pattern.

Fluffy Ruffles. Strain has big flowers (to 6 in.) in a variety of colors, all heavily veined.

PHACELIA campanularia. *Hydrophyllaceae.* DESERT BLUEBELLS. Annual. Native to California deserts. Adaptable to most well-drained soils. Grows 6–18 in. tall, with egg-shaped, coarsely toothed leaves and loose clusters of inch-long, bell-shaped, deep blue flowers. Blooms March–April. Sow where plants are to bloom in fall or earliest spring, or sow in flats and transplant while seedlings are very small.

Phacelia campanularia

PHAEDRANTHUS buccinatorius. See *Distictis buccinatoria.*

PHALAENOPSIS. *Orchidaceae.* MOTH ORCHID. Epiphytic orchids. Greenhouse and house plants. Thick, broad, leathery leaves; no pseudobulbs. Long sprays of 3–6-in.-wide, white, cream, pale yellow, or light lavender pink flowers spring–fall; some are spotted, barred, or have contrasting lip color. Leaves are rather flat, spreading to 1 ft. long. Flower sprays may be 3-ft. long. Cut faded spray back to a node; a secondary spray may form.

Phalaenopsis

Although very popular commercially, moth orchids are more for advanced amateurs than beginners. They require warmer growing conditions than most orchids (minimum 60°–70°F. at night and 70°–85°F. during the day), fairly high humidity, and moist potting medium at all times. Good location is near bathroom or kitchen window with light coming through a gauzelike curtain (foliage burns easily in direct sun). Give them same potting medium as for cattleyas. When cutting flowers, leave part of main stem so another set of flowers can develop from dormant buds. Many lovely, large-flowered hybrids. Some smaller-flowered new hybrids give promise of being easier to grow, taking somewhat lower nighttime temperatures.

PHALARIS arundinacea picta. *Gramineae.* RIBBON GRASS, GARDENER'S GARTERS. All Zones. Tough, tenacious grass that spreads aggressively by underground runners. Leaves form 2–3-ft. spreading clumps. Leaves are deep green striped white, turn buff color in fall. Flowers of no importance. Can take heat or cold, drought or wet soil, sun or partial shade. Confine roots if planted near choice, more delicate plants.

Phalaris arundinacea picta

PHASEOLUS caracalla. See *Vigna caracalla.*

PHILADELPHUS. *Saxifragaceae.* MOCK ORANGE. Deciduous shrubs. White, usually fragrant flowers bloom in late spring (early summer for some species). Most are large, vigorous plants of fountainlike form with medium green foliage. Full sun (part shade in hottest-summer areas), ordinary garden soil and watering. Prune every year just after bloom, cutting out oldest wood and surplus shoots at base. Taller types are striking in lawns or as background and corner plantings; smaller kinds can be planted near foundations or used as low screens or informal hedges.

Philadelphus lemoinei

P. coronarius. SWEET MOCK ORANGE. Zones 1–17. Old favorite. Strong growing, 8–10 ft. tall. Oval leaves 1–4 in. long. Clusters of very fragrant, 1½-in.-wide flowers in June. 'Aureus' has bright golden leaves which turn yellow green in summer, does not grow as tall.

P. gordonianus. See *P. lewisii.*

P. lemoinei. Zones 1–17. This hybrid includes many garden varieties, most to 5–6 ft. tall and all with very fragrant flowers in clusters. Leaves oval, to 2 in. long. Double-flowered 'Enchantment' is best-known variety.

P. lewisii. WILD MOCK ORANGE. Zones 1–17. Native to western North America. Erect and arching habit (tall race from west of the Cascades is often called *P. gordonianus*). Satiny, fragrant blooms nearly 2 in. across; oval leaves 2–4 in. long. Blooms June–July. Somewhat drought tolerant, especially the form native to California. State flower of Idaho.

P. mexicanus. EVERGREEN MOCK ORANGE. Zones 8, 9, 14–24. Best used as vine or bank cover; long, supple stems with 3-in. evergreen leaves will reach 15–20 ft. if given support. Fragrant creamy flowers in small clusters bloom in spring and early summer, or intermittently.

P. purpureomaculatus. Zones 2–17. Group of hybrids including moderate-sized shrubs with flowers showing purple centers. 'Belle Etoile' grows upright to 5 ft. tall; fragrant, fringed, single flowers to 2½ in. Oval leaves to 2 in. long.

P. virginalis. Zones 1–17. Another hybrid which has produced several garden varieties, usually with double flowers. Tall (6–8-ft.) varieties include 'Minnesota Snowflake' and 'Virginal', both double, and 'Natchez', with 2-in. single flowers. Lower growing are double 'Glacier' (3–4 ft.) and 'Dwarf Minnesota Snowflake' (2–3 ft.).

PHILLYREA decora *(Osmanthus decorus).* *Oleaceae.* Evergreen shrub. Zones 4–9, 14–21. Slow growth to 6–8 ft. Neat, glossy leaves 3–5 in. long, dark green above, yellowish green beneath. Small pure white flowers April–May. Male and female flowers on different plants; if both sexes are present, small red fruit follows bloom, turns purplish black in late fall.

(Continued on next page)

P

Has foliage quality of camellia or skimmia but grows well in ordinary garden soils and exposures. Needs little water once established.

Phillyrea decora

PHILODENDRON. *Araceae.* Evergreen vines and shrubs. Philodendrons are tough, durable, fast-growing plants grown for their attractive, leathery, usually glossy leaves. They fall into 2 main classes; each species and variety in list that follows is designated in one of these categories.

Philodendron bipennifolium

Arborescent and relatively hardy. These become big plants 6–8 ft. high (sometimes higher) and as wide. They develop large leaves and sturdy, self-supporting trunks. They will grow indoors, but need much more space than most house plants. They grow outdoors in certain milder climate Zones—see individual descriptions. As outdoor plants, they do best in sun with shade at midday but can survive considerable shade. Use them for tropical jungle effects, or as massive silhouettes against walls or glass. Excellent in large containers; effective near swimming pools.

Vining or self-heading and tender. These forms can only be house plants. There are many kinds, with many different leaf shapes and sizes. Vining types do not really climb and must be tied to or leaned against a support until they eventually shape themselves to it. The support can be almost anything, but certain water-absorbent columns (sections of tree fern stems, wire and sphagnum "totem poles," slabs of redwood bark) serve especially well because they can be kept moist, and moist columns help plants grow better. Self-heading types form short, broad plants with sets of leaves radiating out from central point.

Whether in containers or open ground, a philodendron should grow in rich, loose, well-drained soil. House plant philodendrons grow best in good light (but not direct sun) coming through a window. All prefer moist soil but will not take soggy soil. Feed lightly and frequently for good growth and color. Dust leaves of indoor plants once a month (commercial leaf polishes are available).

It's the nature of most philodendrons—especially when grown in containers—to drop lower leaves, leaving bare stem. To fix a leggy philodendron, you can air-layer leafy top (see page 85) and, when it develops roots, sever it and replant it. Or cut plant back to short stub and let it start over again. Often the best answer is to throw out an overgrown, leggy plant and replace it with a new one. Aerial roots form on stems of some kinds; push them into soil or cut them off—it won't hurt plant.

Flowers may appear on old plants if heat, light, and humidity are high; they somewhat resemble callas, with a boat-shaped bract surrounding a club-shaped, spikelike structure. Bracts are usually greenish, white, or reddish.

Here are the kinds. Note that the great favorite—the so-called "split-leaf philodendron"—is not a philodendron at all, but a *Monstera.*

P. bipennifolium (usually sold as *P. panduriforme).* FIDDLELEAF PHILODENDRON. Vining. Fairly fast climber with rich green, 10-in. leaves oddly lobed to resemble violin (or horse's head; no 2 leaves are exactly alike). Excellent house plant, but sparse foliage on older plants suggests planting in multiples for dense effect.

P. bipinnatifidum. Arborescent. Zones 15–24. Similar to *P. selloum,* but carries more leaves at a time and has more deeply and evenly cut leaves with reddish veins. Next to *P. selloum,* hardiest for outdoor use.

P. cordatum. See *P. scandens oxycardium.*

P. domesticum (usually sold as *P.* 'Hastatum'). Vining. Fairly fast, open growth. Leaves 1 ft. long, arrow shaped, deep green. Subject to leaf spot if kept too warm and moist. A number of selections and hybrids have become available; these are more resistant to leaf spot and tend to be more compact and upright. Some, possibly hybrids with *P. erubescens,* have much red in new foliage and in leaf stalks. 'Emerald Queen' is a choice deep green, 'Royal Queen' a good deep red.

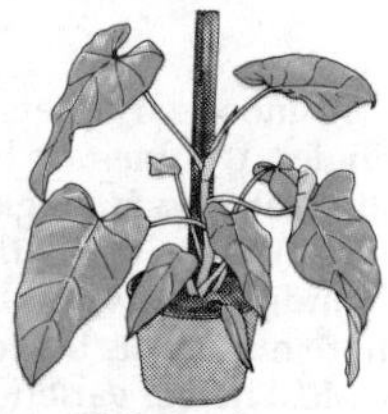

Philodendron domesticum

P. erubescens. Vining. Leaves 9 in. long, arrow shaped, reddish beneath, dark green above, on reddish leaf stalks.

P. 'Florida'. Vining. Hybrid of *P. pedatum* and *P. squamiferum.* Heavy-textured leaves split into 5 broad, sharp-pointed lobes, with pronounced veins and reddish undersurface.

P. 'Florida Compacta'. Vining. Compact, slow to climb. Deep green leaves similar to those of 'Florida' in shape. Red leaf stalks.

P. 'Hastatum'. See *P. domesticum.*

P. laciniatum. See *P. pedatum.*

P. 'Lynette'. Self-heading. Makes close cluster of foot-long, broadish, bright green leaves with strong patterning formed by deeply sunken veins. Good table top plant.

P. oxycardium. See *P. scandens oxycardium.*

P. panduriforme. See *P. bipennifolium.*

P. pedatum (usually sold as *P. laciniatum*). Vining. Dark green, 8-in. leaves, deeply slashed into unequal broad, sharp-pointed lobes. Holds lower leaves well.

P. pertusum. See *Monstera deliciosa.* This is commonly sold as SPLIT-LEAF PHILODENDRON.

P. scandens oxycardium (usually sold as *P. oxycardium* or *P. cordatum*). Vining. Most common philodendron. Heart-shaped, deep green leaves, usually 5 in. or less in length in juvenile plants, up to 1 ft. long on mature plants in greenhouses. Easily grown (cut stems will live and grow for some time in vases of water). Thin stems will trail gracefully or climb fast and high. Grow on moisture-retentive columns or train on strings or wires to frame a window or hang from a rafter.

Philodendron scandens oxycardium

P. selloum. Arborescent. Zones 8, 9, 12–24. Hardiest big-leafed philodendron used outdoors. Deeply cut leaves to 3 ft. long. Variety 'Lundii' is more compact.

P. squamiferum. Vining. Much like *P. pedatum* in appearance, but with red, bristly leaf stalks and deeply sunken leaf veins.

P. wendlandii. Self-heading. Compact clusters of 12 or more deep green, foot-long, broadly lance-shaped leaves on short, broad stalks. Useful where tough, compact foliage plant is needed for table top or low, broad planting area.

Philodendron squamiferum

PHLOMIS fruticosa. *Labiatae.* JERUSALEM SAGE. Shrubby perennial. All Zones. Deserving old-time garden plant, rugged and woody. Coarse, woolly, gray green, wrinkled leaves. Yellow, 1-in.-long flowers in tight, ball-shaped whorls around upper part of 4-ft. stems in early summer. Combine with echinops, eryngium, helenium, helianthus, kniphofia, rudbeckia. Full sun; adapted to poor soil, dry slopes. Resistant to oak root fungus. Stays evergreen in mild winters. Cut back by ⅓ in fall to keep in shape. With summer water, it will produce several waves of bloom; cut back after each flowering for repeat performance.

Phlomis fruticosa

PHLOX. *Polemoniaceae.* Annuals, perennials. Most are natives of North America. Plants in this group show wide variation in growth form. All have showy flower clusters. Give them sun, average garden soil, and water unless otherwise noted.

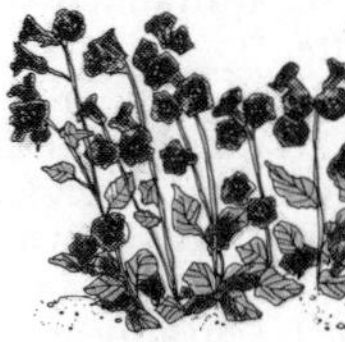

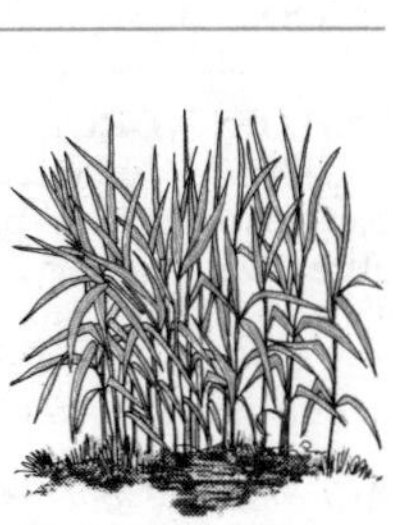

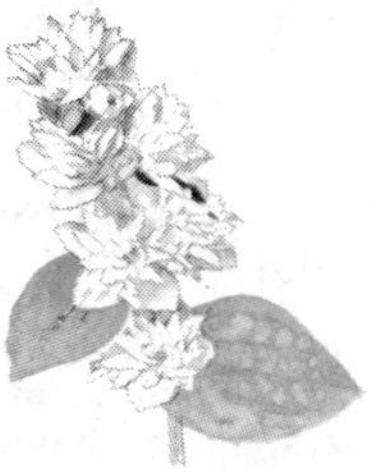

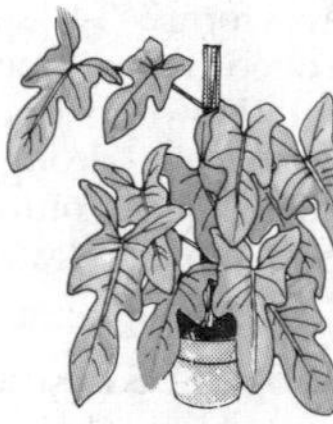

P. carolina ***(P. maculata, P. suffruticosa).*** THICK-LEAF PHLOX. Perennial. Zones 1–14, 18–21. To 3–4 ft. tall. Early flowers about ¾ in. wide, in 15-in.-long clusters. Color varies from white, centered with pale pink eye, to magenta. Shiny foliage, free from mildew and red spider mites (which often attack summer phlox). 'Miss Lingard' is excellent white-flowered variety to 3 ft. tall.

Phlox paniculata

P. divaricata. SWEET WILLIAM PHLOX. Perennial. Zones 1–17. To 1 ft., with slender, leafy stems and creeping underground shoots. Leaves oval, 1–2 in. long, ¾ in. wide. Spring flowers in open clusters; bluish or pinkish blue varying to white, ¾–1½ in. across, somewhat fragrant. Use in rock gardens, as bulb cover (see *Tulipa*). Light shade, good, deep soil, average water. *P. d. laphamii* has best blue color.

P. drummondii. ANNUAL PHLOX. Summer annual. Grows 6–18 in. tall, with erect, leafy stems more or less covered with rather sticky hairs. Flowers numerous, showy, in close clusters at tops of stems. Bright and pastel colors (no blue or orange), some with contrasting eye. Tall strains in mixed colors are Finest and Fordhook Finest. Dwarf strains (6–8 in. tall) include Beauty and Globe, both with rounded flowers, and starry-petaled Petticoat and Twinkle. Bloom lasts from early summer until frost if faded flowers are removed. Plant in spring in colder climates, in fall in mild areas of southern California and desert. Give full sun and light, rich loam.

P. mesoleuca. CHIHUAHUAN PHLOX. Perennial. Zones 4–24. Identification of these rock garden phloxes from Mexico is uncertain; they may be *P. nana* or another species. Grow 6 in. tall, to 1½ ft. wide; growth tends to be straggly if plants are not tip-pinched. Flower color varies from cream to yellow, orange, and red. Hardy to 0°F. Need excellent drainage.

P. nivalis. TRAILING PHLOX. Perennial. Zones 4–7. Trailing plants form loose, 4–6-in.-tall mats of narrow evergreen leaves. Big pink or white flowers in fairly large clusters in late spring or early summer. Excellent in rock gardens. 'Camla' is fine salmon pink variety.

P. paniculata. SUMMER PHLOX. Perennial. Zones 1–14, 18–21. Long lived. Thrives in full sun, but in hottest areas colors may bleach. Leaves 2–5 in. long, narrow and tapering to slender point. Fragrant, 1-in.-wide summer flowers in large, dome-shaped clusters on 3–5-ft. stems. Colors include white, shades of lavender, pink, rose, or red; blooms of some types have a contrasting eye. Many named varieties. Mulch around plants to keep roots cool. Plants subject to mildew at end of blooming season. Divide plants every few years, replanting young shoots from outside of clump. Plants do not come true from seed; most tend toward uncertain purplish pink, though some may be attractive. Plant seed in fall or freeze in ice cubes for month before sowing.

P. subulata. MOSS PINK. Perennial. Zones 1–17. Stiffish, ½-in., needlelike, evergreen leaves on creeping stems; forms mats to 6 in. tall. The ¾-in. flowers range in color from white through pink to rose and lavender blue. Late spring or early summer bloom, according to climate. Makes sheets of brilliant color in rock gardens. Ground cover. Grow in loose, not-too-rich soil. After flowering, cut back halfway. Moderately drought tolerant.

P. suffruticosa. See *P. carolina.*

PHOENIX. *Palmae.* DATE PALM. Mostly large feather palms, but one a dwarf. Trunks patterned with bases of old leaf stalks. Small yellowish flowers in large, hanging sprays followed by clusters of often edible fruit (*P. dactylifera* bears dates of commerce). These palms hybridize freely, so buy from reliable nurseryman who knows his seed or plant source.

Phoenix canariensis

P. canariensis. CANARY ISLAND DATE PALM. Zones 9, 12–24. Big, heavy-trunked plant to 60 ft. tall, with 50-ft. spread composed of a great many gracefully arching fronds. Grows slowly until it forms trunk, then speeds up a little. Young plants do well in pots for many years, looking something like pineapples. Grow on slopes, in parks, big spaces, along wide streets; not for small city lots. Hardy to 20°F. Slow to develop new head of foliage after hard-frost damage.

Phoenix dactylifera

P. dactylifera. DATE PALM. Zones 9, warmer parts of 11, 12–24. The date palm of Indio, California, and of Palm Springs golf courses; classic palm of movie desert oases. Native to Middle East. Very tall (up to 80 ft.), with slender trunk and gray green, waxy leaves; leaflets stiff and sharp pointed. Suckers from base; natural habit is clump of several trunks. Principal commercial variety in California is 'Deglet Noor'. Too stiff and large for most home gardens, but adapts to and does well in seaside, desert gardens. Leaves killed at 20°F. but plants have survived 4°–10°F.

Phoenix roebelenii

P. loureiri ***(P. humilis).*** Zones 9, 12–24. Resembles smaller, more slender and refined Canary Island date palm. Slow grower to 10–18 ft. tall. Leaves dark green, flexible, 10 ft. long. Good in containers or in the garden. Hardy to 20°F.

P. reclinata. SENEGAL DATE PALM. Zones 23, 24. Native to tropical Africa. Makes picturesque clumps from offshoots, with several curving trunks 20–30 ft. high. Offshoots can be removed to make single-trunked trees. Fertilize for fast growth. Expect trouble below 28°F.

P. roebelenii. PIGMY DATE PALM. Outdoors in Zones 23, 24; house plant anywhere. Native to Laos. Fine-leafed, small-scale palm. One stem grows slowly to 6 ft. or so. Curved leaves form dense crown. Good pot plant. Requires moisture. Does best in shade or part shade, but not successful in dark indoor corners.

P. rupicola. CLIFF DATE PALM. Zones 17, 19–24. From India. Stately as Canary Island date palm, but much smaller, reaching only 25 ft. in height. Slender stem; lower leaves droop gracefully. Hardy to 26°F.

P. sylvestris. SILVER DATE PALM. Zones 14–17, 19–24. Native to India. Hardy and beautiful date palm with single trunk to 30 ft., tapering from wide base to narrow top. Trunk covered with old leaf bases. Crown of gray green leaves is thick and round. Hardy to 22°F.

PHORMIUM. *Agavaceae.* NEW ZEALAND FLAX. Evergreen perennials. Zones 7–24; may freeze to ground but regrow in Zones 5, 6. Big, dramatic plants composed of many swordlike, stiffly vertical leaves in fan pattern. Flowers dull red or yellow, 1–2 in. long, in clusters on stems that reach high above leaves. Use as point-of-interest display plant or near swimming pools. Grow in full sun to light shade. Sturdy, fast growing in almost any soil or exposure—heat or cold, salt air or ocean spray. Will take much or little water, even poor drainage to a point (in very poorly drained soil, crown rot can be problem). Subject to summer rot in low desert, but replacement plants set out in fall will grow quickly. Use as windbreak along coast; grow in containers anywhere. Increase by dividing large clumps.

Phormium tenax
'Variegatum'

P. colensoi ***(P. cookianum).*** Leaves 2½ in. wide, to 5 ft. long; less rigid than those of *P. tenax*. Flowers yellow or amber yellow, on 7-ft. spikes. Not common, but useful for its moderate size. With *P. tenax*, a parent of numerous hybrids.

(Continued on next page)

P

P. tenax. NEW ZEALAND FLAX. Large, bold plant tending to spread. Leaves to 9 ft. long, up to 5 in. wide. Nursery plants in containers are deceptively small; allow enough garden room to accommodate mature plant. Reddish brown flower stalks bear many dark red to yellowish flowers. Variants in leaf color are available: 'Atropurpureum' is purple red; 'Bronze' brownish red; 'Rubrum' has deepest coloring, dark purplish red; 'Variegatum' has green leaves striped with creamy white. 'Tiny Tim' grows 3–4 ft. tall, has bronzy leaves striped yellow. A host of varieties from New Zealand have brilliant stripes in a range of colors, including bronze, green, pink, red, orange, and purple. Some have several colors in a single leaf.

PHOTINIA. *Rosaceae.* Evergreen or deciduous shrubs or small trees. Attractive foliage and fruit color. Related to hawthorn, pyracantha. Sun, good garden soil. In Northwest, withhold water in late summer to ripen growth, lessen frost damage. Prune to shape; never allow new growth to get away and make long, bare switches. Use as screens, background.

Photinia fraseri

P. arbutifolia. See *Heteromeles arbutifolia.*

P. fraseri. Evergreen shrub. Zones 4–24. Survives in protected sites Zones 2, 3. Moderate growth to 10 ft. tall, spreading wider. Leaves glossy dark green above, lighter beneath, 2–5 in. long. New growth bright bronzy red, showy. White flower clusters in early spring resemble those of *P. glabra* but are not followed by berries. Attractive to birds. Good espalier or small single-stemmed tree. Cut branches excellent in arrangements. Heat resistant; resists mildew where other kinds susceptible. Sometimes chlorotic in Zones 12, 13. Control aphids.

If *P. fraseri* is too large for your garden, try 'Indian Princess'—compact, dense, and half as tall (6-year-old plants are 5 ft. high). New foliage is more orange than red.

P. glabra. JAPANESE PHOTINIA. Evergreen shrub. Zones 4–24. Broad, dense growth to 6–10 ft. or more. Leaves oval, broadest toward tip, to 3 in. long. New growth coppery; scattered leaves of bright red give touch of color through fall and winter. Summer pruning will restrict size of plant to neat 5 ft. and give continuing show of new foliage. White flowers with hawthorn fragrance in 4-in.-wide clusters. Berries red, turning black. Prolonged freezes may set it back, but it usually recovers.

P. serrulata. CHINESE PHOTINIA. Evergreen shrub or small tree. Zones 4–16, 18–22. Broad, dense growth to 35 ft., but easily held to 10 by 10 ft. Leaves stiff, crisp, deep green, to 8 in. long, prickly along edges. New growth bright copper; scattered crimson leaves in fall, winter. Flowers white, in flat clusters 6 in. across, March–May. Bright red berries often last until December. May freeze badly in continued 0°–10°F. cold but usually recovers. Mildew can be expected almost anywhere. Fairly drought resistant when established. *P. s.* 'Aculeata' (often sold as *P. s.* 'Nova' or *P. s.* 'Nova Lineata') is more compact, has midrib and main leaf veins of ivory yellow.

P. villosa. Deciduous shrub or small tree. Zones 1–6. To 15 ft. tall, with spread of 10 ft. Leaves 1½–3 in. long, dark green. New foliage pale gold with rosy tints when expanding, bright red in fall. White flowers in 1–2-in.-wide clusters in midspring. Bright red fruit nearly ½ in. long decorates plant in fall, early winter.

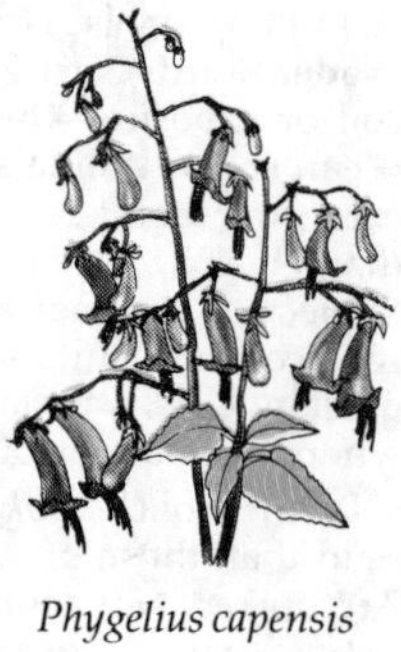

Phygelius capensis

PHYGELIUS capensis. *Scrophulariaceae.* CAPE FUCHSIA. Perennial in Northwest, tending to be shrubby in milder climates. Zones 4–9, 14–24. Perhaps it's called fuchsia because flowers are pendant, but it is really related to penstemons and snapdragons. Stems grow 3–4 ft. high; leaves are 1–5 in. long, scalloped on margins, large at plant base, smaller toward top. Red, tubular, slightly curved flowers, 2 in. long, borne in loosely branched clusters July–September. Looks a bit weedy; use in outskirts of garden. Sun, good garden soil, average water. Spreads by underground roots. Prune for neat appearance. In colder areas, mulch to protect roots. Easy to grow from seed.

PHYLA nodiflora ***(Lippia repens).*** *Verbenaceae.* LIPPIA. Perennial. Zones 8–24. Creeps and spreads to form flat, ground-hugging mat sturdy enough to serve as lawn. Gray green leaves to ¾ in. long. Small lilac to rose flowers in tight, round heads ½ in. across, spring to fall. Flowers attract bees; if you object to this, mow off tops. Full sun, average soil. Dormant, unattractive in winter. Feed regularly, especially in early spring to bring it out of dormancy fast. Drought tolerant once established, but looks best with regular water. Particularly useful in desert areas, but subject to nematodes.

Phyla nodiflora

PHYLLITIS scolopendrium ***(Asplenium scolopendrium).*** *Polypodiaceae.* HART'S TONGUE FERN. Zones 2–24, but difficult in desert and areas with poor water quality. Native to Europe, eastern United States. Needs humus, some limestone chips if soil is poor in calcium. Odd fern with undivided, strap-shaped leaves 9–18 in. long. Fanciers collect various dwarf, crested, or forked varieties. In Pacific Northwest, it is quite hardy and easy to grow in full sun to full shade; hard to grow where summers are long and dry. Striking in woodland gardens, rock gardens, with rhododendrons and azaleas. Durable container plant; grows from tight crown, so may occupy same pot for many years.

Phyllitis scolopendrium

PHYLLOSTACHYS. See Bamboo.

PHYSALIS. *Solanaceae.* Perennials or annuals. Fruit is surrounded by loose, papery husk (enlarged calyx of flower). First species below is ornamental; other 2 are edible.

P. alkekengi ***(P. franchetii).*** CHINESE LANTERN PLANT. Perennial often grown as annual. All Zones. Plant angularly branched, 1–2 ft. high. Long, creeping, whitish, underground stems; may become invasive without control. Long-stalked, light green leaves are 2–3 in. long. Flowers white, rather inconspicuous, appearing in leaf joints. Ornamental part of plant is calyx, which forms around ripened berry as loose, papery, bright orange red, 2-in.-long, inflated envelope shaped like lantern. Dry, leafless stalks hung with these gay lanterns make choice winter arrangements. Sow seed in spring in light soil, in sun or light shade. Grows with minimal water, but plants will be smaller than those receiving regular watering. Increase by root division in fall or winter. 'Pygmy', 8-in. dwarf variety, makes a good pot plant.

Physalis alkekengi

P. ixocarpa. TOMATILLO. Annual of bushy, sprawling growth to 4 ft. Fruit about 2 in. wide, swelling to fill—or sometimes split—the baggy calyx. Fruit yellow to purple and very sweet when ripe, but usually picked green and tart and used (cooked) in Mexican cuisine.

P. peruviana. GROUND CHERRY, POHA. Tender perennial grown as annual. Bushy, 1½ ft. high. Leaves 2–4 in. long. Flowers bell

Phlox paniculata

P. carolina ***(P. maculata, P. suffruticosa).*** THICK-LEAF PHLOX. Perennial. Zones 1–14, 18–21. To 3–4 ft. tall. Early flowers about ¾ in. wide, in 15-in.-long clusters. Color varies from white, centered with pale pink eye, to magenta. Shiny foliage, free from mildew and red spider mites (which often attack summer phlox). 'Miss Lingard' is excellent white-flowered variety to 3 ft. tall.

P. divaricata. SWEET WILLIAM PHLOX. Perennial. Zones 1–17. To 1 ft., with slender, leafy stems and creeping underground shoots. Leaves oval, 1–2 in. long, ¾ in. wide. Spring flowers in open clusters; bluish or pinkish blue varying to white, ¾–1½ in. across, somewhat fragrant. Use in rock gardens, as bulb cover (see *Tulipa*). Light shade, good, deep soil, average water. *P. d. laphamii* has best blue color.

P. drummondii. ANNUAL PHLOX. Summer annual. Grows 6–18 in. tall, with erect, leafy stems more or less covered with rather sticky hairs. Flowers numerous, showy, in close clusters at tops of stems. Bright and pastel colors (no blue or orange), some with contrasting eye. Tall strains in mixed colors are Finest and Fordhook Finest. Dwarf strains (6–8 in. tall) include Beauty and Globe, both with rounded flowers, and starry-petaled Petticoat and Twinkle. Bloom lasts from early summer until frost if faded flowers are removed. Plant in spring in colder climates, in fall in mild areas of southern California and desert. Give full sun and light, rich loam.

P. mesoleuca. CHIHUAHUAN PHLOX. Perennial. Zones 4–24. Identification of these rock garden phloxes from Mexico is uncertain; they may be *P. nana* or another species. Grow 6 in. tall, to 1½ ft. wide; growth tends to be straggly if plants are not tip-pinched. Flower color varies from cream to yellow, orange, and red. Hardy to 0°F. Need excellent drainage.

P. nivalis. TRAILING PHLOX. Perennial. Zones 4–7. Trailing plants form loose, 4–6-in.-tall mats of narrow evergreen leaves. Big pink or white flowers in fairly large clusters in late spring or early summer. Excellent in rock gardens. 'Camla' is fine salmon pink variety.

P. paniculata. SUMMER PHLOX. Perennial. Zones 1–14, 18–21. Long lived. Thrives in full sun, but in hottest areas colors may bleach. Leaves 2–5 in. long, narrow and tapering to slender point. Fragrant, 1-in.-wide summer flowers in large, dome-shaped clusters on 3–5-ft. stems. Colors include white, shades of lavender, pink, rose, or red; blooms of some types have a contrasting eye. Many named varieties. Mulch around plants to keep roots cool. Plants subject to mildew at end of blooming season. Divide plants every few years, replanting young shoots from outside of clump. Plants do not come true from seed; most tend toward uncertain purplish pink, though some may be attractive. Plant seed in fall or freeze in ice cubes for month before sowing.

P. subulata. MOSS PINK. Perennial. Zones 1–17. Stiffish, ½-in., needlelike, evergreen leaves on creeping stems; forms mats to 6 in. tall. The ¾-in. flowers range in color from white through pink to rose and lavender blue. Late spring or early summer bloom, according to climate. Makes sheets of brilliant color in rock gardens. Ground cover. Grow in loose, not-too-rich soil. After flowering, cut back halfway. Moderately drought tolerant.

P. suffruticosa. See *P. carolina.*

PHOENIX. *Palmae.* DATE PALM. Mostly large feather palms, but one a dwarf. Trunks patterned with bases of old leaf stalks. Small yellowish flowers in large, hanging sprays followed by clusters of often edible fruit (*P. dactylifera* bears dates of commerce). These palms hybridize freely, so buy from reliable nurseryman who knows his seed or plant source.

Phoenix canariensis

P. canariensis. CANARY ISLAND DATE PALM. Zones 9, 12–24. Big, heavy-trunked plant to 60 ft. tall, with 50-ft. spread composed of a great many gracefully arching fronds. Grows slowly until it forms trunk, then speeds up a little. Young plants do well in pots for many years, looking something like pineapples. Grow on slopes, in parks, big spaces, along wide streets; not for small city lots. Hardy to 20°F. Slow to develop new head of foliage after hard-frost damage.

Phoenix dactylifera

P. dactylifera. DATE PALM. Zones 9, warmer parts of 11, 12–24. The date palm of Indio, California, and of Palm Springs golf courses; classic palm of movie desert oases. Native to Middle East. Very tall (up to 80 ft.), with slender trunk and gray green, waxy leaves; leaflets stiff and sharp pointed. Suckers from base; natural habit is clump of several trunks. Principal commercial variety in California is 'Deglet Noor'. Too stiff and large for most home gardens, but adapts to and does well in seaside, desert gardens. Leaves killed at 20°F. but plants have survived 4°–10°F.

Phoenix roebelenii

P. loureiri ***(P. humilis).*** Zones 9, 12–24. Resembles smaller, more slender and refined Canary Island date palm. Slow grower to 10–18 ft. tall. Leaves dark green, flexible, 10 ft. long. Good in containers or in the garden. Hardy to 20°F.

P. reclinata. SENEGAL DATE PALM. Zones 23, 24. Native to tropical Africa. Makes picturesque clumps from offshoots, with several curving trunks 20–30 ft. high. Offshoots can be removed to make single-trunked trees. Fertilize for fast growth. Expect trouble below 28°F.

P. roebelenii. PIGMY DATE PALM. Outdoors in Zones 23, 24; house plant anywhere. Native to Laos. Fine-leafed, small-scale palm. One stem grows slowly to 6 ft. or so. Curved leaves form dense crown. Good pot plant. Requires moisture. Does best in shade or part shade, but not successful in dark indoor corners.

P. rupicola. CLIFF DATE PALM. Zones 17, 19–24. From India. Stately as Canary Island date palm, but much smaller, reaching only 25 ft. in height. Slender stem; lower leaves droop gracefully. Hardy to 26°F.

P. sylvestris. SILVER DATE PALM. Zones 14–17, 19–24. Native to India. Hardy and beautiful date palm with single trunk to 30 ft., tapering from wide base to narrow top. Trunk covered with old leaf bases. Crown of gray green leaves is thick and round. Hardy to 22°F.

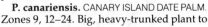

Phormium tenax 'Variegatum'

PHORMIUM. *Agavaceae.* NEW ZEALAND FLAX. Evergreen perennials. Zones 7–24; may freeze to ground but regrow in Zones 5, 6. Big, dramatic plants composed of many swordlike, stiffly vertical leaves in fan pattern. Flowers dull red or yellow, 1–2 in. long, in clusters on stems that reach high above leaves. Use as point-of-interest display plant or near swimming pools. Grow in full sun to light shade. Sturdy, fast growing in almost any soil or exposure—heat or cold, salt air or ocean spray. Will take much or little water, even poor drainage to a point (in very poorly drained soil, crown rot can be problem). Subject to summer rot in low desert, but replacement plants set out in fall will grow quickly. Use as windbreak along coast; grow in containers anywhere. Increase by dividing large clumps.

P. colensoi ***(P. cookianum).*** Leaves 2½ in. wide, to 5 ft. long; less rigid than those of *P. tenax*. Flowers yellow or amber yellow, on 7-ft. spikes. Not common, but useful for its moderate size. With *P. tenax*, a parent of numerous hybrids.

(Continued on next page)

P

P. tenax. NEW ZEALAND FLAX. Large, bold plant tending to spread. Leaves to 9 ft. long, up to 5 in. wide. Nursery plants in containers are deceptively small; allow enough garden room to accommodate mature plant. Reddish brown flower stalks bear many dark red to yellowish flowers. Variants in leaf color are available: 'Atropurpureum' is purple red; 'Bronze' brownish red; 'Rubrum' has deepest coloring, dark purplish red; 'Variegatum' has green leaves striped with creamy white. 'Tiny Tim' grows 3–4 ft. tall, has bronzy leaves striped yellow. A host of varieties from New Zealand have brilliant stripes in a range of colors, including bronze, green, pink, red, orange, and purple. Some have several colors in a single leaf.

PHOTINIA. *Rosaceae.* Evergreen or deciduous shrubs or small trees. Attractive foliage and fruit color. Related to hawthorn, pyracantha. Sun, good garden soil. In Northwest, withhold water in late summer to ripen growth, lessen frost damage. Prune to shape; never allow new growth to get away and make long, bare switches. Use as screens, background.

Photinia fraseri

P. arbutifolia. See *Heteromeles arbutifolia*.

P. fraseri. Evergreen shrub. Zones 4–24. Survives in protected sites Zones 2, 3. Moderate growth to 10 ft. tall, spreading wider. Leaves glossy dark green above, lighter beneath, 2–5 in. long. New growth bright bronzy red, showy. White flower clusters in early spring resemble those of *P. glabra* but are not followed by berries. Attractive to birds. Good espalier or small single-stemmed tree. Cut branches excellent in arrangements. Heat resistant; resists mildew where other kinds susceptible. Sometimes chlorotic in Zones 12, 13. Control aphids.

If *P. fraseri* is too large for your garden, try 'Indian Princess'—compact, dense, and half as tall (6-year-old plants are 5 ft. high). New foliage is more orange than red.

P. glabra. JAPANESE PHOTINIA. Evergreen shrub. Zones 4–24. Broad, dense growth to 6–10 ft. or more. Leaves oval, broadest toward tip, to 3 in. long. New growth coppery; scattered leaves of bright red give touch of color through fall and winter. Summer pruning will restrict size of plant to neat 5 ft. and give continuing show of new foliage. White flowers with hawthorn fragrance in 4-in.-wide clusters. Berries red, turning black. Prolonged freezes may set it back, but it usually recovers.

P. serrulata. CHINESE PHOTINIA. Evergreen shrub or small tree. Zones 4–16, 18–22. Broad, dense growth to 35 ft., but easily held to 10 by 10 ft. Leaves stiff, crisp, deep green, to 8 in. long, prickly along edges. New growth bright copper; scattered crimson leaves in fall, winter. Flowers white, in flat clusters 6 in. across, March–May. Bright red berries often last until December. May freeze badly in continued 0°–10°F. cold but usually recovers. Mildew can be expected almost anywhere. Fairly drought resistant when established. *P. s.* 'Aculeata' (often sold as *P. s.* 'Nova' or *P. s.* 'Nova Lineata') is more compact, has midrib and main leaf veins of ivory yellow.

P. villosa. Deciduous shrub or small tree. Zones 1–6. To 15 ft. tall, with spread of 10 ft. Leaves 1½–3 in. long, dark green. New foliage pale gold with rosy tints when expanding, bright red in fall. White flowers in 1–2-in.-wide clusters in midspring. Bright red fruit nearly ½ in. long decorates plant in fall, early winter.

PHYGELIUS capensis. *Scrophulariaceae.* CAPE FUCHSIA. Perennial in Northwest, tending to be shrubby in milder climates. Zones 4–9, 14–24. Perhaps it's called fuchsia because flowers are pendant, but it is really related to penstemons and snapdragons. Stems grow 3–4 ft. high; leaves are 1–5 in. long, scalloped on margins, large at plant base, smaller toward top. Red, tubular, slightly curved flowers, 2 in. long, borne in loosely branched clusters July–September. Looks a bit weedy; use in outskirts of garden. Sun, good garden soil, average water. Spreads by underground roots. Prune for neat appearance. In colder areas, mulch to protect roots. Easy to grow from seed.

Phygelius capensis

PHYLA nodiflora *(Lippia repens).* *Verbenaceae.* LIPPIA. Perennial. Zones 8–24. Creeps and spreads to form flat, ground-hugging mat sturdy enough to serve as lawn. Gray green leaves to ¾ in. long. Small lilac to rose flowers in tight, round heads ½ in. across, spring to fall. Flowers attract bees; if you object to this, mow off tops. Full sun, average soil. Dormant, unattractive in winter. Feed regularly, especially in early spring to bring it out of dormancy fast. Drought tolerant once established, but looks best with regular water. Particularly useful in desert areas, but subject to nematodes.

Phyla nodiflora

PHYLLITIS scolopendrium *(Asplenium scolopendrium).* *Polypodiaceae.* HART'S TONGUE FERN. Zones 2–24, but difficult in desert and areas with poor water quality. Native to Europe, eastern United States. Needs humus, some limestone chips if soil is poor in calcium. Odd fern with undivided, strap-shaped leaves 9–18 in. long. Fanciers collect various dwarf, crested, or forked varieties. In Pacific Northwest, it is quite hardy and easy to grow in full sun to full shade; hard to grow where summers are long and dry. Striking in woodland gardens, rock gardens, with rhododendrons and azaleas. Durable container plant; grows from tight crown, so may occupy same pot for many years.

Phyllitis scolopendrium

PHYLLOSTACHYS. See Bamboo.

PHYSALIS. *Solanaceae.* Perennials or annuals. Fruit is surrounded by loose, papery husk (enlarged calyx of flower). First species below is ornamental; other 2 are edible.

P. alkekengi *(P. franchetii).* CHINESE LANTERN PLANT. Perennial often grown as annual. All Zones. Plant angularly branched, 1–2 ft. high. Long, creeping, whitish, underground stems; may become invasive without control. Long-stalked, light green leaves are 2–3 in. long. Flowers white, rather inconspicuous, appearing in leaf joints. Ornamental part of plant is calyx, which forms around ripened berry as loose, papery, bright orange red, 2-in.-long, inflated envelope shaped like lantern. Dry, leafless stalks hung with these gay lanterns make choice winter arrangements. Sow seed in spring in light soil, in sun or light shade. Grows with minimal water, but plants will be smaller than those receiving regular watering. Increase by root division in fall or winter. 'Pygmy', 8-in. dwarf variety, makes a good pot plant.

Physalis alkekengi

P. ixocarpa. TOMATILLO. Annual of bushy, sprawling growth to 4 ft. Fruit about 2 in. wide, swelling to fill—or sometimes split—the baggy calyx. Fruit yellow to purple and very sweet when ripe, but usually picked green and tart and used (cooked) in Mexican cuisine.

P. peruviana. GROUND CHERRY, POHA. Tender perennial grown as annual. Bushy, 1½ ft. high. Leaves 2–4 in. long. Flowers bell shaped, ⅜ in. long, whitish yellow marked with 5 brown spots. Seedy yellow fruit is sweet, rather insipid, can be used for pies or preserves (remove papery husks before using in cooking). Grow in same way as tomatoes. Plants sprawl quite a bit and are slow to start bearing, but eventually productive where summers are long and warm. Several species resemble *P. peruviana,* including *P. pruinosa* and *P. pubescens.*

PHYSOCARPUS. *Rosaceae.* NINEBARK. Deciduous shrubs. Zones 1–3, 10. These plants get their common name from their peeling bark, which often shows several layers. They resemble spiraeas and are closely related to them, bearing round clusters of tiny white flowers in spring or early summer. They are not overly fussy about exposure and will tolerate sun or shade. Average soil, average water.

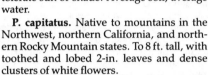

Physocarpus capitatus

P. capitatus. Native to mountains in the Northwest, northern California, and northern Rocky Mountain states. To 8 ft. tall, with toothed and lobed 2-in. leaves and dense clusters of white flowers.

P. monogynus. MOUNTAIN NINEBARK. Rocky Mountain native; 3–4 ft. tall, with 1½-in. leaves and few-flowered clusters of pinkish to white flowers. Brilliant fall colors, mostly orange and red.

P. opulifolius intermedius. DWARF NINEBARK. Grows 4–5 ft. tall. Many white to pinkish flowers in each cluster. Fall color reddish brown. *P. o.* 'Luteus' has leaves that are yellow in sunlight, yellow green in shade. 'Dart's Gold' is similar.

PHYSOSTEGIA virginiana. *Labiatae.* FALSE DRAGONHEAD. Perennial. All Zones. (Sometimes called OBEDIENCE PLANT because flowers, if twisted on stem, remain in position.) Slender, upright, leafy stems to 4 ft. Oblong, 3–5-in.-long, toothed leaves, pointed at tip. Funnel-shaped, 1-in.-long flowers in dense 10-in. spikes, in glistening white, rose pink, or lavender rose. Summer bloom. Spiky form useful in borders, cut arrangements. Combine with taller erigerons, *Scabiosa caucasica,* Michaelmas daisies. Sun or part shade. Any good garden soil, regular watering. Stake taller stems to keep upright. Cut to ground after bloom. Vigorous; divide every 2 years to keep in bounds. 'Vivid', 2 ft. tall, has rose pink flowers. 'Summer Snow', an especially good white form, is least invasive.

Physostegia virginiana

PICEA. *Pinaceae.* SPRUCE. Evergreen trees and shrubs. Zones 1–6, 14–17, except as noted. The large cone-bearing trees take on pyramidal or cone shape. Many kinds have dwarf varieties that, where adapted, are useful in foundation plantings, rock gardens, and containers. Spruces have no special soil requirements. Dwarf forms need reasonably cool location and ample water. Birds are attracted to spruces, and most trees are attacked by small, dull green aphids in late winter. Unless you check plants at that time to see if aphids are on foliage, their attack may not be noticed until weather warms and needles start dropping. Start spraying in February and repeat monthly until May. Pine needle scale (flat and white) may cause sooty mold. Spray when scale insects are in crawler stage in May. In Rocky Mountain states, spruces may be bothered by spider mites (see page 99 for control) and tussock moths.

Picea pungens 'Glauca'

Prune only to shape. If a branch grows too long, cut back to a well-placed side branch. To slow growth and make it more dense, remove part of each year's growth to force side growth. When planting larger spruces, don't place them too close to buildings, fences, or walks; they need space. Except in Zones 1–3, they can be grown in containers for years as living Christmas trees.

P. abies *(P. excelsa).* NORWAY SPRUCE. Native to northern Europe. Not as good as North American native spruces in Rocky Mountain states. Fast growth to 100–150 ft. Stiff, deep green, attractive pyramid in youth; in age, branchlets droop strongly, and oldest branchlets—nearest trunk—die back. Extremely hardy and wind resistant, Norway spruce is valued for windbreaks in cold areas. It has produced a number of varieties; some of the best are:

Picea abies 'Nidiformis'

'Clanbrasiliana'. Very dwarf. Forms tight, compressed ball, 2 ft. across in 20 years.

'Maxwellii'. Picturesque, rounded dwarf with heavy, short twigs, 2 ft. high and 3 ft. wide in 20 years.

'Mucronata'. Dense dwarf, rounded in youth, growing into broad pyramid with age. Reaches 3 ft. in 20 years and has appearance of larger spruces in miniature.

'Nidiformis'. BIRD'S NEST or NEST SPRUCE. Very compact; grows as flattened globe, eventually to 3 ft. high and 4–6 ft. across. Dark green foliage.

'Pendula'. If left to grow naturally, it spreads over ground to cover 10 ft., with height of about 1½ ft. It will cascade downward from rocks or walls. When staked, it becomes dense, irregular column; branches trail downward to 8 ft. or more, with outward-sweeping, recurved tips.

'Procumbens'. Close-branched, irregular growth with upturned branch ends. Slow to 2 ft. high, 5 ft. across.

'Pygmaea'. Broad, rounded cone, very dense, 2 ft. high and 3 ft. across in 20 years.

'Remontii'. Irregular, wide, cone-shaped dwarf, 3 ft. high, 4 ft. wide at base in 20 years, eventually to 20 ft.

'Repens'. Low, irregular, rounded; to 1½ ft. high and 3 ft. wide in 20 years. Fanlike branches held in layers.

'Sherwood Gem'. Dense, heavily foliaged, regular, flattened globe to 2 ft. high, 4 ft. wide.

'Sherwoodii'. Rugged and picturesque, compact but irregular in growth habit. Parent tree, 60 years old, is 5 ft. tall and 10 ft. across.

P. brewerana. BREWER'S WEEPING SPRUCE. Zones 4–7, 14–17. To 100–120 ft. in its native Siskiyou Mountains in California and Oregon. Branchlets are pendulous, hanging vertically to 7–8 ft. or more. Rare in the wilds and in gardens. More tender than most spruces; requires much moisture and cool temperatures.

P. engelmannii. ENGELMANN SPRUCE. Densely pyramidal tree to 150 ft., native from southwest Canada to Oregon and northern California, east to the Rockies. Resembles blue green forms of Colorado spruce, but needles are softer and tree is not so spreading at base. Even 25-ft. specimens will be densely branched to ground. Popular lawn tree in Rocky Mountain area.

P. glauca. WHITE SPRUCE. Native to Canada and northern U.S. Conical tree to 60–70 ft., dense when young, with pendulous twigs and silver green foliage. Best where winters are very cold.

P. g. 'Conica' (often sold as *P. albertiana*). DWARF ALBERTA or DWARF WHITE SPRUCE. Compact pyramidal tree, growing slowly to 7 ft. in 35 years. Short, fine needles are soft to the touch, bright grass green when new, gray green when mature. Handsome tub plant—a miniature Christmas tree for many years. Also makes a fine small formal pyramid for garden. Thoroughly hardy to cold, but needs shelter from hot or cold drying winds and from strong reflected sunlight.

P. g. densata. BLACK HILLS SPRUCE. Slow-growing, dense pyramid; can reach 20 ft. tall in 35 years. Use it in containers, or plant it out in groves for screening or for alpine meadow effects.

P. pungens. COLORADO SPRUCE. Zones 1–10, 14–17. To 80–100 ft. Very stiff, regular, horizontal branches forming broad pyramid.

(Continued on next page)

CLIMATE ZONES, PAGES 33–55

P

Foliage varies in seedlings from dark green through all shades of blue green to steely blue. Often grown outside Zones where it thrives; it survives, but seldom looks its best. Spruce aphid is a serious pest in the Puget Sound area. For control, spray with orthene on March 1. Varieties include:

'Fat Albert'. Compact, erect, broad, formal-looking cone with good blue color. Slow growth (to 10 ft. in 10 years) makes it a good choice for a living Christmas tree.

'Glauca'. COLORADO BLUE SPRUCE. Positive gray blue color.

'Hoopsii'. Considered by many to be the bluest of spruces. Fast growing; needs early training to encourage erect, cone-shaped habit.

'Koster'. KOSTER BLUE SPRUCE. Bluer than 'Glauca', but growth habit sometimes irregular.

'Moerheimii'. Same blue as 'Koster', but tree has more compact and symmetrical shape.

'Pendens'. KOSTER WEEPING BLUE SPRUCE. Gray blue with weeping branchlets.

'Thomsen'. Palest blue white of all spruces. Vigorous, symmetrical habit.

P. sitchensis. SITKA SPRUCE. Zones 4–6, 14–17. Native Alaska to California. Tall, pyramidal tree to 100–150 ft., with wide-spreading, horizontal branches. Short, thin needles are prickly to the touch, bright green and silvery white in color. Requires moist atmosphere and moisture in soil to look its best. Very subject to Cooley spruce gall, a conelike growth on new shoots caused by adelgids, a type of aphid. Treat as for scale.

PICKEREL WEED. See *Pontederia cordata.*

PIERIS. *Ericaceae.* Evergreen shrubs with leathery leaves and clusters of small, white, urn-shaped flowers. Related to rhododendron and azalea, they have the same cultural needs and make good companion plants. Foliage and form are excellent all year. Flower buds in early winter look like strings of tiny greenish pink beads; these begin to open February–April. During (or just after) bloom, tinted new growth begins to appear.

Pieris japonica

Fairly easy to grow in coastal valleys of Northwest, these shrubs become increasingly fussy and often less satisfactory south and inland. Require some shade, particularly in afternoon. Where water is high in salts, they need careful leaching. Protect from wind for maximum beauty. Prune by removing spent flowers. Splendid in containers, in Oriental and woodland gardens, in entryways where year-round quality is essential.

P. floribunda *(Andromeda floribunda).* MOUNTAIN PIERIS. Zones 2–9, 14–17, but needs protection in Zones 2, 3. Compact, rounded shrub 3–6 ft. tall, with elliptical, 1½–3-in. leaves, pale green when new, dull green when mature. Blossoms in upright clusters. Very hardy to cold, and takes hotter, drier air than the others. Takes sun in Zones 4–6.

P. 'Forest Flame' (*P.* 'Flame of the Forest'). Zones 1–9, 14–17; grows satisfactorily in Zones 2, 3, only if sheltered from drying winds and hot sun. Hybrid between *P. japonica* and a form of *P. forrestii* with especially bright red spring foliage; it combines new foliage brilliance of latter with some of hardiness of former. Blooms profusely, with broader, heavier flower clusters than those of *P. japonica.* Grows 6–7 ft. tall and ultimately as wide.

P. forrestii *(P. formosa forrestii).* CHINESE PIERIS. Zones 5–9, 14–17. Dense, broad grower to 10 ft. tall with greater spread. Leaves shiny, leathery, dark green, to 6 in. long. New growth ranges from brilliant scarlet (in best forms) to pale salmon pink. Large, heavy clusters of tiny white flowers on branch tips in April, May. Buy when plants are making new growth; cutting-grown plants from best selections show their quality then. These may be offered as variety 'Bright Red'. Makes good espalier in shaded locations.

P. japonica *(Andromeda japonica).* LILY-OF-THE-VALLEY SHRUB. Zones 1–9, 14–17; in Zones 1–3, it requires protection from sun and wind, generous watering. Upright, dense, tiered growth to 9–10 ft. Mature leaves glossy dark green, 3 in. long; new growth bronzy pink to red. Drooping clusters of flower buds form in autumn and are attractive even before opening to white, pink, or nearly red flowers in February–May. Buds themselves are often dark red. Responds well to frequent feeding—a must in heavy rainfall areas where leaching of nutrients would cause yellowing of foliage. Takes full sun in cool, humid climates, part shade elsewhere. Many horticultural varieties, some rare. For unusual habit or foliage: 'Bert Chandler', with new foliage that turns from salmon pink through cream to white, then pale green; 'Compacta', smaller grower than parent; 'Crispa', smaller grower with wavy-edged leaves of great distinction; 'Mountain Fire', with fiery red new growth; 'Pygmaea', tiny dwarf less than 1 ft. tall, with very few flowers and narrow leaves 1 in. long or less; and 'Variegata', medium-sized, slow-growing, compact plant with leaves prettily marked with creamy white, tinged pink in spring. 'Karenoma' and 'Spring Snow', compact 3–6-ft. plants, have the foliage quality of *P. japonica* combined with the upright flower clusters of *P. floribunda.*

Varieties grown principally for flower characteristics include: 'Christmas Cheer', bicolor white and deep rose red, with rose red flower stalks, early bloom; 'Coleman', pink flowers opening from red flower buds; 'Daisen', similar to 'Christmas Cheer', but with broader leaves; 'Dorothy Wyckoff', white flowers from deep red flower buds; 'Flamingo', heavy bloomer with rose pink flowers; 'Pink', shell pink fading to white; 'Valley Rose', low growing, compact, light pink; and 'White Cascade', an extremely heavy flower producer.

P. taiwanensis. Not completely tested; probably Zones 5–7, 14–17. Similar to *P. japonica,* but with somewhat larger, more erect flower clusters. Hybrid with *P. japonica,* 'Snowdrift', has unusually heavy pure white bloom.

PIGEON BERRY. See *Duranta repens.*

PIGGY-BACK PLANT. See *Tolmiea menziesii.*

PILEA. *Urticaceae.* House or greenhouse plants. Juicy-stemmed foliage plants with inconspicuous flowers. Plant in porous soil mix (1 part sand, 1 part leaf mold, 1 part peat moss). Water thoroughly; don't water again until soil surface is dry. Feed monthly with house plant food. Grow at 65°–70°F. temperature. Light shade or bright light best; plant gets leggy in heavy shade.

Pilea microphylla

P. cadierei. ALUMINUM PLANT. Erect, fast growing to 1–1½ ft. tall. Succulent stems; fleshy, toothed, 3–4-in.-long leaves of vivid green to bluish green with conspicuous silvery blotches. Tiny flowers.

P. depressa. Low, spreading or trailing, rooting where stems touch ground. Roundish leaves, broader toward tips. Used in terrariums, as ground cover in larger mixed plantings.

P. involucrata. PANAMIGA, PANAMIGO. Freely branching plant 6–8 in. tall. Roundish oval leaves to 2 in. long, brownish green above, purplish beneath, heavily veined in seersucker effect.

P. microphylla. ARTILLERY PLANT. Grows 6–18 in. tall, with many spreading branches and fine twigs. Leaves very tiny, thickly set, bright green. Total effect somewhat fernlike. Called artillery plant because flowers forcibly discharge pollen.

P. nummulariifolia. CREEPING CHARLIE (one of several plants so named). Resembles *P. depressa,* but leaves more rounded, more evenly scalloped along edges. Good small hanging basket plant or terrarium ground cover.

PIMELEA prostrata (usually sold as *P. coarctata*). *Thymeleaceae.* Zones 4–7, 14–17. Evergreen shrublet. Forms gray, fine-leafed, compact mat 3–6 in. high, 1 ft. wide or wider. Clusters of tiny white, 4-petaled flowers with faint sweet scent appear over long spring and summer bloom period; they look like tiny daphne flowers (plants are related). White berries follow. Full sun, except in very hot locations where light shade helps. Needs good drainage, nonalkaline soil, average water, light feeding. Use in rock gardens or as small-scale ground cover.

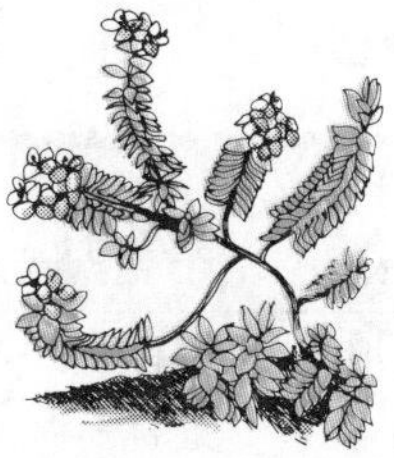
Pimelea prostrata

PIMPERNEL. See *Anagallis.*

PIMPINELLA anisum. *Umbelliferae.* ANISE. Annual herb. All Zones. Bright green, toothed, basal leaves. Tiny white flowers in umbrellalike clusters on 2-ft. stems in June. Start from seed in place when ground warms up in spring. Does not transplant easily. Grow in light soil, full sun; give regular water. Use fresh leaves in salads; use seeds for flavoring cookies, confections.

Pimpinella anisum

Pinaceae. Members of the pine family are evergreen trees with narrow, usually needlelike leaves and seeds borne on the scales of woody cones. Pines, firs, spruces, true cedars, larches, Douglas firs, and hemlocks are examples.

PINCUSHION FLOWER. See *Scabiosa.*

PINCUSHION TREE. See *Hakea laurina.*

PINDO PALM. See *Butia capitata.*

PINE. See *Pinus.*

PINEAPPLE. *Bromeliaceae.* Bold, distinctive house plant that may bear fruit. Plant is rosette of long, narrow leaves with sawtooth edges. To grow it, cut leafy top from market pineapple. Root base of top in water or mixture of damp sand and peat moss. When roots have formed, move to 7–8-in. pot of rich soil. Keep plants in greenhouse or in sunny room where temperatures stay above 68°F. Water overhead when soil gets dry. Feed every 3–4 weeks with liquid fertilizer. Fruit forms, if you're lucky, in 2 years, on top of sturdy stalk at center of clump. Homegrown pineapple fruit is much smaller than commercial fruit. Sometimes available as house plant is a variety with foliage variegated in pink, white, and olive green.

Pineapple

PINEAPPLE FLOWER. See *Eucomis.*

PINEAPPLE GUAVA. See *Feijoa sellowiana.*

PINK. See *Dianthus.*

PINK CEDAR. See *Acrocarpus fraxinifolius.*

PINK POLKA-DOT PLANT. See *Hypoestes phyllostachya.*

PINK POWDER PUFF. See *Calliandra haematocephala.*

PINK TRUMPET VINE. See *Podranea ricasoliana.*

PIÑON. See *Pinus edulis.*

PINUS. *Pinaceae.* PINE. Evergreen trees, rarely shrubs. See chart (pages 466–471) for climate adaptability. Pines are the great individualists of the garden, differing not only among species but also in ways they respond to sun, wind, and soil type. The number of long, slender needles in a bundle and size and shape of cones are the 2 chief characteristics by which pines are classified.

Pinus pinea

Generally speaking, pines grow best in full sun; soil need not be rich, but it should be well drained (many pines naturally grow on rocky slopes or on sandy barrens where fertility is low but drainage excellent). They show effects of bad drainage or overwatering by general poor appearance and unusual number of yellowing needles, especially on older growth. Most pines are fairly to very drought tolerant; general exceptions are the 5-needled species. Polluted air causes abnormal needle drop and poor growth, and can kill trees. Pines require little if any fertilizing; heavy feeding encourages too-rapid, rank growth.

Pines are subject to a number of pests, but healthy, well-grown plants will stay that way with comparatively little attention. Most pines with 5 needles to a bundle are subject to a disease called white pine blister rust. Pines with 2 or 3 needles in a bundle are sometimes attacked by European pine shoot moth in Northwest (symptoms are distorted or dead new shoots). Aphids usually show their presence by sticky secretions, sooty mildew, yellowing needles. Engraver beetles sometimes bore into bark of Monterey, Ponderosa, Bishop, Coulter, Shore, Aleppo, and Torrey pines in California. Healthy trees usually survive with little damage, but trees weakened by drought, smog, or mites and other pests often die.

Birds like to feast on seeds contained in pine cones.

All pines can be shaped, and usually improved, by some pruning. To slow a pine's growth or to fatten up a rangy tree, cut back candles of new growth by half (or even more) when new needles begin to emerge. Leave a few clusters of needles if you want growth to continue along branch. To shape a pine in Oriental manner is trickier, but not really difficult; it's just a matter of cutting out any branches that interfere with the effect, shortening other branches, and creating an upswept look by removing all twigs that grow downward. Cutting vertical main trunk back to well-placed side branch will induce side growth, and wiring or weighting branches will produce cascade effects.

It is unlikely that any one nursery will have *all* pines described in the chart on pages 466–471; in fact, any nursery which has even half of them is remarkably well stocked. Ask a knowledgeable nurseryman for help in locating any of the rare pines you may wish to try, and consult with him concerning local insect, mite, disease, and environmental stress problems. Bonsai specialists and a few mail-order nurseries often stock a wide variety of pines.

PISONIA umbellifera ***(P. brunoniana, Heimerliodendron brunonianum).*** *Nyctaginaceae.* Evergreen shrub in Zones 23, 24; house plant anywhere. Green-leafed wild plant from New Zealand. Can grow from 12–20 ft. tall and spread nearly as wide in frost-free locations. Rare in West. More common is *P. u.* 'Variegata', MAP PLANT, with 4–6-in.-long, oval leaves strongly variegated pale green and creamy white on medium green background. It is not likely to exceed 4–6 ft. in height. Flowers are not showy; fruits (seldom seen in West) are ribbed, 1 in. long, extremely sticky. Indoors or out, plants need regular watering and feeding, warm, even

Pisonia umbellifera

(Continued on page 472)

P

Pine

NAME	GROWTH RATE, SIZE	GROWTH HABIT	NEEDLES AND CONES	CLIMATE ADAPTABILITY	REMARKS
Pinus albicaulis WHITEBARK PINE Native to high mountains of Canada, Washington, Oregon, northern California, and western Nevada, and east into Idaho, western Wyoming, central Montana.	Very slow to 20–40 ft., usually much less.	Prostrate, spreading, or semiupright. Often multitrunked. In youth, slender and symmetrical.	Needles: in 5s, 1½–3 in., dark green, dense. Cones: 3 in., roundish, purple.	Hardy timberline tree. Does well east of Cascades in Northwest. Dislikes warm, low-elevation climates.	Usually dug in mountains and sold by collectors as "alpine" conifer. Good for rock gardens, bonsai.
P. aristata BRISTLECONE PINE Native to high mountains of West; very local and widely scattered.	Very slow to 45 ft., usually not above 20 ft.	Dense, bushy, heavy trunked, with ground-sweeping branches. In youth a symmetrical, narrow-crowned tree with mature look.	Needles: in 5s, 1–1½ in., dark green, whitish beneath flecked with white dots of resin. Cones: 3½ in., dark purplish brown.	Hardy. Does well at sea level in cool-summer areas of coastal California. Somewhat variable in Northwest. Does well along front range of Rocky Mountains. Best as pot plant in southern California.	So slow-growing it is good for years as container plant. Needles persist many years, making crown extremely dense.
P. attenuata KNOBCONE PINE Native to northern and central Cascades in Oregon, Siskiyous, Sierra Nevada foothills in California south to Baja.	Rapid to 20–80 ft.	Open, irregular, and rough. In youth, rounded and regular. Some populations are far more dense, symmetrical. Habit depends on seed source.	Needles: in 3s, 3–5 in., yellow green. Cones: narrowly oval and asymmetrical, light brown, to 6 in.	Quite hardy; adaptable to most areas from Puget Sound south to Baja California.	Very drought tolerant when established. Grows well in poor soils. Holds its cones for many years.
P. balfouriana FOXTAIL PINE Native to California mountains: northern Coast Ranges and southern Sierra.	Very slow to 20–50 ft.	In youth a symmetrical, narrow cone. As it matures, it takes on a more spreading habit, with stout lower branches and irregular upper branches.	Needles: in 5s, to 1½ in., glossy green in dense tufts at branch tips, lasting many years. Cones: narrow, cylindrical, drooping, to 5 in. long.	Hardy; often timberline tree.	Best planted as shrub that in much time can outgrow shrub status. Candidate for container, bonsai, rock garden.
P. banksiana JACK PINE Native to Nova Scotia, New York to Alberta.	Slow to moderate to 70 ft.; often shorter, shrubby.	Crooked, open, picturesque, with slender, spreading branches.	Needles in 2s, 1 in. long, bright green, twisted. Cones 2–2½ in. long, conic-oblong, light brown.	Northernmost pine of North America. Very hardy. Well adapted to areas with long summer days.	Cones persist 12–15 years. Needles yellowish in winter.
P. brutia *(P. halepensis brutia)* CALABRIAN PINE Native to eastern Mediterranean, southern Russia, southern Italy.	Rapid growth, especially in youth, to 30–80 ft.	Denser, more erect than related *P. halepensis*, closer to classic pine tree shape.	Needles: In 2s, 5–6½ in. long, dark green. Cones: like those of *P. halepensis* but not stalked and not bent backward.	Thrives in heat, drought, wind, indifferent soil. Cannot take temperatures much below 0°F.	Faster growing, shapelier tree than *P. halepensis;* form is less interesting in maturity. Good possibilities as commercial Christmas tree.
P. bungeana LACEBARK PINE Native to northern and central China.	Slow to 75 ft.	Often with several trunks, spreading. Sometimes shrubby. Picturesque.	Needles: in 3s, 3 in. long, bright green. Cones: 2–2½ in. long, roundish, light yellowish brown.	Hardy to sub-zero cold, tolerates heat of California's Central Valley.	Smooth, dull gray bark flakes off like sycamore bark to show smooth, creamy white branches and trunk.
P. canariensis CANARY ISLAND PINE Native to Canary Islands.	Fast, to 60–80 ft., sometimes less.	In youth a slender, graceful pyramid. Later a tiered structure; finally a round-crowned tree.	Needles: in 3s, 9–12 in., blue green in youth, dark green when older. Cones: 4–9 in., oval, glossy brown.	Tender in Northwest but excellent in northern coastal and southern California. Has been severely damaged (even killed) at 10°F. Needles freeze at about 20°F.	Resistant to oak root fungus. Very young plants are gawky, but soon outgrow their awkward phase. Drought tolerant, but needs water in southern California.

NAME	GROWTH RATE, SIZE	GROWTH HABIT	NEEDLES AND CONES	CLIMATE ADAPTABILITY	REMARKS
P. cembra SWISS STONE PINE Native to northern Asia, northern Europe.	Extremely slow to 70 ft. or higher.	Spreading, short branches form narrow, dense pyramid, becoming broad, open, and round topped with age.	Needles: in 5s, 3–5 in., dark green. Cones: 3½ in., oval, light brown.	Very hardy (to −35°F.). Good in Northwest and Rocky Mountain region.	Resistant to white pine blister rust. Extremely slow growth and dense, regular foliage make it a good plant for small gardens. Handsome in youth.
P. cembroides MEXICAN PIÑON PINE Native from Arizona to Baja California and northern Mexico.	Slow to 10–25 ft.	Stout, spreading branches form round-topped head. In youth rather rangy.	Needles: in 3s, sometimes 2s, 1–2 in., slender, dark green. Cones: 1–2 in., roundish, yellowish or reddish brown.	Has succeeded in Northwest west of Cascades and in California coastal and valley gardens. Excellent in Rocky Mountains.	Most treelike of piñons. Drought resistant, good in desert soils.
P. contorta BEACH PINE, SHORE PINE Native along coast from Mendocino County, California to Alaska.	Fairly fast to 20–35 ft.	Nursery-grown trees compact, pyramidal, somewhat irregular. Coast trees dwarfed, contorted by winds.	Needles: in 2s, 1¼–2 in., dark green, dense. Cones: 1–2 in., light yellow brown.	Hardy anywhere, but not at its best in hot, dry areas.	Good-looking in youth. Densely foliaged, takes training well. One of best small pines for small gardens. Does well in containers.
P. c. latifolia *(P. c. murrayana)* LODGEPOLE PINE Native to Blue Mountains of eastern Oregon; Cascade Mountains of Washington; throughout Rockies. Plants from California and Oregon mountains have been called *P. c. murrayana*.	Rather slow to 80 ft., sometimes 150 ft.; usually low, bushy tree in cultivation.	In cultivation rather irregular, open branched, attractive. Planted close together, trees are tall, slim trunked. Solitary trees in mountains are heavy trunked, narrow, dense.	Needles: in 2s, 1½–3 in., yellow green. Cones: 1½ in., shiny brown, persist many years.	Hardy. Widely adaptable except in areas of drought and low humidity.	All forms of *P. contorta* excellent in small garden, wild garden, or large rock garden.
P. coulteri COULTER PINE Native to dry, rocky California mountain slopes; Mt. Diablo, Mt. Hamilton, Santa Lucia ranges and mountains of southern California, Baja California.	Moderate to fast, 30–80 ft.	Shapely open growth; lower branches spread widely, persist. Sometimes develops several divergent leaders, producing "oak tree" shape.	Needles: in 3s, 5–10 (even 14) in., deep green, stiff. Cones: 10–13 in., buff colored, heavy, persist many years.	Hardy. Adaptable to area west of Cascades. Resistant to heat, drought, wind. Good in high desert.	Excellent in gardens where not crowded. Too spreading for small gardens. Huge cones attractive but potentially dangerous around play areas, patios, parked cars.
P. densiflora JAPANESE RED PINE Native to Japan.	Rapid when young. May reach 100 ft., usually much less.	Broad, irregular head. Often develops 2 or more trunks at ground level.	Needles: in 2s, 2½–5 in., bright blue green or yellow green, slender. Cones: 2 in., oval or oblong, tawny brown.	Hardy to −20°F., but not tree for desert areas. Will not tolerate hot, dry, or cold winds.	Handsome pine for informal effects, especially if multitrunked. Makes moderate shade for woodland gardens. Variety 'Oculus-draconis', DRAGON EYE PINE, has 2 yellow bands on each needle; seen endwise, branch has concentric green and yellow bands. 'Pendula' is dwarf with sprawling branches, use it in rock garden.
P. d. 'Umbraculifera' TANYOSHO PINE Native to Japan.	Slow to moderate, 12–20 ft.	Broad, flat topped, with numerous trunks from base. Spread greater than height.	Same as above.	Same as above. Has performed well in Denver.	Gallon- and 5-gallon-sized trees frequently bear cones. Good for containers, rock and Oriental gardens.
P. edulis *(P. cembroides edulis)* PIÑON, NUT PINE Native to California's desert mountains, east to Arizona, New Mexico, and Texas, north to Wyoming.	Slow to 10–20 ft.	Horizontal-branching tree. Low, round or flat crowned in age; bushy and symmetrical in youth.	Needles: usually in 2s, dark green, ¾–1½ in., dense, stiff. Cones: 2 in., roundish, light brown.	Hardy. Thrives in coastal California. Northwest, Denver, higher desert areas. Drought resistant.	Beautiful small pine for containers, rock gardens. Collected plants bring look of age into new gardens. Cones contain edible seeds (pine nuts).

(Continued on next page)

P

NAME	GROWTH RATE, SIZE	GROWTH HABIT	NEEDLES AND CONES	CLIMATE ADAPTABILITY	REMARKS
P. eldarica Native to Caucasus Mountains of southern Russia, Afghanistan, Pakistan.	See *P. brutia*.	See *P. brutia*.	See *P. brutia*.	One of best desert pines, it also thrives near coast.	Something of a mystery pine; may be *P. brutia* from Afghanistan and Pakistan.
P. flexilis LIMBER PINE Mountains of northern Arizona, Utah, Nevada, southeastern California, and eastern slope of Rocky Mountains from Alberta to Texas. Grows at 5,000–11,000 ft. elevation.	Slow, to 20–30 ft. in gardens.	Thick trunk, open round top, many limber branches that may droop at decided angle to trunk.	Needles: in 5s, to 3 in., slightly curved or twisted, dark green. Cones: to 5 in. long, ovoid-conic, buff to buff orange.	Hardy. Grows well on hot, dry, rocky slopes. Drought tolerant.	Smaller and more irregular at higher elevations. Young plants rather straggly appearing. Shapes well with shearing, can be used for bonsai. Susceptible to white pine blister rust.
P. halepensis ALEPPO PINE Native to Mediterranean region.	Moderate to rapid growth to 30–60 ft.	Attractive as 2-year-old; rugged character at 5 years; in age, open irregular crown of many short, ascending branches.	Needles: usually in 2s, 2½–4 in., light green. Cones: 3 in., oval to oblong, reddish to yellow brown.	Semihardy. Thrives in desert heat, drought, and wind; good at seashore. Tender when young; established trees can take near-zero temperatures.	Most useful in poor soils and arid climates. Handsomer trees can be found for cooler, moister gardens. Standard desert pine. Sometimes bothered by mites in southern California, temporary dieback in Tucson area.
P. h. brutia See *P. brutia*.					
P. jeffreyi JEFFREY PINE Native to mountains of California, southern Oregon, western Nevada, Baja California.	Moderate to 60–120 ft.	Symmetrical in youth, with straight trunk and short, spreading, often pendulous branches. Upper branches ascending, form open, pyramidal.	Needles: in 3s, 5–8 in., blue green. Cones: 6–12 in., reddish brown, oval. Cone doesn't feel prickly when you hold it in your hand (*P. ponderosa* cone does).	Hardy. High-altitude tree that is not at its best in low areas. Drought resistant. Slow growing in Seattle.	Attractive in youth, with silver gray bark and bluish foliage. One of best natural bonsai trees. Furrows of bark have vanilla odor.
P. lambertiana SUGAR PINE Native to Sierra Nevada and California's higher Coast Ranges; high mountains of southern California, Baja California; north to Cascades of central Oregon.	Slow in youth, then faster, to 200 ft. or higher.	Young trees narrow, open pyramids with spreading, rather pendulous branches. Old trees usually flat topped with wide-spreading, open head.	Needles: in 5s, 3–4 in., dark bluish green. Cones: 10–20 in., cylindrical, light brown.	Hardy but temperamental. Grows well in Seattle.	World's tallest pine. Susceptible to white pine blister rust, but usually safe if no currants or gooseberry bushes (alternate hosts of blister rust) nearby.
P. monophylla SINGLELEAF PIÑON PINE Native to southeastern California south to Baja California, east to Utah, Arizona.	Very slow to 10–25 ft.	Young trees slender, symmetrical, narrow crowned. In maturity a small, round-headed tree with crooked trunk; open and broad topped in great age.	Needles: usually carried singly, ¾–1½ in., gray green, stiff. Cones: 2 in. long, wide, roundish, brown.	Hardy and drought resistant. Only piñon common in southern California.	Good bonsai or rock garden plant—or shrub of great character in dry, rocky places. Cones contain edible seeds (pine nuts).
P. montezumae MONTEZUMA PINE Native from Mexico to Guatemala.	Moderately fast. To 70 ft. or more in the wilds, usually much less in cultivation.	Broad, fairly dense, with horizontal, somewhat drooping branches.	Needles: usually in 5s, but occasionally in clusters of 3–8, to 1 ft., drooping gracefully; deep, often bluish, green. Cones: to 1 ft., conical, yellow, reddish, or dark brown.	Unlikely to survive in low temperatures. Does well in San Francisco Bay Area. Substitute *P. wallichiana* in colder areas.	Striking pine with unusually long needles.

NAME	GROWTH RATE, SIZE	GROWTH HABIT	NEEDLES AND CONES	CLIMATE ADAPTABILITY	REMARKS
P. monticola WESTERN WHITE PINE Native to northern California, north to British Columbia, east to Montana.	Fast first years, then slow to moderate to 60 ft.	Attractive, narrow, open crown in youth; spreading, somewhat drooping branches in age form pyramid.	Needles: in 5s, 1½–4 in., blue green banded with white beneath, fine and soft. Cones: 5–11 in., light brown, slender.	Very hardy.	Susceptible to white pine blister rust throughout Northwest and northern California.
P. mugo *(P. montana)* SWISS MOUNTAIN PINE Native to mountains of Spain, central Europe to Balkans.	Slow to variable heights.	Variable. Prostrate shrub, low shrub, or pyramidal tree of moderate size.	Needles: in 2s, 2 in., dark green, stout, crowded. Cones: 1–2 in., oval, tawny to dark brown.	Hardy but suffers in desert heat.	In nurseries, generally a bushy, twisted, somewhat open pine. *P. m. pumilio* is eastern European form, shrubby and varying from prostrate to 5–10 ft.
P. m. mugo MUGHO PINE Native to eastern Alps and Balkan states.	Slow to 4 ft.	From infancy on a shrubby, symmetrical little pine. May become spreading in age.	Needles: darker green than *P. mugo*. Cones: a little shorter than those of *P. mugo*.	Very hardy but, like *P. mugo*, suffers in desert heat.	One of most widely used pines because of low growth habit. Excellent container plant. Pick plants with dense, pleasing form. Good in rock gardens.
P. muricata BISHOP PINE Native to northern coast of California, Santa Cruz Island, northwestern Baja California.	Rapid to 40–50 ft.	Open, pyramidal when young; dense, rounded in middle life; irregular in age.	Needles: in 2s, 4–6 in., dark green, crowded. Cones: 2–3 in., borne in whorls of 3, 4, or 5; broadly oval, brown.	Takes wind and salt air. Not reliably hardy in Northwest or interior.	Many people prefer *P. muricata* to Monterey pine (*P. radiata*) because of its slower growth rate, greater denseness in youth, all-around better manners.

(Continued on next page)

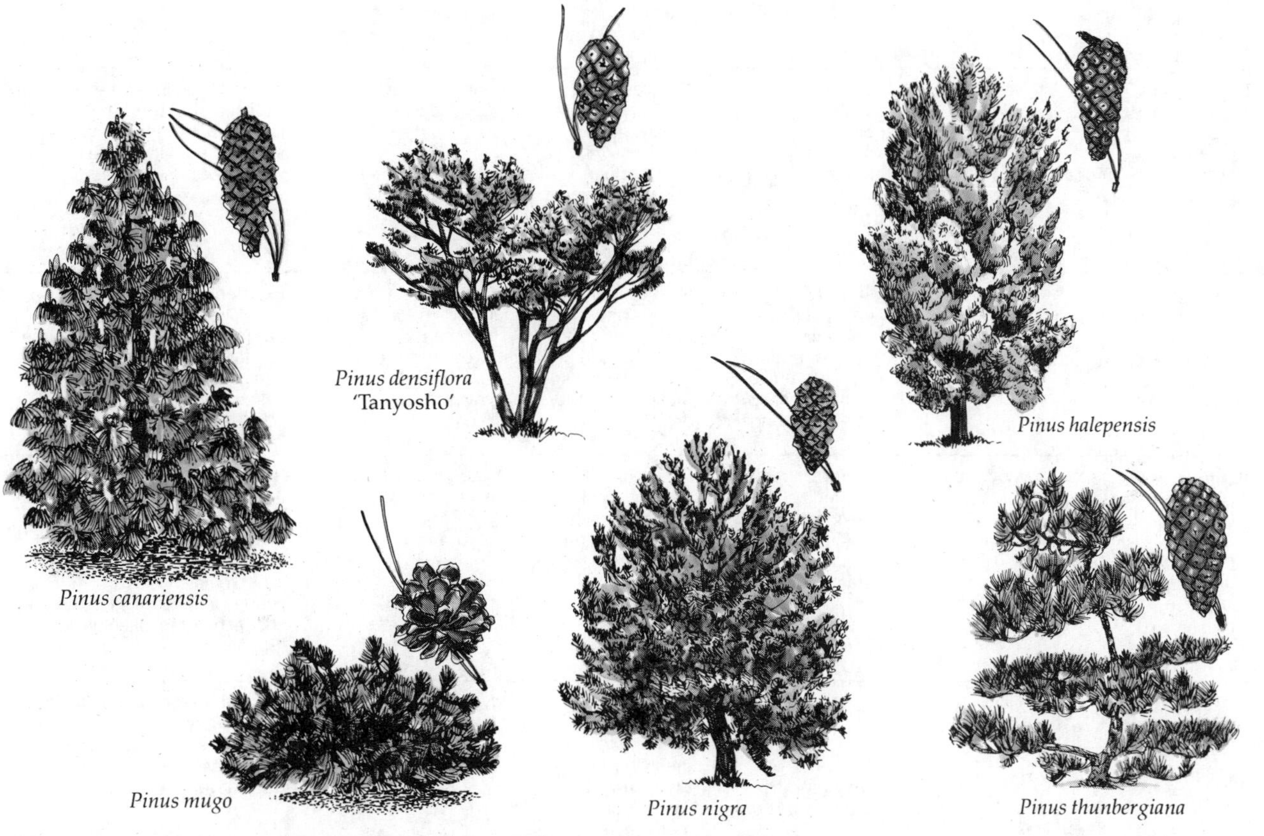

These widely planted pines show great range of outlines and textures.

CLIMATE ZONES, PAGES 33–55

P

NAME	GROWTH RATE, SIZE	GROWTH HABIT	NEEDLES AND CONES	CLIMATE ADAPTABILITY	REMARKS
P. nigra (formerly *P. austriaca*) AUSTRIAN BLACK PINE Native to Europe, western Asia.	Slow to moderate, usually not above 40 ft. in gardens.	Dense, stout pyramid with rather uniform crown. Branches in regular whorls. In age, broad and flat topped.	Needles: in 2s, 3–6½ in., stiff, very dark green. Cones: 2–3½ in., oval, brown.	Very hardy. Adaptable to winter cold and wind.	Tree of strong character which will serve either as landscape decoration or as windbreak in cold regions. Resistant to oak root fungus.
P. palustris LONGLEAF PINE Native to Virginia and Florida to Mississippi; along coast of southeastern United States.	Slow for 5–10 years, then fast to 55–80 ft.	Gaunt, sparse branches ascend to form open, oblong head.	Needles: in 3s, to 1½ ft. on young trees, to 9 in. on mature. Dark green. Cones: 6–10 in., dull brown.	Grows in northern and southern California. In native habitat it occasionally takes frosts down to 5°F. but is accustomed to generally warm winters.	Gallon-sized plants look like fountains of grass, take several years to outgrow this stage. Larger young plants resemble green mops. Good tree for experimenters. Control chlorosis with iron chelates.
P. parviflora JAPANESE WHITE PINE Native to Japan and Formosa.	Slow to moderate to 20–50 ft. or higher.	In open ground a broad pyramid nearly as wide as high.	Needles: in 5s, 1½–2½ in., bluish gray to green. Cones: 2–3 in. long, 1 in. wide, oval, reddish brown.	Hardy. Grows well in Seattle and in northern California. Will survive −20°F.	Widely used for bonsai or container plant.
P. patula JELECOTE PINE Native to Mexico.	Very fast to 40–80 ft.	Symmetrical pyramid with widely spaced tiers of branches.	Needles: in 3s, to 1 ft., grass green, slender, hanging straight down. Cones: to 4½ in., ovoid-conic, lustrous pale brown.	Hardy to 15°F.; a borderline case in Seattle or inland, thriving in coastal California.	Graceful tree casts a light shade, provides handsome silhouette. One of the fastest-growing pines in the world. Treat for chlorosis. Resistant to oak root fungus.
P. peuce MACEDONIAN PINE Native to Yugoslavia, Bulgaria, and Albania.	Slow to moderate growth to 80 ft.	Shapely, dense, erect, narrow cone shape.	Needles: in 5s, slender, 3–4½ in. long, blue green. Cones: slender, curved, 4–6 in. long.	Not widely tested. Hardy to 0°F. and somewhat below. Successful near Denver. Drought tolerant.	Very attractive tree. Similar to *P. wallichiana* but more compact with shorter needles. Rare in nurseries.
P. pinaster CLUSTER PINE, FRENCH TURPENTINE PINE, MARITIME PINE Native to Atlantic coast of France, western Mediterranean, northern Africa.	Very fast to 80–90 ft.	Spreading or sometimes pendulous branches form pyramidal head.	Needles: in 2s, 5–9 in., stiff, glossy green. Cones: 4–7 in., conic-oblong, borne singly or in clusters, glossy light brown.	Hardy to 0°F. Best near coasts, in coastal valleys.	Well-adapted to sandy soil, ocean exposure. Used in San Francisco's Golden Gate Park to help bind sand dunes. May be weak rooted when young.
P. pinea ITALIAN STONE PINE Native to southern Europe and Turkey.	Moderate to 40–80 ft.	In youth, a stout, bushy globe; in middle life, thick trunk topped with umbrella form of many branches. In age, broad and flat topped.	Needles: in 2s, 5–8 in., bright to gray green, stiff. Cones: 4–6 in., glossy, chestnut brown, broadly oval.	Hardy. Takes heat and drought when established. Old trees hardy in Northwest, young ones tender. Good in California valleys, coast; successful in Tucson.	Excellent in beach gardens. Eventually too large for small gardens. Splendid roadside tree. Young trees are handsome, old trees striking.
P. ponderosa PONDEROSA PINE, WESTERN YELLOW PINE Native from British Columbia to Mexico, east to Nebraska, Texas, and northeast Oklahoma.	Moderate to rapid to 50–60 ft. in 50 years, eventually to 150 ft. or more.	In youth, straight trunked and well-branched. Stately in age, with loosely arranged branches in spirelike crown. Handsome plated bark.	Needles: in 3s, 4–11 in., glossy yellow green to dark green, firm, in clusters at branch ends. Cones: 3–5 in., light to red brown, prickly to touch.	Very hardy, but not good in desert heat and wind.	Bushy, attractive tree at all ages. Eventually for large gardens only. Oddly enough, small ones make fine bonsai or large container plants. *P. p. arizonica* has needles in 5s, sometimes 3s and 4s. *P. p. scopulorum* from the Rockies has shorter needles, often drooping branches.
P. pungens TABLE MOUNTAIN PINE Native from New Jersey to Georgia.	Fairly slow to 20–60 ft.	Stout, spreading branches form broad, open, often flat topped or irregular picturesque crown.	Needles: in 2s or 3s, 2–3 in., stiff, prickly, dark green. Cones: 3½ in., bright brown, persist many years.	Hardy. Thriving in Seattle and in northern California.	Somewhat resembles *P. densiflora*. Useful where informal, rather open pine is desirable. Large, abundant, deep purple catkins are decorative.

NAME	GROWTH RATE, SIZE	GROWTH HABIT	NEEDLES AND CONES	CLIMATE ADAPTABILITY	REMARKS
P. radiata MONTEREY PINE Native to California central coast.	Very fast to 80–100 ft.	Shapely, broad cone in youth, then drops lower branches to develop rounded or flattish crown.	Needles: in 3s or 2s, 3–7 in., bright green. Cones: 3–6 in., lopsided, clustered; persist many years.	Most widely planted pine in California even in areas where it is poorly adapted. Not reliably hardy when temperatures drop below 15°F. Best where summers are cool. Not for high or low desert areas nor for California's central valley. Good in sea wind, but not on shallow soils.	Very fast growing, 6 ft. a year when young; 50 ft. in 12 years. Often shallow rooted, subject to blowdown. Prune to maintain denseness (see *Pinus*). In coastal California gets many pests, suffers smog damage, water molds. If you have a tree, keep it healthy with occasional deep watering, feeding. Resistant to oak root fungus.
P. roxburghii *(P. longifolia)* CHIR PINE, INDIAN LONGLEAF PINE Native to Himalayan foothills.	Medium fast to 60–80 ft. or more.	Slender pyramid in youth with long, drooping needles; later broad, spreading, with round-topped, symmetrical head.	Needles: in 3s, 8–13 in., slender, light green. Cones: 4–7 in., ovoid-conic.	Adapted to California coastal areas, lower Oregon coast. Oddly, successful in Tucson.	Rare pine. Similar in many ways to *P. canariensis*.
P. sabiniana DIGGER PINE Native to California foothills.	Fast to 40–50 ft.	Wild trees in dry areas are sparse, open. Main trunk divides into secondary trunks.	Needles: in 3s, 8–12 in., gray green, lacy. Cones: 6–10 in., oblong-oval, contain edible seeds.	Though native to dry foothills, and very drought resistant, thrives in Seattle and is quite hardy there.	Unusual tree for large gardens. Bulky yet lacy, almost transparent crown. Offers little shade. Very ornamental.
P. strobus WHITE PINE, EASTERN WHITE PINE Native Newfoundland to Manitoba, south to Georgia, west to Illinois and Iowa.	Slow in seedling stage, then fast to 100 ft. or more.	Symmetrical cone with horizontal branches in regular whorls. In age, broad, open, irregular.	Needles: in 5s, 2–4 in., blue green, soft. Cones: 3–8 in., slender, often curved.	Hardy in any cold but burns in windy areas. Needs regular water supply.	Fine textured and handsome in form and color. Subject to blister rust. 'Pendula' has weeping, trailing branches. 'Prostrata' is low, spreading shrub with trailing branches.
P. s. 'Nana' DWARF WHITE PINE	Very slow to 3–7 ft.	Broad bush usually twice as wide as tall.	As above but with shorter needles.	Hardy wherever *P. strobus* grows successfully.	Useful in containers or rock gardens.
P. sylvestris SCOTCH PINE Native to northern Europe, Asia.	Moderate to 70–100 ft.	Straight, well-branched pyramid in youth; irregular and picturesque in age, with drooping branches.	Needles: in 2s, 1½–3 in., blue green, stiff. Cones: 2 in., gray to reddish brown.	Very hardy. Not for desert areas; often turns red brown in cold winters, but recovers. Wind resistant.	Popular as Christmas tree and in landscaping. Reddish bark, sparse foliage have own charm. Select young trees with good green winter color; some turn yellowish, even when winter is mild. Excellent in flower arrangements. Many other garden forms: 'Nana' and 'Watereri' are dwarfs, 'Pendula' a weeping tree. All are rare.
P.s. 'Fastigiata'	As above.	Dense, narrow column.	As above.	As above.	Handsome, very densely foliaged plant.
P. thunbergiana *(P. thunbergii)* JAPANESE BLACK PINE Native to Japan.	Fast to 100 ft. in Northwest. Slow to moderate to 20 ft. in southern California and desert.	Spreading branches form broad, conical tree, irregular and spreading in age.	Needles: in 2s, 3–4½ in., bright green, stiff. Cones: 3 in., brown, oval.	Hardy. Widely planted throughout California, in western Washington and Oregon, with watering in intermediate and high desert.	Handsome tree in youth. Takes to pruning like cloth to scissors; shear it into Christmas tree form or make it into cascade. Excellent in planters or as bonsai. Often pruned to open, irregular shape as large container plant or giant bonsai.
P. torreyana TORREY PINE Native to California's San Diego coast and Santa Rosa Island.	Fast to 40–60 ft., sometimes higher.	Broad, open, irregular, picturesque habit when exposed to sea winds.	Needles: in 5s, 8–13 in., light gray green to dark green. Cones: 4–6 in., chocolate brown.	Although native to the coast, it accepts inland, even high desert, conditions, with temperatures as low as 12°F. Stands drought.	Less open growth when grown in heavy soil. Don't prune: cut branches die back to trunk. Resistant to oak root fungus.
P. wallichiana *(P. griffithii, P. excelsa)* HIMALAYAN WHITE PINE Native to Himalayas.	Slow to moderate to 40 ft. in gardens, 150 ft. in wilds.	Broad, conical.	Needles: in 5s, 6–8 in., blue green, slender, drooping. Cones: 6–10 in., light brown.	Hardy to about −10°F. Poor performance in dry, hot areas.	Resistant to blister rust. Eventually large, but good form and color make it good choice for featured pine in big lawn or garden.

temperatures with protection from wind or warm drafts, and good light (but not strong, hot sun). Usually seen as a pot plant 2–3 ft. tall and as wide.

PISTACHE. See *Pistacia.*

PISTACHIO, PISTACHIO NUT. See *Pistacia vera.*

PISTACIA. *Anacardiaceae.* PISTACHE. Deciduous or semievergreen trees. Divided leaves on all species. Flowers not showy. Female trees bear fruit after several years if male trees are nearby. Of species described, only *P. vera* bears edible fruit (nuts). Others are ornamental trees.

Pistacia chinensis

Verticillium wilt (see page 109) may strike established trees. Minimize susceptibility by planting in well-drained soil, watering deeply and infrequently.

P. atlantica. MT. ATLAS PISTACHE. Semievergreen or deciduous. Zones 8–24. Slow to moderate growth to 60 ft. More regular and pyramidal than other pistaches, especially as young tree. Glossy medium green leaves with 7–11 narrow leaflets, rounded at tip. Fruit dark blue or purple. Needs sun, good drainage. Takes desert heat and winds; tolerates drought when established. Holds its foliage very late—all winter in mild climate. Not widely grown as ornamental, but is much used as understock for pistachio (*P. vera*).

P. chinensis. CHINESE PISTACHE. Deciduous. Zones 4–16, 18–23; little grown Zones 4–7. Moderate growth to 60 ft. tall, 50 ft. wide. Young trees often gawky and lopsided, but older trees become dense and shapely with reasonable care. Leaves with 10–16 paired leaflets 2–4 in. long by ¾ in. wide. Foliage colors beautifully in fall—scarlet, crimson, orange, sometimes yellow tones. Only tree to color scarlet in desert. Fruit on female trees bright red, turning dark blue. Not fussy as to soil or water; accepts moderately alkaline conditions, lawn watering (though verticillium wilt is a danger), or no summer watering at all (this only in deep soils). Resistant to oak root fungus. Stake young trees and prune for first few years to develop head high enough to walk under. Reliable tree for street or lawn, patio or garden corner planting.

P. vera. PISTACHIO, PISTACHIO NUT. Deciduous. Zones 7–12, 14, 15, 18–21. Broad, bushy tree to 30 ft. high, with one or several trunks. Leaves have 3–5 roundish, 2–4-in.-long leaflets. Fruit reddish, wrinkled, borne in heavy clusters. Inside husks are hard-shelled pistachio nuts. Be sure to include male tree in your planting. 'Peters' is the male variety most planted, 'Kerman' is principal fruiting (female) variety. When planting, avoid rough handling; budded tops are easily broken away from understock. Pistachios are inclined to spread and droop; stake them and train branches to good framework of 4 or 5 limbs beginning at 4 ft. or so above ground. Established trees will take considerable drought.

PITANGA. See *Eugenia uniflora.*

PITHECELLOBIUM flexicaule. *Leguminosae.* TEXAS EBONY. Tree. Zones 10–13. Grows slowly to 20 ft. (possibly 30 ft.) tall, 15 ft. or more wide. Short, smooth, gray trunk; zigzagging thorny branches and twigs densely set with dark green leaves divided into ½-in. leaflets. Fragrant, creamy yellow flowers in short, feathery spikes appear in spring and early summer. Dark brown, 4–6-in.-long seed pods follow.

Pithecellobium flexicaule

Native to Texas and Mexico, this tree is handsome in desert landscapes, where its dark green color is especially welcome. Don't plant near walks where thorns could cause problems. Needs deep, infrequent watering to thrive; can take more frequent watering.

Pittosporaceae. The pittosporum family consists of evergreen shrubs, trees, or vines from Australia, New Zealand, and eastern Asia. Many have attractive flowers, foliage, or fruit. *Hymenosporum, Pittosporum,* and *Sollya* are representatives.

PITTOSPORUM. *Pittosporaceae.* Evergreen shrubs and trees. Some forms have attractive fragrant flowers and some have pretty fruit, but as a group, pittosporums are valued most by Westerners for their foliage and form. All make basic, dependable shrubs or trees—the kind of plants that can be a garden's all-year backbone. Some make good clipped hedges; all have pleasing outlines when left unclipped. Good as windbreaks.

Pittosporum tobira

Although they are fairly drought resistant, all respond with greener, lusher growth when watered regularly and when fed at least once each spring or summer with nitrogenous or complete fertilizer. All are susceptible to aphids and scale insects. Black sooty covering on leaves (mold growing on insects' honeydew secretions) is a sure sign of infestation. All grow best in full sun to half shade.

P. crassifolium. Zones 9, 14–17, 19–24. Will grow to 25 ft. high in 8–10 years, but can easily be kept 6–10 ft. high and 6–8 ft. wide by yearly pruning. Gray green leaves, 1–2 in. long with rounded ends, densely set on branches. Clusters of little (¼-in.-wide) maroon flowers in late spring. Conspicuous fruit. Notably wind resistant; tolerates even salt-laden ocean winds. Good seaside plant. 'Nana' is dense dwarf form growing 3 ft. tall or a bit taller, and as wide as it's high.

P. eugenioides. Zones 9, 14–17, 19–22. Excellent hedge plant or freestanding shade tree. Good as screen or background plant. Medium glossy, 2–4-in.-long leaves have distinctly wavy edges. Depending on environment, leaf color may be yellow green to medium green. On unpruned plants, clusters of fragrant, yellow, ½-in. flowers form in spring. To grow as hedge, plant gallon-can plants 1½ ft. apart in row. Force bushiness by shearing off 2–6 in. of plant tops several times each year between February and October. Begin clipping sides when necessary. As freestanding tree (to 40 ft. high, 20 ft. wide), develops handsome, curving gray trunk and lush foliage canopy.

P. napaulense *(P. floribundum).* GOLDEN FRAGRANCE. Zones 15–17, 20–24. To 12 ft. high, 8 ft. wide. This shrub is not like the others. Main differences: Leaves are thin, leathery textured, 4–8 in. long, 1–2 in. wide, shiny, pointed at tips; flowers are golden yellow, intensely fragrant, carried in 3-in. clusters protruding beyond branch tips in spring. Use as display plant or fragrance maker, not as hedge or screen plant.

P. phillyraeoides. WILLOW PITTOSPORUM. Zones 9, 12–24. Also different from typical pittosporums. This one's a weeping plant with trailing branches and deep, dusty green leaves, very narrow, 3 in. long. Grows slowly to 15–20 ft. high, 10–15 ft. wide. Always best standing alone; strong structure shouldn't be smothered by other foliage. Good by pool or patio. Small, yellow, bell-shaped, fragrant flowers borne along drooping branches in late winter, early spring, followed by deep yellow fruit. If drainage is poor, water very infrequently but deeply. Tolerates heat and drought better than most other pittosporums, and has even naturalized in some desert areas.

P. ralphii 'Green Globe'. Zones 17, 19–24. The parent species is not grown commercially; it resembles *P. crassifolium.* 'Green Globe' is a dwarf version that grows 1½ ft. tall and as wide. Leaves are only ¼ in. long, bright green when first expanding, then gray green. Tiny, inconspicuous spring flowers are deep blackish purple.

P. rhombifolium. QUEENSLAND PITTOSPORUM. Zones 12–24. Slow-growing shrub or tree, to 15–35 ft. Glossy rich green leaves are nearly diamond shaped, to 4 in. long. Small white flowers in late spring. Growth is open enough that you can see the round, ½-in. fruit that follows: very showy, yellow to orange, in clusters from fall through winter. Fruit contrasts nicely with foliage. As small tree, well suited for patio (if litter of sticky fruit won't pose a problem) or lawn. Or use several as not-too-dense screen that needs little pruning. Resistant to oak root fungus.

P. tenuifolium *(P. nigricans).* Zones 9, 14–17, 19–24. Quite similar in most ways (size, growth habit, uses, culture) to *P. eugenioides,* though more tolerant of beach conditions. Main difference is in leaves and twigs. This one has shorter (1–1½-in.), more oval leaves than *P. eugenioides;* leaf edges are less wavy, and color is deeper green. Small twigs and leaf stems are darker. Altogether, then, *P. tenuifolium* is finer textured, darker, and a little denser than *P. eugenioides.* If pruning allows flowers to form, they will be dark purple, ½ in. wide, in clusters. There are varieties with bronzy purple foliage and variegated leaves.

P. tobira. TOBIRA. Zones 8–24; borderline hardiness in Zones 4–7. Broad, dense shrub or small tree, 6–15 ft. tall, rarely to 30 ft. Can be held to 6 ft. by careful heading back and thinning (tobira does not respond as well to shearing as do some other pittosporums). Clean-looking, dense foliage; leaves leathery, shiny dark green, 2–5 in. long, rounded at ends. Clusters of creamy white flowers at branch tips in early spring have fragrance of orange blossoms. Flowers become round, green fruit that turns brownish in fall and splits to show orange seeds. Best for screens, massing, or individually as crooked-stemmed, freestanding small tree. Effective in containers. Variety 'Variegata', with gray green leaves edged white, is smaller, usually growing to about 5 ft. high and as broad. Sometimes loses many leaves in winter. 'Turner's Variegated Dwarf' has gray green leaves with creamy edges. 'Wheeler's Dwarf' has same handsome leaves as *P. tobira* but on extremely dense-growing, 1–2-ft. shrub. Choice selection for foreground or low boundary plantings, or even small-scale ground cover. Good near swimming pools.

P. undulatum. VICTORIAN BOX. Zones 14 and 15 (in frost-sheltered locations), 16, 17, 21–24. Moderately fast growth to 15 ft., then slow to 30–40 ft. high, equal width. Planted 5–8 ft. apart, can be kept to dense, 10–15-ft. screen by pruning (not shearing). Good background plant. Makes dense single or multitrunked, dome-shaped tree of great beauty. Leaves medium to dark green, glossy, wavy edged, 4–6 in. long. Fragrant creamy white flowers in early spring. Yellowish orange fruit opens in fall to show sticky, golden orange seeds which are messy on lawn or paving. Lawn or street tree, screen, or big container plant. Strong roots become invasive with age.

P. viridiflorum. CAPE PITTOSPORUM. Zones 15–17, 20–24. Shrub or tree to 25 ft. Leaves to 3 in. long, sharp pointed or blunt, often inrolled at edges. Flowers fragrant, yellowish green, in dense clusters. Orange yellow fruit. Resembles large *P. tobira;* serves similar uses, also has great value as street or garden tree. Good as screen.

PITYROGRAMMA. *Polypodiaceae.* GOLDBACK FERN. Finely cut fronds, dark green above, heavily coated beneath with bright golden or silvery white powder. Grow in light shade.

Pityrogramma triangularis

P. hybrida. Zones 23, 24. Large fern of hybrid origin. Broad, finely cut fronds to 2–3 ft. long, backed with brilliant gold. Hardy to 32°F.

P. triangularis. Zones 4–9, 14–24. Native California to Alaska. Small fern with fronds 7 in. long, 6 in. wide, often much smaller in dry woods. Undersides of fronds strikingly golden (silver in some varieties). Dormant in summer, therefore drought tolerant.

PLAID CACTUS. See *Gymnocalycium mihanovichii.*

PLANE TREE. See *Platanus.*

PLANTAIN LILY. See *Hosta.*

PLATANUS. *Platanaceae.* PLANE TREE, SYCAMORE. Deciduous trees. All grow large, have lobed, maplelike leaves. Older bark sheds in patches to reveal pale, smooth, new bark beneath. Brown, ball-like seed clusters hang from branches on long stalks through winter; prized for winter arrangements. Somewhat drought tolerant but better with some deep watering in summer. Subject to blight (anthracnose) which causes early, continued leaf fall; *P. racemosa* especially susceptible. See page 106 for controls. Also rake up and dispose of dead leaves, since fungus spores can overwinter on them. Chlorosis may be a problem in desert.

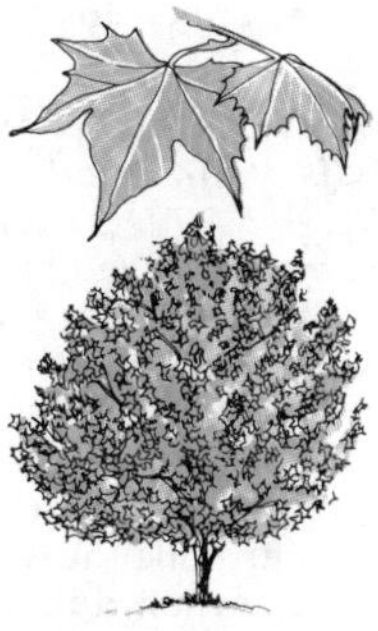

Platanus acerifolia

P. acerifolia (often sold as *P. orientalis*). LONDON PLANE TREE. Zones 2–24. Fast growth to 40–80 ft., with 30–40-ft. spread. Smooth, cream-colored upper trunk and limbs. Leaves are 3–5 lobed, 4–10 in. wide. Tolerates most soils, stands up beautifully under city smog, soot, dust, reflected heat. Can be pollarded to create dense, low canopy.

Watch for spider mites and scale. Good street, park, or lawn tree. Used in lines and blocks for formal plantings—avenues, screens, masses. Powdery mildew can cause premature leaf drop in some seasons. The scarce variety 'Yarwood' is somewhat resistant. 'Bloodgood' has some resistance to anthracnose.

P. occidentalis. AMERICAN SYCAMORE, BUTTONWOOD. All Zones. Similar to London plane tree; new bark is whiter, tree is out of leaf longer. Very hardy. Occasionally grows with multiple or leaning trunks. Old trees near streams sometimes reach huge size and have heavy trunks.

P. racemosa. CALIFORNIA SYCAMORE. Zones 4–24. Native along streams in California foothills and Coast Ranges. Fast growth to robust 50–100 ft. Main trunk often divides into spreading or leaning secondary trunk. Attractive patchy, buff-colored bark. Smooth branches often gracefully twisted and contorted. Deeply lobed, yellowish green leaves 4–9 in. long. Susceptible to leaf miner, red spider mites. Leaves naturally turn dusty brown too early in autumn to be considered as fall color. In mild coastal areas, brown leaves hang on until new leaf growth starts. In winter, the ball-like seed clusters hang 3–7 together along single stalk. Tolerant of much heat, wind. With care in pruning can be trained into picturesque multitrunked clump. For native or wild gardens, or for big informal gardens generally.

P. wrightii *(P. racemosa wrightii).* ARIZONA SYCAMORE. Zones 10–12. To 80 ft. Native along streams and canyons in mountains of south and east Arizona. Needs regular water in dry season. Resembles *P. racemosa,* but leaves are more deeply lobed and seed clusters have individual stalks branching from common stalk.

PLATYCERIUM. *Polypodiaceae.* STAGHORN FERN. Odd epiphytic ferns from tropical regions. In nature, they grow on trees; gardeners grow them on slabs of bark or tree fern stem, occasionally in hanging baskets or on trees. Most should be kept on the dry side and given water only when slab or moss to which plant is attached is actually dry to the touch. Two kinds of fronds. Sterile ones are flat, pale green aging to tan and brown; they support plant and accumulate organic matter to help feed it. Fertile fronds are forked, resembling deer antlers. Striking decoration for lanai, shaded patio.

Platycerium bifurcatum

P. bifurcatum (often sold as *P. alcicorne*). Zones 15–17, 19–24. From Australia and New

Guinea. Surprisingly hardy; survives 20°–22°F. with only lath structures for shelter. Fertile fronds clustered, gray green, to 3 ft. long. Makes numerous offsets which can be used in propagation.

P. grande. Zones 23, 24. From Australia. Fertile and sterile fronds both forked, the former broad but divided somewhat like moose antlers to 6 ft. long. Protect from frosts. Don't overwater.

Platycladus orientalis

PLATYCLADUS orientalis *(Thuja orientalis, Biota orientalis).* *Cupressaceae.* ORIENTAL ARBORVITAE. Evergreen shrubs, trees. All Zones; damaged by severe winters in Zone 1. Shrubby forms common, but tree from which they originate, a 25–50-ft. plant, is very rarely seen. Leaves scalelike, on twigs that are arranged in flat, vertical planes. Juvenile foliage needlelike; some varieties keep juvenile foliage throughout life. Small, fleshy cones become woody when ripe. Less hardy to cold than American arborvitae (*Thuja occidentalis*), but tolerates heat and low humidity better. In Rocky Mountains, grows best when in part shade; shade during winter is especially helpful. Has survived well in nematode-infested soils. Give good drainage, ample water; protect from the reflected heat of light-colored walls or pavement. Blight of leaves and twigs in Northwest is easily controlled by copper sprays in early fall and by pruning out and destroying diseased growth. Spray for spider mites.

Widely used around foundations, in pairs or groups by doorways or gates, singly in lawns or borders, or in formal rows. Most stay small, but some forms often end up bigger than the space they're meant for. Varieties are:

'Aureus' ('Aureus Nana', 'Berckmanii'). DWARF GOLDEN ARBORVITAE, BERCKMAN DWARF ARBORVITAE. Dwarf, compact, golden, globe shaped, usually 3 ft. tall, 2 ft. wide. Can reach 5 ft.

'Bakeri'. Compact, cone shaped, with bright green foliage.

'Beverlyensis'. BEVERLY HILLS ARBORVITAE, GOLDEN PYRAMID ARBORVITAE. Upright, globe shaped to conical; somewhat open habit. Branchlet tips golden yellow. In time, can reach 10 ft. tall, 10 ft. wide. Give it room.

'Blue Cone'. Dense, upright, conical; good blue green color.

'Bonita' ('Bonita Upright', 'Bonita Erecta'). Rounded, full, dense cone to 3 ft. tall. Dark green with slight golden tinting at branch tips.

'Fruitlandii'. FRUITLAND ARBORVITAE. Compact, upright, cone-shaped shrub with deep green foliage.

'Raffles'. Resembles 'Aureus' but is denser in growth, smaller, brighter in color.

Platycodon grandiflorus

PLATYCODON grandiflorus. *Campanulaceae.* BALLOON FLOWER. Perennial. All Zones. Upright branched stems to 3½ ft. Leaves light olive green, 1–3 in. long. Balloonlike buds open into 2-in.-wide, star-shaped flowers in blue violet, white, or soft pink. Bloom June–August if spent flowers (not entire stems) are removed.

Use in borders with astilbe, campanula, francoa, hosta, rehmannia. Plant in sun near coast; light shade in warmer areas. Protect roots from gophers. Good soil, moderate watering. Completely dormant in winter; mark position to avoid digging up fleshy roots. (If you should dig up a root, replant it—or the pieces—at once. Most will grow.) Takes 2–3 years to get well established. Easy to grow from seed. Variety *mariesii* is dwarf form 1–1½ ft. high. 'Apoyama', 2–3-in. dwarf in pots, grows to size of *mariesii* in open ground.

Flowers of 'Komachi' maintain their balloon shape, never opening fully. There are also plants with double flowers.

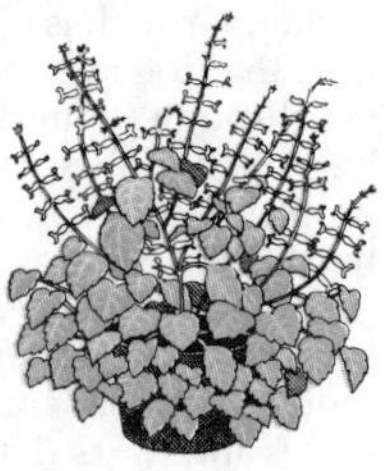

Plectranthus oertendahlii

PLECTRANTHUS. *Labiatae.* SWEDISH IVY. Perennials. Outdoors in Zones 22–24; elsewhere, lathhouse or greenhouse foliage plants. Leaves somewhat thickish, with scalloped edges and prominent veins. Small white or bluish flowers in spikes. Grow as ground cover in small semishady to shady areas, southern California coast. Especially good trailing over wall or edge of planter or raised bed. As indoor or lathhouse plant, grow in hanging pot or wall container. Among easiest plants to grow. Will root in water or soil, take moderate or deep shade (though it prefers good light without direct sun). Requires fairly little water once established. Most people remove flower buds before bloom for more compact plants; alternative method is to allow plant to bloom, then cut it back afterward. Following are the best known of many species and varieties:

P. australis. Shiny dark green leaves. There are white-variegated forms.

P. coleoides 'Marginatus'. Somewhat less trailing in habit than others. Leaves green and gray green with cream edge.

P. oertendahlii. Leaf veins are silvery above, purplish beneath; leaf margins are purplish, scalloped.

Pleione bulbocodioides

PLEIONE. *Orchidaceae.* Terrestrial orchids. Outdoors in Zones 5–9, 14–24. Native to southeast Asia. Many species. All are deciduous. Plant is a pseudobulb bearing 1 or 2 leaves. Leaves to 8 in. long in largest species, narrowly oval and pleated. Flowers resemble those of cattleya, appear before foliage in early spring. Grow them in pots with leaf mold or in peaty soil. Keep on dry side in winter. Shade.

P. bulbocodioides *(P. formosana).* One or two 2½–3-in. flowers on 3–5-in. stem in spring. Lavender sepals and petals, paler lavender lip marked with brown and yellow.

Pleiospilos nelii

PLEIOSPILOS. *Aizoaceae.* SPLIT ROCK. Succulents. Grow in pots. Let them summer outside anywhere. In winter, bring indoors if weather is cold; leave outdoors with overhead protection in Zones 16, 17, 21–24. Plants have 1–3 pairs of leaves that very much resemble gray or gray green rounded pebbles; size varies according to species, from 1 in. long to slightly more than 3 in. Yellow or white flowers large in relation to leaf size, resembling those of ice plants. For culture, see *Lithops*. Of many kinds offered, *P. nelii* and *P. bolusii* are best known.

PLEROMA splendens. See *Tibouchina urvilleana.*

PLOVER EGGS. See *Adromischus festivus.*

PLUM, FLOWERING. See *Prunus.*

Plum

PLUM and PRUNE. *Rosaceae.* Varieties of edible plums and prunes commonly grown in the West are described in the chart on pages 475–476. Noted beneath each variety is group to which it belongs—Japanese (*Prunus salicina*) or European (*P. domestica*). Damson plum (*P. insititia*) is often considered a type of European plum; it intercrosses with European plums freely.

Aside from Japanese and European plums, there is a third category, important only where climate is unusually severe. This is a complex group of hybrids involving Japanese plum, several species of native American wild plums, and the native sand cherry (*P. besseyi*). Originating in Canada, the Dakotas, and Minnesota, this group is exceptionally tolerant of cold and wind. Typical varieties are 'Compass', 'Pipestone', 'Sapa', 'Sapalta', and 'Waneta'. The fruit can be eaten fresh, cooked, or made into preserves. Pollination is often difficult with these hybrids; inquire of local nurserymen about effective and available pollinators.

Plum

As orchard trees, both Japanese and European plums reach a height of 15–20 ft. with somewhat wider spread. Differences in growth habit are discussed below under pruning and thinning. All have white flowers. Leaves to about 3 in. long are broadly oval with serrated edges, turn tawny yellow in fall.

Fruit of Japanese plums ranges in color from green through yellow and brilliant red to deep purple black. With few exceptions, fruit is larger and juicier than that of European plums, with pleasant blend of acid and sugar. Most Japanese plums are used for fresh fruit only. European plums range in color from green and yellow to almost black. Prunes are European plums with a high sugar content, which makes it possible to sun-dry the fruit without it fermenting at the pit. As fresh fruit, prunes are sweeter than other plums.

European plums and prunes bloom late and are better adapted than early-blooming Japanese plums to areas with late frosts or cool, rainy spring weather. Most European varieties have moderately high chilling requirement that rules them out of extremely mild-winter areas. Pollination requirements are listed in the chart; pollinators recommended are not the only combinations possible, but those listed have worked.

You can grow plums in many soil types, but they do best in fertile, well-drained soil. Best growth, fruit development come with periodic deep watering in summer, even though established trees are fairly drought tolerant.

For larger fruit and vigorous growth, fertilize heavily. Orchardists give Japanese plums 1–3 lbs. of actual nitrogen a year, European plums 1–2 lbs.

Train young trees to vase shape. After selecting framework branches, cut back to lateral branches. If tree tends to grow upright, cut to outside branches; if it is spreading, cut to inside branches.

Japanese plums make tremendous shoot growth; rather severe pruning is necessary at all ages. Many varieties tend to produce excessive vertical growth; with these, shorten shoots to outside branchlets. European plums do not branch as freely and selection of framework branches is limited. Prune to avoid formation of V-crotches. Mature trees require little pruning—mainly thinning out annual shoot growth.

Heavy bearing of Japanese varieties results in much small fruit and, possibly, damage to tree. Thin fruit drastically as soon as it is big enough to be seen, spacing fruits 4–6 in. apart. European plums and prunes do not require as heavy fruit thinning as Japanese types.

Control insects and diseases like this: dormant spray for scale, mite eggs, aphids. Or use recommended control (page 100) in early spring to kill scale in crawler stage. Spray when buds show white for twig borer and aphids; use insecticide containing sevin or diazinon. Brown rot and fruit and leaf spot may be severe in humid areas. To control, spray with wettable sulfur weekly as fruit matures. If borers attack, control as for peaches. To control mites and insects after leaves form, use an all-purpose fruit tree insecticide, following the label instructions carefully.

Plumbaginaceae. The leadwort family consists of shrubs and perennials with clustered, funnel-shaped flowers. *Armeria, Ceratostigma,* and *Plumbago* are examples.

Plum and Prune

NAME	ZONES	POLLINATION	FRUIT	REMARKS
'Autumn Rosa' JAPANESE *(Prunus salicina)*	7–12, 14–23	Self-fertile. Good pollinator for 'Mariposa'.	Medium to large. Purplish red skin, yellow flesh with red streaks. Very late.	Ripens over long period, hangs well on tree.
'Beauty' JAPANESE	7–10, 12, 14–20	Self-fertile; yield improved by pollination with 'Santa Rosa'.	Medium sized. Bright red skin, amber flesh streaked with scarlet, good flavor. Very early.	Fruit softens quickly.
'Brooks' EUROPEAN *(P. domestica)*	2–12, 14–22	Self-fertile.	Large blue plum with yellow flesh. Good canned or dried. Midseason.	Most reliable cropper in Northwest.
'Burbank' JAPANESE	2–12, 14–20	'Beauty', 'Santa Rosa'.	Large, red. Amber yellow flesh of excellent flavor. Midseason.	Good choice in regions where hardiness to cold is important.
'Casselman' JAPANESE	2, 3, 7–12, 14–22	Self-fertile.	Resembles 'Late Santa Rosa' but is lighter in color, and ripens later.	Not subject to cracking of skin.
'Damson' ('Blue Damson') EUROPEAN *(P. insititia)*	2–23	Self-fertile.	Small purple or blue black plum with green flesh, very tart flavor.	Makes fine jam and jelly. Strains of this variety sold as 'French Damson', 'Shropshire'.
'Elephant Heart' JAPANESE	2, 3, 7–12, 14–22	'Santa Rosa'.	Very large dark red plum with rich red flesh. Freestone, highly flavored. Midseason to late.	Skin tart; some prefer these plums peeled. Long harvest season.
'French Prune' ('Agen') EUROPEAN	2, 3, 7–12, 14–22	Self-fertile.	Small, red to purplish black. Very sweet and mild. Late.	Standard drying prune of California. Suitable for drying or canning.

(Continued on next page)

CLIMATE ZONES, PAGES 33–55

P

NAME	ZONES	POLLINATION	FRUIT	REMARKS
'Friar' JAPANESE	2–12, 14–20	'Santa Rosa', 'Late Santa Rosa'.	Large black plum with amber flesh. Resists cracking and softens slowly after picking. Late midseason.	Very vigorous, productive tree.
'Golden Nectar' JAPANESE	7–12, 14–22	Self-fertile.	Extra-large yellow plum with yellow flesh, small pit, excellent flavor. Midseason.	Good keeping quality in storage or at room temperature.
'Green Gage' (*P. d. italica*) EUROPEAN	2–12, 14–22	Self-fertile.	Small to medium, greenish yellow, amber fleshed. Good flavor. Midseason.	Very old variety; still a favorite for eating fresh, cooking, canning, or making jam. Selected strain sold as 'Jefferson'.
'Hollywood'	See FLOWERING PLUM under *Prunus*.			
'Howard Miracle' JAPANESE	7–10, 14–20	'Santa Rosa', 'Wickson'.	Medium sized, yellow with red blush. Yellow flesh with spicy, pineapplelike flavor. Midseason.	More acid than most Japanese plums, but truly distinctive in flavor.
'Imperial' ('Imperial Epineuse') EUROPEAN	7–12, 14–18	'French Prune' or other European plums.	Large, red purple to black purple skin, greenish yellow flesh. Sweet, highly flavored, fine quality. Late midseason.	Excellent fresh. Makes a premium dried prune or canned product.
'Italian Prune' ('Fellenburg') EUROPEAN	2–12, 14–18	Self-fertile.	Medium-sized sweet, purplish black prune. Late midseason.	Standard for prunes in the Northwest. Excellent fresh and for canning. Can be dried. 'Early Italian' ripens 2 weeks earlier.
'Kelsey' JAPANESE	7–12, 14–18	Self-fertile.	Large, green to greenish yellow splashed red. Yellow, firm, sweet flesh. Nonjuicy. Late midseason.	Holds for several weeks off tree.
'Late Santa Rosa' JAPANESE	7–12, 14–22	Self-fertile.	Medium to large, purplish crimson. Amber flesh, red near skin; tart-sweet sprightly flavor. Late.	Follows 'Santa Rosa' by a month.
'Mariposa' ('Improved Satsuma') JAPANESE	7–12, 14–22	'Beauty', 'Santa Rosa', 'Wickson', 'Late Santa Rosa'.	Large, purple red skin, deep red flesh. Nearly freestone. Sweet flavor. Midseason.	Good for cooking and eating.
'Nubiana' JAPANESE	2–12, 14–20	Self-fertile.	Large amber-fleshed plum with deep purple black skin. Sweet and firm. Midseason.	Good for cooking and eating. Turns red when cooked. Good keeper.
'President' EUROPEAN	2–12, 14–20	'Imperial'.	Large, purplish blue, amber fleshed, attractive. Flavor not outstanding. Late.	Used for cooking, eating fresh. Not for drying.
'Queen Ann' JAPANESE	7–12, 14–18	'Santa Rosa', 'Wickson'.	Large, dark purple, heart-shaped fruit with amber flesh. Rich flavor when fully ripe. Late.	Holds shape well when cooked.
'Santa Rosa' JAPANESE	2, 3, 7–12, 14–23	Self-fertile.	Medium to large, purplish red with heavy blue bloom. Flesh yellow to dark red near skin; rich, pleasing, tart flavor. Early.	Most important commercial and home variety. Good canned if skin is removed. Makes very strong vertical shoots. Shorten to out-facing branchlets.
'Satsuma' JAPANESE	2–12, 14–22	'Beauty', 'Santa Rosa', 'Wickson'.	Small to medium, dull deep red skin; dark red, solid, meaty flesh. Mild, sweet. Small pit. Early midseason.	Preferred for jams and jellies. Sometimes called blood plum because of its red juice. Spreading habit. Tends to overbear, so thin fruit for best size.
'Stanley' EUROPEAN	2–12, 14–22	Self-fertile.	Large, purplish black with yellow flesh. Sweet and juicy. Midseason.	Good canning variety; resembles larger 'Italian Prune'.
'Sugar' EUROPEAN	2–12, 14–22	Self-fertile.	Medium sized (somewhat larger than 'French Prune'). Very sweet, highly flavored. Early midseason.	Good fresh, for home drying and canning. Trees tend to bear heavily in alternate years.
'Wickson' JAPANESE	2–12, 14–22	'Santa Rosa', 'Beauty'.	Large, showy yellow plum turning yellow red when ripe. Firm yellow flesh of fine flavor. Early midseason.	Good keeper. Makes a fine-textured pink sauce.

PLUMBAGO auriculata *(P. capensis).* *Plumbaginaceae.* CAPE PLUMBAGO. Semievergreen shrub or vine. Zones 8, 9, 12–24. Unsupported, a sprawling, mounding bush to 6 ft. tall, 8–10 ft. wide; with support, can reach 12 ft. or more. In Zone 12 usually a 2-ft. shrub. Fresh-looking, light to medium green leaves, 1–2 in. long. Inch-wide flowers in phloxlike clusters, varying (in seedling plants) from white to clear light blue. Select plants in bloom. Blooms mostly in March–December, throughout year in warm, frost-free areas. Hot desert sun bleaches flowers. Takes poor soil and (once established) very little water, but good drainage is important. Young growth blackens, leaves drop in heavy frosts, but recovery is good. Prune out damaged growth after frost danger is past. In coldest climates, plant in spring so plants have greatest chance to become established before frosts. Propagate from cuttings. Slow to start, but tough. Good cover for bank, fence, hot wall; good background and filler plant. 'Alba' is white-flowered variety.

Plumbago auriculata

For other plants called plumbago, see *Ceratostigma*.

PLUMBAGO larpentae. See *Ceratostigma plumbaginoides*.

PLUME CEDAR, PLUME CRYPTOMERIA. See *Cryptomeria japonica* 'Elegans'.

PLUME HYACINTH. See *Muscari comosum* 'Monstrosum'.

PLUME POPPY. See *Macleaya cordata*.

PLUMERIA. *Apocynaceae.* Evergreen and deciduous shrubs or small trees of open, gaunt character, with thick branches and leathery, pointed leaves clustered near branch tips. Clustered flowers are large, showy, waxy, very fragrant. All are easy to grow from cuttings. Tender to frost; won't take cold, wet soil. Sun near coast, part shade inland. Keep on the dry side in winter. Grow in containers, give shelter from frosts. When frosts can be expected, move container indoors to bright window for continued bloom; or move to frost-free garage or shed, give little water throughout winter. Feeding late in year will result in soft growth that will be nipped by lightest frosts.

Plumeria rubra acutifolia

P. obtusa. SINGAPORE PLUMERIA. Evergreen shrub or small tree. Zone 24. Leaves dark green, 6 in. long, 2 in. wide, very glossy. White, fragrant, 2-in.-wide flowers bloom during warm weather. Very tender.

P. rubra. PLUMERIA, FRANGIPANI. Deciduous shrub or small tree. Zones 12, 13, 19, 21–24. In cold-winter climates, grown in greenhouse or as indoor/outdoor plant. Thick, pointed, 8–16-in.-long leaves drop in winter or early spring. Clusters of 2–2½-in.-wide flowers, red, purple, pink, yellow, or white, bloom June–November. Many varieties available in southern California. Blooms best in full sun (afternoon shade best in desert). Where frosts occur, best grown in containers, moved to shelter when necessary.

PLUM YEW. See *Cephalotaxus*.

POA. *Gramineae.* BLUEGRASS. Perennial or annual grasses. One is the most important cool-season lawn grass, another a sometimes attractive weed; others are meadow grasses (occasionally cultivated). Leaves of all have characteristic boat-prow tip. Must have regular water. They all perform best in maximum available sunlight.

P. annua. ANNUAL BLUEGRASS. Usually considered cool-season weed of lawns, it often furnishes much of the green in winter lawns. Bright green, soft in texture, it would be attractive except for seed heads and propensity to die off just when you need it—when rain lessens in late spring. Discourage it by maintaining thick turf of good grasses.

P. pratensis. KENTUCKY BLUEGRASS. Rich blue green lawn grass, excellent in Zones 1–7. Satisfactory but troublesome in Zones 8–11, 14–17. Difficult and not recommended Zones 12, 13, 18–24. Many selections are available as seed or sod. Mow at 1½–2 in., higher in the summer. Use alone or in mixture with other grasses.

Poa pratensis

P. trivialis. ROUGH-STALKED BLUEGRASS. Fine-textured, bright green grass occasionally used in shady lawn mixtures for its tolerance of shade, damp soil.

PODOCARPUS. *Podocarpaceae.* Evergreen trees, shrubs. Versatile plants grown for good-looking foliage, interesting form; adaptable to many climates, many garden uses. Good screen or background plantings. Foliage generally resembles that of related yews (*Taxus*), but leaves of better-known species are longer, broader, lighter in color.

Grow easily (if slowly) in ordinary garden soil, in sun or partial shade; some shade best in hot valleys. Will grow many years in containers. Not especially drought tolerant. Best with year-round regular water. Practically pest free; sometimes troubled by chlorosis, especially in cold, wet, heavy soil.

Podocarpus gracilior

P. elongatus. See *P. gracilior.*

P. falcatus. Tree. Zones 8, 9, 14–24. Native to South Africa. Slow growth. Differs from *P. gracilior* in technical details. For culture and uses, see *P. gracilior.*

P. gracilior (often sold as *P. elongatus*). FERN PINE. Tree, often grown as espaliered vine, even as hanging basket plant. Zones 8, 9, 12 (warmest areas), 13–24. Native to east Africa, where it grows to 70 ft. Old trees in California reach 60 ft. tall.

Habit and foliage vary with age of plant and method of propagation. Leaves on mature wood are closely spaced, soft grayish or bluish green, 1–2 in. long, narrow. Plants grown from cuttings or grafts taken from such wood will be limber branched and slow to make vertical growth, and will have short, bluish or grayish leaves. Such plants are usually sold as *P. elongatus.*

Leaves on seedlings, vigorous young plants, and unusually vigorous shoots of mature plants are twice as long, more sparsely set on branches, and dark glossy green. Seedlings are more upright in growth than plants grown from cuttings or grafts, and branches are less pendulous, more evenly spaced. Such plants are usually sold as *P. gracilior.* Stake these plants until strong trunk develops. With age, foliage will become more dense, leaves shorter and bluish or grayish green in color.

Cutting-grown and grafted plants are slow to begin upright growth; branches are supple and limber, and dominant, upright trunk is slow to form. Such plants are excellent for espaliering or for growing as vines along fences or eaves. With age they will become trees with single or multiple stems. Stake well to support heavy foliage masses.

Sun or light shade; needs shade in Zone 13. Among cleanest and most pest-free choices for street or lawn tree, patio or flower bed tree, espalier, hedge, big shrub, or container plant. Choice entryway plant or indoor/outdoor plant. Young plants sometimes used in dish gardens.

P. henkelii. LONG-LEAFED YELLOW-WOOD. Tree. Zones 8, 9, 14–24. Handsome, erect, slow-growing tree with masses of drooping foliage. Leaves 5–7 in. long, ⅓ in. wide; leaves are smaller on old trees in their native South Africa. Young trees are strikingly handsome; older, larger ones not yet seen here.

P. macrophyllus. YEW PINE. Shrub or tree. Zones 4–9, 12–24. Has been grown in Zones 3, 11 with shelter from wind, hot sun, deep snow. More tolerant of heat, drought than other species. Ultimately grows to 50 ft. high. Bright green leaves are 4 in. long and are broader than those of *P. gracilior.* Grows indoors or out, in tubs or open ground. Generally narrow and upright, but limber enough to espalier. Easily pruned to shape. Tub plant, large shrub, street or lawn tree (with staking and thinning), screen planting, topiary, clipped hedge.

P. m. maki. SHRUBBY YEW PINE. Smaller, slower growing than yew pine (to 6–8 ft. in 10 years). Dense, upright form. Leaves to 3 in. long, ¼ in. wide. One of the very best container plants for outdoor or indoor use, and fine shrub generally.

P. nagi. Tree. Zones 8, 9, 14–24. Slow growth to 15–20 ft. (80–90 ft. in its native Japan). Branchlets drooping, sometimes to a considerable length. Leaves 1–3 in. long, ½–1½ in. wide, leathery, smooth, sharp pointed. Takes considerable shade or sun, indoors or out. More treelike in youth than other species. Makes decorative foliage pattern against natural wood or masonry. Plant in groves for slender sapling effect. Excellent container plant.

P. nivalis. ALPINE TOTARA. Shrub. Zones 4–9, 14–17. Broad, low, spreading plant, eventually 2–3 ft. tall and 6–10 ft. wide. The dark olive green needles, ¼–¾ in. long, densely clothe branches. Resembles yew (*Taxus*). Attractive ground cover or large rock garden shrub.

P. totara. TOTARA. Tree. Zones 8, 9, 14–24. Reaches 100 ft. in New Zealand; likely to reach 25–30 ft. in gardens. Dense, rather narrow, with leathery, stiff, pointed, gray green leaves to 1 in. long. General appearance like that of yew (*Taxus*).

PODRANEA ricasoliana. *Bignoniaceae.* PINK TRUMPET VINE. Zones 9, 12, 13, 19–24. Twining evergreen vine to 20 ft. May drop leaves in frost, but can recover from root even if tops are frozen. Dark green leaves divided featherwise into 3 or 4 pairs of 2-in. leaflets. Open trumpet-shaped, 2–3-in.-wide summer flowers, pink veined red, in loose clusters at ends of new growth. Slow grower when young, speeding up as it matures. Likes heat, good drainage.

Podranea ricasoliana

POHUTUKAWA. See *Metrosideros excelsus.*

POINCIANA. See *Caesalpinia.*

POINSETTIA. See *Euphorbia pulcherrima.*

POISON OAK. See *Rhus diversiloba.*

POKER PLANT. See *Kniphofia uvaria.*

Polemoniaceae. The phlox family consists mostly of annuals and perennials, including many Western wildflowers (*Gilia, Ipomopsis, Phlox*). One shrubby representative is *Cantua; Cobaea* is a vine.

POLEMONIUM. *Polemoniaceae.* Perennials. Zones 1–11, 14–17. Plants for shaded or half-shaded borders or under trees. Lush rosettes of finely divided, fernlike foliage; clusters of bell-shaped flowers in summer. Combine with bleeding heart, campanulas, ferns, hellebores, hosta, and lilies. Cool, moist conditions; good drainage. Grow from seed, or divide after flowering or in spring. Many species are choice wildflowers from western mountains. Following are the 2 generally available in nurseries.

Polemonium caeruleum

P. caeruleum. JACOB'S LADDER. Clusters of lavender blue, pendulous, 1-in.-long flowers on leafy, 1½–2-ft.-high stems.

P. reptans. Best known is its variety 'Blue Pearl', a dwarf, spreading plant 9 in. tall. Profuse display of blue flowers in April and May. Good in shaded, dampish rock garden.

POLIANTHES tuberosa. *Agavaceae.* TUBEROSE. Tuber. Garden plant in Zone 24; elsewhere planted in containers, moved outdoors after frosts. Native to Mexico. Noted for powerful, heady fragrance. Flowers white, tubular, loosely arranged in spikelike clusters on stems to 3 ft., summer–fall. Basal leaves long, narrow, grasslike. Single forms are graceful, but double variety 'The Pearl' is best known and most widely available.

Polianthes tuberosa

Long, slender, bulblike tubers always show a point of green if alive and healthy. Start indoors like tuberous begonias or plant outside after soil is warm. Plant 2 in. deep, 4–6 in. apart. Needs steady heat, sun or part shade. Water after leaves appear and heavily through growth season. Feed with acid-type fertilizer if soil or water is alkaline. Dry out when leaves yellow in fall; dig and store in a warm place. Or plant 3 tubers in 6-in. pot and treat as above. Tubers will bloom year after year; divide clumps every 4 years.

POLYANTHUS. See *Primula polyantha.*

POLYGALA. *Polygalaceae.* Evergreen shrub, shrublet. Flowers irregular, with slight resemblance to sweet peas. Average water.

P. chamaebuxus. Shrublet. Zones 4–6. To 6–8 in. tall, spreading slowly by underground stems. Leaves dark green, 1–1½ in. long, shaped like those of boxwood. Flowers (April–May, and sporadically throughout year) creamy white or yellow and white, sometimes marked with red. *P. c. grandiflora* has flowers of rosy purple and yellow. Sun or filtered shade. Rock gardens.

P. dalmaisiana. SWEET-PEA SHRUB. Shrub. Zones 8, 9, 12–24. To 5 ft. tall, with spreading habit; usually bare at base. Leaves to 1 in. long. Useful for continuous production of purplish pink, odd-shaped flowers. Sun or light shade. Color is hard to handle; use it with whites or blues, preferably with low, bushy plants which conceal its legginess. May be sheared frequently to promote more compact, bushy growth. Good temporary filler.

Polygala dalmaisiana

Polygonaceae. The buckwheat family consists of annuals, perennials, shrubs, trees, and vines. Flowers lack petals, but sepals are often showy. Stems are jointed. Fruit is small, dry, single seeded. *Eriogonum* is the best-known western representative. Other family members include rhubarb (*Rheum*), *Polygonum*, and *Antigonon.* (True buckwheat—the pancake flour kind—is *Fagopyrum*, a crop plant of no ornamental value.)

POLYGONATUM. *Liliaceae.* SOLOMON'S SEAL. Perennials. Zones 1–7, 15–17. Arching, leafy stems grow from slowly spreading underground rhizomes. Greenish white, bell-shaped blossoms hang down beneath bright green leaves in spring. Plants disappear over winter. Attractive for form and flowers in woodland garden with ferns, hosta, wild

Polygonatum biflorum

ginger. Need loose, woodsy soil, shade, ample water. Attractive in containers. (For the western native FALSE SOLOMON'S SEAL, see *Smilacina.*)

P. biflorum. Stems to 3 ft.; 1–3¾-in. flowers in clusters beneath 4-in. leaves.

P. commutatum. Stems possibly to 6 ft. Leaves to 7 in. long; 2–10 flowers to a cluster.

P. odoratum *(P. japonicum).* To 3½ ft. tall, with 2-flowered clusters beneath 4–6-in. leaves. 'Variegatum' has leaves edged white.

POLYGONUM. *Polygonaceae.* KNOTWEED Evergreen and deciduous perennials and vines. Sturdy, sun-loving plants with jointed stems and small white or pink flowers in open sprays. Some kinds tend to get out of hand and need control.

Polygonum cuspidatum compactum

P. affine. Evergreen perennial. Zones 4–9, 14–17. Tufted plant 1–1½ ft. tall. Leaves mostly basal, 2–4½ in. long, finely toothed, deep green turning to bronze in winter. Bright rose red flowers in dense, erect, 2–3-in.-long spikes, August–October. Informal border or ground cover. Sun or shade, average soil, ample water.

P. aubertii. SILVER LACE VINE. Deciduous in Zones 1–7, 10–12; evergreen in Zones 8, 9, 13–24. Rapid growing; can cover 100 sq. ft. in a season. Leaves heart shaped, glossy, wavy edged, 1½–2½ in. long. Flowers creamy white, small, in frothy mass from late spring to fall. Use as fast-growing screen on fences or arbors, on hillsides, at seashore. Water deeply once a month. You can prune severely (to ground) each year; bloom will be delayed until August. Sun, average soil.

P. baldschuanicum. BOKHARA FLEECEFLOWER. Deciduous vine. All Zones. Much like *P. aubertii* in appearance, growth, vigor, and uses. Flowers are pink, fragrant, and somewhat larger, and grow in large, drooping clusters.

P. capitatum. Evergreen perennial. Zones 8, 9, 12–24. Rugged, tough, trailing ground cover to 6 in. high, spreading to 20 in. Leaves 1½ in. long; new leaves dark green, old leaves tinged pink. Stems and flowers (in small, round heads) also pink. Blooms most of year. Leaves discolor and die below 28°F. Good ground cover for waste places or in confined areas where invasive roots can be held in check. Sun or shade—will even grow under pines. Best with regular water but will endure drought. Seeds freely and can be grown as an annual where winters are cold.

P. cuspidatum. JAPANESE KNOTWEED. Deciduous perennial. All Zones. Tough, vigorous plant forming large clumps of red brown, wiry, 4–8-ft. stems. Leaves nearly heart shaped, to 5 in. long. Greenish white blooms in late summer and fall. Extremely invasive; keep away from choice plants. Useful in untamed parts of garden. Prefers ample water but may survive without irrigation in heavy soils. Cut to ground in late fall or winter. Often called bamboo or Mexican bamboo because of jointed stalks. *P. sachalinense* is even bigger (to 12 ft.) and more aggressive.

P. c. compactum *(P. reynoutria).* Fast-growing ground cover 10–24 in. high with creeping roots. Can become a nuisance near choice plants. Stiff, wiry red stems. Pale green leaves, 3–6 in. long, heart shaped and red veined, turn red in fall. Plants die to ground in winter. Blooms in late summer: dense, showy clusters of small, pale pink flowers opening from red buds. Ground cover for sunny, dry banks, fringe areas of garden. Controls erosion on hillsides.

P. vacciniifolium. Evergreen perennial. Zones 4–7. Prostrate, with slender, leafy, branching stems radiating 2–4 ft. Leaves ½ in. long, oval and shining, turning red in fall. Rose pink late summer flowers in dense, upright, 2–3-in. spikes on 6–9-in. stalks. Excellent bank cover or drapery for boulder in large rock garden. Needs ample summer water. Increase by cuttings.

Polypodiaceae. The polypody family contains by far the majority of ferns. They differ from other ferns only in technical details concerning spore-bearing bodies (*sporangia*).

POLYPODIUM. *Polypodiaceae.* Ferns. Widespread, variable group, some native to West.

Polypodium aureum 'Mandaianum'

P. aureum. HARE'S FOOT FERN. Zones 15–17, 19–24; house plant anywhere. From tropical America. Needs shade and regular heavy watering. Big fern for hanging basket culture. Heavy brown creeping rhizomes, coarse blue green fronds 3–5 ft. long. Fronds drop after frost, but plants recover fast. *P. a.* 'Mandaianum', sometimes called LETTUCE FERN, has frilled and wavy frond edges. Both lettuce fern and the species make showy display plants.

P. coronans. See *Aglaomorpha coronans.*

P. glycyrrhiza *(P. vulgare occidentale).* LICORICE FERN. Zones 4–6, 14–24. Native to coastal strip from Alaska to California. Forms mats with creeping rhizomes. Once-cut fronds resemble smaller (to 1½-ft.) sword ferns. *P. hesperium (P. vulgare columbianum),* which grows from Pacific Coast into Rocky Mountains, is smaller (to 10 in.). In the wilds, these ferns tend to grow on rocks or dead logs; in the garden, give them leaf mold or other organic material and shade (except right on the coast). They grow best with summer water but can survive without it.

P. heracleum. See *Aglaomorpha heracleum.*

P. scouleri. LEATHERY POLYPODY. Zones 4–6, 15–17. Native along seacoast from British Columbia to California. Thick, glossy fronds are once-cut, may reach 1½ ft. long and 6 in. across at base. Often grows on trees and rocks, spreading slightly by short rhizomes. In the ground, it tends to form clumps. Good for woodland gardens, naturalizing. Culture as for *P. glycyrrhiza.*

P. subauriculatum 'Knightiae'. KNIGHT'S POLYPODY. Zone 24; greenhouse and house plant everywhere. Long (to 3 ft. or more and 1 ft. wide), once-cut fronds with fringed edges droop gracefully.

Makes spectacular hanging container specimen when well grown—like a magnified Boston fern. Plants grown outdoors shed old fronds in spring, quickly produce new ones. Needs shade, routine house plant watering.

POLYSCIAS. *Araliaceae.* Evergreen shrubs (small trees in tropics) used as house plants. Like many other aralia relatives, they are grown for their handsomely divided leaves; flowers are unimportant and seldom produced outside tropics. As house plants they grow slowly, maintaining their shapeliness for many years. They are considered fussy, needing fresh air but no drafts, good light but not direct, strong sunlight, and just enough water. Plants that fail usually do so because of overwatering or mite damage. Misting is useful, along with light feeding; if plant is doing well, don't move it. They appreciate warmth and humidity.

Polyscias fruticosa 'Elegans'

P. balfouriana. To 25 ft. tall. Leaves have three 2–4-in., toothed leaflets. Plain green form can grow out of doors in Zones 21–24. 'Marginata', more common than species, has white-edged leaflets. 'Pennockii' has white to pale green leaflets with irregular green spots.

P. fruticosa. MING ARALIA, PARSLEY PANAX. Grows 6–8 ft. tall. Leaves finely divided and redivided into multitude of narrow, toothed segments. 'Elegans' is small-growing, extremely densely foliaged variety.

P. guilfoylei 'Victoriae'. Compact grower with deeply slashed and cut leaflets with white edges.

P

POLYSTICHUM. *Polypodiaceae.* Ferns. Medium-sized, evergreen fronds on hardy symmetrical plants. Among most useful and widely planted ferns in West; they blend well with other plants and are easy to grow.

Polystichum munitum

P. dudleyi. Zones 4–9, 14–24. Native to Coast Ranges of northern California. Resembles *P. munitum* but has broader, shorter, more finely cut fronds. Not always easy to find, but choice. Prefers summer moisture.

P. munitum. SWORD FERN. All Zones. Native from California to Alaska and Montana. Most-seen fern of redwood forests. Leathery, shiny dark green fronds 2–4 ft. long, depending on soil and available moisture. Once-cut fronds with medium coarse texture, long lasting when cut. Old plants may have 75–100 fronds. Good for shady beds, along house walls, as big-scale ground cover, in mixed woodland plantings. Grows best in rich soil with organic matter and ample water.

P. polyblepharum (usually sold as *P. setosum*). JAPANESE LACE FERN, TASSEL FERN. Zones 4–9, 14–24. Handsome, dense, lacy. Resembles *P. setiferum* but is taller, darker green, somewhat coarser; fronds are somewhat more upright (to 2 ft.). Same culture, uses as *P. setiferum*.

P. setiferum. Zones 4–9, 14–24. Low-growing fern with spreading, finely cut fronds, giving effect of dark green lace. Many cultivated varieties. 'Proliferum' makes plantlets on midribs of older fronds; these make for a dense, lacy plant and can be used for propagation. Northwestern specialists offer many fancy varieties as "English ferns." All are splendid in shaded rock gardens or for bedding with tuberous begonias and other shade plants. Regular summer water.

POMEGRANATE. See *Punica granatum.*

POMPON TREE. See *Dais cotinifolia.*

Pontederiaceae. The pickerel weed family contains aquatic or marsh plants with showy, usually blue, flowers, among them *Pontederia* and *Eichhornia.*

PONTEDERIA cordata. *Pontederiaceae.* PICKEREL WEED. Perennial. All Zones. Water plant grown as companion to waterlilies. Roots grow in soil beneath water. Long-stalked leaves stand well above water; these are heart shaped, to 10 in. long and 6 in. wide. Short spikes of bright blue flowers top 4 ft. (or shorter) stems. Best planted in pots of rich soil and sunk in up to 1 ft. of water where leaves will ultimately grow; sun to light shade. Gives wild-pond look to informal garden pool. Dormant in winter.

Pontederia cordata

PONYTAIL. See *Beaucarnea recurvata.*

POOR MAN'S ORCHID. See *Schizanthus pinnatus.*

POOR MAN'S RHODODENDRON. See *Impatiens oliveri.*

POPCORN. See Corn.

POPLAR. See *Populus.*

POPPY. See *Papaver.*

POPPY, HIMALAYAN. See *Meconopsis.*

POPULUS. *Salicaceae.* POPLAR, COTTONWOOD, ASPEN. Deciduous trees. All known for rapid growth. Eminently suitable for country places where fast growth, toughness, and low maintenance are considerations. Although most kinds can grow anywhere in the West, they are grown and appreciated far more in the cold-winter, hot-summer interior regions. Appearance, performance poorer in mild-winter areas and near coast where temperature extremes are minimal. Best with regular deep watering. Some appear to be drought tolerant if roots grow deep enough to tap water table or other underground water. *Do not plant near water lines, sewer lines, or septic tanks or their leach lines.* Roots are invasive—not for city streets, lawns, or small gardens.

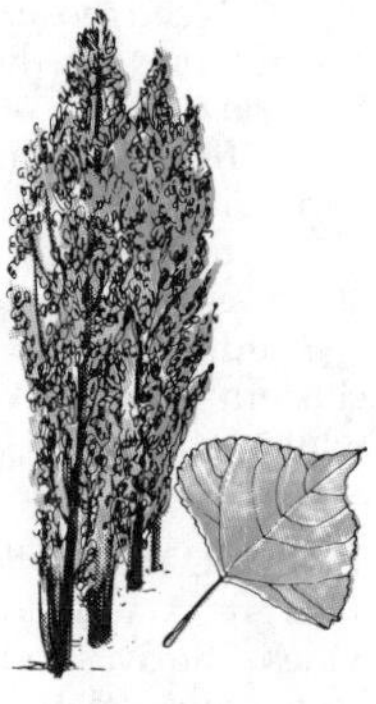

Populus nigra
'Italica'

P. acuminata. LANCELEAF COTTONWOOD. All Zones. Thrives at elevations to 7,500 ft. in Rocky Mountains. To 60 ft. tall, with egg-shaped, sharply pointed leaves to 4 in. long, glossy green above, pale beneath.

P. alba. WHITE POPLAR. All Zones. Fast growth to 40–60 ft., broad and wide spreading. The 5-in.-long leaves, usually with 3–5 lobes, are white and woolly underneath. A "lively" tree, even in light breezes, with flickering white and green highlights. Good tree for desert. Tolerates wide range of soils. Suckers profusely—an advantage if it is planted as windbreak, otherwise a problem.

P. a. 'Pyramidalis' (usually sold as *P. bolleana*). BOLLEANA POPLAR. Narrow, columnar form. Good for country windbreaks or sun screens. Suckers freely; may send up new shoots from roots many feet from main trunk.

P. angustifolia. NARROWLEAF COTTONWOOD. All Zones. Grows at elevations to 8,000 ft. To 60 ft. tall, with narrow leaves 5 in. long, 1½ in. wide.

P. balsamifera *(P. candicans)*. BALM-OF-GILEAD. All Zones. Fast to 30–60 ft., broad topped. Suckers profusely. Triangular leaves 4½–6 in. long, 3–4 in. wide. Two seedless (hence cottonless) selections are 'Idahoensis' ('Idaho Hybrid') and 'Mojave Hybrid', similar fast-growing, large trees. The latter has nearly white bark. The species and its selections all thrive in Zones 11, 12, 13.

P. brandegeei *(P. monticola)*. Zones 12, 13. Desert native tree to 40–60 ft. Resembles *P. fremontii* but has smooth, white bark like quaking aspen. Good to line a long driveway.

P. canadensis. CAROLINA POPLAR. All Zones. Fast growth to 40–150 ft. Triangular, tooth-edged leaves are 4 in. long. Has deservedly bad reputation for invading and breaking sewer lines. *P. c.* 'Eugenei' is somewhat narrower grower. 'Siouxland' is disease-resistant selection.

P. canescens 'Macrophylla'. All Zones. Fast-growing, large tree with exceptionally large leaves (to 9 in. long on vigorous young shoots). Leaves white underneath, bark pale gray on older trees.

P. fremontii. WESTERN or FREMONT COTTONWOOD. Zones 7–24. Fast to 40–60 ft. or more. Thick, glossy yellow green, triangular leaves are 2–4 in. wide, coarsely toothed; turn bright lemon yellow in fall, remain on tree practically all winter in Zones 12, 13. Small greenish yellow flowers in long, slender catkins appear before leaves. Female trees later bear masses of cottony seeds that blow about and become a nuisance; be sure to plant male trees (easily grown from cuttings). Requires little water except in desert, where weekly watering is needed during hot weather if roots haven't tapped underground source. This is the cottonwood of desert waterholes and watercourses.

P. nigra 'Italica'. LOMBARDY POPLAR. All Zones. Fast to 40–100 ft. Beautiful columnar tree with upward-reaching branches. Suckers profusely; invasive roots are a problem. Indispensable to country driveways, valuable both as windbreak and skyline decoration. Bright green, triangular, 4-in.-long leaves turn beautiful golden yellow in fall. Subject to blight of branchlets in many areas. Healthy and attractive in cold, dry, interior climates. *P. n. thevestina* has white bark.

P. tremuloides. QUAKING ASPEN. Zones 1–7. Often tried in warmer areas, where it is usually short lived. Native throughout western mountains. Fast growing to 20–60 ft. Trunk and limbs smooth, pale gray green to whitish. Dainty, light green, round leaves that flutter and quake in slightest air movement. Brilliant golden yellow fall color. Generally performs poorly or grows slowly at low elevations. Needs moist soil. Plants are occasionally offered in nurseries: some are collected, but many are raised from seed or cuttings and are more easily transplanted into gardens. Good background tree for native shrubs and wildflowers. Apt to suffer from sudden dieback or from borers.

P. trichocarpa. BLACK COTTONWOOD. Zones 1–7. Native along mountain streams and wet lowlands west of Cascades, California to Alaska. Tall, spreading tree to 40 ft. in 15 years, 150–180 ft. in age. Heavy limbed, with dark gray, furrowed bark; wood very brittle. Leaves 3–5 in. across, triangular, deep green above and distinctly silver beneath; attractive when ruffled by breeze. Male trees shed quantities of catkins; female trees release myriad cottony seeds if male trees are present.

PORK AND BEANS. See *Sedum rubrotinctum*.

PORT ORFORD CEDAR. See *Chamaecyparis lawsoniana*.

PORTUGAL LAUREL. See *Prunus lusitanica*.

Portulacaceae. The portulaca family contains annuals, perennials, and a few shrubs, usually with succulent foliage and frequently with showy flowers. Examples are *Lewisia, Portulaca,* and *Portulacaria*.

PORTULACA grandiflora. *Portulacaceae.* PORTULACA, ROSE MOSS. Summer annual. Useful warm-weather plants for brilliant color, from early summer until frost. Plants 6 in. high, 1½ ft. across. Leaves fleshy, succulent, cylindrical, pointed, 1 in. long. Trailing, branched reddish stems, also succulent. Flowers roselike, lustrous, in red, cerise, rose pink, orange, yellow, white, pastel shades; single and double strains sold. Flowers open fully only in sun, close in late afternoon. Available as single colors or mixes in either single-flowered or double (Prize Strain, Magic Carpet, Sunglo, Sunkiss) strains. Afternoon Delight and Sundance strains stay open longer in the afternoon than the earlier strains do.

Portulaca grandiflora

Use on hot, dry banks, in parking strips, rock gardens, gravel beds, patio insets, shallow containers, hanging baskets, among succulents, as edgings. Plant in full sun. Any soil; best in sandy loam. Sow seed in place after weather is warm or plant flat-grown plants in late spring. Although drought tolerant, better with occasional watering. Plants self-sow.

P. oleracea. PURSLANE. Essentially a weed with fleshy stems and fleshy leaves, tiny yellow flowers. Warm weather and heavy watering encourage its growth. Control by hoeing or pulling before it goes to seed. Don't allow pulled plants to lie about; they can reroot or ripen seed even if uprooted. If you wish, cook and eat the plants; the French cultivate them as *pourpier,* and people of Mexican extraction gather them as *verdolaga.* In French cultivated variety has yellow green leaves; seed is occasionally offered.

A strain called Wildfire has the broad, plump leaves of the species but displays brightly colored single flowers in red, white, yellow, pink, and orange. Flowers are tiny but profuse. Plants are trailing and can be used in hanging pots. They like sun and heat, average water.

PORTULACARIA afra. *Portulacaceae.* ELEPHANT'S FOOD. Succulent. Outdoors Zones 13, 16, 17, 22–24; outdoors with overhead protection Zones 8, 9, 12, 14, 15, 18–21; house plant anywhere. Native to South Africa. Shrub with thick, juicy stems; to 12 ft. tall and nearly as wide, usually much smaller in pots. Elephant's food looks a bit like jade plant (*Crassula argentea*) and is sometimes sold as "miniature jade plant," but it's faster growing and more loosely branched than jade plant, with more limber, tapering branches and smaller (½-in.-long) leaves. In South Africa, bears tiny pink flowers in clusters; seldom blooms in western U.S.

Portulacaria afra

Small plants are good, easy pot plants; where hardy, can be used as fast-growing informal screen or unclipped hedge, or cut back as high-growing ground cover. Forms with variegated leaves ('Foliis Variegatis' and 'Variegata') are slower growing, smaller than species. Another form has larger, inch-long leaves. All are drought tolerant and fire retardant. Same culture as jade plant; will endure desert sun and heat, which jade plant will not.

POTATO. *Solanaceae.* For ornamental relatives, see *Solanum.* Tuberous-rooted perennial grown as annual. Though not most widely grown of home garden vegetables, potatoes can be most satisfying. Two lbs. of certified seed potatoes (potatoes raised under disease-free conditions) can give you 50 lbs. of potatoes for eating. The many diseases and pests that beleaguer commercial growers are not likely to plague home gardeners. Potatoes need sandy, fast-draining soil; tubers become deformed in heavy, poorly drained soil. Locate in full sun. For early crops, plant in spring as soon as soil can be worked, or in midwinter where frosts are not severe; for fall and winter use, plant from mid-May to mid-June.

Potato

The aboveground potato plant is a sprawling, bushy, dark green plant with much-divided leaves somewhat like a tomato plant's. Clustered inch-wide flowers are pale blue. Round yellow or greenish fruit very rarely seen.

Buy certified (inspected, disease-free) seed potatoes from seed or feed store. Cut potatoes into chunky pieces about 1½ in. square with at least 2 eyes. Place chunks 4 in. deep and 1½ ft. apart. Do not plant if soil is very wet. After top growth appears, give plants an occasional soaking.

Dig early (or new) potatoes when tops begin to flower; dig mature potatoes when tops die down. Dig potatoes carefully to avoid bruises and cuts. Well-matured potatoes free of defects keep best in storage. Store in cool (40°F.), dark place. Where ground doesn't freeze, late potatoes can remain in ground until needed. Dig before spring (or mild winter) temperatures start them into growth again.

Another method of planting is to prepare soil so surface is loose, plant potato eyes ½–1 in. deep, water well, and cover with 1–1½-ft. layer of straw, hay, or dead leaves; surround with fence of chicken wire to keep loose material from blowing away. Potatoes will form on surface of soil or just beneath, need little digging. You can probe with your fingers and harvest potatoes as needed.

POTATO VINE. See *Solanum jasminoides*.

POTENTILLA. *Rosaceae.* CINQUEFOIL. Evergreen and deciduous perennials and shrubs. Hardy plants useful for ground covers and borders. Leaves are bright green or gray green, divided into small leaflets. Small, mostly single, roselike flowers are cream to bright yellow, white or pink to red. Give them full sun (they tolerate part shade in hot-summer areas) and moderate water.

Potentilla fruticosa

(Continued on next page)

P

Evergreen Perennials

P. cinerea. Zones 1–17. Matted stems 2–4 in. high. Leaves divided fanwise into 5 wedge-shaped, gray-hairy leaflets toothed at tip, white and woolly underneath. Flowers are pale yellow, ½ in. wide. Ground cover or rock plants for sun, part shade.

Potentilla fruticosa

P. nepalensis 'Willmottiae' (*P. n.* 'Miss Willmott'). All Zones. Good performance near coast. Grows to 10 in. high, spreads to 1½ ft. Leaves divided fanwise into 5 roundish, 2–3-in.-long, green leaflets. Branching clusters of salmon pink, ½–1-in.-wide flowers. Borders, cut flowers.

P. tabernaemontanii (*P. verna, P. verna* 'Nana'). SPRING CINQUEFOIL. All Zones. Dainty bright green, tufted creeper 2–6 in. high. Leaves divided into 5 leaflets. Butter yellow, ¼-in.-wide flowers, borne in clusters of 3–5, in spring and summer. Stands more moisture than other potentillas. Needs some shade where summers are hot and dry. May turn brown in cold winters. Fast-growing ground cover, bulb cover. Makes good lawn substitute for no-traffic situations. Smothers weeds effectively when well established.

P. tonguei. All Zones. Plant sold under this name is a hybrid between *P. nepalensis* and another species. Plants are evergreen, creeping, with 1-ft.-long stems, leaves with 3–5 leaflets, and ½-in. apricot flowers with red centers. Use in rock garden or foreground of border.

P. warrensii (*P. warrenii,* sometimes sold as *P. warrensii macrantha).* All Zones. Name is properly *P. recta* 'Warrenii'. Grows to 15 in. tall, with leaves of 5–7 leaflets. Flowers 1 in. wide, bright yellow, profuse in May and June. Tolerates a wide range of soils, climates.

Deciduous Shrubby Potentillas

The shrubby potentillas (Zones 1–21) most often sold as named forms of *P. fruticosa,* are native to northern latitudes everywhere, including the Cascade, Olympic, and Rocky mountains. These potentillas all have leaves divided into 3–7 leaflets; some are distinctly green on top, gray beneath, while others look more gray green. In full sun, all bloom cheerfully from June–October despite poor soil, heat, and little water. Best in well-drained soil with moderate water. Cut some of the oldest stems from time to time to make room for new growth.

'Gold Drop' (variety 'Farreri'). To 2 ft. high, 3 ft. wide. Deep yellow, ¾-in.-wide flowers.

'Hollandia Gold'. Deep yellow flowers to 2 in. wide on gray green, 2–3-ft. shrubs.

'Jackman's Variety'. Flowers bright yellow, to 1½ in. wide. Blooms profusely. Shrub to 4 ft. tall, somewhat wider.

'Katherine Dykes'. Can reach 5 feet but usually stays much lower, spreading at least as wide as it is high. Pale yellow, inch-wide flowers.

'Klondike'. Deep yellow, 1½–2-in.-wide flowers on dense-growing, 2-ft. shrub.

'Longacre'. Yellow, inch-wide flowers on bright green, cushiony plants 3 ft. wide, 1 ft. tall.

'Moonlight' ('Maanely's'). Pale yellow to white, 1-in. flowers on 1½-ft. shrubs. Dark blue green, furry foliage.

'Mount Everest'. Pure white, yellow-centered flowers 1½ in. wide on upright, bushy plant to 4½ ft.

'Primrose Beauty'. Consider it a 'Klondike' with pale yellow flowers.

'Red Ace'. Bright red flowers with yellow reverse, 1½ in. wide. Shrub reaches 2 ft. tall by 3–4 ft. wide. Flowers fade to yellow as they age (very quickly in hot-summer climates or under poor growing conditions).

'Snowflake'. Grows 2–4 ft. high. Semidouble white blossoms.

'Sutter's Gold'. Grows 1 ft. high, spreading to 3 ft. Clear yellow flowers an inch wide.

'Tangerine'. Bright yellow orange, 1½-in.-wide flowers on 2½-ft. shrub.

POTERIUM sanguisorba *(Sanguisorba minor).* *Rosaceae.* SMALL BURNET, SALAD BURNET. Perennial herb. All Zones. To 8–12 in. high. Leaves with deeply toothed leaflets grow in rosette close to ground. Unusual thimble-shaped, pinkish white flowers borne on long stems.

Poterium sanguisorba

Grow in sun, poor soil, with adequate moisture, good drainage. Keep blossoms cut. Don't cut plant back more than half. Self-sows almost too freely if flowers are not cut. Also propagated from division of roots (divide each year). Good in containers. Leaves give cucumber aroma to salads, vinegar, cream cheese.

POTHOS aureus. See *Epipremnum aureum.*

POT MARIGOLD. See *Calendula officinalis.*

PRATIA angulata. *Lobeliaceae.* Perennial. Zones 4–9, 12–24. May be killed or badly damaged in coldest Zone 4 winters. New Zealand plant with creeping stems; used as ground cover (no traffic) or rock garden plant. Stems root at joints to form dense, shiny dark green mats. Leaves roundish, ½ in. long, with a few teeth. Flowers oddly shaped, with 2-lobed upper lip and 3-lobed lower lip; white or bluish white, nearly ¾ in. wide, on 2-in. stalks. Likes rich soil and abundant water. Takes full sun in cool climates; needs shade where summer temperatures are high. Thrives even in low desert if growing conditions are right. Plant 6–8 in. apart for fairly fast cover.

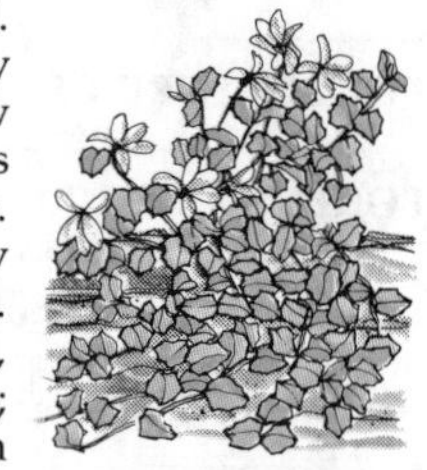

Pratia angulata

PRAYER PLANT. See *Maranta leuconeura.*

PREGNANT ONION. See *Ornithogalum caudatum.*

PRICKLY PEAR. See *Opuntia.*

PRICKLY POPPY. See *Argemone.*

PRIDE OF CALIFORNIA. See *Lathyrus splendens.*

PRIDE OF MADEIRA. See *Echium fastuosum.*

PRIMROSE. See *Primula.*

PRIMROSE TREE. See *Lagunaria patersonii.*

PRIMULA. *Primulaceae.* PRIMROSE. Perennials; a few short-lived perennials treated as annuals. Fanciers reserve the name "primrose" for *Primula vulgaris,* but gardeners generally use "English primrose" to refer to both this plant and polyanthus primroses (*P. polyantha*).

Primula malacoides

Out of some 600 species of primroses, only a few are widely adapted and distributed over the West. Long, hot summers and low humidity are limiting factors. But almost any primrose can be grown to perfection in cool, moist climates of western Oregon and Washington and north coastal California. Most primroses are quite hardy; many thrive

(Continued on page 485)

Primula

NAME	SECTION	ZONES	LEAVES	FLOWERS	REMARKS
Primula acaulis See *P. vulgaris.*					
P. alpicola MOONLIGHT PRIMROSE	Sikkimensis	1–6, 17	Long stalked, wrinkled, forming dense clumps in time.	Sulfur yellow, spreading, bell shaped, in clusters on 20-in. stalk. Summer.	Powerfully fragrant. Flowers sometimes white or purple. Somewhat tender in coldest areas.
P. auricula AURICULA	Auricula	1–6, 17, 22–24 (in shade, preferably in pots)	Evergreen rosettes of broad, leathery leaves, toothed or plain edged, gray green, sometimes with mealy, powdery coating that spots and runs in the rain.	Clusters of yellow, cream, rose, purple, or brownish; white or yellow eye. Fragrant. Early spring.	Three classes: Show Auriculas, usually grown in pots under glass to protect flowers against weather; garden Auriculas, sturdier; and alpine Auriculas. Flowers in shades of white, yellow, orange, pink, red, purple, blue, brownish. Double forms available.
P. beesiana	Candelabra (Proliferae)	1–6, 17	Long leaves taper gradually into leaf stalk. Leaves (including stalks) reach 14 in.	Reddish purple, in 5–7 dense whorls on a 2-ft. flower stem. Mid or late spring.	Somewhat variable in color, but usually reddish purple with yellow eye. Very deep rooted; needs deep watering.
P. bulleyana	Candelabra (Proliferae)	1–6, 15–17	Like *P. beesiana,* but with reddish midribs.	Bright yellow, opening from orange buds. Whorls open in succession over long season in mid and late spring.	Plants disappear in late fall; mark the spot. Older plants can be divided after bloom or in fall. Showy at woodland edge.
P. burmanica	Candelabra (Proliferae)	1–6, 17	Like *P. beesiana,* but broader, longer stalked.	Like *P. beesiana,* but with more densely clustered flowers of deeper purple with yellow eye.	One of best and easiest of Candelabra section.
P. cockburniana	Candelabra (Proliferae)	1–6, 17	Leaves 4–6 in. long, rather few in clump.	Flowers orange scarlet, in 3–5 whorls on 10–14-in. stalks.	Smaller and less vigorous than other Candelabra types. Striking color, most effective when massed.
P. denticulata (often sold as *P. d. cachemiriana* or *P. cachemiriana)*	Denticulata	1–6	Leaves 6–12 in. long, only half grown at flowering time.	Dense, ball-shaped clusters on foot-high, stout stems. Color ranges from blue violet to purple. Very early spring bloom.	Pinkish, lavender, and white varieties are available. Not adapted to warm-winter areas.
P. florindae	Sikkimensis	1–6, 17	Leaves broad, heart shaped, on long stems.	As many as 60 yellow, bell-shaped, nodding flowers top 3-ft. stems in summer. This is the latest-blooming (early July west of the Cascades) and most fragrant primula.	Will grow in a few inches of running water, or in damp, low spot. Plants late to appear in spring. Hybrids have red, orange, or yellow flowers.
P. Inshriach Hybrids	Candelabra	1–6, 17	Typical, lush Candelabra foliage.	Tiered flower clusters in bright and pastel shades of yellow, red, orange, peach, salmon, pink, purple. Midspring to summer.	Easily grown from seed, blooming second year.
P. japonica	Candelabra	1–6, 17	Leaves 6–9 in. long, to 3 in. wide.	Stout stems to 2½ ft. with up to 5 whorls of purple flowers with yellow eyes. May–July. 'Miller's Crimson' is excellent variety.	White and pink varieties are obtainable. One of toughest and hardiest of Candelabras. Needs semishade; lots of water.
P. juliae	Vernales (Julia)	1–6, 17	Smooth, roundish leaves ½–1 in. long rise directly from creeping rootstock.	Flowers ¾–1 in. across, purplish red with yellow eyes, borne singly on 1-in. stems. Bloom in early spring, appearing before or with new leaves.	Makes little flower-covered mats of great beauty.
P. juliae hybrids JULIANA PRIMROSE	Vernales (Vernales-Julia hybrids)	1–6, 17	Tuftlike rosettes of bright green leaves.	Flowers borne singly (cushion type) or in clusters. Very early.	Many named forms in white, blue, yellow, orange red, pink, or purple. Excellent for edging, woodland, rock garden.

(Continued on next page)

P

NAME	SECTION	ZONES	LEAVES	FLOWERS	REMARKS
P. kewensis	Verticillata (Sphondylia)	17; greenhouse, lathhouse, or house plant elsewhere	Leaves 4–8 in. long, coarsely toothed, either deep green or powdered with white.	Borne in whorls on 1½-ft. stems, golden yellow, profuse. Long bloom season in winter, spring; scattered bloom possible any time.	Best as house plant, in lathhouse or greenhouse Zones 15, 16, 18–24. Long-lived with reasonable care. Hybrid between *P. floribunda*, *P. verticillata*.
P. malacoides FAIRY PRIMROSE, BABY PRIMROSE	Malacoides (Monocarpicae)	12–24	Rosettes of soft, pale green, oval, long-stalked leaves 1½–3 in. long. Edges lobed and cut.	Borne in loose, lacy whorls along numerous upright, 12–15 in. stems. White, pink, rose, red, lavender, February–May.	Splendid for winter–spring color in mild-winter areas of California and Arizona. Set out plants in October or November. Use under high-branching trees, with spring bulbs, in containers. Grown as annual; stands light frost. Indoor or cool greenhouse pot plant in cold climates.
P. obconica	Obconica (Obconicolisteri)	15–24	Large, roundish, soft-hairy leaves on long, hairy stems; hairs may irritate skin of some people.	Flowers 1½–2 in. wide in large, broad clusters on stems to 1 ft. tall. Shades of white, pink, lavender, and reddish purple. Nearly everblooming in mild regions.	Perennial, best treated as annual. Use for bedding in shade where winters are mild, as house plant in cold regions.
P. Pagoda Hybrids	Candelabra	1–6, 17	Typical, lush Candelabra foliage.	Tiered clusters of orange, red, yellow, pink, tangerine flowers on 2–3-ft. stems. Late spring through summer.	These are very fine Candelabra hybrids developed near Portland, Oregon.
P. polyantha POLYANTHUS PRIMROSES (often called English primroses; this is a group of hybrids)	Vernales (Primula)	1–10, 12–24	Fresh green leaves in tight clumps.	Flowers 1–2 in. across in large full clusters on stems to 1 ft. high. Almost any color. Blooms from winter to early and midspring. Most adaptable and brilliant of primroses. Usually treated as annuals in desert and other hot-summer areas.	Fine, large-flowered strains are Clarke's, Barnhaven, Pacific, and Santa Barbara. Novelties include Gold Laced, with gold-edged mahogany petals. Miniature Polyanthus have smaller flowers on shorter stalks. All excellent for massing in shade, for planting with bulbs, or in containers.
P. polyneura	Cortusoides	1–6, 17	Leaves long stalked, broad, lobed and toothed, green above, to 4 in. long.	Flower stems 9–18 in. high, with 1, 2, or more whorls of erect rose, purplish, or red flowers with orange yellow eyes. Spring bloom.	Handsome, spreading plant for shade; needs fast drainage, somewhat less water than Candelabra types.
P. prolifera	Candelabra	1–6, 17	Leaves smooth, large, nearly or quite evergreen in mild climates, unlike those of most Candelabra primroses.	5–7 whorls of large, golden yellow flowers in early to midspring. Stalks to 4 ft. tall.	Needs shade, much water. One of the most spectacular and stately for bog, damp woodland, waterside.
P. pulverulenta	Candelabra	1–6, 17	Leaves a foot or more long, deep green, wrinkled.	Flowers red to red purple, purple eyed, in whorls on 3-ft. stems thickly dusted with white meal.	Bartley strain has flowers in pink and salmon range. Also a fine white with orange eye.
P. sieboldii	Cortusoides	1–6, 14–17	Leaves scalloped, toothed, on long, hairy stalks.	Clustered flowers pink, rose, or white, 1–1½ in. across. Stalk 4–8 in. high. Blooms in late spring.	Tolerates more heat and drought than most primroses. Spreads from creeping rootstocks. Often goes dormant in late summer. Easily propagated by cuttings of the rootstock.
P. sikkimensis	Sikkimensis	1–6, 17	Leaves scanty, 3–5 in. long, with short stalks.	Up to 2 dozen yellow, bell shaped, nodding flowers on slender, 20-in.-high stalk. Summer bloom.	Largely supplanted by *P. florindae*, which is taller and somewhat easier to grow.
P. sinensis CHINESE PRIMROSE	Sinenses (Auganthus)	Greenhouse or house plant	Leaves on long stalks, roundish, lobed, toothed, soft, hairy, 2–4 in. long. Hairs irritate skin of some people.	Flowers white, pink, lavender, reddish, coral; 1½ in. or more wide, many in a cluster on 4–8-in. stems. Stellata varieties have star-shaped flowers in whorls.	Tender, scarce. Favorite European pot plant; imported seed available from specialists.

NAME	SECTION	ZONES	LEAVES	FLOWERS	REMARKS
P. veris COWSLIP	Vernales (Primula)	1–6, 17	Leaves similar to those of Polyanthus primroses.	Bright yellow, fragrant flowers ½–1 in. wide in early spring. Stems 4–8 in. high.	Naturalize in wild garden or rock garden. Charming, but not as sturdy as Polyanthus primroses.
P. vialii *(P. littoniana)*	Muscarioides	1–6, 17	Leaves to 8 in. long, 1½–2½ in. wide, hairy, irregularly toothed; disappear in winter.	Flowers violet blue, fragrant, ¼–½ in. across, opening from bright red calyces. Stems erect, 1–2 ft. high. Dense, narrow spikes 3–5 in. long.	Not long lived, but quite easy from seed in cool-winter areas. For collectors. Use in rock gardens.
P. vulgaris *(P. acaulis)* PRIMROSE, ENGLISH PRIMROSE	Vernales (Primula)	1–6, 17	Tufted; leaves much like those of Polyanthus primroses.	Flowers one to a stalk; vigorous garden strains often have 2 or 3 to a stalk. Early spring bloom. White, yellow, red, blue, and shades of bronze, brownish, and wine.	Generally found only in cool, moist climates. Double varieties available. Blues and reds especially desirable. Use in woodland, rock garden, as edging. Nosegay and Biedermeier strains are exceptionally heavy blooming.

east of the Cascades and in the intermountain region.

Specialty nurseries, mainly in the Northwest, offer seeds and plants of many kinds of primroses. Fanciers exchange seeds and plants through primrose societies.

To systematize this large group of plants, specialists have set up sections—groups of species that strongly resemble each other, often hybridize with each other, and usually respond to the same kind of care. Primulas most commonly grown in the West fall into 11 of the 34 primula sections. Following are basic characteristics and requirements of these sections. To learn how to grow a particular species, note which section it belongs to in accompanying chart. (Names of primula sections are now being reviewed by specialists; in the chart, proposed new names are in parentheses.)

Primula polyantha

Accompanying chart does little more than introduce the great primrose group. Enthusiasts will be able to find and grow dozens of other species, some a real challenge to raise to flowering. But primroses in chart are not difficult if you live in the cool, moist primula belt and give plants rich soil, ample water, and shade. Most are splendid companion plants to rhododendrons.

Section Auricula. More than 20 species native to European Alps. Rosettes of thick leaves, often with mealy coating or white margin. Strong, fleshy stems to 8 in. high bear clusters of yellow, cream, purple, rose, or brownish flowers, often fragrant. They grow in full sun in their native habitat, but in most of western U.S. do best in light shade (full sun in coastal areas). Tolerate more sun than polyanthus primroses. Some named varieties show unusual colors and color combinations—green, brown, near-black.

Section Candelabra. Native to and most abundant in meadows, bogs, or open woodland, principally in Himalayan region. Vigorous growing; larger species have semierect leaves. Flowers in whorls, one above another on 2–3-ft. stems. Best in massed plantings. Need rich soil, partial shade, and much water; will take bog conditions.

Section Cortusoides. Called woodland primulas. Spread by underground creeping roots. Leaves long-stalked, oblong and somewhat lobed. Bell-shaped flowers in whorls. After setting seed, plants become dormant and lose their leaves. Extremely hardy; can take somewhat drier conditions than other primroses, but thrive in rich, moist soil with ample humus. Need shade.

Section Denticulata. Native to Himalayan meadows and moist slopes 6,000–14,000 ft. high. These plants winter over as large, scale-covered buds, from which emerge in spring a cluster of leaves and a stout stalk topped with a ball-like cluster of flowers. Grow best where winters are cold; mild days in fall and winter may force blossoms too early.

Section Malacoides. Semihardy primroses from western China, usually treated as annuals. Planted in mild-winter areas in early fall for bloom in winter and early spring. In cold climates, grow in greenhouse. Leaves long stalked, usually lobed. Flowers in whorls.

Section Muscarioides. Short lived, rather difficult, usually treated as biennials. Flowers in this Chinese and Tibetan group are tightly crowded into long clusters resembling miniature red-hot pokers or grape hyacinths. For collectors.

Section Obconica. Semitropical, short-lived primroses from western China. Thick rhizomes; long-stalked, hairy leaves that may irritate skin of some people. Large, showy flower clusters over long period in winter and spring. Good in pots.

Section Sikkimensis. Similar to Candelabra type, but bell-shaped, drooping flowers on long stems are carried in single large cluster, rarely with second, lower whorl. Leaves have distinct stalks. Need abundant water; will take bog conditions.

Section Sinenses. Like Obconica section, includes semitropical, short-lived plants. Best grown indoors in pots, either in greenhouse or cool, bright window.

Section Vernales. Includes familiar species sometimes called English primroses—*P. vulgaris* and *P. polyantha.* Tuftlike rosettes of leaves, with flowers borne singly or in clusters on stiff stems. Grow best in rich soil with lots of humus. Partial shade inland, full sun in coastal fog belt.

Section Verticillata. Densely leafy tufts produce many stems bearing long-tubed yellow flowers. Long lived, with long bloom season. Rather tender plants grown in pots.

New Japanese hybrids sold as late-winter pot plants usually have beautifully colored blooms—but no names on the containers. In the Northwest, treat them as annuals, since most won't make it through even mild frosts. If you want plants that will come back year after year, buy labeled plants so you know exactly what you're getting.

PRINCE'S FEATHER. See *Amaranthus hybridus erythrostachys.*

PRINCESS FLOWER. See *Tibouchina urvilleana.*

P

PRIVET. See *Ligustrum.*

PROSOPIS. *Leguminosae.* MESQUITE. Evergreen or deciduous trees or large shrubs. Zones 10–13 (hardy in other Zones, but rarely planted there). Native to deserts in the Southwest, Mexico, and South America, and among the toughest and most useful trees for the desert. The mesquites hybridize freely; this tendency—and their differing appearance under differing cultural conditions—has made accurate identification of the various kinds difficult.

Prosopis glandulosa torreyana

The following species do have significant differences, although they are similar in many ways. All have dark bark and spreading, picturesque branch canopies that cast light, airy shade. Leaves are composed of many tiny leaflets. Tiny, greenish yellow flowers in catkinlike spikes are followed by flat seed pods 2–6 in. long. Trees may have 1 or many trunks; in poor, rocky soil and without water, they will be shrubby. In deep soil where taproots can go down great distances for water, they can grow rapidly. They tolerate drought, alkaline soil, and lawn watering. Many are spiny when young, but spines usually aren't a problem with older trees.

P. alba. ARGENTINE MESQUITE. Trees sold under this name are vigorous and fast growing, with erect single trunks and rather dense canopies of blue green leaves. They are nearly evergreen, shedding old leaves as new ones appear in spring.

P. chilensis. CHILEAN MESQUITE. Two trees are sold under this name. The commonly sold type (probably a hybrid) is deciduous, with deep green foliage and a spreading crown of branches. The true species from Chile, also vigorous, has a more open foliage mass than the hybrid; it is evergreen in mild winters, deciduous in cold-winter areas.

P. glandulosa. HONEY or TEXAS MESQUITE. Deciduous tree with spreading habit, often with multiple trunks. Bright green leaves and drooping branchlets give it something of the look of California pepper tree (*Schinus molle*). *P. velutina (P. g. velutina)*, ARIZONA MESQUITE, is a smaller, shrubbier tree that is common in Arizona. *P. g. torreyana* ranges westward to California.

PROSTANTHERA rotundifolia. *Labiatae.* ROUND-LEAFED MINT BUSH. Evergreen shrub. Zones 8, 9, 14–24. Dense, rounded growth to 4–10 ft. Tiny, roundish leaves to ⅓ in. long are mint scented, dark green above, paler beneath. Short clusters of blue purple, trumpet-shaped flowers to ½ in. long bloom profusely in April–May. Takes sun or light shade, tolerates some drought.

Prostanthera rotundifolia

PROTEA. *Proteaceae.* Evergreen shrubs. Zones 16, 17, 21–24. Beautiful flowering plants from South Africa. Tubular flowers in large, tight clusters are surrounded by brightly colored bracts; effect is that of large, very colorful artichoke or thistle. Superb cut flowers, they hold their color for weeks and retain their shape even after fading.

Protea cynaroides

Difficult to grow; definitely not for beginners. They need perfect drainage (preferably on slopes), protection from dry winds, good air circulation, full sun. Give moderate summer water until plants are established; thereafter, water only every 2–4 weeks. Most need acid soil; some accept alkaline soil. Smaller species will grow in containers. Young plants tender to cold; older plants of most species hardy to 25°–27°F. They bloom in 3–4 years from seed, but are not long-lived plants. Fertilize lightly with nitrogen; avoid fertilizers with phosphorus (plants will glut themselves, then die of the overdose). Small applications of iron can remedy chlorosis.

Some 150 species grow in South Africa. These 2 seem to do best here:

P. cynaroides. KING PROTEA. To 3–5 ft. tall with open, spreading habit. Leaves oval, leathery. Flower heads to 11–12 in. across. Bracts pale pink to crimson, flowers white (midsummer to winter, early spring). Needs regular watering throughout year. Can be grown in tubs.

P. neriifolia. To 10 ft., 6–8 ft. wide. Leaves narrow, shaped like oleander leaves. Flower heads (autumn, winter) 5 in. long, 3 in. wide. Bracts pink to salmon, with black, furry tips. Will take temperatures as low as 17°F. and grow in alkaline soil.

Proteaceae. The protea family of evergreen shrubs and trees is characterized by leathery leaves and irregular, somewhat tubular flowers in spikelike clusters or heads often surrounded by showy colored bracts. Many are attractive (*Grevillea, Protea*); one has edible nuts (*Macadamia*).

PROVENCE BROOM. See *Cytisus purgans.*

PRUNE. See Plum and Prune.

PRUNUS. *Rosaceae.* Deciduous and evergreen trees and shrubs. Fruit trees that belong to *Prunus* are better known as "stone fruits" and are described individually elsewhere in this encyclopedia under their common names; see Almond, Apricot, Cherry, Peach and Nectarine, Plum and Prune.

Prunus cerasifera

Take away the fruit trees and you have left the ornamentals, of which there are 2 classes: (1) evergreens, used chiefly as structure plants (hedges, screens, shade trees, street trees); and (2) deciduous flowering fruit trees (and shrubs) closely related to fruit trees mentioned above and valued for their springtime flower display as well as for attractive shape and for form and texture of foliage.

Following, in alphabetical order, are descriptions of evergreen forms. After that comes alphabetical listing of the flowering kinds, with certain ones charted.

Evergreen Forms

P. caroliniana. CAROLINA LAUREL CHERRY. Evergreen shrub or tree. Zones 7–24. Native North Carolina to Texas. As upright shrub, it can be well branched from ground up and useful as formal, clipped hedge or tall screen to 20 ft. Can be sheared into formal shapes. Trained as tree, will become broad topped and reach 35–40 ft. Attractive trained as multistemmed tree. Densely foliaged with glossy green, smooth-edged, 2–4-in.-long leaves. Small, creamy white flowers in 1-in. spikes, February–April. Fruit black, ½ in. or less in diameter. Denser, shorter varieties are 'Bright 'n Tight' and 'Compacta'.

Litter from flowers and fruit is problem when tree is planted over paved areas. Appearance best in coastal areas. Often shows salt burn and chlorosis in alkaline soils but does withstand desert heat and wind. Give it average soil, full sun; prune to shape. Once established, it's quite drought tolerant.

P. ilicifolia. HOLLYLEAF CHERRY. Evergreen shrub or small tree. Zones 7–9, 12–24. Native to Coast Ranges and Baja California. Grows at moderate rate to 20–30 ft., usually broader than high. Mature leaves deep, rich green, 1–2 in. long; resemble holly leaves. Light green new leaves (March–May) contrast pleasantly with dark older foliage. Often, leaf color and size vary from plant to plant. Creamy white, ½-in.-wide flowers in 3–6-in.-long spikes appear with new leaves in March. Round fruit, ½–¾ in. wide, turns from green to red, then reddish purple (never as dark or black as fruit of Catalina cherry, *P. lyonii*). Hybrids between hollyleaf and Catalina cherry appear frequently when plants are grown from seeds collected where both grow. Fruits of all these are edible, although the flesh is thin and the pit large.

Hollyleaf cherry can be grown in almost any soil but does best in coarse, well-drained types. May be attacked by whiteflies in moist, shady situations. For control, see pages 101–102. Performs best in sun but will take light shade. Once established, it will require no irrigation in normal rainfall years. Growth rate and appearance are improved by deep but infrequent watering. When buying plants, avoid large, rootbound plants. Gallon-can-size plant, properly grown (no coiled roots), will generally outgrow larger plant in 5-gallon can. Use as small tree, tall screen, or formal clipped hedge of any height from 3–10 ft. (space plants 1–1½ ft. apart, train as described under *Pittosporum eugenioides*). Has unusually high resistance to oak root fungus, like *P. lyonii*. Very large, old trees resemble California live oak (*Quercus agrifolia*).

P. laurocerasus. ENGLISH LAUREL. Evergreen large shrub or small tree. Zones 4–9, 14–24; best performance in Zones 4–6, 15–17. Hardy to 5°F.; varieties listed below hardier. Native from southeastern Europe to Iran. Generally seen as clipped hedge. As tree, fast growing to 30 ft. tall and as wide. Leaves leathery, glossy dark green, 3–7 in. long, 1½–2 in. wide. Creamy white flowers in 3–5-in.-long spikes in summer; often hidden by leaves. Small black fruit in late summer and fall. No special soil requirements. Where adapted, it's a fast-growing, greedy plant that's difficult to garden under or around. Generous watering and fertilizing will speed growth and keep treetop dense. Grows best in part shade in hot-summer areas. Full sun elsewhere. Few pests. May be troubled occasionally by scale (see page 100 for control). Fungus may cause reddish brown spots on leaves. Use combination fungicide-insecticide-miticide to prevent further damage.

Prunus laurocerasus 'Zabeliana'

Stands heavy shearing, but at expense of considerable mutilation of leaves; best pruned not by shearing but 1 cut at a time, cutting overlong twigs just above a leaf. Maintenance of hedge is problem because of fast growth. Best used as tree or tall unclipped screen. Three dwarf forms of *P. laurocerasus* are sold: 'Mt. Vernon', 'Nana', and 'Otto Luyken'. All have leaf size reduced to match their 4–6-ft. (or less) height and spread.

P. l. 'Schipkaensis'. SCHIPKA LAUREL. Zones 2–9, 14–17. Smaller plant than species, with narrow leaves 2–4½ in. long.

P. l. 'Zabeliana'. ZABEL LAUREL. Zones 3–9, 14–21. This narrow-leafed variety has branches which angle upward and outward from base. Eventually reaches 6 ft., with equal or greater spread. More tolerant of full sun than English laurel. Use as low screen, divider, or big foundation plant. With branches pegged down, it makes an effective bank cover. Can be espaliered. If it is planted in narrow strip between house and walk, half the branches will lie on ground and rest will fan up the wall.

P. lusitanica. PORTUGAL LAUREL. Evergreen shrub or tree. Zones 4–9, 14–24. Native to Portugal and Spain. Slower growing than English laurel. Becomes densely branched large shrub 10–20 ft. high or multitrunked spreading tree to 30 ft. or more; trained to single trunk, it is used as formal street tree. Dense-branching habit and attractive dark green foliage make it useful background plant. Glossy dark green leaves to 5 in. long. Small, creamy white flowers in 5–10-in. spikes extend beyond leaves in spring and early summer, followed by long clusters of bright red to dark purple, ⅓-in. fruit. Takes heat, sun, and wind better than English laurel. Reasonably drought tolerant.

P. l. azorica. Native to Azores and Canary Islands, where it grows 60–70 ft. high. In the West, it grows into gigantic columnar bush 20 ft. high and 10 ft. wide. Exceptionally dark green and glossy foliage.

P. lyonii *(P. integrifolia, P. ilicifolia integrifolia).* CATALINA CHERRY. Evergreen shrub or tree. Zones 7–9, 12–24. Native to Channel Islands off southern California. Seen as broad, dense shrub in hedges and screens, clipped and informal. Trained as tree, it will reach 45 ft. tall, over 30 ft. broad, with trunk 6–8 in. in diameter. Leaves 3–5 in. long, dark green, smooth margined or faintly toothed. (Leaves of young plants are more definitely toothed and usually are similar to those of hollyleaf cherry.) Creamy white flowers in clusters 4–6 in. long are borne in profusion in April and May. Black, large-stoned, ¾–1-in. cherries ripen August–September; fruit is sweet but insipid.

When Catalina cherry is used as patio tree or street tree over sidewalks, fallen fruit is objectionable. Best planted in full sun. Quite drought tolerant; may be short lived in heavy soil with regular garden watering. Seldom troubled with diseases, insects, or mites. May be attacked by whiteflies; for control, see pages 101–102. Valuable as tall screen or hedge. Prune to hold to any height desired. Rates high in resistance to oak root fungus.

Flowering Fruit Trees and Shrubs

Flowering Cherry. The several species and many varieties commonly called flowering cherries are described in the chart on page 488. They perform best in Zones 4–6, 15–17. Cold hardy enough for Zones 2 and 3, they suffer severe damage where winters are dry, sunny, and windy. Cultural needs of all varieties are identical. They require full sun and fast-draining, well-aerated soil; if your soil is heavy clay, plant in raised beds. Somewhat drought tolerant but best with moderate summer water. Prune as little as possible. Cut while tree is in bloom and use branches in arrangements. Remove awkward or crossing branches. Pinch back the occasional overly ambitious shoot to force branching.

Pests and diseases are not usually a problem, though infestations of tadpole-shaped slugs and yellowish to greenish caterpillars may skeletonize leaves unless trees are sprayed with insecticide. Plants in heavy soil are sometimes subject to root rot (for which there is no cure) during winter. Affected tree usually will bloom, then send out new leaves which suddenly collapse.

Use flowering cherries as their growth habit indicates. All are good trees to garden under. Large, spreading kinds make good shade trees. Smaller cherries are almost a necessity in Oriental gardens.

Flowering Nectarine. There is one important flowering nectarine: 'Alma Stultz'. It grows quickly to 20 ft. and as wide as high; in early spring, it is covered with deliciously fragrant, 2–2½-in.-wide, waxy-petaled flowers that look somewhat like azalea blossoms. They are rosy white shaded pink; color deepens with age. White-fleshed fruit is sparsely produced. Plant appearance, cultural needs same as peach.

Flowering Peach. Flowering peach is identical to fruiting peach in growth habit and height. But it's more widely adapted than fruiting peach—flowering peach can be grown in Zones 2–24. However, trees may be caught by late frosts in Zones 2, 10, and 11, and suffer from delayed foliation in 13, 23, 24. Heavy pruning necessary for good show of flowers. Cut branches back to 6-in. stubs at flowering time. Multibranched new growth will be luxuriant by summer's end and will flower profusely the following spring. Cultural requirements, insect and disease control are same as for fruiting peaches. Use flowering peaches as giant seasonal bouquets. Place them where they will give maximum effect when in bloom and where they will be fairly unobtrusive out of bloom—behind evergreen shrubs, fence or wall.

Some peach varieties produce showy blossoms and good fruit. These are described under Peach and Nectarine. The following varieties are strictly "flowering" in the sense that their blooms are showy and their fruit is either absent or worthless. Early-flowering varieties are best choices for regions where spring comes early and is hot.

'Early Double Pink'. Very early.

(Continued on page 489)

P

Flowering Cherry

NAME	ZONES	FORM	HEIGHT & SPREAD	FLOWERS & SEASON
Prunus 'Accolade'	2–9, 14–17	Small tree with spreading branches, twiggy growth pattern. Very vigorous.	To 20 ft. or more, equally wide.	Semidouble, pink, 1½ in. wide, in large drooping clusters. Early. Hybrid between *P. sargentii* and *P. subhirtella*.
P. campanulata TAIWAN FLOWERING CHERRY	7–9, 14–23	Graceful, densely branched, bushy, upright, slender small tree. Performs well in California climates where other flowering cherries fail.	To 20–25 ft.; not as wide as high.	Single, bell shaped, drooping, in clusters of 2–5. Strong positive color—electric rose, almost neon purple pink. Blooms early, along with flowering peach.
P. 'Okame'	4–9, 14–23	Upright, oval. Hybrid between *P. campanulata* and *P. incisa*.	To 25 ft. tall, 20 ft. wide.	Early single pink flowers. Dark green, fine-textured foliage. Yellow orange to orange red fall color.
P. sargentii SARGENT CHERRY	1–7, 14–17	Upright, spreading branches form rounded crown. Orange red fall foliage.	To 40–50 ft. or more; not as wide as high.	Single blush pink flowers in clusters of 2–4. Midseason. 'Columnaris' is more narrow and erect than typical *P. sargentii*.
P. serrula BIRCH BARK CHERRY	1–7, 14–16	Valued for beauty of its bark—glossy mahogany red color.	To 30 ft. and as wide.	Small white flowers are almost hidden by new leaves. Midseason.
P. serrulata JAPANESE FLOWERING CHERRY	2–7, 14–20	The species is known through its many cultivated varieties. Best of these are listed below.		
P. s. 'Amanogawa'		Columnar tree. Use as you would small Lombardy poplar.	To 20–25 ft. tall, 8 ft. wide.	Semidouble, light pink with deep pink margins. Early midseason.
P. s. 'Beni Hoshi' ('Pink Star')		Fast grower with arching, spreading branches. Umbrella shaped in outline.	To 20–25 ft. high and as wide.	Vivid pink single flowers with long, slightly twisted petals hang below branches. Midseason.
P. s. 'Kwanzan' ('Kanzan', 'Sekiyama')		Branches stiffly upright, form inverted cone.	To 30 ft. high, 20 ft. wide.	Large, double. Deep rosy pink in pendant clusters displayed before or with red young leaves. Midseason.
P. s. 'Shirofugen'		Wide horizontal branching.	To 25 ft. and as wide.	Double, long stalked, pink, fading to white. Latest to bloom.
P. s. 'Shirotae' ('Mt. Fuji')		Strong horizontal branching.	To 20 ft.; wider than high.	Semidouble, pink in bud, white when fully open, purplish pink as flower ages. Early.
P. s. 'Shogetsu'		Spreading growth, arching branches.	To 15 ft.; wider than high.	Semidouble and very double, pale pink, often with white centers. Late.
P. s. 'Tai Haku'	2–7, 14–20	Vigorous, with rounded crown. Good orange fall color.	To 20–25 ft., equally wide.	Largest blooms of any flowering cherry: pure white, 2½ in. wide, appearing with bronze new foliage.
P. subhirtella 'Autumnalis'	2–7, 14–20	Loose branching, bushy with flattened crown.	To 25–30 ft. and as wide.	Double, white or pinkish white in autumn as well as early spring. Often blooms in warm spells in January and February.
P. s. 'Pendula' SINGLE WEEPING CHERRY		Usually sold grafted at 5–6 ft. high on upright-growing understock. Graceful branches hang down, often to ground.	Slow to 10–12 ft. and as wide.	Single small pale pink blossoms in profusion. Midseason.
P. s. 'Rosea' (usually sold as *P. s.* 'Whitcombii')		Wide-spreading, horizontal branching.	To 20–25 ft., spreading to 30 ft.	Buds almost red, opening to pink single flowers. Profuse, very early bloom. Northwest favorite.
P. s. 'Yae-shidare-higan' DOUBLE WEEPING CHERRY		Same as *P. s.* 'Pendula'.	Same as *P. s.* 'Pendula'.	Double rose pink. Midseason.
P. yedoensis YOSHINO FLOWERING CHERRY	2–7, 14–20	Curving branches; graceful, open pattern.	Fast to 40 ft., with 30-ft. width.	Single, light pink to nearly white, fragrant. Early.
P. y. 'Akebono' (sometimes called 'Daybreak')		Variety is smaller than species.	To 25 ft. and as wide.	Flowers pinker than those of *P. yedoensis*.

'Early Double Red'. Deep purplish red or rose red. Very early and brilliant, but color likely to clash with other pinks or red.

'Early Double White'. Blooms with 'Early Double Pink'.

'Helen Borchers'. Clear pink, 2½-in.-wide flowers. Late.

'Icicle'. Double white flowers. Late.

'Late Double Red'. Later by 3–4 weeks than 'Early Double Red'.

'Peppermint Stick'. Flowers striped red and white; may also bear all-white and all-red flowers on same branch. Midseason.

'Weeping Double Pink'. Smaller than other flowering peaches, with weeping branches. Requires careful staking and tying to develop main stem of suitable height. Midseason.

'Weeping Double Red'. Similar to above, but with deep rose red flowers. Midseason.

'Weeping Double White'. White version of weeping forms listed above.

Flowering Plum. The many species and varieties of flowering plums are grouped in chart form below.

Flowering plums will grow in almost any soil. If soil is wet for long periods, plant 6–12 in. above grade level in raised bed. Expect attacks from aphids, slugs, caterpillars, spider mites. Spray with all-purpose fruit tree spray. Check trunk at and just below ground level for peach tree borers. Spray with dursban (see Peach and Nectarine).

One of the most adaptable and choicest medium-sized flowering trees for lawn, patio, terrace, or small street tree is *P. blireiana*. It also does well in planters and large tubs. In choosing plum to be planted in paved area, check its fruiting habits. When a flowering plum is planted in a patio, prune to establish head at height to walk under. As tree develops, prune out crossing and inward-growing branches.

P. besseyi. WESTERN SAND CHERRY. Deciduous shrub. Zones 1–3, 10. To 3–6 ft. tall. White flowers in spring followed by sweet black cherries nearly ¾ in. in diameter. Used for pies, jams, jellies. Shrubs withstand heat, cold, wind, drought.

P. fruticosa. Like *P. besseyi*, but 2–3 ft. tall, with smaller, red purple fruit.

P. glandulosa. DWARF FLOWERING ALMOND. Deciduous shrub. Zones 1–10, 12, 14–19. Native to Japan, China. Much branched, upright, spreading growth to 6 ft. tall. Leaves light green, narrow and pointed, to 4 in. long. Flowers, set close to slender branches, appear early, before leaves, and turn branches into long wands of blossoms. Species (seldom seen in gardens) has single pink or white flowers only ½ in. wide. Flowers of commonly available varieties are double, 1–1¼ in. across, resembling light fluffy pompon chrysanthemums. Variety 'Alboplena' has double white flowers; 'Sinensis' has double pink flowers. Prune back hard either just after blooming or when in bloom, using cut wands for arrangements. Can be used as flowering hedge.

P. maackii. AMUR CHOKECHERRY. Deciduous tree. Zones 1–3, 10. Native to Manchuria and Siberia; extremely hardy to cold and

Flowering Plum

NAME	ZONE	GROWTH HABIT	LEAF, FLOWER, FRUIT
Prunus americana WILD PLUM, GOOSE PLUM	1–3, 10	Thicket-forming shrub or small tree to 15–20 ft. Extremely tough and hardy.	Dark green foliage follows profusion of 1-in. clustered white flowers. Fruit yellow to red, to 1 in., sour but good for jelly.
P. blireiana Hybrid between *P. cerasifera* 'Atropurpurea' and *P. mume* (page 490).	2–12, 14–22	Graceful, to 25 ft. high, 20 ft. wide. Long, slender branches.	Leaves reddish purple, turning greenish bronze in summer. Flowers double, fragrant, pink to rose, February–April. No or very little fruit.
P. cerasifera CHERRY PLUM, MYROBALAN	2–22	Used as rootstock for various stone fruits. Will grow to 30 ft. and as wide.	Leaves dark green. Flowers pure white, ¾–1 in. wide. Small red plums, 1–1¼ in. thick, are sweet but bland. Self-sows freely; some seedlings bear yellow fruit.
P. c. 'Allred'	2–22	Upright, slightly spreading, 20 ft. tall, 12–15 ft. wide.	Red leaves, white flowers. Red, 1¼-in.-wide, tart fruit is good for preserves, jelly.
P. c. 'Atropurpurea' (*P.* 'Pissardii') PURPLE-LEAF PLUM	2–22	Fast growing to 25–30 ft. high, rounded in form.	New leaves copper red, deepening to dark purple, gradually becoming greenish bronze in late summer. White flowers. Sets heavy crop of small red plums.
P. c. 'Hollywood' Hybrid between *P. c.* 'Atropurpurea' and Japanese plum 'Duarte'.	2–22	Upright grower to 30–40 ft., 25 ft. wide.	Leaves dark green above, red beneath. Flowers are light pink to white, February–March. Good-quality red plums 2–2½ in. wide.
P. c. 'Krauter Vesuvius'	2–22	Smaller growing than *P. c.* 'Atropurpurea', to 18 ft. high, 12 ft. wide; upright, branching habit.	Darkest of flowering plums. Leaves purple black, flowers light pink. February–March. No or little fruit.
P. c. 'Mt. St. Helens'	2–22	Upright, spreading, with rounded crown. Fast growth to 20 by 20 ft.	A sport of 'Newport', it grows faster and leafs out earlier; it has richer leaf color and holds it later in summer.
P. c. 'Newport'	2–22	To 25 ft. high, 20 ft. wide.	Purplish red leaves. Single pink flowers. Will bear a little fruit.
P. c. 'Thundercloud'	2–22	More rounded form than *P. c.* 'Atropurpurea'. To 20 ft. high, 20 ft. wide.	Dark coppery leaves. Flowers light pink to white. Sometimes sets good crop of red fruit.
P. cistena DWARF RED-LEAF PLUM	2–12, 14–22	Dainty, multibranched shrub to 6–10 ft. Can be trained as single-stemmed tree; good for planting in small patios.	Purple leaves; white to pinkish flowers in early spring. Blackish purple fruit in July. 'Big Cis', a sport of *P. cistena*, grows to 14 ft. tall, 12 ft. wide. Form is dense, globular. Flowers are pink.

wind. To 25–30 ft. tall. Bark of trunk is yellowish and peeling, like birch bark. Leaves strongly veined, rather narrow and pointed, to 4 in. long. Small white flowers in narrow clusters 2–3 in. long. Fruit is black, ¼ in. across.

P. mume. JAPANESE FLOWERING APRICOT, JAPANESE FLOWERING PLUM. Deciduous tree. Zones 2–9, 12–22. (Blooms may be frosted in Zones 2, 3.) Neither true apricot nor plum. Considered longest lived of flowering fruit trees, it eventually develops into gnarled, picturesque 20-ft. tree. Leaves to 4½ in. long, broadly oval. Flowers are small, profuse, with clean, spicy fragrance. Blooms January–February in mild areas, February–March in cold-winter areas. Fruit is small, inedible. Prune heavily: let tree grow for a year, then prune back all shoots to 6-in. stubs. The next year, cut back half the young growth to 6-in. stubs; cut back other half the following year, and continue routine in succeeding years.

Varieties are:

'Bonita'. Semidouble rose red.

'Dawn'. Large ruffled double pink.

'Peggy Clarke'. Double deep rose flowers with extremely long stamens and red calyces.

'Rosemary Clarke'. Double white flowers with red calyces. Very early.

'W. B. Clarke'. Double pink flowers on weeping plant. Effective large bonsai or container plant, focus of attention in winter garden.

P. padus. EUROPEAN BIRD CHERRY, MAYDAY TREE, MAYBUSH. Deciduous tree. Zones 1–3, 10. Moderate growth rate to 15–20 ft., occasionally taller, rather thin and open in habit while young. Dark, dull green oval leaves 3–5 in. long are among the first to unfold in spring. Small white flowers in slender, drooping, 3–6-in. clusters make big show in May, nearly hiding foliage. Small black fruit that follows is bitter, but much loved by birds. Any soil, average water. Tolerates much cold.

P. tomentosa. NANKING CHERRY. Like *P. besseyi*, extremely tough, hardy fruiting shrub; grows 6–8 ft. tall. Scarlet, ½-in. fruit.

P. triloba. FLOWERING ALMOND. Deciduous small tree or treelike large shrub. Zones 1–11, 14–20. One of several plants known as "flowering almond." Slow growth to 15 ft., usually 8–10 ft. with equal spread. Rather broad, 1–2½-in.-long leaves and double pink flowers 1 in. wide in very early spring. A white form is sometimes available. Useful where quite hardy small flowering plant of definite tree form is needed. Also is sold as multitrunked shrub.

P. virginiana. CHOKECHERRY. Deciduous shrub or small tree. Zones 1–3, 10. Leaves 2–4 in. long. After leaves have unfolded, tiny white flowers appear in slender, 3–6-in. clusters. Astringent fruit is ½–⅓ in. wide, dark red to black. Gives good display of autumn foliage color. *P. v. demissa*, WESTERN CHOKECHERRY, is native to Pacific Coast, Sierra Nevada, Great Basin area and northern Rockies. It is drought and heat tolerant. *P. v. melanocarpa*, BLACK CHOKECHERRY, has smoother leaves and blacker, sweeter fruit. With average garden watering it grows into 20–25-ft. tree. Its variety 'Canada Red' ('Shubert') has leaves that open green, then turn red as they mature. Tends to sucker freely.

PSEUDOLARIX kaempferi *(Chrysolarix kaempferi, C. amabilis).* *Pinaceae.* GOLDEN LARCH. Deciduous conifer. Zones 2–7, 14–17. Slow growing to 40–70 ft. high, often nearly as broad at base. Wide-spreading branches, pendulous at tips, grow in whorls to form symmetrical, pyramidal tree. Foliage has a feathery look; 1½–2-in.-long, ⅛-in.-wide, bluish green needles (golden yellow in fall) are clustered in tufts except near branch ends, where they are single. Cones and bare branches make interesting winter patterns. Give it sunny, open spot sheltered from cold winds. Best in deep, rich, well-drained, acid or neutral soil. Needs regular supply of moisture. Fine for spacious lawns.

Pseudolarix kaempferi

PSEUDOPANAX. *Araliaceae.* Evergreen shrubs or trees. Slow growing. Leaves of *P. crassifolius, P. ferox* highly variable. Young plants have long, narrow, spiny-toothed leaves; mature plants have divided or undivided leaves of no very remarkable shape. Young plants odd and decorative. Flowers inconspicuous. Take sun or deep shade; respond to average garden water.

Pseudopanax lessonii

P. crassifolius. LANCEWOOD. Zones 16, 17, 21–24. In time, a 50-ft. tree. Usually seen as single-stemmed plant 3–5 ft. tall with rigid, drooping leaves to 3 ft. long, less than 1 in. wide, strongly toothed, reddish bronze in color. Upright growth habit—good choice for narrow areas.

P. ferox. Zones 16, 17, 21–24. Eventually a 20-ft. tree. Young plants with strongly toothed leaves 1–1½ ft. long, 1 in. wide.

P. lessonii. Zones 17, 20–24. Moderate growth to 12–20 ft. tall. In open ground, an effective multistemmed tree. Leaves dark green, leathery, divided into 3–5 leaflets 2–4 in. long. July–August flowers unimportant. Withstands wind. Excellent container plant—confining roots keeps plant shrubby.

PSEUDOSASA. See Bamboo.

PSEUDOTSUGA. *Pinaceae.* Conifers. The 2 species are quite similar but there's a great difference in status—the first is little known and the second is most prominent tree in Pacific Northwest.

Pseudotsuga menziesii

P. macrocarpa. BIGCONE SPRUCE. Zones 1–3, 10, 11, 18, 19. Native to southern California. Stout trunked; grows to about 60 ft. tall. Needles similar to those of *P. menziesii*. Has much larger cones—4–7½ in. long, 2–3 in. wide; 3-pronged bracts on cones barely protrude from each scale. Drought tolerant.

P. menziesii *(P. taxifolia).* DOUGLAS FIR. Zones 1–10, 14–17. Since pioneer days, Northwesterners have been gardening under and near this magnificent native tree. Its entire range not only includes western Oregon and Washington but also extends east to the Rocky Mountains, north to Alaska, and south into many forested parts of California (as far south as Fresno and Monterey Counties).

Sharply pyramidal form when young; widely grown and cherished as Christmas tree. Grows 70–250 ft. in forests. Densely set, soft needles, dark green or blue green, 1–1½ in. long, radiate out in all directions from branches and twigs. Sweet fragrance when crushed. Ends of branches swing up. Pointed wine red buds form at branch tips in winter. These open in spring to apple green tassels of new growth that add considerably to tree's beauty. Reddish brown cones are oval, about 3 in. long, and have obvious 3-pronged bracts. Unlike upright cone of true firs (*Abies*), these hang down.

Best suited to its native areas or to areas with similar summer-winter climates. Will grow in any except undrained, swampy soils. Does well in sun or considerable shade, and can take wind. Environment influences its appearance. Where summers are dry, it is dense with shorter spaces between branches; where there is much moisture or too much shade, it tends to look awkward, thin, and gawky, especially as young tree. As garden tree, its height is difficult to control; you can't keep it down without butchering it. Yet it serves well as 10–12-ft. clipped hedge—plant young trees 2 ft. apart and keep them topped and trimmed. Resistant to oak root fungus.

P. m. glauca is the common form in the Rocky Mountains; it usually has more bluish green needles than the species and is much hardier to winter cold than Pacific Coast trees. Compact, weeping, and other forms exist, but are grown mostly in arboretums and botanic gardens.

PSIDIUM. *Myrtaceae.* GUAVA. Evergreen shrubs or small trees. White flowers (composed principally of brush of stamens). Berrylike fruit, good in jellies, pastes. Best in rich soil, but adaptable, taking some drought when established.

Psidium cattleianum longipes

P. cattleianum ***(P. littorale).*** STRAWBERRY GUAVA. Zones 9, 14 (in sheltered locations), 15–24. Moderate, open growth to 8–10 ft. as shrub; can be trained as multitrunked, 10–15-ft. tree. Especially beautiful bark and trunk—greenish gray to golden brown. Leaves glossy green, to 3 in. long; new growth bronze. Fruit is dark red (nearly black when fully ripe), 1½ in. wide, with white flesh and a sweet-tart, slightly resinous flavor. *P. c.* 'Lucidum', YELLOW STRAWBERRY GUAVA, LEMON GUAVA, has yellow fruit, fairly dense growth.

P. guajava. GUAVA. Zones 23, 24. Taller than strawberry guava, with strongly veined leaves to 6 in. long. Semideciduous briefly in spring; new leaves attractive salmon color. Fruit 1–3 in. across, with white, pink, or yellow flesh, musky and mildly acid flavor.

PSYLLIOSTACHYS suworowii ***(Limonium*** or ***Statice suworowii).*** *Plumbaginaceae.* Summer annual. Rosettes of narrow, 8-in.-long leaves produce 1½-ft.-tall spikes of lavender pink, tiny flowers. Spikes are very slender, single or branched, and cylindrical, reminiscent of slender, furry, highly refined rats' tails. They are excellent in flower arrangements, fresh or dry. Sow seed in pots or open ground seed bed when danger of frost is over; transplant to 1 ft. apart. Needs sun, average soil with good drainage, average water.

Psylliostachys suworowii

PTELEA trifoliata. *Rutaceae.* WAFER ASH, HOP TREE. Deciduous shrub, small tree. Zones 1–3, 10. Slow to moderate growth to 15 ft., but often shrubby. Leaves with 3 leaflets. Summer flowers small, inconspicuous. Seeds are disks up to 1 in. wide—seed surrounded by thin, flat, nearly circular wing. Not related to ash or hop, but to the orange; leaves have tiny oil glands like citrus, and strong scent that most people find pleasant. Once established, it can get along with very little water, even in poor, rocky soil. Yellow fall color.

Ptelea trifoliata

PTERIDIUM aquilinum. *Polypodiaceae.* BRACKEN. Fern. All Zones. Worldwide native. Variety *pubescens* is native to West. Fronds coarse, much divided, rising directly from deep, running rootstocks. Grows from 2 ft. to as tall as 7 ft. under good conditions. Takes full sun to medium shade. Reasonably drought tolerant; goes dormant if it doesn't receive enough water to sustain foliage. Occurs wild in many places and can be tolerated in untamed gardens, but beware of planting it: deep rootstocks can make it tough, invasive weed. Oddly enough, these deep rootstocks make it difficult to transplant. Dead fronds make a good sun screen for broad-leaf evergreens in harsh winter climates.

Pteridium aquilinum pubescens

PTERIS. *Polypodiaceae.* BRAKE. Ferns. Mostly small ferns of subtropical or tropical origin, mostly used in dish gardens or small pots; some are big enough for landscape use. For best garden performance, keep soil moist, but not saturated for any length of time.

P. cretica. Zones 17, 23, 24. To 1½ ft. tall with comparatively few long, narrow leaflets. Numerous varieties exist: some have forked or crested fronds, some are variegated. Variety 'Wimsettii', light green form with forked tips on mature plants, is so dense and frilly that it doesn't look like a fern.

Pteris cretica

P. 'Ouvrardii'. Zones 17, 22–24. Dark green, 1–2½-ft.-tall fronds have extremely long, narrow, ribbonlike divisions.

P. 'Parkeri'. Zones 17, 22–24. To 1–2½ ft. Resembles *P. cretica* and may be a form of it; more vigorous and robust, with broader segments.

P. quadriaurita 'Argyraea'. SILVER FERN. Zone 24. From India. Fronds 2–4 ft. tall, rather coarsely divided, heavily marked white. Showy, but white markings seem out of place on ferns. Protect from frost and snails.

P. 'Rivertoniana'. Zones 17, 22–24. Like *P. cretica,* but with deeply, irregularly cut edges on segments. To 1–2½ ft.

P. tremula. AUSTRALIAN BRAKE. Zones 16, 17, 22–24. Extremely graceful, 2–4-ft. fronds on slender, upright stalks. Good landscape fern with excellent silhouette. Fast growing, but tends to be short lived.

P. 'Wilsonii'. Zones 17, 22–24. Grows 1–2½ ft. tall. Tips of segments are forked and crested.

PTEROCARYA stenoptera. *Juglandaceae.* CHINESE WINGNUT. Deciduous tree. Zones 5–24. Fast to 40–90 ft., with heavy, widespreading limbs. Shows its kinship to walnuts clearly in its leaves: 8–16 in. long and divided into 11–23 finely toothed, oval leaflets. Foot-long clusters of small, single-seeded, winged nuts hang from branches. Good looking, but has only one real virtue: it succeeds well in compacted, poorly aerated soil in play yards and other high-traffic areas. Aggressive roots make it unsuitable in lawn and garden.

P. fraxinifolia, CAUCASIAN WINGNUT, is similar, has slightly larger leaflets, longer nut clusters.

Pterocarya stenoptera

PTEROSTYRAX hispidus. *Styracaceae.* EPAULETTE TREE. Deciduous tree. Zones 5–10, 14–21. Possibly to 40 ft., but more usually held to 15–20 ft. with 10-ft. spread. Trunk single or branched; branches open, spreading at top.

Light green leaves, gray green beneath, 3–8 in. long, rather coarse. Creamy white, fringy, lightly fragrant flowers in drooping clusters 4–9 in. long, 2–3 in. wide. Blooms in early summer. Gray, furry, small fruit in pendant clusters hangs on well into winter, is attractive on bare branches.

Plant in sunny location in well-drained soil, give average garden watering. Prune to control shape, density. Best planted where you can look up into it—on bank beside path, above a bench, or in raised planting bed. It is a choice selection when planted at edge of a woodland area or as focal point in large shrub border.

Pterostyrax hispidus

P

PTYCHOSPERMA macarthuri ***(Actinophloeus macarthuri).*** *Palmae.* Zones 23, 24. Native to New Guinea. Feather palm with several clustered, smooth green stems 10–15 ft. high. Soft green leaflets with jagged ends. Requires part shade in frost-free coastal locations; needs abundant water to look its best.

Ptychosperma macarthuri

PULMONARIA. *Boraginaceae.* LUNGWORT. Perennials. Zones 1–9, 14–17. Long-stalked leaves mostly in basal clumps, with few on flower-bearing stalks. Funnel-shaped, blue or purplish flowers in drooping clusters from April–June. Will grow in shade that discourages most flowering plants. Use with ferns, azaleas, rhododendrons; good under early spring-flowering trees, with blue scillas, pink tulips. Creeping roots. Needs moist, porous soil.

P. angustifolia. COWSLIP LUNGWORT. Tufts of narrowish, dark green leaves. Flowers dark blue, in clusters on 6–12-in. stems. Blooms in spring at same time as primroses. Divide in fall after leaves die down.

P. saccharata. BETHLEHEM SAGE. Grows to 1½ ft., spreads to 2 ft. White-spotted, roundish, evergreen leaves. Flowers reddish violet or white.

Pulmonaria saccharata

PUMMELO. See *Citrus,* Miscellaneous.

PUMPKIN. *Cucurbitaceae.* Annual vine related to gourds, melons, squash. Here's how to grow jumbo-sized pumpkins for Halloween. Varieties that grow to 30–40 in. across are 'Big Tom' (or 'Connecticut Field'), 'Jack O'Lantern', and 'Big Max'. Plant seeds in mid-May or early June. Choose sunny location. Allow vine area of 8–12 ft. in diameter. After soil is cultivated, dig hole 4 in. deep right where you will plant seeds. Put shovelful of manure in hole and cover it with enough soil to make ground level again.

Pumpkin

Plant 6–8 seeds, 1 in. deep, within a circle 6 in. wide. If you want more than one set of vines, plant such circles 8 ft. apart. Water seeds after planting. When plants are 4–6 in. high, remove all but 2 best plants in circle. Water when you see signs of slightest wilting. Try not to wet foliage. When small pumpkins are tennis ball sized, remove all but 3 or 4 on each vine (for extra-large pumpkins, remove all but one). Remove fruit toward ends of vines; save fruit near main stem. Continue removing later flowers. In late summer, slide wooden shingle under pumpkins to protect from wet soil (not necessary if soil is sandy).

Smaller pumpkins with finer-grained, sweeter flesh are 'Small Sugar' or 'Sugar'. Grow 'Trick or Treat' for its seeds; they have no hulls and can be roasted, salted, and eaten as nuts. 'Sweetie Pie' and 'Jack Be Little' are 3-in.-wide miniatures useful as decorations.

PUNICA granatum. *Punicaceae.* POMEGRANATE. Deciduous tree or shrub. Zones 7–24; also Zones 5 and 6 if used against south or west wall. Showy flowers. Some varieties yield fruit. Narrow, glossy bright green to golden green leaves, bronzy new growth, brilliant yellow fall color except in Zone 24. All varieties tolerate great heat and will live and grow well in alkaline soil that would kill most plants. Need sun for best bloom and fruit. When established, nonfruiting varieties need little water, but will take a lot if drainage is good. In desert areas, the leaf-footed plant bug (seriously) may drill holes in fruit, causing it to spoil. Control with spray of diazinon, malathion, or sevin in late spring.

Punica granatum

'Chico'. DWARF CARNATION-FLOWERED POMEGRANATE. Compact bush can be kept to 1½ ft. tall if pruned occasionally. Double orange red flowers over long season. No fruit. Excellent under lower windows, in containers, as edging.

'Legrellei' ('Mme. Legrelle'). Dense 6–8-ft. shrub with double creamy flowers heavily striped coral red. No fruit.

'Nana'. DWARF POMEGRANATE. Dense shrub to 3 ft., nearly evergreen in mild winters. Blooms when a foot tall or less. Orange red single flowers followed by small, dry, red fruit. Excellent garden or container plant; effective bonsai.

'Wonderful'. Best-known fruiting pomegranate. Grow it as 10-ft. fountain-shaped shrub, tree, or espalier. Burnished red fruit in autumn follows orange red single flowers up to 4 in. across. Will not fruit in cool coastal areas. Drought followed by flooding will cause fruit to split. Water deeply and regularly if fruit is important. Other fruiting varieties are rarely seen: 'Fleshman', 'King', 'Phil Arena's', and 'Utah Sweet' have pink flowers and sweet pink pulp.

PURPLE CONEFLOWER. See *Echinacea purpurea.*

PURPLE HEART. See *Setcreasea pallida* 'Purple Heart'.

PURPLE-LEAF PLUM. See *Prunus cerasifera* 'Atropurpurea'.

PURPLE OSIER. See *Salix purpurea.*

PURPLE VELVET PLANT. See *Gynura aurantiaca.*

PURSLANE. See *Portulaca oleracea.*

PUSCHKINIA scilloides. *Liliaceae.* Bulb. All Zones. Closely related to *Scilla* and *Chionodoxa.* Flowers bell-like, pale blue or whitish with darker, greenish blue stripe on each segment, in spikelike clusters on 3–6-in. stems. Leaves broad, strap shaped, upright, bright green, a little shorter than flower stems. Plant bulbs 3 in. deep, 3 in. apart in fall; locate in sun to slight shade. Will grow for years without disturbance. Best in cold climates, will withstand some summer drought. *P. s. libanotica,* a more vigorous plant, is variety usually sold. *P. s.* 'Alba' has white flowers.

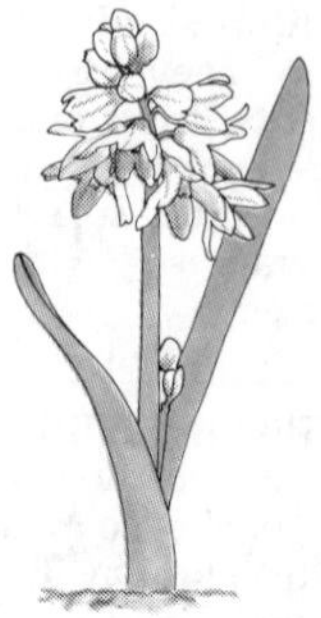

Puschkinia scilloides

PUSSY EARS. See *Calochortus tolmiei, Cyanotis somaliensis.*

PUYA berteroniana (usually sold as *P. alpestris*). *Bromeliaceae.* Evergreen perennial. Zones 9, 13–17, 19–24. Native to Chile. Big, spectacular flowering plant. Massive flower clusters, resembling giant asparagus stalks as they develop, grow from crowded clump of 2-ft.-long, 1-in.-wide, swordlike, gray green leaves with sharp tips and sharp-spined edges. Flower cluster, including stalk, reaches 4–6 ft. high. Blooms late April to early June. Cluster contains 2-in., bell-shaped flowers, metallic blue green and steely turquoise, accented with vivid orange anthers. Stiff, spiky branchlet ends protrude from cluster.

Use in rock gardens, on banks, or in large containers. Good with cactus, succulents, aloes. Full sun. Takes poor soil. Fairly drought tolerant once established.

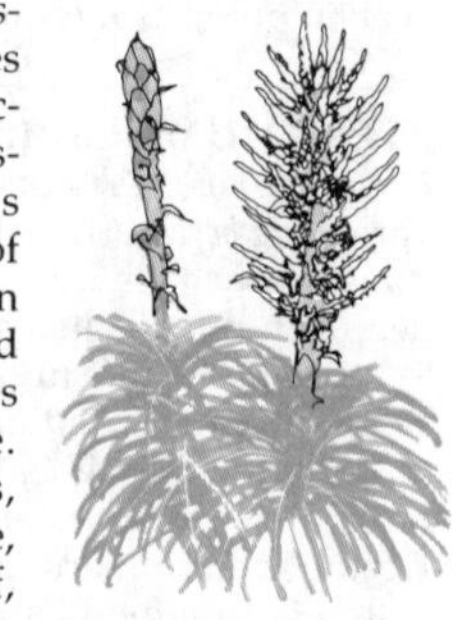

Puya berteroniana

PYRACANTHA. *Rosaceae.* FIRETHORN. Evergreen shrubs. Grown widely for bright fruit, evergreen foliage, variety of landscape uses, and easy culture. All grow fast and vigorously with habit from upright to sprawling; nearly all have thorns. All have glossy green leaves, generally oval or rounded at ends, ½–1 in. wide and 1–4 in. long. All bear flowers and fruit on spurs along wood of last year's growth. Clustered flowers are small, fragrant, dull creamy white, effective because numerous.

Pyracantha coccinea

Fruit varies in color, size, season, and duration. Some types color in late summer; others color late and hang on until cleared out by birds, storms, or decay in late winter. Plants need full sun and do best where soil is not constantly wet; keep them away from lawn sprinklers. Control size and form by pinching young growth or by shortening long branches just before growth starts. Trim branches that have berried, cutting back to well-placed side shoot. Subject to fireblight, scale, woolly aphids, red spider mites. In coastal areas, apple scab is sometimes a problem in early spring and can nearly defoliate plants.

Use as espaliers on wall or fence, as barrier plantings, screens, rough hedgerows or barriers along roads. Can be trained as standards; often clipped into hedges or topiary shapes (which spoils their rugged informality and often their fruit crop). Low-growing kinds are good ground covers. If berry color is important to you, buy plants when they are in fruit. To eliminate old withered or rotted berries, dislodge with a water jet or an old broom.

P. angustifolia 'Gnome'. All Zones except coldest parts of Zone 1. Dwarf, spreading, densely branched shrub with orange fruit. One of the hardiest.

P. coccinea. All Zones except coldest parts of Zone 1. Rounded bush to 8–10 ft. (20 ft. trained against wall). Flowers March–April; red orange berries in October, November. Best known for its varieties 'Fiery Cascade' (to 8 ft.; orange berries turning red), 'Government Red' (red berries), 'Kasan' (red orange, long-lasting berries), 'Lalandei' and 'Lalandei Monrovia' (orange berries), 'Lowboy' (low, spreading; orange fruit), and 'Wyattii' (orange red berries coloring early). Best species for cold-winter areas. 'Lalandei' is hardiest of all.

P. fortuneana *(P. crenatoserrata, P. yunnanensis).* Zones 4–24. Spreading growth to 15 ft. tall, 10 ft. wide. Limber branches make it good espalier plant. Berries orange to coral, lasting through winter. Variety 'Cherri Berri', 10 ft. tall, 8 ft. wide, has deep red berries that last through the winter. 'Graberi' has huge clusters of dark red fruit that colors in midfall, lasts through winter; growth more upright than species.

P. 'Mohave'. Zones 3–24. Shrub to 12 ft. tall and wide. Heavy producer of big orange red fruit that colors in late summer and lasts into winter. One of reddest of the very hardy pyracanthas. Reported to be resistant to fireblight by National Arboretum, its originator.

P. 'Red Elf'. Zones 4–9, 12–24. Low growing, compact, densely branched, with bright red fruit. Small enough for container culture. Less susceptible to fireblight than most pyracanthas. Apparently the same as plant sold as 'Leprechaun'.

P. 'Ruby Mound'. Zones 4–9, 12–24. Long, arching, drooping branches make broad mounds. Bright red fruit.

P. 'Santa Cruz' (*P.* 'Santa Cruz Prostrata'). Zones 4–24. Low growing, branching from base, spreading. Easily kept below 3 ft. by pinching out occasional upright branch. Red fruit. Plant 4–5 ft. apart for ground, bank cover.

P. 'Teton'. Zones 3–24. Columnar growth to 12 ft. tall, 4 ft. wide. Yellow orange fruit. Resistant to fireblight.

P. 'Tiny Tim'. Zones 4–24. Compact plant to 3 ft. tall. Small leaves, few or no thorns. Berries red. Prune once a year when fruit begins to color, shortening any runaway vertical shoots. Informal low hedge, barrier, tub plant.

P. 'Victory'. Zones 4–24. To 10 ft. tall, 8 ft. wide. Dark red fruit colors late and holds on well.

P. 'Walderi' (*P.* 'Walderi Prostrata'). Zones 4–24. Low-growing (to 1½ ft., with a few upright shoots that should be cut out), wide-spreading ground cover plant with red berries. Plant 4–5 ft. apart for fast cover.

P. 'Watereri'. Zones 3–24. To 8 ft. tall, equally wide. Very heavy producer of bright red, long-lasting fruit. Northwest favorite.

P. 'Yukon Belle'. All Zones. Dense, medium-sized, semievergreen shrub with orange berries. Extremely hardy.

PYRETHRUM roseum. See *Chrysanthemum coccineum*.

PYROSTEGIA venusta *(P. ignea, Bignonia venusta).* *Bignoniaceae.* FLAME VINE. Evergreen vine. Zones 13, 16, 21–24. Fast to 20 ft. or more, climbing by tendrils. Leaves with oval, 2–3-in. leaflets. Orange, tubular, 3-in.-long flowers in clusters of 15–20 are impressive sight during fall, early winter. Any soil. Will take some shade, but best in full sun. Thrives in low desert and other hot climates; outstanding against west wall.

Pyrostegia venusta

PYRROSIA lingua. *Polypodiaceae.* JAPANESE FELT FERN. Zones 14–17, 19–24. Dark green, broad, undivided, lance-shaped fronds with feltlike texture grow in dense clusters from creeping rootstocks. Fronds to 15 in. tall. Most often used in baskets, but makes choice ground cover for small areas. Can take full sun along coast, part shade in other areas. Foliage color better with some shade. Requires only moderate watering. Slow grower. Crested and saw-edged forms are collectors' items.

Pyrrosia lingua

PYRUS. *Rosaceae.* ORNAMENTAL PEAR. Deciduous or evergreen trees. Commercial fruiting pear is described under Pear. Following are ornamental species. Most are subject to fireblight (see Pear). All are best in full sun, will get along with no more than moderate summer watering once established.

P. calleryana. Deciduous tree. Zones 2–9, 14–21. Grows to 25–50 ft. Strong horizontal branching pattern. Leaves 1½–3 in. long, broadly oval, scalloped, dark green, very glossy and leathery. Flowers clustered, pure white, ¾–1 in. wide; very early bloom. In coldest areas, flower crop may be destroyed by late freezes in some years. Fruit very small, round, inedible. Fairly resistant to fireblight; rich purplish red fall color.

Pyrus kawakamii

'Bradford', original introduction, has strongly horizontal limbs, has reached 50 ft. in height, 30 ft. in width. 'Aristocrat' is more pyramidal, with upcurving branches. 'Redspire' is similar, with yellow to red fall color. 'Capital' and 'Whitehouse' are narrowly columnar. 'Chanticleer' is narrow but not columnar, about 40 ft. tall by 15 ft. wide. 'Trinity' is a round-headed form.

P. communis. See Pear.

P. kawakamii. EVERGREEN PEAR. Evergreen shrub or tree. Zones 8, 9, 12–24. Partially deciduous in coldest winters in coldest Zones. Branchlets drooping; leaves glossy, oval, pointed. Clustered white flowers appear in sheets and masses in winter and early spring. Small, inedible fruit seldom seen.

Without support, evergreen pear becomes broad, sprawling shrub or, in time, a multitrunked small tree. With willowy young branches fastened to fence or frame, it makes a good-looking espalier. To make tree of it, stake one or several branches, shorten side growth, and keep staked until trunk is self-supporting. Beef up framework branches by shortening (when young) to upward-facing buds or branchlets. Established, well-shaped plants need little pruning or shaping. Heavily pruned evergreen pears, such as those espaliered on small frames, seldom flower.

Tolerant of many soils, easy to grow wherever it doesn't freeze. Spray for aphids and watch for fireblight, which can disfigure or destroy plants.

P. pyrifolia *(P. serotina).* SAND PEAR, JAPANESE SAND PEAR. Deciduous tree. Zones 1–9, 14–21. Like common pear in appearance, but has glossier, more leathery leaves which turn brilliant reddish purple in fall. Fruit small, woody, gritty. Improved forms of this tree, *P. p. culta,* are grown for their fruit by the Japanese and are becoming popular in this country. See page 453 for additional information and a list of Asian pear varieties.

P. salicifolia 'Pendula'. WEEPING WILLOW-LEAFED PEAR. Zones 2–9, 14–21. Attractive tree to 25 ft. with weeping branches. White flowers appear in early spring, at the same time as silvery white leaves that slowly turn to silvery green. Fruit insignificant.

P. ussuriensis. Deciduous tree. Zones 1–3, 10; hardy to any cold, but flowers may be damaged by late freezes. Grows 20–30 ft. tall. Leaves roundish, glossy green turning bright red in fall. Flowers white, 1½ in. across. Fruit 1–1½ in. wide, yellow green, hard, inedible.

QUAIL BUSH. See *Atriplex lentiformis.*

QUAKING GRASS. See *Briza maxima.*

QUAMOCLIT pennata. See *Ipomoea quamoclit.*

QUEEN OF THE PRAIRIE. See *Filipendula rubra.*

QUEEN PALM. See *Arecastrum romanzoffianum.*

QUEENSLAND KAURI. See *Agathis robusta.*

QUEEN'S TEARS. See *Billbergia nutans.*

QUEEN'S WREATH. See *Antigonon leptopus, Petrea volubilis.*

QUERCUS. *Fagaceae.* OAK. Deciduous or evergreen trees. Western homeowners acquire oak trees in either of 2 ways. They may plant the trees themselves, starting from a nursery plant or an acorn (or a jay or squirrel may plant an acorn for them); or they may simply have a native oak tree, left from the days when the land was wild, on their property.

Quercus coccinea

The method of acquisition is quite significant. An oak tree planted in a garden will grow vigorously and fast (1½–4 ft. a year). It probably will not experience poor health or any unusual pest attacks—whether it's a western native or not. Old wild trees, on the other hand, quite frequently cannot handle the surfeit of water and nutrients that they receive in a garden and must be given special treatment.

Special treatment for existing native oaks. If possible, do not raise or lower grade level between trunk and drip line. If you must alter grade, put a well around base of trunk so that grade level there is not changed. Never water within 4 ft. of trunk or allow water to stand within that area. Any of a number of sucking and chewing insects and mites feed upon existing native oaks. Most of the time these creatures are kept in check by other insects and mites, birds, and by insect-and-mite troubles that we don't even know about. Occasionally, though, an outbreak of some organism—usually oak moth larvae—gets bad enough to require artificial control. When that happens, call a commercial arborist or pest control firm to diagnose and treat the problem; oak trees are too big for homeowners to reach with their limited spray equipment.

Oak root fungus (*Armillaria*) is often present in many California neighborhoods that once were oak forests or walnut groves. Get an arborist's advice on how to sustain infected trees. All old oaks, infected or not, can benefit from feeding and deep watering (fertilize and irrigate only out near drip line).

Old native oaks also benefit from periodic grooming to remove dead wood. However, arborists should not cut thick branches unless they have good reasons for doing so, since excessive pruning may stimulate succulent new growth that will be subject to mildew.

How to plant an acorn. Select shiny, plump, fallen acorns, free of worm holes. Remove caps. Plant acorns on or just beneath soil surface and put up screen to protect from jays and squirrels. Surer way is to gather newly sprouted acorns or to sprout fresh ones between layers of damp peat moss (takes 2 weeks). Plant those with strong root sprouts. Make crater deep enough so acorn can be just covered with soil. At bottom of crater poke vertical hole to take sprouted taproot. Insert root and press soil around it. Water. Expect first leaves in 6–8 weeks. If you plant several acorns in a single area, you can thin later to best seedling. After planting, water weekly (when there is no rain) the first 2 months, then monthly.

How to transplant an oak. Oak seedlings of any size up to 5–8 ft. seem not to suffer from having their vertical roots cut in transplanting if root ball is otherwise big and firm enough. Trees may wilt or lose leaves after roots are cut, but if watered well, should show new growth in 4–6 weeks. Oak seedlings from nursery containers usually will not show spiralling of taproots at bottom of containers. The better growers will cut a seedling's taproot when planting into a nursery container so the young oak will develop a branching root system.

How to train a young oak. By nature, many young oaks grow twiggy. Growth is divided among so many twigs that none elongates fast. To promote faster vertical growth, pinch off tips of unwanted small branches, meanwhile retaining all leaf surface possible in order to sustain maximum growth.

Best Oaks for the West

Among the oaks listed below, those native to the western U.S. or to the Mediterranean region need no watering after they are established (but water them through the first 1 or 2 dry seasons).

Q. agrifolia. COAST LIVE OAK. Evergreen tree. Zones 7–10, 12, 14–24. Native to Coast Ranges. Round-headed, wide-spreading tree to 20–70 ft. high, often with greater spread. Smooth, dark gray bark. Dense foliage of rounded, hollylike, 1–3-in.-long leaves, slightly glossy on upper surface. As planted tree from nursery or acorn, it can grow as high as 25 ft. in 10 years, 50 ft. in 25 years. Attractive green all year unless hit by oak moth larvae. Has greedy roots and drops almost all its old leaves in early spring just when gardening time is most valuable. Regardless of these faults, it's a handsome and quite worthwhile shade tree or street tree. Can be sheared into handsome 10–12-ft. hedge.

Quercus agrifolia

Q. bicolor. SWAMP WHITE OAK. Deciduous tree. Zones 1–3, 10. Medium to slow growth to 60 ft., rarely more. Leaves dark shiny green, up to 7 in. long, with shallow lobes or scallops, silvery white underneath. Bark of trunk and branches flakes off in scales. Tolerates wet soil; also thrives where soil is well drained.

Q. chrysolepis. CANYON LIVE OAK. Evergreen. Zones 5–9, 14–24. Native to mountain slopes and canyons of California, southern

Oregon. Handsome round-headed or somewhat spreading tree to 20–60 ft., with smooth, whitish bark. Oval, 1–2-in.-long leaves are shiny medium green above, grayish or whitish beneath. Leaf edges are smooth or toothed. Acorn cups, covered with golden fuzz, look like turbans.

Q. coccinea. SCARLET OAK. Deciduous. All Zones. Native to eastern U.S. Moderate to rapid growth in deep, rich soil. Can reach 60–80 ft. High, light, open-branching habit. Leaves bright green, to 6 in. long, with deeply cut, pointed lobes. Leaves turn bright scarlet in sharp autumn nights (Zones 1–11, 14, 15, 18–20), but color less well where autumn is warm. Roots grow deep. Good street or lawn tree. Fine to garden under.

Q. douglasii. BLUE OAK. Deciduous. All Zones. Native to foothills around California's Central Valley. Low-branching, wide-spreading tree to 50 ft. high. Fine-textured light gray bark and decidedly bluish green leaves, shallowly lobed, oval, almost squarish. Good in dry, hot situations. Fall colors attractive—pastel pink, orange, yellow.

Q. dumosa. CALIFORNIA SCRUB OAK. Evergreen shrub 3–10 ft. tall; rarely small tree. Zones 4–9, 14–24. Evergreen leaves ½–1 in. long, shiny green, smooth edged or lightly spined. Sometimes grown for landscaping wild gardens or for erosion control. Very drought tolerant; thrives in poor, rocky soil. *Q. durata* is similar, but with dull green leaves covered with fine hair.

Q. emoryi. EMORY OAK. Evergreen. Zones 10–13. Handsome tree to 60 ft. (usually smaller in gardens), native to lower mountain slopes in Arizona, New Mexico, Texas, and northern Mexico. Leathery, oval leaves, 2–3 in. long, sometimes turn golden just before new growth starts in late spring. Grows well in low desert, tolerates variety of soils. Needs periodic deep watering during summer.

Q. engelmannii. MESA OAK. Evergreen. Zones 18–24. Native to southern California. Wide-spreading tree of character, to 60 ft. high. Leaves oval or oblong, 2 in. long, usually smooth edged. In its area, it has the same cherished native status as the coast live oak.

Q. frainetto. HUNGARIAN or ITALIAN OAK. Zones 2–12, 14–21. Tall deciduous tree with large (to 8 in. long, 4 in. wide), glossy deep green leaves with deeply cut lobes. Erect, shapely; drought tolerant once established. Attractive but little known.

Q. gambelii *(Q. utahensis).* ROCKY MOUNTAIN WHITE OAK. Deciduous. Zones 1–3, 10. Grows slowly to 20–30 (rarely 50) ft., often in colonies from underground creeping root system. Leaves 3–7 in. long, half as wide, dark green turning to yellow, orange, or red in fall. Characteristic oak of Arizona's Oak Creek Canyon and Colorado foothills south of Denver.

Q. garryana. OREGON WHITE OAK, GARRY OAK. Deciduous. Zones 4–6, 15–17. Native from British Columbia south to Santa Cruz Mountains of California. Slow to moderate growth to 40–90 ft., with wide, rounded crown, branches often twisted. Bark grayish, scaly, checked. Leathery leaves 3–6 in. long, with rounded lobes; dark glossy green above, rusty or downy on lower surface. Casts moderate shade and has deep, nonaggressive root system—good shelter for rhododendrons (but don't plant them within 4 ft. of tree's trunk).

Q. ilex. HOLLY OAK, HOLM OAK. Evergreen. Zones 4–24. Native to Mediterranean region. Grows at a moderate rate to 40–70 ft. high, with equal spread. Leaves vary in shape and size, but are usually 1½–3 in. long, ½–1 in. wide, either toothed or smooth edged, dark, rich green on upper surface, yellowish or silvery below. Tolerates wind and salt air; will grow in constant sea wind, but tends to be shrubby there. Inland, growth rate can be moderately fast but varies with soil and water conditions. Good evergreen street or lawn tree where coast live oak is difficult to maintain, but lacks open grace of coast live oak. Can take hard clipping into formal shapes or hedges.

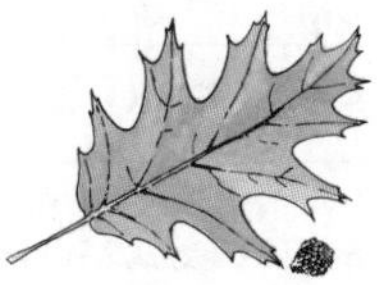

Quercus kelloggii

Q. kelloggii. CALIFORNIA BLACK OAK. Deciduous. Zones 5 (inland portions), 6, 7, 15, 16, 18–21. Native to mountains from southern Oregon to southern California. Moderate growth rate to 30–80 ft. Dark, furrowed and checked bark. Handsome foliage; unfolding leaves are soft pink or dusty rose, becoming bright glossy green and turning yellow or yellow orange in fall. Leaves 4–10 in. long and 2½–6 in. wide, deeply lobed, with lobes ending in bristly points. Good moderate-sized tree for spring and fall color, winter trunk and branch pattern.

Q. lobata. VALLEY OAK, CALIFORNIA WHITE OAK. Deciduous. Zones 1–3, 6–16, 18–21. Native to interior valleys, Sierra foothills, and Coast Ranges away from direct coastal influence. California's mightiest oak, often reaching 70 ft. or more, with equal or greater spread. Trunk and limbs massive, with thick, ashy gray, distinctly checked bark. Limbs often picturesquely twisted; long, drooping outer branches sometimes sweep ground. Deeply lobed leaves, lobes rounded; 3–4 in. long, deep green above, paler beneath.

Quercus lobata

Tolerates high heat and moderate alkalinity in its native range. Best in deep soils where it can tap ground water; in such situations, it can grow fast (2½–3 ft. a year). Magnificent tree for shading really big outdoor living area (debris makes it difficult for beds of small plants or heavily used paved areas). This is the tree that gives much of California's Central Valley its parklike look.

"Oak balls" are lightweight, corky spheres about the size of tennis balls, black and tan when they fall. They result from insect activity but do not harm tree.

Q. macrocarpa. BUR OAK, MOSSY CUP OAK. Deciduous. Zones 1–11, 14–24. Native to eastern U.S. Rugged looking, to 60–75 ft. high, 30 ft. wide. Leaves are glossy green above and whitish beneath, 8–10 in. long, broad at tip, tapered at base, deeply lobed. Large acorns form in mossy cups. Similar to *Q. bicolor* but faster growing, more tolerant of adverse conditions.

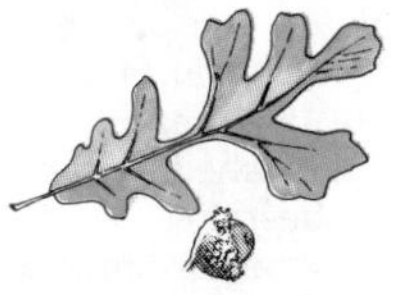

Quercus macrocarpa

Q. myrsinifolia. JAPANESE LIVE OAK. Evergreen. Zones 4–7, 14–24. A 30–50-ft.-tree in its native China and Japan. Leaves 2½–4 in. long, narrow, toothed toward tips, glossy dark green. New foliage purplish. Unlike most oaks, it is graceful rather than sturdy, and is not easily recognized as an oak unless seen with its acorns.

Q. palustris. PIN OAK. Deciduous. All Zones. Native to eastern U.S. Moderate to fairly rapid growth to 50–80 ft. Slender and pyramidal when young, open and round headed at maturity. Brownish gray bark. Lower branches tend to droop almost to ground; if lowest whorl is cut away, branches above will adopt same habit. Only when fairly tall will it have good clearance beneath lowest branches. Glossy dark green leaves are deeply cut into bristle-pointed lobes; in brisk fall weather, leaves turn yellow, red, and finally russet brown. Many hang on in winter.

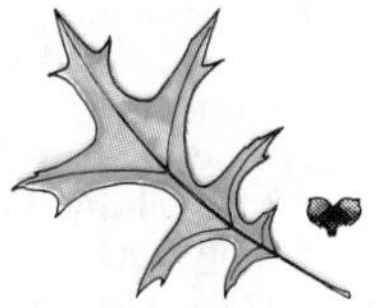

Quercus palustris

Less drought tolerant than most other oaks. Develops chlorosis in alkaline soils; treat with iron chelate. Needs ample water and good drainage. Stake young trees and give only corrective pruning. Plant where its spread will not interfere with walks, drives, or street traffic, or trim it often. Unlike western oaks, it is a fine tree for lawns.

Q. phellos. WILLOW OAK. Deciduous. Zones 1–4, 6–16, 18–21. Native to eastern U.S. To 50–90 ft. Somewhat like pin oak in growth habit and spreading nature, this tree is grown and used the same way as pin oak. Smooth, gray bark. Leaves are unlike those of other common oaks; they somewhat resemble willow leaves—2½–5 in. long, ⅓–1 in. wide, smooth edged. Foliage turns yellowish before falling; in warmer Zones, dead leaves may hang on through winter. Of all oaks, willow oak has most delicate foliage pattern.

Quercus phellos

(Continued on next page)

Q. robur. ENGLISH OAK. Deciduous. Zones 2–12, 14–21. To 90 ft., with rather short trunk and very wide, open head in maturity. Fairly fast growth. Leaves 3–4½ in. long, with 3–7 pairs of rounded lobes. Leaves hold until late in fall and drop without much color change. Variety 'Fastigiata', UPRIGHT ENGLISH OAK, is narrow and upright (like Lombardy poplar) when young, branches out to broad, pyramidal shape when mature. Other varieties are 'Skymaster' (broad pyramid to 50 ft. tall, half as wide, narrower in youth) and 'Westminster Globe' (round crown to 45 by 45 ft.).

Q. rubra *(Q. rubra maxima, Q. borealis).* RED OAK, NORTHERN RED OAK. Deciduous. Zones 1–12, 14–24. Fast growth to 90 ft. Broad, spreading branches and round-topped crown. Leaves 5–8 in. long by 3–5 in. wide, with 3–7 pairs of sharp-pointed lobes. New leaves and leaf stalks are red in spring, turning to dark red, ruddy brown, or orange in fall. Needs fertile soil and plenty of water. Stake young plants. High-branching habit and reasonably open shade make it a good tree for big lawns, parks, broad avenues. Its deep roots make it good to garden under.

Q. shumardii. SHUMARD RED OAK. Deciduous. Zones 4–9, 12, 14–17. Very similar to scarlet oak (*Q. coccinea*), slightly less hardy. Fall color yellow to red. Tolerates acid, poorly drained soil.

Q. suber. CORK OAK. Evergreen. Zones 5–7 (with occasional winter damage), 8–16, 18–23. Native to Mediterranean region. Moderate growth rate to 70–100 ft. high and as wide. Trunk and principal limbs covered with thick, corky bark (cork of commerce). The toothed, 3-in. leaves are shiny dark green above, gray beneath. General effect is fine textured. Needs good drainage. Fairly tolerant of different soil types, but likely to yellow in alkaline soils. Established trees can take considerable drought. One of best oaks for desert.

Quercus suber

Good garden shade tree with interesting contrast between fairly light-textured foliage and massive, fissured trunk. Value as street or park tree diminishes when children find out how easy it is to carve bark.

Q. vacciniifolia. HUCKLEBERRY OAK. Evergreen shrub. Zones 4–7, 14–17. Native to mountains of California. Low (to 2 ft.), with sprawling stems and smooth-edged, gray green leaves ¾–1¼ in. long. Sometimes planted in wild gardens, large rock gardens, mountain summer home gardens.

Q. virginiana. SOUTHERN LIVE OAK. Evergreen, partly or wholly deciduous in cold-winter regions. Zones 4–24. Native to eastern U.S. Moderate to fast growth to eventual 60 ft., with broad, spreading, heavy-limbed crown twice as wide. Smooth-edged leaves 1½–5 in. long, shiny dark green above and whitish beneath. Thrives on ample water and does best in deep, rich soil. In hot interior climates, it's the most attractive of all evergreen oaks. Best oak for lawn planting in low desert. The fast-growing variety 'Heritage' is recommended for low desert areas.

Q. wislizenii. INTERIOR LIVE OAK. Evergreen. Zones 7–9, 14–16, 18–21. Native to Sierra foothills and east side of California's Central Valley. To 30–75 ft. high, often broader than high. Wide-spreading branches form dense crown. Oblong, glossy green leaves to 4 in. long, smooth or spiny edged. Handsome tree for parks and big lawns. Sparse, angular young plants fail to hint at tree's ultimate beauty.

QUILLAJA saponaria. *Rosaceae.* SOAPBARK TREE. Evergreen tree. Zones 8, 9, 14–24. Usually to 25–30 ft.; occasionally to 60 ft. Young plants are dense columns foliaged right down to ground; old trees develop broad, flattened crown. Branchlets are pendulous, especially on younger plants, and general effect of young tree is that of narrow, bushy, weeping live oak. Leaves are 2 in. long, oval to nearly round, rather leathery, shiny green. White flowers are ½ in. across; handsome brown, 1-in. fruit opens into star form. Tends toward multiple trunks and excessive bushiness but responds quickly to pruning. Without firm staking and occasional thinning, younger trees may blow down in strong winds. Fairly tolerant of different soils—and even of drought, once well rooted. Good narrow screening tree. Can be pruned as tall hedge.

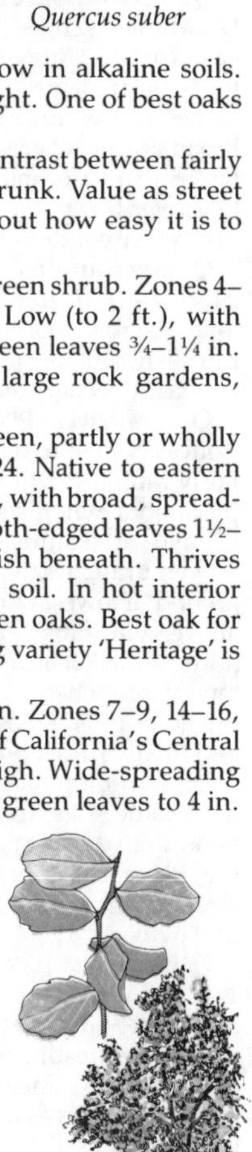

Quillaja saponaria

QUINCE, FLOWERING. See *Chaenomeles.*

QUINCE, FRUITING. *Rosaceae.* Deciduous shrub or small tree. All Zones. Slow to 10–25 ft. Unlike flowering quince (*Chaenomeles*), it has thornless branches.

Generally overlooked by planters of flowering fruit trees and home orchard trees, yet the following virtues make common quince worth considering as an ornamental. Its winter form can be dramatic in pattern of gnarled and twisted branches. In spring, it wears white or pale pink, 2-in.-wide flowers at tips of leafed-out branches. Attractive, oval, 2–4-in. leaves, dark green above, whitish beneath, turn yellow in fall. Fruit is yellow, fragrant. Quince is propagated by hardwood cuttings taken in late fall or winter.

Quince, Fruiting

Best in heavy, well-drained soil but tolerates wet soil. Avoid deep cultivation, which damages shallow roots and causes suckers. Prune only to form trunk and shape frame; thin out and cut back only enough to stimulate new growth. Do not use high-nitrogen fertilizer, as this results in succulent growth which is susceptible to fireblight. Remove suckers that sprout freely around the base of the tree; they rarely fruit, and tend to weaken the tree.

Large, fragrant fruit is inedible when raw but useful in making jams and jellies. Fruit is also made into candy and blended with other fruits in pies. Here are some popular varieties (fruit ripens from late September–October):

'Apple' ('Orange'). Old favorite. Round, golden-skinned fruit. Tender orange yellow flesh.

'Cooke's Jumbo'. Very large yellowish green fruit with white flesh. Can be nearly twice size of other quinces.

'Pineapple'. Roundish, light golden fruit. Tender white flesh; pineapplelike flavor.

'Smyrna'. Round to oblong fruit, lemon yellow skin. Strong quince fragrance.

QUINOA. See *Chenopodium quinoa.*

RABBIT TRACKS. See *Maranta leuconeura.*

RADERMACHERA sinica. *Bignoniaceae.* Evergreen tree. Common as a house plant; rare and risky outdoors Zones 23, 24. In nature, it is a small tree with yellow, trumpet-shaped flowers, but here it's usually seen as a single- or multiple-stemmed potted plant with finely divided, bright green, glossy, rather fernlike leaves. Grows fast and tends to lose lower leaves as it gets taller; tip-pinch occasionally to slow down growth. Provide bright light; fertilize and water regularly.

Radermachera sinica

RADICCHIO. See Chicory.

RADISH. *Cruciferae.* Annual vegetable. All Zones in conditions noted below. You can pull radishes for the table 3 weeks after you sow seed (slowest kinds take 2 months). They need continual moisture and some added nutrients to grow well. Supply nutrients by blending rotted manure into soil before planting, or—about 10 days after planting—feed beside row as for carrots, or feed with liquid fertilizer. Sow seeds in full sun as soon as ground can be worked in spring, and at weekly intervals until warm weather approaches. Can be grown in light shade as weather warms. In mild areas, radishes also make a fall and winter crop.

Radish

Sow seeds ½ in. deep and thin to 1 in. apart when tops are up. Space rows 1 ft. apart. Most familiar kinds are short, round, red or red and white types like 'Cherry Belle', 'Crimson Giant', and 'Scarlet White-tipped'. These should be used just as soon as they reach full size. Slightly slower to reach edible size are long white radishes, of which 'Icicle' is best known. Late radishes 'Long Black Spanish' and 'White Chinese' grow 6–10 in. long, can be stored in moist sand in a frost-free place for winter use.

RANGPUR LIME. See *Citrus,* Sour-Acid Mandarin Oranges.

Ranunculaceae. The immense buttercup family numbers nearly 2,000 species, among them numerous ornamental annuals and perennials, including *Anemone, Aquilegia, Clematis, Delphinium, Helleborus, Ranunculus,* and many others. Many are poisonous if eaten.

RANUNCULUS. *Ranunculaceae.* Tubers, perennials. A very large group (up to 250 species), but the 2 listed are the only ones grown to any extent.

Ranunculus asiaticus

R. asiaticus. PERSIAN RANUNCULUS, TURBAN RANUNCULUS. Tuber. All Zones (tubers lifted and stored after foliage dies down). Leaves bright fresh green, almost fernlike. Flowers are semidouble to fully double, 3–5 in. wide, in many shades of yellow, orange, red, pink, cream, and white. Large tubers produce many 1½-ft-tall or taller stalks, 50–75 blooms (each stalk carries 1–4 blooms). The most popular strain is Tecolote Giants; it includes colors listed above straight or in mixture, as well as picotee (edged) blends. Bloomingdale is a dwarf (8–10-in.) strain. Use in borders with Iceland poppies, snapdragons, nemesias. Plant for follow-up color in daffodil beds. Superb cut flowers.

Planting time depends on climate: November in mild-winter areas, October in desert, November or mid-February in western Washington, Oregon. Later planting gives later bloom. Need perfect drainage, full sun. Set tubers (prongs downward) 6–8 in. apart, 2 in. deep (½–1 in. deep in heavy soil). Tubers come dry and hard, but plump up after absorbing moisture. Water thoroughly after planting; unless weather is very hot and dry, do not water again until sprouts show (10 days–2 weeks). Tubers rot if overwatered before roots form. You can start tubers in flats of moist sand, plant when sprouted and rooted. To protect young sprouts from birds, cover with netting. After blooms fade, let plants dry out; lift tubers, cut off tops, and store in dry, cool place. Flat-grown seedlings are sold in some areas in fall. In coldest climates, grow ranunculus in greenhouse, plant after frosts. Early hot spells may shorten bloom period in such areas.

R. repens 'Pleniflorus'. CREEPING BUTTERCUP. Perennial. All Zones. Vigorous plant with thick, fibrous roots and runners growing several feet in a season, rooting at joints. Leaves glossy, roundish, deeply cut, toothed. Flowers are fully double, button shaped, bright yellow, about 1 in. across, on stems 1–2 ft. high. Spring bloom. Ground cover in moist soil, filtered or deep shade. Can be invasive in flower beds and lawns.

Single-flowered form, *R. repens,* is as aggressive or more so.

RAOULIA australis. *Compositae.* Perennial carpeting plant. Zones 7–9, 13–24. Stems up to 6 in. long form very close mats. Stems are hidden by small gray leaves that overlap them completely. Inconspicuous pale yellow flowers in spring. Useful in dry rockery. Needs sandy soil, full sun, moderate water, perfect drainage.

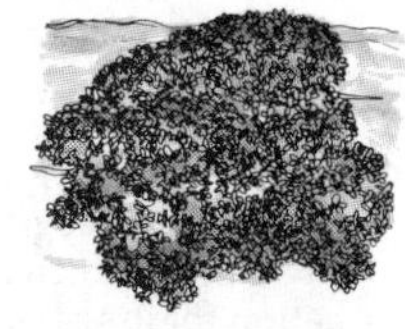
Raoulia australis

RAPHIOLEPIS. See *Rhapiolepis.*

RASPBERRY. *Rosaceae.* Shrubs with biennial stems. For ornamental relatives, see *Rubus.* Best in Zones 4–6, 15–17, but can be grown (perhaps with some setbacks or difficulties) anywhere else in West. Raspberries need slowly warming, lingering springtime to reach perfection. Loose clusters of white flowers; berries ripen in either summer or fall.

Raspberry

Most popular and heaviest bearers are red raspberries. These can be grown as freestanding shrubs and staked, but in Northwest (where they grow tall), they are most easily handled if tied to wires fastened between 2 stout posts. The upper wire should be 4–5 ft. above the ground, the lower 2½ ft.

Set plants 2½–3 ft. apart in rows 7–9 ft. apart. Well-drained soil is essential. Best production is in full sun; in warmer Zones outside of best raspberry climates, satisfactory production may come from plants grown in light shade. Set plants about an inch deeper than they grew originally, and cut back cane that rises from roots, leaving only enough to serve as marker. Plant should produce 3–5 sturdy canes first year; these will bear the next year and should be cut out at ground level after fruiting.

Second-year canes will come up all around parent plant and even between hills and rows. Remove all except 8–12 closely spaced, vigorous canes that come up near crown—be sure to pull up all suckers away from crown. Tie selected canes to top wire. In spring, before growth begins, cut them back to 4½–5½ ft. Fruit-bearing laterals will appear from these canes.

Fall-bearing raspberries differ slightly in pruning needs; these ripen canes earlier in summer, and fruit laterals form and bear fruit near top of cane. Cut off upper portion that has borne fruit; lower parts of cane will fruit next spring. Cut out cane after it has fruited along its whole length. In mild California climates, some growers have had success with handling fall-bearing raspberry canes as annuals. After canes finish fruiting, cut all of them off as close to the ground as possible; use powerful rotary mower in large berry patch. In spring new canes appear to bear new crop. Ease of maintenance helps make up for loss of earliest berries.

Plants need plenty of water, especially during blossoming and fruiting. Feed at blossoming time.

'Bababerry'. Spring- and fall-bearing. Needs little winter chill, stands heat.

'Canby'. Large, bright red berries. Thornless, hardy.

'Cuthbert'. Medium-sized berries of good quality.

'Durham'. Medium-sized, firm berries of good quality. Fall bearing; starts to ripen 2 weeks before 'Indian Summer'.

'Fairview'. Variety for coastal Northwest. Bears young and heavily. Early variety of good quality.

'Heritage'. Small red berries are tasty, a bit dry. Bears in June and again in September.

'Indian Summer'. Small crops of large, red, tasty berries in late spring and again in fall; fall crop often larger.

'Latham'. Older, very hardy variety for intermountain areas. Late. Berries often crumbly. Mildews in humid-summer regions.

'Meeker'. Large, bright red, firm fruit on long, willowy laterals.

'Newberg'. Hardy, late-ripening variety. Large light red berries. Takes heavy soil fairly well.

(Continued on next page)

'New Washington'. Smallish fruit of high quality. Hardy, but needs well-drained soil.

'Puyallup'. For west of the Cascades. Large, soft berries with very good flavor. Midseason.

'Ranere' ('St. Regis'). Bears over a long season, from midspring to frost in California. Berries small, bright red. Needs steady irrigation for long bearing.

'September'. Medium to small berries of good flavor. Some fruit in June, good crop in fall.

'Sumner'. Hardy, with some resistance to root rot in heavy soils. Fine fruit. Early.

'Willamette'. Large, firm, dark red berries which hold color and shape well.

Tasty novelty is 'Golden West', with yellow berries of excellent quality.

RASPBERRY, BLACK or BLACKCAP. *Rosaceae.* Shrub with biennial stems. For ornamental relatives, see *Rubus.* Best Zones 4–6; fails to thrive in California. Resembles regular red raspberry in many ways (see illustration for Raspberry), but blue black fruit is firmer and seedier, with a more distinct flavor. Plants differ from red raspberries in not suckering from roots; new plants form when arching cane tips root in soil. For best crop, plant in good garden soil in sun to light shade; give regular summer water. You need no trellis. Head back new canes at 1½–2 ft. to force laterals. At end of growing season, cut out all weak canes and remove canes that fruited during current season. In late winter or early spring, cut back laterals to 10–15 in. on strong canes, 3–4 in. on weak ones. Fruit is produced on side shoots from these laterals. If you prefer trellising, head new canes at 2–3 ft.

Varieties usually sold are: 'Cumberland', an old variety; 'Morrison', large berry on productive vine; and 'Munger', most popular commercial variety. 'Sodus', purple raspberry, is a vigorous-growing hybrid of red and black raspberry; head new canes at 2½–3 ft.

RATTAN PALM. See *Rhapis humilis.*

RATTLESNAKE GRASS. See *Briza maxima.*

REDBERRY. See *Rhamnus crocea.*

REDBUD. See *Cercis.*

RED CLUSTERBERRY. See *Cotoneaster lacteus.*

RED-FLOWERED MALLEE. See *Eucalyptus erythronema.*

RED FLOWERING GUM. See *Eucalyptus ficifolia.*

RED GUM, RIVER RED GUM. See *Eucalyptus camaldulensis.*

RED-HOT POKER. See *Kniphofia uvaria.*

RED HUCKLEBERRY. See *Vaccinium parvifolium.*

RED IRONBARK. See *Eucalyptus sideroxylon.*

REDONDO CREEPER. See *Lampranthus filicaulis.*

RED-RIBBONS. See *Clarkia concinna.*

RED SPIKE ICE PLANT. See *Cephalophyllum* 'Red Spike'.

REDTOP. See *Agrostis gigantea.*

RED VALERIAN. See *Centranthus ruber.*

REDWOOD, COAST REDWOOD. See *Sequoia sempervirens.*

REDWOOD SORREL. See *Oxalis oregana.*

REHMANNIA elata *(R. angulata).* *Gesneriaceae* or *Scrophulariaceae* (botanists do not agree on proper family for this genus). Perennial. Evergreen where winters are mild; deciduous where winters are colder. Zones 7–10, 12–24. This plant's most impressive trait is its long bloom season: mid-April–November, in sun or shade. Stalks rise to 2–3 ft., loosely set with 3-in.-long, tubular flowers that look something like big, gaping foxgloves. Common form is rose purple with yellow, red-dotted throat; there is a fine white and cream form that must be grown from cuttings or divisions. Coarse, deeply toothed leaves. Spreads by underground roots and forms big clumps. Easy to grow; main requirements are rich soil, ample water, some shade. Handsome, long-lasting cut flowers.

Rehmannia elata

REINWARDTIA indica *(R. trigyna).* *Linaceae.* YELLOW FLAX. Perennial. Zones 8–10, 12–24. Shrublike form to 3–4 ft.; alternate leaves. Brilliant yellow, 2-in. flowers form in great profusion at an unusual season: in late fall and early winter. Blooms do not last long, but for weeks new ones open daily.

Sun or part shade. Pinch to make more compact. Spreads by underground roots. Increase by rooted stems; divide in spring. Good choice for winter color in flower garden or with shrubs.

Reinwardtia indica

RESEDA odorata. *Resedaceae.* MIGNONETTE. Summer annual. To 1–1½ ft. tall; rather sprawling habit. Light green leaves. Not particularly beautiful plant, but well worth growing because of remarkable flower fragrance. Small greenish flowers tinged with copper or yellow, in dense spikes that become loose and open as blossoms mature. Flowers dry up quickly in hot weather.

Sow seed in early spring—or late fall or winter in Zones 15–24. Successive sowings give long bloom period. Best in rich soil with regular watering. Sun in cool sections, part shade inland. Plant in masses to get full effect of fragrance, or spot a few in flower bed to provide fragrance to scentless plantings. Suitable for pots. There are other forms with longer flower spikes and brighter colors, but they are less fragrant.

Reseda odorata

RETINISPORA pisifera. See *Chamaecyparis pisifera.*

Rhamnaceae. The buckthorn family of shrubs and trees has small, usually clustered flowers and fruits which are either drupes (single seeded, juicy) or capsules. Western gardeners grow *Ceanothus, Rhamnus,* and *Ziziphus.*

RHAMNUS. *Rhamnaceae.* Evergreen or deciduous shrubs or trees. Small flowers in clusters are rather inconspicuous; plants are grown for form and foliage, occasionally for show of berrylike fruit.

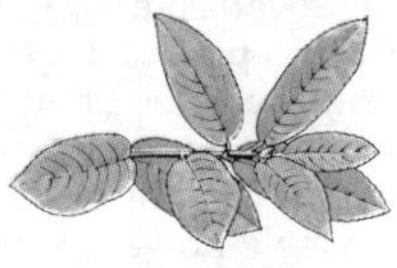

Rhamnus californica

R. alaternus. ITALIAN BUCKTHORN. Evergreen shrub. Zones 4–24. Fast, dense growth to 12–20 ft. or more, spreading as wide. Close planting or pruning will keep it narrow. Easily trained as multistemmed or single-stemmed small tree. Leaves oval to oblong, bright shiny green, ¾–2 in. long. Tiny, greenish yellow April flowers; black, ¼-in.-long fruit.

Rhamnus californica

Easily sheared or shaped. Takes heat, wind, drought or regular watering. Grows in full sun or part shade. Valuable as fast screen or tall clipped hedge. Trained to single stem, makes good plant for tall screen above 6-ft. fence. *R. a.* 'Variegata' (*R. a.* 'Argenteovariegata') has leaves edged with creamy white; striking against dark background. Cut out plain green branches that occasionally appear; if you do not, they will quickly shade out and replace variegated foliage.

R. californica. COFFEEBERRY. Evergreen shrub. Zones 4–24. Native to southwest Oregon, California, Arizona, New Mexico. May have low, spreading habit (especially if growing near ocean) or, in woodlands or hills, upright growth to 3–15 ft. Leaves 1–3 in. long, shiny dark green to dull green above (depending on variety), paler beneath (in some forms gray and hairy beneath). Large berries green, then red, then black when ripe. 'Eve Case', a dense, compact form propagated from cuttings, grows 4–8 ft. tall, with equal spread. Selected coastal form, *R. c.* 'Seaview', can be kept to 1½ ft. high, 6–8 ft. wide if upright growth is pinched out. Both 'Eve Case' and 'Seaview' have foliage that is distinctly broader, flatter, brighter green than that of the species. Coffeeberries grow in full sun to half shade; they are not particular as to soil. Drought tolerant, but the 2 broader-leafed varieties look better with some summer water.

R. cathartica. COMMON BUCKTHORN. Deciduous big shrub or tree. Zones 1–3. To 15–20 ft. Leaves bright glossy green, 1–2½ in. long by half as wide, turning yellow before falling off in autumn. Short twigs often spine tipped. Fruit is black, ¼ in. thick. Useful hedge or small tree in coldest, driest areas. Tolerates drought, poor soil, wind.

R. crocea. REDBERRY. Evergreen shrub. Zones 14–21. Native to Coast Ranges, Lake County to San Diego County, California. To 2–3 ft. high and spreading, with many stiff or spiny branches. Leaves roundish, ½ in. long, glossy dark to pale green above, golden or brownish beneath, often finely toothed. Small bright red fruit, August–October. Full sun to part shade; inland from its native territory, best with some shade. Less drought tolerant than its holly-leaf form, *R. c. ilicifolia.*

R. c. ilicifolia. HOLLY-LEAF REDBERRY. Evergreen shrub. Zones 7–16, 18–21. Native to Coast Ranges and Sierra Nevada foothills, mountains of southern California, Arizona, Baja California. Multistemmed or often treelike, to 3–15 ft. Leaves roundish, ½–1¼ in. long, spiny toothed. Good ornamental plant for dry banks or informal screen in hot-sun areas. Drought resistant.

R. frangula. ALDER BUCKTHORN. Deciduous shrub or small tree. Zones 1–7, 10–13. To 15–18 ft. tall. Leaves roundish, glossy dark green, 1–3 in. long, half as wide. Fruit turns from red to black on ripening. Sun to part shade; established plants need only moderate summer watering. *R. f.* 'Columnaris', TALLHEDGE BUCKTHORN, grows 12–15 ft. tall, 4 ft. wide. Set 2½ ft. apart for tight, narrow hedge that needs minimum of trimming and can be kept as low as 4 ft.

R. purshiana. CASCARA SAGRADA. Deciduous shrub or small tree. Zones 1–9, 14–17. Native from northern California to British Columbia and Montana. To 20–40 ft., with smooth, gray or brownish bark with medicinal value. Dark green, prominently veined leaves are elliptical, 1½–8 in. long, to 2 in. wide, usually somewhat tufted at ends of branches. Foliage turns good yellow in fall. Round black fruit attracts birds. Will grow in dense shade or full sun with ample water. Picturesque branching pattern.

RHAPHIDOPHORA aurea. See *Epipremnum aureum.*

RHAPIDOPHYLLUM hystrix. *Palmae.* NEEDLE PALM. Zones 7–9, 12–24. Hardy, slow-growing fan palm from southeastern U.S. Upright or creeping stems 5 ft. high. Rounded leaves, 3–4 ft. across, dark green above, silvery beneath. Well outfitted with strong black spines. Makes impenetrable hedge. Hardy to 10°F. Tolerates damp soil.

Rhapidophyllum hystrix

RHAPIOLEPIS. *Rosaceae.* Evergreen shrubs. Zones 8–10, 12–24; grown as worthwhile risk in Zones 4–7. With their glossy, leathery leaves, these shrubs make attractive dense background plantings, large-scale ground covers, low dividers, or informal hedges. And they offer more than the constant greenery of most basic landscaping shrubs. From late fall or midwinter to late spring, they carry a profusion of flowers ranging from white to near red. Dark blue, berrylike fruit (not especially showy) follows flowers. New leaves often add to color range with tones of bronze and red.

Rhapiolepis indica

Most stay low. With few exceptions, the taller kinds rarely reach more than 5–6 ft.; pruning can keep them at 3 ft. almost indefinitely. Prune from the beginning if you want sturdy, bushy, compact plants; pinch back tips of branches at least once each year, after flowering. For more open structure, let plants grow naturally and thin out branches occasionally. Encourage spreading by shortening vertical branches. Pinch side branches to encourage upright growth.

It is no accident that rhapiolepis are among the most widely planted of garden shrubs. Most kinds are easy to grow in full sun; in light shade, they are less compact, bloom less. Rhapiolepis stand fairly dry conditions but also tolerate the frequent waterings they get when planted near lawn or flower bed. Aphids occasionally attack. Fungus sometimes causes leaf spotting, especially during cold, wet weather—to control, destroy infected leaves, spray with fungicide, avoid overhead watering. In desert, plants will burn in reflected heat; they need some sheltering shade in Zone 13. Fireblight is a problem in some areas.

R. delacouri. Pink-flowered hybrid of *R. indica* and *R. umbellata.* To 6 ft. tall. Small pink flowers in upright clusters, October–May. Leaves smaller than most. Name is often used incorrectly for many different plants.

R. indica. INDIA HAWTHORN. White flowers tinged with pink are about ½ in. across. Leaves pointed, 1½–3 in. long. Plants grow 4–5 ft. high. The species is rarely grown, but its varieties are widely grown and sold. Varieties differ mainly in color of bloom and in size and form of plant; there is variation even within a variety. Flower color is especially inconsistent: flowers in warmer climates and exposures are usually lighter; bloom is paler in fall than in spring. Varieties include:

'Ballerina'. Deep rosy pink flowers. Stays low (not much taller than 2 ft.) and compact (no wider than 4 ft.). Leaves take on reddish tinge in winter.

'Charisma'. Compact, dense, 3-ft.-tall plant with double pink flowers.

'Clara'. White flowers on compact plants 3–5 ft. high, about as wide. Red new growth.

'Coates Crimson'. Crimson pink flowers. Compact, spreading plants grow slowly, stay small—2–4 ft. high and as wide. Best in part shade and with regular watering.

'Enchantress'. Pink flowers. Faster growing, more vigorous, and taller than 'Coates Crimson'; color not as deep. The white form is called 'White Enchantress'.

'Jack Evans'. Bright pink flowers. To about 4 ft. tall, with wider spread. Compact and spreading. Leaves sometimes have purplish tinge.

'Pink Cloud'. Pink flowers. Compact growth to 3 ft. high, 3–4 ft. wide. Very similar to *R. i.* 'Springtime'.

'Pink Lady'. Deep pink flowers. Vigorous grower 4–5 ft. tall, 4–6 ft. wide. Resembles 'Enchantress'.

'Snow White'. White flowers. Growth habit about like that of 'Jack Evans'. Leaves paler than on most varieties.

'Spring Rapture'. Compact 4-ft.-tall plant with rose red single flowers.

'Springtime'. Deep pink flowers. Vigorous, upright growth to 4–6 ft. high.

R. 'Majestic Beauty'. Fragrant light pink flowers in clusters to 10 in. wide. Leaves 4 in. long. Larger in every detail than other rhapiolepis; can reach 15 ft. Thought by some to be hybrid between *Rhapiolepis* and *Eriobotrya*. Use as background shrub or small tree with single or multiple trunk. Stake tree form carefully until it has formed a sturdy trunk. Thin branches to reduce wind resistance and minimize chances of plant blowing down.

R. umbellata *(R. u. ovata, R. ovata).* Easily distinguished from *R. indica* by its roundish, leathery, dark green leaves, 1–3 in. long. White flowers about ¾ in. wide. Vigorous plants 4–6 ft. tall, sometimes to 10 ft. In full sun, thick and bushy. *R. u.* 'Minor' is a dwarf, slow-growing form.

RHAPIS. *Palmae.* LADY PALM. Fan palms which form bamboolike clumps with deep green foliage. Trunks covered with net of dark, fibrous leaf sheaths. Slow-growing, choice, expensive. Palm specialists sell many variegated forms at very high prices.

Rhapis excelsa

R. excelsa. LADY PALM. Zones 12–17, 19–24. Small, slow, 5–12 ft. tall, often much lower. Best in shade, but will take considerable sun near the beach. In Zones 12–14, needs shade, shelter from heat and cold. Well-drained soil. One of the finest container palms; withstands poor light, dust, and drought, but responds quickly to better light and fertilizer. Hardy to 20°F.

R. humilis. RATTAN PALM, SLENDER LADY PALM. Zones 16, 17, 20–24. Tall, bamboolike stems (to 18 ft.) give charming, graceful, tropical air. Larger, longer-leafed palm than *R. excelsa;* less tolerant of sun and wind. Hardy to 22°F.

RHIPSALIDOPSIS gaertneri *(Schlumbergera gaertneri).* *Cactaceae.* EASTER CACTUS. House plant; lathhouse or covered terrace plant in Zones 16, 17, 21–24. For culture and general description, see *Schlumbergera.* Much like *S. bridgesii,* with the same drooping stems—but more upright, with more rounded stem joints. Bright red flowers to 3 in. long are upright or horizontal rather than drooping. Blooms April, May, often again in September. There are many varieties in shades of pink and red.

Rhipsalidopsis gaertneri

RHODOCHITON atrosanguineum *(R. volubile, Lophospermum atrosanguineum).* *Scrophulariaceae.* Perennial grown as an annual or house plant. Easily grown as a house plant in a 5- or 6-in. pot; twine stems on a wire or bamboo frame. Climbs to 10 ft. (usually less) by clasping leaf stems. Leaves are heart shaped, 3 in. wide. Each blackish red, 2½-in.-long, tubular flower springs from a 5-lobed, pinkish red calyx. Blooms first year from seed. In greenhouse or bright, warm room, will bloom all year. Outdoors, blooms through warm weather.

Rhodochiton volubile

RHODODENDRON (including azalea). *Ericaceae.* Evergreen or deciduous shrubs, rarely trees. Very large group, of approximately 800 species. There are over 10,000 named varieties in the International Register, of which perhaps 2,000 are currently available. Botanists have arranged species into series and subseries; one of these series includes plants called azaleas.

Rhododendron 'Trude Webster'

The climate adaptation pattern of azaleas is very different from that of rhododendrons. For example, evergreen azaleas are planted by the hundreds of thousands in southern California, where rhododendrons are far less frequent and require more special attention.

The West's finest rhododendron climates are found in Zones 4–6, 15–17. However, gardeners in every climate of the West—except deserts and areas of coldest winters–can find ways to grow certain varieties. Even some adventuresome desert gardeners have succeeded with container-grown plants.

Rhododendrons and azaleas have much the same basic soil and water requirements. They require acid soil. They need more air in the root zone than any other garden plants but, at the same time, they need a constant moisture supply. In other words, they need soil that is both fast draining and moisture retentive. Poor drainage can result in root rot, which shows in yellowing, wilting, and collapse of plants. Soils rich in organic matter have the desired qualities; if your soil isn't satisfactory, improve it with liberal quantities of organic matter.

If your garden soil is clay or alkaline, planting in raised beds is the simplest way to give these plants the conditions they need. Make beds 1–2 ft. above soil level. Liberally mix organic materials into top foot of soil beneath raised bed, then fill bed with mixture of 50% organic material (at least half peat moss), 30% soil, 20% sand. This mixture will be well aerated but moisture retentive and will permit alkaline salts to leach through.

Plant azaleas and rhododendrons with top of root ball slightly above soil level. Never allow soil to wash in and bury stems. Plants are surface rooters and benefit from a mulch such as pine needles, oak leaves, and wood by-products (for example, redwood or fir bark or chips). Never cultivate soil around these plants.

Sun tolerance of azaleas and rhododendrons differs by species and varieties. Too much sun causes bleaching or burning in leaf centers, though most can take full sun in cool-summer areas. Ideal location is in filtered shade beneath tall trees; east and north sides of house or fence are next best. Too-dense shade results in lanky plants that bloom sparsely.

Fertilize when growth starts in spring and again at bloom time or immediately afterward; then feed monthly until August. Use commercial acid fertilizer and follow directions carefully; to be extra safe, cut portions in half and feed twice as often.

Both azaleas and rhododendrons need special attention where soil or water is high in dissolved salts—as it is in many areas in California. To avoid damage, plant in containers or raised beds and periodically leach the mix by heavy watering—enough to drain through mix 2 or 3 times. If leaves turn yellow while veins remain green, plants have iron deficiency called chlorosis; apply iron chelate to soil or spray with iron solution.

Insects and diseases are seldom much of a problem. Root weevil larvae feed on roots. Adult weevils notch leaves but damage usually is minor. You can prevent larvae from developing in soil by applying diazinon, orthene, or sevin to soil and working it in to depth of 6 in. at planting time. Or you can kill adults as they emerge from soil (April–May). Use poison bait or spray plant and soil with orthene and repeat every 2 weeks until there is no sign of leaf feeding. The obscure root weevil (gray in color) can be a problem in western Oregon; control with malathion.

Wind and soil salts burn leaf edges; windburn shows up most often on new foliage, saltburn on older leaves. Late frosts often cause deformed leaves.

Prune evergreen azaleas by frequent pinching of tip growth from after flowering to August if you wish a compact plant with maximum flower production.

Prune large-flowered rhododendrons early in spring at bloom time if needed. Early spring pruning will sacrifice some flower buds but is the best time for extensive pruning. Plant's energies will be diverted to dormant growth buds, which will then be ready to push out early in the growing season. Tip-pinch young plants to make them bushy; prune older, leggy plants to restore shape by cutting back to side branch, leaf whorl, or to cluster of dormant buds. (Some varieties will not push new growth from dormant buds.) Prune off faded flower heads or break off spent clusters; take care not to injure new growth just beneath clusters.

Kinds of Rhododendrons

Most people know rhododendrons as big, leathery-leafed shrubs with stunning, rounded clusters (called "trusses") of white, pink, red, or purple blossoms. But there are other types: dwarfs a few inches tall, giants that reach 40 or even 80 ft. in their native Southeast Asia, and a host of species and hybrids in every intermediate size, in a color range including scarlet, yellow, near-blue, and a constellation of blends in the orange-apricot-salmon range.

Listed here are some generally available kinds, representing only a portion of the best species and hybrids grown in the West.

To give some idea of rhododendrons' adaptability to different climates and garden roles, we begin by presenting a few groupings featuring primarily the named varieties described at right and on pages 502–504.

"Ironclad" cold-hardy hybrids that also do well in southern California: 'Anah Kruschke', 'Blue Ensign', 'Cunningham's White', 'Fastuosum Flore Pleno', 'Gomer Waterer', 'Mars', 'Pink Pearl'.

California specials—rhododendrons too tender for Northwest gardens (many are fragrant): *R. burmanicum*, 'Countess of Haddington', 'Countess of Sefton', 'Else Frye', 'Forsterianum', 'Fragrantissimum', 'Saffron Queen'.

Good performers in California, rated low in Northwest: 'Anah Kruschke', 'Antoon Van Welie', 'Rainbow', 'Sappho', 'Unknown Warrior', 'Van Nes Sensation'.

For outdoors in California's frost-free and nearly frostless Zones (17, 23, 24) are the Vireya rhododendrons from the tropics of Southeast Asia. These are also fine container plants (even indoors), so they can be grown in colder Zones if brought inside for the winter. Typically, plants flower on and off throughout the year rather than in one blooming season, bearing waxy-textured flowers in exciting shades of yellow, gold, orange, vermilion, salmon, and pink, plus cream, white, and bicolors. Species, named hybrids, and unnamed seedlings are offered by some specialty growers.

Among the best you're likely to find are: *R. aurigeranum*, an *R. brookeanum* hybrid commonly listed as 'Gracile', *R. javanicum*, *R. konori*, *R. laetum*, *R. lochae*, *R. macgregorae*, and the following hybrids: 'Aravir' (white), 'George Budgen' (orange yellow), 'Ne Plus Ultra' (red), 'Taylori' (pink).

Highly regarded, dependable, popular, easy to grow, widely adapted: 'Anna Rose Whitney', 'Blue Ensign', 'Cotton Candy', 'Crest', 'Hallelujah', 'Loder's White', 'Mrs. G. W. Leak' ('Cottage Gardens Pride'), 'Purple Splendour', 'Ramapo', 'The Hon. Jean Marie de Montague', 'Trude Webster'.

Low-growing species and hybrids of great charm (from their general appearance, you could call them azaleas): *R. chryseum*, *R. impeditum*, *R. keiskei*, *R. moupinense*, *R. pemakoense*, 'Blue Diamond', 'Ocean Lake', 'Sapphire'.

Dwarfs and low growers with distinctive foliage and bell-shaped or funnel-shaped flowers, not in typical trusses: 'Bow Bells', 'Cilpinense', 'Ginny Gee', 'Patty Bee', 'Ramapo', 'Snow Lady'.

Rhododendron Ratings and Hardiness

The American Rhododendron Society has long used 2 numbers for rating rhododendrons (3/3, for example), with flower quality listed first and shrub quality second; 5 is superior, 4 above average, 3 average, 2 below average, 1 poor. But the system is evolving into a 3-number code.

While the first number still represents flower quality, the ARS hasn't decided what the second and third numbers should stand for. Some people use the third number to rate plant performance, while others use the second number to designate foliage quality and the third to rate plant habit. Many oppose any national ratings, since one rating cannot blanket the performance of one rhododendron in a dozen different climates. Regional ratings are on the horizon.

Until the ARS—or popular usage—settles on a firm new code, our ratings will follow the old system. Whenever you encounter a 3-number code, you'll need to find out what the numbers stand for before you make a judgment.

Each plant in the list that follows also has a hardiness rating. It indicates minimum temperatures a mature plant can take without serious injury. Heights given in the list are for plants 10 years old; older plants may be taller, and crowded or heavily shaded plants may reach up faster. Bloom seasons are approximate and vary with weather and location.

'A. Bedford'. 4/3. −5°F. Lavender blue with darker flare. Large trusses. To 6 ft. Late May.

'Anah Kruschke'. 2/3. −10°F. Lavender purple. Color not the best, but plant has good foliage, tolerates heat, is not fussy about soil. To 5 ft. May.

'Anna Rose Whitney'. 4/3. +5°F. Big, rich, deep pink trusses on compact, 5-ft. plant with excellent foliage. May.

'Antoon Van Welie'. 3/3. −5°F. Carmine pink. Big trusses of 'Pink Pearl' type on 6-ft. plant. Late May.

R. augustinii. 4/3. +5°F. Open, moderate growth to 6 ft. Leaves to 3 in. long. Flowers 2–2½ in. wide in clusters of 3 or 4, blue or purple in best named forms. May.

'Autumn Gold'. 3/4. 0°F. Relaxed salmon blooms (not a full domed truss) that come late in the season. Well-branched plant with broad, rather upright growth to about 5 ft. It blooms young.

'Blaney's Blue'. 4/4. −5°F. Covered with pale blue flowers in midseason. To 4–6 ft.; growth is compact, dense, and rounded. Blooms young.

'Blue Diamond'. 5/4. 0°F. Compact, erect growth to 3 ft. Small leaves. Lavender blue flowers cover plant in April. Takes considerable sun in Northwest.

'Blue Ensign'. 4/3. −15°F. Lilac blue flowers have a striking dark spot in the upper petal. Compact, well-branched, rounded plant to 4 ft. Leaves tend to spot. Midseason bloom.

'Blue Peter'. 4/3. −10°F. Broad, sprawling growth to 4 ft.; needs pruning. Large trusses of lavender blue flowers blotched purple. May.

'Bow Bells'. 3/4. 0°F. Compact, rounded growth to 4 ft. Leaves rounded. Flowers bright pink, bell shaped, in loose clusters. May. New growth bronzy.

R. burmanicum. 4/3. 15°F. Sweet-scented yellow to greenish yellow flowers on a 4-ft., upright plant. Leggy, open habit.

R. calophytum. 4/4. −5°F. Small, stocky tree, to 4 ft. Noted for big leaves—4 in. wide. 10–14 in. long. Trusses of white or pink flowers with deep red blotch. Protect from wind. March and April.

'Cary Ann'. 3/4. −5°F. Trumpet-shaped red flowers cover plant in midseason. Habit is low (around 3 ft.) and spreading; foliage looks good all year.

'Christmas Cheer'. 2/4. −5°F. Pink to white flowers in tight trusses. Can take full sun. To 3 ft. Early bloom (February–March) compensates for any lack in flower quality.

R. chryseum. 2/2. −15°F. Dwarf (1-ft.), densely branched plant with 1-in. leaves. Flowers are small, bright yellow bells, 4 or 5 to a cluster. April–May.

'Cilpinense'. 4/4. +5°F. Funnel-shaped flowers of apple blossom pink fading white; loose clusters nearly cover plants in March. Low, spreading growth to 2½ ft.; small leaves. Easy to grow. Effective massed. Protect blossoms from late frosts.

'CIS'. 4/2. +10°F. Flowers (in large trusses) are red in throat to cream yellow at edges of flower. To 3 ft. May.

(Continued on next page)

R

'Cornubia'. 4/3. +15°F. Strong, upright growth to 7 ft. Blood red flowers in large clusters, February–March.

'Cotton Candy'. 4/4. 0°F. Large flowers in soft pink shades carried in tall trusses. Dark green foliage on medium-sized plant. Early May.

'Countess of Haddington'. 4/4. +20°F. Light pink to white, waxy, tubular, fragrant flowers in compact trusses. To 5 ft. May.

'Countess of Sefton'. 3/3. +20°F. Large, tubular, fragrant, white flowers in loose trusses. Not as rangy as 'Fragrantissimum'. To 4 ft. Late April.

'Creamy Chiffon'. 5/4. 0°F. Salmon buds open into ruffled, double, creamy yellow flowers in midseason. Habit is low (to 3 ft.) and compact, leaves rounded.

'Crest'. 5/3. −5°F. Primrose yellow. Outstanding. To 5 ft. April, May.

'Cunningham's White'. 2/3. −15°F. To 4 ft. White with greenish yellow blotch. Hardy old-timer. Late May.

'Cynthia'. 3/3. −10°F. Rosy crimson trusses in May. Dependable, strong grower to 6 ft.

'Dora Amateis'. 4/4. −15°F. Semidwarf, rather small-foliaged plant; compact, spreading, good for foreground. Profuse bloomer with green-spotted white flowers.

'Elizabeth'. 4/4. 0°F. Several forms available. Broad grower to 3 ft. tall with medium-sized leaves. Blooms very young. Bright red, waxy, trumpet-shaped flowers in clusters of 3–6 at branch ends and in upper leaf joints. Main show in April; often reflowers in October. Very susceptible to fertilizer burn, salts in water.

'Else Frye'. 5/3. +15°F. Long, limber growth makes this a natural for informal espalier. Considerable pinching needed for compact plant. Early-season flowers are white with pink flush and gold throats.

Fabia Hybrids. 3/3. +10°F. Group of hybrids with 6–8 nodding flowers to a truss. Early May. Low, spreading growth; to 4 ft. tall. 'Tangerine' has vermilion orange flowers; 'Roman Pottery' terra cotta; 'Exbury' pale apricot tinted pink (not to be confused with Knap Hill-Exbury Hybrid azaleas).

R. falconeri. 3/3. +5°F. One of the unusual tree rhododendrons (others not listed here). To 25 ft. high and wide. Leathery leaves 6–12 in. long, reddish felted beneath. Clusters of 2-in.-wide, creamy white to pale yellow flowers. Blooms when 15–20 years old.

'Fastuosum Flore Pleno'. 3/3. −10°F. Double mauve flowers in May. Dependable, hardy old-timer. To 5 ft.

R. forrestii repens. 3/3. +5°F. Low, spreading dwarf. To 6 in. Tubular, bright red flowers in small clusters, April–May. Not easy to grow. Needs perfect drainage.

'Forsterianum'. 5/4. +20°F. Tubular, frilled, fragrant white flowers tinted pink. March bloom; buds often damaged by frost in colder areas without overhead protection. Open, rangy growth to 5 ft. Attractive glossy, red brown, peeling bark and medium-sized, glossy leaves.

'Fragrantissimum'. 4/3. +20°F. Large, funnel-shaped white flowers touched with pink, April–May. Powerfully fragrant. Loose, open, rangy growth with medium-sized, bright green, bristly leaves. With hard pinching in youth, a 5-ft. shrub. Easily trained as espalier or vine, reaching to 10 ft. or more. Can spill over wall. Grow as container plant in Northwest; overwinter indoors in bright but cool room.

'Ginny Gee'. 5/5. −5°F. Striking 2-ft. plant is covered with 1-in. flowers in midseason. Blooms range from pink to white, with striped and dappled forms. Leaves are small, growth dense.

'Gomer Waterer'. 3/4. −15°F. White flushed lilac. Hardy old-timer. To 5 ft. Late May.

'Graf Zeppelin'. 3/5. −10°F. Late-season, ball-shaped trusses consist of pink flowers that are lighter in the center, spotted with gold in the throat. Dark green, slightly twisted leaves grow on a spreading 5-ft. plant. Vigorous.

'Halfdan Lem'. 5/4. −5°F. Luminous red trusses stand out against deep green foliage in midseason. Well shaped, vigorous, to 5 ft.

'Hallelujah'. 5/5. −15°F. Rose red flowers in midseason stand above beautiful, thick, forest green foliage. To 4 ft. Takes full sun; fine-looking plant with or without leaves. Very strong grower.

'Hotei'. 5/4. 5°F. Canary yellow flowers backed by a prominent calyx come only when plant is 6–8 years old. Midseason. Habit is compact, to about 3 ft. Plant in well-drained soil only, since roots rot easily.

R. impeditum. 2/3. −10°F. Twiggy, dwarf, dense shrub to 1 ft. with closely packed, tiny, gray green leaves. Small flowers mauve to dark blue, April or May. Takes full sun in cooler areas. Needs *excellent* drainage to avoid root rot.

'Janet Blair'. 4/3. −15°F. Ruffled pastel flowers blend pink, cream,

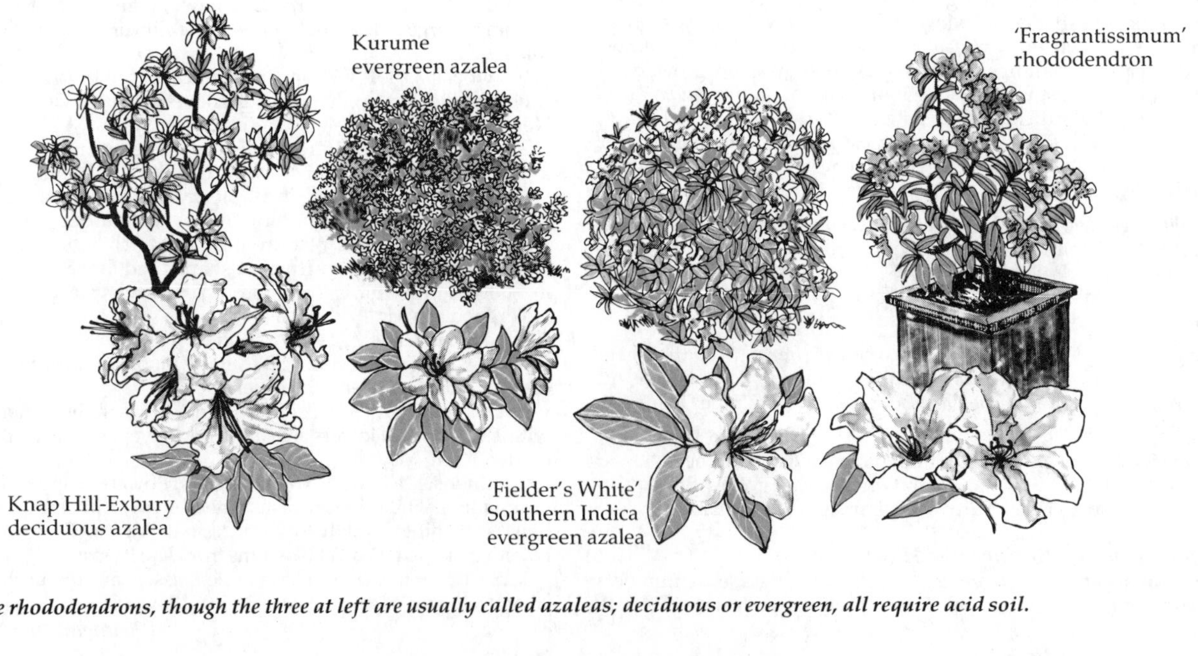

All are rhododendrons, though the three at left are usually called azaleas; deciduous or evergreen, all require acid soil.

white, and gold; large blossoms come in rounded trusses. Vigorous, tall and spreading.

'Jean Marie de Montague'. See 'The Hon. Jean Marie de Montague'.

R. keiskei. 2/1. −5°F. At least 2 forms are sold. The very dwarf, very compact form is a 6-in.-high shrublet. Taller form will reach 3 ft., has more open growth. Both forms produce lovely lemon yellow bells in great profusion, 3–5 in a cluster. March–May.

'Lem's Monarch' ('Pink Walloper'). 5/5. 0°F. Pink flowers, darker at the edges, come in huge round trusses in midseason. Plant grows to 6 ft., takes on a treelike shape. Large, deep green leaves.

'Leo'. 5/3. −5°F. Rounded to dome-shaped trusses are packed with rich cranberry red blooms. Medium-sized plant is well clothed in large dark green leaves.

Loderi Hybrids. 5/4. 0°F. Spectacular group with tall trusses of 6–7-in.-wide flowers in shades of pink or white. Fragrant; early May bloom. Informal, open growth to 8 ft. Too large for small garden. Slow to reach blooming age and not easy to grow. Difficult to maintain good foliage color. Best known are 'King George', with white flowers opening from blush buds; 'Pink Diamond', with blush flowers; and 'Venus', with shell pink flowers.

'Loder's White'. 5/5. 0°F. Big trusses of flowers are white tinged pink when they open, turn pure white as they mature. May. Shapely growth to 5 ft. Blooms freely even when young. Best white for most regions.

'Lord Roberts'. 3/3. −10°F. Handsome dark green foliage and rounded trusses of black-spotted red flowers. Growth is more compact, flowers more profuse in sun.

R. macrophyllum (R. californicum). COAST RHODODENDRON, WESTERN RHODODENDRON. Unrated. +5°F. Native near coast, northern California to British Columbia. Rangy growth to 4–10 ft., to 20 ft. in some locations. Leaves dark green, leathery, 2½–6 in. long; flower trusses rosy, rose purple, rarely white. May–June. Rarely sold; in Northwest, collect only with a permit.

'Madame Mason' ('Madame Masson'). 3/3. −5°F. White with light yellow flare on upper petal. Needs pruning to keep it compact. To 5 ft. Late May.

'Mars'. 4/3. −10°F. Dark red. Outstanding in form, foliage, flowers. To 4 ft. Late May.

'Molly Ann'. 4/5. −10°F. Rose-colored, upright trusses are set against round leaves on a compact 2-ft. plant.

'Moonstone'. 4/4. −5°F. Flaring bells age from pale pink to creamy yellow. April. Attractive dense, dwarf growth to 2 ft. Leaves neat, small, rounded. Fine facing taller rhododendrons, as low foundation planting with 'Bow Bells'.

R. moupinense. 4/2. 0°F. Open, spreading. To 1½ ft. Small (1½-in.-long), oval leaves. White or pink flowers, spotted red. New spring foliage deep red. February–March.

'Mrs. Betty Robertson'. 3/3. +5°F. Pale yellow blossoms in large trusses. May. Low, compact grower to 3 ft. Good foliage, does not burn in sun.

'Mrs. Furnival'. 5/5. −10°F. Clear pink flowers with light brown blotch in upper petals, in tight, round trusses. Late May. Compact growth to 4 ft.

'Mrs. G. W. Leak' ('Cottage Gardens Pride'). 4/4. +5°F. Deep pink with deep brown flare on upper petals. Strong growth to 5 ft. May.

R. mucronulatum. 4/3. −25°F. Deciduous rhododendron with open growth to 5 ft. Makes up for bare branches by flowering in January–February. Flowers generally bright purple; there is a pink form, 'Cornell Pink'.

'Nancy Evans'. 5/4. 5°F. Orange-tinged buds open to yellow in midseason. Each bloom is backed by a calyx that makes it look almost double. New foliage is bronzy. Compact growth to about 3 ft.

Naomi Hybrids. 4/4. −10°F. Top-notch group with trusses of fragrant, 4–5-in. flowers in May. Bloom younger than Loderi Hybrids; lower, more compact, hardier. To 4–5 ft., and leggy unless carefully pruned while young. 'Exbury' (rosy pink blended with yellow), 'Nautilus' (pale pink, frilled, centered with creamy yellow and veined rose), and 'Stella Maris' (pink and yellow) are 3 best known in this outstanding group. Take it easy with fertilizers.

'Nova Zembla'. 3/3. −25°F. Profuse red flowers come late in the season, even in cold country. Takes heat. To about 5 ft.

'Ocean Lake'. 3/3. −5°F. Low, azalealike plant with flowers of deep violet.

'Old Copper'. 4/4. 5°F. Copper orange flowers late in the season. Well-shaped plant to 5 ft.; can take more heat than most rhododendrons.

'Patty Bee'. 5/5. −10°F. Yellow, 2-in., trumpet-shaped flowers cover plant in midseason. Dense, moundlike growth to 1½ ft. Leaves are small, giving plant a fine-textured look.

R. pemakoense. 2/3. 0°F. Compact, spreading. To 1½ ft. Small (1½-in.-long) leaves. Flowers pinkish purple, very free blooming. Useful in rock gardens. March–April.

'Pink Pearl'. 3/3. −5°F. Rose pink, tall trusses in May. To 6 ft. or more. Open, rangy growth without pruning. Dependable grower and bloomer in all except coldest climates.

'PJM'. 4/4. −25°F. To 4 ft. Takes heat as well as cold. Lavender pink blooms come early; foliage turns mahogany in winter.

'Purple Splendour'. 4/3. −10°F. Ruffled, rich deep purple blooms blotched black purple. Informal growth to 4 ft. Hardy and easy to grow. May.

R. racemosum. 3/3. −10°F. Several forms include 6-in. dwarf, 2½-ft. compact upright shrub, and tall 7-footer. Pink, inch-wide flowers in clusters of 3–6 all along stems, March–April. Easy to grow; sun tolerant in cooler areas.

'Rainbow'. 1/2. 0°F. Light pink center, carmine edges. Very showy. Heavy foliage. Strong growth to 5 ft. April bloom.

'Ramapo'. 3/4. −20°F. Violet blue flowers cover plant in midseason. Dense, spreading growth to 2 ft. in sun, taller in shade. New growth is dusty blue green. Fine for rockeries; good choice in California.

'Rosamundi'. 2/3. −5°F. Ball-like trusses of pink flowers appear early in season. Plant is slow growing, compact, to 4 ft. high and wide.

'Saffron Queen'. 4/3. +20°F. Sulfur yellow with darker spots on upper petals. April bloom. Flowers, trusses, foliage smaller than 'Pink Pearl' type. To 3 ft.

'Sapphire'. 4/4. 0°F. Small, bright blue, azalealike flowers in March, April. Twiggy, rounded, dense shrublet to 1½ ft. Foliage gray green, leaves tiny.

'Sappho'. 3/2. −5°F. White with dark purple spot in throat. May. Easy to grow; gangly without pruning. To 6 ft.; use at back of border.

Scarlet King Hybrids. Too recent for rating. +20°F. These New Zealand hybrids thrive in warm-winter conditions, yet perform well in average rhododendron situations. Habit of growth varies. Free flowering. Rich red flowers late April–May.

'Scarlet Wonder'. 5/5. −10°F. Outstanding dwarf (to 2 ft.) of compact growth. Shiny, quilted foliage forms backdrop for many bright red blossoms.

'Scintillation'. 4/5. −10°F. Medium-sized, compact plant covered in lustrous, dark green leaves. Rounded trusses carry gold-throated pink flowers.

'September Song'. 4/4. 0°F. Salmon-edged flowers shade into golden orange throats, giving trusses an overall orange look. Blooms young. Grows to 4 ft.; wider than tall.

'Snow Lady'. 4/4. 0°F. White, black stamens. Wide, fragrant, flat flowers in clusters. To 3 ft. April.

'Sunny Day'. 4/5. −5°F. Medium-sized yellow trusses with red spots on upper lobes of flowers. Midseason bloom starts while plant is still young. Broad, well branched, to 3 ft.

'Susan'. 3/4. −5°F. Silvery lavender flowers in large trusses. May. Handsome foliage. To 4 ft.

'Taurus'. 5/4. 0°F. Brilliant red flowers with black spotting on upper lobes come in large, round trusses. Midseason bloom comes only after plants reach 4–6 years old. Vigorous, upright to 6 ft.; well covered with forest green leaves.

'The Hon. Jean Marie de Montague'. 3/4. 0°F. Brightest scarlet red in May. Good foliage. To 5 ft.

'Top Banana'. 4/4. 0°F. Clear, bright yellow. Midseason bloom. Upright, vase-shaped plant to 4 ft. Buds young (2 years).

(Continued on next page)

'Trilby'. 3/4. −10°F. Dark red flowers are accented by nearly black center spots and complemented by olive to gray green leaves. Compact, upright plant of medium height.

'Trude Webster'. 5/4. −10°F. Huge trusses of clear pink flowers come in midseason on a strong, 5-ft. plant. Fine plant habit, large leaves. One of the best pinks.

'Unique'. 3/5. +5°F. Apricot buds open to deep cream, fade to light yellow; trusses tight, rounded. April, early May. Outstanding neat, rounded, compact habit. To 4 ft.

'Unknown Warrior'. 3/2. +5°F. Light soft red, fades quickly when exposed to bright sun. Easy to grow. To 4 ft. April.

'Van Nes Sensation'. 3/4. 0°F. Pale lilac flowers in large trusses. Strong grower. To 5 ft. May.

'Vulcan'. 3/4. −5°F. Bright brick red flowers in late May, early June. New leaves often grow past flower buds, partially hiding flowers. To 4 ft.

R. yakushimanum. 4/4. −20°F. Clear pink bells changing to white, about 12 in truss. Late May. Dense, spreading growth to 3 ft. New foliage gray felted; older leaves with heavy tan or white felt beneath. Selections range from 'Ken Janeck', a large (and large-leafed) form with very pink flowers, to 'Yaku Angel', with pink-tinged buds opening to pure white. There are also a number of hybrids that are as good in cold country as they are in milder climates, among them 'Anna H. Hall', 'Mardi Gras', and 'Yaku Princess'. (This last is part of a good series of hybrids,all with monarchic names.)

Kinds of Evergreen Azaleas

The evergreen azaleas sold in the West fall into more than a dozen groups and species, though an increasing number of hybrids have such mixed parentage that they don't conveniently fit into any group. But group characteristics are rather elastic. Here are several popular groups:

Belgian Indica. Zones 14–24. This is a group of hybrids originally developed for greenhouse forcing. Where lowest temperatures are 20°–30°F., many of them serve very well as landscape plants. They have lush, full foliage and profuse large blossoms during their flowering season. Among the most widely sold are: 'Albert and Elizabeth' (white and pink), 'California Sunset' (salmon pink with white border), 'Chimes' (dark red), 'Mardi Gras' (salmon with white border), 'Mission Bells' (red semidouble), 'Mme. Alfred Sanders' (cherry red), 'Orange Sanders' (salmon orange), 'Orchidiflora' (orchid pink), 'Paul Schame' (salmon), and 'Red Poppy'. 'Violetta' (deep purple) and 'William Van Orange' (orange red) have pendant growth suitable for hanging baskets.

Brooks Hybrids. Zones 8, 9, 14–24. Bred in Modesto, California, for heat resistance, compactness, and large flowers. Best known are: 'Madonna' (white), 'My Valentine' (rose), 'Pinkie' (pink), and 'Red Wing'.

Gable Hybrids. Zones 4–9, 14–24. Developed to produce azaleas of Kurume type that take 0°F. temperatures. In Zones 4–6, they may lose some leaves, but they bloom heavily from late April through May. Frequently sold are: 'Caroline Gable' (bright pink), 'Herbert' (purple), 'Louise Gable' (pink), 'Pioneer' (pink), 'Purple Splendor', 'Purple Splendor Compacta' (less rangy growth), 'Rosebud' (pink), and 'Rose Greeley' (white). Girard Hybrids, which originated with Gable crosses, are becoming increasingly popular throughout the West.

Glenn Dale Hybrids. Zones 4–9, 14–24. Developed primarily for hardiness, but they do drop some leaves in cold winters. Some grow tall and rangy, others low and compact. Growth rate varies from slow to rapid. Some have small leaves like Kurumes; others have large leaves. Familiar varieties are: 'Anchorite' (orange), 'Aphrodite' (pale pink), 'Buccaneer' (orange red), 'Everest' (white), 'Geisha' (white, striped red), and 'Glacier' (white).

Gold Cup Hybrids. Zones 14–24. Members of this group were originally called Mossholder-Bristow Hybrids. Plants combine large flowers of Belgian Indicas with vigor of Rutherfordianas. Good landscape plants where temperatures don't go below 20°F. Some popular varieties are: 'Easter Parade' (pink and white), 'Sun Valley' (white), and 'White Orchid' (white with red throat).

Greenwood Hybrids. Zones 4–7. Bred in Canby, Oregon, most of these are compact and hardy, with large double flowers. You can make them succeed in colder climates than they're bred for by keeping them from drying out: it's desiccation, not freezing, that does them in. Some of the most popular varieties are: 'Greenwood Orange', 'Greenwood Rosebud' (pink with a slight purple blush), 'Sherry' (very deep red flowers; maroon winter foliage), 'Silver Streak' (reddish purple flowers, white-edged leaves), and 'Sleigh Bells' (single white).

Harris Hybrids. Zones 4–9, 14–22. To date, these relatively new hybrids have received the most attention in the Pacific Northwest, though some California gardeners are using them as well. The offspring of Glenn Dale, Kaempferi, and Satsuki azaleas, most of these extra-large-flowered plants bloom after midseason. Some good ones to look for: 'Bruce Hancock' (3½-in., pink-edged flowers with white centers; low, spreading to 4 ft., a good ground cover); 'Fascination' (4½-in. red flowers with pink centers); and 'Rhonda Stiteler' (double pink flowers, leaves lightly variegated with yellow).

Kaempferi Hybrids. Zones 2–7. Based on *R. kaempferi*, the torch azalea, a hardy plant with orange red flowers. Somewhat hardier than Kurumes, taller and more open in growth. Nearly leafless in coldest winters. Hardy to −15°F. Flowers cover plants in early spring. Similar in every way to Vuykiana Hybrids. Among those sold are: 'Fedora' (salmon rose), 'John Cairns' (orange red), and 'Palestrina' (white).

Kurume. Zones 5–9, 14–24. Compact, twiggy plants, densely foliaged with small leaves. Small flowers borne in incredible profusion. Plants mounded or tiered, handsome even out of bloom. Hardy to 5°–10°F. Grow well outdoors in half sun. Many varieties available; most widespread are: 'Coral Bells' (pink), 'Hexe' (crimson), 'Hino-crimson' (bright red), 'Hinodegiri' (cerise red), 'Sherwood Orchid' (red violet), 'Sherwood Red' (orange red), 'Snow', and 'Ward's Ruby' (dark red).

North Tisbury Hybrids. Zones 4–9, 14–24. You can see the *R. nakaharai* ancestry in most of these plants. Their low, spreading habit and extremely late bloom—into midsummer—make them naturals for hanging baskets and ground covers. Some of the best are: 'Alexander' (red orange flowers, bronze foliage in fall, very hardy), 'Pink Cascade' (pink), and 'Red Fountain' (dark red orange blooms, around July 4th).

Pericat. Zones 4–9, 14–24. Hybrids originally developed for greenhouse forcing, but as hardy as Kurumes. Similar to Kurumes, but flowers tend to be somewhat larger. Varieties sold are: 'Mme. Pericat' (light pink), 'Sweetheart Supreme' (blush pink), and 'Twenty Grand' (rose pink).

Robin Hill Hybrids. Zones 4–9, 14–24. A large group that got its start more than 50 years ago. These medium-sized plants flower late; large blooms have some resemblance to Satsukis. There are so many good ones—several with "Robin Hill" in their names—that it's hard to single out only a few. Try 'Betty Ann Voss' (pink), 'Conversation Piece' (pink with light center), 'Nancy of Robin Hill' (pink with red blotch), 'Robin Hill Gillie' (red orange).

Rutherfordiana. Zones 15–24. Greenhouse plants, good in garden where temperatures don't go below 20°F. Bushy 2–4-ft. plants with handsome foliage. Flowers intermediate between Kurume and Belgian Indica. Available varieties include: 'Alaska' (white), 'Constance' (light orchid pink), 'Dorothy Gish' (brick red), 'Firelight' (rose red), 'L. J. Bobbink' (orchid pink), 'Purity' (white), 'Rose Queen' (deep pink), and 'White Gish' (pure white).

Satsuki. Zones 4–9, 14–24. Includes azaleas sometimes referred to as Gumpo and Macrantha hybrids. Hardy to 5°F. Plants low growing, some true dwarfs; many are pendant enough for hanging baskets. Large flowers late, often in June. Popular varieties are: 'Bunkwa' (blush pink), 'Flame Creeper' (orange red), 'Gumpo' (white), 'Gumpo Pink' (rose pink), 'Hi Gasa' (bright pink), 'Rosaeflora' (rose pink), 'Shinnyo-No-Tsuki' (violet red, white center).

Southern Indica. Zones 8, 9, 14–24. Varieties selected from Belgian Indicas for sun tolerance and vigor. Most take temperatures of 10°–20°F., but some are damaged at 20°F. Generally speaking, they grow faster, more vigorously, and taller than the other kinds. Many varieties are sold, among which are these popular ones: 'Brilliant' (carmine red), 'Duc de Rohan' (salmon pink), 'Fielder's White', 'Formosa' (brilliant rose purple, also sold as 'Coccinea', 'Phoenicia', 'Vanessa'), 'George Lindley Taber' (light pink), 'Imperial Countess' (deep salmon pink), 'Imperial Princess' (rich pink), 'Imperial Queen' (pink), 'Iveryana' (white with orchid streaks), 'Orange Pride' (bright orange), 'Pride of Dorking' (brilliant red), 'Southern Charm' (watermelon pink, sometimes sold as 'Judge Solomon'), and 'White April'.

Vuykiana Hybrids. See description of Kaempferi Hybrids on facing page. Varieties sold are: 'Blue Danube' (violet blue), 'Vuyk's Rosy Red', and 'Vuyk's Scarlet'.

R. mucronatum ('Indica Alba', 'Ledifolia Alba'). Zones 4–9, 14–24. Spreading growth to 6 ft. (but usually 3 ft.); large, hairy leaves. White or greenish flowers 2½–3 in. across, March–April. Variety 'Sekidera' ('Indica Rosea', 'Ledifolia Rosea') has white flowers flushed and blotched rose in February, March.

Kinds of Deciduous Azaleas

Very few deciduous shrubs can equal deciduous azaleas in show and range of color. Their evergreen relatives can't match them in yellow, orange, and flame red range or in bicolor contrasts. They are at their best in Zones 4–7, 15–17. Also perform well in coastal valley Zone 14 (even in full sun) if well watered. Deciduous types tend to be less particular about soil, watering than most evergreen sorts. Fall foliage color is often brilliant orange red to maroon.

Ghent Hybrids. Extremely hardy. Many will take −25°F. temperatures. Upright growth variable in height. Flowers generally smaller than those of Mollis Hybrids. Colors include shades of yellow, orange, umber, pink, and red. May flowering.

Knap Hill-Exbury Hybrids. Plants vary from spreading to upright, from 4–6 ft. tall. Flowers are large (3–5 in. across), in clusters of 7–18, sometimes ruffled or fragrant, white through pink and yellow to orange and red, often with contrasting blotches.

Both Knap Hill and Exbury azaleas come from same original crosses; first crosses were made at Knap Hill, and subsequent improvements were made at both Exbury and Knap Hill. The "Rothschild" azaleas are Exbury plants. Ilam Hybrids are from same original stock, further improved in New Zealand.

A hundred or more named varieties are available in the Northwest and northern California. They make up perhaps half of all deciduous azaleas sold in the Pacific Northwest. If you want to be sure of color and size of flower of plant you buy, choose from named varieties. Some of the best are: 'Cannon's Double' (pink), 'Gibraltar' (orange), 'Homebush' (double deep pink), 'Klondyke' (golden tangerine), and 'Oxydol' (white with yellow markings). But don't consider all seedlings as inferior plants. Generally it's best to select seedlings in bloom.

Mollis Hybrids. Hybrids of *R. molle* and *R. japonicum*. Upright growth to 4–5 ft.; 2½–4-in. flowers in clusters of 7–13. Colors range from chrome yellow through poppy red. Some people don't like the light skunky fragrance of the new growth, but everybody seems to love the yellow to orange fall foliage color. Very heavy bloom in May.

Northern Lights Hybrids. Developed by the University of Minnesota, these are hardy to −40°F. They grow 2–4 ft. tall, produce ball-shaped trusses of fragrant, sterile flowers (they won't set seed) in late spring. The most widely available now are: 'Orchid Lights', 'Rosy Lights', and 'White Lights'. Foliage can have the skunky odor of the hybrids' Mollis Hybrid ancestors.

Occidentale Hybrids. Hybrids between *R. occidentale* and Mollis Hybrids. Flowers same size as those of Mollis Hybrids; plants taller, to 8 ft. Colors range from white flushed rose and blotched yellow to red with orange blotch.

Viscosum Hybrids. Hybrids between Mollis azaleas and *R. viscosum*. Deciduous shrubs with color range of Mollis but with added fragrance from *R. viscosum*.

R. japonicum. JAPANESE AZALEA. Hardy to −10°F. Upright, fast growth to 6 ft. Salmon red flowers, 2–3 in. wide, in clusters of 6–12. Variety *aureum* has rich yellow flowers. Blooms in May.

R. luteum (R. flavum). PONTIC AZALEA. To 8 ft. Fragrant flowers are single yellow with darker blotch. Blooms in May.

R. occidentale. WESTERN AZALEA. Hardy to −5°F. Zones 4–24. Native to mountains and foothills of California and Oregon. Erect growth to 6–10 ft. Funnel-shaped flowers in clusters, May–June. Color varies from white to pinkish white with yellow blotch; some are heavily marked carmine rose. Fragrant.

R. schlippenbachii. ROYAL AZALEA. Hardy to −20°F. Native to Korea. Densely branched shrub to 6–8 ft. Leaves in whorls of 5 at tips of branches. Large (2–4-in.), pure light pink flowers in clusters of 3–6, April–May. A white form is also available. Good fall color: yellow, orange, scarlet, crimson. Protect from full sun.

R. vaseyi. PINKSHELL AZALEA. Hardy to −20°F. Upright, irregular, spreading to 15 ft. Light pink flowers in clusters of 5–8 in May.

RHODOHYPOXIS baurii. *Hypoxidaceae.* Bulb. Zones 4–7, 14–24. Tufts of narrow, 2–3-in. leaves are nearly obscured by masses of 1-in., white, pink, or rose red flowers over a long spring–summer season. Dormant in winter. Bulbs multiply quickly with good drainage, adequate water. In cold-winter climates, protect from winter rains with pane of glass or shingle. If grown in pots, turn pots on side in winter or store over winter in cold frame. Excellent plant for rock garden, stone sink garden, or pots.

Rhodohypoxis baurii

RHOEO spathacea ***(R. discolor).*** *Commelinaceae.* MOSES-IN-THE-CRADLE, MOSES-IN-THE-BOAT. Perennial. Outdoor plant in Zones 16, 17, 20–24; sheltered spots in Zones 12–15, 18, 19. House plant everywhere. Stems to 8 in. high. Leaf tufts grow to 6–12 in. wide, with dozen or so broad, sword-shaped, rather erect leaves which are dark green above and deep purple underneath. Flowers are interesting rather than beautiful. Small, white, 3-petaled, they are crowded into boat-shaped bracts borne down among leaves. Best used as pot plant or in hanging basket. Tough plant which will take high or low light intensity and casual watering, low humidity and heat on a desert patio. Avoid overwatering; keep water out of leaf axils. Variety 'Variegata' has leaves striped red and yellowish green.

Rhoeo spathacea

RHOICISSUS capensis ***(Cissus capensis).*** *Vitaceae.* EVERGREEN GRAPE. Evergreen vine with tuberous roots. Outdoors in Zones 16, 17, 21–24; house plant anywhere. Leaves roundish to kidney shaped, scallop toothed, something like those of true grape in size and appearance. New stems and leaves are a rosy rust color, covered with red hairs; mature leaves are strong light green tinged with copper, with rusty, hairy undersides. Flowers insignificant. Takes full sun outdoors, but roots need shade, moisture. Will take heavy shade as house plant. Good overhead screen or ground cover in milder regions. Slow growing.

Rhoicissus capensis

R

RHOPALOSTYLIS. *Palmae.* Zones 17, 23, 24. Feather palms with long, clean trunks. Moderate growth rate. Need shade and ample water; do best in frost-free gardens.

R. baueri. From Norfolk Island. Grows to 50 ft.; beautiful curving, arching leaves 6–9 ft. long.

R. sapida. NIKAU PALM, SHAVING BRUSH PALM. From New Zealand. Grows to 30 ft. Good pot plant where small space dictates upright palm. On outdoor plants, feathers 4–8 ft. long stand upright from prominent bulge at top of trunk.

Rhopalostylis sapida

RHUBARB. *Polygonaceae.* Unconventional perennial vegetable growing from large, fleshy rhizomes. Best in Zones 1–11; also grown in 14–24. In Zones 10, 11, it is treated as an annual and set out in fall for winter, spring harvest (plant tends to rot in heat of late spring, early summer). Big, elongated, heart-shaped, crinkled leaves and red-tinted leaf stalks are showy enough to qualify for display spot in garden. Delicious leaf stalks are used like fruit in sauces and pies. The leaves themselves are poisonous; always discard them when preparing rhubarb. Flowers are insignificant, in spikelike clusters. Preferred varieties are 'Victoria', with greenish stalks, and 'Cherry' ('Crimson Cherry'), 'MacDonald', and 'Strawberry' (red stalks).

Rhubarb

Plant in late winter or early spring. Divisions should contain at least one bud. Soil should be deep, rich, and well drained. Place tops of divisions at soil line. Space divisions 3–4 ft. apart. Give plants some shade in hot inland gardens. Irrigate freely when active top growth indicates that roots are growing. Permit plants to grow 2 full seasons before harvesting. During next spring you can pull off leaf stalks (to cook) for 4 or 5 weeks; older, huskier plants will take up to 8 weeks of pulling. Harvest stalks by grasping near base and pulling sideways and outward; cutting with knife will leave stub that will decay. Never remove all leaves from a single plant. Stop harvesting when slender leaf stalks appear. After harvest, feed and water freely. Cut out any blossom stalks that appear.

RHUS. *Anacardiaceae.* SUMAC. Evergreen or deciduous shrubs or trees. Of the ornamental sumacs, deciduous kinds are hardy anywhere and thrive in poor soils. They tend to produce suckers, especially if their roots are disturbed by soil cultivation. They need some water. Evergreen sumacs are not as hardy as the deciduous kinds, but they will grow in almost any soil as long as it is well drained (soggy soils may kill them). They are fire retardant if fairly well watered.

Rhus typhina

Rhus includes poison oak and poison ivy, both of which may cause severe dermatitis on contact; even breathing smoke from burning plants is harmful. If you have either plant on your property, destroy it with chemical brush killer.

Poison oak *(R. diversiloba)* is most common in California, western Oregon, and western Washington. In the open or in filtered sun, it grows as a dense, leafy shrub. Where shaded, as in coast redwood country, it becomes a tall-climbing vine. Its leaves are divided into 3 leaflets, edges of which are scalloped, toothed, or lobed. Very similar is poison ivy *(R. radicans),* which grows in eastern Oregon, eastern Washington (and eastward), but it's more sprawling in growth habit and rarely climbs. Foliage of both turns bright orange or scarlet in the fall—beautiful but to be avoided. It's hardest to identify bare branches in winter and early spring; even brushing against these can cause typical rash.

R. aromatica. FRAGRANT SUMAC. Deciduous shrub. Zones 1–3, 10. Fast growing, 3–5 ft. tall, spreading much wider. Leaves divided into 3 leaflets, fragrant when brushed against or crushed. Tiny yellowish flowers in spring. Chief use: coarse bank cover, ground cover for poor, dry soils. Red fall color. Two available varieties are 'Low Grow' (to about 2 ft.) and 'Green Mound' (to 4 ft.).

R. cotinus. See *Cotinus coggygria.*

R. glabra. SMOOTH SUMAC. Deciduous large shrub or small tree. Zones 1–10, 14–17. Native to eastern Oregon, eastern Washington, British Columbia, and eastward in North America. Upright to 10 ft., or sometimes treelike to 20 ft. In the wilds, it spreads by underground roots to form large patches. Looks very much like staghorn sumac *(R. typhina),* but usually grows lower and does not have velvety branches.

Leaves are divided into 11–23 rather narrow, 2–5-in.-long, toothed leaflets, deep green above, whitish beneath; turn brilliant scarlet in fall. Inconspicuous greenish flowers followed by showy autumn display of scarlet fruit in conical clusters which last on bare branches well into winter. Very tolerant of drought and heat. Garden use same as for *R. typhina. R. g. cismontana,* dwarf variety that grows in Rocky Mountains, is 3–4 ft. tall, has smaller leaves with fewer leaflets. *R. g.* 'Laciniata' has deeply cut and slashed leaflets, giving it a fernlike appearance.

R. integrifolia. LEMONADE BERRY. Evergreen shrub. Zones 15–17, 20–24. Native to coastal southern California, Channel Islands, and Baja California. Generally 3–10 ft. high and as wide, rarely treelike to 30 ft. Oval to nearly round, leathery dark green leaves, 1–2½ in. long, with smooth or shallowly toothed edges. White or pinkish flowers in dense clusters February–March, sometimes January–July. Small, flat, clustered fruit is reddish and gummy, with acid pulp which can be used to flavor drinks—hence common name.

Set plants out in fall or winter. Although drought resistant, they perform best if watered deeply once a month during summer. They will also take normal garden watering if drainage is good.

Lemonade berry grows best near coast. Makes wonderful ground cover on rocky slopes exposed to salt-laden winds; one plant eventually sprawls over wide area, even down cliffs. In less windy places, use it as a tall screen or background. Makes excellent espalier against fences and walls. Can be trimmed to dense formal hedge and kept only 10 in. wide. Useful in erosion control. Very susceptible to verticillium wilt.

R. lancea. AFRICAN SUMAC. Evergreen tree. Zones 8, 9, 12–24. Slow growing to 25 ft. Open, spreading habit; graceful weeping outer branchlets. Leaves divided into 3 willowlike, dark green leaflets 4–5 in. long. Pea-sized, berrylike, yellow or red fruit grows in clusters on female tree, can be messy on pavement.

Because it can take high summer heat African sumac is popular in Zones 12, 13, although it is susceptible to Texas root rot there. Established plants are drought resistant, but will also thrive in lawns. Hardy to 12°F. Stake and prune to establish form you want. Makes attractive, airy tree with interesting branch pattern and effective dark red, rough bark. You can train it to a single trunk or let it grow as multitrunked tree that looks somewhat like olive. Also useful for screens, clipped hedges, or background plantings. Old plants easy to transplant if grown under dry conditions.

R. laurina. LAUREL SUMAC. Evergreen shrub. Zones 20–24, Native mostly to coastal foothills of southern California and Baja California. Grows rapidly to 6–15 ft.; sometimes almost treelike, with rounded crown. Gets rangy unless pruned and trimmed. Attractive reddish branchlets. Laurel-like leaves, 2–4 in. long, light green, often with pink margins and pink leaf stalks; foliage pleasantly aromatic. Small whitish flowers in dense, branched, 2–6-in.-long clusters bloom May–July, sometimes to December. Berrylike white fruit attracts birds. More tender to frost than native sugar bush or lemonade berry. Sometimes freezes in its native range but comes back quickly from stump. Very drought tolerant. Useful as espalier plant or as clipped hedge. Good bank cover where frost is rare. Aids in erosion control.

R. ovata. SUGAR BUSH. Evergreen shrub. Zones 7–24. Native to dry slopes away from coast in southern California, Baja California,

Arizona. Upright or spreading shrub 2½–10 ft. high. Glossy, leathery leaves, 1½–3 in. long, differ from those of *R. integrifolia* in being somewhat trough shaped and pointed rather than rounded at the tips. White or pinkish flowers in dense clusters, March–May, followed by small, reddish, hairy fruit coated with sugary secretion. For culture and use, see lemonade berry *(R. integrifolia)*; sugar bush can substitute for lemonade berry in inland areas. Can be used along coast but not where exposed to salt spray and sea winds. In desert, plant in fall or winter; hard to establish in hot weather. Very heat and drought tolerant.

R. trilobata. SQUAWBUSH, SKUNKBUSH. Deciduous shrub. Zones 1–3, 10. Similar in most details to *R. aromatica,* but scent of bruised leaves considered unpleasant by most people. Clumping habit makes it a natural low hedge. Brilliant yellow to red fall color. Very tolerant of heat and drought.

R. typhina. STAGHORN SUMAC. Deciduous shrub or small tree. Zones 1–10, 14–17. Upright growing to 15 (sometimes to 30) ft., spreading wider. Very similar to *R. glabra,* but branches are covered with velvety short brown hairs, like deer's antler "in velvet." Leaves divided into 11–31 toothed, 5-in.-long leaflets deep green above, grayish beneath; they turn rich red in fall. Tiny greenish flowers in 4–8-in.-long clusters in June–July are followed by clusters of fuzzy crimson fruit that lasts all winter, gradually turns brown. *R. t.* 'Laciniata' has deeply cut leaflets; it doesn't grow quite as big as the species and is said to have richer color in fall.

Both staghorn sumac and smooth sumac *(R. glabra)* take extreme heat and cold and will grow in any except the most alkaline soils. Big divided leaves give tropical effect; when they turn color, show is brilliant. Bare branches make fine winter silhouette; fruit is decorative. Good among evergreens, where they can show off their bright fall foliage color. Can also grow in large containers.

RHYNCHOSPERMUM. See *Trachelospermum.*

RIBBON BUSH. See *Homalocladium platycladum.*

RIBBON GRASS. See *Phalaris arundinacea picta.*

RIBES. *Saxifragaceae.* CURRANT, GOOSEBERRY. (See Currant and Gooseberry for fruiting currants and gooseberries.) Deciduous and evergreen shrubs. Those without spines are called currants; those with spines, gooseberries. A number of native species are ornamental; 4 are sold in nurseries. Fruit attracts birds.

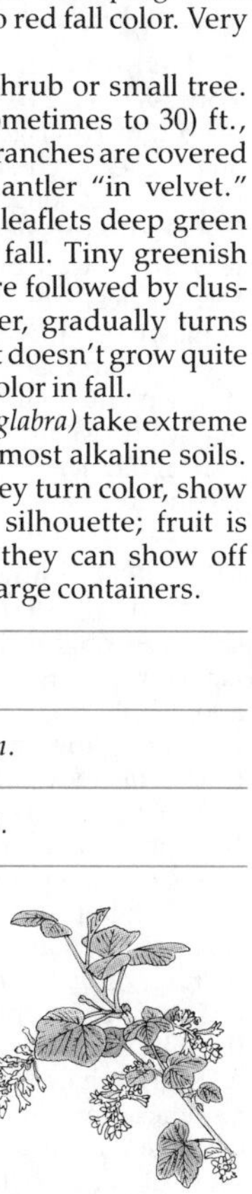

Ribes sanguineum

R. alpinum. ALPINE CURRANT. Deciduous shrub. Zones 1–3, 10. Spineless shrub 4–5 ft. tall (rarely taller) of dense, twiggy growth. Roundish, toothed and lobed leaves ½–1½ in. across appear very early in spring. Flowers and fruit inconspicuous. Good hedge plant. Sun or shade, average water.

R. aureum. GOLDEN CURRANT. Deciduous shrub. All Zones. Native to inland regions of West. Erect growth, 3–6 ft. tall. Light green, lobed, toothed leaves. Clusters of small, bright yellow spring flowers, usually with spicy fragrance, are 1–2½ in. long. Summer berries are yellow to red to black. Plant in full sun to part shade. Prefers moderate summer watering.

R. nigrum. BLACK CURRANT. Deciduous shrub. Zones 1–7. Most varieties are banned because the plant is an alternate host to white pine blister rust, but the hybrid variety 'Consort' is immune to the disease. Thornless plants grow to 6 ft. Leaves are 3 lobed, deep green, oddly scented. Drooping clusters of whitish flowers turn to juicy, shiny, black fruits with blackberry-currant flavor. Fruit used in jams, jellies, sauces.

R. odoratum. Deciduous shrub. All Zones. Similar to *R. aureum* but native to the Midwest and high plains. Flowers have carnation fragrance. The variety 'Crandall' has large, shiny black fruit that has the rich, sweet-tart flavor of European black currant (*R. nigrum*). Resistant to white pine blister rust.

R. sanguineum. PINK WINTER CURRANT, RED FLOWERING CURRANT. Deciduous shrub. Zones 4–9, 14–24. Native to Coast Ranges from California to British Columbia. To 4–12 ft. tall. Leaves are 2½ in. wide, maplelike. Small, deep pink to red flowers, 10–30 to each drooping, 2–4-in.-long cluster, bloom March–June. Berries blue black, with whitish bloom. Variety *glutinosum* (more southerly in origin) is the most common in nurseries; it has 15–40 flowers to a cluster, generally deep or pale pink. 'Elk River Red', occasionally sold in Northwest, has rich red flowers. 'King Edward VII' is lower-growing variety with red flowers. A white-flowered form is occasionally seen. Plant in sun to light shade. Fairly drought tolerant, but best with moderate water, some shade where summer is hot and dry.

R. speciosum. FUCHSIA-FLOWERING GOOSEBERRY. Nearly evergreen shrub. Zones 8, 9, 14–24. Native near coast from Santa Clara County south to Baja California. Erect, 3–6 ft. tall, with spiny, often bristly stems. Thick, green, 1-in. leaves resemble those of fruiting gooseberry. Drooping, deep crimson to cherry red flowers are fuchsialike, with long, protruding stamens. January–May bloom. Berries gummy, bristly. Excellent barrier planting. Sun near coast, light shade inland. Tolerates much drought and heat when established, but loses leaves in summer through fall (with a little summer water, though, it is nearly evergreen).

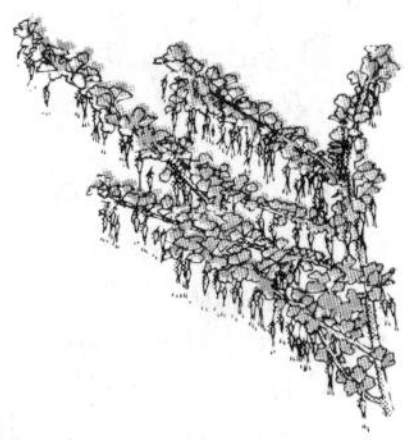

Ribes speciosum

R. viburnifolium. CATALINA PERFUME, EVERGREEN CURRANT. Spreading evergreen shrub. Zones 8, 9, 14–24. Native to Catalina Island, Baja California. Low-growing plant. To 3 ft. tall and much wider (to 12 ft.). Low-arching or half-trailing wine red stems may root in moist soil. Leaves leathery, roundish, dark green, an inch across, fragrant (some say like pine, others like apples) after rain or when crushed. Light pink to purplish flowers, February–April; red berries.

Ground or bank cover for sun or half shade on coast, part shade inland. Useful in erosion control. Foliage turns yellow in hot sun. Spider mites are sometimes a problem in coastal areas. Drought tolerant when established. Excellent ground cover under native oaks where heavy watering is undesirable. To keep plants low, cut out upright-growing stems.

RICE PAPER PLANT. See *Tetrapanax papyriferus.*

RICINUS communis. *Euphorbiaceae.* CASTOR BEAN. Summer annual. Bold and striking shrublike plant. Can provide tall screen or leafy background in a hurry; grows to 6–15 ft. in a season with full sun, plenty of heat and moisture. Where winters are mild, will live over and become quite woody and treelike. Has naturalized in small areas in many climates.

Should not be planted in areas where small children play—large, mottled, attractive, shiny seeds are poisonous. To prevent seeds, pinch off the burrlike seed capsules while they are small. Also, foliage or seeds occasionally cause severe contact allergies.

Ricinus communis

Large-lobed leaves are 1–3 ft. across on vigorous young plants, smaller on older plants. Unimpressive small, white flowers are borne in clusters on foot-high stalks, followed by attractive prickly husks which contain seeds.Grown commercially for castor oil extracted from seeds. Many horticultural varieties: 'Zanzibarensis' has very large green leaves; 'Dwarf Red Spire' is lower-growing plant (to 6 ft.) with red leaves and seed pods.

RIVER RED GUM. See *Eucalyptus camaldulensis.*

R

ROBINIA. *Leguminosae.* LOCUST. Deciduous trees or shrubs. All Zones. Leaves divided like feathers into many roundish leaflets; clusters of sweet pea–shaped, white or pink flowers midspring to early summer. They are hardy everywhere, fairly fast growing, and well adapted to dry hot regions. Will take poor soil, much drought when established. Drawbacks: wood is brittle, roots aggressive, plants often spread by suckers.

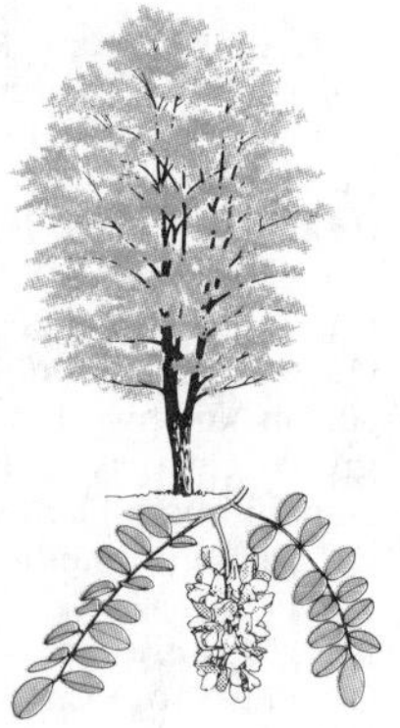

Robinia pseudoacacia

R. ambigua. Name given to hybrids between *R. pseudoacacia* and *R. viscosa,* a seldom-grown pink-flowering locust. Best-known varieties are:

'Decaisneana'. To 40–50 ft. tall, 20 ft. wide. Flowers like those of black locust, but pale pink.

'Idahoensis'. IDAHO LOCUST. Tree of moderately fast growth to shapely 40 ft. Flowers bright magenta rose in 8-in. clusters; one of showiest of locusts in bloom. Good flowering tree for Rocky Mountain gardens.

'Purple Robe'. Resembles Idaho locust but has darker, purple pink flowers, reddish bronze new growth; blooms 2 weeks earlier and over a longer period.

R. pseudoacacia. BLACK LOCUST. Tree. Fast growth to 75 ft., with rather open, sparse-branching habit. Deeply furrowed brown bark. Thorny branchlets. Leaves divided into 7–19 leaflets 1–2 in. long. Flowers white, fragrant, ½–¾ in. long, in dense, hanging clusters 4–8 in. long. Beanlike, 4-in.-long pods turn brown and hang on tree all winter.

Emigrants brought seeds with them from eastern U. S., and black locust is now common everywhere in West. In California's Gold Country it has gone native. Very drought tolerant. With pruning and training in its early years, it is a truly handsome flowering tree—but it is so common, and so commonly neglected, that it's often overlooked.

Has been used as street tree, but not good in narrow parking strips or under power lines. Wood is extremely hard, tough; trees difficult to prune out where not wanted. Varieties include:

'Frisia'. Leaves yellow; new growth nearly orange. Thorns, new wood red.

'Pyramidalis' ('Fastigiata'). Very narrow, columnar tree.

'Tortuosa'. Slow growing, with twisted branches. Few-flowered blossom clusters.

'Umbraculifera'. Dense, round headed. Usually grafted 6–8 ft. high on another locust. Very few flowers.

ROCHEA coccinea *(Crassula coccinea).* *Crassulaceae.* Succulent. Outdoors in Zones 17, 23, 24; greenhouse plant anywhere. From South Africa. Shrubby, well-branched plant 1–2 ft. tall. Leaves 1–1½ in. long by half as wide, closely set on stems. Flowers once a year in late spring or summer. Fragrant, bright scarlet blooms are 2 in. long, in flat clusters at tops of stems.

Rochea coccinea

In greenhouse, give plants rich, porous soil. Keep cool, in bright light, and on dryish side until January; then increase warmth, water. In mild-winter gardens, root cuttings in late spring or very early summer; grow rooted plants in porous, peaty soil with feeding. Plants will flower following summer.

ROCKCRESS. See *Arabis.*

ROCKROSE. See *Cistus.*

ROCK SPIRAEA. See *Holodiscus dumosus.*

RODGERSIA. *Saxifragaceae.* Perennials. Zones 2–9, 14–17. Large perennials with imposing leaves and clustered tiny flowers somewhat like those of astilbe. They need rich soil, plenty of moisture, and, in hot summer climates, shade. Dormant in winter. Showy in woodland or bog gardens.

Rodgersia aesculifolia

R. aesculifolia. To 6 ft. Leaves nearly round, divided handwise into 5–7 toothed, 10-in. leaflets. White flowers.

R. podophylla. To 5 ft. Leaves divided into five 10-in. leaflets, green in spring, bronzy in summer. Creamy flowers.

ROHDEA japonica. *Liliaceae.* Perennial. Zones 4–9, 14–24. Grown for its dense clumps of evergreen foliage. Broad, dark green, strap-shaped leaves, usually arched and recurving, to 2 ft. long and 3 in. wide. Cream-colored flowers in thick, short spike among leaves followed by short, dense cluster of red berries. Spreads slowly by thick rhizomes; old plants have many foliage clumps.

Rohdea japonica

Grow it in shade outdoors or pot it up as a house plant. Tough and sturdy. Needs average water. Many varieties with crested and variegated leaves are collector's items in Japan. Some are available from specialists here.

ROMNEYA coulteri. *Papaveraceae.* MATILIJA POPPY. Perennial. All Zones. Native to southern California, Baja California. Spectacular plant growing to 8 ft. or more. Stems and deeply cut leaves are gray green. White flowers up to 9 in. wide; 5 or 6 petals with texture of crepe paper surround round mass of golden stamens. Fragrant. Blooms May–July, on into fall if watered. Flowers handsome in arrangements.

Romneya coulteri

Use on hillsides as soil binder, along roadsides and in marginal areas, in wide borders. Invasive, spreading by underground rhizomes; don't plant near less vigorous plants. Needs sun; tolerates varying amounts of water, varying soils (including loose, gravelly soil). Withhold summer irrigation to keep growth in check. Cut nearly to ground in late fall. New shoots emerge after first rains in winter. Although easy to grow once established, it's very difficult to propagate. Easiest way to grow more plants is to dig up rooted suckers from spreading roots, but you can try taking cuttings from thickest roots. To make seeds germinate, mix them with potting soil in a foil-lined flat, burn pine needles on top of flat for 30 minutes, water, and hope for sprouting.

RONDELETIA. *Rubiaceae.* Evergreen shrubs. Borderline in Zones 8, 9, 18; reasonably safe in Zones 14–17, 19–24. Tubular flowers in clusters are brightly colored, sometimes fragrant. Best in slightly acid soil in part shade (sun along coast). Feed and water generously. Prune when young to make compact. Remove spent flowers. Shelter from hard frosts.

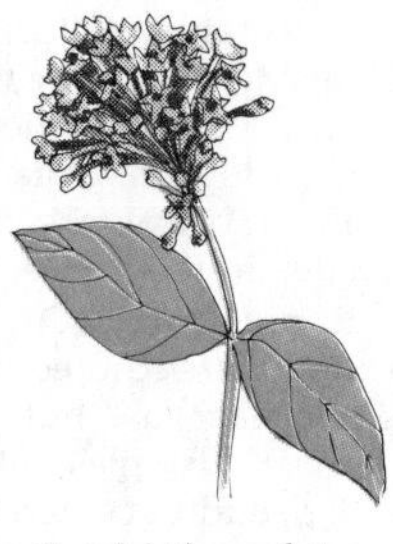

Rondeletia cordata

R. amoena. Medium to fast growth to 6–8 (possibly 15) ft. Glossy golden green to dark red green, 5-in., oval leaves. New growth bronzy. Clustered flowers light salmon pink, yellow in throat. Late winter, spring, and intermittently later on.

R. cordata. Similar to *R. amoena,* but with smooth, shiny green leaves. Blooms February–March, often into June; flowers near red in bud, opening to salmon pink.

ROSA. ROSE. *Rosaceae.* Deciduous, bushy or climbing shrubs (a few are evergreen in mildest Zones). Undoubtedly the best-loved and most widely planted shrubs in the West and all other temperate parts of world. Although the most popular kinds are not completely hardy in Zones 1–3, they will survive cold winters with some protection and perform year after year.

Hybrid Tea rose 'Seashell'

It is not difficult to grow roses well, but to be successful, you must follow certain guidelines:

1. Select varieties suited to your climate.
2. Buy the best plants available (No. 1 grade is tops).
3. Locate and plant them properly.
4. Attend to their basic needs: water, nutrients, any necessary pest and disease control, and pruning.
5. In Zones 1–3, provide some sort of winter protection.

Climate

The American Rose Society rates modern roses on a scale of 1–10. The higher the rating based on a national average of scores, the better the rose. The highest-rated roses generally will perform well in most climates and are good choices for the novice grower. But rating does not always tell the entire story: lower-rated roses may do especially well in certain regions and fail in others. The following general tips will guide your selection.

In cool-summer areas, you should, if possible, avoid varieties having an unusually great number of petals; many of these tend to "ball" (open poorly or not at all). Also note that varieties with deep color tones tend to appear "muddy" in cool summers, while pastel colors seldom appear off-color or unattractive. Choose varieties noted as being disease resistant and plant them in open areas where air circulation is good. Watch for foliage diseases—primarily mildew, rust, and black spot—and control them with appropriate fungicide sprays.

In hot-summer areas, rose plants grow vigorously, but hot sun causes flowers to open quickly, fade, and sometimes sunburn. In these regions, best flowering is in spring and fall (sometimes winter, too), with plants going nearly dormant in summer. Varieties with few petals (under 30) are usually disappointing in hottest weather, when they can go from bud to flat-open bloom in several hours; fuller-petaled flowers open more slowly and last longer. In such areas, any rose flowers will last longer if plants are located where they will receive midday or afternoon shade in summer. Also avoid planting roses where they will receive reflected heat from light-colored walls or fences—especially in south or west exposures.

In cold-winter areas (Zones 1–3), most modern roses will not survive winter low temperatures unless given some sort of protection. Certain old roses, species, and modern shrub roses will endure winter freezing in coldest Zones without sustaining much damage.

In any region, your best guide to suitable roses is a nearby municipal or private rose garden. The varieties you see performing well are the safest choices for your garden.

Buying Plants

All roses are available as bare-root plants from late fall through early spring. In Zones 4–24, they may be planted throughout winter, but in Zones 1–3, plant in fall or spring—before ground freezes or after it has thawed. Bare-root plants are always the best buy, and they are graded according to strict standards: Nos. 1, 1½, and 2. Nos. 1 and 1½ are most satisfactory (in that order); No. 2 plants can develop into decent bushes, but it may take them several years longer than the huskier Nos. 1 and 1½. Retail nurseries and specialist growers of modern roses who sell by mail order usually offer No. 1 plants, and they will often replace plants that fail to grow. Old roses (usually sold by mail order) may be available as budded plants that conform to the 1, 1½, and 2 grading standard, but some growers offer own-root (not budded) plants that may or may not be up to No. 1 size. The catalogues usually state what size of plant to expect.

Frequently you will find packaged bare-root roses sold at attractive prices in supermarkets and department stores. These can be good buys if you purchase them as soon as they appear for sale, but the longer you wait, the more the high temperatures in market or store will encourage premature growth or dry out the plants. Be prepared, too, for a number of these bargain roses to be mislabeled.

If you wish to plant roses during their growing season, you can buy roses growing in containers (these are more expensive than bare-root plants). This way, you can see the flowers of an unfamiliar variety before you buy, and you can be assured that the plant has put on healthy root and top growth following its bare-root transplanting. Look for plants growing in large (preferably 5-gallon) containers; this guarantees that the minimum possible amount of the root system was cut off to fit in the container. Also try to buy only roses that were planted in containers toward the end of the most recent dormant season; they will generally be in better condition than plants container grown for a year or more. Avoid plants showing considerable dead or twiggy growth. Container-grown roses may be planted out any time after rooting is sufficiently advanced to hold soil ball together—usually 3 months after being planted in containers.

The advent of molded paper containers has added a new wrinkle to planting of container-grown roses: you can plant the pot without having to disturb the rose. Cut or tear holes in the sides and bottom of paper pot so roots can easily grow into garden soil. Then dig a hole and plant the container with rose, making sure plant is at proper depth as described under bare-root planting. Within a year, the pot will have decomposed.

The presence of a plant patent number on a variety's tag is no assurance of quality. It simply means that for a variety's first 17 years, the patent holder receives a royalty on each sale. Many of these are excellent roses; many without patents are also excellent. Quite a number of the latter were once patented.

Location and Planting

For best results, plant roses where they will receive full sun all day (exceptions noted under "Climate"). Avoid planting where roots of trees or shrubs will steal water and nutrients intended for roses. To lessen any problem with foliage diseases, plant roses where air circulates freely (but not in path of regular, strong winds). Generous spacing between plants will also aid air circulation. How far apart to plant varies according to growth habit of roses and according to climate. The colder the winter and shorter the growing season, the smaller the bushes will be; where growing season is long and winters are mild, bushes can attain greater size. But some varieties are naturally small, others tall and massive—and those relative size differences will hold in any climate. In Zones 1–3, you might plant most vigorous sorts 3 ft. apart, whereas the same roses might require 6-ft. spacing in milder Zones.

Soil for roses should drain reasonably well; if it does not, the best alternative is to plant in raised beds. Dig soil deeply, incorporating organic matter such as ground bark, peat moss, or compost; this preparation will help aerate dense clay soils and will improve moisture retention of sandy soils. Add complete fertilizer to soil at the same time, and dig supplemental phosphorus and potash into planting holes; this gets nutrients down at the level where roots can use them.

Healthy, ready-to-plant bare-root roses should have plump, fresh-looking canes (branches) and roots. Plants that have dried out slightly in shipping or in nursery can be revived by burying them, tops and all, for a few days in moist soil, sand, or sawdust. Just before planting any bare-root rose, it is a good idea to immerse entire plant in water for several hours to be certain all canes and roots are plumped up. Plant according to directions for bare-root planting on pages 64–66, being sure to make holes large enough to spread out roots without bending or cutting back. Just before planting, cut broken canes and broken roots back to below breaks. Set plant in hole so that bud union ("knob" from which canes grow) is just above soil level. Even growers in Zones 1–3 find this successful, and plants produce more canes when planted this way, as long as plants are well protected during winter. After you have planted a rose and watered it well, mound soil, damp peat moss, or sawdust over bud union and around canes to conserve moisture. Gradually (and carefully) remove soil or other material when leaves begin to expand.

Basic Needs

All roses require water, nutrients, some pruning, and, at some point in their lifetime, pest and disease control.

Water is needed at all times during growing season for best performance of most popular garden roses. Inadequate water slows or halts growth and bloom. Water deeply so that entire root system is moistened. How often to water depends on soil type and weather; refer to watering section, pages 68–72, for guidelines. Big, well-established plants need more water than newly set plants, but you will need to pay closer attention to watering frequency of new plants in order to get them well established.

Basin flooding is a simple way to water individual rose plants, and if you have a drip irrigation system (see page 70–71), many plants can be watered this way at one time. Overhead sprinkling, often practiced in hot, dry regions, helps remove dust and freshen foliage, and provides partial control for aphids and spider mites; on the minus side, it washes off spray residues, may leave mineral deposits on foliage if water is hard, and in some areas may encourage foliage diseases by keeping foliage and atmosphere damp. If you sprinkle, do it early in the day to be sure foliage dries off by nightfall. Even if you irrigate in basins, give plants an occasional sprinkling to clean dust off foliage.

Mulch, spread 2–3 in. deep, will help save water, prevent soil surface from baking hard, keep soil cool in summer, deter weed growth, and build healthy soil structure (well aerated, permeable by water and roots). See page 72 for mulch suggestions.

Nutrients, applied fairly regularly, will produce the most gratifying results. In mild-winter climates, begin feeding established plants with complete commercial fertilizer in February. Elsewhere, give first feeding just as growth begins. Fertilizer application should be timed in relation to bloom period. Ideal time to make subsequent feedings is when a blooming period has come to an end and new growth is just beginning for next cycle of bloom. Depending on expected arrival of freezing temperatures, stop feeding in late summer or fall—generally about 6 weeks before earliest normal hard frost. In Zones 1–3, last application may be around August 1; in Zones 4–7 and 10, last feeding may be from early to late September. In milder Zones, fertilizing may continue until mid-October for crop of late fall flowers.

Dry commercial fertilizer, applied to soil, is most frequently used. A variation on that type is slow-release fertilizer that provides nutrients over prolonged period; follow directions on package for amount and frequency of applications. Liquid fertilizers are useful in smaller gardens in which roses are basin watered. Most liquids can also be used as foliage fertilizers—sprayed on rose leaves, which absorb nutrients immediately for quick tonic.

Pest and disease control may not constitute a regular part of your rose-growing activities, but certain controls are usually needed during growing season. Descriptions of pests and diseases, along with recommended controls, appear on pages 96–109.

Principal rose pests are aphids, spider mites, and (in some areas) thrips. If you don't want to rely on natural predators, begin aphid control when aphids first appear and repeat as needed until they are gone or their numbers are severely reduced. Spring is prime aphid time. Spider mites are hot-weather pests, capable of inflicting severe damage—especially to underwatered plants and weak bushes. They work on leaf undersides, stippling leaves and giving them a silvery cast; in severe infestations, leaves fall off. Spider mites also can sap growth to the point that flower production stops. Thrips do their damage inside rose buds, making brown streaks on petals, browning petals completely, or turning entire buds brown; buds may also be so misshapen that they cannot open. Control is difficult because tiny thrips are hidden in rose petals, difficult to reach by contact insecticides; systemic insecticides are usually most successful for thrips control.

Mildew, rust, and black spot are the "big 3" of rose foliage diseases. First line of defense for all 3 is thorough dormant season cleanup of all dead leaves and other debris from previous season; this is simplest right after you have pruned plants. Then, before new growth begins, spray plants and soil with dormant season spray of oil or lime sulfur (calcium polysulfide). This will destroy many disease organisms that otherwise might live over winter to reinfect plants in spring; overwintering insect eggs are also dispatched.

Mildew, a gray to white furry coating on leaves, thrives under conditions of high humidity but no rain; it needs dry leaves on which to grow. Poor air circulation—typical when plants are crowded or grown against a wall—encourages mildew development in regions where it is likely to occur. Rose varieties differ in their susceptibility to mildew; degree of mildew resistance is noted in detailed descriptions in *Sunset's* book *How to Grow Roses.*

Rust usually appears first in late spring as small bright orange spots beneath leaves. In severe infestations, entire leaf undersurface will be covered with orange powder and leaves may drop off. Rust is easily spread by air currents and by rain or sprinkling; it needs damp leaves on which to grow.

Black spot is the most devastating of the 3 foliage diseases. It is present in parts of the Northwest and in the Rocky Mountain states, and is increasing in frequency in California (especially in the northern part of the state). Because black spot spreads in water, it is naturally found in areas with summer rainfall, but overhead watering will spread the disease where it is present. Leaves (and sometimes stems) of infected plants will show black spots with irregular, fringed margins; leaves turn yellow around the spots, and if the disease is unchecked, the entire plant will defoliate. Replacing all its leaves is a strain on a plant, and a rose weakened by the effort is likely to suffer more winter damage in Zones 1–3.

Chlorosis—leaves turning light green to yellow, with veins remaining dark green—is not a disease, but usually a symptom of iron deficiency. This condition can be a major problem in Zones 12 and 13. Iron chelate corrects the problem most quickly; iron sulfate is also effective, but slower acting.

Pruning, done properly each year, will contribute to the health and longevity of your rose plants. Sensible pruning is based on these facts about growth of roses:

A. Blooms are produced on new growth. Unless pruning promotes strong new growth, flowers will come on spindly outer twigs and be of poor quality.

B. The more healthy wood you retain, the bigger the plant will be; and the bigger the plant, the more flowers it can produce. Also, nutrients are stored in woody canes (branches), so a larger plant is a stronger plant. Therefore, prune conservatively; *never* chop down vigorous 6-ft. bush to 1½-ft. stubs unless you want only a few huge blooms for exhibition. (Exception: in Zones 1–3, where plant freezes back to its winter protection, you will remove dead wood in spring and be left with equivalent of severely pruned plant.)

C. Best pruning time for most roses (certain climbers and shrub types excepted) is at the end of dormant season when growth buds begin to swell. Exact time will vary according to locality.

General pruning guidelines. The following 5 pruning practices apply to all roses except certain shrub and species roses, for which special instructions are indicated in their descriptions.

1. Use sharp pruning shears; make all cuts as shown on pages 77–78.

2. Remove wood that is obviously dead and wood that has no healthy growth coming from it; branches that cross through plant's center and any that rub against larger canes; branches that make bush appear lopsided; and any old and unproductive canes that have been replaced by strong new ones during past season.

3. Cut back growth produced during previous year, usually making cuts above outward-facing buds (except for very spreading varieties where some cuts to inside buds will promote more height without producing many crossing branches). As a general rule,

remove ⅓ to no more than ½ the length of previous season's growth (exception for Zones 1–3 is noted in point B above). The ideal result is a V-shaped bush with relatively open center.

4. If any suckers (growth produced from rootstock instead of from rose variety growing on it) have grown, completely remove them. Dig down to where suckers grow from rootstock and pull them off with downward motion; that removes growth buds that would produce additional suckers in subsequent years. Let wound air dry before you replace soil around it.

Be certain you are removing a sucker rather than a new cane growing from the bud union of the budded variety. Usually you can note a distinct difference in foliage size and shape, and size of thorns, on sucker growth. If in doubt, let the presumed sucker grow until you can establish its difference from budded rose. A sucker's flowers will be different; a flowerless, climbing cane from a shrub rose is almost certainly a sucker.

5. Consider cutting flowers as a form of pruning. Cut off enough stem to support flower in vase, but don't deprive plant of too much foliage. Leave on plant a stem with at least 2 sets of 5-leaflet leaves.

The most widely planted modern roses—Hybrid Teas and Grandifloras—can be pruned successfully according to guidelines above. A few additional tips apply to 4 other popular types:

Floribunda and Polyantha roses are grown for quantities of flowers they produce in clusters, so amount of bloom rather than quality of individual flower is the objective. Cut back previous season's growth only by ¼, and leave as many strong new canes and stems as plant produced. Most produce more canes per bush than do Hybrid Teas and Grandifloras. If you grow Floribundas or Polyanthas as hedge or border of one variety, cut back all plants to uniform height.

Climbing roses divide into 2 general types: those that bloom in spring only (including a large category known as natural climbers, discussed on page 512), and those that bloom off and on in other seasons as well as in spring (including the very popular climbing sports of Hybrid Tea roses). All climbers should be left unpruned for first 2–3 years after planting; remove only dead and weak, twiggy wood, and allow plants to get established and produce their long, flexible canes. Most bloom comes from lateral branches that grow from long canes, and most of those flowering branches develop when long canes are spread out horizontally (as along a fence). Types that bloom only in spring produce strong new growth after they flower, and that new growth bears flowers the following spring. Prune these climbers just *after* they bloom, removing oldest canes that show no signs of producing strong new growth. Repeat-flowering climbers (many are climbing sports of bush varieties) are pruned at the same time you'd prune bush roses in your locality. Remove oldest, unproductive canes and any weak, twiggy growth; cut back lateral branches on remaining canes to within 2 or 3 buds from canes.

Pillar roses are not quite bush or climber. They produce tall, somewhat flexible canes that bloom profusely without having to be trained horizontally. Prune pillar roses according to general guidelines for bush roses.

Tree roses, more properly called "standards," are an artificial creation: a bush rose budded onto a 2–3-ft.-high understock stem. Most important is to stake trunk securely to prevent its breaking from weight of bush it supports. A ½-in. metal pipe makes good permanent stake; use cross "X" tie between stake and trunk to hold secure. General pruning guidelines apply, with particular attention to maintaining symmetrical plant.

Winter protection. Where winter low temperatures regularly reach 10°F. and lower, some amount of protection is needed for all modern roses—bushes, climbers, and standards. A healthy, well-ripened plant will withstand winter better than a weak, actively growing one; your first step to protection is preparation. Time your last fertilizer application so that bushes will have ceased putting on new growth by expected date of first sharp frosts; leave last crop of blooms on plants to form hips (fruits), which will help ripening process by stopping growth. Keep plants well watered until soil freezes.

After a couple of hard freezes have occurred and night temperatures seem to remain consistently below freezing, mound soil over base of each bush to height of 1 ft. Get soil from another part of garden; do *not* scoop soil from around roses, exposing surface roots. Cut excessively long canes back to about 4 ft.; then, with soft twine, tie canes together to keep them from whipping around in wind. When mound has frozen, cover it with evergreen boughs, straw, or other fairly lightweight material that will act as insulation to keep mounds frozen. Your objective is to prevent alternate freezing and thawing of mound (and canes it covers), maintaining plant at constant temperature of 15°–20°F. A cylinder of wire mesh around soil mound will help keep it and insulating material in place.

Remove protection in early spring when you are reasonably certain hard frosts will not recur. Gradually remove soil mounds as they thaw; do it carefully to avoid breaking new growth that may have begun under the soil.

Use of manufactured styrofoam rose cones eliminates the labor of mounding and unmounding; just a bit of soil over the cone's base plus a rock or brick on top will hold it in place over the bush. Disadvantages are: cost and availability; need to cut rose down to fit cone over it, perhaps pruning more severely than if plant were mounded to endure winter cold; moisture condensation inside cone as days begin warming. To avoid condensation problem, get cones with removable tops that can be opened for air circulation on warm late-winter days.

Climbing roses should be mounded in same manner, but in addition you will have to protect all of their canes. Where winter lows are in −10° to +5°F. range, wrap canes in burlap stuffed with straw for insulation. Where temperatures normally go below −10°F., remove canes from their support, gently bend them to ground, secure them in that position and cover with soil. A wiser plan in such climates is to plant only climbers known to be successful in your area or reputed to be hardy in similar climates.

Standards (tree roses) may be insulated as described for climbers, but it is still a gamble: the part you want—the head of the tree—is the most exposed. Some rosarians wrap with straw and burlap, then construct a plywood box to cover insulated plant. Others dig their standards each year and heel them in a cool garage, basement, or shed, then replant in spring. A simpler technique is to grow standards in large containers, then move them in fall to cool shed or garage where temperature won't drop below 10°F.

Modern Roses

Types described below constitute majority of roses offered for sale and planted by hundreds of thousands each year. Those that have been All-America Rose Selections, recognized on basis of performance in nationwide test gardens, are indicated by AARS; those with an asterisk (*) in front of their names are rated 8.0 or higher by the American Rose Society.

Hybrid Teas. This, the most popular class of rose, outsells all other types combined. Flowers are large and shapely, generally produced one to a stem on plants that range from 2 ft. to 6 ft. or more, depending on the variety. Many thousands of varieties have been produced since the class first appeared in 1867; hundreds are catalogued, and new ones appear each year. The most popular Hybrid Teas are listed in the color groups that follow.

Red. *'Chrysler Imperial' (AARS), *'Mr. Lincoln' (AARS), 'Oklahoma', *'Olympiad' (AARS), *'Precious Platinum', 'Red Devil', *'Red Jacket'.

Pink. 'Bewitched' (AARS), *'Century Two', *'Color Magic', *'Dainty Bess' (single), *'Duet' (AARS), 'First Love', *'First Prize' (AARS), 'Friendship' (AARS), 'Milestone', *'Miss All-American Beauty' (AARS), 'Perfume Delight' (AARS), 'Princesse de Monaco', *'Royal Highness' (AARS), *'Swarthmore', 'Sweet Surrender' (AARS), *'Tiffany' (AARS), 'Touch of Class' (AARS).

Multicolors, Blends. 'Broadway' (AARS), *'Chicago Peace', *'Double Delight' (AARS), *'Granada' (AARS), 'Just Joey', *'Lady Rose', 'Medallion' (AARS), 'Mon Cheri' (AARS), 'Seashell' (AARS), 'Snowfire', 'Voodoo' (AARS).

(Continued on next page)

R

Orange, Orange Tones. 'Brandy' (AARS), *'Folklore', *'Fragrant Cloud', 'Las Vegas', 'Matador', *'Tropicana' (AARS).

Yellow. 'Eclipse', 'King's Ransom' (AARS), 'Lowell Thomas' (AARS), 'Oregold' (AARS), *'Peace' (AARS), 'Summer Sunshine', 'Sunbright', 'Sutter's Gold' (AARS).

White. *'Garden Party' (AARS), 'Honor', 'Ivory Tower', 'John F. Kennedy', *'Pascali' (AARS), *'Pristine', 'Virgo', 'White Masterpiece'.

Lavender. 'Blue Girl', 'Heirloom', *'Lady X', *'Paradise' (AARS).

Grandifloras. Vigorous plants, sometimes 8–10 ft. tall, with Hybrid Tea–type flowers borne singly or in long-stemmed clusters. This class is very close to Hybrid Teas, and some varieties have been switched from one class to the other. Valuable for large number of cuttable flowers per plant and mass color effect in garden. Good barrier plants.

Grandiflora rose 'Camelot'

Red. 'Carrousel', 'John S. Armstrong' (AARS), 'Love' (AARS), 'Olé'.

Pink, Pink Blends. 'Aquarius', 'Camelot' (AARS), *'Pink Parfait' (AARS), *'Queen Elizabeth' (AARS), *'Sonia'.

Orange, Blends. 'Arizona' (AARS), 'Montezuma', 'Prominent', 'Sundowner' (AARS).

Yellow. 'Gold Medal'.

White. 'Mount Shasta', 'White Lightnin'' (AARS).

Floribundas. Originally developed from Hybrid Teas and Polyanthas, these are noted for producing quantities of flowers in clusters on vigorous and bushy plants. Flowers and plants generally are smaller than most Hybrid Teas. Excellent for providing masses of color in landscape: informal hedges, borders, barriers, massing, containers. Some varieties have climbing forms.

Floribunda rose 'Cathedral'

Red. 'Charisma' (AARS), 'Double Talk', *'Europeana' (AARS), 'Eye Paint' (single), 'Frensham', 'Happy Talk', 'Impatient', 'Interama', 'Merci', 'Sarabande' (AARS), 'Town Talk', 'Trumpeter'.

Pink. *'Betty Prior' (single), *'Cherish' (AARS), *'Gene Boerner', 'Rose Parade' (AARS), 'Sea Pearl', 'Simplicity'.

Orange, Blends. *'Apricot Nectar' (AARS), 'Cathedral', *'First Edition', 'Ginger', 'Gingersnap', *'Little Darling', 'Marina', *'Orangeade', 'Redgold' (AARS), 'Sunfire'.

Yellow. 'Sun Flair', *'Sunsprite'.

White. *'Evening Star', 'French Lace' (AARS), *'Iceberg', *'Ivory Fashion'.

Lavender. *'Angel Face' (AARS), 'Deep Purple' (AARS), *'Escapade', 'Intrigue' (AARS).

Polyanthas. Small flowers (less than 2 in. wide) are carried in large sprays. Plants are vigorous, many-caned, nearly everblooming, and quite disease resistant. Uses are same as for Floribundas, but color range is more limited. Five varieties are most often sold: 'Cecile Brunner' (often called the "Sweetheart Rose") has light pink flowers that are of best Hybrid Tea form; 'Perle d'Or' is similar but color is apricot orange; 'Margo Koster' has coral orange, very double flowers that resemble ranunculus; 'The Fairy' produces huge clusters of small light pink flowers; 'China Doll' has larger, deeper pink flowers in smaller clusters.

Polyantha rose 'Margo Koster'

Miniature roses. True roses 6–12 in. tall or a little taller, with miniature canes, foliage, and flowers. They are derived in part from *R. chinensis minima (R. rouletii)* and come in all colors of modern Hybrid Tea roses. Plants are everblooming and can even be grown indoors in a cool, bright window (use 6-in. or larger pot and rich potting soil). Use outdoors in rock gardens, window boxes, or containers, or as border plants. Miniatures are hardier than Hybrid Teas, but their shallow roots demand regular water, regular fertilizing, and mulch. Nearly all miniatures are grown from cuttings.

Miniature rose

Many new varieties are put on the market each year. Among the best are these, all rated 8.0 or higher.

Red, Red Blends. 'Beauty Secret', 'Dreamglo', 'Kathy', 'Magic Carrousel', 'Over the Rainbow', 'Rose Hills Red', 'Sheri Anne', 'Starina', 'Toy Clown'.

Pink. 'Baby Betsy McCall', 'Baby Cecile Brunner', 'Cuddles', 'Cupcake', 'Fresh Pink', 'Judy Fischer', 'Opal Jewel', 'Swedish Doll', 'Willie Winkie'.

Orange, Blends. 'Baby Darling', 'Caribe', 'Holy Toledo', 'Kathy Robinson', 'Mary Marshall', 'Minnie Pearl', 'Orange Sunblaze', 'Party Girl', 'Peaches 'n Cream', 'Puppy Love', 'Rainbow's End', 'Rosmarin'.

Yellow. 'Rise 'n Shine', 'Yellow Doll'.

White. 'Cinderella', 'Little Eskimo', 'Popcorn', 'Simplex', 'Snow Bride', 'Starglo', 'White Angel'.

Lavender. 'Lavender Jewel'.

Climbing roses. Two general categories comprise climbing roses: natural climbers (large flowered except for Miniatures) and climbing sports of bush roses (Hybrid Teas, Floribundas, Grandifloras, Polyanthas, Miniatures). See "Pruning," page 510, for a description of pruning procedure. Here are the most popular varieties in the 2 categories.

Climbing rose 'Climbing Mrs. Sam McGredy'

Natural Climbers

Red. *'Altissimo' (single), 'Blaze', *'Don Juan', *'Dortmund' (single), 'Dublin Bay', 'Paul's Scarlet Climber', 'Solo', 'Spectacular', 'Tempo'.

Pink. *'Blossomtime', 'Clair Matin', *'Galway Bay', *'Hi Ho' (Mini.), *'Jeanne Lajoie', 'New Dawn', 'Parade', 'Pink Cameo' (Mini.), 'Rhonda'.

Orange, Blends. 'America' (AARS), *'Handel', 'Joseph's Coat', 'Piñata', 'Royal Sunset'.

Yellow. 'Golden Showers' (AARS), 'Royal Gold'.

White. 'White Dawn'.

Climbing Sports

Red. 'Cl. Chrysler Imperial' (HT), 'Cl. Crimson Glory' (HT), 'Cl. Etoile de Hollande' (HT), 'Cl. Over the Rainbow' (Mini.).

Pink. 'Cl. Cecile Brunner' (Poly.), 'Cl. Dainty Bess' (HT, single), *'Cl. First Prize' (HT).

Orange, Blends. 'Cl. Double Delight' (HT), 'Cl. Mrs. Sam McGredy' (HT), 'Cl. Shot Silk' (HT).

Yellow. 'Cl. Peace' (HT).

White. 'Cl. Snowbird' (HT).

Old Roses

Some of the wild or species roses and their immediate hybrid offspring are still grown by fanciers and sold by specialists. Many are valuable landscape or flowering shrubs. All are as hardy as modern Hybrid Teas, except where noted. Three old rose garden types (Hybrid Perpetual, Tea, China) are an important source of vigor, delicate form, and everblooming quality in modern roses. Refer to "Climate" on page 509.

Shrub roses. As the name implies, these are roses that can serve as flowering landscape shrubs. They are not as widely available as the roses in the preceding 6 categories; most are sold by mail-order, usually by specialist growers of old roses.

Shrub roses vary greatly in ancestry and appearance. Some are primary species hybrids with single or semidouble blooms of simple, wildflower charm; 'Golden Wings' and 'Nevada' (white) are examples. Others are more complex derivatives of species hybrids and modern Hybrid Teas, Grandifloras, and Floribundas;

many of these result from breeding programs designed to produce winter-hardy plants bearing flowers in the style and color range of modern roses. Still others, popularized as "English roses"(from their country of origin), are derived from modern roses and old types such as Albas, Gallicas, Damasks, and so forth. These flower repeatedly during the growing season, their blossoms combining full, old-rose-style form with modern colors.

For more on modern shrub roses, see HYBRID MUSKS under *R. moschata* (page 514).

Hybrid Perpetuals. Before Hybrid Teas became popular, these were *the* garden roses. Plants are big, vigorous, and hardy to about −30°F. if cut back to 1½ ft. when ground freezes and mounded with soil until new growth pushes out in spring. Often very susceptible to rust. They need more frequent feeding and watering than Hybrid Teas to produce repeated bursts of bloom. Prune high and thin out oldest canes. Flowers are big (to 7 in. wide), opulent, and full petaled, and have strong old-rose fragrance. Buds often are shorter and plumper than average Hybrid Tea bud. Colors range from white through many shades of pink to deep red. Examples are 'Paul Neyron', 'Ulrich Brunner', 'American Beauty'. Though now officially classed as a Hybrid Tea, the old favorite white 'Frau Karl Druschki' typifies Hybrid Perpetual growth and flower.

Tea roses. One of the parents of Hybrid Teas. Primarily adapted to climates of little seasonal change, with short rest periods (best in Zones 8, 9, 12–24). All resent heavy pruning; thin out weak growth and let plants develop into large shrubs. Flowers are refined, well formed, in tones of soft cream, light yellow, apricot, buff, pink, and rosy red, produced throughout warm weather. 'Maman Cochet', 'Duchesse de Brabant', and 'Catherine Mermet' are among those currently available. Hybrids with Noisette roses (below) were responsible for Tea-Noisette climbers. An ancestor of the Tea rose, *R. gigantea,* produced the celebrated rampant pale pink climber 'Belle Portugaise' ("Belle of Portugal").

China roses. The first 2 China roses to reach Europe (around 1800) were really cultivated forms of *R. chinensis* that had been selected and maintained by Chinese horticulturists. Flowers were pink or red, on the small side, in small clusters, on 2–4-ft.-high plants. 'Old Blush' ('Parson's Pink China'), one of the original 2, is still available from old rose specialists. China roses were the primary source of repeat-flowering habit in later 19th- and 20th-century roses. *R. chinensis minima (R. rouletii)* is the chief source of small size in modern miniature roses. It is, in effect, a dwarf version of 'Old Blush', growing 10–18 in. high. A famous China-Bourbon hybrid, 'Gloire des Rosomanes' (better known as "Ragged Robin"), was once widely used as an understock and still may be offered as a plant for hedges.

Bourbon roses. The original Bourbon rose was a hybrid between *R. chinensis* and the Autumn Damask (*R. damascena bifera*). Later developments were shrubs, semiclimbers, and climbers in white, pink shades, and red, usually quite fragrant; they resembled the Hybrid Perpetuals and were largely supplanted by them. Best known today are: 'La Reine Victoria', 'Madame Ernst Calvat', 'Madame Pierre Oger', 'Souvenir de la Malmaison' (all pink), and 'Madame Isaac Pereire' (magenta red).

Noisette roses. The union of *R. chinensis* and *R. moschata* (page 514) produced the first Noisette rose: a repeat-flowering shrubby climber with small pink flowers in medium-sized clusters. Crossed with itself and China roses, it led to a race of similar roses in white, pink shades, and red tones; crossed with Tea roses, it yielded large-flowered, climbing Tea-Noisettes. Old rose specialists offer a limited assortment of both types, including 'Blush Noisette' (small flowered, pink) and Tea-Noisettes 'Lamarque' (white), 'Marechal Niel' (yellow), and 'Rêve d'Or' (buff).

Other old garden rose types available from nursery rose specialists are:

R. alba. WHITE or YORK ROSE. Deciduous shrub. All Zones. Associated with England's War of the Roses. Semidouble, flat, ivory white flowers. Garden hybrids grow vigorously, make erect shrubs. Smooth, green wood; gray green, cool-looking leaves. Garden varieties are pink 'Celestial', 'Königin von Dänemark', 'Maiden's Blush'.

R. banksiae. LADY BANKS' ROSE. Evergreen climber (deciduous in cold winters). Zones 4–24. Vigorous grower to 20 ft. or more. Aphid resistant, almost immune to disease. Stems have almost no prickles; leaves with 3–5 leaflets to 2½ in. long, glossy and leathery. Large clusters of small, yellow or white flowers in late spring to midsummer, depending on Zone and season. Good for covering banks, ground, fence, or arbor in mild climates. The 2 varieties sold are 'Alba Plena', with double white, violet-scented flowers; and 'Lutea', with scentless double yellow flowers.

R. bracteata. Climbing shrub with large, single creamy white blossoms. Zones 4–24. Naturalized in southeastern U.S. Its celebrated offspring is 'Mermaid', evergreen or semievergreen climber. Vigorous (to 30 ft.), thorny, with glossy, leathery, dark green leaves and many single, creamy yellow, lightly fragrant flowers, 5 in. across, in summer, fall, and intermittently through winter in mildest Zones. Tough, disease resistant, thrives in sun or part shade, beach or inland. Plant 8 ft. apart for quick ground cover; or use to climb wall (will need tying), run along fence, or climb tree.

R. centifolia. CABBAGE ROSE. Deciduous shrub. All Zones. Rose of Dutch painters. Open growing, to 6 ft. tall, with prickly stems. Flowers pink, double, nodding, very fragrant. Blooms in late spring, early summer. Selections range from pale pink to purplish. *R. c. muscosa,* MOSS ROSE, is grown in many named kinds. Moss roses, a Victorian favorite, have flower stalks and bases covered with hairy, green "moss." Flowers are mostly double, in pink, white, or red, with intense old-rose fragrance. Some varieties bloom only one season each year; others, such as 'Salet', bloom repeatedly.

R. damascena. DAMASK ROSE. Deciduous shrubs. All Zones. To 6 ft. or more, with pale green, downy foliage, long, arching canes, and loosely double, very fragrant blooms in clusters. Autumn Damask (*R. damascena bifera*) flowers more than once in a year; this is the "Rose of Castile" of Spanish missions. Summer damasks flower in spring only; forms of these are source of attar of roses. Available spring-flowering damasks include white hybrid 'Madame Hardy', blush pink 'Celsiana', and the celebrated 'York and Lancaster', with blooms that may be pink, white, or a pink-white blend.

R. eglanteria *(R. rubiginosa).* SWEET BRIAR, EGLANTINE. Deciduous shrub or climber. All Zones. Vigorous growth to 8–12 ft. Prickly stems. Dark green leaves are fragrant (like apples), especially after rain. Flowers single, pink, 1½ in. across, appearing singly or in clusters in late spring. Fruit red orange. Can be used as hedge, barrier, screen; plant 3–4 ft. apart and prune once a year in early spring. Can be held to 3–4 ft. Naturalized in some parts of West. Good hybrid forms: 'Lady Penzance', 'Lord Penzance'.

R. foetida *(R. lutea).* AUSTRIAN BRIER. Deciduous shrub. All Zones. Slender, prickly stems 5–10 ft. long, erect or arching. Leaves dark green, smooth or slightly hairy; may drop early in fall. Flowers (May–June) single, bright yellow, 2–3 in. across, with odd scent. This species and its well-known variety 'Bicolor', AUSTRIAN COPPER ROSE, are the source of orange and yellow in modern roses. 'Bicolor' is a 4–5-ft.-tall shrub with brilliant coppery red flowers, their petals backed with yellow.

Austrian brier does best in warm, fairly dry, well-drained soil and in full sun. Needs reflected heat in Zones 4–6. Prune only to remove dead or worn-out wood.

R. gallica. FRENCH ROSE. Deciduous shrub. All Zones. Prickly, often bristly stems to 3–4 ft. tall from creeping rootstocks. Leaves smooth, dark green. Flowers red, fragrant, 2–2½ in. across. All have old rose fragrance, and some, like 'Rosa Mundi', are strikingly striped red on white. Flowers pink through slate blue and purple, often mottled with these colors.

R. harisonii. HARISON'S YELLOW ROSE. Deciduous shrub. All Zones. Thickets of thorny stems to 6–8 ft.; fine-textured foliage; flowers (in late spring) profuse, semidouble, bright yellow, fragrant. Occasionally reblooms in fall in warmer climates. Showy fruit. Hybrid between *R. foetida* and *R. spinosissima.* Very old rose that came west with pioneers and still persists in California's gold country and around old farm houses. Vigorous growing, disease free, hardy to cold, and (once established) resistant to drought. Useful deciduous landscaping shrub.

R. hugonis. FATHER HUGO'S ROSE, GOLDEN ROSE OF CHINA. Deciduous shrub. All Zones. Dense growth to 8 ft. Stems arching or straight, with bristles near base. Handsome foliage; leaves deep green, 1–4 in. long, with 5–11 tiny leaflets. Flowers profusely in May–June; branches become garlands of 2-in.-wide, bright yellow, faintly scented flowers. Useful in borders, for screen or barrier plantings, against fence, trained as fan on trellis. Will take high filtered afternoon shade. Prune out oldest wood to ground each year to shape plant, get maximum bloom.

R. moschata. MUSK ROSE. Deciduous shrub. Zones 4–24. Vigorous, arching, with clustered ivory white flowers of musky odor. Parent of Tea-Noisettes. Available are many HYBRID MUSKS, large 6–8-ft. shrubs or semiclimbers. Heavily fragrant flowers, in clusters or large trusses, are almost everblooming, in red, pinks, buff, yellow, and white. Some produce decorative orange or red hips in fall. Musks grow and bloom in afternoon shade or broken shade as well as in sun. Popular varieties are 'Belinda' and 'Cornelia' (pink); 'Nymphenburg' and 'Penelope' (salmon); 'Buff Beauty' (buff apricot); 'Will Scarlet' (single red); and 'Kathleen' (single pink, like apple blossoms).

R. multiflora. Deciduous shrub. All Zones. Arching growth on dense, vigorous plant 8–10 ft. tall and as wide. Susceptible to mildew, spider mites. Many clustered, small white flowers (like blackberry blossoms) in June; profusion of ¼-in. red fruit, much loved by birds, in fall. Promoted as hedge but truly useful for this purpose only on largest acreage—far too large and vigorous for most gardens. Spiny and smooth forms available; spiny form best for barrier hedge. Set plants 2 ft. apart for fast fill-in. Can help control erosion.

R. roxburghii. CHESTNUT ROSE. Deciduous. Zones 2–24. Spreading plant with prickly stems 8–10 ft. long. Bark gray, peeling. Light green, very fine-textured, ferny foliage; new growth bronze and gold tipped. Immune to mildew. Buds and fruit are spiny like chestnut burrs. Flowers generally double, soft rose pink, very fragrant; appear in June. Normally a big shrub for screen or border, but if stems are pegged down, makes good bank cover, useful in preventing erosion.

R. rugosa. RAMANAS ROSE, SEA TOMATO. Deciduous shrub. All Zones. Vigorous, very hardy shrub with prickly stems. To 3–8 ft. tall. Leaves bright glossy green, with distinctive heavy veining which gives them crinkled appearance. Flowers are 3–4 in. across and, in the many varieties, range from single to double and from pure white and creamy yellow through pink to deep purplish red, all wonderfully fragrant. Bright red, tomato-shaped fruit, an inch or more across, edible but seedy; sometimes used for preserves.

All Rugosas are extremely tough and hardy, withstanding hard freezes, wind, drought, salt spray at ocean. They make fine hedges and will help prevent erosion. Foliage remains quite free of diseases and insects, except possibly aphids. Among most widely sold are 'Blanc Double de Coubert' (double white), 'Frau Dagmar Hastrup' (single pink), 'Hansa' (double purplish red), 'Will Alderman' (double pink). Two unusual Rugosa hybrids are 'F. J. Grootendorst' and 'Grootendorst Supreme'; their double flowers with deeply fringed petals resemble carnations more than roses.

R. sericea pteracantha. Deciduous shrub. Zones 4–24. Single, 1½–2-in., white, mostly 4-petaled flowers. A rose to grow for its decorative thorns: new shoots have inch-long, winged, bright red prickles that are actually translucent.

R. spinosissima *(R. pimpinellifolia).* SCOTCH ROSE, BURNET ROSE. Deciduous shrub. All Zones. Suckering, spreading shrub 3–4 ft. tall. Stems upright, spiny and bristly, closely set with small, ferny leaves. Handsome bank cover on good soil; helps prevent erosion. Spring flowers white to pink, 1½–2 in. across. Fruit dark brown or blackish. Many varieties range to deep rose or yellow. 'Frühlingsgold', 'Frühlingsmorgen', 'Stanwell Perpetual' are among most widely sold. Best-known variety is *R. s. altaica,* sometimes 6 ft. tall with larger leaves and 3-in. white flowers garlanding branches.

R. wichuraiana. MEMORIAL ROSE. Vine. All Zones; evergreen or partially evergreen in Zones 4–24. Trailing stems grow 10–12 ft. long in one season, root in contact with moist soil. Leaves 2–4 in. long, with 5–9 smooth, shiny ¼–1-in. leaflets. Midsummer flowers are white, to 2 in. across, in clusters of 6–10. Good ground cover, even in relatively poor soil. Wichuraiana ramblers, produced in the first 20 years of this century, are group of hybrids between the species and various garden roses. They flower lavishly once in late spring, then put out much new growth for next year's bloom. 'Dorothy Perkins' (pink), 'Excelsa' (red), and 'Alberic Barbier' (white) are among those offered by old rose specialists.

Rosaceae. The rose family contains an immense number of plants of horticultural importance. In addition to ornamental shrubs such as rose, family members include strawberries, bramble fruits, many flowering and fruiting trees, *Photinia, Pyracantha,* and *Spiraea,* and other ornamental trees, shrubs, and perennials.

ROSA DE MONTANA. See *Antigonon leptopus.*

ROSARY VINE. See *Ceropegia woodii.*

ROSE. See *Rosa.*

ROSE APPLE. See *Syzygium jambos.*

ROSELLE. See *Hibiscus sabdariffa.*

ROSE-MALLOW. See *Hibiscus moscheutos.*

ROSEMARY. See *Rosmarinus officinalis.*

ROSE MOSS. See *Portulaca grandiflora.*

ROSE OF SHARON. See *Hibiscus syriacus.*

ROSMARINUS officinalis. *Labiatae.* ROSEMARY. Evergreen shrub, herb. Zones 4–24. Rugged, picturesque, to 2–6 ft. high. Narrow, aromatic leaves glossy dark green above, grayish white beneath. Small clusters of light lavender blue, ¼–½-in. flowers in winter, spring; bloom occasionally repeats in fall. Flowers attract birds, bees. Leaves widely used as seasoning.

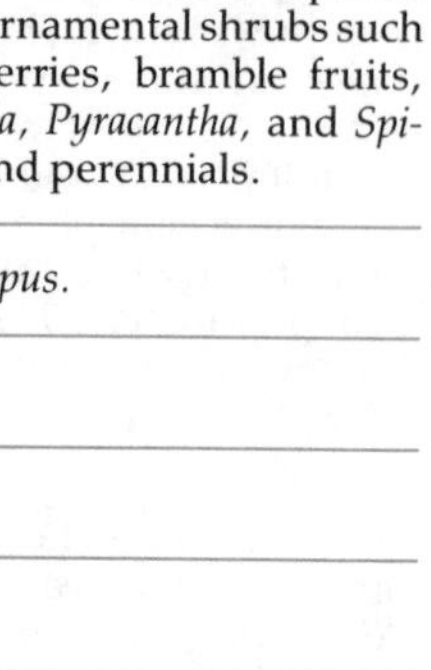

Rosmarinus officinalis

Endures hot sun and poor soil, but good drainage is a must. Once established, needs some watering in desert, little or no watering elsewhere. Feeding and excess water result in rank growth, subsequent woodiness. Control growth by frequent tip-pinching when plants are small. Prune older plants lightly; cut to side branch or shear.

Some taller varieties are useful as clipped hedges or in dry borders with native and gray-leafed plants. Greatest use for lower-growing varieties is as ground or bank covers. Set container-grown plants or rooted cuttings 2 ft. apart for moderately quick cover. Feed lightly, thin occasionally, and head back gently to encourage new growth. Useful in erosion control.

'Collingwood Ingram' *(R. ingramii).* To 2–2½ ft. tall, spreading to 4 ft. or more. Branches curve gracefully. Flowers rich, bright blue violet. Tallish bank or ground cover with high color value. Proper name is probably 'Benenden Blue'.

'Huntington Blue'. Grows to 1½ ft. tall, spreads quickly yet maintains dense center. Deep blue flowers.

'Lockwood de Forest' *(R. lockwoodii, R. forrestii).* Resembles 'Prostratus', but has lighter, bright foliage, bluer flowers.

'Prostratus'. DWARF ROSEMARY. To 2 ft. tall with 4–8-ft. spread. Will trail over wall or edge of raised bed to make curtain of green. Pale lavender blue flowers. Fire retardant if reasonably well watered.

'Tuscan Blue'. Rigid, upright branches to 6 ft. tall grow directly from base of plant. Leaves are rich green, flowers blue violet. Makes an attractive tall, narrow screen. Correct name may be 'Fastigiatus'.

ROYAL FERN. See *Osmunda regalis.*

ROYAL TRUMPET VINE. See *Distictis* 'Rivers'.

RUBBER PLANT. See *Ficus elastica.*

Rubiaceae. This widespread and varied family contains herbs, shrubs, and trees with opposite or whorled leaves and clustered flowers (usually). Among its members are *Bouvardia, Coffea* (coffee), *Galium, Gardenia,* and *Rondeletia.*

RUBUS. *Rosaceae.* BRAMBLE. Best known for edible members blackberry and raspberry (see separate entries), the brambles include many ornamental plants, generally little known and not much resembling their thornier relations.

Rubus deliciosus

R. calycinoides. Evergreen shrub. Zones 4–6, 14–17. Creeping stems make mat that spreads 1 ft. a year. Densely packed shiny green leaves, felted beneath, look crinkled on upper surface; 1½ in. across, nearly round, ruffled. Small white flowers resemble strawberry flowers; salmon-colored berries are rarely seen. Needs good drainage, average soil; takes sun or light shade. Attractive ground cover, rock garden plant. Some drought tolerance. 'Emerald Carpet' is a cutting-grown selection of merit.

R. deliciosus. ROCKY MOUNTAIN THIMBLEBERRY, BOULDER RASPBERRY. Deciduous shrub. Zones 1–5, 10. Graceful plant with arching, thornless branches; reaches 3–5 ft. Leaves bright green, nearly round, lobed. Flowers, 2–3 in. across, look like single white roses. May–June bloom. Fruit attracts birds. Good drainage, dryish soil, sun or light shade.

RUDBECKIA. *Compositae.* Annuals, biennials, perennials. All Zones. Garden rudbeckias are descendants of wild plants from eastern United States. All are tough, easy-to-grow plants which thrive in full sun and any except soggy soils. Showy flowers are good for cutting and brighten summer and autumn borders.

Rudbeckia hirta

R. hirta. GLORIOSA DAISY, BLACK-EYED SUSAN. Biennial or short-lived perennial; can be grown as annual, blooming first summer from seed sown in early spring. To 3–4 ft., with upright branching habit, rough, hairy stems and leaves. Wild black-eyed Susan has daisylike single flowers 2–4 in. across, with orange yellow rays and black purple center.

Gloriosa Daisy strain has single daisies 5–7 in. wide in shades of yellow, orange, russet, or mahogany, often zoned or banded. 'Irish Eyes' has golden yellow flowers with light green centers that turn brown as they mature. 'Pinwheel' has mahogany and gold flowers. Gloriosa Double Daisy strain has somewhat smaller (to 4½-in.) double flower heads, nearly all in lighter yellow and orange shades. 'Marmalade' (2 ft.) and 'Goldilocks' (8–10 in.) are lower growing, can be used at front of border or as ground cover.

R. laciniata 'Hortensia'. GOLDEN GLOW. Perennial to 6–7 ft. tall. Spreads (sometimes aggressively) by underground stems. Leaves deeply lobed, light green. Flowers (summer and fall) double, bright yellow. Tolerates heat remarkably well. Good summer screen or tall border plant. Does not seed, but spreads rapidly, is easily divided. Spray to control aphids. Variety 'Goldquelle' grows to 2½ ft., is less aggressive.

R. purpurea. See *Echinacea.*

RUE. See *Ruta graveolens.*

RUELLIA peninsularis. *Acanthaceae.* Shrub. Zones 12, 13. Native to Sonora. Grows 2–4 ft. tall and as wide; leaves are bright green, about 1 in. long. In mild-winter areas, it is evergreen and blooms heavily in summer, with scattered blooms throughout the year. Loses leaves in sharp frosts. Flowers are pale purple, bell shaped, ¾–1 in. wide. Hardy to about 20°F. Drought tolerant when established, but needs frequent watering to start. Background or clipped hedge.

Ruellia peninsularis

RUMOHRA adiantiformis (usually sold as *Aspidium capense*). *Polypodiaceae.* LEATHERLEAF FERN. Zones 14–17, 19–24. Fronds are deep glossy green, triangular, finely cut, to 3 ft. tall. They are firm textured and last well when cut for arrangements. Although it does best in partial shade, this fern will grow in full sun. Hardy to 24°F. Moderate water.

Rumohra adiantiformis

RUPTURE WORT. See *Herniaria glabra.*

RUSCUS. *Liliaceae.* BUTCHER'S BROOM. Evergreen shrublets. Zones 4–24. Will grow indoors. Unusual plants with some value as small-scale ground cover, curiosity, or source of dry arrangement material and Christmas greens. Flattened leaflike branches do work of leaves. They bear tiny greenish white flowers in centers of upper surfaces. If male and female plants are present, or if you have plant with male and female flowers, bright red (sometimes yellow), marble-sized fruit follows flowers. Plants spread by underground stems. Best in shade but will take sun except in desert. They tolerate water, drought, competition from tree roots. Subject to chlorosis in desert. Will grow indoors.

Ruscus hypoglossum

R. aculeatus. To 1–4 ft. tall with branched stems. Spine-tipped "leaves" are 1–3 in. long, a third as wide, leathery, dull dark green. Fruit ½ in. across, red or yellow.

R. hypoglossum. To 1½ ft.; unbranched stems. "Leaves" to 4 in. long, 1½ in. wide, glossy green, not spine tipped. Fruit ¼–½ in. across. Spreads faster than *R. aculeatus.* Superior as small-scale ground cover. Shade tolerant.

RUSSELIA equisetiformis. *Scrophulariaceae.* CORAL FOUNTAIN. Perennial. Outdoors in sheltered locations Zones 19–24; house plant or indoor/outdoor plant anywhere. Hardy to temperatures of about 32°F. Shrubby plant with trailing, bright green, practically leafless stems that look attractive spilling from a wall or hanging basket; stems can also be fastened to a trellis or wall. Many side branches bear a profusion of bright red, narrowly tubular flowers that look like little firecrackers; bloom lasts all spring and summer outdoors, goes on continuously in house or greenhouse. Needs steady watering, and regular fertilizing. Easy to propagate with pencil-sized cuttings taken in spring.

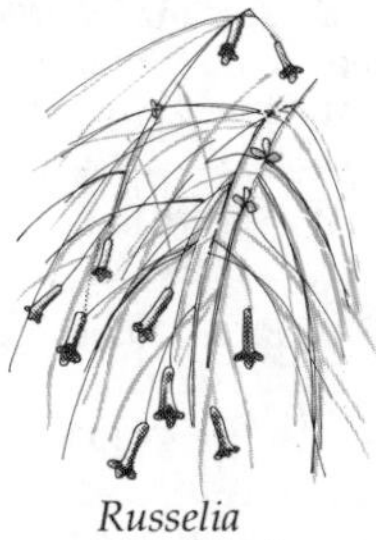
Russelia equisetiformis

R

RUSSIAN OLIVE. See *Elaeagnus angustifolia.*

RUSSIAN SAGE. See *Perovskia atriplicifolia.*

RUTABAGA. See Turnip and Rutabaga.

Rutaceae. The rue family includes, besides rue *(Ruta),* a large number of perennials, shrubs, and trees, most important of which are the citrus clan. Most members of the family have oil glands in leaves or other plant parts and are aromatic. *Boronia, Choisya, Coleonema, Geijera,* and *Skimmia* are other important members.

RUTA graveolens. *Rutaceae.* RUE, HERB-OF-GRACE. Perennial herb. All Zones. To 2–3 ft. Aromatic, fernlike blue green leaves; small, greenish yellow flowers; decorative brown seed capsules. Sow seeds in flats, transplant to 1 ft. apart. Good garden soil with additions of lime to strongly acid soil. Full sun; average to minimal water. Plant at back of border. Dry seed clusters for use in wreaths or swags. 'Jackman's Blue' is dense, compact, and fine gray blue in color.

Ruta graveolens

Rue is accorded herb status for its history and legend rather than for any use. It was once thought to ward off disease, to guard against poisons, and aid the sight. It was also used to make brushes for sprinkling holy water.

RYEGRASS. See *Lolium.*

SABAL. *Palmae.* PALMETTO. Zones 12–17, 19–24. Native from North Carolina to South America. Large, slow-growing fan palms, some with trunks, some without. Large clusters of inconspicuous flowers appear among leaves when plants are mature. Hardy, all withstanding 20°–22°F., some even lower temperatures. Take sun in youth. Average garden water except *S. uresana.*

Sabal palmetto

S. blackburniana *(S. domingensis, S. umbraculifera).* HISPANIOLAN PALMETTO. Largest palmetto, ultimately 80 ft. or more, with immense green fans 9 ft. across.

S. mexicana *(S. texana).* OAXACA PALMETTO. Leaf stems hang on trunk in early life, then fall to show attractive, slender trunk. Grows 30–50 ft. high.

S. minor. Leafy green palm, usually trunkless, but sometimes with trunk to 6 ft. Old leaves fold at base, hang down like closed umbrella.

S. palmetto. CABBAGE PALM. Zones 10, 12–17, 19–24. Trunk grows slowly to 20 ft., much taller in its native southeastern states. Big (5–8-ft.) green leaves grow in dense, globular head.

S. uresana. SONORAN PALMETTO. Native to northwestern Mexico. To 30 ft.; faster growing than most palmettos. Drought tolerant. Silver gray to blue gray leaves are 6 ft. wide.

SAFFLOWER. See *Carthamus tinctorius.*

SAGE. See *Salvia.*

SAGE, RUSSIAN. See *Perovskia atriplicifolia.*

SAGEBRUSH. See *Artemisia tridentata.*

SAGINA subulata. *Caryophyllaceae.* IRISH MOSS, SCOTCH MOSS. Perennial. Zones 1–11, 14–24. *Sagina subulata* is the more common of 2 different plants (the other is *Arenaria verna,* usually called *A. v. caespitosa*) of similar appearance. Both make dense, compact, mosslike masses of very slender leaves on slender stems. But *Arenaria verna* has tiny white flowers in few-flowered clusters, while *Sagina subulata* bears flowers singly and differs in other technical details. In common usage, however, green forms of the 2 species are called IRISH MOSS, and golden green forms (*Arenaria verna* 'Aurea' and *Sagina subulata* 'Aurea') are called SCOTCH MOSS.

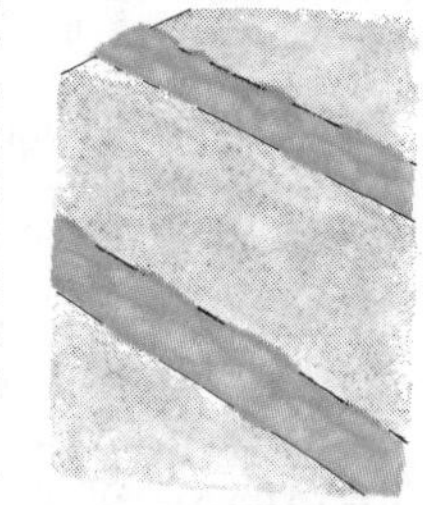

Sagina subulata

Both *Sagina* and *Arenaria* are grown primarily as ground covers for limited areas in full sun or semishade; they're useful for filling gaps between paving blocks. In cool coastal gardens, they can seed themselves and become pests.

Although they look like moss, these plants won't grow well under conditions that suit true mosses. They need good soil, good drainage, ample water, and occasional feeding with slow-acting, nonburning fertilizer. In hot places, give partial shade; they don't do well in deep shade. They take some foot traffic and tend to hump up in time; control humping by occasionally cutting out narrow strips, then pressing or rolling lightly. Control snails, slugs, cutworms. Cut squares from flats and set 6 in. apart for fast cover. To avoid lumpiness, plant so that soil line of squares is at or slightly below planted soil surface.

SAGO PALM. See *Cycas revoluta.*

SAGUARO. See *Carnegiea gigantea.*

ST. AUGUSTINE GRASS. See *Stenotaphrum secundatum.*

ST. CATHERINE'S LACE. See *Eriogonum giganteum.*

SAINTPAULIA ionantha. *Gesneriaceae.* AFRICAN VIOLET. Evergreen perennial. Probably most popular house plant in the United States. Fuzzy, heart-shaped leaves with smooth edges grow in rosettes up to 1 ft. wide. Pale lavender flowers grow in clusters of 3 or more. Hybrids and named varieties have leaves that are plain or scalloped, green or variegated; flowers are purple, violet, pink, white, or bicolored. Best in east window with roof overhang or filtered morning sun. Keep where temperatures average 60°–70°F. Preferably humidity should be high; if house air is quite dry, increase humidity around plants by setting each plant on a saucer filled with wet gravel.

Saintpaulia ionantha

African violets won't take just any potting mix. They need acid conditions (use plenty of leaf mold); suitable soil conditioner such as builder's sand or vermiculite; good loam (preferably sterilized if you use garden soil); and small amount of slow-acting fertilizer such as bone meal or manure. One good mix is 3 parts leaf mold, 1 part loam, ½ part builder's sand, and small amount of bone meal. (For a number of other good mixes, see the *Sunset* book *How to Grow African Violets.*) Don't use too large a pot—African violets bloom best when roots are crowded.

Water plants from top or below, but avoid watering crown or leaves. Wick-irrigated pots work well. Use water at room temperature or slightly warmer, wet soil thoroughly, let potting mixture become dry to the touch before watering again. Don't let water stand in pot saucers for more than 2 hours after watering plants. If plant is well established, feed—only when soil is moist—with slightly acid fertilizer once every 2–4 weeks. Propagate from seeds, leaf cuttings, or divisions. Most common pests are aphids, cyclamen mites, thrips, and mealybugs.

SALAL. See *Gaultheria shallon.*

Salicaceae. The willow family consists of deciduous trees or shrubs with flowers in catkins and (generally) with silk-tufted seeds that blow about. Cottonwood, poplar, and willow are examples.

SALIX. *Salicaceae.* WILLOW. Deciduous trees or shrubs. All Zones, but best, most useful where there are pronounced winters. Very fast growing. Will take any soil; most kinds will even tolerate poor drainage. One important need is plenty of water. All have invasive roots and are hard to garden under. Most are subject to tent caterpillars, aphids, borers, and spider mites.

Salix babylonica

Weeping willows are best used as single trees near stream or lake. With training, they can become satisfactory shade trees for patio or terrace. All leaf out very early in spring, hold leaves late (until Christmas in milder climates).

Shrubby willows are grown principally for their catkins ("pussy willows") or colored twigs, as screen plants, or for erosion control on stream or river banks.

S. alba tristis (***S. babylonica aurea,*** 'Niobe'). GOLDEN WEEPING WILLOW. Tree. To 80 ft. or more, with greater spread. One-year-old twigs are bright yellow, quite pendulous. Leaves are bright green or yellow green, paler beneath.

Left to go its own way, this (and other weeping willows) will head too low to furnish usable shade. Stake up main stem and keep it staked—right up to 15–18 ft. Shorten side branches and remove them as they lose their vigor; keep early growth directed into a tall main stem and high-branching scaffold limbs. This treatment will make a tree you can walk under. Subject to twig blight in Northwest; use copper spray on new foliage. Texas root rot a problem in desert.

S. alba vitellina is an upright form with brilliant yellow winter twigs. Hard pruning will keep tree size down and yield an abundance of twigs for winter color.

S. babylonica. WEEPING WILLOW. Tree. To 30–50 ft. with equal or greater spread. Smaller than golden weeping willow, with longer (3–6-in.) leaves and even more pronounced weeping habit. Greenish or brown branchlets. Train to be full-fledged weeper as described for *S. alba tristis*.

Variety 'Crispa' ('Annularis'), RINGLEAF or CORKSCREW WILLOW, is an interesting oddity with leaves twisted and curled into rings or circles. It is somewhat narrower in spread than the species.

S. blanda. WISCONSIN WEEPING WILLOW. Tree. To 40–50 ft. or more, spreading wider. Less strongly weeping habit than *S. babylonica;* leaves broader, more bluish green. 'Fan', FAN GIANT BLUE WEEPING WILLOW, is resistant to borers and blight.

S. caprea. FRENCH PUSSY WILLOW, PINK PUSSY WILLOW. Shrub or small tree. All Zones. To 25 ft. Broad leaves 3–6 in. long, dark green above, gray and hairy beneath. Fat, inch-long, pinkish gray, woolly catkins before leaves in very early spring. Forces easily indoors, and can be cut for winter arrangements. For large gardens that can spare room for unusual shrubs, or for naturalizing. Can be kept to shrub size by cutting to ground every few years.

S. discolor. PUSSY WILLOW. Shrub or small tree. To 20 ft., with slender, red brown stems and bright green, 2–4-in.-long, oval leaves, bluish beneath. Catkins of male plants (usually only kind sold) are feature attraction—soft, silky, pearl gray, and up to 1½ in. long. Branches can be cut in winter for early bouquets.

S. gracilistyla. ROSE-GOLD PUSSY WILLOW. Upright spreading shrub. To 6–10 ft. tall; 2–4-in.-long, ½–1¼-in.-wide leaves are gray green above, bluish green beneath. Plump, 1½-in.-long, furry gray catkins show numerous stamens with rose and gold anthers. Good-looking in garden or in arrangements. Cutting branches for indoor use will help curb shrub size; every 3 or 4 years, cut back whole plant to short stubs. You'll be rewarded by especially vigorous shoots with large catkins. *S. g. melanostachys* has black catkins with red anthers—weird but attractive in arrangements.

S. matsudana. HANKOW WILLOW. Tree. Upright, pyramidal growth to 40–50 ft. Leaves narrow, bright green, 2–4 in. long, ½ in. wide. Can thrive on less water than most willows. This plant and its varieties are popular in high desert and plateau areas.

S. m. 'Navajo'. GLOBE NAVAJO WILLOW. Large, spreading, round-topped tree to 70 ft. tall, equally wide. Very tough and hardy.

S. m. 'Tortuosa'. TWISTED HANKOW WILLOW, CORKSCREW WILLOW. To 30 ft. high, with 20-ft. spread. Branches and branchlets fantastically twisted into upright, spiralling patterns, attractive in summer and showy even in winter. Use for silhouette value; cut branches good in arrangements.

S. m. 'Umbraculifera'. GLOBE WILLOW. To 35 ft. with equal spread. Round, umbrella-shaped head with upright branches, drooping branchlets.

S. purpurea. PURPLE OSIER, ALASKA BLUE WILLOW. Shrub. To 10–18 ft. high with purple branches and dark green, 1–3-in.-long leaves that are markedly bluish underneath. Variety 'Gracilis' ('Nana'), DWARF PURPLE OSIER, often seen in cold-winter regions, has slimmer branches and narrower leaves; it is usually grown as clipped hedge and kept 1–3 ft. high and equally wide. General effect is fine textured; color effect blue gray. Grows easily from cuttings. Good background plant.

S. sachalinensis 'Sekka' (***S. s.*** 'Setsuka'). Shrub or small tree. Leaves 2–4 in. long, ½ in. wide, green above, silvery beneath. Catkins silvery, up to 2 in. long. Big feature: flattened branches often 1–2 in. wide, twisted and curled, picturesque in arrangements.

SALPIGLOSSIS sinuata. *Solanaceae.* PAINTED-TONGUE. Summer annual. Upright, open habit, to 2–3 ft. tall. Sticky leaves and stems. Leaves to 4 in. long, narrowly oblong. Flowers much like petunias in shape and size (2–2½ in. wide), but more unusual in color—shades of mahogany red, reddish orange, yellow, purple and pink tones, marbled and penciled with contrasting color. Bolero (2 ft.), Friendship (15 in.), and Splash (2 ft.) are compact strains.

Salpiglossis sinuata

Seeds are rather difficult to start, especially when sown directly in garden bed. Good method: In late winter or early spring, plant in potting mixture in peat pots, several seeds to pot. Keep in warm, protected location; seeds should sprout in 7–10 days. Thin to one seedling per pot. Later, when young plants are well established and all danger of frost is past, plant in sunny location. Best in rich soil; don't overwater. Pinch out tips of growing plants to induce branching. Best bloom in late spring and early summer, but plants will endure until frost. Good background plant for border; handsome cut flowers.

SALSIFY. OYSTER PLANT. *Compositae.* Hardy biennial. All Zones. Grown for its edible root which looks something like parsnip and has creamy white flesh that tastes a little like oysters. Plant grows to 4 ft. tall; leaves are narrow, grasslike. Plant in rich, deep, sandy soil, spaded deep. Culture is same as for parsnips. It takes 150 days to grow to maturity. Cooked, mashed salsify, mixed with butter and beaten egg, can be made into patties and sautéed until brown to make mock oysters. If plant is allowed to overwinter, it will produce flower stalk topped by large head of lavender purple, dandelionlike flowers followed by white, cottony seeds.

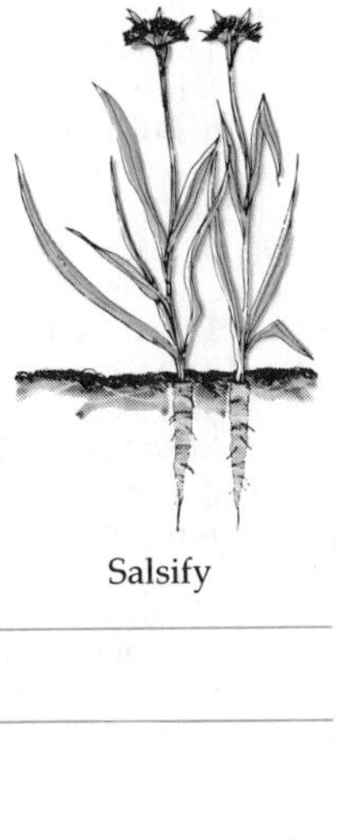

Salsify

SALTBUSH. See *Atriplex*.

SALT CEDAR. See *Tamarix chinensis.*

SALVIA. *Labiatae.* SAGE. Annuals, biennials, perennials, evergreen shrubs. Flowers in whorls, sometimes distinctly spaced, sometimes pushed close together so they appear as one dense spike. Tubular flowers vary in color from white through a range of pinks and lavenders to true blue and scarlet.

Salvia officinalis

Dozens of lesser-known species from Mexico, South America, and Eurasia have been introduced at botanical gardens; look for them at arboretum plant sales or check specialists' seed lists. Some are large, spectacular shrubs. Many additional native salvias are obtainable from native plant specialists.

S. argentea. SILVER SAGE. Biennial. All Zones. First-year rosettes are 1 ft. or more across, the leaves 6–8 in. long, white with silvery hairs. Branched flowering stems reach 4 ft.; flowers white tinged pink or yellow. Striking foliage plant.

S. azurea grandiflora ***(S. pitcheri).*** Perennial. Zones 1–11, 14–24. To 5 ft. tall with hairy, 2–4-in.-long leaves. Gentian blue flowers, ½ in. long, provide mass of color from early July to frost. Full sun.

S. clevelandii. Shrub. Zones 10–24. Native to chaparral slopes of San Diego County. Rounded form to 4 ft. tall. Foliage and flowers have delightful fragrance. Smooth, gray green leaves about an inch long. Blue, ¾-in. flowers May–August. Sun, well-drained soil, practically no water in summer. For best appearance, prune after frosts have passed. Use with plants that have similar cultural requirements.

S. elegans ***(S. gracilistyla, S. rutilans).*** PINEAPPLE SAGE. Perennial herb. Zones 8–24. To 2–3 ft. Use woolly light green leaves fresh or dried as seasoning; milder, more fruity scent and taste than garden sage. Scarlet flowers in fall. Tender to frost, otherwise same care as garden sage.

S. farinacea. MEALY-CUP SAGE. Perennial; annual where winters are cold. All Zones. Fast growth to 3-ft. mound. Gray green, 4-in.-long leaves. Spikes of violet blue, ½-in.-long flowers rise well above mound. Use with other annuals and perennials or by itself as foundation plant. Favorite of flower arrangers. 'Blue Bedder' and 'Victoria' are blue varieties; 'White Porcelain' and 'Silver White' are white selections.

S. greggii. Shrub. Zones 8–24. Upright-branching, bushy plant to 3–4 ft. tall. Leaves ½–1 in. long, medium green. Flowers an inch long, rosy red, in loose, spikelike clusters in late spring and summer (heaviest fall through spring in the desert). Ordinary garden soil and watering, full sun or light shade. Drought tolerant near coast. Can be sheared into a hedge. Pink and salmon forms exist.

S. leucantha. MEXICAN BUSH SAGE. Shrub. Zones 10–24. To 3–4 ft. tall and as wide; graceful habit. Long, slender, velvety purple or deep rose spikes with small white flowers; blooms summer and fall. Tolerates drought. Cut old stems to the ground; new ones bloom continuously. Grow from pieces of old clumps with roots attached. Sun or light shade.

S. leucophylla. PURPLE SAGE. Shrub. Zones 10–24. Native to southern Coast Ranges and mountains of southern California. To 2–6 ft. tall with white stems and gray, crinkly, 1–3-in. leaves which drop in dry seasons. Flowers light purple, ½ in. long, in 3–5-whorled clusters, May–June. Tolerates heat and drought.

S. officinalis. GARDEN SAGE. Perennial herb. All Zones. To 1½–2 ft. high. Narrow, gray green, 1–2-in.-long leaves. Tall spikes of violet blue (rarely red or white) flowers attractive to bees in early summer. Variety 'Tricolor' has leaves variegated with white and purple red; 'Icterina' has golden yellow leaves. Poor but well-drained soil, full sun. Fairly drought resistant. Cut back after bloom; fertilize if you cut continually. Divide every 3–4 years. Propagate from cuttings, layers, or seeds. Excellent for rock gardens and containers. Fragrant, colorful cut flower. Use leaves (fresh or dried) for seasoning meat, sausage, cheese, poultry.

S. patens. GENTIAN SAGE. Perennial, evergreen in mild climates; use as annual where winters are cold. All Zones. Stems to 2½ ft.; arrow-shaped, hairy, 2–5-in.-long, green leaves. Deep dark blue flowers 2 in. long. Sun or part shade.

S. splendens. SCARLET SAGE. Annual. Sturdy plant 1–3 ft. high (depends on variety) with dark green leaves topped by tall, dense clusters of magnificent scarlet flowers. Also rose, lavender, white varieties. Blooms early summer to frost. 'Scarlet Pygmy' and 'St. John's Fire' are extremely dwarf varieties. Start from seed (slow) or buy young plants from nursery. Thrives in full sun, but will also flower in part shade. Any soil; generous water. Cut flowers don't last. Strong color is best with gray foliage or white flowers.

S. viridis ***(S. horminum).*** Annual. Upright plants to 1½ ft. tall with showy inflorescences: actual flowers are insignificant, but beneath them are leaflike bracts in shades of pink, white, or blue. Attractive for arrangements; use fresh or dried. Claryssa strain is compact (to 15 in.) and branches freely.

SAMBUCUS. *Caprifoliaceae.* ELDERBERRY. Deciduous shrubs or trees. In their natural state, these western natives are rampant, fast growing, wild looking. But they can be tamed to a degree. Use them in same way as spiraea or other large deciduous shrubs. In large gardens, they can be effective as screen or windbreak. To keep them dense and shrubby, prune hard every dormant season. New growth sprouts readily from stumps. Sun or light shade, average water. Will take wet conditions with good drainage.

Sambucus caerulea neomexicana

Elders are a confusing lot, and botanists in different regions tend to assign different names to the same plant. Generally speaking, there are black-, blue-, and red-fruited elders; birds eat the fruit of all types, but red elderberries can cause nausea in humans if consumed raw in large quantities.

S. caerulea ***(S. glauca).*** BLUE ELDERBERRY. All Zones. Native from California north to British Columbia, east to Rockies. Shrub 4–10 ft. tall or spreading tree to 50 ft. Leaves 5–8 in. long, divided into 5–9 rather firm, toothed, 1–6-in.-long leaflets. Small white or creamy white flowers in flat-topped clusters 2–8 in. wide, April–August. Clusters of blue to nearly black, ¼-in. berries, usually covered with whitish powder. Berries edible, often used in jams, jellies, pies, and wine—if birds don't get them first. Forms from southern California and desert states (*S. c. mexicana* and *S. c. neomexicana*) have fewer leaflets of grayer green, and berries are fewer, smaller, drier.

S. callicarpa ***(S. racemosa callicarpa).*** COAST RED ELDERBERRY, RED ELDERBERRY. Zones 4–7, 14–17. Native to coastal regions, northern California to British Columbia. Shrub to 8 ft. or small tree to 20 ft. Leaves 3–6 in. long, divided into 5–7 smooth, sharply toothed leaflets. Flowers creamy white, in dome-shaped clusters 2–5 in. across. Small, bright red berries are probably poisonous. Requires ample water.

S. canadensis. AMERICAN ELDERBERRY. Zones 1–7, 14–17. Spreading, suckering shrub to 6–8 ft., seldom grown except in cold-winter climates. Almost tropical looking in foliage, each leaf having 7 leaflets up to 6 in. long. Flat, creamy white flower clusters to 10 in. wide in summer are followed by purple black fruit of good flavor. Fruit used for pies; both flowers and fruit used for wine. Needs sun, good soil, ample water, hard pruning each year. In March, cut back all last year's growth to a few inches. Named fruiting varieties include 'Adams', 'Johns', and many more. Plant any 2 varieties for pollination.

Ornamental varieties include 'Aurea', with golden green foliage, golden in full sun; and 'Laciniata', CUTLEAF or FERNLEAF ELDER, with finely cut foliage.

S. pubens. Zones 1–3. Shrubby, usually 2–4 ft. tall, possibly to 15 ft. Loose, tall flower clusters followed by bright red fruit later in season.

S. racemosa. RED ELDERBERRY, EUROPEAN RED ELDERBERRY. Zones 1–3. Native to northern latitudes in North America, Europe,

Asia. Bushy shrub 8–10 ft. tall; leaves 3–6 in. long, divided into 5 or 7 smooth, sharply toothed leaflets. Small, creamy white flowers in dome-shaped clusters to 2½ in. wide, May–July, followed by bright red berries. Golden variety with finely divided leaves is called 'Plumosa Aurea'.

SAND CHERRY. See Plum and Prune.

SANDHILL SAGE. See *Artemisia pycnocephala*.

SAND PEAR. See *Pyrus pyrifolia*.

SAND STRAWBERRY. See *Fragaria chiloensis*.

SAND VERBENA. See *Abronia*.

SANGUINARIA canadensis. *Papaveraceae.* BLOODROOT. Perennial. Zones 1–6. This member of the poppy family gets its common name because of the orange red juice that seeps from cut roots and stems. Big, deeply lobed grayish leaves. In early spring, 1½-in., white or pink-tinged flowers are borne singly on 8-in. stalks. For damp, shaded rock garden where it can spread, or for leafy soil beneath trees or open shrubs. 'Multiplex' has double flowers.

Sanguinaria canadensis

SANGUISORBA minor. See *Poterium sanguisorba*.

SANSEVIERIA trifasciata (often sold as *S. zeylanica*). *Agavaceae.* BOWSTRING HEMP, SNAKE PLANT, MOTHER-IN-LAW'S TONGUE. Evergreen perennials. Outdoors Zones 13–24, protected locations Zone 12. House plants everywhere. Appreciated for thick, patterned leaves that grow in rosettes from thick rhizomes. Leaves 1–4 ft. tall, 2 in. wide, rigidly upright or spreading slightly at top, dark green banded gray green. *S. t.* 'Laurentii' is identical, but with broad, creamy yellow stripes on leaf edges. Dwarf variety 'Hahnii' has rosettes of broad, triangular, 6-in.-long leaves, dark green with silvery banding. Plant piles up to make mass 1 ft. tall, equally wide. Serves as good small pot plant or focus for dish garden.

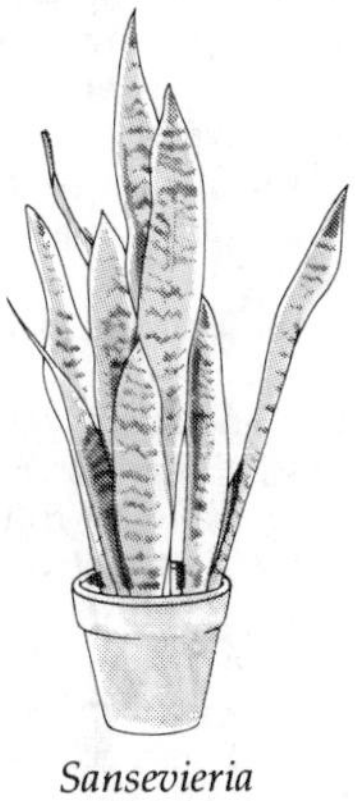

Sansevieria trifasciata 'Laurentii'

First common name comes from use of tough leaf fibers as bowstrings; second comes from banding or mottling on leaves, which resembles some snakeskins; third probably comes from toughness of leaves and plants' persistence under neglect. Erect, narrow clusters of greenish white, fragrant flowers seldom appear.

No special soil requirements; water seldom but thoroughly. If grown outdoors, shelter from midday sun, which makes leaves pale and unsightly. Indoors, plants will grow in much or little light, seldom need repotting, and withstand considerable neglect—dry air, uneven temperatures, and light, capricious watering.

Other *Sansevieria* varieties and species are collectors' items; scores can be found in catalogues of succulent plant dealers.

SANTA BARBARA DAISY. See *Erigeron karvinskianus*.

SANTOLINA. *Compositae.* Herbs, evergreen subshrubs. All Zones. These have attractive foliage, a profusion of little round flower heads, and stout constitutions. Good as ground covers, bank covers, or low clipped hedges. Grow in any soil in full sun. Both species are aromatic if bruised, and both look best if kept low by pruning. Clip off spent flowers. Cut back in early spring. May die to ground in coldest areas, but roots will live and resume growth. Needs little or no water where summers are cool.

S. chamaecyparissus. LAVENDER COTTON. Can reach 2 ft., but looks best clipped to 1 ft. or less. Brittle, woody stems densely clothed with rough, finely divided, whitish gray leaves. Bright yellow, buttonlike flower heads in summer on unclipped plants. Plant 3 ft. apart as ground cover, closer as edging for walks, borders, foreground plantings. Replace if woodiness takes over.

Santolina chamaecyparissus

S. virens. Similar to lavender cotton, but narrower, deep green leaves of striking texture; plants look something like puffs of green smoke. Creamy chartreuse flowers. Faster growing than *S. chamaecyparissus*, tolerates more water. Fire retardant.

SANVITALIA procumbens. *Compositae.* CREEPING ZINNIA. Summer annual. Not really a zinnia, but looks enough like it to fool most people. Plants grow only 4–6 in. high, but spread or trail 1 ft. or more. Leaves are like miniature (to 2-in.-long) zinnia leaves. Flower heads nearly 1 in. wide, with dark purple brown centers and bright yellow or orange rays. Bloom lasts from midsummer until frost. Plants take much drought and heat once established; need sun and good drainage. Sow seeds from mid-March (low desert) to May or even June (where soil is slow to warm up). Good hanging basket or pot plants, temporary fillers in borders, slope and bank covers, edgings. Avoid overhead watering. 'Gold Braid' (yellow) and 'Mandarin Orange' are doubles.

Sanvitalia procumbens

Sapindaceae. The soapberry family contains trees and shrubs with (usually) divided leaves, clustered small flowers (sometimes showy), and fruit which is berrylike, sometimes with inflated husks, often showy. Some have edible fruit. Examples are *Cupaniopsis, Dodonaea, Koelreuteria,* and *Litchi.*

SAPIUM sebiferum. *Euphorbiaceae.* CHINESE TALLOW TREE. Deciduous tree. Zones 8, 9, 12–16, 18–21. To 35 ft. with dense round or conical crown of equal width. Outstanding fall color. Tends toward shrubbiness, multiple trunks, suckering, but easily trained to single trunk. In colder areas, unripened branch tips freeze back each winter; new growth quickly covers damage, but may require thinning. Leaves are poplarlike, roundish, tapering to slender point, light green. Foliage is dense, but general effect is airy; leaves flutter in lightest breeze. If tree is in full sun and has moderate autumn chill, its foliage turns brilliant, translucent, neon red. Some trees color plum purple, yellow, orange, or mixture of colors. If possible, select your tree while it is in fall color; a few specimens have shown nondescript yellow instead of flaming red. Tiny yellowish flowers in spikes at branch tips; fruit small, clustered, grayish white; they are covered by a waxy coating.

Sapium sebiferum

Hardy to 10°–15°F. Grows in most soils, but does somewhat better in mildly acid conditions. Give it ample water for fast growth and prune only to correct shape. Stake young plants securely. Good lawn or street tree, patio or terrace shade tree. Resistant to oak root fungus. Good screening against low summer sun or objectionable view. Gives light to moderate shade.

S

SAPONARIA ocymoides. *Caryophyllaceae.* Perennial. All Zones. Trailing habit, to 1 ft. high and 3 ft. across. Dark green, oval leaves; in spring, plants are covered with small pink flowers in loose bunches shaped much like phlox. Any soil; easy to grow. Useful for covering walls and as ground cover in little-used areas.

Saponaria ocymoides

SAPOTE, WHITE. See *Casimiroa.*

SARCOCOCCA. *Buxaceae.* Evergreen shrubs. Zones 4–9, 14–24. Native to Himalayas, China. Of great value in landscaping shaded areas—under overhangs, in entryways, beneath low-branching, evergreen trees. They maintain slow, orderly growth and polished appearance in deepest shade. Will take sun in cool-summer areas. Grow best in soil rich in organic matter. Add peat moss, ground bark, or the like to planting bed. Average garden water. Scale insects only pests.

Sarcococca ruscifolia

S. confusa. Very similar to (and generally sold as) *S. ruscifolia.* However, latter has red fruit, while that of *S. confusa* is black.

S. hookerana humilis *(S. humilis).* Low growing, seldom more than 1½ ft. high; spreads by underground runners to 8 ft. or more. Dark green, glossy, narrow oval, pointed leaves (1–3 in. long, ½–¾ in. wide) closely set on branches. Tiny, fragrant white flowers, hidden in foliage in early spring, are followed by glossy blue black fruit. Good ground cover in shade.

S. ruscifolia. Slow growth (6 in. a year) to 4–6 ft., with 3–7-ft. spread. Will form natural espalier against wall, branches fanning out to form dark patterns. Glossy, waxy, deep green, wavy-edged leaves, 2 in. long, densely set on branches. Flowers (in early spring) are small, white, nearly hidden in foliage, but fragrant enough to be noticed many feet away. Flowers are followed by red fruit.

SARGENT CHERRY. See *Prunus sargentii.*

SARRACENIA. *Sarraceniaceae.* PITCHER PLANT. Perennials. Zones 4–7; house plants (or terrarium plants) nearly anywhere. Leaves rise from creeping rhizomes, look like hollow tubes or "pitchers." These leaves trap and digest insects in same manner as our western native pitcher plant (see *Darlingtonia*). Not easy to grow; require boggy, acid soil and high humidity. Will not tolerate hot, dry air, strong fertilizers, or extended irrigation with hard water. Grow in bogs, in pots of wet sand–sphagnum mix; or try in terrariums or enclosed, humid glass frames. Give rainwater or distilled water.

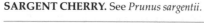

Sarracenia flava

S. flava. Leaves 1–2 ft. tall, erect, yellowish green veined red. Yellow, 4–5-in. flowers borne singly on 1–2-ft. stalks.

S. purpurea. Green to purple red leaves 6–10 in. tall, rather plump. Purple red or greenish flowers to 2 in. across.

Sarraceniaceae. The pitcher plant family is easily identified by its leaves, which have been modified into hollow structures partially filled with liquid. These trap insects, which contribute to the plant's food supply. Examples are *Darlingtonia* and *Sarracenia.*

SASA. See Bamboo.

SASSAFRAS albidum. *Lauraceae.* SASSAFRAS. Deciduous tree. Zones 4–6, 10–12, 14–17. Fast to 20–25 ft., then slower to eventual 50–60 ft. Dense and pyramidal, with heavy trunk and rather short branches. Sometimes shrubby. Pleasantly aromatic tree; bark of roots sometimes used for making tea. Leaves 3–7 in. long, 2–4 in. wide; shape may be oval, lobed on one side (mitten shaped), or lobed on both sides. Orange and scarlet fall color, better some years than others. Inconspicuous flowers. Best in sandy, well-drained soil; won't take long summer drought or alkaline soil. Hard to transplant. Suckers badly if roots are cut during cultivation.

Sassafras albidum

SATUREJA. *Labiatae.* Annual and perennial herbs, sometimes shrublike. Aromatic foliage.

S. douglasii *(Micromeria chamissonis).* YERBA BUENA. Creeping perennial. Zones 4–9, 14–24. Native from Los Angeles County to British Columbia. Plant for which San Francisco was given its original name of Yerba Buena. Slender stems root as they grow, spreading to 3 ft. Roundish, 1-in.-long leaves with scalloped edges have strong minty scent. Small white or lavender-tinted flowers April–September. Needs rich, moist soil for best appearance. Give sun along coast, part shade inland. Dried leaves make pleasant tea.

Satureja montana

S. hortensis. SUMMER SAVORY. Summer annual. Upright to 1½ ft. with loose, open habit. Rather narrow, ½–1½-in.-long, aromatic leaves. Delicate, ⅛-in.-long, pinkish white to rose flowers in whorls. Grow in light soil rich in humus. Full sun; average water. Excellent container plant. Sow seed where plants are to be grown; thin to 1½ ft. apart. Use fresh or dried leaves as mild seasoning for meats, fish, eggs, soups, vegetables; favorite with beans (German name *Bohnenkraut* means "bean herb"). Some believe that planting it among beans will keep whiteflies away.

S. montana. WINTER SAVORY. Perennial or subshrub. All Zones. Low, spreading, 6–15 in. high. Stiff, narrow to roundish, ½–1-in.-long leaves. Profusion of white to lilac, ⅜-in.-long blooms in whorls, attractive to bees. Grow in sun, in sandy, well-drained soil; give little to moderate water. Fire retardant if fairly well watered. Keep clipped. Space plants 1½ ft. apart in rows. Use as edging in herb border, or in rock garden. Use leaves fresh or dried. Clip at start of flowering season for drying. Propagate from seed (germinates slowly), cuttings, divisions. Not as delicate in flavor as summer savory.

SAUROMATUM venosum *(S. guttatum, Arum cornutum).* *Araceae.* VOODOO LILY. Tuber. Zones 5, 6, 8, 9, 14–24; also grown as house plant. Flower is composed of 1-ft.-long bract, greenish yellow with deep purple markings, surrounding long, blackish purple central spike. Bloom has extremely strong, unpleasant odor for a brief time after opening. Large, deeply lobed, fanlike, tropical-looking leaves on 3-ft. stalks appear after flowers. Tuber will bloom without planting if it is large enough; just place it on window sill or table. After bloom, plant in big pot or in garden. Loose, slightly acid soil. Light shade or sun, average water.

Sauromatum venosum

SAVIN. See *Juniperus sabina.*

SAVORY. See *Satureja.*

SAXIFRAGA. *Saxifragaceae.* SAXIFRAGE. Perennials. Some native to western mountains and foothills, most from Europe. They thrive best in rock gardens of Northwest, where specialists grow dozens of kinds. Most saxifrages grow in full sun or light shade in cooler regions. They require good drainage and light soil; they are easily rotted by soggy soil, but can't take drought. Bergenias, once classified as saxifrages, are still often sold as such.

Saxifraga umbrosa

S. rosacea ***(S. decipiens, S. sternbergii).*** Zones 1–7, 14–17. Cushion-forming, spreading plant—typical "mossy saxifrage." Spreads fairly rapidly; narrow, fleshy leaves are divided into 3–5 narrow lobes. In Northwest, foliage turns crimson in late fall. In spring, flower stalks to 8–9 in. tall display wide-open white flowers. Afternoon shade best in cool-summer areas; shade essential where summers are hot. Many named varieties and hybrids exist, with flowers of pink, rose, and red.

S. stolonifera ***(S. sarmentosa).*** STRAWBERRY GERANIUM. Zones 1–9, 14–24; house plant everywhere. Creeping plant that makes runners like strawberry. Nearly round, white-veined leaves to 4 in. across, pink underneath, blend well with pink azaleas. Flowers white, to 1 in. across, in loose, open clusters to 2 ft. tall. Used as house plant in hanging baskets or pots. Ground cover where hard freezes are infrequent. Shade or part shade, considerable moisture.

Saxifraga stolonifera

S. umbrosa. LONDON PRIDE. Zones 1–7, 14–17. Rosettes of green, shiny, tongue-shaped leaves 1½ in. long. Blooms in May, with open cluster of pink flowers on wine red flower stalk. Does best in shade. Good ground cover for small areas; effective near rocks, stream beds. Needs ample water.

Saxifragaceae. The large saxifrage family includes annuals, perennials, shrubs, some vines and small trees. So varied are its characteristics that a simple description is scarcely possible. Among its members are *Astilbe, Carpenteria, Escallonia, Hydrangea, Heuchera, Philadelphus, Ribes* (including currants and gooseberries), and of course *Saxifraga.*

SCABIOSA. *Dipsaceae.* PINCUSHION FLOWER. Annuals, perennials. Stamens protrude beyond curved surface of flower cluster, giving illusion of pins stuck into a cushion. Easy to grow; need sun. Bloom begins in midsummer, continues until winter if flowers are cut. Good in mixed or mass plantings. Excellent for arrangements.

Scabiosa columbaria

S. atropurpurea (usually sold as *S. grandiflora*). PINCUSHION FLOWER, MOURNING BRIDE. Annual; may persist as perennial where winters are mild. Grows to 2½–3 ft. tall. Oblong, coarsely toothed leaves. Many long, wiry-stemmed flower clusters 2 in. or more across, in colors from blackish purple to salmon pink, rose, white.

S. caucasica. PERENNIAL PINCUSHION FLOWER. Perennial. All Zones. To 2½ ft. high. Leaves vary from finely cut to uncut. Flower clusters 2½–3 in. across appear from June to frost. Depending on variety, color may be blue to bluish lavender or white. Excellent plant for cut flowers.

S. columbaria. Perennial. Zones 4–24. Does particularly well in Zones 22–24. To 2½ ft. tall. Leaves gray green, finely cut. Flowers to 3 in. across; lavender blue, pink, white varieties.

S. ochroleuca. Biennial or short-lived perennial. All Zones. To 2 ft. tall, with light yellow flowers.

S. stellata. Annual to 1½ ft. with many heads of pale blue flowers that quickly turn to papery bronze drumsticks useful in dry arrangements.

SCAEVOLA 'Mauve Clusters'. *Goodeniaceae.* Shrubby perennial. Zones 8–9, 14–24. Evergreen, nearly everblooming (in mild climates) ground cover or rock garden plant from Australia. Forms mats 4–6 in. tall, eventually 3–5 ft. across. Lilac mauve flowers in clusters are ½ in. wide, fan shaped (all petals on one side). Has no particular pests, takes moderate drought once established; 2 soakings a month are adequate. Set plants 3 ft. apart for ground cover, or try in hanging basket. Needs little fertilizer, but iron sulfate deepens flower color.

Scaevola

SCARLET LARKSPUR. See *Delphinium cardinale, D. nudicaule.*

SCARLET WISTERIA TREE. See *Sesbania tripetii.*

SCHEFFLERA. *Araliaceae.* Evergreen large shrubs, small trees. Outdoors in Zones 16, 17, 21–24; house plants everywhere. Fast-growing, tropical-looking plants; long-stalked leaves divided into leaflets which spread like fingers of hand. Useful near swimming pools. All need rich soil, routine watering, full sun or light shade near coast, light shade inland.

Schefflera actinophylla

S. actinophylla ***(Brassaia actinophylla).*** QUEENSLAND UMBRELLA TREE, OCTOPUS TREE, SCHEFFLERA. Outdoors Zones 21–24; precariously hardy Zones 16–20 with protection of overhang. As garden plant, grows fast to 20 ft. or more. "Umbrella" name comes from way giant leaves are held. Horizontal tiers of long-stalked leaves are divided into 7–16 large (to 1-ft.-long) leaflets that radiate outward like ribs of umbrella. "Octopus" comes from curious arrangement of flowers in narrow, horizontally spreading clusters to 3 ft. long. Color changes from greenish yellow to pink to dark red. Tiny dark purple fruit. Use for striking tropical effects, for silhouette, and for foliage contrast with ferns and other foliage plants. Cut out tips occasionally to keep plants from becoming leggy. Overgrown plants can be cut nearly to ground; they will branch and take better form.

As house plant, give standard rich potting mix, occasional feeding, bright light. Let mix become dry between waterings. Wash leaves occasionally; mist plants to discourage mites.

S. arboricola ***(Heptapleurum arboricolum).*** HAWAIIAN ELF SCHEFFLERA. Outdoors Zones 23, 24. As outdoor plant can reach 20 ft. or more, with equal or greater spread, but easily pruned to smaller dimensions. Leaves very dark green, much smaller than those of *S. actinophylla,* with 3-in. leaflets which broaden toward rounded tips. If stems are planted at angle, they continue to grow at that angle, which can give attractive multistemmed effects. Flowers clustered in flattened spheres 1 ft. wide, yellowish aging to bronze. General plant effect denser, darker, less treelike than *S. actinophylla.* Same care as *S. actinophylla.* Loves humidity.

Schefflera arboricola

SCHINUS. PEPPER TREE. Evergreen trees. Commonly planted in lowland parts of California and Arizona. Pepper trees are praised

S

by some gardeners, heartily disliked by others. Fruit attracts birds. Actually, the 2 species discussed here are quite different from one another, and each should be judged on its own merits.

S. molle. CALIFORNIA PEPPER TREE. Zones 8, 9, 12–24. Fast to 25–40 ft. tall and wide. Trunks of old trees are heavy and fantastically gnarled, with knots and burls that frequently sprout leaves or small branches. Bark is light brown, rough. Limbs heavy, branchlets light and gracefully drooping. Bright green leaves are divided into many narrow, 1½–2-in.-long leaflets. Numerous tiny, yellowish white summer flowers in drooping 4–6-in. clusters give way to pendant clusters of rose-colored berries in fall, winter. (Some trees have nearly all male flowers; these will not fruit.) Grows in any soil, tolerates drought when established, and will even get along with poor drainage.

Schinus molle

Stake young plants; prune for high branching if you wish to walk under them. To avoid heart rot, keep large pruning cuts sealed until well healed over. Spray for psyllids and scale. Subject to root rot diseases in infected soils—especially Texas root rot in the desert.

There's room for argument when it comes to usefulness. Some gardeners object to these trees' messy litter, scale infestation, and greedy surface roots; and yet many newcomers to California consider them to be one of our most strikingly handsome trees. Probably the brightest green of desert-tolerant trees. Fire retardant if reasonably well watered. Properly used, they are splendid. Don't plant them between sidewalk and curb, near house foundations, patio paving or entrances, in lawns, or near sewers or drains. Do plant them along roads or rustic streets without curbs—if you can give them room to spread. They are fine trees for shading play area or gravel-surfaced, informal lounging area. One different use: plant young pepper trees 2 ft. apart and prune into a graceful, billowy hedge. California pepper was introduced to California early, and is a characteristic tree of mission gardens.

S. terebinthifolius. BRAZILIAN PEPPER. Zones 13, 14 (sheltered), 15–17, 19–24. Moderate growth rate to 30 ft., with equal spread. Differs from California pepper in its nonpendulous growth; in its darker green, coarser, glossy leaves with only 5–13 leaflets instead of many; and in bright red berries that are very showy in winter.

With very little training, Brazilian pepper tree makes a broad, umbrella-shaped crown. Stake young trees well and prune to make fairly high crown. Also popular as multitrunked tree. Variations in foliage and growth habit are often pronounced. When selecting tree, try to choose one that has rich foliage and that has already set berries. The dried berries are sold as pink peppercorns; some people are allergic to them.

Feed and water infrequently and deeply to discourage surface roots. To reduce possibility of storm breakage, shorten overlong limbs and do some late-summer thinning so wind can pass through. Subject to verticillium wilt. Good shade tree for patio or small garden.

SCHIZANTHUS pinnatus. *Solanaceae.* POOR MAN'S ORCHID, BUTTERFLY FLOWER. Winter-spring annual in Zones 15–17, 21–24; summer annual in Zones 1–6. To 1½ ft. high. Great quantities of small orchidlike flowers. Flowers have varicolored markings on pink, rose, lilac, purple, or white background and are quite showy against the ferny foliage. Sensitive to frost and to heat. Buy plants in pots, or start seeds indoors about 4 weeks ahead of planting time (germination is slow). Plant in filtered shade.

Combines well with *Primula malacoides* and cineraria, and has the same cultural requirements. Good pot subject. Often grown in greenhouses and conservatories.

Schizanthus pinnatus

SCHIZOCENTRON elegans. See *Heterocentron elegans.*

SCHIZOSTYLIS coccinea. *Iridaceae.* CRIMSON FLAG, KAFFIR LILY. Rhizome. Zones 5–9, 14–24; best in mild-winter climates. Narrow, evergreen leaves, 1½ ft. tall, resemble those of gladiolus. Spikes of showy, crimson, starlike, 2½-in. flowers bloom on slender 1½–2-ft. stems in October–November. Variety 'Mrs. Hegarty' has rose pink flowers. Excellent cut flower spikes—each flower lasts 4 days, others follow.

Plant in sun. Provide light shade in hot areas. Add peat moss or leaf mold to soil; water freely during growth. Divide overgrown clumps.

Schizostylis coccinea

SCHLUMBERGERA. *Cactaceae.* House plants; lathhouse or covered terrace plants in Zones 16, 17, 21–24. In nature, these cacti live on trees like certain orchids. Plants often confused in nursery trade; many hybrids, selections differ principally in color. Remember, they come from the jungle—give them rich, porous soil with plenty of leaf mold and sand. Water frequently (but avoid soggy soil) and feed frequently—as often as every 7–10 days—with liquid fertilizer. If grown outdoors in summer, give half shade.

Schlumbergera bridgesii

S. bridgesii (often sold as *Zygocactus truncatus*). CHRISTMAS CACTUS. Old favorite. Arching, drooping branches are made up of flattened, scallop-edged, smooth, bright green, spineless, 1½-in. joints. Grown right, plants may be 3 ft. across and may have hundreds of many-petaled, long-tubed, 3-in.-long, rosy purplish red flowers at Christmas time. To ensure bud set for late December bloom, keep plant where it will receive cool night temperatures (50°–55°F.) and 12–14 hours of darkness per day during November.

S. gaertneri. See *Rhipsalidopsis gaertneri.*

S. truncata *(Zygocactus truncatus).* CRAB CACTUS. Joints 1–2 in. long, sharply toothed, with 2 large teeth at end of last joint. Short-tubed scarlet flowers with spreading, pointed petals, November–March. Many varieties in white, pink, salmon, orange.

Schlumbergera truncata

SCIADOPITYS verticillata. *Pinaceae.* UMBRELLA PINE. Evergreen tree. Zones 4–9, 14–24; borderline Zones 1–3. To 100–120 ft. in its native Japan, but not likely to exceed 25–40 ft. in western gardens. Very slow grower. Young plants are symmetrical, dense, rather narrow; older plants open up and branches tend to droop. Small, scalelike leaves grow scattered along branches, bunched at branch ends. At branch and twig ends grow whorls of 20–30 long (3–6-in.), narrow, flattened, firm, fleshy needles of glossy dark green (they radiate out like spokes of umbrella). In time, 3–5-in.-long woody cones may appear.

Plant in rich, well-drained, neutral or slightly acid soil. Full sun in cool-summer

Sciadopitys verticillata

areas or near coast; afternoon shade in interior valleys. Give ample water. Watch for mites in hot, dry weather. Can be left unpruned or can be thinned to create Oriental effect. Choice decorative tree for open ground or container use. Good bonsai subject. Boughs are beautiful and long lasting in arrangements.

SCIADOXUS. See *Haemanthus.*

SCILLA. *Liliaceae.* SQUILL, BLUEBELL. Bulbs. All Zones; exceptions noted below. All have basal, strap-shaped leaves and bell-shaped or starlike flowers in clusters on leafless stalks. Best planted in informal drifts among shrubs, under deciduous trees, among low-growing spring perennials. Good in pots, for cutting. Dormant in summer.

Scilla peruviana

S. bifolia. First to bloom. Carries up to 8 turquoise blue, inch-wide, starlike flowers on each 8-in. stem. White, pale purplish pink, and violet blue varieties. Plant 2 in. deep, 3–5 in. apart.

S. hispanica. See *Endymion hispanicus.*

S. nonscripta. See *Endymion non-scriptus.*

S. peruviana. PERUVIAN SCILLA. Outdoors all year in Zones 14–17, 19–24; in colder climates, grow in pots (1 to a 6-in. pot, 3 to a 9–10-in. pot). Despite its common name, Peruvian scilla is actually native to Mediterranean. Bluish purple, starlike flowers—50 or more in large, dome-shaped cluster, on 10–12-in. stalks. Long, floppy, strap-shaped leaves die down after flowers bloom in May–June. Plant 4–6 in. deep. Bulbs dormant only short time after leaves wither; replant then, if necessary.

S. siberica. SIBERIAN SQUILL. Zones 1–7, 10. Very early blooming, with loose spikes of intense blue flowers on 3–6-in. stems. 'Spring Beauty', with darker blue stripes, is choice. Also comes in white, purplish pink, and violet blue varieties.

S. tubergeniana. Blooms in January, at same time as snowdrops (*Galanthus*). Pale blue flowers, 4 or more to each 4-in. stalk; 3 or more stalks to each bulb. Plant 2–3 in. deep.

SCINDAPSUS pictus. *Araceae.* Perennial vine grown as house or greenhouse plant. Resembles more familiar green and yellow pothos (*Epipremnum aureum*) in appearance, but the egg-shaped leaves are dark green mottled with gray green. Leaves are also thinner in texture and usually somewhat larger (to 6 in., compared with 2–4-in. leaves of pot-grown pothos). Flowers insignificant. Variety 'Argyraeus' is most often grown; its markings are more prominent, larger, nearly silver, and leaves have a silky sheen. Needs same care as pothos and other philodendron relatives, but is fussier about drainage, good atmospheric humidity, careful watering and feeding, and bright (but not strong) light.

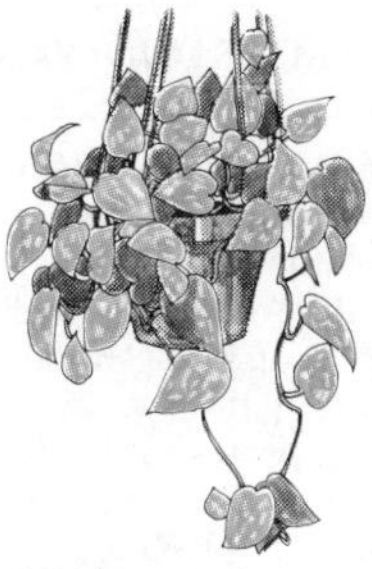
Scindapsus pictus

SCIRPUS cernuus *(Isolepis gracilis).* *Cyperaceae.* LOW BULRUSH. Grasslike perennial. Zones 7–24. To 6–10 in. high, usually less. Drooping, green, threadlike stems topped by small brown flower spikelets. Ample moisture is all it needs to grow; occasional division and resetting will keep it small. Ideal for edge of shallow pond; highly attractive for streamside effect in Japanese gardens. Good pot subject.

Scirpus cernuus

SCOTCH BROOM. See *Cytisus scoparius.*

SCOTCH HEATHER. See *Calluna vulgaris.*

SCOTCH MOSS. See *Sagina subulata.*

Scrophulariaceae. The figwort family consists principally of annuals and perennials. Most have irregular flowers, with 4 or 5 lobes often arranged as 2 lips. Examples are *Antirrhinum* (snapdragon), *Calceolaria, Digitalis* (foxglove), *Nemesia, Penstemon,* and *Torenia.*

SEAFORTHIA elegans. See *Archontophoenix cunninghamiana.*

SEA HOLLY. See *Eryngium amethystinum.*

SEA LAVENDER. See *Limonium.*

SEA PINK. See *Armeria.*

SEA POPPY. See *Glaucium.*

SEASHORE PASPALUM. See *Paspalum vaginatum.*

SEASIDE DAISY. See *Erigeron glaucus.*

SEA URCHIN. See *Hakea laurina.*

SEA URCHIN CACTUS. See *Echinopsis.*

SEDUM. *Crassulaceae.* STONECROP. Succulent perennials or subshrubs. They come from many parts of the world and vary in hardiness, cultural needs; some are among hardiest succulent plants. Some are tiny and trailing, others upright. Leaves fleshy, highly variable in size, shape, and color; evergreen unless otherwise noted. Flowers usually small, starlike, in fairly large clusters, sometimes brightly colored.

Sedum rubrotinctum

Smaller sedums are useful in rock gardens, as ground or bank cover, in small areas where unusual texture, color are needed. Some of the smaller types are prized by collectors of succulents, who grow them as pot or dish garden plants. Larger kinds good in borders or containers, as shrubs. Most kinds propagate very easily by stem cuttings—even detached leaves will root and form new plants. Soft and easily crushed, they will not take foot traffic; otherwise they are tough, low-maintenance plants. Set ground cover kinds 10–12 in. apart. Sedums take full sun or considerable shade, need little water in summer.

S. acre. GOLDMOSS SEDUM. All Zones. Evergreen plant 2–5 in. tall, with upright branchlets from trailing, rooting stems. Tiny light green leaves; clustered yellow flowers in mid or late spring. Extremely hardy but can get out of bounds, become a weed. Use as a ground cover, between stepping stones, or on dry walls.

S. album (often sold as *S. brevifolium*). All Zones. Creeping evergreen plant 2–6 in. tall. Fleshy leaves ¼–½ in. long, light to medium green, sometimes red tinted. Flowers white or pinkish white. Ground cover. Roots from smallest fragment; beware of placing it near choice, delicate rock garden plants.

S. altissimum. See *S. sediforme, S. reflexum.*

S. amecamecanum. See *S. confusum* for plant sold under this name. True *S. amecamecanum (Sedadia amecamecana)* resembles *S. confusum,* but is rare in gardens.

S. anglicum. All Zones. Low, spreading plants 2–4 in. tall. Dark green, fleshy leaves to ⅛ in. long. Pinkish white spring flowers. Ground cover.

S. brevifolium. Zones 8, 9, 14–24. Europe, north Africa. Tiny, slowly spreading plants to 2–3 in. high, with tightly packed, fleshy leaves less than ⅛ in. long. Gray white leaves flushed with red; pinkish or white flowers. Sunburns in hot, dry places. Needs good drainage. Best in rock garden or with larger succulents in pots, containers, or miniature gardens.

S. confusum. Zones 8, 9, 14–24. Native to Mexico. Plants spreading, branching, 6–12 in. tall. Fleshy, shiny light green leaves, ¾–1½ in. long, tend to cluster in rosettes toward branch ends. Dense clusters of yellow flowers in spring. Good ground cover, but sometimes plagued by dieback in wet soils, hot weather; looks best during cooler weather. Use in borders, pots, or containers, as edging, in miniature gardens.

S. dendroideum. Zones 8, 9, 12, 14–24. Native to Mexico. To 2 ft. Branching, spreading plant with rounded, fleshy leaves 2 in. long, yellow green, often bronze tinted. Flowers deep yellow, in spring and early summer.

S. d. praealtum *(S. praealtum).* Like the species but taller (to 3–5 ft.), with lighter yellow flowers and less bronze tinting on leaves. Both plants good for low-maintenance informal hedge or space divider; especially useful along semirural streets or lanes where watering is difficult.

S. guatemalense. See *S. rubrotinctum.*

S. lineare (often sold as *S. sarmentosum*). All Zones. Spreading, trailing, rooting stems to 1 ft. long, closely set with very narrow, fleshy, light green leaves 1 in. long. Flowers yellow, star shaped, profuse in late spring, early summer. Ground cover. Vigorous spreader. 'Variegatum', with white-edged leaves, is favorite pot or herbarium plant.

S. morganianum. DONKEY TAIL, BURRO TAIL. Safely outdoors in Zones 17, 22–24; much used under protection of lath or eaves in Zones 13–16, 18–21. House plant everywhere. Makes long, trailing stems that grow to 3–4 ft. in 6–8 years. Thick, fleshy, light gray green leaves overlap each other along stems to give braided or ropelike effect. Flowers (rarely seen) pink to deep red. Choice plant if well grown. Because it grows such long, pendulous stems, most practical place to grow it is in hanging pot or wall pot. In mildest areas near coast, try it at top of walls or high up in rock garden. Rich, fast-draining soil. Protect from wind and give half shade; water freely and feed 2 or 3 times during summer with liquid fertilizer. Relatives that have same culture and same uses: *S.* 'Burrito', with fat tails 1 in. thick composed of densely packed ½-in. leaves; GIANT DONKEY TAIL (often sold as *S. orpetii*), with somewhat shorter, thicker tails; and *Sedeveria* 'Super Giant Donkey Tail', with still thicker, shorter tails.

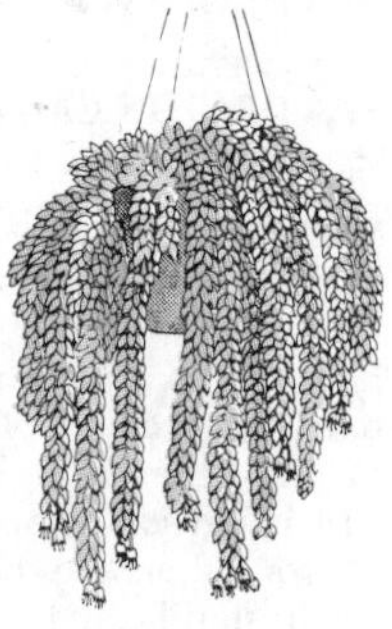

Sedum morganianum

S. oxypetalum. Zones 16, 17, 21–24. Native to Mexico. Grows to 3 ft. high, usually much less. Even tiny plants have look of a gnarled tree. Leaves 1–1½ in. long; flowers dull red, fragrant. Evergreen or semievergreen in mildest areas, deciduous elsewhere. Handsome pot plant.

S. reflexum (often sold as *S. altissimum*). Zones 8–24. Much like *S. sediforme,* but with shorter leaves, yellow flowers. Ground cover.

S. rubrotinctum *(S. guatemalense).* PORK AND BEANS. Zones 8, 9, 12 (with a little shade and water), 14–24. Sprawling, leaning stems 6–8 in. tall. Leaves like jelly beans, ¾ in. long, green with reddish brown tips, often entirely bronze red in sun. Flowers reddish yellow. Easily detached leaves root readily. Rock garden or pot subject, small-scale ground cover.

S. sarmentosum. See *S. lineare.*

S. sediforme *(S. altissimum).* Zones 8–24. Native to Mediterranean region. Spreading, creeping plants to 16 in. tall. Leaves light blue gray, fleshy, to 1½ in. long, narrow, closely set on stems. Flowers small, greenish white. Use in rock garden, for blue green effects in carpet or pattern planting, as small-scale ground cover.

S. sieboldii. All Zones. Native to Japan. Spreading, trailing, unbranched stems to 8–9 in. long. Fleshy leaves in 3s, nearly round, stalkless, toothed in upper half, blue gray edged red. Plant turns coppery red in fall, dies to ground in winter. Each stem shows a broad, dense, flat cluster of dusty pink flowers in autumn. *S. s.* 'Variegatum' has leaves marked yellowish white. Beautiful rock garden or hanging basket plant. Light shade, occasional water in hot interior gardens.

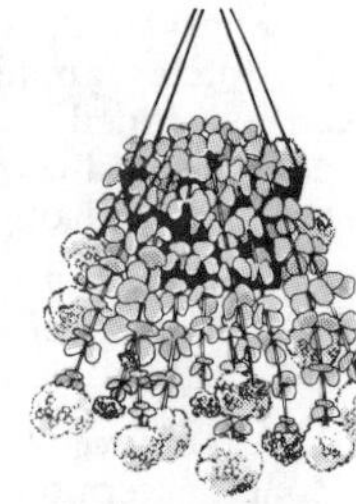

Sedum sieboldii

S. spathulifolium. All Zones. Native from California's Coast Ranges and Sierra Nevada north to British Columbia. Leaves blue green tinged reddish purple, spoon shaped, fleshy, packed into rosettes on short, trailing stems. Flowers light yellow, spring–summer. Ground cover. 'Cape Blanco' is a selected form with good leaf color. 'Purpureum' has deep purple leaves. Good in sunny or partially shaded rock gardens. After it's rooted, needs no water in cool-summer climates.

Sedum spathulifolium

S. spectabile. All Zones. China, Japan. Upright or slightly spreading stems to 1½ ft. tall, well set with blue green, roundish, fleshy, 3-in. leaves. Pink flowers in broad, dense clusters atop stems in late summer, autumn. Dies down in winter. 'Brilliant' has deep rose red flowers, 'Carmen' is soft rose, and 'Meteor', brightest, has carmine red flowers. Sun, average garden water.

S. spurium. All Zones. Evergreen perennial plant with trailing stems. Leaves thick, an inch or so long, nearly as wide, dark green or bronzy tinted. Flowers pink, in dense clusters at ends of 4–5-in. stems in summer. Garden variety called 'Dragon's Blood' has bronzy leaves and rosy red flowers. Rock garden, pattern planting subject, ground cover.

S. telephium. All Zones. To 2 ft. Resembles *S. spectabile,* but leaves somewhat narrower. If stalks are not cut after bloom, 6-in., dome-shaped flower clusters turn to purple clusters of seeds on top of bare stalks. Garden varieties: 'Autumn Joy', to 2½ ft., with coppery rose blooms; 'Indian Chief', coppery red flowers.

SEGO LILY. See *Calochortus nuttallii.*

SEMIARUNDINARIA. See Bamboo.

SEMPERVIVUM. *Crassulaceae.* HOUSELEEK. Succulents. All Zones. Evergreen perennial plants with tightly packed rosettes of leaves. Little offsets cluster around parent rosette. Flowers star shaped, in tight or loose clusters, white, yellowish, pink, red, or greenish, pretty in detail but not showy. Summer bloom. Blooming rosettes die after setting seed, but easily planted offsets carry on. Good in rock gardens, containers, even in pockets on boulders or pieces of porous rock. All need sun in most climates, shade in Zones 12, 13; good drainage, and generous summer watering (except on coast). Many species, all good; these are fairly common:

Sempervivum tectorum

S. arachnoideum. COBWEB HOUSELEEK. Europe. Tiny gray green rosettes, ¾ in. across, of many leaves joined by fine hairs which give a cobweb-covered look to plant. Spreads slowly to make dense mats. Bright red flowers on 4-in. stems; seldom blooms.

S. tectorum. HEN AND CHICKENS. Rosettes gray green, 4–6 in. across, spreading quickly by offsets. Leaves tipped red brown, bristle pointed. Flowers red or reddish in clusters on stems to 2 ft. tall. Easy to grow in rock gardens, borders, pattern planting.

SENECIO. *Compositae.* Perennials, shrubs, vines. Daisy relatives which range from garden cineraria and dusty miller to vines, shrubs, perennials, succulents, even a few weeds. Succulents are often sold as *Kleinia,* an earlier name.

S. cineraria. DUSTY MILLER. Shrubby perennial. All Zones (needs protection Zones 1–3). Spreading plant to 2–2½ ft.; woolly, white leaves cut into many blunt-tipped lobes. Clustered heads of yellow or creamy yellow flowers at almost any season. Plant gets leggy unless sheared occasionally. Easy to grow; needs only light watering. Fire retardant if fairly well watered. Use in combination with bright-flowered, sun-loving annuals and perennials. Striking in night garden.

Senecio cineraria

S. confusus. MEXICAN FLAME VINE. Evergreen or deciduous vine. Zones 13, 16–24. Sometimes grown as annual or perennial in colder climates. Twines to 8–10 ft. in frost-free areas; dies back to ground in mild frost, comes back fast from roots. Leaves light green, rather fleshy, 1–4 in. long, ½–1 in. wide, coarsely toothed. Daisylike flowers in large clusters at ends of branches, ¾–1 in. wide, startling orange red with golden centers. 'Sao Paulo' is deeper orange, almost brick red.

Blooms all year where winters are mild. Sun or light shade; moist, light soil. Use on trellis, column, to cascade over bank or wall, or in hanging basket.

S. greyi. Evergreen shrub. Zones 5–9, 14–24. Spreading plant that grows 4–5 ft. high. Stiff, slightly curving stems bear 3½-in.-long, leathery leaves of gray green outlined in silvery white. Blooms profusely in summer; 1-in.-wide, yellow daisies in 5-in.-wide, flattish clusters contrast effectively with gray foliage. Plants usually sold as *S. greyi* are similar but somewhat smaller *S. compactus* or hybrids between the 2.

Senecio greyi

Full sun, not-too-rich soil, good drainage, little or moderate water. Prune yearly to remove oldest or damaged growth, stimulate new wood. Attractive with geraniums, zauschneria, cistus, rosemary, purple- or red-leafed shrubs. Cut branches effective in arrangements, especially with scarlet and orange flowers; long lasting.

S. hybridus *(S. cruentus)*. CINERARIA. Perennial in Zones 16, 17, 22–24; grown as summer annual elsewhere. Valuable for bright colors in cool, shady places; not for hot, dry climates. Most commonly grown are the large-flowered, dwarf kinds generally sold as Multiflora Nana or Hybrida Grandiflora. These are compact, 12–15-in.-tall plants with lush, broad, green leaves and broad clusters of 3–5-in.-wide daisies that cover top of plant. Will self-sow where adapted. Colors range from white through pink and purplish red to sensational blues and purples, often with contrasting eyes or bands. Bloom late winter and early spring in mild regions, spring and early summer elsewhere. Plants sold as *Cineraria stellata* are taller (to 2½–3 ft.), with looser clusters of smaller, starlike daisies; these often self-sow in shaded gardens that get regular (even if infrequent) irrigation.

Senecio hybridus

Frost is a hazard to fall-planted cinerarias; plant in spring or protect by planting under shrubs, trees, overhang, or lath. Plant in shade in cool, moist, loose, rich soil. Water generously and often, but avoid soggy soil, which brings on stem rot. Principal pests are leaf miners, spider mites, slugs, snails.

To grow in large pots for patio display, begin by setting transplants in 3–4-in. pots in mixture of rich soil, leaf mold, sand. After several weeks (or before they become potbound), shift into 5–6-in. pots. Feed every 2 weeks with liquid fertilizer. Never let plants dry out.

Effective in mass plantings or combined with ferns, tuberous or other begonias, foliage plants. Use to decorate lanais, shaded terraces, sitting areas. Usually discarded after bloom.

S. leucostachys. See *S. vira-vira.*

S. macroglossus. KENYA IVY, NATAL IVY, WAX VINE. Evergreen vine. House plant. *S. macroglossus* can grow out of doors in Zones 12, 13 if given north or east exposure. 'Variegatum' has leaves sharply splashed with creamy white. Twining or trailing vine with thin, succulent stems and thick, waxy or rubbery leaves 2–3 in. across. Leaves are shaped like ivy leaves with 3, 5, or 7 shallow lobes. Flowers are tiny yellow daisies. Grow in sunny window and water only when soil becomes dry.

S. mandraliscae *(Kleinia mandraliscae)*. Succulent perennial. Zones 12 (protected spots), 13, 16, 17, 21–24. Somewhat shrubby, with branches to 1–1½ ft. tall, spreading wider. Leaves cylindrical, 3–3½ in. long, slightly curved, strikingly blue gray. Widely used as a ground cover where blue gray effect is desired.

Senecio mandraliscae

S. mikanioides. GERMAN IVY. Perennial vine. Zones 14–24. Evergreen in mildest areas, deciduous elsewhere. Twines to 18–20 ft. Leaves roundish, with 5–7 sharply pointed lobes, ivylike, ½–3 in. long. Winter flowers are small yellow daisies without rays. Trailer in window boxes, or screening vine. Plant in sun to semi-shade. Water sparingly. Has become a weed in coastal California where it can grow into or smother choicer plants.

S. petasitis. VELVET GROUNDSEL, CALIFORNIA GERANIUM. Perennial or shrubby perennial. Zones 15–17, 21–24, greenhouse plant anywhere. Bulky plant 6–8 (or more) ft. tall, equally wide. Leaves evergreen, tropical looking, large, lobed, fanlike, velvety to touch, to 8 in. across. Blooms in midwinter, with large clusters of small, daisylike, bright yellow flowers standing well above mass of plant. Best in sheltered locations in full sun. Needs ample water, some feeding. Prune hard after bloom to limit height and sprawl. Can be kept 2–4 ft. tall in big pots or tubs. Good filler in tropical garden.

S. rowleyanus. STRING OF BEADS. Succulent. Zones 15–17, 21–24. Trailing stems to 6–8 ft. set with spherical green leaves ½ in. wide. Small, white, carnation-scented flowers. Hanging basket. Sun or shade near coast, shade inland. Moderate water. Hardy to 25°F.

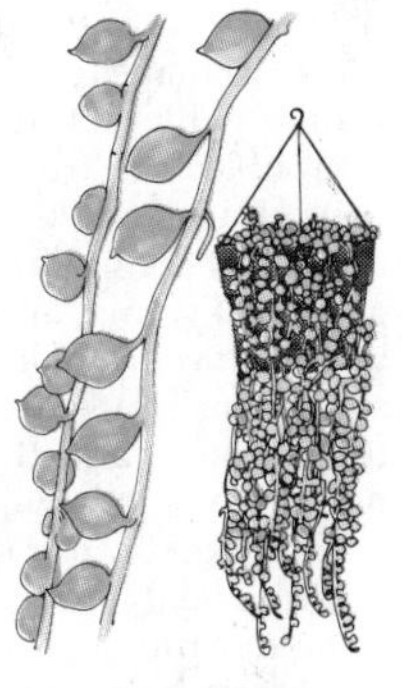

Senecio rowleyanus

S. serpens *(Kleinia repens)*. Succulent perennial. Zones 16, 17, 21–24. Like *S. mandraliscae,* but grows 1 ft. tall, has 1½-in.-long, light gray or bluish leaves.

S. vira-vira *(S. leucostachys, S. cineraria* 'Candissimus'). Subshrub. All Zones. To 4 ft. tall; broad, sprawling habit. Leaves like those of *S. cineraria* but whiter and more finely cut into much narrower, pointed segments. Creamy white summer flowers are not showy. In full sun brilliantly white, densely leafy; in part shade looser, more sparsely foliaged, with larger, greener leaves. Tip-pinch young plants to keep them compact. Needs light watering.

Senecio serpens

SENSITIVE FERN. See *Onoclea sensibilis.*

SENSITIVE PLANT. See *Mimosa pudica.*

SENTRY PALM. See *Howea belmoreana.*

SEQUOIA sempervirens. *Taxodiaceae.* COAST REDWOOD. Evergreen tree. Zones 4–9, 14–24. Native to parts of Coast Ranges from Curry County, Oregon, to Monterey County, California. Tallest of

S

the world's trees, and one of West's most famous native trees (equally famous is its close relative *Sequoiadendron*, GIANT SEQUOIA or BIG TREE). Fine landscaping tree—fast growing (3–5 ft. a year), substantial, pest free, and almost always fresh looking and woodsy smelling.

Sequoia sempervirens

Its red brown, fibrous-barked trunk goes straight up (unless injured). Nearly parallel sides on redwood's trunk indicate tree has fared well (if redwoods struggle, they develop trunks with noticeable taper). Branchlets hang down slightly from branches. Flat, pointed, narrow leaves (½–1 in. long) grow in one plane on both sides of stem like feathers. Leaves are medium green on top, grayish underneath. Small round cones are 1 in. long.

Plant in full sun to half shade. One of best growing places is in or directly next to a lawn, since redwood thrives on generous watering (in 10–20 years, however, tree may defeat lawn). Away from lawns it needs occasional feeding and regular summer watering (at least for first 5 years). Resistant to oak root fungus.

Here's a planting mix recipe for a 1- or 5-gallon-size redwood. It makes a redwood grow well in just about any soil—it's especially useful in Zones 7–9, 14–16, 18–24. Dig a hole 1½ ft. wide and 3 ft. deep. Pile the excavated soil and thoroughly mix into it 1 lb. of iron sulfate and 2 cubic ft. of cattle manure. Throw the blended mix back into the hole and saturate it (to leach out salts and ammonia). After mix dries enough to be workable, remove enough from the center to make room for the root ball. Use removed mix to make a watering dike about 10 in. out from the tree trunk.

Troubles the tree encounters are mostly physiological: (1) not enough water or hot, dry sites make it sulk and grow slowly; (2) too much competition from bigger trees and structures makes it grow lanky, thin, and open; (3) lack of available iron makes needles turn yellow every summer, especially on new growth—apply iron sulfate or chelated iron. (It's normal for oldest leaves to turn yellow, then brown, and then drop in late summer and early fall; it is normal for short twigs to brown and fall also.)

Count on branch spread at base (tip to tip) of 14–30 ft. Mature, centuries-old natives surpass 350 ft. in height, but 70–90 ft. seems to be most to expect in garden in one owner's lifetime; trees can reach this height in 25 years. Use redwood singly as shade tree, tree to look up into or to hang a swing from, or tree to be seen from 2 blocks away. Or plant several in a grove or in a 40-ft.-diameter circle—inside it's cool, fragrant, and a fine spot for fuchsias, begonias, and people on hot summer days. For grove or circle planting, space trees 7 ft. apart. Trees can be planted 3–4 ft. apart and topped at least once a year to make beautiful hedge.

Redwoods vary greatly in form, texture, and color. Some are dense and some are open; some are pendulous, others bristly; foliage colors may be any shade from light green to deep blue green; branch angles vary from a slight up-tilt to straight out from the trunk and cupping a little at the outer ends to almost straight down. These characteristics are determined mostly by heredity—a tree will have them all its life.

Until the 1970s, all redwoods at nurseries were grown from seed, with each seedling inheriting a slightly different set of characteristics. But now there are named varieties available, vegetatively propagated, with certain definite growth and color characteristics. 'Aptos Blue' has dense blue green foliage on nearly horizontal branches with branchlets hanging down. 'Santa Cruz' has light green foliage, soft texture, branches pointing slightly down. 'Soquel' has fine texture, somewhat bluish green foliage, horizontal branches that turn up at tips, and a sturdy, stout trunk with little suckering. 'Los Altos' has deep green foliage of heavy texture on horizontal, arching branches.

Variety 'Adpressa' ('Albo spica') is a dwarf for rock garden use—up to 3 ft. high and 6 ft. wide; its new growth is tipped white, which deepens to green as summer advances. 'Filoli' and 'Woodside', similar, possibly identical varieties, are distinctively blue—almost like blue spruce. These need careful training when young to establish good form.

SEQUOIADENDRON giganteum *(Sequoia gigantea).* *Taxodiaceae.* BIG TREE, GIANT SEQUOIA. Evergreen tree. All Zones. Native to west slope of the Sierra Nevada from Placer County to Tulare County. Most massive trunk in the world and one of tallest trees, reaching 325 ft. in height with 30-ft. trunk diameter. It has always shared fame and comparisons with its close relative, the coast redwood (*Sequoia*). Horticulturally, however, similarities are rather few.

Sequoiadendron giganteum

Dense foliage of giant sequoia (more bushy than coast redwood) is gray green; branchlets are clothed with short, overlapping, scalelike leaves with sharp points. It's a somewhat prickly tree to reach into. Dark reddish brown cones, 2–3½ in. long. Bark is reddish brown and generally similar to that of coast redwood.

Giant sequoia is hardier to cold than coast redwood. It grows a little more slowly—2–3 ft. a year. It also needs less water. Plant in deep soil, preferably in full sun, and water deeply but infrequently once trees are established.

Primary use is as featured tree in large lawn (roots may surface there in due time) or other open space. Trees hold lower branches throughout their long youth, and are likely to get too broad for the small garden. In essence, then, giant sequoia is easier to grow than coast redwood and more widely adaptable to cold, dry climates, but it doesn't have as many landscape uses. Variety 'Pendulum' has drooping branches and must be staked to coax it into vertical habit.

SERISSA foetida. *Rubiaceae.* Evergreen shrub. Outdoors Zones 14–24; house plant anywhere. To 2 ft. tall, somewhat wider. Egg-shaped, ½-in.-long leaves; white, ½-in.-wide flowers. A thin, spreading shrub when grown in the garden, it is chiefly used as a bonsai subject. Specialists supply named varieties with variegated leaves, double flowers, or pink flowers.

Serissa foetida

SERVICEBERRY. See *Amelanchier.*

SESBANIA tripetii *(Daubentonia tripetii).* *Leguminosae.* SCARLET WISTERIA TREE. Deciduous shrub or small tree. Zones 7–9, 12–16, 18–23. Native to Argentina. Neither a wisteria nor a tree, and flower color is more burnt orange than scarlet. Fast growing to 8–10 ft. high and 6–8 ft. wide, with fernlike leaves. Showy, drooping clusters of yellow and orange red, sweet pea–shaped flowers from May through summer; winged, 4-angled pods follow. To prolong flowering, remove pods as they form.

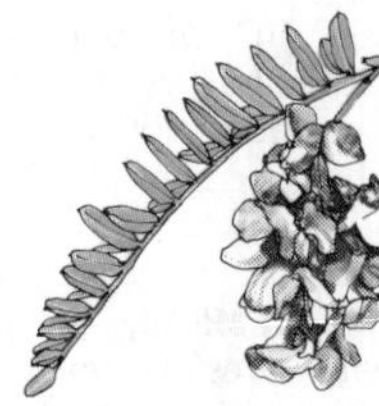

Sesbania tripetii

Give full sun and warmest spot in garden. Prune severely in early spring to thin and shorten side branches to stubs. Average water.

Not long-lived plant and appears a little out of place with glossy-leafed, refined plants, but valued for exciting color and quick effects. Most often seen trained into flat-topped standard tree on 6-ft. trunk. Can be grown in containers, blooming quite heavily in 1-ft. pots.

SETCREASEA pallida 'Purple Heart'. *Commelinaceae.* PURPLE HEART. Perennial. Zones 12–24. Freezes, recovers from roots Zones 12–18;

house plant anywhere. Stems a foot or more high, inclined to flop over. Leaves rather narrowly oval and pointed, very strongly shaded with purple, particularly underneath. Use discretion in planting, or the vivid foliage may create a harsh effect (pale or deep purple flowers are inconspicuous). Pinch back after bloom. Plants are generally unattractive in winter. Will take light shade; color best in sun. Frosts may kill tops, but in warm weather recovery is fast.

Setcreasea pallida 'Purple Heart'

SHADBLOW, SHADBUSH. See *Amelanchier.*

SHALLOT. *Liliaceae.* Small onionlike plant that produces cluster of edible bulbs from single bulb. Prized in cooking for its distinctive flavor. Plant either sets (small dry bulbs) or nursery plants in fall in mild climates, early spring in cold-winter areas. Leaves 1–1½ ft. high develop from each bulb. Tiny lavender or white flowers sometimes appear. Ultimately 2–8 bulbs will grow from each original set. At maturity (early summer if fall planted, late summer if spring planted), bulbs are formed and tops yellow and die. Harvest by pulling clumps and dividing bulbs. Let outer skin dry for about a month so that shallots can be stored for 4–6 months. Some seed firms sell sets; nurseries with stocks of herbs may sell growing plants. If you use sets, plant so that tips are just covered. Golden brown skins of Dutch shallots enclose white cloves. Coppery skins of red shallots conceal purple cloves.

Shallot

SHAMROCK. Around St. Patrick's Day, nurseries and florists sell "shamrocks." These are small potted plants of *Medicago lupulina* (hop clover, yellow trefoil, black medick), an annual plant; *Oxalis acetosella* (wood sorrel); or *Trifolium repens* (white clover), both perennials. The last is most common.

All have in common leaves divided into 3 leaflets (symbolic of the Trinity). They can be kept on a sunny window sill or planted out, but have little ornamental value and are likely to become weeds.

SHASTA DAISY. See *Chrysanthemum maximum.*

SHELL FLOWER. See *Alpinia zerumbet, Moluccella laevis.*

SHELL GINGER. See *Alpinia zerumbet.*

SHE-OAK. See *Casuarina.*

SHEPHERDIA argentea. *Elaeagnaceae.* SILVER BUFFALOBERRY. Deciduous shrub. Zones 1–3, 10. Native to many western habitats, from the plains of Canada and the Midwest to California. Spreading, suckering shrub 5–6 ft. tall (rarely to 12 ft.) with spine-tipped branchlets. Longish oval leaves to 1 in., silvery on both upper and lower surfaces. Plants either male or female; if both are present, latter bear ¼-in. berries of bright red or orange, sour but edible and used for jams and jellies. Flowers not showy. Good plant for attracting birds. Withstands any amount of cold and wind, takes most soils (including considerable alkali), and puts up with drought once established.

Shepherdia argentea

SHIBATAEA. See Bamboo.

SHIMPAKU. See *Juniperus chinensis sargentii.*

SHISO. See *Perilla frutescens.*

SHOOTING STAR. See *Dodecatheon.*

SHORTIA. *Diapensiaceae.* Perennials. Zones 1–7. Beautiful small evergreen plants. Spread slowly by underground stems. Need shade, moisture, and acid, leafy or peaty soil. Grow with azaleas or rhododendrons. All are choice pot or alpine house plants.

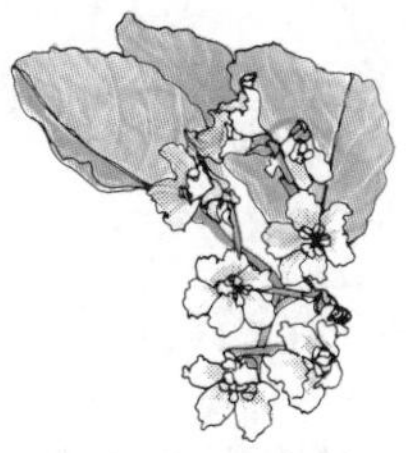
Shortia galacifolia

S. galacifolia. OCONEE BELLS. Forms clump of round or oval, glossy green leaves 1–3 in. long, with scallop-toothed edges. Single, nodding white bell, 1-in.-wide, with toothed edges, tops each of the many 4–6-in.-high stems in March–April.

S. soldanelloides. FRINGE BELLS. Round, coarsely toothed leaves form clumps similar to those of *S. galacifolia,* but flowers are pink to rose in color, with deeply fringed edges.

S. uniflora 'Grandiflora'. Like *S. galacifolia* but with indented and wavy-edged leaves and flowers that are large fringed bells of clear soft pink.

SHRIMP PLANT. See *Justicia brandegeana.*

SIBERIAN WALLFLOWER. See *Erysimum hieraciifolium.*

SIERRA LAUREL. See *Leucothoe davisiae.*

SILENE. *Caryophyllaceae.* Perennials. Many species, some with erect growth habit, others cushionlike. Sun, part shade.

S. acaulis. CUSHION PINK, MOSS CAMPION. Zones 1–11, 14–16, 18–21. Mosslike mat of bright green, narrow leaves about ⅝ in. long. Reddish purple flowers, ½ in. across, borne singly, March–April. Good choice for gravelly, damp but well-drained spot in rock garden.

Silene californica

S. californica. CALIFORNIA INDIAN PINK. Zones 7–11, 14–24. Native to California and southern Oregon foothills. Loosely branching plant to 6–16 in. tall. Foliage somewhat sticky. Flaming red, 1¼-in.-wide flowers, with petals cleft and fringed, bloom during spring. *S. californica* is occasionally sold in seed packets. Needs well-drained soil; let it dry off in the summer months.

S. coeli-rosa. See *Lychnis coeli-rosa.*

S. schafta. MOSS CAMPION. Zones 1–9, 14–16, 18–21. Forms tufts of upright-growing, rather wiry stems to 6–12 in. high. Leaves are small, and tongue shaped. Rose purple flowers, 1 or 2 to each blossomed stalk, bloom from late summer into autumn. Average water requirements.

SILK OAK. See *Grevillea robusta.*

SILKTASSEL. See *Garrya.*

SILK TREE. See *Albizia julibrissin.*

SILVER BELL. See *Halesia carolina.*

S

SILVERBERRY. See *Elaeagnus commutata, E. pungens.*

SILVER BUFFALOBERRY. See *Shepherdia argentea.*

SILVER DOLLAR GUM. See *Eucalyptus polyanthemos.*

SILVER FERN. See *Pteris quadriaurita* 'Argyraea'.

SILVER LACE VINE. See *Polygonum aubertii.*

SILVER SAGE. See *Salvia argentea.*

SILVER SPREADER. See *Artemisia caucasica.*

SILVER TREE. See *Leucodendron argenteum.*

SIMMONDSIA chinensis. *Buxaceae.* JOJOBA, GOATNUT. Evergreen shrub. Zones 10–13, 19–24. Native to deserts of southern California, Arizona, Mexico. Dense, rigid-branching, spreading shrub 3–6 (rarely to 16) ft. tall. Dull gray green, leathery leaves are 1–2 in. long, to ½ in. wide. Flowers are inconspicuous. Male and female blooms are borne on different plants; if both are present, female plants bear edible, nutlike fruit about ¾ in. long. Flavor like filbert, slightly bitter until cured. High oil content of fruit gives plant commercial value as crop for marginal land. Such plantings are chancy in soil infested with verticillium or Texas root rot.

Simmondsia chinensis

Young plants rather tender; when established, will take 15°F. Needs little water. Likes full sun, heat. Of particular value as clipped hedge, foundation planting in desert garden.

SINARUNDINARIA. See Bamboo.

SINNINGIA speciosa *(Gloxinia speciosa).* *Gesneriaceae.* GLOXINIA. Tuber. House plant; pot plant for shaded terrace or patio. Leaves oblong, dark green, toothed, fuzzy, 6 in. or longer. Flowers are spectacular—large, velvety, bell shaped, ruffled on edges, in blue, purple, violet, pink, red, or white. Some flowers have dark dots or blotches, others contrasting bands at the flower rims. Leaves occasionally white veined. Tubers usually available December–March. Plant 1 in. deep in rich, loose mix. Water sparingly until first leaves appear; increase watering after roots form. Apply water around base of plant or from below; don't water on top of leaves. When roots fill pot, shift to larger pot. Feed regularly during growth. After bloom has finished, gradually dry off plants and store tubers in cool dark place with just enough moisture to keep them from shriveling or store tubers, soil and all, in pots until new growth starts. Repot in January–February.

Sinningia speciosa

SISYRINCHIUM. *Iridaceae.* Perennials. Zones 4–24. Related to iris. Narrow, rather grasslike leaves. Small flowers, made up of 6 segments, open in sunshine. Pretty but not showy, best suited for informal gardens or naturalizing. Sun or light shade, average water. Will endure some drought.

S. bellum. BLUE-EYED GRASS. Native to coastal California. To 4–16 in. tall. Narrow green or bluish green leaves. Flowers purple to bluish purple, ½ in. across, bloom early to midspring.

S. californicum. YELLOW-EYED GRASS. Native to coast of California and Oregon. Dull green leaves, broader, slightly taller than those of blue-eyed grass. Yellow flowers open May–June. Can grow in wet, low, or poorly drained places.

S. macounii. Native to Northwest. Grows 12–20 in. tall with short, broad leaves and blue, 1-in. flowers. Plant sold as *S. macounii* 'Album' (probably a form of *S. bellum*) has inch-wide white flowers on 6-in. stems.

S. striatum. Larger than other sisyrinchiums; attractive gray green leaves are irislike, 1 ft. long, up to 1 in. wide. Spikelike flower clusters grow to 2½ ft., with many pale yellow, brown-streaked, ½-in. flowers in spring. Useful for foliage clumps of gray, with old leaves fading to black.

Sisyrinchium bellum

SKIMMIA. *Rutaceae.* Evergreen shrubs. Zones 4–9, 14–22 (grows best in Zones 4–6, 17; needs special handling elsewhere). Slow growing and compact, with glossy, rich green leaves neatly arranged. In April and May, tiny white flowers open from clusters of pinkish buds held well above foliage. Red hollylike fruit in fall and through December if pollination requirements are met.

When massed, forms level surface of leaves; individual plants are dense mounds. Light to moderate shade preferable; full sun yellows leaves, heavy shade makes plants lanky, inhibits bloom.

Skimmia japonica

No special soil requirement in Northwest. In California's alkaline soils, add at least 50 percent peat moss or the like to planting soil. In Northwest, skimmia is attacked by a skimmia mite that gives leaves sunburned look. Also expect attacks by thrips and red spider mites. Plants need ample water, but water mold is a problem in hot regions. Good shrub under low windows, beside shaded walks, flanking entryways, in containers. Blends well with all shade plants.

S. foremanii. Hybrid between following 2 species. Resembles *S. japonica* but is more compact, with broader, heavier, darker green leaves. Seems to take northern California conditions better than either parent. Plants may be male, female, or self-fertile.

S. japonica. Variable in size. Slow growth to 2–5 ft. tall, 3–6 ft. wide. Leaves 3–4 in. long, an inch wide, oval, blunt ended, mostly clustered near twig ends. Flowers fragrant, in 2–3-in. clusters. Female plants bear bright red berries if male plant present; berries are attractive enough to be worth the effort of planting both male and female shrubs. Form with ivory white berries is available. *S. j.* 'Macrophylla' is a male form—rounded, spreading shrub to 5–6 ft., with large leaves and flowers.

S. reevesiana *(S. fortunei).* Dwarf, dense-growing shrub 2 ft. tall. Self-fertile, with dull crimson fruit. Fragrant flowers.

SKUNKBUSH. See *Rhus trilobata.*

SKY FLOWER. See *Duranta repens, Thunbergia grandiflora.*

SMILACINA racemosa. *Liliaceae.* FALSE SOLOMON'S SEAL. Perennial. Zones 1–7, 15–17. Commonly seen in shaded woods—California to British Columbia, east to Rockies. Grows 1–3 ft. tall. Each single, arching stalk has several 3–10-in.-long leaves, hairy beneath. Stalks topped by fluffy, conical clusters of small, fragrant, creamy white flowers in March–May, followed by red, purple-spotted berries. Most common form in West is variety *amplexicaulis,* with leaves sheathing stem at base. Sun or shade, water during spring growth.

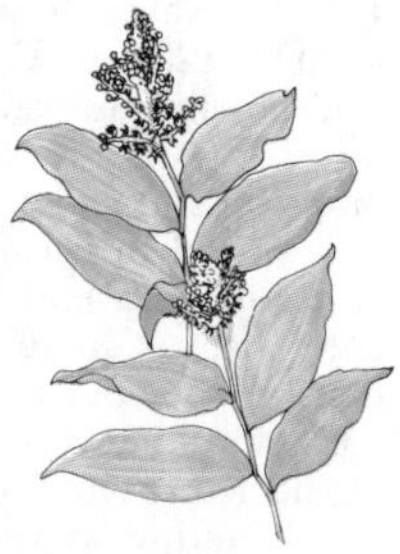
Smilacina racemosa

SMOKE TREE. See *Cotinus coggygria, Dalea spinosa.*

SNAIL VINE. See *Vigna caracalla.*

SNAKE PLANT. See *Sansevieria.*

SNAKESHEAD. See *Fritillaria meleagris.*

SNAPDRAGON. See *Antirrhinum majus.*

SNAPWEED. See *Impatiens.*

SNEEZEWEED. See *Helenium.*

SNOWBALL. See *Viburnum.*

SNOWBELL. See *Styrax.*

SNOWBERRY. See *Symphoricarpos.*

SNOWDROP. See *Galanthus.*

SNOWDROP TREE. See *Halesia carolina.*

SNOWFLAKE. See *Leucojum.*

SNOW GUM. See *Eucalyptus niphophila.*

SNOW-IN-SUMMER. See *Cerastium tomentosum.*

SNOW-ON-THE-MOUNTAIN. See *Euphorbia marginata.*

SOAPBARK TREE. See *Quillaja saponaria.*

SOCIETY GARLIC. See *Tulbaghia violacea.*

Solanaceae. Members of the potato family bear flowers that are nearly always star or saucer shaped and 5 petaled; fruits are berries or capsules. Plants are frequently rank smelling or even poisonous, but many are important food crops—eggplant, pepper, potato, tomato. Others are garden annuals, perennials, shrubs, or vines—*Browallia, Cestrum, Nicotiana,* and *Petunia,* to name a few.

SOLANDRA maxima (usually sold as *S. guttata*). *Solanaceae.* CUP-OF-GOLD VINE. Evergreen vine. Zones 17, 21–24; with overhead protection in Zones 15, 16, 18–20. Fast, sprawling, rampant growth to 40 ft. Fasten to support. Large, broad, glossy leaves 4–6 in. long. Blooms February–April and intermittently at other times. Bowl-shaped flowers are 6–8 in. wide, golden yellow striped brownish purple.

Solandra maxima

Full sun near coast; needs cool, shaded roots in hot inland valleys. Prune to induce laterals and more flowers. Can be cut back to make rough hedge. Takes salt spray directly above tide line; stands wind, fog. Use on big walls, pergolas, along eaves, or as bank cover. For easy viewing inside the big flowers, encourage growth low on plant by tip-pinching. This vine is spectacular trained along swimming pool fence.

SOLANUM. *Solanaceae.* Evergreen and deciduous shrubs and vines. In addition to potato and eggplant (described under those names), the group includes a number of ornamental plants. Ordinary garden care suits most of them.

Solanum pseudocapsicum

S. aviculare. Evergreen shrub. Zones 17, 21–24. Fast growing to 6–10 ft., with deeply cut smooth deep green leaves to 1 ft. long. Purple 1-in. flowers.

S. jasminoides. POTATO VINE. Evergreen or deciduous vine. Zones 8, 9, 12–24. Fast growth to 30 ft.; twining habit. Leaves 1½–3 in. long, evergreen in milder winters, medium to purplish green. Flowers pure white, or white tinged blue, an inch across, in clusters of 8–12. Nearly perpetual bloom; heaviest in spring. Sun or part shade. Grown for flowers or for light overhead shade. Cut back severely at any time to prevent tangling, promote vigorous new growth; control rampant runners that grow along ground.

S. muricatum. PEPINO. Evergreen perennial. Zones 17, 24; with shelter in Zones 15, 16, 20–23, but fruiting inconsistent there. Sprawling plant to 2 ft. tall, several feet across. Tapering bright green leaves are 3 in. long. Blue flowers are followed by football-shaped, greenish yellow fruits striped with purple. Fruits weigh from 4 oz. to 1 lb. and taste like a cross between melon and cucumber. Named varieties grown from cuttings. Grow like tomatoes.

S. pseudocapsicum. JERUSALEM CHERRY. Evergreen shrub. Zones 23, 24; pot or container plant for indoor use, outdoor summer decoration in all Zones. Grows 3–4 ft. high. Foliage deep green; leaves 4 in. long, smooth, shiny. White, ½-in.-wide flowers. Fine show of scarlet (rarely yellow), ½-in. fruit like miniature tomatoes, October–December. Fruit may be poisonous; caution children against eating it. Usually grown as annual. In Zones 23, 24, blooms, fruits, and seeds itself through year. The many dwarf strains (to 1 ft. high) are more popular than taller kinds, have larger fruit (to 1 in.).

S. rantonnetii. See *Lycianthes rantonnei.*

S. seaforthianum. BRAZILIAN NIGHTSHADE. Vine. Zones 16, 21–24. Evergreen in mildest winter areas. Leaves to 8 in. long, some undivided, others divided featherwise into leaflets. Clusters of violet blue, star-shaped, inch-wide flowers are followed by small red fruits (inedible except to birds).

S. wendlandii. COSTA RICAN NIGHTSHADE. Deciduous vine. Zones 16, 21–24. Tall, twining vine with prickly stems. Leaves larger than those of other species (4–10 in. long), lower ones divided into leaflets. Leaves drop in low temperatures even without frost. Slow to leaf out in spring. Big clusters of 2½-in., lilac blue flowers. Use to clamber into tall trees, to cover a pergola, to decorate eaves of large house.

S. xantii. Evergreen shrub. Zones 7–9, 14–24. California native. Erect or sprawling to 2 ft., with leaves to 1¾ in. long and purple 1-in. flowers late winter, spring. Superior forms sometimes seen in California native plant gardens.

SOLEIROLIA soleirolii *(Helxine soleirolii).* *Urticaceae.* BABY'S TEARS, ANGEL'S TEARS. Perennial. Zones 8–24; in Zones 4–7, a summer cover that renews itself from root fragments and seeds. Creeping plants with tiny round leaves make lush, medium green mats 1–4 in. high. Flowers inconspicuous. Tender, juicy leaves and stems are easily injured, but aggressive growth habit quickly repairs damage. Roots easily from pieces of stem and can become an invasive pest.

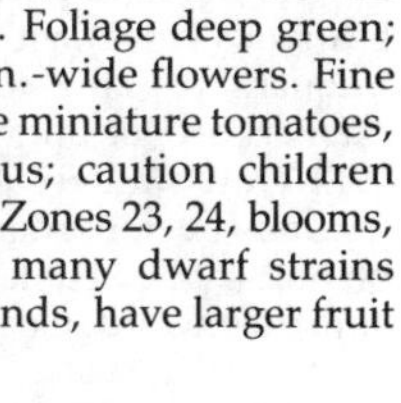

Soleirolia soleirolii

Grows best in shade, but takes full sun near coast if water supply is ample. Freezes to black mush in hard frosts, but comes back fast. Cool-looking, neat cover for ferns or other shade-loving plants. Can be used to carpet terrariums or space under greenhouse benches. There is a golden green variety.

S

SOLIDAGO. *Compositae.* GOLDENROD. Perennial. All Zones. Not as widely known and grown in far West as Rockies and eastward. A few can be grown here. Varieties of garden origin are sometimes sold. They grow 1–3 ft. high (sometimes to 5 ft.), with characteristic goldenrod plume of yellow flowers topping leafy stems. Varieties differ chiefly in size and in depth of yellow shading. 'Golden Mosa', to 3 ft., has light yellow flowers the color of "mimosa" (*Acacia baileyana*). Plants grow best in not-too-rich soil, in full sun or light shade. Average water requirement. Good meadow planting with black-eyed Susan and Michaelmas daisies, or can be used in border for summer–fall color.

Solidago

SOLLYA heterophylla ***(S. fusiformis).*** *Pittosporaceae.* AUSTRALIAN BLUEBELL CREEPER. Evergreen shrub or vine. Zones 8, 9, 14–24. Grows 2–3 ft. tall as loose, spreading shrub; given support and training, climbs to 6–8 ft. Foliage light and delicate; leaves narrow, glossy green, 1–2 in. long. Clusters of ½-in.-long, brilliant blue, bell-shaped flowers appear through most of summer.

Full or part sun in coastal areas, part shade inland. Drought tolerant when established, but looks better with regular watering and frequent pruning to fatten it up. Dies if drainage is poor. Spray to control scale insects. Will grow under eucalyptus trees. Use as ground cover, border planting, along steps, on half-shaded banks. Plant over low wall, where its branches can spill downward. Good container plant.

Sollya heterophylla

SOLOMON'S SEAL. See *Polygonatum.*

SOPHORA. *Leguminosae.* Deciduous or evergreen trees or shrubs. Leaves divided into numerous leaflets. Drooping clusters of sweet pea–shaped flowers are followed by pods bearing seeds.

S. arizonica. Evergreen shrub. Zones 10, 11 (possibly), 12, 13. To 6–10 ft. Gray green foliage, clusters of lavender, 1-in. flowers. Takes heat and drought, prefers occasional deep irrigation. Slow growing.

S. japonica. JAPANESE PAGODA TREE, CHINESE SCHOLAR TREE. Deciduous tree. All Zones. Unreliable bloom where summers are cold and damp. Moderate growth to 20 ft.; from this point it grows slowly to 40 ft., with equal or greater spread. Young wood smooth, dark gray green. Old branches and trunk gradually take on rugged look of oak. Dark green, 6–10-in. leaves divided into 7–17 oval, 1–2-in.-long leaflets. Long, open, 8–12-in. clusters of yellowish white, ½-in.-long flowers, July–September. Pods are 2–3½ in. long, narrowed between big seeds in bead necklace effect. Not fussy as to soil, water; no special pests or diseases. Resistant to oak root fungus. 'Regent' is exceptionally vigorous, uniform grower. One of best spreading trees for giving shade to lawn or patio. Good tree for Rocky Mountain area, but subject there to damage from ice storms.

Sophora japonica

S. secundiflora. MESCAL BEAN, TEXAS MOUNTAIN LAUREL. Evergreen shrub or tree. Zones 8–16, 18–24. Can be trained into 25-ft. tree with short, slender trunk or multiple trunks, narrow crown, and upright branches. Very slow growth, especially in cool-summer regions. Leaves 4–6 in. long, divided into 7–9 glossy, dark green, oval leaflets, 1–2 in. long. Blooms February–April; inch-wide, violet blue, wisterialike, sweet-scented flowers are carried in drooping 4–8-in. clusters. A white-flowered form rarely appears. Silvery gray, woody, 1–8-in.-long seed pods open on ripening to show bright red ½-in. seeds which are decorative but poisonous—remove pods before they mature. Thrives in hot sun and alkaline soil, but needs good drainage and some water. Choice small tree for street, lawn, or patio. Untrained, it is good large screen, bank cover, or espalier.

S. tetraptera. KOWHAI, YELLOW KOWHAI. Evergreen or deciduous shrub or small tree. Zones 15–17. Slow growing to 15–20 ft. Slender, open, rather narrow tree which drops its leaves in spring just before blooming. Leaves 3–6 in. long, divided into 20–40 tiny leaflets. Flowers bright golden yellow, 2 in. long, in hanging clusters of 4–8. Seed pods with 4 wings, narrowed between seeds, grow 2–8 in. long. Rather tender; doesn't take drought and low humidity. Well-drained soil, ample water, full sun or partial shade.

SORBARIA sorbifolia ***(Spiraea sorbifolia).*** *Rosaceae.* FALSE SPIRAEA. Deciduous shrub. Zones 1–10, 14–21. Spreads by suckering to cover large areas if not curbed. Grows 3–8 ft. tall, less in poor, dry soil. Leaves are fern-like, 6–12 in. long, with up to 23 toothed, deep green leaflets. Stems topped in summer by branching clusters (to 1 ft. long) of tiny white flowers. These should be cut off after they have faded.

General effect is lush, almost tropical, especially in rich, moist soil. Sun or light shade. Tolerates some drought when established. Thin clumps drastically or cut back near ground in earliest spring; plants bloom on new wood.

Sorbaria sorbifolia

SORBUS. *Rosaceae.* MOUNTAIN ASH. Deciduous trees, rarely shrubs. Zones 1–10, 14–17. Grown for finely cut, somewhat fernlike foliage, clustered white flowers, and bright fruit. All stand winter cold, can endure strong winds, low humidity, extreme heat. Average garden soil, sun or light shade, good drainage, average garden watering. Where adapted, good small garden or street trees, though fruit can be messy over paving. Fruit is generally red, but white, pink, and golden varieties and species are occasionally available. All are attractive to birds. Some may be difficult to transplant. Cankers a problem when trees are under stress. Watch for fireblight.

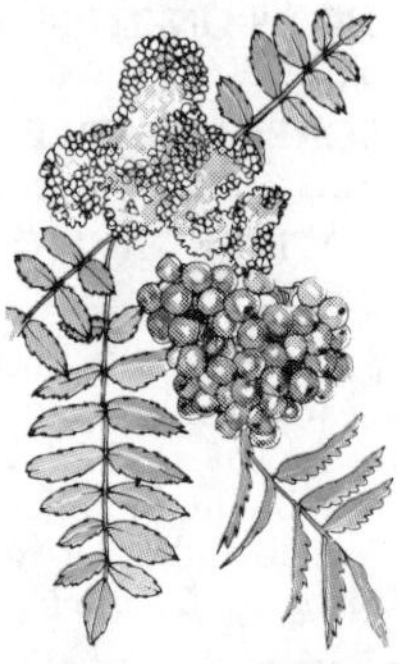
Sorbus aucuparia

S. alnifolia. KOREAN MOUNTAIN ASH. Unlike others, has simple, undivided leaves like those of alder. Broad, dense tree, eventually to 60 ft., with small, loose clusters of flowers, red and yellow fruit, yellow to orange fall color.

S. aucuparia. EUROPEAN MOUNTAIN ASH. Moderate to rapid growth to 20–30 ft. with 15–20-ft. spread; may grow much larger. Sharply rising branches make dense, oval to round crown. ('Black Hawk' is columnar in form.) Leaves have 9–15 leaflets to 1–2 in. long, dull green above, gray green below, turning yellow, orange, or red in fall. Flat, 3–5-in.-wide clusters of tiny white flowers bloom in late spring; these are followed by orange red, berrylike, ¼-in. fruit which colors in midsummer and may hang until spring unless birds eat it. Fruit especially attractive against background of conifers. 'Cardinal Royal' has especially large bright red berries that color early.

S. hupehensis. Eventually 50 ft. tall, usually much less. Leaves to 7 in. long, with 4–8 pairs of 1–2-in. leaflets. Fruit clusters are white or coral red; the form in cultivation is fireblight-resistant 'Coral Cascade', with red fruit and red fall foliage.

S. hybrida. Erect tree to 20–30 ft. tall; leaves are divided into leaflets at the base, but tips are merely lobed, like oak leaves. Fruit is red, ½–⅝ in. across.

S. reducta. Shrub ½–2 ft. tall, 3 ft. wide, spreading by underground runners. Leaves to 4-in. long, with 4–7 pairs of leaflets. Spring flowers white, in loose clusters. Fruit pink. Rock garden shrub or bonsai subject.

S. thuringiaca. Tree to 40 ft. tall. Hybrid between European mountain ash and a species with undivided leaves. Leaves either deeply lobed and toothed, or having one pair of leaflets beneath a large terminal leaflet. Spring flowers are white, in clusters 3–5 in. wide. Berries bright red, ¼–⅜ in. in diameter.

S. tianshanica. TURKESTAN MOUNTAIN ASH. Large shrub or small tree to 16 ft. Leaves 5–6 in. long, with 9–15 leaflets to 2 in. long, ½ in. wide. Loose, 3–5-in.-wide clusters of ¾-in. flowers are followed by bright red fruit. Neat form, slow growth; excellent plant for small garden. 'Red Cascade' is a compact, oval-crowned variety.

SORREL, WOOD or REDWOOD. See *Oxalis.*

SOTOL. See *Dasylirion wheeleri.*

SOUR GUM. See *Nyssa sylvatica.*

SOURWOOD. See *Oxydendrum arboreum.*

SOUTHERNWOOD. See *Artemisia abrotanum.*

SPANISH BAYONET. See *Yucca aloifolia.*

SPANISH BLUEBELL. See *Endymion hispanicus.*

SPANISH BROOM. See *Genista hispanica, Spartium junceum.*

SPANISH DAGGER. See *Yucca gloriosa.*

SPARAXIS tricolor. *Iridaceae.* HARLEQUIN FLOWER. Corm. Zones 9, 13–24. Native to South Africa. Closely related to ixia and similar to it in uses and culture. Sword-shaped leaves; small, funnel-shaped flowers in spikelike clusters on 1-ft. stems. Flowers come in yellow, pink, purple, red, and white. Usually blotched and splashed with contrasting colors. Blooms over long period in late spring. Use in borders, rock gardens, containers, for cutting. Plant in full sun in fall; set corms 2 in. deep, 2–3 in. apart.

Sparaxis tricolor

SPARMANNIA africana. *Tiliaceae.* AFRICAN LINDEN. Evergreen shrub, tree. Zones 17, 21–24; with special protection 15, 16, 18–20; house plant anywhere. Fast to 10–20 ft., usually as thicket, multitrunked from base, especially if frosted back or pruned to control size; slower, smaller in container or as house plant. Dense, coarse foliage. Leaves broad, angled, to 9 in. across, light green, heavily veined, velvety with coarse hairs. Flowers white with brush of yellow stamens, 1–1½ in. across, clustered, borne in midwinter to early spring.

Sparmannia africana

Ample water and feeding, sun or shade. Susceptible to spider mites. Prune heavily every few years to give desired height and control legginess. Best used for furnishing bulk and mass near entryways, screening, combining with tropical foliage plants. Big leaves, easy cleanup make it a good choice near pools. Easily propagated by cuttings.

SPARTIUM junceum. *Leguminosae.* SPANISH BROOM. Evergreen shrub. Zones 5–9, 11–24. Grows to 6–10 ft., forming a shrub of many green, erect, almost leafless stems. Bright yellow, fragrant, 1-in.-long flowers in clusters at branch ends bloom continuously from July to frost in north, March–August in south. Flowers followed by hairy seed pods. All parts of plant are poisonous if eaten.

Spartium junceum

Gaunt-looking woody shrub, but pruning will fatten it up. Does best with little water, in full sun. Takes poor, rocky soil. Has naturalized many places in West. Good rough bank cover with native shrubs, but where best adapted is capable of crowding out desirable native plants. Easily controlled in garden.

In southern California (especially Zone 24), Spanish broom is extremely subject to caterpillars in summer; by fall, they often leave plants without flowers or stems. (Stems may resprout at base in winter.) Aphids are a problem at blooming time.

SPATHIPHYLLUM. *Araceae.* Evergreen perennial. House plant. Dark green leaves are large, oval or elliptical and narrowed to a point, erect on slender leaf stalks that rise directly from soil. Flowers resemble calla lilies or anthuriums—central column of closely set tiny flowers surrounded by leaflike white flower bract.

Spathiphyllum 'Mauna Loa'

Loose, fibrous potting mixture; weekly feedings of dilute liquid fertilizer. Grow in good light, but avoid hot, sunny windows; they can endure low light. They like ample water. One of the few flowering plants that grows and blooms readily indoors. Many varieties include: 'Mauna Loa', 3½ ft.; 'St. Mary', 6 ft.; 'Silver Streak', 1½ ft., with matte-finished leaves with a silvery midrib; 'Supreme', 2½ ft.; 'Tasson', 2 ft. (considered by some the surest bloomer); and 'Wallisii', 20 in. 'Silver Streak' has insignificant flowers, but foliage is attractive.

SPATHODEA campanulata. *Bignoniaceae.* AFRICAN TULIP TREE. Zones 21–24. Fast-growing evergreen tree (deciduous with frost). Glossy leaves divided into 4–8 pairs of leaflets. Branches end in clusters of spectacular tulip-shaped, 4-in., orange scarlet flowers edged with yellow; typical bloom time is spring, but flowers may appear in any season. Plants grow rapidly and bloom young, but can be devastated by frosts. Give good drainage and a warm site. Can reach 40–70 ft., but such height is unlikely in California because of frost damage.

Spathodea campanulata

SPEARMINT. See *Mentha spicata.*

SPEEDWELL. See *Veronica.*

SPHAEROPTERIS cooperi. See *Cyathea cooperi.*

SPICE BUSH. See *Calycanthus occidentalis.*

SPIDER FLOWER. See *Cleome spinosa.*

SPIDER LILY. See *Lycoris.*

SPIDER PLANT. See *Chlorophytum comosum.*

SPIDERWORT. See *Tradescantia andersoniana.*

SPINACH. *Chenopodiaceae.* Annual vegetable. All Zones. Sow according to schedules on pages 194–197 to mature during fall, winter, and spring; long daylight of late spring and heat of summer make it go to seed too fast. It requires rich, fast-draining soil. Make small sowings at weekly intervals to get succession. Grow in sun. Space rows 1½ ft. apart.

After seedlings start growing, thin plants to 6 in. apart. Give plants plenty of water; one feeding will encourage lush foliage. When plants have reached full size, harvest by cutting off entire clump at ground level.

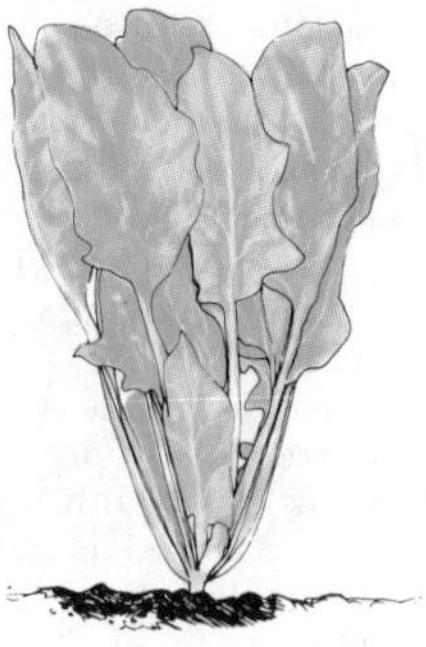
Spinach

SPIRAEA. *Rosaceae.* Deciduous shrubs. Zones 1–11, 14–21. Easy to grow in all kinds of soils, in sun or light shade, average water. Form, height, and flowering season vary; all provide generous quantities of white, pink, or red flowers.

Prune according to form and time of bloom. Those with loose, graceful look need annual renewal of new growth. Remove old wood that has produced flowers—cutting it back to ground. Most shrubby types require less severe pruning. Prune spring-flowering kinds when they finish blooming—or better yet, cut flowering branches for arrangements; they have graceful lines and last well. Prune summer-flowering species in late winter or very early spring.

Spiraea bumalda
'Anthony Waterer'

S. bumalda. Blooms June to fall. Includes hybrids between *S. japonica* and *S. albiflora.* Varieties include 'Anthony Waterer', 2–3 ft. tall, with flat-topped, bright carmine flower clusters and maroon-tinged foliage; 'Froebelii', similar, but taller (3–4 ft.), with rosy red flower clusters; 'Goldflame', like 'Froebelii' but with bronzy leaves that turn yellow as they expand; and 'Limemound', dense and dwarf, with pink flowers and lime green leaves that turn orange red in fall.

S. cantoniensis *(S. reevesiana).* Upright, to 5–6 ft., with arching branches. Small dark green leaves turn red in fall. White flowers wreathe branches in June and July. Pinch back occasionally to limit growth.

S. douglasii. WESTERN SPIRAEA. Suckering, clump-forming shrub 4–8 ft. tall. Native West Coast to Rocky Mountains. Leaves are dark green above, velvety white beneath; pale to deep pink flowers form 8-in.-tall clusters at branch ends in July, August. Useful for wild plantings near streams.

S. japonica. Upright-growing shrub with flat clusters of pink flowers to 8 in. wide at branch tips. Varieties, better known than the species, include 'Fortunei', taller, with markedly saw-toothed leaves and pink summer flowers; 'Alpina' and 'Little Princess', under 20 in. tall, with long summer bloom in pink; and 'Shirobana', 2–3 ft. tall, with flowers of white, pink, and red on same plant.

S. nipponica tosaensis 'Snowmound'. Compact, spreading, 2–3-ft.-tall plant with a profusion of white flowers in early summer.

S. prunifolia 'Plena'. BRIDAL WREATH SPIRAEA, SHOE BUTTON SPIRAEA. Graceful, arching branches on a 6- by 6-ft. plant. Small dark green leaves turn rich red in fall. Small double white flowers like tiny roses line branches in April and May.

S. thunbergii. Showy, billowy, graceful shrub with many arching branches. To 5 ft. Blue green leaves turn soft reddish brown in fall; round clusters of small single white flowers appear all along branches in April.

S. trilobata 'Swan Lake'. Like a smaller bridal wreath. Grows to 3–4 ft., gives massive show of tiny white flowers in May and June.

S. vanhouttei. Widely planted hybrid between *S. cantoniensis* and *S. trilobata.* Forms a 6-ft. fountain of arching branches covered with white flower clusters in June, July.

SPLIT-LEAF PHILODENDRON. See *Monstera deliciosa.*

SPLIT ROCK. See *Pleiospilos.*

SPREKELIA formosissima (often sold as *Amaryllis formosissima*). *Amaryllidaceae.* JACOBEAN LILY, ST. JAMES LILY, AZTEC LILY. Bulb. Zones 9, 12–24 as all-year garden plants; everywhere in pots or as spring–fall garden plants. Native to Mexico. Foliage looks like that of daffodils. Stems 1 ft. tall, topped with dark crimson blooms resembling orchids: 3 erect upper segments and 3 lower ones rolled together into tube at base, then separating again into drooping segments. Plant in fall, setting bulbs 3–4 in. deep and 8 in. apart in full sun. Blooms 6–8 weeks after planting. Most effective in groups. In mild climates, may flower several times a year, with alternating moisture and drying out. Where winters are cold, plant outdoors in spring; lift plants in fall when foliage yellows and store over winter (leave dry tops on). Or grow in pots like amaryllis (*Hippeastrum*), giving slightly cooler conditions. Repot every 3–4 years.

Sprekelia formosissima

SPRING STAR FLOWER. See *Ipheion uniflorum.*

SPRUCE. See *Picea.*

SPURGE. See *Euphorbia.*

SQUASH. *Cucurbitaceae.* This edible annual comes in 2 forms. Those that are harvested and cooked in the immature state are called summer squash; this group includes scalloped white squash, yellow crookneck and straightneck varieties, and cylindrical, green or gray zucchini or Italian squash. Winter squash varieties have hard rinds and firm, close-grained, fine-flavored flesh. They store well and are used for baking and for pies. They come in a variety of shapes—turban, acorn, and banana are a few—and a variety of sizes and colors.

Crookneck squash

Many summer squashes grow on broad, squat bushes rather than on vines; these help save garden space. 'Early Summer Crookneck' and 'Early Prolific Straightneck' are good yellow summer squash. 'Early White Bush' (white) and 'Scallopini Hybrid' (green) are fine scalloped varieties. 'Ambassador Hybrid', 'Aristocrat Hybrid', and 'Burpee Hybrid' are productive zucchini varieties. Zucchini and scalloped squash also come in golden yellow variants. Novelties include 'Gourmet Globe', a round, striped zucchini, and 'Kuta', a whitish squash that can be eaten like summer squash at 6 in. or permitted to ripen into a 1-ft. winter squash.

Fall and winter squash for storing are the small 'Bush Table Queen', 'Acorn', 'Butternut', and 'Buttercup', and the large 'Hubbard', 'Blue Hubbard', and 'Jumbo Pink Banana'. Spaghetti squash looks like any other winter squash, but when you cook (bake or boil) and open it, you find that the flesh is made up of long, spaghettilike strands. It has a nutty flavor.

Bush varieties of summer squash can be planted 2 ft. apart in rows. If planted in circles ("hills"), they need more room, so space hills 4 by 4 ft. Runner-type winter squash needs 5-ft. spacing in rows, 8 by 8 ft. in hills. Roots will need ample water, but keep leaves and stems as dry as possible; irrigate in basins or furrows. Plant summer squash in full sun; winter squash tolerates light shade but does better in full sun. Harvest summer squash when they are still small and tender; seeds should still be soft and you should be able to pierce rind easily with your thumbnail. Common complaint concerning summer squash is that immature fruits rot at blossom end while still tiny; usual reason is that blossom has not been pollinated, due to poor weather, lack of bees, or lack of open male blossoms. Late squash should stay on vines until thoroughly hardened; harvest these with an inch of stem and store in cool (55°F.), frost-free place.

SQUAWBUSH, SKUNKBUSH. See *Rhus trilobata.*

SQUILL. See *Scilla.*

SQUIRREL'S FOOT FERN. See *Davallia trichomanoides.*

STACHYS byzantina ***(S. lanata, S. olympica).*** *Labiatae.* LAMB'S EARS. Perennial. All Zones. Soft, thick, white-woolly, rather tongue-shaped leaves grow densely on spreading, 1–1½-ft. stems. Flower stalks with many whorls of small purplish flowers form in June–July, but plant is most useful for foliage effect. Rain smashes it down, makes it mushy. Frost damages leaves. Cut back in spring. Use for contrast with dark green and different-shaped leaves such as those of strawberry or some sedums. Good edging plant for paths, flower bed borders; highly effective edging for bearded iris. Excellent ground cover under high-branching oaks. Average soil, sun or light shade, light water but not absolute drought, good drainage.

Stachys byzantina

STACHYURUS praecox. *Stachyuraceae.* Deciduous shrub. Zones 4–6 best; also 14–17. Slow to 10 ft., with spreading, slender, polished chestnut brown branches. Pendulous flower stalks 3–4 in. long, each with 12–20 unopened buds, hang from branches in fall–winter. These open in February–March into pale yellow or greenish yellow, bell-shaped flowers ⅓ in. wide. Berrylike fruit in August–September. Bright green, toothed leaves, 3–7 in. long, taper to sharp tip. Leaves often somewhat sparse. Fall color pleasant (but not bright) rosy red and yellowish.

Stachyurus praecox

Grow under deciduous trees to shelter winter buds from heavy freezes. With ample water, takes full sunshine.

STAGHORN FERN. See *Platycerium.*

STAPELIA. *Asclepiadaceae.* STARFISH FLOWER, CARRION FLOWER. Succulents. Outdoors Zone 24; Zones 12, 13, 16–23 with lath or some other shelter. House plants everywhere. Plants resemble cacti, with clumps of 4-sided, spineless stems. Flowers (summer) are large, fleshy, shaped like 5-pointed stars; they usually have elaborate circular fleshy disk in center. Most smell like carrion, but odor is not usually offensive on plants blooming outside in summer. They need cool, dry rest period in winter, sun and moderate water in summer. Best managed in pots. Good desert succulent, tolerating extreme heat.

Stapelia variegata

S. gigantea. Grow this plant as a remarkable novelty. Stems 9 in. tall. Flowers 10–16 in. wide, fringy edged, brown purple marked yellow.

S. variegata. Most common. Stems to 6 in. Flowers to 3 in. across, yellow heavily spotted and barred dark purple brown. There are many hybrids and color variants. Flowers not strongly scented; plant takes light frost.

STAR BUSH. See *Turraea obtusifolia.*

STAR CLUSTERS. See *Pentas lanceolata.*

STARFISH FLOWER. See *Stapelia.*

STAR JASMINE. See *Trachelospermum.*

STAR OF BETHLEHEM. See *Campanula isophylla, Ornithogalum arabicum.*

STAR TULIP. See *Calochortus uniflorus.*

STATICE. See *Limonium.*

STENOCARPUS sinuatus. *Proteaceae.* FIREWHEEL TREE. Evergreen tree. Zones 16, 17, 20–24. Slow to 30 ft., with a spread of 15 ft. Foliage dense, shiny. Leaves on young plants to 1 ft. long, lobed like oak leaves; on older plants, leaves are smaller and usually unlobed. Tubular, 2–3-in., scarlet and yellow flowers arranged in clusters like spokes of wheel. Has been adopted by Rotary Clubs as mascot. Plants will not bloom until established for several years. Bloom season varies; plants may flower at any time, but early fall is usually peak season. Blooms sometimes come out of the trunk's bark, giving most unusual effect.

Stenocarpus sinuatus

Rather tender, especially when young. Best in deep, rich, well-drained, acid soil. Needs occasional deep watering even when well established. Prune to shape in early years. Where climate, soil, and water are right, it can be a showy flowering tree for use near patio or terrace. Good lawn tree. Good near swimming pools; has little leaf drop. Beautiful juvenile leaves make it popular as an indoor pot plant.

STENOLOBIUM stans. See *Tecoma stans.*

STENOTAPHRUM secundatum. *Gramineae.* ST. AUGUSTINE GRASS. Perennial lawn grass. Zones 12, 13, 18–24. Tropical or subtropical coarse-textured grass that spreads fast by surface runners that root at joints. Leaves very dark green, up to ⅜ in. wide, on coarse, wiry, flattened stems. Turns brown during short winter dormancy, can creep into flower beds or other plantings, requires power mower to deal with heavy blades, produces thick thatch. On the plus side, it is easily removed from flower beds because of shallow roots, tolerates much wear, has few pests, is fairly salt tolerant, and endures shade better than other subtropical grasses. Moderate to high water requirement. Plant from sod, plugs, or stolons. Mow 1 in. high once a week.

Stenotaphrum secundatum

Will grow in Zones 14–16, but long dormant season limits use. Needs somewhat less water than bluegrass. A variegated form exists and is sometimes seen as a hanging basket plant.

S

STEPHANOTIS floribunda. *Asclepiadaceae.* MADAGASCAR JASMINE. Evergreen vine. Zones 23, 24; house or indoor/outdoor plant everywhere. Moderate growth to 10–15 ft. (more if grown in open ground). Can be kept small in pots. Waxy, glossy green leaves to 4 in. long. Funnel-shaped flowers are white, waxy, very fragrant, 1–2 in. long in open clusters. Blooms June through summer as outdoor plant; grown indoors and properly rested by some drying out, will bloom 6 weeks after resuming growth. Favorite flower in bridal bouquets.

Stephanotis floribunda

Grown outdoors, does best with roots in shade, tops in filtered sun. Needs warmth, support of frame or trellis. As indoor/outdoor plant, feed and water liberally, but dry out somewhat before bringing indoors. Grow in bright light out of direct sun. Watch for scale, mealybugs.

STERCULIA. See *Brachychiton.*

Sterculiaceae. The sterculia family of shrubs and trees has flowers in which the calyx (usually bowl shaped and 5 lobed) replaces the corolla as the conspicuous element. Examples are *Brachychiton* and *Firmiana.*

STERNBERGIA lutea. *Amaryllidaceae.* Bulb. All Zones. Narrow, 6–12-in. leaves appear in fall simultaneously with flowers and remain green for several months after blooms have gone. Golden yellow, 1½-in.-long flowers resemble large crocuses on 6–9-in. stems, provide a pleasant autumn surprise in borders, in rock gardens, near pools. Good cut flowers. Plant bulbs as soon as available—August or September. Set 4 in. deep, 6 in. apart, in sun. In coldest climates, give sheltered location. When bulbs become crowded, lift, divide, and replant in August.

Sternbergia lutea

STEWARTIA. *Theaceae.* Deciduous shrubs or trees. Zones 4–6, 14–17, 20, 21. These are all-season performers: distinctive pattern of bare branches in winter, fresh green leaves in spring, white flowers like single camellias in summer, and colored foliage in autumn. Slow growing. Best in moist, acid soil with high content of organic matter. Need ample moisture when young, otherwise leaves burn. Take sun, but prefer partial shade in warm climates.

Stewartia koreana

S. koreana. KOREAN STEWARTIA. Tree. To 20–25 ft.; may eventually reach 50 ft. Rather narrow pyramidal habit. Leaves dark green, to 4 in. long, somewhat silky underneath, turning orange or orange red in fall. Blooms in June–July: white flowers with yellow orange stamens, to 3 in. across, on short stalks among leaves. Possibly only a variety of Japanese stewartia.

S. monadelpha. TALL STEWARTIA. Tree. To 25 ft., with upward-angled slender branches, 1½–2½-in.-long leaves. Summer flowers 1½ in. across, the stamens with violet anthers. Outstanding red leaf color in fall.

S. ovata. MOUNTAIN STEWARTIA. Shrub or small tree. To 15 ft. Slender habit. The 2½–5-in., grayish green leaves turn brilliant orange in fall. Three-inch flowers with frilled petals bloom in summer. *S. o. grandiflora* has 4-in. flowers with lavender anthers. It will bloom even as a young plant.

S. pseudocamellia. JAPANESE STEWARTIA. Tree. To 60 ft. Leaves 1–3 in. long, turning bronze to dark purple in fall. July–August flowers to 2½ in. across, with orange anthers.

STIGMAPHYLLON. *Malpighiaceae.* ORCHID VINE. Evergreen or partially deciduous vines. Tall twiners of fairly fast growth to 20–30 ft. Leaves borne in pairs. Long-stalked clusters of bright yellow flowers of irregular shape, somewhat resembling oncidium orchids, spring from upper portions of stems. Heaviest bloom July–September, but may carry some bloom all year in mildest climates. Do best in rich soil, with shade at roots and ample water. Furnish support and prune out dead or straggling growth.

Stigmaphyllon ciliatum

S. ciliatum. Zones 19–24. Foliage open and delicate, and plants easily kept small. Leaves heart shaped, 1–3 in. long, with a few long, bristly teeth on edges. Clusters of 3–7 flowers 1½ in. across.

S.littorale *(Heteropteris glabra).* Zones 15–24. Larger, coarser vine than *S. ciliatum,* with larger (to 5 in. long) oval leaves and larger clusters (10–20) of smaller flowers (1 in. across). Extremely vigorous; can climb to tops of tall trees if allowed to do so.

STIPA gigantea. *Gramineae.* GIANT FEATHER GRASS. Perennial. Zones 4–9, 14–24. Clumps of narrow, arching leaves grow 2–3 ft. tall. Open, airy sheaves of yellowish flowers shimmer in a broad cloud reaching 6 ft. tall and as wide. Full sun. Needs ample water until established; after that, it will take some drought.

Stipa gigantea

STOCK. See *Matthiola.*

STOKESIA laevis. *Compositae.* STOKES ASTER. Perennial. Zones 1–9, 12–24. Rugged and most adaptable plant. Much branched, with stiff erect stems 1½–2 ft. high. Smooth, firm-textured, medium green leaves, 2–8 in. long, spiny, toothed at bottom. Asterlike flower heads in blue, purplish blue, or white, 3–4 in. across. Composed of button of small flowers in center, surrounded by ring of larger flowers. Blooms summer, early autumn. Leafy, curved, finely toothed bracts surround tight flower buds. Several varieties; 'Blue Danube' is selected form. Sun, average water, good drainage. Good in pots. Long-lasting cut flower.

Stokesia laevis

STONECRESS. See *Aethionema.*

STONECROP. See *Sedum.*

STONE PLANTS. See *Lithops, Pleiospilos.*

STORAX, CALIFORNIA. See *Styrax officinalis californicus.*

STRANVAESIA davidiana. *Rosaceae.* Evergreen shrub or small tree. Zones 4–11, 14–17. Informal, wide-spreading, 6–20 ft. high; moderate growth rate. Leaves oblong, smooth edged, to 4 in. long; new foliage reddish. Some leaves turn bronze or purple in late fall and winter—good foil for clusters of showy red berries that form at same time. White flowers in 4-in. clusters, June.

Stranvaesia davidiana

Best if given plenty of room, sun, not-too-rich soil. In hot interior gardens, protect from hot winds and supply adequate water. Subject to fireblight. Looks good with strong-growing native plants, or as screen or background. Berried branches are handsome as holiday cut foliage.

S. d. undulata ***(S. undulata).*** Lower growing than the species, to irregularly shaped 5-ft. shrub. New foliage and branch tips are colorful bronzy red. Leaves are wavy along edges.

STRAWBERRY. *Rosaceae.* All Zones. Plants are 6–8 in. tall, spreading about 1 ft. across with long runners. Toothed, roundish, medium green leaves, white flowers. Plant strawberries in sunny location, in well-drained, fairly rich soil.

Strawberry

You'll find that strawberries are often labeled as day neutral, everbearing, or June bearing. June-bearing types produce one crop per year, in late spring or early summer. Plant these for preserving or freezing, since they give you all their fruit at once. Generally speaking, June-bearing types are the highest-quality strawberries you can grow.

Everbearing kinds include the day neutrals, which flower and set fruit with little regard for day length. Instead of coming all at once, the everbearing harvest tends to peak in early summer, then continue on (often unevenly) through fall; the exact fruiting pattern depends on the variety.

To harvest just a few berries, you can simply plant a dozen or so plants, spaced 14–18 in. apart, in sunny patch within flower or vegetable garden, or even in boxes or tubs on patio.

To bring in big crop of berries, plant in rows. If soil is heavy or poorly drained, set plants in rows along raised mounds 5–6 in. high and 28 in. from center to center. Use furrows between mounds for irrigation and feeding. Set plants 14–16 in. apart.

If your soil drains well or if furrow irrigation would be difficult, plant on flat ground, 14–18 in. apart, in rows 1½ ft. apart, and irrigate by overhead sprinkler. Flat-ground method is best where salinity is a problem. Strawberries are difficult to grow in desert or other regions where soil and water salinity are very high.

In Northwest, most gardeners set plants 2–3 ft. apart in rows 4–5 ft. apart, let runners fill in until plants are 7–10 in. apart, then keep additional runners pinched off. Keep the rows 20–30 in. wide.

Planting season is usually determined by when your nursery can offer plants. In mild-winter areas, plants set out in late summer or fall produce a crop the following spring. Other than that, rule is to plant in early spring. Everbearers will give summer and fall crop from spring plantings; pinch off earliest blossoms to increase plant strength.

Set plants carefully; crown should be above soil level, topmost roots ¼ in. beneath soil level (buried crowns rot; exposed roots dry

Strawberry

NAME	DESCRIPTION	ADAPTABILITY	RESISTANCE
'Benton'	June-bearing variety that produces a good crop of firm, flavorful berries.	Outstanding in Northwest, especially in mountain and intermountain areas.	Virus tolerant, mildew resistant.
'Brighton'	Everbearing. Showy flowers and big, beautiful berries make this good for hanging baskets. Fruit flavor not as intense as many others.	Best in California, but hardy enough for mountain and intermountain states.	Resists verticillium wilt and viruses; some mildew resistance.
'Douglas'	June bearing. Heavy producer of early, flavorful berries. Grows and flowers in low temperatures.	At its best in California.	Resistant to viruses and leaf spot, but gets botrytis; gets red stele in Pacific Northwest.
'Fern'	Everbearing. Sweet, medium-sized, wedge-shaped berries are good fresh, canned.	Good throughout the West, except in coldest regions east of the mountains.	Susceptible to viruses, red stele.
'Fort Laramie'	Everbearing. Good yield of large, bright red berries over long season. Excellent flavor.	Tolerates −30°F. without mulch. Hardy in mountain states, high plains.	
'Hecker'	Everbearing. Smallish berries are very flavorful, a little soft.	Bred on the mild California coast, this one is the equal of 'Fort Laramie' in its ability to handle extreme cold.	Good virus and wilt resistance, but gets red stele.
'Hood'	Berry is large, cone shaped, bright red. Bears same time as 'Northwest'. Fine for jam, fresh use. Not best freezer.	Similar to 'Northwest'.	Resists mildew.
'Lassen'	Medium-large berry with spring and fall crops. Use fresh or for freezing.	Good in southern California, inland valleys. Takes warm winters.	Moderate resistance to alkalinity. Highly subject to yellows.
'Northwest'	Big, good-looking berry for use fresh, frozen, in preserves. June–July in Northwest.	Very popular in Washington, Oregon.	Resistant to yellows. Susceptible to red stele; give good drainage.
'Ogallala'	Everbearing. Hybrid with wild Rocky Mountain berry.	Very cold tolerant. Blossoms fairly frost resistant.	
'Olympus'	Average-sized light red fruit in midseason. No runners; vigorous plants bear on branching crowns.	Good in southwestern Washington and northwestern Oregon.	Some botrytis resistance. Resists red stele where best adapted; susceptible in northwestern Washington.

(Continued on next page)

S

NAME	DESCRIPTION	ADAPTABILITY	RESISTANCE
'Ozark Beauty'	Everbearing. Large, long-necked berries. Mild, sweet flavor. Produces many runners.	Wide climate adaptability. Tolerates much cold.	
'Puget Beauty'	Sweet, glossy red. Good fresh, frozen, and for jam. Main crop June; light crop in August.	Good variety for heavy soils in Northwest.	Some resistance to red stele and mildew.
'Quinault'	Everbearing. Fruit is large, attractive, tasty, rather soft. Good producer of runners.	Developed for Northwest.	Resistant to viruses and red stele, but susceptible to botrytis.
'Rainier'	Good-sized red berries that hold size throughout long main crop season. Fine flavor; fine home garden variety. Vigorous plant producer.	Best in Northwest, west of Cascades.	Fair tolerance to root rot.
'Selva'	Everbearing. First flush of fruit comes as late as July, but produces heavily through fall. Fruit huge for day-neutral type, very sweet.	Perfectly hardy; great in California, not so good in the Northwest.	Gets red spider mites, leaf spotting in mild parts of the Northwest, but appears to be red stele resistant.
'Sequoia'	Medium to large red fruit. Tastiest of modern strawberries. Prolific. Bears for many months.	Developed in and for coastal California, but with wide climate adaptability, even in coldest winters.	Resistant to alkalinity, yellows, and most leaf diseases.
'Shuksan'	Medium-sized dark red, soft, mealy berries in midseason.	Very cold hardy, tolerant of alkalinity. Good east of Cascades.	Resistant to botrytis fruit rot.
'Tillikum'	Everbearing. Because it's such a heavy producer, its soft berries are small. Flavor is mild.	Best in western Oregon and Washington.	Good virus tolerance, no problem with mildew.
'Tioga'	Yield, size, and appearance better than 'Lassen'.	Grows well in all strawberry areas of California.	Resistant to yellows. Susceptible to wilt.
'Totem'	June bearing. Very productive; juicy, flavorful fruit is on the soft side.	Good, flavorful berries for western Oregon, Washington, but since it flowers early, late frosts can impair fruit set.	Resistant to red stele; virus tolerant. Holds berries up off ground, so fruit rot is rarely a problem.
'Tristar'	Everbearing. Large fruit has best flavor of any everbearing type but 'Quinault'. Bears well the first year.	Good throughout the West.	Resists red stele and mildew, but moderately susceptible to viruses.

out). Mulch to keep down weeds, conserve moisture, keep berries clean.

Strawberries need frequent deep soaking, especially in bearing season. In summer-arid areas they may need water every 2 or 3 days if soil is sandy, every 7–10 days if soil is heavy. In humid Northwest, early berries may ripen without irrigation, but everbearers will need summer water.

Feed plants twice a year—once when growth begins, again after first crop. In California and Southwest, nitrogen is especially necessary. Northwest growers usually apply superphosphate at planting time and use complete fertilizers high in phosphorus.

Most varieties are reproduced by offset plants at ends of runners. You can (a) pinch off all runners, which will give large plants and small yields of big berries; or (b) permit offset plants to grow 7–10 in. apart or even closer, which will give heavy yields of somewhat smaller berries. When your plants have made enough offsets, pinch off further runners. (Some varieties make few or no offsets.)

Strawberries are subject to red stele (root rot), yellows (virus), and verticillium wilt (soil-borne fungus). Spray or dust to control aphids and spider mites; do not use chemicals if fruit has set. Control snails and slugs. Replace plants every 3 years (everbearers every other year). Use your own runner-grown plants only if they are disease free.

See variety chart for choices in regular strawberries.

Alpine strawberries. Also called wild strawberries or *fraises de bois,* these are worthwhile garden plants, although it takes lots of them to get much fruit. Plants produce no runners, but bear numerous tiny, long, slender berries from spring to fall. Fruit is fragrant and tasty. Raise from seed sown in early spring to fruit first summer. Extend plantings by dividing older plants. Often naturalize in partially shaded, well-watered gardens. Attractive informal low edging plant. Varieties are 'Alexandria', 'Baron Solemacher', and 'Harzland'. Occasionally seed of white or yellow forms is offered.

STRAWBERRY GERANIUM. See *Saxifraga stolonifera.*

STRAWBERRY TREE. See *Arbutus unedo.*

STRAWFLOWER. See *Helichrysum bracteatum.*

STREAM ORCHID. See *Epipactis gigantea.*

STRELITZIA. *Strelitziaceae.* BIRD OF PARADISE. Evergreen perennials. Tropical plants of extremely individual character. Need full sun in coastal areas, light shade inland. Both kinds are good to use by pools—make no litter and seem to withstand some splashing.

Strelitzia reginae

S. nicolai. GIANT BIRD OF PARADISE. Zones 22–24; with protection, Zones 12, 13. This one is grown for its dramatic display of leaves (similar to those of banana plants); flowers are incidental. Treelike, clumping, many stalks to 30 ft. Gray green, leathery, 5–10-ft. leaves are arranged fanwise on erect or curving trunks. Floral envelope is purplish gray, flower is white with dark blue tongue.

Feed young plants frequently to push to full dramatic size, then give little or no feeding. Goal is to acquire and maintain size without lush growth and need for dividing. Keep dead leaves cut off and thin out surplus growth. Endures temperatures to 28°F.

S. reginae. BIRD OF PARADISE. Outdoors in Zones 22–24; under overhangs where heat can be trapped, Zones 9, 12–21. Damaged at 28°–29°F. and recovers slowly; do not attempt where frost is likely. This one is grown for its spectacular flowers, startlingly like tropical birds. Orange, blue, and white flowers on long, stiff stems bloom intermittently throughout year, but best in cool season. Extremely long lasting. Official city flower of Los Angeles. Trunkless plants grow 5 ft. high with leathery, long-stalked, blue green, 1½-ft.-long leaves, 4–6 in. wide. Benefits greatly from frequent and heavy feedings. Divide infrequently, since large crowded clumps bloom best. Good in containers.

STREPTOCARPUS. *Gesneriaceae.* CAPE PRIMROSE. Evergreen perennials. Outdoors in Zones 17, 22–24; house plants everywhere. Related to African violets and gloxinias (*Sinningia*), and look something like a cross between the 2. Leaves are fleshy, sometimes velvety. Flowers are trumpet shaped, with long tube and spreading mouth. Long bloom season; some flower intermittently all year. Indoors, handle like African violets. Outdoors, give shady, cool, moist situation. Many species and hybrids of interest to fanciers; most widely available kinds are hybrids.

Streptocarpus hybrid

Large-flowered Hybrids (Giant Hybrids). Clumps of long, narrow leaves and 1-ft.-tall stems with long-tubed, 1½–2-in.-wide flowers in white, blue, pink, rose, red, often with contrasting blotches. Usually bloom after 1 year from seed.

Nymph series. Long-blooming plants grown from leaf cuttings. 'Constant Nymph', midblue, is best known; other named sorts available in purple, rose, red, white, pink. Flowers resemble those of Large-flowered Hybrids.

Wiesmoor Hybrids. Flowers fringed and crested, to 4–5 in. wide, on 2-ft. stems. Grow from seed.

S. saxorum. Unlike others; shrubby, much-branched perennial making spreading mound of furry, gray green, 1½-in.-long, fleshy leaves. Long-stemmed flowers appear in waves over much of year, pale blue and white, 1½ in. wide. Makes splendid hanging pot plant. Give African violet conditions, perhaps a bit more light. Among the hybrids, 'Concord Blue', with large flowers, blooms continuously.

STREPTOSOLEN jamesonii. *Solanaceae.* MARMALADE BUSH. Evergreen vining shrub. Outdoors in Zones 17, 23, 24; indoor/outdoor plant or with careful protection, Zones 13, 15, 16, 18–22. To 4–6 ft. tall and as wide (to 10–15 ft. trained against wall, bank, trellis). Leaves ribbed, oval, 1½ in. long. Flowers are 1 in. across, carried in large, loose clusters at branch ends. Color ranges from yellow to brilliant orange, but most types have orange flowers.

Streptosolen jamesonii

Big bloom season April–October (in most frost-free parts of Zones 23, 24, plants are occasionally everblooming, with good display in midwinter). Grow in warm spot with ample water, fast drainage.

In colder areas, protect plants from frost; cut back dead wood after last frost, thin and prune to shape. Good hanging basket plant (needs some protection from hottest sun). Strikingly effective spilling over a wall or lining garden stairs.

STRING OF BEADS. See *Senecio rowleyanus.*

Styracaceae. The storax family includes trees and shrubs with bell-shaped, usually white flowers. Members are *Halesia, Pterostyrax,* and *Styrax.*

STYRAX. *Styracaceae.* Deciduous trees, shrub. Pretty white bell-like flowers in hanging clusters.

S. japonicus. JAPANESE SNOWDROP TREE, JAPANESE SNOWBELL. Tree. Zones 3–10, 14–21. Slow to moderate growth to 30 ft. Slender, graceful trunk; branches often strongly horizontal, giving the tree a broad, flat top. Leaves oval, scallop edged, to 3 in. long; turn from dark green to red or yellow in fall. White, faintly fragrant flowers ¾ in. long hang on short side branches in June. Leaves angle upward from branches while flowers hang down, giving parallel green and white tiers.

Styrax japonicus

Needs reasonably good, well-drained garden soil. Full sun or part shade. Plenty of water. Prune to control shape; tends to be shrubby unless lower side branches suppressed. Splendid tree to look up into; plant it in raised beds near outdoor entertaining areas, or on high bank above path. Roots are not aggressive. 'Pendula' is a rare shrubby variety with weeping branches. 'Pink Chimes' is rarer still; it has pink flowers on a normal-sized tree.

S. obassia. FRAGRANT SNOWBELL. Tree. Zones 3–10, 14–21. To 20–30 ft. tall, rather narrow in spread. Roundish leaves 3–8 in. long, deep green. June flowers fragrant, ¾–1 in. long, carried in drooping, 6–8-in. clusters at ends of branches. Culture same as for *S. japonica.* Good against background of evergreens, or for height and contrast above border of rhododendrons and azaleas.

S. officinalis californicus (*S. californica*). CALIFORNIA STORAX. Zones 8, 9, 14–24. Shrub to 4–12 ft. Native to foothills of Sierra Nevada, inner Coast Ranges. Trunks gray, leaves 1–2 in. long, green above, gray underneath. Flowers (April–June) fragrant, white, drooping in clusters of 2 or 3, about an inch long. *S. o. fulvescens,* very similar, is native to mountains of southern California. Endures drought, heat, rocky soil.

SUCCULENT. Strictly speaking, a succulent is any plant that stores water in juicy leaves, stems, or roots to withstand periodic drought. Practically speaking, fanciers of succulents exclude such fleshy plants as epiphytic orchids and include in their collections many desert plants (yuccas, puyas) which are not fleshy. Although cacti are succulents, common consent sets them up as a separate category (see Cactus).

Most succulents come from desert or semidesert areas in warmer parts of the world. Mexico and South Africa are 2 very important sources. Some (notably sedums and sempervivums) come from colder climates, where they grow on sunny, rocky slopes and ledges.

Succulents are grown everywhere as house plants; in milder western climates, many are useful and decorative as landscaping plants, either in open ground or in containers. When well grown and well groomed, they look good all year, in bloom or out. Although considered low-maintenance plants, they look shabby if neglected; they may live through extended drought but will drop leaves, shrivel, or lose color. Amount of irrigation needed depends on summer heat, humidity of atmosphere. Plants in interior valleys may need water every 1–2 weeks; near the coast, water less. Give plants just enough water to keep them healthy, plump of leaf, and attractive.

One light feeding at start of growing season should be enough for plants in open ground. Larger-growing and later-blooming kinds may require additional feeding.

Some succulents make good ground covers. Some are sturdy and quick growing enough for erosion control on large banks.

(Continued on next page)

S

Other smaller kinds are useful among stepping stones or for creating patterns in small gardens. Most of these come easily from stem or leaf cuttings, and a stock can quickly be grown from a few plants. See: *Echeveria*, Ice Plant, *Portulacaria*, *Sedum*, *Senecio*.

Large-growing succulents have decorative value in themselves. See: *Aeonium*, *Agave*, *Aloe*, *Cotyledon*, *Crassula*, *Doryanthes*, *Dudleya*, *Echeveria*, *Kalanchoe*, *Portulacaria*, *Yucca*.

Many succulents have showy flowers. For some of the best, see: *Aloe*, some species of *Crassula*, *Hoya*, Ice Plant, *Kalanchoe*, *Rochea*.

Some smaller succulents are primarily collectors' items, grown for odd form or flowers. See: smaller species of *Aloe*, *Ceropegia*, *Crassula*, *Echeveria*, *Euphorbia*, *Haworthia*, *Lithops*, *Stapelia*.

A few words of caution to growers of succulents:

1. Not all succulents like hot sun; read species descriptions carefully. Some do not thrive in interior valley or desert summer heat, even if given some shade.
2. Variety of forms, colors, textures offers many possibilities for handsome combinations, but there's a fine line between successful grouping and jumbled medley. Beware of using too many kinds in one planting. Mass a few species instead of putting in one of each.
3. You can combine succulents with other types of plants, but plan combinations carefully. Not all plants look right with them. Consider also different cultural requirements.

SUGAR BUSH. See *Rhus ovata*.

SUGAR GUM. See *Eucalyptus cladocalyx*.

SULFUR FLOWER. See *Eriogonum umbellatum*.

SUMAC. See *Rhus*.

SUMMER CYPRESS. See *Kochia scoparia*.

SUMMER FORGET-ME-NOT. See *Anchusa capensis*.

SUMMER HOLLY. See *Comarostaphylis diversifolia*.

SUMMER HYACINTH. See *Galtonia candicans*.

SUMMER LILAC. See *Buddleia davidii*.

SUMMERSWEET. See *Clethra alnifolia*.

SUNDROPS. See *Oenothera tetragona*.

SUNFLOWER. See *Helianthus*.

SUNROSE. See *Helianthemum nummularium*, *Halimium*.

SURINAM CHERRY. See *Eugenia uniflora*.

SWAMP MAHOGANY. See *Eucalyptus robusta*.

SWAMP MALLEE. See *Eucalyptus spathulata*.

SWAN PLANT. See *Asclepias fruticosa*.

SWAN RIVER DAISY. See *Brachycome*.

SWAN RIVER PEA SHRUB. See *Brachysema lanceolatum*.

SWEDISH IVY. See *Plectranthus*.

SWEET ALYSSUM. See *Lobularia maritima*.

SWEET BALM. See *Melissa*.

SWEET BAY. See *Laurus nobilis*, *Magnolia virginiana*.

SWEET BRIAR. See *Rosa eglanteria*.

SWEET BRUSH. See *Cercocarpus betuloides*.

SWEET CICELY. See *Myrrhis odorata*.

SWEET GUM. See *Liquidambar*.

SWEET OLIVE. See *Osmanthus fragrans*.

SWEET PEA. See *Lathyrus odoratus*.

SWEET-PEA SHRUB. See *Polygala dalmaisiana*.

SWEET POTATO. *Convolvulaceae*. This vegetable is the thickened root of a trailing tropical vine closely related to morning glory (*Ipomoea*). Zones 8, 9, 14, 18–21; 12, 13 if well watered. Requires long frost-free season; much space; warm, well-drained, preferably sandy loam soil; and considerable work in getting started. The tubers are, moreover, tricky to store. All in all, only devoted gardeners will take trouble to order plants from specialist growers. Mark off rows 3 ft. apart, and ditch between them to form planting ridges 6–9 in. high. Set shoots with roots 5–6 in. deep so that only stem tips and leaves are exposed. Plants should be 14–16 in. apart. They tolerate dry soil once established. Harvest before first frost; dig carefully to avoid cutting or bruising roots. Dry in sun, then cure by storing 10–14 days in dry place at temperatures between 85°–95°F. Then store in cool (not below 55°F.) place to await use. Sometimes grown for its attractive foliage; handsome vine in hanging basket.

Sweet Potato

To grow sweet potato vine as house plant, push 3 toothpicks firmly into sweet potato at equal distances around tuber; these will support potato within rim of glass or jar of water. Adjust water level so it just touches tip end of tuber; it doesn't matter which end. Keep water touching base. Sprouts will grow from tuber and in 6 weeks you'll have lush vine with very attractive foliage. Vine will continue to grow until tuber shrivels. If nothing happens for several weeks, your sweet potato probably has been kiln dried or treated to prevent sprouting. Occasionally planted to cascade from high raised beds.

SWEETSHADE. See *Hymenosporum flavum*.

SWEET SULTAN. See *Centaurea moschata*.

SWEET WILLIAM. See *Dianthus barbatus*.

SWEET WOODRUFF. See *Galium odoratum*.

SWISS CHARD. *Chenopodiaceae*. One of the easiest and most practical of vegetables for home gardens in all Zones. Sow big, crinkly, tan seeds ½–¾ in. deep in spaded soil, in sunny position, any time from early spring to early summer. Thin seedlings to 1 ft. apart. Water enough to keep them growing. About

Swiss Chard

2 months after sowing (plants are generally 1–1½ ft. tall) you can begin to cut outside leaves from plants as needed for meals. New leaves grow up in center of plants. Yield all summer and seldom bolt to seed (if one does, pull it up and throw it away). In desert, plant in fall; doesn't stand up to summer heat there.

Regular green and white chard looks presentable in flower garden. Rhubarb chard has red stems, reddish green leaves, and makes attractive plant in garden beds or containers. Its leaves are valuable in floral arranging and tasty when cooked, too—sweeter and stronger flavored than green chard. Both leaves and leaf stalks are edible, but best cooked separately. Stems take longer to cook. Swiss chard is actually a form of beet.

SWISS CHEESE PLANT. See *Monstera friedrichsthalii.*

SWORD FERN. See *Nephrolepis, Polystichum munitum.*

SYCAMORE. See *Platanus.*

SYDNEY BLUE GUM. See *Eucalyptus saligna.*

SYMPHORICARPOS. *Caprifoliaceae.* Deciduous shrubs. North American natives. Low growing, often spreading by root suckers. Small, pink-tinged or white flowers in clusters or spikes. Attractive round, berrylike fruit remains on stems after leaves fall; nice in winter arrangements, attracts birds. Best used as wild thicket in sun or shade for erosion control on steep banks.

Symphoricarpos albus

S. albus *(S. racemosus).* COMMON SNOWBERRY. All Zones. Upright or spreading shrub 2–6 ft. tall. Leaves roundish, dull green, ¾–2 in. long (to 4 in. and often lobed on sucker shoots). Pink flowers May–June; white, ½-in.-wide fruit from late summer to winter. Drought tolerant. Best fruit production in sun. Not a first-rank shrub, but useful in its tolerance of poor soil, urban air, and shade. Withstands neglect.

S. chenaultii. All Zones. Hybrid of garden origin. Resembles *S. orbiculatus,* but red fruit is lightly spotted white and leaves are larger. *S. c.* 'Hancock' is 1-ft. dwarf of special value as woodland ground or bank cover.

S. mollis. CREEPING SNOWBERRY, SPREADING SNOWBERRY. Zones 4–24. Like *S. albus,* but usually less than 1½ ft. high, earlier flowering, fewer flowers, smaller fruit. Spreads like ground cover. Best in part shade; tolerates drought.

S. orbiculatus *(S. vulgaris).* CORAL BERRY, INDIAN CURRANT. All Zones. Resembles *S. albus,* but with profusion of small purplish red fruit in clusters. These are bright enough and plentiful enough to provide a good fall-winter show.

SYMPHYTUM officinale. *Boraginaceae.* COMFREY. Perennial. All Zones. Deep-rooted, clumping perennial to 3 ft. Basal leaves 8 in. or more in length, upper leaves smaller, all furry with stiff hairs. Flowers not showy, ½ in. long, usually dull rose, sometimes white, creamy, or purple. Leaves have been used as food for people or livestock, or dried as medicinal tea—but they contain a poison, pyrrolizidine, and should not be eaten. Plants take full sun or partial shade, average garden water. Leaves grow all year in coastal southern California. Plants go dormant elsewhere. To keep leaf production high, cut out flowering stalks and mulch each spring with compost. Grow from root cuttings.

Symphytum officinale

Although comfrey has a long history as food and as a folk remedy, think hard before establishing it in your garden. Plants spread freely from roots and are difficult to eradicate. Herb enthusiasts claim that comfrey accumulates minerals, enriches compost.

SYNADENIUM grantii. *Euphorbiaceae.* Evergreen shrub. Zones 21–24; indoor/outdoor plant anywhere. Can reach 12 ft. in warm, frost-free location, but is usually much lower. Thick stems filled with milky, poisonous sap are clothed with dark green leaves to 7 in. long and half as wide. More widely grown than the species is *S. g.* 'Rubra', with deep purplish red leaves. Flowers are insignificant. Resembles *Euphorbia cotinifolia,* but easily distinguished by leaves that taper toward the main stems and are stalkless; leaves of *E. cotinifolia* have long stalks.

Synadenium grantii

Showy container plant for a hot, sunny terrace.

SYNGONIUM podophyllum (often sold as *Nephthytis afzelii*). *Araceae.* Evergreen climbing perennial grown as house plant. Succeeds outdoors in sheltered patios in Zones 13, 23, 24. Dwarf, slow growing. Related to philodendron. It has long-stalked, arrow-shaped, dull green leaves, sometimes lobed. Flowers insignificant. Easy to grow in pots of rich house plant mix. Useful in terrarium, dish garden, as a trailer, or trained against support in manner of vining philodendron. Can grow to 10–15 ft. with support. Many varieties, including 'Ruth Fraser', silvery leaves bordered green; 'Trileaf Wonder', green leaves covered with whitish powder; 'California Silver Wonder', narrow, silvery leaves.

Syngonium podophyllum

SYRINGA. *Oleaceae.* LILAC. Deciduous shrubs, rarely small trees. Best known are common lilac (*S. vulgaris*) and its many named varieties, but there are other species of great usefulness. Best where winter brings pronounced chill, but some bloom well with light chilling. Sun; light shade in hottest areas. All like alkaline soil; in areas where soils are strongly acid, add lime and cultivate into soil beneath drip line of plants. Average watering best, but can take some drought when established. Do not, however, limit water when plants are coming into bloom and making new growth. Control growth during early years by pinching and shaping. Flower buds for next year form in pairs where leaves join stems. After bloom, remove spent flower clusters just above points where buds are forming. Heavy pruning results in loss of much of next year's bloom. Thin out dead and weak wood at same time.

Syringa vulgaris

Renovate old, overgrown plants by cutting a few of oldest stems to the ground each year. Leaf miner, scale, and stem borer are the only important pests; bacterial blight, leaf spot, downy mildew are occasional problems.

S. chinensis *(S. rothomagensis).* CHINESE LILAC. Zones 1–11, 14–16, 18–21. Hybrid between common and Persian lilacs. Moderate growth rate to 15 ft., usually much less. More graceful than common lilac, with finer-textured foliage. Airy, open clusters of fragrant rose purple flowers in May (April in warmer Zones). Profuse bloom. Does well in mild-winter, hot-summer climates. Variety 'Alba' has white flowers.

S. hyacinthiflora. Zones 1–12, 14–16, 18–22. Hybrids between common lilac and *S. oblata,* a Chinese species. 'Excel' and 'Grace McKenzie' (both single lilac) can bloom as early as March 1. Other varieties are 'Alice Eastwood' (double magenta), 'Blue Hyacinth' (single lavender blue), 'Clarke's Giant' (single lavender blue, large flowers), 'Esther Staley' (single magenta), 'Gertrude Leslie' (double white), 'Pocahontas' (single purple), 'Purple Heart' (single purple), and 'White Hyacinth' (single white).

(Continued on next page)

S

S. josikaea. HUNGARIAN LILAC. Zones 1–11, 14–16, 18–21. Dense, upright growth to 12 ft. Dark green foliage. Flowers lilac purple, slightly fragrant, in narrow clusters 4–7 in. long. Blooms in May (April in warmer Zones).

S. laciniata *(S. persica laciniata)*. Zones 1–12, 14–16, 18–21. Moderate growth to 8 ft. tall, open habit, good rich green foliage color. Leaves to 2½ in. long, divided nearly to midrib into 3–9 segments. Many small clusters of fragrant lilac flowers in April, May.

S. patula *(S. palibiniana, S. velutina)*. KOREAN LILAC. Zones 1–9, 14–16. Dense, twiggy growth to eventual 8–9 ft., but stays at 3 ft. many years. Flowers pink to lavender, in clusters to 5 in. long. Blooms April–May. Sometimes grafted high to make 3-ft. standard tree. 'Miss Kim' is dwarf (to 3-ft.) lavender blue variety.

S. persica. PERSIAN LILAC. Zones 1–12, 14–16, 18–21. Graceful, loose form to 6 ft., with arching branches and 2½-in.-long leaves. Many clusters of fragrant pale violet flowers appear all along branches in May (April in warmer areas).

S. prestoniae. Zones 1–12, 14–16. To 10–15 ft. tall. Group of extra-hardy hybrids developed in Canada. Medium to large shrubs that bloom on new spring growth after other lilacs have finished. 'Isabella' (single lilac), 'Jessica' (single violet), 'Nocturne' (blue), and 'Royalty' (purple to violet) are good selections. For 'James MacFarlane' (sometimes sold as member of this group), see *S. swegiflexa*.

S. reticulata *(S. japonica, S. amurensis japonica)*. JAPANESE TREE LILAC. Large shrub easily trained as single-stemmed 30-ft. tree. Zones 1–12, 14–16. Bark smooth, something like cherry in its gloss. Large leaves (to 5 in. long). White flower clusters to 1 ft. appear in late spring, early summer. Flowers showy, but not fragrant; they smell like privet flowers. Useful small shade or street tree in difficult climates.

S. swegiflexa. Zones 1–9, 14–16. To 12 ft. Single pink flowers open from deep reddish buds. Clusters to 8 in. long. Blooms 3 weeks after common lilac. Sometimes sold as PINK PEARL LILAC. Hybrid between 2 hardy Chinese species, *S. reflexa* and *S. sweginzowii*. 'James MacFarlane' is best-known variety.

S. vulgaris. COMMON LILAC. Zones 1–12. In Zones 14–16, 18–22, plants often bloom irregularly because of failure to break dormancy after mild winters. It was once recommended that plants be gradually but completely dried off beginning in August. It is now felt that such treatment can harm the plant, possibly kill it. Water may be restricted at this time, but should always be available. To accept mild winters, and perform exeptionally well in Zones 18–22, the Descanso Hybrids were developed in southern California. Best known is 'Lavender Lady' (lavender); other varieties are 'Blue Skies' and 'Blue Boy' (blue), 'Chiffon' (lavender), 'Forrest K. Smith' (light lavender), 'Sylvan Beauty' (rose lavender), and 'White Angel' (or 'Angel White').

Common lilacs can eventually reach 20 ft. tall, with nearly equal spread. Leaves roundish oval, pointed, dark green, to 5 in. long. Pinkish or bluish lavender flowers ('Alba' has pure white flowers) in clusters to 10 in. long or more. Flowers in May; fragrance is legendary. Excellent cut flowers. Lilac fanciers swear these are more fragrant than newer varieties.

Varieties, often called French hybrids, number in the hundreds. They generally flower a little later than species and have larger clusters of single or double flowers in wide range of colors. Singles are often as showy as doubles, sometimes more so. All lilacs require 2–3 years to settle down and produce flowers of full size and true color. Here are just a few of the many choice varieties:

'Charles Joly' (double dark purplish red), 'Miss Ellen Willmott' (double pure white), 'Ludwig Spaeth' (single reddish purple to dark purple), 'President Lincoln' (single Wedgwood blue), 'President Poincare' (double 2-tone purple), 'Sensation' (single wine red with white picotee edge), 'William Robinson' (double pink).

Some experts call hybrids between *S. vulgaris* and *S. oblata* *S. hyacinthiflora*. These bloom earlier than the French hybrids by a week or 10 days. 'Blue Hyacinth' and 'Clarke's Giant' (blue) and 'Esther Staley' (deep pink) are typical.

SYZYGIUM. *Myrtaceae.* Evergreen shrubs or trees. Closely related to *Eugenia* and usually sold as such in nurseries. Foliage rich green, often tinted coppery; new foliage brightly tinted. Flowers conspicuous for tufts of stamens that look like little brushes. Fruit is soft, edible, handsomely colored. Grow best in sun with ample water. Tolerate shade.

Syzygium paniculatum

S. jambos *(Eugenia jambos)*. ROSE APPLE. Zones 18–24. Slow growth to 25–30 ft., usually much smaller and shrubby. Leaves 5–8 in. long, narrow, thick, shiny, coppery green; new growth pinkish. Greenish white flower brushes 2–3 in. across in clusters at branch ends. Spring bloom. Fruit greenish or yellow (sometimes blushed pink), 1–2 in. wide; sweetish, with mild flavor, fragrance of rosewater. Slow growth means little or no pruning.

S. paniculatum *(Eugenia myrtifolia, E. paniculata)*. BRUSH CHERRY, AUSTRALIAN BRUSH CHERRY. Zones 16, 17, 19–24. Unclipped, a handsome, narrowish tree, to 30–60 ft. tall. Single or multitrunked, with dense foliage crown. Usually clipped into formal shapes and hedges, and a most popular hedging, background, and screening plant in mild, nearly frost-free areas. Young foliage reddish bronze; mature leaves oblong, 1½–3 in. long, rich glossy green, often bronze tinged. Flowers white or creamy, ½ in. wide, with feathery tufts of stamens. Fruit is rose purple, showy, ¾ in. long, edible but insipid.

Will not stand heavy frost; foliage burns at 25°–26°F., and even old plants may die if temperature drops much lower. Thrives in well-drained garden soil. Hedges need frequent clipping to stay neat, and heavy root systems make it hard to grow other plants nearby; new red foliage, showy fruit make it worth the effort. Don't plant where dropping fruit will squash on pavement.

Variety 'Compacta' is smaller, denser in growth. Very popular hedging plant. 'Brea' and 'Globulus' are also dwarf and compact, with bronzy amber foliage color. Tiniest of all is 'Teenie Genie'; it grows very slowly to 4 ft. 'Red Flame' has new growth of exceptionally bright red.

TABEBUIA. *Bignoniaceae.* Briefly deciduous, sometimes evergreen trees. Zones 15, 16, 20–24; in warm locations, Zones 12, 13. Fast growth to 25–30 ft. Very showy, 2–4-in.-long, trumpet-shaped flowers grow in rounded clusters which become larger (up to 23 flowers) and more profuse as trees mature. Leaves dark olive green, usually divided into 3–7 leaflets arranged like fingers of hand.

Tabebuia chrysotricha

Useful as patio trees or as free-standing flowering trees for display. Tolerate many soils and degrees of maintenance, but respond well to feeding and frequent watering. Once established, can also take much drought. Good drainage essential. Stake while young and keep plants to single leading shoot until 6–8 ft. tall, then allow to develop freely. Hardy to about 24°F.

T. avellanedae *(T. ipe)*. More erect, larger growing than *T. chrysotricha*. Leaves dark green, smooth. Tree usually evergreen. Flowers 2–3 in. long, lavender pink with white throat banded yellow. Blooms late winter, sometimes again late summer to fall. Does not bloom as young tree.

T. chrysotricha (sometimes sold as *T. pulcherrima*). GOLDEN TRUMPET TREE. Rounded, spreading growth to 25 ft. Leaves with 5 leaflets (2–4 in. long, 1–2 in. wide); young twigs, undersides of leaves covered with tawny fuzz. Flowers are 3–4 in. long, golden yellow, often with maroon stripes in throat. Bloom heaviest April–May, when trees lose leaves for brief period. Sometimes blooms lightly at other times with leaves present. Blooms young.

TAGETES. *Compositae.* MARIGOLD. Summer annuals, perennials. Robust, free-branching, nearly trouble-free plants ranging from 6 in.–4 ft. tall, with flowers from pale yellow through gold to orange and brown maroon. Leaves finely divided, ferny, usually strongly scented. Plants will bloom early summer to frost if old flowers are picked off; in desert, they bloom best in fall, until frost. Handsome, long-lasting cut flowers; strong scent permeates a room, but some odorless varieties are available. Easy to grow from seed, which sprouts in a few days in warm soil; to get earlier bloom, start seeds in flats or buy flat-grown plants. Full sun, ample water. Smog will damage tender young plants, but they toughen up.

Tagetes erecta

It is widely believed that marigold roots can entrap, destroy, or repel nematodes. University tests discount this belief.

T. erecta. AMERICAN MARIGOLD, AFRICAN MARIGOLD (often sold simply as TALL MARIGOLD). Original strains were plants 3–4 ft. tall with single flowers. Modern strains are more varied, and most have fully double flowers. They range from dwarf Guys and Dolls and Inca series (12–14 in.) through Galore, Lady, and Perfection (16–20 in.) to Climax (2½–3 ft.). Novelty tall strains are Odorless and First Whites (28–30 in.). 'Snowbird' (1½ ft.) is a white marigold with uniform habit and color.

Triploid Hybrids, crosses between African and French marigolds, have exceptional vigor and a long bloom season. They are generally shorter than other *T. erecta* strains and bear an enormous profusion of 2-in. flowers. They range from the 10-in. Nugget to the 12–14-in. Fireworks, H-G, Solar, and Sundance.

Avoid overhead watering on taller kinds, or stems will sag and perhaps break. To make tall plants stand as firmly as possible (perhaps stoutly enough to do without staking), dig planting holes extra deep, strip any leaves off lower 1–3 in. of stem, and plant with stripped portion below soil line.

T. filifolia. IRISH LACE. Mounds of bright green, finely divided foliage, 6 in. tall and as wide, resemble unusually fluffy round ferns. Used primarily as edging plant for foliage effect, but tiny white flowers in late summer and fall are attractive.

T. lemmonii. Shrubby perennial. Zones 8–10, 12–24. Native from southeastern Arizona (where it can reach 3 ft.) to southern Mexico and Central America, where it is a shrub to 6 ft. or taller, spreading as wide as it's high. Finely divided 4-in. leaves are aromatic when brushed against or rubbed—a strongly fragrant blend of marigold, mint, and lemon. To some people the odor of the foliage is too strong; it will not trouble you if you don't brush against the plant. Golden orange flower heads are carried in broad sheaves at ends of branches. Bloom is scattered throughout the year, heaviest winter–spring. Damaged by frost in open situations; cut back to remove damaged growth or to correct shape and limit size.

T. lucida. MEXICAN TARRAGON. Perennial in Zones 8, 9, 14–24 (but usually grown as an annual); annual elsewhere. Single, usually unbranched stems grow to 2–2½ ft. Narrow, uncut, smooth dark green leaves have strong scent and flavor of tarragon. Unimpressive yellow flowers are less than ½ in. wide.

T. patula. FRENCH MARIGOLD. Varieties from 6–18 in. tall, in flower colors from yellow to rich maroon brown; flowers may be fully double or single, and many are strongly bicolored. Best for edging are the dwarf, very double Janie (8 in.), Bonanza (10 in.), and Hero (10–12 in.) series in a range of colors from yellow through orange to red and brownish red. The Aurora and Sophia series have flowers that are larger (2½ in. wide) but not as double.

T. tenuifolia *(T. signata).* SIGNET MARIGOLD. Relatively infrequently planted species. Smaller flower heads than French marigold, but incredibly profuse in bloom. Finely cut foliage. Golden orange 'Golden Gem' ('Ursula') and bright yellow 'Lemon Gem' both grow 8 in. tall.

TALLHEDGE BUCKTHORN. See *Rhamnus frangula* 'Columnaris'.

TAM. See *Juniperus sabina* 'Tamariscifolia'.

TAMARACK. See *Larix occidentalis.* Lodgepole pine (*Pinus contorta latifolia*) is also called tamarack in some regions.

TAMARIX. *Tamaricaceae.* TAMARISK. Deciduous and evergreen-appearing shrubs and trees. In deserts of California and Arizona, they have no equal in resistance to wind and drought, and they will grow in saline soils that are toxic to other plants. Fire retardant if reasonably well watered. Nurseries can't keep them in containers long because they form deep taproots. But they are easy to grow from ½–1-in.-thick cuttings set in place and kept watered.

Tamarix aphylla

There is much confusion in labeling of tamarisks in the nurseries. There is almost equal confusion among botanists; these plants are simply very difficult to classify. Leaves and flowers are individually tiny, and hand lens is necessary to see flower details. As far as the gardener is concerned, there are 3 kinds—evergreen-appearing, spring-flowering, and spring-through-summer-flowering trees.

Evergreen-appearing Tree

T. aphylla *(T. articulata).* ATHEL TREE. Widely used in Zones 10–13; useful in some difficult situations in Zones 7–9, 14–24. Heavily damaged at 0°F. but comes back rapidly. Excellent windbreak tree. Fast growth from planted cuttings to 10 ft. or more in 3 years; eventually 30–50 ft. and more in 15 years with deep soil and water.

Greenish jointed branchlets give tree its evergreen appearance. Takes on grayish look in late summer where soils are saline, due to secretions of salt. True leaves are minute. White to pinkish, very small flowers grow in clusters at ends of branches in late summer, but tree is not as spectacular in bloom as other tamarisks. Not a good selection for highly cultivated gardens; its roots are too competitive.

Spring-flowering Tamarisks

These are hardy and adapted in all Zones. Fast growth to 6–15 ft., depending on culture. Graceful, airy, arching branches with reddish bark. Pink flowers in clusters on branches of previous year. Prune after bloom in spring to maintain graceful effect, limit height, and produce new flowering wood.

T. africana. Bears its flowers in upright, 1–2-in.-long clusters of white or very pale pink. For plants sold and widely used under this name in California, see *T. parviflora.*

T. parviflora (often sold as *T. tetrandra;* sold as *T. africana* in California). Profuse display of pink, 4-petaled flowers. These turn to tan, then brown; prune hard after bloom to remove.

Spring-through-summer-flowering Tamarisks

T. chinensis *(T. pentandra, T. juniperina, T. ramosissima, T. japonica).* SALT CEDAR. The many names result from the variability in flower color, bloom season, and plant habit. Blooms may come from March to October and vary from white through cream and various pinks to deep purple; they may bloom on last year's wood before growth begins or later in summer on new wood. Looks best if pruned to ground in early spring; if so treated, will remain 6–12-ft. shrub and bloom heavily July to fall, giving masses of large plumes. Unpruned, it can become 20–30-ft. rank-growing shrub with highly competitive root system. Tiny leaves are pale blue green. This plant, a native of China, has under certain circumstances become an aggressive weed in the Southwest. Its deep, thirsty roots use ground water at a remarkable rate.

TAMPALA. See *Amaranthus tricolor.*

T

TANACETUM vulgare. *Compositae.* COMMON TANSY. Perennial herb. All Zones. Coarse garden plant with history of medicinal use. To 3 ft. Finely cut, bright green, aromatic leaves; small, buttonlike yellow flowers. Any soil, full sun. Fairly drought tolerant. Start from seed or division of roots. Thin clumps yearly to keep in bounds. Foliage and flowers keep well in bouquets.

T. v. crispum. FERN-LEAF TANSY. To 2½ ft.; more decorative than the species.

Tanacetum vulgare

TANBARK OAK. See *Lithocarpus densiflorus.*

TANGELO. See *Citrus.*

TANGERINE. See *Citrus.*

TANGOR. See *Citrus.*

TANSY. See *Tanacetum vulgare.*

TARO. See *Colocasia esculenta.*

TARRAGON, FRENCH or TRUE. See *Artemisia dracunculus.*

TARRAGON, MEXICAN. See *Tagetes lucida.*

TASMANIAN TREE FERN. See *Dicksonia antarctica.*

TASSEL FERN. See *Polystichum polyblepharum.*

Taxaceae. The yew family contains needle-leafed evergreens with single-seeded fruit surrounded by a fleshy coat. Yew (*Taxus*) and California nutmeg (*Torreya*) are examples.

Taxodiaceae. The taxodium family contains evergreen (rarely deciduous) coniferous trees, usually with small cones containing 2–6 seeds on each scale. Bald cypress and Montezuma cypress (*Taxodium*) give the group its name. *Cryptomeria,* redwood, and giant sequoia are other examples.

TAXODIUM. *Taxodiaceae.* Deciduous or evergreen trees. Conifers of considerable size bearing short, narrow, flat, needlelike leaves in graceful sprays. Cones are scented. One of the trees below is native to the southeastern U.S., the other to Mexico, but both show remarkably wide adaptation to colder and drier climates.

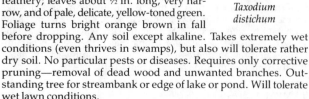

Taxodium distichum

T. distichum. BALD CYPRESS. Deciduous tree. Zones 2–9, 14–24. Also thrives in wet places in Zones 10, 12, 13. Can grow into 100-ft.-tall, broad-topped tree in the wild, but young and middle-aged garden trees are pyramidal. Foliage sprays very delicate and feathery; leaves about ½ in. long, very narrow, and of pale, delicate, yellow-toned green. Foliage turns bright orange brown in fall before dropping. Any soil except alkaline. Takes extremely wet conditions (even thrives in swamps), but also will tolerate rather dry soil. No particular pests or diseases. Requires only corrective pruning—removal of dead wood and unwanted branches. Outstanding tree for streambank or edge of lake or pond. Will tolerate wet lawn conditions.

T. mucronatum. MONTEZUMA CYPRESS. Evergreen tree in mild climates; partially or wholly deciduous in cold regions. Zones 5, 6, 8–10, 12–14. Has strongly weeping branches. Fast grower in its youth; with ample water will reach 40 ft. in 14 years, and is likely to reach eventual 75 ft. in gardens. Established plants are fairly drought tolerant, but growth is slow under drought conditions. Extremely graceful, fine-textured evergreen for large lawns.

TAXUS. *Taxaceae.* YEW. Evergreen shrubs or trees. Zones 3–9, 14–24. Conifers, but instead of cones they bear fleshy, scarlet (rarely yellow), cup-shaped, single-seeded fruit. Fruit (seeds) and foliage poisonous if eaten. In general, yews are more formal, darker green, and more tolerant of shade and moisture than most cultivated conifers. Slow growing, long lived, tolerant of much shearing and pruning. Excellent basic landscape plants for hedges, screens.

Taxus baccata 'Stricta'

Easily moved even when large, but slow growth makes big plants a luxury item. Take many soil conditions, but will not thrive in strongly alkaline or strongly acid soils. Once established, fairly drought tolerant. Grow well in shade or sun, but reflected light and heat from hot south or west wall will burn foliage. Even cold-hardy kinds show needle damage when exposed to bright winter sun, dry winds, very low temperatures.

Only female plants produce berries, but many do so without male plants nearby. Considered disease free; the few pests include vine weevils, scale, and spider mites. All yews benefit from being washed off with water from hose every 2 weeks during hot, dry weather.

T. baccata. ENGLISH YEW. Slow growth to 25–40 ft., with wide-spreading branches forming broad, low crown. Needles ½–1½ in. long, dark green and glossy above, pale underneath. Red fruit has poisonous seeds. Garden varieties are far more common than the species.

T. b. 'Adpressa' (usually sold as *T. brevifolia,* which is really the native western yew). Wide-spreading, dense shrub to 4–5 ft. high; leaves about ½ in. long.

T. b. 'Aurea'. More compact than the species. New foliage is golden yellow spring to autumn, then turns green.

T. b. 'Erecta'. Erect and formal. Less compact than *T. b.* 'Stricta', and with smaller leaves.

T. b. 'Repandens'. SPREADING ENGLISH YEW. Long, horizontal, spreading branches make 2-ft.-high ground cover. Useful low foundation plant. Will arch over wall.

T. b. 'Repandens Aurea'. Golden new growth; otherwise like *T. b.* 'Repandens'.

T. b. 'Stricta' ('Fastigiata'). IRISH YEW. Makes column of very dark green. Slow growing to 20 ft. or higher. Needles larger than those of English yew. Many crowded upright branches tend to spread near top, especially in snowy regions or where water is ample, growth lush. Branches can be tied together with wire. Plants that outgrow their space can be reduced by heading back and thinning; old wood sprouts freely. Striking against big wall, in corner plantings, or as background planting. Very drought tolerant once established.

T. b. 'Stricta Aurea'. New foliage has golden color.

T. b. 'Stricta Variegata'. Like Irish yew, but leaves show yellowish white variegations.

T. brevifolia. WESTERN or OREGON YEW. Zones 1–6, 14–17. Native to moist places, California north to Alaska, inland to Montana. Tree of loose, open growth to 50–60 ft. with dark yellowish green needles 1 in. or less in length. Not common in nature and very difficult to grow. Most plants sold under this name are *T. baccata* 'Adpressa' or *T. cuspidata* 'Nana'.

T. cuspidata. JAPANESE YEW. Zones 1–6, 14–17. Tree to 50 ft. in Japan. Most useful yew in cold-winter areas east of the Cascades. Varieties will grow in shaded areas of Rocky Mountain gardens. Usually grown as compact, spreading shrub. Needles ½–1 in.

long, usually in 2 rows along twigs, making flat or V-shaped spray. Foliage dark green above, tinged yellowish underneath.

T. c. 'Capitata'. Plants sold under this name are probably ordinary *T. cuspidata* in its upright, pyramidal form. Dense, slow growth to 10–25 ft. Can be held lower by pinching new growth. Fruits heavily.

T. c. 'Densiformis'. Much-branched, very low, dense, spreading plant with dark green foliage.

T. c. 'Nana' (often sold as *T. brevifolia*). Grows slowly (1–4 in. a year) to 3 ft. tall and spreads to 6 ft. (in 20 years). Good low barrier or foundation plant.

T. media. Group of hybrids between Japanese and English yew. Intermediate between the 2 in color and texture.

T. m. 'Brownii'. Slow-growing, compact, rounded yew eventually 4–8 ft. tall. Good for low, dense hedge.

T. m. 'Hatfieldii'. Broad columnar or pyramidal yew of good dark green color. Grows 10 ft. or taller.

T. m. 'Hicksii'. Narrow, upright yew, slightly broader at center than at top and bottom; to 10–12 ft.

TEA. See *Camellia sinensis*.

TEABERRY. See *Gaultheria procumbens*.

TEA TREE. See *Leptospermum*.

TECOMA. *Bignoniaceae*. Various trumpet vines once lumped together as *Tecoma* now have different names. What remains is a showy large shrub or small tree.

T. australis. See *Pandorea pandorana*.

T. capensis. See *Tecomaria capensis*.

T. jasminoides. See *Pandorea jasminoides*.

T. stans *(Stenolobium stans).* YELLOW BELLS, YELLOW TRUMPET FLOWER, YELLOW ELDER. Evergreen shrub or small tree. Zones 12, 13, 21–24. In mildest-winter areas, can be trained as tree. Where frosts are common, it is usually a large shrub. Much of wood may die back in winter, but recovery is quick in warm weather: very rapid, bushy growth to 20 ft. Leaves divided into 5–13 toothed, 1½–4-in.-long leaflets. Flowers (June–January) bright yellow, bell shaped, 2 in. across, in large clusters. Needs heat, water, deep soil, fairly heavy feeding. Cut faded flowers to prolong bloom; prune to remove dead and brushy growth. Very showy mass in large garden. Boundary plantings, big shrub borders, screening. *T. s. angustata*, with narrow leaflets, is kind best adapted to Zones 12 and 13; it needs less water and feeding. June–October bloom.

Tecoma stans

TECOMARIA capensis *(Tecoma capensis).* *Bignoniaceae*. CAPE HONEYSUCKLE. Evergreen vine or shrub. Zones 12, 13, 16, 18–24; Zones 14, 15 with protection. Native to South Africa. Can scramble to 15–25 ft. if tied to support. With hard pruning, a 6–8-ft. upright shrub. Leaves divided into many glistening dark green leaflets. Total foliage effect is informal and fine textured. Brilliant orange red, tubular, 2-in. blossoms grow in compact clusters, October through winter.

Tecomaria capensis

Needs good drainage. Takes sun, heat, wind, salt air, some drought when established. Tolerates light shade. Use as espalier, bank cover (especially good on hot, steep slopes), coarse barrier hedge.

Variety 'Aurea' has yellow flowers and lighter green foliage; it's smaller growing and less showy. Requires more heat to perform well.

TEDDYBEAR CACTUS. See *Opuntia bigelovii*.

TELLIMA grandiflora. *Saxifragaceae*. FRINGECUPS. Perennial. Zones 4–9, 14–17. Creeping rootstocks send up roundish, lobed leaves to 4 in. across on leaf stalks up to 8 in. long. Leaves are light green, softly hairy, somewhat like those of piggyback plant (*Tolmiea*). Small, urn-shaped flowers with tiny fringed petals open green, age to deep red; these are not showy, but are attractively disposed along tall (to 2½-ft.), slender stems. Evergreen where winters are mild, deciduous in colder parts of its native range—central California north to southern Alaska. Choice with ferns in woodland garden. Needs water when growing. Takes summer drought if shaded.

Tellima grandiflora

TERNSTROEMIA gymnanthera *(T. japonica).* *Theaceae*. Evergreen shrub. Zones 4–9, 12–24. It takes a long time to reach 6–8 ft. and is usually seen as rounded plant 3–4 ft. tall and 4–6 ft. wide. Its appeal lies in its glossy, leathery foliage. Red-stalked, rounded oval to narrow oval leaves are 1½–3 in. long, bronzy red when new; when mature, they turn deep green to bronzy green to purplish red, depending on season, exposure, and plant itself. Plants in deep shade tend to be dark green; with some sun, leaves may be bronzy green to nearly purple red. Red tints are deeper in cold weather.

Ternstroemia gymnanthera

Summer flowers are ½ in. wide, creamy yellow, fragrant but not showy. Fruit (uncommon on small plants) resembles little yellow to red orange holly berries or cherries, splits open to reveal shiny black seeds.

Full sun to partial shade (full shade in Zones 12, 13). Ample moisture—and the more sun plants get, the greater the water need. Leaves turn yellow if soil isn't acid enough—feed with acid plant food. Pinch out tip growth to encourage compact growth. Use as basic landscaping shrub, informal hedge, tub plant. Good near pools. Grows well and blends well with camellias (to which it is related), azaleas, nandina, pieris, ferns. Cut foliage keeps well.

TETRAPANAX papyriferus *(Aralia papyrifera).* *Araliaceae*. RICE PAPER PLANT. Evergreen shrub. Zones 15–24. Fast growing to 10–15 ft., often multitrunked. Big, bold, long-stalked leaves are 1–2 ft. wide, deeply lobed, gray green above, white-felted beneath, carried in clusters at ends of stems. Fuzz on new growth irritating if it gets in eyes or down the neck. Tan trunks often curve or lean. Big, branched clusters of creamy white flowers on furry tan stems show in December.

Sun or shade (midday shade in hottest summer areas). Young plants sunburn easily, older ones adapt. Nearly any soil. Needs only average garden watering, but for best appearance, should never be drought stressed. Few pests; seems to suffer only from high winds (which break or tatter leaves) and frost (foliage severely damaged at 22°F., but plants recover fast from freezes, often put up suckers to form thickets). Digging around roots stimulates sucker formation; suckers may arise 20 ft. from parent plant.

Tetrapanax papyriferus

Use as silhouette against walls, in patios; combine with other sturdy, bold-leafed plants for tropical effect. Name comes from the thick pith of the stems, used to make Chinese rice paper.

T

TETRASTIGMA voinieranum *(Cissus voinierana).* *Vitaceae.* Evergreen vine. Zones 13 (shade only), 17, 20–24. Climbs by tendrils or covers ground rapidly to 50–60 ft. Thick, fleshy stems. New growth covered with silvery fuzz. Leaves glossy, dark green, up to 1 ft. across, divided fanwise into 3–5 oval, leathery leaflets with toothed edges. Flowers and fruit are rarely seen. Needs ample water; feed until well established. Plant so roots are shaded while top can run out or up to sun. Good eave-line decoration. Large-scale bank or ground cover in Zones 17, 23, 24. Good near swimming pools.

Tetrastigma voinieranum

TEUCRIUM. *Labiatae.* GERMANDER. Evergreen shrubs or subshrubs. Tough plants for sun and heat, enduring poor, rocky soils; established plants are quite drought tolerant. They can't stand wet or poorly drained soils, but will take ordinary garden watering where drainage is good.

T. chamaedrys. All Zones. Low growing (to 1 ft. tall), spreading to 2 ft., with many upright, woody-based stems densely set with toothed, dark green, ¾-in.-long leaves. In summer, red purple or white, ¾-in. flowers form in loose spikes (white-flowered form is looser). Attractive to bees. Use as edging, foreground, low clipped hedge, or small-scale ground cover. To keep neat, shear back once or twice a year to force side branching. As ground cover, set plants 2 ft. apart. Fire-retardant if reasonably well watered.

Teucrium chamaedrys

T. c. 'Prostratum'. Leaves and flowers similar to those of *T. chamaedrys*, but growth habit is very prostrate (4–6 in. high and spreading to 3 ft. or more).

T. fruticans. BUSH GERMANDER. Zones 4–24. Loose, silvery-stemmed shrub to 4–8 ft. tall and as wide or wider. Leaves 1¼ in. long, gray green above, silvery white beneath, giving overall silvery gray effect. Lavender blue, ¾-in.-long flowers in spikes at branch ends through most of year. Thin and cut back in late winter, early spring.

Use as an informal hedge, against a fence or screen, in mass at end of lawn area, but far enough from sprinklers to avoid overwatering. Attractive with reddish- or purplish-leafed plants.

TEXAS MOUNTAIN LAUREL. See *Sophora secundiflora*.

TEXAS RANGER. See *Leucophyllum frutescens*.

TEXAS UMBRELLA TREE. See *Melia azedarach* 'Umbraculiformis'.

THALICTRUM. *Ranunculaceae.* MEADOW RUE. Perennials. All Zones; most species short lived in Zones 18–24. Basal foliage clumps resemble those of columbines; sparsely leafed stems on most species are 3–6 ft. tall, topped by airy clusters of small flowers in summer. Give wind-protected location, plenty of moisture, light shade. Superb for airy effect; delicate tracery of leaves and flowers is particularly effective against dark green background. Pleasing contrast to sturdier perennials. Foliage good in flower arrangements.

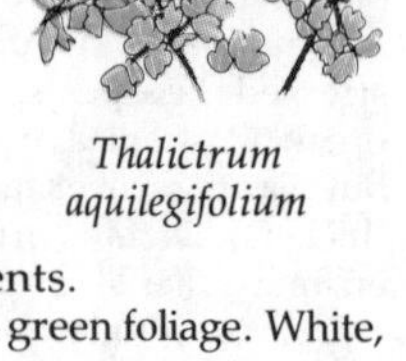

Thalictrum aquilegifolium

T. aquilegifolium. Grows 2–3 ft. tall. Bluish green foliage. White, lilac, or purple flowers.

T. dipterocarpum. CHINESE MEADOW RUE. To 3–6 ft. Lavender to violet flowers, yellow stamens. Long lived everywhere.

T. minus. A somewhat variable species. The form most often sold reaches to 3 ft. when in flower. Bluish green foliage; yellow flowers, consisting mostly of stamens.

T. rochebrunianum. Clumps grow to 4–6 ft. tall. White flowers with pale yellow stamens. Variety *T. r.* 'Lavender Mist' has lavender flowers.

Theaceae. The tea family consists of evergreen or deciduous trees and shrubs with leathery leaves and 5-petaled flowers with a large number of stamens. *Camellia, Franklinia,* and *Stewartia* are important representatives.

THEA sinensis. See *Camellia sinensis.*

THEVETIA. *Apocynaceae.* Evergreen shrubs, small trees. Fast-growing plants with narrow leaves and showy, funnel-shaped, yellow or apricot flowers in clusters. They thrive in heat, take full sun, very little frost. Like their relatives the oleanders (*Nerium*), they are poisonous.

T. peruviana *(T. neriifolia).* YELLOW OLEANDER. Zones 12 (with careful protection), 13, 14 (sheltered locations), 21–24. Fast growth typically to 6–8 ft. or more. Leaves 3–6 in. long, very narrow, with edges rolled under. Leaves are deep green, glossy, with inconspicuous veins. Fragrant flowers bloom any time (mostly June–November); yellow to apricot, 2–3 in. long, in clusters at branch ends.

Thevetia peruviana

Takes any amount of heat and sun. Best with ample water, good drainage. Shallow rooted. Protect from wind or prune to lessen wind resistance. Can be grown (with training) as 20-ft. tree or pruned into 6–8-ft. hedge, background planting, or screen. In cold-winter areas, mound dry sand 6–12 in. deep around base of stem. If top is frozen, new growth will bloom same year.

T. thevetioides. GIANT THEVETIA. Zones 12 and 13 (with winter protection), 22–24. Fast, open growth to 12 ft. tall, 12 ft. wide. Leaves, darker green than those of *T. peruviana*, resemble oleander leaves but are corrugated, heavily veined beneath. Flowers brilliant yellow, to 4 in. across, in large clusters, June–July and into winter. Desert heat wilts summer flowers.

THREADLEAF FALSE ARALIA. See *Dizygotheca*.

THRIFT. See *Armeria*.

THUJA (sometimes spelled "Thuya," and always so pronounced). *Cupressaceae.* ARBORVITAE. Evergreen shrubs or trees. Neat, symmetrical, even, geometrical plants which run to globes, cones, or cylinders. Scalelike leaves in flat sprays; juvenile foliage feathery, with small, needlelike leaves. Small cones with few scales. Foliage in better-known varieties is often yellow green or bright golden yellow.

T. occidentalis. AMERICAN ARBORVITAE. Tree. Zones 2–9, 15–17, 21–24. Native to eastern U.S. Upright, open growth to 40–60 ft. with branches that tend to turn up at ends. Leaf sprays bright green to yellowish green. Foliage turns brown in severe cold, will scorch badly in winter in coldest, windiest Rocky Mountain gardens unless plants are shaded, watered. Needs moist soil, moist air to look its best. Spray for red spider mites.

Thuja plicata

The species itself is seldom seen, but certain garden varieties are fairly common. Among them, taller kinds make good unclipped or clipped screens. Lower-growing kinds often planted around foundations, along walks or walls, as hedges. Some good varieties are:

'Douglasii Pyramidalis'. Tall, vigorous green pyramid of fairly fast growth.

'Emerald' ('Emerald Green', 'Smaragd'). Neat, dense-growing, cone-shaped plant that holds its color through the winter.

'Fastigiata' ('Pyramidalis', 'Columnaris'). Tall, narrow, dense, columnar plant to 25 ft. high, 5 ft. wide; can be kept lower by pruning. Good plant for tall (6-ft. or more) hedges and screens, especially in cold regions and damp soils. Set 4 ft. apart for neat, low-maintenance screen.

'Globosa' ('Little Gem', 'Little Giant', and 'Nana' are very similar varieties). GLOBE ARBORVITAE, TOM THUMB ARBORVITAE. Small, dense, rounded, with bright green foliage. Usually 2–3 ft. tall with equal spread, but eventually larger.

'Little Gem' ('Pumila'). Dense, dark green; slow growth to 2 ft. tall, 4 ft. across. Larger in great old age.

'Little Giant'. Dwarf, slow growing, globular, dark green.

'Nana'. Small, round, dense, to 1½–2 ft. in height.

'Nigra'. Tall, dense, dark green cone.

'Rheingold' ('Improved Ellwangeriana Aurea'). Cone-shaped, slow-growing, bright golden plant with a mixture of scalelike and needlelike leaves. Even very old plants seldom exceed 6 ft.

'Umbraculifera'. Globe shaped in youth, gradually becoming flat topped. At 10 years it should be 4 by 4 ft.

'Woodwardii'. Widely grown dense, globular shrub of rich green color. May attain considerable size with age, but it's a small plant over reasonably long period. If you can wait 72 years, it may be 8 ft. high by 18 ft. wide.

T. orientalis. See *Platycladus*.

T. plicata. WESTERN RED CEDAR. Tree. Zones 1–9, 14–24. Native from coastal northern California north to Alaska and inland to Montana. In Zones with hot summers, must have summer shade to avoid foliage burn. Plants from inland seed are hardy anywhere in West; those from coastal seed less hardy to cold. Can reach over 200 ft. in coastal belt of Washington, but usually much less in gardens. Slender, drooping branchlets, set closely with dark green, scalelike leaves, form flat, graceful, lacy sprays. Cones are ½ in. across, cinnamon brown. Prefers cool, moist (but not soggy) soil. In their native areas, established plants may get along with little or no summer water.

Single trees are magnificent on large lawns, but lower branches spread quite broadly and trees lose their characteristic beauty when these are cut off.

Here are a few varieties:

'Aurea'. Younger branch tips golden green.

'Fastigiata'. HOGAN CEDAR. Very dense, narrow, erect; fine for tall screen.

'Hillieri'. Irregularly shaped dense, broad shrub with thick, short, heavy branches.

'Stoneham Gold'. Dense, slow growing dwarf; new growth orange.

'Striblingii'. Dense, thick column 10–12 ft. tall, 2–3 ft. wide. For moderate-height screen planting or use as an upright sentinel.

THUJOPSIS dolabrata. *Cupressaceae.* FALSE ARBORVITAE, DEERHORN CEDAR, HIBA CEDAR. Evergreen tree. Zones 1–7, 14–17. Needs part shade in Zone 14, warmest parts of 15. Pyramidal, coniferous, of very slow growth to 50 ft. high, often shrubby. Foliage resembles that of *Thuja*, but twigs are coarser, very glossy, branching in staghorn effect. Will grow in part shade. Best where summers are cool, humid; may get by with little summer water there. Where summers are hotter and drier, requires more shade and moisture. Plant as single tree where foliage details can be appreciated. Slow growth makes it good container plant. 'Nana' is a dwarf variety; 'Variegata' has white branch tips.

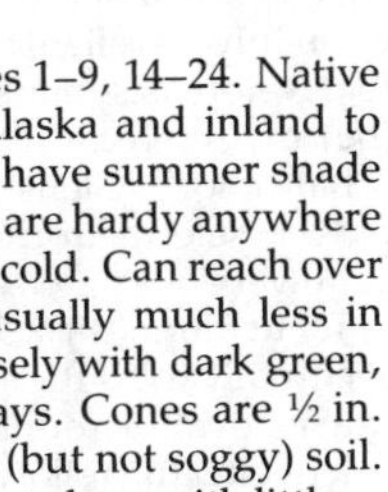

Thujopsis dolabrata

THUNBERGIA. *Acanthaceae.* Perennial vines. Noted for showy flowers. Tropical in origin, but some are hardy in milder parts of California and Zone 13. Others grow fast enough to bloom the first season and thus to be treated as annuals. Best with regular garden watering.

Thunbergia alata

T. alata. BLACK-EYED SUSAN VINE. Perennial, grown as summer annual. May live over in mild climates. Small, trailing or twining plant with triangular, 3-in. leaves. Flowers are flaring tubes to 1 in. wide, orange, yellow, or white, all with purple black throat. Start seed indoors, set plants out in good soil in sunny spot as soon as weather warms. Use in hanging baskets or window boxes or as ground cover in small, sunny spots; or train on strings or low trellis.

T. grandiflora. SKY FLOWER. Zones 16, 21–24. Vigorous twiner to 20 ft. or more, with lush, green, 8-in., heart-shaped leaves. Slightly drooping clusters of tubular, flaring, 2½–3-in., delicate pure blue flowers. Blooms fall, winter, spring. Takes a year to get started, then grows rapidly. Comes back to bloom in a year if frozen. Full sun near coast, part shade inland. Use to cover arbor, lathhouse, or fence; makes dense shade. There is a white variety. *T. laurifolia* is nearly identical to *T. grandiflora* in appearance and needs.

T. gregorii *(T. gibsonii)*. ORANGE CLOCK VINE. Zones 21–24; warm lathhouse or greenhouse in Zones 13, 16, 17; or grow as summer annual. Twines to 6 ft. tall or sprawls over ground to cover 6-ft. circle. Leaves 3 in. long, toothed, evergreen. Flowers tubular, flaring, bright orange, borne singly on 4-in. stems. Blooms nearly all year in mildest areas, in summer where winters are cool. Plant 3–4 ft. apart to cover wire fence, 6 ft. apart as ground cover. Plant above wall, over which vine will cascade, or grow in hanging basket. Showy and easy to grow; watch color conflicts with pink and red flowers.

T. mysorensis. Zones 16, 21–24. Tall-climbing vine with spectacular hanging clusters of gaping flowers which are red on the outside, yellow within. Clusters can reach several feet in length. Vine should be trained to overhead pergola or other support to permit flowers to hang unimpeded.

THYME. See *Thymus*.

THYMOPHYLLA tenuiloba. See *Dyssodia*.

THYMUS. *Labiatae.* THYME. Ground covers, erect shrubby perennial herbs. All Zones. Foliage usually heavily scented. Plants attract bees. Grow in warm, light, well-drained soil that is fairly dry. Full sun to light shade. Stands some neglect but will need periodic summer watering in hottest Zones. Restrain plants as needed by clipping back growing tips. Propagate from cuttings taken early in summer, or sow seed. Plant ground cover kinds 6–12 in. apart in fall or spring.

Thymus vulgaris

T. citriodorus. LEMON THYME. Small shrub, erect or spreading, 4–12 in. tall. Tiny leaves (to ⅜ in.) have lemon scent. Flowers palest purple. Variegated forms are 'Argenteus' (silver) and 'Aureus' (gold).

T. herba-barona. CARAWAY-SCENTED THYME. Ground cover. Fast growing; forms thick, flat mat of dark green, ¼-in.-long leaves with caraway fragrance. Rose pink flowers in headlike clusters. Leaves can be used to flavor vegetable dishes.

T. lanuginosus. See *T. pseudolanuginosus*.

T. praecox arcticus *(T. serpyllum, T. drucei)*. MOTHER-OF-THYME, CREEPING THYME. Ground cover. Forms flat mat, the upright branches 2–6 in. high. Roundish, ¼-in.-long, dark green, aromatic leaves.

(Continued on next page)

T

Small purplish white flowers (white in one form) in headlike clusters, June–September. Good for small areas or filler between stepping stones where foot traffic is light. Soft and fragrant underfoot. Leaves can be used in seasoning and in potpourris. Rose red variety is sold as 'Reiter's'.

T. pseudolanuginosus *(T. lanuginosus).* WOOLLY THYME. Ground cover. Forms flat to undulating mat 2–3 in. high. Stems densely clothed with small, gray, woolly leaves. Seldom shows its pinkish flowers. Plants become slightly rangy in winter. Use in rock crevices, between stepping stones, to spill over bank or raised bed, to cover small patches of ground.

T. vulgaris. COMMON THYME. Shrubby perennial herb. To 6–12 in. high. Narrow to oval, ¼-in.-long, fragrant, gray green leaves. Tiny lilac flowers in dense whorls, June–July. Low edging for flower, vegetable, or herb garden. Good container plant. Use leaves fresh or dried for seasoning fish, shellfish, poultry stuffing, soups, vegetables, vegetable juices.

T. v. 'Argenteus'. SILVER THYME. Has leaves variegated with silver.

TI. See *Cordyline terminalis.*

TIBOUCHINA urvilleana *(T. semidecandra, Pleroma splendens).* *Melastomataceae.* PRINCESS FLOWER. Evergreen shrub or small tree. Zones 14 and 15 (sheltered locations), 16, 17, 21–24; excellent greenhouse plant anywhere. Native to Brazil. Fast, rather open growth to 5–18 ft. Branch tips, buds, new growth shaded with velvety, orange and bronze red hairs. Oval, velvety, 3–6-in.-long green leaves are strongly ribbed, often edged red; older leaves add spots of red, orange, or yellow, especially in winter. Brilliant royal purple, 3-in.-wide flowers in clusters at ends of branches appear intermittently May–January.

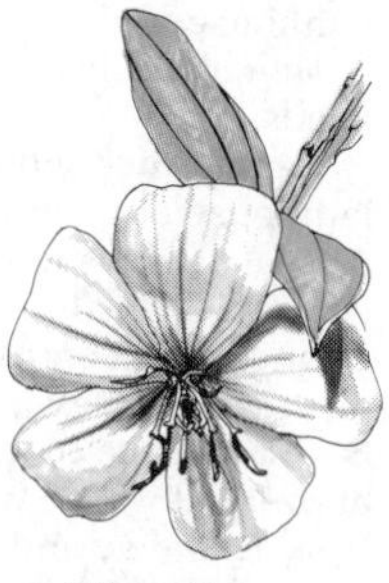

Tibouchina urvilleana

Best in somewhat acid, well-drained soil with roots in shade, top in sun. Give average water; protect from strong wind. Minimize legginess by light pruning after each bloom cycle, heavier pruning in early spring. Resprouts quickly after heavy pruning. Pinch tips of young plants to encourage bushiness. Feed after spring pruning and lightly after each bloom cycle. If buds fail to open, look for geranium (tobacco) budworm.

TIDYTIPS. See *Layia platyglossa.*

TIGER FLOWER. See *Tigridia pavonia.*

TIGER ORCHID. See *Odontoglossum grande.*

TIGRIDIA pavonia. *Iridaceae.* TIGER FLOWER, MEXICAN SHELL FLOWER. Bulb. All Zones if treated like gladiolus; leave bulbs in ground only in mild-winter areas. Leaves narrow, ribbed, swordlike, 1–1½ ft. long; leaves are shorter on 1½–2½-ft. flower stalks. Showy, 3–6-in.-wide flowers have 3 large segments forming triangle, joined with 3 smaller segments to form center cup. Larger segments usually vivid solid color–orange, pink, red, yellow–or white. Smaller segments usually spotted or blotched with darker colors. (Immaculata strain features solid colors, unspotted.) Plants bloom July–August; each flower lasts one day, but others follow for several weeks.

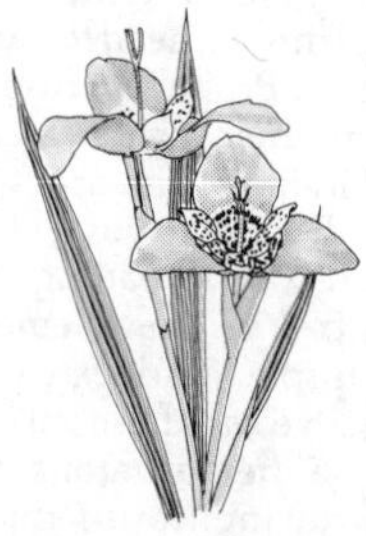

Tigridia pavonia

Plant after weather warms in rich, porous soil in groups of 10–12. Set bulbs 2–4 in. deep, 4–8 in. apart. Full sun near coast, afternoon shade in warmer areas. Or plant 6–8 bulbs in 9-in. pot. During active growth, water regularly and feed every 2 weeks with mild solution of liquid fertilizer. In colder areas, dig and store after foliage ripens. Do not break bulbs apart until just before planting in spring. Plants in open ground require division every 3–4 years. Easily grown from seed; may bloom first year. Control red spider mites, starting when leaves are a few inches tall.

TILIA. *Tiliaceae.* LINDEN. Deciduous trees. Dense, compact crowns. Much used for street and park planting in Europe. All have small, quite fragrant, yellowish white flowers in drooping clusters. All respond well to deep, rich soil and plenty of water. All grow at slow to moderate rate. Young trees need staking and shaping. Older trees need only corrective pruning. Under certain circumstances, aphids cause disagreeable drip of honeydew and accompanying sooty mildew.

Tilia cordata

T. americana. AMERICAN LINDEN, BASSWOOD. Zones 1–17. To 40–60 ft. with 20–25-ft. spread. Straight trunk; dense, compact, narrow crown. Heart-shaped, dull dark green leaves to 4–6 in. long, 3–4 in. wide (sometimes larger). Loose clusters of fragrant, yellowish white flowers in June–July. 'Redmond' is a pyramidal form with glossy foliage.

T. cordata. LITTLE-LEAF LINDEN. Zones 1–17. To 30–50 ft. with 15–30-ft. spread. Form densely pyramidal. Leaves 1½–3 in. long, equally broad or broader, dark green above, silvery beneath. Flowers in July. Excellent medium-sized lawn or street tree. Given space to develop its symmetrical crown, it can be a fine patio shade tree (but expect bees in flowering season). It is the hardiest linden. 'Chancellor', 'Glenleven', 'Greenspire', 'June Bride', and 'Olympic' are selected forms. 'June Bride' has an especially heavy show of flowers.

T. euchlora. CRIMEAN LINDEN. Zones 1–17. To 25–35 ft., perhaps eventually to 50 ft., almost as wide. Branches slightly pendulous. Leaves oval or roundish, 2–4 in. long, rich glossy green above, paler beneath. Yellowish white flowers in July. Use in same way as little-leaf linden—form is broader, shade and foliage less dense. 'Redmond' is pyramidal in habit.

T. tomentosa. SILVER LINDEN. Zones 1–21. To 40–50 ft. high, 20–30 ft. wide. Light green, 3–5-in.-long leaves, silvery beneath, turn and ripple in the slightest breeze. Drought resistant when well established.

Tiliaceae. The linden family of trees and shrubs includes *Grewia, Sparmannia* (African linden), and *Tilia.*

TILLANDSIA. *Bromeliaceae.* Perennials. Outdoors Zones 22–24; house plants anywhere. Bromeliads grown in pots of loose, fast-draining soil mix or as epiphytes on tree branches or slabs of bark. Best known is *T. usneoides,* the "Spanish moss" of the South. Similar is Arizona native *T. recurvata.*

Leaf rosettes of some are bright green, of others gray and scaly or scurfy; the latter require bright light and are drought resistant. They are often mounted on plaques of wood or bark and used as wall ornaments indoors or outside (where hardy). Let potting mix dry out between waterings.

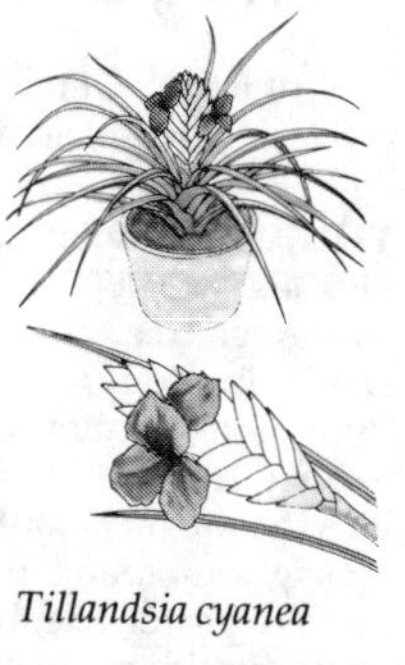

Tillandsia cyanea

T. cyanea. Rosette of bright green, arching, 1-ft. leaves produces showy flower cluster–flattened plume of deep pink or red bracts from which violet blue flowers emerge 1 or 2 at a time for a long period.

T. ionantha. Miniature rosettes of 2-in.-long leaves covered with a silvery gray fuzz. Small, tubular flowers are violet; at bloom time, center of rosette turns red. Tough and undemanding plant.

T. lindenii (*Vriesea lindenii*). Like *T. cyanea*, but plume is green or green marked rose. As with other bromeliads, each rosette produces just one long-lasting in florescence. Offsets replace original plant.

TIPUANA tipu. *Leguminosae.* TIPU TREE. Deciduous or semievergreen tree. Zones 12 (warmest locations), 13–16, 18–24. Fast growing to 25 ft.; can reach eventual 35–50 ft. Hardy to 25°F.; well-ripened wood will take 18°F. with minor damage. Broad silhouette with flattened crown that is usually wider than high; can be pruned to umbrella shape to make narrower, denser crown. Leaves divided into 11–21 oblong, 1½-in.-long, light green leaflets. Blooms June–July, bearing clusters of apricot to yellow, sweet pea–shaped flowers. Blooms followed by 2½-in. pods. Any soil except strongly alkaline. Established trees need occasional deep soaking, young plants more frequent irrigation. Flowers best in warm-summer areas out of immediate ocean influence. Good street or lawn tree. Useful shade canopy for patio or terrace, although flower litter can be slight nuisance.

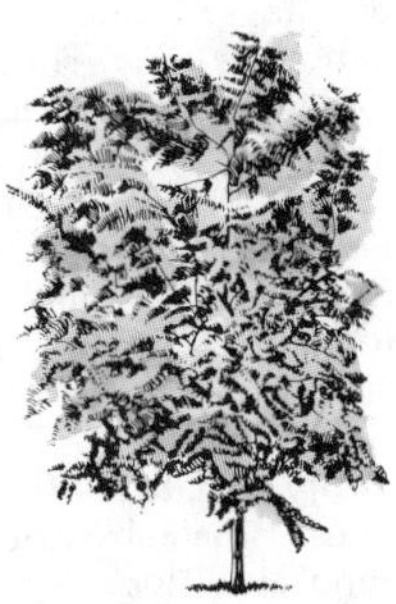

Tipuana tipu

TIPU TREE. See *Tipuana tipu.*

TITHONIA rotundifolia (*T. speciosa*). *Compositae.* MEXICAN SUNFLOWER. Perennial grown as summer annual. Husky, gaudy, rather coarse plant; rapid growth to 6 ft. tall. Spectacular 3–4-in.-wide flower heads with orange scarlet rays and tufted yellow centers bloom July to frost. Inflated hollow stems; cut with care for bouquets to avoid bending stalks. Velvety green leaves. Sow seed in place in spring, in not-too-rich soil. Full sun. Tolerates drought and heat; good choice for desert gardens. Belongs in background where flowers can be seen above other plants. 'Torch', lower-growing variety to 4 ft., makes bushy summer hedge.

Tithonia rotundifolia

TOADFLAX. See *Linaria.*

TOBIRA. See *Pittosporum tobira.*

TOLMIEA menziesii. *Saxifragaceae.* PIGGY-BACK PLANT. Zones 5–9, 12–24; house plant everywhere. Native to Coast Ranges from northern California northward to Alaska. Chief asset is abundant production of attractive 5-in.-wide basal leaves—shallowly lobed and toothed, rather hairy. Leaves can produce new plantlets at junction of leaf stalk and blade. Tiny, rather inconspicuous reddish brown flowers top 1–2-ft.-high stems. Tolerates wet soil. Good ground cover for shade. As house plant, needs filtered light, cool temperatures, frequent watering. Mealybugs, spider mites are occasional pests. Makes handsome hanging basket plant. Start new plants any time of year. Take leaf with plantlet and insert in moist potting mix so base of plantlet contacts soil. Or float leaf with plantlet in bowl of water—roots will form.

Tolmiea menziesii

TOMATILLO. See *Physalis ixocarpa.*

TOMATO. *Solanaceae.* Easy to grow and prolific, tomatoes are just about the most widely grown of all garden plants, edible or otherwise. Amateur and commercial growers have varying ideas about how best to grow tomatoes; if you have developed your own particular scheme, continue to follow it. But if you're a novice or you're dissatisfied with your previous attempts, you may find the following information useful.

First, choose varieties suited to your climate that will yield the kind of tomatoes you like on the kind of vines that you can handle. (Though the tomato plant is really a sprawling plant incapable of climbing, it is commonly referred to as a "vine.") Plant a few each of early, midseason, and late varieties for production over a long period; some good varieties for the West are described on page 548.

Tomato

To grow your own tomato plants from seed, sow in early March in pots of light soil mix or in a ready-made seed starter (sold at garden supply stores). Cover seed in pots with ½ in. of fine soil. Firm soil over seeds. Keep soil surface damp. Place seed container in cold frame or sunny window. (A temperature of 65°–70°F. is ideal, although range of 50°F. at night to 85°F. in the day will give acceptable results.) When seedlings are 2 in. tall, transplant them into 3- or 4-in. pots. Keep in sunny area until seedlings reach transplant size.

The time to plant tomato seedlings, whether grown from seed (above) or purchased from a nursery or garden store, depends on where you live. Plant in February or early March in Zones 12, 13; April, May, or early June in Zones 7–9, 14–24; May or early June in Zones 1–6, 10, 11. Typically, 6 plants can supply a family with fresh fruit and some for processing.

Plant in a sunny location in well-drained soil. Space plants 1½–3 ft. apart (staked or trained) to 3–4 ft. apart (untrained). Make planting hole extra deep. Set seedlings in hole so lowest leaves are just above soil level. Additional roots will form on buried stem and provide stronger root system.

When selecting tomato varieties, you may find some noted as *determinate*, others as *indeterminate*. Determinate types are bushier and not as suitable for staking or trellising. Indeterminate ones are more vinelike, need more training, and generally have a longer bearing period.

Tomato management and harvest will be most satisfying if you train plants to keep them mostly off the ground (left alone, they will sprawl and some fruit will lie on soil, often causing rot, pest damage, and discoloration). Most common training method for indeterminate varieties is to drive a 6-ft.-long stake (at least 1-by-1-in. size) into ground a foot from each plant. Tie plants to these stakes as they grow.

Slightly easier in the long run, but more work at planting time, is to grow each plant in wire cylinder made of concrete reinforcing screen (6-in. mesh). Form cylinder with 1½-ft. diameter. Screen is manufactured 7 ft. wide, which is just right for cylinder height; most indeterminate vines can grow to top of such a cylinder. Put stakes at opposite sides of cylinder and tie cylinder firmly to them. As vine grows, poke protruding branches back inside cylinder every week. Reach through screen to pick fruit.

For a novelty, you may also plant in a large suspended container and let vine cascade down (quite useful and practical with small-fruited tomatoes).

Irrigate tomato plants often during early part of the season, less frequently after fruit begins to ripen. Tomato plants are deep rooted, so water heavily when you do water.

If soil is fairly rich, you won't need to fertilize at all. But in ordinary soils, give light application of fertilizer every 2 weeks from the time first blossoms set until end of harvest.

If diseases or insects trouble or threaten tomatoes, protect plants with all-purpose vegetable dust or spray—a mixture that contains both an insecticide and a fungicide.

(Continued on next page)

T

If your plants grow, set fruit, and then shrivel, wilt, and die, they may have been sabotaged by gophers. If no gopher evidence is found, plants probably are suffering from verticillium or fusarium wilt or both. Pull and dispose of such plants. Diseases live over in soil, so the next year plant in different location and try one of the wilt-resistant varieties suited to your climate. Some tomato problems—leaf roll, blossom-end rot, cracked fruit—are physiological, usually corrected (or prevented) by maintaining uniform soil moisture. A mulch will help.

If you have done everything right and your tomatoes have failed to set fruit in the spring, use hormone spray on blossoms. Tomatoes often fail to set fruit when night temperatures drop below 55°F. In chilly-night areas, select cold-tolerant varieties (especially small-fruited strains). Fruit-setting hormone often speeds up bearing in the earlier part of the season. Tomatoes can also fail to set fruit when temperatures rise above 100°F., but hormones are not effective under those conditions.

Harvest fruit when it is fully red and juicy; keep ripe fruit picked to extend season. When frost is predicted, harvest all fruit, both green and partly ripe. Store at 58°F. and bring into 70°F. to ripen as needed.

Tomato Varieties

Following are kinds of tomatoes you can buy as seeds or started plants—listings are arranged according to fruit and vine types. Several varieties are valued especially for their resistance to verticillium or fusarium wilt. Varieties with VF after their names tolerate verticillium and fusarium; those marked VFN also tolerate nematodes. Additional keys to disease resistance include FF (resistant to Race 1 and Race 2 fusarium), T (tobacco mosaic virus), A (alternaria leaf spot), and L (septoria leafspot).

Main crop or standard tomatoes. 'Ace' and 'Ace' types are large tomatoes of very fine flavor that bear well in California's interior and inner coastal valleys. 'Pearson' and 'Pearson Improved' will set fruit under wide range of temperatures and produce well in California's coastal and interior valleys. 'Stone' is a late-maturing variety with globular scarlet fruit on large vines; it is a southern California favorite. 'Manalucie' is another good main crop variety for warm areas. 'Pritchard' produces fairly early main crop and is useful in northwestern gardens.

Early tomatoes. "Early" means more than early harvest. Early varieties set fruit at lower night temperatures than midseason or late varieties; most will ripen fruit in cool-summer climates. Name 'Earliana' covers several varieties such as 'Early Market', 'First Early', 'Morse's 498', and 'Pennheart'. 'Early Girl' gives high yield of medium-small tomatoes beginning early and lasting through season. Early types grown in Oregon and Washington include: 'Bonny Best', 'John Baer', and 'Valiant', all large-vine types; and 'Willamette', a small-vine type.

Cool-summer tomatoes. Where summers are unusually cool, nurseries offer locally adapted varieties. In Seattle, you'll find 'Seattle Best of All'; in San Francisco, tests suggest that 'Early Girl' performs better than the traditional 'Frisco Fogger'.

Hybrid tomatoes. Hybrid vigor makes these tomatoes grow more strongly and rapidly, and produce larger and more uniform fruit than other varieties. And, except for the large-fruited kinds, they produce fruit in climate extremes. Of many hybrids, 'Beefmaster' (VFN); 'Burpee Hybrid', a medium to large main crop variety; 'Big Boy', a very large, thick, round red tomato; 'Better Boy' (VFN); 'Wonder Boy'; and 'Spring Giant' (VF) are well known.

Yellow orange tomatoes. 'Jubilee' and 'Sunray' are strikingly handsome golden orange tomatoes. They taste just like good red tomatoes and look good too, especially sliced and mixed with sliced red tomatoes. (There are even white tomatoes; 'New Snowball' and 'White Beauty' are interesting novelties with very low acid content.)

Large-fruited tomatoes. These are home gardener's specials. They are poor shippers. Unless they are grown locally, you won't find them at your produce market. Among the best are 'Ponderosa', 'Beefsteak' ('Crimson Cushion'), 'Big Boy', 'Big Girl' (VF), 'Beefmaster' (VFN), 'Bragger', 'Spring Giant' (VF). Fruit is large, broad, rather shallow, meaty, and mild. All varieties need moderate heat and rarely thrive in cool-night or coastal areas. Vines are large.

Small-fruited tomatoes. Ripe fruits are size of large marbles or small plums, but there's nothing small about vines of small-fruited tomatoes. Trained against a wall, they will reach 8 ft. and spread almost as wide. These varieties set fruit well under greater climate extremes than do larger-fruited varieties. Many shapes and colors are available, as indicated by their names: 'Red Cherry', 'Red Plum', 'Red Pear', 'Yellow Cherry', 'Yellow Pear', 'Yellow Peach'. Extra-heavy producers of small, very sweet tomatoes are 'Sugar Lump', 'Sweet 100', and 'Sweet Million'. 'Basket Pak' produces tomatoes to 1½ in. wide. Dwarf varieties for pots or containers are 'Tiny Tim', 'Small Fry' (VFN), 'Pixie', 'Toy Boy', 'Patio', 'Salad Top', 'Tumbling Tom', 'Early Salad', 'Atom'. A special type of extra-meaty tomato is often grown for making tomato paste and purée. These smallish varieties with little seed pulp include 'San Marzano' and 'Roma'.

TORCH-LILY. See *Kniphofia uvaria.*

TORENIA fournieri. *Scrophulariaceae.* WISHBONE FLOWER. Summer annual. Compact, bushy, to 1 ft. high. Light blue flowers with deeper blue markings and bright yellow throats look like miniature gloxinias. Stamens are arranged in shape of a wishbone. A white-flowered form is also available. Blooms summer and fall. Full sun where summers are cool and short, part shade elsewhere. Needs lots of water. Sow seed in flats; transplant to garden when frosts are over. Good for borders, pots, window boxes.

Torenia fournieri

TORREYA californica. *Taxodiaceae.* CALIFORNIA NUTMEG. Evergreen tree. Zones 7–9, 14–24. Conifer native to cool, shaded canyons in scattered California mountain regions below 4,500 ft. elevation. Slow growing to 15–50 ft. high with trunk 1–3 ft. in diameter. Wide, open pyramidal crown, becoming domelike with age. Branches are horizontal, slender, somewhat drooping at tips. Leaves dark green with 2 whitish bands underneath, flat, rigid, sharp pointed, 1¼–2½ in. long, ⅛ in. wide, in flat sprays. Plumlike fruit is pale green with purplish markings. Easy to grow; needs occasional watering.

Torreya californica

TOTARA. See *Podocarpus totara.*

TOUCH-ME-NOT. See *Impatiens.*

TOWER OF JEWELS. See *Echium wildpretii.*

TOYON. See *Heteromeles arbutifolia.*

TRACHELIUM caeruleum. *Campanulaceae.* Perennial. Zones 7–9, 14–24; annual elsewhere. Grows to 2½ ft. tall and as wide; clumps of stems are clothed with narrow, sharply toothed dark green leaves and topped by broad, dome-shaped clusters of tiny bluish violet flowers (good for cutting) over a long season. Sown early, will bloom first year; may self-sow in mild climates. Tough, undemanding plant with average water needs.

Trachelium caeruleum

TRACHELOSPERMUM *(Rhynchospermum).* *Apocynaceae.* STAR JASMINE. Evergreen vines or sprawling shrubs. Used as ground covers, spillers, or climbers.

T. asiaticum. Zones 6–24. Twines to 15 ft. or sprawls on the ground with branchlets rising erect. Leaves smaller, darker, duller green than those of *T. jasminoides;* flowers smaller, creamy yellow or yellowish white, fragrant, blooming April–June. Regular watering, sun (best with part shade in desert to avoid foliage burn).

Trachelospermum jasminoides

T. jasminoides. STAR JASMINE. Zones 8–24. One of most widely used plants in California and Arizona. Given support, is twining vine to 20 ft.; growth rate slow at first but eventually moderately fast. Without support and with some tip-pinching, a spreading shrub or ground cover 1½–2 ft. tall, 4–5 ft. wide. New foliage glossy light green; mature leaves lustrous dark green, to 3 in. long. White, sweet-scented flowers to 1 in. across, profuse in small clusters on short side branches. Blooms June–July; May–June in desert. Attractive to bees. Rare variety *T. j.* 'Variegatum' has leaves variegated with white.

To grow as vine, start with plant that has been staked, or that at least has not been tip-pinched to make it shrubby. Provide support immediately. Use heavy cord to lead vine in direction you wish it to take. Train on posts, baffles, walls, fences, trellises, wherever its fragrance can be enjoyed or where night lighting can pick out white blossoms. Give some shade in hottest areas. Cut back older plants by about ⅓ each year to prevent inner growth from becoming too woody and bare.

To grow as bank or ground cover, set plants 1½–3 ft. apart (depending on how fast you want cover). Cut back upright shoots. Feed in spring, late summer. Spray if necessary for scale, mealybugs, red spider mites. Keep well watered and weeded. In 3–4 years, growth is thick enough to discourage most annual weeds.

Use in raised beds, entry gardens, for edging along walks or drives, to extend lawn, or as ground cover under trees and shrubs that need summer water.

TRACHYCARPUS. *Palmae.* Fan-leafed palms of moderate size and great hardiness. Characteristic blackish fiber grows at least at tops of all but oldest trunks. Need regular watering.

Trachycarpus fortunei

T. fortunei (sometimes sold as *Chamaerops excelsa*). WINDMILL PALM. Outdoors Zones 4–24; indoor potted palm anywhere. Native to China. Hardy to 10°F. or lower. Moderate to fast growth to 30 ft. in warm-winter areas. Trunk is dark, usually thicker at top than at bottom, covered with dense, hairy-looking fiber. Leaves 3 ft. across on toothed, 1½-ft. stalks. Responds to water and feeding, but isn't demanding. Sometimes becomes untidy and ruffled in high winds.

T. martianus. Zones 15–17, 19–24. Native to Himalayas. Hardy to 22°F. Slower growing, taller, more slender than *T. fortunei.* Trunk covered with fiber only at top, ringed with leaf scars.

T. takil. Zones 15–17, 19–24. Native to western Himalayas. Very slow grower with heavy, inclined trunk. Can reach 20 ft., but is dwarf for many years.

TRACHYMENE coerulea *(Didiscus coeruleus).* *Umbelliferae.* BLUE LACE FLOWER. Late spring annual; blooms in summer where weather is cool. To 2 ft. tall. Numerous small, lavender blue flowers in flat-topped, 2–3-in.-wide clusters that are quite lacy in appearance, as are divided leaves. Sow seeds in place in spring for summer bloom. Regular watering. Needs sunny location but won't take too much heat.

Trachymene coerulea

TRADESCANTIA. *Commelinaceae.* Perennials. Long-trailing, indestructible plants often grown indoors, or outdoors as ground cover for shaded areas. Most are used as pot plants or hanging basket plants; these can also be used as ground covers, but are likely to prove invasive. The long-stemmed, rambling kind is often called INCH PLANT or WANDERING JEW—a name also often applied to related *Callisia, Tripogandra,* and especially *Zebrina.*

Tradescantia fluminensis

T. albiflora. WANDERING JEW, GIANT INCH PLANT. Zones 12–24. Trailing, or sprawling and rooting at joints. Leaves 2–3 in. long. Flowers small, white. 'Albovittata' has leaves finely and evenly streaked with white; 'Aurea' ('Gold Leaf') has chartreuse yellow foliage; 'Laekenensis' ('Rainbow') has bandings of white and pale lavender. Variegated forms are unstable and tend to revert to green; keep solid green growth pinched out. Easiest care in well-drained soil with average water and strong light but not hot, direct sunlight. Can take considerable shade. Trailing stems will live a long time in water, rooting quickly and easily. Renovate overgrown plants by cutting back severely or by starting new pots with fresh tip growth.

T. andersoniana (usually sold as *T. virginiana*). SPIDERWORT. All Zones. Grows in clumps 1½–3 ft. tall, with long, deep green, erect or arching grasslike foliage. Three-petaled flowers open for only a day, but buds come in large clusters and plants are seldom out of bloom during summer. Named garden varieties come in white and shades of blue, lavender, purple, pink, and purplish rose to near red. Needs ample water and tolerates boggy conditions. Any soil. Sun or shade. Propagate by division.

T. blossfeldiana. Zones 12–24. Fleshy, furry stems spread and lean, but do not really hang. Leaves to 4 in. long are shiny dark green above, purple and furry underneath. Flowers showier than those of most trailing or semitrailing tradescantias: clusters of furry purplish buds open into ½-in., white-centered pink flowers. Grow in full sun in coastal valleys, full sun or partial shade inland. Average water requirement.

T. fluminensis. WANDERING JEW. Zones 12–24; house plant everywhere. Prostrate or trailing habit. Fast growing. Succulent stems have swollen joints where 2½-in.-long, dark green, oval or oblong leaves are attached ('Variegata' has leaves striped yellow or white). Tiny white flowers are not showy. Very easy to grow. In mild-winter areas can be grown in shade as ground cover. Excellent for window boxes and dish gardens, or for under greenhouse bench. A few stems placed in glass of water will live for a long time and will even make some growth.

T. multiflora. See *Tripogandra multiflora.*

T. navicularis. CHAIN PLANT. House plant. Compact plant with short, barely trailing branches packed with fleshy, folded, brownish purple leaves. Miniature plants form along stems, detach for propagation. Tiny purple red flowers. Treat as succulent.

T. sillamontana. House plant. Short trailing or ascending branches with 2–2½-in. leaves densely coated with soft white fur. Tiny rose purple flowers. Avoid overwatering.

TRAILING AFRICAN DAISY. See *Osteospermum fruticosum.*

TRAILING ARBUTUS. See *Epigaea repens.*

TRANSVAAL DAISY. See *Gerbera.*

TREE FERN. See *Blechnum, Cibotium, Cyathea, Dicksonia.*

T

TREE MALLOW. See *Lavatera*.

TREE-OF-HEAVEN. See *Ailanthus altissima*.

TREE TOMATO. See *Cyphomandra betacea*.

TREVESIA. *Araliaceae.* SNOWFLAKE TREE. Evergreen shrubs or small trees. Zones 21–24; house plants everywhere. Resemble *Fatsia japonica* in growth habit, but taller (10–20 ft.), more treelike. Long-stalked leaves are 1–2 ft. across, deeply lobed like those of fatsia, but each lobe is deeply cut. Leaves have lacy look resembling outline of enormous snowflake. Flowers unimportant. Several have been cultivated; best known is *T. palmata* 'Micholitzii'.

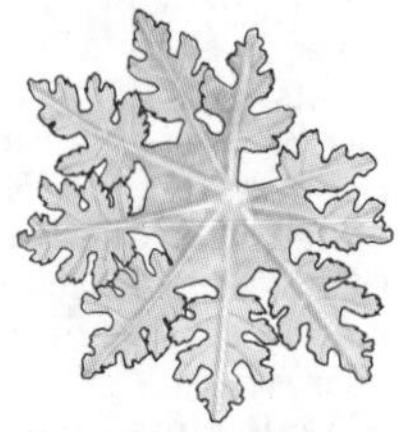

Trevesia palmata 'Micholitzii'

Take filtered sun or afternoon shade; loose, leafy, fast-draining soil with liberal water and feeding. Watch for mealybugs, spider mites. Indoors, give good light but not hot sun from west or south window. Young plants are good tub subjects, indoors or outdoors. Serves well near pools.

TRICHOSPORUM. See *Aeschynanthus*.

TRICHOSTEMA lanatum. *Labiatae.* WOOLLY BLUE CURLS. Evergreen shrub. Zones 14–24. Native to dry, sunny slopes of Coast Ranges, California. Much-branched, neat plant, 3–5 ft. high. Narrow, 1¼–2-in.-long leaves, pungently aromatic when bruised, are shiny dark green on upper surface, white and woolly beneath; leaf edges are rolled under. Flowers, in separated clusters along a long stalk, are blue with conspicuous arching stamens. Stalks and parts of flowers are covered with blue, pink, or whitish wool. Blooms April–June; throughout summer and early fall if old flower stems are cut back. Needs excellent drainage. Do not water in summer. Good choice for sunny hillsides.

Trichostema lanatum

TRICUSPIDARIA dependens. See *Crinodendron patagua*.

TRICYRTIS. *Liliaceae.* TOAD LILY. Perennials. Zones 1–9, 14–17. Woodland plants that somewhat resemble false Solomon's seal (*Smilacina*) in foliage. Flowers are complex in structure and heavily spotted, not showy but fascinating close up. Plants need partial shade, soil with plenty of organic material, and ample water. Fall bloom.

T. formosana. To 2½ ft. tall, with green leaves mottled with deeper green. Clusters of brown or maroon buds open to inch-wide white flowers spotted purple.

T. hirta. To 3 ft., with white, purple-spotted flowers set all along the stems in leaf joints.

Tricyrtis

TRIFOLIUM. *Leguminosae.* CLOVER. Scores of species, most of them field crops. Two are perennials of garden importance.

T. fragiferum. STRAWBERRY CLOVER. Zones 4–24. O'Connor's Legume, an Australian strain of this forage crop, is used as a ground or bank cover for its deep rooting (6–7 ft.) and tolerance of heat, drought, and moderate salinity. Sow seed at 2–8 oz. per 1,000 sq. ft. and water well until established. With average water, makes 6–7-in. mat of green.

Trifolium repens

T. repens. WHITE CLOVER, WHITE DUTCH CLOVER. All Zones. Sometimes used to mix with lawn grass or dichondra seed. Useful for deep rooting (with some drought resistance) and ability to take nitrogen from air and put it into the soil through root bacteria action. Can stain clothing of children who play on it; white flower heads attract bees. Prostrate stems root freely and send up lush cover of 3-part leaves with ¾-in. leaflets. Thrives in full sun to half shade. *T. r. minus* is one of the shamrocks.

TRILLIUM. *Liliaceae.* WAKE ROBIN. Perennials. Early spring-blooming plants. Whorl of 3 leaves tops each stem, and from center of these springs a single flower with 3 maroon or white petals. Plant the thick, deep-growing, fleshy rhizomes in shady, woodsy location. Never let plants completely dry out. Let them alone; they will gradually increase.

Trillium ovatum

T. chloropetalum *(T. sessile californicum).* Zones 4–9, 14–17. Western native. To 1–1½ ft. high. Flower, with greenish white to yellowish petals about 2½ in. long, sits without a stalk on the 3 large (6-in.-long), mottled leaves. *T. c. giganteum* has deep maroon petals.

T. grandiflorum. Zones 1–6. Stout stems 8–18 in. long; leaves 2½–6 in. long. Flower is stalked, nodding, white aging to rose.

T. ovatum *(T. californicum).* Zones 1–6, 14–17. Western native similar to *T. grandiflorum* but with narrower petals; flowers are usually upright on stalks. Effective in shady part of wildflower garden or among ferns, azaleas, or Polyanthus primroses.

TRINIDAD FLAME BUSH. See *Calliandra tweedii*.

TRIPOGANDRA multiflora *(Tradescantia multiflora).* *Commelinaceae.* BRIDAL VEIL, FERNLEAF WANDERING JEW. Perennial used as house plant, usually in hanging pot or basket. Resembles common wandering Jews (*Tradescantia* and *Zebrina*) in most details and in culture, but is finer in texture, with smaller (1–2-in.-long), narrower leaves, thinner stems. Leaves dark green above, purple underneath. Tiny white flowers are freely produced on slender, almost hairlike stalks. Stems can trail to considerable length—a yard or even more. Plants need same culture and conditions as *Tradescantia albiflora* and *T. fluminensis* but are less hardy to cold and low humidity.

Tripogandra multiflora

TRISTANIA. *Myrtaceae.* Evergreen trees. Zones 19–24; also grown in Zones 15–18, but hardiness is questionable where temperatures drop below 26°F. Related to eucalyptus. The 2 species grown in California are of manageable size, and both have brightly colored, shedding bark in addition to handsome evergreen foliage.

T. conferta. BRISBANE BOX. Moderate to fast growth rate to 30–60 ft. Trunk and limbs resemble those of madrone, with reddish brown bark peeling away to show smooth, light-colored new bark underneath. Growth habit is rather upright, crown eventually broad and rounded. Leaves are 4–6 in. long, oval, leathery, bright green; they tend to cluster toward tips of branchlets. White to creamy, ¾-in.-wide flowers in clusters of 3–7 in summer. Fruit is woody capsule something like that of eucalyptus. 'Variegata' has brilliant yellow leaf markings.

Tristania conferta

Takes almost any soil, but young plants get better start with good soil and liberal watering; established plants are quite drought resistant. Pinch and prune to get more twiggy growth. Not bothered by insects or diseases, but chlorosis is sometimes a problem in Los Angeles area. Good street or lawn tree.

T. laurina. Slow-growing, rather formal-looking small tree or shrub. Trees 8 years old are 10 ft. tall and 5 ft. across, with remarkably dense and rounded crown. Trunk is covered with mahogany-colored bark which peels to show satiny white new bark. Leaves to 4 in. long, usually narrow, but varying to somewhat broader, heavy textured, glossy medium green. Clusters of small yellow flowers are borne in sufficient profusion to put on good show in late spring or early summer. Fruit similar to that of *T. conferta* but smaller (only ¼ in. across). Young plants are densely shrubby and can be kept that way with a little pinching. May be trained, like olives, as multistemmed trees. To make a single-stemmed tree, stake plant and shorten side branches. Remove shortened side branches when treelike growth pattern is established; thereafter, only light shaping will be necessary. Good tub subject. Variety 'Elegant' has broad leaves that open red and hold color until shaded by newer growth; they then turn green.

Both species and variety make excellent tall screens or boundary and background plantings.

TRITELEIA. *Amaryllidaceae.* Corms. Plants under this name were formerly known as *Brodiaea.* General descriptions and culture are same as for *Brodiaea,* which differs only in technicalities. Species below are quite tolerant of heat and drought.

Triteleia laxa

T. grandiflora *(Brodiaea douglasii, B. grandiflora).* Flowering stalk to 2 ft. tall; many 1¼-in.-long, blue to white trumpets.

T. hyacinthina *(Brodiea hyacinthina).* *White Brodiaea.* Clusters of 10–40 white, purple-tinged flowers with greenish veins, papery in texture top 9–20 in. stems in June, July.

T. ixioides *(B. ixioides).* PRETTY FACE, GOLDEN BRODIAEA. Flower stalk to 2 ft.; flowers 1 in. long, golden yellow with purple black midrib and veins.

T. laxa *(B. laxa).* ITHURIEL'S SPEAR. Flower stalk to 2½ ft.; purple blue, 1½-in. trumpets.

T. 'Queen Fabiola'. Flower stalk to 2½ ft. tall; flowers deep violet. Good cut flower.

T. tubergenii. Flower stalk to 2½ ft. tall; flowers light blue.

T. uniflora. See *Ipheion uniflorum.*

TRITOMA uvaria. See *Kniphofia uvaria.*

TRITONIA *(Montbretia).* *Iridaceae.* Corms. Zones 9, 13–24. Native to South Africa. Related to freesia, ixia, and sparaxis. Narrow, sword-shaped leaves. Branched flower stems carry short, spikelike clusters of brilliant flowers. Grow in sun. Give regular watering through blooming period, after which foliage dies down and plants will withstand drought. Good in rock gardens, borders, pots. Long-lasting cut flowers.

Tritonia crocata

T. crocata. Often called flame freesia. Flower stems to 1–1½ ft. Flowers orange red, funnel shaped, 2 in. long. Variety *T. c. miniata* has bright red blooms; 'Princess Beatrix' has deep orange flowers. Others come in white and shades of pink, salmon, yellow, and apricot.

T. hyalina. Flowers bright orange; narrower segments than *T. crocata,* with transparent area near base. More dwarf than *T. crocata.*

TROLLIUS. *Ranunculaceae.* GLOBEFLOWER. Perennials. All Zones. Shiny, finely cut, dark green leaves. Yellow to orange flowers resemble those of ranunculus. Bloom season late spring to late summer. Need shade or part shade, rich soil, plenty of moisture. Subject to aphids. Valuable for bringing bright color to shady area; particularly happy choice near garden pool. Excellent cut flowers.

Trollius ledebouri

T. europaeus. To 1–2 ft. tall. Flowers yellow, 1½ in. across. Some varieties are orange.

T. ledebouri. Plant so called by nurseries grows to 2 ft. tall. Flowers gold orange, 2 in. across. Variety 'Golden Queen' reaches 4 ft., has 4-in.-wide flowers.

TROPAEOLUM. *Tropaeolaceae.* NASTURTIUM. Perennials in Zones 15–24; generally grown as annuals in other Zones. Distinctive appearance, rapid growth, and easy culture are 3 of nasturtiums' many strong points. Less conspicuous, but odd and pretty, is *T. peregrinum,* the canary bird flower.

Tropaeolum majus

T. majus. GARDEN NASTURTIUM. Two main kinds. Climbing types trail over the ground or climb to 6 ft. by coiling leaf stalks; dwarf kinds are compact, up to 15 in. tall. Both have round, shield shaped, bright green leaves on long stalks. Broad, long-spurred flowers have a refreshing fragrance, come in colors ranging through maroon, red brown, orange, yellow, and red to creamy white. Young leaves, flowers, and unripe seed pods have peppery flavor like watercress and may be used in salads.

Easy to grow in most well-drained soils in sun; best in sandy soil. Should have regular summer watering. Sow early spring. Grows and blooms quickly, often reseeds itself. In Zones 12 and 13, plant seeds in fall against sunny wall; plants will bloom from winter until heat of late spring. If hard frosts kill seedlings, just plant more seeds. Has become naturalized in some Zone 17 areas. Needs no feeding in average soils.

Climbing or trailing kinds will cover fences, banks, stumps, rocks. Use dwarf kinds for bedding, to cover fading bulb foliage, for quick flower color in ground or in pots. Good cut flowers.

Dwarf forms are most widely sold. You can get seeds of mixed colors in several strains, or a few separate colors, including cherry rose, mahogany, gold. Both single- and double-flowered forms are available.

T. peregrinum. CANARY BIRD FLOWER. Climbs to 10–15 ft. Leaves are deeply 5-lobed. Flowers ¾–1 in. across, canary yellow, frilled and fringed, with green curved spur. Light shade, moist soil.

TRUMPET CREEPER. See *Campsis.*

TRUMPET VINE. See *Campsis.*

TSUGA. *Pinaceae.* HEMLOCK. Coniferous evergreen trees and shrubs. Zones 1–7, 14 (part shade only), 15–17, except *T. canadensis.* These are mostly gigantic trees with unusually graceful foliage. Branches horizontal to drooping; needlelike leaves flattened and narrowed at the base to form distinct, short stalks. Small, medium brown cones hang down from branches. Best in acid soil, with ample moisture, high summer humidity, protection from hot sun and wind.

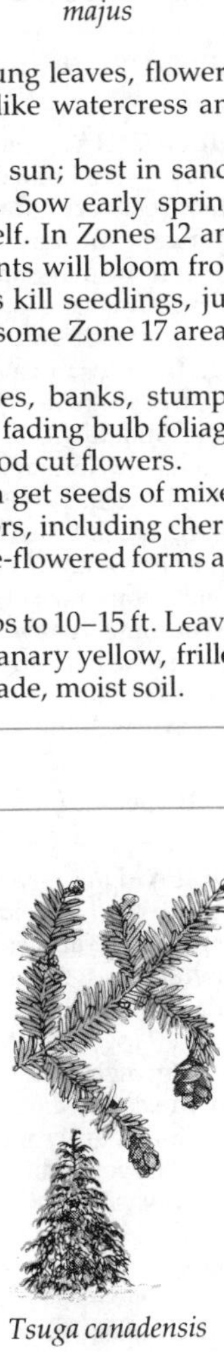

Tsuga canadensis

T. canadensis. CANADA HEMLOCK. Zones 3–7, 17. Dense, pyramidal tree to 90 ft. tall in its native eastern states, much smaller here.

(Continued on next page)

T

Has tendency to grow 2 or more trunks. Outer branchlets droop gracefully. Dark green needles, white banded beneath, about ½ in. long, are mostly arranged in opposite rows on branchlets. Oval cones about ¾ in. long grow on short stalks. Fine lawn tree or background planting. Can be clipped into outstandingly beautiful hedge, screen. One variety, 'Pendula', SARGENT WEEPING HEMLOCK, is low, broad plant 2–3 ft. high and twice as wide, with pendulous branches; it is good in large rock gardens. Many other dwarf or pendulous varieties exist.

T. heterophylla. WESTERN HEMLOCK. Native along coast from Alaska to northern California, inland to northern Idaho and Montana. Handsome tree with narrow, pyramidal crown. Grows fairly fast to 125–200 ft. high. Somewhat drooping branchlets and fine-textured, dark green to yellowish green foliage give fernlike quality. Short needles (¼–¾ in. long) with whitish bands beneath grow in 2 rows. Many 1-in. cones droop gracefully from branch tips. Needs water in dry seasons. Picturesque large conifer for background use, hedges, or screens.

T. mertensiana. MOUNTAIN HEMLOCK. Native to high mountains from Alaska south through the higher Sierra Nevada in California and to northern Idaho and Montana. Grows to 50–90 ft. high in the wilds but is much shorter and slower growing in home gardens. Blue green foliage with a silvery cast; ½–1-in.-long needles grow all around stems to give branchlets plump, tufty appearance. Cones 1½–3 in. long. Trees at timberline frequently grow in horizontal or twisted fashion. Slow growing under lowland conditions. Thrives on cool slope with plenty of organic matter in soil. Least adapted to lowland, hot-summer areas. Decorative in large rock garden. Good for containers, bonsai.

TUBEROSE. See *Polianthes tuberosa*.

TULBAGHIA. *Amaryllidaceae.* Perennials. Zones 13–24. Frost damage at 20°–25°F. with quick recovery. Many narrow leaves grow from central point to make broad clumps. Clusters of star-shaped flowers rise above clumps on long stems. Full sun, average watering. Evergreen in mild climates.

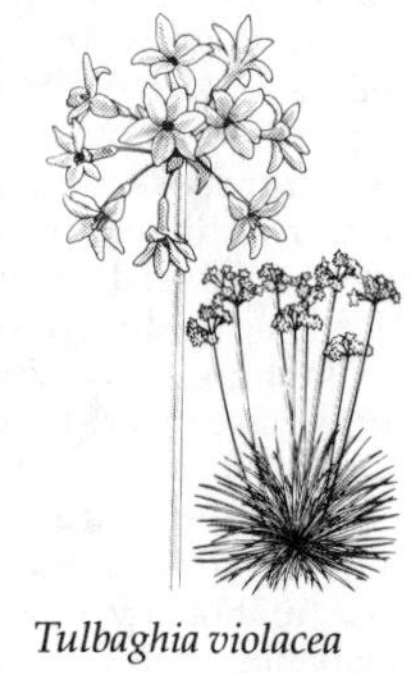

Tulbaghia violacea

T. fragrans. Leaves to 12–14 in. long or longer, 1-in. wide, gray green. Fragrant, lavender pink flowers, 20–30 on 1½–2-ft. stalk. Blooms in winter. Good cut flower.

T. violacea. SOCIETY GARLIC. Leaves bluish green, narrow, to 1 ft. long. Flowers rosy lavender, 8–20 in cluster on 1–2-ft. stems. Some bloom most of year, with peak in spring and summer. Leaves, flower stems have onion or garlic odor if cut or crushed. Unsatisfactory cut flower for this reason (but can be used as seasoning). One form has creamy stripe down the center of each leaf. Variety 'Silver Lace' has white-margined leaves.

TULIP. See *Tulipa*.

TULIPA. *Liliaceae.* TULIP. Bulbs. All Zones. Best adapted to cold-winter climates. Tulips vary considerably in color, form, height, and general character. Some look stately and formal, others dainty and whimsical; a few are bizarre. Together, the species (the same as those growing in the wilds) and hybrids provide color March–May in the garden, in containers, and for cutting.

Darwin Hybrid tulip

Use larger tulips in colonies or masses with low, spring-blooming perennials such as arabis, aubrieta, aurinia, iberis, or *Phlox divaricata*, or with annuals such as forget-me-not, sweet alyssum, pansies, or violas. Plant smaller, lower-growing species in rock gardens, near paths, in raised beds, or in patio or terrace insets for close-up viewing. Tulips are superb container plants; see pages 182–183 for container culture. More unusual kinds, such as Double Early, Rembrandt, and Parrot strains, seem more appropriate in containers than in garden.

Need sun most of the day while in bloom; can be planted under deciduous trees that leaf out after tulips fade (good practice in hot-summer areas). Light shade helps prolong bloom of late-blooming kinds. Good light should come from overhead; otherwise, stems will lean toward light source. Rich, sandy soil is ideal, although tulips will grow in any good soil with fast drainage. Plant bulbs 2½ times as deep as they are wide, and 4–8 in. apart depending on ultimate size of plant. Plant bulbs in October except where weather is still warm. In Southwest, store tulip bulbs at 40°–45°F. for 6–8 weeks before planting in November or December (or even as late as end of January). Plant bulbs at least 6–8 in. deep in warmer areas to provide necessary cool root run. Give plants ample water during growing and flowering period. Need is much less after flowering, particularly if bulbs are deeply planted or shaded in summer.

Gophers, field mice, and aphids consider tulips a great delicacy. To protect from rodents, plant bulbs in baskets of ¼-in. wire mesh. To control aphids, spray twice a month in growing season or use systemic insecticide.

Tulips have been classified into many divisions; the most important of these are listed below, in approximate order of bloom.

Single Early tulips. Large single flowers of red, yellow, or white grow on 10–16-in. stems. Much used for growing or forcing indoors in pots. Also grown outdoors, blooming in March to mid-April, except in warm-winter climates.

Double Early tulips. Double peonylike flowers to 4 in. across bloom on 6–12-in. stems. Same colors, same bloom season as Single Early tulips. In rainy areas, mulch around plants or surround with ground cover to keep mud from splashing short-stemmed flowers. In colder climates, effective massed in borders for early bloom.

Darwin Hybrids. Spectacular group bred from Darwin tulips and huge, brilliant species *T. fosterana*. Bloom before Darwins; have enormous, brightly colored flowers on 24–28-in. stems. Most are in scarlet orange to red range; some have contrasting eyes or penciling; some measure 7 in. across.

Mendel tulips. Single flowers grow on stems to 20 in. tall. Bloom after Single Early and Double Early kinds, before Darwin tulips. Shades of white, rose, red, orange, yellow.

Triumph tulips. Single flowers on medium-tall (20-in.), very sturdy stems. Bloom earlier than Darwin tulips and (like Mendel tulips) are valuable in providing continuity of bloom.

Darwin tulips. Most popular of late April–May-flowering tulips. Graceful, stately plants with large oval or egg-shaped flowers, square at base, usually with stems to 2½ ft. tall. Clear, beautiful colors of white, cream, yellow, pink, red, mauve, lilac, purple, maroon, and near black.

Breeder tulips. Large oval to globular flowers on stems to 35 in. tall. May blooming. Unusual colors include orange, bronze, purplish, mahogany—often overlaid with flush of contrasting shade. Called Breeders because Dutch growers once grew them primarily to breed the much admired "broken" (variegated) tulips.

Lily-flowered tulips. Once included in Cottage division; now separate group. Flowers are long and narrow, with long, pointed segments. Graceful, slender stemmed, fine in garden (where they blend well with other flowers) or for cutting. Stems 20–26 in. tall. May blooming. Full range of tulip colors.

Cottage tulips (often called May-flowering tulips). About same size and height as Darwins. Flower form variable, long oval to egg shaped to vase shaped, often with pointed segments. May blooming.

Double Late tulips (often called Peony-flowered). Large, heavy blooms like peonies. They range from 18–22 in. tall; flowers may be damaged by rain or wind in exposed locations.

NOTE: The 10 divisions above have recently been reclassified (and somewhat simplified), and you may now find tulips sold under the following names:

Single Early and *Double Early.* The earliest large tulips.

Triumph and *Darwin Hybrids.* Midseason bloomers.

Single Late or *May-flowering.* Now includes Darwin and Cottage classes.

Double Late, Lily-flowered, and *Parrot* classes wind up the season. Novelty tulips (described below) include Rembrandt, Bizarre, Bybloems, and Parrot types.

Rembrandt tulips. "Broken" (variegated) Darwin tulips. Scarlet striped white, white flamed lilac purple, white edged red are characteristic patterns. Color variegation due to transmittable virus disease; don't plant near valued solid-color tulips or lilies.

Bizarre tulips. "Broken" Breeder or Cottage tulips. Flowers have yellow background marked bronze, brown, maroon, or purple. See planting caution under Rembrandt tulips.

Bybloems (Bijbloemens). "Broken" Breeder or Cottage tulips with white background marked rose, lilac, or purple. See planting caution under Rembrandt tulips.

Parrot tulips. May-flowering tulips with large, long, deeply fringed and ruffled blooms striped and feathered in various colors. Many have descriptive names, e.g. 'Blue Parrot', 'Red Parrot'. Good in containers, unusual cut flowers. See planting caution under Rembrandt tulips.

Three fairly new novelty groups include: *Fringed* tulips, variations from Single Early, Double Early, and Darwin tulips, finely fringed on edges of segments; *Viridiflora* tulips, 10–20 in. tall, flowers edged or blended green with other colors—white, yellow, rose, red, or buff; and *Multiflowered*, 3–6 flowers on each 20–27-in. stem, flowers white, yellow, pink, and red, May bloom.

Seven divisions include varieties and hybrids of *I. batalinii, I. eichleri, T. fosterana, T. greigii, T. kaufmanniana,* and *T. marjolettii,* and another division that includes all other species. Most important:

Hybrids and varieties of *T. fosterana,* including huge, fiery red variety 'Red Emperor' ('Mme. Lefeber'), 16 in. tall.

Varieties and hybrids of *T. kaufmanniana,* 5–10 in. tall, very early blooming, in white, pink, orange, and red, often with markings, some with leaves patterned brown.

Most species tulips—wild tulips—are low growing and early blooming with shorter, narrower leaves than garden hybrids, but there are exceptions. Generally best in rock gardens or wild gardens where plantings can remain undisturbed for many years. Those noted as being "easy" are also good container subjects.

Following are outstanding species:

T. acuminata. Flowers have long, twisted, spidery segments of red and yellow on 1½-ft. stems. May. Easy.

T. batalinii. Single, soft yellow flowers on 6–10-in. stems. Very narrow leaves. April.

T. biflora. Small flowers, off-white inside, greenish gray purple outside, yellow at base; several blooms on each 8-in. stem. March.

T. clusiana. LADY or CANDY TULIP. Slender, medium-sized flowers on 9-in. stems. Rosy red on outside, white inside. Easy; grows well in mild-winter areas. Give sheltered position in colder areas. April–May.

T. c. chrysantha *(T. stellata chrysantha).* To 6 in. tall. Outer segments rose carmine shading to buff at base; inner segments bright yellow. April.

T. eichleri. Big scarlet flowers with black bases margined buff on 1-ft. stems. Blooms late March.

T. greigii. Scarlet flowers 6 in. across, on 10-in. stems. Foliage mottled or striped with brown. Early flowering.

T. kaufmanniana. WATERLILY TULIP. Medium-large creamy yellow flowers marked red on outside and yellow at center. Stems 6 in. tall. Very early bloom. Easy, permanent in gardens. Many choice named varieties.

T. linifolia. Scarlet, black-based, yellow-centered flowers on 6-in. stems in late April. Handsome with *T. batalinii.*

T. praestans. Cup-shaped, orange scarlet flowers, 2–4 to 10–12-in. stem, in early April. Variety 'Fusilier' is shorter, has 4–6 flowers to a stem.

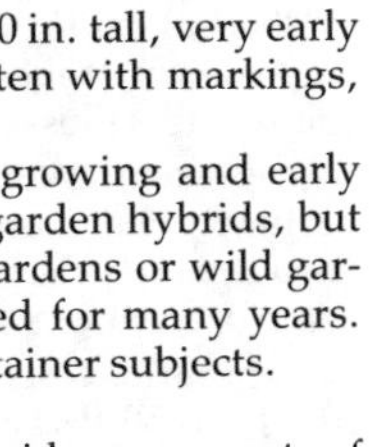

Tulipa kaufmanniana

T. saxatilis. Fragrant, yellow-based pale lilac flowers open nearly flat, 1–3 to each 1-ft. stem. Early bloom. Dependable in warm-winter areas.

T. stellata chrysantha. See *T. clusiana chrysantha.*

T. sylvestris. Yellow, 2-in. flowers, 1 or 2 on 1-ft. stem. Late flowering. Good in warm-winter areas.

T. tarda *(T. dasystemon).* Each 3-in. stem has 3–6 upward-facing, star-shaped flowers with golden yellow centers, white-tipped segments.

T. turkestanica. Vigorous tulip with up to 8 flowers on each slender, 1-ft. stem. Flowers slender in bud, star shaped when open, gray green on the outside, off-white with yellow base inside. Early March bloom. Easy.

TULIP TREE. See *Liriodendron tulipifera, Magnolia soulangiana.*

TUPELO. See *Nyssa sylvatica.*

TUPIDANTHUS calyptratus. *Araliaceae.* Evergreen shrub or small tree. Zones 19–24. Grows to 20 ft. Single or multiple trunk. Leaves to 20 in. wide, divided fanwise into 7–9 leathery, glossy bright green, stalked leaflets about 7 in. long by 2½ in. wide. Resembles the better known schefflera, but branches from base and makes broader, denser shrub.

Needs rich, well-drained soil, plenty of food, moderate water, and sheltered location. Best in partial shade but will take full sun in cooler coastal gardens. Can be pruned into almost any form. Good small tree for sheltered lanai, entryway, or patio. Grows well near pools. Splendid plant for large tubs and containers. As container plant indoors, give same care as *Schefflera actinophylla.* Effective when grown against fence or wall as triple-trunked small tree.

Tupidanthus calyptratus

TURNIP and RUTABAGA. *Cruciferae.* Biennial vegetables grown as cool-season annuals for their colorful, flavorful roots. Foliage of turnips is also a useful green vegetable. Different varieties give a nice choice of colors (white, white topped with purple, creamy yellow) and shapes (globe, flattened globe). Rutabaga is tasty kind of turnip with large yellowish roots. It's a late-maturing crop that stores well in the ground; turnips are quick growing and should be harvested and used as soon as they are big enough. Plant in full sun. Roots are milder flavored if soil is kept moist, become more pungent under drier conditions.

Turnip

In cold-winter areas, plant turnips or rutabagas in April for early summer harvest, or in July or August for fall harvest. In mild-winter areas, grow as winter crop by planting September through March.

TURRAEA obtusifolia. *Meliaceae.* STAR BUSH. Evergreen shrub. Outdoors in Zones 22–24; with protection from frosts in Zones 15, 16, 19–21. Native to South Africa. Slow growth to 4–5 ft. tall, 4 ft. wide; many drooping branchlets, some lower branches nearly prostrate. Leaves 2 in. long, dark green, glossy, polished. Many star-shaped, narrow-petaled, pure white flowers, 1½ in. across, in loose clusters. Long bloom season reaches peak in September, October. Tem-

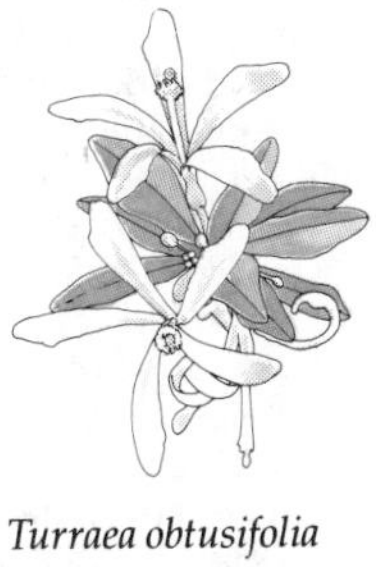

Turraea obtusifolia

T

peramental: needs good drainage and either light shade of high-branched trees or eastern exposure without strong reflected heat. Hardy to 26°F. Water deeply.

TWINFLOWER. See *Linnaea borealis.*

TWINSPUR. See *Diascia barberae.*

UGNI molinae *(Myrtus ugni).* *Myrtaceae.* CHILEAN GUAVA. Evergreen shrub. Zones 14–24. Slow to moderate growth to 3–6 ft. tall. Scraggly and open in youth, it matures into compact, rounded plant. Foliage is dark green with bronze tints; leaves are oval, leathery, ½ in. long, whitish beneath, with edges slightly rolled under. White, rose-tinted flowers in late spring, early summer; they are principally little brushes of stamens. Purplish or reddish, pleasant-tasting, ½-in. fruits follow; they smell like baking apples and can be used fresh or in jams and jellies.

Ugni molinae

Takes sun near coast, part shade in hot areas. Neutral to acid soil; ample water. Tidy, restrained plant for patios, terraces, near walks and paths where passers-by can pick and sample fruit, enjoy its fragrance.

Ulmaceae. The elm family contains trees and shrubs, usually deciduous, with inconspicuous flowers and fruits that may be nutlike, single-seeded and fleshy, or winged. Elm, hackberry, and zelkova are representative.

ULMUS. *Ulmaceae.* ELM. Deciduous or partially evergreen trees. Easy to grow in any fairly good soil; will survive in most poor ones. Best with normal watering, but will tolerate low moisture conditions at expense of good growth, plant health. Root systems are aggressive and close to surface; you'll have trouble growing other plants under these trees. Branch crotches often narrow, easily split. Many of the larger elms are tasty to leaf beetles, bark beetles, leafhoppers, aphids, and scale, making them either time-consuming to care for or messy (or both). Dutch elm disease, formerly a problem in the East and Midwest, has reached western states. For description, measures to take, see page 105.

Ulmus americana

U. americana. AMERICAN ELM. Zones 1–11, 14–21. Fast-growing tree which can reach 100 ft. or more with nearly equal—sometimes even greater—spread. Form is stately, with stout trunk dividing into many upright main branches at same height; outer branches are pendulous, silhouette vase shaped. Rough-surfaced, toothed leaves are 3–6 in. long. Leafs out very late where winters are mild. Yellow fall color. Pale green, papery seeds in spring blow about, are messy.

Grows best in deep soil, with 70–75-ft. circle to spread in. Roots send up suckers, can make thickets; will lift pavement if crowded. Leaf and bark beetles weaken and disfigure trees; scale causes drip and sooty mildew. Until the 1970s the only really recommendable use for such a tree was for very large gardens, out-of-the-way places, on broad boulevards unencumbered by utility lines, or in parks. Since then its attack by Dutch elm disease in the West has ruled out recommendation for planting under any circumstances.

U. carpinifolia. SMOOTH-LEAFED ELM. Zones 1–11, 14–21. To 100 ft. Wide-spreading branches, weeping branchlets. Leaves 2–3½ in. long, shiny deep green above. Culture, uses, precautions same as for American elm.

U. glabra. SCOTCH ELM. Zones 1–11, 14–21. To 120 ft. tall. Non-suckering. Leaves 3–6 in. long, oval, sharply toothed, rough surfaced, on very short stalks. Old trees sometimes seen, but scarcely grown now. Variety 'Camperdownii', CAMPERDOWN ELM, generally 10–20 ft. tall, has weeping branches that reach to ground, making tent of shade.

U. hollandica. DUTCH ELM. Zones 1–11, 14–21. To 100 ft. or more. Suckers freely. Name covers a number of hybrids between Scotch elm and smooth-leafed elm.

U. parvifolia (often sold as *U. p.* 'Sempervirens'). CHINESE ELM, CHINESE EVERGREEN ELM. Zones 8, 9, 12–24. Evergreen or deciduous according to winter temperatures and tree's individual heredity. So-called evergreen elm usually sold as 'Sempervirens'; this may be evergreen most winters, lose its leaves in unusual cold snap (new leaves come on fast). Very fast growth to 40–60 ft., with 50–70-ft. spread. Often reaches 30 ft. in 5 years. Extremely variable in form, but generally spreading, with long, arching, eventually weeping branchlets. Trunks of older trees have bark which sheds in patches somewhat like sycamore. Leaves leathery, ¾–2½ in. long, ⅓–1⅓ in. wide, oval, evenly toothed. Round fruit forms in fall while leaves are still on tree.

Stake young trees until trunks can carry weight of branches. Stake and head leading shoot higher than other shade trees to compensate for weeping. Rub or cut out small branches along trunk for first few years. Shorten overlong branches or strongly weeping branches to strengthen tree scaffolding. Older trees may need thinning to lessen chance of storm damage. Very little bothered by pests or diseases except Texas root rot in desert.

Good for patio shade in milder portions of West. Useful for sun screening. With careful pruning, useful as a street tree.

Varieties are 'Brea', with larger leaves, more upright habit; and 'Drake', with small leaves, weeping habit. Both are more or less evergreen. 'True Green' has small deep green leaves, is round headed, more evergreen than others.

Word of caution: Siberian elm (*U. pumila*) is sometimes sold as Chinese elm. Siberian elm flowers in spring, has stiffer habit and thinner, less glossy leaves.

U. procera. ENGLISH ELM. Zones 1–11, 14–21. To 120 ft. Suckers profusely. Tall trunk with broad or tall, dense crown of branches. Foliage holds dark green color later in fall than American elm. Same precautions apply to this tree as to American elm.

U. pumila. SIBERIAN ELM. All Zones; most useful in Zones 1–3, 10, 11. To 50 ft. Leaves ¾–2 in. long, ⅓–1 in. wide, dark green, smooth. Extremely hardy and tough, enduring cold, heat, drought, and poor soil. Under worst conditions grows slowly, may even be shrub. As fast-growing tree, it is suitable for windbreaks or shelterbelts. Has brittle wood, weak crotches, and is not desirable as single garden tree. Root system troublesome in gardens, but possibly useful in holding soil in problem areas against wind or water erosion. Papery, winged seeds disperse seedlings over wide area.

UMBELLULARIA californica. *Lauraceae.* CALIFORNIA LAUREL, CALIFORNIA BAY, OREGON MYRTLE, PEPPERWOOD. Evergreen tree. Zones 4–10, 12–24. Native to southwestern Oregon, California Coast Ranges, lower elevations of Sierra Nevada. In the wilds, it varies from a huge, gumdrop-shaped shrub (on windy hillsides near coast) to a tall and free-ranging tree 75 ft. high and over 100 ft. wide (in forests). Leaves are 3–5 in. long, 1 in. wide, pointed at tip, medium to deep yellow green and glossy on top, dull light green beneath.

Umbellularia californica

As sure identification, crush a leaf—if it's this plant it will be powerfully aromatic. A little of the fragrance is pleasant, but too much can cause a headache. Leaves are sometimes used as more potent substitute for true bay leaves (*Laurus nobilis*) in soups and stews. Tiny yellowish flowers in clusters give plant yellowish cast in spring. They are followed by olivelike, inedible green fruit that turns purple. Each fruit contains a large seed, and volunteer seedlings occasionally turn up in suburban gardens; they can be transplanted if no more than 6 inches tall.

In gardens, California laurel tends to grow slowly (about 1 ft. a year) to 20–25 ft. high and as wide. Grows best and fastest in deep soil with ample water, but tolerates many other conditions, including drought. Will grow in deep shade and ultimately get big enough to become shade maker itself (casts very dense shade unless thinned). Always neat. Good for screening, background plantings, or tall hedges. Often multitrunked. Good patio or street tree when thinned to one or a few trunks.

UMBRELLA PINE. See *Sciadopitys verticillata.*

UMBRELLA PLANT. See *Cyperus alternifolius.*

UMBRELLA TREE. See *Schefflera actinophylla.*

URBINIA agavoides. See *Echeveria agavoides.*

Urticaceae. The nettle family, best known for stinging nettles (*Urtica*), also contains such ornamentals as artillery plant (*Pilea*) and baby's tears (*Soleirolia*).

VACCINIUM. *Ericaceae.* Evergreen and deciduous shrubs. Excellent ornamental shrubs with clusters of bell-shaped flowers and colorful, edible fruit that attracts birds. All require acid soil and ample leaf mold, peat moss, or ground bark. Good woodland garden subjects.

Vaccinium ovatum

V. corymbosum. See Blueberry.

V. ovatum. EVERGREEN HUCKLEBERRY. Evergreen shrub. Zones 4–7, 14–17. Native Santa Barbara County north to British Columbia. Erect shrub to 2–3 ft. in sun, to 8–10 ft. in shade. Young plants spreading, older plants taller than wide, compact. Leathery, lustrous dark green leaves, ½–1¼ in. long; bronzy new growth. Flowers (March–May) are white or pinkish. Black berries with whitish bloom, good in pies, jams, jellies, syrups.

Best in partial shade; will take full sun in cool-summer areas. Can be trimmed into hedge or grown in container. Cut branches popular for arrangements.

V. parvifolium. RED HUCKLEBERRY. Deciduous shrub. Zones 2–7, 14–17. Native Sierra Nevada and northern California Coast Ranges to Alaska. Slow growth to 4–12, rarely 18 ft. Thin, green branches with spreading or cascading habit provide intricate, filmy winter silhouette. Light green leaves are thin, oval, ½–¾ in. long, light green. Greenish or whitish flowers, fine for arrangements, bloom April–May. Clear, bright red, showy berries are delicious in jams, jellies, and pies. Needs highly acid humus soil, moisture, partial shade.

V. vitis-idaea. COWBERRY, FOXBERRY. Evergreen shrub. Zones 2–7, 14–17. Slow growth to 1 ft. tall, spreading by underground runners to 3 ft. Leaves glossy, dark green, ⅓–1 in. long; new growth often brightly tinged red, orange. Clustered white or pinkish flowers bloom in May. Sour red berries, something like tiny cranberries, are esteemed for preserves, syrups. Handsome little plants for small-scale ground cover, informal edging around larger acid-soil plantings. Good in wet areas. With ample water, will take full sun in cool-summer areas. *V. v. minus,* LINGONBERRY, is smaller, with leaves ⅛–½ in. long. Attractive container plant.

Valerianaceae. The valerian family of perennial herbs (rarely shrubs) has clustered small flowers. False valerian (*Centranthus*) and valerian are the only representatives in western gardens.

VALERIANA officinalis. *Valerianaceae.* VALERIAN, GARDEN HELIOTROPE. Perennial herb. All Zones.

Valeriana officinalis

Both true heliotrope (*Heliotropium*) and RED VALERIAN (*Centranthus ruber*) are more common than *Valeriana officinalis.* Tall, straight stems grow to about 4 ft. high; most leaves remain fairly close to ground. Leaves are light green, borne in pairs that are further divided into 8–10 pairs of narrow leaflets. Tiny, fragrant flowers are white, pink, red, or lavender blue, in rounded clusters at ends of stems. Plant spreads and can become invasive. Roots are strong smelling.

Plant in sun or part shade. Start new plants from seeds or divisions. Grow in mixed herb or flower borders but don't allow it to crowd other plants. Use cut flowers in arrangements.

V. rubra. See *Centranthus ruber.*

VALLOTA speciosa. *Amaryllidaceae.* SCARBOROUGH LILY. Bulb. Outdoors Zones 16, 17, 23, 24; anywhere in containers. Native to South Africa. Strap-shaped evergreen leaves are 1–2 ft. long. Clusters of bright orange vermilion, funnel-shaped, 2½–3-in.-wide flowers grow on 2-ft. stalks. Blooms summer and early fall. White-flowered form rarely available. Survives outdoors where frosts are very light and infrequent, even succeeding in competition with tree roots. Excellent container plant. Plant June–July or just after flowering. Set bulbs with tips just below surface. Use smallest pots possible; repot or divide only when absolutely necessary, since plant blooms best when roots are crowded. Prefers light shade, tolerates full sun along coast. Fertilize monthly during active growth. Water regularly except during semidormant period in winter and spring, but never let plant dry out completely.

Vallota speciosa

VANCOUVERIA. *Berberidaceae.* Deciduous and evergreen perennials. These close relatives of *Epimedium* have the same uses in garden. Leaves are divided into numerous leaflets. Flowers in late spring, early summer. In cool-summer areas, will grow with little summer water; elsewhere, prefers regular watering. Attractive ground cover for tree-shaded beds. Cut foliage is attractive in bouquets.

Vancouveria planipetala

V. chrysantha. Evergreen. Zones 5, 6, 14–17. Native to Siskiyou Mountains. To 8–16 in. tall. Bronzed, gray green leaves, 1½ in. long and wide. Small yellow flowers, 4–15 to the stalk, each flower ½ in. wide.

V. hexandra. Deciduous. Zones 4–6, 14–17. Native to coastal forests from northern California to Washington. To 4–16 in. tall. Leaflets 1–2½ in. long, light green; fresh appearance all summer. Flower stalks usually topped with 3 drooping white flowers to ½ in. across, petals and sepals sharply bent backward.

V. planipetala *(V. parviflora).* INSIDE-OUT FLOWER. Evergreen, sometimes deciduous in cold-winter areas. Zones 4–6, 14–17. To 2 ft. in height. Light to medium green leaflets, shallowly lobed, 1½ in. long and wide. White flowers are even smaller than those of *V. hexandra,* but are carried in clusters of 25–50.

VANDA. *Orchidaceae.* Epiphytic orchids. Greenhouse or indoors. Beautiful orchids, but it's hard to get them to flower in coastal fog belts where light is limited. Plants grow erect, with leaves arranged opposite each other up the stem. Flowers grow on stalk formed in leaf joints.

Plant in osmunda fiber, tree fern fiber, or ground bark. Support stem against stake of tree fern stem about ⅔ height of plant to provide anchor for aerial roots. Vandas fall into 2 general groups according to leaf type. Those with pencil-like leaves require much light, high humidity, night temperatures above 50°F. Only tropical greenhouse conditions are suitable. Kinds with strap-shaped leaves require less light, lower temperatures, will grow and flower under more usual cool greenhouse atmosphere. Water very lightly during winter. They need plenty of light all year, but especially from November–February in order to set flower buds. Many species, hybrids may be grown.

Vanda coerulea

V. coerulea. India. Pale to dark blue, 3–4-in. flowers on 1–2-ft.-long stems in late summer, early fall. Plants grow 1–2 ft. high with rigid, dark green, 6–10-in.-long, strap-shaped leaves.

V. teres. Burma. Blooms May–September, bearing 3–4-in.-wide flowers, 2–5 per stalk. This is the orchid so frequently used in making leis; it is often flown in from Hawaii. Blossoms have deep rose petals and white sepals with a rosy tinge; side lobes of lip are yellow, lower lobe rose with yellow lines and spots. Cylindrical, slightly tapered leaves clothe slender, 2–7-ft. climbing stems. Needs winter rest, much light.

VANILLA TRUMPET VINE. See *Distictis laxiflora*.

VARIEGATED GINGER. See *Alpinia sanderae*.

VAUQUELINIA californica. *Rosaceae.* ARIZONA ROSEWOOD. Evergreen shrub or small tree. Zones 10–13. Upright, sometimes rather contorted growth to as much as 20 ft., with dark gray to reddish brown bark. Lance-shaped leaves with lightly toothed edges, to 3 in. long and ½ in. wide, leathery bright green with slightly woolly undersides. White, 5-petaled, ¼-in.-wide flowers grow in loose, flattened clusters at branch tips in late spring. Woody seed capsules, about ¼ in. long, develop in summer, persist through fall, winter.

Rather open-growing shrub or small tree for desert landscapes, dry margins of cultivated desert gardens.

Vauquelinia californica

VELTHEIMIA bracteata. *Liliaceae.* Bulb. Zones 23, 24 outdoors; Zones 13, 16–22 outdoors with winter shelter; anywhere in containers as house plant or summer patio plant. Native to South Africa. There is some name confusion in the nursery trade; some plants sold as *V. capensis* or *V. viridifolia* are really *V. bracteata*. The true *V. capensis* has bluish green leaves and pale pink flowers, while *V. bracteata* has pinkish purple flowers and shiny deep green, wavy-margined leaves to 1 ft. long, 3 in. wide. It is probable that all sold are *V. bracteata* or a variety of it.

Veltheimia bracteata

Foliage makes *V. bracteata* a beautiful plant even when not in bloom. Flowers appear in winter and early spring: heavy clusters of green-tipped, tubular, drooping blooms, resembling those of red-hot poker (*Kniphofia*), on 1-ft., stout, brown-marked stems. Set bulbs with upper ⅓ above surface. Keep cool and barely moist until roots start to form. Increase watering, light, and warmth as growth begins. Fertilize every 2 weeks through growing season. Dry off as foliage ripens in summer; resume watering in September when new growth begins. Outdoors, protect from hot sun and wind.

VELVET GROUNDSEL. See *Senecio petasitis*.

VELVET PLANT. See *Gynura aurantiaca*.

VERBASCUM. *Scrophulariaceae.* MULLEIN. Biennials, perennials. All Zones. Stately, sun-loving, summer-blooming plants. Broad leaves closely set on stems. Shallow-dished flowers in straight spikes. A large group, some of them weedy. They self-sow freely. Start biennial sorts from seed in spring; sow in place or in containers (but transplant to ground when 2 in. high). Drought tolerant when established, but best flower show with some water, fertilizer. *V. thapsus*, COMMON MULLEIN, is an attractive pasture or roadside weed.

Verbascum bombyciferum 'Arctic Summer'

V. blattaria. MOTH MULLEIN. Biennial. Low clumps of smooth, dark green, cut or toothed leaves. Flower spikes 1½–2½ ft. high with pale yellow or white blooms, purple stamens. Flowers open with morning light.

V. bombyciferum 'Arctic Summer'. Biennial. Foot-high rosettes of furry, gray green, oval leaves. Powdery white stems to 6 ft. or more bear yellow, 1½-in. flowers.

V. dumulosum. Perennial. Dwarf, to 1 ft., with velvety white leaves and spikes of yellow, purple-eyed flowers in midsummer. A hybrid, 'Letitia', has a long summer bloom season.

V. olympicum. Perennial. Stems to 5 ft. high. Large white leaves, 2 ft. or more long, with soft, downy hairs. Bright yellow, 1-in. flowers clustered in many long spikes.

V. phoeniceum. PURPLE MULLEIN. Perennial. Stems 2–4 ft. high. Leaves smooth on top, hairy on underside. Purple flowers in slender spikes half the height of plant or more. The Cotswold Hybrids are similar to the species and come in shades of pink, white, purple, and cream.

VERBENA. *Verbenaceae.* Perennials, some grown as annuals. They need sun and heat in order to thrive, and are drought resistant. Set 2 ft. apart for ground cover; growth is fast. Species listed below adjust effectively to planting in parking strips, along sides of driveways, and on dry banks, walls, and rock crevices where they display their colors all summer. All like good air circulation, dislike wet foliage.

Verbena peruviana

V. bipinnatifida. Perennial. All Zones. Native western Great Plains to Mexico. Grows 8–15 in. tall. Very finely divided leaves; blue flowers all summer. Spreads by self-sowing in most climates.

V. gooddingii. Short-lived perennial. All Zones. Native to Southwest. To 1½ ft. high, spreading. Oval, deeply cut leaves. Heads of flowers, usually pinkish lavender, top short spikes. Sow in early spring for summer bloom. Can reseed where moisture is adequate. Good performer in desert heat.

V. hybrida *(V. hortensis)*. GARDEN VERBENA. Short-lived perennial in Zones 8–24; usually grown as annual. Many-branched plants 6–12 in. high and spreading 1½–3 ft. Oblong, 2–4-in.-long leaves are bright green or gray green, with toothed margins. Flowers in flat, compact clusters, 2–3 in. wide. Colors include white, pink, bright red, purple, blue, and combinations. Romance (6 in.) and Showtime (10 in.) are superior strains. 'Showtime Trinidad', deep rose pink, is hardy enough to withstand light frosts. Subject to mildew; there will be less chance of it if you water deeply and not too often. If used as perennial, prune severely in winter or early spring. Good ground cover in Zones 12, 13 if Bermuda grass can be kept out of it.

V. peruviana *(V. chamaedryfolia)*. Perennial, often grown as annual. Zones 8–24. Spreads rapidly, forms very flat mat. (Planted

2 ft. apart, can make solid cover in a season.) Leaves are neat, small, closely set. Flat-topped flower clusters on slender stems lavishly cover foliage. In original form, corolla tube is white, spreading lobes rich scarlet. Hybrids spread somewhat more slowly, have slightly larger leaves and stouter stems, and are available in several colors: 'Starfire' (red); 'Appleblossom', 'Cherry Pink', 'Princess Gloria', 'Little Pinkie', 'Raspberry Rose', 'St. Paul' (pink and rose tones); many purplish varieties; and a very fine pure white. Especially popular in southern California and the desert.

V. pulchella gracilior. MOSS VERBENA. Perennial. Zones 8–24. Very finely cut leaves; rose violet to pink flowers. A form of *V. p. gracilior* widely sold as *V. tenuisecta* is similar, but with white flowers.

V. rigida *(V. venosa).* Perennial. All Zones. Spreading plants, 10–20 in. tall. Leaves rough, dark green, 2–4 in. long, strongly toothed. Lilac to purple blue flowers in cylindrical clusters on tall, stiff stems summer and fall. Takes considerable drought; useful in low-maintenance gardens. Can be grown as annual; blooms in 4 months from seed.

V. tenera maonettii. Creeping perennial. Zones 8–24. Leaves cut to midrib and lobes cut again. Flat clusters of pink flowers with distinct white margins.

VERBENA, LEMON. See *Aloysia triphylla.*

Verbenaceae. The immense verbena family contains annuals, perennials, shrubs, and a few trees and vines. Leaves are usually opposite or in whorls, flowers in spikes or spikelike clusters. Fruits may be berries or dry. *Clerodendrum, Lantana, Verbena,* and *Vitex* are examples.

VERONICA. *Scrophulariaceae.* SPEEDWELL. Perennials (for shrubby plants sold as *Veronica,* see *Hebe*). All Zones. Handsome plants ranging from 4 in.–2½ ft. in height. Small flowers (¼–½ in. across) are massed to display effectively the white, rose, pink, pale or deep blue color. Use in sunny borders and rock gardens. Most need regular watering; prostrate, mat-forming kinds will tolerate less frequent attention.

Veronica hybrid

V. grandis holophylla. Many stems to 2 ft. high are densely clothed with dark green, very glossy leaves. Long stalks of rich deep blue flowers show above foliage.

V. hybrids. These include a number of midsummer-blooming, upright bushy perennials ranging from 10–18 in. high. Choice varieties: 'Barcarole', to 10 in. tall, rose pink flowers; 'Crater Lake Blue', prostrate with flower stems to 10 in. tall, bright blue flower spikes; 'Icicle', 15–18 in. tall, white flower spikes.

V. longifolia subsessilis. Clumps of upright stems to 2 ft. tall topped by close-flowered spikes of deep blue flowers about ½ in. across in midsummer. Stems are leafy and rather closely set with narrow, pointed leaves.

V. pectinata. Forms prostrate mats that spread by creeping stems which root at joints. Roundish, ½-in.-long leaves with scallop-toothed or deeply cut edges. Flowers are profuse, deep blue with white center, in 5–6-in. spikes among the leaves. Good as a rock plant or in wall crevices.

V. prostrata *(V. rupestris).* Has tufted, hairy stems, some of which are prostrate. Leaves ½–¾ in. long. Flower stems to 8 in. high are topped by short cluster of pale blue flowers. 'Heavenly Blue' is almost entirely prostrate, with flower stems reaching up to 6 in. high. Bright blue flowers.

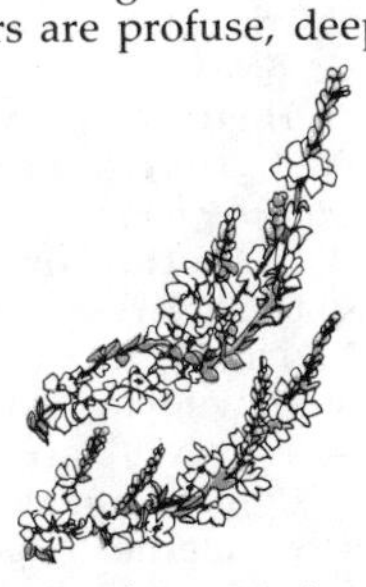

Veronica prostrata

V. repens. Shiny green, ½-in.-long leaves clothe prostrate stems, give mosslike effect. Flowers ¼ in. wide, lavender to white in few-flowered clusters in spring. Takes sun or some shade; fast growing with regular watering. Good as a small-scale ground cover, paving plant, or cover for small bulbs.

V. saturejoides. Many-tufted stems spread by creeping roots. Roundish, ½-in.-long leaves closely overlap on stems. Dark blue flowers in short, compact spikes appear in May. Fine rock plant.

V. spicata. Much like *V. longifolia subsessilis* but less robust and with shorter flower spikes. Miniature variety 'Nana' grows 6 in. high, with violet blue flowers June–July.

VIBURNUM. *Caprifoliaceae.* Deciduous or evergreen shrubs, rarely small trees. Large and diverse group of plants with clustered, often fragrant flowers and clusters of single-seeded, often brilliantly colored fruit much liked by birds. Some are valuable for winter flowers. They tend to fall into groups determined by landscape use.

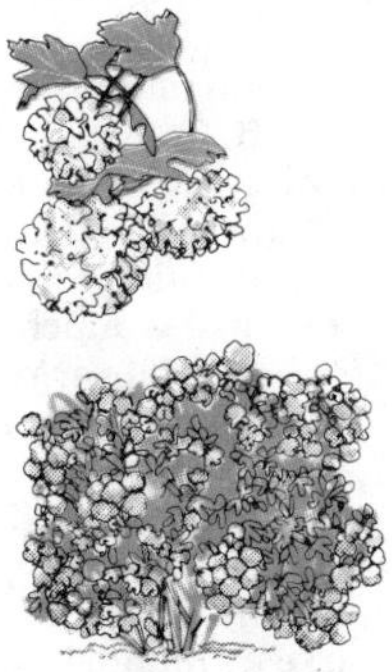

Viburnum opulus 'Roseum'

Evergreen viburnums used principally as foliage plants are *V. cinnamomifolium, V. davidii, V. japonicum, V. propinquum,* and *V. rhytidophyllum.*

Evergreen viburnums used as foliage and flowering plants are *V. odoratissimum, V. suspensum, V. rigidum,* and *V. tinus.*

Partially deciduous viburnums grown for their flowers are *V. burkwoodii* and *V. macrocephalum macrocephalum.* They are nearly evergreen in mild climates and have showy flowers.

Deciduous viburnums grown for fragrant flowers are *V. bitchiuense, V. bodnantense, V. carlcephalum, V. carlesii, V. burkwoodii* 'Chenault', *V. farreri,* and *V. juddii.*

Deciduous viburnums for showy flowers, fall leaf color include *V. dentatum, V. lentago, V. opulus* (also has showy fruit), *V. o.* 'Roseum', *V. plicatum plicatum, V. p. tomentosum, V. prunifolium,* and *V. trilobum.*

Deciduous viburnums valued for fruit color are *V. dilatatum* and *V. wrightii.*

With few exceptions noted in descriptions, viburnums tolerate alkaline and acid soils. They do well in heavy, rich soils with ample moisture, though many are somewhat tolerant of drought. Useful near swimming pools. Many have unusually wide range in climate adaptability; note *V. burkwoodii* and *V. tinus* 'Robustum'. They grow in sun or shade. Most evergreen kinds look better with some protection from sun where summers are hot and long. Prune to shape to prevent legginess; some evergreen kinds can be sheared. Aphids, thrips, spider mites, and scale are likely to be problems. Use an all-purpose insecticide-miticide spray in early spring at 2-week intervals. Keep sulfur sprays off viburnum foliage.

V. bitchiuense. Deciduous shrub. Zones 4–9, 14–24. To 10 ft. Leaves oval, 1½–3½ in. long, downy. Flowers (May) pink aging white, very fragrant. Fruit black, not showy. Somewhat more open habit than *V. carlesii.*

V. bodnantense. Deciduous shrub. Zones 4–9, 14–24. To 10 ft. or more. Oval leaves 1½–4 in. long are deeply veined, turn dark scarlet in fall. Flowers deep pink fading paler, very fragrant, in loose clusters October–April. Fruit red, not showy. This plant is a hybrid; there are several varieties. Best known is 'Dawn' ('Pink Dawn'). Flower buds freeze in coldest Northwest winters.

V. burkwoodii. Deciduous shrub in coldest areas, nearly evergreen elsewhere. Zones 1–10, 14–24. To 6–12 ft. tall, 4–5 ft. wide. Leaves to 3½ in. long, glossy dark green above, white and hairy beneath; purplish in cold weather. Very fragrant white flowers open from dense 4-in. clusters of pink buds. Blooms February–March. Fruit blue black, not showy. Early growth is straggly; mature plants are dense. Can be trained as espalier.

V. b. 'Chenault' ***(V. chenaultii).*** Deciduous shrub. Zones 1–9, 14–24. To 4–6 ft. tall, 3–4 ft. wide. Leaves and flowers are much like those of *V. burkwoodii,* though plant is more compact, more deciduous than the species.

(Continued on next page)

V

V. carlcephalum. FRAGRANT SNOWBALL. Deciduous shrub. Zones 1–11, 14–24. To 8–10 ft. tall, 4–5 ft. wide. Leaves dull grayish green, downy beneath, 2–3½ in. long. Flowers long-lasting, waxy white, fragrant; bloom in dense 4–5-in. clusters in spring, early summer. No fruit. Showy as common snowball (*V. opulus* 'Roseum') but has added fragrance.

V. carlesii. KOREAN SPICE VIBURNUM. Deciduous shrub. Zones 1–11, 14–24. To 4–8 ft.tall, 4–5 ft. broad. Leaves are like those of *V. carlcephalum*. Flowers pink in bud, opening white, in 2–3-in.-wide clusters, sweetly fragrant, March–May. Blue black fruit in summer. Loose, open habit. Best in part shade during summer, in sun during spring, winter.

V. chenaultii. See *V. burkwoodii* 'Chenault'.

V. cinnamomifolium. Evergreen shrub. Zones 5–9, 14–24. To 10–20 ft. tall, equally wide. Leaves 3–6 in. long, 1–3 in. wide, leathery, glossy dark green, strongly 3-veined. White, individually tiny flowers, in flattish clusters 6 in. across, open from pink buds in April. Faintly honey scented. Fruit is shiny blue black, small. Looks like a much-magnified *V. davidii*. Use in screens, background. Best in acid soil with plenty of water.

V. davidii. Evergreen shrub. Zones 4–9, 14–24. To 1–3 ft. tall, 3–4 ft. wide. Leaves are glossy dark green, deeply veined, to 6 in. long. White flowers in 3-in.-wide clusters open from dull pinkish red buds; not showy. Metallic turquoise blue fruit. For abundant berry production, set out more than one plant.

Use as foundation shrub, in foreground plantings, with ferns, azaleas, other acid soil plants in part shade. Extremely valuable in Zones 4–6, 17.

V. dentatum. ARROWWOOD. Deciduous shrub. Zones 1–9, 14–21. To 15 ft. with many stems from base tending to form clumps or thickets. Oval, coarsely toothed leaves to 3 in. long turn glossy red in autumn. White spring flowers in flattish 4-in. clusters; blue black fruit, relished by birds, in late spring to summer. Use in woodland plantings, as background or screen shrub. Grows well in sun or shade, moist or dry soil.

V. dilatatum. LINDEN VIBURNUM. Deciduous shrub. Zones 3–9, 14–16. Compact shrub to 6, possibly 10 ft. tall. Leaves nearly round, 2–5 in. long, gray green. Flowers are tiny, creamy white, in 5-in.-wide clusters in early summer. Showy bright red fruits are produced best where summers are warm; they ripen in September, hang on into winter.

V. farreri *(V. fragrans)*. Deciduous shrub. Zones 4–9, 14–24. To 10–15 ft. tall and as wide. Smooth green leaves are oval, heavily veined, 1½–3 in. long; turn soft russet red in fall. Fragrant white to pink flowers in 2-in. clusters, November–March. Blossoms will stand to 20°–22°F., freeze in colder temperatures. Fruit bright red. Prune to prevent leggy growth. *V. f.* 'Album' (*V. f.* 'Candidissimum') has pure white flowers. *V. f.* 'Nanum' is lower growing (to 2 ft.), with pink flowers.

V. japonicum. Evergreen shrub or small tree. Zones 5–10, 12, 14–24. To 10–20 ft. tall. Leaves are leathery, glossy dark green, to 6 in. long. Sparse bloom in spring: fragrant white flowers in 4-in. clusters. Red fruit is sparse but very attractive. Big, bulky shrub or small tree for background plantings. Best with some shade in warmer areas. Control aphids.

V. juddii. Deciduous shrub. Zones 3–9, 14–24. To 4–8 ft. tall. Hybrid between *V. carlesii* and *V. bitchiuense*. More spreading and bushy than *V. carlesii*, but otherwise similar to it.

V. lantana. WAYFARING TREE. Deciduous shrub or small tree. Zones 1–12, 14–20. To 8–15 ft. tall. Leaves are broadly oval, to 5 in. long, downy on both sides; turn red in fall. Tiny white flowers in 2–4-in. clusters, May or June. Showy, bright scarlet fruit turning black. Variety 'Mohican' is smaller, to 6 ft. high and 8 ft. wide; fruit remains orange red. Use in woodland or background plantings. Will take dryish conditions.

V. lentago. NANNYBERRY. Deciduous shrub or small tree. Zones 1–9, 14–21. Will grow as single-trunked tree up to 30 ft. or as massive shrub to lesser height. Creamy white spring flowers in flat clusters to 4–5 in. across. Edible fruit red at first, changing to blue black, remaining on plant into winter. Glossy foliage turns purplish red in fall.

Grows in shade as well as sun. Use as large background shrub, small tree. Good in shade of taller trees, at woodland edge.

V. macrocephalum macrocephalum (***V. m.*** 'Sterile'). CHINESE SNOWBALL. Deciduous shrub in coldest areas, nearly evergreen elsewhere. Zones 1–9, 14–24. To 12–20 ft. tall, with broad, rounded habit. Leaves oval to oblong, dull green, 2–4 in. long. Spectacular big, rounded flower clusters to 6–8 in. are composed of sterile flowers. Blooms April–May. No fruit. Good for espaliers, display.

V. odoratissimum. SWEET VIBURNUM. Evergreen shrub (briefly deciduous in colder-winter areas). Risky in coldest winters in Zones 8, 9, 14; reliable in Zones 15–24. To 10–20 ft. tall, broader than tall. Bright green leaves, 3–8 in. long, with glossy, varnished-looking surface. Conical, 3–6-in. clusters of white, lightly fragrant flowers, May. Red fruit ripening to black. Variety 'Emerald Lustre' has larger leaves. Use as big screen or single plant.

V. opulus. EUROPEAN CRANBERRY BUSH. Deciduous shrub. Zones 1–9, 14–24. To 10–20 ft. Lobed dark green leaves shaped like maple leaves; 2–4 in. long and wider, turn red in fall. Blooms in May: white flower clusters 2–4 in. across, rimmed with ¾-in.-wide, white sterile flowers in lace cap effect. Large, showy red fruit. Needs careful spraying to control aphids. Varieties include:

'Aureum'. To 10 ft. Golden yellow foliage needs some shade to prevent sunburn. Red fruit.

'Compactum'. Same as *V. opulus* but smaller: 4–5 ft. high and wide.

'Nanum'. Dwarf form of *V. opulus*. To 2 ft. tall, 2 ft. wide. Needs no trimming as low hedge. Can take poor, wet soils. No flowers, fruit.

'Roseum' ***(V. o.*** 'Sterile'). COMMON SNOWBALL. To 10–15 ft. Resembles *V. opulus*, but flower clusters resemble snowballs: 2–2½ in. across, composed entirely of sterile flowers (so no fruit).

V. plicatum plicatum *(V. tomentosum* 'Sterile'). JAPANESE SNOWBALL. Deciduous shrub. Zones 1–9, 14–24. To 15 ft. tall and as wide. Oval, dull dark green, strongly veined leaves 3–6 in. long. Leaves turn purplish red in fall. Snowball clusters of white sterile flowers 2–3 in. across, borne in opposite rows along horizontal branches, May. Less subject to aphids than *V. opulus*. Horizontal branching pattern, fall color, flowers all attractive.

V. p. tomentosum. DOUBLEFILE VIBURNUM. Resembles plant above, but flat flower clusters are 2–4 in. wide, edged with 1–1½-in.-wide sterile flowers in lace cap effect. Fruit red, showy, not always profuse. Selections include: 'Cascade', a smaller grower; 'Mariesii', with larger sterile flowers; 'Shasta', with even more horizontal habit (6 ft. tall, 12 ft. wide); and 'Watanabe', a dwarf (4- by 6-ft.), nearly everblooming variety.

V. propinquum. Evergreen shrub. Zones 5–9, 14–24. To 4 ft. tall. Leaves narrowish oval, 3 veined, 2–3½ in. long, dark glossy green. Bronzy new growth. Greenish white flowers bloom in 1½–3-in.-wide clusters. Small blue black fruit. Resembles a bushier *V. davidii* with twiggier outline, smaller leaves.

V. prunifolium. BLACK HAW. Deciduous shrub. Zones 1–9, 14–21. Upright to 15 ft. and spreading as wide. Can be trained as small tree. Common name comes from dark fruit and plant's resemblance to hawthorn (*Crataegus*). Oval leaves, to 3 in. long and finely toothed, turn red in autumn. Abundant clusters of creamy white flowers in spring are followed by edible blue black fruit to ½ in. long in fall, winter. Use as dense screen or barrier, attractive specimen shrub, or small tree. Best in sun.

V. rhytidocarpum. See *V. rhytidophyllum*.

V. rhytidophylloides. See *V. rhytidophyllum*.

V. rhytidophyllum. LEATHERLEAF VIBURNUM. Evergreen shrub. Zones 2–9, 14–24. Narrow, upright shrub to 6–15 ft. tall; fast growing in colder areas, slow in Zones 18–24. Leaves narrowish, to 4–10 in. long, deep green and wrinkled above, densely fuzzy underneath. Off-white spring flowers in 4–8-in.-wide clusters. Fruit scarlet, turn-

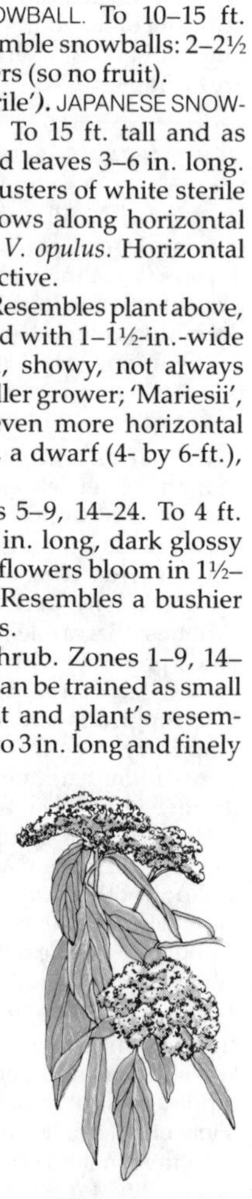

Viburnum rhytidophyllum

ing black. Cold hardy, but tattered looking where cold winds blow. Some think it striking, others merely coarse. Several hybrids include 'Alleghany', 'Pragense', and 'Willowwood', all similar to the *V. rhytidophyllum;* some have been called *V. rhytidocarpum.*

V. rigidum. CANARY ISLAND VIBURNUM. Evergreen shrub. Zones 15–24. Resembles *V. tinus* but has larger flower clusters, larger leaves to 6 in. long. Grows upright to 6–10 ft. with equal or greater spread. Flowers in late winter, early spring are followed by blue fruit that later turns black. Uses same as for *V. tinus.*

V. suspensum. SANDANKWA VIBURNUM. Evergreen shrub. Risky in coldest winters Zones 8–10, 12, 14; reliable in Zones 13, 15–24. To 8–10 ft. tall and as broad. Leathery, oval, 2–4-in.-long leaves; glossy deep green above, paler beneath. Flowers white, in loose 2–4-in. clusters in early spring. Fragrance objectionable to some people. Fruit red turning black, not long lasting. Takes sun or considerable shade. Serviceable screen, hedge, with dense foliage. Watch for thrips, spider mites, aphids.

V. tinus. LAURUSTINUS. Evergreen shrub or small narrow tree. Zones 4–10, 12, 13 (in coolest locations), 14–23. To 6–12 ft. tall, half as wide. Leaves dark green, oval, leathery, slightly rolled under at edges, 2–3 in. long. New stems wine red. Tight clusters of pink buds open to white flowers, November–spring. Lightly fragrant. Bright metallic blue fruit lasts through summer. Dense foliage right to ground makes it good plant for screens, hedges, clipped topiary shapes. Mildews near ocean. May be bothered by spider mites.

V. t. 'Dwarf'. Similar to above, but grows only 3–5 ft. tall, equally wide. Low screens, hedges, foundation plantings.

V. t. 'Lucidum'. SHINING LAURUSTINUS. Leaves larger than those of *V. tinus;* plant less hardy, but more resistant to mildew near coast.

V. t. 'Robustum'. ROUNDLEAF LAURUSTINUS. Leaves coarser, rougher than those of *V. tinus;* flowers less pink. More resistant to mildew. Makes excellent, small narrow tree.

V. t. 'Spring Bouquet' (also sold as *V. t.* 'Compactum'). Foliage is slightly smaller, darker green than that of *V. tinus.* Plant is fairly compact, upright to about 6 ft.; good for hedges.

V. t. 'Variegatum'. Zones 4–9, 14–23. Like *V. tinus,* but leaves are variegated with white and pale yellow.

V. trilobum. CRANBERRY BUSH. Deciduous shrub. Zones 1–11, 14–20. To 10–15 ft. tall. Leaves are much like those of *V. opulus;* turn red in fall. Lace cap flowers and fruit (edible) similar to those of *V. opulus.* Less susceptible to aphid damage than *V. opulus.*

V. wrightii. Deciduous shrub. Zones 4–9, 14–17. To 6–10 ft. tall, with narrow, erect habit. Leaves smooth, bright green, oval, 2–5 in. long, 1–2½ in. wide. Flowers small, white, in 2–4-in.-wide clusters, May. Fruit is showy, bright red, lasts many months.

VICTORIAN BOX. See *Pittosporum undulatum.*

VIGNA caracalla *(Phaseolus caracalla;* often sold as ***P. gigantea).*** *Leguminosae.* SNAIL VINE. Perennial vine. Zones 12–24. Looks much like pole bean in foliage and general appearance. Climbs to 10–20 ft. Flowers (spring and summer) are fragrant, cream marked purple or pale purple. Common name comes from twisted keel petals which are coiled like snail shell. Odd and pretty. Cut to ground when frost kills tops. Plant in full sun. Will accept overwatering. Summer screen or bank cover.

Vigna caracalla

VINCA. *Apocynaceae.* PERIWINKLE, MYRTLE. Evergreen perennials. Trailing habit; extensively used as ground covers, for pattern plantings, and for rough slopes and otherwise unused areas. Both species can be extremely invasive in sheltered and forested areas.

Vinca minor

V. major. Zones 5–24. Long, trailing stems root as they spread, carry many 1–3-in., somewhat broad-based, oval, dark green, glossy leaves (white-variegated form also common). Short flowering branches with lavender blue flowers 1–2 in. across. Will mound up 6–12 in., possibly to 2 ft. high. Tough plant, quite easy to grow. Needs shade and some moisture to look its best, but will take sun if watered generously. If used as ground cover, shear close to ground occasionally to bring on fresh new growth.

V. minor. DWARF PERIWINKLE. All Zones; in Zones 1–3, 7, 10–13, grow only in shade. Perfect miniature of *V. major,* except leaves are more often oblong, have shorter stalks, are more closely spaced. Also requires more care—2 or 3 good soakings per month and feeding several times a year. Lavender blue flowers an inch across; also forms with white, double blue, and deeper blue flowers and with variegated foliage. 'Bowles' Variety' has larger blue flowers.

V. rosea. See *Catharanthus roseus.*

VIOLA. *Violaceae.* VIOLA, VIOLET, PANSY. Perennials; some treated as annuals. Botanically speaking, violas, pansies, and violets are all perennials belonging to genus *Viola.* Pansies and violas, however, are generally treated as annuals, especially in mild-winter areas.

Viola wittrockiana

All 3 grow best in rich, moist soil. Plant violas and pansies in full sun in coastal areas, in partial shade in warmer sections. Violets need shade from hot afternoon sun; in desert and other hot-summer climates, plant in full shade.

Violas and pansies are invaluable for winter and spring color in mild regions, from spring through summer in cooler areas. They provide mass color in borders and edgings, as ground covers for spring-flowering bulbs, and in containers outdoors. Pansies also give colorful displays in pots and boxes. Sweet violets are notorious hosts to spider mites.

V. alba. PARMA VIOLET. Zones 4–9, 14–24. Small, sweetly fragrant, double blue purple flowers. Resembles *V. odorata* in plant form and growth habit. Give it rich soil, cool location, regular water. Individual plants send out runners that form new crowns. Use as small-scale ground cover in woodland gardens.

V. cornuta. VIOLA, TUFTED PANSY. All Zones. Tufted plants 6–8 in. high. Smooth, wavy-toothed, ovalish leaves. Purple, pansylike flowers, about 1½ in. across, have slender spur. Newer strains and varieties have larger flowers with shorter spurs, in solid colors of purple, blue, yellow, apricot, ruby red, and white. Crystal strain has especially large flowers in clear colors.

In mild-winter climates, sow seed of violas in late summer, set out plants in fall for color from late winter or early spring to summer. In cold regions, sow seed in September or early spring; transplant September-sown seedlings to cold frame, keep there over winter, set plants outside in spring. Named varieties of violas such as 'Maggie Mott' and 'Pride of Victoria' also increased by division or cuttings.

V. hederacea. AUSTRALIAN VIOLET. Zones 8, 9, 14–24. Tufted plant 1–4 in. high, spreads by stolons at slow to moderate rate to several feet in time. Leaves kidney shaped. Flowers, ¼–¾ in. across, nearly spurless, are white or blue fading to white at petal tips. Summer bloom; plant goes dormant at about 30°F. Use as ground cover in shade or in sun with abundant water.

V. labradorica. Perennial. All Zones. Tiny violet 3 in. tall or less, with roundish, 1-in. leaves tinged purple and tiny lavender blue violets in spring. Spreads aggressively by runners and can invade choice small perennials. Useful for small-scale ground cover in shade or for filler between stepping stones or paving blocks.

V. odorata. SWEET VIOLET. All Zones. The violet of song and story. Tufted, long runners root at joints. Leaves dark green, heart shaped, toothed on margins. Flowers are fragrant, short spurred, deep violet, bluish rose, or white. Large, long-stemmed (to 6 in.), deep purple 'Royal Robe' is widely used. 'Royal Elk' has single, fragrant, long-stemmed violet-colored flowers; 'Charm' grows in clumps, has small white flowers; 'Rosina' is pink flowered. Plant size varies from 2 in. for smallest varieties to 8–10 in. for largest.

(Continued on next page)

V

Plants spread by runners at moderate rate. Take full sun near coast and in cool-summer areas.

Remove runners and shear rank growth in late fall for better spring flower display. For heavy bloom, feed in very early spring, before flowering, with complete fertilizer.

V. priceana. See *V. sororia.*

V. sororia *(V. priceana).* CONFEDERATE VIOLET. All Zones. Leaves, blossoms rise directly from sturdy rootstock. Leaves are somewhat heart shaped, to 5 in. wide. Flowers ½–¾ in. across, white, heavily veined with violet blue, flat-faced like pansies. Self-sows readily; best in woodland garden. Good ground cover among rhododendrons.

V. tricolor. JOHNNY-JUMP-UP. Annual or short-lived perennial. To 6–12 in. tall with oval, deeply lobed leaves. Tufted habit. Purple and yellow flowers resemble miniature pansies. Color forms available in blue or in mix including yellow, lavender, mauve, apricot, red. Spring bloom. Self-sows profusely.

V. t. hortensis. See *V. wittrockiana.*

V. wittrockiana *(V. tricolor hortensis).* PANSY. Excellent strains with flowers 2–4 in. across, in white, blue, mahogany red, rose, yellow, apricot, purple; also bicolors. Petals often striped or blotched; Crown and Crystal Bowl strains have unblotched flowers. Plants grow to about 8 in. high. F_1 and F_2 hybrids more free flowering, heat tolerant.

Sow pansy seed from mid-July to mid-August. In mild-winter areas, set out plants in fall for bloom from late winter or early spring to summer. In cold sections, transplant seedlings into cold frame, set out plants in spring; or sow seed indoors in January or February, plant outdoors in spring. Or plant nursery plants in spring. Pansies need rich, cool, moist soil with protection from hottest sun. To prolong bloom, pick flowers (with some foliage) regularly, remove faded blooms before they set seed. In warmer climates, plants get ragged by midsummer and should be removed.

VIOLET. See *Viola.*

VIOLET TRUMPET VINE. See *Clytostoma callistegioides.*

VIRGINIA BLUEBELLS. See *Mertensia virginica.*

VIRGINIA CREEPER. See *Parthenocissus inserta, P. quinquefolia.*

VIRGINIAN STOCK. See *Malcolmia maritima.*

VISCARIA coeli-rosa. See *Lychnis coeli-rosa.*

Vitaceae. The grape family contains vines that climb by tendrils and produce berries. Grape, Boston ivy, and Virginia creeper are the best-known representatives.

VITEX. *Verbenaceae.* CHASTE TREE. Deciduous and evergreen shrubs or trees. Two species are sold in the West; both have divided leaves and clustered flowers.

Vitex agnus-castus

V. agnus-castus. CHASTE TREE. Deciduous shrub or small tree. Zones 4–24. Growth is slow in cold climates, fast in warmer areas. Size varies from 6 ft. in Northwest to 25 ft. in low desert. Habit broad and spreading, usually multitrunked. Leaves are divided fanwise into 5–7 narrow, 2–6-in.-long leaflets that are dark green above, gray beneath. Conspicuous 7-in. spikes of lavender blue flowers appear in summer and fall.

Tolerates many types of soils, but requires plenty of summer heat for richly colored, profuse bloom. In rich, moist soils it grows luxuriantly, but has paler flowers. Good for summer flower color in shrub border. If trained high, makes good small shade tree. Resistant to oak root fungus. Varieties are: 'Alba', white flowers; 'Latifolia' (often sold as *V. macrophylla*), sturdy, with large leaflets; and 'Rosea', with pinkish flowers.

V. lucens. NEW ZEALAND CHASTE TREE. Evergreen tree. Zones 16, 17, 22–24. Slow to moderate growth to 40–60 ft. Leaves with 3–5 shining, glossy, corrugated-looking, roundish, 5-in.-long leaflets. Pink winter buds open to lavender pink, 1-in. flowers in loose clusters. Bright red fruit resembles small cherries. Needs deep, rich soil, ample water, and protection from frost while young. Luxuriant near coast; tolerates sea breezes.

VITIS. See *Grape.*

VOODOO LILY. See *Sauromatum venosum.*

VRIESEA. *Bromeliaceae.* Perennial. Outdoors in most frost-free parts of Zones 22–24; house plant anywhere. Bromeliads with rosettes of long, leathery leaves and oddly shaped flower clusters. Grow as epiphytes in pockets of sphagnum moss on branches or in pots of loose, highly organic mix. Keep leaf bases filled with water, and water mix occasionally. Mist if grown in hot, dry rooms. Feed lightly and often. Give strong light, but not direct, hot sun.

Vriesea hieroglyphica

V. hieroglyphica. Rosettes of 30–40 leaves, each 3 ft. long, 3 in. wide, dark green with pronounced cross-banding of blackish purple. Greenish flower spike with dull yellow flowers.

V. lindenii. See *Tillandsia lindenii.*

V. splendens. FLAMING SWORD. Rosettes of up to 20 dark green, 1½-ft. leaves barred transversely with blackish purple. Flower stalk like a 1½–2-ft.-wide feather of bright red bracts from which small yellow flowers emerge. 'Chantrierei' is brightly colored selection.

WAFER ASH. See *Ptelea trifoliata.*

WAKE ROBIN. See *Trillium.*

WALDSTEINIA fragarioides. *Rosaceae.* BARREN STRAWBERRY. Zones 2–9, 14–17. Evergreen strawberrylike ground cover 2–3 in. high, spreading to 6–8 in. Leaves consist of 3 wedge-shaped leaflets to 2 in. long, glossy green turning bronze in autumn. Yellow, 5-petaled spring flowers to ¾ in. across. Full sun to light shade, ordinary garden watering.

Waldsteinia fragarioides

WALLFLOWER. See *Cheiranthus cheiri, Erysimum.*

WALNUT *(Juglans).* *Juglandaceae.* Deciduous trees. Usually large and spreading, with leaves divided into leaflets. Oval or round nuts in fleshy husks. English walnut (*J. regia*) is a well-known orchard tree in many parts of the West; American native species are sometimes planted as shade trees with incidental bonus of edible nuts or are used as understock for grafting English walnut. English and California black walnut trees are notorious as hosts to aphids. The pests and their honeydew exudation are inevitable, so you should not plant either tree where branches will arch over patio or automobile parking place.

Walnut

J. californica. SOUTHERN CALIFORNIA BLACK WALNUT. Zones 18–24. Native to southern California. Treelike shrub or small tree to 15–30 ft., usually with several stems from ground. Leaves 6–12 in., with 9–19 leaflets to 2¼ in. long. Roundish, ¾-in. nuts have good flavor but extremely hard, thick shells. Tree is not commercially grown, but worth saving if it grows as native. Takes drought and poor soil. Resistant to oak root fungus.

J. cinerea. BUTTERNUT. Zones 1–9, 14–17. Native to eastern U.S. To 50–60 ft., with broad, spreading head. Resembles black walnut (*J. nigra*), but is smaller; leaves have fewer leaflets; nuts are oval or elongated rather than round. Flavor is good, but shells are thick and hard. Needs only moderate amount of summer water.

J. hindsii. CALIFORNIA BLACK WALNUT. Zones 5–9, 14–20. Native to scattered localities in northern California. To 30–60 ft. tall, with single trunk and broad crown. Leaves have 15–19 leaflets, each 3–5 in. long. Widely used as rootstock for English walnut in California. Tree is drought tolerant and resistant to oak root fungus.

J. major (*J. rupestris major*). NOGAL, ARIZONA WALNUT. Zones 10, 12, 13. Native to Arizona, New Mexico, northern Mexico. Broad tree to 50 ft. Leaves have 9–13 leaflets. Round, small, thick-shelled nuts in husks that dry on tree. Takes desert heat and wind; needs deep soil, some water.

J. nigra. BLACK WALNUT. Zones 1–9, 14–21. Native to eastern U.S. High-branched tree grows to 150 ft. (usually not over 100 ft. in the West) with round crown, furrowed blackish brown bark. Leaves have 15–23 leaflets, each 2½–5 in. long. Nuts 1–1½ in. across, thick shelled and very hard, but with rich flavor. Improved varieties (scarce) with thinner shells are: 'Thomas', 'Stabler', and 'Ohio'. Big, hardy shade tree for big places. Fairly drought tolerant. Don't plant near vegetable or flower gardens, rhododendrons or azaleas; black walnut inhibits these plants' growth, either through root competition or by secreting a substance that inhibits growth of other plants. Long dormant season.

J. regia. ENGLISH WALNUT. Zones 4–9, 14–23; some varieties in Zones 1–3. Native to southwest Asia, southeast Europe. To 60 ft. high, with equal spread; fast growing, especially when young. Smooth, gray bark on trunk and heavy, horizontal or upward-angled branches. Leaves with 5–7 leaflets, rarely more, 3–6 in. long. The tree is hardy to −5°F., but certain varieties are injured by late and early frosts in colder regions. Strains from the Carpathian mountains of eastern Europe are hardy in all but the coldest mountain areas.

English walnut should not be planted as landscape tree except on very large lots. It's out of leaf a long time, messy when in leaf (drip and sooty mildew from aphid exudations), and messy in fruit (husks can stain). It needs deep soil and deep watering. Many people are allergic to the wind-borne pollen.

To thrive, trees need deep soil moisture; bases of trunks must be kept dry to prevent fungus attack and rot. Deep, slow irrigation in basins is ideal; where tree must grow with lawn sprinkling, keep base of trunk dry by digging away earth down to level of first roots, replacing it with coarse gravel or rock. Or pave area near trunk with brick or stone on sand. Keep other plants out under drip line where feeder roots grow.

Established plants take some drought, but in dry-summer areas need deep, regular watering for top-quality nuts. Old plants need pruning only to remove dead wood or correct shape. Young plants grow fast, should be trained to make central leading shoot and branch high enough for comfortable foot traffic. Shorten overlong side branches.

Spray for aphids, scale insects, codling moths, spider mites. Walnut husk fly attacks husks, making them adhere to and disfigure nuts. Control with repeated malathion sprays.

Walnut husks open in fall, dropping nuts to ground. Hasten drop by knocking nuts from tree. Pick up nuts immediately. Remove any adhering husks. Dry in single layer spread out in airy shade until kernels become brittle; then store.

Two varieties with exceptionally large, thin-shelled nuts are 'Cooke's Giant Sweet' and 'Carmelo'. Kernels do not entirely fill the shells, but are large nevertheless.

In Zones 1–3, grow walnuts described as Carpathian or Hardy Persian. Most offered are seedlings, but grafted, named varieties do exist. 'Ambassador' is hardy to −25°F. In Zones 4–7, 'Adams', 'Cooke's Giant Sweet', 'Franquette', 'Idaho', and 'Mayette' bloom late enough to escape spring frosts, yield high-quality nuts. Gardeners in Zones 8, 9 can grow 'Carmelo', 'Cooke's Giant Sweet', 'Drummond', 'Eureka', 'Hartley', 'Payne', 'Idaho', or 'Serr' (bears at early age). Best varieties for Zones 14–16 are 'Carmelo', 'Concord', 'Cooke's Giant Sweet', 'Franquette', 'Hartley', 'Mayette', 'Payne', 'Serr', and 'Wasson'. In Zones 18–20, grow 'Drummond', 'Payne', or 'Placentia'. In Zones 21–23, best choice is 'Placentia'. Variety 'Laciniata', with deeply cut leaflets, is occasionally sold.

WANDERING JEW. See *Callisia, Tradescantia, Tripogandra, Zebrina.*

WARMINSTER BROOM. See *Cytisus praecox.*

WASHINGTONIA. *Palmae.* Palms. Zones 8, 9, 11–24. Native to California, Arizona, northern Mexico. Fan-shaped leaves. Following 2 species are the most widely planted palms in California.

Washingtonia robusta

W. filifera. CALIFORNIA FAN PALM. Fast grower to 60 ft. In native stands in Southwest deserts, it always grows near springs or other moist spots. Takes desert heat and some drought, but thrives on moisture in well-drained soil. Long-stalked leaves stand well apart in open crown. As leaves mature, they bend down to form a petticoat of thatch which develops in straight lines, tapering inward toward trunk at lowest edge of petticoat. Trunk is much more robust than that of its Mexican cousin, even though cousin's specific name is *robusta*. Hardy to around 18°F.

Use young trees in containers. In landscape, can serve as street or parkway planting, in groves, or in large gardens as single trees or in groups.

W. robusta. MEXICAN FAN PALM. Taller (to 100 ft.), more slender, more widely sold than California fan palm. Leaf stalks are shorter, with distinguishing reddish streak on undersides. More compact crown, rougher thatch. Very fast growing. Old plants take on natural curvature; young ones started at an angle will grow upright to produce a bend. Hardy to 20°F. Takes poor soil or drought, but grows faster with good conditions. This is the tall palm that is widely used as an avenue tree in Southern California.

WASHINGTON THORN. See *Crataegus phaenopyrum.*

WATERCRESS. *Cruciferae.* Perennial. All Zones. This plant grows naturally in running streams. You can plant seed in flats or pots and transplant seedlings to moist banks, where they will grow rapidly. Or insert cuttings of watercress from the market into wet soil in or near the stream; these root readily. Be quite certain the stream is free from pollution before planting out in such a location. Watercress can also be grown in wet place in garden, but requires some shade in warm inland gardens. Or grow it in pots of soil placed in tub of water; water should be changed at least weekly by running hose slowly into tub. Plant grows to 10–15 in. with small, roundish leaflets. Flowers are insignificant.

Watercress

WATER HAWTHORN. See *Aponogeton distachyus.*

WATER HYACINTH. See *Eichhornia crassipes.*

W

WATER LILY. See *Nymphaea*.

WATERMELON. *Cucurbitaceae.* Annuals. These need a long growing season, more heat than most other melons, and more space than other vine crops—space hills (circles of seed) 8 ft. by 8 ft. Other than that, culture is as described under Melon. If you garden in a commercial watermelon-growing area—Zones 8, 9, 12–14, 18–21—choose any variety that suits your fancy. If your summers are short or cool (Zones 1–6, 15–17, 22–24), choose one of the fast-maturing ("early") varieties. Those listed in catalogues and on seed packets at 70–75 days to harvest are best.

Watermelon

WATSONIA. *Iridaceae.* Deciduous and evergreen perennials growing from corms. Zones 4–9, 12–24. Gardeners in Zones 1–3 can experiment growing them like gladiolus, lifting and storing corms over winter. Native to South Africa. Flowers are smaller, generally more tubular than gladiolus, on taller, branched stems. They grow in fall and winter and hence are of limited use where winters are severe. All are good cut flowers. Plant in late summer or early fall; plants produce foliage in autumn. Full sun, little to moderate summer water except for newly planted corms. Stake tall stems of pot-grown plants. In mild climates, they can remain undisturbed for many years. Lift overcrowded clumps in summer after bloom; divide and replant as quickly as possible.

Watsonia pyramidata

Of about 70 species, these two are best known:

W. beatricis. Evergreen. Leaves 2½ ft. long; July–August flowers 3 in. long, bright apricot red, on somewhat branched, 3½-ft. stems. Selected hybrids in colors from peach to nearly scarlet.

W. pyramidata. Deciduous. Blooms late spring, early summer. Rose pink to rose red, 2½-in. flowers in spikelike clusters on branched, 4–6-ft. stems. Leaves are 2½ ft. long, 1 in. wide. Many excellent large-flowered hybrids in pink, white, lavender, red. *W. p. ardernei* (often listed as *W. ardernei*) is pure white.

WATTLE. See *Acacia*.

WAXFLOWER, GERALDTON. See *Chamelaucium uncinatum*.

WAX FLOWER, WAX PLANT. See *Hoya*.

WAX MYRTLE, PACIFIC. See *Myrica californica*.

WAX VINE. See *Senecio macroglossus*.

WAYFARING TREE. See *Viburnum lantana*.

WEDELIA trilobata. *Compositae.* WEDELIA. Perennial. Zones 12, 13, 21–24. Trailing plant that roots wherever stems touch damp earth. Fleshy evergreen leaves are dark glossy green, to 4 in. long and half as wide, with a few coarse teeth or shallow lobes toward tips. Inch-wide flower heads resemble tiny yellow zinnias or marigolds. Blooms nearly throughout the year in sun; blooms sparsely in shade. Spreads fast by creeping, rooting stems; easily propagated by lifting rooted pieces or by placing tip cuttings in moist soil. Best in sandy, fast-draining soils but will take others if drainage is acceptable. Reasonably salt tolerant. Killed to ground by frost, it makes fast comeback. Tolerates high heat of desert. Plant 1½ ft. apart, water regularly, feed lightly. Cut back hard if plantings mound up or become stemmy.

Wedelia trilobata

WEIGELA. *Caprifoliaceae.* Deciduous shrubs. Zones 1–11, 14–17. Valuable for voluminous flower display late in spring season (May–June in Northwest, earlier in California). Funnel-shaped flowers grow singly or in short clusters all along previous season's shoots. When weigelas finish blooming, their charm fades—they aren't outstandingly attractive out of bloom. Most are rather coarse leafed and stiff, becoming rangy unless pruned.

Weigela florida

After flowering, cut back branches that have bloomed to unflowered side branches. Leave only 1 or 2 of these to each stem. Cut some of the oldest stems to ground. Thin new suckers to a few of the most vigorous. A simpler method you can employ every other year is to cut back entire plant about halfway just after blooms fade. Resulting dense new growth will provide plenty of flowers the next spring.

Use as backgrounds for flower borders, as summer screens, in mixed shrub borders. Can grow in full sun to part shade. Need at least moderate summer watering.

Many garden varieties are complex hybrids of 4 species; names are often mixed in nursery trade.

W. 'Bristol Ruby'. To 6–7 ft. tall, nearly as wide. Ruby red flowers in late spring; some repeat bloom midsummer and fall.

W. 'Bristol Snowflake'. Resembles 'Bristol Ruby', but has white flowers.

W. 'Eva Supreme'. Compact shrub to 5 ft. Deep red flowers. Needs little pruning to maintain size, form.

W. florida ***(W. rosea).*** Fast growth to 8–10 ft. tall. Flowers pink to rose red, 1 in. long, in May and June.

W. f. 'Variegata'. Bright green foliage variegated with cream. Popular and showy.

W. 'Java Red'. Compact, mounding plant to 6 ft. or wider. Deep pink flowers open from red buds. Foliage deep green tinted purple.

W. middendorffiana. Dense, broad shrub to 3–4 ft. tall. Leaves 2–3 in. long, 1–1½ in. wide, wrinkled, dark green. Flowers (April, May) are sulfur yellow marked orange, an inch long and as wide, clustered at ends of branches. Best in cool, moist place; less rugged than other weigelas.

W. 'Newport Red' (also sold as *W.* 'Vanicekii', 'Cardinal', 'Rhode Island Red'). To 6 ft. tall, with brilliant red flowers 1–1½ in. across in May–June.

W. praecox. Similar to *W. florida* but blooms several weeks earlier and grows to about 6 ft. tall. Flowers pink to rose with yellow throats.

WELSH POPPY. See *Meconopsis cambrica*.

WESTERN RED CEDAR. See *Thuja plicata*.

WESTERN SAND CHERRY. See *Prunus besseyi*.

WESTRINGIA rosmariniformis. *Labiatae.* Evergreen shrub. Zones 14 (damaged in coldest winters), 15–17, 19–24. Native to Australia. Spreading, rather loose growth to 3–6 ft. tall, half again as wide. Leaves medium green to gray green above, white beneath, slightly finer and filmier in texture than rosemary leaves. Small white flowers Feb-

Westringia rosmariniformis

ruary through spring in colder areas, all year in milder climates.

Needs light, well-drained soil in sun. Little to average water. Good near coast; very wind tolerant. Effective on sunny banks and in borders with lavender; charming with *Podocarpus gracilior.*

WHEATGRASS. See *Agropyron.*

WHITE CEDAR. See *Chamaecyparis thyoides.*

WHITE CLOVER, WHITE DUTCH CLOVER. See *Trifolium repens.*

WHITE FORSYTHIA. See *Abeliophyllum distichum.*

WHITE IRONBARK. See *Eucalyptus leucoxylon.*

WHITE MUGWORT. See *Artemisia lactiflora.*

WHITE PEPPERMINT. See *Eucalyptus pulchella.*

WHITE SAPOTE. See *Casimiroa edulis.*

WHITE TRAILING ICE PLANT. See *Delosperma* 'Alba'.

WILD GINGER. See *Asarum caudatum.*

WILD HYACINTH. See *Dichelostemma pulchellum.*

WILD INDIGO. See *Baptisia australis.*

WILD LILAC. See *Ceanothus.*

WILD MARJORAM. See *Origanum vulgare.*

WILD PLUM. See *Prunus americana.*

WILD STRAWBERRY. See *Fragaria chiloensis.*

WILGA. See *Geijera parviflora.*

WILLOW. See *Salix.*

WILLOW-LEAFED JESSAMINE. See *Cestrum parqui.*

WINDFLOWER. See *Anemone.*

WINDMILL PALM. See *Trachycarpus fortunei.*

WINTER ACONITE. See *Eranthis hyemalis.*

WINTER CREEPER. See *Euonymus fortunei.*

WINTERGREEN. See *Gaultheria procumbens.*

WINTER HAZEL. See *Corylopsis.*

WINTER'S BARK. See *Drimys winteri.*

WINTERSWEET. See *Chimonanthus praecox.*

WIRE VINE. See *Muehlenbeckia.*

WISHBONE FLOWER. See *Torenia.*

WISTERIA. *Leguminosae.* Deciduous vines. All Zones (but some flower buds damaged in cold winters in coldest parts of Zone 1). Twining, woody vines of great size, long life, and exceptional beauty in flower. So adaptable they can be grown as trees, shrubs, or vines.

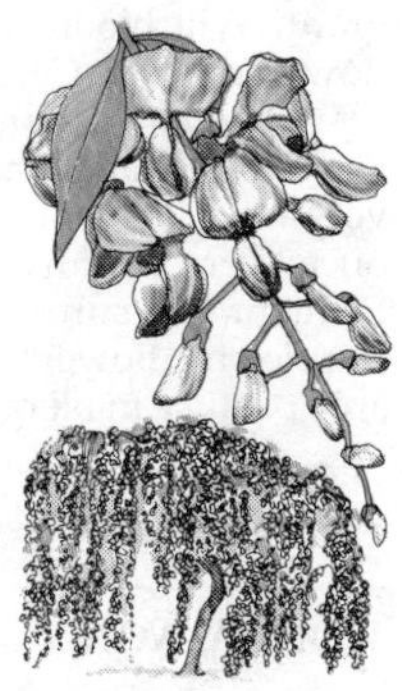

Wisteria sinensis

To get off to a good start, buy cutting-grown or grafted wisteria; seedlings may not bloom for many years. With grafted plants, keep suckers removed or they may take over. Wisterias are not fussy about soil, but they need good drainage and ample water during bloom and growth. In alkaline soil, watch for chlorosis and treat with iron chelates or iron sulfate.

Pruning and training are important for bloom production and control of plant's size, shape. Let newly set plants grow to establish framework you desire, either single or multitrunked. Remove stems that interfere with desired framework, pinch back side stems and long streamers, rub off buds that develop on trunk for single-trunked specimens. For multiple trunks, select as many vigorous stems as you wish and let them develop. If plant has only one stem, pinch it back to encourage others to develop. Remember that main stem will become good-sized trunk, and that weight of mature vine is considerable. Give firm support, and tie developing stems where you want them.

Tree wisterias can be bought ready-trained; or you can train your own. Remove all but one main stem, and stake this one securely. Tie stem to stake at frequent intervals, using plastic tape to prevent girdling. When plant has reached height at which you wish head to form, pinch or prune out tip to force branching. Shorten branches to beef them up. Pinch back long streamers and rub off all buds that form below head. Replace stakes and ties as needed.

Wisterias can be trained as big shrubs or multistemmed, small, semiweeping trees; permit well-spaced branches to form the framework, shorten side branches, and nip long streamers. Unsupported plants make vigorous bank cover.

Young plants should be well fed and watered; blooming-size, established plants flower better with less food and water. Prune blooming plants every winter, cutting back or thinning out side shoots from main or structural stems and shortening back to 2 or 3 buds the flower-producing spurs that grow from these shoots. You'll have no trouble recognizing fat flower buds on these spurs.

In summer, cut back long streamers before they tangle up in main body of vine; save those you want to use to extend height or length of vine and tie them to support—eaves, wall, trellis, arbor. If old plants grow rampantly but fail to bloom, withhold all nitrogen fertilizers for an entire growing season (buds for the next season's bloom are started in early summer). If that fails to produce bloom the next year, you can try pruning roots in spring—after you're sure no flowers will be produced—by cutting vertically with spade into plant's root zone.

W. floribunda (often sold as *W. multijuga*). JAPANESE WISTERIA. Leaves are 12–16 in. long, divided into 15–19 leaflets. Violet or violet blue, fragrant flowers in 1½-ft. clusters appear with leaves in April–May. Flowers begin to open at base of cluster, gradually open toward tip, prolonging bloom season but making less spectacular burst of color than Chinese wisteria. Long clusters give extreme beauty of line. Many varieties obtainable in white, pink, and shades of blue, purple, lavender, usually marked with yellow and white. 'Longissima' ('Macrobotrys') has very long (1½–3-ft.) clusters of violet flowers; 'Longissima Alba' bears white flowers in 2-ft. clusters. 'Ivory Tower' is similar. A good lavender pink variety is 'Rosea'. 'Plena' has very full clusters of double, deep blue violet flowers.

Japanese wisteria blooms best in full sun.

W. sinensis. CHINESE WISTERIA. Most widely planted throughout West. Leaves divided into 7–13 leaflets. Plants bloom before leaves

W

expand in April–May. Flower clusters are shorter (to 1 ft.) than those of Japanese wisteria, but make quite a show by opening nearly full length of cluster at one time. Violet blue, slightly fragrant. Will bloom in considerable shade. *W. s.* 'Alba' is white-flowered form. 'Caroline' and 'Cooke's Special' are grafted forms.

W. venusta (often sold as *W. v.* 'Alba'). SILKY WISTERIA. Broad leaves and leaflets have silky hairs. Individual flowers are white, very large, long-stalked, in short, heavy clusters that open all at once. Very profuse bloom when leaves begin to open in April. Plant in full sun for best bloom. *W. v.* 'Violacea' has fragrant, purple blue flowers. Older plants (especially in tree form) remarkably profuse in bloom.

WITCH HAZEL. See *Hamamelis.*

WONGA-WONGA VINE. See *Pandorea pandorana.*

WOODBINE. See *Parthenocissus, Lonicera periclymenum.*

WOOD FERN. See *Dryopteris.*

WOOD HYACINTH. See *Endymion non-scriptus.*

WOODRUFF. See *Galium odoratum.*

WOOD SORREL. See *Oxalis acetosella.*

WOODWARDIA. *Polypodiaceae.* CHAIN FERN. Large, strong-growing ferns. The only common species in cultivation is native giant chain fern.

Woodwardia fimbriata

W. fimbriata (often sold as *W. chamissoi* or *W. radicans*). GIANT CHAIN FERN. Zones 4–9, 14–24. Native British Columbia to Mexico, always in moist places. The largest native fern, it can reach 9 ft. tall in wet coastal forests. Fronds twice cut, rather coarse in texture, with strong upright or spreading silhouette. Excellent near pool or brook, against shaded wall, in woodland gardens. Slow to establish if dug from clumps; nursery plants grown from spores or tissue culture are vigorous and rapid. Ultimately withstands neglect.

W. orientalis. Zones 17, 22–24. Native to Japan, Formosa. Hardy to 26°F. Broad, arching, drooping, leathery-textured fronds to 8 ft. long, quite red when immature, deep green later. Produces many plantlets on fronds. Stunning in shaded, moist raised beds, where its fronds will cascade, or massed at woodland edge. Needs partial shade.

W. radicans. EUROPEAN CHAIN FERN. Zones 15–17, 19–24. Native to southern Europe to China. Resembles *W. fimbriata* but more arching and drooping, the fronds broader at the base. Forms bulblets at tips of fronds; these root while attached to plant. To 3 ft. tall; fronds 4–6 ft. long, 1½–2 ft. wide. Uses, culture same as for *W. orientalis.*

WOOLLY BLUE CURLS. See *Trichostema lanatum.*

WOOLLY SENNA. See *Cassia tomentosa.*

WORMWOOD. See *Artemisia.*

Xanthorrhoea preissii

XANTHORRHOEA. *Liliaceae.* GRASS TREE. Perennials. Zones 16, 17, 20–24. Native to Australia. Dense tufts of narrow, long, grasslike leaves radiate out from top of thick, woody, nearly black, very slow-growing stem. White flowers grow in dense, narrow spike on tall stem. Drought resistant. Best used with yuccas, century plants, succulents in full sun and dry, loose, sandy soil.

X. preissii. BLACKBOY. Stem is slow growing, but in age may reach 15 ft. Leaves 2–4 ft. long, about ⅛ in. wide. Flower spike 1–3 ft. long, on stem of equal length.

X. quadrangulata. Trunk reaches several feet high. Leaves 1½ ft. long. Spike and its stem may reach 12–15 ft.

XANTHOSOMA. *Araceae.* Cormlike tubers. Best adapted Zones 23, 24; in protected gardens Zones 12, 13, 16, 17, 21, 22; or anywhere as indoor or greenhouse plant in winter, outdoors in summer. Tropical foliage plants related to *Alocasia.* All have big, arrow-shaped leaves on long stalks. Flowers clustered on spike surrounded by callalike bract (spathe), usually greenish or yellowish and more curious than attractive. Rich soil, ample water. Use with ferns, begonias, schefflera in warm filtered shade, humus soil. Protect from hard frosts.

Xanthosoma violaceum

X. sagittifolium. Trunklike stem to 3 ft. Dark green leaves 3 ft. long on 3-ft. stems. Spathes greenish white, 7–9 in. long.

X. violaceum. Stemless, forming clumps by offsets. Leaves to 2 ft. long, 1½ ft. wide, dark green above, lighter beneath, with purplish veins and margins, powdery appearance. Purple, 2½-ft. leaf stalks with heavy, waxy, bluish or grayish cast. Large, yellowish white spathes.

XERANTHEMUM annuum. *Compositae.* COMMON IMMORTELLE. Summer annual. To 2½ ft. tall. Everlasting flower; fluffy heads of papery bracts up to 1½ in. across in pink, lavender, white, shades of violet purple. Scant foliage is silvery green. Sow seed in spring in place in full sun. Accepts almost any soil, regular watering. Cut flowers dried for winter bouquets.

Xeranthemum annuum

XYLOSMA congestum *(X. senticosum).* *Flacourtiaceae.* Evergreen or deciduous shrub or small tree. Zones 8–24. Usually loose, graceful, spreading shrub 8–10 ft. tall and as wide or wider. Height is easily controlled. Leaves are shiny, yellowish green, long-pointed oval in shape, clean and attractive. New growth bronzy. Flowers insignificant, rarely seen. Some plants are spiny.

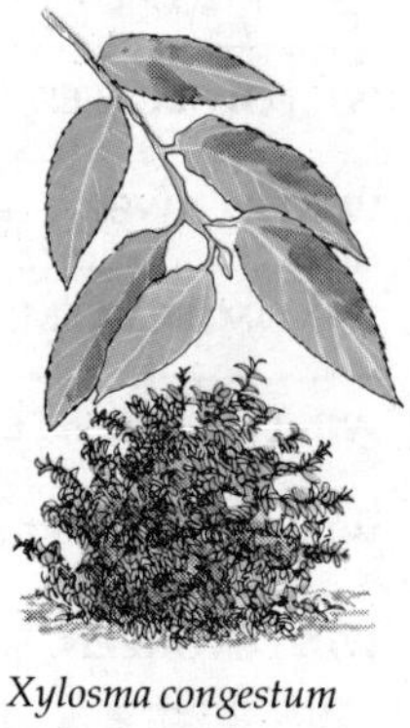
Xylosma congestum

Left alone, plants develop angular main stem that takes its time zigzagging upward. Meanwhile, side branches grow long and graceful, arching or drooping, sometimes lying on the ground. Easily trained as espalier. If shrub is staked and side growth pruned, can be made into 15–30-ft., spreading tree. Variety 'Compacta' grows more slowly, reaches half the size of species.

Adaptable to most soils; heat tolerant. Established plants survive with little water but look better with adequate water, moderate feeding. Best growth in full sun or filtered shade. Spray as necessary to control occasional scale or red spider mites. Apply iron chelates or iron sulfate for chlorosis.

One of the handsomest, easiest, and most versatile of the all-foliage, landscape structure plants. Unattractive appearance in nursery cans (especially in winter, when plants may be nearly bare of leaves) and slow start in ground may discourage the gardener.

Plants actually are hardy to 10°F., but may lose many (or all) leaves in sharp frosts. Plant normally sheds many old leaves in April when new growth begins. Frost at that time will kill new growth. Well-established plants usually evergreen except in coldest seasons, and new leaves come fast.

Use as single or multitrunked tree, arching shrub, ground or bank cover (prune out erect growth), espalier on wall or fence, clipped or unclipped hedge (twine long branches together to fill in gaps faster), container shrub in large (1½-ft.-wide or wider) container.

YARROW. See *Achillea.*

YAUPON. See *Ilex vomitoria.*

YELLOW BELLS. See *Tecoma stans.*

YELLOW ELDER. See *Tecoma stans.*

YELLOW-EYED GRASS. See *Sisyrinchium californicum.*

YELLOW FLAX. See *Linum flavum, Reinwardtia indica.*

YELLOW OLEANDER. See *Thevetia peruviana.*

YELLOW TRUMPET FLOWER. See *Tecoma stans.*

YELLOW TRUMPET VINE. See *Anemopaegma chamberlaynii, Macfadyena unguis-cati.*

YELLOW WOOD. See *Cladrastis lutea.*

YERBA BUENA. See *Satureja douglasii.*

YESTERDAY-TODAY-AND-TOMORROW. See *Brunfelsia pauciflora* 'Floribunda'.

YEW. See *Taxus.*

YEW PINE. See *Podocarpus macrophyllus.*

YOUNGBERRY. See Blackberry.

YUCCA. *Agavaceae.* Evergreen perennials, shrubs, trees. Yuccas grow over much of North America, and hardiness depends on species. All have clusters of tough, sword-shaped leaves and large clusters of white or whitish flowers. Some are stemless, while others reach tree size. Best in full sun in well-drained soil. Most take considerable drought when established—many are true desert plants. Most will accept garden watering. Useful near swimming pools. Fire retardant if reasonably well watered.

Yucca whipplei

Group with agaves, cacti, or succulents in desert gardens, or grow with various softer-leafed tropical foliage plants. Taller kinds make striking silhouettes, and even stemless species provide important and vertical effects when in bloom. Some have stiff, sharp-pointed leaves; keep these away from walks, terraces, and other well-traveled areas. (Some people clip off the sharp tips with nail clippers.)

Young plants of some species can be used as indoor plants. They withstand dry indoor atmosphere and will grow well in hot, sunny windows. Buy gallon-can size or smaller; set out in garden ground when plants become too large for house. Successful indoors are *Y. aloifolia* (but beware of sharp-pointed leaves), *Y. elephantipes, Y. filamentosa, Y. gloriosa, Y. recurvifolia.*

Y. aloifolia. SPANISH BAYONET. Zones 7–24. Native to southern U.S. Slow growth to 10 ft. or more; trunk either single or branched, or sprawling in picturesque effect. Sharp-pointed leaves to 2½ ft. long and 2 in. wide densely clothe stems. Leaves are dark green; in *Y. a.* 'Variegata', they are marked yellow or white. White flowers (sometimes tinged purple) to 4 in. across in dense, erect clusters to 2 ft. tall. Summer bloom. Sharp-spined leaf tips a hazard if plant is near walkway.

Y. baccata. DATIL YUCCA. All Zones. Native to deserts of southern California and Nevada to Colorado and Texas. Grow as single stemless rosettes or sometimes in clumps with short, leaning trunks to 3 ft. Leaves 2 ft. long, 2 in. wide. Flowers (May–June) fleshy, red brown outside, white inside, in dense clusters 2 ft. long. Fleshy fruit was eaten by Indians.

Y. brevifolia. JOSHUA TREE. Zones 8–24. Native to deserts of southern California, Nevada, Utah, Arizona. Tree of slow growth to 15–30 ft. with heavy trunk and few, heavy branches. Short, broad, sword-shaped leaves clustered near ends of branches. Old, dead leaves hang on a long time. Flowers (February–April) greenish white, in dense, heavy, foot-long clusters.

Collected plants sometimes available; nursery plants are very slow to make trunks. Best in dry, well-drained soil in desert gardens. Difficult under average garden conditions.

Y. elata. SOAPTREE YUCCA. Zones 7–24. Native to Arizona, New Mexico, west Texas, and northern Mexico. Slow growth to 6–20 ft. with single or branched trunk. Leaves to 4 ft. long, ½ in. wide. White summer flowers bloom in very tall spikes.

Y. elephantipes *(Y. gigantea).* GIANT YUCCA. Zones 12 and 13 (protected from sun, hard frosts), 16, 17, 19–24. Native to Mexico. Fast growing (to 2 ft. a year), eventually 15–30 ft. tall, usually with several trunks. Leaves 4 ft. long, 3 in. wide, dark rich green, not spine tipped. Striking silhouette alone or combined with other big-scale foliage plants; out of scale in smaller gardens. Large spikes of creamy white flowers in spring. Does best in good, well-drained soil with ample water.

Y. filamentosa. All Zones. Native to southeastern U.S. Much like *Y. flaccida,* but with stiffer, narrower leaves, narrower flower clusters. Variety 'Bright Eagle' has leaves margined in creamy white.

Y. flaccida. Zones 1–9, 14–24. Native to southeastern U.S. Stemless. Leaves to 2½ ft. long, 1 in. wide, with long, loose fibers at edges of leaves. White flowers in tall, branching clusters to 4–7 ft. or more in height. Lightly fragrant in the evening. One of hardiest, most widely planted in colder regions.

Y. glauca. SMALL SOAPWEED. All Zones. Native Texas, New Mexico to Montana, South Dakota. Stemless or short stemmed. Leaves 1–2½ ft. long. Greenish white summer flowers in tall, narrow clusters.

Y. gloriosa. SPANISH DAGGER, SOFT-TIP YUCCA. Zones 7–9, 12 and 13 (protected from frost, reflected heat), 14–24. Much like *Y. aloifolia,* generally multitrunked to 10 ft. tall. Blooms late summer. Leaf points soft, will not penetrate skin. Good green color blends well with lush, tropical-looking plants. Easy garden plant, but overwatering may produce black areas on leaf margins. There is a variegated form.

Y. harrimaniae. All Zones. Native to Colorado and Southwest. Short stemmed or stemless; clumps single or clustered. Leaves yellowish or bluish green, 4–18 in. long, ½–1½ in. wide. Summer flowers greenish white, 2–2½ in. across, in erect, unbranched clusters 1–3 ft. tall. May be slow to bloom in coldest climates.

Y. recurvifolia *(Y. pendula).* Zones 7–10, 12–24. Native to southeastern U.S. Single, unbranching trunk to 6–10 ft. tall, or lightly branched in age. Can be cut back to keep single trunked. Spreads by offsets to make large groups. Leaves, 2–3 ft. long, 2 in. wide, beautiful blue gray green, are spine tipped, sharply bent downward. Leaf tips bend to touch, are not dangerous. Less stiff and metallic looking than most yuccas. Flowers (in June) are large and

Y

white, in loose, open clusters 3–5 ft. tall. Easy to grow under all garden conditions.

Y. rostrata. Zones 7–24. Native to Mexico, extreme southwestern Texas. Notable feature is the trunk, 6–12 ft. tall, 5–8 in. thick, covered with soft gray fuzz (fibers remaining from old leaf bases). Needle-pointed leaves to 2 ft.long, ½ in. wide. White flowers in 2-ft. clusters on a 2-ft. stalk.

Y. schidigera *(Y. mohavensis).* Zones 10–24. Native to deserts of California, Nevada, Arizona, Baja California. Trunk 3–12 ft. tall, single or branched. Tough, sharp-tipped leaves 2–3 ft. long, 1–2½ in. wide, yellowish green. Creamy or purple-tinted flowers (April–May) in 2-ft. clusters.

Y. schottii *(Y. macrocarpa).* Zones 7–9, 11–24. Native to Arizona, New Mexico, northern Mexico. Treelike, with unbranched or branched trunk 6–20 ft. tall. Leaves gray green to yellow green, 1½–3 ft. long, 1½ in. wide, tipped with sharp spines. Summer flowers are white, 1–2 in. long, in branched clusters 1–3 ft. long.

Y. torreyi. TORREY YUCCA. Zones 7–24. Native to west Texas. Trunk to 10–15 ft., usually not branched. Stiff, sharp-pointed leaves to 3 ft. long. White summer flowers in dense, heavy, fat-looking clusters partially hidden by leaves.

Y. whipplei. OUR LORD'S CANDLE. Zones 2–24. Native to southern California mountains, California coast, Baja California. Stemless, with dense cluster of rigid, gray green leaves 12–21 in. long. These are needle tipped; don't plant where people can walk into them. Flowering stems to 6–14 ft. long. Drooping, bell-shaped, 1–2-in., creamy white blossoms in large, branched spikes 3–6 ft. long. Plants die after blooming and producing seed; new plants come from seeds or offsets.

YUSHANIA. See *Otatea* under Bamboo.

ZABEL LAUREL. See *Prunus laurocerasus* 'Zabeliana'.

Zamiaceae. This family is closely related to the *Cycadaceae,* differing only in technical details; both families are generally considered to be cycads. *Ceratozamia, Dioon,* and *Zamia* are representatives.

ZAMIA pumila (*Z. furfuracea*). *Zamiaceae.* Cycad relative. Zones 21–24; house plant anywhere. Native to Florida, Mexico. Short (6-in.) or completely buried trunk and 2–4-ft.-wide crown of leaves. Each leaf has up to 13 pairs of oval leaflets with inrolled edges. Effect is that of a coarse, leathery fern. Very slow growing, choice container plant. Profits from strong light but some overhead shade. Needs ample water, light feeding.

Zamia pumila

ZANTEDESCHIA. *Araceae.* CALLA. Rhizomes. Zones 5, 6, 8, 9, 14–24. Native to South Africa. Basal clumps of long-stalked, shiny, rich green, arrow- or lance-shaped leaves, sometimes spotted white. Flower bract (spathe) surrounds central spike (spadix) that is tightly covered with tiny true flowers.

Common calla tolerates many soils. Full sun near coast, partial shade in hot-summer areas. Thrives on heavy watering, even grows in bogs. Nearly evergreen in mild areas, deciduous where winters are cold. Set rhizomes 4–6 in. deep, 1–2 ft. apart.

Zantedeschia aethiopica

Golden, red or pink, and spotted callas need slightly acid soil, moderate water with drainage, and a resting season. Plant 2 in. deep, 1 ft. apart. In mild climates, they survive in well-drained, open-ground beds. If drainage is poor or frosts heavy, dry off gradually in late summer, dig, and store at 40°–50°F. in dry soil, sawdust, or peat moss. To grow in pots, set 2 in. deep (1 rhizome to 6-in. pot) and water sparingly until leaves appear. Then water freely, feed weekly with mild solution of complete fertilizer. Reduce watering after bloom to dry off plants, then withhold entirely until new growth begins.

Z. aethiopica. COMMON CALLA. Forms large clump of leaves 1½ ft. long, 10 in. wide. Pure white or creamy white, 8-in.-long spathes on 3-ft. stems appear mostly spring and early summer. 'Green Goddess' is a robust variety with very large spathes which are white at the base, green toward the tip. 'Hercules', larger than species, has big spathes that open flat, curve backward. 'Childsiana' is 1 ft. tall. 'Minor' grows 1½ ft. tall, with 4-in. spathes.

Z. albomaculata. SPOTTED CALLA. Grows to 2 ft. Leaves spotted white. Spathes 4–5 in. long, creamy yellow or white with purplish crimson blotch at base. Spring–summer bloom.

Z. elliottiana. GOLDEN CALLA. To 1½–2 ft., with bright green, white-spotted leaves 10 in. long by 6 in. wide. Spathes 4–5 in. long, changing from greenish yellow to rich golden yellow, June–July. Tolerates full sun, even in hot-summer areas.

Z. pentlandii. Resembles *Z. albomaculata,* but leaves are unspotted and large spathes (to 5 in. long) are deep golden yellow with a purple blotch at the base.

Z. rehmannii. RED or PINK CALLA. To 1–1½ ft., with narrow, lance-shaped, unspotted green leaves 1 ft. long. Pink or rosy pink spathes to 4 in. long. Blooms May. 'Superba', a deeper pink, improved variety, is generally sold rather than species. Hybrids of this and other callas available; flowers range through pinks and yellows to orange and buff tones, with some purplish and lavender tones on yellow grounds.

ZANTHOXYLUM piperitum. *Rutaceae.* JAPAN PEPPER. Deciduous shrub or small tree. Zones 6–9, 14–17. Dense, to 20 ft. Leaves 3–6 in. long, divided into 7–11 oval, 2-in.-long leaflets. Prickly main leaf stalk. Form sometimes seen in California nurseries has yellow main leaf stalk, yellow blotches at base of each leaflet. Green flowers are inconspicuous. Small, black, aromatic fruit is ground and used as seasoning in Japan.

Ordinary garden soil, full sun, moderate water.

Zanthoxylum piperitum

ZAUSCHNERIA. *Onagraceae.* CALIFORNIA FUCHSIA, HUMMINGBIRD FLOWER. Perennials or subshrubs. Zones 2–10, 12–24. These California natives can take dry, hot summers and will produce many pretty red flowers against gray foliage from summer to fall, but they never will become completely domesticated. Most grow a bit rangy, spread into other garden beds with invasive roots, go to seed and reseed themselves, and become twiggy and ungroomed through the winter. Use them in full sun in informal gardens, at summer cabins, on banks or hillsides. All have ½–1½-in.-long, gray or gray green, narrow leaves and bright scarlet, trumpet-shaped, 1½–2-in.-long flowers. The flowers attract birds. Some botanists have placed *Zauschneria* within *Epilobium* (fireweed). Most gardeners ignore this change.

Zauschneria californica

Z. californica. Stems upright or somewhat arching, 1–2 ft. tall. Plants sometimes shrubby at base. Evergreen in mild-winter climates. There are pure white forms.

Z. c. latifolia (***Z. septentrionalis,*** often sold as *Z. latifolia* 'Etteri'). Perennial that makes mats of closely set stems about 6 in. high. Dies to ground in winter. There is a bright pink variety named 'Solidarity Pink'.

Z. cana. Stems woody at base, sprawling. Foliage dense; leaves very narrow, silvery. Evergreen in mild-winter climates.

Z

ZEBRA PLANT. See *Calathea zebrina.*

ZEBRINA pendula. *Commelinaceae.* WANDERING JEW. House plant. Has much the same growth habit and leaf shape as *Tradescantia fluminensis,* but is not as hardy. Small clusters of flowers are purplish rose and white. Known mostly in its variegated forms. *Z. p.* 'Quadricolor' has purplish green leaves with longitudinal bands of white, pink, and carmine red; 'Purpusii' has leaves of dark red or greenish red. Other varieties add white, pink, and cream to prevailing colors. When selecting a location indoors, remember that variegated plants need more light than all-green ones.

Zebrina pendula

ZELKOVA serrata. *Ulmaceae.* SAWLEAF ZELKOVA. Deciduous tree. Zones 3–21. A good shade tree, it grows at moderate to fast rate, eventually to 60 ft. or higher, and equally wide. Smooth, gray bark like that of beech. Leaves similar to those of elm (2–3½ in. long by 1½ in. wide) but rougher textured, with sawtooth margins. Carefully train young trees to develop strong framework—head back excessively long pendulous branches to force side growth, thin competing branches to permit full development of the strongest. Water deeply to encourage deep rooting. Very pest resistant, but sometimes gets red spider mites.

Zelkova serrata

Fall foliage color varies from yellow to dark red to dull reddish brown. Three grafted selections are sold; 'Halka', the fastest growing, resembles American elm more than do 'Green Vase' and 'Village Green'. All are good substitutes for the elm.

ZENOBIA pulverulenta *(Andromeda speciosa).* *Ericaceae.* Deciduous shrub. Zones 4–7, 14–17. Native to southeastern U.S. Slow growth to 2–4, possibly 6 ft. Open, loose growth. Leaves pale green, 1–2 in. long, half as wide; new growth heavily dusted with bluish white powder in pearly gray effect. White, bell-shaped, ½-in.-wide flowers grow in loose clusters at ends of branches. Blooms June–July in Northwest. Sometimes spreads by underground stems.

Related to heaths and heathers; needs acid, uniformly moist soil, partial shade in warm exposures.

Zenobia pulverulenta

ZEPHYRANTHES. *Amaryllidaceae.* ZEPHYR FLOWER, FAIRY LILY. Bulbs. Zones 1–9, 14–24. Bright green, rushlike leaves. Funnel-shaped flowers with 6 similarly shaped segments appear singly on hollow stems, usually in late summer or early fall, often throughout the year if plants are kept alternately wet and dry. In the wilds, flowers appear a few days after a rain (hence, often called RAIN LILY).

Use in rock garden or foreground of border. Good in pots. Plant late summer or early fall; set bulbs 1–2 in. deep, 3 in. apart. Full sun, although *Z. candida* takes light shade. In cold climates, plant in spring and lift in fall; or mulch heavily over winter months.

Zephyranthes candida

Z. ajax. Hybrid between *Z. candida* and *Z. citrina.* Free flowering, light yellow. Evergreen. Leaves to 8 in. long.

Z. candida. Large clumps of rushlike, glossy evergreen leaves to 1 ft. long. Crocuslike flowers 2 in. long, glossy textured, pure white outside, tinged rose inside, borne singly on stems as long as leaves; blooms in late summer, autumn.

Z. citrina. Fragrant, lemon yellow, 2-in. flowers; narrow, ridged leaves. Stems 10 in. tall.

Z. grandiflora. Rose pink, 4-in.-wide flowers look like small amaryllis; 8-in. stems. Leaves 1 ft. long, appearing with flowers in late spring, early summer.

Z. hybrids. 'Alamo' has deep rose pink flowers flushed yellow. 'Apricot Queen', low growing, has yellow flowers stained pink. 'Prairie Sunset' has large, light yellow flowers suffused with pink that appear after rain or a watering. 'Ruth Page' is rich pink. These are usually available only from mail-order specialists.

ZEPHYR FLOWER. See *Zephyranthes.*

Zingiberaceae. The ginger family contains tropical or subtropical perennials with fleshy rhizomes and canelike stems that are clothed with sheathing leaf stalks and usually bear large leaves. Flowers are irregular in form, in spikes or heads, often showy or with showy bracts. Many are aromatic or have fragrant flowers. Representatives are *Alpinia, Hedychium,* and *Zingiber.*

ZINGIBER officinale. *Zingiberaceae.* TRUE GINGER. Perennial with thick rhizomes. Zones 9, 14–24. Rhizomes are the source of ginger used in cooking. Stems 2–4 ft. tall. Narrow, glossy bright green leaves to 1 ft. long. Summer flowers (rarely seen) are yellowish green, with purple lip marked yellow; not especially showy. Tropical in origin, ginger needs heat and humidity, shade from hottest sun. Buy roots (fresh, not dried) at grocery store in early spring; cut into 1–2-in.-long sections with well-developed growth buds. Let cut ends dry, then plant just underground in rich, moist soil. Water cautiously until top and root growth are active; then water heavily. Feed once a month.

Zingiber officinale

Plants are dormant in winter; rhizomes may rot in cold, wet soil. Plant with tree ferns, camellias, fuchsias, begonias. Harvest roots at any time—but allow several months for them to reach some size.

ZINNIA. *Compositae.* Summer annuals, perennial. Long-time garden favorites for colorful, round flower heads in summer and early fall. Distinctly hot-weather plants, they do not gain from being planted early, but merely stand still until weather warms up. Subject to mildew in foggy places, if given overhead water, and when autumn brings longer nights, more dew, and more shade. Sow seeds where plants are to grow (or set out nursery plants) May–July. Give plants good garden soil in sunny place. Feed and water generously, but always water by soaking soil, not by overhead sprinkling.

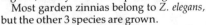

Zinnia elegans

Most garden zinnias belong to *Z. elegans,* but the other 3 species are grown.

Z. angustifolia. Annual. Compact plants to 8 in. tall. Leaves very narrow. Inch-wide flower heads orange, each ray with a paler stripe. Blooms in 6 weeks from seed, continues late into fall. 'Classic' grows 8–12 in. tall, spreads to 2 ft. Can be perennial where winters are mild. Good in hanging baskets.

Z. elegans. Annual. Plant height ranges from 1–3 ft., leaves to 5 in., flower head size from less than 1 in. to as much as 5–7 in. across. Forms include full doubles, cactus flowered (with quilled rays), and crested (cushion center surrounded by rows of broad

Z

rays); colors include white, pink, salmon, rose, red, yellow, orange, lavender, purple, and green.

Many strains are available, from dwarf plants with small flowers to 3-ft. sorts with 5-in. blooms. Extra dwarf (to 6 in. tall) are the Mini series and Thumbelina strain. Other small-flowered kinds on larger (1-ft.) but still compact plants are Cupid and Buttons; still taller (to 2 ft.) but small flowered are the Lilliputs. Dreamland and Peter Pan strains have 3-in. blooms on bushy dwarf plants to 1 ft.; Whirligig has large bicolored flowers on 1½-ft. plants. Large-flowered strains with 2–3-ft. plants include Border Beauty and Burpeeana California Giants, Dahlia-flowered, Giant Cactus-flowered, Ruffles, State Fair, and Zenith. 'Rose Pinwheel', a single (daisy-type) rose pink zinnia, represents a breakthrough: a hybrid between *Z. elegans* and *Z. angustifolia,* it is apparently resistant to mildew. Grows 1½ ft. tall, 2 ft. wide; has 2½–3-in. flowers.

Z. grandiflora. Perennial. All Zones. Native to high plains, the Southwest, Mexico. Grows to 10 in. tall and spreads by seeds or runners. Leaves very narrow (⅛ in. wide), to 1 in. long. Flower heads orange eyed, bright yellow, 1½ in. wide. Blooms spring–fall if watered, but drought tolerant once established.

Z. haageana. Annual. Plants compact, 1–1½ ft. tall; 3-in. leaves narrower than on common zinnias. Double strains Persian Carpet (1 ft. tall) and Old Mexico (16 in. tall) have flowers in strong shades of mahogany red, yellow, and orange, usually mixed in the same flower head. Colorful, long blooming.

ZIZIPHUS jujuba. *Rhamnaceae.* CHINESE JUJUBE. Deciduous tree. Zones 7–16, 18–24; it grows in Zones 4–6, 17, but fruit ripens only in warmest summers. Slow to moderate growth to 20–30 ft. Branches spiny, gnarled, somewhat pendulous. Leaves glossy bright green, 1–2 in.long, with 3 prominent veins. Clusters of small yellowish flowers in May–June. Shiny, reddish brown, datelike fruit in fall has sweet, applelike flavor; candied and dried, fruits resemble dates.

Ziziphus jujuba

Tree is deep rooted and takes well to desert conditions, tolerating drought, saline and alkaline soils. Grows better in good garden soil with regular, deep watering. Thrives in lawns. No serious pests, but subject to Texas root rot in deserts. Prune in winter to shape, encourage weeping habit, or reduce size. Attractive silhouette, foliage, fruit, and toughness make it a good decorative tree, especially for high desert. Foliage turns a good yellow in fall.

Fruit of seedlings is ½–1 in. long. Two cultivated varieties are 'Lang' (1½–2-in.-long fruit, bears young) and 'Li' (2-in.-long fruit).

ZOYSIA. *Gramineae.* Perennial grasses used for lawns and ground covers. They tend to spread slowly, are fairly deep rooted and drought tolerant. Thrive in sun but tolerate some shade. Dormant and straw-colored during the winter; turn green in spring. Plant using sod, sprigs, stolons, or plugs. (Stolons give much faster cover than plugs.) Cut lawns ¾ in. high.

Z. japonica 'Meyer'. MEYER ZOYSIA. Zones 12, 13. Resembles bluegrass in appearance and texture. Turns brown earliest in winter, turns green latest in spring.

Zoysia tenuifolia

Z. matrella. MANILA GRASS. Zones 8, 9, 12–14, 18–24. Also similar to bluegrass in appearance. Holds color a little better than Meyer.

Z. tenuifolia. KOREAN GRASS. Hardy in Zones 8, 9, 12–24; best in Zones 18–24. Creeping, fine textured, bumpy. Makes a beautiful grassy meadow or gives mossy Oriental effect in areas impossible to mow or water often. The farther inland, the longer the dormant season.

Z. t. 'Emerald'. EMERALD ZOYSIA. Zones 8, 9, 12–14, 18–24. Wiry, dark green, prickly-looking turf. Dense, wiry blades hard to cut. More frost tolerant than other zoysias.

ZUCCHINI. See Squash.

Glossary

To prepare a comprehensive gardening book, it is necessary to use a number of special words common to the art of horticulture and the science of botany. These gardening terms serve as a sort of shorthand in explanations and descriptions. Grouped in this glossary are the special words and phrases used in this book. Some are particular to the world of plants; others are familiar words that take on new meanings when applied to gardening.

In addition to these gardening terms, certain other words describe specific large groups of plants—bamboo, bromeliad, cycad, cactus, fern, herb, orchid, palm, succulent. These words are fully explained in the alphabetical listings in the Western Plant Encyclopedia.

Acid soil, alkaline soil. Acidity and alkalinity describe one aspect of the soil's chemical composition: the concentration of hydrogen ions (an ion is an electrically charged atom or molecule). The relative concentration of hydrogen ions is represented by the symbol *p*H followed by a number. A *p*H of 7 means that the soil is neutral, neither acid nor alkaline. A *p*H below 7 indicates acidity; one above 7 indicates alkalinity.

Many plants will grow well over a range of *p*H from slightly acid to slightly alkaline; some garden favorites are more particular. Usually they need an acid soil (most rhododendrons, azaleas, and heathers, for example). Soils in areas with high rainfall tend to be acid. Areas where rainfall is light tend to have alkaline soils which require treatment if you wish to grow acid-loving plants in them. For more information, see page 62.

Actual (as in actual nitrogen). Sometimes we recommend a certain amount of actual nitrogen; to calculate it, multiply the total weight of fertilizer by the percentage of the particular nutrient. For example, a 25-lb. bag of fertilizer that contains 5 percent nitrogen will yield 1¼ lbs. actual nitrogen (25 lbs. × .05 = 1.25 lbs.). The same formula will allow you to calculate actual phosphorus or potash. It will also allow you to calculate the real nutritive value of a given fertilizer.

Alkaline soil. See **Acid soil.**

Annual. A plant that completes its life cycle in a year or less is called an annual. Seed germinates and the plant grows, blooms, sets seed, and dies—all in one growing season. Examples are most marigolds (*Tagetes*) and zinnias. The phrase "grow as an annual" or "treat as an annual" means to sow seed or set out a plant in spring after the last frost, enjoy it from spring through fall, and pull it out or let the frosts kill it at the end of the year. (Some plants that desert gardeners treat as annuals are planted in fall, grow and bloom during winter and spring, and then are killed by summer heat.)

Axil, axillary. The inner angle between a leaf or other organ of a plant and the stem from which it springs. (The anatomical name for armpit is axilla.) Axillary means arising from an axil; the principal bud types are axillary (in the axil of a leaf) or terminal (at the end of a shoot).

Backfill. Backfill soil is returned to a planting hole after a plant's roots have been positioned. Sometimes backfill is simply the soil dug out to create the planting hole; often it is mixed with some organic soil amendments to improve its texture.

Balled and burlapped (sometimes abbreviated B and B). From late fall to early spring, some nurseries sell shrubs and trees with a large *ball* of soil around the roots, wrapped in *burlap* to hold the soil together. Usually these are plants that cannot be offered **Bare root.**

Bare root. In winter and early spring, nurseries offer many deciduous shrubs and trees, and some perennials, with all soil removed from their roots. These are dormant plants dug from growing fields, trimmed and freed of soil, and then protected against drying out until planting.

Biennial. This type of plant completes its life cycle in 2 years. Two familiar biennials are foxglove (*Digitalis*) and Canterbury bells (*Campanula medium*). Typically, you plant seeds in spring or set out the seedling plants in summer or fall. The plants bloom the following spring, then set seed and die.

Bolt. Annual flowers and vegetables that grow quickly to flowering stage at the expense of good overall development are said to *bolt*. This happens most often when plants are set out too late in the year or when unseasonably hot weather rushes the growth.

Bonsai. *Bonsai* (the word is Japanese) is one of the fine arts of gardening: growing carefully trained, dwarfed plants in containers selected to harmonize with the plants. The objective is to create in miniature scale a tree or landscape; often the dwarfed trees take on the appearance of very old, gnarled specimens. To get the desired effect the bonsai craftsman meticulously wires and prunes branches, and trims roots.

Bracts. These modified leaves may grow just below a flower or flower cluster (not all flowers have bracts). Usually bracts are green, but in some cases they are conspicuous and colorful, constituting what people regard as "flowers"; examples are bougainvillea, dogwood, and poinsettia.

Broadcast. To broadcast means to scatter seed by hand over the soil surface; the ground may be a prepared surface, as for a lawn, or uncultivated, as in scattering wildflower seed.

Broad-leafed. The phrase "broad-leafed evergreen" refers to a plant that has green foliage all year but is not an evergreen **Conifer** (such as a juniper) with needlelike or scalelike foliage. A broad-leafed weed is any weed that is not a grass.

Bud. This word has several definitions. A flower bud is one that develops into a blossom. A growth bud may be at the tip of a stem (*terminal*) or along the sides of a stem (*lateral*); these buds will produce new leafy growth (see page 76). Finally, to *bud* a plant is to propagate by a process similar to grafting (see pages 86–87).

Bulb. In everyday conversation, any plant that grows from a thickened underground structure is referred to as a "bulb." But a true bulb is one particular type of underground stem. (Others, defined in this glossary and on pages 184–186, are **Corms, Rhizomes, Tubers,** and **Tuberous roots.**) The true bulb is more or less rounded and composed of fleshy scales (actually modified leaves) that store food and protect the developing plant inside. The outer scales dry to form a papery covering. Slice an onion in half from top to bottom to see a typical example.

Caliche. A soil condition found in some areas of the arid Southwest, caliche is a deposit of calcium carbonate (lime) beneath the soil surface. For help in dealing with it, see "Shallow soil" (page 62).

Calyx. See **Anatomy of a Flower,** page 59.

Catkin. A catkin is a slender, spikelike, and often drooping flower cluster. Catkins are either male or female; in some plants, the male catkins are borne on one individual plant, the female on another (cottonwoods, willows); or both male and female catkins may be produced on each individual plant (alders, birches).

Chilling requirement. Many deciduous shrubs and trees (fruit trees in particular) and perennials need certain amounts of cold weather in winter in order to grow and bloom well during the following year. Where winters are mild and these plants do not get the necessary winter chill, their performance will be disappointing: plants leaf out late, fail to flower or fruit well, and often decline in health and vigor even to the point of dying. With some of these plants (apples and lilacs, for example), varieties have been developed that require less winter cold than is normal for the type. Gardeners in milder winter areas should choose varieties with low chilling requirements. (Chilling requirement is measured in hours required at temperatures below 45°F.)

Chlorosis. When a leaf looks yellower than it should (especially between the leaf veins), it often is chlorotic or suffering from *chlorosis.* Chlorosis is frequently caused by a plant's inability to obtain the iron it needs to produce green coloring. For one way to correct this condition, see **Iron chelate.**

Complete fertilizer. Any plant food that contains all three of the primary nutrient elements—nitrogen, phosphorus, potassium—is a complete fertilizer.

Complete flower. See **Anatomy of a Flower,** page 59.

Composite family (Compositae). This enormous family of plants includes all the flowers known as daisies—and many more. What appears to be an individual flower is actually many small flowers tightly grouped into a head and surrounded by **Bracts** that form a cup (*involucre*). A typical daisy is composed of two kinds of flowers. *Disk flowers* are the small tubular flowers that usually are tightly packed together to form the round, cushionlike center of a daisy; *ray flowers* are those that appear to be petals (each "petal" is an individual ray flower) surrounding the central disk flowers. Some composites have disk flowers only (chamomile and santolina, for example); others, such as most dahlias, marigolds, and zinnias, have blossoms that consist only of ray flowers.

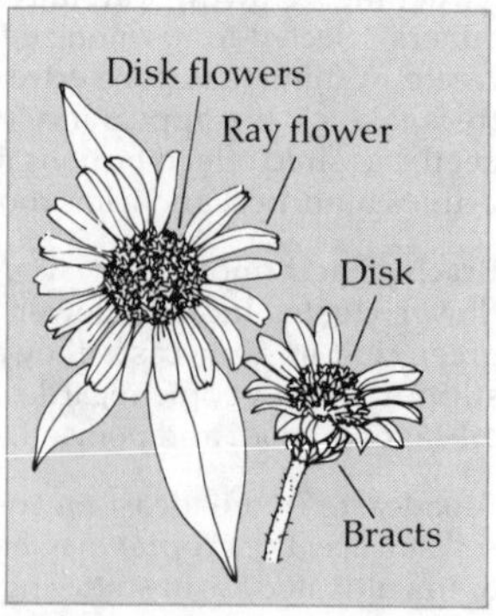

Conifer. Conifer is a more precise word for the plants many people call "evergreens," such as cedars, cypresses, junipers, and pines. Leaves on most are narrow and needlelike or tiny and scalelike. Not all conifers are evergreen, but all bear their seeds in cones or in modified conelike structures.

Conservatory. Originally a conservatory was a greenhouse for displaying rather than growing plants; now it is simply a fancy greenhouse.

Corm. Technically, a corm is a thickened underground stem capable of producing roots, leaves, and flowers during the growing season. Gladiolus and crocus are two familiar plants that grow from corms. A corm differs from a bulb in that food is stored in the solid center tissue, whereas in bulbs food is stored in scales. See also **Bulb** and pages 184–186.

Corolla. See **Anatomy of a Flower,** page 59.

Crown. The crown of a tree is its entire branch structure, including foliage. In other usage, "crown" refers to the point at which a plant's roots and top structure join (usually at or near the soil line).

Culm. The hollow, jointed stem of a grass (especially the giant grass bamboo) is called a culm.

Cuttings. These are portions of leaf, stem, or root, sometimes called "slips," that can be induced to form roots and develop into new plants. Also see pages 83–85.

Daisy flower. See **Composite family.**

Damping off. This plant disease, caused by fungi in the soil, makes small seedlings rot, wilt, or fall over and die, just before or soon after they break through the soil.

Deciduous. Any plant that sheds all of its leaves at one time each year (usually in fall) is deciduous.

Defoliation. This refers to the unnatural loss of a plant's leaves, usually to the detriment of the plant's health. Defoliation may result from high winds that strip foliage away, intense heat (especially if accompanied by wind) that critically wilts leaves, drought, unusually early or late frosts that strike a plant still in active growth, or severe damage by chemicals, insects, or diseases.

Dieback. In dieback, a plant's stems die, beginning at the tips, for a part of their length. Causes are various: not enough water, nutrient deficiency, plant not adapted to climate in which it is growing, or severe insect, mite, or disease injury.

Disk flower. See **Composite family.**

Dissected. A leaf is said to be dissected when it is divided into many narrow segments.

Divided. A leaf is said to be divided when it is separated into sections entirely to its stalk or nearly to its stalk. In the first case the sections are called leaflets; in the second, they are called lobes.

Dividing. This is the easiest way to increase perennials, bulbs, and shrubs that form clumps of stems with rooted bases. Procedural information is on pages 82–83.

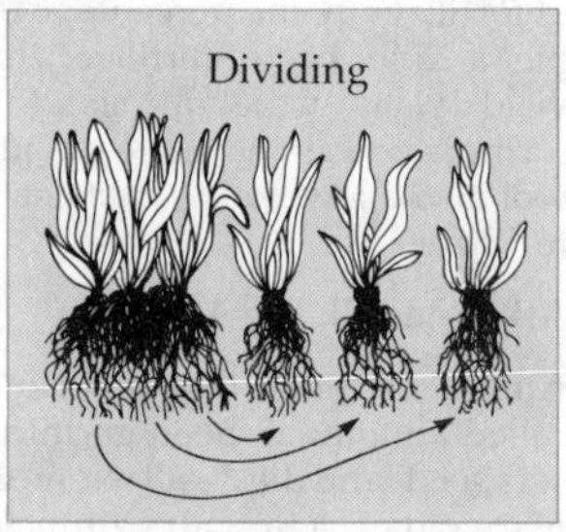

Double flower. A double flower has an indefinite number (usually large) of petals that give the blossom an unusually full appearance.

Drainage. Drainage refers to the movement of water through the soil in a plant's root area. When this happens quickly, the drainage is "good" or "fast," and the soil is "well drained"; when it happens slowly, the drainage is said to be "slow" or "bad," and the soil is "poorly drained." For plants to grow, water must pass through soil. Plant roots need oxygen as well as water, and soil that remains saturated deprives roots of necessary oxygen. Fast drainage (water disappears from a shrub planting hole in 10 minutes or less) is typical of sandy soils; slow drainage (water still remains in planting hole after an hour) is found in clay soils and where hardpan exists. Refer to pages 60–62 for more information on soils and drainage.

Drip line. The circle that you would draw on the soil around a tree directly under its outermost branch tips is called a drip line. Rainwater tends to drip from the tree at this point. The term is used in connection with feeding, watering, and grading around existing trees and shrubs.

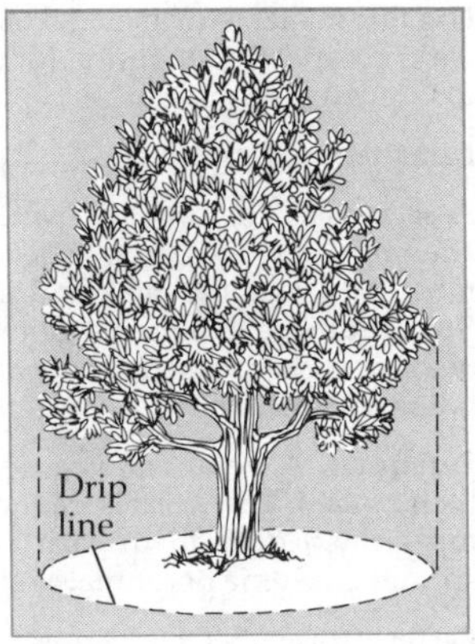

Dust. This word defines a type of insecticide or fungicide and its method of application. Several insecticides and fungicides are manufactured as powders so finely ground that they are *dust*. You put the product into a special applicator (sometimes the container is the applicator) and *dust* it onto the plants. If you do this in early morning when air is still, the dust makes a large cloud, the particles of which slowly settle as a thin, even coating over everything. The advantage of dusting over spraying is convenience: no mixing, fast application, and easy clean-up.

Epiphyte. These plants grow on another plant for support but receive no nourishment from the host plant. Familiar examples are cattleya orchids and staghorn ferns. These are often mistakenly called *parasites;* true parasites steal nourishment from the host.

Espalier. This is a tree or shrub trained so its branches grow in a flat pattern—against a wall or fence, on a trellis, along horizontal wires. Espaliers may be formal and geometric, or informal.

Evergreen. This kind of plant never loses all its leaves at one time. For plants many people call "evergreens," see **Conifer.** Also refer to **Broad-leafed.**

Eye. This undeveloped growth bud ultimately will produce a new plant or new growth. The "eyes" on a potato will, when planted, produce new potato plants. "Eye" is synonymous with one definition of **Bud.**

Family. See **Plant classification.**

Fanwise, featherwise. Leaves divided into leaflets fall into two classes: palmate, in which the leaflets are arranged like fingers of a hand (fanwise), and pinnate, in which they are arranged like the divisions of a feather (featherwise).

Fertilize. In popular usage, this word has two definitions. To fertilize a flower is to apply pollen (the male element) to a flower's pistil (the female element) for the purpose of setting seed. (See Pollination on page 59.) To fertilize a plant is to apply nutrients (plant food, usually referred to as fertilizer).

Flower, flower parts. See **Anatomy of a Flower,** page 59.

Forcing. Forcing is a process of hastening a plant along to maturity or a marketable state, or of growing a plant to the flowering or fruiting stage out of its normal season, usually by growing it under shelter, as in a greenhouse, where temperature, humidity, and light can be controlled.

Formal. The term *formal* means regular, rigid, and geometric. In gardening, it is variously applied to flowers, methods of training, and styles of garden design. A formal double flower, as in some camellias, consists of layers of regularly overlapping petals. Examples of formal plant training are rigidly and geometrically structured espaliers and evenly clipped hedges. Formal gardens are those laid out in precise geometric patterns; they often contain formal hedges and espaliers.

Foundation plant. This outmoded but persistent term originally described a plant used to hide the foundation of a house. Since many of today's homes lack high or even visible foundations, the term has come to mean any shrub you plant near the house walls.

Frond. In the strictest sense, fronds are the foliage of ferns. Often, however, the word is also applied to the leaves of palms and is even used to designate any foliage that looks fernlike.

Genus. See **Plant classification.**

Girdling. This refers to the choking of a branch by a wire, rope, or other inflexible material. It occurs most often in woody plants that have been tightly tied to a stake or support. As the tied limb increases in girth, the tie fails to expand in diameter and cuts off supplies of nutrients and water to the part of the plant above the tie; if girdling goes unnoticed, the part of the plant above the constriction will die.

The word girdling also applies to an encircling cut made through the bark of a trunk or branch.

Grafting. With this method of plant propagation, a section of one plant (called the *scion*) is inserted into a branch of another plant (the *stock*). The procedure is explained on pages 86–87.

Ground bark. The bark of trees, ground up or shredded for use as a mulch or soil amendment, is known as ground bark. It may have other names in some areas.

Harden off. This process adapts a plant that has been grown in a greenhouse, indoors, or under protective shelter to full outdoor exposure. The plant is exposed, over a week or more, to increasing intervals of time outdoors, so that when it is planted out in the garden it can make the transition with a minimum of shock.

Hardy. This term describes a plant's resistance to, or tolerance of, frost or freezing temperatures (as in "hardy to −20°F."). The word does not mean tough, pest resistant, or disease resistant. A half-hardy plant is hardy in a given situation in normal years, but subject to freezing in coldest winters.

Heading back. This is cutting a branch back to a side branch or bud to promote more compact growth. Also see page 77.

Heavy soil. This rather imprecise term refers to dense soil made up of extremely fine particles packed closely together. The term is used interchangeably with "clay" and "adobe." See page 60.

Heeling in. This term refers to a means of preventing roots of bare-root plants from drying out before you can set them out in the garden. Simplest is to dig a shallow trench, lay the plant on its side so that roots are in the trench, then cover roots with soil, sawdust, or other material, moistened to keep roots damp.

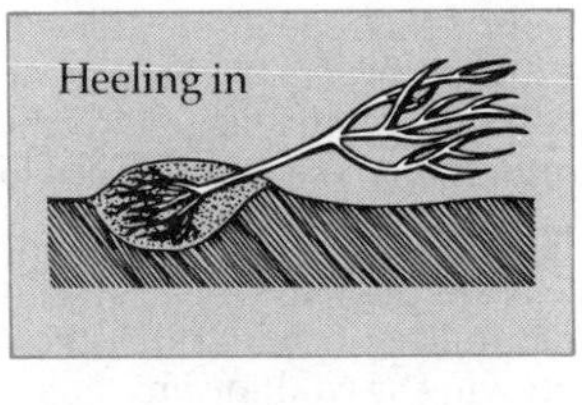

Herbaceous. Herbaceous, the opposite of *woody,* describes a plant with soft (nonwoody) tissues. In the strictest sense, it refers to plants that die to the ground each year and regrow stems the following growing season. In the broadest sense, it refers to any nonwoody plant—annual, perennial, or bulb.

Honeydew. Aphids, as well as several other sucking insects, secrete a sticky substance called *honeydew;* certain ants and fungi feed on honeydew, adding to the mess. Often honeydew from a tree will drip onto whatever is below: car, patio, or other plants.

Humus. The soft brown or black substance formed in the last stages of decomposition of animal or vegetable matter is called humus. Common usage has incorrectly applied the word to almost all organic materials that eventually would decompose into humus—sawdust, ground bark, leaf mold, and animal manures, for example.

Hybrid. See **Plant classification.**

Iron chelate (pronounced *key*-late). This chemical remedy for plants that show signs of **Chlorosis** is a combination of iron and a complex organic substance that makes the iron readily available to roots.

Lath. In gardening, this word designates any overhead plant-protecting structure (originally a roof of spaced laths) that reduces the amount of sunlight that shines on plants beneath or protects them from frost.

Layering. In this method of propagating plants, a branch is rooted while it is still attached to the plant. See page 85–86.

Leaching. Think of brewing tea or coffee. When you pour hot water through tea leaves or ground coffee you are *leaching*. You leach soil with water when you want to remove excess salts (see **Salinity**). In high-rainfall areas, rain water leaches good as well as bad substances from the soil.

Leader. In a single-trunked shrub or tree, this is the central, upward-growing stem.

Leaflet. If a leaf is divided into completely separated divisions, these are called leaflets. They may be arranged like the fingers of a hand (palmate, fanwise) or like the divisions of a feather (pinnate, featherwise).

Leaf mold. This term refers to partially decomposed leaves that can be dug into the soil as an organic amendment. Most familiar is oak leaf mold.

Leaf scar. This usually rounded or crescent shaped mark on a branch indicates where a leaf stalk once was attached.

Light soil. The opposite of **Heavy soil,** this is an imprecise term referring to soil composed of relatively large particles loosely packed together. The term is often synonymous with "sandy soil" (see page 60). Although such soils are well supplied with oxygen, water and nutrients quickly drain through them.

Lip. Irregular flowers (flowers in which the segments are not equal in size and arrangement) often show two divisions, an upper and a lower, each bearing one or more of the segments. Each division is known as a lip. Familiar examples are honeysuckle (*Lonicera*) and snapdragon (*Antirrhinum*).

Mulch. Any loose, usually organic material placed over the soil, such as ground bark, sawdust, straw, or leaves, is a mulch. The process of applying such materials is called *mulching*. A mulch can serve various functions. It may reduce evaporation of moisture from soil; reduce or prevent weed growth; insulate soil from extreme or rapid changes of temperature; prevent mud from splashing onto foliage and other surfaces; protect falling fruit from injury; or make a garden bed look tidy.

Naturalize. To plant out randomly, without precise pattern, and leave in place to spread at will. Some plants have the capability to naturalize, meaning that they can spread or reseed themselves, growing as wildflowers.

Node. The joint in a stem where a leaf starts to grow. The area of stem between joints is the *internode*.

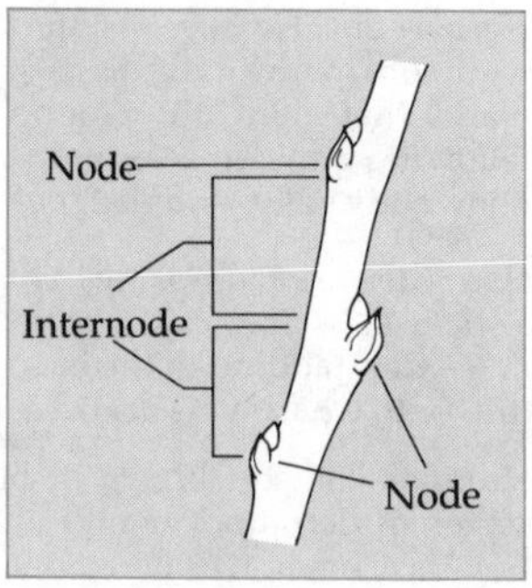

Offset. Some mature perennials may send out from the base a short stem, at the end of which a small new plant develops. The new plant is the offset. Familiar examples are hen and chicks (*Echeveria*), hen and chickens (*Sempervivum*), and strawberry. See also **Stolon.**

Opposite, alternate. Leaves are said to be opposite when they spring from the same point on a stem but on opposite sides. When they arise from different points and on opposite sides they are called alternate. The buds in the drawing for **Node** (above) will give rise to alternate leaves. A group of three or more leaves arising at a single point is called a **Whorl.**

Organic matter. Any material of organic origin—peat moss, ground bark, compost, or manure, for example—that can be dug into soil to improve its condition.

Parasite. See **Epiphyte.**

Peat moss. This highly water-retentive, spongy organic soil amendment is the partially decomposed remains of any of several mosses. It is somewhat acid in reaction, adding to soil acidity. **Sphagnum** peat moss is generally considered to be highest in quality. There is a sedge peat, not composed of mosses, which is not necessarily acid.

Perennial. A perennial is a nonwoody plant that lives for more than 2 years. The word is frequently used to refer to a plant whose top growth dies down each winter and regrows the following spring, but some perennials keep their leaves all year long.

Perfect flower. See **Flowers & Fruit,** pages 58–59.

Perlite. A mineral expanded by heating to form white, very light-weight, porous granules useful in container soil mixes for enhancing the retention of moisture and air.

Petals. See **Anatomy of a Flower,** page 59.

Pinching back. Simply using thumb and forefinger to nip off the tips of branches. This basic pruning technique forces side growth, making the plant more compact and dense.

Pistils. See **Anatomy of a Flower,** page 59.

Plant classification. Botanists have classified plants into an orderly, ranked system reflecting similarities among the world's plants. The plant kingdom is broken down into groups that are less and less inclusive: division, class, order, and then the groups defined below, which are the ones of most significance to gardeners.

Family. Each plant belongs to a family, members of which share certain broad characteristics that are not always immediately evident. The rose family, for instance, includes such diverse plants as the rose, the apple tree, and the familiar perennial *Geum*. Family names such as *Rosaceae* (rose family) and *Liliaceae* (lily family) are not as important to gardeners as the names of the smaller divisions into which families are divided, but knowing the family does sometimes help one to recall a plant or make an educated guess about its cultural needs.

Genus. A plant family is divided into groups of more closely related plants; each group is called a genus (the plural is *genera*). Sometimes a family will contain only one genus: for example, *Ginkgoaceae* contains only the genus *Ginkgo*. At the other extreme, the composite family (*Compositae*) contains around 950 genera. The first word in a plant's botanical name is the name of the genus to which the plant belongs: for example, *Ginkgo, Liquidambar, Primula*.

Species. Each genus is subdivided into groups of individuals called species; the second word in a plant's botanical name designates the species. A few genera contain only one species (the genus *Ginkgo* consists only of the species *Ginkgo biloba*), but more often a genus contains two or more species. Each species is a generally distinct entity, reproducing from seed with only a small amount of variation. Species in a genus share many common features but differ in at least one characteristic.

Subspecies, variety. A third word in a botanical name indicates a subspecies or variety. In the strictest sense, a subspecies is more inclusive than a variety. "Subspecies" is often used to denote a geographical variant of a species, but in general usage, "subspecies" and "variety" have become virtually interchangeable. Subspecies or varieties retain most characteristics of their species while differing in some particular way, such as flower color or leaf size. The name may appear in either of two ways: *Juniperus chinensis sargentii* (subspecies) or *Juniperus chinensis* 'San Jose' (a variety).

Horticultural variety (clone or cultivar). These often are of hybrid origin. They are usually listed by genus name followed by cultivar name, as *Rosa* 'Chrysler Imperial'. Some have been found as wild plants but have been perpetuated by cuttings or other means of vegetative propagation.

Hybrid. This is a distinct plant resulting from a cross between two species, subspecies, varieties, cultivars, strains—or any combination of the above—or even between two plants belonging to different genera. Some occur in the wild (such as *Halimiocistus,* a hybrid between a species of *Halimium* and a species of *Cistus*), but more often hybrids are deliberate crosses.

Strain. Many popular annuals and some perennials are sold as strains, such as State Fair zinnias. Plants in a strain usually share similar growth characteristics but are variable in some way—usually in flower color.

Pleaching. This is a method of training plant growth where branches are interwoven and plaited together to form a hedge or arbor. Subsequent pruning merely keeps a neat, rather formal pattern.

Pollarding. In this pruning style, the main limbs of a young tree are drastically cut back to short lengths. Each dormant season following, the growth from these branch stubs is cut back to one or two buds. In time, branch ends become large and knobby. The result is a compact, leafy dome during the growing season and a somewhat grotesque branch structure during the dormant months. London plane tree (*Platanus acerifolia*) is most often subjected to this treatment.

Pollination. See page 59.

Potbound. See **Rootbound.**

Pseudobulb. This thickened, above-ground modified stem, found in some orchids such as *Cymbidium,* serves as a storage organ for nutrients.

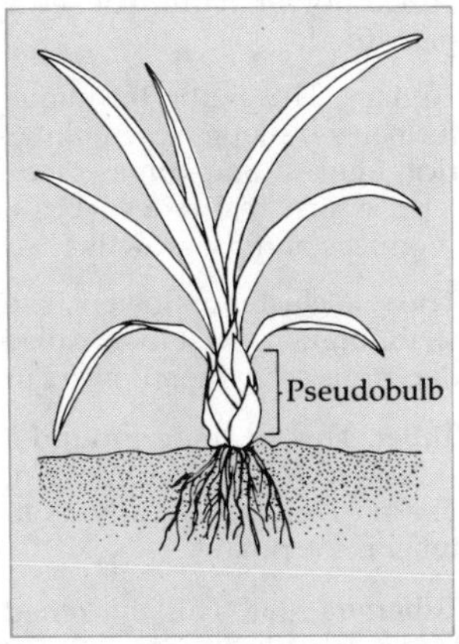

Ray flower. See **Composite family.**

Rhizome. This thickened, modified stem grows horizontally along or under the soil surface. It may be long and slender, as in some lawn grasses, or thick and fleshy, as in many irises.

Rock garden. Usually a man-made landscape, often on sloping ground, a rock garden contains natural-appearing rock outcrops and rocky soil surfaces. Plants grown in a rock garden are generally low-growing, spreading or mat-forming types that conform to the rocky terrain. A special type of rock garden is the alpine garden, in which plants from high altitudes are grown in a replica of their native setting. Many favorite rock garden plants require fast drainage and full sun, and are somewhat drought tolerant.

Rootbound. This condition develops when a plant grows for too long in its container. With no room for additional growth, roots become tangled, matted, and grow in circles. Rootbound plants placed in the ground without having roots untangled often fail to outgrow their choked condition and don't grow well—or don't grow at all.

Rootstock. This is the part of a budded or grafted plant (see **Bud, Grafting**) that furnishes the root system and sometimes part of the branch structure. *Understock* has the same meaning.

Rosette. Plants are said to grow in rosettes if the leaves are closely set around a crown or center—as in the case of hen and chicks (*Echeveria*), hen and chickens (*Sempervivum*).

Runner. In common usage, this imprecise term has come to refer either to **Offsets** or **Stolons.** A runner is a slender stem sent out from the bases of certain perennials, at the end of which an **Offset** develops.

Salinity. Gardeners use this word when speaking of an excessive salt content in the soil. Frequently a buildup of salts occurs in deserts and semiarid regions, resulting from continued light watering with low-quality water containing sodium. If plants are to thrive in such regions, gardeners must periodically wash (leach) accumulated salts out of the plant root zone (see **Leaching**). High salinity can do great harm to many plants, scorching and yellowing leaves and stunting plant growth.

Scree. These are the fragmented rocks and pebbles found in nature at the base of a cliff or around large rocks in a rocky landscape. Some gardeners create their own artificial scree as a place for growing choice alpine plants. Also see **Rock garden.**

Self-branching. This term describes certain annuals that produce numerous side growths and grow compactly without having to be pinched back.

Semidouble flower. This flower form has a few more than the basic minimum number of petals for its kind (see **Single flower**), but not so many petals that the stamens and pistils are obscured. (*Petals, stamens,* and *pistils* are defined under **Anatomy of a Flower,** page 59.)

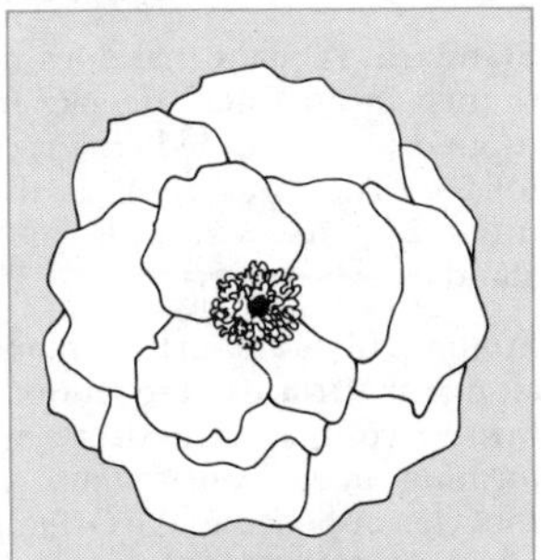

Semidouble flower

Sepals. See **Anatomy of a Flower,** page 59.

Single flower. This flower type has the minimum number of petals for its kind, usually four, five, or six (basic number for roses, for example, is five).

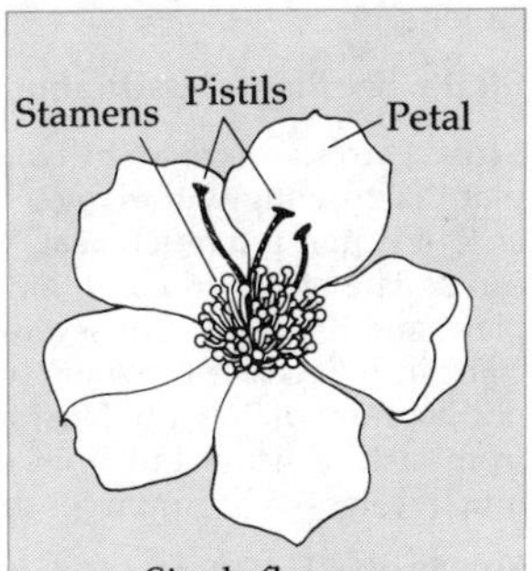

Single flower

Spadix. A thick, fleshy spike containing many small (usually) flowers. Usually it is partially enclosed by a spathe. Members of the Arum family have their flowers so arranged.

Spathe. A large bract (leaflike organ), often conspicuously colored or shaped, that surrounds a spadix. A heavy, woody spathe surrounds the inflorescences of many palms.

Species. See **Plant classification.**

Specimen. As used by nurserymen, this term refers to a tree or shrub large enough to make an immediate, significant contribution to a planting. "Specimen" may also refer to a single large plant in a conspicuous location.

Sphagnum. Various mosses native to bogs are called sphagnum. Much of the **Peat moss** sold in the West is composed partly or entirely of sphagnum mosses in a partially decomposed state. These mosses also are collected live and packaged in whole pieces, fresh or dried, and used in planting certain orchids, for lining hanging baskets, and for air layering.

Spike. This is a flowering stem with flowers directly attached (without any short flower stems) along the upper portion of its length. The flowers open in sequence, beginning at the bottom of the spike. Familiar examples are *Gladiolus* and red hot poker (*Kniphofia*). The term is often applied loosely to inflorescences that resemble spikes—especially to racems, which differ in that each individual flower has its own short stem.

Spore. A spore is a simple type of reproductive cell capable of producing a new plant. Certain kinds of plants (such as algae, fungi, mosses, and ferns) reproduce by spores.

Sport. A mutation—a spontaneous variation from the normal pattern. In horticulture, a sport is usually seen as a branch that differs notably from its parent plant. Examples include the spurred apple varieties that occur as limb sports on standard apple varieties and camellias propagated from branches which have shown changes in color or form of flowers.

Spur. Some fruit trees, particularly apples and cherries, bear their blossoms on a specialized short twig called a spur.

Spurs. These are short and saclike or long and tubular projections from a flower (the columbine, *Aquilegia*, is a familiar example). Spurs can arise from either sepals or petals.

Stamens. See **Anatomy of a Flower,** page 59.

Standard. A plant that does not naturally grow as a tree can be trained into a small treelike form, with a single, upright trunk topped by a rounded crown of foliage. The "tree rose" is the most familiar example of a standard.

Stolon. This is a stem that creeps along the surface of the ground, taking root at intervals and forming new plants where it roots (as opposed to the **Offsets** which may form at the ends of **Runners**). Bermuda and St. Augustine grasses spread by stolons.

Strain. See **Plant classification.**

Stress. Stress refers to the condition or conditions under which a plant is growing with danger to its health. Stress may stem from lack of water; too much heat, wind, or moisture; or low temperatures. The stressful condition varies according to the particular plant and its needs. Stress shows up as wilting, loss or dulling of color in foliage, or browning of leaf edges. Causes of stress may not be immediately obvious; for instance, wilting may result not from lack of water but from destruction of roots caused by too much water—a common condition in house plants.

Subshrub. This type of plant, usually under 3 ft. high and with more or less woody stems, is sometimes grown and used as a perennial, sometimes grown and used as a shrub.

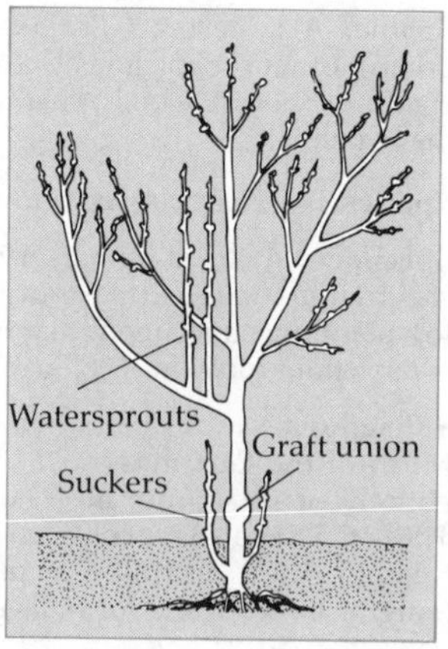

Subspecies. See **Plant classification.**

Sucker. In a grafted or budded plant, sucker growth originates from the **Rootstock** rather than from the desired grafted or budded part of the plant. In trees, any strong vertical shoot growing from the main framework of trunk and branches is sometimes called a sucker, although the more proper term for such growth is *watersprout*.

Sweet pea shaped. This term describes the flowers of most members of the pea family (*Leguminosae*). The flower has a broad uppermost petal (the banner or standard), two lateral petals (wings), and two lower petals united into a hollow structure called the keel. The keel encloses the stamens and pistil.

Systemic. A systemic is any chemical that is absorbed into a plant's system, either to kill organisms that feed on the plant or to kill the plant itself. There are systemic insecticides, fungicides, and weed killers.

Taproot. This main root grows straight down, like the root of a carrot or dandelion. In dry areas, some plants have very deep taproots to reach a deep water table.

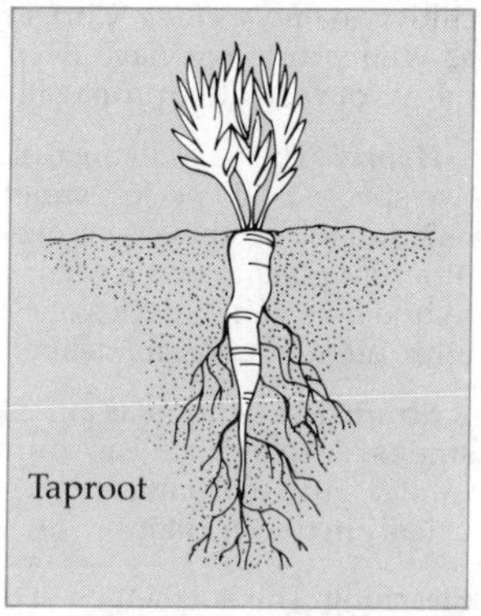

Tender. Tender is the opposite of **Hardy.** It denotes low tolerance of freezing temperatures.

Tendrils. These twisting, threadlike projections are found on some vines. Tendrils enable vines to cling to supports and climb.

Thinning out. This pruning term means to remove entire branches—large or small—back to the main trunk, a side branch, or the ground. The object is to give the plant a more open structure. Also see pages 76–77.

In growing plants from seed, thinning out means removing excess plants so those remaining are spaced far enough apart to develop well.

Topdress. To topdress means to apply on the surface, usually referring to the spreading of an organic material such as ground bark or manure on the soil as a mulch. Sometimes it refers to application of manure or sewage sludge on a lawn as a low-grade plant food.

Topiary. This is the technique of shaping shrubs and trees into formalized shapes resembling such things as animals and geometrical figures. Sometimes inaccurately called "poodle pruning," a term which really describes only the sort of topiary work that produces puffs of growth.

Truss. A cluster of flowers, usually rather compact, at the end of a stem, branch, or stalk is called a truss. The most familiar rhododendrons carry their flowers in trusses.

Tuber. This fat underground stem, from which a plant grows, is similar to a **Rhizome,** but it is usually shorter and thicker, and doesn't lengthen greatly as it grows. The world's most famous tuber is the potato.

Tuberous root. This thickened underground food storage structure is actually a root rather than a true tuber, which is a modified stem. Growth buds are in the old stems at the upper end of the root. The dahlia is a familiar example.

Underplanting. Planting one plant beneath another, such as a ground cover under a tree.

Understock. See **Rootstock.**

Variety. See **Plant classification.**

Vermiculite. The mineral mica is heated and puffed up to form spongelike, lightweight granules useful in conditioning container soils. Vermiculite granules hold both water and air.

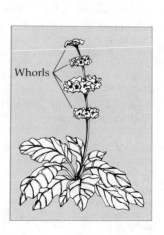

Watersprout. See **Sucker.**

Wettable powder. This finely ground pesticide can be mixed in water and sprayed onto plants. Some kinds also can be dusted on, as described under **Dust.**

Whorl. Whorls are composed of three or more leaves, branches, or flowers growing in a circle from a joint (node) on a stem or trunk.

A guide to understanding botanical names

Botanical names are in Latin, the universal language of scholars at the time plant classification was formalized. The genus name of a plant (see **Plant classification**) may be the classical name of the plant, a Latinized version of a vernacular name, or a classical word of general application. The species name usually is descriptive (color, form, leaf structure), commemorative (named after a person), or geographical (signifying the region where the plant grows or was discovered).

The following words occur frequently in the botanical names of plants. All (except -dendron) are descriptive adjectives.

Color of flowers or foliage

albus—white
argenteus—silvery
aureus—golden
azureus—azure, sky blue
caesius—blue gray
coeruleus—dark blue
candidus—pure white, shiny
canus—ashy gray, hoary
carneus—flesh colored
cereus—waxy
citrinus—yellow
coccineus—scarlet
concolor—one color
croceus—yellow
cruentus—bloody
discolor—two colors, separate colors
glaucus—covered with gray bloom
incanus—gray, hoary
luteus—reddish yellow
purpureus—purple
rubens, ruber—red, ruddy
rufus—ruddy

Form of leaf

acerifolius—maplelike leaves
angustifolius—narrow leaves
aquifolius—spiny leaves
buxifolius—leaves like boxwood
ilicifolius—hollylike leaves
laurifolius—laurel-like leaves
parvifolius—small leaves
populifolius—poplarlike leaves
salicifolius—willowlike leaves

Shape of plants

adpressus—pressing against, hugging
altus—tall
arboreus—treelike
capitatus—headlike
compactus—compact, dense
confertus—crowded, pressed together
contortus—twisted
decumbens—lying down
depressus—pressed down
elegans—elegant; slender, willowy
fastigiatus—branches erect and close together
humifusus—sprawling on the ground
humilis—low, small, humble
impressus—impressed upon
nanus—dwarf
procumbens—trailing
prostratus—prostrate
pumilus—dwarfish, small
pusillus—puny, insignificant
repens—creeping
reptans—creeping
scandens—climbing

Where it came from

The suffix *-ensis* (of a place) is added to place names to specify the habitat where the plant was first discovered.

australis—southern
borealis—northern
campestris—of the field or plains
canadensis—of Canada
canariensis—of the Canary Islands
capensis—of the Cape of Good Hope area
chilensis—of Chile
chinensis—of China
hortensis—of gardens
insularis—of the island
littoralis—of the seashore
montanus—of the mountains
riparius—of river banks
rivalis, rivularis—of brooks
saxatilis—inhabiting rocks

Plant peculiarities

armatus—armed
baccatus—berried, berrylike
barbatus—barbed or bearded
campanulatus—bell or cup shaped
ciliaris—fringed
cordatus—heart shaped
cornutus—horned
crassus—thick, fleshy
decurrens—running down the stem
-dendron—tree
diversi—varying
edulis—edible
floridus—free flowering
fruticosus—shrubby
fulgens—shiny
gracilis—slender, thin, small
grandis—large, showy
-ifer, -iferus—bearing or having. For example, *stoloniferus*, having stolons
laciniatus—fringed or with torn edges
laevigatus—smooth
lobatus—lobed
maculatus—spotted
mollis—soft, soft hairy
mucronatus—pointed
nutans—nodding, swaying
officinalis—medicinal
obtusus—blunt or flattened
-oides—like or resembling. For example: *jasminoides*, like a jasmine
patens—open spreading growth
pinnatus—constructed like a feather
plenus—double, full
plumosus—feathery
praecox—precocious
pungens—piercing
radicans—rooting, especially along the stem
reticulatus—net-veined
retusus—notched at blunt apex
rugosus—wrinkled, rough
saccharatus—sweet, sugary
sagittalis—arrowlike
scabrus—rough feeling
scoparius—broomlike

Index to general subject matter

Index to botanical & common names

Boldface numerals refer to entries in the encyclopedic chapter.

F

G

H

Photographers

William C. Aplin: 13 top left. **Carolyn Caddas:** 19 top left. **Glenn Christiansen:** 12, 29 top right, 134. **Stephen Cridland:** 10 bottom. **Derek Fell:** 139, 153. **Gerald R. Fredrick:** 11 top right, 21 bottom left, 25 top right, 29 bottom left, 147. **Pamela Harper:** 120. **Michael McKinley:** 31 bottom, 119. **Carol Malcolm:** 9 bottom. **Stephen Marley:** 29 bottom right, 128. **Ells Marugg:** 14 top right, 15 top left, 18 top, 23 bottom left, 23 right, 25 bottom right, 115, 121, 148, 159, 167. **Don Normark:** 17 bottom, 20 top, 23 top left, 137. **Norman A. Plate:** 10 top, 11 left, 13 bottom left, 15 right, 16, 18 bottom, 21 top left, 31 top, 32, 113, 116 right, 142, 150, 152, 161. **Bill Ross/West Light:** 11 bottom right, 15 bottom left, 19 bottom right, 24 bottom right, 25 top left, 27 bottom left, 114, 117 left, 126, 129, 133, 138, 141, 143 top, 154, 163, 165, 168, 173 right. **Teri Sandison:** 14 bottom right, 125, 158. **Chad Slattery:** 8, 24 top right. **David Stubbs:** 9 top, 160. **Jeff Teeter:** 173 left. **Michael Thompson:** 2, 19 top right, 24 left, 26, 29 top left, 140, 144, 149, 151, 156. **Darrow M. Watt:** 13 right, 14 left, 17 top, 20 bottom, 21 right, 22, 30, 135, 143 bottom, 145, 169. **Russ Widstrand:** 164. **Tom Wyatt:** 1, 27 top left, 27 top right, 28, 116 left, 117 right, 118, 122, 131, 166, 174.